THE
GLADSTONE
DIARIES

Gladstone in 1857, aged forty-seven

THE
GLADSTONE
DIARIES

VOLUME V · 1855–1860

Edited by

H. C. G. MATTHEW

STUDENT
OF
CHRIST CHURCH, OXFORD

CLARENDON PRESS · OXFORD
1978

Oxford University Press, Walton Street, Oxford OX2 6DP

OXFORD LONDON GLASGOW
NEW YORK TORONTO MELBOURNE WELLINGTON
IBADAN NAIROBI DAR ES SALAAM LUSAKA CAPE TOWN
KUALA LUMPUR SINGAPORE JAKARTA HONG KONG TOKYO
DELHI BOMBAY CALCUTTA MADRAS KARACHI

THIS EDITION © OXFORD UNIVERSITY PRESS 1978

British Library Cataloguing in Publication Data

Gladstone, William Ewart
  The Gladstone diaries.
    Vol. 5: 1855–1860; [and], Vol. 6: 1861–1868
    1. Gladstone, William Ewart
    I. Matthew, Henry Colin Gray
    941.081′092′4   DA563.4
    ISBN 0–19–822445–1

1478
1978

PRINTED IN GREAT BRITAIN
BY WILLIAM CLOWES & SONS LIMITED
LONDON, BECCLES AND COLCHESTER

PREFACE

The main Gladstone Diary and its ancillary papers are owned by the Archbishop of Canterbury, and once again thanks are due to him for permission for publication. Similar thanks are due to Sir William Gladstone for permission to publish material from the British Library and St Deiniol's collections, for his generous provision of illustrations and for his help with research.

The editor has been greatly assisted by the *ad hoc* committee at Oxford which, under the chairmanship of Lord Blake, supervises the publication of this edition; its other members are Mr. E. G. W. Bill, Lord Bullock, Dr. J. F. A. Mason and Mr. A. F. Thompson. Mr. D. M. Davin of the Oxford University Press has been its secretary and he, together with Mr. A. H. Gye and Dr. A. B. Tayler of St. Catherine's College (the project's academic sponsor), have relieved the editor of many bureaucratic chores.

Finance for the research for these volumes has been provided by the Archbishop of Canterbury, the Calouste Gulbenkian Foundation, the British Academy, All Souls College, the Marc Fitch Fund, The Pilgrim Trust; the Rhodes Trust by its timely help in difficult times has given a very considerable measure of security to the project. The committee and the editor are most grateful to all these for their generous support.

Christ Church, Oxford, has provided a home for the preparation for the publication of the diaries of one of the most distinguished of its *alumni*; the college has also sustained the editor, materially and intellectually, by the generosity of its assistance and by the comradeship of its senior and junior members. The elevation of the editor to an especially created Studentship at Christ Church was a high honour for him and a notable compliment to the project.

The burden of editorial research for these two volumes was very considerably alleviated by the assistance, especially in matters bibliographical, first of Dr. Perry Butler, and then of Mrs. Francis Phillips. Dr. Butler worked on the years 1855–1859. Mrs. Phillips worked on the concluding years of volume V and on the whole of the long reaches of the 1860s which comprise volume VI. She also assisted in transcribing and in seeing these two volumes through the press. Collaboration in research on a work which is both so detailed and so wide ranging as Gladstone's diaries is not easy, but both of these assistants bore the editor's demands upon them without complaint, and considerably compensated his extensive areas of ignorance.

The librarian of Christ Church (Dr. J. F. A. Mason), of Lambeth Palace (Mr. E. G. W. Bill) and of All Souls College (Mr. J. S. G. Simmons) and their staffs, have offered ready and generous help, as have those of the Bodleian and the British Library. Mr. Geoffrey Veysey and Mr. Christopher Williams of the Clwyd Record Office at Hawarden have answered many queries about the Gladstone and Glynne family papers which are deposited at St. Deiniol's Library at Hawarden, and the excellent handlist which they have prepared for this important collection will be of great value to all historians of the nineteenth century.

Thanks are also due to Sir Robert Mackworth-Young, Keeper of the Royal Archives at Windsor, and to the staffs of the National Library of Scotland and of the many county record offices who have dealt with enquiries which by their expertise they make appear routine.

The manuscript diaries have been on temporary deposit in the Bodleian Library, where special arrangements were made for them. Access to the unpublished Lambeth diary and to its ancillary papers remains restricted to the editor. Addenda, corrigenda and enquiries should be sent to him at Christ Church, Oxford.

Some of the text of these volumes has been printed from the typed transcript made long ago by Professor H. W. Lawton and amended and checked by the editor. The transcripts of the other sections, and all the notes, were typed by Mrs. Doris Hopkins, except for the list of *Dramatis Personae* which was typed by Lady Sarah Russell.

Gladstone's eclecticism leads the editor and the reader down many strange paths and by-ways; the charting of the routes can only be done by enquiry. The many colleagues in Oxford who have willingly responded to obscure questions have shown that the idea of a literary culture is not dead; in particular, Dr. Daniel Bueno de Mesquita, Mr. Peter Parsons and Mr. Denis Mack Smith may be mentioned in this context.

In writing the Introduction, I have been much obliged to Lord Blake for his comments, and to Mr. A. F. Thompson for his trenchant, demanding, and generous criticism, and I am again grateful to Dr. Perry Butler and Dr. Boyd Hilton for discussions about the religion and politics of the period.

'Will he never die?' is my long-suffering family's question about, I hope, the author rather than the editor of this diary. The answer must merely be that Gladstone has, with these two volumes, at least now run half his course, in years if not in volumes.

COLIN MATTHEW

Christ Church,
Oxford
June 1977

CONTENTS

VOLUME V

VOLUME VI

LIST OF ILLUSTRATIONS

ABBREVIATED CHRISTIAN AND SURNAMES

in diary text of Volumes V and VI

(*prefixed or suffixed to a name in a footnote indicates an article
in the *Dictionary of National Biography*)

A.	Agnes Gladstone, *daughter*, or the duke of Argyll
A., D. of	duke of Argyll
A., Ld	Lord Aberdeen
Abn, Ld	the same
Agnes	Agnes Gladstone, *daughter*
A.G.	*the same*
A.K.	A. Kinnaird
Arthur	A. Gordon
Arthur, Ld	Clinton
B., Miss	Miss Browne, *governess*
B., Lord	Lord Brougham
B., Count	Count Bernstorff
B., Mrs.	Mrs. Bennett, *cousin*
B. & B.	Bickers & Bush, *booksellers*
B.H.	Archdeacon Harrison
Bob	Robertson Gladstone, *brother*
C.	Catherine Gladstone, *née* Glynne, *wife*
C., Ld	Lord Clarendon
C., Ld F.	Lord Frederick Cavendish
C., Lucy	Lady Frederick Cavendish, *née* Lucy Lyttelton
C.E.T., Sir	Sir Charles Trevelyan
C.G.	Catherine Gladstone
C.N.G., Lady	Lady Charlotte Neville Grenville
Colin, Cousin	C. C. F. Robertson
D.	B. Disraeli *or* S. Darbishire
D., Aunt	*wife of next*
D., Uncle	David Gladstone *or* Divie Robertson
D., Ld	Lord Derby *or* Lord Devon
D., Mr.	Mr. Darlington *or* Darbishire
D.G.	David Gladstone *or deo gratia*
D. of N.	fourth or fifth duke of Newcastle
D.R.	Divie Robertson, *uncle*
E.	Elizabeth Honoria Gladstone, *née* Bateson, *sister-in-law*

E., Aunt	Elizabeth Robertson
E., Lord and Lady	Lord and Lady Ellesmere
E.C.	Edward Cardwell *or* Elizabeth Collins *or* Emma Clifton
E.K., Sir	Sir E. Kerrison
F., Sir T.	Sir T. Fremantle
F., Mr.	Mr. *or* Dr. Fergusson
F.E., Ld or Ly	Lord *or* Lady F. Egerton
F.C., Ld	Lord Frederick Cavendish
F.H.D.	Sir F. H. Doyle
F.L.	Frank Lawley
Frank	*the same*
G.	George Lyttelton, *wife's brother-in-law*, *or* Lord Granville
G.A.S.	(Bishop) G. A. Selwyn
Gertrude	Gertrude Glynne
G.L.	George Lyttelton
G., Lady	Lady Glynne, *mother-in-law*
H.	(Bishop) W. K. Hamilton *or* Helen Jane Gladstone, *sister*, *or* Sidney Herbert
H., Lord	Lord Hardinge
H., Lady	Lady Herbert of Lea
H., Mr. and Mrs.	Mr. and Mrs. Hampton, *the butler and his wife.*
Harry	Henry Neville Gladstone, *son*
Helen	Helen Jane Gladstone, *sister*, *or* Helen Gladstone, *daughter*
Henry	Henry Glynne, *brother-in-law*
H.G.	Helen Jane Gladstone, *sister*
H.J.G.	*the same*
Hs., the two	Herbert and Harry, *sons*
J.	John Neilson Gladstone, *brother*, *or* Johnnie Gladstone, *nephew*
J., Aunt	Johanna Robertson
Jim	James Hope(-Scott)
J.L. & co.	Johnson, Longden & Co., *stockbrokers*
J., Lord	Lord John Russell
J.G., Sir	Sir James Graham
J.M., Lord	Lord John Manners
J.M.G.	James Milnes Gaskell, *or* John Murray Gladstone, *cousin*
J.M.G.(R.)	J. M. G. Robertson, *cousin*
J.N.G.	John Neilson Gladstone, *brother*
John	*the same*

Johnnie	John Gladstone, *nephew*
J.R.	J.M.G. Robertson, *cousin or* Lord John Russell
J.S.H., Sir	Sir J. S. H. Forbes
J.S.W.	James Stuart-Wortley
K.	A. Kinnaird
Kate *or* Katie	Catherine Glynne, *wife's niece, or* Katherine Gladstone, *niece*
L.	Lyttelton *or, occasionally* Lacaita *or* Marquis of Lorne
L., Mr	J. Lacaita
L., Lord	Lord Lansdowne
L., Sir E.B.	Sir E. Bulwer-Lytton
Lavinia	Lavinia Glynne, *née* Lyttelton, *wife's sister-in-law*
Lena	Helen Gladstone, *daughter*
L.L.	Lucy Lyttelton
Ln	Lord Lyttelton *or, occasionally* W. H. Lyttelton
Louisa	Louisa Gladstone, *née* Fellowes, *sister-in-law*
Lucy	Lucy Lyttelton, *wife's niece*
M.	Meriel Sarah Lyttelton, *wife's niece*
M., Aunt	Mary Robertson
M., Sir R.	Sir Roderick Murchison
Mamma	Catherine Gladstone, *wife*
Mary	Lady Lyttelton, *née* Glynne, *sister-in-law*
Mary Ellen	Mrs. Robertson Gladstone, *née* Jones, *sister-in-law*
May	Mary Lyttelton, *wife's niece*
Mazie *or* Mary	Mary Gladstone, *daughter*, or Mary Lyttelton, *wife's niece*
M.E.	Mrs. Robertson Gladstone, *sister-in-law*
Meriel	Meriel S. Lyttelton, *wife's niece*
M.G., Mrs.	Mrs. Milnes Gaskell
Molly	Mary Glynne, *wife's niece*
M.S.	M. Summerhayes, *rescue*
Murray, John	John Murray Gladstone, *cousin*
N., D. of	duke of Newcastle
N.	N. G. Lyttelton, *wife's nephew*
Neville	*the same*
Nina	Helen Gladstone, *daughter*
Nora	Honora Glynne, *wife's niece*
O.B.C.	O. B. Cole
P. *or* Pn.	Lord Palmerston
P., Mr.	(Sir) Charles Pressly
R.	Robertson Gladstone, *brother*

R., Lord	Lord Ripon
R., Miss	Miss Rose
R.G.	Robertson Gladstone, *brother*
R.I., Sir	Sir R. H. Inglis
Rn (G.)	Robertson Gladstone, *brother*
Robn	*as above*
R.P.	(Sir) Robert Phillimore
S.	A. P. Sanders *or* (Bishop) G. A. Selwyn *or* Sir Stephen Glynne, *brother-in-law*, or Stephen Edward Gladstone, *son*
S., dowager Duchess of	Sutherland
S.	Summerhayes, *rescue*
S. of A.	Lord Stanley of Alderley
S.E.G.	Stephen Gladstone, *son*
S.G.	*the same*
S.H.	Sidney Herbert
S.R.G.	Sir Stephen Glynne, *brother-in-law*
Stephy	Stephen Gladstone, *son*
T.	(Sir) Thomas Gladstone, *brother*
T., Mr.	W. E. Tallents
T., Mrs.	Laura Thistlethwayte
T.G.	Sir Thomas Gladstone, *brother*
Tom	*the same*
T.S.G.	T. S. Godfrey
W.	William Henry Gladstone, *son*
W., Lady	Lady Wenlock
W., Lord	Lord Ward
Walter	Sir W. R. Farquhar *or* (Bishop) W. K. Hamilton
Willy	William Henry Gladstone, *son*
Winny	Lavinia Lyttelton, *wife's niece*
W.H.L.	William Lyttelton
W.K.H.	(Bishop) W. K. Hamilton
W.L.	William Lyttelton
W.W., Sir	Sir Watkin Williams Wynn
Xt	Christ.

ABBREVIATED BOOK TITLES, ETC.

Used in Volumes V and VI

Acton-Simpson Correspondence	The correspondence of Lord Acton and Richard Simpson, edited by J. L. Altholz, D. McElrath and J. C. Holland, 3v. (1971–5)
Add MS(S)	*Additional Manuscript(s), British Museum*
Argyll	Eighth duke of Argyll, *Autobiography and memoirs*, 2 v. (1906)
Autobiographica	John Brooke and Mary Sorensen, eds., *The prime minister's papers: W. E. Gladstone. I and II* (1971–4)
Bassett	A. Tilney Bassett, ed., *Gladstone to his wife* (1936)
Bassett, *Speeches*	A. Tilney Bassett, ed., *Gladstone's speeches: descriptive index and bibliography* (1916)
Battiscombe	Georgina Battiscombe, *Mrs. Gladstone* (1956)
Beales, *England and Italy*	D. E. D. Beales, *England and Italy, 1859–60* (1961)
BFSP	*British and Foreign State Papers*
Blake	Robert Blake, *Disraeli* (1966)
Brand MSS	The papers of Sir H. B. W. Brand, first Viscount Hampden, in the Record Office of the House of Lords
Broadlands MSS	The papers of H. J. Temple, Lord Palmerston, in the National Registry of Archives
Buckle	W. F. Monypenny and G. E. Buckle, *Life of Benjamin Disraeli*, 6 v. (1910–20)
Buxton, *Finance and Politics*	Sydney Buxton, *Finance and politics: an historical study, 1783–1885*, 2 v. (1888)
Carlingford MSS	Papers of Chichester Fortescue, Lord Carlingford, in the Somerset County Record Office
Chadwick	Owen Chadwick, *The Victorian church*, pt. 1 (1966)
Checkland	S. G. Checkland, *The Gladstones, a family biography, 1764–1851* (1971)
Clapham, *Bank of England*	Sir J. H. Clapham, *The Bank of England: a history*, 2v. (1944)
Clarendon MSS	Papers of George Villiers, Lord Clarendon, in the Bodleian Library
Conacher	J. B. Conacher, *The Aberdeen coalition, 1852–1855: a study in mid-nineteenth-century party politics* (1968)

Costin, *Great Britain and China*	W. C. Costin, *Great Britain and China, 1833–1860* (1937)
Cowling, *1867*	M. J. Cowling, *1867, Disraeli, Gladstone and revolution: the passing of the second Reform Bill* (1967)
Denison, *Journal*	J. E. Denison, Viscount Ossington, *Notes from my journal when Speaker of the House of Commons* (1899)
DLFC	J. Bailey, ed., *Diary of Lady Frederick Cavendish*, 2 v. (1927)
Derby Papers	The papers of E. G. G. S. Stanley, fourteenth earl of Derby, in keeping of Lord Blake, The Queen's College, Oxford
DNB	*Dictionary of National Biography*, 71 v. (1885–1957)
EHR	*English Historical Review* (from 1886)
Elwin MSS	Papers of W. Whitwell Elwin in the National Library of Scotland
Fitzmaurice	Lord E. Fitzmaurice, *Life of Earl Granville*, 2 v. (1905)
Gardiner	A. G. Gardiner, *Life of Sir William Harcourt*, 2 v. (1923)
Gleanings	W. E. Gladstone, *Gleanings of past years*, 7 v. (1879)
Greville	Lytton Strachey and R. Fulford, eds., *The Greville memoirs*, 8 v. (1938)
Guedalla, *P*	P. Guedalla, ed., *Gladstone and Palmerston* (1928)
Guedalla, *Q*	P. Guedalla, ed., *The Queen and Mr Gladstone*, 2 v. (1933)
H	*Hansard's Parliamentary Debates*, third series (1830–91)
Harrison, *Drink and the Victorians*	B. H. Harrison, *Drink and the Victorians* (1971)
Hawn P	Hawarden Papers (deposited in St Deiniol's Library, Hawarden)
Hewett	'. . . and Mr. Fortescue'. A selection from the diaries from 1851 to 1862 of Chichester Fortescue, Lord Carlingford, K.P., edited by O. W. Hewett (1958)
Juventus Mundi	W. E. Gladstone, *Juventus Mundi, The Gods and Men of the Heroic Age* (1869)

Kimberley	*A Journal of Events during the Gladstone Ministry 1868–1874, by John, first Earl of Kimberley,* edited by E. Drus, *Camden Miscellany,* vol. XXI (1957)
Kirkwall, *Four Years*	G. W. H. Fitzmaurice, Viscount Kirkwall, *Four Years in the Ionian Islands,* 2 v. (1864)
Knaplund, *Imperial policy*	P. Knaplund, *Gladstone and Britain's imperial policy* (1927)
Lathbury	D. C. Lathbury, *Correspondence on church and religion of W. E. Gladstone,* 2 v. (1910)
LQV	A. C. Benson, Viscount Esher, and G. E. Buckle, *Letters of Queen Victoria,* 9 v. (1907–32) in three series each of three v.: I series 1837–61; 2 s., 1862–85; 3 s., 1886–1901.
Lytton MSS	Papers of Sir E. G. E. L. Bulwer-Lytton, first Baron Lytton of Knebworth, in the Hertfordshire County Record Office
Magnus	Sir Philip Magnus, *Gladstone* (1954)
Masterman	C. F. G. Masterman, ed. and abridged J. Morley, *Life of Gladstone* (1927)
Migne, *PG*	J.-P. Migne, *Patrologiae Cursus Completus, series Graeca,* 161 v. (1857–66)
Migne, *PL*	J.-P. Migne, *Patrologiae Cursus Completus series Latina,* 221 v. (1844–64)
Mirror	J. H. Barrow, ed., *Mirror of Parliament* (1828–42)
Morley	J. Morley, *Life of William Ewart Gladstone,* 3 v. (1903)
Newman	*The Letters and Diaries of John Henry Newman,* edited by C. S. Dessain and T. Gornall (1961ff.)
NSH	T. C. Hansard, ed., *Parliamentary Debates,* new series (1820–30)
Perry, *Forbes*	W. Perry, *Alexander Penrose Forbes* (1939)
Phillimore MSS	Papers of Sir R. I. Phillimore in Christ Church Library, Oxford
Ponsonby	A. Ponsonby, *Henry Ponsonby* (1943)
PP	*Parliamentary Papers*
PRO	Public Record Office
Purcell	E. S. Purcell, *Life of Cardinal Manning,* 2 v. (1896)
Reid, *F*	(Sir) T. Wemyss Reid, *Life of . . . William Edward Forster,* 2 v. (1888)
Reid, *G*	Sir T. Wemyss Reid, ed., *Life of W. E. Gladstone* (1899)
Robbins	A. F. Robbins, *Early public life of Gladstone* (1894)

Selborne, I	Earl of Selborne, *Memorials family and personal*, 2 v. (1896)
Selborne, II	Earl of Selborne, *Memorials personal and political*, 2 v. (1898)
Smith	F. B. Smith, *The Making of the Second Reform Bill* (1966)
Stanmore	Lord Stanmore, *Sidney Herbert*, 2 v. (1906)
Steele, *Irish Land*	E. D. Steele, *Irish Land and British Politics. Tenant-Right and Nationality 1865–1870* (1974)
Stirling, *Richmond*	A. M. W. Stirling, *The Richmond Papers, from the correspondence and manuscripts of George Richmond, R. A., and his son Sir William Richmond, R.A., K.C.B.* (1926)
Studies on Homer	W. E. Gladstone, *Studies on Homer and the Homeric Age*, 3 v. (1858)
T.A.P.S.	*Transactions of the American Philosophical Society*
Translations	*Translations by Lord Lyttelton and the Right Hon. W. E. Gladstone* (1861)
VCH	*Victoria History of the Counties of England*
Walpole	S. Walpole, *Life of Lord John Russell*, 2 v. (1889)
Ward	W. R. Ward, *Victorian Oxford* (1965)
Wilberforce	A. R. Ashwell and R. G. Wilberforce, *Life of the rt. rev. Samuel Wilberforce*, 3 v. (1881)
Wolf, *Ripon*	L. Wolf, *Life of the first Marquess of Ripon*, 2 v. (1921)
Woodward	E. L. Woodward, *The age of reform, 1815–1870* (2nd ed., 1962)

OTHER ABBREVIATIONS

ab.	about
abp.	archbishop
acct.	account
aft(n).	afternoon
agst.	against
agt.	against
amdt.	amendment
Anc. Mus.	Ancient Music group
appt.	appointment
apptd.	appointed
arr.	arrived
b.	book *or* born *or* brother
B.	board of trade
bart.	baronet
Bd.	board of trade
B.I.R.	board of inland revenue
bkfst.	breakfast
B.N. *or* B.N.I.	Bank Notes Issue Bill
B.N.A.	British North America
B. of T.	board of trade
bp.	bishop
br.	brother
B.S.	Bedford *or* Berkeley Square
B.T.	board of trade
ca.	*circa*
cd.	could
C.G.	Carlton Gardens
Ch.	church *or* Chester
Ch. of Exchr.	Chancellor of the Exchequer
C.H.T.	Carlton House Terrace
C.O.	colonial office
co.	county
Col. Ch.	Colonial Church
commee.	committee
commn.	commission
cons.	conservative
conv.	conversation
cp.	compare
C.R.	Caledonian Railway

cr.	created
ctd.	continued
cttee.	committee
cum	with
d.	died
da.	daughter
deb.	debate
deptn. *or* dpn.	deputation
dft.	draft
div.	division
do.	ditto
Dowr.	Dowager
Dr.	doctor *or* dowager
E.	earl
E.C.	ecclesiastical courts
eccl.	ecclesiastical
ed.	edited *or* edition *or* editor *or* educational
E.I.	East Indies *or* East Indian
E.I. Assn.	East India Association of Liverpool
E p.	epistle
evg.	evening
f.	father *or* folio
F.	father *or* Fettercairn *or* Fasque
fa.	father
ff.	folios *or* following
F. House.	Fettercairn House
F.O.	foreign office
1°R	first reading
G. & co.	Gladstone and company
gd.	granddaughter
gf.	grandfather
G.J.R.	Grand Junction Railway
Gk.	Greek
gm.	grandmother
govt.	government
gs.	grandson
G.W.R.	Great Western Railway
H.C.	holy communion
Hn.	Hawarden
Ho.	house of commons
H.O.	home office
H. of C.	house of commons

H. of L.	house of lords
H.S.	holy scripture
Ibid.	*ibidem*, in the same place
J.S.	joint stock
k.	killed
l.	letter
Ld.	lord
lect.	lecture
lib.	liberal
Lkirk	Laurencekirk
Ln.	London
Lpool.	Liverpool
L.S.	*Liverpool Standard*
L.S.W.R.R.	London South-Western Railway
Ly.	lady
m.	married *or* mother
mem.	memorandum
mg.	morning
M.S.F.	Merchant Seamen's Fund
Nk.	Newark
N.S.	National Society
N.S.W.	New South Wales
nt.	night
n.y.n	not yet numbered
N.Z.	New Zealand
No. 6	6 Carlton Gardens
No. 11	11 Carlton House Terrace
No. 13	13 Carlton House Terrace
O. and C.	Oxford and Cambridge Club
O.F.	Oak Farm
O. and W.R.R.	Oxford, Worcester, Wolverhampton Railway
p., pp.	page(s)
P.D.R.	Perth Dundee Railway
P.O.	post office
P.P.	poetry professorship
pr. *or* priv.	private
pt.	part
rec(d).	receive(d)
ref(s).	reference(s)

resp.	respecting
Rev(d).	reverend
R.R.	railway
2°R	second reading
S.	son *or* series *or* sister
Sact.	sacrament
S.B.	Savings Banks
Seb.	Sebastopol
Sec. Euch.	Secreta Eucharistica
sd. *or* shd.	should
soc.	society
Sol. Gen.	solictor-general
sp.	speech
S.P.G.	Society for the Propagation of the Gospel
succ.	succeeded
T.	Treasury
tel.	telegram
3°R	third reading
tr.	translated *or* translation
U.C.C.	Upper Canada Clergy
Univ.	university
v.	verso *or* very *or* volume
V.C.	vice-chancellor
V.D.L.	Van Diemen's Land
V.I.	Vancouver's Island
Vicar, the	Henry Mackenzie
vol.	volume
vss.	verses
vy.	very
w.	wife
wd.	would
wh.	which
W.I.	West Indies
W.L.	Wine Licences
Xtn.	Christian
Y.N.B.R.	York, Newcastle, Berwick Railway
yesty.	yesterday

Signs used by the diarist

X	rescue work done this day
+	prayer, usually when on a charitable visit
♄	the use of a scourge
﷼	million

Signs inserted into the text editorially

[R] follows names of subjects of diarist's rescue work

INTRODUCTION

I

But I feel like a man under a burden under which he must fall and be crushed if he looks to the right or left, or fails from any cause to concentrate mind and muscle upon his progress step by step. This absorption, this excess, this constant ἄγαν is the fault of political life with its insatiable demands which do not leave the smallest stock of moral energy unexhausted and available for other purposes.

They certainly however have this merit: they drive home the sense that I am poor, and naked, and blind and miserable: and they make forgetfulness of God not a whit less unintelligible than it is excusable, though it is one thing to remember and another to obey.

Swimming for his life, a man does not see much of the country through which the river winds, and I probably know little of these years through which I busily work and live, beyond this, how sin and frailty deface them, and how mercy crowns them.[1]

Thus Gladstone, twenty six days after kissing hands as first lord of the treasury for the first time, celebrated his arrival at 'the top of the greasy pole'. It had not for him been a difficult climb, though there had been the odd slip and loss of grip. Nor had the conditions been especially arduous in the fourteen years these volumes cover. The crises of 'the hungry forties' gave way to the spectacular prosperity of the 1850s and 1860s. Britain moved towards democracy by the rule book, recalcitrant theorists proving a worse problem for the government than the demonstrations of loyal artisans, eager to ally themselves with political democracy. Problems of public order, the chief feature of the earlier years of Gladstone's career, gave way to the limited adjustment of relationships between unalienated groups: whereas the Chartists had wished to overturn the political order, the Reform League merely wished to associate itself with it.

The 1850s and early 1860s showed the Victorian constitution working in its most characteristic form, in a context of economic progress at which contemporaries wondered, though without complacency. By the late 1860s the propertied classes were becoming disconcerted by the re-emergence of those 'great social forces' which suggested that the mid-Victorian settlement might not, after all, hold. But the majority of the years covered by these volumes were those in which the achievement of progress—material, moral, intellectual—seemed to be Britain's contribution to an envious and ad-

---

[1] 31 Dec. 68 (cross references to the diary text are all in this abbreviated form). A description of the form and physical appearance of the diary, and of its history, will be found in the introduction to volume i of this edition. A list of the diarist's movements, 'Where Was He?' will be found at the end of volume iii and subsequent volumes. In volume v and in subsequent volumes the diarist's changing nightly location has been indicated in square brackets following the daily heading in the diary text.

miring world. 'Greater World' was Gladstone's slip of the pen when
Dilke's 'Greater Britain' was intended: it characterised a generation.[1]

For Gladstone personally most of these years offered a similar tranquillity. The great crises of his public and private life described in the
previous two volumes had been largely resolved. The tensions in what he
saw as political and sexual temptations became the tensions of tactical not
of strategic decision: the path of his life seemed finally charted, the set of his
thought consolidated.

This is not to say that the problems of political tactics were not extremely complex, as we shall see; but the great questions for Gladstone of
the 1830s and 1840s, of whether politics was for him a legitimate career,
of the nature of the Christian State, and of the relationship between ambition and duty, no longer form the central themes of the diary.

Politically, the diary of these years records a series of decisions and
manoeuvres whose context is quite different from that in which Gladstone
could seriously offer to Peel the amalgamation of two Welsh sees as a
reason for not joining the cabinet. For Gladstone, the relationships of
Church and State had ceased to be a chief point of theoretical controversy:
his decisions about the abolition of compulsory church rates[2] and Irish
disestablishment were decisions about timing and tactics, no longer about
great moral issues; the latter, he believed, had already been settled by the
failure of the Oxford movement in the 1840s to convert the nation.[3]

However, in purely tactical political terms, the years 1855–1859 were
the most personally complex in Gladstone's career. The success of the
Peelite-Liberal coalition of 1852 was from Gladstone's point of view broken
by the events of January and February 1855, which he records in very
great detail. But no great ideological difference separated Gladstone from
the Palmerston government (in which some Peelites, notably Argyll,
continued to serve) except the character of its leader. On the other hand,
no great question of policy seemed to bar his return to the tory party. As
he put it, anonymously, in the *Quarterly Review*:

> The interval between the two parties has, by the practical solution of so many
> congested questions, been very greatly narrowed. He who turns from Pall Mall
> towards the Park between the Reform and Carlton Clubs will perceive that

---

[1] 11 Nov. 68.

[2] See, e.g. 7 June 61. As in volumes iii and iv, a selection of Gladstone's theological,
political and personal memoranda and addenda to the diary, has been printed in nine
point type to supplement, illustrate and amplify the main diary (see further details
above, iii. xxiv). Some of these have been previously quoted by Morley, Lathbury,
Guedalla and the Historical Manuscript Commission's series *The prime ministers' papers*.
The practice below has been to present this material as nearly as possible as Gladstone
wrote it, not, as Morley and other editors have done, as he might have written it if preparing it for publication. This is particularly important with respect to (a) punctuation:
Gladstone quite clearly put inverted commas round direct speech only when he remembered the exact words spoken: there is therefore an important difference between
passages of direct speech in inverted commas and those not in inverted commas.
(b) abbreviations. The expansion of abbreviations, including the allocation of names to
initials (not always self-evident in their identification) gives, together with inserted
punctuation, a quite false, over-polished, impression of the often rough-hewn fragments which Gladstone left.

[3] See introduction above, iii. xxxiii.

each of those stately fabrics is mirrored in the windows of the other, and it may occur to him, with horror and amusement, according to his temper, that those mutual reflections of images set up in rank antagonism to one another, constitute a kind of parable, that offers to us its meaning as we read with conscience and intelligence the history of the time.[1]

The Peelites found themselves standing in the street, exiles from one club, fearful to join the other, though willing to visit it.

Thus while there was a tendency to cooperation with the liberal party, as in 1852, when, as Gladstone told Aberdeen in 1857, 'the act was done, which would probably have led to a real & final amalgamation with the Liberal party',[2] there was also a tendency to reunion with the mass of the conservatives who appeared to have abandoned the fiscal views which after 1846 had made continued cooperation with them impossible.[3]

In his attempt to reassess his notion of a moral organic society, Gladstone had in the late 1840s travelled a very considerable distance in certain aspects of his thought towards a liberal position.[4] His difficulty was that politics had not continued to divide on the question of free trade on which this liberalism was founded, and the national dedication to free trade seemed belied by the later stages of the Crimean war and the disasters of the general election in 1857 in which many of the free trade radicals lost their seats. Foreign policy during Palmerston's government of 1855 to 1858 had certainly not followed what Gladstone regarded as moral policies, and that government had in his view also been misguided in its financial and immoral in its divorce policy.[5] Gladstone thus found it easier to work on some questions with the radicals, on others with the conservatives, but rarely with the whigs.

However, the position of a politician assessing motion by motion on its merits was not congenial to Gladstone's executive turn of mind: 'He must be a very bad minister indeed, who does not do ten times the good to the country when he is in office, that he would do when he is out of it'.[6] The radicals he found irresponsible, in the sense that they were critics with no desire to become actors. He could work with them on specific issues, but they could offer no solution to the question of the execution of policy. Similarly the conservatives, much though he might appreciate Derby's probity, offered no prospect of a satisfactory executive position, for Gladstone believed, very probably rightly, that the Peelites did not constitute a political grouping substantial enough to assist the conservatives to a working majority in the Commons. Moreover, Gladstone found that cooperation with the conservatives on financial matters broke down on the important question of the social implications of different types of taxation,

[1] [W. E. Gladstone], 'The declining efficiency of parliament', *Quarterly Review*, xcix. 562 (September 1856); this important and neglected article, an expansion of Gladstone's letter to Aberdeen (quoted at 13 Mar. 56), written in the light of his memorandum at 16 Feb. 56, gives a clear and revealing account of Gladstone's views about the proper development of British politics.
[2] 31 Mar. 57.   [3] ibid.
[4] See *ante*, iii. xxxff.
[5] See 17 June 57.
[6] *Quarterly Review*, xcix. 530 (September 1856).

an issue which in 1856 raised the question whether the apparent agreement between the Peelites, the radicals and the conservatives on the defects of Cornewall Lewis's financial policy, could in the long term be maintained.[1]

Gladstone had become essentially an executive politician. As he told Samuel Wilberforce in 1857, 'I greatly felt being turned out of office, I saw great things to do. I longed to do them. I am losing the best years of my life out of my natural service . . .'[2] This was by no means a characteristic attitude for a mid-Victorian politician. Even more uncharacteristic was Gladstone's action in drawing up in opposition (in February 1856) a programme of measures to be passed through when next in office.

This programme of twenty one financial measures included, amongst other measures, what became the Exchequer and Audit Act of 1866, the assertion of treasury control over all other departments, a reappraisal of the role and profits of the Bank of England, the abolition of the paper duties, the reduction of the wine, malt, sugar, coffee, insurance and stamp duties, the reform of the taxation system, and a series of technical measures.[3] Where Peel had moved hesitantly and experimentally, Gladstone codified a large but miscellaneous body of fiscal and departmental reforms into a coherent plan for an all-powerful 'ministry of finance', and one which only his formidable political will was likely to be able to translate into legislative and administrative reality.

Not surprisingly, therefore, Gladstone regarded his period of opposition after 1855 as an anomaly to be ended by entry to the cabinet of either a whig-liberal or a conservative administration. Although he does not say so, he must have realised that his choice of party must now be final: he could hardly expect forgiveness from either side a second time. This may well account for his caution. His personal inclination in the period 1855 to 1859 lay on the whole with the conservatives, whom he saw as less capricious than Palmerston; but, apart from Derby and Spencer Walpole, he had little intimacy with conservatives of cabinet rank. The conservatives, for their part, while keen to capture Gladstone, made it clear to him that the extent of demand for office within their own party would leave no room for a general occupancy of senior cabinet posts by the Peelite group.[4]

Gladstone, however, consistently argued that the problem of party after the break-up of the coalition in 1855 could not be solved by men, but by measures. By measures, he meant the fulfilment of the programme of financial reform which he worked out in February 1856. Other Peelites, however, without exception worked to push him away from Derby and appear on several occasions to have exercised at least a decisive negative influence upon him. His failure to join Derby in 1858 was crucial, for, if he was again to hold office, there was no alternative left for him but to join the government of 1859, consequent upon the overthrow of the Derby cabinet.

[1] Gladstone's argument (see 13 Mar. 56) that finance benefited from having the conservatives in office because the liberals were more effective retrenchers when in opposition hardly offered a long-term solution.
[2] Wilberforce, ii. 349; Gladstone added that this did not outweigh his relief not to be in office with Palmerston.
[3] 16 and 20 Feb. 56.   [4] 17 and 26 Apr. 56.

The Ionian Islands commissionership extraordinary, held by Gladstone in 1858–9 at the request of the conservative government, was not from his point of view a move towards the tories, though it was so intended by them.[1] Gladstone had never, by his votes or speeches in the 1850s, hidden his view that the conservatives deserved respect and, when possible, support. Though accepting the position from a conservative ministry might seem to suggest a movement towards holding domestic office in that ministry, this was not the consequence seen by Gladstone's subtle mind. In Gladstone's analysis of the political situation it added nothing and subtracted nothing: it did not involve the Peelites as a group, and it did not involve 'measures'. If he had found insufficient reason to join the Derby ministry at its outset, there was no further reason to contemplate joining later, for the life of the ministry was agreed by all to be certain to be short. The Ionian interlude is certainly of interest, but not in the party political context; it will be discussed later in this introduction.

There was also 'the difficulty of Disraeli', by the late 1850s firmly established as the leading conservative in the Commons and the probable Leader of the House in any conservative ministry. As Sir James Graham said to Gladstone, the Peelites could not expect Derby to throw Disraeli away 'like a sucked orange'.[2] Gladstone personally felt 'unable to enter into any squabble or competition with him for the possession of a post of prominence'.[3] To join with Disraeli was, in the Peelites' view, to place political morality at the service of chicanery, though in Gladstone's opinion Palmerston was not much better, having 'dishonour as the great characteristic of [his] Government'.[4]

By biding his time and accepting Peelite cautions against conservatism, Gladstone solved the problem by elimination. Always reluctant to admit the role of ambition in politics, Gladstone was nonetheless aware of his abilities and their lack of application since 1855; his entry to Palmerston's cabinet in 1859 thus involved no great moral choice and produced no great passage of self-analysis in the diary.[5] It was the hard-headed response of an able politician with a programme for action, invited to join a cabinet at the outset of its formation.[6] In discussing political contingencies in 1856

[1] And seen as such: see Hayward's report of Carnarvon; see H. E. Carlisle, *A selection from the correspondence of Abraham Hayward* (1886), ii. 14.
[2] 14 Feb. 57.   [3] ibid.
[4] Gladstone to W. Whitwell Elwin, 27 March 1857, NLS 2262, f.66.
[5] The aftermath of the general election of April–May 1859 did, however, occasion one night of self-flagellation (25 May 59) and a half-sleepless night (3 June 59).
[6] Palmerston had been confident Gladstone would join, and hopeful that he could be kept out of the Exchequer. On 30 March 1859 he had listed Gladstone for the Colonial Office, as he also did on an undated list, and for the India Office on another (undated) list. On these lists he had put Lewis down for the Exchequer (Broadlands MS GMG/136 and 138). But Gladstone apparently saw Palmerston, knowing that Lewis would cede the Exchequer to him; see A. Hayward (to his sisters, 16 June 1859) *Correspondence* (1886) ii. 34: 'It was through me that Sir George Lewis communicated to Gladstone his readiness to give up the Chancellorship of the Exchequer to him if he wished and it was I who first told Lord Palmerston that Gladstone would join.' This is probably the meeting recorded by Gladstone on 2 June 59, i.e. before the vote of 10 June which felled Derby's government, in which Gladstone voted against the motion of want of confidence. Gladstone told Herbert he would only have accepted the Exchequer; see 13 June 59.

with Heathcote, a conservative and his colleague as M.P. for Oxford University, Gladstone remarked:

> That as to union, it was quite impossible to treat it as a matter of mere choice or will: whether it were a question of rejoining our late colleagues, or any other persons, our proceeding to be warrantable, must be founded on convictions of the public interest & on community of views evinced to the world by co-operation on great questions of the day which as they arose would speak for themselves & would open the path of duty.[1]

Robertson Gladstone, the diarist's brother and a leader of radicalism in Liverpool, put the political point more directly:

> No one, who knows you, if he ever thinks, can suppose, that you would coalesce with D'Israeli: when *you* join with another, that move, we know, will have some sort of principle, at least, to boast of.[2]

Italy was, or could be made to seem, such a question in 1859. But in the general context of Gladstone's position in the years after 1855, of his failure to find a similar basis for cooperation with the conservatives despite his violent and publicly voiced hostility to whig foreign policy, of his persistently expressed criticisms of the financial policies of successive governments, of his own solution to financial ills, and of his demand in 1859 for the exchequer alone,[3] it is hard to see Italy as more than a convenient issue on which to combine with the whigs on their own ground of foreign policy. This is not to say that Gladstone was using the Italian question deceitfully: he undoubtedly believed in the policy to which in the latter part of 1859 he contributed, but he can hardly have seen Italy as the basis for a government, and it did not figure in the list of public questions which he believed in 1857 to be of primary parliamentary significance.[4]

Gladstone's visit to Venetia and Piedmont in the spring of 1859 on his way back from the Ionian islands undoubtedly quickened his interest in the subject,[5] though his view of what should happen there was largely negative and even anti-Piedmontian: Austria should be removed, but not to Piedmont's advantage, and the temporal power of the Pope diminished.[6] Despite his opportunities, Gladstone did not much encourage the Italianate sympathies of the English radicals, with their republican overtones, and his behaviour during Garibaldi's visit to England in 1864 can only be described as shuffling.[7]

---

[1] 17 Apr. 56.
[2] R. Gladstone to W. E. Gladstone, 20 October 1855, Add MS 56445, nf.
[3] See 13 June 59n.
[4] 31 Mar. 57.
[5] See 23 Feb.–4 Mar. 59.
[6] 30 June 59.
[7] See April 64, especially 17 Apr. 64 which shows that, despite his later claims, Gladstone played an important part in persuading Garibaldi to abandon his planned provincial tour. Gladstone to Clarendon, 23 April 1864, Bodleian Clarendon dep. c. 523, shows the extent of Gladstone's involvement in persuading Garibaldi of the cabinet's embarrassment at his presence in Britain.

Appalling though Gladstone believed Palmerston's policies to have been between 1855 and 1858, their direction had advantages from his point of view. Gladstone argued that Palmerston's

> stock in trade as a Peace Minister was wholly inadequate, or rather nearly null. It followed that he could only be a Peace Minister by keeping alive the passions, maintaining the sentences, and thus ever walking on the giddy brink of war.[1]

But, to last, a peace-time government must offer more than this; it must offer a substantial programme of domestic legislation. This Gladstone could provide. There was 'a policy going a'begging', already prepared in some detail, which could provide the basis for the domestic programme of the government. A prime minister whose chief interest was bound to be in the area of foreign policy could have advantages for a chancellor of the exchequer with his own programme of legislation, and a programme it was. Gladstone as chancellor between 1859 and 1866 introduced step by step, the items of the programme he had drawn up in 1856, the last item, the Exchequer and Audit Act, being passed shortly before the government resigned in 1866. This was a remarkable, perhaps unique, achievement in Victorian politics, and one which showed that, at least for Gladstone, the construction of policy could be something more than the accidental product of the politics of personality.

Gladstone was chancellor of the exchequer from June 1859 until July 1866, the longest continuous tenure between Vansittart and Lloyd George.[2] Naturally exchequer business bulks large in the diaries, though not in a coherent or reflective form. It may be useful, therefore to set out the chief aims and activities of Gladstone's chancellorship, with some reference to his earlier tenure from 1852 to 1855, the end of which is covered in the early part of volume V.

A Victorian chancellor was not much troubled by the sort of crises characteristic of British history since 1914; the only peace-time occasion on which Gladstone had to act unexpectedly was the 1866 financial crisis caused by the failure of Overend and Gurney's bank,[3] and even this was, from the chancellor's point of view, intrusive only for a weekend: 'Although the case was perplexing at the onset, & will be so in the *hereafter*, yet when we obtained the facts of the operations of the day our course became at once perfectly clear.'[4] For the most part the chancellor was concerned with strategy, with the construction of an efficient 'Ministry of Finance',[5] as Gladstone usually called it, and with the measured preparation of the annual budget. This pattern was disturbed only by the spasmodic need for extra revenue for imperial exploits, and by sudden calls for extra domestic defence expenditure through last minute changes in the departmental

[1] *Quarterly Review*, civ. 522 (October 1858).
[2] Gladstone beat Hicks Beach (1895–1902) by five days, and was beaten by Lloyd George (1908–15) by a month.
[3] See 11 May 66.
[4] 11 May 66.
[5] See his legislative programme at 20 Feb. 56.

estimates. As chancellor, Gladstone was rarely involved in the day-to-day activities of the treasury. The sort of detailed work which at the board of trade he had done himself, such as the day-to-day correspondence with other departments, was the responsibility of the financial secretary to the treasury. It would seem that Gladstone involved himself more in departmental matters than most chancellors,[1] but even this involvement was chiefly in the area of contract negotiations, especially as they affected overseas communications, for example the Red Sea telegraph and the Galway packet contract for postal communication with North America.[2]

Gladstone usually drew up the heads of his spring budget the previous Christmas,[3] at Hawarden, and without any reference to the treasury. On one occasion he began earlier, in August: 'I dreamt of the next Estimates: with a dour sense of the work I have to do.'[4] He would then request information from the various departments, such as the board of inland revenue and the national debt commissions, about the likely effect on revenue of changes in taxation which he contemplated introducing. He did not consult the treasury or the departments on questions of policy, but merely on administration, nor did the treasury or the departments propose policy changes to him. Least of all did he involve his cabinet colleagues. As he told Cornewall Lewis when Lewis succeeded him as chancellor in 1855: 'I advised him to keep his own Counsel & let the Cabinet as a whole not know his plans till his mind was made up in the main, & the time close at hand'.[5]

As chancellor, therefore, Gladstone acted independently. He also acted aggressively. His years at the treasury coincided with reform of that institution from within which Gladstone both shared in and encouraged.[6] The treasury was asserting its right to control the activities and personnel of the civil service as a whole; Gladstone asserted the political position of the chancellor in cabinet, in parliament and hence in the country generally. Hitherto the exchequer had either been held by a man of importance, but not of the first importance, or by the first lord of the treasury himself. Peel had between 1841 to 1846 used Goulburn more as a financial secretary than a chancellor, and had prepared and introduced budgets almost without reference to his chancellor. Whig chancellors had been second rank men without aspirations to real power. Disraeli had been the first chancellor also to be the obvious second man in the government.

By deliberately asserting the overall suzerainty of the treasury, Gladstone not surprisingly clashed with the spending departments, particularly the admiralty and the war office, for army and navy estimates constituted 43% of all government spending in 1861. In the cabinet battles of the early 1860s, Gladstone tried to force the defence departments to work

---

[1] See J. W. Cell, *British colonial administration in the mid-nineteenth century* (1970), ch. vii.
[2] See ibid. and 17 Nov. 62 etc.
[3] See 1 Jan. 63, 9 Jan. 65.
[4] 10 Aug. 64.
[5] 3 Mar. 55.
[6] See M. Wright, *Treasury control of the civil service, 1854–1874* (1969).

within the treasury's framework of taxation reform; that is, he appeared to give priority over imperial considerations to a financial programme of mainly domestic political importance. But this was to a considerable extent only appearance. Because Gladstone could not decide whether spending on imperialism was chronic or merely spasmodic, he failed to develop a policy to deal with it, save the negative one of making colonies of predominantly European settlement pay for their own defence.[1] Thus he found himself treating each imperial crisis in non-white areas separately and in its own terms only, and, as each imperial action could be made to seem plausible, Gladstone, as Cobden so often complained, found himself raising funds for imperialism as effectively as any whig or tory. The other contentious item was the plan to fortify the Southern coast against French invasion. Here Gladstone had an alternative policy: the French commercial treaty, and on this question time proved him right. The fact that the war secretary was his close and already ailing friend, Sidney Herbert, made no difference to Gladstone, who relentlessly exposed Herbert to a full-scale battle by correspondence. But Herbert had behind him the duke of Somerset, first lord of the admiralty, and, more important, Palmerston, one of the very few men who could equal Gladstone in political stamina.

Gladstone pressed his hostility to the brink of resignation, but not over it. 'My resignation *all but* settled': the significance lay in the italics.[2] Gladstone, unlike Randolph Churchill in 1886, never offered resignation formally. Moreover Palmerston, unlike Salisbury with Churchill, did not wish him to go, and went to considerable lengths to keep him in the cabinet, the duke of Argyll acting as mediator.[3] In these protracted struggles, each side convinced itself that it had won at least the odd battle.[4] In the sense that imperialism was paid for and some of the fortifications built, the admiralty and war office gained most of their objectives. Gladstone pressed through the French treaty and, eventually, the repeal of the paper duties. He gained politically what he lost fiscally, and, by not resigning, remained to realise the programme of treasury control which, if unsuccessful in the short term of the 1860s, in the long term seemed to triumph.

Gladstone aggressively and consistently politicized the chancellorship, through the preparation and prosecution of budgets. In 1853 he immediately established almost complete independence from his old department, the board of trade, remembering perhaps the way it had, under his direction, influenced budgetary preparation in the 1840s. The 1853 and 1860 budgets were of course in large measure tariff budgets, but in their preparation the board of trade was consulted merely on technicalities.

The 1860 French treaty, a central feature of that year's budget, was negotiated almost independently of the foreign office, and largely independently of the cabinet. The 1860 treaty was a quite deliberate interference in whig foreign policy. It was presented politically as a further step

[1] In practical terms this meant Canada; see 14 Dec. 61, 10 Apr. 62, May–June 64, 20 Jan. 65 etc.
[2] 2 June 60.   [3] 4 June 60.
[4] See the amusing juxtapositions at 21 July 60n.

towards free trade, though technically it was a reciprocity treaty and criticised as such by some theoretical free traders. Its financial importance was
chiefly confined to its effect on the English silk and glove trades, and to
Gladstone's plan to solve the drink problem by creating a nation of wine
drinkers consuming their cheap 'Gladstone claret', as it came to be called,
in decorous cafés which paid their licence fees to the government, instead
of in public houses under the licence of local and often independently minded
magistrates.[1] The French treaty was the first of several such treaties in the
1860s, but it was the only one to which Gladstone attached much political
importance.[2] To counter whig suspicions of France and the consequent
construction of massive fortifications along the English south coast, Gladstone was determined to get a commercial treaty with France, at almost
any cost. He told Cobden, who negotiated the treaty in Paris, of

> . . . the great aim—the moral and political significance of the act, and its
> probable and desired fruit in binding the two countries together by interest
> and affection.[3]

> Neither you nor I attach for the moment any superlative value to this Treaty
> for the sake of the extension of British trade . . . What I look to is the social
> good, the benefit to the relations of the two countries, and the effect on the
> peace of Europe.[4]

Similarly the repeal of the paper duties in 1860 and 1861, involving the
first major institutional row between the two Houses of Parliament since
1832, deliberately allied the chancellor with political radicalism. Both
Gladstone's most famous budgets, of 1853 and 1860, were pressed through
an unwilling cabinet. Gladstone's finesse in getting eventual cabinet acceptance for his 1853 budget has been referred to in an earlier volume.[5] In 1860,
on the paper duties question, Gladstone was only supported by
Gibson and Argyll in the cabinet, and in 1861 only by Gibson, yet he was
eventually able to prevail.[6] Moreover, since it became quite clear from the
press, and from the behaviour of Palmerston in parliamentary debates,[7]
that paper duty repeal was at cabinet level very much Gladstone's own
policy, the political advantages to Gladstone of the eventual success of the
repeal and of the outflanking of the House of Lords were all the greater.
    Much of Gladstone's work as chancellor was self-consciously in the
tradition of Peel, but it was executed in a political style more dramatic,
more rhetorical and less discreet than the Peelite reforms of the 1840s.
This was not accidental or merely the result of personal differences. Gladstone believed that big bills and budgets were a necessary feature not

---

[1] See Harrison, *Drink and the Victorians*, 248ff. I am obliged to Dr. Harrison for showing me his unpublished paper on this subject.
[2] See 13 Feb., 13 Nov. 65.
[3] Gladstone to Cobden, 26 November 1859; Add MS 44135, f. 60.
[4] ibid., 10 January 1860; Add MS 44135, f. 167.
[5] See above, iii. xl.
[6] See 2 July 60n. and 11–13 Apr. 61.
[7] 30 May 61n.

merely of executive government but of post-1832 politics. He attacked
Macaulay for articulating the eighteenth–century view that it was not the
function of the executive persistently to initiate legislation,[1] and he denounced Palmerston between 1855 and 1858 for acting like the eighteenth–
century duke of Newcastle—a domestic programme of quiescence designed
to placate placemen.

This was therefore not merely the Pitt-Peel argument that there were
reforms to be done and abuses to be remedied, but a much more political
argument that it was politically essential that reforms should persistently
be seen to be done, for 'it is rapid growth in the body politic that renders
stereotyped law intolerable.' 'Public opinion,' Gladstone argued, 'is disposed to view with great favour all active and efficient government.'[2] In
this sense Gladstone's chancellorships represented the politicization of
Peelism. For Gladstone, therefore, big bills and big budgets[3] represented a
means of regular renewal of the legitimacy of Parliament and the political
system; for Palmerston and the whigs they represented a continuous threat
to stability and moderation.

Gladstone's programme of legislation was, as has been mentioned above,
set out in 1856 and carried through between 1859 and 1866. Its aim was the
construction of an independent and controlling treasury, represented at
cabinet level by a powerful 'minister of finance', supported in the legislature
by annual inquiry through the Public Accounts Committee, set up in 1861,
and by a House of Commons dedicated to vigilance.

Gladstone is well known for his phrase that money should 'fructify in
the pockets of the people', but what he actually meant was that it should
fructify in the deposit vaults of the National Debt Commissioners. Much
though he extolled the virtues of self-help, his actions as chancellor were
consistently *étatist*.[4] While Gladstone often used pluralist free trade arguments to justify the use of exchange as an impartial arbiter of social
morality,[5] in practice as chancellor he often returned to the organic, almost
corporatist view of the State which he had set out in his first book. The
aim of his Post Office Savings Banks plan was to give the treasury more
independence from the Bank of England. His Working Class Annuities Act,
passed against strong hostility from the friendly societies, was in direct
competition with them, and denounced by them as quite contrary to the
self-help ethos, but was welcomed by trade unionists anxious to associate
themselves with the State.[6]

The aim of his Country Bank Notes Issue Bill, which had to be withdrawn, was to speed up the working of the issue centralising clauses of the

---

[1] *Quarterly Review*, xcix. 521 (September 1856).   [2] ibid. 567.
[3] Ironically, the Queen, later to be so alarmed by the Gladstonian policy of big bills,
encouraged Gladstone in this direction, telling him in 1859 that a big budget was required; 14 Nov. 59.
[4] Gladstone is aptly compared with Turgot in the compelling essay in J. R. Vincent,
The formation of the liberal party, (1966). His solution to the problem of dockyard prostitution was thoroughgoingly *étatist*; see 18 Feb. 63.
[5] See e.g. 1 Jan. 55.
[6] In practice, the working classes almost completely ignored this offer of govt. annuities.

Bank Charter Act of 1844. But the strengthened Bank of England was to make less money from its role as the government's bank, and was to be less firmly entrenched as the pivot of fiscal crisis, for Gladstone contemplated a radical alteration to the 1844 Bank Act, by which an issue of Bonds, controlled by the Treasury, would expand the money supply in times of crisis, controlled by an ever increasing rate of interest. The failure of the Country Notes Bill showed the strength of the lobby for the existing banking system[1], and the plan for the revision of the 1844 Act, also strongly opposed within the treasury, never became more than a privately canvassed proposal.

Gladstone's mistrust of the existing banking system stemmed from his experiences after his wife's family business had been bankrupted in the fiscal crisis of 1847. Partly as a result of this, partly in keeping with a general change of view characteristic of mid-Victorian Britain, Gladstone came to believe, at least in the 1860s, that market forces could not produce a just society. Moreover, he had never been an out-and-out Ricardian. His youthful Idealist approach to the organic nation had been in direct contrast to Ricardianism and though in the late 1840s he had abandoned as un-workable the view of State-Church relations set out in his first book, he had specifically not forsworn his view of the organic nature of the State.[2]

As chancellor, he compared himself to an architect altering a fine but decaying eighteenth–century mansion to a form fitted for the industrial age, designing the new building, controlling its construction, modifying its form as the years passed.[3] Technically put, the function of the chancellor was to create a model of international free trade and then to interfere at the margin of the domestic economy on grounds of social justice:

> Once security has been taken that an entire society shall not be forced to pay an artificial price to some of its members for their production, we may safely commit the question [of cheapness of goods] to the action of competition among manufacturers, and of what we term the laws of supply and demand. As to the condition of the workpeople, experience has shown, especially in the case of the Factory Acts, that we should do wrong in laying down any abstract maxim as an invariable rule.[4]

But this absence of 'abstract maxim' led in practice to considerable flexi-bility, for

> There is no one, I should imagine—at least I know of none—who thinks that savings banks, or the grant of annuities or assurances for the people, are matters with which it is desirable abstractedly for Government to deal. If it could be said that the operation of the great law of supply and demand is generally satisfactory and sufficient, and that the failures which occur are incidental to the principles on which commerce must be conducted, that would merely be a

[1] See 11 May 65.   [2] See above, iii.xxxiv.
[3] Speech to the men of M'Corquodale & Co., Liverpool printers, 22 July 65, in *The Guardian*, 26 July 1865, 775.
[4] Address to the employees of the Wedgwood factory at Burslem, in *Gleanings*, ii. 184; see 26 Oct. 63.

conclusive condemnation, not merely of the law you passed two years ago for Post Office Savings Banks . . . and also of the laws as to the grant of annuities and the old savings banks.[1]

Government interference could be of three kinds:

The highest form in which it has been carried out is that of positive regulations requiring this thing and that thing to be done in the course of private commercial arrangements, for the sake of obviating social, moral or political evils . . the second kind of Government interference . . . has been interference by sheer naked prohibition . . . the third and . . . mildest description of Government interference . . . [is] that by the interference of the Government you enjoin nothing and you prohibit nothing, but you offer to such members of the community as may be disposed to avail themselves of your proposal certain facilities for what I may call self-help.[2]

To permit movement towards freer trade for Britain, Peel's government had in 1842 imposed income tax: a spectacular departure, since the previous income tax had been a war measure, removed with indecent haste and with little concern for a fair balance of taxation, in 1816. At the board of trade in 1842, Gladstone had regretted the imposition of income tax, favouring instead an increase in a different form of direct tax, the house tax.[3] He had not, however, disagreed with Peel's view, that the balance of contributions to government revenue was too far weighted to the disadvantage of the indirect tax payers.

In the arguments about the income tax in the 1850s and 1860s, this concern for the balance between the direct and indirect tax payers had continued to be of central importance, and Gladstone's attempts to remove the income tax must always be seen in the context of that concern. In 1853 his chief aim had been to prevent the existing tax being discredited, as he saw it, by differentiation (that is, the taxation of different forms of income at different rates).

This he had triumphantly done. The Aberdeen coalition, defeated in the Commons three times in the week before the budget in 1853, was not again seriously threatened until the worst days of the Crimean war. Gladstone's budget in 1853 retained the income tax but did not reform it; his 1860 budget confirmed this position.[4] In maintaining the income tax unreformed Gladstone strove to achieve a balance. On the one side, the radicals through the Liverpool Financial Reform Association called for abolition of all indirect taxes and the raising of government revenue only through the income tax, but an income tax differentiated to accommodate the claims of 'precarious' professional income tax payers. On the other side the landed interest favoured indirect taxation and, if there was to be an income tax, one not altered to favour the professions. Gladstone's

---

[1] Speech of 7 March 1864, *H* clxxiii. 1551.
[2] ibid.
[3] See Gladstone to Peel, 4 November 1841, Parker, *Peel*, ii. 502.
[4] In 1856 Gladstone considered replacing the income tax with his 1842 solution, the house tax, a self-regulating graduated tax; see 16 Feb. 56, points 14 and 15.

budgets struck a balance between the two. In 1853 he imposed income tax for seven years (three had previously been the maximum) and by allowing a rebate for life insurance he gave a form of differentiation without actually altering the schedules of the tax.[1] To the opponents of income tax he offered the prospect of its abolition by a sliding scale of reduction by which in 1859 its contribution to the government's revenue would be much less significant.

We may however note that in 1853 the phased reduction of the income tax to permit its abolition in 1860 was hedged about by many conditions. First, it assumed that the *pari passu* reduction and abolition of customs and excise duties would be offset by an increase in consumption by which those duties remaining—especially tea, drink and sugar—would produce more revenue; in other words it assumed at the least no economic recession. Second, it assumed no intervening disaster requiring a large increase in government expenditure. Third, it assumed that the succession duties, another direct tax, imposed for the first time in 1853, would yield substantial amounts. Finally it assumed a diminution of ordinary government expenditure.

It was unlikely that all of these conditions could be met, and they were not met, even if the Crimean war is discounted. Faced in 1860 with continuing the income tax or substantially increasing the burden of indirect taxation as a necessary consequence of repealing the income tax, Gladstone unhesitatingly chose to continue income tax.[2] Throughout the 1850s and 1860s he paid close attention to the social balance of taxation. In the year after the Crimean war, he consistently supported reduction of customs and excise duties. In 1857, during what was potentially the most successful of his various negotiations with the conservative party in these years, he broke off the negotiation rather than give way on this point. In the Commons the difference between them was made clear: Disraeli moved the reduction of the income tax, Gladstone proposed to move the reduction of the tea and sugar duties.[3] Derby told Gladstone that his Resolutions

> not only point distinctly to an infraction of the *implied* engagement that the Income Tax should terminate in 1860 but also to an alteration of its positive enactment during the term of its continuance; and this, not to meet any sudden and unforeseen emergency, but to enable the Government to reduce other Taxes, by again raising the Income Tax to its original amount.[4]

As chancellor of the exchequer the need for a balanced reduction of direct and indirect taxation was one of Gladstone's chief concerns.[5] But since the maintenance of the balance greatly increased the difficulty of abolishing income tax, and since its abolition depended on the substantial reduction of government expenditure, Gladstone determined to increase equally sub-

[1] Professional men with 'precarious' incomes particularly benefited from the insurance exemption.

[2] A third possibility would have been further increases in the succession duties, but this was, at least before the 1867 Reform Act extended the electorate, hardly possible politically.

[3] See especially 6 Mar. 57. For Gladstone's resolutions, see Derby MSS Box 135, in care of Lord Blake.

[4] Derby to Gladstone, 11 February 1857, Derby MSS Box 135.

[5] See, for example, 21 Mar. 63, 22 Apr. 65.

stantially the number of income tax payers. For he believed that the more persons made to pay the tax, the greater would be the demand for the reduction in expenditure which would permit its eventual abolition. His budget in 1853, therefore, reduced from £150 to £100 the amount at which incomes became liable to pay the tax, a drop which doubled the number of income tax payers on Schedule D. The £100 line was, Gladstone argued, 'the dividing line . . . between the educated and the labouring part of the community'.[1] There was thus intended to be a rough correlation between the income tax payers and the electorate.

The experiences of the 1857 general election,[2] when Gladstone campaigned unsuccessfully on an anti-expenditure basis in Flintshire for his brother-in-law, Sir Stephen Glynne, and when most of the anti-expenditure Radicals lost their seats, and of the long battle with Palmerston and the service ministries over military and naval estimates between 1860 and 1863,[3] showed that the House of Commons as at present constituted, was not an effective check against government expenditure, however many of its electors also paid income tax. Moreover, Gladstone came to see income tax not as the restrainer of expenditure through its unpopularity, but as the creator of expenditure through the ease with which it could be levied, and the predictability of its return.[4]

This left two possibilities: abolish the income tax, or reform the House of Commons. In the winter of 1863, Gladstone toyed with both. The arguments against income tax abolition had been resolved, and the contacts Gladstone had with trade unionist artisans during the preparation of the Government Annuities Bill in the spring of 1864 encouraged him in the view that a moderate increase in the electorate through the addition of articulate artisans would strengthen the economical wing of the liberal party in the House of Commons. Gladstone's 'pale of the constitution' speech of 1864,[5] and his subsequent strict adherence to the £7 level of qualification in the Reform Bill crisis of 1866 and 1867, have therefore to be seen in the context of his views on the role of taxation in politics.

The effect of Disraeli's Reform Acts of 1867–8, which introduced a much wider (if still quite limited) urban franchise than the abortive liberal Reform Bill of 1866 would have allowed, was to remove the basis of the 1860s settlement which Gladstone had helped to create. For the extended franchise of 1867 introduced problems of political communication, organization and policy of a quite new order. Gladstone's franchise proposals of 1866 were designed to consolidate an existing order; Disraeli's destroyed it.

II

Gladstone's budgets represented a compromise and a balance—a settlement in accord with the House of Commons as it was between the first and

---

[1] *H* cxxxvii. 1592 (20 April 1855). [2] 7 and 8 Apr. 57.
[3] See especially May–July 60.
[4] Gladstone to Cobden, 22 December 1863, Add MS 44136, f. 200, hints at this; the income tax's role in promoting expenditure is discussed in the 1864 budget speech, *H* clxxiv. 595.
[5] 11 May 64.

second reform acts. As such, they gave Gladstone a central place in the success of the whig-liberal ministries between 1859 and 1866. They also allowed him to construct a new kind of constituency in the country. Gladstone had no personal political base of the sort normal in post-1832 politics. He could not even get his brother-in-law elected[1] in the small county constituency in which they were together important land and coal-owners. His position in his own university seat—which had no constituency in the normal sense of the word—was increasingly uncertain.

After he joined Palmerston's ministry it was evident that his candidacy at Oxford would always be contested (a contest in a university seat was in itself a grave mark of disfavour)[2] and few doubted it would soon be defeated. In 1860, Gladstone drafted an address stating his intention not to contest the Oxford seat again, though he did not send it.[3] In the early 1860s he rejected a number of offers of alternative seats,[4] though he did not wholly disavow his selection by the liberals for the new, third, seat in South Lancashire, and his candidacy for Oxford in 1865 was, especially after his statement in 1865 on Irish disestablishment,[5] virtually a challenge to the university to throw him out. Gladstone's rejection in 1865, and his famous arrival 'unmuzzled' in Lancashire,[6] dramatised the role of popular politician which he had cultivated during the 1860s with considerable skill. Defeat in a wholly Anglican and largely clerical constituency also made Gladstone's position in the liberal party much simpler. As he told Sir Walter James:

> These good people, my opponents, have been resolved, in their blind antagonism, to *force* me into the confidence of the Liberal party, and it really seems they are succeeding.[7]

It has rightly been emphasised that changes in the nature of national and local politics in the 1850s and 1860s made possible the emergence of a new kind of popular politician.[8] We may notice here, however, Gladstone's own contribution to his success, since his emergence as the chief beneficiary of the changing political order was not accidental.

Gladstone had made himself a national politician in a literal sense. He travelled frequently, widely and conspicuously, and he kept his friendships warm. There were few parts of the mainland of the United Kingdom with which he did not have intimate links and powerful friends.[9]

---

[1] 7, 8 Apr. 57, although he was unapologetically feudal, referring to 'my tenants'; 24 May 61n.

[2] After Gladstone's defeat in 1865, there was no contest for either Oxford university seat at a general election until 1918, and only one at a by-election (1878).

[3] 10 Nov. 60.

[4] Resignation was contemplated from November 1860; see 10 Nov. 60. South Lancashire was discussed from June 61; see 9 June 61. Rothschild offered his city of London seat; this would have meant being harnessed with Russell; see 13 June, 12 July 61.

[5] 28 Mar. 65.

[6] 18 July 65.

[7] Gladstone to Sir W. James, 24 July 1865, Add MS 44535, f. 93.

[8] J. R. Vincent, *The formation of the liberal party* (1966), especially ch. II.

[9] Ireland was of course the exception. A visit contemplated in 1865 came to nothing.

In Scotland the Gladstone family was of course well known. In this period, as rector of Edinburgh University from 1859,[1] Gladstone made annual visits. Appointments to chairs were made jointly by the university and the city corporation under the rector's chairmanship. Gladstone in this capacity made several political friendships, and laid the base to which he returned for the Midlothian Campaign in 1879. He could, and did, remind his audiences of his family's roots in the Borders and Lothians and in the port of Leith.[2] In Glasgow, his stockbroker, Sir James Watson, was a powerful member of the corporation, and soon to be lord provost. In Wales, Gladstone could and did show himself as an important landowner in a rich farming area,[3] an encourager of industrial development in the Dee estuary,[4] a well-known holiday maker[5] and local personality.

In England, Gladstone's areas of contact were numerous. He could tell his Lancastrian audiences of his youth on the sandhills of the Mersey,[6] and almost all his speeches in his Lancastrian campaigns showed local knowledge. In the Midlands his contacts with the duke and duchess of Sutherland,[7] with the earl of Dudley (his creditor in the Oak Farm disaster, also a tractarian friend), his relationship to the Lytteltons of Hagley, and his links with sundry influential local solicitors (many of them started by Oak Farm correspondence but now maintained on a political basis),[8] his experience with Midland capitalists during his arbitrations of railway disputes,[9] all these made him familiar and prominent in the heartland of industrial expansion. In the capital Gladstone was a noted pedestrian by day and night, a trustee of the British Museum and of the National Portrait Gallery, a governor of King's college and of Charterhouse, a founder of the London Library, a commissioner of the 1851 Exhibition, as well as being one of the best known lay Christians in the city, whose appearance in church could of itself abate an anti-ritualist riot.[10]

Such a geographical range of interests might be forced upon a great whig landlord by the accident of heredity. In Gladstone it was present largely by the assiduous nourishment of interests which, not being landed, would otherwise soon have withered. Railways allowed politicians to treat the British mainland as a single political constituency in a way physically impossible in the pre-railway age. But if Gladstone was the beneficiary of this new national political community, it was in large measure because he

[1] See 10–15 Dec. 59, 16 Apr. 60 etc. He was defeated when standing as Chancellor of Edinburgh University in 1868; see 16 May 68n. and 21 Nov. 68n. His proposal (included in a permissive clause of the 1858 Universities (Scotland) Act) that the Scottish universities would use their resources more efficiently if they became colleges of one Scottish National University, was not popular; see 5 July 58.

[2] See e.g. his speech laying the foundation stone of St. James's, Leith, 11 Jan. 62, in *Scottish Ecclesiastical Journal*, supplement, xii. 2.

[3] Chester Agricultural Show, 21–2 July 58; 11 Dec. 56.

[4] 15 Oct. 57, 6 Aug. 63.

[5] See section III of this introduction.

[6] Speech at Bootle, 13 Nov. 68, quoted in W. E. Williams, *The rise of Gladstone to the leadership of the liberal party, 1859–68* (1934), 169.

[7] See 8 Dec. 60.

[8] For example W. B. Collis of Stourbridge.

[9] See 6 Jan., 22 Apr., 13 July, 7 Dec. 57.

[10] 14 Oct. 60.

imposed himself upon public attention not merely in the metropolis, but also at many points on the periphery.

The nurturing of these regional acquaintances could encourage an impression of national reputation, but it could not bring that reputation to influence the practicalities of power. This could be done more directly first by the impact of things done at the periphery upon Westminster politics, second by astute use of the press, third by the control and demonstration of executive power. These three prerequisites of Gladstone's political success will now be discussed.

Gladstone's use of extra-parliamentary speech-making, dormant in the late 1850s save for addresses to societies such as the Society for the Propagation of the Gospel, was recommenced in 1862 with tours of Lancashire and Tyneside.[1] Public orations increased his reputation in the regions in which he spoke, in the newspaper reading nation as a whole through verbatim reports of his speeches, and at Westminster, for one result of his platform speeches was to emphasise his separation from the conventional whiggery of the rest of the ministry's leadership. The extent of Gladstone's platform activities of the 1860s should not be exaggerated —he turned down many more invitations to speak than he accepted[2]—but they were large in comparison with his previous platform appearances, with his ministerial colleagues, and with his own behaviour as prime minister in his first ministry. By these speeches Gladstone, hitherto known mainly at Westminster, at Court and amongst the intelligentsia, became a national figure, a household name among the middle class families which attended the meetings or, a far larger number, read the six columns of closely set type, reporting the speech in the morning newspapers.

Gladstone's relationship with the middle classes in the provinces, and also with the working classes, is to be seen, from his point of view, primarily in terms of his fiscal strategy. He visited factories and he marvelled at the achievement of the middle class: he hoped Samuel Smiles would write his father's biography.[3] Similarly he assessed groups of working people according to the extent to which they complemented and buttressed that strategy, which to a considerable degree they did.

Viewed *en masse*, Gladstone found the working classes amorphous, obscure in their tendencies and potentially dangerous. He noted on Harrison Ainsworth's historical novel: 'Finished that singular and for the masses dangerous book Jack Sheppard',[4] and just after the débâcle of the Reform Bill in 1866 George Eliot's reconstruction of the riots in 1832 disconcerted him: 'Finished Felix Holt: a most inharmonious book. It jars and discomposes me.'[5] But when 'the masses' were presented to him in an organized and particularized form, his reaction was almost always enthusiastic.

As chancellor, Gladstone received deputations from working people.[6]

[1] See 21–24 Apr., 6–9 Oct. 62.
[2] For an important example, see 28 Apr. 67. See also 16, 19 July 61n., 20 Nov. 62n., 21 Mar. 65n., 2 July 66.
[3] 19 Apr. 60. Nothing came of this.   [4] 11 Sept. 61.   [5] 7 Aug. 66.
[6] Another important source of contact with London artizans were the exhibitions organized by Newman Hall and patronized by Gladstone; see 31 Mar. 64.

As is well known, these deputations had a considerable effect upon his views on working class 'responsibility'. What is rarely emphasised is that these were trade union deputations. In particular, the trade unions requested the privilege of using the new Post Office Savings Banks, a concession expressly conceded,[1] and in 1864 the well known deputation in favour of the Annuities Bill, which spurred Gladstone to his 'pale of the constitution' speech, was a deputation from the 'Junta' offering the support of the new unionism for the government's proposals.[2]

The consequence of this was that, when in 1867 and 1868 trade unionism became a question of primarily political discussion, Gladstone defended the 'Junta' as being a useful adjunct to the consolidation of the 1860s economic settlement. In an important speech opening a Mechanics Institute in Oldham in 1867 he declared himself not hostile to the right to strike and while arguing an orthodox Millite view of the wages fund, he did not 'deny, in principle, that it is perfectly fair, as an economical question, for the labouring man to get as good a share of it as he can'.[3] In saying this, Gladstone placed himself in an advanced position in the intense debate about the labour question in the late 1860s. But he did so believing that the 'Junta' and its moderate policy represented the likely development of the trade union movement; he rejected the more extreme demands of George Potter when Potter led a deputation hostile to what he saw as the moderation of the Oldham speech,[4] and in his contacts with working class support for the 1866 Reform Bill, he declined contact with the Potter faction.[5]

Gladstone confirmed his advanced position and his optimistic view of union moderation when he was chairman of a remarkable meeting of the National Association for the Promotion of Social Science in July 1868. At this meeting he stated his conclusion reached through his contacts with those of the 'Junta' who favoured cooperation rather than confrontation with capitalism: 'Experience convinces me that with respect to those from whom perhaps we might anticipate the greatest difficulties, viz. the artisans

[1] See S. and B. Webb, *The history of trade unionism* (1902 ed.), 245. An echo of this request is to be found in the only 'fancy franchise' of the Liberal Reform Bill of 1866— a right of registration for holders of a savings bank account of £50 for two years, in lieu of qualification through the property qualification; this would chiefly assist those in the counties whose houses were under the £14 qualification; see *H* clxxxii. 31 (12 March 1866).

[2] Characteristically, Morley describes the 'Junta' deputation merely as 'a deputation of workmen'; Morley, ii. 125. The 'Junta's' support for the Bill was bitterly denounced by Potter, who was in turn disavowed by the London Trades Council; see Webb, op. cit., 230.

[3] Gladstone in Oldham, *Daily Telegraph*, 19 December 1867, 2. On the other hand, Gladstone also argued that the capitalist should improve his machinery and 'make himself independent of those who resort to strikes', thus anticipating the 1871 Criminal Law Amendment Act. He also opposed 'restraint in industry' and restrictions on piece work.

[4] Gladstone told Potter that the employer's right of dismissal was 'a natural mode . . . of self defence in that friendly strife which must always go on between the capitalist and the labourer'; see 15 and 18 Feb. 68 and *The Times*, 19 February 1868, 10. See also Gladstone to G. Potter, 6 January 1868, in *Daily Telegraph*, 15 January 1868, 2b.

[5] See 2 July 66.

and skilled labourers of this country, we have only to approach these in the right way, in order to find them thoroughly amenable to reason.'[1]

Gladstone's call, therefore, was for working people's allegiance to the economic order of a marginally modified free trade society. Working class movements that buttressed that order he encouraged, those that challenged it he disparaged. Thus he approved of cooperative ownership, because 'in the cooperative mill the operative becomes a capitalist', but the cooperative store could be commended only insofar as it encouraged a more competitive retail system, for the existence of the cooperative store could only be 'indicative of some defect, removal of which would restore things to their natural course' of capitalist entrepreneurship.[2]

The great tours of Tyneside and Lancashire[3] were celebrations of achievements, not campaigns for a better future: free trade, the French Treaty, the repeal of the paper duties, these were the themes of speeches which were already by 1868 retrospective. Criticism was confined to government expenditure, and the need for the new electorate to reduce it. As we have seen, Gladstone's call for reform in 1866 was for a carefully limited addition of frugally minded artisans to the franchise. Frustrated in this, he attempted to enroll the household suffrage of 1867 under the same colours: 'There are those who tell us that a Parliament more highly popularised would become more extravagant than Parliaments resting upon a more limited suffrage. It depends upon you to falsify that adverse prediction (Cheers)'.[4]

The 'Cheers' may have caused a moment of optimism in the ex-chancellor's mind, but it was not to last. Gladstone believed that the extension of the franchise to thinking and articulate artisans would force the Commons to reduce expenditure; Cobden had likewise believed that it would reduce militarism. But the experiment was never tried, and Gladstone soon found after 1867 that appeals to frugality were incompatible with the *étatist* measures which as chancellor in the 1860s he had begun to introduce. His appointment of the rigidly orthodox Robert Lowe as his chancellor of the exchequer in 1868 suggests that he had already made his choice in favour of frugality.

'God knows I have not courted them: I hope I do not rely on them' recorded Gladstone after a Lancastrian tour in 1864.[5] But the courting lay in the very existence of the tours. Many contemporaries supposed that the novelty of Gladstone's electioneering must also involve a novelty of message to the electorate. In fact Gladstone consistently used such occasions as an

[1] See 4 July 68; the remarkable assembly, in addition to 'advanced' employers such as A. J. Mundella and T. Brassey, included John Ruskin, W. Allen, R. Applegarth, Frederick Harrison, J. G. Holyoake, Lloyd Jones, and J. M. Ludlow; the meeting was to set up a cttee., of which Gladstone was elected chairman, 'to diffuse information as to the natural laws regulating the rate of wages and the demand for and supply of labour, and to promote industrial partnership and the formation of courts of conciliation'.
[2] Gladstone in Oldham, *Daily Telegraph*, 19 December 1867, 2.
[3] See Oct. 62, Oct. 64 etc.
[4] Gladstone in Werneth, *Daily Telegraph*, 19 December 1867, 2.
[5] 14 Oct. 64. Gladstone had reflected on the relationship of leadership to oratory; see quotation on flyleaf of diary at 1 May 62.

appeal for support for an already existing order;[1] only three times did he appeal for popular support for a novelty: in 1862, 1866 and 1867.

In 1862 on his visit to Newcastle he made his famous claim that the Confederate leaders had 'made a nation'. [2] Much repented later, this claim was both premeditated and popular. Gladstone had used the same phrase three weeks before in a letter to Arthur Gordon,[3] and the same sentiments, less dramatically expressed, in a speech in Manchester in April.[4] The speech was well received in Newcastle; Gladstone's view was not as heretical in liberal and northern circles as was subsequently made out.[5] If Gladstone's aim in making this speech was to use extra-parliamentary oratory to force the cabinet into recognition of the confederacy, it was unsuccessful.

In 1866 Gladstone appealed for popular support for reform, but for reform as expressed in the very limited Bill with the £7 limit. Even so, extra-parliamentary oratory had little effect on the Adullamites.[6] Gladstone, though offered many opportunities, declined the next logical step, public collaboration with the Reform League.[7]

In 1867, in his speech at Southport, he raised the general questions of Irish land and the Irish Church, but with no specific proposals, no personal commitment save by implication, but with an appeal for popular involvement and awareness: 'Ireland is at your doors. Providence placed her there; law and Legislature have made a compact between you; you must face these obligations: you must deal with them and discharge them.'[8] The Southport speech and its exhortation suggested a departure from a mere appeal for consolidation but its consequences are not to be found in the pages of these volumes. Radical activity in the 1860s consisted chiefly of groups appealing for inclusion in the working of the political community. It was such groups that Gladstone addressed; it is not therefore surprising that his consolidatory appeals met so enthusiastic a response. It was his aim to encourage the disaffected Irish to behave similarly: 'What we want is that those sympathies in Ireland which now hang and float bewildered between law and lawlessness shall be brought into active alliance with it.'[9]

Consolidatory though Gladstone's public appeal might be, his enunciation of it on platforms in industrial towns in vast speeches, nationally reported, created an unprecedented focus of popular interest in an executive politician, which in turn gave him in a parliamentary context a patina of strangeness, even of menace. As yet Gladstone had not tried to use his

[1] The 1868 election campaign was retrospective, in the sense that it requested popular support for an Irish Church policy already approved by the House of Commons.
[2] 7 Oct. 62.
[3] '. . . it has long been (I think) clear that Secession is virtually an established fact & that Jeff. Davis & his comrades have made a nation.' Gladstone to Gordon, 22 September 1862, in *T.A.P.S.* n.s. li part 4, 41. The diary at 30 July 62 shows Gladstone offering cabinet confederate views without disclosing them as such; see also 7, 18 July 62.
[4] 24 Apr. 62.
[5] M. Ellison, *Support for secession: Lancashire and the American civil war* (1972), *passim*, especially pp. 116, 126–7, 207. For Gladstone's subsequent interview with Spence, the confederate agent, see 15 Oct. 62.
[6] 5 and 6 Apr. 66.   [7] 2 July 66.
[8] Gladstone in Southport, *Daily Telegraph*, 20 December 1867, 3.
[9] ibid.

popular following against the Commons; but the threat existed, exemplified in the London crowds which followed him daily in the streets during the 1866 debates, that he might do so.

A further result of these speeches may be noted. They were the chief means by which free trade, for long associated with radicalism and in a vaguer way with whiggery, became an absolute article of faith for the liberal party as a whole. It has been argued that the liberal party was made up of groups whose chief point of identification was religious or parochial, that liberalism was not an exact creed and that most liberal M.P.s were not much more than men of good will.[1] Nonetheless, the 1860s was the decade in which the liberal party moved from being the party amongst which free traders were most likely to be found, to being the chief free trade party in European politics, with an absolute commitment to the doctrine which survived as the article of party faith virtually unchallenged until 1929.

Through Gladstone's chancellorships free trade became an administrative reality, but also something much more remarkable, for through his oratory the creed of the Cobdenites became the orthodoxy of the electorate. Further, the years of Gladstone's chancellorships came to be generally regarded as 'normal' years, the point of reference by which subsequent decades in the period before 1914 were measured. The early 1860s represented for the nineteenth century, as the 1950s did for the twentieth, the period in which the British economy behaved 'naturally', the years in which capitalism seemed to have created a balanced society.

Public appreciation of Gladstone as a new kind of executive politician had depended greatly on the rapidly expanding provincial and metropolitan daily press. Gladstone's awareness and use of the newspaper press was much more acute than has hitherto been allowed. He was of course the benefactor of the popular quality provincial and London dailies by his repeal of the paper duties in 1861, which made possible the development of the penny press. He exploited this advantage deliberately. When J. A. Froude wrote in 1861 to criticize Gladstone's handling of the press, he replied:

> The whole subject of working through the press for the support of the measures of the financial departments is very new to me: I have commonly been too much absorbed in the business of the offices I have held to consider as much as I ought of the modes in which my proceedings or those of others could be commended favourably to the public notice. I will with your permission bear the subject in mind.[2]

Gladstone found a remedy with little difficulty. The chief London paper to benefit from the repeal of the 'taxes on knowledge' was the *Daily Telegraph*, owned by the Levy-Lawson family. Virtually restarted as a penny daily in 1855, it had reached a circulation of nearly 200,000 by 1871, far outdistancing *The Times*.[3] Gladstone had come in contact in 1860 with one of

---

[1] See Vincent, op. cit., *passim*.

[2] Gladstone to J. A. Froude, 16 February 1861, Add MS 44531, f. 121.

[3] See A. P. Wadsworth, 'Newspaper circulations, 1800–1954', *Manchester Statistical Society Transactions*, 1954. The *Telegraph* withdrew its support from Gladstone over the Eastern question in the 1870s.

its reporters, Thornton Leigh Hunt,[1] son of the essayist, J. H. Leigh Hunt. In 1861 they corresponded on the paper duty repeal.[2] By 1862 Gladstone was helping Hunt gain access to details about the Ecclesiastical Commissioners, and a spasmodic but substantial flow of information passed from Gladstone to Hunt during the later years of Palmerston's government. In 1865, for example, Gladstone sent papers on the annuities legislation with encouragement to write on it, but with instructions about not disclosing the name of Scudamore, the source of the information.[3] Hunt organised at Gladstone's request an Irish visit in 1866 by the oldest Gladstone boy, Willy,[4] as a result of which some of Willy's articles on Ireland were published in the *Telegraph*.[5]

During the reform bill crisis, Hunt's name is very frequently mentioned in the diary, as it is during the Irish Church resolutions and Church rate debates in 1868.[6] The *Telegraph* was a strong supporter of Gladstone through the crises of the 1860s, and this appears to have been largely encouraged by his links with Hunt; certainly there is little evidence of contact with its proprietors.[7]

The *Telegraph*'s view that Gladstone was the coming man was persistently pressed from at least 1862 onwards:

> We have enshrined Free Trade at last in a permanent act . . . The time must come, though patriotism wishes it far away, when the failing hand of the Premier will relinquish the helm of state. It would be ill for England, in prospect of such a day, if she had not one pilot at least to whom she could look with proud and happy confidence. She can, she does, so look to Mr. GLADSTONE, because in all a long career of public life he has never swerved from the path of manly and straightforward policy. His words and deeds alike have confuted the fools who hold that statemanship is intrigue, and diplomacy chicanery. His words and deeds have alike confuted the cynics who think religion and morality are well in every place but a Cabinet. In his person it is not only a grand commercial theorem that has been triumphantly vindicated, but the sterling worth of veracity and the irresistible strength of honour.[8]

Since much of the provincial press followed the *Telegraph*'s lead respecting Westminster politics, these contacts between Gladstone and the *Telegraph* are of great importance. As W. T. Stead pointed out, it was the *Telegraph* which created the 'People's William'.[9]

[1] See 26 Apr. 60. He was also in touch with G. Sala on *Telegraph* business; (see 9 July 60), and with E. Arnold, the *Telegraph*'s leader writer, just after the Newcastle speech (see 16, 24 Oct. 62).
[2] Add MS 44531, f. 178.
[3] Gladstone to Hunt, 13 September 1865, Add MS 44535, f. 123.
[4] See 2 Aug. 66.   [5] See 16 Jan. 68.
[6] See e.g. 27 Jan., 3 Feb., 14, 21 Mar., 9, 11, 27, 28 Apr., 15, 29 May, 23 June 66 etc., and 25 Feb., 6 Mar., 11 Mar., 14 Mar., 25 Mar., 17 July 68. It seems likely that Frank Lawley (for whom see later, p. lxviii) also dealt with Hunt.
[7] Levy-Lawson is first mentioned at 11 June 61, but not subsequently frequently until 1869. Unfortunately there are no *Daily Telegraph* archives for this period.
[8] *Daily Telegraph*, first leader, 13 October 1862.
[9] W. T. Stead, "*Lest We Forget*" (n.d., 1901?), 87.

Gladstone's attention to publicity in the 1860s was always exact, from instructions to his secretary about the release of budget figures, to his insistence on his photograph being sold for 6d. or under.[1] That this was combined with an appearance of unworldliness was particularly irritating to opponents. Even during his commissionership in Ionia in 1858–9 the flow of copy for the press was undiminished, provoking Disraeli's exasperated complaint to Lytton, the colonial secretary: 'The daily advertisements respecting Gladstone, his intentions & movements, are becoming ridiculous. Pray give direction, that it should be stopped.'[2] But this was a futile plea: Gladstone had reached that point when his own efforts as a publicist were no longer fundamental to his persistent appearance in the press: an action or a speech was news because he did or said it, regardless of its intrinsic interest. This enabled Gladstone sometimes to appear uninterested in publicity, but this unworldliness should not be allowed wholly to mask an acute and purposeful flair.

Gladstone's relationships with regional politics and the press were characteristic of a radical; as such, they caused dismay and distrust among the leaders of the whig-liberal party; they were certainly not sufficient in themselves to carry him to the party leadership. The informal but tight group of whig elders—if Palmerston may by the 1850s be so included—still played a role of great importance. But the ability of the whigs to control the liberal party fully was uncertain. In 1855, in the last great political crisis of the closet in the eighteenth–century style, the true whigs had, between them, failed to form a ministry, thus letting in Palmerston. In 1859, a liberal ministry only became a certainty after a party meeting. But if the whigs' patronage was in decline and their hereditary right to rule in question, party had not yet risen in a formal sense. The prediction of divisions was risky, and a ministry could expect to be defeated quite frequently on minor questions and even, on occasion, on major ones, without being expected to resign or dissolve. Nor was the size of the electorate yet such as to require the strict party allegiance of individual M.P.s, many of whom still expected to be returned almost regardless of how they voted in the House.

Gladstone stood to benefit from this Parliamentary situation. By the 1860s, while not rivalling the whigs in executive service, he was, of the non-whig cabinet members, much the most experienced. Italy had been the question which sustained the unity of the ministry at its formation, but Italy could not have more than a passing effect on party politics. Gladstonian finance provided the staple legislation around which the whig-radical-Peelite coalition of 1859 could coalesce. The technical aspects of Gladstone's work as chancellor have already been discussed. Politically, his 1853 budget stabilised the Aberdeen coalition. The defection of the senior Peelites in 1855 was caused by the personal loyalty of Gladstone, Herbert and Graham to Aberdeen and Newcastle, not by differences on general

[1] See 1 Apr. 62, 22 Sept. 64 and 16 July 67.
[2] Disraeli to Lytton, n.d. (early January 1859), Lytton MS D/EK 024.

policy.[1] The budgets of the 1860s and the gradual fulfilment of Gladstone's programme of treasury legislation constituted the main domestic achievement of Palmerston's government. Cobden told Gladstone in 1863, 'I consider that you alone have kept the party together so long by your great budgets'.[2]

By his combination of administrative achievement and political moralising, Gladstone appealed, not merely to the established radicals such as John Bright, but to the leaders of the coming generation of liberal M.P.s, men of moderate but none the less firmly held radicalism, such as H.A. Bruce, H. C. E. Childers, W. E. Forster, James Stansfeld, W. P. Adam, G. J. Shaw-Lefevre, Lyon Playfair: representatives of the moderate but committed readership of the *Telegraph*, men who were to epitomise the non-whig element and to be the work-horses of the liberal party in the 1870s. For his part, Gladstone gave these men their chance in his first administration. They were mostly men more interested in policy than in party, and this accorded with Gladstone's own view.

Gladstone's successes as chancellor balanced the mistrust which his tractarianism caused amongst many of the whigs. His church policy was always liable to lead to conflict. In July 1857 he had prolonged the session to prevent the Divorce Bill then being passed from forcing Anglican priests against their consciences to remarry divorced persons.[3] But in Palmerston's 1859 ministry Gladstone avoided religious wrangles. His interference in episcopal appointments was cautious[4] and he refrained from playing a public role in the Colenso case and in the outcry about *Essays and Reviews*.[5] Although Gladstone's personal beliefs remained resolutely 'catholic', in the sense that he used the word in his book on *Church Principles* (1840), he enlarged his experience by a series of meetings with methodists and congregationalists, organised by Christopher Newman Hall. Though Newman Hall carefully balanced the denominational membership of these meetings, Gladstone regarded them all as 'Dissenters': 'A conclave of Dissenters chiefly Ministers: the teeth and claws not very terrible'.[6] These meetings did not encourage intimacy, but they developed respect on both sides. A potentially important barrier to Gladstone's party leadership was being removed. At a personal level, the many meetings at Penmaenmawr with unitarian guests of Samuel Darbishire were of importance.

Developments within the coalition hierarchy fell favourably for Gladstone. Cornewall Lewis, the ablest of the younger whigs of cabinet rank, regarded by some as a likely successor to the Palmerston-Russell duumvirate, died in 1863. Of the Peelites, Lord Aberdeen died in 1860, Sidney Herbert and Sir James Graham (already retired) died in 1861, the fifth duke of Newcastle, once regarded by Gladstone as a future prime minister, died in 1864, his mind, his family and his estates in chaos.[7]

[1] See Gladstone's detailed description in the diary, Jan.–Mar. 55.
[2] Cobden to Gladstone, 19 December 1863, Add MS 44136, f. 196.
[3] 1–16 Aug. 57.
[4] On one occasion Catherine Gladstone was used as intermediary; see 9 Mar. 60.
[5] He was active, but privately, in the Forbes heresy case in Scotland; see 13 Oct. 67.
[6] 25 Jan. 66 and 15 Nov. 64.
[7] 26–9 Oct. 64; as one of his executors, Gladstone had much difficulty with his dissolute children; see e.g. 23–4 Jan. 65.

With the death of Palmerston in 1865, this left only Russell and Gladstone in obvious contention for the premiership; Granville and Clarendon, the other possible candidates, would have to challenge in order to be considered. Some of Gladstone's friends had encouraged him to bid for the post-Palmerstonian leadership.[1] But the circumstances of Palmerston's sudden death found Gladstone quite unprepared and 'giddy';[2] the Queen told Russell to be ready even before Palmerston died, and Gladstone, isolated at Clumber sorting out Newcastle's chaotic estate,[3] sent an unsolicited letter of allegiance to Russell, who insisted on his taking the leadership of the Commons in addition to the chancellorship. Gladstone's position of heir-apparent to Russell was thus reached without any explicit struggle for power. His formidable political skills were known; they did not have to be directly employed.

The serious commitment of the liberal cabinet to a reform bill in the autumn of 1865 to some extent altered this. Gladstone's great measures of the 1850s and 1860s had all been carefully balanced compromises: the Oxford University Bill of 1854 which achieved a middle way between the liberal reformers and the college traditionalists, the budgets of 1853 and 1860 which satisfied both radicals and whigs. Once Gladstone had achieved what he regarded as a balance, he stuck to it with obduracy. This was particularly noticeable in the case of the Taxation of Charities Bill of 1863. Gladstone believed that many charities were inefficient, corrupt and misnamed, and that bequests by the dead which went untaxed, encouraged posthumous vanity, while donations by the living, made regularly and unspectacularly, came out of income which was taxed. To round off his reform of the income tax, already extended in 1853 to Ireland, he wished to extend it to charities. Gladstone saw this as a reasonable and fair bill, a logical part of his great series of reforms. He saw the Reform Bill as introduced in 1866 in the same light. His limited extension of the franchise was based on arguments about the declining efficiency of parliament and the virtues of the labour aristocracy which seemed to him self-evident: there were self-evident reasons why reform was needed, and self-evident reasons why reform should be limited to the £7 rate payer.[4] Moreover, this was just the sort of balanced measure which had stood the coalition well in the past.

This is not the place to trace the complex débâcle of the 1866 Reform Bill. Certain aspects of it as it affected Gladstone and his political position may however be noted. Unlike previous major legislative measures for which he had been responsible in the Commons, Gladstone had only partial control of the drawing up of the Bill. His usual exhaustive mustering of figures and facts gave way to confused discussions in a committee of cabinet working with rushed and inaccurate data.[5] It became clear to Gladstone at an early stage that the bill was in difficulties; he told his tractarian friend

[1] Particularly Samuel Wilberforce; see 20 Oct. 63.
[2] 18 Oct. 65.   [3] ibid.
[4] Gladstone argued that his 'pale of the constitution' speech of May 1864 went no further than his vote for Baines' Borough Franchise Bill of 1861 (see 10 Apr. 61) or the various tory and whig bills of 1859–60; see 11 May 64.
[5] See 12 Jan. 66n., 22 Jan., 29 Jan., 2 Feb., 15 Feb. 66.

and legal adviser Sir Robert Phillimore even before the bill was introduced: 'I cannot see how I am to succeed or how I am to be beaten'.[1] He began to bring into play alternative political forces.

First, in early February[2] he raised in cabinet the question of a compromise on the long standing dissenter grievance on church rates. By the time the reform bill was in serious difficulties, agreement had been reached with the dissenters and a bill was introduced.[3] Gladstone ran church rates side by side with the reform question from the drafting of the reform bill early in 1866 until his church rates bill emerged in its final form to confirm his links with radicalism in 1868.[4]

Second, once the bill was seen to be in danger, he made two speeches in Liverpool attacking the Adullamite minority, an unprecedented extra-parliamentary appeal by a cabinet minister on behalf of legislation before the Commons, ensuring that, whatever the fate of the Bill, he would have been popularly seen heading the 'fight for the future'.[5] His support for dissolution and a 'purge' of the party, rather than resignation,[6] in June 1866 followed from this activity. The cabinet's over-ruling of Gladstone's and Russell's calls for dissolution saved Gladstone from what was potential-ly the biggest set-back of his career: a poor general election result, fought on an issue at that time intensely divisive for the liberal party, might have created the circumstances for an organised opposition to his succession to Russell. Resignation, removal from British politics by a winter in Rome, and the extraordinary passage of the Derby-Disraeli bill in 1867, did not. Indeed, in the crisis of April 1867, it was Gladstone who considered a letter threatening resignation from leadership in the Commons, while Granville and Brand, the chief liberal whip, begged him not to send it.[7]

The 'smash perhaps without example'[8] of April 1867, when forty five liberals paired or voted against Gladstone's amendment, certainly was a 'smash' in the short term in the Commons. But what was smashed was not Glad-stone's position of liberal leader in the Commons, but rather his attempt to keep reform to the moderate £5 limit. Gladstone's political ferocity had been a ferocity of consistent moderation. The effect of Disraeli's intricate manoeuvres was, as Gladstone told a 'Monster Deputation' of the Reform Union after the 'smash', to cut Gladstone loose from moderation: 'my proposal of the £5 is gone (cheers). I do not see the circumstances under which I am likely to revive it. I must reserve to myself perfect liberty . . .'[9] It was not difficult for Gladstone then to move quickly to support, before Disraeli's unexpected acceptance of it, Hodgkinson's amendment which

---

[1] See 7 Mar. 66n.   [2] See 4 Feb. 66.
[3] See 4 and 6 May 66, 1 Aug. 66.
[4] For the details, see O. Anderson, 'Gladstone's abolition of compulsory church rates', *Journal of Ecclesiastical History*, xxv. 187 (1974); the Act was a characteristic compromise, seeming more radical than it was.
[5] See 5 and 6 Apr. 66, and 20 and 21 Mar. 66nn.
[6] See 19 to 26 June 66.
[7] 16 Apr. 67.
[8] 12 Apr. 67.
[9] 11 May 67. Gladstone remained one of the few politicians actually giving priority to a properly constructed bill; see 16 May 67.

seemed to lead the way to thoroughgoing household suffrage.[1] Nor, given the extraordinary complexity of the implications of the various amendments, incomprehensible to many M.P.s, let alone electors, was it difficult for Gladstone to be presented in the country as the champion of the bill, the man who forced reform upon the Commons. On the other hand at Westminster he could be known as the proponent of that bill which the Adullamite whigs would have preferred if they could have seen the end at the beginning. Disraeli's desire for any bill at any price so long as it was his bill, for any amendment so long as it was not Gladstone's amendment, could discompose the latter but not displace him.

In December 1867 Russell announced his intention that he would not again take office. By telling Gladstone a week before he told Granville, his successor in the Lords, he effectively made Gladstone his heir.[2] Gladstone heard the news in bed at Hawarden, almost blinded by a stray splinter of wood, a hazard of his hobby.[3] Russell's parting gift to British radicalism was a pamphlet series on the Irish church, calling for not merely disestablishment but almost complete disendowment as well.[4]

Gladstone's Irish Church Resolutions of 1868[5] had therefore an immediate and impeccable whig as well as radical pedigree: indeed in the context of such proposals as Russell's and of those of the Liberation Society, Gladstone could even present his Resolutions as being a compromise to save the Irish church, rather than to break it. The Resolutions, added to the Church Rates Bill already in the Commons, allowed Gladstone to continue to behave as he had behaved since the ministry's resignation in June 1866, as if he were a government minister rather than an opposition leader. Gladstone's first ministry had in a legislative sense started with the beginning of the autumn session of 1867. He brought forward and successfully pressed through the Commons legislation and resolutions in 1868 as if he were in office and sitting on the government rather than the opposition front bench. He introduced his Suspensory Bill for the Irish Church exactly as if he were leader of the House,[6] and indeed it was soon assumed, and has often been assumed since, that the Church Rates Bill was passed by his government and that therefore his first ministry must have begun early in 1868, rather than in December.[7]

This appearance of competence and control consolidated Gladstone's position within his party. Disraeli was caught in his own web: he could not put Gladstone's confused position of 1867 quickly to an electoral test

---

[1] 16 and 17 May 67.
[2] Russell made it plain that he already had Gladstone's reply before writing to Granville; Fitzmaurice, i. 518.
[3] 23–26 Dec. 67.
[4] Earl Russell, 'A letter to the Right Hon. Chichester Fortescue on the state of Ireland' (3 February 1868), 'A second letter . . .' (1868), 'A third letter . . .' (18 January 1869).   [5] 30 Apr. 68.   [6] 14 May 68.
[7] See O. Anderson, art. cit., *passim*. The fact that the tory budget of 1867 was largely and admittedly based on Gladstone's debt proposals of the previous year reminded M.P.s of his executive importance even during his worst humiliations in the spring of 1867; see 20 Apr. 66.

because the tail-ends of the reform legislation,—Scotland, Ireland, re-distribution, corrupt practices—took as long to pass as the England and Wales Act on which most interest had been centred.

As soon as Derby resigned through ill-health in February 1868, Gladstone began to consider 'the personnel of our party with a view to contingencies.'[1] In July he reached what appear to have been amicable agreements with the whig leaders—first Granville, then Clarendon—about the distribution of offices, Clarendon being promised the foreign office.[2] These conversations insured, so far as possible, against any move by the Crown to form a whig-led ministry.[3]

Such a move was unlikely. Gladstone's standing at Court was still good. During Albert's life he had been a Court favourite.[4] Certainly his reverential manner had been in marked contrast to that of Palmerston and Russell. After Albert's death he had had an important and intimate audience with the Queen. His account of it shows the start of that unbendingness which Disraeli so adroitly exploited.[5] The reserve this caused on the part of Victoria was apparent to Gladstone at Osborne in 1865;[6] but so great was his reverence for the institution of monarchy that he seems to have been unable to adapt himself to the needs of its holder. Gladstone had had considerable opportunities as minister in residence at Balmoral in 1863 and 1864.[7] He seems to have got on well, but not very well. Lady Augusta Stanley recorded the effect: 'Mr. Gladstone left us today, to our sorrow. He is most pleasant, but perhaps a thought too systematic.'[8] But these were as yet minor, largely personal difficulties. Gladstone had handled the batch of royal marriage financial settlements in the early 1860s with skill. He had been the leader of the 'peace' party in the Schleswig-Holstein affair, his Reform Bill had had strong royal support. The Queen disapproved of the liberal party's Irish Church policy, but, since the whole party was committed to it, this was not a question on which the choice of leader could have an effect. The summons from the Queen in December 1868[9] was therefore surprising only in the sense that Disraeli's resignation without meeting the Commons was unprecedented. From the point of view of the liberal party it merely recognised a supremacy unchallenged, if not universally welcomed.

[1] 28 Feb. 68.
[2] 10 and 13 July, 2 Dec. 68.
[3] The court was ignorant of these mid-summer talks and decisions, General Grey, the Queen's secretary, thinking in November 1868 in terms of preventing an offer of the foreign office to Clarendon; see Grey to Victoria, undated (but late November 1868), *LQV*, 2nd series, i. 555.
[4] See, e.g. 4 Jan., 1–2 Dec. 60. As a member of the 1851 Commission which met often throughout the 1850s, Gladstone maintained his contacts with Albert even when not in office; see 24 Apr. 58.
[5] 19 Mar. 62. He was aware of this deficiency, see 16 Mar. 62.
[6] 25 July 65 and 19 Mar. 67; other factors besides Gladstone's personal deficiences were at work by 1867.
[7] 25 Sept.–9 Oct. 63, 25 Sept.–8 Oct. 64.
[8] *Letters of Lady Augusta Stanley* (1927), 297.
[9] Victoria appears to have summoned Gladstone immediately and without hesitation, being concerned more with keeping salacious whigs—Clarendon and de Tabley—out of office than with Gladstone; *LQV*, 2nd series, i. 559.

Certainly Ireland had played a large part in consolidating that supremacy, and these observations on some of the aspects of Gladstone's political life in the 1860s may fittingly close with a comment on his Irish policy.

On 23 November 1868, when the general election was virtually over,[1] Gladstone published 'A Chapter of Autobiography'. The 'Chapter' explained Gladstone's changing views about establishment, but it did so first, almost entirely in terms of the effect on Gladstone's political development in the late 1830s, Peel's ministry of 1841–6, and the Maynooth Grant of 1845, second, almost entirely in terms of changes in the 1840s in Gladstone's own position on State and Church. These developments have been discussed in the introduction to earlier volumes of these *Diaries*, where it was seen that by the late 1840s Gladstone had indeed significantly changed the orientation of his political views.[2] It can easily be seen why the 'Chapter' was originally intended as an election tract: its effect was to concentrate discussion of the Irish establishment on Gladstone, on the Gladstone of the 1840s, and on the Oxford Movement.

By its compelling prose—it is the best written of Gladstone's pamphlets, with several passages reminiscent of Newman's artful simplicity—'A Chapter of Autobiography' deflected attention from Ireland to England, and from the policies of the liberal party in the 1860s to the problems of the conservative party and the Oxford Movement in the 1840s. Though it alluded to 'silent changes, which are advancing in the very bed and basis of modern society', it placed these changes in the England of the 1840s. But if, from the late 1840s 'that principle—the application of a true religious equality to Ireland—was biding its time', why was 1868 the moment when that time had come? 'A Chapter of Autobiography' gave no analysis of Gladstone's assessment of the 1860s, save for documentation of his statements in 1863 and 1865. It gave no clue to the part that the parliamentary situation, Fenianism, and agitation for tenant right, played in Gladstone's conclusion that Irish disestablishment had ceased to be 'a remote question'. 'A Chapter of Autobiography' answered the immediate political questions of the day as obliquely as Newman's *Apologia* answered Charles Kingsley.

The *Diaries* contain no analytic treatment of the Irish question in the 1860s. Spasmodic comment, however, helps to establish a chronology. In 1857, rather surprisingly, Gladstone told Aberdeen that 'Ecclesiastical questions in Ireland' were one of the 'great subjects of public policy, which may be said to lie within reach'.[3] Before the election in 1865 Gladstone, apparently with the desire of not deceiving his Oxford constituents, made a statement that the Irish establishment was in principle indefensible, but he committed neither the government nor himself to any action.[4] But as

---

[1] It was originally intended as a contribution to the election, but was 'delayed until after the stress of the General Election'; see the 'Chapter's' introduction, and 26 Oct. 68 and n. Quotations in these two paragraphs are all from 'A Chapter of Autobiography'.
[2] See above, iii. xxix. ff.   [3] 31 Mar. 57.
[4] 2 and 28 Mar. 65; see also 'A Chapter of Autobiography', 40; ironically, Gladstone's speech on Dillwyn's motion immediately followed that of Gathorne-Hardy, his subsequent opponent at Oxford.

Gladstone had believed this since the late 1840s, standing in the meantime at three contested and three uncontested elections for the university constituency, his need to state it publicly must mean that he anticipated imminent circumstances in which secret belief would have to become public practice.[1] Three days after making this statement, Gladstone notes on the question of a select committee on Irish land tenure: 'We *persuaded* Lord Palmerston'.[2] In 1865, therefore, Gladstone was moving towards an active policy on what he perceived were the twin remediable evils of the Irish question: the church establishment and the land tenure system.

Gladstone was by no means unique in this; indeed he had hardly reached the position held by the whigs since 1835, let alone that of the radicals. The difference was that he alone held a position which could offer success on both wings of the policy; he could throw behind disestablishment—the question which would immediately involve public opinion—the widely based range of political skills discussed earlier, and behind a new land settlement—involving the dislocation of an interest group—the formidable executive capacity which his years as chancellor had demonstrated. In February 1866 a large 'Budget' of possible Irish legislation was sent to him by Chichester Fortescue, the whig with whom at this time he had a close relationship second only to, and perhaps equal with, Granville. From this, Gladstone strongly pressed for a large scale extension of the 1860 Irish Land Act, urging Fortescue, 'if progress can be made in such a question as Landlord and Tenant I quite think it should be done by a Bill'.[3]

The 1866 Land Bill, caught in the breakdown of party business and discipline caused by the Reform Bill, had to be withdrawn, though Gladstone was seen publicly attached to it.[4] Gladstone had therefore given priority to land over disestablishment, arguing that the latter was too contentious and 'unripe'. The heat of Fenianism seems to have caused a sufficient ripening of both points, bitter though they might be. Gladstone explained his views to Fortescue in December 1867:

I am going into Western Lancashire next week,[5] & I have just had an intimation that the *Liberal* Farmers are for maintaining the Irish Church as it is! This I suppose is the tendency which Fenian manifestations make on stupid men. Of course I do not mean my constituents.

The Irish question which has long been grave is growing *awful*. In my opinion this Empire has but one danger. It is the danger expressed by the combination of the three names Ireland, United States and Canada. English policy should set its face two ways like a flint: to support public order, and to make the laws of Ireland such as they should be. This is what we must try:

---

[1] His statement in his letter to Hannah, sent on 9 June 1865, (which Gladstone knew would be widely circulated if not immediately printed), that 'the question is remote, and apparently out of all bearing on the practical politics of the day' apparently showed little awareness of the activities of the nonconformists and Irish, until it is noted that Gladstone wrote in 'A Chapter of Autobiography' that by 'remote' he meant 'Heaven knows, perhaps it will be five years, perhaps it will be ten'.

[2] 31 Mar. 65.

[3] Gladstone to Fortescue, 13 February 1866, Carlingford MSS, CP 1/4.

[4] *H* clxxxiii. 1123, 1126; ibid. clxxxiv. 1475 (17 May and 25 July 1866).

[5] His visit to Scarisbrick Hall, Ormskirk and Southport; see 16 and 19 Dec. 67.

but I believe we shall have to go to martyrdom upon it, which is a graver consideration for men of your age than of mine.

   ... Maguire has given notice of his Resolution only to occupy the ground— so at least I understood him.

   I hope you will use every effort to come to an understanding with him & with others perhaps through him, as to a new Land Bill. Except the quantities which may be afforded by loans of public money to the Landlords, I do not *know* in what the Bill of 1866 can be greatly improved.

   It would have been with the utmost difficulty that we should have got that Bill well supported by the Cabinet & our friends and a more ultra measure would only mean more splitting.[1]

Gladstone's views on Irish land were thus only loosely formed and he was as yet engaged in the question in principle rather than in detail. Moreover, the tender condition of the liberal party did not allow an attempt in opposition to bring forward land proposals: that could only be achieved with the full panoply of executive authority. Resolutions of principle on the Irish church, however, both unified the party[2] and were possible within the limitations of opposition. It was towards these that the liberal leadership moved in the winter of 1867–68, Russell's pamphlet giving the clarion call.[3]

Gladstone summed up the position in February 1868 to Clarendon, who was well known for his caution on the land question:

I have not yet seen Lord Russell's pamphlet but it is in the act of being born. It recommends I understand distribution of the Irish Church Revenue among the different bodies—this may be reasonable, but it appears to me to be impossible. The Irish land question becomes more and more complicated with delay. I am afraid it is passing from the stage of compensation for improvement into the very dangerous and unsound one of fixity of tenure in some form or other. In truth the aspect of affairs is to my mind more gloomy than it has been for a quarter of a century.[4]

Gladstone's Irish Church Resolutions of March 1868 should therefore be seen not merely as an individual initiative on a single Irish issue, but as part of a general move by the liberal leadership to solve both their party and their policy problems, Gladstone wishing to preserve more of an equality of urgency between church and land than the propertied whigs.

III

As a politician Gladstone was well known, even notorious, for hard work. His diary shows, however, that even a life lived at full stretch by the

[1] Gladstone to Fortescue, 11 December 1867, Carlingford MSS, CP 1/10. Fragments of this letter, with a useful gloss, are in Steele, *Irish Land*, 62, 67. Gladstone to Bright, 10 December 1867 (in W. E. Williams, *The rise of Gladstone to the leadership of the liberal party 1859 to 1868* (1934)) is less revealing.

[2] See 19, 20, 23 Mar., 3 Apr. 68.

[3] Russell also prepared, shortly before announcing his intention to retire, an initiative on education, in which Gladstone was not included; Gladstone would certainly not have been able to unify the party on the education issue: see Fitzmaurice, i. 516.

[4] Gladstone to Clarendon, 17 February 1868, Bodleian Library, MS Clarendon dep. c. 523.

standards of the day left a considerable time for relaxation and activities not directly political—writing, holidaying and week–ending. By the 1860s the week–end had become an established form of relaxation, combining comfort in the great houses of England with the development of political relationships. Gladstone's week–ends were spent almost entirely at whig houses, particularly with the Sutherland family and their relations the Argylls, at their great houses of Chiswick and Cliveden;[1] during the holidays he also visited Trentham,[2] Dunrobin[3] and Inveraray.[4] He was also a fairly frequent visitor to Lady Waldegrave[5] and Chichester Fortescue at Strawberry Hill in Twickenham. Chislehurst, Chatsworth, Mentmore Towers, Woburn, Brougham Hall, Eaton Hall, Pembroke Lodge and Broadlands (after Palmerston's death) were the other main whig houses visited.[6] The only tory roofs under which Gladstone slept were those of Lord Penrhyn in Wales, where courtships between Penrhyn's daughters and the Gladstone boys were proceeding,[7] the duke of Marlborough at Blenheim, an odd and unexplained visit in 1861, and, curiously, Lord Salisbury at Hatfield, where he stayed as his administration was being completed in December 1868.[8]

Certainly politics was a chief reason for many of these visits but, especially at Chiswick and Cliveden, politics often took second place to religion and literature.[9] A characteristic extract is, 'Off with the Argylls and others to Cliveden. Conversation with Argyll on Future Punishment. We had a delightful evening'.[10] Tennyson was also a friend of the dowager duchess of Sutherland and read his poems to the company.[11]

Life at Hawarden and holidays in North Wales constituted the chief relaxation. In the autumn Gladstone usually spent several months in the country. When chancellor, for example, he was away from London in 1863 between 31 July and 10 November, in 1864 from 2 August until 7 November. Business was conducted by letter from Hawarden, but heavy though the correspondence was—one day when his secretary was away Gladstone had to open forty-four envelopes[12]—it could almost always be dealt with in the morning.

[1] A glance at the table 'Where Was He' (which shows only *nights* spent, not day visits) at the end of volumes v and vi will show the frequency of these week–end visits—nine to Chiswick or Cliveden between February and July 1863; he also went quite often for the day or to dine without staying the night.

[2] See 8 Dec. 59.   [3] See 11 Sept. 58.

[4] See 25 Sept. 65; the visit was cut short by a death in the family.

[5] See, e.g. 7 July 57.

[6] Chislehurst (Lord F. Cavendish): 11 June 64 and frequently thereafter; Chatsworth (Devonshire): 14 Nov. 61; Mentmore (Rothschild): 19 Mar. 64; Woburn (Bedford): 13 Sept. 66; Brougham Hall (Brougham): 22 Oct. 57, 1 Sept. 58, 4 Oct. 62, 10 Oct. 64; Eaton Hall (Grosvenor): 22 Nov. 55, 10 Dec. 61, 9 Jan. 65; Pembroke Lodge (Russell): 5 Jan. 60; Broadlands (Cowper-Temple): 22 July 68.

[7] 13 Sept. 62.

[8] See 23 Nov. 61 (Marlborough), 11–15 Dec. 68 (Salisbury).

[9] See, e.g., 23 Apr., 18 May 61.   [10] 2 Apr. 64.

[11] 4 May 62. Gladstone also attended a pre-publication reading of 'Enoch Arden' organized by Palgrave and Woolner; see 30 Apr. 62.

[12] See 21 Aug. 60. It may be convenient here to list the private secretaries active between 1859 and 1866; C. L. Ryan (June 1859–?May 1865), J. F. Stuart-Wortley (from

In mid-August the family usually took a house for three or four weeks on the North Wales coast at Penmaenmawr, near to where Dean Liddell owned a house for holidaying.[1] At Penmaenmawr business was confined mainly to letters with leading politicians; administrative correspondence seems to have been occasional. While on holiday Gladstone worked on his classical studies, walked and swam daily,—'I find it a very *powerful* agent'[2] —noting the number of times, and days missed, in his diary. He liked the water astringent, complaining at Brighton that the sea on Whit Monday was 'over-warm'.[3]

In North Wales Gladstone led his family great distances over the mountains of Snowdonia, though he suffered from vertigo, much to Henry Liddell's amusement (and perhaps relief in finding a chink in the armour). A crisis on the Great Orme ended with these two Christ Church dignitaries clutching each other on the heights, 'the Dean leading Mr. Gladstone along, with eyes closed, while the rest of the party formed a sort of buttress to protect him on the seaward side'.[4] Gladstone also took his family frequently to church, in Penmaenmawr on occasion to a service in Welsh, though he was not impressed by the language.[5] At Hawarden the boys joined in silviculture—mostly cutting, but also planting—a regular occupation from 1858.[6] Cataloguing the already vast collection of books, pamphlets and private papers, including 'a bonfire of papers on private business to 1866 inclusive',[7] took up much time, as did the servicing of the porcelain collection, which was lent out to exhibitions. In the diaries 'worked on China' almost always refers in the 1850s and 1860s to the collection rather than the country, even at the height of the Canton crisis.

Gladstone did not try to make Hawarden a centre of political activity. There were some visitors of political importance. There was an important visit in 1855 from Lord Stanley, later 15th earl of Derby;[8] the French Treaty was suggested by Cobden in the Hawarden garden,[9] Bagehot made a visit to discuss the country banks issue question,[10] Lord Clarence Paget

January 1860), W. H. Gladstone (20 May 1865–June 1866), W. B. Gurdon (20 May 1865–June 1866), S. E. Gladstone (13 July 1865–?). The chancellor had two paid private secretaries; members of the family often also acted unofficially. See J. C. Sainty, *Treasury Officials 1660–1870* (1972), 78. When in office, the private secretaries recorded most outgoing letters in letter books, but since Gladstone had at this time no formal secretarial help out of office, the letter books were not then kept up. Identification of correspondents mentioned in the diary is therefore more difficult when he was out of office, especially in the great bulk of correspondence in 1866–8. Problems of identification are eased by the hand list made by the staff of the Clwyd Record Office of 'minor' correspondents in the papers which were kept back from the British Museum by Tilney Bassett, and now at St. Deiniol's; many of these 'minor' correspondents would in any lesser collection be of major importance. Identification is made more difficult by the 'bonfire' of private business papers on 6 Sept. 67.
  [1] The Gladstones were at Penmaenmawr in 1855, 1859, 1860–4, 1867–8.
  [2] 8 Sept. 59.
  [3] 16 May 64. See also 4 Oct. 56.
  [4] H. L. Thompson, *Henry George Liddell* (1899), 253. Probably the expedition described at 23 Aug. 61. See also 31 Aug. 64n.
  [5] 23 Sept. 55, 2 Sept. 60.   [6] 23 Sept. 55, 31 July 58.
  [7] 6 Sept. 67.   [8] 8 Nov. 55.
  [9] 12–13 Sept. 59; Robertson Gladstone was also present.
  [10] 18 Dec. 65.

came to arrange a compromise on the fortifications issue,[1] an attempt at reconciliation with Northcote included a visit by the latter to Hawarden,[2] Anderson of the treasury came to discuss treasury matters,[3] and there were visits from Lancashire liberal organisers such as George Melly.[4] But Hawarden Castle was not on the great house circuit, and Gladstone did not attempt to put it there. Gladstone's many visits to the great houses of the Sutherlands and the Argylls were reciprocated only twice, in 1855 and 1867.[5] Indeed he bore most visitors only with reluctance and because they pleased his brother-in-law, Sir Stephen Glynne, still the nominal owner of the Castle.[6] Visitors whom he enjoyed were usually academic or ecclesiastical, or close friends such as Robert Phillimore and Sidney Herbert.[7] Hawarden was a family home, with 'ordinarily a family song or dance after dinner',[8] not, as yet, a political headquarters.

Gladstone built on to the Castle the famous 'Temple of Peace'—a library and working room—into which books were moved in October 1860,[9] and it was at Hawarden that most of his literary work in these years was done. Before joining the Aberdeen coalition in 1852, Gladstone's books and articles had been very largely theological or at least ecclesiastical. Out of office in 1855, his attention turned to the classics, and in the years covered in these volumes he hardly published on church questions at all, though, as the diary shows, there was little slackening in his religious reading. The exception was his extremely influential review of Seeley's Ecce Homo.[10]

Between 1855 and 1868 Gladstone published seven long articles on classical topics, a book of *Translations* (with Lord Lyttelton) of classical and romantic poetry, a three volume work, *Studies on Homer and the Homeric Age* (1858),[11] and prepared a popularised version of it, *Juventus Mundi*, published in 1869. Gladstone's abstinence from theological composition is to be accounted for partly by the fact that his earlier writings had led him into an impasse, partly perhaps because open conflict with the liberalism of *Essays and Reviews* (1860) and bishop Colenso's publications on the Pentateuch[12]—the two theological storms of the 1860s—would have led to political complications, partly because, as his review of *Ecce Homo* showed, Gladstone had reached a position of some ambivalence on theological modernism, but partly also because he believed classical writings, and especially Homer, made a real and neglected contribution to European civilization.

[1] 27–9 Dec. 60.   [2] 10 Aug. 65.   [3] 3–4 Oct. 60.
[4] 28 Apr. 67.   [5] 22 Dec. 55 and 5 Nov. 67.
[6] See, e.g. 27 July 58. See also 20 Oct. 56.
[7] Though see 27 Sept. 56.
[8] 24 Aug. 58.
[9] When it is first recorded as such; see 27 Oct. 60. See also 22 Oct. 64.
[10] 21 Dec. 65, 20 Oct. 67.
[11] For its genesis see 7 July, 6 Aug. 55. The proofs were read by Connop Thirlwall, see 17 Oct. 57.
[12] Gladstone was publicly though not spectacularly involved in the Colenso case, being sued, as one of the trustees of the Colonial Bishopric Fund, by Colenso; the Fund had cut off his salary. See 20 June 65. He was involved in the case of archdeacon Denison, found heretical on the eucharist; he wrote, with Phillimore, Denison's statement for appeal; see 24–26 Aug., 1 Sept. 56.

He believed that the neglect of Homer at Eton and Oxford during his years there was similar and parallel to the neglect of true religion. In Gladstone's mind the two were inseparably linked. The ideal of the Christian gentleman was in his view not the erastian pentameter–construing cynic of the late eighteenth century, but the tractarian suffused with the civic qualities of the Homeric world. His concern touched upon a fundamental problem for Victorian middle and upper class education: if the aim of education was to produce godliness and good living, how could the predominance, at school and university, of the study of a pagan society be justified?

Briefly put, Gladstone's argument was that civilization was 'a thing distinct from religion, but destined to combine and coalesce with it. The power derived from this source was to stand in subordinate conjunction to the Gospel, and to contribute its own share towards the training of mankind'. Thus the Old Testament was a guide to man's relationship to God, a 'master-relation'; it was not intended to present 'a picture of human society, or of our nature drawn at large'.[1] The earliest statement of the values and organization of a civilised society was to be found in ancient Greece, and especially in the works of Homer. Greece had therefore a special place in the 'providential order of the world',[2] and it was the duty of those involved in the construction of a modern society to study and expand its lessons.[3]

Homeric writings were therefore not an alternative but a supplement to religious works. Gladstone noted on the day he finished the MS of *Studies on Homer*: 'If it were even tolerably done, it would be a good service to religion as well as to literature: and I mistrustfully offer it up to God'.[4] Vast effort was lavished on these works, even when in office. A translation of the Iliad (never published), a translation of and concordance to Aristotle's Politics,[5] and a 'Trochaic Version' of Homer, worked on 'even in Crewe waiting room at midnight'[6] were attempted while Gladstone was chancellor. He noted: 'This attempt is of the utmost interest & attraction: it threatens to be a snare. I think of beginning to inhibit myself from touching it except after dinner. This will pretty well starve it.'[7] But in 1864 he started work on the 'Shield of Achilles' instead.[8] Not surprisingly, Gladstone was aware of the clash between his literary and political work: 'Worked on Translation in German & English: an agreeable way for a C. of E. to pass his time'.[9] He was also aware why, as chancellor, he did it: 'Restlessness drives me to this'.[10] In 1868 the preparation of *Juventus Mundi* was a clear

---

[1] W. E. Gladstone, 'On the place of Homer in classical education and in historical inquiry', *Oxford Essays* (1857), 3–5. An examination of Gladstone's competence as a classicist and of his place in classical historiography will be found in Hugh Lloyd-Jones, 'Gladstone on Homer', *Times Literary Supplement*, 3 January 1975.

[2] The title of his last rectorial address in Edinburgh; see 3 Nov. 65.

[3] This exposition of Homer coincided with Gladstone's increasing interest in the Orthodox church; see H. C. G. Matthew, 'Gladstone, Vaticanism and the question of the East', in D. Baker, ed., *Studies in Church History* (1978).

[4] 9 Feb. 58.   [5] 10 Sept. 60.   [6] 9 Jan. 62.   [7] 22 Jan. 62.
[8] 23 Dec. 64.   [9] 25 Oct. 59.   [10] 28 Jan. 62.

antidote to rising political excitement as the result of the election became clear.[1]

Classical studies were therefore both a vocation and a distraction. But they were doomed to fulfil the second role more effectively than the first. For Gladstone's studies of the society of the ancient world, while contributing to the eclecticism of Victorian culture, were not much more than an *ex post facto* justification of that culture. Gladstone used classicism to buttress tractarianism: his habits of thought were at bottom apologetic (in the sense of being a vindication): he could never have seriously considered an intellectual framework alternative to Christianity. The implications of his views of comparative myth could have led him towards *The Golden Bough*, but instead they did not amount to much more than a plea for more Homer at Eton and Oxford. *Studies on Homer* showed that John Gladstone had been wise in his choice of his son's profession.

If classical studies in the 1850s and 1860s represent an alternative to theological writings, Gladstone's religious activities after 1855 also show considerable change. While religious activity remained very important to him, religious experience appears to have become less intense. The diary in these volumes dwells little on preparation for communion, failures in observing Lent (though this was partly on doctor's orders)[2] or on the obsessive distinctions between godly and worldly activity, hitherto a persistent characteristic of the diary. The dimension of the secret male fraternity of the 'engagement' has wholly disappeared.[3] Of the lay tractarian generation of the 1830s, only Sir Walter James continued in intimate contact with Gladstone, and even in this case, their fund for charitable work in Leicester Square was wound up in 1855.[4] Contact was renewed with H. E. Manning and James Hope-Scott, the two catalysts of the great sexual crisis of the summer of 1851[5] (described above in the introduction to volume iii) but with nostalgia rather than intensity:

> Saw Manning: a great event: all was smooth: but quantum mutatus: Under external smoothness and conscientious kindness, there lay a chill indescribable. I hope I on my side did not affect him so. He sat where Kossuth sat on Friday: How different![6]

Liberal politics encouraged Manning and Gladstone to establish a working relationship, and this was done. But Manning's inflexible ultramontanism meant intimacy was impossible.[7]

If less intense, Gladstone's religious observances were as regular as ever. Church daily, whenever possible, remained the rule; 'ejaculatory

[1] 24 Nov., 1 Dec. 68.
[2] 6 Apr. 60.
[3] See the introduction to volume iii passim. See 23 Mar. 62 for an unusual repetition of his work in London refuges, a notable feature in vols. iii and iv.
[4] 2 Apr. 55.
[5] See 12 June 55 and 25 Oct. 61 for Gladstone's continued preoccupation about this.
[6] 20 Mar. 61.
[7] See 12 June 55; 28 Apr., 25 Oct. 61; 26 June, 23 July 64; 30 July, 27 and 28 Aug. 66. See also H. C. G. Matthew, 'Gladstone, Vaticanism and the question of the East', in D. Baker, ed., *Studies in Church History* (1978).

prayer', described in a fascinating little note, was to be secretly practised at odd moments, such as the striking of the clock.[1] W. E. Heygate's *The Good Shepherd*, a popular anglo-catholic work of the period, whose subtitle, 'meditations for the clergy', is a reminder of Gladstone's youthful desire to be ordained, was read daily as he dressed in the morning and for dinner.[2] Less obviously predictable is an interest in Jansenism; the works of Nicole, the sisters Agnès and Angélique Arnauld, and of others of the seventeenth century Port-Royal group were studied in French in considerable detail.[3] Gladstone's evangelical origins, still discernible in some of his notes ('The hours of our mirth are not the hours in which we live . . . the hours in which we live are the hours of trial sorrow care evil & struggle'[4]), may account for this interest in Jansenism, but his interest in ecumenicalism and his growing horror of ultramontanism in the 1850s and 1860s also led him to investigate any form of catholicism which was unsullied by Rome. This was certainly the reason for his growing interest in the 1850s and 1860s in the Orthodox religion of the Eastern churches.[5]

As with politics, Gladstone appears to have become tougher and less vulnerable in religion. His religious charity work with prostitutes caused, or was the occasion for, much less highly charged encounters than between 1850 and 1853. The sign for flagellation (λ) occurs only once in these volumes, on 25 May 1859, and the comments in the diary on prostitutes are on the whole formulaic and routine rather than agonised. This is not to say that there was any diminution in rescue work. It remained persistent and regular whenever Gladstone was in London, spasmodic but prominent when elsewhere,[6] except at Hawarden. To a certain extent 'rescue work' had become a habit. If anything his success rate seems to have declined. Nowhere in these volumes does Gladstone analyse its usefulness or its results, nor does he seem to have made any link between his own 'rescue work' which was conducted on strictly individualist principles, and his early and determined support in cabinet for state control of dock-town prostitution through the Contagious Diseases Act.[7]

Most of the girls to whom he talked appear to have been common prostitutes met on the streets and appealed to there. However, there were exceptions. On 30 July 1859 Gladstone met an artist's model named Summerhayes, who also seems to have been a courtesan, a common enough situation; she was 'full in the highest degree both of interest and of beauty'.[8] After Gladstone returned from Hawarden in September, without his wife, although he realised his thoughts 'require to be limited and purged',[9] there were several highly-charged meetings: 'a scene of rebuke

---

[1] 12 Oct. 56.   [2] 6 Sept. 63.
[3] See, e.g., 5 Sept. 58, 21 Apr. 61, 9 Oct. 64, 23 Dec. 66.
[4] 30 Nov. 56.
[5] See Matthew, art. cit.
[6] See encounters in Paris, 23 Jan. 67; Dresden, 14 Nov. 58; Ionia, 7 Jan. 59; Turin, 3 Mar. 59; Brighton, 9 Apr. 60.
[7] See 18 Feb. 63.
[8] 30 July 59. See also 26 Sept. 59.   [9] 1 Sept. 59.

not to be easily forgotten'.[1] Miss Summerhayes was a striking beauty in the pre-Raphaelite style. Gladstone introduced her to his friend, the painter William Dyce, and arranged for her portrait to be painted.[2] Dyce painted her as 'Lady with the Coronet of Jasmine', reproduced in this volume.[3] The picture certainly bears out Gladstone's remark that 'Altogether she is no common specimen of womanhood'.[4] Later when she had changed her name and perhaps her station to Mrs. Dale, Gladstone met her at a meeting of the Fine Arts Club held in his house,[5] and their meetings continued fitfully until 1867.[6]

Lucy Sinclair, also known as Phillips, was a courtesan of some substance —she had a housekeeper.[7] Gladstone met her in August 1866. They appear to have got on convivially ('singing, luncheon'),[8] but though on occasion they had a 'smart contest',[9] Gladstone's feelings about her do not seem to have become intense. The same was true with H. Hastings, to whom he 'read the whole of [Tennyson's] Guinevere aloud'[10] and Miss Rigby, to whom he 'gave Shakespeare' (The Tempest, perhaps?) 'for a practical purpose & advised to think of emigration'.[11] Miss Cowper, a courtesan 'at the very top of the tree . . . she has driven her open carriage and pair daily all this year in the Park',[12] did constitute a success, at least for a time. Gladstone arranged for her to go to Harriet Monsell's House at Clewer, the responsibility for the welfare her King Charles spaniel falling upon the Chancellor.[13]

Laura Thistlethwayte was to prove a very different case. Gladstone probably met her in 1864, riding in Rotten Row where he often rode,[14] and where she was well-known.[15] She was the daughter of Captain Bell of Bellbrook, county Antrim, and the wife of Augustus Frederick Thistlethwayte, a gentleman of means, with a house in Grosvenor Square a few doors from Lord Shaftesbury, a brother at Eton and Christ Church, and a lineage in Burke's Landed Gentry.[16] Gladstone always referred to her in his diary as 'Mrs. Thistlethwayte', or 'Mrs. T.', not giving merely a surname (perhaps

[1] 17 Sept. 59. On 16 Sept. 59 he read Tennyson's 'Princess' with her: 'much and variously moved'.
[2] 6 Aug. 59.
[3] See plate 3. Gladstone met her two days after speaking to Thomas Combe, the pre-Raphaelite patron. See also M. Pointon, 'W. E. Gladstone as an art patron and collector', Victorian Studies, xix. 73.
[4] 17 July 61.
[5] 17 July 61. Gladstone did not take rescue cases' claims of marriage at face value; he unsuccessfully searched Somerset House for E. Collins' marriage certificate; see 26 June, 19 July 58.
[6] See, e.g., 5 Mar. 62, 14 and 20 June 67.
[7] 3 Jan. 68.   [8] 27 Sept. 66.   [9] 30 Nov. 67.
[10] 16 Mar. 65.   [11] 29 June 59.
[12] Bassett, 146. She was also known as Throckmorton.
[13] 31 July 63.
[14] See 9 July 64, and 4 Apr. 63 for a bad fall.
[15] The first diary reference to her is to a letter, suggesting an already established acquaintance; see 10 Dec. 64. There are some details about her in C. Pearl, The girl on the swansdown seat (1955), 142–5.
[16] Gladstone dined at their house on 22 Mar. 65 and 4 Mar. 67; letters to Mr. Thistlethwayte were recorded in the usual way in the secretary's letter books. This was not the case with letters to Mrs. Thistlethwayte.

with an initial) as was done with regular rescue cases. She was not therefore a
'rescue case', but she had been well-known, even notorious, in the demi-
monde.[1] In 1869 she wrote a lengthy autobiography to show Gladstone that
her reputation had been unfairly treated, but unfortunately this work has
not survived. It is clear, however, that, probably some time after her
marriage in 1852, she experienced a religious conversion to a nondenomina-
tional ethical Christianity, about which she lectured at the London Poly-
technic. Gladstone attended one of these lectures and noted: 'I do not much
wish to repeat it'.[2] After her conversion, she became a friend of the duke of
Newcastle and Arthur Kinnaird,[3] and it was in this context that her early
conversations with Gladstone occurred.[4] At first their relationship was
one of interested acquaintance. They met and corresponded on occasion,
but not very regularly.[5] It was not until Gladstone was prime minister,
in the autumn of 1869, that there occurred one of those Gladstonian
emotional explosions of extraordinary force and danger. Very much more
will be found about Laura Thistlethwayte in subsequent volumes of this
diary, for she died in 1894, her friendship with Gladstone maintained until
the end. But since their relationship in the 1860s can only be understood
in terms of the crisis of 1869, something may be said about that here.

In October 1869, Mrs. Thistlethwayte made a move towards great intimacy with the prime minister, accusing him of misunderstanding and
mockery. In response Gladstone wrote describing their relationship since
1864:[6]

In my ragged letter of yesterday, I did not get *through* my answer to your
question 'had you knowledge of all this when you came to see me'? Yet it
may be short—No!

I told you some things I did perceive;[7] and I proceed. The modesty (so to
call it) struck me, with which, when I rather thrust open your door (I fear)
after one friend's death [i.e. the duke of Newcastle in 1864], you did not hasten
to call me in; it struck and pleased me. With regard to myself afterwards, I
thought you interpreted me too favourably, and in all things seemed to dress
me (so to speak) in colours agreeable to yourself. But I did not dream that, as
among your *friends*, I was drawn into any inner circle. I have not a good
opinion of myself. And, if I see kindness from any one gushing out upon me, it

[1] Though see 28 Dec. 68. Her photograph is not flattering, but her portrait by Girard
is (for both, see below vi, plate 3), bearing out the observation of the pre-Raphaelite
artist J. R. Herbert that she was 'half sybil, half prophetess, with beauty enough at
times to make one secretly offer praises and thanks to the great Maker of it'; J. R.
Herbert to Gladstone, 12 October 1874, Add MS 44444, f. 303. I am obliged to Mr. A.
F. Thompson for bringing this portrait to my notice.
[2] 30 Apr. 65.   [3] See 6 Feb. 65n.
[4] See 5 Feb. 65. His first recorded letter to her was written from Clumber; see 10 Dec. 64.
[5] Usually about religion; Gladstone's first long letter to her is on 30 July 1865, on her
misunderstanding of the Anglican church. Gladstone's letters to Mrs. Thistlethwayte
(which he had explicitly requested her to keep (letter of 18 October 1869)) were recovered
by the Gladstone family solicitors after her death and are, together with her letters to
him, in Lambeth Palace Library. They will be available for consultation when publication
of the diary is completed.
[6] Gladstone to Mrs. Thistlethwayte, 'Oct. 19 (also Oct. 20, 21, 22) 1869'.
[7] In particular 'her large and most catholic spirit in a form of religion which (forgive
me) is apt to be too much individualised'; letter of 18 October 1869.

mainly strikes me what a fund of it they must have, to spend so liberally. Again, you ask did kindness (in, not to, me) draw me to see you? There was enough in what all knew of you, to draw me, without kindness: a sheep, or a lamb rather, that had been astray; (I omit what you do not wish to be mentioned but what, I do not deny, enhances interest—), and that had come back to the Shepherd's Fold, and to the Father's arms . . . I fretted, as oftentimes I have done, at my want of time and free mind for the cultivation of friendship; but there was no period at which I should not have been very sorry to think I was seeing you for the last time.

Yet I did not then know you as I know you now through your tale, and what accompanies the tale.

In Mrs. Thistlethwayte Gladstone had found an ideal object of fascination: educated enough to understand something of his mind, young enough to offer beauty, religious enough to seem redeemed, but exotic enough to stand outside the ring of society women with whom he usually corresponded on religion.[1] 'It is like a story from the Arabian Nights, with much added to it' was his comment on her autobiography.[2]

The dramatic but apparently resolved nature of Mrs. Thistlethwayte's life and religion called forth a response from Gladstone:

> There is a *region* beyond that of interest in your tale, beyond bewilderment, beyond gratitude for an open-hearted confidence: but the first step into that region prompts me to remember as a sacred trust what is for your peace and weal. If in speaking thus I seem mysterious and strange it is because I am so. My life is a battle between inclination and duty. Inclination calls me to repose, duty leads me into conflict: I have high aspirations, and mean tendencies. But a voice above the din orders me to study your peace and your weal.[3]

Her bid for attention had come at a timely moment; Gladstone needed the friendship and attention of a woman outside his family circle. In volumes V and VI this role was fulfilled occasionally by Lady Waldegrave,[4] but chiefly by the dowager duchess of Sutherland, to whom Gladstone wrote very regularly when they were apart, letters usually on literature, with some politics added.[5] The dowager duchess died in October 1868;[6] Gladstone was one of her pall-bearers. Mrs. Thistlethwayte was hardly the dowager duchess, but Gladstone saw her in the same context: 'You were never to me simply a common acquaintance. Friendships with women have contributed no small portion of my existence. I know the meaning of the words "weakness is power": apparent weakness is real power.'[7] And again: 'what could lead you to tell me I was made much of by women. I fear only

---

[1] E.g. Miss Stanley and Lady Dunraven; Gladstone frequently comments to Mrs. Thistlethwayte that his prose style and cultural background are more complex than hers, but that she can nonetheless understand him.

[2] To Mrs. Thistlethwayte, 18 October 1869.

[3] To Mrs. Thistlethwayte, 4 November 1869.

[4] See 19 May 60.

[5] His letters to her do not appear to have survived. A selection will be found in Morley, ii, ch. xii, and in Add MS 44324–9; his letters to his wife are much franker on politics, but the dowager duchess offered occasional whiggish advice; see 14 May 60.

[6] 28 Oct., 3 Nov. 68.

[7] To Mrs. Thistlethwayte, 25 October 1869.

my own declaration, that valued and precious friendships with women had formed no small part of my life. That is true. In every principal case they were women older than myself. To be prized by women in general is in my opinion a great glory, because of their gift of judging character: but it is a glory I cannot claim and do not deserve'.[1] This friendship with a woman was to lead Gladstone into comic, almost ludicrous situations. His letters to her did not show him at his best: after October 1869 he began his letters to her 'Dear Spirit', though ending 'Ever yours, W.E.G.' He wanted to wear a ring she had given him: 'A ring is a bond: and in it I will have engraved "L.T. to W.E.G.".'[2] She, with more circumspection, insisted on a mere 'L'. On the other hand, Gladstone just kept his head; his letters never became mawkish and, though Mrs. Thistlethwayte took up much time, he never reached the degree of dependence of H. H. Asquith upon Venetia Stanley.

Through Gladstone's rescue work ran a strong pre-Raphaelite streak. He read 'The Princess' and 'Guinevere' to rescue cases; he compared Mrs. Thistlethwayte to the second; he was reading Tennyson and Malory when he suggested that Miss Summerhayes should be painted as 'Lady with the Coronet of Jasmine'. The blend of duty and romance of the Arthurian knights was recreated in alleys, on street corners and in Rotten Row. 'Lofty example in comprehensive forms is, without doubt, one of the great standing needs of our race' is Gladstone's opening comment in his review of Tennyson's *Idylls*.[3] London accommodated this easily enough. The controlled and perceivable relationships of provincial towns with their respectable nonconformity meant nothing there.

Together with the image of womanhood, Gladstone wondered at the image of London and the relationship in it of two worlds: 'the west and the east ... I wish that those who inhabit the western portions of this great metropolis could, each for himself, endeavour to realise their immense responsibilities towards the vast masses of population which are as completely unknown to the inhabitants of the magnificent squares and streets of London as if they were neither fellow-countrymen nor even fellow Christians. Aye, they might be better known if they inhabited the remotest quarters of the globe.'[4] Courtesans, prostitutes and servants lived in both these worlds, hence, in part, their fascination.

Gladstone agreed to Laura Thistlethwayte's request that she should have a veto on what he told his wife about their relationship: 'I shall say no more to my wife, except it be with your free and full concurrence, and approval.'[5] This placed their relationship in the same category as the flagellating rather than the charitable side of the rescue work: the only

[1] ibid. 3 November 1869.   [2] ibid. 28 October 1869.
[3] *Quarterly Review*, cvi. 465 (October 1859); this review is usually recalled for its criticism of 'Maud', but most of the review is a highly favourable appraisal of Tennyson's Arthurian poetry and of the Arthurian legend and its social implications: 'The Arthurian Romance has every recommendation that should win its way to the homage of a great poet. It is national: it is Christian . . . and, though highly national, it is universal.'
[4] Speech at St. Thomas, Charterhouse; see 8 May 56.
[5] Gladstone to Mrs. Thistlethwayte, 11 January 1870.

topic on which Gladstone did not consult his wife.[1] It is clear that his relationship with Catherine Gladstone, while stable and very affectionate, had a clear limit to intimacy. Gladstone spent a good deal of time away from her, and she from him. He noted that his weekends at Cliveden without her were 'selfish', but did not remedy this. He told Mrs. Thistlethwayte: 'from morning to night, all my life is pressure, pressure to get on, to dispatch the thing I have in hand, that I may go to the next, urgently waiting for me. Not for years past have I written except in haste a letter to my wife. As for my children, they rarely get any.'[2]

Gladstone's expectations of his wife in her post-child-bearing years seem unclear. He noted in 1862 when he had been reading *Tannhäuser*: 'Dearest C's. birthday. How much might I say of her as a hero-woman'.[3] Certainly she often offered advice, on politics[4] as well as family affairs. She handled Arthur Gordon's proposal to Agnes[5] and helped the boys with theirs. 'Walk with C.—now rare'[6] exemplifies the references of Gladstone to his wife in these volumes: he took it for granted that she would be on hand when needed, valued her advice and energy, but did not go much out of his way on her behalf.[7]

On the occasion of her great need—the lingering death of her sister Mary Lyttelton in 1857—Gladstone paid only fleeting visits to the Lyttelton's house at Hagley, remaining in London to oppose and amend the government's Divorce Bill.[8] After Mary's death, Catherine suffered a severe breakdown in health, the doctor finding 'her whole system much deranged'.[9] This may also have been linked to her menopause (she was forty–six in 1858), though Gladstone says nothing directly on this point. The decision to go to Ionia later in 1858 may have been influenced by a desire to improve Catherine's health, as the visit to Rome in 1850 had been to help his daughter Mary's.

By 1868 Willy Gladstone was twenty–eight, and Herbert, the youngest of the seven living children, sixteen. No serious illness afflicted the children in these years, and their upbringing was on the whole uneventful. Willy bore the brunt of his father's expectations as he worked his way through Eton and Christ Church, never short of admonition and instruction. Encouraged, even forced into a political career,[10] he was not even allowed to write his own election address.[11] 'Most satisfactory though taciturn',[12]

---

[1] See Introduction above, iii. xlvii-viii.
[2] To Mrs. Thistlethwayte, 22 October 1869. It was true he did not often write to his children, but when he did the letter was substantial; see Lathbury, ii, chapter v.
[3] 6 Jan. 62.   [4] See, e.g., 8 Oct. 68.
[5] 4 Oct. 61.   [6] 5 July 63.
[7] Her energetic charitable activities in Lancashire during the cotton distress are given one, retrospective, mention. Gladstone did, however, attend some of the meetings for raising funds for her London children's home charities; see 21 Nov. 67.
[8] See June–Aug. 57.
[9] See 6 Jan.–10 Feb. 58.
[10] 6 Sept. 64; 'a satisfactory conversation with Willy, whose disinclination to try Parliament seems to be removed'.
[11] See 12, 23–4 Apr., 24 May 65.
[12] 9 Sept. 65.

he acted as his father's secretary in 1865, as did his brother Stephen. Stephen at the age of eleven announced his intention to enter the church,[1] and apparently never deviated from it; he was ordained deacon in 1868. Harry, aged twelve, said he would be a merchant,[2] which he later became. Herbert already showed signs of an easy relationship with his father, whom he also puzzled: 'Herbert's [eighth] birthday: he will hardly be an ordinary man, seems to have both breadth and depth'.[3]

The three girls, Agnes, Mary and Helen, figure in these volumes chiefly as objects of education—unlike the boys, they were educated entirely at home by governesses and by their father. Although Agnes, the oldest girl, was twenty–eight by the end of these volumes, there seems to have been only one (unsuccessful) proposal of marriage, that by Arthur Gordon, who had fallen in love with her when he was Gladstone's secretary in Ionia.[4] Lucy Lyttelton, Catherine Gladstone's niece, became almost one of the family after her mother's death. She often stayed at Hawarden or Carlton House Terrace, rode with Gladstone in Rotten Row, and listened to his speeches in the Commons. Her marriage to Lord Frederick Cavendish, which was not without important political implications for the Gladstone family, was the chief moment of formal family rejoicing recorded in these volumes.[5]

Much more worrying than the immediate family were the affairs of the Glynnes and George Lyttelton. Lyttelton was melancholic after the death in 1857 of his wife Mary, who died almost certainly from bearing their twelfth child. Gladstone tried to draw him out of himself by joining him in authorship of a volume, *Translations*, published after several delays by Quaritch in 1861, and by encouraging him in his educational activities. Lyttelton found some consolation in a liaison with Sybella, wife of Humphrey St. John Mildmay, the liberal M.P. The Gladstones did not discourage this, and Lyttelton married her after her husband's death.[6]

Sir Stephen Glynne's business affairs improve in these volumes, but the prosperity hoped for from the coal mines opened on the Hawarden estates in the late 1850s[7] was not realised. However, the mining finances were conducted by Burnett, the agent, with none of the abandon of Boydell at the Oak Farm fifteen years earlier, and the estate finances were not over-extended. The residual problems of the Oak Farm disaster were no longer acute and by the 1860s the way to an eventual solution was clear, so much so that funds were available for the development of the estuary of the Dee.[8]

More dramatic were the personal affairs of the widowed Henry Glynne, Catherine Gladstone's brother and rector of Hawarden, who became entangled first with a Miss Lowder, then with a Miss Rose, daughter of a local pit owner and for a time governess to his motherless daughters. Henry

---

[1] 13 Jan. 56.   [2] 17 Aug. 64.

[3] 7 Jan. 62; see also 15 May 59. The chief problem recorded about Harry and Herbert was swearing; see 10 Apr. 63.

[4] 4 Oct. 61.   [5] See 7 June 64.   [6] See 29 July 61.

[7] See 12 Aug. 56, 7 Jan. 57, 8 Aug. 62.

[8] 6 Aug. 63. For Gladstone's statement of Glynne's and his own finances see 26 Dec. 56 and 19 Dec. 65.

Glynne's remarriage was of great potential importance, for, should he have a male heir, Hawarden would not pass to the Gladstone family, and the intricate structure of mortgages and loans, constructed in the aftermath of the Oak Farm crash on the assumption that Willy Gladstone would ultimately inherit, would be overturned.[1] The Gladstones were strongly opposed to a marriage to either lady, as becomes clear from the diary, though no reason for this hostility is given.[2]

Unfortunately full documentation of the Lowder and the Rose affairs has not come to light. It seems, however, that a breach of promise action against Henry Glynne was only avoided by a payment by Gladstone to either Miss Lowder or Miss Rose, probably the latter. The affair was publicly referred to in the *Cork Constitution* in 1861 when the paper, trying to discredit the chancellor because of his part in cancelling the government contract with the Galway steam boat packet company for postal services to the United States, stated that he had paid £5000 to avoid summons as a co-respondent in a divorce case.[3] Gladstone told his solicitor:

> In the present case it happens that some circumstances have happened to a relative of mine which recently caused me to be the medium of transmitting to a lady through a London Bank a sum of money: it is possible that this may have grown without any intentional falsehood into the fiction we now have to deal with.
>
> When your contradiction has been inserted into the *Cork Constitution* I should prefer not taking steps to inquire whether other papers have carried the paragraph. It seems to me that with a public denial my duty terminates, if the idea of legal punishment or redress is not to be entertained.[4]

This was the end of the matter publicly and privately; there was no legal action,[5] and Henry Glynne did not remarry.

Gladstone saw more of the Glynnes and the Lytteltons than he did of his own kin, who were met chiefly at deathbeds. His brother Robertson was an exception to this, though, already in decline, he played less of a part in Gladstone's electioneering in Lancashire than might have been expected from a former radical mayor of Liverpool. Two of Gladstone's brothers' wives died during these years, Elizabeth,[6] wife of John Neilson Gladstone, and Mary Ellen,[7] wife of Robertson Gladstone. John Neilson Gladstone did not long survive his wife.[8] At her funeral Gladstone noted: 'There I found my three brothers & sister. I think not assembled since my Father's death.'[9]

---

[1] The passage at 27 June 55 reveals a tender conscience on the succession question; but, as long as Henry Glynne had no male heir, Willy's eventual succession was never really in doubt, Catherine Gladstone being the older of the two daughters, although in his mem. of 3 July 1855 (Hawn P) for R. Barker, the Chester solicitor, Gladstone raised the question of a succession involving Henry Glynne's daughters.

[2] See 2–13 Feb., 15–18 Mar. 60 (Lowder) and 3 and 6 Sept., 3 Nov. 60 (Rose).

[3] See 3 June 61.

[4] Gladstone to Freshfield, 3 June 1861, Add MS 44531, f. 170.

[5] Gladstone told Phillimore (5 June 1861, Add MS 44531, f. 171): 'There is a subsequent utterance in the *Cork Constitution* which I suppose closes the question. The *causis* instrumental we seem to know; but the *causa causans* seems after all to be what last night gave Baron de Bode his majority—the Galway Contract'.

[6] 11–12 Feb. 62.   [7] See 29 Sept. 65.   [8] 6 Feb. 63.   [9] 19 Feb. 62.

Despite this family disintegration, two important relationships were restored. The visit of Sir Thomas Gladstone and his family to Hawarden in 1856[1] was reciprocated by a nostalgic trip to Fasque, now Thomas's house, in 1858;[2] the brothers were not intimate, and Tom continued to vote against William at Oxford University elections, but the hostility of the early 1850s declined. Helen Gladstone, whose harrowing experiences consequent upon her apostasy were of such central importance to her brother William in the 1840s, and who had largely disappeared from the diary in the 1850s,[3] appears in the 1860s considerably restored: 'Helen's birthday. Well, it is brighter than once it was'.[4] He visited her at St. Helen's Convent on the Isle of Wight[5] and she became quite a regular visitor to the family. She remained a source of political embarrassment, being the only convincing evidence for the many charges of Popery levelled at Gladstone in Lancashire, especially in the 1868 election campaign.

One figure on the fringe of the family circle is revealed by the diary as deserving some attention: Frank Lawley. Lawley resigned his seat and his position as Gladstone's secretary in 1854 after being caught gambling with the funds. This lapse of probity by no means discredited him with Gladstone who assisted in his financial rehabilitation[6] and subsequently employed him as a less spectacular version of Disraeli's political factotum, Ralph Earle.[7] Lawley sent information from Virginia about the attitude of the Confederate cabinet during the Civil War[8] and, on his return from America, he acted as Gladstone's intermediary with the Adullamites during the Reform Bill crises, during which Gladstone records seeing him almost daily.[9] Gladstone clearly tried to use Lawley to counter the chief weakness in his political armoury: his relationship with the party in the Commons, and with its organisation. But if he had identified a problem, he had not solved it.

Gladstone knew cabinets and the executive machine and he had to a considerable extent outflanked the party by his development of extraparliamentary appearances. But, though he accorded party an important, indeed crucial, constitutional role, he had given little attention to the details of its management.

It is true that he might be called the first psephologist, for in 1857 he calculated the median percentage swing for five polling stations in the Flintshire and Flint boroughs constituences at the general election,[10] but this was not an interest followed up in his post-Oxford elections. At Oxford, tradition compelled him not to interest himself directly in the details of political management. In Lancashire and Greenwich in 1865 and 1868, he was content to continue this practice, leaving the details of campaigning

[1] 21 July 56.
[2] 7 Oct. 58 (see also 8 Oct. 64); Gladstone earlier contemplated buying an estate near Fasque; see 27 Aug., 3 Sept. 56.
[3] See 20 Feb. 58 for their first meeting for some years.
[4] 28 June 63.   [5] 12 Aug. 59.   [6] See 12 July 56.   [7] See, e.g. 10 July 68.
[8] See 30 Dec. 62. For Gladstone's meeting with Confederate notables at the Lawley dinner-table, see 14 Nov. 65.
[9] See particularly 10 Feb. 66n. and Cowling, *1867*, 185.
[10] Add MS 44747, ff. 31–42.

almost entirely to the local experts, in Lancashire to George Melly and the Heywood family, in Greenwich to Alderman Salomons.

Though he had thought about the nature of the new electorate, and though he had a perception and active awareness of the dynamic economic and social condition of the nation, Gladstone had not developed any view of the relationship of the liberal party as such to it.[1] His technique as chancellor had been to gather the party in parliament and in the country around 'measures'. But the specific financial reform measures used for this purpose were now almost all achieved. 'Measures' could be divisive as well as integrative, as 1866 showed. Gladstone had not developed any counter-vailing force to this divisiveness; his solution was more but different 'measures', presented as Gladstonian initiatives. The liberal whips of the period, Brand and G. G. Glynn, were, as members of great banking families now also landed, well placed to manage the parliamentary party of the 1860s.[2] But they had no answer to the constituency problems implied by the Reform Act of 1867. Certainly Frank Lawley, Willy Gladstone, William Gurdon, Algernon West and the others who formed the immediate group of personal assistants around Gladstone when he became prime minister were not the sort of men to answer or even to address themselves to this problem.[3]

Gladstone took his family on continental journeys twice in these volumes—to Ionia in 1858–9, to Italy in 1866–7. Both are of considerable interest. For the first time on a long continental trip, Gladstone in 1858 did not keep a separate travel diary—indeed he never kept one after 1852—and the daily journal entries are therefore more detailed and livelier for these months.

Gladstone went to Ionia first to act as commissioner extraordinary alongside Sir John Young, a well known Peelite of the second rank who had failed to deal constructively with the Risospast ('union with Greece') movement. He then recommended Young's replacement and acted briefly as lord high commissioner until Sir Henry Storks arrived to take his place. His function was therefore to offer a means by which Young, regarded by Derby as incompetent well before Gladstone was sent,[4] could be eased out without a scene, and to make recommendations about the future of a potentially important strategic Protectorate[5]—the islands being with Gibraltar and Malta the only British bases in the Mediterranean.

As well as their general strategic importance (limited for want of a good harbour), the islands were one of the many factors in the Eastern question;

[1] A tentative start is suggested in Gladstone's speech arguing the need for returning officers' expenses to be borne by the local authority, so as to encourage working class candidates; see 18 July 68.

[2] For them, see A. F. Thompson, 'Gladstone's whips and the general election of 1868', *E.H.R.*, lxiii. 189 (1948).

[3] Another relative, Stuart-Wortley, had been with Ryan his private secretary 1860–65; see 21 Dec. 59.

[4] See Col. Talbot to Sir E. Lytton, 30 September 1858, Lytton MS D/EK 0.12. The removal of Young, unusual though it was, led to no lasting bitterness; see 18 Jan. 61.

[5] Important in the sense of being denied to the Russians, though the union with Greece was regarded as dangerous because Greek politics were so unstable as to be unable to prevent Russian penetration of the islands, should they be annexed to Greece.

'this small question,' Gladstone correctly observed, 'is the narrow corner of a very great question, one no less, in all likelihood, than the reconstruction of all political society in South-Eastern Europe.'[1] Gladstone's appointment thus directly confronted him with a problem involving questions of strategy, imperialism and nationalism, and in a crisis in which he had to act. As so often, his instinct was consolidatory. Though he went to the islands with some predisposition for their partial union with Greece,[2] familiarization with the situation decided him in favour of a bold attempt to convert 'the abstract sentiment of nationality', which he found to be 'universal', to an acceptance of the benefits of an imperial protectorate. This was to be achieved by 'Responsible Government', which 'may now be said to form the fixed rule of the policy of the British Empire' in all areas 'not stamped with an exceptional character, either as purely military Possessions, or as being in mere infancy, or as being too critically divided between dominant and subject races.' Nationalism, Gladstone argued, subsumed all grievances, whether strictly related to national feeling or not; approached, however, 'by reason rather than by reproach', nationalism could be contained, since 'free institutions' would create an educated class receptive to imperial considerations.[3] Even after the loss of the islands was certain, he was anxious to avoid the Ionians being seen 'as "deciding" on their destiny.'[4] Not too much should be made of the obvious comparisons which can be drawn from this analysis; Ionian nationalism was pro-Greek and pre-imperial, rather than primarily anti-imperial and anti-British. Nonetheless, Gladstone made it clear in a remarkable despatch to Lytton that he saw the Ionian question in a general imperial context, and that comparisons with problems about the compatibility of nations within the United Kingdom were also in his mind. His analysis of Ionian nationalism was acute, and, as can be seen, over-ran his conclusions in the earlier part of the despatch: he did not succeed in showing that his proposals for constitutional reform were in practice likely to woo middle class Ionians from their Risospast (unionist) position. It is unfortunate that Gladstone never attempted to set down in similar detail his thoughts on Irish nationalism which, as he hints, were in his mind as he wrote the despatch. Had he done so, he would have had to think more exactly about the relationship of practical reform to nationalist sentiment in the United Kingdom, and about the precise meaning of the 'justice' he claimed for Ireland.

Gladstone took his mission to Ionia seriously: no sense of irony is to be found in his observation that his work in the Islands had absorbed him as much as any Parliamentary business.[5] But despite his pains and intensive lobbying, his proposals were completely rejected by the Ionian Assembly, which petitioned for union with Greece instead—an instructive lesson to which Gladstone seems to have paid little attention. Also while in Ionia, his interest in the Greek Orthodox church, hitherto theoretic, received a practical impetus at a time when his view of Roman Catholicism was increasingly pessimistic.[6]

[1] 28 Dec. 58.   [2] 7 Oct. 58n.   [3] 28 Dec. 58.   [4] 7 July 63.
[5] 31 Dec. 58.   [6] See H. C. G. Matthew, art. cit.

While returning from Ionia in 1859, Gladstone passed through northern Italy, which was virtually in a state of war.[1] In Milan he met Cavour and other Risorgimentist leaders who took him into their confidence about their plans,[2] as a result of which Gladstone arrived in London sympathetic to change in Italy, a sympathy reflected in his article in the *Quarterly*[3] and in his early activity in Palmerston's ministry.[4] This sympathy was chiefly for moves against Austria and against the Pope's temporal power; Gladstone did not in principle favour major increases in Sardinia's territory.[5]

Gladstone visited Italy again in 1866, to recover and to distance himself from English reform politics. While in Rome he had two audiences with the Pope,[6] observed the making of the Vatican Council of 1870, and was dismayed, a feeling shared by Sir John Acton, also in Rome at that time. During this visit, Gladstone's relationship with Acton considerably deepened. Hitherto it had centred round exchanges of letters and meetings in company at Gladstone's breakfast parties. When they had met more privately, as at Cliveden, Gladstone had been much impressed: 'the more I see the more I like. *Si sic omnes.*'[7] Drives and dinner parties in Rome allowed Gladstone's opinion of Acton to be confirmed. One of Gladstone's aims in visiting Italy at this time was to assist his friend Father Tosti in saving the monastery of Monte Cassino,[8] then in the process of being secularized. The exact details of Gladstone's part in the compromise reached are not clear; he raised the matter when visiting Florence (then the Italian capital) on his way home, when he also advised Scialoja on the preparation of the Italian Budget.[9]

These two foreign journeys occasioned none of the emotional crises which characterised all Gladstone's previous expeditions abroad. They did however confront him with two of the problems which were to be in the forefront of his mind in the early years of his first ministry: nationalism and ultramontanism.

Gladstone's diary in these years contains no single theme to which the diarist returns, almost obsessively, as was the case in volumes three and four. That there was no such theme accounts for the length of this introduction, and perhaps also for Gladstone's feeling of suspension: 'the horizon enlarges, the sky drifts around me'[10] and 'a man does not see much of the country through which the river winds'.[11] This introduction has suggested that for most of the years covered by these volumes, Gladstone used his financial policy, interpreted in its widest sense, to stabilise and check this feeling of drift, and that he was remarkably successful in suggesting to himself and to his countrymen an illusion of stability and, following it in the second half of the 1860s, of change to consolidate that stability. Whether Gladstone's view of the State, a strange mixture of organic and

[1] See 28 Feb. 59.   [2] 3–4 Mar. 59.   [3] 11 Apr. 59.
[4] See 30 June, 31 Aug. 59.
[5] ibid. He shifted his view on this, see 26 Mar. 61.
[6] 22, 26 Oct. 66.
[7] See 4 Apr. 64 and especially Dec. 66; see also 2 May 61.
[8] For his visit to the monastery, see 27–8 Dec. 66.
[9] 7–15 Jan. 67.   [10] 29 Dec. 60.   [11] 31 Dec. 68.

pluralist practice and theory, could offer a permanent solution will be seen
in subsequent volumes. What is clear is that Gladstone faced the world
bleakly and increasingly alone:

> There is a resistance to the passage of Time as if I could lay hands on it &
> stop it: as if youth were yet in me & life and youth were one.[1]

> All the world seems to lie before me, none behind.[2]

> I feel within me the rebellious unspoken word, I will not be old.[3]

> The strangest though not the worst of all in me is a rebellion (I know not what
> else to call it) against growing old.[4]

Above all, these volumes show Gladstone progressively isolated but
persistently resilient. Resilient, in that the years after 1865 showed him
flexible and inventive enough to move from the settled and predictable
field of government trade and finance to a central point in the increasingly
volatile and complex politics of British liberal-radicalism in such a way as
both to encourage and control them. Isolated, in that he lived on, both the
only survivor of the tractarian politicians of the 1830s, and the only relic
of the Peelite conservatives, still described in *Dod's Parliamentary Companion* (until 1870) as a liberal-conservative. He noted in 1864:

> Newcastle's death removes the very last of those contemporaries who were also
> my political friends. How it speaks to me!
>   'Be doing: and be done'.[5]

To 'be doing' was never a problem for Gladstone; to 'be done' was to prove
a painful process, for him and for others.

---

[1] 29 Dec. 59.   [2] 31 Dec. 64.   [3] 29 Dec. 60.   [4] 29 Dec. 61.
[5] 19 Oct. 64. See also 11 July 68: 'Visited the [National] Portrait Gallery. Its two or
three last rooms were indeed for me a meeting of the dead: I seemed to know everyone.'

Hawarden
Monday Jan. One[1] 1855.
The Circumcision

Ch. 11 A.M. Wrote to Earl of Aberdeen—Sir T.G.—Sir H. Vavasour—Scotts—and minutes. Worked on my books: of which the last arrival actually came on Saturday. Read Watson's Memoirs[2]—Monti's Galeotto Manfredi[3]—Foreign Legion papers[4] Wrote MS Theol.

Th[eology]. Our Lord loves to represent the gifts accorded to the Christian under the figure of commodities in the hands of a trader. And why does he thus fetch his forms of teaching from the manner of unrighteousness? Surely these among others may be reasons. Because where there is a real interest and desire, as there certainly is in the pursuit of money, men proceed with activity, with earnestness, with precision: they apply all their powers, whatever they may be: they do not make much of small difficulties but little of great ones: they venture the present for the sake of the future: they thrust aside out of their path every thing that is frivolous and trivial with reference to the main object: their whole life falls into order & discipline, all the movements of it have a purpose, and the consciousness of that purpose shapes and governs all those movements either sensibly or if insensibly yet not less truly. And further it is in money and merchandise that we best appreciate the manners of great and small, and the application of means to ends without waste, in the quantities exactly adapted to produce them. Now what is all this but the framework of a Christian discipline ready to be applied to the Christian end? Hence it is conversely that we hear a worldly man talk of money, it has become a common phrase, as the one thing needful. And our work what is it but to study with his earnestness the science of spiritual exchanges, of the exchange of time, thought, money, health, influence, against the inward gifts of God & the likeness of Christ?[5]

2. T.

Ch. 8½ A.M. Wrote to Sir A. Spearman—Mr Glyn—Mr Anderson—C.A. Wood—Mr MacMahon MP—Sir J. Young and minutes. Read Watson's Memoirs—and Martial. Worked on my books. Attended the rent dinner 1½–4½. Tea at the Rectory.

3. Wed.

Ch. 8½ A.M. Wrote to M. Duveyrier—Mr G. Smith—& minutes. Worked on my books—finished the whole affair: & found them (Theology & Literature)

[1] Lambeth MS 1482 continued.
[2] See 29 Dec. 54.
[3] By V. Monti (1788); a tragedy.
[4] Probably the returns on foreign troop employment: *PP* 1855, xxxii. 407.
[5] Dated 1 January 1855, Add MS 44745, f. 1.

5185 Vols. Children's play in evg. Read Watson's Memoirs Vol 2—Butler's d'Aguesseau[1]—Victoria Ch. Confer. Report.[2] Saw Mrs. Read.[3]

4. Th.

Ch. 8½ A.M. Wrote to Sir C. Trevelyan—Jas Wilson—R. Wilbraham—T. Moffatt[4]—G. Burnett—C. Skeet[5]—and minutes. Walk with C. Worked on accounts. Read Watson's Memoirs—Butler's D'Aguesseau—Conv. with Willy on his arrangements.[6] Hawarden Concert (most creditable) at 7½ P.M. Supper at the Rectory afterwards. I got among the Professional singers. Home at midnight.

5. Fr.

Ch. 8½ A.M. Wrote to D. of Newcastle[7]—Ld Cowley—D. of Buccleuch— Sir J. Graham—E. of Aberdeen—Mr Wilson—Mr Read—and minutes. Saw Mr Burnett. Walk with C. & alone. Read Butler on the Roman Law— Newland's acct of Norwegian Church[8]—Watson's Memoirs (finished). Conv. with C: on Willy's arrangements.

6. Sat. Epiph[any]

Church 11 A.M. and C.s birthday: may the blessing of God be with her. Wrote to Earl of Aberdeen—Robn. G—Sir A. Spearman—J.N.G.—Mr Moffat—R. Barker—Supt. Chester Station—and minutes. Read Butler on Rom. Law (finished)—Woods office papers[9]—Goldsmith's Poems.[10] Arranged for departure on Monday.

7. 1 S. Epiph.

Hn. Ch. mg (& H.C.) also evg. The Talbot children went to Broughton. Wrote to R. Wilbraham—O.B. Cole—& minutes. Read Doctr. St C. Borromoei[11]—Tiers Ordre de S. Francois[12]—Lindsay's Xtn Idolatry[13]— and Tracts. Nitzsch Christliche Lehre.[14] Packing at night.

[1] C. *Butler, *Memoir of . . . Henry Francis d'Aguesseau . . . and an historical and literary account of the Roman and canon law* (1830).
[2] On bill then being passed in Victoria to give local autonomy to the anglican church in Victoria; the bill was similar to the private member's bill which Gladstone had proposed in 1852: *PP* 1856, xliv. 137.
[3] Probably the wife of T. Read, the local shoemaker.
[4] The Hawarden surgeon.
[5] Charles Joseph Skeet, 1812–92; bookseller and publisher in the Strand.
[6] His allowance, see 11 Jan. 55.
[7] Some in Conacher, 382.
[8] H. G. *Newland, *Forest life: a fisherman's sketches in Norway and Sweden* (1854); ch. xiii.
[9] On the Kennedy affair, see 6 June 53n.
[10] *The poetical works of Oliver *Goldsmith. With a biographical sketch of the author* (1855).
[11] Probably G. B. Castiglione, *Sentimenti dir S. Carlo Borromeo intorno agli spettacoli* (1759).
[12] See 17 Sept. 48.
[13] T. *Lindsey, *Conversations on Christian Idolatry* (1792).
[14] C. I. Nitzsch, *System der christlichen Lehre für academische Vorlesungen* (1831).

8. M. [*London*]

Wrote to Mr Vardon—and minutes. Saw Lord Aberdeen—do *cum* Sir J. Graham—Mr Jackson MP. Off at 10 with a party of 17: reached D[owning] St at 4½. Worked on business & clearing my chaos. Read D'Anquetil[1]—La Guerronnière.[2]

9. T.

Wrote to Ld Blayney[3]—Rev Mr Dowding—& minutes. Read La Guerronnière. Dined with the Herberts. Cabinet 2¾–6½. Saw Sir A. Spearman—Duke of Argyll—Bp of London—S. Herbert.

10. Wed.

Wrote to Sir R. Peel—Ld Lyttelton—Mr R. Scott—H. Glynne—and minutes. Read La Guerronnière. Dined with the Herberts. Tasso with W. & A. Worked on preparing Bills.[4] Saw Sir A. Spearman—Mr Arbuthnot —Sir C. Trevelyan—Mr G. Thorp—Mr R. Herbert—Mr Vardon (H of C.)— Mr Wilson—Lord Aberdeen *cum* Sir J. Graham—Mr Herbert.

11. Th.

Wrote to Rev Dr Wolff—S.R.G.—J.E. Denison—Mr Wood—Mr D. Gladstone—J.N.G.—Sir J. Young—T.G.—Mr Wilson—Macinroy—& minutes. Read de la Guerronnière. Settled with Willy the matter of his allowance. Saw Mr Freshfield—Mr Lacaita. Mr L. & R. Herbert dined. Cabinet 3¼–6½. Tasso with W. & A.

12. Fr.

Wrote to Mr Wilson and minutes. Read De La Guerronnière—and L. Faucher on Engl. & French Finance.[5] Saw Mr Roebuck MP.—Mr Wood cum Timm & R Hill—Mr Goulburn—Mr [L.A.] Jones (Treasury)—Sir A. Spearman—Ld Abn. with Sir J. Graham. Worked on Superann[uatio]n question & wrote Mem. with a plan.[6] Tasso with W. A., & Stephen by way of experiment.

13. Sat.

Wrote to Leightons—Sir J. Graham—D of Argyll—Sir C. Wood—Rev W. Jelf—Rev Mr Powell—Rev P.H. Morgan[7]—Sir C. Trevelyan & minutes.

[1] Probably A. H. Anquetil Duperron, *Dignité du commerce, et de l'état de commerçant* (1789).

[2] A. de la Gueronnière, *Les Hommes d'État de l'Angleterre au xixe siècle* (1855); see 22 Feb. 55n.

[3] Cadwallader Davis Blayney, 1802–74; 12th Baron Blayney 1834; an Irish representative peer from 1841; had written on an appt.: Add MS 44530, f. 10.

[4] See 12, 19 Jan. 55.

[5] L. Faucher, *Economie politique* (1855), i, ch. vi, on war finance.

[6] With a draft of the Bill: Add MS 44745, f. 2.

[7] Philip Howell Morgan, b. ? 1816; perpetual curate of Bettws Penpont, Brecon, from 1842; declining preferment: Add MS 44530, f. 12.

Tasso with the children as usual. Saw Sir C. Trevelyan—Mr Wilson—Baron Usedom[1]—Earl of Ellesmere—Duchess of Sutherland—Mr Timm & Mr R. Hill—Mr J.D. Cooke—F. Lawley. Read de la Guerronnière—Quarterly on Conduct of War[2]—L. Faucher (finished).

14. 2. S.Epiph.

Whitehall m̤ St A[ndrews] Wells St aftn. MS on 12 Rom 1. aloud in evg. Conv. with children on ἀγάπη ἀνυπόκριτος.[3] Wrote to S. Herbert. Saw Ld Abn. cum Sir J. Graham—Sir W. James. Read V. Mildert Bampton L[ectures][4]—Cassandri Dialogus[5]—Memoria di Marcet (Gesuita).[6] Mazie had one of her crouplike attacks. C. with admirable forethought & a mother's instinct had sent her to bed & taken measures very early: there was a fight during the night but thank God all went well.

15. M.

Wrote to Sir A. Spearman—Mr Wilson—Ld Clarendon—Mr J. Wood—Ld Lyttelton—Robn. G.—Bp of Argyll—Sir G. Clerk—Jas Watson—Mr Timm —D of Newcastle—Capt Neville[7]—D of Argyll—and minutes. Saw Mr Westcott (sat)[8]—Earl of Aberdeen—Mr Sandars (dentist). Tasso with the children. Read De la Guerronnière—Quarty (part) on the Campaign.[9]

16. T.

Wrote to M. Duveyrier—J. Jones—E. Clarendon(2)[10]—G. Burnett & minutes. Cabinet 3¼-7. Dined with Sir C. Trevelyan. Saw Sir C. Trevelyan (Commt.)—do *cum* Sir S. Northcote—Mr Arbuthnot—Mr Timm (Newsp. Bill)—Mr Macaulay. Read Q.R. on Campaign (finished)—'The Book'.[11]

17. W.

Wrote to V.C. Oxford—H. Lees—Sir C. Trevelyan—Robn. G.—Sir A. Spearman—Mr Barnes—Mr 'J. Gladstone'—Scotts—Sir Geo. Grey—Ld Elcho—& minutes.[12] Saw Mr Wilson. Called to see Wolff (2): absent[R]. Worked on papers & accts. Read Ed. Rev. on the War.[13] Br Quarterly on do[14]—De La Guerronnière—Tasso with the children.

[1] Count Karl Georg Ludwig Guido von Usedom, 1805–84; Prussian diplomat, then without a post; earlier in Rome.
[2] *Quarterly Review*, xcvi. 277 (December 1854).   [3] 'undisguised brotherly love'.
[4] W. *Van Mildert, *An inquiry into the general principle of scripture interpretation* (1815).
[5] See 10 Dec. 54.
[6] Italian tr. of M. Marcet de la Roche-Arnaud, *Mémoires d'un jeune Jésuite* (1828).
[7] Edward Neville, 1824–1908, nephew of 3rd Baron Braybrooke; A.D.C. to Sir R. *England in Crimea; had sent enclosures on the war; Add MS 44550, f. 13.
[8] See 25, 29 Nov. 54; picture untraced.
[9] *Quarterly Review*, xcvi. 200 (December 1854).
[10] Hostile to *Clarendon's plans for war subsidies to Sardinia; Add MS 44530, f. 13v.
[11] L.N.R. [Ellen H. *Ranyard], *The book and its story: a narrative for the young* (1852); on the bible society.
[12] Circulating copies of Newspaper Stamp Bill: Add MS 44745, f. 16.
[13] *Edinburgh Review*, ci. 261 (January 1855).
[14] *British Quarterly Review*, xxi. 182 (January 1855); 'Our foreign policy, who is to blame'.

18. *Th.*

Wrote to E. of Clarendon—[H.] Mont[agu] Villiers—Sir J. Graham—A. Gordon—V. Chancellor Oxf—J.N.G.—Ld Chancellor—and minutes. Saw Mr A. Gordon (Comn.)—Sir A. Spearman *cum* Mr Anderson—and one late [R]. Again missed finding Wolff[R]. Eight to dinner. Cabinet 3½–7. Read Fraser's Magazine[1]—De la Guerronnière. Worked on private arrangements.

19. *Fr.*

Wrote to Stanistreets—A. Oswald—Rev D Robertson—A. Gordon—Ld Aberdeen—& minutes. Saw Bp of NZ: a farewell—Baron Usedom— Gombier (for butler)[2]—S. Herbert. Dined with the Herberts. Tasso with the children. Worked on private arrangements. Educ. Commee. 1½–3. Cabinet 3–6. (Opened the Examining Board affair & closed the Newsp. Stamp.)[3]—Read Fox's Memoirs[4]—De la Guerronnière.

20 *Sat.*

Wrote to E. Hammond[5]—Mr Waters[6]—E. Cardwell—Robn. G.—Bp of N Scotia—Sir C.E.T[revelyan]—& minutes. Worked on priv. matters. Eight to dinner. Saw Mr Wilson—Sir C. Trevelyan—Marq. d'Azeglio—Mr Arbuthnot *cum* Mr Greenwood—Lord Aberdeen—Lord Granville—A. Gordon. Read de la Guerronnière—Fox's Correspondence. Cabinet 3½–6¾. Exam[inin]g Board agreed to: Also War Board: & Transport Do.

21. *3 S.Epiph.*

Whitehall mg & St James's Evg. MS for 6 S Epiph. aloud. Wrote 'reasons' on the matter of Kennedy & the Committee.[7] Read Cassander & Calixtus— Xtn Remembr. on the Eirenic writers & on Chr. Education[8]—Monro's Sermons on the War[9]—Bennet's Life of Bogue.[10] Saw Bp of Argyll.

22. *M.*

Wrote to The Speaker—Mr Wilson(2)—Ld Canning—Miss Slade—Mr Jowett[11]—Sir C. Trevelyan—Jas Watson—Ld A. Hervey—Mr Rawson— and minutes. Dined with the Wortleys. Saw Mr J. Wood—Sir A. Spearman —City (Conservancy) Deputation—Sir C. Trevelyan—Mr Hayter—Rev. D.

---

[1] *Fraser's Magazine*, lii. 1 (January 1855).
[2] See 6 Feb. 55.
[3] The draft order in council for civil service examinations and the Newspaper Stamp Bill, abolishing stamp duty; both executed by Palmerston's govt.; see M. Wright, *Treasury control* (1969), 63 and 3 Mar. 55.
[4] Lord J. *Russell, ed., *Memorials . . . of C. J. *Fox*, 4v. (1853–7).
[5] Edmund *Hammond, 1802–90; permanent undersecretary at foreign office 1854–73; cr. Baron 1874.
[6] George Waters, Irish distiller; in correspondence on spirit duties.
[7] Add MS 44654, f. 35.
[8] *Christian Remembrancer*, xxix. 192, 215 (January 1855).
[9] E. *Monro, *Leonard and Dennis; or the soldier's tale* (1855), 38–54; sermons and prayers.
[10] See 26 June 53.
[11] Appointing him civil service examiner: Add MS 44530, f. 16.

Robertson—Ld A. Hervey—Earl of Aberdeen—Mr S. Herbert(2). Also saw one[R]. Read Fox Mem—Leslie's Hand Book[1]—Clinton's Remains.[2]

23. T.

Wrote to Mr Rawlinson—Sir C. Wood—Ld Aberdeen—Mr H. Raikes—D of Newcastle—Robn G.—Mr J. Blundell[3]—Mr Burgon—& minutes. Sir J. Hanmer dined. Read Fox's Memoirs. H of C. $4\frac{1}{4}$–$6\frac{1}{4}$.[4] Wrote Mem. on Col. Ch. Legisln.[5] Saw Mr Goulburn—Earl of Aberdeen—Hon F. Lawley—Duke of Newcastle—Lord Granville—Audit Commissioners.—also —West[R].

24. Wed.

Wrote to Sir C. Trevelyan—S.R.G.—E. of Aberdeen—E. Granville—and minutes. Read Maitland on Convn[6]—Ch. Defence Report—Fox's Memoirs. Saw Earl of Aberdeen—Mr S. Herbert—Mr Wilson—Sir C. Trevelyan—Rev D. Robertson—Mr Jowett—Hon A. Gordon—Saw M.M. Dumin[R]. Cabinet $3\frac{1}{4}$–$6\frac{3}{4}$: and at Ld Aberdeens $10\frac{1}{4}$–1.

Cabinet. Jan. 24. 55.

Earl of Aberdeen read a letter[7] from Lord J. Russell stating that Mr. Roebuck had given notice of a motion—that he did not see how it could be resisted—that as it implied a censure on the conduct of colleagues he had no course but to resign. On receiving this letter last night his first impression was that it involved the breaking up of the Government. On further consideration however feeling how desirable it was that the Govt. shd. continue in office if it cd. be done with[8] propriety, dignity & utility, he was disposed to think they should do so.

D. of Newcastle apologised for speaking first but did so as well knowing that he was alluded to in the letter & by the general voice his was now declared, whether justly or unjustly, to be the weak place in the Govt.[9] This being so, he had to consider on the other hand how important it was to avert the evils wh. wd. attend on the formation of such a Govt. as was likely to succeed us—with Malmesbury for its F[oreign] Secretary & Ellenborough, notwithstanding his great talents, for its War Minister. The country wanted a victim however, & he was most willing to be the victim & thought he ought to be so. On these terms if he might presume to make a suggestion he thought he could show how the Govt. might be carried on with credit & strength: namely that he shd. resign & Ld Palmerston should take his place.

Ld. Palmerston argued that the feeling of the country whether rightly or wrongly was favourable to his having the Dept. of War. That he considered Newcastle liable to no blame in his administration of it: on the contrary N. had done & thought of many things wh. he P. should have omitted to think of. But he was prepared to place himself at the disposal of the Cabinet for this or any

---

[1] C. R. *Leslie, *Handbook for young painters* (1855).
[2] *Literary remains of Henry Fynes *Clinton*, ed. C. J. F. Clinton (1854).
[3] John Blundell, 1824–96, of Crook Hall, Chorley.
[4] Public Health Amdt. Act: *H* cxxxvi. 912.
[5] On colonial diocesan synods: Add MS 44745, f. 18.
[6] S. R. Maitland, *Convocation. Remarks on the Charge recently delivered by the Bishop of Oxford* (1855).
[7] Printed in S. *Walpole, *Life of . . . Russell* (1889) ii. 237.
[8] 'any degree' deleted.   [9] Half a page here blank.

purpose, if they thought he could be useful: as he agreed in the opinion that the formation of any other Govt. from whatever men or combination of men wd. under the circs. be an evil to the country.

Ld. Abn. expressed his willingness to adopt the proposal wh. the D. of Newcastle had made in the most highminded manner, the manner thoroughly in keeping with his character.

Sir Geo. Grey said he as at present (thus far at the time—resumed Mch. 9. 55) advised thought resignation absolutely necessary after the secession of Lord J. Russell: he did justice to D. of N. and believed he had done & thought of many things wh. wd. have wholly escaped him Sir G. Grey.

Sir C. Wood, Lansdowne, Clarendon, & I do not recollect whether any others (Whigs if any) spoke in a similar sense.

Sir J. Graham thought N.s resignation cd. not be accepted absolutely but did not see why he should not take another office & continue in the Cabinet.

I said I could not see that it was less difficult for N. to accept the change of office than the absolute resignation—that upon that subject I felt the greatest difficulty in forming a judgment—that I did not however think the resignation of the Cabinet would be justified by Lord John's resignation, although I fully saw and admitted that if a part of the Cabinet thought so this might justify & require the resignation of the rest. Clarendon indicated a desire that as Newcastle wished to resign Lord J. Russell might come back. I with others treated this mode of handling the subject as quite out of the question: & the idea fell still born.

A sort of message came from Lord John to know whether he should attend the Cabinet!!

It was determined that Lord Abn. should carry our resignations to the Queen. Charles Wood was commissioned to let Lord John know. I objected to his being informed that we had resigned on account of his resignation—we resigned as a body because some of us thought it necessary to resign on account of his resignation, & the rest of the Cabinet cd. not remain without this portion of their colleagues.

It was agreed that C. Wood should simply state the fact & no more.[1]

25. *Th.*

Wrote to Lord Aberdeen—Sir C. Trevelyan—R.M. Bromley—Mr Cowan—Rev D. Robertson—H. Glynne—Dr Jeune—Mr Rawlinson—and minutes. S. Herbert dined. Saw Sir C. Trevelyan—Rev Mr Jowett—Mr A. Gordon—Mr Wilson—Sir C. Wood—Sir J. Graham—Mr S. Herbert—E. Cardwell & J. Young. Cabinet 12½–4¼. Then to the House.[2] Ld Abns. (with N[ewcastle], S. H[erbert], Sir J. G[raham]) 10–1. Read Rawlinson's sermon.[3] To Bed at 3.

Jan. 25. Thursday. Lord Aberdeen announced that the Queen declined to receive our resignations and urged with the greatest earnestness that the decision should be reconsidered.

This wish of the Queen's produced a remarkable effect. Grey led the way in retiring from his position of the preceding[4] day: & the Government as a body were saved from the very questionable position in which the course thus taken by Grey and his friends on the preceding[4] day would have placed them, that of flying

---

[1] Dated, at the end, 9 March 1855, Add MS 44745, f. 22.

[2] Misc. business: *H* cxxxvi. 940.

[3] G. Rawlinson, 'Thoughts on the closing year' (1855).   [4] 'yesterday' deleted.

from Roebuck's motion. We all seemed to feel (what Argyll had if I remember right expressed on the previous occasion) that we were bound to abide the sentence of the House of Commons.[1]

Accordingly [rest blank]

26. *Fr.*

Wrote to Ld Palmerston[2]—Rev Mr [blank] & minutes. Cabinet 3–4¼ before the Debate. Saw Mr Wood *cum* Mr Timm—Mr Wood (resp. K[ennedy])— Mr Hayter—Mr Wilson—Ld Canning—Mr Gordon—Earl of Abn. (bef. Cabinet). H of C. 4¼–12.[3] Read Virgil Æn IV—Fox's Memoirs—Also *the* [Kennedy] Correspce. & noted the dates.

Lord John's explanation, which was very untrue in its general effect though I believe kindly conceived in feeling as well as tempered with some grains of policy & a contemplation of another possible Premiership,[4] carried the House with him as Herbert observed while he was speaking. Palmerston's reply to him was wretched. It produced in the House that is in so much of the House as wd. otherwise have been favourable, a flatness & deadness of spirit towards the Govt., wh. was indescribable: & Charles Wood with a marked expression of face said while it was going on 'And this is to be our leader!' I was myself so painfully full of the scene that when P. himself sat down I was on the very point of saying to him unconsciously [']Can anything more be said'? But no one wd. rise in the adverse sense & therefore there was no opening for a Minister.

P. had written to ask me to follow Lord J. on account of his being a *party*.[5] But it was justly thought in the Cabinet that there were good reasons against my taking this part upon me & so the arrangement was changed.

In the evening I went up to the Ladies' Gallery. Lady John was there in a box apart from the other wives & sent for me. She seemed shy & embarrassed as well she might. She hated she said these political crises.—I told her Lord John's speech was very kind but that I did not agree in his mode of viewing or putting the facts.[6]

27. *Sat.*

Wrote to Ld Granville—Mr Shaw—Lord Aberdeen—Dr Jeune—E. Romilly—Sir G. Clerk—Hon F. Lawley—Duke of Newcastle, & minutes. Cabinet 2¼–5½. Saw Lord Aberdeen—Ld Elcho—Sir C. Trevelyan—S. Herbert. Dined with the Herberts. Read Walcheren Debates[7]—Fox's Memoirs Vol. 2.

28. *4 S.Epiph.* X

St James mg. St George aft. MS. for Sexa[gesima] aloud in evg. Saw Ld

---

[1] Begun on 26 Jan., but dated at end 9 march 1855; Add MS 44745, f. 28.

[2] In Guedalla, *P*, 100.

[3] *Russell's resignation statement, followed by *Roebuck's motion for a select cttee. to inquire into the condition of the army at Sebastopol and of the conduct of govt. departments: *H* cxxxvi. 960, 979. Roebuck collapsed during his speech.

[4] 'produced' here deleted.   [5] Guedalla, *P*. 100.

[6] Dated and initialled 9 March 1855; Add MS 44745, f. 31.

[7] I series *H* xv. 162, quoted by him defending the govt. two days later.

Abn. *cum* Sir J. Graham & alone. Read Calixtus &c—Anti Montlorier[1]—
Bennett's Bogue. Saw West[R].

29. M.

Wrote to S. Herbert—Sir C. Trevelyan—Ld Lyttelton—and minutes. Read
'the Book'. The Herberts dined. Worked on the subject of Debate. Saw S.
Herbert—Ld Hardinge Sir A. Spearman—Mr Wilson—Wilson Patten (aft.
H. of C.). H of C. 4½–7 and 8½–1¾. Spoke (1½ h) on the Committee: hard &
heavy work: especially as to the cases of three persons Lord J.R., D. of
Newcastle, & Lord Raglan.[2]

30. T.

Wrote to J. Bramston—Sir C. Trevelyan(3)—Mr Wood —Mr J. D. Cook—
Mr H. Raikes—R Phillimore—F R Bonham—R.W. Rawson—Sol. General
—and minutes. Read Fox's Memoirs. Saw Sir J. Young—Earl of Aberdeen[3]
—Mr Wilson—Duke of Argyll—Capt. Gladstone—Sir Wm. Heathcote—
D[uche]ss of Sutherland &c.—S. Herbert—Rev Mr Temple. Cabinet 1–2.
We exchanged friendly adieus. Dined with the Herberts.

This was a day of personal lightheartedness: but the problem for the
nation is no small one.[4]

31. Wed.

Wrote to Lady Graham—Mr L B Dykes[5] —Mr M'Culloch—R. Phillimore—
Rev Mr Daniells—Ld Derby (after drafts)[6]—and minutes. Dined at
Grillions. Read Fox's Memoirs—Rep. on Poor in Knoidart.[7] Saw Sir A.
Spearman—Mr Wilson—Mr T. Green M.P.—Robn. G.—Ld Aberdeen day
& in evg.—Ld Abn. *cum* S. Herbert—Ld Canning—Ld Wenlock—Sir J.
Graham (cum S.H.)—Ld Palmerston (before & after Clarendon). Worked
on Treas. papers. This day must have a separate Memm.

Jan. 31. Ld. Palmerston came to see me between 3 & 4 with a proposal from Ld.
Derby that he & I with S. Herbert should take office under him: P. to be President
of the Council & lead the H. of C.—Not finding me when he called before[,] he
had gone to S.H. who seemed to be disinclined. I inquired 1. whether Derby
mentioned Graham? 2. Whether he had told Ld. P. if his persevering with the
Commission he had received would depend on the answer to this proposal. 3. How
he was himself inclined. He answered the two first questions in the negative, &
said as to the third, though not keenly, that he felt disinclined, but that if he
refused it wd. be attributed to his contemplating another result which other result
he considered wd. be agreeable to the country.

[1] Untraced.
[2] He argued the proposed cttee. had 'no foundation either in the constitution or in the
practice of preceding Parliaments': *H* cxxxvi. 1205. The ministry was defeated in 305 to
148; annotated div. lists in Add MS 44586, f. 1, speech notes in Add MS 44654, f. 1.
[3] See Conacher, 548.   [4] Morley, i. 525.
[5] J. B. *Dykes had written to defend *Herbert: Add MS 44530, f. 1.
[6] Stating 'his sincere desire to offer' a *Derby administration 'an independent Parliamentary support', quoted in *H* cxxxvi. 1822 (23 February 1855).
[7] On destitute females in Glenelg: *PP* 1855 xlvi. 105.

I then argued strongly with him that though he might form a Govt., & though if he formed it he would certainly start it amidst immense clapping of hands, yet he could not have any reasonable prospect of stable Parliamentary support: on the one hand wd. stand Derby with his phalanx, on the other Lord J. Russell of necessity a centre & nucleus of discontent, & between these two there wd. & could be no room for a Parliamentary majority such as wd. uphold his Government. He argued only rather faintly the other way & seemed rather to come to my way of thinking.

I said that even if the proposition were entertained there wd. be much to consider—that I thought it clear, whatever else was doubtful, that we cd. not join without him, for in his absence the wound would not heal kindly—again, that I cd. not act without Lord Aberdeen's approval, nor should I willingly separate myself from Graham—that if we joined, we must join in force, but I was disposed to wish that if all details cd. be arranged we should join in that manner rather than that Derby shd. give up the Commission, though I thought the best thing of all wd. be his forming a Ministry of his own men, provided only he could get a good or fair Foreign Secretary instead of Clarendon who in any case wd. be an immense loss.

Herbert came in & gave a more adverse turn to the conversation saying the change wd. be too sharp & sudden, but that Derby shd. go on & wd. have great advantages for making peace, while we ought to give him a real support.

I went off to speak to Lord Abn. & Pn. went to speak to Clarendon: with respect to whom he had told D. that he cd. hardly enter any Govt. wh. had not C. at the Foreign Office.

When we reassembled I asked Lord P. whether he had made up his mind for himself independently of us, inasmuch as I thought that if he had that was enough to close the whole question?

He answered yes that he should tell D. he did not think he could render useful service in his Admn. He then left—it was perhaps 6½. Herbert & I sat down to write but thought it well to send off nothing till after dinner & we went to Grillions where we had a small but merry party, H. even beyond himself amusing. At night we went to Lord Abn., & Graham's, & so my letter came through some slight emendations to the form in which it went.[1] I had doubts in my own mind whether D[erby] had even intended to propose to H. & me *except* in conjunction with P., though I had no doubt that without P. it could not do: and I framed my letter so as not to assume that I had had an independent proposal but to make my refusal a part of his.[2]

Thurs. Feb. One. 1855.

H of C. & H. of L. 4½–7.[3] Wrote to Rev R.W. Brown—Mr Wilson—Ld Palmerston (& copy[4]—Sir J. Graham—G. & Co—Bp of Man—E. Clarendon —Sir A. Spearman—Solr. General—Sig. Cas. di Lieto—and minutes. Saw Robn. G.—Sir J. Graham—Mr Bonham—Mr S. Herbert—Bp of Oxford— A. Gordon—Mr J.E. Denison—C. Walewski—Mr Arbuthnot—Ld Palmerston—Mr Cardwell—Earl of Aberdeen. Saw Cary + 1[R]. Dined with the

[1] Add MS 44140, f. 192.
[2] Dated apparently 21 February 1855 (2 February may be intended); Add MS 44745, f. 79. This, and parts of mema. until 28 February, in Morley, i. 525–41.
[3] *Aberdeen's resignation statement: *H* cxxxvi. 1234.
[4] Some in Guedalla, *P*, 101.

Wenlocks. Read Fox—Battle Pieces[1]—Napoleons letters to Joseph.[2] Saw Mr Disraeli in H. of L. & put out my hand wh was very kindly accepted.[3]

F.1.55. I went to Cardwell, recited the proceedings of yesterday & found him to be altogether in the same sense with myself in regard to them. He considered that if our Coalition had failed or was run out we could not attempt a new form of it but that we ought to hold together.

In the afternoon I saw Lord Aberdeen on his way to the H. of Lords for the purpose of entreating him not to say anything that wd. make it impracticable for him to resume the Govt. It had only impressed itself on my mind today that a failure among the Whigs was very far from impossible and that if this took place following upon Derby's it might make it quite practicable for Lord Aberdeen's Govt. to continue in office with such changes, under him, as might appear desirable. He said as I understood him that he shd. have a further opportunity of speaking to the Queen: and his words in the H. of L. by no means closed up the future.[4]

I yesterday also called on Lord P. & read him my letter to Lord Derby. He said 'Nothing can be better.'[5]

2. *Fr. Purification*

Wrote to Rob. Phillimore—Jas Watson—Ld Lansdowne—G.F. Bowen— Ld Clarendon—Robn G.—Mr Wilson—and minutes. Luncheon at Ld Overstone's & saw his pictures. Saw Lord Lansdowne—Mr S. Herbert— Mr J.E. Denison—Sir J. Graham—Earl of Aberdeen—Mr Goulburn—Mr Wilson—R. Phillimore—Mr A. Gordon—D. of Argyll—Sir J. Young—E. Granville. Dined at Stafford House. Wrote Pol. Mema. Read Fox's Memoirs.

Feb. 2. 55 In consequence of a commun[icatio]n from Ld. Lansdowne I went to him in the forenoon & found him just returned from Windsor.

He told me [he] had undertaken to make inquiries on the Queen's behalf among such public men as he thought most likely to be of service, without giving Her any expectation but intending to advise Her if he found himself able to do so. He trusted I should not mind speaking freely to him & I engaged to do it only promising that in so crude & dark a state of facts it was impossible to go beyond first impressions. We then conversed on various combinations as 1. Ld. J. Russell Premier 2. Ld. Palmerston 3. Ld. Clarendon 4. Ld. Lansdowne himself. Of the first I said I doubted whether in the present state of feeling he could get a ministry on its legs. In answer to a question from him I added that I thought viewing my relations to Ld. Abn. & to Newcastle, & *his* to them also, the public feeling would be offended & it wd. not be for the public interest if I were to form part of his Govt. Of the second I said that it appeared to me Lord P. could not obtain a Parly. majority. Aloof from him wd. stand on the one hand Derby & his party, on the other Lord J. Russell—who I took it for granted wd. never serve under him—whatever the impression made by his recent conduct yet his high personal character & station, forty years career, one half of it in the leadership of his party,

---

[1] H. and F. Lushington, *Two battle-pieces* (1855).
[2] *The confidential correspondence of Napoleon Bonaparte with his brother Joseph*, 2v. (1855), tr. from P. E. A. Du Casse, *Mémoires et correspondance politique et militaire du Roi Joseph* (1853) (also read by Gladstone, see 22 Mar. 55).
[3] Morley, i. 528.   [4] Dated here 2 February 1855.
[5] Dated 2 February [1855]; Add MS 44745, f. 85.

and the close association of his name with all the great legislative changes of the period, must ever make him a Power in the State & render it impossible for a Government depending on the Liberal Party to live independently of him. I also hinted at injurious effects wh. the substitution of P. for Lord A. wd. produce on foreign Powers at this critical moment but dwelt chiefly on the impossibility of his having a majority. In this Lord L. seemed to agree.

He mentioned Ld. Clarendon as First Minister either moving to the Treasury or remaining at the F.O. which we agreed it was of great importance to the country he should do. I said that I wd. not[1] venture to say anything on this wh. wd. in some respects be a preferable arrangement to the others but should wish to reflect on it and to consult Ld. Abn. & Sir J. Graham. But see below.

Lastly I said that if Ld. L. himself could venture to risk his health & strength by taking the Govt. this wd. be the best arrangement. My opinion was that at this crisis Derby if he cd. have formed an administration wd. have had advantages with regard to the absorbing questions of the war & of a peace to follow it such as no other combination could possess. Failing this I wished for a homogeneous Whig Government: or as I believe I called it to Ld. L. [a] Govt. formed from among those with whom he had acted during his political life. The best form of it would be under him. He said he might dare it provisionally if he cd. see his way to a permanent arrangement at the end of a short term: but he cd. see nothing of the sort at present.

He looked to collecting under one of the heads I have named most of the *disjecta membra* of the Aberdeen Admn. and I thought on the whole with a preference for Ld. John founded on personal loyalty & recollection of the past, for he strongly disapproved of his late conduct. But I told him strongly and repeatedly that I thought a Coalition Govt. as such had peculiar sources of weakness—that the idea was at present under the discredit of failure—that if the endeavour to make a homogeneous Govt. should fail we might get back to it but in that case I was of opinion that the old Coalition would be preferable to a new one: meaning by the old form of it, a Govt. with Lord Aberdeen at the head though it might be modified in its members: by the new, a Govt. with a head other than Lord Aberdeen tho' it might contain many of his colleagues. The former would only be the prolongation of the old experiment, the latter would be a new one, with a fresh stake, and a greater venture.

At the same time it was clear I said that this could not come about until something had been tried under a commission from the Queen to a chief such as we had named. If that failed, *then.* Ld. L. did not express concurrence in the idea that the Govt. cd. revert to Ld. Abn.

I went from him to S. Herbert & told him the sum of the conversation before Lord L. came to him.

Then I went to Graham & did the same. He expressed very strongly his intention to stand by Ld. Abn. and this both as a matter of public policy with reference to his general wisdom & especially to peace, and likewise with reference to Lord A's feelings which he thought would be wounded by abandonment. It was plain that Lord A. whether he knew it or not felt an interest in retaining office and he (G) now thought it quite possible that his turn might again arrive.[2]

3. Sat.

Wrote to D of Newcastle—Rev Dr Worthington—Rev Mr Haddan &

[1] 'speak absolutely' here deleted.
[2] Initialled and dated 2 February [1855]; Add MS 44745, f. 87.

minutes. Dined at the Speaker's. Sat to Mr Westcott. Saw Earl of Aberdeen(2)—Sir J. Young—Lord J. Russell—Mr S. Herbert (2)—Duke of Argyll—Mr Wilson—Sir C. Wood—Sir Geo. Grey—Sir R. Bethell—D of Newcastle—Miss Eden. Wrote Pol. Mema. Read Fox's Memoirs.

Feb. 3. I called on Ld. Abn. acc[ordingl]y. His commun[icatio]n was this. Last night Col. Phipps came by the Prince's desire. Ld L[ansdowne] had advised the Queen to see Ld. J.R. and he had been to her to explain his conduct. In the course of the conversation he had managed to state that he was ready to undertake the formation of a Government. But she did not avail herself of this intimation: & it was arranged that J.R. should meet L[ansdowne] & P[almerston] in the evening, out of whose commun[ication]ns Ld. A. thought it likely that a commission to Clarendon to form a Govt. might proceed.

Today for the first time Lord Aberdeen let drop a sort of opinion on our duties in the crisis as to one point: heretofore he had restrained himself. He said 'certainly the most natural thing under the circs., if it could have been brought about in a satisfactory form, would have been that you should have joined Derby.'

At half past two today Lord John Russell was announced: and sat till three—his hat shaking in his hand. A communication had reached him late last night from the Queen charging him with the formation of a Govt. & he had thought it his duty to make the endeavour.[1] I said perhaps Lord L. had told him what had fallen from me yesterday & he replied yes: but he wished to say what importance he attached to my continuing to hold my office. On Sidney Herbert's being mentioned he said it was fair to tell me he had seen him and had had no reason to expect his aid. I repeated to him what I had urged on Lord Lansdowne—that a coalition with advantages has also weaknesses of its own—that the late Coalition was I thought fully justified by the circumstances under which it took place, but at this juncture it had broken down—this being so I thought what is called a homogeneous Govt. would be best for the public & most likely to command approval—that Derby if he cd. get a good Foreign Minister would have had immense advantages with respect to the great questions of war & peace—he however had failed but I adhered to my opinion that an homogeneous Govt. would be the best—and it wd. be a great advantage to such a Govt. that Clarendon wd. continue in the F.O. He said he was not able to assure himself of having that advantage. He had seen Clarendon & made the proposal but C. had only promised to take time to consider.[2]

If however I said the country was to continue under a Coalition Govt. it was in my opinion better to continue the old Coalition under Lord Abn. than to form a new one. To Ld. A. I was attached closely by both political & personal ties, & I had ever been so. I could not look on him as condemned either by Parlt. or by the country—and I was not prepared to acquiesce in his exclusion or in anything to act without his full concurrence. Such I thought was Graham's view, whom I supposed he would see? He did not seem to have intended it before but then gave me to understand he might do it.

I told him that independently of all other matters & though I was glad to see neither a division nor even the germ of a division in the ideas of the Cabinet respecting negotiation & peace, yet I preferred a Cabinet *weighted* as the Aberdeen Cabinet was in this matter to one without Lord A. He said Clarendon's views

---

[1] '(Through Sir J. Graham) it appears he said the Queen laid this upon him as a duty incumbent on him in consequence of his having contributed so largely to the downfall of the late administration'; note added in margin on 4 February.

[2] 'Lord John agreed as to Derby: thought that every one must have supported him, & that he ought to have persevered'; note in margin added on 4 February.

would determine the foreign policy of the Cabinet. I held to my point adding that I did not think Ld. Abn. & Ld. Palmerston represented opposite principles, but rather distinct forms of the same principles connected with different habits and temperaments.

He said that Ld. P. had agreed to lead the H. of Commons for him, he going as First Minister to the Lords: but he did not mention any other adhesion.

He inquired about the State of Finance and prospects of a Budget. I said that if in April it was necessary to propose a War Budget I did not think the entire provision cd. be made by fresh taxes: though as much ought to be done as it was in fairness possible to ask of Parlt. & the country in that line. I told him in answer to queries I thought the excess of expenditure at the end of the Financial year would be about 6₥ of which probably 4₥ might be covered by taxes due but not collected by that time.

Upon the whole his tone was low and doubtful.

I told him that my doctrine that the old Coalition was preferable to a new one did not refer to any one person as Prime Minister in particular: at the same time I did not enter upon the question whether particular objections applied to him when I described our position as a false one in the event of our joining him as Minister.

He asked whether my answer was to be considered as given or whether I would take time: but I said that as there was no probability that my ideas would be modified by reflection it would not be fair by him to ask any delay.

He therefore departed *re infectâ*[1] my promise however being that I would gladly aid my successor to the best of my power & would endeavour to regulate my relations to his Govt. if formed in the same spirit by wh. I had been governed as his Colleague.[2]

4. *Septua[gesima] Sunday.*

Chapel Royal mg (H.C.) & aft. Wrote to Sir J. Graham—S. Herbert—Hon A. Gordon. Saw Sir J. Graham—S. Herbert—Ld Palmerston—10¼–11¼ PM —Ld Abn.—11½–12¾ (P.M.) Dined with the Wortleys. Read Bennet's Bogue. Wrote Pol. Mema. A rather sad Sunday! Bed at 3 A.M.

F. 4. 55. I went to Graham at 3 to report progress, and especially to let him know as clearly as I could the views of Wood & Sir Geo. Grey. For as we must anticipate Lord John's failure (of which indeed I heard immediately after quitting Graham) and as Palmerston's turn must come next to whom we I apprehended must clearly answer in the negative, it was desirable to meditate on what was to follow: inasmuch as Lord Aberdeen if again sent for by the Queen would probably at once apply to his late colleagues & would be met by them with a refusal. What was to follow?

He was quite determined not to separate from Lord Aberdeen & *therefore* not to serve in a Palmerston Govt.: he also believed its chief had very dangerous ideas on the subject of war and peace. He said that if the task came back to Lord Abn. & his late colleagues would not support him then he ought to strengthen himself in any & every quarter where he could *non obstante* the difficulty of Disraeli.

He regretted to hear that S. Herbert rather inclined to Lord L[ansdowne] as premier and said that in his interview on Friday Lord L. twice threw out intima-

[1] 'without accomplishing his object'.
[2] Initialled and dated 3 February [1855]; Add MS 44745, f. 97.

tions that *he* might undertake the Govt. but drew no favourable response from Graham: while he G. on his side twice signified that Ld. Abn. might continue at the head of the Govt. without the slightest sign of assent from Lord L.

He went over his conversation with Lord J. [Russell] in which he declared adhesion to Ld. A. and preference of the old coalition to a new one: he told Lord J. that in reviewing his career he found that versatility was the rock on which he had split: & he would now keep with Ld. A. and change no more. What he asked was said of Reuben? 'Unstable as water thou shalt not excel'[1] I replied: & he said 'that was what my old tutor said to me when I was a boy.' 'With a personal application'? I asked. Yes, he said, he applied it to me then: waving his hand with glee.

I told him my chief object was to give him the information of the views of some of Lord John's friends wh. I had communicated: I wished to deposit it as a seed in his mind, that he might ruminate upon it, with a view to our being prepared for the next *step but one.*[2]

Herbert came to me soon after I left him & told me Palmerston had [at] last got the commission. He considered that this disposed of Lord Lansdowne: and seemed himself to be disposed to join. He said *we* must take care what we were about & that we should be looked upon by the country as too nice if we declined to join Palmerston: who he believed (& in this I inclined to agree) would probably form a government.

He argued that Lord Aberdeen was out of the question: that the vote of Thursday night was against him: that the country would not stand him.

I said I was confident nothing would bring Graham into the P. Cabinet as matters now stand & that I hoped we should all act together—just as the Derby overture had been dealt with upon that principle[.]

No new coalition ought to be formed I said without a prospect of stability: and joining Lord P.'s Cabinet would be a new Coalition.

He said he rather applied that phrase to junction with Derby.

I quite agreed we could not join Derby except under conditions which might not be realised: but if we *did* it, it would be a reunion not a coalition—in coalition the separate existence is retained. I referred to the great instances of change of party in our times: Palmerston himself, & Stanley with Graham: but these took place when parties were divided by great questions of principle—there were none such now, & no one could say that the two sides of the House were divided by anything more than this, that one was rather more stationary the other rather more moveable.

He said true, the differences are on the back benches. We agreed that Derby's chance is now a good one: & that not improbably if he gets the turn he may now form his Govt. of his own friends alone.[3]

I said I had now for two years been holding my mind in suspense upon the question I used to debate with Newcastle who used to argue that we should grow into the natural leaders of the Liberal Party. I said it is now plain this will not be: we get on very well with the independent liberals, but the Whigs stand as an opaque body between us and others & moreover thus they will stand & ought to stand.

He was uneasy but seemed not to be prepared to urge the junction with Lord P. to whom I stated some of the objections: & I said that in consenting as we

[1] Genesis xlix. 4.
[2] This para. added on the previous page, dated this day, linked to this place with an arrow.
[3] This sentence added in the margin.

cheerfully did to act under him as leader in H. of C. we were like the Light Cavalry at Balaklava—we saw our doom. Still *that* was a risk that might be run.[1]

Sir J. Young called & I told him P. had the commission. He seemed to favour this: & I gave him four reasons against it. 1. That the P. Govt. would have no Parliamentary majority 2. That it wd. cause alarm abroad at this very peculiar juncture. 3. That P. is not fit for the duties of the office of Prime Minister. 4. That Ld. Abn. has not been condemned & may others having failed go on. He agreed with all but the last.

Ld. Palmerston came at little after two and remained perhaps an hour. Ld. Lansdowne had promised to join him if he formed an admn. on a basis sufficiently broad. He wished me to retain my office: & dwelt on the satisfactory nature of my relations with the Liberal Party. He argued that Ld. Abn. was excluded by the vote of Monday night: & that there was now no other Govt. in view.

My argument was adverse tho' without going to a positive conclusion. I referred to my conversation of Wedy. in favour of homogeneous govt. at this juncture: and spoke in the sense of my adjoined Memorandum A except that No. 6 and 7 were of course differently turned. Comparing the old coalition with the new I contended that there would be a loss of former strength, and nothing real to replace it, such as the cordial & united support of a party: admitting that he would start off with much popular favour but holding that this wd. not enable him to carry on a Govt.

At half past eleven I went to Lord Aberdeen's & staid above an hour. His being in the P. Cabinet which had been proposed was he said out of the question: but his *velleities*[2] seemed to lean rather to *our* joining wh. surprised me. He was afraid of the position we should occupy in the public eye if we declined. I argued at some length on the question of peace policy as against a Palmerston Cabinet, the impression abroad, unfitness for the office, and the want of any fair expectation of a parliamentary majority. He only desired that we should *meet* tomorrow to consider the matter which I was glad to do. I had promised Lord P. I would consult him & then see or write to him.[3]

A.

1. I think Ld. Aberdeen the fittest man to be Minister. 2. I do not recognise the vote of Monday as condemning and excluding him. 3. But *if* it excludes him, it excludes him for the sin of clinging to peace: in which I partook. 4. A Palmerston Govt., with Derby & J. Russell aloof, has no prospect of stability. 5. For us it would have the character of a new coalition:[4] & we ought not to enter into a new coalition without a prospect of stability. This also wd. be liable to all the jealousies from without that beset the old one. 6. Especially when it has no merit in itself but is got up to serve the purpose of the moment. 7. Lord Palmerston is in no way equal to the duties which fall upon a Prime Minister. 8. I look with apprehension to the effect which would be produced abroad at this juncture by the proposed changes in the Cabinet. 9. I cannot say I am altogether satisfied with the composition of it in regard to the prospects of maintaining such a financial policy as I think requisite.[5] 10. I am deeply responsible to Lord Aberdeen, perhaps more so

---

[1] Initialled and dated here 4 February 1855.　　　[2] 'inclinations'.
[3] Dated 4 February 1855; Add MS 44745, f. 108. 'I think the *nearer* prospect of its coming back to him if Lord P. failed had something to do with the semi-inclination shown tonight'; note added in the margin.
[4] 'or combination' here deleted.
[5] Initialled and dated here 4 February 1855; Add MS 44745, f. 118.

than any other man for having induced him to take office: & I shd. not feel my
obligations to him fulfilled were I now to act without his concurrence. 11. Not
wishing to shift responsibility on others, I still feel that here, as with Lord Derby,
we the friends of Sir R. Peel must act in unison: & I am sure we cannot remain
together in joining Ld. P. I cannot act as an individual. 12. Much of the strength
of the Cabinet would have departed & it would not be replaced.

B

1. If Ld. Abn. is to be shut out of his own Cabinet it is for causes wh. are applicable
to me. 2. I feel a confidence in that Cabinet with regard to the great question of
peace & war, as it was lately constituted, wh. I could not extend in the same
degree to the allied Cabinet wh. it is proposed to form. 3. I entirely reject the idea
that without Lord Aberdeen those who may have sympathised with him could
give the same weight to the cause of peace as it had when he was present. 4.
Neither have I the same[1] confidence in the Cabinet as it is proposed to be altered
with reference to domestic questions. 5. I am fearful of the effect of the change
abroad with reference to pending negotiations. 6. I see no prospect of Parliamentary stability for a government between & apart from Ld. Derby on the one
side & Lord J. Russell on the other. 7. The coalition will be weakened as a
Coalition by the loss of some of its most important members, & it will have
acquired men of that kind of strength which appertains to an homogeneous
Government. 8. I do not think that if the commission reverts to Lord Derby
this is to be viewed as a national evil: & I hope he may be encouraged to form a
Govt. from his own party.[2]

Considering the circs. under wh. the late Govt. was broken up I think it was
to be desired when that event had taken place that the attempt shd. be made to
direct public affairs by means of an administration taken either from Lord
Derby's party alone or from the Liberal party alone rather than by any new
form of the old coalition, which in my opinion would in all the elements of permanent strength be inferior to the late administration.[3]

But in answer to this it is said the vote of Monday [29th January] was aimed
in great part at Ld. Aberdeen, and he cannot any longer therefore be Minister:
whereas the popular voice calls for Lord P. to become the head of the Govt.

In referring to Lord Abn. I shall not enter upon the question of personal feeling,
for I am sure that he would himself be the first to desire me to put it out of view.

Neither will I enter on the inquiry whether it is really impossible that he should
continue Minister: as even I can grant that the opinions of those who say so can
make it impossible.

But if I assume the fact that he is ostracised, when I ask myself the cause I
cannot find it in his domestic policy. I at least am bound to remember that,
generally & cordially as I have at all times been treated by my Colleagues without
exception, there is perhaps no one member of the late Cabinet from whom I have
received such uniform & effective support.

His condemnation must rest on other grounds: on his tenacious[4] adherence to
peace, to the retention of it, the recollection of it, & the hope of it: & on his
opinions respecting the Turkish Empire. But as to peace my sympathies have been
in the main the same: & as to the Turkish Empire I believe that if not content
with repelling Russian aggression we attempt to maintain the predominance of

---

[1] Word illegibly deleted.   [2] Dated 4 February [1855]; Add MS 44745, f. 33.
[3] 'old Coalition under Ld. Aberdeen' deleted.   [4] 'obstinate' deleted.

Mahometan institutions in Europe we shall undertake both a mischievous & a hopeless task.

Upon what principle then am I to separate myself from the condemnation passed upon Lord Aberdeen and as it were affirmed by reconstructing his Cabinet without himself?[1]

5. M. X

Wrote to Ld Palmerston (& drafts)[2]—A. Gordon—Ld Aberdeen—Sir J. Graham—Newcastle—S. Herbert and minutes. Saw D. of Newcastle—S. Herbert—Mr Monteith—Duke of Argyll—Ld Elcho—Mr G. Harcourt— Sir John Young—Sir J. Graham (late)—Ld Canning—J. Wortley—E. Cardwell—Ld Ellesmere. We were at Graham's from 10¾ to 2: at first S.H. & I: then Ld Abn.: then Argyll also. H of C. 4¼–6. Spoke in reply to Ld J.R.s explanatory statement.[3] Wrote Pol. Mema. Dined at Ld Elles-meres: at Admiralty &c. afterwards. Saw one X[R]. Read Fox.

Feb. 5. 55. The most irksome & painful of these days: beginning with many hours of anxious consultation to the best of our power, & ending amidst a storm of disapproval almost unanimous not only from the generality but from [my] own immediate political friends.

At 10½ I went to Sir Jas Graham who is still in bed and told him the point to which by hard struggles I had come. It is one which I have stated today in a letter to Newcastle.[4] The case with me was briefly thus. I was ready to make the sacrifice of personal feeling: ready to see him expelled from the Premiership by a censure equally applicable to myself, & yet to remain in my office: ready to overlook not merely the inferior fitness but the real & manifest unfitness of P. for that office: ready to enter upon a new venture with him although in my opinion without any reasonable prospect of Parliamentary support such as is absolutely necessary for the credit & stability of a Government: upon the sole & all embracing ground that the prosecution of the war with vigour and the prosecution of it to & for peace was now the question of the day to which every other must give way. But then it was absolutely necessary that if we joined a Cabinet after over-looking all this & more it should be a Cabinet in wh. confidence cd. be placed with reference to war & peace. Was the Aberdeen Cabinet without Lord Aberdeen one in which I could place confidence? I answer no. He was vital to it: his love of peace was necessary to its right & steady pursuit of that great end: if then *he* could belong to a Palmerston Cabinet, I might, but without him I could not.

In all this Sir J. Graham concurred. He also had great fears of the French influence over & through Palmerston. We agreed that the Foreign Policy must be in the hands of Palmerston more than anyone, next to him Clarendon & Ld. Lansdowne, both of whom would take their cue from him. In such a Cabinet we should be part of the mob with reference to Foreign policy. It was in vain to talk of similarity of view in others such as Granville & Grey: mere numbers without a centre would not & could not secure justice to peace.

Herbert came full of doubts & fears but on the whole adopted the same con-

---

[1] Dated 4 February 1855, Add MS 44745, f. 35; docketed on back: 'My mind Feb. 4. 55 *in re* Palm. Premier. and F. 5.'

[2] Refusing office: in Guedalla, *P*, 101–3.

[3] *Russell attacked *Newcastle, whom Gladstone defended: *H* cxxxvi. 1283.

[4] An account substantially the same as that which follows: Aberdeen 'recommended us to join, but after this his recommendation was, for me, still born.' Add MS 44262, f. 181.

clusion. Lord Aberdeen sent to say he could not come but I wrote to beg him & he appeared. On hearing how we stood he said his remaining in the Cabinet was quite out of the question: & that he had told P. so yesterday when he glanced at it. But he thought we should incur great blame if we did not: which indeed was plain beyond all dispute.

The Duke of Argyll called & was asked to come in. He had in his mind the idea of a concordat by which the Govt. should be bound to ask at this time for no more than certain terms of peace. We all I think held that no written terms could guide a course through the tangled ground of negotiations, & that the personal composition of the Cabinet, not any attempt to fetter freedom of action was the proper & only security.

He also came to our point: and we tried it over & over again in a conversation of three hours & more.

At length when I had written & read aloud the rough draft of an answer, Lord Abn. said he must strongly advise our joining. I said to him

Lord Aberdeen, when we have joined the P. Cabinet, you standing aloof from it, will you rise in your place in the H. of Lords & say that you give that Cabinet your confidence with regard to the question of war and peace?

He replied I will express my hope that it will do right but not my confidence which is a different thing.

Certainly I answered & that which you have now said is my justification. The unconquerable honesty of your mind has saved us. Ninetynine men of a hundred in your position at the moment would have said Oh yes I shall express my confidence: but you would not deviate an inch to the right or to the left.

This nearly ended the matter. Herbert ventured faintly to recommend his joining the P. Cabinet. I said it would be the height of presumption for me to form a judgment: that it was impossible for me really to get his point of view, but on the whole now that he had declared himself I could not wonder at his decision.

Herbert & I went to my house & dispatched our answers.[1] Then began the storm. Granville met us driving to Newcastles. Sorry beyond expression: he almost looked displeased which for him is much. Newcastle: I incline to think you are wrong. Canning: my impression is you are wrong. G. Harcourt, Sir J. Young, Elcho, Ld. Ellesmere, J. Wortley, & various letters streaming in all portending condemnation & disaster. Herbert became more & more uneasy: Young when I had read my letter to him seemed to think there was matter in it. A note from Arthur Gordon was in the opposite sense: and Cardwell this morning before the fact seemed to lean that way. The truth is the world is drunk about a P. Government: and if we humour it in its drunkenness it will rightly refuse to admit the excuse when restored to soberness it condemns what we have done.

God grant it may be right: I think I see the reason of what we have done clear and broad before me. I saw Graham again at night: he did not recede.[2]

6. T.

Wrote to A. Gordon—S. Herbert—Duke of Argyll—Mr J. Moss—Ld Palmerston (2) (and drafts)—Sir A. Spearman—J.S. Wortley—Mr Moffatt —G.E.H. Vernon—Lord Ellesmere—Dss of Sutherland—Eg. Harcourt— Sir W.C. James—Robn G.—Mr Goulburn—Mr Wylie—Mr H. Drummond & minutes. Saw Sir J. Young—Lord A. Hervey—Lord Canning—Mr A.

[1] Guedalla, *P.* 101.
[2] Initialled and dated 5 February 1855; Add MS 44745, f. 39.

Gordon—Mr Anderson—E. Cardwell (2)—S. Herbert (3)—Sir J. Johnstone
—Ld Elcho—R.M. Milnes—D. of Newcastle—W. Cowper—D. of Argyll—
R M Milnes—and at night visited Lord Palmerston. Admy. Conclave 12–2¼.
10 to dinner. Wrote Pol. Mema. Discussions abt the new Butler: C. decided
to take him.[1] A great event with us.

Feb. 6. 55. The last day I hope of these tangled records: in which we have seen,
to say nothing of the lesser sacrifice, one noble victim struck down, and are set
to feast over the remains. The thing is bad & the mode worse.

Arthur [Gordon] came early in the day with a most urgent letter from Ld.
Aberdeen addressed virtually to us and urging us to join.[2] He had seen both P.
and Clarendon & derived much satisfaction from what they said.

We met at the Admiralty at twelve: where Graham lay much knocked up with
the fatigue and anxiety of yesterday. I read to him & Lord Abn. Palmerston's
letter of today to me.[3] Herbert came in & made arguments in his sense. I told
him I was at the point of yesterday & was immovable by cons[ideratio]ns of the
class he urged. The only security worth having lies in men: the man is Lord
Aberdeen: moral union & association with him must continue & must be publicly
known to continue. This will define our standing ground for the case of need in
the Cabinet and will supply both the *point d'appui* and the ensign not to be mis-
taken without. Canning gives an extra strength but not one that could enable us
to dispense with the other. I therefore repeated my question to Lord Aberdeen
whether he would in his place as a Peer declare if we joined the Cabinet that it
had his confidence with respect to war and peace? He said much moved that he
felt the weight of the responsibility but that after the explanations & assurances
he had received he would. He was even more moved when Graham said that
though the leaning of his judgment was adverse he would place himself absolutely in the hands of Lord Aberdeen. To Herbert of course it was a simple
release from a difficulty. Palmerston had told Cardwell 'Gladstone feels a difficulty
first infused into him by Graham: Duke of Argyll and Herbert have made up
their minds to do what Gladstone does.' Newcastle joined us and was in Herbert's
sense. I repeated again that Lord Aberdeen's declaration of confidence enabled me
to see my way to joining. I hoped also that the formation of the Cabinet in this
manner on the strength and by the means of his expressed judgment would tend
to place him before the public eye in the high position he deserves to hold.

Something said by Canning had given me alarm as to what he had learned
from P. about the fleet in the Black Sea: and Lord Aberdeen went away from us
to have this explained. It appeared when he returned & came to Downing Street
that P. had been quite misunderstood. I went, after he had left us to write my
draft of letter to Lord Palmerston.[4] Graham, far from well, was quite affectionate
in his demeanour. There is a strain of exaggeration in his feelings but they are
thoroughly warm and pure. He said it was a strain upon him after having served
three Prime Ministers in whom he reposed implicit confidence & whom he loved
to serve one whom certainly he did not love.[5]

Canning had been with us in the morning and heard a further statement of our
case which he said he would consider & then make up his mind.

He went afterwards to Palmerston and agreed to join him on condition of being

---

[1] An assistant for W. Hampton, who stayed in service.
[2] See *T.A.P.S.*, n.s. li part 4, p. 21.   [3] Guedalla, *P*, 104.
[4] Guedalla, P. 106.   [5] *Graham stayed at the Admiralty.

in the Cabinet: to which Palmerston agreed. This was apart from and independent of us: but I imagine he had Lord Aberdeen's approval or something near it.

My letter to Palmerston was written in anticipation of Lord Aberdeen's return. He highly approved of it as did Sidney Herbert: and the Duke of Argyll to whom I gave it after sending it off.

We have thus escaped the storm: but we did not move in order to escape it. I told Lord Aberdeen that no consideration upon earth should move us to enter this Cabinet except under circumstances which would fully and visibly maintain my union with him. To this Graham would have adhered: nor did I today enter into discussion but only carried the matter to a point. But I think it not impossible that had Lord Ab. continued to decline stating his confidence in the Govt., Graham & I should have been left alone.

I went to Ld. Aberdeen in his official room after his return from Palmerston. It was only when I left that room today that I began to realise the pang of parting. There he stood, struck down from his eminence by a vote that did not dare to avow its own purpose, and for his wisdom and his virtue: there he stood endeavouring to cure the ill consequences to the public of the wrong inflicted upon himself: and as to the point immediately within reach successful in the endeavour. I ventured however to tell him that I hoped our conduct and reliance on him would tend to his eminence and honour: and said 'you are not to be of the Cabinet, but you are to be its tutelary deity'.

I had a message from P. that he would answer me but at night I went up to him. I told him that Cardwell's claim to the Cabinet had been viewed by Lord Abn. as parallel to Canning's: but learned to my regret that he believed he was *full*. I told him, as he gave me the opportunity, that I was sure S. Herbert would greatly prefer the Colonies to the Home Office: and he promised to propose the change to Sir G. Grey.[1] He assured me, with reference to my letter, that he knew what an University Constituency was and that he quite agreed, and would bring me into no trouble, with reference to the Established Church. He did not speak to me of the noble conduct of Lord Aberdeen: but as Herbert told me he had done so to him.[2] He spoke of various arrangements and proposed for consideration whether Layard should be made Under Secretary for the Department of War. I expressed some doubt whether he would submit himself to the views & policy of the Govt.— & advised that there should be some mention of this in the Cabinet.[3]

7. Wed.

Wrote to Robn. G.—Mr J. Blundell—J.N.G.—Ld Chancellor—W. James —E. of Aberdeen—W.H.G.—Mr Hayter—J. Gurney—Sir J. Young—& minutes. H. of C. 12–1¼ for Finance business.[4] Saw Sir J. Young—E. Cardwell—Sir C. Wood—Mr Hayter—Lord A. Hervey—Sir C. Trevelyan—Mr Horsfall MP.—Mr S. Herbert—Mr. A. Gordon—Sir J. Graham. Dined at Lord Overstone's: a small & very pleasant party. Wrote Pol. Mema.[5] Read La Guerronnière.

[1] *Herbert moved to the colonial office from the secretaryship at war.
[2] 'I inquired his intentions as to Mr. Roebuck's motion & found he was of opinion that it should be resisted'; note in margin added on 21 February 1855.
[3] Confirming this by letter, Guedalla, *P*, 107. Initialled and dated 6 February 1855; Add MS 44745, f. 47.
[4] Introduced a supplementary ordnance estimate: *H* cxxxvi. 1309.
[5] Talks with Peelites: Add MS 44745, f. 57.

8. *Th.* X

Wrote to S. Herbert, & minutes. Saw Geo. Hope—A. Gordon—Sir J. Graham—Ld Lansdowne—Ld Palmerston—Ld Canning—Ld Aberdeen—Mr S. Herbert—Sir C. Wood (cum Mr Wilson & Mr Anderson) Read La Guerronnière—H. of C. $4\frac{1}{4}$-to 6 and Lords to $7\frac{3}{4}$.[1] To Council at Windsor $11\frac{1}{4}$-$3\frac{3}{4}$: for the new appts. Saw Car & missed Cary[R]. Read De La Guerronnière.

9. *Fr*

Wrote to W.C. James—Dss of Sutherland(2)—R M Fox—Mr Ironside[2]—& minutes. Also (late) Draft to Ld Abn. Cabinet $3\frac{1}{4}$-$6\frac{3}{4}$. Read Rickards Pol. Ec.[3] Saw Mr Monsell—Mr Hayter—Mr Pressly—Aunt J.—S. Herbert (Col. matters)—Sir J. Graham. Saw one[R]. H of C. 12–1.[4]

Feb. 8 and 9. The rush of events was somewhat slackened. On Thursday Sir J. Graham told me of Ld. J. Russell's singular visit to him last night: at which he dissuaded the recall of Ld. Raglan—recommended sending out a Chef d'Etat Major—& complained of the Peelites for having selfishly sought too many offices, alluding to what Canning had done, & imputing the same to Cardwell. He also thought they had made a great mistake in joining Palmerston. He seemed sore about me: & told Graham Christopher had said that if I joined Ld. Derby, 100 of the party wd. withdraw their allegiance. He appeared to wish to establish a ground of friendly relations with Graham.

I ought to have mentioned before that during our Conferences at the Admiralty Ld. Abn. expressed great compunction for having allowed the country without adequate cause to be dragged into the war. So long as he lived he said with his own depth & force it wd. be a weight upon his conscience. He had held similar language to me lately at Argyll House: but when I asked him at what point *after* the fleet went to Besika Bay it wd. have been possible to stop short, he alluded to the *sommation* which we were encouraged however as he added by Austria to send: & thought *this* was the false step: yet he did not seem quite firm in the opinion.

Yesterday we had our first Cabinet. It did not relieve the gloom of my impressions. Though it was a first Cabinet we were as I reported to Graham in the evening more Acephalous than ever; less order, less unity of purpose: Charles Wood had twice cried '*Will* the Cabinet decide *something* upon *some* point?' Palmerston, though he had appeared more *eveillé*[5] than usual, had taken no lead. He introduced to the Cabinet three subjects: one the recal of Lord Raglan, which he tossed among us, without clear broad or strong views of his own, as if for what chance might bring: another the Roebuck Committee on wh. he said he thought the House would give it up, if we undertook or promised an investigation under the authority of the Crown—and here he gave me the idea that Wood or some one had been with him to prepare him: the other subject astonished me: it was a question whether 25000 rifles should or should not, after being arranged for by Sir C. Fox, be had from America: such a subject to be brought before a

---

[1] Statement on the new ministry by *Granville; Gladstone spoke on the army: *H* cxxxvi. 1329, 1388.
[2] Isaac Ironside of Sheffield.   [3] See 30 Mar. 53.
[4] Spoke on supplementary estimates: *H* cxxxvi. 1395.
[5] 'attentive' or 'sprightly'.

Cabinet by a Prime Minister I never knew: he talked of political considerations as involved, but could not tell what they were: he said it was a small point, now it was not precisely small, but it was purely administrative & as little fit to be brought to Cabinet as any question I ever [1] remember.

Cowley wrote from Paris about the avoidance! of negotiations in a tone which showed the impression made on him by the change of Govt. I hope however that we took sufficien⁺ security for pulling him up.

Lord Palmerston made a feeble argument for delay in the matter of negotiations. 'Either we shall take Sebastopol & then we shall get better terms or we shall fail & then we shall stand excused for asking less.' It is plain that this might be exactly turned inside out & used as a reason the other way. 'Either we shall take S. & be compelled to ask more, or we shall fail & then we shall get less'. I said however that I deeply felt the immense responsibility of delay without a clear & definite reason for it. Looking to the condition of our army & the possibility of our losing it, I could conceive nothing more fearful than if we dawdled about these negotiations and then upon its being lost it should hereafter appear that we might have brought them into activity & perhaps attained a successful issue.[2]

10. Sat.

Wrote to Mr Wilson—E. of Aberdeen—Mr R. Hill—Rev Ld C. Hervey—Stephy—Williams & Co—& minutes. 14 to dinner: official. Lady Waldegrave's in evg. Saw Mrs Greene—Ld Mahon—Mr Harcourt—Sir J. Herschel. Read Fox's Memoirs.

11. Sexa[gesima] S.

Whitehall mg. Chapel Royal evg. MS. on Ep. aloud at night. Saw Mr Monsell—Sir W.C. James—Bp of Oxford. Saw Cary[R]. Read Calixtus—Bogue's Life (finished)—Webers Acatholischen Secten[3]—Stanley's Becket.[4]

12. M.

Wrote to Bp of Oxford—Rev D. Robertson—Ld Granville—W.R. Farquhar—R. M. Milnes—Ld Palmerston—Mr Wilson—and minutes. Cabinet 2½–4½. Dined with Mr G. Harcourt. Saw Dumin(38)[R]—Saw Ld Shaftesbury—Sir A. Spearman—Mr Roberts—Mr G. Glyn—Sir W. Farquhar—Sir C. Trevelyan—Mr Anderson—Mr Wilson—Ld Granville *cum* Mr Temple—C.G. resp. Lyttelton. Read By Loans or by Taxes?[5]

13. T.

Wrote to Sir W. Farquhar—H.J.G.—Mr Anderson—J. Caird—& minutes. Eight to dinner. Read 'By Loans or by Taxes'—Sydney Smith's Letters.[6]

---

[1] 'knew' deleted.   [2] Dated 10 February [1855]; Add MS. 44745, f. 61.
[3] G. Weber, *Geschichte der akatholischen Kirchen und Secten von Grossbritannien* (1845).
[4] See 25 Aug. 54.
[5] W. *Newmarch, *Should the money required to pay the expenses of the War be raised by loans or taxes?* (1855).
[6] *Selections from the letters of Sydney *Smith,* 2v. (1854).

Attended Treas. Board, reading in. Saw Scotts—Westcott (sat to him)—
A. Gordon. Arranging letters.

14. Wed.

Wrote to R. Neville—Mr Arbuthnot—Mr Oliveira—Ld Monteagle—S.
Herbert—Bp of Exeter—Ld Palmerston—Master of Pembroke—Mr R. Hill
—Ld J. Russell—Mr Panizzi—and minutes. Cabinet 3–6 and Cabinet din-
ner: broke up at 12. Saw Mr Wilson—Mr Anderson—Ld A. Hervey—Sir A.
Spearman—Sir J. Graham—Saw Dumin[R] & another, gent. incert.[1] Read
Sydney Smith.

15. Th.

Wrote to Sir G. Grey—Ld Panmure—G.W. Hope—Mr R. Walker—Ld
Mahon—and minutes. Dined with the Jameses. Lady Granville's afterwards. Read Sydney Smith. Bills & Housebusiness with Hampton. Saw
Sir C. Trevelyan—Mr Delane—Mr Oliveira M.P.—Mr Monsell—Mr Rowland Hill—Mrs Herbert—Sir J. Young—E. Cardwell—Captain Addison.[2]

16. Fr. X.

Wrote to Mr Reynolds—Ld Palmerston—Mr J. Wood—and minutes. H of
C. $4\frac{1}{4}$–$8\frac{1}{4}$ & $10\frac{3}{4}$–$12\frac{1}{4}$.[3] Read Sydney Smith. Saw Mr Wood *cum* Mr Pressly
(Fin[ancial] plans) 11–2—Mr Anderson—Sir A. Spearman—J.N. Gladstone
—Sir J. Graham—Mr A' Court—Mr S. Herbert.

Saw Louis: missed West[R]. Ld P.s statement was in many respects a
good one: but there was not in it the stuff to confront the difficulties in
immediate view: & our throw off was worse than even I had anticipated.

17. Sat.

Wrote to Mr Symonds[4]—Mr M'Mahon—& minutes. Dined at the Palace.
Cabinet 3–7. (See [next day's] mema.). Lady Palmerston's at night—Read
S. Smith. Walk with C. buying spoons &c. Saw Mr A'Court—Lord J.
Thynne—Mr Kirk MP—Sir C. Trevelyan—Clarendon—Canning—Gran-
ville—& others, on the Roebuck question.

18. Quinqua[gesima] S.

St James's mg and H.S.: an excellent Sermon from the Rector. Chapel
Royal aftn. MS of 44 aloud at night. Dined with the Herberts. Wrote
Pol. Mema. Saw Ld Abn. *cum* Sir J. Graham—S. Herbert. Read Harvey on
the Creeds[5]—Catherine de Suède.[6]

[1] 'of uncertain race'.
[2] Perhaps Major Joseph Edward Addison, of the adjutant general's office.
[3] Statement by *Palmerston, not excluding the appt. of the *Roebuck cttee, but
offering the inquiries of the new govt. as an alternative: *H* cxxxvi. 1425.
[4] Arthur Symonds, registrar of metropolitan buildings, had written on civil service
reform: Add MS 44530, f. 27.
[5] W. W. *Harvey, *The history and theology of the creeds*, 2v. (1854).
[6] French tr. of Ulpho's *Incipit vita sive legenda cum miraculis divae Chaterinae* (1557),
life of Catherine of Sweden, St. Bridget's da.

[1] At yesterday's cabinet after some foreign questions we discussed the Roebuck Committee.

Ld. Palmerston (I think) opened, said it was plain from the feeling last night [i.e. on the 16th] that the House were set upon it, and was disposed simply to stand for a fairly composed Committee but having secured this to allow the inquiry to proceed.

Wood had communicated with many members of Parlt. & thought the Committee should be appointed by the c[ommittee] of Selection,[2] & that they should by Instruction be confined 'in the first instance' to the conduct of the Govt. Departments at home.

Sir G. Grey agreed that this was the proper course: and urged that it wd. be very difficult for us to resign in consequence of the appt. of this Committee as it stood affirmed by a large majority when we accepted our offices in the reconstructed Cabinet.

Sir J. Graham said he felt the force of this argument: and he did not think the instruction wd. be effectual to limit the inquiries of the Committee: the question was whether it should be granted.

Granville said he was himself opposed to granting it & thought that after refusing it we might in case of need dissolve standing on the inquiries we had ourselves ordered, & as being the 'only possible' Government: but as he perceived this was not the general feeling of the Cabinet he did not persist & was disposed to agree with those who thought that the limitation wd. fail to exclude the question of the state of the army in the Crimea, & that we should make it our sole object to have a fairly constituted Committee.

I contended that the limitation might be made if not literally yet really to take effect—if it would not, then I must fall back on objecting to the Committee altogether. In any view I was quite prepared to concur in that course with the rest of the Cabinet: but if that was not to be our choice then I thought we shd. have the limitation for I thought it impossible to agree to an inquiry by Committee into the state of the army in the Crimea while the expedition is in progress: & I argued at some length & with vehemence upon the breach of duty which it wd. involve on our part towards those holding responsible commands there if we without ourselves condemning them were to allow them to be brought before another tribunal such as a Select Committee of the H. of C.

Molesworth said the H. of C. would have the Committee & would have it practically unlimited—but wd. agree to its being chosen by the C. of Selection.

Herbert & Argyll both spoke with feelings of strong disinclination to the Committee.

The Chancellor, Ld. Lansdowne, Clarendon, Canning, were very silent: Panmure said that if the Committee were granted he wd. not answer for it that the army would not be in a state of mutiny in a month & he would say this in his place in the H. of Lords.

At one time it seemed as if we were about to agree to the Committee with a limitation, either absolute or 'in the first instance' to inquire & report only upon the war departments at home: but Ld. P. whose mind seemed made up to giving way—(after what he had said the night before!)—obstructed this & said it was agreed that we shd. take till Tuesday to consider.

[1] Follows description of a talk about the meeting of Convocation.
[2] Consisting of the chairman of the standing orders cttee., and five nominated members.

I went so far as to say that if the inquiry into the state of the army were allowed by this Govt. it neither could nor ought to enjoy a week's credit or authority in the H. of C. & intimated that I cd. not see my way to this concession under any circs.

In the evening at the Palace I had conversation on the subject both with the Queen and with the Prince. The latter compared the appointment of a Committee to the proceedings of the Convention of France: but still seemed to wish that the Govt. shd. submit rather than retire. The Queen spoke openly in that sense: & trusted that she shd. not be given over into the hands of those 'who are the least fit to govern'. Without any positive & final declaration I intimated to each that I did not think I cd. bring my mind to acquiesce in the proposition for an inquiry by a Select Committee into the state of the army in the Crimea.[1]

19. M.

Wrote to Sir J. Graham(2)—J.N.G.—Ld Palmerston[2]—Mr Anderson— W.F. Campbell—Sir C. Trevelyan, & minutes. Worked on Newsp. Stamp papers. Stafford House in evg. H of C. $4\frac{1}{2}$–$7\frac{3}{4}$, 9–$9\frac{3}{4}$, $11\frac{3}{4}$–$1\frac{3}{4}$.[3] Saw Sir W. Farquhar—Ld Palmerston—Mr Timm—Sir J. Graham—E. of Aberdeen— Duke of Argyll—E. Cardwell—Sir J. Young. Read Sydney Smith. The Roebuck Committee was the constant subject of my thoughts.

A.

1. As to French alliance. 2. As to obedience & discipline of the army. 3. As to justice to the General & others in command. 4. As to efficiency & celerity in providing remedies. 5. As to the principle that no Government should exist under the censure or without the confidence of Parliament. 6. As to the intrinsic fitness of the tribunal which it is proposed to appoint. 7. As to the impossibility of regarding this Committee in the light of a general one, or in any other light than as carrying over the authority of the Crown into the hands of another power. 8. As to the dangers inherent in a precedent which so transfers under critical circumstances the authority vested in the Crown.[4]

20. T.

Wrote to Duke of Argyll—Mr Reynolds—Ld Chanc[ello]r—Mr Fitzerald— & minutes. Cabinet $2\frac{1}{2}$–$4\frac{3}{4}$. H of C. $4\frac{3}{4}$–6.[5] Read S. Smith—Smollet on Byng (1756)[6]. Saw R. Phillimore(2)—Duke of Argyll—Sir C. Trevelyan—Sir J. Graham *cum* Ld Abn—S. Herbert and Mr. Whitcombe.[7] Wrote Pol. Mema.

Feb. 20. Today I met Ld. Abn. at Sir J. Graham's in the forenoon & we talked through the question of the Committee. Lord Aberdeen's opinion was that the whole Govt. should resign: he was more doubtful whether we should do so if our Colleagues refused: but leaned on the whole to the affirmative.

---

[1] Dated 18 February 1855; Add MS 44745, f. 72.   [2] Guedalla, *P*, 108.
[3] Deb. on the new govt.: *H* cxxxvi, 1514.
[4] Initialled and dated 19 February 1855; Add MS 44745, f. 120.
[5] Russian trade: *H* cxxxvi. 1659.
[6] For *Smollett's opinion of Admiral John Byng, see his *Continuation of the complete history of England*, i, 470–80.
[7] Robert Henry Whitcombe, attorney with W. N. Marcy in Bewdley, Worcestershire (see 26 June, 16 Aug. 55).

At the Cabinet (which Herbert could not attend from illness) Lord Palmerston said that the House of Commons was becoming unruly from the doubts which had gone abroad as to the intentions of Govt. with respect to the Committee: that the House was determined to have it: that if we opposed it we should be beaten by an overwhelming majority: to dissolve upon it would be ruinous: to resign a fortnight after taking office would make us the laughing stock of the country.[1]

I dwelt mainly on these points 1. That the proposed transfer of the functions of the Executive to a Select Committee of the House of Commons, with respect to an army in the face of the enemy and by the side of our French allies, & the recognition of this transfer by the Executive Govt. was an evil greater than any that cd. arise from a total or partial resignation—and 2. That it was clear that we did not, as we stood, possess the confidence of a majority of the House.

I glanced at the points in Memm. A except No. 7.[2] I said that the Committee was itself a Censure on the Govt.: it might be urged that though so meant at first it had dropped this significance & had become a motion only for inquiry: that even if this would hold provided it were clear that we had the confidence of Parlt., it wd. be a pure assumption as matters now stand, when all evidence is the other way: I objected to Sir G. Grey's argument of Saturday and contended that we had a right to believe that Parlt. wd. not inflict this Committee on a Govt. which had its confidence—recited my having ascertained from Pn.[3] on the 6th before our adhesion was declared his intention to oppose the Committee, my subsequent conversation with Ld. Lansdowne & others at Windsor—my proposal of a Commission to him, then to Sir J. Graham, then to the Cabinet, who I thought entertained it favourably—my conviction that this instrument might have been worked so as to keep inquiry in the hands of the Crown, & regret for the change of plan arranged I presumed by Lord Pn. & Panmure who substituted several minor measures for our principal one.

The argument on the other side, wh. proceeded principally from Ld. Lansdowne, Clarendon, Granville, & C. Wood, was all to the effect that if we did not grant the Committee Derby wd. come in, & wd. dissolve upon the cry of inquiry & wd. obtain an immense majority—& whereas if we appointed the Committee we might keep it within bounds, after a Dissolution the inquiry would be far more formidable.

Sir J. Graham & I both urged that we ought not to be governed by these mere speculations on Derby's probable conduct but that there were rules & principles of the Constitution lying much nearer hand for our guidance. I ventured to express the opinion that Derby wd. not be the man to dissolve upon this cry of inquiry, for he wd. see & be the first to fear the dangers of such a measure: and that *he* might without our aid still be enabled to keep the inquiry in the hands of the Crown & so keep the evil & inconvenience within bounds & avoid the main mischief namely the transfer to the H. of Commons.

Sir J. Graham stated the strong feeling he entertained of Ld. Palmerston's friendly conduct in forming this Govt. as well as previously & his earnest desire in consequence to have cooperated with him after ascertaining that on the great question of Foreign Policy there was nothing to prevent it. This I reechoed.

I stated that former experience (viz. 1851, the Ecc. Titles Bill) had shown me how the determined resistance of a few could cripple a serious measure & practically reduce it to a nullity though they might not be able at the first moment to stay its progress.

---

[1] Graham's views omitted.   [2] See 19 Feb. 55.
[3] 'upon on this recital we were agreed'; note added in margin.

There was a desire to make a declaration today but as Sir J. Graham said he could only promise to consider the matter yet further it was agreed that it should stand over until tomorrow.

He told me after the Cabinet that nothing had been said to shake his judgment. I saw Herbert in the evening & begged him to see Graham too.[1]

21. Ash Wednesday

St James's mg: and also evg. but neither service entire. Wrote to Rev Mr Warter—Mr Timm—Mr Grenfell MP[2]—J.N.G.—Sir C. Trevelyan—T.G.— Solr. General—D W Harvey—V.C. of Oxford—C.S. Hardinge—& minutes. Saw Lord A. Hervey—R. Phillimore—Mr Whitcombe—Mr Prince[3]— Graham *cum* Herbert—D. of Argyll—E. Cardwell. Cabinet $12\frac{3}{4}$–$4\frac{1}{4}$. Wrote Pol. Mema. Read Anon. Journalism[4] and divers pamphlets.

Feb. 21. Ash Wedy. At 12 o'clock on returning from Church I found a note from the Prince & went off at once to the Palace.

He told me the Queen was most anxious that we should fully weigh our position and bear in mind that the choice is only a choice of evils as we have no course before us that is free from great embarrassment: while She regarded our being in the Cabinet as a great advantage.

I replied I could not speak fully & finally except for myself but I believed Graham & Herbert more or less concurred—

That we were fully sensible of the gravity of the situation, that no personal or party consideration entered into the question before us & that we should endeavour as I hoped HRH would convey to HM. to consider it with a single eye to the honour & advantage of the Crown wh. were deeply engaged.

That trying the question by the practical test of the greater evil I was convinced that the proposed transfer of the power of the Executive, & the proposed recognition of that transfer, were greater evils than any that cd. arise from political dislocation & disruption.

That though by quitting office we might not be able to stop the evil in its first stage we should by this means lay the ground for firm & probably hereafter more effective resistance.

That I likewise felt the Govt. had not the confidence of the H. of C. wh. I had never expected it wd. keep but had hoped it wd. at any rate commence with.

That I did not judge of the evil of this transfer of power in the abstract but with reference to the fact that it touched the army in the midst of a gigantic operation, the enemy in its face, the French by its side, & the whole of the proposed enquiry at any point running up directly into the question of the relation of Lord Raglan to the French.

That as to the foreign policy it was already secured in the right line, so far as the case admitted, independently of our remaining, by what had taken place at the formation of the Pn. Cabinet.

That I feared H.M. would have little peace until Parlt. had again resolved itself into the old form of two parties.

He observed on the great practical mischiefs that resulted from having one party overcharged with Right Honourables i.e. Candidates for ministerial offices,

[1] Initialled and dated 20 February 1855; Add MS 44745, f. 121.
[2] Charles William Grenfell, 1823–61; liberal M. P. Windsor 1852–9.
[3] Perhaps A. Prince and co., of the patent office.
[4] *Anonymous journalism* (1855).

& I replied that first it enfeebled & disorganised the action of the supporters of an Administration which the Opposition not being in a state to assume power had not the due sense of its responsibilities & became reckless accordingly.

I thought however that Lord P. without us would have a firmer support from the Liberal Party than he could have while we remained in his Govt.

I said Ld. P.s conduct had been very honourable both under Lord Abn. & since the disruption: here his dislike broke out & he seemed to intimate doubt as to the first part but afterwards limited himself to this that his friends assailed & vilified Ld. Abn.

He said Ld. P. had written to the Q. to state his apprehensions but added that he expected to be able to fill up the places and continue in the Govt. The Q. had given him her accession accordingly which he seemed to hint was in order to avoid suspicion but I at once said there could not be a doubt of the strict propriety & wisdom of such a course.

Our time was short & he did not say much but my impression was that he approved of the step proposed.

From the P[rince] I went to the Cabinet.

Lord P. began by proposing that the Govt. should accept the Committee fairly nominated by the House but shd. intimate our expectation that it wd. be careful to do nothing wh. wd. tend to injure the French alliance! To this he again expressed the hope that as the lesser of two evils we would agree.

Graham began & repeated the statements of yesterday founding himself mainly on the want of confidence wh. he saw to prevail & wh. fixed on this Committee the character of censure . . .[1]

I followed Graham & dwelt chiefly on the evils inherent in the appointment of the Committee:[2] put against it the use of the powers of the Crown: said I agreed with G. as to dividing, but shd. reserve to myself to consider whether to record my views by moving an amendment for fear of misunderstanding: considered that *even* if it were possible after admitting the vicious principle of the Committee to limit its operation, this cd. only be done by a Govt. having a commanding position in the House & the full confidence of a majority, wh. this Govt., as now constituted had not: protested against Ld. P's proposal to warn the Committee off the ground of relations with the French inasmuch as that wd. in effect stop & nullify the whole inquiry into the state of the army in the Crimea, for every question of difficulty turned upon these relations: allowed that H. of C. was entitled to inquire by way of calling to account but that this shd. not be while the operation was going on: inquiry for mere information without reasons of the facts or remedy for the evils wd. be nobody's view: inquiry with a view to remedy wd. be ineffective in the hands of the Committee but effective in those of the Crown.

Sir G. Grey asked whether we did not admit that the Committee was now inevitable: I answered perhaps it now had become so with this Govt.: that last Friday it certainly was not so: that it wd. not now be so were Derby in power & we supporting him properly in the matter.[3]

I adverted, at some moment, to the fact that the measures announced last Friday had not been before the Cabinet & that what we had heard of before was a Committee by the Crown.

[1] Rest of *Graham's statement omitted.
[2] *Argyll records this as 'the only occasion in my public life with Gladstone when he did for a moment show some considerable irritation'; Argyll, ii. 537.
[3] Views of others omitted.

Afterwards I had a conv. with G. & H. who were disinclined to my notion of moving an amendment [1] for fear of a forced division on it.[2]

22. *Th.*

Wrote to R. Phillimore (2)—Sir G. Grey—V.C. Oxford—T.L. Hodges—Willis (Books[eller])—Robn. G(2)—D[uche]ss of Sutherland—[Miss] L. Gladstone—E. Cardwell—S. Herbert—Govr. Higginson—Rev Mr Harvey—Sir T. Tancred—Ld Palmerston—Cte A. de la Guerronniere [3]—Rev. Mr Trench—Mr Bright—Sir W. Heathcote—Sir J. Graham—& minutes. Saw Ld A. Hervey—Mr Wilson—Sir W. Heathcote—J.N.G.—A. Gordon—R. Phillimore—Sir J. Graham—do cum E. Cardwell—Ld Palmerston & Sir C. Wood—Ld Aberdeen—Sir J. Graham *cum* Herbert—also Herbert. Dined with Herbert. Read Fox.

Feb. 22. Sir J. Graham & Herbert on the whole dissuaded me from moving the Resolutions [4] which I had prepared by way of draft: from their fear of being driven into a division so small as to make the *cause* ridiculous—& wh. wd. place friendly persons in a position of difficulty. I yielded to them.

After considering various *sites*, we determined to ask the Manchester School to yield us, at any rate for tomorrow, the old place devoted to Ex ministers.[5]

23. *Fr.*

Wrote to V.C. Oxford—W.C. James—Mr Trench—Scotts—& minutes. Thought on the difficult subject of the debate: dined early: sat $4\frac{1}{2}$–2 & spoke (I fear) $1\frac{1}{2}$ hour: but much satisfied with the feeling of the House.[6] Saw J.N.G.(2)—Sir W. Heathcote—Sir J. Graham—Mr Cardwell. Tea at home after House: Mrs A. Gordon [7] our guest: then read Fox, & to bed.

24. *Sat.*

Wrote to Sir J. Graham—Ld Monteagle—J.N.G.—Sir C. Wood—Willy—and minutes. Dined at Ld Ellesmere's: Lady Palmerston's afr & many conversations. Saw Lord A. Hervey—Sir C. Trevelyan—Sir A. Spearman—Mr Wilson—Mr Wood—Mr Pressly—Jas Wortley—Sir J. Young—E. Cardwell—Sir J. Graham—Earl of Aberdeen & do *cum* Sir J.G. Read Fox's Memoirs—'One Thing Needful'.[8]

---

[1] Draft of this at Add MS 44745, f. 141.

[2] Marginal notes of *Grey and *Panmure's observations omitted; dated 21 February [1855]; Add MS 44745, f. 140.

[3] Count Alfred de la Gueronnière, 1810–84; legitimist politician and publicist; described diarist in *Les Hommes d'État de l'Angleterre au xixᵉ siècle* (1855). Gladstone sent amendments on his fa. for the 2nd edition: Add MS 44530, f. 30.

[4] Add MS 44745, f. 141.

[5] Details of Palmerston's cabinet making omitted; initialled and dated 22 February 1855; Add MS 44745, f. 143.

[6] Explaining his resignation, notes in Add MS 44654, f. 15; *Bright earlier made his 'angel of death' speech: *H* cxxxvi. 1820.

[7] Caroline Emelia Mary, *née* Herschell, m. 1852 A. H. Gordon (see 22 July 55) and d. 1909.

[8] By W. R. *Greg (1855), on the army.

[Pasted to the back inside cover are two sheets of paper which contain:—]

[In W.E. Gladstone's handwriting:—]

Copy. Miss Clough—(taken by Lady Canning). 6 M.–N.E. 42.

A well judging person	a good Classic
considerate	is apt to mistrust himself
undecided—	if to choose a profession wd
has much application.	prefer the Church
a great reasoner	very affectionate & tender in
has a good deal of pride	his domestic relations
and determination, or	is very fond of society
rather obstinacy—	particularly ladies'—
neat	fond of reading

[In W.E. Gladstone's handwriting:—]

Copy. Oct. 1854. Miss Clough.[1] *per* Hon. Miss Lyttelton.

[In another handwriting:—]

Highly educated, & has very good common sense. Is wedded to his own opinions—& though he would go very quietly to work, he would contrive to gain his own ends. Is careful in money matters, & cautious in most things— Much to be depended upon—very sincere—strict & honorable, & fond of having all things in good order. Very firm in friendship—Difficult to convince—Is fond too of literary pursuits.[2]

[1] A governess, apparently not employed by the Gladstones.
[2] Possibly a reference for the butler; see 6 Feb. 55.

[VOLUME XIX]¹

[The inside front cover contains:]

NO 19.

FEB. 25. 55 TO DEC. 31. 1856

καὶ μὴν ἔμοιγε ζῶντι μὲν καθ' ἡμέραν,
κἐι σμίκρ' ἔχοιμι παντ' ἂν ἀρκούντως ἔχοι.
τύμβον δὲ βουλόιμην ἂν ἀξιουμενον
τὸν ἐμὸν ὁρᾶσθαι διὰ μακροῦ γὰρ ἡ χάρις.²

Eurip. Hecuba. [317—20]

London February 1855

25. 1 S. Lent.

Whitehall mg & Chapel Royal Evg. Wrote to Sir W. Heathcote. Saw Sir G. Lewis.—E. Cardwell—S. Herbert. Read Harvey on the Creeds—Cath. de Suede—Ms of 41 on Ps 139 aloud at night.

26. M.

Wrote to Sir G. Lewis—Mr Hayter—Sir C. Trevelyan—Sir C. Wood—Lady Pembroke—Rev. Dr Wolff—Sir A. Spearman—Willy—Rev W. Selwyn—and minutes. H. of C. 4½–7 and 10½–12¾.³ Saw Sir W. Heathcote—Mr A' Court—Duke of Argyll(2)—Mr S. Herbert—Mr Trevor—Lord Ward. Read S. Smith's Letters—Bowring on Russian trade⁴—Ld Raglan's defence.

27. T.

Wrote to Rev. A. Stanley—Mrs Andrew—C. A. Hope⁵—Miss Scott—C. Marriott—Ld Panmure—& minutes. H. of C. 4½–10¼. Spoke 1¾ hour in reply to Shelleys (still worse) 3 h.⁶ Saw Sir Geo. Lewis—Sir S.H. Northcote—Mr Arbuthnot. Worked up the Kennedy papers—J. Wortley's in evg. Read S. Smith—Napoleon letters.

---

¹ Lambeth MS 1433, ff. 138.
² 'While I live, anything at all, however little I had, would satisfy my daily need. But my tomb I should wish conspicuously honoured: for that is a tribute which endures.'
³ Admiralty and supply: *H* cxxxvi. 1891.
⁴ Untraced.   ⁵ Minister in Edinburgh.
⁶ Defending himself against Shelley's motion for a select cttee. on the *Kennedy affair (see *supra* iii. lii): *H* cxxxvi. 1991; notes in Add MS 44654, f. 23.

28. Feb.

Wrote to Sir C. Trevelyan—Sir Geo. Grey—Mrs Goalen—Mr Hayter—J.S. Buckingham—Mr A B Hope—Bp of Oxford—Robn G.—and minutes. Dictated Pol. Mema. & arranged former ones to date. Saw Mr Wilson—Mr Westcott(sat)—Mr S. Herbert—Sir J. Graham—Mr Mowbray—Sir T. Fremantle. Read S. Smith. Attended [1851] Royal Commission 12½–2. At the Palace at 2.45 for Audience to resign.

On[1] Sunday Sir George Lewis called on me & said my office had been offered him: this was after being refused by Cardwell & Baring: he asked my advice as to accepting it: this I told him I could not give, he asked if I would assist him with information in case of his accepting. I answered that he might command me precisely as if instead of resigning I had only removed to another department. I then went over some of the matters needful to be made known: on Tuesday he came again acquainted me with his acceptance, & told me he had been mainly influenced by my promise. This day at a quarter to three I attended at the Palace to resign the seals & had an audience of about twenty minutes. The Queen in taking them over was pleased to say that she received them with great pain. I answered that the decision which had required me to surrender them had been the most painful effort of my public life. The Queen said she was afraid on Saturday night last from the language I then used that this was about to happen. I answered that we had then already had a discussion in the Cabinet which pointed to this result & that I spoke as I did because I thought that to have no reserve whatever with H.M. was the first duty of all those who had the honor and happiness of being her servants.[2]

Thurs. Mch One 55.

Wrote to V. Chancr. of Oxford—Mr A. Russel—Solr. General—Provost of Eton—Sir W.R. Farquhar—Mr Jas. Watson—Mr R.M. Bromley—Ld Aberdeen—Galt. Gent & Co[3] & minutes. Read S. Smith. Worked on papers & packing up. Saw Chr. of Exr. (2½ hour on Budget) Miss Scott—R. Herbert —Sir F. Rogers—Mr Anderson—Mr Monsell M.P.—Sir J. Graham—Mr Wilson—General Peel[4]—Mr A. Gordon. H. of C. 4½–7 and 10½–1.[5]

2. Fr.

Wrote to Mr Monsell—Hon A. Gordon—Ld Brougham—Mr G. Smith—Sir J. Young—Mast. Pembroke—Bp of Moray and minutes. Dined with the Herberts. H. of C. 4¾–8½. Secrecy well knocked on the head.[6] Read the Peel MS.[7] Saw Rev. Mr Lake—Mr Wilson Patten—(2)—Mr A Gordon—Mr Anderson *cum* Spearman[8]—Sir A. Spearman—Ld Granville—Sir C.

[1] Follows reports of *Palmerston's cabinet making.
[2] Rest omitted: Add MS 44745, f. 149. Mem. dictated to Catherine Gladstone with some additions in diarist's hand.
[3] Galt, Kerruish and Gent, printers and owners of *Manchester Weekly Advertiser*.
[4] i.e. J. *Peel; cp. 8 Jan. 35n.
[5] Army promotion: *H* cxxxvi. 2091.
[6] *Roebuck withdrew his motion to make the Sebastopol cttee. proceedings secret as the first report of his cttee. had proposed: *PP* 1855, ix. 3 and *H* cxxxvii. 18.
[7] Untraced.
[8] About Spearman's retirement pension: Add MS 44530, f. 33v.

Trevelyan—Sir J. Graham + Herbert & Cardwell. Mr Monsell (2)—S. Herbert. Worked on packing & putting away: a most serious affair.

3. Sat.

Wrote to Rev. Mr Mills[1]—Mast. of Pembroke—Mr Roche M.P.—V.C. of Oxford—Mrs Goalen—and minutes. Visited Munro's Studio & the Bernal Collection[2]—Eleven to dinner. Music in evg. Read Peel MS. Worked on moving & putting by. Saw Sir A. Spearman—The Provost of Eton—Sir C. Trevelyan—Mr Wilson—Lord Ward—Sir J. Graham—Mr Cardwell — Hon. A. Gordon.

I have gone at great length with Sir G. Lewis[3] into the state of finance & my embryo plans for the coming year. I have named to him near 30 ₥ as the excess of military expenditure over that of 53–4 for wh. he will have to provide if the war continue: & of wh. 12 ₥ have already been supplied by the measures of 54. Of the remainder I told him I thought ⅓ must be raised by taxes & I gave him particulars. He seemed to shrink from this & feared that so large a proportion could scarcely be got in this form. I told him that upon this my mind was very much made up: so that he might understand that if he did less he must not count on me.[4] I also told him that if he proposed less than this he would very probably be run in upon & get nothing. I advised him to keep his own Counsel & let the Cabinet as a whole not know his plans till his mind was made up in the main, & the time close at hand. I thought him ready of comprehension and sound in his principles.

I warned him that the Newspaper Stamp Bill[5] might very probably cause trouble, not only directly but in indirect & unavowed forms.[6]

4. 2. S. Lent.

Chapel Royal & H.C. mg: St James's evg. MS of 46 aloud. Saw W.C. James —Aunt J. Read S. Cath de Suéde—Foulkes's Pamphlet[7]—S. Smith Memoirs—Harvey on [blank] [the creed].

5. M.

Wrote to Dr Jacobson—Ld Brougham—Rev. Mr Michell—Sir S. Northcote —Sir W. James. and minutes. H. of C 4¾–7 and 9–1.[8] Sat to Mr Westcott. Read Peel MS. Saw Sir A. Spearman—Earl of Aberdeen—Mr Wilson—Mr R. Herbert—Sir Jas. Graham—Robn. G.—Mr Ball—Mr. [blank] and Sir J. Paxton. Worked up the stamp question—moving operations advanced.

[1] Robert Twyford Mills, d. 1874; rector of Halse 1844; wrote on poor rates, Add MS 44530, f. 35.

[2] Ralph *Bernal's art collection, sold for £71,000. See 12 Mar. 55.

[3] See 25, 27 Feb. 55.

[4] *Lewis's willingness to borrow led to violent hostility from Gladstone; see 20 Feb. 57.

[5] Bill abolishing newspaper stamp as such, originally drawn up by Gladstone (see 19 Jan. and 20 Mar. 55) got royal assent in June 1855.

[6] Rest, news of *Palmerston's cabinet making, omitted; dated 3 March 1855, Add MS 44778, f. 196.

[7] E. S. Ffoulkes, *One more return from captivity; or my submission to the Catholic Church vindicated and explained*, (1855).

[8] Supply: *H* cxxxvii. 111.

6. *T.*

Wrote to V.C. Oxford—Willy—Mr Barclay—T.G. Saw R. Herbert (fare-well)[1]—Ld Granville—Robn. G. Worked on Bank papers.[2] Worked on moving & arranging in my new sitting-room upstairs. H. of C. $4\frac{3}{4}$–$6\frac{1}{2}$.[3] Dined at Stafford House. Read Greg 'The way out'[4]—S. Smith's Life. Peel MS.

7. *Wed.*

Wrote to Mr G. Cree[5]—Rev. A. Spooner[6]—S. Rose[7] —V. Princ. Magd. Hall[8]—Mr A. Allaidier[9]—Mr R. Watson.[10] Worked on books, papers, & turning out of dressing-room. Saw S. Herbert—Sir W. Heathcote (Oxford &c)—Sir G. Grey—Bp of Oxford—Earl Granville. Rode in mg. Attended the (first) Levee. Dined with the Farquhars—Read S. Smith's Life (finished) & the Peel MS (finished).

8. *Th.*

Wrote to V. Chancr. Oxford—Willis (books)—Warden H. of Charity[11]—Rev. Mr Meek—Mr. Hampton—Rode in mg. Dined with the Granville Vernons. Saw Ld Granville—Sir W. Heathcote—Chancr. of Exchequer—Mr Barclay—Ld Hatherton—Read Fox's Corresp. (finished II.) H. of C. $4\frac{1}{2}$–$7\frac{1}{2}$ and $11\frac{3}{4}$–$12\frac{1}{2}$.[12]

9. *Fr.*

Wrote to Mr G. Dundas—J. Bannister—W.W. Clark—C.A. Wood—Mr Maiden[13]—Mrs Uwins—Rev. Mr Mathews[14]—Mr Betts[15]—Sir T.G. Saw Chancr. of Exr.—Newcastle—Mr Ellice. Read Trevor's Wm III[16]—A Lancashire man on the War.[17]—M. Arnold's Rustum & Sohrab.[18] Six to dinner (from H.) Worked on my papers &c Wrote Pol. Mema.[19]

10. *Sat.*

Wrote to Jas. Watson—Chancr. of Exchr.—Mr Willis—Rev. J. O. Powell—

[1] As his private secretary.
[2] The monthly bank bullion returns: *PP* 1855, xxx. 361.
[3] Misc. business: *H* cxxxvii. 189.
[4] By W. R. *Greg (1855), on administrative reform.
[5] Possibly Edward David Cree, author of devotional books.
[6] None found; probably *sc.* George Spooner, curate of St. Mary, Dunstall, 1853, vicar of Inglesham 1857.
[7] Perhaps Samuel Rose, London yarn merchant.   [8] R. Michell.
[9] Unidentified.   [10] Perhaps Ralph Watson, London attorney.
[11] Henry Augustus *Rawes, 1826–85; warden of St. Barnabas, Soho, 1855–6; became Roman catholic 1856.
[12] Baltic naval operations: *H* cxxxvii. 261.
[13] Possibly George Augustus Maiden, London diamond merchant.
[14] George Fraser Mathews; priest 1849, vicar of Bungay 1861.
[15] Probably John Thomas Betts, brandy distiller.
[16] A. H. *Trevor, *The life and times of William III*, 2v. (1835–6).
[17] By J. A. Nicholls, who wrote several pamphlets under this pseudonym.
[18] Published (1853).   [19] Completing those begun earlier; see 24, 25 Jan. 55.

Mr E. White—Rev. Mr Tremlett[1]—Rev. A.W. Haddan. Paying bills: &
continued the work of restoring order. Sat to Mr Westcott. Saw Ld Aberdeen—Ditto *cum* A. Gordon.

$$\left.\begin{array}{l}\text{Chancr. of Exchr.}\\ \text{Count Colloredo}\\ \text{Ld Grey—}\\ \text{Ld Stanley Ald[erley]}\end{array}\right\}\ \text{Evg.}$$

Dined at Ld Clarendon's. Read Memoires &c. de Joseph[2]—Peter Plymley[3]

11. 3. S. Lent.

St James's mg. Bedfordbury evg. MS of 42 aloud. Late dinner with the
Wortleys. Wrote to Bp of Argyll—Marquis d'Azeglio—Mr O'Brien—Read
Allocuzione &c[4]—Sydney Smith's Sermons.—Wathen[5]—Bp of Glasgow on
Unity.[6] Wrote on 'Parable'[7]—

12. M. X.

Wrote to Mr E.F. Collins[8]—Robn. G.—Rector of Exeter[9]—Mr G.H.
Wathen[10]—Rowland Hill & minutes. Read P. Plymley's Letters (finished)—
Wathen's Golden Colony. Saw Dumin[R]—Saw Ld Granville—Chancr. of
Exchequer—Sir J. Graham—H. of C. $4\frac{1}{2}$–$7\frac{1}{2}$.[11] Dined with Lady Hope to
meet Jim [Hope-Scott]. Not as in other days! But all was kind & kindly.
Sat (a while) to Mr Munro & fixed on design for Relief of Agnes & baby[12]—
thence to Aunt J.s—Thence to the Bernal sale.

13. T.

Wrote to Rev. Wilson Pedder[13]—J. Griffiths—Visc. Palmerston—Mrs S.
Brown—R. Wilbraham—Mr O'Brien—Chr. of Exchr.—E. Sharpe. Worked
5 h. on pamphlets & made a beginning. H. of C. $4\frac{1}{2}$–$8\frac{3}{4}$[14] Saw Bp of Salisbury

---

[1] Dr. Francis William Tremlett, emissary in Britain for bps. of Southern United
States; vicar of St. Peter's, Hampstead 1859.
[2] See 1 Feb. 55.
[3] See 6 Aug. 40.
[4] *Allocuzione della Santità di nostro Signore Pio Papa ix del 22 Gennaio, 1855* (1855);
reviewed in his *Quarterly* article, see 29 May 55.
[5] G. H. Wathen, *The golden colony; or Victoria in 1854* (1855).
[6] W. J. Trower, 'Pastoral letter . . . chiefly on the present divided state of the church'
(1855).
[7] Not found.
[8] Edward Francis Collins, 1807–72; edited *Hull Advertiser* 1842–66; a Roman catholic.
[9] John Prideaux Lightfoot, 1803–87; rector of Exeter, Oxford, from 1854; vice-chancellor 1862–6.
[10] George H. Wathen, author.
[11] Spoke briefly on Scottish affairs: *H* cxxxvii. 417.
[12] Done in marble by A. *Monro, now at Hawarden.
[13] Wilson Pedder, b. 1816?; Brasenose; vice-principal Wells theological college 1842;
vicar of Garsang, Lancashire, 1859.
[14] *Heywood's Deceased Wife's Sister Bill: *H* cxxxvii. 486.

—Sir Jas. Graham. Six to dinner: Bp of S. & Mrs H[amilton] came after. Read Durando's Speech.[1]

14. Wed.

Wrote to Ld Monteagle—G. Burnett—and copy. Mast. Pembroke—Mr J.B. Hume—Ld Clarendon. Dined at Ld Overstones. Lady Palmerston's afterwards. 5 h. more on pamphlets. Saw Robn. Gladstone—do. *cum* Mr Jeffery[2] —Duke of Argyll—Mr Geo Hope—Sir W. Heathcote—Sir H. Holland[3]— Duke of Newcastle—A. Panizzi. Read Debate at Turin on the Treaty.[4]

15. T.

Wrote to Mrs Goalen—Chr. of Exchequer—A. Wylie—B.B. Williams— G.W. Hope—A. White. Rode in mg. Saw Chancr. of Exchequer[5]—Mr Wilson—Sir W. Clay—Sir James Graham—Sir S. Northcote—Mr Gibson *cum* Mr Bright (H of C)—T.S. Gladstone. Worked on pamphlets. Read Sard. Debate—Wathen's Golden Colony. Arranged & Indexed my own 'Tracts' to 53.—&c.

16. Fr.

Wrote to Ld Monteagle (2)—Ld Granville—Rev. Mr Lawrence—Ld Blayney—J. Cunningham—W.C. James—Rowland Hill—Chr. of Exchr.— H. Tayleur—Saw Chr. of Exchr.—Sir J. Graham—Mr Wilson. Rode in aftn. Worked on Joint Fund: plan of division.[6] Five to dinner. Read Newmarch on Pitt's Loans.[7] H. of C. 4½–7½[8]

17. Sat.

Wrote to Mr P. Nagle[9]—Rev Mr. Surtees[10]—J.T. Totty[11]—H. M'Cormac—[12] J.W. Cowell—Jas Henderson—J. Boodle[13] and others. Warden Trin Coll.[14] W.A. Byron[15]—Ld Monteagle—Sat to Mr Westcott

---

[1] Perhaps G. Durando, *Schiarimenti sulla condotta del General Durando comandante le truppe pontifique nel Veneto* (1848), or a more recent untraced speech.
[2] See 30 Jan. 54.
[3] Sir Henry *Holland, 1788–1873; physician and traveller; cr. bart, 1853.
[4] Sardinian assembly debates on the British loan, discussed by Gladstone on 24 May 1855: *H* cxxxviii. 1066–7.
[5] See 20 Mar. 55.
[6] See 2 Apr. 55.
[7] W. *Newmarch, *On the loans raised by Mr. *Pitt . . . 1793–1801* (1855); disputed at length by Gladstone on 20 April 1855: *H* cxxxvii. 1593.
[8] Education Bill: *H* cxxxvii. 640.
[9] P. J. Nagle, pamphleteer.
[10] Scott Frederick Surtees, 1813?–89; vicar of Richmond 1843–50; rector of Banham, Norfolk, 1850–6, of Sprotborough, Yorkshire, 1856–79.
[11] Possibly John William Tottie, gentleman, of Down Street, off Piccadilly.
[12] Henry M'Cormick was blacksmith of Toxteth Park.
[13] Of Boodle and Partington, London surveyors.
[14] J. *Hannah.
[15] Perhaps of Byron & Selfe, London commission agents.

12–2¼. Saw Scotts—Mr J.D. Cook—Sir James Graham—Mr R. Wilbraham—Mr A. Gordon—

Mr A. Court M.P.⎫
Sir F. Baring   ⎪
Sir C. Wood   ⎬ at Sp[eaker's] Levee
General Peel   ⎪
Mr Miles   ⎭

Speaker's Levee in evg. Read (finished) Mr Newmarch. Meditated & began
Genl. Tom Thumb.¹

18. 4. S.L.

Whitehall mg. & Ch. Royal aft.—MS of 49 aloud at night. Wrote to Bp of
Salisbury. Saw Lady Hope—Sir C. Anderson. Walk with C. Read the
Heathcote MS. on Reunion²—Howe on the Living Temple³—Hook on H.
Eucharist.⁴ Arranged some Tracts.

19. M.

Wrote to W. Newmarch⁵—Mr R. Hill—Ld Monteagle—J. Murray (& copy)
—Warden Trin. Coll.—Sir W. James—Worked on Stamp & Fin[ance] pa-
pers. H. of C. 4½–11: and spoke on these questions.⁶ Saw Mr J. D. Cook—Sir
Jas. Graham—Mr J. Griffiths—J. MacCulloch—Mr Smythe (Methven)—
Mr Gibson—Mr Laing. Read Ld Abns. dispatches.⁷

20. T.

Wrote to H. Tayleur—Sir S. Scott & Co—Mr Jas M'Kear⁸—W.P. Brookes⁹
—Jas Wilson—Mr Tremlett. Rode aftn. Dined at Mrs Talbots—H. of C.
4½–7¾ and 9¾–1¼. Voted agt. Walmsley.¹⁰ Saw Earl of Aberdeen—F.Calvert¹¹
—A. Gordon.

On Thursday last I saw Lewis about his Newspaper Stamp Bill¹²—regretted the
changes—& predicted that his Clauses respecting Registration & Securities would
not pass.
I took the opportunity of telling him that I thought they cd. not defend the
arrangement under which they had an Absentee Colonial Minister¹³ & that I was

¹ C. S. Stratton, *An account of . . . General Tom Thumb* (1844).
² Not found; see 27 Mar. 55; but Heathcote also later acted as go-between Gladstone
and *Derby in a reconciliation attempt; see Add MS 43071, ff. 330, 335.
³ See 13 Dec. 46.   ⁴ See 21 Feb. 47.
⁵ William *Newmarch, 1820–82; statistician and economist; see 12 Feb., 16 Mar. 55n.
⁶ Defending the continuation of the temporary Exchequer Bills of March 1854: *H*
cxxxvii. 826.
⁷ See 16 Apr. 55.
⁸ Perhaps James Haslen M'Kean, gentleman, of Altrincham.
⁹ Probably W. G. Brooks of the Bank of England's Liverpool branch.
¹⁰ Sir J. *Walmsley's motion to open the National Gallery & British Museum on
Sundays: *H* cxxxvii. 915.
¹¹ Lt. General Felix Calvert, of the board of general officers.
¹² See 3 Mar. 55n.   ¹³ i.e. *Russell, in Vienna at the Conference.

in fear & trembling lest Pakington shd. give notice of an Address. He said at once he entirely agreed with me. I hoped they wd. anticipate a possible & (if made) formidable motion by doing something freely.[1]

21. Wed.

St Margaret's at 12: Melville preached a brilliant & powerful sermon. Chapel Royal aft. MS of 47 aloud in evg. Read Churton's Sermon[2]— Documenti. Wrote to J. Murray—Hatchards. Saw S. Herbert—the Jameses. I am now able to operate a little on my diet: & today complied in part.

22. Th.

Wrote to N. Higinbotham[3]—Sir J. Bowring—Vicar of Newark[4]—V.C. Oxford—Mast. Pembroke—W. Smythe—J.N.G. Dined at Lady Wenlock's. Saw M. Dumin. Saw Marquis d'Azeglio—Rev. N. Woodard—Bp of Salisbury —Mr Anderson—Mr Hayter—Read Documenti—and Memoires de Joseph.

23. Fr.

Wrote to Baron d'Azein[5]—Mr A. Hunter—Sir W. Heathcote—Mr Ramfitt[6] —Sir S. Northcote—Mr J[ohn] Patch[7]—Prov. of Oriel—Jas Watson— Dined at D. of Argyll's—H. of C 4½–7.[8] Worked on pamphlets &c. Saw Master of Pembroke—Sir B. Hall—Chr. of Exr.—Mr Neate—Mr Jas Durham—J.N.G.—S.H. Northcote. Read Memoirs du Roi Joseph— Haydn's Autobiography[9]—Allocuzione &c.

24. Sat. [Richmond]

Wrote to Mr Whatman—Dep. Paymaster[10]—Mr C. Perks[11]—Sir W. Heathcote—C. S. Barker[12]—Mr R. V[ernon] Smith—Mrs Oldfield.[13] My last sitting to Mr Westcott. Saw Ld Aberdeen—do cum Sir J. Graham. Worked long in preparation for the binder. Dined with the Cardwell's. Off at 11 to Richmond & sat up talking with Bp N.Z. till two. Read Scudamore's Engl. & Rome.[14]

25. Annunc. & 5. S. Lent.

Parish Ch mg. (Bp preached) & Kew aftn. Walked in the gardens. Wrote Mem. on Trin Coll.[15] Read Scudamore—Wordsworth's Lecture &c.[16] Sat with Bp in evg.

[1] Dated 20 March 1855; Add MS 44778, f. 201.
[2] E. *Churton, 'The Gifts of God to the Good' (1855).
[3] Newburgh Higinbotham, of the Woods and Forests office.   [4] J. G. Bussell.
[5] Baron P. d'Azene of Paris had written on French affairs (Hawn P).
[6] Untraced; reading uncertain   [7] London barrister.
[8] Crimean transport: H cxxxvii. 1016.
[9] *The Life of Benjamin Robert *Haydon ed. T. Taylor, 3v. (1853).
[10] E. A. Hoffay, see 22 Feb. 54.   [11] Charles Perks, bookseller in St. Martin's Lane.
[12] Charles Spackman Barker, 1806–79; organ builder.
[13] Mrs. E. O. Oldfield of Hyde Park; Hawn P.
[14] By W. E. *Scudamore (1855).   [15] Not found; but see 3 Oct. 55.
[16] Charles *Wordsworth, 'What is national humiliation without national repentance?' (1855).

26. M. [London]

After breakfast we bade farewell & drove back to town: home about $10\frac{3}{4}$.—
The Bp sails tomorrow for his noble work. Finished my laborious job for the
bookbinder. Wrote to Mr Petheran—Dingwall Library.[1] Read Haydn's
Autobiography. Six to dinner. H. of C. $4\frac{1}{2}$–8: spoke on Sardinian Treaty.
and $9\frac{3}{4}$–1: voted in 215: 161 on the Newsp. Stamp.[2] Saw Mr Woollcombe—
Mr J. Wood—Miss M.N. Gladstone—Creswick (foreman).

27. T.

Wrote to R. Wilbraham—J. Palmer—R. Whitaker[3]—Sir A[lexander]
Gordon—R.V. Smith—A.W. Haddan—Sir W. Heathcote—Rev. G.
Buller[4] —Mr Murray—Bickers—W. Smythe. Dined with Bp of Salisbury
to meet Mr Heathcote: we had a long conversation respecting reunions &
the Roman See. Rode in forenoon. Saw Mr Rowsell—Sir J. Young—Mr
Anderson—Mr H. Roberts—Mr Smythe (Methven)—Sir Chas. Wood—
R.V. Smith. Read Educn. Bills[5]—A Commoner on the War.[6]

28. Wed.

Wrote to Sir R. Napier[7] and Ld Brougham. Dined with the Attorney
General. H. of C. $12\frac{1}{4}$–$4\frac{3}{4}$.[8] Failed in inquiries for Osborne & Wolf: probably
my last[R]. Read Capefigue[9]—Haydn. Saw Chr. of Exchequer—Lord
Aberdeen—Duke of Newcastle—Mr. H. Roberts—Mr Walpole—Mr Glynn
—Solr. General.

29. Th.

Wrote to Chr. of Exchequer—W.C. James—Jones & Yarrell—Rev. Mr
Tibbs[10]—Mr W. Toogood—Mr G. Smith—Miss M.N. Gladstone[11]—Mr
Betts. Countess Colloredo's in evg. Saw Tilburn (38)[R]. Read Haydn—&
Pamphlets. Attended the Drawingroom. Worked on Joint Fund Accounts.
Saw B. Usedom—Count Colloredo—Ld Aberdeen—Ld St. Germans.

30. Fr.

Wrote to Mr J. Esh Shellaby[12]—H. Tayleur—Mr Rathbone—Rev. Mr
Price—Rev. Mr Pusey. The Herberts dined. Willy & Stephy came home

[1] Probably on the Mackenzie collection; see 12 Jan. 48n.
[2] Defending loan to Sardinia, and voting for 2°R of bill to remove stamp duty on
newspapers: *H* cxxxvii. 1085, 1109.
[3] Robert Whitaker, commission agent in Liverpool.
[4] Unidentified nonconformist?
[5] Two govt. education bills brought in in February and March: *PP* 1855 ii. 235.
[6] 'The warnings of the War . . . by "a British Commoner" [E. R. Humphreys]' (1855).
[7] Sir Robert John Milliken Napier, 1818–84; soldier; 9th bart. 1852.
[8] Exchequer Bills: *H* cxxxvii. 1249.
[9] J. B. Capefigue, perhaps his *Les diplomates européens*, 4v. (1843–47).
[10] Henry Wall Tibbs; Trinity, Dublin; priest 1842; curate of Oxton, Nottinghamshire,
1856–9; vicar of Shelford from 1859; theologian.
[11] Margaret Neilson Gladstone, 1820–71, cousin, daughter of Hugh; d. unmarried.
[12] Possibly G. Eshelby, London courier.

both well and happy. Rode in forenoon. Saw Mr B. Williams—Mr Goldwin Smith—Mr H. Roberts—Mr Walpole—Mr S. Herbert—Mr Gibson—Ld Granville. H. of C. 4½–6¾.[1] Wrote on the Two Decades.[2] Began to consider our plans for moving. Read Haydn.

31. Sat.

Wrote to H.T. Stainton[3]—Rev. Mr Gruggen.[4] Dined with the Cannings. Rode in aftn. Saw Chancr. of Excr.—Ellisons—Mr Anderson—Mr Westcott (another *last* sitting)—Mr [W.M.H.] Church (resp. W. & Stephy—it looked like S.s going to Eton)—Mrs Tyler—Earl of Aberdeen—Ld Canning. Wrote on the Two Decades. Read Capefigue. Calls.

Palm Sunday. Ap. 1/55.

Whitehall Chapel & Holy Commn. with C. & Willy mg. St Andrews Wells St aftn. Wrote MS on the day & read (in part) aloud. Wrote to Bp of Salisbury. Saw R. Cavendish—S. Herbert. Dined with the Herberts. Read Scudamore.

2. M.

Wrote to H. Tayleur—Robn. G—Mrs Coultast[5]—R. Hill—C. Paskin—Scotts—Wms. Deacon & Co. Marg. Chapel 5 P.M. Corrected Report (part) of Feb 23. Saw Mr Bonham—Judge Coleridge—Mr H. Roberts—Mr Jas. Wilson—Mr Grogan—Sir W. James—with whom I finally arranged the division of our Joint Fund.[6] It has greatly prospered, thank God, in our hands. Wrote on the Two Decades. Read N. Ferrar's Life[7]—Wilson's MS.[8]

3. T.

Italian Service Bloomsbury 11 a.m. Wrote to Mr J. Moss—R. Wilbraham—Mr R. Browning[9]—Goldwin Smith—Jas Watson—Sir W. James—Wms. Deacon & Co.—Rev. Mr Haddan—Overends—Mr W. Linton—Robn. G.—W. Sorbrett[10]—Govr. Wodehouse. Worked on my papers. Read Mayor's N. Ferrar—& Strickland's Travel Thoughts.[11] Saw Sir A. Spearman—Mr

[1] Wills: *H* cxxxvii. 1429.
[2] Marked in pencil on the cover, 'Party as it was and as it is. A sketch of the Political History of Twenty years'; not published: Add MS 44745, ff. 173–222. A very interesting and important article; Gladstone does not seem to have approached *Elwin (see 19 Apr. 55) about its publication; see N. L. S. Elwin Papers.
[3] Henry Tibbats *Stainton, 1822–92, entomologist.
[4] Frederick James Gruggen, 1820–72; headmaster of Pocklington school, Yorkshire, from 1848.
[5] Unidentified.
[6] Originally started to finance the abortive Leicester square church project, the fund had been used for the Bedfordbury chapel of ease and other projects; details of its dissolution in Hawn P.
[7] N. *Ferrar, *Two Lives by his brother John and by Dr. Jebb*, ed. J. E. B. Mayor (1855).
[8] T. *Wilson, *Sacra Privata from the original manuscripts*, ed. W. Denton (1853).
[9] Reuben Browning, writer on finance.   [10] Unidentified.
[11] H. Strickland pseud. [H. S. Constable], *Travel Thoughts and Travel Fancies* (1854).

Farquhar Matheson[1]—Govr. of the Bank—Mr Colnaghi—Mr E. Bunsen.[2] Worked on P.O. Stamp papers. Continued that incredibly wearisome task of correcting the (Explanation) Speech.[3]

4. Wed.

Westm[inste]r Abbey 10 a.m. Wrote to Messrs Overend—Robn. G.—H. Tayleur—J.N.G.—Baron Usedom—H. Slatter[4]—Sir W. Molesworth— Cocks & Co.—M. Lyttelton. We went over to Mr Ellisons to tea in the evg. Saw Mr G.ogan—Chancr. of Exchequer—Sir W.C. James. Worked on papers & accts. Finished that truly penal operation the correcting the Report of my Speech. Read Robertson's America[5]—Rode: my last; I am glad to get quit of a personal luxury and indulgence.

5. Th.

Marg. Chapel & H.C. 11–1 a.m. Wrote to Williams D[eacon] & Co—J. Murray—Rev. S. Surtees—Mrs Ellison—Rev. R. Daniell—H. Tayleur— T. C. Hansard—W.G. Anderson—Jas. Macgregor M.P.—Jas. Watson—Jas. Robertson. Wrote MS. on the day & read it in family. Saw Ld Aberdeen— Mr A. Gordon—Mr Godley. Read Nicholas Ferrar—The Aberdeen Correspondence.

6. Good Friday

Chapel Royal mg.—where we were disappointed of H.C.—St Paul's (with W[illy] A[gnes] & S[tephen]) aftn.—MS of 41 aloud in evg. Bible conv. with W. & A. when S. was gone at his own particular desire a 3d time to Church. Worked on H.S. Read N. Ferrar—pamphlets—and Aberdeen Correspondence. Saw D. of Newcastle. Wrote to Canning.

7. S. Easter Eve.

Westmr. Abbey 10 a.m. and the impressive Service at Marg. Chapel with W.A. & S. at 8 P.M. Wrote to Lord Elphinstone[6]—Sir Jamsetjee[7]—Sig. Casimiro di Lieto—Ld Wodehouse—Mr Deale—R. Wilbraham—Mr Brough[8] —C. had a day of great pain with brow ague. Read the Abn Dipl. Correspondence—N. Ferrar (with wh Willy is delighted). Worked on the Two Decades.

8. Easter Day.

Chapel Royal & H.C. at 12. Marg. Chapel (with Willy) at 7. MS on Zech 9.

[1] ?1808–90, of Lochalsh; episcopalian incumbent of Lairg, Sutherland; ? at 30 Aug. 44.
[2] Ernest Bunsen, s. of C.C.J.   [3] Of 23 February.
[4] Of the London coach and harness firm.
[5] W. *Robertson, The history of America, 2v. (1777).
[6] John *Elphinstone, 1807–60; governed Madras 1837–42, Bombay 1853–9; 13th Baron Elphinstone 1813 in Scottish peerage, 1st in U.K. peerage 1859.
[7] Sir Jamsetjee Jejeebhoy, 1783–1859; Parsee merchant and philanthropist in Bombay; kt. 1842; in London to receive its freedom April 1855; cr. bart. 1857.
[8] Perhaps Thomas Brough, Liverpool merchant and shipper.

aloud to family. Wrote on Luke XXII. 44. Saw Bp of Oxford. Read N. Ferrar (finished)—Bp O.s (Univ.) Sermon[1]—Scudamore's England & Rome[2]—Chr. Remembr.[3]

9. M.

Marg. Chapel 5 P.M. Wrote to Mr Herbert Stack—Mr Tupper—Mr Anderson. Virgil with W. & S. Visited the Carlton at night, second time this year. Visited the Richmonds' to see his pictures. Worked on the Decades. Worked on arranging books papers &c: & discussed household plans. Saw Chancr. of Exchequer—Mr Edw. Hamilton[4]—Mr Grogan. Read Le Moinne on the Committee[5]—Aberdeen Correspondence.

10. T.

St Mary's Crown St 8½ P.M. Wrote to Williams Deacon & Co—Mr Deale—King's Coll. Hospital—Mr W. Smythe—Rev. Mr Greene. Saw E. Cavendish. Worked much on the Two Decades. Virgil with W. & Stephy. Read The Female Jesuit abroad.[6]

11. Wed. X

Wrote to C.A. Wood—Bp of Moray. Dined at the Dow[age]r Ly Wharncliffe's. Worked much on the Two Decades. Saw Sir G. Clerk—M.F. Tupper—J. Wortley—Saw one[R]. Read the Abn. Correspondence.

12. Th. X.

St Stephen's 6 P.M. Wrote to C.G. Saw Duke of Argyll—J.E. Denison—resp Ministry. Saw Horton—things not better[R]. Finished the writing & revising of the Two Decades. I still want a title. Read 'Female Jesuit abroad'—Aberdeen's Correspondence.

13. Fr.

Marg. Chapel 5 P.M. Wrote to Cocks & Co —Lyttelton (Ly G[lynne']s Estate)—Robn. Gladstone—Duke of Newcastle—Sir A. Spearman—Mayor of Oxford[7]—Mr J. Cowell. Worked on accts & papers. C. returned—refreshed. Read Abn. Corr[espondence]—Female Jesuit Abroad. Saw Chancr. of Exchr.—Mr H. Roberts (2).

The Chancr. of the Exchequer came to me to tell me he had arranged to receive tenders for a Loan on Monday—in conformity with the decision of the last Cabinet—but the amount was not yet fixed—he had however almost decided on taking the money in Consols with an annuity to raise the sum to par[8]—and he

---

[1] S. *Wilberforce, 'Rome her new dogma and our duties' (1855).
[2] See 24 Mar. 55.　　　[3] *Christian Remembrancer*, xxix. 1 (April 1855).
[4] i.e. W. K.'s* brother (see 2 June 34).
[5] J. Lemoinne, 'L'enquête parlementaire en Angleterre' in *Revue des Deux Mondes* n.s. x. 149 (1855).
[6] By Charles *Seager (1853); see 24 Sept. 63.　　　[7] James Pike.
[8] In April 1855 *Lewis raised £16m. in 3% Consols, raised with terminable annuities of 14/6 per £100; see O. Anderson, 'Loans *versus* Taxes', *Ec. Hist. Rev.*, xvi. 317.

thought of taking the whole at once, instead of a minor Loan in the first instance. I told him

1. That I thought he was right in not dividing his operation, if it was to be a *Loan* in the proper sense, into two parts.

2. That with me the only question would have been whether he could get on for the present by some temporary supply until he saw his way positively as to the Vienna Conferences, and, so far, as to war and peace.

3. I hinted my doubts as to Consols if a lower stock were practicable.

4. I suggested that he should consider whether he could acquaint the bidders that he meant to raise whatever might be required over & above the Loan to be balance[d] next week by means of Taxes—as they would probably bid better under such circumstances than if they supposed that Loans were now to be adopted as a *system*.[1]

I suggested to him the three farthing Book Post. He did not disapprove but was not inclined to move. He told me to my great regret that his intention was only to give a Book Post at the rate of 1d. per 2 oz.[2]

14. Sat.

Wrote to Rev. Mr Peake[3]—Mrs Goalen—Robn. G—Mr Smythe. Saw Mr H. Roberts—Ld Canning—Mr G. Smith—Mr Greene. Read Abn. Correspondence—Seagers Female Jesuit (finished)—Westmr. Review on Palmerston[4]—Quart. Rev. on Public affairs.[5] Sixteen to dinner—Arranging books, &c.

15. 1 S. E[aster].

Chapel Royal mg & Marg Chapel Evg. Wrote to Rev. Dr Hessey—Rev. F. Meyrick. Saw Aunt J. Read Chr. Rem. on Wilberforce and on Law of Marriage[6]—Pamphlets on ditto[7]—Johnstone on Sunday.[8]

16. M.

Wrote to H. Tayleur—D. of Newcastle—Saw Mr S. Herbert—Lord Aberdeen. Saw one[R]. Eight to dinner. We were all much of one mind with regard to the adulation lavished on Louis Napoleon: about whom London is all agog today.[9] Music in evg. Made up with some labour a set of the Two corrected Fin[ancia]l Speeches of 1854. Finished the Abn. Levant Correspondence & made Extracts from it.[10] Virgil with W. & S.

---

[1] Dated here 13 April 1855.

[2] Dated here 13 April 1855; Add MS 44778, f. 203.

[3] Thomas Cross Peake, 1817–89; Sidney Sussex, Cambridge; rector of Hallaton from 1843.

[4] *Westminster Review*, n.s. vii. 398 (April 1855), denounced *Palmerston: 'not a man of progress'.

[5] *Quarterly Review*, clvi. 568 (March 1855).

[6] *Christian Remembrancer*, xxix. 369, 458 (April 1855).

[7] James Gibson, 'Some brief conclusions' (1855) and J. A. Hessey, 'A scripture argument against permitting marriage with a wife's sister' (1855); both annotated in Add MS 44586, f. 17. 25.

[8] W. H. Johnstone, *Sunday and the Sabbath* (1853).   [9] On a state visit.

[10] On the correspondence between *Wellington and *Aberdeen, 1828–29: Add MS 44745, f. 159ff.

17. T.

Wrote to Mr Goldwin Smith—Mr R.M. Fox M.P.—Sir W.C. James—Rev. Mr Lea[1]—Mr H. Slatter—Hon A. Gordon. Saw Mr G.G. Tyler—Mr W. Forbes—Capt. Gordon—Also saw one Allem[R]. Finished Extracts from Abn. Corresp. Dined at Mrs Talbots. Read Sebastopol Committee's Evidence[2]—Espinasse on Authorship[3]—&c. Virgil with W. & S.

18. Wed.

Wrote to Overends—R. Barker—R. Andrews[4]—Hon A. Gordon—Chr. of Exchr. Saw J.N.G.—S. Herbert—Molesworth—Ld Canning. Arranged all my prints in portfolios &c.—my forenoons work. Read Committee's Evidence. Off at 8 to Windsor. We made our bow to the Emperor & Empress. The whole was as slight as it could be & therefore as well. I am depressed & grieved to the heart at our position & prospects acc. to present news & surmise. Back at $1\frac{1}{4}$.

19. Th.

Wrote to Rev. W. Elwin[5]—Robn. G. Worked on my Chests of papers. Read Sebastopol Evidence. Saw R. Cavendish—Mr Hayter—Mr Moffatt—Mr A. Gordon —E. Cardwell. 6–$10\frac{1}{2}$ dined at Pol. Ec Club, & heard discussions on National Issue & Small Notes.[6]

20. Fr.

Wrote to The Speaker. Read Sebastopol Evidence—Phillips on the Solar System[7]—Haydns Autobiography.[8] Worked on books & papers. Saw Ld Aberdeen—Mr Anderson—Mr Gibson M.P. H. of C. $4\frac{1}{4}$–$8\frac{1}{4}$: spoke on the budget—mainly with a view to War & Peace.[9] H. of C. also $9\frac{3}{4}$–11. Stephen went off. He is thank God most satisfactory: indeed our treasure in children is rare. Continuing preparations.

21. Sat.

Wrote to Rev. Mr Cureton—Sir J. Graham—G.H. Forbes—Mr C. Gray[10] and [blank]. Read Sebastopol Evidence—Br. Q.R. on Italian Literature[11]—

---

[1] Frederick Simcox Lea, 1823–93; fellow of Brasenose 1853; curate in Stepney 1855; rector of Tedstone from 1873.
[2] Evidence of the March hearings, including *Cardigan's, S. G. Osborne's and Lucan's: *PP* 1855 ix. part 1.
[3] F. Espinasse, *What reading and writing have become* (1850).
[4] Richard Andrews, 1798–1859; Southampton coach manufacturer and radical, contested it 1857.
[5] Whitwell *Elwin, 1816–1900; rector of Booton from 1849; succ. *Lockhart as editor of *Quarterly Review*, 1853–60; see Add MS 44152.
[6] Led by J. W. Cowell; see *Political Economy Club* (1860), 99.
[7] M. L. Phillips, *Worlds beyond the earth* (1855).   [8] See 23 Mar. 55.
[9] And on income tax: *H* cxxxvii. 1589; notes in Add MS 44654, f. 66.
[10] Of C. and B. Gray, Liverpool merchants.
[11] *British Quarterly Review*, xxi. 317 (April 1855), on Gioberti.

Arranged my letters. Saw Mr Goldwin Smith—Mr Walker (Marg. St)[1]—Ld Canning—Mr Goulburn. Saw one aet. 18[R]. Dined with the Herberts.

22. 2 S.E[aster].

Whitehall mg: St Andrews aft.—Finished MS on Luke XXII. 44 & read it aloud at night. Finished my papers for Willy's Confirmation Time.[2] Saw S. Herbert—Read Bromley on Pakington's Bill[3]—Colquhoun on do[4]—Arthur to Ld Stanley[5]—Drummond's Reply to Wilberforce.[6]

23. M.

Wrote to J.A. Hope. Saw Mr Toogood—Mr Stanistreet—Mr Maitland—Read Sebastopol Evidence—Worked on books & putting away for departure—H. of C. $4\frac{1}{2}$–$7\frac{1}{2}$ and 9–$11\frac{1}{4}$. Finance & Stamp Newsp. Bill.[7] Saw three.[R] & at Lady Lyttelton's.

24. T.

Wrote to Col. Phipps.—Mr Rawlinson—Mr J. Wood—Ld Canning—Mr V. Smith—H. of C. $4\frac{1}{2}$–$7\frac{3}{4}$ (& H. of L.): Mr Heywood's motion.[8] Dined with Mrs Talbot. Breakfast with the Dean of St Paul's. Went on to the City & saw Mr [D.B.] Chapman (Overends)—Mr Longden—Mr Freshfield—Lord Canning—Missed two: saw one[R]—Fervet opus:[9] the house all agog with moving. Read Sebastopol Evidence.

25. Wed. X

Wrote to Overends—Johnson L & Co—Rev. H.L. Baker—Sir A. Gordon—Mr T. Rathbone—Mr F. Hincks—Rev. Mr Jackson—Robn. G—Rev. Dr Cook—Mr Barber—Rev. Hugh Bennett[10]—Mr Curry[11]—Mr Betts—R. Wilbraham. Saw Mr Grogan Mr Walpole—J.N.G.[12] Saw Warwick 3[R]. Dined with Lady Wenlock. Read Sebastopol Evidence—'Our Consul's in the East'.[13] H. of C. $12\frac{1}{4}$–2 and $2\frac{3}{4}$–$5\frac{3}{4}$ on Marriage Bill.[14]

[1] The engraver (see 30 Jan. 44), lived in Margaret Street.
[2] In Lathbury, ii. 415.
[3] Untraced pamphlet, perhaps by James Bromley, on *Pakington's Education Bill, introduced March 1855.
[4] J. C. Colquhoun, 'Remarks on Sir John *Pakington's Education Bill' (1855).
[5] W. Arthur, '"The people's day." An appeal to Lord *Stanley against his advocacy of a French Sunday' (1855).
[6] H. *Drummond, 'Reply to Rev. R. Wilberforce's Principles of Church Authority' (1855).
[7] Spoke on periodicals: *H* cxxxvi. 1677.
[8] Defending the religious test clauses of 1854 Oxford Act against Heywood: *H* cxxxvii. 1733.
[9] 'The work thrives'.
[10] Hugh Bennett, b. ? 1818; fellow of Worcester 1853; rector of Pirton, Worcestershire, 1878.
[11] Perhaps Peter Finch Curry, Liverpool attorney.
[12] John Gladstone had been added to the *Roebuck cttee. on 23 April.
[13] *Our consuls in the East: a parliamentary inquiry into their proceedings imperative; by an Anglo Levantine* (1855).
[14] *H* cxxxvii. 1743.

26. Th.

Wrote to Ed. Guardian[1]—Robn. G—J. Flanedy[2]—Mr Hatch.[3] Saw Lord Aberdeen—A. Gordon. Busy with our packing and putting away. H. of C. $4\frac{1}{2}$–8 and $9\frac{1}{2}$–10. Spoke of the Budget by way of warning.[4] Read Sebastopol Evidence—Burgess on Education Bills.[5] Dined at Mrs Talbots.

27. Fr.

Wrote to [H.] Mont[agu] Villiers—E.A. Bowring—Fortnum & Mason. H. of C. $4\frac{1}{2}$–$7\frac{3}{4}$ (Loan Bill &c): and 2d R. Scots Edn. Bill $11\frac{1}{4}$–1: voted in majority having learned from Ld Advocate that Episcns. are not to be indemnified.[6] Saw Mr Walker—Mr Munro—Scots Ch. Deputn 1–2. Read Kingscote on Edn. Bill[7]—Sebastopol Evidence. Continued at work in moving. Dined at Stafford House: & had a stiff argument with Argyll resp. the conditions of peace.[8]

28. Sat.

Marg. Chapel 5 P.M. Wrote to Mrs Domvile[9]—Solr. General—Mr Beadnell[10]—Mr C. Gray—Rev. Chr. Martin[11]—Rev. E. Lowe[12]—Saw Ld Aberdeen—Mr A. Gordon—Mr Sebbons (Pictures)[13]—Mr Walker. Read Sebastopol Evidence. Preparations ended per force, & we moved to Lady Wenlock's. After dinner discussed Newcastle's strange evidence about absence.[14] Lady Palmerston's afterwards. Saw Azeglio—Thackeray—Sat to Mr Mayall for photograph.[15] Visited Thos. Foster at King's Coll. Hospital.

29. 3 S. E[aster].

St Georges mg. St Paul's aftn. Saw Aunt J. the Herberts. Read Heartley

---

[1] Not published; it had the previous day praised *Lewis's budget; *The Guardian*, 25 April 1855, 316.

[2] John Flanedy, journalist, of Everton had written about newspaper stamp duty (Hawn P).

[3] Probably Henry John Hatch, chaplain of the Surrey house of correction.

[4] Warning of dangers of funding and protective taxes: *H* cxxxvii. 1800.

[5] R. Burgess, 'National education, by rates or taxes' (1855).

[6] Voted for 2°R Scottish Education Bill: *H* cxxxvii. 1931.

[7] H. *Kingscote, *Sir John Pakington's plan. A reply to the ' Remarks of J. C. Colquhoun'*, (1855).

[8] The previous day Westmorland, British plenipotentiary in Vienna, had declared that his instructions were exhausted.

[9] Mary Anne, *née* Orde, m. 1848 (Sir) James Graham Domville (cp. 29 May 37) and d. 1890.

[10] Probably James Beadell, surveyors.

[11] Charles Herbert Martin, 1804?–65; perpetual curate of Maismore, Gloucestershire, from 1829.

[12] Edward Clarke Lowe, 1823–1912; headmaster of St. John's, Hurstfield point, 1850–73; provost of Denstone 1873–91; canon of Ely 1873; critic.

[13] Unidentified agent.

[14] *Newcastle was questioned in the Roebuck cttee. by General *Peel and *Layard about members of cabinet absent from London at start of the war and refused to answer: *PP* 1854–5 ix. part 2, 205.

[15] John Edwin Mayall, d. 1867; studios in Regent street.

on Cathedrals.[1] Scudamore's Engl. & Rome[2]—Drummond's Reply to R.W.[3]

30. M.

Wrote to Mr Hartley[4]—Sir J. Graham—Maish & Beattie[5]—Ed. N.B. Review. Read N.B.R. on Civil Service[6]—Sebastopol Evidence. Saw Fortnum—Mr Grogan—Sir T.G.—Mr Anderson—A. Gordon—S. Herbert. Business at D[owning] St. House. Saw German Exhibition. Dined with the Herberts. H. of C. 4½–7¾ on Loan Bill &c.[7]

Tues. May One. SS. Philip & James.

Wrote to Sig. Jos. Massari—Mr J. Curry—Mr M.C. Terry[8]—Robn. G.— Mr W. Smythe. Read Sebastopol Evidence—Memoirs of Jeffreys.[9] Visited Lady C. Guest's House[10]—Saw Mr. Stansbury[11]—Mr H. Roberts. Rev. Mr. Richards—Lord Granville—Mrs Herbert—S. Herbert—Ld Hardinge— Lord Aberdeen—D. of Newcastle—Duke of Argyll—Mr Bright. H. of C. 4½–5½ + late.[12] Attended the children's Ball at the Palace: a really beautiful sight: no small trial morally to such as Agnes.

2. Wed.

Wrote to Ld Aberdeen—Judge Coleridge (& copy) Mr Goldwin Smith (& copy)—Mr Meredith—Cattermole[13]—Johnson L. & Co. Saw Lord Canning —Mr S. Herbert—Ld Abn. cum S.H. and Sir James Graham. Sir S.H. Northcote—Baron de Cetto—Mr Packe—Read Sebast. Evidence. N. Gallery Protest[14]—H. of C. 4–6.[15] Dined with the Ch. of the Exr. Mad. Colloredo's in evg.

3. Th.

Wrote to W. Hampton—Mr J. Ball—Jas. Watson—Mr J. Smith—Mr M.J. Horne[16]—Saw Lord Aberdeen—Mr Packe—Sir J. Graham—Bp of Oxford—

[1] C. T. Heartley, *Our Cathedrals and their Mission* (1855).
[2] See 24 Mar. 55.   [3] See 22 Apr. 55.   [4] *Sc.* Heartley.
[5] Print publishers and varnishers in Fleet Street.
[6] *North British Review*, xxiii. 137 (May 1855).
[7] Opposing the Bank's hoarding of public funds: *H* cxxxvii. 1961.
[8] Unidentified.
[9] H. Jeffreys, *Sentiments of the late Archdeacon Jeffreys with a brief memoir* (1854).
[10] Lady Charlotte Elizabeth *Schreiber, 1812–95, da. of 9th earl of Lindsey, m. 1833 Sir Josiah John Guest, d. 1852, 1st bart. and 1855 Charles Schreiber, 1826–84, tory M.P. Cheltenham 1865–8, Poole from 1880; she managed her 1st husband's iron works, ed. Welsh MSS, and collected china.
[11] Charles Frederick Stansbury, London patent agent.
[12] Maynooth: *H* cxxxvii. 2060.
[13] Probably Richard *Cattermole, 1795–1858; vicar of Little Marlow from 1848; poet and essayist.
[14] Untraced; see 1 May 56n.   [15] English education: *H* cxxxvii. 2112.
[16] Perhaps of M. C. W. Horne, surveyors and architects.

Mr Lee (Bounty Board)[1]—Read Sebast. Evidence[2]—Ed. Rev. on Army Reform[3] —Luncheon at 37 G[rosvenor] Square & went over the house.[4] Dinner party at Lady W[enlock']s.

4. Fr.

Wrote to Rev. Mr Dalton[5]—R. Barker—Mr Gardiner—R. Andrews. Read Sebastopol Evidence—Porter's & other pamphlets on the War.[6] Napier's Hist. Penins. War.[7] Saw Ld Aberdeen—Johnson Longden & Co. Dined at Mr Moffats. Stafford House afterwards. Saw Bearn[8]—Then H. of C.[9]

5. Sat. X

Wrote to R. Wilbraham—Scotts—Mrs Comyns—Captain G[ladstone]— Mr R. Greig[10]—Robn. G. Read Red Tapeism[11]—Sebastopol Ev. Appx (finished)—N. Br. Rev. on the War.[12] 3h at the Exhibitn. & attended the dinner.[13] Saw one 23[R].

6. 4 S. E[aster].

St Georges mg & H.C.—Wells St aftn. Saw Ld Granville—Ld Aberdeen— Ill tidings! Read Joyce's Sacred Synods[14]—Scudamore's Rome—Sydney Smith Mor. Phil.[15]

7. M.

Wrote to Rev. Mr Boyle[16]—Rev. Mr Joyce[17]—Mr Whitehead[18]—Mr Rawlinson. Dinner party in B. Square.

Breakfasted with Milnes. Dinner party. Saw Ld Stanhope. Mr Bright— Mr Blackburn M.P.[19] Read Med. Commn. Report[20]—Nelson's Life[21]— Amelia[22]—Napier. H. of C. $4\frac{1}{2}$–7.[23]

[1] J. B. Lee of the Queen Anne's Bounty Board, about the Seaforth church deeds (Hawn P).
[2] On the April hearings, including Sir C. E. *Trevelyan's, who gave evidence for the treasury and the commissariat, and *Newcastle's; published this day: *PP* 1855 ix. part 2.
[3] *Edinburgh Review*, ci. 537 (April 1855).   [4] Wenlock's house.
[5] Charles Browne Dalton, 1810–94; prebendary of St. Paul's from 1845.
[6] W. *Porter, *Life in the trenches before Sebastopol* (1856).   [7] See 11 May 41.
[8] Probably a rescue case.   [9] Misc. business: *H* cxxxviii. 100.
[10] Robert Greig, builder.
[11] *Red-tapeism: its cause; by one behind the scenes* (1855).
[12] *North British Review*, xxiii. 266 (May 1855).   [13] The Royal Academy exhibition.
[14] J. W. Joyce, *England's sacred synods* (1855).
[15] S. *Smith, *Elementary Sketches of Moral Philosophy* (1850).
[16] Probably John Boyle, d. 1866; curate in Staffordshire 1854–8.
[17] James Wayland Joyce, 1812–87; rector of Burford, Shropshire, from 1843; prebendary of Hereford from 1868.
[18] Thomas Whitehead; Oxfordshire curacies 1850–70; vicar of Stoke Newington 1870–86.
[19] Peter Blackburn, 1811–70; tory M.P. Stirlingshire 1855–65; treasury lord 1859.
[20] Reports on the medical commissariat in the Crimea: *PP* 1855 xxxiii. 1.
[21] R. *Southey, *Life of Nelson* (1813).
[22] See 6 Sept. 42.   [23] Estimates: *H* cxxxviii. 197.

8. T.

Wrote to R.W. Wilbraham—T.M. Gladstone—Sec. Bounty Board[1]—Mr A. Munro—Ld Overstone—Mr Stanistreet—Rev. H.B. Barry[2]—Archd. Sinclair—Rev. W. Rawson—Jas. Watson—Mr Wm. Smythe—W.C. James —Mr Christopher. Saw Mr Lee—(B[ounty] Board)—Mr A. Munro (Studio) —Dined at S. Herberts. Read Med. Commn. Report (finished) Ann. Reg. 1794. Grenville Correspondence.[3]

9. Wed.

Wrote to Mr Hutchins—Mr D. Masson[4]—J.D. Coleridge—Saw Mr Ricardo —Mr Adderley—Ld Aberdeen—S. Herbert—

Breakfast Bp of Oxfords⎫
Dined at Ld Aberdeen's ⎬ ! !
Queen's Ball in Evg.   ⎭

Read Grenville Correspondence—D. of Buckingham—H. of C. 12¾—6. Spoke agt Marriage Bill & voted in 157:164.[5]

10. Th.

Wrote to Sir W. Heathcote—Dr Kynaston—Ld Ellesmere—Jas Watson— E. Humphrey. Read the Vienna Protocols[6]—Sebastopol Evidence (2). Dined at Ld Lansdowne's. H. of C. 4½–7.[7] Saw Lady Wenlock (her affairs)— Lord Aberdeen (cum Sir J.G. & 2)—Sir James Graham—J.E. Denison—G. Harcourt—G.C. Glyn—Sol. General.—E.V. Harcourt—Bp of Edin. & Scots Deputn.[8] Saw Langsford (Denbigh 9)[R].

11. Fr.

Wrote to Rev. W. Rawson—Miss H. Forbes[9]—J. Herbert Coe[10]—D. of Argyll—Rev. C. Eckersall[11]—W. M. Goalen. H. of C. 4½–7.[12] Dined at Ld Stanhope's. House aft. Saw A. Munro. D. of Argyll. (Saw Leicester 15 & another)[R]—Ld Stanhope—Mr [Milner] Gibson (H. of C). J.E. Denison—

[1] C. Hodgson, secretary of Queen Anne's Bounty.
[2] Henry Boothby Barry; Queen's, Oxford; priest 1848; an inspector of schools.
[3] *Annual Register 1794* (1808) contained correspondence of *Grenville on American shipping and the commercial treaty. See also 14 May 52.
[4] David *Masson, 1822–1907, professor of English literature in London 1853–65, in Edinburgh 1865–95; first ed. *Macmillan's Magazine* 1859–67.
[5] Start of a long campaign by Gladstone, *Heathcote, *Palmer and others against a series of marriage bills: *H* cxxxviii. 269.
[6] Part xii of the protocols, published in instalments: *PP* 1855 lv. 65.
[7] Indian army: *H* cxxxviii. 302.
[8] Protesting against episcopalians' exclusion from benefits of the Scottish Education Bill; see *Scottish Ecclesiastical Journal*, v. 81 (May 1855).
[9] Harriet Williamina, da. of Sir J. S. H. Forbes; m. 1858 Charles Henry Rolle Trefusis, 1834–1904, Peelite M.P. N. Devon 1857–66, when he succ. as 20th Baron Clinton; minor office 1867–8. She d. 1869.
[10] Perhaps James Herbert Coe; see J. G. Bartlett, *Robert Coe* (1911) index.
[11] Charles Eckersall, 1797?–1863; Corpus, Oxford; rector of All Saints, Worcester.
[12] Misc. business: *H* cxxxviii. 420.

Scots Episc. Depn. Read Annual Registers—Sebastopol Evidence (2)—
Vienna Protocols.

12. Sat.

Wrote to Jas. Wilson—J.D. Coleridge—D. of Argyll—E. of Clarendon—Ld
Herbert—Sir J.E. Tennent—Willy—Mrs Reilly—Mr Dilke.[1] Dined at
Spencer House. Lady Palmerston's afterwards. Read Eastern papers[2]—
Napier—Sebastopol Evidence. Saw Mr Lacaita. Sir W. Heathcote. Lord
Canning—Sir [G]. Hamilton Seymour (S[pencer] House).

13. 5 S. E[aster]

St Mary Magd. & H.C. morning. Ch. Ch. Broadway (part) evg. Wrote to Mr
Reynolds. Read Drummond's Reply[3]—Pusey on Real Presence[4]—Joyce's
Sacred Synods.

14. M. X.

Wrote to Sir C. Trevelyan—Robn. G. (2)—Duke of Argyll—J. Murray—(&
draft). Read Napier Pen. War.—Valentini on Turkey[5]—A Looker on (A.
Gordon)[6]—Sebastopol Evidence—Origin of the War.[7] Attended Committee
at 2—to hear Ld A. *but* he was put off.[8]

H. of C. at 5. Saw Mr Gibson (H. of C.) & Cobden, resp. Mr G.s motion.[9]
Missed Morgan & others: saw Tillnen & another [R].

15. T.[10]

Wrote to Bp of Aberdeen—R.V. Smith—Saw Ld Aberdeen—Bp of Oxford
—Bp of Edinburgh—Sir Jas. Graham—E. Cardwell—J.E. Denison—H. of
C. $4\frac{3}{4}$–6.[11] Seb. Committee $12\frac{1}{4}$–$1\frac{1}{4}$.[12] Read Sebastopol Evidence—Eastern
papers. (& worked on them)—Grenville papers. Vol. IV.

16. Wed.

Wrote to Ld A. Hervey—Jas. Watson—Robn. G.—Mrs Johnson—Thos.

[1] (Sir) Charles Wentworth *Dilke, 1810–69; horticulturalist and chairman of royal
society of arts; cr. bart. 1862; liberal M.P. Wallingford 1865–9; fa. of C.W.*
[2] Probably *House of Lords Sessional Papers*, xvii; *Canning's circular, published 7 May
1855.
[3] See 22 Apr. 55.
[4] E. B. *Pusey, *The Doctrine of the Real Presence* (1855).
[5] Baron de Valentini, *Description of the seat of war in European Turkey* (1854).
[6] Perhaps Alexander Gordon, 'Remarks on national defence' (1853), or an untraced
pamphlet by him on the Crimea.
[7] Probably *Newcastle's evidence, *PP* 1854–5 ix. part 2, 182.
[8] *Graham's evidence took the whole of the day, *Aberdeen gave his on the 15th.: *PP*
1855 ix. part 3, 293.
[9] *Gibson's motion on a negotiated peace: see 21 May 55n.
[10] This and next page of MS headed '29 Berkeley Square', the Wenlocks' house.
[11] Screw propellers: *H* cxxxviii. 639.
[12] *Layard's cross-examination of *Aberdeen, who denied negligence in summoning
cabinets: *PP* ix. part 3, 293.

Scott[1]—Dr Acland. Dined at Sir F.[2] Johnstones[3]—Bridgewater House aft.[4] Saw one [R]. Saw Sir W. Heathcote—R. Phillimore—Mr F. Baring—Adm. Walcot[5]—Ld Abn *cum* Sir J. Graham—E. Cardwell.—Earl Grey—Jas. Wortley—G.G. Harcourt—Count Strzelecki.[6] Read Eastern Papers—Seb. Evidence—Fate of Xtendom.[7]

17. Th. Ascension Day.

St Mary Magd. & H.C. $10\frac{1}{2}$–$12\frac{3}{4}$. Wrote to Mr Dundas (Arniston)[8]—Mr Lucas—Robn. G.—Mr Meredith—Rev. Mr Short—Sir Jas. Graham—Mr J. Harrison.[9] Read Buck[ingha]m papers.[10]—Seb. Evidence. Saw Lord Aberdeen—Sir James Graham—J.S.Wortley—Lord A. Hervey. Dined at Ellisons. H. of C. $4\frac{1}{2}$–$6\frac{1}{2}$.[11]

18. Fr.

Wrote to Mr Griffiths—Mr Pressly—Jas. Watson—Overends—Rector of Sefton.[12] Read Wilkins on Camb. Reform.[13] Buckingham Papers. Saw D. of Argyll—E. Granville—D. of Newcastle—Ld Aberdeen cum Sir J. Graham —Rev. Mr Wayte—Mr Miall[14]—Mr Macaulay—Ld Grey. H. of C. $4\frac{1}{2}$–7.[15]

19. Sat.

Wrote to J.W. Wilkins[16]—Robn. G.—Provost of Oriel—Scotts—Miss H. Forbes.—A. Tudor[17]—Ld Clarendon—Read Sebastopol Evidence[18]—Memoirs of Fox[19]—Breakfast at Milnes's. Saw Bp of Oxford—G.H. Vernon M.P. Ld Aberdeen—Attended the Drawingroom—Ld Palmerston's dinner —Ld Lansdowne's party.

[1] Thomas *Scott, 1808–78, freethinker and pamphleteer; corresponded frequently with Gladstone in 1870s.
[2] Written over 'Lady'.   [3] *sc.* Sir J. Johnstone.
[4] Ellesmere's house in Cleveland Square.
[5] John Edward Walcott, 1790–1868; rear admiral 1852; tory M.P. Christchurch from 1852.
[6] (Sir) Paul Edmund de *Strzelecki, 1796–1873; explored Australia; K.C.M.G. 1869; close friend of *Herbert.
[7] H. *Drummond, *The Fate of Christendom* (1854).
[8] i.e. W. P. Dundas.   [9] See 3 Aug. 55n.
[10] R. P. T. N. B. C. *Grenville, duke of Buckingham, *Memoirs of the court and cabinets of George III . . .*, 2v. (1853).
[11] Misc. business: *H* cxxxviii. 697.
[12] Richard Rainshaw Rothwell, 1772–1863; rector of Sefton from 1803; in dispute with diarist about the Toxteth Park church advowson.
[13] J. W. Wilkins, 'A letter . . . to . . . Viscount *Palmerston . . . on Cambridge University reform' (1855).
[14] Edward *Miall, 1809–81; nonconformist minister and liberal M.P. Rochdale 1852–7, Bradford 1869–74; leading disestablishmentarian.
[15] Scottish education: *H* cxxxviii. 790.
[16] John William Wilkins, b. 1829; Trinity hall, Cambridge; called to the bar 1857. See previous day.
[17] Augustus Tudor of Ryde.
[18] Of the May hearings, including *Herbert's, *Graham's and *Aberdeen's: *PP* ix. part 3.
[19] See 9 Nov. 54.

20. S. aft. Ascension

Hanover chapel mg: Wells St aft. At Ld Aberdeen's conclave (Sir J.G., S.H., Cardwell) 2½–3½.[1] Saw R. Phillimore. Read Scudamore's England & Rome. Wrote to M'Kenzie & Baillie—W. Smythe. Lord Aberdeen. Worked (evg.) on Eastern Papers[2] & Debates for tomorrow.

21. M.

Saw Gen. Lindsay[3]—Sir C. Trevelyan—Mr Heywood—Sir W. Heathcote— Mr Cobden. Then Herbert called & to my amazement told me his plan, all arranged.[4] I went off to Sir J. Graham—Mr Gibson—& Lord Aberdeen: a painful & anxious morning. At last it ended in H. of C. well for the cause of peace but certainly with very suspicious appearances. Dined at Mrs Talbots. Saw Carn[R].[5] Read Sebast. Evidence. Unwell in evg.

22. T.

Wrote to Dean of Ch. Ch.—Rev. J. Crabb[6]—Mr D. Black[7]—Mr E. M'Donnell—Mr M'Kean—G. Burnett—J. Freshfield. Read Sebast. Evidence. Dinner party here. The Herberts were of it: strange to feel a jar with them. Saw Ld Aberdeen—Ly Pembroke—A. Gordon—Sir H. Verney— Mr Adderley—Jas. Wortley—E. Ellice jun. calls. H. of C. 6–7¼ and 10¾–12¾.[8]

23. Wed.

Wrote to Provost of Eton—C.E.X.[9]—Mr Toogood—E.V. Harcourt—Bp of Edinbro'—Dr Jeune—Rev. Mr Woodgate—Rev. Mr Rothwell. Read Sebast. Evidence. Mem. & copy for Mrs Herbert.[10] Visited Noble's Studio.[11] Saw Sir W. Heathcote—E. Cardwell—Count Montalembert—Mr Wilson. Dined at Mr Wilson's—Then Bridgwater House—Then Lady Granville's —but missed G.

24. Th.

Wrote to Sir W. Heathcote—Mr A. Hayward—J. Graham—Jas Watson— Saw Lord Granville (2) Sir J. Graham—E. Cardwell—Ld Aberdeen & conclave. Sir W. Heathcote. Worked on Eastern Question papers. H. of C.

[1] See next day.

[2] Part xiii of the Vienna protocols, just published: *PP* lv. 155.

[3] (Sir) Alexander *Lindsay 1785–1872; served in India; lieutenant general 1851, general 1859; K. C. B. 1862.

[4] *Gibson's resolutions deplored the break-off of negotiations and supported Russian proposals as a basis for resumption. As negotiations had already resumed, *Herbert, supported by Gladstone, appealed to *Gibson to withdraw his motion. *Disraeli declared this 'extraordinary and . . . impolitic' but *Gibson agreed to delay his motion, never in fact moved: *H* cxxxviii. 837.

[5] MS smudged.

[6] James Crabb; priest 1854, episcopal incumbent of St. Andrews', Brechin, 1866.

[7] Unidentified.   [8] Voted against the ballot: *H* cxxxviii. 947.

[9] Perhaps Mrs. C. E. Bramwell, a rescue case whom he later assisted.

[10] Not found.   [11] In Bruton street.

$4\frac{1}{2}$–7. (dinner at Mrs Talbots) & $7\frac{3}{4}$ –$1\frac{1}{2}$. Spoke with my whole heart in the sense of peace 10–12.[1] Read Sebastopol Evidence.

25. Fr.

Wrote to Ed. Guardian (2)—Geo. Hancock—M.F. Tupper—J. Murray—Cte. Montalembert—Dined at Lady Wenlock's. H. of C. $4\frac{3}{4}$–7 and $10\frac{1}{2}$–3. Voted in 319:219 agt Disraeli.[2] Radcliffe Trust Meeting $11\frac{1}{4}$–1.[3] Saw Earl Granville—Ld Aberdeen & conclave—Robn. G—(Seaforth &c) Ld De Tabley—Ld Elcho—Jas. Wortley.

26. Sat. [Hawarden]

Wrote to Ld Canning. Off at $9\frac{3}{4}$: reached Hawarden $5\frac{1}{2}$ & found all the children blooming: baby much come on. A delightful change from London & such subjects. Read Mad. de Sevigné[4]—Sheridan's 'Critic', & 'Camp'[5].

27. Whitsunday

Hn. Church 11 (and H.C.) and $6\frac{1}{2}$. Read Litton on Church.[6] Life of Lindsay.[7] Rectory in evg.

28. M.

Church 11 A.M. (rather $11\frac{1}{2}$). Wrote to Sir W. Heathcote—Rev. A. Lendrum —R. Phillimore—Rev. E. Coleridge—R. Dalyell—Rev. J.S. Hadow[8]—S. Boult—O.B. Cole—Bp of Oxford—Chancr. of Exr. Children's tea on the lawn to the North: they were intensely happy. Read Cic[ero] de Republicâ. —Sheridan's Rivals[9]—Piedmontese Debates.[10]—

29. T.

Church 11 a.m. Saw Griffiths Collis & Blackwell $11\frac{3}{4}$–2. Wrote to Lady Wenlock—Scotts—Jas. Heywood—Mrs Goalen—Mr Mackinnan—A. Hunter—Sec. Bounty Board. Wrote (a little) for Q.R.[11]—Dined at the Rectory—Read the School for Scandal[12]—Cic. de Republicâ—

[1] Supporting *Heathcote's amnd. to *Disraeli's motion on the negotiations: H cxxxviii 1036, reprinted as 'War with Russia'.
[2] H cxxxviii. 1296; leading Peelites supported the govt.
[3] In S. *Herbert's house; Gladstone was appointed a trustee of the Radcliffe trust, which administered the Radcliffe observatory, camera, library etc. in Oxford, on 20 June 1854; its minutes are in Bodleian MSS dd. Radcl. c. 54. He was its chairman 1856–80.
[4] M. de R. Chantal, Marquise de Sévigné, Letters (1725, often reprinted).
[5] R. B. *Sheridan, The Critic (first performed 1779) and The Camp (first performed 1778).
[6] See 24 Dec. 54.
[7] T. Belsham, Memoirs of the late Revd. Theophilus Lindsey (1812).
[8] Perhaps a nonconformist; no anglican of this name found.
[9] First performed 1775.
[10] Speech by Cavour of 17 February, quoted in his Quarterly article; see next day.
[11] 'Sardinia and Rome', Quarterly Review, xcvii. 41 (June 1855).
[12] First performed 1777.

30. *Wed.*

Ch 8½ a.m. Wrote to Earl of Aberdeen—Dr Bampt[1]—S. Herbert (2)—S. Triscoll[2]—Rev. R. Montgomery—W. Hampton—Rev. W. Rawson—Robn. G.—Rev. S. Arnott[3]—Sir A.D. Gordon—Saw Mr G. Burnett. Breakfast & dinner at the Rectory. C. & a party went to Liverpool. Read Sardinian Documents. Midsummer Night's Dream.

31. *Th.*

Ch. 8¼ a.m. Wrote to Lord Canning—Robn. G—Chancr. of Exr.—Dr Acland. Wrote on Sardinian affairs—Read Allocuzione[4] &c—Mids. Night's Dream (finished)—Orlandino.[5] Arranged letters.

Fr. June One. 1855.

Church at 8¼ a.m. Wrote to Sir J. Graham—Dr Acland—J. Murray—A. Gordon—Count Corti—Willy—Johnson L[ongden] & Co. Read Orlandino—The Humours of Oxford(?)[6]—Merchant of Venice—Walk with C. Miss L.[7] here & music in evg. Wrote on Sardinian affairs.

2. *Sat.*

Ch 8¼ a.m. Wrote to R. Phillimore—Bp Edinburgh—Rev. C. Warner.[8] Read Colloquia Erasmi[9]—Allocuzione &c.

Humours of Oxford ⎫
Merchant of Venice ⎬ Finished
⎭

Wrote on Sard. Eccl. Affairs.

3. *Trin. S.*

Ch. 11 a.m. (H.C.) & 6¼ P.M. Wrote to Sir J. Graham. Wrote on Sard. Eccl. Affairs. Read Allocuzione &c—Life of Lindsey—C. & the children had an escape by God's mercy in the Park when one of the Carriage horses fell with the staggers. Willy's Birthday: God bless him.

4. *M.*

Ch. 8½ a.m. Wrote to Chancr. of Exchr—A. Masson[10]—W.B. Collis. Read

---

[1] Unidentified.

[2] Samuel Triscoll, storekeeper at Plymouth, corresponded occasionally on politics (Hawn P).

[3] Samuel Arnott, d. 1904; vicar of Chatham 1858–65; rector of Hollington 1867–70, of Turnham Green from 1870; contributor to *Notes & Queries*.

[4] See 10 Mar. 55.

[5] M. *Edgeworth, *Orlandino* (1848).

[6] A. Danvers, *Academia: or, The humours of the University of Oxford* (1691).

[7] Lucy Lyttelton.

[8] Charles Warner, 1818–1900; curate of Kidderminster 1849; rector of Henley 1863; vicar of Clun, Shropshire, 1868–97.

[9] D. Erasmus, *Colloquia* (1527).   [10] Probably a slip for D. *Masson.

Allocuz. & worked long on my Sardinian paper. Read Orlandino. Walk to
C.s ride.

5. *T.* [*London*]

Church 8½ a.m. Wrote to A. Williams—Col. Phipps—Rev. Jas. Murray.
Finished my Sard. paper & began to correct it. Prepared for journey & off
to London at one. Read the Times & Sebast. Comme. on my way up: a
proof that my eyes thank God are stronger than heretofore. Reached H. of C.
at 10.45, for the latter part of the Debate.[1] Saw G. Wood—R. Phillimore—
S. Herbert. Worked on letters & papers till 2½ a.m.

6. *Wed.* X

Wrote to Clowes & Sons—A Panizzi—Stanistreet—J.N.G.—Dr Pusey—
C.G.—Wm. Gladstone—Robn. G.—Mr M'Culloch—J. Mill. Saw T.M. Gladstone—Rev. Jas. Murray—Rev. Dr Todd. Dined with the Dunravens & had
much interesting conv. with Lady D. Saw Car. & two [R]. Finished correcting Sard. paper. House 3½–4½.[2]Read Pamphlets on War. & Church Rates.

7. *Th.*

Wrote to Ld. Canning—Ed. Empire[3]—Dean Ramsay—Jas. Watson—J.
Freshfield—Mrs Edwards—Rev. E. Hawkins—Mr Conolly—Rev. H.
Kynaston—T.H. Foster[4]—Rev. J. Jenkinson[5]—Lord Advocate—Rev. T.
Stooks—Scotts—Rev. D. Hulbert[6]—C.G. Saw Mr H. Roberts—Hon A.
Gordon—Lord Aberdeen cum G[ranville] & H[erbert]—Duke of Argyll—
J. Murray—Col. Phipps. Dined with the Herberts. H. of C. 4¾–7¼ and 9–
11¾.[7] Read Elton on the War. &c.[8]

8. *Fr.*

Wrote to Mr E. Webber—Lord J. Russell—W.E. Price[9]—Mr Hugh Hope[10]
—Rev. C. Marriott—W. Jordan[11]—Miss F. Dorr[12]—C.G.—Dr Acland—
Lady Dunraven. Drove with Duchess of Suth[erlan]d to the Crystal Palace. I
never had such a view of London. Calls & business. Saw Mr Heywood—H.
of C. 5¼–7½ and 8½–2½. I forbore to speak.[13]

---

[1] Prosecution of the war: *H* cxxxviii. 1438.   [2] Maynooth: *H* cxxxviii. 1488.

[3] Independent whiggish weekly; none published (see 16 June, 24 July 55).

[4] Thomas Hay Forster, unbeneficed priest.

[5] John Simon Jenkinson, 1798–1871; vicar of Battersea 1847; hymnist.

[6] Daniel Paul Meek Hulbert, 1816–94?; curacies 1840–55; missionary in Australia
1855–84.

[7] *Herbert, *inter alia*, on prosecution of the war: *H* cxxxviii. 1560.

[8] Sir A. H. Elton, 'Where are we drifting? or, a plain question for the British people
on the war with Russia' (1855).

[9] Probably William Philip Price, 1817–91; timber merchant and liberal M.P. Gloucester 1852–9, 1865–73.

[10] 1813–76, parliamentary agent in Fludyer street.

[11] William J. Jordan, London wine and spirit merchant.   [12] Unidentified.

[13] He did speak, regretting time had eroded the relevance of *Heathcote's amndt.: *H*
cxxxviii. 1757.

9. Sat. [Hawarden]

Wrote to Ld Aberdeen—Robn. G—Scotts—Rev. G. Rawlinson. Read Grant on the Crimea[1]—Elton on the War (finished). Off at 5¾ for Hawarden wh I reached before one: some sleep in aftn. All well D.G.

10. 1 S. Trin.

Hn. mg. & St John's evg. Julienne went & was pleased.[2] Read Lindsey's Life.[3] —Scudamore's Engl. & Rome.[4] Looked over some of my books in Theol.

11. M. St Barn[abas].

Ch 11 a.m. Wrote to Sir J. Kingsmill—Hugh Hope—Rev. L. Owen—Mr Betts—Rev. W. Thorpe[5]—Mr Spencer. Read Cic[ero] de Republ. As You Like It—and Ovid's Tristia. Italian lesson with Agnes. Began unpacking fresh arrivals of books & papers. Music in evg.

12. T.

Ch. 8½ a.m. Wrote to Messrs. Overend—Sir S. Scott & Co—Robn. G—and Provost of Oriel. Read Cic. de Rep.—As You Like It (finished)—Singing in evg. Worked much on arranging my letters. In selecting Manning's through the long years of our intercourse I again go through that sad experience.[6]

13. Wed.

(No Ch. H[enry Glynne] absent) Wrote to Robn. G. Read Lyttelton on Educn.[7] Love's Labour Lost. Worked all day upon my letters. I find 216 of Manning's, near 100 of Sir R. Peel's. Singing in evg.

14. Th.

Off to Liverpool at 11 where I worked with Rn. G. & Breakenridge on my own affairs & went over the Seaforth plans. Dined and slept at Courthey. Read K. Henry IV. Wrote to Rev. Mr Rawlinson—Overends—Mr Lomax[8] —J. Talbot—Rev. Mr Rowsell, & [blank]

15. Fr. [London]

Off at 8.30 for London—Reached H. of C. before five, & in time for Mr Otway.[9] Also spoke in the Layard debate.[10] Saw R. Phillimore—J.N.G.—

[1] A. *Grant, An historical sketch of the Crimea (1855).   [2] Unidentified visitor.
[3] See 27 May 55.   [4] See 24 Mar. 55.
[5] William Thorpe, 1778–1865; minister and owner of Belgrave chapel, Pimlico, from 1832.
[6] See May–July 51.   [7] G. W. *Lyttelton, 'Thoughts on national education' (1855).
[8] Probably Thomas Lomax, barrister in Lincoln's Inn.
[9] A. J. Otway accused the Peelites of treason: Gladstone objected and the Speaker ruled Otway out of order, H cxxxviii. 2036.
[10] On administrative reform; ibid. 2098.

Sir J. Paxton—J. Heywood—Lord Canning—Mr Bright—young Breakenridge[1]—Worked on letters & papers. Read the closing Protocol. Colq.[2]

16. Sat. [Oxford]

Read Ch Disc[ipline] Bill.[3] Breakfast at Stafford House—Saw Bp of Oxford—Duke of Argyll—E. of Aberdeen—J. Murray—Scotts. Off at 2 for Oxford. Saw Dr Jacobson—Dr Acland—Mr Marriott—Dined with my kind host the Provost of Oriel. Wrote to the Earl of Derby—Editor of the Empire—W. Monsell M.P.—R. Phillimore—Hon. A. Gordon.

17. 2 S. Trin.

Ch. Ch. mg & aft. Univ. Sermon mg. & aft. Read Jowett on St Paul's Epistles[4]—Stephen's Opinion.[5] Visited Philip Pusey. Also saw Mr Rawlinson—Dr Jacobson Mr Bode & others of my constituents at the Provosts. Wrote to C.G.

18. M.

Oriel Chapel 8 a.m. and Magd. Chapel 4 P.M. Wrote to Archd. Harrison—Mr C. Paskin. Dean of Peterborough and [blank]. Dinner at Oriel. Ball in evg. Saw Dr Scott—Ward[en of] Merton—Mr Greswell—Mr Haddan—Mr Lake—Mr Butler—Dr Pusey—Bp of Brechin—Pres. Magdn.—Sir W. Heathcote. Read Bentley & Middleton Controversey[6]—Harrison on Ch Rates.[7] Pamphlets on Admin[istrativ]e Reform.

19. T.

Radcliffe Service 10½ a.m. Wrote to Ld Aberdeen—P. Rolandi[8]—Ld Canning—Rev. J. Wilkinson—Archdn. Grant—Messrs. M'Kenzie & Baillie[9]—Messrs. Burden & Dunning[10]—R. Phillimore. Saw Bp of Brechin—Vice Chancellor—Mr Woollcombe—Archdeacon Clerke—Dr Pusey. Dined at Exeter. Breakf. Oriel Common R. Dr Acland's meeting at 8¾—Town Hall Ball afterwards.

20. Wed.

Wrote to Agnes.—Sir A. Gordon—Mr Broster. Breakfast at Mast. of Pembroke's. Commem[oratio]n 10½–1½. I was less hooted than cheered: & glad of this, because of the War. Saw Philip Pusey—M. Montalembert[10]—Sir W. Heathcote—Mr Lake—Mr Tennyson[11]—T. Acland. Museum

---

[1] i.e. E. Brackenbridge's son.   [2] PP 1854–5 lv.

[3] Bill to continue temporary provisions for ecclesiastical jurisdiction: PP 1855 ii. 187.

[4] B. *Jowett, The Epistles of St. Paul to the Thessalonians, Galatians, Romans (1855).

[5] A. C. Stephens, Adelaide Diocesan Constitutions (1854).

[6] R. *Bentley, 'Proposals for printing a new edition of the Greek testament' (1721) and C. Middleton, 'Remarks, paragraph by paragraph' on Bentley's proposals, etc.

[7] See 18 June 54.   [8] F. Rolandi sold foreign books in Berners Street.

[9] Edinburgh W.S.; doubtless dealing with the Glenalmond loan, see 3 Oct. 55.

[10] London parliamentary agents.

[11] Recieving honorary degrees; The Guardian (27 June 1855, 497) reported Gladstone and *Aberdeen had a 'dubious reception'.

Ceremonial 2.45. Luncheon at All Souls. Dinner at Oriel. Magdalen evening party. Read the Roebuck Report[1] & Bentley Correspondence.

21. Th. [Hawarden]

Wrote to The Lord Mayor[2]—Mr W. Monsell—Rev. Whitwell Elwin—Robn. G—(from Hawarden). Dined with Henry Glynne. Saw Sir W. Heathcote— 9.50 to 4.20 to Hawarden by Bletchley. The first three hours in close conversation with Montalembert whom I was so happy as to have for a fellow traveller. Read Henry IV P. 2.

22. Fr.

Ch. 8½ a.m. Wrote to W. Woodgate[3]—C.G.—Willy—Mr Elwin—J.N.G.— Sir W. Molesworth. Worked much on my letters & papers. Also on correcting and revising Proofs of Article.[4] Read Henry IV.

23. Sat.

Ch 8½ a.m. Wrote to C.G.—S. Herbert—Jas. Robertson—O.B. Cole— D[owage]r Lady Wenlock—Sir C. Trevelyan—J. Murray. Dined at the Rectory & much & pleasant conv. on poetry & criticism. Read Martial. Whewell on Cambridge Bill[5]—Piedmontese Debates. Finished correcting Article on Sardinia. Tasso with Agnes.

24. St John Baptist & 3 S. Trin.

Hawarden Ch mg. & evg. Conv. with Agnes on St John Bapt. Wrote to Mr Woodgate—E. Breakenridge. Read Life of Lindsay[6]—Brief History of Socinians[7]—Proceedings agt. Foster.[8]

25. M.

Church 8½ a.m. Wrote to Count Corti—Robn. G.—Rev. B. Jowett. Saw Mr Burnett—Mr Austin. Finished arranging my papers; Music in evg. Read Shakespeare H. IV. & V.—Cic. de Republicâ—Sebastopol Rep. & proc. Went to meet C.—She came at 5.

26. T.

Church 8½ a.m. Wrote to Earl of Aberdeen—Mr Fergusson—Rev. R.L. Brown[9]—Lady Beauchamp[10]—J.T. Rowsell[11]—Mr Marcy.[12] Read Henry V

[1] Final report of the Roebuck cttee. exonerating the army, blaming the cabinet for want of information, foresight and coordination: *PP* ix. part 3, 387.

[2] i.e. F. G. *Moon (see 6 Nov. 43).

[3] Solicitor with Currie, Woodgate and Williams in London.

[4] See 29 May 55.   [5] Untraced; MS?   [6] See 27 May 55.

[7] S. Nye, *A brief history of the Unitarians, called also Socinians* (1687).

[8] One of the many attacks (on James *Foster (1697–1753) for his description of *Kilmarnock's death) arguing *Foster's perfidy.

[9] Richard Lewis Brown, 1811–?84; King's, Cambridge; chaplain to marquis of Downside from 1848.

[10] Catherine, *née* Otway-Cave, widow of 3rd Earl Beauchamp; she d. 1875.

[11] i.e. T. J. Rowsell.

[12] William Nichols Marcy, 1810–94; clerk of the peace for Worcestershire from 1844.

—Cic. de Republ.—Quetelet sur l'Homme[1]—Dined at the Rectory. Walk to C.s ride.

27. Wed.

Ch 8½ a.m. Wrote to Chancr. of Exchr.—R. Barker—M'Kenzie & Baillie—W. Goryle[2]—Mr Marcy altered from yesty.—J.N.G. Read Henry V.—Cic. de Republ.—Quetelet sur l'Homme. Tasso with Agnes. Rode with her & C. Music in evg. Saw R. Barker. He (uninvited) made known to me Stephen's Testamentary arrangements.[3] They are of very deep interest to me on Willy's account: but I do not feel satisfied either that all has been done wh might be done in the way of charging the Estate for Henry's daughters; or even on the main point that he is right in passing from Henry's male issue to C.s. I must consider carefully whether I can take any step to obtain a clearer view in this matter; for it touches both honour & justice very nearly. I have no doubt whatever on the point that he is right in taking measures to prevent the cutting up & sale of the property after Henry's demise. C. & I talked over this matter & agreed that it should be kept deeply secret by *us*: Mary [Lyttelton] the only exception, if even Mary.

28. Th.

Ch 8½ a.m. Wrote to Ld A. Hervey—E. Breakenridge—Earl of Aberdeen—Rev. A. Gordon—Read Henry V.—Quetelet sur l'Homme—Cic[ero] de Republicâ. Tasso's Aminta & Canzoni.[4] Campbell on Engl. Poetry.[5] Tasso with Agnes. Saw Mr Theakstone[6]—Music in evg.

29. Fr. St Peter

Ch 11 a.m. Wrote to Mr Barwick[7]—Sir W.C. James—T.G.—Tasso with Agnes. Read Athenaeus.[8] Cic. de Rep. (finished). Quetelet sur l'Homme—Henry VI Part 1. Rode with Agnes—Saw Mr Burnett—Began correcting my speech.[9]

30. Sat.

Ch 8½ a.m. Wrote to R. Barker—E.A. Bowring—Mr J. Hamilton—Mrs Cleaver.[10] Read Athenaeus—Quetelet—Shakespeare H[enry] VI. Tasso with Agnes. Continued corr. of Speech—with infinite repugnance.

---

[1] L. A. J. Quetelet, *Sur l'homme et le developpement de ses facultés, ou essai de physique sociale*, 2 v. (1835).
[2] Perhaps J. Gorle, who wrote *Analysis of Butler's ' Analogy'* (1855).
[3] Sketch of these in Morley, i. 343n.; Willy was to succeed on decease of last male Glynne. See 16 Dec. 67 for the signing of the deed.
[4] By T. Tasso (1572). [5] T. Campbell, *An essay on English poetry* (1848).
[6] Henry Theakstone, Liverpool stockbroker, lived at Seaforth.
[7] Perhaps John Barwick, London goldsmith.
[8] Probably the rhetorician's *Deiprosophistai*.
[9] See 24 May 55. [10] Harriet Cleaver, Piccadilly bookseller.

Jul. 1. 55. 4 S. Trin.

Hn. Ch mg. with H.C. Broughton 6½ P.M. Wrote to Mr L. Evelyn. Read Life of Lindsay. Gilbert on the Atonement[1]—Magee on do[2]—Priestley's Tracts.[3]

Xty. B. Constant observes of Spain that it fell through the decay of its liberties: but that it lived for a considerable time after their extinction upon the capital wh. they had enabled it to accumulate.

Even so society is living & even in many ways improving, out of the results of Christianity, while its hold upon the essence becomes weaker & weaker.[4]

2. *M.*

Ch. 8½ a.m. Wrote to Mr A. de Boinville[5]—W.G. Anderson—S. Herbert— Read Athenaeus—B.XIII. Quetelet sur l'Homme—Shakesp. H[enry] VI. P.2. Constant on Filangieri[6]—Filangieri Scienza della Leg.[7] Walk with C. & Mrs T[heakstone] to explore the Park for a drive. Saw Mr Burnett (mineral).

3. *T.*

Church 8½ a.m. Wrote to E. Breakenridge—Scotts—J. Ryman—Robn. G. Read Quetelet—Athenaeus—Henry VI. Wrote (for Cons[ideration]n) Mem. on Stephen's Testamentary dispositions.[8] Worked on Speech—Rode with Stephen.

4. *Wed.*

Church 8½ a.m. Wrote to E.A. Bowring—V. Scully M.P.—Mrs H. Marsh.[9] Read Canti Carnascialeschi[10]—Athenaeus—Fox's Speeches[11]—Quetelet —Henry VI. Rode with Agnes. Worked on Speech—Saw Mr Burnett.

5. *Th.*

Church 8½ a.m. Wrote to Sir J. Graham—Jas. Watson —& H. Lees. School feast 4–8. Read Athenaeus—Canti Carnascialeschi—Henry VI. P.III—Quetelet sur l'Homme. Worked on private business—Discussed the subject of Tuesday's Memm. with C.

6. *Fr.*

Ch 8½ a.m. Wrote to T.W. Rathbone—Hon. A. Gordon—W. Scott—Tasso

[1] See 22 Oct. 53.
[2] W. *Magee, Discourse on the Scriptural doctrines of Atonement and Sacrifice* (1801).
[3] J. *Priestley, Three Tracts* (1791).
[4] Dated 1 July 1855; Add MS 44745, f. 253.
[5] Charles Alfred Chastel de Boinville, wrote *De la théologie naturelle* (1857).
[6] B. H. Constant de Rebecque, *Commentaire sur l'ouvrage de Filangieri* (1822).
[7] G. Filangieri, *La Scienza della legislazione* (1804).   [8] Not found.
[9] Eliza Mary Anne, wife of [Matthew] Henry Marsh, 1810–81; barrister and liberal M.P. Salisbury 1857–68 (see 14 July 55).
[10] Ed. R. M. Bracci (1750).
[11] *The Speeches of . . . C. J. *Fox*, 6v., ed. H. Wright (1815).

with Agnes. Read Henry VI (P. 3) finished.—Quetelet—Athenaeus. Saw Mr Burnett (bis). Rode with Map to mark the boundaries of my property.

7. Sat.

Ch. 8½ a.m. Wrote to Earl of Aberdeen—Mr G. Smith—Mr R. Calvert—E. Breakenridge. Read Richard II—Quetelet—Athenaeus B.1. V, XIII (finished). Looked into my papers on Homer:[1] & I am strongly tempted to undertake something, avoiding Scholarship however on account of inability.[2] Read the Debate of last night with astonishment.[3] Tasso with Agnes. Walk with a family party.

8. 5 S. Trin.

Hn. Ch mg & evg. Wrote to Sir J. Graham. Read Lindsay (finished)— Secret Policy of the Jansenists[4]—Quakerism.[5]

9. M.

Ch 8½ a.m. Wrote to Witherly[6]—Willy—Child & Co—Mr Linton. Tasso with Agnes. Read Quetelet—Richard II. Hobhouse on Ital. Literature.[7] Arranging books & papers. Worked on Pol. papers. Saw R. Barker: & attended the 'Peculiar' Court awhile.[8] I showed Mr Barker the Memorandum I had drawn respecting Sir Stephen's Testamentary Arrangements: & corrected the recital of facts it contained in one minor point. He stated to us his belief that the plan adopted is the most wise & equitable of wh. the case, doubtless a difficult one, admits. I told him I should be glad to submit the Mem. to Mr Freshfield, with his authority: but he said he was on the whole disinclined. I told him I should make a note of our conversation. He observed that the dispositions might lead to remark. My opinion is that as the Estate now stands there is scarcely a choice if it is to be kept: but that if the case should greatly mend, it would then become a question whether these dispositions—with wh C. has indirectly at least had to do—should be reconsidered.

10. T. [London]

Wrote to Earl Granville—C.G.—Jas. Watson—Overends—Mrs Cleaver— Read Macbeth—V. Lushington on the War.[9] Off at 8¾ to London. Saw Ld Aberdeen—R. Phillimore—Mr Cobden. Worked on letters & papers. H. of

---

[1] Those of 1847 and 1848.   [2] Genesis of *Studies on Homer*, see above v. lvii–lix.
[3] *Russell's statement on why he had not resigned when his proposals as plenipotentiary were overruled: *H* cxxxviii. 559.
[4] *The secret policy of the Jansenists and the present state of the Sorbon* (1667).
[5] [S. D. Greer] *Quakerism; or the story of my life* (1851).
[6] Probably Arthur Witherby, London stock broker.
[7] J. C. *Hobhouse, *Historical Illustrations of the Fourth Canto of Childe Harold* (1818).
[8] Ecclesiastical court not subject to the bp.'s jurisdiction; its powers mostly abolished in 10 & 11 Vict. c. 98.
[9] V. Lushington, *How shall the strong man use his strength? or the right and duty of war, with application to the present crisis* (1855).

C. 6–7½ & 8–1. Spoke for Competition & Voted in 125: 140. alike surprised & pleased at the largeness of the minority: also voted for Roebuck's Call.[1]

11. Wed.

Wrote to Rev. Mr Ironside[2]—Temple—C. Moody—Clarkson[3]—Goodwin[4] —R. Rice[5]—J.T. Gordon[6]—J. Hayward[7]—J. Palmer—C.G.—Mr Copeland —J.N.G.—Sir Wm. Molesworth. H. of C. 1½–3 and 4¼–6.[8] Saw Earl of Aberdeen—Worked on letters & papers, the usual accumulation. Went to hear Gavazzi at 8. Missed West[R]. Saw Dupré[R]. Read Howe's Speech[9]— M'Culloch's Life of A. Smith.[10]

12. Th.

Wrote to C.G.—Sir James Stephen. Saw Canning—J. Wortley—Duke of Argyll—Ld A. Hervey—Sir W. Heathcote—Mr Cobden—Mr V. Scully—G. Harcourt—Molesworth—Sir W. Gallwey.[11] Dined with the Wortley's— conv. with Wharncliffe—& General Buller.[12] Made various calls. Luncheon at Stafford House & went with Duchess of S[utherland] to Sebastopol Panorama & to Marochetti's Studio which is richly worth a visit.[13] Read Sir A. Hervey's Suggestion[14]—Hopwood Case.[15]

13. Fr.

Wrote to Sir W.C. James—J. Griffiths—Count Corti—C.G. Sir J. Graham— J. Herbert Coe—Dr Pusey—Whitlock[16] & de Gex.[17] Dined with the Hey-woods. Read Quarterly on War.[18]—Eastern papers. Saw Mr F. Hincks. Rev. C. Moody (Cathedrals &c) Lord Aberdeen—Lord A. Hervey—Chancr. of Exchequer. H. of C. 6–7½.[19]

[1] Scully's motion to abolish civil service patronage; *Roebuck's motion for a call was defeated: H cxxxix. 723.

[2] Not identified.

[3] Probably Thomas Clarkson, d. 1882; priest 1841; rector of Chillenden, Kent, 1852–5, of Wyverstone, Suffolk, from 1855.

[4] Harvey *Goodwin, 1818–91; fellow of Gonville and Caius 1841; dean of Ely 1858; bp. of Carlisle from 1869.

[5] Richard Rice, 1793?–1868; rector of Eaton Hastings, Berkshire.

[6] John Thomson Gordon, 1813–65; sheriff of Midlothian from 1848.

[7] Perhaps John Curtis Hayward, 1804–74; barrister, Gloucestershire landowner and magistrate.

[8] Church rates: H cxxxix. 753.

[9] J. Howe, 'Speech on the union of North American provinces and on the right of British colonists to representation in the imperial parliament' (1855).

[10] See 15 Aug. 46.

[11] Sir William Payne-Gallwey, 1807–81; 2nd bart. 1831; tory M.P. Thirsk 1851–80.

[12] Sir George *Buller, 1802–84; commanded 2nd brigade in Crimea, wounded at Inker-man; commanded troops in Ionian Isles 1856–62.

[13] Carlo *Marochetti, 1805–67, sculptor; studio in Onslow square; carved Inkerman memorial in St. Paul's and bust of Gladstone; see 18 May 57.

[14] Lord A. C. *Hervey, 'A suggestion for supplying the literary, scientific and mechanics institutes . . . with lecturers from the Universities' (1855).

[15] Earl of Sefton v. Hopwood. A report of the Hopwood Will Case (1855).

[16] George Stewart Whitlock, b. 1824?; rector of Milton Bryant 1854–65; vicar of Chelsea 1865–86.

[17] One of the family of solicitors; probably Edward Peter de Gex.

[18] Quarterly Review, xcvii. 245 (June 1855).   [19] Misc. business: H cxxxix. 860.

14. Sat.

Wrote to D. of Argyll—Mr Bohn[1]—Jas. Watson—Sir A. Elton[2]—J.N.G.—
Mr Frölich[3]—Sir A. Gordon—Robn. G—Sec. Treasury—Mr Lewin—
Messrs. G. & Co—S. Bannister[4]—M'Kenzie Dick[5]—E. Ellis—Rev. Mr
Tweed—T. Wright—H. Marsh. Saw Mr Goldwin Smith—E. Cardwell—
Scotts. Missed Ld Abn. Lady T. Lewis's party in evg. Missed Trains. Read
Quarterly on Archd. Hare[6]—finished Eastern Papers. Read Powell on
Unity of World.[7]

15. 6 S. Trin

St Barnabas (& H.C.) mg. Chapel Royal aft. Wrote to Chancr. of Exr.—Jas.
Wilson. Read Chr. Remembr.[8] Q.R. on Imm[aculate] Conception. Archd.
Hale's Charge.

16. M.

Wrote to Mr Dyce—Bp of Oxford. Conclave at Lord Aberdeen's at 12.
Worked on Eastern Papers. H. of C. $4\frac{3}{4}$–$8\frac{3}{4}$. Spoke briefly on bye points in
the negotiations.[9] Read Quetelet Sur l'Homme (finished). Phillimore on
Internat. Law.[10] Lushington Poems & Preface.[11]

17. T.

Wrote to Earl Granville—Sir G.C. Lewis—Rev. Mr Wood—Rev. Mr White
—H. of C. 6–$12\frac{1}{2}$: $\frac{1}{2}$h. to dinner. We finally agreed to oppose Govt. on
Peel's motion.[12] Saw Mr Anderson—Mr J. Griffiths—Count Corti—E.
Cardwell—Meeting at Lord Aberdeen's 12–$2\frac{1}{4}$. Read Rickards, 1st Lecture.[13]

18. Wed. X.

Wrote to Robn. G—Rev. Ld A. Hervey—Sir A. Elton Bt. and [blank]
Worked on accounts & papers also out book buying. H. of C. $12\frac{1}{2}$–2.[14] Saw
Mr V. Scully. Mr Grogan—Sir S. Northcote—R. Phillimore—Mr Liddell
M.P.—Scotts—Earl of Aberdeen. Lord Hardinge with Herbert and E.

[1] Henry George *Bohn, 1796–1884, bookseller and publisher.
[2] Sir Arthur Hallam Elton, 1818–83; 7th bart. 1853; poet; liberal M.P. Bath 1857–9.
[3] Count D. Frölich was in correspondence in September on French affairs (Hawn P).
[4] Saxe *Bannister, 1790–1877, barrister, author and traveller.
[5] Colin MacKenzie Dick, phrenologist in Oxford Street.
[6] *Quarterly Review*, xcvii. 1. (June 1855).
[7] Baden *Powell, *Essays on the spirit of the Inductive Philosophy, the Unity of the Worlds, and the Philosophy of Creation* (1855).
[8] *Christian Remembrancer*, xxx. 1 (July 1855).
[9] Debate on *Russell's resignation statement: *H* cxxxix. 939.
[10] See 21 Dec. 52.
[11] H. Lushington, *La Nation Boutiquière and other poems chiefly political* (1855).
[12] General *Peel moved the previous question to *Roebuck's motion criticizing all members of the war cabinet: *H* cxxxix. 966.
[13] J. Rickards, *Lectures on mental philosophy and theology* (1846).
[14] Misc. business: *H* cxxxix. 1024.

Cardwell. Saw Tilburn[R]. Dined with the Hardinges. Read 'Whom shall we hang'[1]—Richards on Loans.

19. Th. X.

Wrote to J. Murray—J. Griffiths—Mr Collis—Sir C. Roney[2]—F. Morrell.[3] H. of C. 6–8¾ and 9¼–2¾: Voted in 182:289 agt. General Peel's previous question.[4] Saw Sir W. Heathcote—Rev. Mr Greswell—Mr Robinson (St. Petersburg.)[5]—Mr Geo. Hope—Sir A. Gordon—Mr Bouverie—Mr V. Scully—Mr Ricardo. Saw Wolf: missed Collins[R]. Read Maxwell 'Whom shall we hang'—Mem. of A. Smith.

20.

Wrote to W.B. Collis—Mr Toogood—Worked in H. of C. Library on Treaty & Guarantee papers.[6] H. of C. 4¼–9 and 9½–12½: voted in 132:135 agt. Turkish guarantee: a significant division.[7] Saw Mr Griffiths—J.N.G.— Bp of Oxford—Mr Walpole (bis)—Sir S. Northcote. Read Lushington Poems.

21. Sat. X.

Wrote to Mr Bentley—Sir W. Heathcote—Dr Acland—A.F. Montague[8]— Dr Hannah—D[uche]ss Sutherland—Mr Wade—Rev Wh[itwell] Elwin— Mr Hansard. Calls & business with C. Read Adm. Reform Tracts.[9] Dragged myself to work, late, on revising Speech. Saw Mr Walker—Mr S. Herbert— Mr Dunning (Burder & D.)[10] Dr Hessey (resp. M[erchant] T[aylors] School) —Earl of Aberdeen. Missed Morgan, saw another[R].

22. 7 S. Trin

St James mg & Chapel Royal Evg. A circuit to Mrs Wadd's & Mr Goulburn's. Saw Mrs W. also Col. Gordon.[11] Wrote to Sir J. Graham—Mr Mackenzie—Mr Browne (Braintree)[12] Mrs Smith. Read T.A. Kempis— Cases of Conscience[13]—Butler Mem. & Sermon.[14]

[1] [P. B. Maxwell] 'Whom shall we hang? The Sebastopol Inquiry' (1855); cp. Add MS 44384, f. 113.
[2] Sir Cusack Patrick Roney, 1810–68; railway secretary; secretary to Dublin exhibition 1853; managed Canadian Grand Trunk railway 1853–60.
[3] Frederick Joseph Morrell, 1811–83; solicitor to Oxford university from 1853.
[4] Much cross-party voting: H cxxxix. 1186; annotated div. lists in Add MS. 44586, f. 84.
[5] Unidentified, not in the foreign Office List.
[6] Convention signed by Britain, France and Turkey to guarantee a loan raised by Turkey: PP 1854–5 lv. 49.
[7] Spoke against the loan to Turkey: H cxxxix. 1226; see O. Anderson, 'Great Britain and the beginnings of the Ottoman public debt, 1854–5', Hist. Journal, vii. 55.
[8] Perhaps Andrew Fountain Wilson Montagu of Melton Park, Doncaster.
[9] 'Official Papers of the Administrative Reform Association' (1855).
[10] Simon Dunning, of Burder, Son, & Dunning, London attorneys.
[11] (Sir) Alexander [Bertie] Hamilton-Gordon, 1817–90, *Aberdeen's 2nd s.; as deputy quarter master general in Crimea, severely criticized by the MacNeill commission; general 1873; won E. Aberdeenshire as a tory 1874, liberal 1880.
[12] i.e. Rev. J. D. Browne.   [13] See 28 Sept. 51.
[14] W. Archer Butler, Sermons, first series, with a memoir (1855?).

23. M.

Wrote to W.B. Collis—Duchess of Sutherland—H. of C. 2–3, 6–9, 10½–12. Spoke in defence of Friday night's proceedings.[1] Read Massey's History of England.[2] Worked on revision of Speech. Saw W. Hampton (bills &c)—J₀ Griffiths (S.R.G.)—Mr Henley—Mr Walpole—Sir E. Bulwer Lytton[3]—Mr Labouchere —Mr Cardwell—Sir Jas. Graham—Captain G.

24. T.

Wrote to Ed[ito]r Empire—Ld Canning—Mr K. Smith—Mr Dowding— Mr Wilkins—Mr Gibson—Thos. Cole. H. of C. 3–4.[4] Saw Morgan[R]—Saw Sir A. Elton—Earl of Aberdeen—Mr Walker—Earl Granville—Sir W. Heathcote. Read Massey's Hist England—Bancroft's Hist Amn. Revn.[5] Finished that most irksome work of correction of my Speech. In my increasing difficulties with respect to doing what I dislike I trace the greater weakness of the brain *relatively* to its work than ten years back [sic].

25. Wed. St James

Westmr. Abbey 3 P.M. Wrote to Robn. G.—Mr Browne—Mr Hodgskin—P. Pickering. Stafford House & French Exhibn.[6] mg. Read Blackwell, on Homer[7]—Massey's Hist. Engl. H. of C. 1–2 and 4–6.[8] Saw Duke of Argyll— Ld Mulgrave—Mr Hubbard—Mr Hamilton M.P.—Mr Walpole—Dined at Lady Wenlock's.

26. Th.

Write to S. Herbert—Sir James Graham—Read Massey's Hist. and Blackwell's Homer. Lady Granville's party evg. Saw Mr Grogan (resp. Houses.)[9] A. Panizzi (bis)—Mr Walpole—Ld Redesdale. Visited No 8 Spring Gardens.[10] Saw H. of L. Library—H. of C. 1–3½ & the evg.[11]

27. Fr.

Wrote to Mr C. Ingram[12]—Duchess of Sutherland—Earl Stanhope—Mr Grogan (with offer)—Mr F. Fowler[13]—Mr A Strettell—Provost of Eton.

[1] Defended himself against violent denunciation by *Layard; notes in Add MS 44654, f. 153: *H* cxxxix. 1301.

[2] W. N. *Massey, *A history of England during the reign of George the Third*, 4v. (1855–1863).

[3] Sir Edward George Earle Lytton Bulwer-*Lytton, 1803–91; novelist; tory M.P. Hertfordshire 1852–66; colonial secretary 1858–9; cr. bart. 1838, Baron Lytton 1866. See Add MS 44241.

[4] Misc. business: *H* cxxxix. 1338.

[5] G. Bancroft, *History of the American Revolution*, 3v. (1852–4).

[6] French school of fine arts 2nd annual exhibition, in 131 Pall Mall.

[7] T. Blackwell, *An Enquiry into the Life and writings of Homer*, (1735).

[8] Misc. business: *H* cxxxix. 1362.

[9] He moved into 4 Carlton House Terrace, previously occupied by the duke of *Argyll.

[10] Lady Charlotte Guest's house; see 1 May 55.

[11] Limited Liability Bill: *H* cxxxix. 1378.

[12] C. T. Ingram of Cambridge Terrace; Gladstone developed a slight acquaintance; see 4 July 56.

[13] Frederic Cooke Fowler, 1802–97; rector of Gunton, Suffolk, 1837–95.

Saw Duchess of Sutherland & Solr. General—H. of C. 12–1¾ and 6–12½ (45 m[inutes] to dinner) working the Turkish Loan Guarantee.[1] Read Massey's Hist. & Hinck's reply to Howe.[2]

28. Sat. [Chevening, Kent]

Wrote to Mr Whyte (Forfar)—Solicitor General—Mr Sandars. After much confabulation about the journey off at 3 by Bromley & Westerham to Chevening[3] where we passed a very pleasant evening with music & discourse: Saw Cardwell, late. Read Chevening letters[4]—Massey's History.

29. 8 S. Trin.

Ch mg. & evg. Walk with the Stanhopes & C[ardwell]s. Read T.A. Kempis —Chr. Remembr. on Dogm. Theoly.[5]

30. M.

Copied out my letter to Sol. Gen.[6] & sent it by C[ardwell]. We drove to Knowle & Wilderness.[7] The former is indeed a great rarity: trees, pictures, & living rooms of near 300 years back compete with one another in interest. Read Abelard & Heloissa, orig & Pope's (far inferior & more earthy)[8] & divers books in Library. Walked about the place with Stanhope. I had no proper idea of its beauty.

31. T. [London]

9–12. Journey to London. Wrote to Jas. Watson—F. Fowler—Sir A. Elton—Rev. H. Reed.[9] Read Pamphlet on Dec. Coinage +[10] Saw Sir W. Heathcote—Mr Swainson—R. Phillimore—Sir R. Bethell. Chancellor of Exchequer. H. of C. 1½–4, 6½–7½, 10–2½.[11]

Wed. Aug. One 55.

Wrote to E.A. Bowring—Chancr. of Exchequer—Rev. E. Coleridge. Attended Ld Canning's dinner: he spoke admirably. I returned thanks for the House of Commons.[12] Saw Mr Panizzi—Mr Gibson—Ld Chancellor— Sir E. Ryan[13]—Sir G. Lewis. Read Massey—Ed. Rev. on Dryden[14]—Willy's verses.

[1] *H.* cxxxix. 1438, 1474.
[2] Sir F. Hincks, 'Reply to the Speech of the Hon. J. Howe'; see 11 July 55.
[3] Seat of the Stanhopes, by Sevenoaks, Kent.
[4] *The earl of Chatham at Chevening in 1769*, privately printed by *Stanhope (1855).
[5] *Christian Remembrancer*, xxx. 101 (July 1855).   [6] i.e. to R. *Bethell.
[7] Knole, the Sackville-Wests' place in Kent.
[8] *Letters of Abelard and Heloise*, tr. J. Hughes with (from 10th ed. 1765) *Pope's 'Poem of Eloisa to Abaelardus'.
[9] See 12 Sept. 45, apparently still alive.
[10] 'Decimal Coinage. A short and easy method . . .' (1854).
[11] Estimates: *H* cxxxix. 1558.   [12] See *The Times*, 2 August 1855, 10b.
[13] Sir Edward *Ryan, 1793–1875; judge in India 1826; civil service commissioner 1855; wrote on law.
[14] *Edinburgh Review*, cii. 1 (August 1855).

2. Th.

Wrote to Ld Canning—V. Ch.[W.P.] Wood—Jas. Watson—W. Marshall[1]—
Sir A. Elton. Saw Earl of Aberdeen cum Sir J.G.—Scotts—Ld Palmerston
—Sir Geo. Lewis—Mr Laing—J.E. Denison—Shopping. H. of C. 3–4 and
$8\frac{1}{2}$–$12\frac{1}{2}$. Spoke on Kensington vote & on ways & means.[2] Read Massey.
Worked on books.

3. Fr.

Wrote to Rev. Mr Davis—Ld Wodehouse. Worked on Eastern Papers,
preparing for Debate. H. of C. $8\frac{1}{4}$–$1\frac{1}{2}$: spoke $\frac{3}{4}$ h. on the War & negotiations.[3]
Saw Mr Grogan. Lord Lyttelton (& M[ary] L.) Sat up to finish Massey.
Preparations for journey.

4. Sat. [Hawarden]

Wrote to Mrs Cleaver. To Chester by 10 A.M. Train. Found all well D.G. &
all but Lena bloomingly well. Read King John—Upton on Shakespeare.[4]

5. 9. S. Trin.

Hawarden Ch mg. (with H.C.) and evg. Tea at the Rectory. Wrote to
Chester Sup[erintenden]t. Read Robinson's Life[5]—Hampden's Introduction.[6]

6. M.

Wrote to Messrs. Overend—T.G.—Mr Anderson—Robn. G.—R. Phillimore
—J.N.G. Jas. Watson—G. & Co—Rev. Mr Cameron[7]—Sir J.G.s Ex[ecut]-
ors.—G.H. Forbes. Saw Mr Burnett. Began the Iliad: with serious intentions of working out something on old Homer if I can.[8] Read Upton on
Shakespeare—Blackwell's Homer. Construed Virgil with W. & S. Tasso
for W. & Agnes. Reluctantly began the correction of my Speech.

7. T.

Church $8\frac{1}{2}$ a.m. Wrote to Mr J. Hamilton—Mr W. Grogan—Rev. W. Malet
—Mr C. Ross. Worked on correcting Speech. On Homer: for wh I hope to
reserve the forenoons as a general rule. Family music. Read Othello—
Blackwell's Homer. Virgil with W. & S. Tasso with W. & A.

8. Wed.

Ch. $8\frac{1}{2}$ a.m. Wrote to Robn G.—G. Burnett. Worked on Homer l. II. Il.—

---

[1] Perhaps William Burton Marshall, Liverpool merchant.
[2] On museums at Kensington-gore: *H* cxxxix. 1685.
[3] *H* cxxxix. 1794; notes in Add MS 44654, f. 164; reprinted as 'Speech . . . on the war
and the negotiations' (1855).
[4] J. Upton, *Critical observations on Shakespeare* (1746).
[5] *Autobiography of Matthew Robinson* (1855).
[6] See 11 Feb. 49.   [7] i.e. C. R. Cameron; see 5 Jan. 31.
[8] Start of serious work on his essay on Homer, and of *Studies on Homer*; see 7 July 55
and 15 Dec. 56.

Read Iliad—Blackwell's Homer—Othello: the beauty of the latter part is almost superhuman. Virgil Æn 2 with W. & S. Tasso with W. & A. Family Music in evg. Worked on correcting speech.

Drive to Sandicroft & *round* to see the crops: the heaviest are sadly laid: little progress in the last 4 weeks.

9. Th.

Ch 8½ a.m. Wrote to Earl of Aberdeen—Mr T. Wright—Mr A. Simson[1]—Mr Samson.[2] Worked on correcting Speech. Read Iliad—Herodotus—Blackwell (finished)—Virgil & Tasso as usual. Music as usual. Worked on Homer. Walk to C'.s ride.

10. Fr.

Ch 8½ a.m. Wrote to G. Burnett—Mr Hamilton—M. Chamaillard[3]— Worked on & read Iliad—Read Gell, Plain of Troy[4]—Virgil & Tasso as usual. Finished correcting Speech.

11. Sat.

Ch 8½ a.m. Wrote to Mr Grogan—Rev. Mr Neale[5]—Worked on & read Iliad—Plut. de Aud. Poet[6]—Gell's Plain of Troy—Virgil & Tasso as usual. Family singing as usual. Worked on accounts.

12. 10 S. Trin.

Hawarden Ch mg. & evg. Wrote Tent. Butl. Read Butler—Hunter's Preface to More's Works[7]—and Robinson's Life.

13. M.

Ch 8½ a.m. Neuralgia came on: grew in aft. & towards night. Read Plutarch: read & worked on Iliad.

14. T.

An invalid's day. I thought, but not so much as I ought, of the war, & what it suggests. Chloroform & laudanum enabled me to get some sleep. Read Haydon's Journal[8]—Lesseps on the Isthmus of Suez[9]—and the Odyssey B.1.

[1] Alexander Simson, Scottish law agent in London.
[2] Possibly Blum Samson, fancy toy dealer in Lowther arcade, London.
[3] Henri Pierre Charles de Chamaillard, French royalist advocate; representative 1871.
[4] W. *Gell, *The topography of Troy and its vicinity* (1804).
[5] John Mason *Neale, 1818–66; ecclesiologist and hymnist; warden of Sackville college, E. Grinstead, 1846.
[6] *De audiendis poetis.*
[7] J. Hunter, ed., *The life of Sir Thomas *More, by Cresacre More with a biographical preface, notes and other illustrations.* (1828).
[8] See 23 Mar. 55.   [9] F. M. de Lesseps, *The isthmus of Suez question* (1855).

15. *Wed.*

Woke entirely relieved. Wrote to Mr J. Hamilton—Robn G—Mrs Loraine[1] —W. Muirhead[2]—M. de Lesseps[3]—Rev. G. Cole[4]—Rev. P. Hedgeland.[5] Corrected proofs of Speech May 24. Read Acland on Agric. Chemistry[6]— Odyss. & Iliad. Drive to St John's [Pentrobin] with Acland & much conv. at intervals. Virgil with W.& S. + guests.

16. *Th.*

Ch 8½ a.m. Wrote to Miss J. Robertson—Mr W. Marcy & Whitcombe. Read & worked on Il & Od.—Donaldson's Gatylus.[7] Virgil with W.& S. & W. Selwyn.[8] Tasso with W. & A. Drove with Acland through a line of farms. Saw Mr Burnett. Conv. with Acland on Politics & his destination.

17. *Fr.*

Ch 8½ a.m. Wrote to Sir S. Scott & Co—Mr W. Grogan—Mrs E. Bourne[9]— Mr Jas. Watson. Worked on Homer: read Iliad & Od.—Virgil with a conclave—Tasso with W. & A.—Haydon's Autobiogr. Music in evg.

18. *Sat.*

Ch 8½ a.m. Wrote to Mr J. Hamilton—Rev. J.O. Powell—Messrs. G. & Co. Worked on Homer. Read Iliad—Virgil with W, S, & W. Selwyn. Tasso with W. & A. Corrected proofs of my second speech. Music in evg. conversations with Acland: also with Stephen on Homer.

19. 11 *S. Trin.*

Ch. mg & evg. Read Catholicism without Popery.[10] Robinson's Life. More's Life. Conv. with Willy on St. Matt. 16. With Acland on the controv resp. revelation & a living authority.

20. *M.*

No Church, the day of the expedition to the Bridges.[11] Wrote to Rev. Mr Neale—Rev. A. Tarbull—and B. Quaritch. Worked πανημέριος[12] nearly on Homer & went down to Q[ueen's] F[erry] to meet the party.

---

[1] Of London, had sent comments on a book of verses; Hawn P.

[2] Liverpool food supplier.

[3] Ferdinand de Lesseps, 1805–94, canal builder; importuned for funds in England in 1850s and early 60s.

[4] George Cole, d.? 1876; Corpus, Cambridge; curacies 1831–66; vicar of Bethersden, 1866–9, perpetual curate of St. Michael's, Toxteth Park, 1869–75.

[5] Philip Hedgeland, priest 1850; assistant curate, Madron, Cornwall.

[6] MS or early proof of T. D. *Acland, *The chemistry of farming* (1857).

[7] J. W. Donaldson, *The New Gatylus, or contributions towards a more accurate knowledge of the Greek language* (1839).

[8] His godson; see 6 May 40.   [9] Charity worker?

[10] *Catholicism without popery; an essay to render the Church of England a means and a pattern of union to the Christian world* (1699).

[11] Over the Menai Straits.   [12] 'All the day long'.

21. T.

Ch. 8½ a.m. Worked on & read Il & Od. Read Essays on Homer. Virgil with the boys. Tasso with W. & Agnes. Wrote to Duke of Argyll—Mr Stanistreet —Sir T.G.—T.C. Hansard.

22. Wed.

Church 8½ a.m. Wrote to Mr J. Hamilton—Worked on Homer—Read Homeric Tracts. Expedition to the top of Moel Famma: a large party & great extent of view.[1]

23. Th.

Church 8½ a.m. Wrote to Mr Mayor[2]—Saw Mr Burnett. Attended Vestry meeting. Virgil with W, S, & W. Selwyn. Tasso with W. & Agnes. Worked on Homeric MS.

24. Fr. St Barthol.

Ch. 11 a.m. Virgil with W, S, & W. Selwyn. Tasso with W. & Agnes. Read Homer & Homeric Tracts. Worked at MS on do.

25. Sat.

Ch 8½ a.m. Wrote to Mr Hansard—Mr Hamilton—Worked on proofs of Sp[eech]. Virgil and Tasso as yesty. Worked nearly the day through & late on ἄναξ ἀνδρῶν.[3]

26. 12 S. Trin.

Ch 11 & 6½ P.M. Wrote to Ld Powis—Rev. W. Selwyn. Wrote on Hom. Theology.

The day was painfully occupied for the most part about the sad conduct of W. Selwyn.[4] But all evil in others should with me principally have the effect of deepening the sense of my own, deeper & more rooted, & more varied. Conv. with Willy on the Epistle.

27. M.

Ch 8½ a.m. Read & worked much on my Homer. Rode with Agnes & C. Read Thucyd. (in illustrn.).

28. T.

Ch. 8½ a.m. Wrote to Mr J. Hamilton—Mr Uwins—Mr [J.R.] Herbert R.A. —Creswicks. Music in evg (with the Andersons).[5] Went to the Sandycroft

---

[1] 4 miles W. of Mold; the highest point on the Clwydian range.
[2] John Eyton Bickersteth *Mayor, 1825–1910; fellow of St. John's, Cambridge, from 1849; classicist and editor.
[3] For *Studies on Homer*, i.   [4] His godson.   [5] See 3 Sept. 55.

(non) launch,[1] and walked through the fields. Virgil with W. & S. Read & worked on Homer.

29. Wed.

Ch 8½ a.m. Wrote to C. Roach Smith[2]—Mr J. Watt[3]—Sig. Gadaleta—R. Barker—Mrs Loftus. Rode with A. & Miss F. Anderson. Music in evg. Read and worked on my Homer. Virgil with W. & S. Tasso with W. & A.

30. Th.

Ch 8½ a.m. Wrote to Ld Lyttelton—Rev. J. Browne—J.P. Edward.[4] Read Hom. Il. & Rennell[5]—Worked on Homer. Saw Mr J. Griffiths. Virgil & Tasso as usual.

31. Fr.

Ch 8½ a.m. Wrote to Ld Lyttelton—Mrs Loftus—H. Raikes—J.N.G. Virgil with W. & S. Tasso with W. & A. Read Il. & Rennell. Worked on Homer.

Sat. Sept. One 55

Wrote to Dean Ramsay—Scotts—Lord Holland—Robn. G—E. Clarkson[6] —Hatchards—H. Garnett[7]—Cleaver—S. Hatherley[8]—J. Moor[9]—Banting & Sons.—Jas. Hulton—Marcy & Whitchurch and W. Grogan. Worked on accounts, letters and papers. Read Mure[10]—Hom. Il. Worked on Hom. Il.

2. 13 S. Trin

Ch 11 (H.C.) & 6½ P.M. Read Shaw's Sermon[11] &c Madan's Letters to Priestley[12]—More's Life of More. Got some of my small Theol books into order. Preparations for departure in evg. Conv. with Agnes on Gospel.

3. M. [Penmaenmawr]

Off with Agnes at 8¾ to St Asaph at 12, and 2–3 to Abergele thence by train to Conway & again to Pen-maen-mawr[13]. At St. Asaph we stayed with the

[1] Works on the Dee.
[2] Charles Roach *Smith, 1807–90; authority on Greek and Roman antiquities.
[3] Perhaps James Henry *Watt, 1799–1867; engraver, especially of ancient subjects.
[4] Unidentified; see perhaps 18 Mar. 56.
[5] J. Rennell, *Observations on the topography of the plain of Troy* . . . (1814).
[6] Edward Clarkson of Highbury Vale had sent verses; Hawn P.
[7] Of York, had written on the war; Hawn P.
[8] S. G. Hatherley of Solihull had sent an anti-Turkish pamphlet, of which he published several (Hawn P).
[9] Perhaps James Hoare Christopher Moor, had just published *Sermons* (1855).
[10] Colonel W. *Mure, *A critical history of the language and literature of ancient Greece*, 5v. (1850–7), defends, agst. the Germans, notion of an individual Homer.
[11] W. Shaw, *Sermon before . . . J. Phillott* (1810).
[12] M. Madan, *Letters to J. Priestley* (1786).
[13] Watering place 4 miles SW. Conway; the Gladstones took Plas Mariandir, on the sea front, owned by John Harrison of Plas Glanymor; Robert Frost, Chester coal merchant, also seems to have had an interest in the house.

Bp[1] & went into the Cathedral. He was *warlike* to a degree & in a manner which carries the mark of belonging to a general distemper.

At Conway we met the Andersons & went over the very striking Castle of the 14th Cent. & the Palace House of 1576. The spot is very lovely. We found at our journey's end a soft & pretty nook under the stern & grand though not high mountain: & a healthy happy party. Set my little goods to rights: and worked on Homer.

4. T.

Wrote to Lyttelton. A short walk with C. a mountain walk with Willy, and a bathe made a good first day. Read Col. Mure—Iliad—worked on Iliad—Construed Virgil for Stephen.

5. Wed.

Wrote to Overends—Sir A. Elton—Robn. G.—J.N.G. Read Iliad—Rennell Geogr.—Maclaren's do.[2] Worked on Homer—Tasso with W. & A.—Virgil with W. & S. Walked the old Conway road to C.s ride & bathed.

6. Th.

We made an expedition to the fall above Aber,[3] well worth it. Tasso with W. & A. Read Il & Od.—Maclaren on the Plain of Troy. Worked on Homer.

7. Fr.

Wrote to Messrs. Overends—R. Barker—Messrs. Williams (Ch[este]r)—Robn. G.—Count Frölich—Scotts (3)—Mr Anderson. Finishing my arrangements for the £20000 with wh I am to take up S.R.G.s O[ak] F[arm]. Mortgage next Wedy. Walked up the hill with Willy. Bathed. Read Maclaren—Rennell—Hom. Il. Worked on Homer.

8. Sat.

Wrote to Dean Ramsay—Mr W. Pelton[4] (Hansard)—Mr C. Simms.[5] Walked with Willy up Pen Maen Mawr.[6] Settled with S.R.G. the plan of our tour for next week. Worked on Homer. Read Iliad—Maclaren.

9. 14 S. Trin.

Prayers & Sermon at home mg. Parish Ch aft. Walk with C. Read Burder's Life[7]—Bp Hamilton's Charge[8]—Manning & Meyrick Correspondence.[9]

---

[1] T. V. *Short (see 14 Oct. 28n).

[2] C. *Maclaren, *A dissertation on the topography of the Plain of Troy* (1822).

[3] 9 miles SW. of Conway, with waterfalls over 180 feet.   [4] One of the reporters?

[5] Charles Samuel Simms, 1809–72; bookseller in Manchester; poet, later tr. the Iliad.

[6] 1550 feet, behind the town, the northern buttress of the Snowdon range.

[7] Perhaps H. F. *Burder, *Memoir of the Rev. G. Burder* (1833).

[8] By W. K. *Hamilton (1855).

[9] H. E. *Manning and F. *Meyrick, *Moral theology of the Church of Rome* (1855); on Liguori.

Th[eology] Both the righteousness and the sufferings of our Blessed Lord operate for our salvation: yet diversely: for by our union with Him His sufferings stand in the stead of and dispense with ours: but His righteousness on the contrary procures and engenders ours. Yet to our first acceptance in the Beloved both concur and our Father seeing us in Him the lack of our righteousness is supplied by the fulness of His.[1]

10. M. [Llanrwst]

Wrote to Lady Fitzgerald[2]—Robn. G—(2)—R. Barker—J. Griffiths— Messrs. Overend and [blank]. Tasso with W. & A. Read Iliad—Bathed in forenoon.

Started at 3.25 for Llanrwst[3] 16 miles over the hills: a beautiful walk: took 3 h. 35m. reached at dusk. C. & Co an hour later. Four miles with a self sufficient but straightforward & intelligent pedlar: most warlike. Read two short books of Odyssey in evg. Eagles Inn. good eating: not dear: not clean.

11. T. [Dolgelly]

Off with Willy at 9: forty miles (one astray) to Bettys-y-Coed. Penmachno Festiniog, Transfynnydd and Dolgelly.[4] The first eight & last ten miles lovely. C. & Co arrived very late after all sorts of miscarriages. Read Odyssey—Inn Golden Lion: Good.

12. Wed [Barmouth]

After a good night we gave up Machynlleth[5] but tried Cader Idris: saw a grand precipice & beautiful views but the clouds prevented our reaching the top.[6] We went in afternoon down to Barmouth[7] where we found the Inn excellent: the drive lovely. Read Odyssey.

13. Th. [Beddgelert]

An early bathe at Barmouth. 10 long miles [north] to Harlech: where we saw a grand old Castle nobly situated. Our weather was at first doubtful and wet; as we went on to Tanybwlch, a most beautiful drive, it became fair and even fine. I walked over to Beddgelert:[8] Willy riding with me. Pont Aber Glaslyn surpassed all my expectations.[9] At Tanybwlch we went to Mrs Oakeley's terrace: liberally opened. Here also I saw my old Agent at Newark Mr R. Caparn entirely blind: & heard much from him of my old acquaintants. Read Odyssey.

[1] Dated 9 September 1855; Add MS 44745, f. 257.
[2] Jean, née Ogilvy, m. 1829 Sir J. F. Fitzgerald.
[3] On the river Conway, 10 miles S. of Conway.
[4] The walk took them almost due south, most of the way across Merioneth.
[5] Village 10 miles S. of Dolgelly.   [6] 2927 feet S. of Dolgelly.
[7] Watering place on the Mawddach estuary.
[8] On the south side of Snowdon, the highest of the Welsh hills.
[9] Bridge over the Glaslyn which there passes through a spectacular gorge.

14. *Fr.* [*Capel Curig*]

Goat at Beddgelert very good. We drove to Llanberris[1] through the grand base & beneath the base of Snowdon, which was an approach to the sublime in character far exceeding its dimensions. We did not like the Llanberris Inn (Victoria) overmuch but the situation at the mouth of the deep vale is pretty. We saw the Fall & Dolbadern Castle[2] wh is curious. I then walked up the [Llanberis] pass & we drove down to Capel Curig:[3] a bad approach though between high mountains.

15. *Sat.* [*Penmaenmawr*]

Capel Curig Hotel: good. C.s urgency took us backwards on our line for Snowdon: the view of wh was grand but from the masses of rolling clouds which circled round the peaks. We started at 10½. I took (walking) 1h. 12m. to the point of leaving the road.[4] We went slowly to the top by the two Llyns and arrived (some of the last part both steep & giddy) at 1.55. We could not see beyond arms length: & waited for the chance of better things till 3.15, employing ourselves upon luncheon, the materials of wh at the hut were good. (They made a charge of 5/– for bed supper & breakfast: moderate enough). We came down by the highest route: I took 1h. 20m. to the road & then walked 8½m. along the road by C[apel] C[urig] towards Llyn Ogwyn[5] The two basins are very grand. In Scotland they would I think be called Corries: the upper one is the finest as a whole, the lower one has the grander precipice. Lake Ogwyn and Nant F[f]rangon[6] below it are quite worthy of the Snowdon group. In the midst of the Cabinet—mountain scenery wh makes these counties so beautiful, Snowdon & its family form an island of real grandeur in character. We baited & had tea in a tolerable Inn at Bethesda: & reached home[7] at 11 P.M. I reckon it 10m. from C.C. to the top: two fives.

16. *15 S. Trin.*

Prayers at home mg. Parish church Evg. Read Burder's Life—the Manning & Meyrick Correspondence: this latter with extreme pain.

17. *M.*

Wrote to Sir W.C. James—Sir T.G.—Messrs. Overend—J. Wilson—Mr J. Hamilton—Mr Grogan—Rev. Dr Hannah. Bathed & walked with S.R.G. over the shoulder of P[en] M[aen] M[awr] to Llanfairvechan.[8] Read Edwards on the War.[9] Odyssey—Made up accounts of our tour for settlement.

[1] On the north side of Snowdon.   [2] An ancient circular tower.
[3] About 12 miles E. of Llanberis.
[4] The path from the Capel Curig road is the steepest of the non-mountaineering routes to the summit. It passes the lakes Lydaw and Glaslyn and, below the summit, a refreshment hut. This is not the path with the plaque marking the place of Gladstone's mass-meeting in September 1892.
[5] N.E. of Snowdon.   [6] Valley leading down to Bethesda and Bangor.
[7] i.e. Penmaenmawr.   [8] A village 1½ miles S.
[9] John Passmore *Edwards, 1823–1911, progressive journalist and philanthropist, had sent his anti-war pamphlet, *The war, a blunder and a crime* (1855); Hawn P.

18. T.

Read & worked on Il. & Od. Read Maclaren—Browne on Ithaca.[1] Tasso
with W. & A. Bathe—& with C. on the Conway Pass.

19. Wed.

Wrote to E. Coleridge—Overends—Rev. Mr Richards—Williams (Chester).
Read Il. (finished)—Od. (B.16). Maclaren (finished)—U. Service Mag. on
Ld Raglan.[2] Took C. & some of the children up our nearest hill. Bathed as
usual.

20. Th.

Wrote to W. Hampton—Worked on Homer. Read Odyssey—Col. Mure's
History.[3] Walk to C.s ride up the hill. Bathed. We kept Willy on account
of a bad boil: probably the result of over exertion. Tasso with him & Agnes.
Arranged a letter to Lady Stuart: who gives us trouble.[4]

21. Fr. St Matth. (Agnes 1847)[5]

Wrote to Messrs Stanistreet—Stephen—Mr Pressly—Robn. G. Worked on
Homer. Read Odyssey—Col. Mure—Count Frölich on Money[6]—Maj.
Court on Income Tax.[7] Up the hill to Col. Macdonald's[8] nest with C.—
Bathed—Willy went in evg. (we hope quite well) to Hawarden on his way.
Put off from our visit to Penrhyn Castle.[9]

22. Sat.

Wrote to Robn. G—Read Od. & worked on Homer. Read Col Mure. Drove
to Penrhyn Castle for luncheon & went over it & the place: it is a great
curiosity; probably unique.

23. 16. S. Trin.

Parish Ch mg & evg. The evening service was in Welsh: gross total of the
congregation 30: the clergyman (a stranger) seemingly not to blame: I saw
some irreverence of kinds wh wd not occur in England. The language does
not make favourable impressions. Read Burder's Life (finished): Sutton's
excellent Disce Vivere:[10] Spect. de l'Or. on C. Lucar, &c. Chillon.[11]

[1] In R. W. Browne, *A history of Greece* (1852).
[2] *United Service Magazine* (1855) part II, 515.   [3] See 1 Sept. 55.
[4] Perhaps Theresa Pauline, *née* Ott, supposed wife of 1st Baron Stuart de Decies; her
marriage was finally not recognised 1876 (*G.E.C.*, xii. part I, 409).
[5] The start of her erysipelas; cp. 17 Sept. 47.
[6] D. Frölich, *Sketch of a plan for the reform of the laws and regulations respecting money
and currency* (1855).
[7] See 10 June 53.
[8] Probably John MacDonald, lived at Plas Uchaf, Penmaenmawr.
[9] Seat by Bangor of Edward Gordon Douglas-Pennant, 1800–86; tory M.P. Carnarvon-
shire 1841–66; cr. Baron Penrhyn 1866; future fa.-in-law of Gertrude Glynne (cp.24
Sept. 50). His slate quarries at Penrhyn then the largest in the world.
[10] See 16 Feb. 40.
[11] *Le Spectateur de l'orient*, periodical published in Athens 1853–7.

24. M.

Worked on Homer. Read Odyssey & Col. Mure. Went up the hills walking to H. Glynne's & Col. Macdonald's ride: improved my acquaintance with them. Tea & evg. at Col. Macdonald's.

25. T.

Wrote to Mr T. Rathbone—Bathed. Took C. & four little girls up Pen Maen Mawr—they drove by Llanfairvechan & did their walking (five miles or more) very gallantly. Read Odyssey & Mure.

26. Wed.

Wrote to Mrs Cleaver—Bathed—Calls: arrangements for leaving. Read Odyssey—Col. Mure Vol. 1. An admirable book: in some parts incomparable.

27. Th [Bodelwyddan]

Wrote to J. M'Culloch—Willy—Robn. G.—J.H. Parker. One farewell bathe. Read Odyssey—Col. Mure. Packing & arrangements. Off at half past 12 from this pleasant sojourn: where I have lived too happily for one who thinks as I do about the course of events & the responsibilities of needless war. Drove C. to Abergele:[1] walked on through Kinmall Park[2] to Bodelwyddan[3] where we were most kindly received. We saw the beautiful Stove, in wh I had sadly to lament my ignorance. We found here Lady A. Fitzclarence[4] & Miss Gordon; excellent company. Sat up late reading the detailed accounts from Sebastopol: wh were for England grievous.[5]

28. Fr.

Wrote to Robn. G—Hon. A. Gordon. Read Pliny's Epistles—Hist. of Woman[6]—Marryatt's Little Savage.[7] We drove to see the beautiful & very satisfactory Church built by Mrs Mainwaring.[8] Read Miss [sc. Mrs.] Thrale (Mrs Piozzi)'s Letters to Bodelwyddan.[9]

[1] 5 miles W. of Rhyl.
[2] 3 miles SE. of Abergele.
[3] 5 miles SW. of Rhyl: seat of Sir John Hay-Williams Hay, 1794–1859; 2nd bart. 1830; added name of Hay 1842; deputy-lieutenant of Flintshire.
[4] Lady Adelaide Georgiana Fitzclarence, 1820–83, da. of 1st earl of Munster (illegitimate s. of William IV).
[5] The Pyrrhic victory at Sebastopol was won on 8 September, British forces storming the Redan with great loss.
[6] L. M. Child, *The history of the condition of women in various ages and nations*, 2v. (1835).
[7] F. *Marryat, *The Little Savage*, 2v. (1848–9).
[8] Holy Trinity, Trefnant, built by Mrs. Townshend Mainwaring of Galltfaenan and Mrs. Mainwaring of Otley Park (see 16 Sept. 56).
[9] Unpublished letters by Mrs. *Piozzi to the Williams family; see J. L. Clifford, *Hester Lynch Piozzi* (1952 ed.), 467.

29. Sat. St Michael. [Hawarden]

Church (Hawarden) 7 P.M. Read the Little Savage. Saw Mr Crawford (with Sir J.W[illiams]) off at 10.45 drove to Bodfarry[1] to the 'Rising Sun' then ten miles on foot, which took me a trifle under two hours; overtaken & so home. Wrote to Mr J. Griffiths—Mr Blackwell—Mr J. Hamilton. Worked on letters & papers.

30. 17 S. Trin.

Ch mg & evg. Lesson on the Epistle to Agnes. Read Bp Wilson's Life[2]— Mad. de la Valliere's Life & Meditations.[3]

Monday Oct. 1 1855

Church 8½ a.m. Wrote to Count Montalembert—Sir W. James—J.G. Hubbard—W. Hampton—S. Herbert. Willy—Mr Grogan—Finished the Little Savage. Worked on transfer to my new Table. Bp of Salisbury & Mrs H[amilton]. Walk with him.

2. T.

Church 8½ a.m. Busy all the morning in preparing for post some 80 copies of each of my two War Speeches. Saw Mr Burnett. Drove to Caergwrle Castle[4] & Pont Blyddyn. Walk with the Bp. His society is delightful: & his wife is worthy of him. Read Mure Vol. 2.

3. Wed.

Ch 8½ a.m. Wrote to Bp of Aberdeen—J.N.G.—Duke of Argyll—Robn. G— T.W. Rathbone—Circular—J.H. Parker—J. Griffiths—Butler of Ch.Ch.[5] Mem. on Trin. Col. Loan and copy.[6] Took the Bp to St John's [Pentrobin]; & much conv. with him. Saw Mr Troughton. Read Col. Mure—Mr Heathcotes letter to the Bp.[7]

4. Th.

Church 8½ a.m. Wrote to Mr G. Wilson[8]—R. Barker—Manager Union Bank—Scotts & Co. Saw Mr Burnett. Much conv. with Bp on Ch matters as usual. Read Odyssey—& Col Mure. Still busy getting into order.

---

[1] Bodfari, village 4 miles NE. Denbigh.
[2] C. Cruttwell, *The works of . . . Thomas Wilson . . . With his life* (1782).
[3] See 17 July 53.
[4] Ruined castle about 8 miles S. of Hawarden.   [5] i.e. Henry Grant; see 19 Dec. 51.
[6] He had loaned Trinity college, Glenalmond, £3500; see G. St. Quintin, *History of Glenalmond* (1956), 52.
[7] Untraced MS.
[8] George *Wilson, 1808–70; Manchester corn merchant, chairman of A. C. L. L. 1841; president of National Reform Union 1864; one of diarist's chief sponsors in Manchester, 1865; see 18 July 65 and Hawn P.

5. *Fr.*

Ch 8½ a.m. Read Q.R. on Mure[1]—Mure Vol II—(& Od.) Saw the Bp off early; his visit has been a delightful obstruction to Studies also delightful. Our room[2] is growing characteristic: & we think of having in it our own furniture. Finished the Odyssey: but I must go over & over again both poems, as indeed I have been doing. C. busy reducing to order.

6. *Sat.* [*Courthey, Liverpool*]

Ch. 8½ a.m. Wrote to Mr Baillie—Mr Evans jun. Off at 2.10 to Liverpool & Courthey. Read Col Mure—Isocrates Enc.[3]

7. *18 S. Trin.*

St Thomas Toxteth[4] & H.C. mg. St Philip's aft. & walked out to Courthey. Saw Mr [J.O.] Powell & went over his schools. I was pleased with his seemingly earnest & laborious character. The Church was quite half full: strong choir, little responding, about 32 Communicants: the element of Bread delivered to four at once, the Chalice (two) each to one. Wrote to C.G. —Read Bp Wilson's Life. Scandret on Sacrifice &c.[5] Conv. with Robn. on St Thoms. Toxteth & on Helen's matters.

8. *M.*

Wrote to C.G.—Mr Smythe of Methven—Mr Paviso[6] (Birmm.). Read Ed Rev. on Col. Mure—Ed. Rev. on Colonies.[7] Bp Thirlwall Appx 1.[8] Tennyson's Maud[9] & Poems. Col. Mure. Saw Mr Moss—The Mayor (& excused myself from dining tomorrow)[10]—Mr Tayleur's Assistant—E. Breakenridge —A. Gladstone. A family party at Courthey.

9. *T.* [*Hawarden*]

Back to L'pool & Hawarden. Wrote to J.G. Hubbard—J.H. Parker—and [blank space] Read Col. Mure—H. Coleridge—Introd. to Poets.[11] Music in evg. Busy on Bookcases &c.

10. *Wed.*

Somewhat unwell. Wrote to T. Nimmo—Sec. Empire Comme.[12] Read Doctor Antonio[13]—Col. Mure—K.O. Muller (Hist. Gr. Lit.)[14] and H. Coleridge on Homer: also Turgot on Free Trade & on Amn. War.[15] Worked on Books. A short walk in aft.

---

[1] *Quarterly Review*, xcvii. 378 (September 1855).   [2] Not yet the 'temple of peace'.
[3] Isocrates, *Helenae encomium.*   [4] i.e. his own church.   [5] See 20 Aug. 48.
[6] Probably Benno Paraviso, general commission agent in Birmingham.
[7] *Edinburgh Review*, cii. 542 (October 1855).   [8] On Homer; see 5 Jan. 47.
[9] Recently published. Gladstone later denounced the warlike stanzas of the poem which he found as a whole 'unintelligible'; see 14 July 59 and *Gleanings*, ii. 146.
[10] John Stewart, mayor of Liverpool 1855.   [11] See 20 Nov. 53.
[12] Untraced.   [13] [G. Ruffini], *Doctor Antonio; a tale* (1855).
[14] K. O. Müller, *A history of the literature of ancient Greece*, tr. G. C. *Lewis (1840–2).
[15] See 17 Aug. 48.

11. Th.

Wrote to Mr Collis—Duchess of Sutherland—Mr Lacaita—Mr M. Bernard. Worked on Homer: with scissors and otherwise, having obtained waste copies for the purpose. Read Col. Mure—H. Coleridge—Canada MS papers.[1]

12. Fr.

Ch 8½ a.m. Wrote to E. of Aberdeen—Saw Mr Burnett & wrote Mem resp. Mr Ashworth's Farm.[2] Read Doctor Antonio—N.Z. Bill Speech of 1852.[3] Worked on Homer—made notes of figures &c. for the evening. Lecture on Colonies at 7½; about an hour and twenty minutes, in the Parish Schoolroom.[4] Tea at the Rectory.

13. Sat.

Ch 8½ a.m. Wrote to Robn G. New bookcases put up; much work on moving & arranging my books. Also worked on Homer—cutting. Dinner party in evg. Conv. with Phillimore. Read National Review on British Statesmen.[5]

14. 19 S. Trin.

Ch mg, aft (Confirmation) and Evg. Read Bp Wilson's Life (finished)—Scandret on Sacrifice & Nat. Rev. on St Paul.[6]

15. M.

Ch 8½ a.m. Wrote to Sir Thos. G.—R.M. Milnes—Worked some hours on arranging my books—Also much on Homer: this is $\dot{o}\mu\eta\rho\hat{\epsilon}\iota\nu$[7] with a vengeance: Walk with C.

16. T.

Ch 8½ a.m. Wrote to Bp of Salisbury—Mr Capper—Dr Goodford—Mr Mason.[8] Saw Mr Burnett. Conv. with E. Neville on the Sebastopol winter.[9] With R. P[hillimore] on Ch, & Politics & Homer. Dined at the Rectory—Singing. Read Doctor Antonio. Worked resolutely on Homer—cutting.

17. Wed.

Ch 8½ a.m. Worked much on Homer. Read Hymn to Venus.[10] Col. Mure—Doctor Antonio.

[1] He discussed the 1837 rebellion in his speech next day.
[2] Farm purchase resulting in an evicted tenant; Gladstone asked Phillimore to take him on at Henley (Phillimore MSS).
[3] See 21 May 52.
[4] Report in *Liverpool Mercury*, reprinted in *The Guardian*, 24 October 1855, 798; notes in Add MS 44654, f. 169.
[5] *National Review*, i. 411 (October 1855).   [6] ibid., i. 438 (October 1855).
[7] 'to meet'; here used punningly on name of Homer.
[8] sc. Masson.   [9] See 15 Jan. 55.   [10] i.e. *Pervigilium Veneris*.

18. Th. St Luke

Ch 11 a.m. Agnes's birthday: I spoke to her shortly on the character & use of such recurring seasons. Finished my scissor work upon the Iliad. Wrote to Robn. G., Duke of Argyll—& copy. Walk with the party. Singing in evg. Read Coleridge on Homer.

19. Fr.

Ch 8½ a.m. Wrote to Sec. Union Bank[1]—Warden Trin. College—Mr W. Grogan. Saw Mr Burnett on numerous arrangements connected with the purchase of Moor Farm & S.R.G.s affairs. Worked on Odyssey. Read Doctor Antonio. Milnes arrived: talks thunder & conflagration but gives up the War on its old grounds. Planned new bookcases for London.

20. Sat.

Ch 8½ a.m. Wrote to Mr Burnett—Worked on Homeric papers. Read Doctor Antonio—Letzten Stunden des Kaisers Nic. I.[2] French play got up with dancing by Suzie[3] & the children—a very creditable affair. Walk with Bp of Oxford & conv. on Ch affairs. S. Herbert came.

21. 20. S. Trin

Ch 11 a.m. (when Bp of O[xford] gave us one of his beautiful sermons) and 6½ P.M. Conv. with Agnes. Walk & conv. with the Bp. Read Wards Letter to Archdeacon of Dorset[4]—Life of Dr Comber[5]—Breviary. Wrote to Sir T.G.

22. M.

Ch 8½ a.m. Wrote to Robn. G—Aunt Johanna. Began my perusal of Il. & Od. anew for classification of passages. Dined at the Rectory: Music—Conv. with Herbert on the War. We seem to be at nearly the same point, to my great satisfaction. With the Bp & R. Phillimore on Clergy Discipline & Court of Appeal. With Milnes on the War. Read Doctor Antonio.

23. T. [Tabley]

Ch 8½ a.m. Wrote to W. Grogan—Mr Axon (Chester Mech. Inst.)[6]—Mr G. Burnett—Mr T. Scott—Conv. with S.R.G. on the Ashworth purchase. Our company went off: & we followed driving to Tabley[7] through the Forest 1½–5½. Discussed the War there. Read Berni's Orlando[8]—Dr Antonio.

[1] Walter Laurie, secretary of the Union Bank of London.
[2] *Die letzten Lebensstunden des Kaisers Nicolaus des Ersten. Nebst seinem Testament* (1855).
[3] Unidentified; presumably not Lady (Susan) Lincoln.
[4] W. H. P. Ward, *Divine Service. A letter to . . . the archdeacon of Dorset* (1855).
[5] *Memoirs of the life . . . of Thomas Comber* (1799).
[6] About the meeting on 12 Nov. 55.
[7] Eighteenth century seat of the De Tableys, by Knutsford, Cheshire.
[8] F. Berni, *Orlando innamorato* (1541).

24. Wed.

Drove to see Ashley & the Warburtons.[1] Also saw the Hall & Chapel here.[2] Dinner party. Wrote to Willy and J.N.G. Read Berni—Doctor Antonio—Mrs Norton's Letter to the Queen.[3]

25. Th.

Wrote to Lady Pembroke—Finished Mrs Norton—Doctor Antonio—much of it I fear 'an over true Tale[']—Read MS of Sir P. Leicester[4]—saw the Pictures—& 'Nelly's'[5] remarkable work in the schoolroom: where there is self-government in a wonderful form.

26. Fr.

Wrote to M. Benj. Consolo—Mr J. Hamilton—Rev. T. Jones—Rev. W. Malet—Ld Lyttelton—Again visited the Hall & Chapel. 2–5¼ Drive by Middlewich to Crewe. Conv with Bp of Oxford. Read Berni's Orlando.

27. Sat.

Wrote to Mrs Southey[6]—Read Berni's Orlando—Hom. Iliad—Holland's Physiology.[7] Drove to Audley & Barthomley Churches. Walk in the grounds. Conv. with Bp of Oxford on the War.

28. 21. S. Trin. & SS. Simon & Jude

Chapel 11 a.m. Aftn. service in school at Crewe Green. Wrote to Warden Trin. Coll. Read Suckling on Relig. & Reason[8]—Waldgraves Sermons.[9] Robins on the Supremacy[10]—Case of Honorius I.[11]—Sermons on Sebastopol.[12]

29. M. [Hawarden]

Wrote to Mr Hamilton M.P. 2.40 Left for Hawarden wh we reached at 5.30. Read Berni's Orlando VI & VII—Domenichi's Ditto (which I much prefer)

[1] The Egerton Warburtons at Arley Hall.
[2] Tabley Old Hall, fourteenth century house on an island in a lake.
[3] Mrs. G. C. Norton, *A letter to the Queen on Lord Chancellor Cranworth's Marriage and Divorce Bill* (1855).
[4] Perhaps that printed as *Tracts written in the controversy respecting the legitimacy of Amicia, daughter of . . . the earl of Chester, by Sir P. Leicester*, ed. W. Beamont (1869).
[5] Eleanor Leicester, née Warren, 1841–1914, da. of 2nd Baron De Tabley, m. 1864 Sir Baldwyn Leighton 1836–95, 8th bart.; she succ. to the Tabley properties 1895, taking name of Warren 1900.
[6] Perhaps she who had been nurse to the royal children; see C. Hibbert, *Edward VII* (1976), 4.
[7] G. C. Holland, *The physiology of the foetus, liver and spleen* (1831).
[8] Sir J. *Suckling, 'An account of religion by reason' in *Fragmenta Aurea* (1646).
[9] S. Waldegrave, *New Testament Millennarianism. Bampton Lectures 1854* (1855).
[10] S. *Robins, 'The whole evidence against the claims of the Roman church' (1855); cp. Add MS 44384, f. 201.
[11] J. Garnerius, 'De causa Honorii Summi Pontificis et VI Synodi' from *Liber diurnus Romanorum Pontificum* (1680).
[12] Many on this, including 'The siege of Gibeah, a parallel to the siege of Sebastopol' (1855).

1 & 11[1]—Panizzi's Introductory Essay. We found the children well thank God.

30. T.

Ch 8½ a.m. Wrote to Duke of Argyll—Robn. G.—Duchess of Sutherland Mr W.G. Anderson—Mr W.H. Pinfield.[2] Read Amadigi of B. Tasso—Panizzi's Essay & Life of Bojardo—Domenichi's Bojardo—and Bojardo himself. Worked on Iliad.

31. Wed.

Ch. 8½ a.m. Wrote to Brothers (Circ[ular])—W. Hampton—Ivalls—Ld Overstone—J.N.G.—T.W. Rathbone—W. Grogan—W. Monsell—R. Smith. Worked on Iliad. Saw Mr Burnett. Read Panizzi—Bojardo and Berni—Tiraboschi on them & on P. Aretino[3]—Ricciardetto.[4]

Thurs. Nov One All Saints.

Church 11 A.M. Worked on Iliad. Wrote to Sir W.C. James—Williams Deacon & Co.—Dr Moffatt—Miss Christie[5]—Aunt J. Read Ricciardetto—Panizzi's Life of Ariosto.[6]

A retrospect from this day shows me how deeply unworthy I am of the company of those whom it celebrates. In the point perhaps of all my worst this year shows perhaps a faint improvement as compared with the last four: but what is it as compared with not only what it ought to be but with what the life of others, & of others too without pretension makes their years to be!

Again I find feebleness & timidity for duty, & a disposition to Epicurean self-indulgence is growing upon me. Of this my public cares have been the excuse perhaps in some degree the occasion: but as I now am the time for trying to brace myself somewhat has arrived. In some points however I think that the weakness I lament is a real admonition from nature.

2. Fr.

Confined by cold. Wrote to Mr Jas Freshfield—Mrs Herbert. Read Ricciardetto—Panizzi's Life of Arisoto—Diversions of Purley[7]—Orlandino. Worked a little on Iliad.

3. Sat.

Again confined except a short half hour. Wrote to Earl of Aberdeen—Earl

---

[1] See 5 Apr. 50.   [2] Liverpool accountant.
[3] G. Tiraboschi, probably his *Compendium of the literary history of Italy until the formation of the modern Italian language*, tr. F. V. Barbacori (1835).
[4] Ricciardetto, *Richardet, Poëme*, tr. A. F. Duperrier Dumouriez (1781).
[5] Unidentified.
[6] A. *Panizzi, *Orlando furioso di Ariosto with memoirs and notes*, 4v. (1834).
[7] J. H. *Tooke, Επεα πτεροεντα or, the Diversions of Purley (1786).

Stanhope—Mr Roundell Palmer. Read Ricciardetto—Pope's Preface to Iliad & Satires[1]—Orlandino.

4. 22 S. Trin.

Ch. & H.C. 11 A.M. Not out in evg. Lesson to Agnes on the Gospel. To Mary & Lena respecting David. Read Life of Comber—Theol. Germanica with Introductory Matter[2]—Bp of Ossory's Charge[3]—Memoir of Raikes.[4]

5. M.

Wrote to Sir A. Elton—Ld Overstone—Archdeacon Jones[5]—Mr H. Raikes —Robn. G.—Captain G. Saw Mr Burnett. Worked on Homer—Read Ricciardetto—Orlandino—Evans on Jamaica.[6]

6. T.

Resumed *well* habits. Ch. $8\frac{1}{2}$ A.M. Wrote to Robn. G.—Mr Panizzi—Rev R Hunt—T.D. Acland—H. Roberts—Rev S. Robins[7]—Rich. Smith. Saw Messrs. Burnett & Barker. Worked on Iliad. Read Acland on the Plain of Troy[8]—Euripides Troades—and Ricciardetto.

7. Wed.

Ch. $8\frac{1}{2}$ A.M. Wrote to Dean Ramsay—M'Kenzie & Baillie—Rev Mr Ander[9] —Mr M.T. Baines—T.A. Hope.[10] Worked on Iliad. Walk with S. & to C.s ride, to meet Lady W[enlock]. Read Aristot. Poetica—Orlandino (finished) —Eurip. Troades—and Iphig. in Aulis.[11]

8. Th.

Ch. $8\frac{1}{2}$ A.M. Wrote to Ld Canning—Messrs. Overend—Rev Mr Church— Rev Mr Tweed—Ed. Lpool Daily Post.[12] Worked on Iliad. Read Troades (finished)—Arist. Poet.—Q.R. on Pitt & Fox.[13] Dinnerparty.

9. Fr.

Ch. $8\frac{1}{2}$ A.M. Wrote to Mrs Herbert. Worked on Homer. Read Iphig. in Aulis—Arist. Poet.—Ricciardetto. Conv. with Rev Mr Wilbraham,[14] mg: & walked Sir E. Cust with Mr Taylor to St John's. Dinner party.

[1] A. *Pope, *Preface to the translation of the Iliad* (1715).
[2] See 18 June 54.   [3] See 25 Apr. 52.
[4] Probably *Memoir of Sir J. Brenton* by H. Raikes (1855), to whom Gladstone wrote next day.
[5] i.e. John *Jones, cp. 16 Aug. 25.
[6] H. B. Evans, *Our West Indian Colonies* (1855).
[7] Sanderson *Robins, 1801–62; rector of Shaftesbury 1840–54, of Dover, 1854–6; vicar of St. Peter's, Isle of Thanet from 1856; broad church educationalist.
[8] H. W. *Acland, *The plains of Troy* (1839).
[9] Henry Smith Anders (see 19 Aug. 40), d. 1877, rector of Asgarby from 1854.
[10] Thomas Arthur Hope, Liverpool merchant, d. 1897; bought Seaforth House.
[11] C. G. Fienhaber, *Euripidis Iphigenia in Aulis. Mit deutschem Commentar* (1841).
[12] Not published.   [13] *Quarterly Review*, xcvii. 513 (September 1855).
[14] Charles Philip Wilbraham, 1810–79; vicar of Audley 1844–74.

10. Sat.

Ch. 8½ A.M. Wrote to Willy—R. Barker—M'Kenzie & Baillie—Mr J. Murray. Worked on Homer. Read Aristot. Poetica—Iphig. in Aulis— finished Q.R. on Pitt and Fox—Ricciardetto.

11. 23 S. Trin.

Church 11 A.M. & 6½ P.M. Conv. with Agnes on the Gospel. Wrote to J.N.G.—Willy (further). Read De Honorio Primo[1]—Comber's Life— Berington's Abelard & Heloisa[2]—Paradise Regained.

12. M.

Ch 8½ A.M. Read Mr Greg on Modern Cabinet-making[3]—Iphig. in Aulis (finished)—and luxuriated in Burke. Walking & at home, threw my thoughts into order & made notes for the evening. 14 to dinner—conv. with Adderley and (mg) with Mrs Wilbraham. 7–11 to Chester where I delivered a lecture on Colonies. 1 h. 50 m. Much below what it shd have been.[4]

13. T.

Ch. 8½ A.M. Wrote to Sir James Graham—Rev. J. Macmillan[5]—Rev. Jenkin Davies[6]—R.E.E. Warburton. Read Aristot. Poet.—Ricciardetto. Walk & much conv. with Mr Wilbraham who is alike good & delightful.

14. Wed.

Ch 8½ A.M. Wrote to Overends—Mr Goldwin Smith—T.D. Acland—Justin M'Carthy[7]—Robn. G. Saw Mr Burnett—Park walk with C. & Lady Wenlock to talk about a possible green drive. Read Hecuba of Eurip[ides]— Parad. Regained (finished)—Ricciardetto. Worked on the Iliad.

15. Th.

Ch. 8½ A.M. Wrote to Rev. Mr Church—Bp of Argyll—Stephen E. G[lad-stone]—E. Coleridge—S.O. Mahony[8]—J. Murray. Read Hecuba—Milton —Marlowe—Ricciardetto. Read & worked on Iliad. Dinner party: singing in evg.

[1] See 28 Oct. 55.

[2] J. *Berington, *History of the lives of Abeillard and Heloisa* (1787).

[3] [W. R. *Greg], 'Cabinets and statesmen', *North British Review*, xxiv. 183 (November 1855).

[4] Published as 'Our colonies' (1855); notes in Add MS 44654, f. 177. Most of the text is in *The Guardian*, 21 November 1855, 854.

[5] Episcopalian incumbent at Dunkeld.

[6] Jenkin Davies; St. David's college, Lampeter; vicar of Mold 1854–72.

[7] Justin *M'Carthy (1830–1912); as *Liverpool Daily Times* reporter attended the speech and arranged its publication (see 12 Nov. 55, Add MS 44384, f. 222, and his *Reminiscences* (1899) ii. 444–6); journalist in London 1859; home rule M.P. co. (N.) Longford, 1879–86, 1892–1900, Londonderry 1886–92; led anti-Parnellites 1890.

[8] Wrote 'On the study of modern languages in public schools' (1853).

16. Fr.

Ch. 8½ A.M. Wrote to J. M'Carthy—D.B. Chapman—Henry Taylor—Mrs (Major) Leigh[1]—Mr W.R. Greg. Read Hecuba (finished)—Herodotus—Ricciardetto. Read & worked on Iliad—Saw Mr Barker—Dinner party: singing in evg.

17. Sat.

Ch. 8½ A.M. Wrote to Robn. G.—G. & Co—J. Caldecott[2]—Scotts—Mast. Pembroke—Sec. Greenock & Glasg. Co—Saw Mary Hazelhurst. Read Caldecott on Double Entry[3]—Arist. Poet. (finished)—Johnson on Paradise Lost[4]—Eurip. Helena.

18. 24 S. Trin.

Ch mg. & evg. Conv. with Agnes. Read Comber's Life (finished)—Sir T. More's Life[5]—Burgon on St John[6]—Paradise Lost B I.

19. M.

Ch. 8½ A.M. Wrote to Earl of Aberdeen—Rev Mr Burgon—T.W. Rathbone —J.G. Talbot—Robn. G. Worked on Iliad ἄναξ ἀνδρῶν &c. Read the Gerusalemme (for critical purposes)[7]—Ricciardetto—Iliad. Walk to C.s ride.

20. T.

Ch. 8½ A.M. Wrote to S. Herbert (& fair copy)—Marcy & Whitcombe—Rev E. Coleridge—Willy. Walk to C.s ride. Saw Mrs Ducker:[8] a patient Christian sufferer indeed. Worked on & read Iliad. Read Ricciardetto—Gerus. Liberata—Pycroft's Course of Reading.[9]

21. Wed.

Ch. 8½ A.M. Worked on Proof Sheets of Address.[10] Wrote to A. Somerville[11] —J. Hamilton—W.G. Anderson—Jas Freshfield—Dow[age]r C[ounte]ss Pembroke[12]—Ld Canning—Sutherland Greene[13]—J. M'Carthy. Worked on

---

[1] Lydia Rachel, née Wright, d. 1893; m. 1842 Egerton Leigh fils, 1815–76, Cheshire landowner and major, later colonel, in dragoons, tory M.P. Mid Cheshire 1873–6.

[2] John Caldecott, Chester accountant.

[3] J. Caldecott, A practical guide for retail tradesmen and others to bookkeeping by double entry (1851).

[4] S. *Johnson, 'Life of Milton' in Prefaces biographical and critical to the works of the English poets, 10 v. (1779–81).

[5] By W. Roper (1626, probably the 1835 ed.).

[6] J. W. *Burgon, A plain commentary on the four holy gospels (1855).

[7] By Tasso, see 28 May 53.   [8] A villager.

[9] J. Pycroft, A course of English reading, adapted to every taste and capacity (1844).

[10] See 14 Nov. 55n.

[11] Alexander *Somerville, 1811–85; on Manchester Examiner 1844–58; wrote free-trade pamphlets; see 28 Jan. 43n.

[12] Catherine, née Woronzow, d. 1856; Sidney *Herbert's mother.

[13] Unidentified; perhaps two people.

& read Iliad. Read Electric Psychology[1]—and Tasso Ger. Lib. Dinner party & singing.

22. Th. [Eaton Hall]

Ch. 8½ A.M. Wrote to Sir J. Hanmer—G. Burnett—R. Barker—Read Tasso Ger. Lib.—Ricciardetto—Eurip. Hel[en]—Worked on Iliad. Went over to Eaton. Singing mg with Mrs Owen[2] (whose playing is a treat) & evg. at Eaton.[3] Lost half my night by a cup of strong coffee.

23. Fr.

Morning walk at Eaton with D[uche]ss of Sutherland & a party. Wrote to Resid. Legatees—Robn. G (2)—G. Burnett—W. Walker[4]—W. Murgatroyd —C.R. Hall[5]—J. M'Carthy. Dinner party in evg. Read Ricciardetto. Worked on Proof sheets. And through a great packet of letters from London —To bed for 2 hours. My dear Mazie's birthday: may God ever bless the dear little soul.

24. Sat. [London]

3½–11¼ A.M. to 4 C[arlton] H[ouse] Terrace. Wrote to C.G.—Lord J. Russell —Mr Frank Curzon.[6] Saw Ld Canning (my purpose in coming)—Mrs Talbot—Mr W.G. Anderson—Sir C. Trevelyan—Mr Bonham—Chancr. of Exchequer—Mrs Hampton. Missed Wolf [R]. Dined with the Wortleys. Read Tasso Ger. Lib.

25. Preadv. Sunday

Chapel Royal mg & aft. Saw F. Bonham—E. Cardwell—Ld E. Bruce—Mr Hillyard MP.[7]—Rev A.P. Stanley—Lady Canning (2).[8] Wrote to Bp of Oxford—Mr Snell—Mr Bonham. Read S. Bern[ard]—Horsley Serm[9]—Q.R. on Huet[10]—Whately's Cautions.[11]

26. M. [Hawarden]

Wrote to Mrs Anstice—Ly Canning—Mr P. Maxwell[12]—Dr Acland—Mr Horton—Mr Jessop[13]—Wms & Norgate[14]—Mrs Monk. Saw W. Hampton—

---

[1] By J. B. Dods and I. S. Grimes (1851).   [2] Not further identified.
[3] Gothic seat of the Westminsters.   [4] The engraver; see 30 Jan. 44.
[5] Possibly Charles Radclyffe Hall, 1819–79; Cheshire physician; practised in Torquay from 1850.
[6] Author of *The Gift of Life* (1853); not of the noble family.
[7] Robert Charles Hildyard, 1800–57; barrister; tory M.P. Whitehaven from 1847.
[8] See 13 Feb. 36.   [9] See 18 Aug. 50.
[10] *Quarterly Review*, xcvii. 291 (September 1855).
[11] R. *Whately, *Cautions for the times* (1853).
[12] (Sir) Peter Benson *Maxwell, 1817–93; recorder of Penang 1856, of Singapore 1866; chief justice Straits Settlements 1867–71; kt. 1856.
[13] Perhaps William Henry Bowlestone Jessop, d. 1865; wrote pamphlet on decimal coinage (1855).
[14] Booksellers in Henrietta street, Covent Garden.

J. Griffiths—Hon. Mrs Stanley—D.B. Chapman (in City)—Mr Walker (sat)
—Mr Robinson (Bank)[1]—W.F. Larkins[2]—Mr Godley & others. Packed
books &c. for Hawarden. Shopping. Read Tasso Ger. Lib. Off by Express
8.45 P.M.

27. T.

Reached Hn. at 3 A.M. Wrote to Mary Hazelhurst—Miss Stanley & copy[3]
—J. Jones. Draft for C. to Lady S[tuart]. S. Herbert—G. Burnett—Signora
Pistrucci[4]—T. Webb Gilbert[5]—Rev. H. Howard. Conv. & cons[ultatio]n
on Lady Stuart's case wh is annoying.[6] Music in evg. Arranged letters.
Read Tasso Ger. Lib. —Robinson on the Thames.[7]

28. Wed.

Ch 8½ A.M. Saw Mr G. Burnett—Wrote to Rev. N.J. Moody[8]—Mr
Snell & copy—F.R. Bonham & copy—M.F. Tupper & copy—Robn. G.—
J. Griffith—R.G. Gammage[9]—H.J. Rollo[10]—A. Baillie Cochrane—G.
Arbuthnot. R. Cavendish came. We planned & laid out the Park walk to
Church with Wray.[11] Read Canada Finance[12]—Gerus. Liberata.[13]

29. Th.

Ch. 8½ A.M. Wrote to Duke of Argyll (& copy)—Sec. Free Library[14]—Hon.
Mrs Wilbraham—J. M'Carthy—A. Panizzi. Read Hallam—Tasso's Life
by R. Milman[15]—Tasso. Worked on Iliad—Walk with L[yttelto]n & R.
Cavendish.

30. Fr. St Andrew

Ch 11 A.M. Wrote to Earl of Aberdeen—W. Grogan—R.M. Milnes MP.—
S. Herbert—Jas Crook MP[16]—J.N.G.—G. Burnett. Read Tiraboschi—Tasso
—Ricciardetto—Milman's Life of Tasso. Worked on the Iliad. Walk with
L[yttelto]n & Cavendish.

---

[1] John Robinson, chief clerk in the issue dept.; perhaps the pseud. author of Rusticus,
'The world on the Thames' (1855); see next day.
[2] Walter F. Larkins, a distant relative (see 22 Aug. 25), senior clerk in the board of
trade.
[3] In Lathbury, ii. 27.   [4] Perhaps her later met in Rome; see 1 Jan. 67.
[5] Thomas Webb Gilbert, oil man in Peerless Place, London.
[6] See 20 Sept. 55.   [7] See 26 Nov. 55.
[8] Draft, on Sebastopol, in Add MS 44384, f. 248.
[9] Robert George *Gammage, 1815–88; Northampton chartist and historian of the
movement; later a physician.
[10] Hugh J. Rollo, Edinburgh W.S. and episcopalian, fund-raising for Trinity college,
Glenalmond.
[11] The walks of Hawarden Park, which were finished by Lancashire factory workers
during the 1862–3 distress.
[12] Imports and exports: PP 1855 li. 242.   [13] See 28 May 53.
[14] Probably the Free Library in Southampton Buildings, Chancery Lane.
[15] R. Milman, The life of Torquato Tasso, 2v. (1850).
[16] Joseph Crook, 1809–84; Bolton cotton manufacturer; liberal M.P. Bolton 1852–61.

Sat. Dec. One. 1855

Church 8½ A.M. Wrote to Duke of Argyll—Sir T.G.—Rev. M. Bayly—R. Barker—W. Hampton—Stephy—Mr F. Davis. Dined at the Rectory: George's Lecture,[1] & music afr. Walk with him & Homeric talk. Wrote on φίλον ἦτορ[2] &c. Read Tasso—Ricciardetto—finished—such a 'Classic'!

2. Adv. Sunday

Ch. 11 A.M. & H.C.—also 6½ A.M. Wrote to Miss Stanley—Lord Aberdeen —W. Hampton. Conv. with Agnes. Read More's Life & Appx. (finished)— Fisher's Life (began)[3]—Bp of Oxfords 5 Novr. Sermon.[4]

3. M. [Windsor]

Off at 8.20 for Windsor which I reached at 4.15. Saw Coleridge—Willy— Duchess of Sutherland—Count Cavour.[5] Wrote to C.G.[6]—Mass. d'Azeglio— Johnson Longden & Co—Mr Labouchere—W. Grogan—Cav. Nigra[7]—Jas Freshfield—Mr Labouchere [sic]—Duke of Argyll—R. Barker. Read Tasso Cantos 13 & 14. A Dinner party of 80 in St George's Hall. Nothing could be more splendid.

4. T.

Prayers at nine. Wrote to Rev. E. Hobhouse—Mr H. Lees. Conv. with Ld Malmesbury—Provost of Eton—Rev E. Coleridge—Willy—S. Herbert— Ld Wodehouse—Mr Baines—Ld Aberdeen. Dinner as yesterday. Walked with the Speaker & a party to the Garden & Farm.

5. Wed. X. [London]

Prayers at nine. Read de Roos on the Crimea.[8] Wrote to Overends—M. Froment[9]—Ld Drumlanrig—C.G.[10]—Mr Hay Mackenzie[11]—Scotts. Saw D[uche]ss of Sutherland—Count Cavour—Ld Aberdeen—Gen. Peel—Gen. Grey[12]—Mr Trevor—Overends—Johnson Longden & Co—Duke of Argyll[13] —Mr Grogan. Saw three incl. Langton [R]. Up late.

[1] Probably on 'National education', in G. W. *Lyttelton, *Ephemera* (1865).
[2] 'his dear heart'; a common Homeric formula.
[3] J. Lewis, *Life of John Fisher, bp. of Rochester*, 2v. (1855) with introduction by T. H. Turner.
[4] S. *Wilberforce, *The principles of the English reformation*; a sermon on 2 Kings XXII. v. 11. (1855).
[5] Accompanying Victor Emmanuel's state visit, and failing to gain guarantee of territorial compensation for Piedmont; see A. J. Whyte, *The political life and letters of Cavour* (1930), 191 and *The Times*, 4 December 1855, 7a.
[6] Bassett, 112.   [7] Accompanying Victor Emmanuel.
[8] W. L. L. Fitzgerald, Baron de Ros, *Journal of a tour in the Principalities, Crimea, and countries adjacent to the Black Sea in the years 1835–6* (1855).
[9] Perhaps of the French royalist family; see *Dict. des Parlementairs Français* (1891) iii. 78.
[10] Bassett, 112.   [11] James Hay MacKenzie, Edinburgh W.S.
[12] Sir John *Grey, 1780?–1856; served in India and the Peninsula; lieut.-general 1851.
[13] See Argyll, i. 601.

6. *Th.*

St Paul's Kn[ightsbridge] 5 P.M. Wrote to Mr Rowsell—Mr White—Mr Archer Gurney—Mr Archer—Capt. Fowke[1]—Dr Mitchell.[2] Saw G. Hope & J. Hope Scott—Miss Stanley: twice—Lord Aberdeen: Dr Hessey. Calls & business & packing. Read Tegoborsky.[3]

7. *Fr.* [*Hawarden*]

Up at 5. Off by 6.15 train: reached Hawarden 12.45. Wrote to Mr Rollo W.S.—Robn. G.—Mrs Wilbraham—J. M'Carthy. Saw Mr Hignett (Chester). Finished proof sheets of Address on Colonies. Read Grote's Greece[4]— Tasso Ger. Lib. Singing in evg.

8. *Sat.*

Ch. 8½ A.M. Wrote to Rev W. Elwin—Mr C. M'Gregor[5]—W. Hampton— Mary Hazelhurst. Read Tasso Ger. Lib.—Grote—Worked on Homer. Ld Stanley came: we had much conversation.

9. *2 S. Adv.*

Ch. 11 (Parish) and 3 P.M. (Broughton). Walks & much conv. with Ld S[tanley] on Church & other matters. Read Jowett (Introd & Comm)[6]— Life of Fisher—Wix on Reunion.[7] Stephen with Agnes on Acts IX.

10. *M.*

Ch. 8½ A.M. Wrote to Earl of Aberdeen—Duchess of Sutherland—J.G. Hubbard—Messrs. Overend—Sir S. Scott & Co. Saw Mr G. Burnett— Mr Ffoulkes. Worked on books. Music in evg. Long walk with Ld S. & most of the morning too. Read Grote—Tasso Ger. Lib.—& Lushington's Judgment.[8]

11. *T.*

Ch. 8½ A.M. Wrote to Earl Stanhope—Very Rev. Jas Smith[9]—Miss Stanley. Walk with L[yttelto]n & Lord Stanley. Worked on my books (from Ln.) Read Ger. Lib.—Dean Elliott's Letter to Ld Palmerston[10]—Grote's Hist— Troilus & Cressida.

[1] Francis *Fowke, 1823–65; captain of royal engineers; sec. to English commission to Paris exhibition 1855–7; architect and inventor.
[2] Perhaps Samuel Mitchell, physician at St. Bartholomew's.
[3] L. Tegoborski, probably *Commentaries on the productive forces of Russia*, 2v. (1855).
[4] Further volumes; see 19 Mar. 47.
[5] See 14 Jan. 33; sending contribution to a memorial (Hawn P).
[6] See 17 June 55.   [7] See 20 Feb. 42.
[8] S. *Lushington, 'Judgment . . . in the case of Westerton against Liddell and Horne and others . . .' (1855).
[9] Probably James Smith, d. 1865; archdeacon of Connor from 1849.
[10] G. *Elliot, *Letter to Viscount Palmerston . . . on the address voted by Convocation on June 29th 1855* (1855).

12. Wed.

Ch. 8½ A.M. Wrote to Messrs. Overend—Robn. G—W. Grogan—W. Forbes. Walk with S. & De Tabley. Exhibited my room &c. to Stanley before (to our regret) he left us. He will if spared write his name on the page of Engl. History.[1] Wrote on Homer. Read Tasso Ger. Lib.—Brownells Ephemeron[2] —Grote's Hist.—Troilus & Cressida (finished).

13. Th.

Ch. 8½ A.M. Wrote to W. Lyttelton—Rev H. Pye[3]—Rev J. Ferguson. Read Ger. Lib. (finished)—Grote—Brownell's Poems (finished). Dined at the Rectory—Singing. Work with Willy —& arranging for Stephen's lessons. Worked on Homer.

14. Fr.

Ch. 8½ A.M. Wrote to Earl of Aberdeen—Mr Panizzi—H. Glynne. Saw Mr Burnett. Worked on Homer. Read Monk's Bentley[4]—Grote's Greece— Iliad—Thirlwall's Hist.[5] Tasso with W. & A.

15. Sat.

Ch. 8½ A.M. Wrote to Sec. Lanc. & Yorksh. Co.—Dean of St Asaph[6]— Johnson Longden & Co—Dr Moffatt. Saw Mr Ffoulkes. Read Thirlwall— Swift's Battle of the Books[7]—Monk's Bentley—P. Knight's Prolegomena[8] —Worked on Homer. Prepared a note of the state of my property.

16. 3 S. Adv.

Ch. 11 & 6¼. Mazie better thank God. Had the three eldest for Holy Scripture. Read Bentley on Popery—on Atheism[9]—Wix on Reunion—& Baxter's Life.[10] Long conferences with Phillimore on the Lushington Judgment.[11] Perused my will & paper of directions.

17. M.

Ch. 8½ A.M. Mrs Talbot went. Saw Mr Burnett—R. Phillimore—Mr Austin. Wrote to A. Panizzi—Rector of Exeter Coll.—Robn. G. Tasso with W. & A.

---

[1] 'I am very greatly struck, and scarcely less pleased with him. The force and vigour of his mind, combined with the adaptation of its general construction to the demands of the nineteenth century as it moves towards his [sic] close, mark him out, especially when his lineage and social position are taken into view, for a high but perhaps agitated destiny'; to Aberdeen, 10 Dec. 1855, Add MS 43071, f. 275.
[2] H. H. Brownell, *Ephemeron. A poem* (1855).
[3] Henry John Pye, *fils*, 1827–1903; rector of Clifton Camville 1851–68 when he seceded to Rome; then a barrister; m. 1851 Emily Charlotte, da. of S. *Wilberforce.
[4] J. H. Monk, *The Life of Richard *Bentley* (1830).
[5] See 5 Jan. 47.   [6] Charles Butler Clough, 1793–1859; dean of St. Asaph from 1854.
[7] J. *Swift, *Battle of the Books* (1704).
[8] R. P. Knight, *Prolegomena in carmina Homerica* (1808).
[9] R. *Bentley 'A confutation of atheism' (1692) and 'A sermon upon popery' (1715).
[10] J. Napier, *Richard *Baxter and his times* (1855).   [11] See 10 Dec. 55n.

Began Anacreon with Stephy. Worked on Homer. Read Mitford's Greece[1]
—Life of Bentley.

18. T.

Ch. 8½ A.M. Wrote to Judge Coleridge—Mr Kilgour[2]—Mr J. M'Carthy—
G. & Co—Mr Street.[3] Worked on Homer. Tasso with W. & A. Anacreon
with Stephy. Read Thirlwall—Macaulay Vol. III[4] wh I thought quite equal
to England's expectation.

19. Wed.

Ch. 8½ A.M. Anacreon with Stephy. Tasso with W. & A. Wrote to Mr
Lacaita—Mr J. Griffith. Worked on Homer. Read Grote's Greece—
Macaulay. Singing after luncheon. Attended Mr Hawkins's Lecture on
Geology.[5] Rectory afterwards. Family arrangements discussed.

20. Th.

Ch. 8½ A.M. Tasso with W. & A. Anacr. with Stephy. Wrote to Mr A.
M'Lellan[6]—Mr Frere[7] & Goodford—Major Neville. Worked on Homer.
Read Macaulay's Hist—Grote's Hist—Cramer's Greece[8]—Darling's Psy-
chology.[9] Conv. with Miss L. on the future State.

21. Fr. St Thomas

Ch. 11 A.M. Wrote to Ld Lyttelton—Miss Kohn[10]—Mr Blackwell—Mr
Keble. Anacreon with Stephy. Tasso with W. & A. Also turned a letter into
Latin & made some beginnings towards helping Willy in that line: in wh
he is backward. Read Macaulay—Wachsmuth's Antiq. of Greece.[11]

22. Sat.

Ch. 8½ A.M. Anacreon with S. Tasso with W. & A. Worked on Homer.
Read Macaulay—Iliad—Cramer's Greece. Duchess of Sutherland with
D. & Dss. of Argyll came in aftn.: & we passed most of the rest of the day
with them.[12]

23. S. 4 S. Adv.

Hawarden Ch. mg & Buckley aftn. Walk & drive with Duchess of S.

---

[1] W. *Mitford, *A history of Greece*, 5v. (1784).
[2] H. Kilgour of Edinburgh had written on colonial reform (Hawn P).
[3] George Edmund *Street, 1824–81, ecclesiastical architect.
[4] See 2 Feb. 49 and *Gleanings*, ii. 265.
[5] Perhaps by Thomas Hawkins, 1810–89, collected fossils in S.W. England and wrote
on them.
[6] See 9 Nov. 54.
[7] Probably Charles Frere, examiner of petitions to the Commons.
[8] J. A. *Cramer, *A geographical and historical description of ancient Greece*, 3v. (1828).
[9] See 21 Nov. 55.   [10] Unidentified.
[11] E. W. G. Wachsmuth, *The historical antiquities of the Greeks with reference to their
political constitutions*, tr. E. Woolrych, 2v. (1837).
[12] *Argyll's description in Argyll, ii. 2.

Church conv. with D. of A. for 2½ hours: the evening went in conversation with a little singing. Read Buckland[1]—Wix on Reunion.

24. M.

Ch. 8½ A.M. Wrote to J. Tollemache—Jas Wilson—Saxe Bannister— H. Lees—A. M'Lellan. Saw Mr Burnett. The Sutherland party went off at 11¼: leaving every kindly & genial recollection behind them. Read Macaulay—Cramer—Electric Biology[2]—finished. Worked on Homer.

25. Xmas Day. Tu.

Church (& H.C.) 11 A.M.—7 P.M. Wrote to J.N.G. Read Wix on Reunion —Dante Vita Nuova[3]—Parad. Lost—Macaulay.

26. Wed. St Stephen.

Ch 11 A.M. Wrote to J. M'Carthy—Ld Ward—Mr Burnett—Mr Pressly. Worked on Homer. Read Macaulay—Electric Psychology.[4] Anacreon with S. Tasso with W. & A.

27. Th. St John.

Ch. 11 A.M. Wrote to Robn. G.—Mr H. Lees (3). Worked on Homer— Tasso with W. & A. Read Macaulay Vol. IV—Sir W. Gell's Argolis.[5] Walk with the party.

28. Fr. H. Innocents.

Ch. 11 A.M. Wrote Earl of Elgin—Mr R. Hill—J.W. Williams[6]—Rev. H. Owen.[7] Worked on Homer—Anacreon with Stephy—Tasso with W. & A. Dined at the Rectory. Read Macaulay.

29. Sat.

Ch. 8½ A.M. Wrote to Mrs Baker—Mr Axon[8]—Read Macaulay—Mitford— the French Congress Pamphlet in M. Post[9]—Worked much on Homer— Anacreon with Stephy—Tasso with W. & A.—Conv. on Latin prose with W.

And so passes my 46th birthday: the 46 first years of my eternity are

[1] W. Buckland, *Geology and mineralogy considered with reference to natural theology*, 2v. (1836).
[2] J. B. Dods, *Philosophy of Electro-Biology*, ed. G. W. Stone (1852).
[3] Poem written on death of Beatrice.   [4] See 21 Nov. 55.
[5] W. *Gell, *Itinerary of Greece: with a commentary on Pausanias and Strabo, and an account of . . . Argolis* (1810).
[6] Perhaps Joseph William Williams, London auctioneer.
[7] Hugh Owen, incumbent of St. Mary's, Llanerchymedd, from 1853, corresponded on the classics (Hawn P).
[8] John William Axon, bookbinder in Bartholomew Close, London.
[9] 'De la nécessité d'un Congrés pour pacifier l'Europe', *Morning Post*, 29 December 1855; supposedly by Napoleon III.

complete. I see amidst a good deal of evil some miserable snail's paced movement towards what is better: my only hope is that *One* has caused it to be written 'Thou hast in love to my soul delivered it from the pit of corruption: for thou hast cast all my sins behind thy back'.[1] And that He can cause those words to be written for me also.

30. S. after Xmas.

Church & H.C. 11 A.M.—again 6½ P.M. W.A. & S. for the Gospel. Conv. with W. on the Eastern Church. Wrote to Bp of Oxford—R. Cavendish. Read Theologia Germanica[2]—Proceedings agt. Foster[3]—Wix on Reunion.

31. M.

Ch. 8½ A.M. Wrote to Jas Watson—J. Hamilton—Williams & Co Chester. Anacreon with Stephy. Tasso with W. & A. Saw Mr Burnett. Worked on Homer much. Read Macaulay—& Homeric books.

　　And so dies the old year: laden with his burden which do thou O Saviour bear.

[1] Isaiah, xxxviii. 17.　　　[2] See 4 Dec. 55.　　　[3] See 24 June 55.

Hawarden Jan One 1856.
The Circumcision.
Tues.

Ch. 11 A.M. Worked on Homer. Wrote to J.N.G.—Mrs M.A. Smith[1]—Mr W. Ffoulkes[2]—A. Hayward—Mr M'Glashan.[3] Saw Mr Burnett—J. M'Culloch[4]—& made the arrangements needed for him.

2. Wed.

Ch. 8½ A.M. Wrote to J. Griffiths—Jas Watson—Griffiths jun—Ld Ward— J. Freshfield—[J]. W. Axon—Johnson L[ongden] & Co—Robn. G. Worked on Homer—Tasso with W. & A. Anacreon with Stephy. Read Macaulay —Payne Knight Prolegom.[5]

3. Th.

Ch. 8½ A.M. Wrote to Rev. A. Harper[6]—Rev. P. Freeman. Arranging letters & papers—Worked on Homer—Anacreon with S. Gave Willy my Nizolius[7] & such promptings as I could to more Latin writing. Read Wachsmuth—Cramer—Macaulay—Dinner party today.

4. Fr.

Ch. 8½ A.M. Wrote to Mr G. Burnett—Ld Ward—Mr W. Hampton—Robn. G.—Ld Aberdeen—Scotts—Sir J. Graham—Cleaver—Sir C. Trevelyan— Johnson L. & Co. Anacreon with Stephen. Latin prose writing with W. Worked on Books & papers. Read Macaulay—Montalembert on England.[8]

5. Sat.

Ch. 8½ A.M. Anacreon with Stephen. The children acted 'When shall I dine'; W.A. & Lena with most promise. Worked on Homer—& Tasso. Read Macaulay (finished Vol 4)—Tasso—Donaldson's Cratylus.[9]

6. Epiphany.

Church 11 AM. (and H.C.)—6½ P.M. Dearest C.s birthday: may it be ever blessed. Wrote to Miss Stanley: a bewildering case. She is already in feeling

[1] Stationer off Piccadilly.
[2] William Wynne Ffoulkes, 1821–83, of the Denbighshire family; barrister and judge on Birkenhead circuit.
[3] Perhaps H. McGlashan, London papermaker.   [4] The coachman's son.
[5] See 15 Dec. 1855.   [6] A nonconformist.
[7] Italian renaissance humanist and philosopher.
[8] C. F. R. de Montalembert, *The political future of England* (1856), intr. by J. W. *Croker.
[9] See 14 Aug. 55.

Roman & something more.[1] Read Pusey's Sermon[2]—B. Price's do[3]—Bp Glasgow's Charge[4]—Many other Tracts. Scripture with the children.

7. M.

Ch. 8½ A.M. Wrote to D[uche]ss of Sutherland—S. Herbert—Mrs Smith—J. Watson. Agnes's measles out: our plans are broken up. Anacreon with Stephy. Worked on Homer. Attended the tenants' dinner & spoke on the War. They were not a hostile audience. Read Monk's Bentley—Finished Montalembert.

8. T.

Ch. 8½ A.M. Wrote to W. Grogan—Stephen R.G. left us. Worked much on Homer. Read Wachsmuth—Monk's Bentley—Tooke on the Bank Charter Act.[5]

9. Wed.

Ch. 8½ A.M. Wrote to J. M'Culloch—W. Brown—J. Griffiths—Ld Ward— Rev. J. Anderson—Sir T.G. Worked on Homer. Anacreon with Stephy. Read Tooke on Bank Charter—Monk's Life of Bentley—Wachsmuth— Strabo.[6]

10. Th.

Ch. 8½ A.M. Wrote to A. Hayward—Robn. G.—Sir J. Graham—Messrs. Parker. Worked on Homer. Anacreon with Stephy. Latin prose with Willy. Journey arrangements. Read Tooke (finished)—Monk's Bentley.

11. Fr.

Ch. 8½ A.M. Wrote to J.G. Hubbard—S. Herbert—Rev Mr Verschoyle[7]— Rev Mr Barnes.[8] Saw Mr Burnett. Worked on accounts & Worked on Homer—Anacreon with Stephy. Read Hesiod—Monk's Bentley—Barnes's Letters—P. Knight's Prolegom.

12. Sat.

Ch. 8½ A.M. The 4 younger were dispatched to London. Wrote to S.H. Blackwell—Ld Ward—Warden Trin Coll—Miss Stanley. Saw J. Griffiths— Worked on arranging my books. Greek lesson with Stephy. Latin prose

---

[1] She became a Roman catholic later this year; see 25 Nov. 54.
[2] E. B. *Pusey, 'All faith the gift of God. Real faith entire. Two sermons' (1855).
[3] B. *Price, 'The presence of God in the creation' (1855).
[4] By W. J. Trower (1855).
[5] T. *Tooke, *On the Bank Charter Act of 1844, its principles and operation; with suggestions for an improved administration of the Bank of England* (1856).
[6] Strabo of Amasya, floruit 40 B.C., Greek geographer and historian.
[7] Hamilton Verschoyle, chancellor of Christ Church, Dublin.
[8] Richard William Barnes, 1811?–85; vicar of Probus, Cornwall, from 1849, had sent his 'Public opinion considered in letters between one of his friends and R. W. Barnes' (1855).

with Willy. Calls on Farmers. Read Hesiod—Monk's Bentley—Cobden on the War.[1]

13. 1 S. Epiph.

Ch. 11 AM., & 3 P.M. (St John's). Rectory in evg. Stephy said he wd like to be a Clergyman if he cd. see how to manage the Sermons. Arranging some books. Read Parker's Correspondence[2]—Toogood's Dissent Justified[3]—Consecr. of Cemeteries[4]—Theol. Germanica (finished) a noble book—Xt Remembrr.[5]

14. M.

Ch. 8½ A.M. Wrote to Duchess of Sutherland—G. & Co.—G. Crawshay[6]—Rn. G. Finished work on my books, wh (here about 6000) are now I hope in tolerable order. Read Hesiod ἔργα[7]—Monk's Bentley—Cobden on the War.

15. T.

Ch 8½ A.M. The boys went. Wrote to Earl of Elgin—Robn. G—Rev E. Coleridge—A. Panizzi. Saw Mr Austin—Mr G. Burnett—Mr [W.] Smith (Cop [House Farm])—Mr Swindley.[8] Read Hill on Currency[9]—Wachsmuth on Greeks[10]—Monk's Bentley—Swann on Bread Question.[11]

16. Wed.

Ch. 8½ A.M. Wrote to Sec. Nightingale Fund[12]—A. Hayward—Rowland Hill—Robn. G.—J. Griffiths—J. Hamilton. Read Strabo—Monk's Bentley—Hill on Currency—Bp of Exeters Letter to Dr Lushington.[13] Worked on my Library.

17. Th.

Ch. 8½ A.M. Wrote to Earl of Aberdeen—A. Panizzi—Jas Watson—F. Cortazzi.[14] Saw Sheen.[15] Worked on accounts. Read Cortazzi on Currency—

[1] R. *Cobden, *What next and next?* (1856).
[2] *Correspondence of Matthew *Parker*, ed. J. Bruce and T.T. Perowne (1853).
[3] M. Towgood, *A Dissent from the Church of England fully justified* (1753).
[4] Probably 'Consecration versus Desecration. An appeal to the Bishop of London against the bill for the destruction of City Churches and the sale of burial grounds' (1854).
[5] *Christian Remembrancer*, xxxi. 1 (January 1856).
[6] George Crawshay, Gateshead ironmaster; financed *Urquhart's *The Free Press* (1855); some correspondence on politics in Hawn P.
[7] Hesiod's *Works*, probably in T. Gaisford's ed. (1814).   [8] Probably a villager.
[9] E. *Hill, 'Principles of currency. Means of ensuring uniformity of value and adequacy of supply' (1856).
[10] See 21 Dec. 55.
[11] E. G. Swann, 'The Bread Question; or, when the shoe pinches' (1855).
[12] Sidney *Herbert was joint secretary with S. C. Hall of the fund started in November 1855 to raise money for schools of nurses.
[13] H. *Phillpotts, 'A letter to . . . *Lushington, on his judgement in the case of *Westerton v. Liddell*' (1856).
[14] Frederick Cortazzi, writer on economic topics, had sent untraced pamphlet or MS.
[15] One of the Hawarden Shone family; locally the names are interchangable.

Monk's Bentley (finished this remarkable book)—Wachsmuth Histor. Antiq.—Goethe's Faust—Worked on Homer.

18. Fr.

Ch. 8½ A.M. Wrote to Mr Leslie—Mr Burnett—Mr Lawrence—Messrs. Williams & Co—Ld Ward—Duke of Argyll—R. Barker—Miss Stanley— Robn G.—Johnson L[ongden] & Co—G. & Co—J.N.G. Saw Mr Burnett: a long sederunt on S.s matters & my own. Worked on Library. Packing: & arrangements for departure. Read Goethe's Faust—&c. Worked on Homer.

19. Sat. [London]

Ch. 8½ A.M. Visits, paying bills, & other arrangements in mg: saw Mac-Culloch. Off at 11 to London. Arrived all well about 8 in a scene of utter chaos. Read Berington Hist. Mid. Ages.[1] Went to work at 9 PM on my books & worked till 2 AM.

20. Septa. S.

St James's mg (& H.C.)—Chapel Royal aftn. Saw Ld Aberdeen—Mr Bonham. Read MS on Jer. 12. aloud at night. Lena sharply ill with liver &c: the rest seem to have much improved upon change of air. Read Freeman on Divine Service[2]—Statutes of Guild of St Alban[3]—Chr. Rem. on Dulwich College.[4]

21. M.

Wrote to J. Griffiths—J. Leslie—Rev Mr Keble—Jones & Yarrell. Saw Mr Cook—Johnson L[ongden] & Co.—Mr Panizzi (at Museum)—Messrs. Johnson L. & Co—Leslie, & Quaritch—book buying. Up early & had a hardish day on books papers &c. Read Reade's poems.[5]

22. T.

Wrote to S. Herbert—Ld Ward (& copy)[6]—Jas Watson. Another day on books & papers. Saw Lord Ward—R. Phillimore—A. Hayward. Evening on Oak Farm Work. Read Hutton's Modern Warfare.[7]

23. Wed.

Wrote to A. Gibbon—J. Farrow[8]—T. Towsey[9]—A. Johnson—Dr Hessey—

---

[1] J. *Berington, A literary history of the Middle Ages (1814).
[2] P. *Freeman, The principles of divine service (1855).
[3] The Constitution of the Guild of St. Alban (1854).
[4] Christian Remembrancer, xxxi. 84 (January 1856).
[5] J. E. *Reade, Poetical works, 2v. (1852).
[6] Add MS 44385: very long, on Oak Farm.
[7] H. D. Hutton, Modern warfare: its positive theory and true policy (1855).
[8] Perhaps the tailor in Upper Seymour Street.
[9] Perhaps of W. Towsey & Co., London florists.

J. Newman[1]—W. Rogers[2]—H. Snell.[3] Saw J. Griffiths—Lord Hardinge—
Lord Stanhope. Another day upon pictures, books & papers, working &
superintending. Read Maitland on the Income Tax.[4]

24. Th.

Wrote to Lady Molesworth[5]—Leightons—Jas Watson—Ld A. Hervey—
Johnson L. & Co—F.R. Bonham. Saw S. Herbert—Mr Keble (to whom I
spoke fully on Parlty. Churchmatters: how few are like him!) Dined with
the Jameses—More housework: but we now see progress. Read Letter to
Ld J. Russell[6]—Blackwood on War, Westmr. on Do, Br. Quarterly on Do.,
all alike, & all mad[7]—Reid on Bank.[8]

25. Fr. Conv. St. Paul.

Wrote to J. Griffiths—W.M. Wilkinson[9]—C. Morgan—E.B. Carter[10]—T.
Falconer[11]—Mr Towsey—Rev Mr Canney[12]—R. Hill—W. Bennion[13]—S.
Herbert—R. Phillimore—Ld Granville. Saw Chancellor of the Exchr.—A.
Hayward—Sir A. Gordon. Read Quarterly on the War[14]—Unter Dem
Doppel Adler[15]—Civil Service Admission Papers[16]—Montalembert on
England (finished).[17] The house improves upon us, & the appearance mends.

26. Sat.

Wrote to Mr H. Lees—D. of Newcastle—W.C. James—Robn. G. Read
Doppel Adler—Germ. Nation.[18] Saw Mr Morley and Civil Service Admn
Deputation [19]—Mr Grogan. Worked on books—Dined with the Wortleys.

---

[1] If J. H.*, no other record of the letter found.
[2] William 'hang theology' *Rogers, 1819–96; curate in the Charterhouse and educationalist, founded secular middle-class schools; see 8 May 56.
[3] Of the house-agents' firm; see 25 Feb. 49.
[4] See 8 Dec. 52 and 15 Feb. 53.
[5] Andalusia Grant, née Carstairs, m. 1844 Sir W. *Molesworth and d. 1888.
[6] Probably 'Strike, but hear . . . being a second letter to . . . *Russell . . . by the
author of "Russian, Turkey, or a Greek Empire"' (1856).
[7] Westminster Review, ix. 91, Blackwood's, lxxix. 20, British Quarterly, xxiii. 219 (all
January 1856).
[8] W. Reid, The life and adventures of the Old Lady of Threadneedle Street (1832).
[9] Probably William Arthur Wilkinson, 1795–1865; liberal M.P. Lambeth 1852–7;
railway director.
[10] Probably E. J. Carter, see 9 Mar. 62.
[11] Probably Thomas Falkner, 1828–1910; curate of W. Lavington 1853–6, of Hawton
1856–7; later in Yorkshire.
[12] A. S. Canney, licenciate; curate of All Saints, St. Pancras.
[13] Grocer and corn factor at Queen's Ferry, near Hawarden.
[14] Quarterly Review, xcviii. 249 (December 1855).
[15] F. Pflug, Unter dem doppeladler (1855).
[16] Order in council introducing modified form of the Northcote–Trevelyan report: PP
1855 xli. 1.
[17] See 4 Jan. 56.
[18] G. Diezel, The formation of a national party in Germany, a necessity of the present crisis
in Europe, (1855).
[19] The deputation coincided with a large meeting of the Administrative Reform
Association, chaired by S. *Morley; The Times, 28 January 1856, 5a.

27. Sexa[gesima] S.

St James's mg—St Peter's Mile End[1] evg—dinner with Dr Hessey before, & tea with Mr Rowsell after: I am alike pleased with both in their several capacities. Read Bunsen's Briefe[2]—Xtn Remembr. on Dulwich—Freeman's Principles.[3] Wrote to Miss Stanley.[4] Saw Bertram[R].

28. M.

Wrote to Sir J. Graham—Sir T.G.—Ld Ward—Watson & Smith[5]—Saw Earl of Aberdeen—Mr J. Griffiths (O[ak]F[arm])—Mr Ellice. Saw Tilburn [R]—Dined with Hayward. Read U[nter] dem Doppeladler.

29. T.

Wrote to Mr W. Potter[6]—J.N.G.—Mr C. Attwood[7]—T.S. Gladstone—Bp of Oxford. Worked on books &c: the rooms are now in decent order. Read U.dem Doppeladler. Eight to dinner: our first effort. Saw R. Phillimore— Ld Aberdeen—Rev. Wm. Selwyn. Out book buying at Westall's[8] &c. Saw Tilburn[R].

30. Wed.

Wrote to Mr G. Grant—Bp of Glasgow—Robn. G—Rev. E. Elton[9]—Rev G. Trevor—Rev. Mr Mayhew[10]—Mr Farrow—Rev Mr Westmacott[11]—Mr Reid—C.A. Wood—Sir G. Prevost—Rev J Wilkinson—Mr Leslie—A. Hayward—Sir W. Heathcote—Sir J.B. East[12]—Borthwick & Co[13]—Miss Stanley—Mast. Pembroke—Mr Dyce—Johnson L. & Co. Saw Rev Mr Lake —Bar. Rothschild—Ct Vitzthum[14]—Dr Sandwith[15]—Gen. La Marmora[16]— Finished Diezel on German National party—Read U.dem Doppel Adler— Twiss on Law Studies.[17] Ly Granville's in evening.

[1] Built in Cephas Road, Mile End, 1838; T. J. Rowsell was its incumbent.
[2] C. C. J. von Bunsen, *Die Zeichen der Zeit. Briefe an Freunde*, 2 v. (1855).
[3] See 20 Jan. 56.   [4] In Lathbury, ii. 29.
[5] James Watson's stockbroking firm in Glasgow, which handled most of Gladstone's railway shares.
[6] Unidentified.
[7] C. M. Attwood of Darlington had written about Russia (Hawn P).
[8] Off Tottenham Court Road.
[9] Edward Elton, 1817?–*ca*. 1900; perpetual curate of Wheatley, Oxfordshire, 1849–84.
[10] Thomas Rabett Mayhew, b. 1817; vicar of Darsham, Suffolk, 1851–66; rector of Warehorne from 1866.
[11] Horatio Westmacott, d. 1862; Corpus, Cambridge; rector of Chastleton, Oxfordshire, from 1838.
[12] Sir James Buller East, 1789–1878; tory M.P. Winchester 1830–32, 1835–64; 2nd bart. 1847.
[13] Borthwick, Wark & Co., London Stock-brokers.
[14] Count Carl Friedrich Vitzthum von Eckstaedt, Saxon minister in London 1853–66; his *St. Petersburg and London*, 2v. (1887) describes conversations with Gladstone, but not this one.
[15] Humphrey *Sandwith, 1822–81; physician, in near east 1854; captured at Kars 1855 and released; in colonies; Serbian propagandist 1877; see 7 Feb. 56.
[16] Count Alessandro Ferrero de la Marmora, 1799–1856; Piedmontese general, created the bersaglieri and d. in the Crimea.
[17] Sir T. *Twiss, 'A letter to the Vice-Chancellor of the University of Oxford on the law studies of the university' (1856).

31. Th.

Wrote to Watson & Smith—Scotts—G. Burnett—Ld Wodehouse—Dined
at Mrs Talbots. Meeting at Ld Abns 12½–2¼. Saw T.S. Gladstone—S. Herbert—H. of C. 4¼–7½. A very satisfactory evening. I thanked Ld P. privately
for his speech.[1] Read U.dem Doppeladler—Walpole's George II[2]—Saw
Wood[R].

Friday Feb. One. 56.

Wrote to Johnson L. & Co—Rev. G. Trevor—Rector of Exeter—J.
Griffiths—J. Griffiths jun—G. Crawshay—P. Sec. Ld Palmerston.[3] Saw Bp
of Oxford (to breakfast)—Goldwin Smith (Oxf. Comm[issio]n)—Ld Ward—
O[ak] F[arm] & Politics—J.N.G. Resid[uary] Estate &c.—S.R.G. &
H.G. (O.F).—Roundell Palmer—R. Phillimore—Mr Geo. Glyn. Read U.
dem Doppel Adler—Duberley's Journal of the War—a poor affair.[4]

Sat. Feb. 2. Purification.

Twelve to dinner. Wrote to Panizzi—Sir W. James—R.L. Chance—Willy
—W. Potter—Robn. G.—A. Fletcher B.I.R.[5]—W. Davies.[6] Saw Sir H.L.
Bulwer[7]—Ld Sandon—J. Freshfield—Mr Harcourt—Mr Chapman jun[8]—
R. Cavendish—Mr Longden. Lady Palmerston's in evg. Read U. dem
Doppel Adler—Sir J. Macneill's Report.[9]

3. Quinqua[gesima] S.

St James's & H.C. mg—do prayers only evg—MS. on Gospel aloud. Saw
Sir T.G. Wrote to Miss Stanley. Read Hervey on Bolingbroke[10]—Zeichen
der Zeit[11]—R. Williams's Rational Godliness.[12]

4. M.

Wrote to J. Griffiths—F.R. Saye—C. Pressly—Ld Ward—Rev Dr Barry[13] &
[blank]. Dined at Mrs Talbots. Spent the morning on my accounts &

[1] Unwontedly pacific, on the Address: *H* cxl. 75.

[2] H. *Walpole, *Memoirs of the reign of King George the second* (1846).

[3] William Law, treasury official and *Palmerston's private secretary 1855–October
1856.

[4] F. I. Duberly, *Journal kept during the Russian war* (1855).

[5] Angus Fletcher, comptroller and solicitor to Scottish inland revenue board.

[6] Probably John Davies of Lawton, in correspondence on the Parishes Bill (Hawn P).

[7] Sir William Henry Lytton Earle *Bulwer 1801–72; diplomatic posts; negotiated
Bulwer-Clayton treaty 1850; ambassador at Constantinople 1858–65; liberal M.P. sundry
constituencies, Tamworth 1868; cr. Baron Dalling 1871.

[8] David Ward Chapman, 1828–1921, eldest s. of D.B., the banker.

[9] *MacNeill and Tulloch's report on the working of the commissariat in the Crimea
(the treasury had refused them finance for a secretary): *PP* 1856 xx.

[10] J. *Hervey, 'Remarks on Lord *Bolingbroke's letters on the study and use of history'
(1756).

[11] See 27 Jan. 56.

[12] R. *Williams, *Rational godliness after the mind of Christ and the written voices of his
Church* (1855).

[13] Probably Henry Boothby Barry, though never D.D., fellow of Queen's Oxford,
with whom he had been corresponding on education.

relative papers wh require much looking up: & on letters. H of C. 4¾–7.[1]
Saw Graham & Herbert—Lord R. Cecil[2]—Northcote. Read U.dem Doppel
Adler—Gilbart's Banking.[3]

5. *T.*

Wrote to 1st Commr. Works[4]—G.H. Drewe[5]—Rev Geo Trevor. Saw S.H.
Northcote—Sir W. James—S. Laing—Tom & his family—Sir J. Graham—
Duke of Newcastle. Eleven to dinner. Worked on accounts. Read U.dem
Doppel Adler—Macneill's & Tullochs 2d Report &c.[6]

6. *Ash Wedy.*

St James's 11 A.M. and 5½ P.M. Wrote to Miss Stanley—Mr V. King—Bp
of Moray. Saw Sir J. Graham—Sir T. Gladstone—'Edr. S. London News'.[7]
Kept the day. MS on Matt VI aloud at night. Read U.dem Doppel Adler—
Wheat on Phillimore[8]—Martens on Embassies.[9] Gilbart's Hist. of Banking.

7. *Th.*

St James's 8 A.M. Wrote to E. Breakenridge—H.J.G.—J. Griffiths—G.
Burnett—joint l. to ditto & draft—Rev. Sir G. Prevost—J.N.G.—C.
Mathieson.[10] Saw Mr R L Chance (cum SRG)—T.S. Gladstone—with T.G.
H. of C. and H. of Lords 4½–1:[11] but home to tea—& found Clements.[12] The
first part of Lord Lyndhurst's Speech, which he called the dry part was a
wonderful exhibition of keen and clear intellect. Read U.dem Doppeladler—
Sandwith's Siege of Kars[13]—Vansittart on Currency.[14]

8. *Fr.*

St James's 8 A.M. Wrote to Sir C. Trevelyan—Mr J. Whyte—R. Wilbraham
—Robn. G.—W. Wickham (Ballot Society)[15]—Rev H. Venn. Saw T.G.—
Sir J. Graham—Do *cum* Lord Brougham—Dined at Phillimores: a party
of old friends & contemporaries. Read U.dem Doppeladler—Lord Brougham's Characters.[16] In the morning we had a great alarm & sent in all directions. Dixon our nurse gave C. an embrocation containing lead instead of a

---

[1] Shipping dues; *H* cxl. 153.
[2] Lord Robert Arthur Talbot Gascoyne *Cecil, 1830–1903; journalist; tory M.P.
Stamford 1853–68; styled Viscount Cranborne 1865; sec. for India 1866–7, 1874–8, for
foreign affairs 1878–80, 1885, 1886–92, 1895–1900; 3rd marquis of Salisbury 1868; prime
minister 1885, 1886–92, 1895–1902.
[3] J. W. *Gilbart, *The history and principles of banking* (1834).
[4] i.e. Sir B. *Hall (see 14 May 35).
[5] George Henry Drew, 1816?–1906; solicitor; taxing master in Chancery 1870–91.
[6] See 2 Feb. 56.   [7] Not found published.
[8] Not found.   [9] Probably C. von Martens, *Guide diplomatique* (1832).
[10] Charles Frederick Mathieson, merchant in Crutchedfriars.
[11] In the Lords, start of the Wensleydale life peerage deb., in the Commons, naval
administration: *H* cxl. 263.
[12] Probably a charity case.
[13] H. *Sandwith, *A narrative of the siege of Kars* (1856).
[14] N. *Vansittart, *Outlines of a plan of finance*, (1813).
[15] William Wickham, secretary of the Vote by Ballot Society.   [16] See 4 Sept. 43.

draft. Locock came quickly: but we had already been assured that there was nothing dangerous: a signal mercy indeed.

9. Sat.

St James's 8 A.M. Wrote to Mr J. Hamilton—Mr A. Gibbon—Rev G.H. Forbes—Mr J. Severn. Read Wood Campaign in Crimea[1]—U.dem Deppel-adler (finished). Bookbuying—Household affairs discussed. Saw Lord Aberdeen.

10. 1 S. Lent.

St James's mg. Chapel Royal aft. MS. on Eccl. 3. aloud in evg. Saw R. Herbert. Wrote to Miss Stanley (& draft)[2]—Sir W.C. James. Wrote on Character of Judas.[3] Read Bunsen's Zeichen[4]—Sidney's Life of Hill[5]—Freeman on Divine Service.[6]

11. M.

St James's 8 A.M. Wrote to Mr G. Hadfield MP—Rev A. Buller[7]—Mr Wrenfordsley[8]—Rev W. Denton. Book buying: & also did some scissors work on Homer. Read Gilbart on Banking—Head on Defence of Engl.[9]—Blandford's letter to Sir G. Grey.[10] Saw J. Murray—Scotts—Mr G. Spencer[11]—J.N.G.—E. Cardwell—G. Hadfield—Col. Boldero.

12. T.

(Overslept myself). Wrote to Sir J. Graham—R. Barker—Bp of Argyll—W. Deering[12]—J. Griffiths. The Talbots dined. Attended meeting Radcliffe Trust.[13]—Saw Mr Severn (& Mr Gale)[14]—The Speaker—Mr Hallam—S. Herbert—E. Cardwell—Also A. Gordon. H of C. $4\frac{1}{4}$–7, 10–$11\frac{1}{4}$.[15] Read Sandwith's book—Paget on the Talbot case[16]—Head on Defences—Saw Aldis—Madens[R].

13. Wed.

St James's 8 A.M. Wrote to R.L. Chance—Dow[age]r Ly. Wenlock—Mrs

---

[1] N. A. Woods, *The past campaign: the war in the East*, 2v. (1855).
[2] Add MS 44385, f. 77: on her persistent requests for 'answers to questions that have occupied volumes'.
[3] Not found.   [4] See 27 Jan. 56.   [5] See 6 Jan. 50.
[6] See 20 and 27 Jan. 50.   [7] See 30 Sept. 26.
[8] Probably (Sir) Henry Thomas Wrenfordsley, d. 1908; barrister; liberal candidate at Peterborough 1868, 1874; judge in colonies from 1877; kt. 1883.
[9] Sir F. B. *Head, *The defenceless state of Great Britain* (1850).
[10] J. W. S. Churchill, Lord Blandford, 'A letter to . . . *Grey, on some points connected with past and proposed legislation for the Church of England' (1856).
[11] George English Spencer, London barrister.
[12] W. W. Deering, incumbent of Bishopswood, Herefordshire; disappears from *Crockford* 1860.
[13] See 25 May 55.   [14] Richard Gale, picture dealer in High Holborn.
[15] Law Amendment: *H* cxl. 619.
[16] J. *Paget, *Ecclesiastical Courts, A report of the judgement delivered by Dr. Radcliffe, in the case of Talbot* v. *Talbot* (1854).

Key[1]—Rev J.D. Browne—H. of C. 1–2½.[2] Visited Wolf—Madens[R]. Saw J. Griffiths—Mr Jackson—R. Phillimore—Read Sandwith—Talbot v. Talbot—Head on Defences—Bowles on the Navy.[3]

14. Th.

Ch 8 A.M. Wrote to Rev E. Hawkins—Sir J. Young—R. Wilbraham—Sir W. James—Col. Short—Mr J. Daniell[4]—Saw Lord Overstone—Archdeacon Thorp—V. Chancellor's Messenger—Ld Blandford. Read Thelyphthora— Letters on Do[5]—Clayton-Bulwer Correspondence[6]—Annuaire Rev. des Deux M.[7]—Sandwith's Kars—Phillips on the Bank Charter[8]—H. of C. 10– 11½. Came away advisedly.[9] Worked on papers arr.

15. Fr.

St James's 8 A.M. Wrote to Jas Watson & Smith—J.N.G.—Mrs Wallis[10]— W. Dyce—Miss Stanley—Mr Hansard—H. of C. 4½–6¾ and 10–11½.[11] Saw M.F. Tupper—Scotts—Mr Severn—J. Walker—Sir W.C. James—S. Herbert—Duchess of Suthd.—Sir J. Graham—R. Phillimore. Read Educational Crisis[12]—Sandwith's Kars—P. Urquhart on Nat. Debt.[13]

16. Sat.

St James's 8 A.M. Wrote to Sir J. Bowring—Rev Mr Keith[14]—Mr Stanistreet—Rev Mr Davis—F.H. Dickinson—R. Hanby. Saw Lord Aberdeen— A. Gordon—Mrs Larkins.[15] Read Sandwith's Kars—Cole's Russia[16]— Thompson's Army of G. Britain.[17] Dined with the Granville Vernons.

Memorandum of Finance[18]
Secret

1. To abolish the Exchequer, at the same time strengthening and accelerating Audit?

[1] Not identified.   [2] Spoke on Parishes Bill: *H* cxl. 689.
[3] W. Bowles, *Pamphlets on naval subjects* (1854).
[4] John Jeremiah Daniell, 1818–98; many curacies 1848–77; rector of Langley Burrell from 1879; antiquary.
[5] M. Madan, *Thelyphthora; or a treatise on female ruin, its causes, effects, consequences, prevention and remedy* (1780); *Letters on Thelyphthora* (1792).
[6] See next day n.
[7] Probably Rémusat on *Fox, *Revue des Deux Mondes*, 2nd series i. 103 (January 1856).
[8] E. Phillips, 'Bank of England charter, currency, limited liability companies, and free trade' (1856).
[9] Attacks on Pennefather, an allegedly blind Irish judge: *H* cxl. 760.
[10] Unidentified.
[11] Relations with U.S.A.; spoke on Carlisle canonries: *H* cxl. 837, 897.
[12] [E. R. Humphreys] 'England's educational crisis: a letter to . . . *Palmerston' (1856).
[13] Essay 5 of W. P. Urquhart, *Essays on subjects in political economy* (1850).
[14] William Alexander Keith, d. 1888; curacies 1855–68; vicar of Burham, Kent, from 1868.
[15] Mother of W. F. Larkins (Hawn P).   [16] J. W. Cole, *Russia and the Russians* (1854).
[17] H. B. Thomson, *Military forces and institutions of Great Britain* (1855).
[18] This mem., unnoticed by Morley, outlines almost all the major policy, accounting and institutional reforms attempted by Gladstone as chancellor 1859–66, except the French treaty as such (though see n. 11); this is a unique example of mid-Victorian political planning, see above, introduction, vol. v. xxvi, xxix.

2. To bring the Chancery & all other accounts for which the public are virtually liable under the controul of the Finance Department?

3. To apply to the miscellaneous Estimates the same rules of voting & revoting as have already been applied to the Military Estimates?

4. To define the position of the Bank as the Agent of the State with respect to Dividends & management of the Debt?

5. To make further provision for true periodical statements of the Debt of the country on Saving Bank & other like accounts and for the liquidation of the same in case of need?

6. To regulate & limit the powers of the Minister of Finance in regard to the use of Deficiency Bills & Cons. Fund Bills & the monies of the Comm[issione]rs for the redemption of the National Debt?

7. To make further provision for efficient departmental aid & counsel to the Minister of Finance & for the compilation & continuance of proper Financial Records?

8. To investigate the question what nearer relation shd. be established between the British Govt. & the management of Indian Finance?

9. To provide for the extension of the existing ($3\frac{1}{2}$ and?) $2\frac{1}{2}$ per cent Stocks?

10. For the abolition of the Paper Duty?

11. For the reduction of the Wine Duty?

12. For the reduction of the Malt Sugar & Coffee Duties?[1]

13. For the reduction & equalisation of duties of Insurance & other Stamp Duties?

14. For the increase of Income Tax 1857–60 but with descent and extinction in the latter year?

15. For the extension & increase of the House Duty upon the determination of the Income Tax?

16. To make further provision for the absorption of the Private Note Circulation?

17. To authorise at certain rates of interest the issue of Notes upon the deposit of Govt. Securities in lieu of the deposit of Bullion?

18. To pay off the Bank Debt by an issue of Notes & to put an end to the Privileges of the Bank in regard to issue, retaining its agency & machinery for a public issue?

19. To authorise issue of Notes for the public account to a certain limit beyond the present one without deposit?

20. To investigate the practicability & economy of resuming the issue of notes below £5 convertible into gold at the Bank & its branches, & to be legal tender in payment of taxes?[2]

21. To approximate to an equalisation of the issues at the different periods of the year as far as may be by relieving the ends/beginnings of each quarter.[3]

Sir J. Graham's Notes.[4] 1. Yes. reorganise Audit. 2. Yes. Expect Chancery opposition. 3. Important—should not be delayed. 4. Yes. But Bank will resist rallying the money Interest to its aid. 5. Yes, think *Legislation* may be needless, administrative authority sufficient. 6. 'I doubt the policy of stringent legislative

---

[1] 'i.e. from the War Standard. This is done *1856*' added in margin.

[2] Initialled and dated 16 February 1856; Add MS 44746, f. 1; marginal note states '(20) probably supersedes (19)'.

[3] This para. added later.

[4] Gladstone sent *Graham his mem. on 4 December 1856 and transcribed Graham's subsequent comments in the margin; see 15 Dec. 56 and Bodley MS Film 127.

prohibitions. Unforeseen circs. may render the prompt exercise of these powers necessary: but when exercised early publicity with its attendant responsibilities shd. be enforced by law[']. 7. Is against Bureaucratic. Wishes the C. of E. to have the aid of 'efficient subordinates'. 8. 'Indian receipt & expenditure virtually British in the last resort & should be so regarded & controuled['.] 9. If without serious shock to credit 3% cd. be converted into $2\frac{1}{2}$,the advantage wd. be very important: especially as the present tendency of money is to increase in quantity & to decrease in value. 10. Desirable. 11. If reduction small, the effect will be insignificant: if large, malt & Spirits revenue will be affected. Wine will be for this generation the luxury of the rich: does not feel the necessity urgent. 13. Cries aloud for immediate cons[ideratio]n. 14. 'To insure a pacific policy & an economical Expenditure, the early cessation of the Income Tax is the best security & the most powerful lever for operating on the public mind in this direction. If we are not involved in a fresh war this will be the grand subject for debate in the approaching Session'. 15. 'If the Inc. Tax be remitted a duty on H[ouses] to a larger extent is a fair substitute. Graduation in an I.T. is the incline wh. hurries to spoliation. Graduation in an H.T. is self imposed acc. to the means of the occupant & a tax on the dwelling acc. to valuation within moderate limits is the fairest & best mode of getting at 'the means & substance' of each head of a family['.] '16–19 bear on the double question of Banking & of Currency. I am disposed to think that the time has arrived when a new settlement with the B. of E. is necessary & the whole of these questions must be duly consd. & determined. A *strong* Govt. would legislate without a Commn. of Inquiry: a weak one will seek for time.'

17. S. Lent.

St James's mg & Holy Commn.—[St. Andrews] Wells St aftn—MS of 44 aloud at night. Saw Lady Lyttelton—R. Cavendish. Read Sidney's Sir R. Hill—Denison's Saravia[1]—Caird's Sermon[2]—W. Wilks's Irving.[3]

18. M.

St Martin's 8 A.M. Wrote to Ld Derby (& copy)—Mr Toogood—Hon C. Neville[4]—R. Barker—Rev Mr Cowan—Ld Ward—Robn. G. Read Gondon's Letters[5]—Lucan & Cardigan Letters.[6] Saw Mayor of Lpool & Deputn.[7] —Mr T.C. Hansard—Mr Goldwin Smith—Chancr. of Exchr.—R. Phillimore—Ld Blandford—Ld Goderich—Sir J. Graham—A. Kinnaird. Dined with the Granvilles.

19. T.

St James's 8 A.M. Wrote to Dr Kynaston—M.F. Tupper—Mr R[euben] Browning—C. Frost—Rev. J.R. Tweed—Judge Coleridge. Saw Ld Derby

---

[1] *Saravia on the Holy Eucharist*, tr. G. A. *Denison (1855).
[2] J. *Caird, 'Religion in common life, a sermon on Rom. xii. 11' (1855).
[3] W. Wilks, *Edward *Irving: an ecclesiastical and literary biography* (1854).
[4] Charles Cornwallis Neville, 1823–1902; 5th Baron Braybrooke 1861.
[5] J. Gondon, *De l'état des choses à Naples et en Italie; lettres à Georges Bowyer esq.* (1855).
[6] Probably those in *PP* 1856 xx.
[7] On Liverpool aspects of the Local Dues on Shipping Bill; correspondence on the Bill and the deputation with his br. Robertson in Hawn P.

with Sir W. H[eathcote])—Sir W. Heathcote—Gr[anville] Vernon—Mr Walpole—Scotts—J.N.G.—Mrs Hagart. Five to dinner. Finished Sandwith's
Kars—Read Lorient's Memoir[1]—Gondon's Letters to Bowyer.

20. Wed.

St James's 8 AM. Wrote to G. Burnett—W.H.G.—J. Griffiths—H. of C.
12½–1½[2] Attended the Levee. Saw Sir Wm. Heathcote—M.F. Tupper—Mr
Walpole—Solr. General—J.N.G.—Prov. of Eton—Mr Liddell MP.[3]
Worked on outlines of Bills. Bookbuying &c. Read Lorient on Oxford
(finished)—Potter on Glossop[4]—Gondon's Letters—Thorp on the Lord's
Day.[5]

   1. To complete the construction of a real department of Finance.
   2. To determine and define the position of the Bank as the Agent of the State in
regard to public account Loans & dividends.
   3. To determine the rules of Issue.
   4. To readjust Taxation—especially with reference to the juncture of 1860.
   3. To bring all really public accounts under the controul of the Treasury.
   6. To make further provision for the custody & management of monies in the
hands of the public: & for the security of depositors in Savings Banks & the like.
   Permanent advisers.   1. Master of the Mint. 2. Comptroller of the N.D. Office.
3. First Clerk (hereafter Sec. or A[ssistant] Sec.) Revenue Room.[6]

21. Th.

St James's 8 AM. Wrote to Messrs. Tatham—Ld Ward—Mr Hooper—
Mr F. Sims—Rev Mr Cox. Saw Hull Deputation—Bp of Salisbury—J.N.G.
Ld Blandford's Commee. 3½.[7] H. of C. 3¾–6¾ and 9½–11.[8] Read Cole on
Russia—Gondon's Letters (finished)—Brougham on Republic.[9]

22. Fr.

St James's 8 AM. Wrote to Bp of Ripon—C.A. Wood—Dean [John] Torry
—Rev Mr Shortland. Read Brougham on Republic—Davies on Lancashire
History.[10] Worked on arranging books & room. H. of C. 4½–9½: & H. of L.
Spoke on the Loan: heard Ld Lyndhurst from the steps of the Throne—
imperfectly.[11] Worked on Draft of Cathedral Schemes Bill.[12]

[1] P. Lorain, *Mémoir sur l'Université d'Oxford* (1850).   [2] Misc. business: *H* cxl. 979.
[3] Henry George Liddell, 1821–1903; tory M.P. S. Northumberland 1852–78; styled
Lord Eslington 1874; 2nd earl of Ravensworth 1878.
[4] E. Potter, *A picture of a manufacturing district* (1856).
[5] W. Thorpe, *An argument in behalf of the Christian Sabbath, or Lord's day* (1856).
[6] Undated; probably the list referred to this day, resulting from the mem. of 16
February; Add MS 44746, f. 4.
[7] Select cttee. chaired by Lord Blandford on Division of Parishes Bill on which Gladstone sat: *PP* 1856 iii. 427 and vii. 293.
[8] Museum Sunday opening: *H* cxl. 1053.
[9] *Brougham discussed republics in 'Aristocratic governments', in his *Political
philosophy*, ii (1843).
[10] Not found.
[11] *Lyndhurst on the Wensleydale peerage; Gladstone on *Lewis's budget: *H* cxl. 1153,
1246.
[12] See 17 Mar. 56n.

23. Sat.

St James 8 AM. Wrote to Bp of Salisbury.—J. Wilson—Dr Pusey. Dined with the Speaker. At Ly. Palmerstons afterwards. Worked on books: shopping with C. Saw Mr Sturge—Ld Grey—Sig. Consolo jun.[1]—Speaker— Mr Grogan—E. Cardwell—Bp of Salisbury—Sir W. Heathcote. Read Head on Defences—Hugh Miller on his Schools &c.[2]

24. 3 S. Lent and St Matthias.

St James 8 AM(HC) and 11—Quebec Chapel[3] 3 P.M.—Walk with Mrs G. Malcolm—Saw Ld Aberdeen—MS of/41 aloud. Wrote on Thy will be done.[4] Read Paix de l'Ame[5]—Life of Sir R. Hill—Wilks's Irving.

25. M.

St Martin's 8 A.M. Wrote to L.H. Evelyn—J.H. Simpson[6]—Mr Wilkinson MP.—Rev J. Hildyard—Robn. G. Div. Parishes Commee.[7] 1¼–4 H. of C. 4½–7½ and 11¼–12.[8] Saw R. Phillimore—Rev. E. Hawkins—J.N.G.—F.R. Bonham. We dined at the Palace where I had a conv. with the Prince on peace—& the U.S. Questions—Dean of Windsor on Episcopal Appointments—Ct. Bernstorff,[9] on the peace. I was greatly pleased with Miss Bulteel.[10] Read Head on Defence.

26. T.

Wrote to Sir J. Graham—Mrs Wallis—J. Needham[11]—Tatham & Co—Ld Chandos—Rev. J. Innes[12]—Mr W. Green—Rev A.P. Stanley. Dined at Stafford House: a family party (chiefly) of men 20. Saw Rev G. Nugee— Manchester Deputation[13]—Earl of Aberdeen—S. Herbert—Scotts—J.N.G. —J. Griffith . . . Do cum [S.H.] Blackwell.—D. of Argyll. H of C. 4½–7½.[14] Read Wilk's Irving—Lincoln Coll. Statutes. (awake late).

27. Wed.

Wrote to Mr Pressly—Professor Cole[15]—S.R.G.—F.W. Mackenzie[16]—T.G.

---

[1] Son of B.; see 10 May 54.
[2] H. Miller, 'My schools and schoolmasters, or, the story of my education' (1854).
[3] In Quebec Street.   [4] Not found.
[5] Jean de Bonilla, *Traité de la paix de l'âme* (1675), originally published as *Sentiero del Paradiso* (1660); see M. Olphe Galliard, ed., J.-P. de Caussade, *Lettres Spirituelles*, (1964) ii. 12n.
[6] James Harvey Simpson, 1825–1915; curate of Bexhill 1852, rector there 1857–1905; worked for S.P.G.
[7] See 21 Feb. 56n.
[8] Local Dues on Shipping Bill: *H* cxl. 1314; see 18 Feb. 56 and n.
[9] Albrecht Graf von Bernstorff, 1809–73; Prussian minister in London 1854–61, 1862–7, after which he represented the confederation and empire.
[10] Mary Bulteel, one of *Victoria's maids of honour.
[11] Joseph Needham, London barrister.
[12] John Clarke Innes, studied in Scotland and Germany; priest 1850; curate of Holy Trinity, Lambeth.
[13] On the Shipping Dues Bill.   [14] Shipping Bill: *H* cxl. 1412.
[15] i.e. (Sir) Henry *Cole.
[16] Frederick William MacKenzie, 1816?–65; London physician and accoucheur.

(2)—T. Mainwaring[1]—Rev Mr Davis—Rev Mr Barton[2]—Bp of Exeter—
Scotts. Sir R. Murchison's & Ly Wodehouse's Evg. Saw Coalwhippers Depn.
—Hon Col. Gordon—Bp of Salisbury—Bp of Exeter—Earl of Aberdeen.
Worked on Cathedrals Plan. Read Wilks's Irving.

28. Th.

St James's 8 AM. Wrote to J. Griffiths. Saw S. Herbert—Ld Mulgrave[3]—
J. Wortley—Mr Geo Glyn—S.H. Northcote—Mr Lowe—R. Phillimore—
Parishes Commee. & House 2–10$\frac{1}{4}$.[4] Read Colportage[5]—Parl. Debates.
Sadly perplexed about the pending motions.

29. Fr.

St James 8 A.M. Saw Mr Safe—Earl of Aberdeen—S. Herbert. Finished
draft of Chapters Bill. Read Quelques mots sur les Communions Occiden-
tales[6]—H of C. 4$\frac{1}{4}$–7$\frac{1}{2}$ and 8–11$\frac{1}{2}$. Spoke on Roebuck's motion.[7]

Sat. March One 1856.

Wrote to Earl Stanhope—Saw J.N.G.—E. Cardwell—S. Herbert—H.
Labouchere—A. Panizzi—D. of Newcastle—Ly. Malcolm—Dean Milman—
Earl of Elgin. Dined with the Laboucheres[8]—Mad. Van de Weyer's aft.
Worked on Ch Rate Bill. Read St Arnaud's Letters[9]—Quelque Mots
finished—Rogers Table Talk.[10]

2. 4 S. Lent.

St James & H.C. mg.—Ch. Royal aft. MS of 44 aloud at night. Wrote to
Bp of Oxford—Madens[R]—Mrs Aldis.[11] Saw Chr. of Exchr. Read Wilks's
Irving (finished)—Paix de l'Âme—Sidney's Life of Rich. Hill.[12]

3. M.

St James's 8 A.M. Wrote to Rector of Exeter—Sir G. Grey—Mr Goldwin
Smith—Lord Grey—Vice Ch. Oxford—Mr Santon[13]—Syed Abdoollah—

---

[1] Townshend Mainwaring, d. 1883; tory M.P. Denbigh 1841–7, 1857–68.

[2] Probably Henry Jonas Barton, d. 1872; rector of Wicken, Buckinghamshire, from 1838.

[3] Sir George Augustus Constantine *Phipps, 1819–90; styled Lord Mulgrave; liberal M.P. Scarborough 1847–57; governed colonies 1858–84; 2nd marquis of Normanby 1863; unionist 1886.

[4] Talbot v. Talbot: *H* cxl. 1544.

[5] C. Nisard, *Histoire des livres populaires ou de la littérature du colportage*, 2v. (1854).

[6] A. S. Khomyakov (pseud. Ignotus), *Quelques mots sur les communions Occidentales . . . par un Chrétien Orthodoxe* (1855).

[7] On the war commissioners' report: *H* cxl. 1649.

[8] Mary Matilda Georgiana, da. of 6th earl of Carlisle m. as his 2nd wife 1852 H. *Labouchere, and d. 1892; see 11 Feb. 36n.

[9] *Lettres du Maréchal de Saint-Arnaud*, ed. L. A. Leroy de Saint-Arnaud (1855).

[10] *Recollections of the table talk of Samuel *Rogers*, ed. A. Dyce (1856).

[11] Possibly a charitable worker.   [12] E. Sidney, *The life of Sir R. Hill* (1839).

[13] Probably P. Santon of Cork Street, London; business untraced.

Saw Mr G. Smith—Sir G. Grey—Chancr. of Exchr.—Sir J. Graham—R. Phillimore—S. Herbert—Sir W. Heathcote—S.H. Walpole. Parishes Comm. 1–4. H of C. $4\frac{1}{2}$–$7\frac{3}{4}$ and 9–$11\frac{3}{4}$[1] Read St Arnaud's letters—Oxford(Coll) Statutes.[2]

4. T. X.

St James 8 AM. Wrote to Rector of Exeter—A. White—Rector of Lincoln —Mr Roberts—Pres[iden]t of Corpus[3]—Sir W. James—Dr [James] Booth —G. Burnett—Sir E. Wilmot—Copied L. for Sir G. Grey. Saw Sir E. Kerrison—Mr Goldwin Smith (Oxf. affairs. & Homer)—Sol. General—Sir W. Heathcote cum Mr Walpole & Mr Henley—Chancr. of Exchr. Saw two [R]. Read St Arnaud's Letters—Close on Education.[4] Awake very late.

5. Wed.

Wrote to Mr Knott—Rect. of Exeter—Rev J.L. Ross—Rect. of Lincoln —President of C.C.C. 11–$12\frac{1}{2}$ at Ld Derby's with Heathcote & Walpole, Henley, Sir J. Pakington; on Oxf. Statutes.[5] Saw Sir W. Heathcote—Mr H. Hope (executed Deed)[6]—Sir G. Grey—Sir J. Graham—Mr Ince of Exeter.[7] H. of C. $12\frac{3}{4}$–6.[8] Dined with Dow[age]r Lady Wharncliffe. Admiralty afterwards. Saw one(hest)[R]. Read Arnaud's Letters.

6. Th.

St James's 8 A.M. Wrote to Rev Mr Church and Stephy—& Mr G.E. Cole. Commee. 2–4. H of C. $5\frac{1}{4}$–8: and 11–$1\frac{1}{2}$. Spoke on Heywood's motion: wh we disposed of pretty well.[9] Dined with the Woods. Saw Sir W. Heathcote— Mr Goldwin Smith—Do cum Rector of Exeter & others from Oxford—Col. Tulloch[10]—Ld Stanhope—R. Phillimore—Ld Carnarvon. Read Letter on Carlisle Scheme[11]—Roger's Table Talk.

7. Fr.

Wrote to Ld Stanley—Sir S. Scott & Co. Dined at Ld Overstone's. H. of C. $4\frac{1}{2}$–7.[12] Read St Arnaud's Letters. Saw Syed Abdoollah—Rev Dr Trench— Lord Duncan—Sir W. C. James—Sub-rector of Exeter Coll.[13]—S. Herbert—

[1] Army estimates: H clx. 1726.   [2] See 20 Apr. 54.
[3] James Norris, 1796–1872, president of Corpus, Oxford, from 1843.
[4] F. *Close, 'Christian Education. A lecture' (1854).   [5] See next day.
[6] Hugh Hope of Connell & Hope, parliamentary agents; deed of trust for loan to Trinity college, Glenalmond.
[7] William *Ince, 1825–1910; fellow of Exeter, Oxford, 1847; proctor 1856; regius professor of divinity 1878; an evangelical.
[8] Voted against Church Rates Abolition Bill 2°R: H cxl. 1860.
[9] Opposed Heywood's motion to withhold approval of amndts. to sundry college statutes: H cxl. 2032.
[10] (Sir) Alexander Murray *Tulloch, 1803–64; colonel 1854; investigated commissariat in Crimea with *McNeill; K.C.B. 1857; major-general 1859.
[11] Not found; presumably on the current Carlisle Canonries Bill.
[12] Army estimates: H cxl. 2054.
[13] George Herbert Curteis, 1824–94; sub-rector of Exeter, Oxford, 1855–7, principal of Lichfield 1857–80, professor at King's, London, from 1881.

Earl of Aberdeen—Bp of Exeter—S.H. Walpole—Mr Raikes Currie—J.G. Hubbard.

8. Sat.

St James's 8 A.M. Wrote to Messrs. Tatham—Mr Phillott—U. Sec. For. Dept.[1]—Mr Woodgate—Bp of Brechin—Read 'Our Tent'[2]—Hawkin's Letter[3]—Kars papers.[4] Arranging letters. Christie's Sale[5]—Saw Mr Grogan—Ld Overstone. Dined with the Argylls: where we had a melée on Epic and other poets.

9. 5 S. Lent.

St Martins 8½ A.M. (H.C.) St Jamess 11 AM. Chapel Royal 5.30. MS of 42 evg. Wrote to Provost of Oriel. Read Saravia[6]—Sidney's Hill—Hist. Eglise des Freres[7]—Paix de l'Ame.

10. M. (X).

St James's 8 A.M. Wrote to Mr G. Burnett—Mr Bramwell[8]—Rev Mr Cockett[9]—Ld Ward—Robn. G.—Read Kars Papers—St Arnaud. Arranged my letters. Commee. & H of C. 2–7¼.[10] 7 to dinner: Homeric discussion till 11. Saw M. Eugen— . . . forgotten names[11][R].

11. T. (X)

St James 8 A.M. Wrote to Mr W. Brown—Saw C. A. Wood—Earl of Aberdeen—R. Phillimore—Mr Norton. Read Kars papers—Paul Ferrol[12]—Southgate's Turkey.[13] Saw Milligan[R].

12. Wed. (X)

St James 8 AM. Wrote draft of a long letter to Ld Aberdeen—Also wrote to Mr Cooke—B. Quaritch—Mr Green—V.C. Oxford—H. Glynne—Mr T. Woollcombe[14]—Rev F. Wade.[15] Read Southgate—Vansittart on Cur-

---

[1] *Wodehouse.

[2] 'Our tent in the Crimea and wanderings in Sebastopol' (1856).

[3] C. E. *Eardley, *The rights of the laity in the universities, a letter to Lord *Monteagle, and a correspondence with the Rev. Dr. *Hawkins 1854–5* (1856).

[4] Siege of Kars: *PP* 1856 lxi. 459.   [5] See 15 Mar. 56.   [6] See 17 Feb. 1856.

[7] Probably *Brième et fidèle exposition de l'origine, de la doctrine, des constitutions, usages et cérémonies ecclésiastiques de l'Église de l'Unité des Frères* (1758).

[8] George William Wilshere *Bramwell, 1808–92; judge of exchequer and kt. 1856; lord justice 1876–81; cr. baron 1882.

[9] William Cockett; vicar of Upperby, Cumberland, from 1846.

[10] Police Bill: *H* cxl. 2113.   [11] This phrase in pencil.

[12] Novel (1855) by Mrs C. A. *Clive.

[13] H. Southgate, *Narrative of a tour through Armenia, Kurdistan, Persia and Mesopotamia*, 2v. (1840).

[14] Thomas Woollcombe, 1800–76; Devonport town clerk from 1837; chairman of S. Devon railway from 1844.

[15] Frederick Tobias Wade, d. 1884; vicar of Kidsgrove, Staffordshire, 1837–80; prebendary of Lichfield 1855; wrote on parish reorganisation.

rency—Paul Ferroll. H. of C. at 12½.[1] Nat. Gallery 4½ PM. Five to dinner. Saw Mr Horsfall—Mr Burnett—Do cum Mr Griffiths—Saw Milligan[R].

13. Th.

St James's 8 AM. Wrote to Robn. G.—Ld Aberdeen—concluded & copied my political letter to Ld Aberdeen. Read Southgate—Committee on Parishes 2–4¼. House to 7¼ and 9½–12.[2] Saw Mr Horsfall—S. Herbert—Sir G. Grey—Seeing pictures at Christie's.

My dear Lord Aberdeen,

Although I am conscious of the difficulty of giving a practical consideration to political contingencies before they arrive, especially as they may never arrive at all, yet under the present circumstances I cannot help thinking that equal difficulty, & far greater evil, might arise from being taken unawares.

For the present are not ordinary circumstances, whether we look to the actual state of the instruments of government, or to the exigencies of public affairs.

To take the latter first; the return from war to a state of peace, which it seems may now happily be assumed at least for the purposes of argument, of itself constitutes a great civil juncture: and the importance of that juncture is on this occasion enhanced, because of the sudden, enormous, and practically uncontrouled extension of our establishments: and because, after making every allowance for the effect of forty years of peace, it must I think be admitted & deplored that we have during the war suffered great calamities & even more than corresponding discredit, from causes which were in no small degree avoidable.

The rate at which we are to reduce, the manner in which we are not only to get quit of vast establishments but to satisfy corresponding claims, & that reconsideration of our entire military system for peace, which the nation feels to be imperatively required, are questions demanding a determined and vigorous policy.

A firm resistance should in my opinion be offered to the fashion, that has lately gained strength, of laying the blame of all our evils on parsimony. There can be no scape-goat so convenient as this same parsimony: for we at once punish the guilty, and rid ourselves of what is disagreeable. But even if parsimony has killed its tens, other causes have killed their thousands.

It is not less true than startling, that the whole Expenditure of the State, excepting the fixed charges of that great mortgage the Debt, stands trebled within a period of less than three years; having passed (to use round numbers) from twenty odd millions to more than sixty.

The equilibrium of our finances has been of necessity entirely destroyed; and its re-establishment will involve many subjects of the utmost moment.

Besides this, the whole department of finance still remains in a very backward state: & much has yet to be done to bring it up to the ordinary level of our departments.

The duties connected with our establishments & our finances are in my opinion the primary and urgent duties to be performed upon a return from war to peace.

Next, as to the instruments of Government. The disorganisation of political parties has for the last ten years greatly impaired the strength of the Executive; and previously it had none to spare. This capital evil discredits government,

---

[1] Education: *H* cxli. 2.   [2] Baltic operations: *H* cxli. 48.

encourages faction, retards legislation, diminishes the respect necessary for the efficiency of Parliament, and is thus unfavourable, by a sure though circuitous process, to the stability of our institutions.

All men would agree, abstractedly, that, whatever Government we are to have in the next coming political crisis, it ought to be a strong Government.

In many, perhaps most periods of our recent history, it has appeared that a strong Government might be formed, if only certain persons would agree to unite together for the purpose.

Such is not our present position. There is no practicable combination of men, which of itself would form a strong Government. The truth of this negative is not dependent on the personal inclination of those who might be invited or expected to enter into such a combination. If we suppose their willingness so far extended, as to pass beyond all limitations of party, yet the greater disposition on their part to forget former differences would be more than counteracted by less of compactness among their followers, more of feeble and half-hearted support, if they unite as men only, upon the strength of their traditions, & with a policy to seek.

I come to the conclusion that, though a Government may be patched now or hereafter, and though the every day work of administrators will doubtless be in some manner carried on with or without a policy, yet though there should be an entire forgetfulness, among all public men, of selfish and ambitious aims—no Government can at the moment be formed, that will even for the moment check the now chronic evil of Executive weakness, unless it be in a marked manner founded upon a policy.

Thus the actual exigencies of public affairs, and the peculiar state of Parliament and of parties, lead up to the very same point. There is a third element in the case. Public feeling has been irritated and wounded: and public opinion will not be at rest, unless under the consciousness that those who are to govern recognise the nature & magnitude of the work they will have to perform.

Although, in short, Mr Canning's phrase of 'men not measures' may for other times have had, and may again have, no small degree of force and truth, the present moment is one that calls for measures, and that will estimate men chiefly with reference to measures.

It seems to be universally assumed, that the present Government has come close upon a crisis, with the usual three courses open to them; resignation, reconstruction, dissolution. I will proceed then upon the assumption that such a crisis is near at hand.

Whatever form it may take. I do not think it can be one that would either falsify the foregoing conclusion, or render it inapplicable to the time.

We who belonged to your Government, or some of us, may perhaps not be touched by the proceedings to which this crisis would give rise: but it is better to be prepared for the opposite alternative, as far as preparation can go in such a case, which I grant is not very far.

In all that has preceded, I have been suggesting rather than removing difficulty. And I must confess that it is not diminished, when we pass from the abstract to the concrete. For, so far as I am able to judge, when we look at the names of those persons, who would be publicly regarded as most likely to be at the head of an administration after the crisis we have supposed, I am very doubtful whether they are men, whose ready and cordial adoption of such a policy, & whose adherence to it as a matter of life and death for their Cabinet, could be safely taken for granted.

And here it is not immaterial to observe a difference between the several positions of the head of a Conservative and of a Liberal Government. The Liberal party, it may perhaps be allowed, are, when in Opposition, the most effective champions of public economy and administrative reforms. But when a Liberal Government is in office, with a head not disposed to be over active or firm in this direction, that quality of the party, which perhaps constitutes its best claim with the public, is in a great degree neutralised by a pardonable unwillingness on the part of many or most its members to disturb a Ministry that has their general confidence. But, when a Conservative party is in power, there is no restraint put upon the natural bias of the Opposition in favour of economy & of administrative improvements. Presuming therefore that a given Minister on the Liberal side is personally no better than the rival who would be taken from the Conservative benches, he will in all likelihood practically be worse; for he will be worse kept in order.

Next I do not see how it could be our duty, or as it may be more proper to use the singular, my own duty, as public matters now stand, to take office upon either of two very common grounds. The first of them is, that of preventing the public inconvenience that attends a change of Government. The second is, that of preventing the public inconvenience of protracted suspense about the formation of a Government. Any resolution now taken must be subject to review when the particular form of the emergency is known: but, with this reserve, I for one am inclined to resolve to enter no Government, actual or possible, without an adequate assurance, that it will take its stand upon a policy, & upon such a policy as I have generally indicated.

It would be better, as it seems to me, to decline taking any part in public affairs upon such an occasion as the next turn of the wheel is likely to present, and to wait for an opportunity when arrangements more advantageous to the nation could be made, than to enter a weak Government in the rather presumptuous hope of making it by personal adhesion one degree less weak; after all the evidence we have had, that adequate strength for the purposes of Government is not now to be drawn from the names & reputations of men, but must rest upon the doings & practical intentions of the Minister, and upon a corresponding conviction wrought by them in the public mind.

Thus far & thus far only does my political vision at the present moment extend. I hope others may be more far sighted.

To whatever cause these speculations & inclinations may be due, let me assure you they are not owing to any mere antipathies in any direction whatever. I find it one of the chief comforts of public life, amidst many discomforts, that, as years pass away, antipathies also and resentments if they have existed, disappear; and one of the chief comforts of the present time in particular, that all the motives and considerations, bearing upon personal conduct, are so evidently and directly summed up in the answer to the one question, What do the public interests require?

I remain my dear Lord Aberdeen,[1]

Most sincerely yours,

W.E. Gladstone.[2]

---

[1] *Aberdeen replied recommending Gladstone 'to adopt no position or specific resolution, until the nature of the contingency shall be apparent under which you may be called upon to act'; Add MS 43071, f. 292.

[2] Marked ' *Private*'; Add MS 43071, f. 285. The main points of this letter are expanded in Gladstone's article, 'The declining efficiency of Parliament', *Quarterly Review*, see 19 Sept. 56. See also 31 Mar. 57.

14. Fr.

St James's 8 A.M. Wrote to Rev N.J. Moody—R.B. Jones[1]—T. Macknight. Dined with the Stanhopes: a remarkable party. Worked on books. Saw Mr Gibson & Depn.—Mr T. Rossetti.[2] Parishes Commee. 2–4½. House to 7½: spoke a little on the Persian Squabble.[3] Read Southgate.

15. Sat.

St James's 8 A.M. Wrote to W.C. James—Messrs. Child—J. Griffiths—Sec. Office Works[4]—Rector of Exeter Coll. At Christie's: bought a pair of Venetian pictures.[5] Saw J.N.G. —Ld Ward—Mr Walpole—Saw M. Eugen [R]. Visited Ld Ward's Gallery.

16. Palm Sunday.

Chapel Royal mg. Broad Court Evg.[6] Wrote on Rom 12.7 & read aloud in Evg. Scripture conv. with the elder children. Saw W.C. James—R. Cavendish. Read Sidney's Rich. Hill finished—Paix de l'Âme—Penity. Report.[7]

17. M.

All Saints (Marg) 8 AM. Wrote to Sir C. Trevelyan—Ld Ward—Sec S.P.G. —Robn. G—Sec. L[ondon] & Y[ork] RR. Co—Rev J.L. Ross—J.G.S. Lefevre. Wrote Memm. on Cathl. Draft.[8] Saw W. Hampton—J. Griffiths (2 h on O[ak] F[arm])—Mrs Herbert. Walk & shopping with C. Read Tolla[9] —Jervis on the Poor Condition of the Clergy[10]—Italian with W. & Agnes.[11]

18. T.

St James's 8 A.M. Wrote to Rev. Mr Borton[12]—Slatter—Rev. Mr Edwards —A. Williams—J.A. Langford[13]—Hatchard—Mr Köber[14]—T.G. Saw Sir James Graham—Rev. Mr Tweed—Mr Hildyard—Worked on accounts.

---

[1] Of London, had written about the immaculate conception (Hawn P).

[2] Neapolitan candidate for the Italian professorship being established by the curators of the Taylorian, Oxford; brought to Gladstone's attention by De Tabley: Add MS 44385, f. 257.

[3] Supporting *Layard against the govt. for raising the question of responsibility of payments for operations in Persia: H cxl. 166.

[4] Alfred Austin, 1805–84; secretary to office of works 1854–68.

[5] Giving £27 for Giorgione's 'Noah's sacrifice' and 'Noah and his sons' (Hawn P).

[6] St. John's episcopal chapel, off Bow Street.

[7] Annual report of the Church Penitentiary Society; he was on the council.

[8] 'The *principle* of the accompanying draft is that, without violation of vested interests, Cathedral emoluments should hereafter only be enjoyed in consideration of the discharge of adequate duties': Add MS 44746, f. 6.

[9] E. About, *Tolla, a tale of modern Rome* (1855).

[10] W. G. Jervis, 'The poor condition of the clergy and the causes considered, with suggestions for remedying the same' (1856).

[11] Probably William Key Borton, 1806–82; rector of Wickham St. Paul, Essex, 1835–76.

[12] Joseph Charles Edwards, d. 1896; anglican priest and author; continually in trouble with ecclesiastic and civil authorities.

[13] Of Ann Street, London, later of Birmingham, had asked about publishing (Hawn P).

[14] Perhaps Charles Koeber, London woolen draper.

Homer (Il. 12) with Willy. Tasso with W. & Agnes. Read Tolla (finished)—Filder's Letter[1]—Curzon's Erzeroum[2]—Cough with headach & threatened sore throat obliged me to take measures at night.

19. Wed.

Rose at midday. St James's 5½ P.M. Wrote to Rector of Exeter—Sir G. Grey (2)—Rev Mr Jennings. Arranging lists for entertainments. Saw Adm. Reform Deputn.[3] Saw Ld Aberdeen—Dined with Dowr. (1) Ly. Wharncliffe. Read Prescott's Philip II[4]—Curzon's Erzeroum. Tasso with W. & A. Homer with W.

20. Th.

Chapel Royal 11½ AM. Wrote to Rev J.C. Edwards—Mr J. Hales[5]—J. M'Culloch—Dr Henderson—Mrs Davenport—Rect. of Exeter—J.A. Milligan[6] NB. Saw Mr Lacaita—Mr Panizzi—Mr A. Gordon—Ld Hardwicke.[7] Tasso with W. & A. Homer with W. Read Curzon's Erzeroum—Hales's Appeal from Bp to Ch.[8]—Ruskin's Mod. Painters V. 3.[9]

21. Good Friday.

St James's 11 AM and H.C. (with Willy). Tenison's Chapel Evg. MS. of 40 aloud. Saw S. Herbert. Read Rundle's Life & Letters[10]—Paix de l'Ame—Usher's life[11]—Pinkerton on Russian Church, & Platon's Doctrine.[12] Looked at accounts.

22. Easter Eve.

St Andrew's Wells St 5 P.M. Wrote to Ld Goderich—C.G.—Rev Mr Stonhouse[13]—Sir G. Grey—Sir J. H. Maxwell—Received in the morning the unwelcome news of Mazie's scarlet fever: but D.G. with all circs. favourable. Saw F.R. Bonham—Dean of St Paul's. B. Museum, meeting of Trustees, at 1 PM. Aunt J., Miss Scott, & the children, dined. Read Lewin

---

[1] W. Filder, 'The Commissariat in the Crimea' (1856).

[2] R. *Curzon, *Armenia; a year at Erzeroom, and on the frontiers of Russia, Turkey, and Persia* (1854).

[3] No account found.

[4] W. H. Prescott, *History of the reign of Philip the Second, King of Spain*, 3v. (1855–9).

[5] John Dixon Hales, vicar of St. John's, Richmond, from 1837.

[6] Glasgow commission agent.

[7] Charles Philip *Yorke, 1799–1873, 4th earl of Hardwicke 1834; sailor; minor office 1852, 1858–9.

[8] F. Hales '"Tell it to the Church". An appeal from the Bishop [of Melbourne, C. Perry] to the Church' (1853).

[9] Just published.

[10] *Letters of Thomas Rundle . . . to Mrs. Barbara Sandys, with introductory memoirs by James Dalloway*, 2v. (1789).

[11] N. Bernard, *The Life of James *Usher* (1837).

[12] Metropolitan Platon, *The present state of the Greek church in Russia*, tr. R. Pinkerton (1814).

[13] Arthur Stonehouse, vicar of Walford from 1842 (Hawn P).

on Torture[1]—Civil Service Commee. Report[2]—Paix de l'Ame—Letters of Columbanus.[3]

23. Easter Day.

Holy Commn. (with W) St Martins 8.30. St Jamess 11 AM. All Saints (Marg[aret Street]) 7 P.M. Instruction to the children. MS. of 40 aloud. Wrote MSS Theol.[4] Read Usher's Life & Appx—Blair's Life[5]—Flower Address & Serm.[6]

24. Easter M. X

All Saints 5 P.M. Wrote to Rev E. Hobhouse—Mrs Herbert—Sec. L.N.W. Co[7]—C.G.—Mrs Hancock—H. Glynne—J.N.G. Read L'Orient devant L'Occident. Worked on accounts. Saw Bp of Oxford. Ld Goderich (drew Address dft).[8] Saw Thompson 29. A strange form of our poor humanity[R]. Attended Ld Mayor's dinner: & spoke; glancing at the D. of Cambridge.[9] Worked on arranging books. Tasso with W. & A. Caesar with Stephen.

25. Easter T. & Annunciation.

St James's at 3 failed me. Took the boys to Ld Ward's Gallery—Homer with Willy. Dined at Sir W. James's. Worked on books: shopping. Saw Mr Burnett 10–12: do, & Messrs. Robertson & Darby.[10] on the Hawarden Coalfield, $4\frac{3}{4}$–$6\frac{3}{4}$. Saw Sir J. Kirkland—Mr Lacaita. Read Langdale's Mrs Fitzherbert[11]—Taylor on Currency.[12] Wrote to Mr A. Symonds—C.G.—Mrs Goalen.[13]

26. Wed. X

Wrote to Ld Blandford—Ld Ward—Rev J. Bramston—C.G.—Jas Watson —Dr Irons[14]—Mrs Davenport. Read Orient devant l'Occident.[15] Ride with Willy. Saw Mr Grogan—Mr Ruttley—Messrs Jaffir Alee & Ally Akbar[16]—

[1] M. Lewin, *Torture in Madras* (1855).
[2] Select cttee. on Civil Service Superannuation Bill of which Gladstone was a member, though he infrequently attended: *PP* 1856 ix. 1.
[3] See 13 Aug. 45.   [4] Not found.
[5] *Life of Mr. Robert Blair*, ed. T. MacCrie (1848).
[6] W. B. Flower, 'Choral Services and Ritual observances. Two sermons' (1856).
[7] See 19 Aug. 49n.   [8] Not found; see Wolf, *Ripon*, i. 124.
[9] The duke said he hoped the expanded army and navy would be maintained; Gladstone urged retrenchment: *The Times*, 25 March 1856, 10c.
[10] They leased parts of the estate for mining; see 12 Aug. 56; the latter was W. H. Darby of the Brymbo Iron works.
[11] C. *Langdale, *Memoirs of Mrs. Fitzherbert* (1856).
[12] J. Taylor, probably *A catechism of the currency* (1835).
[13] Helen Goalen, wife of Thomas and da. of James Gladstone, Sir J.G.'s brother; she lived in Oxford, where the diarist paid part of university fees of her son Alexander, (d. 1872) Brasenose 1853, later lecturer in natural science; she d. 1869.
[14] William Josiah *Irons, 1812–83; priest; strong establishmentarian; supported compulsory education; vicar of Brompton 1872; rector of St. Mary Woolnoth (Gladstone's presentation) 1872.
[15] Not found.
[16] Perhaps emissaries of the King of Oude, who came in August to oppose the annexation of his kingdom.

Ld Aberdeen—E. Cardwell—Mr Robinson (Scotts)[1]—Mr Burnett. Saw Milligan[R]. Dined with the Ellisons. Æsop with Stephy. Tasso with W. & A.

27. Th.

Wrote to Mr Pressly—C.G. (2)—Mr H. Cole—Sir T.G.—Mr Gardiner—Messrs. Leighton—Mr J. Wilson—Hon Mrs Wilbraham. Rode with Willy. Lady Pembroke at length released.[2] Read Huskisson's Speeches[3]—Huskisson on Depreciation[4]—Parl. Papers—Langdale's Mrs Fitzherbert—Gasparin's Liberalisme[5]—Æsop with Stephy—Tasso with W. & A. Went over the house No 11 [Carlton House Terrace] & saw Mr Grogan about it.

28 Fr.

Wrote to Ly. Lyttelton—W. Hancock—G. Burnett—S.R.G.—C.G.—J.E. Roe[6]—M. Gladstone—Mrs Langton[R]. Rode with Stephy. Saw Mr H. Robertson—& (I hope) concluded with him resp. the H[awarde]n Coal Field—Mrs Kersley[7]—Rev. J. Bramston—Mr Trevor. Tasso with W. & A. Æsop with Stephy. Read Bazancourt's Narrative[8]—Ireland & her Rulers[9] Huskisson on Depreciation—Rundle's Letters (finished)—L'Orient devant l'Occident.

29. Sat.

All Saints 5 P.M. Wrote to Scotts—C.G.—J.N.G.—Ld Granville—Mr Pressly—Mr Grogan. Tasso with W. & A. Caesar with Stephy. Rode with Willy. Read the U.S. Trials.[10] Took the boys to see the Stamping operations at S. House.[11] Tea at Lady Granville's. Again visited No 11.

30. 1 S. E[aster][12]

Found St Martin's closed at 8.30 AM. Chapel Royal mg—All S. evg. MS of 45 aloud. Lesson with the 3 children. Wrote to Sec. Penitentiary.[13] Saw R. Cavendish—P. Lightfoot [R]—J. Gordon[14]—Missed Langton [R]. Read Paix de l'Ame—Life of Bp Low[15]—Tracts & Sermons—Life of Ussher.

[1] i.e. of Scotts bank in Cavendish Square.   [2] She died that day.
[3] *The speeches of the Rt. Hon. W. *Huskisson, with a biographical memoir*, 3v. (1831).
[4] W. *Huskisson, 'The question concerning the depreciation of our currency stated and examined' (1810).
[5] Cte A-E de Gasparin, 'Après la paix. Considérations sur le libéralisme et la guerre d'Orient' (1856).
[6] John Erasmus Roe, London barrister.   [7] Unidentified.
[8] C. de Bazancourt, *The Crimean Expedition, to the capture of Sebastopol*, tr. R. H. Gould, 2v. (1856).
[9] *Ireland and its rulers; since 1829*, 3v. (1843–4); ascribed to D. O. Madden.
[10] Perhaps the Dred Scott case, then in the federal courts.
[11] Presumably the final count of the quarterly customs and excise duties, then being made at Somerset House, see *The Guardian*, 2 April 1856, 256.
[12] News of the signing of the peace treaty reached London this evening.
[13] T. H. Greene, secretary of the Church Penitentiary Society; see 6 Feb. 52 and 16 Mar. 56n.
[14] Perhaps 'Gondon'.   [15] W. Blatch, *A memoir of the Rt. Rev. David Low* (1855).

31. M.

Wrote to Jane C. Robertson—S.R.G.—Jane Gordon—C.G.—Rev C.H. Davis[1]—A.W. Cole—Rev. E. Hawkins—T.M. Gladstone—Ld Delamere. Rode with Agnes: her first. Saw Mr Caffin (Worc Coll.)[2]—Mr G. Goode—Mr Geo. Glyn—Sir J. Graham—Ld Goderich. Took the boys to the Haymarket Theatre at 9 P.M.[3] Read Thompson on the Army.[4] H. of C. $4\frac{1}{4}$–$6\frac{3}{4}$.[5]

Tues. April 1. 1856.

Wrote to J. Hamilton—Ld Ward—Sec. L[ondon] & Y[ork] Railw. Co.—Mr Grogan—C.G.—Aunt J. Read Curzon's Erzeroum—Huskisson on Depreciation. Rode with Agnes. Saw S. Herbert—Rev. Mr Thomas—Sir J. Graham—Sir E.L. Bulwer. H of C. 4.15–7.15. Disraeli did good service.[6] Saw a Spaniard: & had a warning[R].

2. Wed.

Wrote to Mr Grogan—V.C. Oxford—Aunt J.—Mlle. Españ[7]—C.G.—Sec. Bd Works. Dined at Grillions. H of C. 4–$5\frac{3}{4}$.[8] Rode with Stephy. I had to speak most seriously to little Lena: in more things than one she has been tempted & overcome. It seems so hollow to speak to her of her sins & pray with her, & then think of my own. Saw Mr Grogan—Mr J. Hamilton—Mr Jelf—E. Cardwell—Sir W. Heathcote. Hom[er] with Willy—Tasso with W. & A. Read Bowyer on Span. Ch.[9]—M'Culloch on Lim[ited] Liability[10] and [blank space]

3. Th.

Wrote to Provost of Oriel—Aunt J.—Sir C. Trevelyan—S. Herbert—C.G.—Mr J. Craufurd. Dined at Ld Duncan's. Saw Mr Jelf jun[11]—Mr Grogan—Rev. D. Robertson—Sir J. Graham—Sir W. Heathcote—Mr Butt. Tasso with W. & A. Æsop with Stephy. Rode with Agnes. Read Statham's

[1] Charles Henry Davis; chaplain of Stroud union 1851; rector of Littleton Drew, Wiltshire, 1875; pamphleteer.

[2] Benjamin Charles Caffin, b. 1826?; fellow of Worcester, Oxford, 1852; vicar of Northallerton 1877.

[3] *The Evil Genius*, followed by *El Gambusino* and *A Daughter to Marry*.

[4] See 16 Feb. 56.

[5] *Palmerston's statement on the peace; Gladstone later spoke on cathedral entry charges: *H* cxli. 221.

[6] He spoke against raising county court judges' salaries: *H* cxli. 307.

[7] Presumably the Spanish prostitute of the previous day.

[8] Factories Bill, for inspection of machinery, opposed by *Cobden: *H* cxli. 358.

[9] G. *Bowyer, *The differences between the Holy See and the Spanish Government* (1856).

[10] J. R. *McCulloch, *Considerations on partnerships with limited liability* (1856).

[11] George Edward *Jelf, 1834–1908, s. of R.W.*; then up at Christ Church; anglican priest and extensive writer of moderate high church devotional studies.

Pamphlets[1]—Unwin's Letter on Edn.[2]—Central American papers[3]—Report &c. on St James's Park.[4]

4. Fr.

Wrote to S.R. Glynne—C.G.—Rev. T.F. Barker[5]—R.G.—Rev E. Hawkins—G. & Co.—Ld Overstone. H of C. $4\frac{1}{2}$–$7\frac{1}{2}$ and 10–$12\frac{1}{2}$.[6] Shopping. Tasso with W. & A. Rode with Stephy. It is his birthday. We have every reason to love him: & as regards mere intellect I am impressed with the idea that there is much yet to grow out of him. Saw General Grey—W. Hampton—Mr Laing—Sir J. Graham. Read India Bill Debates of 1783[7]—Curzon's Erzeroum—papers on Dec. Coinage.[8]

5. Sat.

Wrote to C.G. Homer with Willy. Br. Museum Meeting at 12. Then to Mrs Tyler's: & on to Delarues[9] with Mr Pressly & the boys where we had a most interesting aftn. We then missed Sir E. Landseer[10] at his house. I talked to Agnes after she had a great tooth out: & she was most satisfactory. A dinner party of 12. Finished Curzon's Erzeroum. Saw Ld Aberdeen—R. Phillimore—Españ[R].

6. 2 S.E[aster].

St James's mg & H.C. with Willy. All Saints evg with both boys. Conv. of the Gospel [sic]. MS. of 40 on Col. 3.1. (2) aloud. Saw Sir J. Graham. Wrote MS. Theol.[11] Wrote to Españ. Saw Gordon[R]. Read Paix de l'Âme[12]—Chr. Remembrancer[13]—Blatch's Bp Low.

7. M.

Wrote to Messrs. Banting—S. Herbert—J. Griffiths—Dr Wess[14]—Messrs. Leighton—W. Lewis—Gen. Mercer[15]—J. Berry—Messrs. Banting. Saw Col. Tulloch—J. M'Culloch—Hon W.F. Campbell—Mr Panizzi—Mr Grogan &

---

[1] F. F. Statham, *Our Protestant faith as distinguished from the corruption and superstitions of Popery* (1851).

[2] W. J. Unwin, 'Education and work of the people. A letter to . . . Russell' (1856).

[3] Probably *PP* 1856 lx. 1; correspondence with U.S.A. on central America, issued on 24 Apr.

[4] Select cttee.'s report on proposed road across St. James's Park: *PP* 1856 vii. 387.

[5] Thomas Francis Barker, 1810?–78; Christ Church and Brasenose; vicar of Thornton-le-Moors from 1849.

[6] Called for more amicable approach to differences with U.S.A. in central America: *H* cxli. 475. G.M. Dallas (see 2 June 56) on hearing this speech, thought Gladstone would soon supercede *Palmerston: Letters from London* (1870) i. 11.

[7] On *Fox's Bill: Hansard's Parliamentary History* xxiv. 1.   [8] See 25 Nov. 53.

[9] Shop and factory in Bunhill Row of Thomas Delarue, 1793–1866, card, paper and straw hat manufacturer.

[10] Sir Edwin Henry *Landseer, 1802–73, artist, lived in St. John's Wood Road.

[11] Not found.   [12] See 24 Feb. 56.

[13] *Christian Remembrancer*, xxxi. 1 (April 1856).

[14] Probably Ludwig Weis, German author on philosophy.

[15] Alexander Cavalie Mercer, major-general 1854, general 1865.

signed for No 11.[1] C.G. returned—House business. H. of C. $4\frac{1}{2}$–$7\frac{1}{4}$ and $9\frac{1}{2}$–12.[2] Read Custine's Russia.[3]

8. *T.*

Wrote to Rector of Exeter—Rev G. Venables[4]—J.N.G.—A. Panizzi—A. Consolo—Mr W. Irvine—Sec. B. of Works. Saw Sir J. Graham cum Cardwell(bis)—Sir W. Heathcote MP—Mr G. Hadfield MP—Mr S. Laing MP—Mr Grogan—Mr Hammond—Ld Wodehouse. Exhib. Finance Commee. at 2. S.P.G.Ch.Commee. at 3.[5] H. of C. $4\frac{1}{2}$–$7\frac{1}{2}$.[6] Read Campbell's Letters[7]—Gassiot on Adm. Reform.[8]

9. *Wed.*

Wrote to Scotts—Warden Trin Coll.—Mr J. Butt[9]—Rev. W. Pattinson[10]—D. Meehan.[11] Rode with Agnes. Saw Mr Grogan—Mr Wilson MP—Ld President (?D. MacNeill).[12] H of C. $3\frac{1}{4}$–6.[13] Read Thompson on the Army—Female Life among the Mormons[14]—Higgins on Military Education[15]—Close and Bains on Education'[16]

10. *Th.*

Wrote to Gen. Mercer—Mrs Bennett—Rev Mr Platt[17]—Rector of Exeter. Rode with Agnes—Nine to dinner—H of C. $4\frac{3}{4}$–$7\frac{1}{2}$ and $9\frac{1}{2}$–12.[18] Surveying at No 11. Read Sandhurst Report[19]—Educn. papers.[20] Saw Mr Greswell—Mr Grogan—Sir S. Northcote—Sir B. Hall.

11. *Fr.*

Wrote to Scotts—Sir T.G. Tasso with Willy & Agnes. H of C. $4\frac{1}{2}$–$7\frac{1}{4}$ and

[1] The purchase from the earl of Arundel of 11 Carlton House Terrace.
[2] Supply: *H* cxli. 589.　　[3] See 11 Dec. 43.
[4] George Venables, 1821–1908; vicar of St. Paul's, Chatham, 1854–8, of Friezland, Yorkshire, 1858–69, of St. Matthew's, Leicester, 1869–74, of Great Yarmouth 1874–86.
[5] Raising money for memorial church at Constantinople: prospectus in Add MS 44385, f. 293.
[6] *Muntz's motion on income tax: *H* cxli. 640.
[7] T. *Campbell, *Letters from the south*, 2v. (1837).
[8] J. P. *Gassiot, *Second Letter to J. A. *Roebuck* (1856).
[9] Perhaps John Butt, 1826–99; Roman catholic chaplain in Crimea, then to dukes of Norfolk.
[10] William Pattinson, 1817–91; rector of Kirkbampton 1845–78, of Patterdale 1878–91.
[11] Of Spitalfields, receiving help from Gladstone (Hawn P).
[12] i.e. *Granville, probably on an 1851 exhibition question.
[13] Gibson's Oath of Abjuration Bill: *H* cxli. 703.
[14] *Female life among the Mormons: by the wife of a Mormon elder* (1855).
[15] Jacob Omnium [M. J. *Higgins], *Letters on military education* (1856).
[16] F. Close, 'A few more words on Education Bills' (1856), E. *Baines, 'National education. Remarks on . . . *Russell' (1856).
[17] George Platt, 1807–83; Trinity, Cambridge; vicar of Sedbergh, Yorkshire, from 1841.
[18] National Education; Henley moved the chairman leave the chair: *H* cxli. 780.
[19] Select cttee. on Sandhurst Royal Military College: *PP* 1855 xii. 311.
[20] Preparing for next day's debate.

8–1. Some perplexity in the debate: it ended well. I spoke 11–11.50.[1] Saw
Mr R. Barker—The Danish Minister[2]—Edw. Ellis (Manning)[3]—Mr & Mrs
D. Robertson. Rode with Willy.

12. Sat.

Wrote to Baron Brunnow—Sir W. Heathcote. Saw Ld Aberdeen cum Sir
J. Graham & Cardwell—Sir W. Heathcote—Scotts. Royal Commn. Meeting
11–2¾. We doctored the Report a little.[4] Rode with Willy. Made inquiry
for Langton[R]. Read . . . [blank] Worked on No 11 (Carlton House Terrace)
for furnishing &c.

13. 3 S. E[aster]

St James's H.C. 8 A.M. and mg 11 A.M. Chapel Royal aftn. MS of 1841
aloud in evg. Conv. with the children. Reperused my letters to Willy. Saw
Sir W. Heathcote—Earl of Aberdeen—R. Cavendish—Langton: with
whom I had a satisfactory conversation[R]. Read Blatch's Low[5]—Ld A.
Hervey's Sermons.[6] Wrote to Rev Mr Greene—Rev Mr Lee.

14. M.

Wrote to Ld Ward—Sec. L[ondon] & Y[ork] Compy—E. Ellis—Sir W.
Heathcote—Rev W. Pound—Lady Macmahon.[7] H of C. 4½–7½ and 10–12¾.[8]
Dined with Mrs Talbot. Saw Mr J. Griffiths—Ld Ward cum Mr Smith &
Mr Griffiths 12½–3½—Sir W. Heathcote—Sir J. Graham. Read Amn.
Edition of the recruiting papers.[9]

15. T. X

Wrote to Ld Granville—Mr Jacob—Wm. Gladstone—Robn. G.—Rev Mr
Caparn—G. & Co—Rev W. Scott. Dined with the Denisons. Saw Canville
[R]. Saw B. Benjamin[10]—Mr Grogan—Mr A. Munro (at Studio)—Col.
Tulloch—Sir T.G.—Sir J. Graham—Ld St Germains—Mr Stephenson.[11]
H of C. 4¾–5¾ & paired.[12] Rode with Willy. Read U.S. recruiting papers—
Sardinian (Congress) papers.[13]

---

[1] Supporting existing voluntary system of national education: *H* cxli. 941, notes in
Add MS 44654, f. 190; the govt. was defeated in 260:158, the Peelites voting with the
tories.
[2] General Waldemar Tully d'Oxholm, 1805–76; minister in London 1854–7.
[3] Obscure.
[4] Third report of 1851 exhibition commissioners: *PP* 1856 xxiv. 501.
[5] See 30 Mar. 56.
[6] Lord A. C. *Hervey, *The Inspiration of Holy Scripture. Five Sermons* (1856).
[7] Maria Catherine, *née* Bateson, Captain J. N. Gladstone's sister-in-law, m. 1838 Sir
Beresford Burston McMahon, 1808–73, soldier, 2nd bart. 1837; she d. 1876.
[8] Estimates: *H* cxli. 1001.
[9] 'Messages of the President' on American recruiting, reprinted in *PP* 1856 lx. 687.
[10] Antique dealer in Duke Street.
[11] Robert *Stephenson, 1803–59; civil engineer; tory M.P. Whitby 1847–59; see next
day.
[12] Maynooth: *H* cxli. 1049.   [13] Sardinian papers on the Paris congress.

16. Wed.

Wrote to Rev Mr Gleig—H.R. Sandbach—Rev. E. Coleridge—W.E. Corner.[1] Saw Sir [T.] E. Perry—Ld Granville—Mr W.G. Anderson—Mr Grogan—Sir W. Heathcote. bis—Mr Reeve[2]—R. Phillimore—Sir S. Northcote—Dr Jelf. Caesar with Stephen. Rode with him: & bid him goodbye for Eton, with a cheerful confidence in his well doing there. Read Stephenson's address.[3] Dined with Mrs Talbot: large evening party at home, over about 12.40: rather well attended by Ld Derby's friends. H. of C. 3¼–6.[4]

17. Th.

Wrote to Edw. Ellis—Sec. L. & Y. Co.—Mrs Chisholm—Ld Aberdeen—Rev Mr Foster. Rode with Willy. Wrote Mem. (French) on Continental Policy.[5] Saw Sir W. Heathcote—Mr Bonham—Mr Panizzi—Mr G. Smith—Bp of Oxford. Wrote Pol. Mema. Read Sardinian papers (finished)—Nat Rev. on Peace & on Macaulay.[6] At No 11 where there is great hurry.

In connection with a letter which I addressed to Ld. Aberdeen on the [13] of March,[7] I conversed with him, with Graham & with Herbert, adding names to my general indications: to the effect that neither Ld. John nor Ld. Palmerston would be satisfactory as ministers with reference to the administrative work to be done—that possibly a question might arise whether the so-called Peelites could return to office with the controul of all the spending & financial departments or with full confidence in the holders of them, even with Palmerston as Head—that if both P. & J.R. could disappear & Clarendon come to the top it might be more practicable to conduct the Govt. in a satisfactory manner: that more might be hoped from him[,] at least as to permitting the administrative work to be done[,] than from the others, but at the same time that it did not appear in what work they could make way & C. be brought forward.

A few days afterwards Graham told me, quite unexpectedly, that he had given confidentially to C. Greville as an old friend not my conversation as such but his own idea of my present views.[8] In his version of it he had adverted to P. as out of the question—Lord J.R. as a case for the House of Lords—& he did not appear to have dwelt on the difficulties in the way of Clarendon's coming to the head. He had warned Greville against indiscreet repetition, but without binding him to absolute secrecy, on the contrary he seemed to contemplate that G. would turn the conversation to account. Greville had asked whether I objected to Lewis as a colleague: Graham said he believed I liked & esteemed him: but took it for granted that the question referred to some Cabinet Office other than his present one.

In some points Sir J. Graham had certainly gone beyond the mark in stating to Greville his estimate of my opinions. My reference for instance to Clarendon as a

[1] William Elgie Corner, ship owner; business with him untraced.
[2] Henry *Reeve, 1813–95; ed. *Edinburgh Review* from 1855 and influenced *The Times* foreign policy; known as Puffendorf.
[3] *Address of R. *Stephenson on his election as President of the Institution of Civil Engineers* (1856).
[4] Ireland: *H* cxli. 1113.   [5] In Add MS 44746.
[6] *National Review*, ii. 468, 357 (April 1856).   [7] See 11 and 13 Mar. 56.
[8] According to *Greville (*Memoirs*, ed. L. Strachey and R. Fulford (1938), vii. 223–6), *Graham said 'Gladstone would have nothing to do with any Government unless he were leader in the H. of C.' and that Gladstone's religious views 'approach nearly to Rome'.

possible Premier had been no more than negative & abstract. But as he had *done* it, & had purported to speak his own opinions only, it did not seem necessary to make any remark to this effect.

I have kept a copy of a note[1] which soon after I addressed to Mr. Ellice about a suggestion of his that a Committee of Finance should be appointed, with Graham in the Chair, F. Baring, myself & others upon it to consider the whole subject of expenditure & establishments. His reply to my note is curious.[2]

Next in order of time came the Education debate. This was a spontaneous combination. We first saw Henley's notice given. We then tried to suggest a Resolution in lieu of it: but I found it difficult to draw, & Henley's course was fixed. So we fell into the ranks, Herbert came up & found us pledged.[3]

Next to this, we considered the notice of motion given by Mr. Baillie for a censure, in extreme terms, upon the Govt. with reference to recruiting abroad standing for last Monday before the papers on the subject were in the hands of the House of Commons.[4]

Disapproving of the conduct of Govt. in both branches of the American question, and obliged to hope that the public interests might be rescued and defended by the Opposition we were unwilling to find ourselves in opposition to Baillie with his leaders, or even to see Baillie with a section open & discredit so great a question in opposition to his leaders, desiring that the force which might become available for it shd. remain unbroken.

It was agreed that as in the last named case I should see Heathcote & suggest his conveying to Ld Derby's friends our idea of the dangers impending & to be avoided. He saw Ld Derby on Sunday who proceeded accordingly: & hence the postponement of the motion on Monday last the 14th.

The same evening Heathcote told me Derby had requested to see him on Tuesday at eleven. On Wednesday he reported to me the substance of Derby's conversation.

He thanked Heathcote for being willing to speak confidentially with him; adverted to the uneasy state of politics & weakness of the Govt: observed that it might almost any day be overturned and that it was among the possibilities of the case that he might then be sent for, so that he was anxious as far as he could to be prepared: he adverted to the difficulties he had encountered with his party last year, & added that he was naturally unwilling to encounter such difficulties afresh without having any reasonable hope of success to warrant it: said he must not be understood as sending any message or as being able to speak for any other persons but that knowing Heathcote to be intimate with me he was desirous to learn from him as far as he might be able & disposed to give the information what he thought my views were on the possibility of political cooperation. That as to me individually he conceived I might have no vital objection to it, and apparently without using any determinate language he gave H. to understand it would be agreeable to him. This was his first point. His second was an inquiry as to the nature of my relations with other members of the Peel Govt. who had also been in the Cabinet of Ld. Aberdeen. Did we systematically communicate? Were we a party, & did we intend to hold & act together? On this part of the question he observed about the difficulty which arose in respect to personal claims from recent disruptions: men were of necessity promoted from the ranks to high office who had not looked for it, but having been so promoted they had

[1] Add MS 44385, f. 285, dated 4 April 1856.
[2] *ibid.* f. 291, dated 5 April 1856, ambiguous about the cttee.   [3] See 11 Apr. 56.
[4] Henry James Baillie, 1804–85, tory M.P. Inverness-shire 1840–68, eventually withdrew his motion on relations with America: *H* cxlii. 1660 (18 June 1856).

their position to maintain & could not be summarily discarded. Lastly he glanced at Parliamentary cooperation as a proper antecedent to any junction properly so called; and said this must of course depend on the views we might take. He adverted to the question of Kars, and considered that Whiteside would have much to say in support of his motion,[1] i.e. as I understood wd. make a strong case agt. the Govt. not wholly sparing Ld. Stratford.

On all this Heathcote wished to know what I had to say to him, what he was to carry to Lord Derby, and whether I would reflect upon the matter in order to consult with friends before giving him any authority to speak to Ld Derby at all.

I thought that considering the necessary vagueness & inconclusiveness of Ld Derby's own conversation, and the position he took in it as speaking better for himself, it was best for me to answer Heathcote from myself alone for the time: that he again should carry no message from me but should carry his own impressions on the three points which he had put to me, while in order to assist his means of judgement I should not confine myself in my conversation to those points but would give him all the light I could leaving it to his discretion to judge whether any part of what I said should enter into any further conversation he might have with Derby.

On the first point I said you cannot better describe my views for the present purpose than by saying that they are much like Lord Derby's own as I understand them—there was nothing in them to prevent a further consideration of the subject, if public affairs should assume such a shape as to recommend it.

On the second I said that Graham Herbert Cardwell & I communicated together habitually & confidentially: that we did not seek to act but rather eschewed acting as a party: that our habits of communication were founded on long political association, general agreement & personal friendship: that they were not however a covenant for the future but a natural growth & result of the past & that as such I presumed they would continue unless interrupted by conscientious difference of opinion on some vital question.

As to the third point I said that such knowledge as I possessed of the question of Kars led me to think that there was no case for a censure on the Govt. That it was impossible to dismiss from view on the one hand that to defend Kars through action on the Turkish Govt. was like defending it through acting on a corpse: while on the other hand France had a keen & able jealousy of anything that could raise a barrier on the way between Russia & British India. I believed Graham's views to be much the same: & asked him whether he was not inclined to think with us: he answered in the affirmative.

I pointed to the American question on which also I thought myself in possession more or less of Sir J. Graham's views. I declared myself deeply dissatisfied with the conduct of Govt. on the Central American branch of it, and also on the Crampton affair so far as it was yet known to us. I thought we both regarded it as of vital consequence and not much trusting in the Govt. to bring it right we looked with anxiety to the House of Commons, & to those independent of the Govt. there to preserve the public interests from jeopardy. I thought it probable that upon this question we might find our convictions more or less in the same line with those of Ld Derby and his friends.

Besides these three points I touched upon various other matters with Heathcote. I read him the letter of [13] March to Ld. Aberdeen: told him that I deeply deplored the broken & disorganised state of the H. of Commons: felt that we, the

---

[1] Whiteside's motion condemned govt. 'want of foresight and energy' in surrendering Kars: *H* cxlii. 1594 (28 April 1856).

friends of Lord Aberdeen, were though I hoped not by our own fault yet de facto a main cause of disunion & weakness in the Executive Govt. & must be so, from whichever side the Govt. were formed so long as we continued in a separate position or were not absolutely incorporated into one or the other of the two great parties: for though we had few positively & regularly following us yet we had indirect relations with others on both sides of the house which tended to relax, & so far disable party connection, & that our existence as a section encouraged the formation of other sections all working with similar efforts. That I carried my feeling individually so far upon the subject as even to be ready, if I had to act alone, to surrender my seat in Parlt. rather than continue a course of disturbance to any Govt. to which I might generally wish well. That I admitted that any pledge of more general favour & independent support even if it cd. be given of wh. nothing cd. now be said, might still be utterly rejected by Ld Derby who might still reasonably say he could not undertake the Govt. with us remaining as outlaws in the H. of Commons. That as to union, it was quite impossible to treat it as a matter of mere choice or will: whether it were a question of rejoining our late colleagues, or any other persons, our proceeding to be warrantable, must be founded on convictions of the public interest & on community of views evinced to the world by cooperation on great questions of the day which as they arose would speak for themselves & would open the path of duty. I dwelt strongly on the impossibility of meeting the main want of the country & forming a strong Govt. except upon the basis of a decided & well understood policy: no mere association of names would do: & I indicated the subjects to wh such a policy should have reference.

No names except of Commoners were mentioned in the conversation. I may add that Heathcote told me he had told Ld Derby from his own observation that he thought Sir J. Graham might not be unfavourably inclined: at wh D. expressed surprise, adding that they had been most intimate, that he might have some reason to complain but that he felt no sort of animosity or ill-feeling on the subject. He seemed also to be under the impression that Herbert from health or otherwise might not be looking to office at the present moment. On this I said, with reference to the three, that in my view it was not simply a question of personal wishes: the present juncture was one when men of administrative capacity were required and that these three, to put them together, were among the very best whose services the country could command.[1]

18. Fr.

Wrote to Rev Mr Purchas[2]—Willy—D. of Norfolk—W. Rogers—Sir G. Grey—Marq. Azeglio—Rector of Exeter—V. Chancr. Superann. Comm. 12–3. H of C. $4\frac{1}{2}$–$7\frac{3}{4}$ and $11\frac{1}{2}$–1.[3] Dined at Mr Harcourt's—Lady Jersey's afr. Saw Mr Panizzi—Sir J. Graham—Mr Wilson. Read Neales Bp Torry.[4]

19. Sat.

Wrote to Sir C. Wood—Mrs Bennett—Col Short—R. Stephenson—Mr Hawkins—Rev Mr Simpson. Rode with Agnes. Sat to Mayall: little fruit.

[1] Initialled and dated 17 April 1856; Add MS 44778, f. 206.
[2] John *Purchas, 1823–72; held sundry curacies; suspended for ritualism after a long case just before his death.
[3] Indian revenues: *H* cxli. 1189.
[4] J. M. *Neale, *The life and times of Patrick *Torry* (1856).

Read Paul Ferroll.[1] Eighteen to dinner. Saw E. Cardwell—Sir W. Heathcote —Earl of Elgin—Sir S. Scott & Co—Earl of Aberdeen *cum* Sir J. Graham, S. Herbert, E. Cardwell[2]—Count Cavour—Ld Ellesmere—M. de Lesseps.

20. 4 S. E[aster].

St James's mg (H.C.) All Saints aftn.—Pt MS of 42 aloud in evg. Read Paix de l'Ame—Neale's Life of Torry—Hervey on Inspiration (finished).[3] Saw Geo. Hope—Ld Abn. cum Sir J. Graham. Wrote to Dean of Ch Ch— Rector of Exeter—Master of Pembroke.

21. M.

Wrote to Sir C. Trevelyan—R. Barker (2)—Archdn. Bickersteth[4]—Robn. G—V. Chancr. Oxford—H. Bruce[5]—Rev. E.C. Lowe—H. Tayleur—Wm. Gladstone. H of C. & H. of L. 4–9½.[6] Read Paul Ferroll (finished)—Canada papers.[7] Saw B. Benjamin—Mr Grogan—Sir W. Heathcote—J. Wilson Patten—Marq. of Blandford. Visited the Rogers Collection.[8]

22. T.

Wrote to S. Herbert—W.W. Neville[9]—W. Lyle[10]—W. Deering. Dined at Mrs Talbot's: that C. might nurse her. Rode with Agnes. Saw Mr Grogan (let No 4)[11]—Bp of Salisbury—G. Dundas—R. Phillimore—T.G. & J.N.G. Read Kars Papers[12]—Canada Ch. Papers—De Quincey's Autobiogr. Sketches.[13]

23. Wed.

Wrote to Chr. of Exchr.—Mrs Bolter—Dean of Ch Ch—Mr Ormsby.[14] Rode with Agnes. Worked much upon a careful perusal & examn. of the Kars papers. Saw Ld St Leonards—W. Hampton—Mr Fellowes—H.K. Seymer— T.G. Visited the Mammoth Tree.[15] Dined with the Thesigers.[16] Visited the Rogers Collection. Read Traill's Letter to Ld Blandford.[17]

---

[1] See 11 Mar. 56.   [2] See 26 Apr. 56.   [3] See 15 Apr. 56.
[4] Edward *Bickersteth, 1814–92; archdeacon of Buckinghamshire 1853; dean of Lichfield 1875.
[5] Henry Austin *Bruce, 1815–95; liberal M.P. Merthyr 1852–68, Renfrewshire 1869–73; minor office 1862–4, 1866; home secretary 1868–73; lord president 1873–4; cr. Baron Aberdare 1873; chaired Royal Niger company. See Add MSS 44086–7.
[6] Estimates, and Church Discipline Bill: *H* cxli. 1344, 1251.
[7] Probably on colonial church there: *PP* 1856 xliv. 126.
[8] Exhibition of Samuel *Rogers' pictures before sale; see 2 May 56.
[9] William Wyndham Neville, 1834–58, 6th s. of G. Neville Grenville; see 25 Dec. 58.
[10] William Lyle, shorthand reporter; wrote *Government situations handbook* (1856).
[11] Carlton House Terrace; he was moving into number 11.
[12] See 8 Mar. 56.   [13] See 20 Oct. 54.
[14] Perhaps William Arthur Ormsby, rector of Smallburgh, Norfolk, from 1853.
[15] Washingtonea from California, 363 ft. high in the Adelaide gallery.
[16] Anna Maria, *née* Tinling, m. 1822 Sir F. *Thesiger, Lord Chelmsford, and d. 1875.
[17] J. C. Traill, *A letter to the marquis of Blandford, on the management of Church property* (1856).

24. Th.

Breakf. with Bp of Oxford—Saw S. Herbert—Sir W. Heathcote—Sir J. Graham—Ld Elgin—Mr Bonham—Mr Wilson—Mr Hadfield—J.N.G. (resid. Estate). Worked on Kars papers. Read Combe on Currency.[1] H. of C. $4\frac{1}{2}$–8 and $8\frac{3}{4}$–$12\frac{1}{4}$. Spoke on Goderich's motion: when we had a good vote.[2]

25. Fr. St Mark.

Wrote to Jas Freshfield—Jas Wilson—Rev. Mr Barnes. H of C. $4\frac{1}{2}$–7.[3] Rode with Willy. Saw Mr Stuart (B. Guiana)[4]—Rev. C. Christie—Sir W. Heathcote—Ld Clarendon—Ld Wodehouse—Dss. of Sutherland—Ld Derby *cum* Ld Harrowby—Ld Stanhope—Aunt J. At Christie's: saw Mr Farrer[5] & Mr [George] Richmond. Queen's (Child) Ball 9–$12\frac{1}{4}$: the most beautiful sight of the (London) year.[6] Read Mills on Colonies.[7]

26. Sat.

Wrote to Mr A. Mills—Rev J. Watson Reid[8]—Bp of Oxford—Wm. Gladstone—Jas Brown[9]—A. Panizzi—A. Gordon—Sir H. Dukinfield. Rode with Willy. Took C to the Rogers pictures. 11–$1\frac{3}{4}$ Committee of Royal Exhibition Commn. Saw R. Phillimore—Dean of Christ Church—Wm. Gladstone—Sir W. Heathcote. Wrote Pol. Mema. Dined at Ld J. Thynne's. Read Kars papers (finished)—Culling Eardley Correspce.[10]—Mills on Colonies.

On Saturday Ap. 19 at my request Ld Aberdeen summoned Sir J. Graham Herbert and Cardwell. Newcastle was to have come but did not appear. I recounted to them the whole substance of my communications with Heathcote as put in my memorandum [11] & invited them to refresh my memory by questions. Not a great deal was said but I made a clean breast & said so. There was nothing said that was adverse to the ideas I had expressed. Graham thanked me for replying without first consulting them: suggested that there was an apparent desire to deal with me alone: I told him this was not my construction, nor as I thought Heathcote's: and observed that the question was of the most vital consequence, who should lead the House of Commons? This he thought must come to me, & could not be with Disraeli. I had said & repeated that I thought we could not bargain Disraeli out of the saddle, that it must rest with him (as far as we were concerned) to hold the lead if he pleased, that besides my looking to it with doubt and dread I felt he had this right, and that I took it as one of the *data* in the case before us upon which we might have to consider the question of political junction & which might be seriously affected by it.

[1] G. *Combe, 'The currency question, considered in relation to . . . the Bank Restriction Act' (1856).
[2] *Goderich's motion on competitive examinations, lukewarmly opposed by the govt., was only narrowly defeated: *H* cxli. 1421.
[3] Misc. business: *H* cxli. 1536.   [4] See 7 Aug. 38?
[5] Henry Farrer, picture restorer and dealer.
[6] Long report in *DFLC*, i. 31–3.   [7] A. Mills, *Colonial constitutions* (1856).
[8] James Watson Reid, episcopalian incumbent in Glasgow.
[9] Perhaps James Brown of Arniston, wrote on forestry.
[10] Sir C. *Eardley, *Christianity in Turkey. Correspondence . . . relating to executions in Turkey for apostacy from Islam* (1855).
[11] See 17 Apr. 56.

I saw Heathcote afterwards & he told me that when he saw Lord Derby after the conversation with me, Lord D. had asked him whether it was possible that without being able to take office we might nevertheless be able to give him a friendly support? especially with a view to the case of the overturn of the Govt. without our cooperation or even in opposition to our votes. He alluded in touching on this point to the case of himself & Sir J. Graham in 1835 which he observed grew into political identification.

Upon this subject I told Heathcote that it would not have been well for me to have made the suggestion as it would have appeared to be like a trap, after what happened in 1852: but that I was glad Ld Derby had started it for I thought the case a possible one, and even could conceive circumstances in which it might be the best of the alternatives before us.

H. who is most earnest as well as most intelligent & judicious in this business told me also that Jolliffe had assured him that he was doing all in his power to prevent opposition to us at the Election whenever it might come but he regretted he had not been able to prevail upon Lord Bath. Col. Tayler from Ireland wrote that in deference to him he was working to the same effect. I said this was kind & generous but I feared it might be premature as it was not yet possible to forecast the shape which matters might take.

Since Sat. Ap. 19 I have discussed with Heathcote the question of Kars which appears to me to be very variously viewed even among Lord Derby's friends & to be unhappily put forward at the present moment. I understood from him yesterday that many principal men among them were quite aware of this & were labouring on some arrangement to get rid of the debate for the present.[1]

27. 5 S. E[aster].

St James's mg. All Saints Evg. MS. of 42 on Ep. aloud to servants. Conv. on do with Agnes. At Ld Abns. with Sir J.G., S.H., & Cardwell. Saw Milligan & gave Bible & Pr[ayer Book][R]. Read Neales Bp Torry—Paix de l'Âme—Clewer Papers & Carter's Sermons.[2]

28. M.

Wrote to Mrs Nimmo—Mr Labouchere—Mr W. Irvine—Rev A. Gurney. Read Central Amn. papers—Combe on Currency. Rode with Lucy [Lyttelton]. Saw Coalwhippers Deputn—A. Panizzi—R. Phillimore—Mr Grogan—Sir W. Heathcote—Ld Goderich. H. of C. 4¼-8¼ and 9¼-12¼.[3]

29. T.

Wrote to E.A. Bowring—Dr Acland—Alex. Goalen—Sir T.G.—A. Doiree[4]—R. Barker. Dined with the Mildmays. Worked on papers. Busy with house & family arrangements. Saw Sir W. Heathcote—Mr B. Benjamin—Mr Farrer (at Christie's)—Geo. Hadfield. Read Central Am. papers—Peace Protocols & Peace—[5] Crowe's pamphlets.[6] H of C. 4¼-7½ and 10½-1.

[1] Initialled and dated 26 April 1956; Add MS 44778, f. 223.
[2] T. T. Carter, *The first five years of the House of Mercy, Clewer* (1855).
[3] Whiteside's motion on fall of Kars: *H* cxli. 1594; see 17 Apr. 56.
[4] Unidentified.
[5] The treaty signed at Paris on 30 March 1856 and its protocols, published this day in *PP* 1856 lxi. 1.
[6] J. W. Crowe, 'Our army' and 'Yesterday and tomorrow; or Shadows of the war' (1856).

Voted agt. Palmerston on Adjournment mainly moved by his insolent speech.[1]

30. Wed.

Wrote to Mr M. Jones—City Remembrr.—W. Linton (2)—T.C. Sandars[2]—E.S. Cayley—G. Nicoll[3]—Ld Lyttelton—Mr Farrer. H. of C. $1\frac{3}{4}$–6.[4] Saw Ld Aberdeen—R. Phillimore—Sir W. Heathcote—Sir Jas Graham—J.N.G.—Mr Farrer (at his Gallery)—M. Van de Weyer—Mr J.W. Knott. Concert at the Palace $9\frac{3}{4}$–$12\frac{1}{4}$. Read Eastern Papers Parts 17 & 18—Peace Protocols.

Thurs. May One. 1856.
Ascension Day.

All Saints Holy C. at 8 A.M. Exhibn. Commee. Meeting 11–$12\frac{1}{4}$. We went wrong: I dissenting.[5] Wrote to Dr Acland—Rev C. Lowder[6]—Mr J. Farrer[7]—Mr Grogan—Scotts—Ld Overstone—Ld Lyttelton—City Remembrancer—Rector of Exeter—Read Johnson on Falkl. Isl[8]—Swainson on N.Z.[9] Saw Ld Overstone—Sir C. Trevelyan—J.N.G.—Mr Grogan—Mr Bonham. H of C. $4\frac{1}{2}$–$7\frac{1}{4}$ and $9\frac{1}{4}$–$1\frac{1}{2}$. A very well sustained debate. Voted in 303:178 agt. Mr Whiteside.[10]

2. Fr.

Wrote to Ld J. Thynne—Mr Farrer (cancelled)—Ld Lyttelton—Dr Kynaston. Read Col. Ch. papers.[11] H of C. 5–$7\frac{3}{4}$ and $11\frac{1}{2}$–$1\frac{1}{2}$.[12] Attended the Rogers Sale from $1\frac{1}{2}$ to $4\frac{1}{2}$: my *convoitise*[13] was not gratified. Rode with L[ucy] L[yttelton]. Saw M. Van de Weyer—Sir W. Heathcote—Mr Denison—Hon A. Kinnaird—Mr Liddell. The Herberts dined & we had much conversation.

3. Sat.

Wrote to Count Strzelecki—T. Nimmo—Mr Newland—S. Bannister—T.M. Gladstone—Rev. Mr. Berry. Read U.S. Papers. Breakfasted at Grillions.

---

[1] On the fall of Kars; the govt. easily survived: H cxli. 1781.

[2] Thomas Collett *Sandars, 1825–94; barrister, civil service commissioner and editor of Justinian.

[3] Accountant in Mincing Lane.   [4] Housing: H cxli. 1786.

[5] 1851 Exhibition cttee. supported moving the National Gallery to S. Kensington.

[6] Charles Fuge *Lowder, 1820–80, curate of St. Barnabas, Pimlico, 1851–6, of St. Peter's, London docks, from 1866; worked in tractarian missions in London, provoking anti-ritualist riots.

[7] Picture dealer in New Bond Street; see next day.

[8] S. *Johnson, *Thoughts on the late transactions respecting the Falkland Islands* (1771).

[9] W. *Swainson, *New Zealand* (1856).

[10] On the fall of Kars; the tories voted with *Whiteside: H cxli. 1903.

[11] PP 1856 xliv. 137; see 3 Jan. 55.

[12] Argued all art collections should be scrutinized by Parliament before being sold: H cxli. 1946.

[13] 'covetousness'. Sale of Samuel *Rogers' pictures, from 28 April to 10 May.

Attended the French Exhibn. 12–1.[1] The Academy Exhibition 2–5 and remained after dinner till 10½. Many pictures remarkable: Hunt's awful.[2] Saw Mr Herbert—Mr Dyce—& other artists.—Mr J. Lefevre—Sir P.G. Egerton—Lady Dunmore—Ld John Thynne.

4. S. aft. Ascension.

St James's 11 A.M. (H.C.) & 7 P.M. MS of 1840 aloud evg. At Ld Aberdeens 3–5. Saw Mrs Langton—R. Phillimore—Read Neales Bp Torry (finished)—Paix de l'Âme.

5. M.

Wrote to W.M. Goalen—E. Thornton[3]—Chancr. of Exchr.—Robn. G. Rode with Agnes. Dined with the Woods. Tea at Lady C. Russells.[4] H. of C. 4½–7¾ and 9¾–12. (minus 20 m. to tea).[5] Saw R. Phillimore—Mr J. Robertson—Hon. A. Kinnaird (bis)—Sir Wm. Heathcote—Mr Goldwin Smith—Sir J. Graham—Sir W.C. James. Read Recruiting Papers U.S.

6. Tu.

Wrote to P. Norton—Read U.S. Recruiting Papers—Johnson's Falkl. Islands.[6] Nine to breakfast. Rode with Agnes. Saw Sir C. Barry—Mr J.R. Herbert—Mr F.R. Bonham—Jas Wilson—A. Kinnaird—Sir J. Graham. Dined at Mrs Talbots. H of C. 4–7½ and 8¼–1¼. Spoke (1 hour) on the Peace & Protocols, particularly the Belgian case, dangerous but not to be avoided.[7]

7. Wed.

Wrote to P. Norton—Christie & Manson—W. Linton—Sec. Nightingale F[und]—J. Leslie—Dean Torry—Sir C. Barry—G.C. Stanfield.[8] H. of C. 1–5¼: spoke on Phillimore's Bill.[9] Saw London Corpn. Deputn.—Lyttelton —Sir W. Riddell & their party. Attended Superannn. Commn. Nine to dinner & large evening party: Van de Weyer[10] spoke to me in strong terms. Read Recruiting papers & Prescott's Philip II.[11]

8. Th.

Wrote to J. Freshfield—P. Norton. 12¼–4¼ went to lay the foundation stone of the Golden Lane Schools for Mr Rogers.[12] Saw Mr Grogan—Sir W.

---

[1] Charles Okey's exhibition, 'Paris', in the Regent gallery.
[2] *The Scapegoat* by Holman *Hunt, which provoked much clerical hostility.
[3] Edward Thornton, tr. Schiller's *Wallenstein* (1854).
[4] Caroline Alicia Diana, da. of 1st earl of Limerick, m. 1834 George Lake Russell, 1802–78, and d. 1890.
[5] Peace concluded: *H* cxli. 2037.   [6] See 1 Mar. 56.
[7] Condemning attacks on the Belgian press in the peace protocols: *H* cxlii. 103.
[8] George Clarkson *Stanfield, 1828–78, artist (Hawn P).
[9] Supporting *Phillimore's Tithe Commutation Bill: *H* cxlii. 162.
[10] i.e. the Belgian ambassador; see previous day.   [11] See 19 Mar. 56.
[12] See 'Report of the proceedings at the ceremony of laying the foundation stone of St. Thomas, Charterhouse', with William *Rogers.

Heathcote—H. Baillie—Mr Miles—R. Palmer—Count Vizthum—Mr
Whiteside[1]—Mr Dyce—Mr R Lowe (Oxf.)—Sir J. Graham—Count
Lavradio & Bernstorff[2] spoke to me in very different senses ab. my speech
of Tuesday. H of C. 5–7¼. To the Queen's Ball at 9¼. Read U.S. papers—
Rogers on Costermongria.[3]

9. Fr.

H. of C. 4½–7, 9½–11 and again at 12½.[4] Began seriously preparations for
departure. Rode with Agnes: made calls. Dined at Mrs Talbots: charades.
Saw M. Tricoupi—R. Phillimore—E. Cardwell—Sir J. Graham—Col.
Gordon—Hon A. Kinnaird.

10. Sat.

Wrote to Mr Stonehouse—Ld Lyttelton. Saw R. Phillimore—Mr & Mrs
Hughes[5]—Mr Whiteside. Dined at Baron Rothschild's[6] where I had much
conversation with Ld Lyndhurst. Lady Derby's afterwards. A stiff day's
work in movings to No 11 and preparations for putting away.

11. Whits.

St James's mg (& H.C.)—Chapel Royal aft: MS of 47 aloud. Saw A.
Kinnaird—Bp of Oxford & Bp of St David's.[7] Read Paix de l'Ame—
Clewer pamphlets—Bp of Exeter's Speech[8]—Stansfeld on Lord's Day.[9]
Wrote to Rev Mr Ridley[10]—R. Phillimore—and [blank]

12. Whitmonday.

Wrote to Robn. G—Col Bertie Gordon[11]—Rev W. Rawson—Supt Xt
Knowl Depot[12]—Sir W. James—C.H. Butcher[13]—J.N.G. Dined at Lady
Wenlock's. Finished U.S. Recruiting papers. A day of tumult in arranging
for departure. Saw Edw. Ellis—Sir S. Scott & Co—Ld Braybrooke—Ld
Lyndhurst—Geo. Nicoll—Earl of Aberdeen—Ld Lyttelton—Hon Mrs
Stuart Wortley.

---

[1] James *Whiteside, 1804–76; defended *O'Connell 1843; tory M.P. Enniskillen 1851–9,
Dublin university 1859–66; minor office 1858–9, 1865–6; lord chief justice, Ireland, 1866;
wrote on Italy. See 17 Apr. 56.
[2] i.e. The Portuguese and Prussian ambassadors.
[3] Untraced pamphlet by W. *Rogers on his parish; see his *Reminiscences* (1888) 51, 75.
[4] Misc. business: *H* cxlii. 258.
[5] Elizabeth, *née* Wormald, m. 1825 W. B. Hughes, Peelite M.P. (cp. 16 Oct. 47).
[6] At 148 Piccadilly.   [7] i.e. Connop *Thirlwall.
[8] H. *Phillpotts, 'Speech . . . on the Church Discipline Bill' (1856).
[9] Untraced pamphlet by J. or H. Stansfeld.
[10] William Henry *Ridley, 1816–82; student of Christ Church 1836–41; rector of
Hambledon from 1840; wrote on clerical incomes; see Add MS 44385, f. 340.
[11] See 22 July 55.
[12] George Cox, d. 1857; the S.P.C.K. depository was in Great Queen Street.
[13] Charles Henry Butcher, 1833–1907, curate of St. Clement Danes, London, 1856–8,
of St. Paul's, Hammersmith 1858–63; then missionary in China.

13. *Whit Tues.* [*Albury*]

After three hours of very hard work in packing, righting, orders, & accounts, we got off at 12 & had a sweet & most tranquil journey to Albury[1] by Leatherhead. We were most kindly received. Read De Quincey's Autobiogr. Sketches[2]—Seymour on Russia.[3] Conv. with Rev Mr Portal on Church matters & hopes.[4]

14. *Wed.*

Wrote to Sir J. Graham—Duke of Newcastle. Read Autobiogr. Sketches—Ruskin's Modern Painters—Q.R. on Eastern Question—Do on Montalembert[5]—Dorans Men & Habits.[6] Ld Lovaine took us a delightful Park Wood & heath walk. Music in evg. Conv. with Miss Alderson:[7] a remarkable person: & with our host on his Bowyer controversy.[8]

15. *Th.*

Wrote to Willy & Stephy—Mrs Bibby[9]—Rev Mr Nihill—Rev Mr West—Rev Mr Yates[10]—Read De Quincey—Amn. Recruiting Pamphlet—Palmer's Trial[11]—Autobiography of a Beggar Boy.[12] Walk in Weston Woods.[13] Music in evg.

16. *Fr.*

Wrote to J.E. Jones[14]—Ld Blandford. Walk &c. to St Martha's[15] wh has a glorious view: & saw the Tuppers. Also enjoyed the garden here. Saw Mr Drummond's 'Church' with its light, incense, & confessional.[16] Music in evg. Read De Quincey—Autobiogr. of Beggar Boy—Palmer's Trial—Mozley's Preface.[17] Read the melancholy MS. wh tells the tale of Lady Gage.[18]

[1] Seat of Henry *Drummond, 3½ miles SE. of Guildford; when he d. 1860 it passed to Lord Lovaine, his son-in-law. *Drummond built two Irvingite chapels in the grounds, which became the movement's centre.
[2] See 22 Apr. 56.
[3] H. D. Seymour, *Russia on the Black Sea and the Sea of Azof* (1855).
[4] George Raymond Portal, 1827–89; curate of St. Barnabas, Pimlico, 1852–7; rector of Albury 1858–71, of Burghclere from 1871; friend of *Drummond who, as patron of the living, fulfilled his hopes.
[5] *Quarterly Review*, xcviii. 502, 535 (March 1856).
[6] J. *Doran, *Habits and men, with records on makers of both* (1855).
[7] Georgina Alderson, a strong tractarian, m. 1857 Lord R. Cecil, Lord Salisbury.
[8] (Sir) G. *Bowyer, Roman catholic lawyer, who had recently published pamphlets on the papacy, see 2 Apr. 56.
[9] Unidentified.
[10] Probably James Yates, 1822?–68; fellow of Sidney Sussex, Cambridge, 1846; taught at King Edward's, Birmingham 1849.
[11] Just started; see 25 May 56.
[12] [J. D. Burn], *Autobiography of a Beggar Boy* (1855).
[13] On a ridge to the NE. of the park.
[14] John Edward Jones, 1806–62; society sculptor, mostly of busts.
[15] An ancient church on the hill between Albury and Guildford, restored by M. F. *Tupper 1848. The Tuppers lived at Albury House, by the park, and had quarrelled with *Drummond; see D. Hudson, *Tupper* (1949) 76–9.
[16] *Drummond's Irvingite chapel.
[17] J. B. *Mozley, *The primitive doctrine of baptismal regeneration* (1856).
[18] Not found.

17. Sat. [Polesden Park]

At 10.45 we drove off to Wotton[1] where Mr Evelyn showed us his curiosities: of the place we saw little. Then on to Polesden[2] by Dorking. In the aftn. we had a walk over Ranmore Common[3] & enjoyed the views. Music in evg. read De Quincey.

18. Trin S.

Gt Bookham Ch[4] (with its singular monuments) mg and aftn. Read Tyndale's Brief Declaration, & answer to More resp. H. Eucharist: wretched doctrine.[5] Also Zurich letters Vol. 2.[6]—Paix de l'Ame. My walks were four of 2 m. each, to Church twice & back: with F[arquhar] & Lady M[ary]—We conversed about his son.[7]

19. M. [London]

Wrote to Rector of Exeter Coll—S. Herbert—Saw Sir J. Graham—R. Phillimore. Left Polesden 10.30 and reached Maurigys Hotel[8] before 3, conveying Lady G. Bathurst,[9] and stopping $1\frac{1}{4}$ hour at Hampton Court for the palace & pictures. H. of C. $4\frac{1}{2}$–$8\frac{1}{2}$ and 9.–1. Spoke on the Budget & Sardinia.[10]

20. T.

Wrote to J. Griffiths—Rev Mr Browne—Luxmore—Hutchinson—Rector of Exeter—Mrs Stonehouse[11]—T. Cadwallader[12]—W. Scholefield[13]—Mrs Cruden.[14] Saw Mr Stanistreet—Mr J. Griffiths—Sir W. Farquhar & conclave on the bequest[15]—Sir J. Graham—Jas Wortley—Sir W. Heathcote—

M. Van de Weyer⎫
   Azeglio   ⎬ at Mad.
   Vitzthum   ⎭ Persigny's.[16]

—Mr Hildyard—Mr Liddell. Dined at the French Embassy. H of C. $4\frac{1}{2}$–$7\frac{1}{2}$.

---

[1] Wotton House, Evelyn's place, with many of the diarist's relics.
[2] Polesden Park, seat of Sir W. R. Farquhar, $2\frac{1}{4}$ miles NW. of Dorking; see 5 Aug. 54.
[3] Between Polesden and Dorking.   [4] See 6 Aug. 54.
[5] W. *Tyndale, *A brief declaration of the Sacraments* (1536) and *An answer to Sir Thomas *More's Dialogue The Supper of the Lord* (1536), reprinted ed. H. Walter (1848).
[6] See 8 Feb. 46.
[7] (Sir) Henry Thomas Farquhar, 1838–1916; Gladstone's god-son; 4th bart. 1900; he went to Harrow, but was not further educated.
[8] At 1 Regent Street.
[9] Lady Louisa Georgiana Bathurst, d. 1874, da. of the politician; she held minor court offices.
[10] On the Sardinian loan proposed in the budget: *H* cxlii. 374.
[11] She kept a house of refuge, see 3 July 56.
[12] James Cadwallader, curate of Old Sodbury; rector of Littleton-on-Severn 1884.
[13] William *Scholefield, 1809-67: Birmingham business man and liberal M.P. there from 1847.
[14] Unidentified.   [15] No clue as to its nature in Add MS 44155.
[16] The French Ambassador's wife.

Spoke on the Eccl. Court Bills.[1] Read Abp of Armagh's Letter[2]—Powys on Liturgy Reform.[3] Family arrangements.

21. Wed.

Wrote to Robn. Gladstone—Wm. Gladstone—Rev Mr How[4]—A. Hayward —Rev Mr Simpson—R. Phillimore. Saw Lady S. Ramsay[5]—Ld Aberdeen— do with Sir J. Graham—J.N.G.—Mr Gibson (U.S. papers)—Mr Stanistreet. H. of C. 2–4.[6] Visited National Gallery. Dined with the R. Palmers: an excellent party. Spencer House afterwards.[7] Read Modern Society in Rome[8] —Creasy's Turks Vol II.

22. Th.

Wrote to Mr Pitman—S. Price[9]—Rev Mr Ridley—J. Grinsted[10]—Rector of Exeter—W. Muter[11]—Archd. Harrison—Willy and Stephy. Read Ridley on Clergy Rating[12]—D. of Buckm. on the Regency.[13] Dined with the Oswalds. Saw Mr G. Smith—Sir W. Heathcote (bis)—Ld Blandford—E. Cardwell: and Mr Bonham. H of C. $4\frac{1}{2}$–$7\frac{3}{4}$ and 11–$1\frac{1}{2}$ (Ld Blandford's [Parishes] Bill.)[14]

23. Fr. X

Wrote to Mr R. Eliot—S. Cave[15]—Flynn[16]—Rev Mr Woodgate—Rector of Exeter—Rev Mr Hamilton—Mr W. Emery.[17] Dined at Lady Wenlocks. Saw Bp of Salisbury—Mr H. Baillie—Sir J. Graham—Ld Blandford—A. Gordon—R. Phillimore & Ld A. Hervey. H of C. 4–$7\frac{1}{2}$ and at $10\frac{1}{2}$.[18] Saw Milligan[R]. Read Peltier's Trial[19]—Froude's Hist. Engl.[20]

[1] And voted against the ballot: *H* cxlii. 454.
[2] J. G. *Beresford, 'A letter to [Phillpotts] on the Church Discipline Bill' (1856).
[3] A. L. Powys, 'Liturgical revision and church reform the only remaining remedy for the spread of Romanism' (1856).
[4] William Walsham *How, 1823–97; bp. of Bedford 1879, of Wakefield 1888; humanitarian, worked much in London's East End.
[5] Lady Susan Georgiana Broun-Ramsay, da. of 1st marquis of *Dalhousie, m. 1863 Robert *Bourke, 1st Baron Connemara, and divorced him 1890; she m. 1894 W. H. Broun and d. 1898.
[6] Church Rates: *H* cxlii. 467.   [7] Earl Spencer's town house in St. James's Place.
[8] J. R. Best, *Modern Society in Rome*, 3v. (1856).   [9] Unidentified.
[10] John Grinsted, financial journalist.   [11] Not found.
[12] W. H. *Ridley, 'Clerical incomes and clerical taxation. A letter to W. E. Gladstone' (1856); on *Phillimore's tithe bill.
[13] R. *Grenville, Duke of Buckingham, *Memoirs of the Court of England, during the Regency 1811–20*, 2v. (1856).
[14] *H* cxlii. 576.
[15] (Sir) Stephen *Cave, 1820–80; barrister; tory M.P. New Shoreham from 1859; paymaster 1866–8, 1874–80; chaired West India cttee.; G.C.B. 1880.
[16] Unidentified.
[17] William *Emery, 1825–1910; fellow of Corpus, Cambridge, 1847–65; archdeacon of Ely 1864–1907; Church Congress organiser.
[18] Misc. business: *H* cxlii. 555.
[19] J. G. Peltier, 'The trial of John Peltier, Esq. for a libel against Napoleon Buonaparte' (1803).
[20] J. A. *Froude, *History of England from the fall of Wolsey to the death of Elizabeth*, 12v. (1856–70).

24. Sat.

Wrote to Rev Mr Stonehouse—Rev Mr A. Bruce[1]—Rev Mr Russell and to Rev. Mr Pattison.[2] Dined with the Wortleys: Lady Derby's party afterwards. Again we missed Landseer. Saw Mr G. Smith—Rev Mr Ludlow—R. Phillimore—Provost of Eton—Geo.W. Hope—Ld Barrington[3]—J. Wortley (U.S.) Read Peltier's Trial—Pennant's Journey.[4]

25. 1 S. Trin.

St James mg & Ch. Royal aftn. 3–5¼ at Ld Abns. on U.S. affairs: somewhat to my dissatisfaction as far as the day was concerned. Saw Mrs Langton[R]. Wrote to Mrs Langton and [blank]. Read Wodrow Publications[5]—Paix de l'Ame—Bp of Moray's Sermon.[6] & other pamphlets.

26. M. X.

Breakf. with J. Wortley & off to Palmer's Trial.[7] Heard Ld Campbell[8] till 5½: sitting between Serj. Shee & Mr James.[9] I liked ill both the looks & the demeanour of the prisoner. H of C. 5¾–7.[10] Wrote to Rev Mr Rogers—J.H. Parker—J.R. Godley. Dined with the Jameses. Saw R. Phillimore—Eugen[R]. Read Stephen's Letter to Ld Derby.[11]

27. T.

Wrote to Rev C.H. Davis—Mr Grogan—R Barker—T. Russell—R[euben] Browning—J. Ormsby—Robn. G—F. Cortazzi—J. Nunn. Worked on letters & accts. Saw Sir W. Heathcote—Mr F.R. Bonham—Mr Dignan[12]—Lord Aberdeen—Scotts & Co. H of C. 4¼–7 and 8¼–1½.[13] Read De Quincey's Sketches—Froude's History of England.

---

[1] Alexander Bruce, ordained 1810, episcopal incumbent at Banff.

[2] Mark *Pattison, 1813–84; gradually abandoned youthful tractarianism; fellow of Lincoln, Oxford, 1843, resigned 1855; journalist and educationalist; rector of Lincoln 1861. Prototype of Squire Wendover in *Robert Elsmere* and, in part, of Casaubon in *Middlemarch*.

[3] William Keppel Barrington, 1793–1867; 6th Viscount Barrington (Irish peerage) 1829; tory M.P. Berkshire 1837–57.

[4] See 19 Sept. 53.

[5] Society formed in Edinburgh in 1843 for publishing Church of Scotland founders' works.

[6] R. Eden, 'The path of the youthful minister in days of controversy' (1856).

[7] Sensational case of William *Palmer, the Rugeley poisoner, convicted on circumstantial evidence and hanged 14 June 1856. The trial lasted from 14 to 27 May, many peers and M.P.s attending.

[8] John *Campbell, 1779–1861; lord chief justice 1850; lord chancellor 1859; wrote *Lives of the lord chancellors* (see 15 Aug. 46).

[9] (Sir) William *Shee, (1808–68, liberal M.P. co. Kilkenny 1852–7, first Roman catholic judge since reformation 1863; kt. 1864) defended. Edwin John *James (1812–22, liberal M.P. Marylebone 1859–61, bankrupt and emigrated 1861) assisted Sir A. J. E. *Cockburn, attorney general, in prosecuting.

[10] Joint Stock Bills: *H* cxlii. 633.

[11] Probably C. A. Stevens, 'Remarks on the rating of tithe commutation rent-charge' (1856), though not addressed to Derby.

[12] Perhaps Thomas Dignam, solicitor in Sise Lane.

[13] Irish church: *H* cxlii. 715.

28. Wed.

Wrote to Mr Hadlow—Willy. Dined with the Beresford Hopes. Lady Wood's afterwards. Saw Mr Hallam—Mr Ruttley—S. Herbert. Read De Quincey's Sketches—Bazancourts Memoirs[1]—Creagh's Letter[2]—Italie.[3] C. was laid up with giddiness.

29. Th.

Wrote to M.F. Tupper—S. Samuel[4]—J.W. Williams—Rev J.L. Ross—E.H. Tripp.[5] We went to the birthday drawing room: & the fireworks in the evening we saw from the roof of Stafford House. We had grand material but much poverty of invention in the use of it. Willy came up. Saw Duke of Argyll—Bp of Rochester—Bp Spencer. Read Froudes Hist. of England—Peltier's Address.

30. Fr. X

Wrote to A. Panizzi. H of C. $4\frac{1}{2}$–$7\frac{1}{2}$ and $11\frac{1}{4}$–$12\frac{1}{4}$.[6] Attended Radcliffe Trust Meeting at $12\frac{1}{2}$–Ch Building Socy. at 2. Read Lords Evidence (Appeals)[7]—Froude's Hist of England—Elliot on Suffr. Bps.[8] Saw Mr [Norman] Macdonald—Rev. Mr Hobhouse—Sir J. Graham—Sir W. Heathcote—Bp of Salisbury—Ld H. Vane. Dined at Ld Harry Vane's. Saw M. Felicn: bad indeed[R].

31. Sat.

Wrote to A. Williams—Mr Labouchere—Mr Woodgate—Ly Lyttelton—Mr Pitman—Mr L. Barber—Rev. O. Gordon—Rev J.L. Ross—Rev Mr Hollinsed.[9] Arranged letters. Luncheon at Stafford House: & long conv. with the Duke of Argyll on the U.S. questions. Visited Christie's. Dined with the Herberts & again on U.S. matters. Read Froude's Hist.—Lords Evidence on Appeals.

2 S. Trin. June 1. 56.

St James & H.C. mg. Broad Court Ch. evg. Explained St Luk. 14.v.—to servants in evg: quatenus eheu miser potui.[10] Read Mozley on Bapt Reg.[11]—Froude Vol 2. Chap 1.—Paix de l'Ame. Walk with C. Saw R. Cavendish.

---

[1] C. de Bazancourt, *The Crimean Expedition, to the capture of Sebastopol*, tr. R. H. Gould, 2v. (1856).

[2] Perhaps by James Creagh, whose memoirs *Sparks from camp fires* (1901) describe the war.

[3] Perhaps G. Briano, *La politique française en Italie* (1856).

[4] Sylvester Samuel, Liverpool merchant, lived in Rodney Street.

[5] Edwin H. Tripp, stockbroker in Castle Court.

[6] Cambridge University Bill: *H* cxlii. 807.

[7] Select cttee. of the lords on appellate jurisdiction: *PP* 1856 viii. 401.

[8] G. Elliot, 'Observations on the Marquis of Blandford's Question, May 23rd 1856. (Concerning the appointment of suffragen Bishops)' (1856).

[9] Richard Edward Hollingsed, b. 1821?; Queen's, Oxford; vicar of North Moreton, Berkshire; n.i. *Crockford* (1860).

[10] On Sabbatarianism; 'so far alas as I, poor thing, was able'.   [11] See 16 May 56.

2. M. X

Wrote to R. Browning—Willy—Mr Ruttley. Dined at Mr Moffatt's to meet Dallas[1] & Clarendon—our party was anything but political. 8.30–10.15 A.M. With C. to the Exhibition.[2] At 12 to Benjamin's. 12.45–3 Attended Christie's Sale: bought the Bonifazio.[3] Saw Sir W. Heathcote—Rev. Mr Woodgate—Sir J. Graham—R. Phillimore—Mr Bouverie—Lady Cremorne[4]—Mr Massey.[5] Saw Lightfoot[R]. Lady Jersey's in evg. Read Froude's Hist. H of C. $4\frac{1}{2}$–$7\frac{1}{2}$.[6]

3. T. X.

Wrote to R. Browning—W.R. Farquhar—S. Herbert—Earl of Aberdeen. Saw Milligan[R]. Dined with Mrs Speirs. Attended Christie's. Saw Bp of Oxford—Ld Lovaine—Duke of Newcastle—Lady Cremorne—Mr Whiteside. Read Froude's Hist (Finished 1)—Doubleday's Peel, & Appx[7]— Lords Appellate Evidence. Willy's [sixteenth] birthday: may he be blessed in all things.

4. Wed. X.

Wrote to Mr Ruttley. H. of C. 3–$5\frac{3}{4}$. Spoke in Comm. on Dissrs. Marriages Bill.[8] Dined at Ld Mayor's: spoke for Oxford.[9] Saw Bp of Oxford—Mr Knight M.P.—Mr H. Baillie M.P.—R. Phillimore—Archdn. Sinclair—Ld J. Russell (at the dinner)—R. Palmer. Read Froude's Hist.—Peltier Address & papers—Lords Appellate Evidence—Saw Mate [R].

5. Th.

Wrote to Mate.[R]. Went to the Palace with Oxford Delegacy:[10] then to (an early) dinner with Ld Derby as Chancellor. Saw Sir W. Heathcote— Mr Powell—Earl of Aberdeen—Master of Pembroke—Mr Liddell—Wilson Patten—Ld Delamere—Ld Ely[11] resp. America. H. of C. $5\frac{1}{2}$–$10\frac{3}{4}$ (& H. of L.)[12] Read Froude—U.S. papers. Breakf. with Stafford.

---

[1] George Mifflin Dallas, 1792–1864; democratic lawyer and senator; U.S. minister in London 1856–61; negotiated settlement of Nicaragua with *Clarendon. The dismissal of the British minister in Washington had endangered relations; see 16 June 56.

[2] Exhibition of American plants in Ashburnham Park.

[3] Later sold, no longer at Hawarden.

[4] Augusta, *née* Stanley, m. 1841 Richard Dawson, 1817–97, liberal, later a unionist; 2nd Baron Cremorne 1827, cr. earl of Dartrey 1866; she d. 1887.

[5] William Nathaniel *Massey, 1809–81; liberal M.P. Newport 1852–7, Salford 1857–65, Tiverton 1872–81; under-sec. home office 1855–8; chaired Commons cttees. 1859–65; historian.

[6] Supply: *H* cxlii. 865.

[7] T. Doubleday, *The political life of the Rt. Hon. Sir Robert *Peel*, 2v. (1856).

[8] *H* cxlii. 944.

[9] Urging the expansion of Oxford's influence in commerce: *The Times*, 5 June 1856, 10b.

[10] To congratulate the Queen on the peace.

[11] John Henry Loftus, 1814–57; tory M.P. Woodstock 1845; 3rd marquess of Ely 1845.

[12] Army education: *H* cxlii. 980.

6. *Fr.*

Wrote to H. Baillie (2)—Mrs Bennett—Rev E. Hawkins—M.F. Tupper. 11–1 at Ld Aberdeen's. Saw Scotts—Mr Cheetham[1]—E. Cardwell—Sir W. Heathcote(bis)—R. Phillimore—J.S. Wortley—Mr Liddell—Ld Elcho— Mr Forster[2]—resp. U.S.[3] Dined at Sir J. Walsh's.[4] H of C. $4\frac{1}{4}$–$7\frac{1}{2}$ and $10\frac{1}{2}$– $12\frac{1}{4}$.[5] Col. Bprics meeting 3 P.M. At Christie's: ἄπρακτος.[6]

Memorandum of June 6 given by W.E.G. to Sir W. Heathcote for confidential use on his own part & on that of those present at Ld Aberdeen's. *Private*

1. No motion should be made unless with a prospect of very extensive support.
2. As to its terms, it should contemplate peace as the first & paramount object —but the conduct of affairs as disclosed in the correspondence on Recruiting cannot be justified.
3. On account of the immense importance of the subject & its critical circs. it wd. be of the greatest advantage if some gentleman known not to be a candidate for power as well as otherwise highly qualified could be induced to make the motion; but Mr. Baillie's official character need not in our view be an obstacle to his being the seconder if he think fit.[7] If however the mover is a person in opposition, it appears to us that it would be most expedient that an independent member in high position, & not ordinarily in opposition to the Govt. should second it if such can be found.[8]

7. *Sat.*

Wrote to Coalwhippers—R. Lowe—S. Herbert—J.H. Parker. Read (further) U.S. papers[9]—Papers on Italy. Saw Sir W. Heathcote—Mr S. Fitzgerald[10]—Mr Stanistreet—Mr Christie—Sir C. Burrell. Br. Museum 2–4. British Institn. $12\frac{1}{4}$–$1\frac{3}{4}$. Visited Miss Eden. Dined with Sir W. Heathcote to meet Mr Dallas.

8. *3 S. Trin.*

St James's 8 A.M. (H.C.) 11 A.M. & 7 P.M. Wrote to Sir W. Heathcote— Mrs Langton[R]. Saw Ld Abn. & Sir J. Graham $1\frac{1}{2}$–$4\frac{1}{2}$. —Lady Dunraven & Ly Cremorne—J.S. Wortley—Sir W. Heathcote—Ld E. Bruce. Dined

[1] John Cheetham, 1802–86; Staleybridge manufacturer; liberal M.P. S. Lancashire 1852–9, Salford 1865–8.
[2] Possibly W. E. *Forster (see 9 May 62) already known for his interest in U.S.A., but no record of this meeting in Reid, *F*.
[3] Draft resolution effectively supporting U.S. complaints about recruiting; Add MS 44746, f. 28.
[4] Sir John Benn *Walsh, 1798–1881; 2nd bart. 1825; tory M.P. Sudbury 1830–4, 1837–40, Radnorshire 1840–68, when cr. Baron Ormathwaite.
[5] Supply: *H* cxlii. 1127.
[6] 'effecting nothing'.
[7] See 17 Apr. 56 for Baillie's motion.
[8] 'Mr T. Baring. Ld Harry Vane. June 6. 56' added later at bottom of note; Add MS 44746, f. 31.
[9] *PP* 1856 1x. 329, issued previous day, on Guatemala.
[10] Sir [William Robert] Seymour Vesey-*Fitzgerald, 1818–85; tory M.P. Horsham 1848, 1852–65, 1874–5; under-sec. F.O. 1858–9; governed Bombay 1867–72; kt. 1867.

with the J. Wortleys. Read Paix de l'Ame—Bp Nixon's Charge[1]—Archdn. Hale's Charge.[2]

9. M.

Wrote to R. Palmer—Watson & Smith—Mr Cowell—J.C. Robinson[3]—Mr Rees—Mr Davidson—Mr [T.H.] Mayhew—Mr H. Smith. Saw Col. Boldero —Mr Dering—R. Phillimore—Mr Hayter—Sir W. Heathcote(bis)—Mr Baillie—Mr Christie—Ld Abn. cum Graham & Cardwell—Lady Dunraven. Read Froude's Hist H. of C. $4\frac{1}{2}$–8 and $10\frac{3}{4}$–$1\frac{1}{4}$.[4]

10. T.

Wrote to Mr Williamson—Rev Mr Lake—Wm. Gladstone—Robn. G—Mr M. Lothian[5]—Mr A. Black[6]—C.W. Sikes[7]—W. Sherlock[8]—Ed. Common-wealth.[9] Saw Mrs Loftus—Ld Dalhousie—R. Phillimore—Dean Ramsay— Sir J. Graham—Messrs. Scott—Rev. Dr Hessey—Mrs Walker(sat)[10]—Ld Granville—Mr Wm. Brown—Mr Christie. The U.S. accounts looked better. Dined with Lady Wenlock: Lady Granville's afr. H of C. $4\frac{1}{2}$–$7\frac{3}{4}$ and late.[11] Saw two [R]. Read Froude.

11. Wed.

Wrote to Mr W.J. Smith[12]—Mr Chambers. Dined with Mr Wilson Patten. H. of C. 3–6.[13] Saw B. Benjamin—Ld Aberdeen—Mr Christie—Mr J.C. Robinson (Marlb. Ho)—J. Wilson Patten. Meeting at Ld Abns. at night to consider further the dft. Address & the U.S. question. Read Palmer's Letter to Ld Campbell[14]—Worked on U.S. papers.

12. Th.

Wrote to J.H. Parker—Rev G.B. Morris[15]—Sir C. Barry—Mr H. Jones— Mr G. Brown. Saw Mr D. Gibb[16]—Mr H. Baillie(bis)—Rev Mr Lake—Rev Mr Kennaway—Sir W. Heathcote—Mr Panizzi—J. Wilson—Mr Lacaita—

---

[1] F. R. Nixon, 'A charge delivered at the visitation held in May 1851' (1851).
[2] W. H. Hale, 'The office of the suffragan, or titular bishop in the Church of England' (1856).
[3] (Sir) John Charles *Robinson, 1824–1913; first superintendent of S. Kensington museum art collections 1852–69; kt. 1887; often consulted by Gladstone on potential picture and china purchases.
[4] Spoke on Cambridge University Bill: *H* cxlii. 1214.
[5] Maurice Lothian of Edinburgh.
[6] Adam *Black, 1784–1874; Edinburgh publisher; liberal M.P. Edinburgh 1856–65.
[7] (Sir) Charles William *Sikes, 1818–89; Huddersfield banker; proposed savings bank scheme effected by Gladstone's 1860 budget; kt. 1881.
[8] William Sherlock, Birmingham knife manufacturer.
[9] Glasgow weekly; not published.   [10] The engraver, see 30 Jan. 44.
[11] Voted for death penalty: *H* cxlii. 1262.
[12] William John Bernhard Smith, barrister.   [13] Misc. business: *H* cxlii. 1297.
[14] T. Palmer, pseud., 'A letter to the lord chief justice Campbell' (?1856); on the Rugeley poisoner's case.
[15] Apparently a nonconformist.
[16] Of T. A. Gibb and co., East India merchants.

Mr Henley—Ld R. Cecil—Sir J. Graham. Dined with Sir C. Wood. Worked on U.S. papers. H. of C. 4½–8 and 10¾–12¾.[1] At C. Wood's we learned Lord P. was at Ascot. His absence from H of C. had been put down to a long Cabinet!

13. Fr.

Wrote to A. Panizzi—H. Baillie (& dft.)[2]—J. Cole—J. Griffiths—Rector of Exeter—J. Freshfield—Jafir Alee—Ld Perth.[3] H of C. 4½–7½ and again late for Oxford Bill &c.[4] Saw Sir W. Heathcote—Mr Baillie—Mr R. Phillimore—Mr Lacaita—Mr N.W. Senior—Mr Henley—Ld A. Hervey. After consultn. with Graham Ld Abn. & Cardwell, & hearing the answers in Parlt. we made an end of our address & I gave it to Baillie (who was eager for it) at 7½. He adopted it bodily as I saw by the Notes next morning.[5] Dined at Lady Clinton's.

14. Sat. [Dropmore]

Wrote to J. Watson & Smith—G. Burnett—Rev E. Hawkins. Saw R. Phillimore—C.B. Adderley. Add Sir T.G.—Mrs Langton[R].[6] Morning given to packing & arrangements. Off at 12¼ to Dropmore:[7] which we found in the greatest beauty & even glory. *Here* learn how to use Rhododendrons. Homeric discussions with Doyle. Read Moore's Journal[8]—Senior's MS Journal (Cairo &c.)[9]

15. 4 S. Trin.

Burnham Ch. mg; & prayers aftn. Willy & Stephy enjoy their visit much. Lady G[renville] wears wonderfully & has all her old quiet courtesy & kindliness. Read Fabiola[10]—Denison's Arg.[11] Conv. on Denison's Argum.

16. M. [London]

The boys went to Eton early. We used the forenoon in walking: Doyle & I again went to Homeric discourse. Read Seniors Journal—Bowring Debate of 1840.[12] Reached London about 3. Saw Ld Abn. (who gave me the news

[1] Spoke on drafting Oxford University Bill: *H* cxlii. 1341.
[2] Draft motion on American enlistment: Add MS 44386, f. 13.
[3] George Drummond, 1807–1902; recognised as 14th earl of Perth by Act 1853; a Roman catholic.
[4] *H* cxlii. 1572.
[5] Baillie's motion for 19 June on Anglo-American negotiations, withdrawn on 18 June: *H* cxlii. 1660.
[6] These two names added at foot of page.
[7] See 7 June 45; still occupied by Lady Grenville.
[8] J. Moore, *A Journal during a residence in France from . . . August to December 1792*, 2v. (1793).
[9] N. W. *Senior, *Conversations and journals in Egypt and Malta*, written 1855, ed. M. C. M. Simpson, 2v. (1882).
[10] N. P. S. *Wiseman, *Fabiola* (1855).
[11] Probably G. A. *Denison, 'Paper delivered into the Registry of the Diocese of Bath and Wells' (1856); on his refusal to recant.
[12] See 18–24 Mar. and 8 Apr. 40.

that Dallas remains)[1]—Sir J. Graham & Cardwell—H. Baillie—who showed me his new motion[2]—H. Seymer—A. Gordon—R. Phillimore—A. Kinnaird—Sir W. Heathcote. We were received by Mrs Talbot with her well known hospitality: she showed me the letters about Lady Victoria Talbot; lovely in her life & in her death more lovely still.[3] Her sister Gertrude's[4] letter struck me as most remarkable.

17. T.

Wrote to J. Wilson—J. Severn—J. Napier (& draft)—Rev Mr. Pattinson—Mr Davies—Mr. Ross—Rev. Dr Hessey—R. Heathfield[5]—F. Peel MP—Scotts—A. Kinnaird—J. Freshfield—M. Rangabé—Rev Mr Marks.[6] Wrote MS Mema. Read Senior's Journal. Unpacking & arranging papers, &c. Working on accounts. Saw Sir J. Graham—do cum Ld Aberdeen—H. Baillie—Sir W. Heathcote—Solr. General—Sir G. Grey (Oxf. Bill)[7]—Ld Stanley—R. Phillimore. H. of C. $6\frac{1}{2}$–$7\frac{1}{2}$ and $9\frac{3}{4}$–$12\frac{3}{4}$.[8] At Ruttleys, Benjamin's &c.

Yesterday at $7\frac{1}{2}$ after the explanations in the House Mr. Baillie told me he must alter the terms of his motion and produced the paper annexed which he said he was about to give in. I received the communication in the manner described in the accompanying note to Sir J. Graham:[9] & I also sent an account of the conversation to Ld Aberdeen.[10]

. . .[11]Mr Baillie sent me a note which follows:[12] and I answered that I should be happy to see him. He asked me for advice as to his course. I told him that giving advice belonged rather to the leaders of his party than to me: that however I should speak to him with perfect freedom: that the Govt. had not explained the retention of Dallas, & that for me it meant little unexplained: it might be provisional, or might be exhibited as a new act of magnanimity and longsuffering on our part, or the guilt might be thrown on Crampton. None of these things would satisfy me, but I adhered to the declaration of Cartwright that if the Govt. by word or act did frankly & at once what was needful to settle the question I could not join in a vote against them. In turn, I was in the dark & could come to no decision for myself, standing as I do, until I knew what the intentions & policy of the Govt. really were. Later in the evg. Heathcote came to me on a similar errand from Jolliffe asking however my intentions rather than advice—& adding that Baillie's persevering wd probably depend on them. I said to him that it was a pity to act first & deliberate afterwards—that it wd. have been nice to consider the declarations of Govt. last night & then determine whether they could

[1] President Pierce had dismissed Crampton, the British envoy in Washington, for enlisting Americans, and cessation of Anglo-American diplomatic relations was anticipated.
[2] See *H* cxlii. 1660 and next day.
[3] She d. on 8 June 1856, aged twenty-five.
[4] Lady Gertrude Talbot, da. of 18th earl of Shrewsbury, m. 1874 George Robert Charles, 1850–95, S. *Herbert's son; 13th earl of Pembroke 1862. She d. 1906.
[5] Richard Heathfield, published on taxation.
[6] Probably Edward Marks, minor canon of Dublin.
[7] The Bill had by now passed all its stages, see *H* cxlii. 1771.
[8] Irish education: *H* cxlii. 1580.   [9] In Add MS 44164.
[10] Not in Add MSS 44089 or 43071.
[11] Follows omitted account of talk with *Graham.   [12] Add MS 44386, f. 16.

proceed without an explanation of motions which is not yet forthcoming. That for myself I was in the dark, and so forth as I had said to Baillie.[1]

18. Wed.

Wrote to D. of Argyll—Jas Watson & Co—Johnson L[ongden] & Co—Rev L. Paige—Rev Mr Simpson—Rev. W. Elwin—Chancr. of Exchr.—J. Murray—Mr Jafer Alee. Saw Mr Fitzgerald—Sir J. Graham—R. Phillimore—Ld Abn. cum Sir J. G. & E. C[ardwell]—E. Cardwell—Mr Fortescue—Mr Granville Vernon MP. Read U.S. papers. Spoke at S.P.G. meeting.[2] H of C 12¼-2½ and 4-6.[3] Went with C & Mrs Talbot to see Ristori: who is great.[4] Worked on priv. affairs.

19. Th.

Wrote to Sec. Comm Woods[5]—C.A. Wood—Mr G. Burnett—Mr Flyer[6]—Mr Goodfellow. Saw A. Kinnaird—Mr S. Fitzgerald—Sir R.G. Booth[7]—Mr R. Palmer *cum* Sir R.G.B., & Mr Frere—Mr Lowe—Coalwhippers' Deputation[8]—Rev Mr Ridley—R. Phillimore—Sir J. Graham—Duke of Argyll. Breakfast at Stafford House with royalties. The Prince of Prussia makes an agreeable impression.[9] Read Senior's Journals—U.S. Enlistment Pamphlets. Attended Christie's.

20. Fr.

Wrote to Archdeacon Hill[10]—Mr Niblett[11]—Rev J. Bramston—W.J. Smith—Ed Morning Post[12]—Messrs. Farrer—Mr Mickleham[13]—Mr Brophey—Rev A. Gurney—J. Murray—Blackadder & Co.[14] Calls & business. Finished Senior's Journals. Saw Sir R.G. Booth—Mr R. Palmer—R. Phillimore—A. Kinnaird—Sir Jas Graham—Earl of Aberdeen—Sir E. Bulwer—Scotts. Packing. H. of C. 4½-8 and 10½-12¾. Spoke on Cambr. Bill Clauses, & asked for U.S. dispatch.[15]

21. Sat [Hawarden]

Off by 10 A.M. train for Hawarden where we found Lena convalescent &

---

[1] Dated 17 June 1856; Add MS 44778, f. 229.

[2] Anniversary meeting in Willis's Rooms.

[3] Baillie's statement on his motion: *H* cxlii. 1660.

[4] Adelaide Ristori, 1822-1906; Italian tragedienne, in Schiller's *Maria Stuarda* at the Lyceum.

[5] Probably Richard Rotton, chief clerk to commissioners for woods and forests.

[6] Probably John Floyer, 1811-87; tory M.P. Dorset 1846-57, 1864-85.

[7] Sir Robert Gore Booth, 1805-76; 3rd bart. 1814; tory M.P. Sligo from 1850.

[8] Spoke this day on Coalwhippers (Port of London) Bill urging employers' assurances should be put in writing: *H* cxlii 1729.

[9] Frederick William Ludwig, 1797-1888; prince of Prussia; regent 1858; William I 1861; emperor 1871.

[10] Thomas Hill, 1790?-1875; archdeacon of Derby 1847-73; biographer.

[11] Possibly Alfred N. Niblett, published commercial dictionaries.

[12] Announcing departure.   [13] Probably Thomas Micklem, London solicitor.

[14] Booksellers in Paternoster Row.

[15] Against Heywood's motion on dissenters, and calling for papers: *H* cxlii. 1737, 1741.

the rest blooming: so good is God to us! We had Wilson Patten for a fellow
traveller: & then joined the Duchess of Sutherland. Read Massinger's Virgin
Martyr:[1] & began an (intending) Article for Q.R. on the Recruiting
question.[2] Unpacking. Wrote on U.S.

22. 5 S. Trin.

H[awarde]n Ch. mg & evg. Conv. with Agnes & Mazie: the latter joined her
sister for the first time: gave a very good account of the Gospel for the day.
Read Basire on Br. Church[3]—Fr. Barnes on Councils[4] &c.—Acaster's Ch.
in danger[5]—Overton's Apology[6]—Erskine's Sketches[7]—Sc. Eccl. Journals.
Tea at the Rectory.

23. M.

Ch. 8½ A.M. Wrote to Mr Brophey—Dean of Peterborough. Read Virgin
Martyr (finished)—Marsh's Pelasgians[8]—Burn's Poems. Worked on letters
—arranging drawers—unpacking books. Music in evg. Wrote on U.S.

24. St John Bapt.

Ch. 8½ AM. Wrote to Earl of Aberdeen—Jas Watson—W. Deering. Read
Ariosto. Dined at the Rectory. Worked on arranging my books: & papers.
Singing.

25. Wed.

Overslept myself, shamefully enough. Wrote to Mrs Langton—C.A. Wood
Warden Trin Coll—Mr Darby—G.H. Christie—Rev W. Elwin—Sir R.G.
Booth. Worked on Homer. Read Selden's Titles of Honour[9]—Orl Furioso.
Music. The Lytteltons dined. Worked on books.

26. Th.

Church 8½ A.M. Wrote to Barker & Co—Earl of Aberdeen(2)—E. Ellis—
Mr J. Collier[10]—J. Gye—J. Emery.[11] Worked on Homer. Read Heyne[12]—

[1] P. Massinger, *The Virgin Martyr, a tragedy* (1622).
[2] *Elwin turned down the article, on the 'error' of the Foreign Enlistment Act, Add
MS 44746, f. 38; see Gladstone to Elwin, 25 June 1856, National Library of Scotland; see
also 19, 21 July 56.
[3] I. *Basire, *The ancient liberty of the Britannick Church* (1661).
[4] J. Barnes, *Select discourses concerning Councils, the pope, schism* (1661).
[5] J. Acaster, 'The church in danger from herself: or, the causes of her present declining
state explained' (1827).
[6] See 29 Oct. 54.
[7] J. Erskine, *Sketches and hints of Church history, and theological controversy*, 2v.
(1790, 97).
[8] H. *Marsh, *Horae Pelasgicae ... containing an inquiry into the language of the Pelasgi,
or ancient inhabitants of Greece* (1815), much quoted in *Studies on Homer.*
[9] J. Selden, *Titles of honour* (1614).
[10] Probably John Payne *Collier, 1789–1883, editor and Shakespearean forger.
[11] Probably sc. Amery.
[12] One of many works on philology by Christian Gottlob Heyne (1729–1820).

Mure[1]—Proclus[2]—Diodorus Sic.[3]—Odyssey B I—and Or [lando] Fur[ioso] Music in evg. Worked on books: & domestic plans. The new walk called mine gives a road to Church a very little longer & opens the park delightfully.[4]

27. Fr.

Ch. 8½ A.M. Wrote to Sir J. Wilmot—G. & Co—D[owage]r Lady Wenlock Robn. G.—Mr W. Stacy—G. Burnett—Mr J.H. Rippe.[5] Saw Lady L. on her affairs. Dined at the Rectory: singing. Agnes played me 'The old Clock', accompanying. Read Odyssey—Orl Furioso—Worked on Homer.

28. Sat.

Ch. 8½ AM. Wrote to Willy—Sir J. Graham—H. Tayleur—A. Kinnaird. Read & noted the new U.S. papers.[6] Worked on Homer—Read Odyssey— Orl Furioso—Marsh on Pelasgi—Poor Helen's birthday must not pass unnoticed.

29. S. Peter & 6 S. Trin.

Hn. Ch mg & evg. Conv. with the children. A Summons to London for tomorrow disturbed me: I had to write to Jas Watson—Sir J.S. Pakington Ld A. Hervey. Read Voies de la Croix[7]—Overton's Apology—Acaster (finished) &c.

30. M [London]

Wrote to C.G.—Rev. J.L. Ross—Rt Hon W. Cowper. Up at 3 & reached London (10 George St) at 11¼. Read Odyssey—Froude's H. VIII Vol. 2.[8] Saw Sir J. Graham—F.R. Bonham—H.K. Seymer—Ld Aberdeen—Ld Stanley—Sir W. Heathcote—Scotts—Ld A. Hervey. Worked on U.S. question. H. of C. 4¼–7½ & 8¼–1¼: U.S. Debate wh perplexes me much as to all but the subject.[9]

Tues. July One. 1856.

Wrote to C.G. Saw Ly. Blantyre—Mr Labouchere—Dss. of Sutherland— D[owage]r Lady Wenlock—Ld Abn. cum Graham & Cardwell—Mr Farrer (D. of N.s trust)[10]—Mr Freshfield—Mr Longden. Read Odyssey: for a little calm. Made up my mind not to part from Graham: & then found at the

---

[1] See 2 Aug. 51.   [2] Proclus (A.D. 410–485), neoplatonist theologian.
[3] Diodorus Siculus, (ca. 40 B.C.) Sicilian historian.
[4] The walk from the front of the castle through the grounds to the cross roads in the village.
[5] Rippe (see also 16 July 56) and Stacy probably both involved in Lyttelton business.
[6] Those consequent upon his request in the Commons (see 20 June 56): PP 1856 lx. 317.
[7] Untraced.   [8] See 23 May 56.
[9] Motion of lack of confidence in the govt.'s handling of Anglo-American differences: H cxliii. 40.
[10] Gladstone was one of *Newcastle's executors and trustees.

House that from the non appearance of Opposition in the field this was the obvious course. I spoke at great length in the debate: & then gave the Govt. a worthless vote.[1] At the House till 2¼ (from 6) opposing J. Phillimore's Bill.[2] Then walk & conv with R. Cecil.

2. Wed.

Wrote to C.G.—Sir C. Eastlake—Robn. G.—and E.A. Bowring. H of C. & Commee. 2–5½ (Superannuations).[3] Saw Sir G.C. Lewis (Ch of Exr.)— Robn. G—Mr Bonham—Ld Lyttelton—Mr Irton[4]—Ld Lyndhurst—Mr G. Dundas[5]—Ld Aberdeen—Ld Overstone—Maj. C. Bruce[6]—Ld Stanley— Mr Walpole—Saw two [R]. Dined at Grillions. Then went to Queen's Concert where Ld Palmerston had some conv. with me in great good humour. Read Odyssey.

3. Th.

Wrote to Warden of Wadham—Rev N. Woodard—Rector of Exeter— Rev J.T. Boyle—Mr J. Griffiths—Mr Jas Wylde[7]—Mr E. Slater[8]—C.G.[9]— Goldwin Smith. Saw Geo. Hope—Sir J. Graham—Aunt J.—Sir R. Gore Booth—

Mrs Terry
E. Langton } at Mrs Stonehouse [R].

Read Odyssey—Froude. Princess's Theatre 9–11 to see the Winter's Tale. H of C. at 3–6–8¾ and 11½–1.[10]

4. Fr. X.

Wrote to Rev J.O. Powell. Breakfast at Milnes's: late from oversleeping. Then went to see Mr T. Baring's fine Collection. Superann. Comm. 1¾–4. H of C. 4–8¼ and 10¾–11¾. Spoke ab. Bp of N.Z—Voted agt. Scots Edn. Bill as impracticable, & an *un*settlement only.[11] Dined with Sir R.G. Booth. Went to Mrs M. Ingram's Concert.[12] Saw Bp of Oxford—Marquis Azeglio— Mr Aubrey de Vere—Mr G. Bunsen[13]—Mr J.E. Denison—Mr Dering—Mr J. Wilson—Mr Leeman—Saw E. Smith[R].

[1] H cxliii. 141. The Peelites were in much agitation about Gladstone's vote, see Argyll, ii. 51–2.
[2] sc. R. *Phillimore; in cttee.; see 11 July 56n.
[3] Misc. business: H cxliii. 210.
[4] Samuel Irton, 1796–1866; tory M.P. West Cumberland 1833–47, 1852–7.
[5] George Dundas, 1819–80; tory M.P. Linlithgowshire 1847–58, then governed colonies.
[6] Charles Lennox Cumming-Bruce, 1790–1875; tory M.P. Inverness burghs 1831–7 Elginshire 1837–68.
[7] sc. James *Wylde, tory M.P., cp. 27 Dec. 48.
[8] Edward Slater, a London curate, had sent his 'Biblical Revision' (1856).
[9] In Bassett, 113.   [10] Supply: H cxliii. 272.
[11] On bp. of New Zealand's salary: H cxliii. 326 and see 10 May 55.
[12] The wife of C. T. Ingram; see 27 July 55.   [13] George, son of C. C. J. Bunsen.

5. *Sat.* X

Wrote to Mr Mayne[1]—J. Griffiths—Rev Mr Sweet. Saw Mr Smith (Naturalist)[2]—Mr Panizzi—Sir W. Heathcote—Mr Emery—Mr H.K. Seymer—Sir J. Graham—E. Smith[R]. C.G. came & I transferred myself to 29 B[erkeley] Square.[3] Attended the Harveian oration: & dined at the College of Physicians.

6. *7 S. Trin.*

St Jamess & H.C.mg. Chapel Royal aftn. Read The Paradise Regained. Conv. with Lady Wenlock.

7. *M.*

In bed till 3 P.M. from bowel complaint. H of C. $4\frac{1}{2}$–$7\frac{3}{4}$: & paired on the Appellate Jurisdiction Bill.[4] Read the Odyssey—Milton's Lycidas.— M'Queen on App Jur.[5]

8. *T.*

Wrote to Bp of Oxford—J. Devey[6]—Jas Freshfield—Mr H. Cole—Miss Johnstone[7]—R. Barker—Rev J. Bramston—D. Meehan—Mr Robinson— T.A. Hope—Sir C. Eastlake—Jas Watson—E. Breakenridge—Mr Dering —Warden Trin Coll (2)—Messrs. Edwards. Still somewhat invalided. Read the Odyssey. Saw Sir G. Bowen—Sir J. Graham—Chancr. of Exchr.

9. *Wed.*

Wrote to E. Langton—Mrs Terry[R]. H of Commons at $3\frac{1}{2}$: saw Ld Goderich ab. his motion.[8] In bed until two: the liver now seems deranged. Read the Odyssey—Hermann's Opuscula[9]—Samson Agonistes.[10]

10. *Th.*

Wrote to Ld Wenlock—W. Forbes (Med.)—Mr Willock[11]—D. Meehan—H. Barthorp. H. of C. $2\frac{3}{4}$–$3\frac{3}{4}$ and 6–8, $9\frac{1}{2}$–1. Spoke (40 m) & voted in a majority agt. Appellate Jurisdiction Bill.[12] Much conv. in the morning with Frank [Lawley], & with Lady W[enlock]—then with the Recorder[13]—about summoning the family. Read Hermann's Homer u. Sappho.—Iliad B.13.—

---

[1] Henry Blair Mayne, 1813–92; barrister 1845; commons clerk; chief clerk for private bills 1858–70.
[2] Perhaps William Smith, 1808–57, professor of natural history at Cork from 1854.
[3] Lady Wenlock's house.   [4] *H* cxliii. 407.
[5] J. F. MacQueen, *A practical treatise on the Appellate Jurisdiction of the House of Lords and Privy Council* (1842).
[6] Had written on Gladstone's speech of 1 July (Hawn P).   [7] Unidentified.
[8] Motion to go into Cttee. to discuss civil service reform: *H* cxliii. 525.
[9] By J. G. J. Hermann, 7v (1827–39).   [10] By *Milton (1671).
[11] William Alexander Willock, wrote on Scottish religion and education.
[12] *H* cxliii. 597; notes in Add MS 44654, f. 219.
[13] i.e. James Stuart *Wortley, Frank Lawley's br.-in-law.

11. Fr.

Wrote to Mr Toogood—Sir E.E. Wilmot—Hon. Rev. R. Liddell—& others.—Mr D. Bell[1]—Mr F.W. Lewis.[2] H of C. $4\frac{1}{4}$-$2\frac{3}{4}$. Spoke on Res. resp. County Courts Charges—and again on the Judge's Salaries—where the House unexpectedly rallied, & ended by rejecting the increase.[3] Saw Rob[ertso]n G[ladstone)—Mr Gregory—Lord Braybrooke—Hon W.F. Campbell—Ld Aberdeen—Mr Mowbray—Mr Grogan—Sir J. Graham—Sir W. Heathcote—Ld Blandford—R. Phillimore (his Bill).[4]

12. Sat.

Wrote to D. of Newcastle—S. Herbert—Bp of Oxford—Robn. G.—Chr. of Exchr. Saw F.R. Bonham—Mr Lacaita—Bp of Oxford—Scotts—Earl of Aberdeen—Sir Jas Graham—Sir Wm. Heathcote. Attended Br. Museum 2 P.M. At No 29 we discussed fully Frank's case & decided on advising Lady W[enlock] to urge Frank's return at the proper time. *We* means S. Lawley & J. Wortley with Robert [Lawley] & myself. Shopping, paying Bills, & packing. Off by Mail Train at 8. Read Ld Abn. Essay on Greek Architecture.[5]

13. 8 S. Trin. [Hawarden]

Rose at $9\frac{1}{2}$ having arrived safely at 3 A.M. Church mg & aft. Conv. with Ag. M. & Lena on the Gospel. Wrote to Mr Emery—Mr J. Murray. Read Birch's Tillotson[6]—Stanley's Faith & Practice—Eden's Introd. Essay(!)[7]—Ellison's 'Protestant Errors'.[8] We found D.G. all the children in great bloom. Evg. conv. with Mr Hartmann.[9] The only thing that seems wanting there is fineness of touch.

14. M.

Ch. $8\frac{1}{2}$ AM. Wrote to Sir W.C. James—Jas Watson & Smith—Mr Francillon[10]—Mr S. Triscoll—Mr R.L. Chance. Unpacking: arranging letters, & doing accounts. Walk with C. & alone. Read Odyssey—Orlando Furioso—Goldsmith's Poems. Worked on Homer—Music.

15. T.

Church $8\frac{1}{2}$ AM. Wrote to Rev J.O. Powell—Mr W. Grogan—Attorney

---

[1] David Bell of Liverpool had written about an address there: Hawn P.
[2] Untraced.   [3] *H* cxliii. 704.
[4] His Tithe Commutation Bill; *Phillimore abandoned the Bill on 14 July: *H* cxliii. 811.
[5] G. H. *Gordon, 4th earl of Aberdeen, *An inquiry into the principles of beauty in Grecian architecture* (1822).
[6] T. Birch, *The life of John Tillotson* (1752).
[7] R. Eden's strongly protestant introduction to the 2nd ed. of W. Stanley, *The faith and practice of a Church of England-man* (1848).
[8] N. T. Ellison, *Protestant errors and Roman Catholic truths; a tale* (1829).
[9] Husband of the governess; see 27 Oct. 57.
[10] Probably Henry James Francillon, solicitor in Gloucestershire.

General—Mr Maund[1]—Mr C. Butler. Saw Mr Burnett. Read Gell's Ithaca[2] —Strabo—Goldsmith's Poems (finished)—Odyssey. Saw Mr Burnett. Worked on Homer—the Pelasgians.[3] Began my diggings.

16. *Wed.*

Ch. 8½ A.M. Wrote to Sir T. Gladstone—J.K. Ripp—Mrs Fanny Cole[4]— Chas Rogers (Wallace Mon.)[5] Visited the Austins.[6] Worked on Homer. Read Q.R. on Grote's Greece—and on Police[7]—also Grote[8]—Strabo.

17.

Ch. 8½ A.M. Wrote to Sir James Graham—Jas Watson and Provost of Eton. Dined at the Rectory. Worked on Homer. Read Q.R. on Guizot's Chas I[9] —Mitford's Hist[10]—Plato's Minos—Herodotus. My second digging. Examined M. & Lena in their geogr. which I thought good.

18. *Fr.*

Ch. 8½ AM. Wrote to Sir W. Heathcote—T.M. Gladstone—Saxe Bannister. Worked on Homer. Read Marsh's Pelasgi—Mitford—Ld Aberdeen—Sir R. Adrey's [*sic*] Addresses.[11] The T.G. family came: and H.G. dined.

19. *Sat.*

Ch. 8½ A.M. Wrote to J. Griffiths—Bp of Aberdeen. Saw T.M. Gladstone —on his O.F. proposal.[12] Walk & conversations with Tom. Resumed Sketch for Gent. Mag. on Russian War.[13] Music in evg. Read Cramer[14]—Ld Aberdeen on Greek Architecture.

20. *9 S. Trin.*

Ch mg & aft. Conv. on the Gospel with Agnes & (my niece) Mary. Walk with Tom. Read Birch's Tillotson—Overton's Apology.

21. *M.*

Wrote to Mr W. Grogan—Wms. & Co (Chester)—Messrs. G. & Co.— Chambers & Co[15]—J.H. Parker + ∧

---

[1] Benjamin Maund, 1790–1863, publisher and botanist.
[2] Sir W. Gell, *The geography and antiquities of Ithaca* (1807).
[3] See 23 June 56.   [4] Slip of the pen for Lady Fanny Cole; see 24 May 36.
[5] Charles *Rogers, 1825–90; when presbyterian chaplain to Stirling garrison (1855–63) erected the Wallace monument by Stirling 1861; antiquarian.
[6] At Broughton; see 6 Dec. 53.   [7] *Quarterly Review*, cxiv. 60, 160 (June 1856).
[8] See 19 Mar. 47.   [9] *Quarterly Review*, xciv. 105 (June 1856).
[10] W. Mitford, *The History of Greece* (1822).
[11] Sir R. Airey, *Opening address . . . before the board of General Officers assembled at the Royal Hospital, Chelsea . . .* (1856).
[12] Not found.
[13] 'The war and the peace', *Gentleman's Magazine*, August 1856.
[14] See 20 Dec. 55.   [15] Edinburgh booksellers and publishers.

[At foot of page:—] + B. Blundell[1]—E. Whitty.[2]
Worked much on my Article, wh threatens to split into two. Walk with
Tom: this visit has been good in many ways: we are much pleased with our
nieces: painfully struck with the state of Louisa's health. Left at 10.15 for
London—Read Odyssey.

22. T. X [London]

Reached Mrs Talbots at 5.30: bed for 3 hours. Wrote to Rev Mr Jowett—
C.G.—Rev Mr Maul[3]—Mr Toogood—Mr Blackadder—Jas Watson—Mr B.
Maund. Worked on Article. Saw J. Milligan (late)[R]—Mr Grogan—Mr
Whitaker (Parker)[4]—Mr W. Forbes—Mr Jas Wilson. Read Froude's Hist.
—Cochrane's letter.[5] H. of C. 12–3¾ and 10½–11¼.[6] Worked on letters &
papers.

23. Wed.

Wrote to C.G.—Mrs Alderson—H. Thring—Mrs Davenport—J. Inman[7]—
M.F. Tupper—Miss Green—Sig. Filice[8]—J. Milligan—Rev. Mr Surtees—
Stephy—Mr Strangways. Saw Mr Freshfield—Mr D. Chapman—Messrs
Johnson L[ongden] & Co—Mr W. Forbes—Sir J. Graham—Mr Henley—
Sir W. Heathcote—Ld Advocate. Dined at Lady Wenlock's & much conv.
with her & Jane on Frank's matters. H. of C. 12¼–6 opposing the Bps
Resignations Bill.[9]

24. Th.

Wrote to Mr Heath—Dr Cullen—Mr Dyce RA—Mr Mathew—J.H. Parker.
H of C. 12–4 and 6–7½, 8½–10: again at work on the Bps Bill both in debate
& in commn. with the Govt. to prevent the omission of the words 'duly &
canonically'.[10] Saw Sir W. Heathcote—Mr Wilson—Duke of Buccleuch—
Mr Hamilton MP. Read Odyssey. Finished Article.

25. Fr. St James.

Wrote to G.B. Mathew—Robn. G—Rev H M'Kenzie—J. Craufurd—Jas
Watson—J. Murray. Saw Mr & Mrs Hampton (No 4)—Scotts—Ld Aber-

---

[1] Benson Blundell, Lincoln's Inn barrister.
[2] Edward Michael Whitty, 1827–60; ed. *Northern Whig* 1857–8; wrote *Times* parliamentary summaries and political works.
[3] Richard Graham Maul, 1820–95; St. John's, Cambridge; vicar of St. John's, Drury Lane, 1855–82.
[4] Joseph *Whitaker, 1820–95; J. H. *Parker's London agent; publisher, founded his *Almanac* 1869.
[5] A. Baillie *Cochrane, *The map of Italy* (1856).
[6] Spoke on payment of education officials: *H* cxliii. 1210.
[7] James Williams Inman, d. 1899; fellow of St. John's, Cambridge, 1835–7; schoolmaster, priest and editor.
[8] This and preceding, unidentified.   [9] Bill to enable bps. to retire: *H* cxliii. 1326.
[10] The amnd. substituted 'under his hand and seal' for 'duly and canonically': *H* cxliii.
1415.

deen (Pol. & Homer)—Lady Wenlock—Dss Sutherland. Saw M. Theret[1] 12 Broad St—J. Milligan[R]. Saw Rev Mr Lake—Mr G. Smith—Homer &c. Read Niebuhr[2]—Odyssey. H of C. 4½–7½: Disraeli made a mess of it: he was vilipended in the Carlton at nt.[3] This day must not be forgotten for family anniversaries as well as its sacred one. Cretâ notandus.[4]

26. Sat.

Wrote to Bp of Aberdeen—Read Odyssey—H. of C. 12–1½: spoke on Scots Bps, & on Mathew's case[5]—Worked hard on removal from No 4 to No 11— about books pictures &c. Saw Lady Wenlock—Mrs Macknight[6]—Ld Redesdale. We had Stephy's operation performed at 4 P.M. by Mr Bowman.[7] Nature appeared repugnant to the Chloroform but it was we were assured only a muscular resistance: & he was not sick. Mr Bowman afterwards explained the operation of dividing the muscle. The dear boy had sharp twinges of pain at intervals in the evg, with general depression & little appetite: but he slept much.

27. 10 S. Trin.

Vauxhall Br. Ch. 11 A.M. Westmr. Abbey (near 2 h) aftn. Read Chr. Rem. on Religious Biography[8]—England before Reformation &c.[9]—Anderdon's Life of Ken[10]—Mill's Lecture on H. Eucharist.[11] Saw Lady Wenlock. Stephy got up in the afternoon much better.

28. M.

Worked hard at No 11 upon my books & on other arrangements: espy. considering how to place pictures. Stephy had his second operation performed: Mr Bowman was pleased with the result. Saw Sir G.C.Lewis—Mr Grogan—Dean Ramsay—Mr Bowman (mg). Read Odyssey—Arbuthnot on the Bank Act.[12]

29. T.

Wrote to Mr Sandbach—Mr Aitchison—Mr Shirley[13]—Miss Amphlett—

[1] Probably a rescue case, as is the next name; 12 Broad Street, Golden Square, was a coffee house.
[2] B. G. Niebuhr, *Griechische Heroengeschichten* (1842).
[3] Review of the Session. Palmerston vigorously asserted his superiority: *H* cxliii. 1461.
[4] His wedding anniversary; 'a red letter day', after Horace, *Sat.* 2.3.246.
[5] Opposing end of govt. grant to episcopal church in Scotland, and on case of G. B. Mathew (see 6 Apr. 44); *H* cxliii. 1481, 1488.
[6] Of Notting Hill, a charitable case in whom Gladstone was interested (Hawn P).
[7] An eye operation by (Sir) William *Bowman, 1816–92, ophthalmologist, cr. bart. by Gladstone 1884.
[8] *Christian Remembrancer*, xxxii. 141 (July 1857).
[9] Perhaps C. Ullman, *Reformers before the Reformation*, tr. in 2v. (1854).
[10] J. L. Anderdon, *The life of Thomas *Ken* (1851).
[11] W. H. Mill, *Lectures on the Catechism*, ed. B. Webb (1856); xlviii.
[12] Privately printed pamphlet (no copy found) by G. Arbuthnot of the treasury on the working of the 1844 Act; see Add MS 44096, f. 120.
[13] Evelyn Philip *Shirley, 1812–82; genealogist and tory M.P., S. Warwicks, 1853–65.

Sir T.G.—Messrs. Freeman[1]—J. Watson. Saw Mr Grogan—Mr Cantwell (Assistant)—Mr Bowman—Saw M. Eugen—J. Milligan[R]. Attended the Prorogation. Worked at No 11. Read Odyssey.

30. Wed.

Wrote to Milligan—Read Odyssey—Mr Bowman came & allowed us to go tomorrow. Shopping. Arrangements at No 11. Saw Panizzi: & spent 2 h. at Museum with Messrs. Newton,[2] [blank], and Oldfield,[3] who were most intelligent & kind, upon Inscriptions. In evg, went with J. Wortley to the Royal Academy—Saw Mr Grogan—M. Bratiano (on the Principalities.)[4] Packing books & clothes at night.

31. Th. [Hawarden]

Wrote to Overends—G. Burnett. Up at 4.45 and off by 6.15 train with C. & Stephy. We reached Hawarden all right at 12.45 after a little business in Chester: & found all well & blooming thank God: a very happy day. Some part however was given to sleep as we had little in the night from heat. Read Odyssey—Q.R. on America[5]—N. British on Crimean Campaign.[6]

Friday Aug. One, 1856.

Church 8.30 A.M. Tasso & Ital. lesson with W & A. A great improvement visible in Stephy's eyes. Wrote to Jas Watson—Earl of Aberdeen—Mrs Hampton—Mr Westell[7]—R.L. Chance—Jas Freshfield—Author of 'Currency Regulated'.[8] Saw Mr G. Burnett. Worked on Homer—Read Odyssey —Apollodorus.

2. Sat.

Ch. 8½ A.M. Wrote to A. Munro .... Tasso with W. & A. Worked & wrote on Homer—Read Odyssey—& accompaniments. Finished Q.R. on America—Read N. British on Oude.[9]

3. 11 S. Trin.

Ch. 11 AM (& H.C.) and 7 P.M. Conv. on Ep. & Gospel with the three eldest. Read Overton's Apology—Birch's Tillotson—Hey's Lectures.[10]

---

[1] Perhaps Arthur Freeman & sons, wine merchants, but several firms of this name.

[2] (Sir) Charles Thomas *Newton, 1816–94; assistant in antiquities department 1840, keeper 1861–85; excavated Calymnos 1854–5; K.C.B. 1877.

[3] Edmund Oldfield, 1816–85; Trinity, Cambridge; assistant in antiquities department 1848–61; *Layard's private secretary 1868–9.

[4] Demetrius Bratiano, Rumanian publicist; diarist's comments on him in Add MS 43071, f. 293ff.; see 4 Apr. 58.

[5] *Quarterly Review*, xcix. 235 (June 1856).

[6] *North British Review*, xxv. 493 (Aug. 1856).   [7] Of the bookshop.

[8] [P. MacCulloch] author of *Currency self-regulating and elastic, explained in a letter to . . . the duke of Argyll* (1855); see Hawn P.

[9] *North British Review*, xxv. 515 (Aug. 1856).

[10] J. Hey, *Lectures in Divinity, delivered in the University of Cambridge*, 4v. (1796–98).

Q.R. on Savonarola.[1] Great heat continues: Earth dresses her yellow hair (Propert).[2]

4. M.

Ch. 8½ A.M. Wrote to Scotts—Bp of Brechin[3]—A. Hayward—Mr Geo. Nicol. Tasso & It. Ex[ercises] with W. & A. Worked on Homer; with Grote, Thirlwall,[4] Dionys[ius] Halicarn[assus],[5] Strabo, Herod., Thucydides (the prince of them i.e. of the auxiliaries) also Müller's Orchomenos.[6] Read Odyssey—Marsh's Horae Pelasg.

5. T.

Ch. 8½ A.M. Wrote to M. Bratiano—Earl of Aberdeen—Rector of Liverpool[7]—Mr T. Bowater.[8] Madame Bourgeau[9] came. Worked on Homer: with much the same auxiliaries incl. Cramer[10]—and finished Marsh. Read Odyssey—North Br.Qu. on Rogers.[11]

6. Wed.

Ch. 8½ AM. Wrote to Robn G—Mrs Trotter[12]—Bickers & Bush—Saw Mr G. Burnett—Rev Mr Williams (Nannerch).[13] Worked on Homer. Read Clinton's Fasti[14]—Odyssey. Finished Lord Aberdeen's Essay. Tasso & Itn. with W. & A. Singing—We were much pleased with Mad. Bourgeau: & French now reigns supreme at the early dinner.

7. Th.

Ch. 8½ A.M. Wrote to Rev. E. Hawkins—Rev Ld Charles Hervey—Count Corti[15]—Worked on Homer: finished a new cast of my Introduction: set to rewriting my Pelasgians.[16] Finished Odyssey. Tasso & It. with W. & A. Horace with Stephen. His outright earnestness of purpose must make its way.

8. Fr.

Ch 8½ A.M. Saw Mr Burnett (mines &c)—Rev. Mr Jones (from Lady

[1] *Quarterly Review*, xcix. 1 (June 1856).
[2] Presumably a tr. from Propertius.   [3] A. P. *Forbes.
[4] See 5 Jan. 47.   [5] First century B.C. Greek rhetorician and historian.
[6] C. O. Müller, 'Orchomenos und die Minyer', vol. i of *Hellenischer Stämme und Städte*, 3v. (1820–4).
[7] A. Campbell.   [8] Lived in Camden Town; not further identified.
[9] French governess.   [10] See 20 Dec. 55.
[11] *North British Review*, xxv. 399 (August 1856).
[12] Perhaps she who kept a seminary in London.
[13] David Williams, d. 1882; rector of Nannerch, Flintshire, 1845–72, of Castle Careinion from 1872.
[14] H. F. Clinton, *Fasti Hellenici*, 3v. (1824–30).
[15] Cavour had asked him to forward Gladstone's 1853 budget speech; see Add MS 44386, f. 85.
[16] *Studies on Homer*, i. 311ff.

Dunraven on her distressing case)[1]—Mr Voller[2]—whose fine young horse (3 years old) I bought for £57.15. + 5/ = £58. Tasso & It. with W. & A. Read Harvey on Trees[3]—National Currency[4]—Worked on Homer—particularly the Catalogue.[5]

9. Sat.

Ch. 8½ A.M. Wrote to R.M. Milnes—Duchess of Sutherland—Mr W. Grogan —Scotts. Worked on Homer—the Catalogue. Read Cramer—Strabo B[ook]V.—Castile's Delcanetto[6]—Arbuthnot on Act of 1844.[7] Did some varnishing.

10. 12 S. Trin.

Hawarden Ch mg and evg. Conv. on Acts VIII with W., A., & S. Wrote to Count Corti. Read Harrison's Charge[8]—Grueber[9]—Birch's Tillotson— Magee's Discourses[10]—Overton (finished)—Lyttelton's 'Commentary'.[11]

11. M.

Ch. 8½ A.M. Wrote to G. Arbuthnot—Ld Lyttelton—J.N.G. River Dee Trust Meeting 12–1¼. Saw Mr Barker. Worked on Homer. Read Grote— Muller's Orchomenos.

12. T.

Ch 8½ A.M. Read Grote—Athenaeus VI. Worked on Homer. Saw Mr Burnett—Four hours with the Darby & Robertson party on the Coal Lease: which we settled.[12]

13. Wed.

Ch 8½ A.M. Wrote to Ld Abn., & copy: having just seen Phillimore who gave me a disastrous account from Bath.[13] But oh! what manner of persons

---

[1] Her husband, a Roman catholic, wished to employ a Roman catholic governess to convert his children; she sent her clergyman to get Gladstone's advice; see Add MS 44386, f. 80.

[2] Unidentified.   [3] A. Harvey, *Trees and their nature* (1856).

[4] See, probably, 1 Aug. 56n.

[5] Probably the grammatical catalogue of Pelasgian words: *Studies on Homer*, i. 299ff.

[6] Hippolyte Castille, 1820–86; French novelist and controversialist, had sent his 'Le Marquis Delcanetto', one of his *Portraits politiques au dix-neuvième siècle* (1856–9) (Hawn P).

[7] See 28 July 56.

[8] B. Harrison, 'The heritage of England, and the dangers which threaten it, a charge' (1856).

[9] C. S. Grueber, 'Article xxix, considered in reference to the three sermons of the archdeacon of Taunton' (1855).

[10] W. Magee, *Discourses on the scriptural doctrines of Atonement and Sacrifice* (1801).

[11] G. W. *Lyttelton, *The four Gospels and . . . Acts of the Apostles, with explanatory notes* (1856).

[12] For the development of mines on the Hawarden estate.

[13] The previous day G. A. *Denison's views on the eucharist were declared contrary to articles 28 and 29 by Sumner's court at Bath; his appeal eventually succeeded.

ought we to be in all holy conversation, who have such things to encounter. Tasso & It. with W. & A. Dined at Mr R. Eaton's.[1] Worked on my books—Worked on Homer—Read Grote.

14. Th.

Ch 8½ A.M. Wrote to Bp of Oxford—Mr A. Ross—Rev. J. Armitstead—Miss Hathway[2]—B. Quaritch. Worked on books—Worked on Homer—Read Ar[istotle] Pol[itics]—Herod.—Bp Thirlwall—Gell's Journey in the Morea.[3] Saw R. Phillimore. Tasso & It. with W. & A.

15. Fr.

Ch 8½ A.M. Wrote to R.H. Dana[4]—Robn G . . . . R. Phillimore—W. Forbes (Medwyn)[5]—Mrs Hampton. Worked much on books. Tasso & It. with W. & A. Did a turn with the spade. Saw R. Phillimore. Worked on Homer. Read *relative* books.

16. Sat.

Ch. 8½ A.M. Wrote to Jas Watson & Smith—Saw R. Phillimore—Worked on Homer—Read . . . . . Much on the cricket ground: to see Willy play: he was ἀριδείκετος.[6]

17. 13 S. Trin.

Hawarden Ch mg & aft. Conv. on Acts XV with the three eldest. Saw R. Phillimore. Read Hey's Lectures—& much on the Holy Eucharist—Beveridge[7]—Palmer[8]—Macbride[9]—Arnauld[10]—Tillotson.

18. M.

Ch. 8½ A.M. Wrote to Rev. J. Keble—on Robn. G—Lady Cremorne—Bp of Oxford—Worked on Homer—A little digging. Tasso &c. with W. & A. Horace with Stephy. Singing in Evg. Read Inquiry into the Liturgy[11]—Saw R. Phillimore—Mr Burnett.

19. T.

Ch 8½ A.M. Wrote to Dr Roskelly—Mr Roskelly [*sic*]—Mr C. Lucey.[12] Saw Mr Burnett—Do with Mr Darlington[13]—R. Phillimore. Tasso with W. & A. Horace with S., & E. Talbot.[14] Worked on Homer. Read Knox's Observations on the Liturgy.[15] Dined at the Rectory.

[1] Robert Wynne Eyton, 1787?–1865; vicar of Northop, Flint, from 1849.
[2] Writing obscure.   [3] Sir W. Gell, *Narrative of a journey in the Morea* (1823).
[4] Richard Henry Dana, 1815–82; American lawyer, writer and antislaver; prosecuted Jefferson Davis 1867–8; not confirmed by Senate as minister to Britain 1876.
[5] See 3 Sept. 45.   [6] 'famous' or, as in Homer, 'most renowned'.
[7] Probably W. *Beveridge's contribution to *The pascal lamb* (1707).
[8] Perhaps in W. *Palmer of Worcester, *Origines Liturgicae*, 2v. (1832); see 5 July 40.
[9] J. D. Macbride, *Observations on the nature of the sacrament of the Lord's Supper* (1832).
[10] See 16 Apr. 48.   [11] Perhaps Knox, see next day.
[12] Oak Farm business.   [13] Joseph Darlington, Hawarden blacksmith.
[14] E. S. *Talbot, see 3 Feb. 49n.   [15] By W. Knox (1789).

20. W.

Ch. 8½ A.M. Wrote to Rev. J. Keble—Mr G. Arbuthnot—Mr W. Emery.
Tasso with W. & A. Horace with St., & E. Talbot. Worked on Homer—
Read Grote.

21. Th.

Ch 8½ A.M. Wrote to Robn. G.—Sir S. Scott & Co—G.C. Farrant[1]—
Captain Frere[2]—Mr J. Sawers.[3] Attended the Vestry Meeting. Saw Mr
Burnett. Tasso with W. & A. Horace with S., & E. Talbot. Worked on
Homer. Went late in evg to consult Moffatt about Baby's (intermittent)
fever. Thank God there is no special sign to cause alarm.

22. Fr.

(Missed Ch. from cold) Wrote to Alex. B. Cochrane—Sir Thos. G.—Bp of
Aberdeen. Tasso with W. & A. Horace with S., & E. Talbot. Worked an
hour at my walk. Worked on Homer. Read Müller's Orchom.—Grote's
Greece. Early to bed.

23. Sat.

Late up. Wrote to Bp of Oxford—Rev J. Keble—R. Phillimore. Saw
Phillimore: & wrote a Draft of such a reply as it seemed to me Archd.
Denison might make.[4] Worked a little on Homer—Tasso &c. with W. & A.
Read Müller's Orchom—Grote's Hist.

24. S. Barth. & 14 S. Trin.

Ch 11 A.M. Bible conv. with the 3 eldest—another with M. & Lena. Conv.
with Mr [J.H.] Parker. Saw Phillimore & amended my Draft. Read Mayhew
& Apthorp Tracts—1764.[5] Radcliffe's Two Letters. 1773[6]—Ansr to View of
Internal Evidence.[7]

25. M.

Rose just before noon. Baby thank God much better. Wrote to J.N.G.—
Countess Clarendon—Countess Dunraven—Mr Blackadder—Mr Cuzner[8]
—Worked on Homer—Tasso &c. with W. & A. Saw Mr Parker, with whom
I had much Oxford, Book, & Ch. convn. Saw R. Phillimore who sent for
Archdn. Denison. Read Grote.

---

[1] Probably George Binstead Farrant, London barrister.
[2] (Sir) Henry Bartle Edward *Frere, 1815–84, commissioner for Sind 1850–9 (in U.K.
1856–April 1857), governed Bombay 1862–7, the Cape 1877–80, criticized by Gladstone
in Midlothian campaign; K.C.B. 1859; see 6 Mar. 57.
[3] Shipwright in Toxteth Park.   [4] Not found; see 13 Aug. 56.
[5] Controversy about S.P.G. affairs by E. Apthorp and J. Mayhew, 1763–4.
[6] E. Radcliff, 'Two letters addressed to the Rt. Rev. Prelates, who a second time
rejected the Dissenters Bill' (1773).
[7] Untraced.
[8] John Henry Cuzner of Shore Road, Hackney; business untraced.

26. T.

(Still an absentee [from church]). Wrote to Sir W. Heathcote—Mrs Bennett —Rev J. Marshall—Earl Powis. Worked on Homer—Horace with Stephen: Tasso &c. with W. & A. Saw R. Phillimore with Archdn. Denison when we went over the subject of his answer. Visited St John's & saw Mr T[roughton']s remarkable works there. Dined at the Rectory.

27. Wed.

Ch. 8½ A.M. Wrote to Bp of Oxford—Mr J.C. Dean (Manchr.)[1]—Mr W. Grogan—Horace with Stephen: and Tasso with W. & A. Saw Mr Brand (Drumt.)[2]—Mr Burnett with Mr Darlington. Worked on Homer. Read Dryden, Absalom & Achitophel.

28. Th.

Ch. 8½ A.M. Wrote to Mr Whitwell Elwin—Baron Alderson—Mr Tyler. Saw Mr Burnett & went on the ground with him—Saw R. Phillimore. Worked on Homer—Tasso with W. & A. Lena's seventh birthday: an eminently earnest child, with deep feelings, & rapid & strong perceptions, she only calls on us to thank God for what she is, & to pray that she may grow up such as she has begun. Dined at the Rectory: much conv. with Mr Carey[3] resp. Sir W. Molesworth.

29. Fr.

Ch. 8¼ A.M. Wrote to Countess Stanhope[4]—Sir J. Hanmer. Saw R. Phillimore. Made our arrangements for a Welsh tour on the children's account: & some visits. Worked on Homer—Tasso & It. with Willy & A.— Horace with Stephy. Read Dryden. The Rectory party dined—Music in evg.

30. Sat.

Ch. 8½ A.M. Wrote to J. Watson & Smith—Edwards & Ball[5]—Mrs Hampton—Swift & Wagstaff[6]—I[b]id. *cum* Johnston [Longden] & Co. Saw R. Phillimore. Worked on Homer: got thro' the Races, & into the

---

[1] John Connellan Deane, 1816–87; exhibition organizer, had written about the 1857 Great Exhibition at Manchester (Hawn P); see 29 June 57.
[2] He contemplated purchasing a Scottish estate; this one is Drumtochty, just N.E. of Fasque; doubtless he negotiated through *Brand, (whose da. Alice m. 1862 (Sir) H. T. Farquhar with land in the area) as Sir T. Gladstone might well have opposed the plan, of which nothing came.
[3] Perhaps Adolphus Frederick Carey, vicar of Brixham, Devon, where *Molesworth held advowsons.
[4] See 15 Aug. 35.
[5] Unidentified.
[6] John Swift's attorney's firm; see 18 Mar. 44.

ἄναξ[1] ἀνδ[ρῶν]. Read Lower on Surnames[2]—Farini's Letter[3]—Müller on Dorians[4]—Rode with Agnes.

31. 15 S. Trin.

Hn. Ch. mg & evg. Conv. with the children on Ep. & Gosp. Saw R. Phillimore. Read Birch's Tillotson—Wordsworth's Sir J. Oldcastle[5]—Berault on Church of Rome[6]—Hist. Clause in Art. 20.[7]

Hawarden Sept One 1856. M[onday].

Wrote to Robn G.—J. Rowsell—Rev. L. Paige—Executed & dispatched deeds. Ch. 8½ A.M. Worked on Homer—Horace with Stephy—Tasso with W. & A. Saw Phillimore (as usual) on the Bath case. His client is if possible worse than his Judges! Read Hardwicke on the Articles[8]—and [blank]

2. T.

Ch. 8½ A.M. Wrote to Bp of Moray (?)—M.F. Tupper—Horace with Stephy—Tasso with W. & A. Worked on Homer—Worked on the walk aided by S. Read Mrs Stowe's 'Dred'[9]: wh sent me irresistibly to sleep. Saw R. Phillimore.

3. Wed.

Ch. 8½ A.M. Wrote to Sir T.G.—Lumsden & Grant[10]—Rev H.P. Ffoulkes— Archdn. Denison (& copy). Saw Mr Burnett—Also Mr Brand—resp. Tilwhiller.[11] Tasso with W. & A. Read Farini's Letter—& 'Dred'. My work on Homer was almost wholly stopped by an explosion among the men— servants, & inquiries connected with it. Worked on the walk, aided by the boys. C. & I consulted on the question of a purchase in Scotland.

4. Th.

Ch. 8½ A.M. Wrote to Jas Watson & Smith—R. Phillimore—J. Rowsell— Lambert Marshall[12]—Mr C.W. Sikes.—Mr Geo. Arbuthnot. Worked on arranging letters & papers. Almost a blank day for Homer. Tasso & Itn.

[1] Translated by Gladstone as 'Chieftain' or 'Patriarch', considered at length in *Studies on Homer*, i. 440ff.

[2] M. A. Lower, *English surnames* (1842).

[3] L. C. Farini, 'La diplomazia e la quistione Italiana; lettera . . . al Signor G. Gladstone' (1856).

[4] C. O. Müller, *Account of the Dorians* (1839).

[5] Perhaps untraced pamphlet by Charles *Wordsworth, who published on Shakespeare and the bible.

[6] P. Berault, *The Church of England evidently proved the holy catholick church* (1683).

[7] G. A. *Denison's case hung on the interpretation of the articles, especially the 28th and 29th.

[8] C. Hardwick, *A history of the articles of religion* (1851).

[9] H. B. Stow, *Dred, a tale*, 2v. (1856).   [10] Untraced; *re* the Scottish estate?

[11] Tilquhilly castle, Kincardineshire; see 27 Aug. 56.

[12] A destitute artist, living in Brighton, had asked Gladstone's help (Hawn P).

with W. & A. More investigation. Finished Farini. R. Lawley came & gave advice resp. the young horse.

5. Fr.

Ch. 8½ A.M. Wrote to G. Burnett—Master of University—Mr R. Roberts —Mr H. Grant—Jones & Yarrell—Mr J. Lavis[1]—M. Hippolyte Castille— J.N.G.—A. Panizzi—Sig. L.C. Farini. Horace with Stephy—Tasso with W. & A. The children acted (French) Blue Beard very creditably. Arranging plans for journey and packing. More conv. with Lawley: and we had a trial ride. Read Greenwood's Instructions[2]—Grote's Hist. Again all but a blank day in Homer.

6. Sat. [Corwen]

Wrote to J. Ellis—Rev. Whitwell Elwin—Roundell Palmer M.P.—Mr Swift (Sol[icito]r)—Rev. L. Paige. We set off at 11 A.M. by Ruthin[3] to Corwen (Owen Glendower).[4] We found very interesting objects in the Ruthin Ch. (roof, books, brasses): and the whole drive from Mold was beautiful. Read Iliad (began)—Orsini's Account.[5]

7. 16 S. Trin. [Bala]

We went off at 7½ A.M. to Bala (White Lion): a very beautiful drive 13 m. by the Dee road.[6]—Walk up the hills in aftn. Church at the old village 11 A.M. & H.C.—Litany & Psalms at house—Bala Ch. aftn.—Wrote to Sir T.G—A. Panizzi. Read Huddlestone's Way to Faith,[7] &c. Ld G. Digby's Corresp. with Sir K. Digby[8]—Life of Stonehouse.[9]

8. M. [Mallwyd]

We left Bala at 11 delighted with the Inn and the place. We went 20 m. by the Bwlch y Groes pass to Mallwyd.[10] The ascent was steep the descent far steeper & the surface of the road bad. But the descending scenery was very fine. We also went up the valley of the Mowddy on foot: a scene of most beautiful detail. At Mallwydd we found a very good Inn. On our way we saw Llangwm Church.[11] In the Church yard an yewtree 18 to 20 f. girth. We

[1] James Lavis, blockmaker in Toxteth Park.
[2] Perhaps G. W. Greenwood, *A manual of the practice of conveyancing* (1856); the standard nineteenth century text book.
[3] On the Clwyd, 8 miles SE. of Denbigh.
[4] i.e. they stayed at the Owen Glendower hotel at Corwen, about 15 miles south of Denbigh.
[5] F. Orsini, 'The Austrian dungeons in Italy. A narrative of fifteen months' imprisonment and final escape from the fortress of S. Giorgio', tr. J. M. White (1856).
[6] SW. from Corwen.
[7] R. Hudleston, *A short and plain way to the faith and church* (1688, reprinted 1844).
[8] 'Letters between the Ld George Digby, and Sir Kenelm Digby. Kt. concerning religion' (1651); his wife's ancestors.
[9] W. A. Greenhill, *Life of Sir J. Stonhouse* (1844).
[10] By the Dovey, on the Merioneth–Montgomery border.
[11] Near which Henry Raikes lived.

saw Mallwyd Ch. too: well renovated. An yew tree more to pieces but I think near 25 feet girth. Read Hom. Il.—Orsini's Austrian Dungeons.

9. T. [Aberdovey]

Stephy was unwell: overdone with walking yesterday. We started at 11 for Machynlleth[1] and saw Kemmis & Penigos Churches on our way.[2] S. & I. walked on most of the stage to Aber Dovey wh was done by car for the rest. Both stages were exceedingly beautiful in their different ways. In the morning we visited the Dovey at M[achynlleth] & in aftn bathed at Aberdovey. Stephy was better—We were dispersed here & there to find lodging but dined at the Corbet Arms an excellent Hotel. Read Hom. Il. Saw Phillimore. Distance 12m + 10 m.

10. Wed. [Aberystwyth]

Off at 8.15 with Willy & Henry across the marsh & Garrig Ferry to the mouth of the Lyffnant Glen $7\frac{1}{2}$ m: I went up, alone, 6 m to the Falls.[3] 1 h. 40 m. up, & finding my way: 1 h. 17 m. down. This glen is of extraordinary beauty: the head is wild & grand but the fall very scanty in water. I joined the carriage (wh remained at Machynlleth for the night) at 2.30 reached Aberystwyth 4.30 (14 m) bathed. Belle Vue Hotel excellent. The Talbots came in as we were dining: but the boys were heavy with the presentiment of departure early in the morning. Read Hom. Il—Æneid B. IV.

11. Th.

Wrote to Mrs Hughes (Hn.)[4] and Robn. G. Also Scotts. Bathed: explored town, port & junction; also shopping. The boys off early with Henry. Read Hom. Il. and Æneid. At night I had a violent attack of diarrhoea.

12. [Llanidloes]

Skilfully nursed by C. I was relieved by strong sal-volatile wh acted as an emetic: & got up at $10\frac{1}{2}$, just able to have an altercation with a landlady yet more yellow about the Bill. 30 miles to the D[evil's] Bridge and Llanidloes[5] (Queen's Head, comfortable & moderate). The first few miles the least interesting part of our drive. We were greatly delighted with the Bridge scenery & falls: but especially with the descent close above the Bridge itself. A blank day for books & nearly so for food.

13. Sat. [Powis Castle]

Wrote (at P[owis] Castle) to SRG—Rev. Canon Blomfield—Rev. D.

---

[1] On the Dovey, about 5 miles from the estuary.
[2] Cemmes and Penegoes, villages in the Dovey valley.
[3] To the south of the Dovey–Machynlleth road.
[4] A nurse or governess; see 16 Sept. 56.
[5] About 22 miles east of Aberystwyth, as the crow flies.

Williams—J. Hamilton Geale—J.A. Shipton.[1] Read Iliad—Æneid finished B.V.—We had a delightful drive of 28 miles to Powis Castle[2] by Newtown where I went to the new Church. We found an exceeding beautiful place, a very kind welcome, & much Crimean & Army conversation, Col. Herbert[3] being here.

14. *17 S. Trin.*

Wrote to Archdn. Denison—Mrs Phillimore—Mr L. Marshall—Lady Cremorne—Read Asnio Paleario—Babington's Introduction[4]—Ld G. Digby's Letters—Harper on Cler. Incomes.[5] Welshpool Ch mg—New Ch aftn—Walks in the Park.

15. *M.*

Read Leake's Morea[6]—Iliad 5. We had a long ride first about the place then to Mr Naylor's Church & Farm Buildings.[7] Wrote a little for Q.R. Saw Sir W. Wynn[8] whom I was much pleased with & his brother Col Wynn[9] whom I also liked. At dinner another Eton acquaintance appeared Mr Mytton[10] whom I had not seen for 33 years. We were & more & more pleased with the family & the place.

16. *T.* [*Oteley Park*]

Wrote to Mr Grogan—J.S. Wortley—S. Herbert. Read Iliad—Æneid— After seeing Castle &c Books, left at 11¼: drove 18 m to Whittington[11] where we sent Agnes off to Hawarden (Mrs Hughes meeting her) and on 7 more to Oteley Park[12] where we went over the Gardens & met a party including 3 excellent clergymen.

17. *Wed.* [*Bettisfield, Shropshire*]

Wrote to Mrs F. Shone—W.F. Larkins (on his Father's death).[13] Read Iliad —Æneid—Ch. (Litany) at noon: at Ellesmere. We went over the Ch &

[1] Possibly John Noble Shipton, 1788–1864; rector of Othery, Somerset, from 1832.
[2] Norman seat of the earls of Powis, 1 mile SW. of Welshpool.
[3] (Sir) Percy Egerton *Herbert, 1822–76, br. of 3rd earl of Powis; wounded at the Alma, fought in Indian mutiny; tory M.P. Ludlow 1854–60, S. Salop 1865–76; K.C.B. 1869.
[4] A. Paleario, *The benefit of Christ's Death,* . . . *with an introduction by C. Babington* (1543, 1855).
[5] F. W. Harper, 'The incomes of the clergy: what they ought to be' (1856).
[6] See 22 July 50.
[7] John Naylor, 1813–89, of Leighton Hall, 2 miles east of Powis Castle.
[8] Sir Watkin Williams-Wynn, 1820–85; 6th bart. 1840; tory M.P. Denbighshire 1845–85.
[9] Herbert Watkin Williams-Wynn, 1822–62; lt. colonel 1854; tory M.P. Montgomery-shire (which the Wynns held 1832–80) 1850–62.
[10] Richard Herbert Mytton of Garth, Montgomeryshire, 1808–69; Eton and Hailey-bury; judge in Calcutta, retired 1853.
[11] 3 miles NE. of Oswestry.
[12] Seat, a mile east of Ellesmere, of Charles Kynaston Mainwaring, d. 1861; see 28 Sept. 55n.
[13] See 22 Aug. 25n. and 1 May 33.

School Buildings. In aftn. 5 m. to Bettisfield.[1] thence to Hanmer where we saw the Church & went over the mere. Music in evg & a party. We had a most kind reception.

18. Th. [*Hawarden*]

Wrote to Capt. Clarke[2]—Countess of Dunraven—Mr J. Phillips. Saw the house vine & pictures including the fine Venetian frescoes: & went off at 11 by Wrexham to Hawarden 24 miles making 226 for our tour. We were welcomed on the road by all our darling children in full health: & God has made joyful 'our going out & our coming in'. Saw Mr Whalley (at Wrexham)[3]—Mr Littleboy[4] and the Coalpit after reaching Hawarden. Tried to settle down. Read Iliad—Virgil—Leopardi's Narrazioni.[5]

19. Fr.

Wrote to J. Watson & Smith—Rev. J. Keble—Sir J.S. Forbes—Rev. A. Grant—G. Bramwell Esq—Rev. J.R. Byrne[6]—Mr L. Marshall. Saw Burnett (Rigby &c. lease)—Mr Littleboy (at the pit). Read Iliad—Æneid —Pamphlets on Army & Administrative Reform. Arranging papers &c: worked a little on Homer but could scarcely touch my intended Article for Q.R.[7]

20. Sat.

Ch. 8½ A.M. Wrote to Mr W. Grogan—Rector of Liverpool—Read Iliad— Æneid—and ...... Music in evg. Worked on MS. for Quarterly—Went to the pit again.

21. 18 S. Trin.

Broughton Ch. & H.C. mg. Mr Austin's luncheon afterwards. Hn. Ch in evg. Wrote to Bp of Brechin. Much conv. with R. Phillimore. Read Collins on Articles[8]—Lamb's Hist of do[9]—Stonehouse's Life.

22. M.

Ch. 8½ AM. Wrote to Earl Stanhope—Rev Whitwell Elwin—Robn. G. Saw Mr Burnett—Mr Dunstan—R. Phillimore—Sir W. Heathcote (came in evg). Worked hard on my MS. Read Iliad and Æneid.

[1] Sir John *Hanmer's place, 5 miles NE. of Ellesmere.
[2] Captain J. Walround Clarke, lived in Beaufort Gardens, London.
[3] George Hampden Whalley of Ruabon, d. 1878; liberal M.P. Peterborough 1852–3, 1859–78.
[4] John Littleboy of Brymbo, by Wrexham; had local coal interests, but also corresponded on national politics (Hawn P).
[5] P. S. Leopardi, *Narrazioni storiche . . . con molti documenti inediti relativi alla guerra dell' indipendenza d'Italia* (1856).
[6] John Rice Byrne, b. 1828?; curate of St. James's, Westminster; later inspector of schools.
[7] 'The declining efficiency of Parliament', *Quarterly Review*, xcix. 521 (September 1856); ventilating at length the views of his letter to *Aberdeen; see 13 Mar. 56.
[8] A. Collins, 'An historical and critical essay on the thirty-nine articles' (1724).
[9] J. Lamb, 'An historical account of the thirty nine articles' (1829).

23. T.

Ch. 8½ A.M. Wrote to Mrs Hampton—Mr Dorrell[1]—E. Ellis. Worked much on MS: corrected & sent off one half. Read Dryden's Homer[2]—Anecdotes of Johnson[3]—Music in evg. Saw Sir W. Heathcote—R. Phillimore.

24. Wed.

Ch. 8½ A.M. Wrote to Mr Dorrell—Mr Swift. Finished & sent off my MS.—Walk, & conversations with my admirable friend and colleague. We heard of Lady Braybrooke's death: may God be with her afflicted husband. Read Homer. Much discussion on the curious history of Art 29 in evg.[4] The Herberts came at midnight.

25. Th.

Ch. 8¼ A.M. Wrote to Jones & Yarrell—Earl Stanhope—Sir Thos G—Mr J. Hamilton—Mr E. Thornton. Morning spent with Herbert, Heathcote, & Phillimore, on the Ch. Rate & other questions of Church matters. Visited the Coal Pit. Walked with Herbert. Homeric convv. with Heathcote—Read Iliad.

26. Fr.

Ch. 8¼ A.M. Wrote to Rev. E. Hawkins (2)—Sir Edw. Cust—Canon Trevor —Goldwin Smith—Mr C.R. Hall. Worked on Homer—Conv. with Heathcote—Walk & politics with Herbert—Heathcotes went & Stanhopes came. Visited the pit—& Mr Smith's [Cop] Farm. Read Lessings Laocoon[5]—Boileau v. Perrault on Homer.[6]

27. Sat.

Ch. 8½ A.M. Wrote to Earl of Aberdeen—Jones & Yarrell—Geo. Bennett—G. Grant—Robn. G. Walked with Herbert & Stanhope. The latter goes from hence to Knowsley & promises to write to us after his visit.[7] Worked on Homer. Read Il. & Æn: & Guizot on Peel.[8]

28. 18 S. Trin.

Hn. Ch mg & St John's [Pentrobin] aftn. Conv. with Agnes. Walk with

---

[1] Printer, probably for Clowes, who printed the *Quarterly*.
[2] *Fables ancient and modern; translated into verse, from Homer, Ovid, Boccace and Chaucer* (1700); see *Studies on Homer*, iii. 608.
[3] See 23 July 52.   [4] See 31 Aug. 56n.
[5] G. E. Lessing, *Laokoon; oder über die Grenzen der Mahlerey und Poesie* (1766).
[6] The controversy between N. Boileau-Despréaux (1636–1711) and C. Perrault (1628–1703) over the latter's *Parallèle des anciens et des modernes*, 4v. (1688–96), which started modern study of Homer.
[7] *Stanhope wrote (3 October 1856, Add MS 44317, f. 129): '. . . He [Derby] and I were rather shy I think of present politics & had no conversation at all on any point of them, except only & that very shortly on Naples'.
[8] F. P. G. Guizot, *Sir Robert *Peel: étude d'histoire contemporaine* (1856); see 17 Mar. 57.

Stanhope & Herbert. Read Hawkins's Hist.[1]—Life of Stonehouse—S.P.G. Report.[2] Wrote to Rev Mr Elwin & the Rector of Mold.[3]

29. St. Mich[ael] [Courthey]

Mold Ch. 11 A.M. Conv. with Herbert on Church & other measures & saw him off. Mold S.P.G. meeting 12–2 where I spoke: then drove to Sutton, reached Liverpool at 4½, saw Rn. G., dined with Mr Grant, & at 6½ went to a crowded S.P.G. meeting at the Collegiate Institution wh lasted till near 10 & where I again spoke.[4] But the assumption of this function is very painful to me: it is the proper work of saints. Went afterwards to Courthey: Read Æneid.

30. Tues.

Wrote to Rev Mr Keble—Rev Mr Hawkins—Lord Braybrooke—and C.G. Saw E. Breakenridge—ditto with Robn. G.—Mr Moss[5]—Mr Stanistreet— Shopping & calls—Dinner party at Courthey. Read Cranford.[6]

Wed. Oct. One 1856. [Hawarden]

In Lpool at 10: went with Mr Bright to the new Docks, then on board & all over the Royal Charter & down the River with her.[7] Saw E. Breakenridge —Mr Pearson[8]—Wrote to Messrs. G. & Co—Williams & Co Chester—Jas Watson & Smith—Dr A. Ruge.[9] 3–5¼ Lpool to Hawarden by Sutton and the Ferry. Read Æneid.—De Tocqueville on the Revolution & ancien Regime[10]—The Rectory party dined: music in evg.

2. Th.

Ch. 8½ AM. Wrote to Sir W. James—Mr A. Polson[11]—Rev. Whitwell Elwin —Rev Warden of Ruthin[12]—Captain Gladstone. Music with C[harles] Lyttelton—Worked on letters—accounts of debts & securities—& on proofsheets of MS Article. Also discussed the Homeric question with Lyttelton. Saw Mr Burnett—Read De Tocqueville—Æn IX—Cranford.

3. Fr.

Ch. 8½ A.M. Wrote to Mr T.C. Sandars—Mr Hudson (Manchr.)[13]—Rev Mr

[1] Probably F. B. Hawkins, Germany: the spirit of her history, literature, social condition and national economy (1838).
    [2] See next day.   [3] Jenkin Davies; vicar of Mold, Flintshire, from 1854.
    [4] Full report in the Guardian, 8 October 1856, 777.   [5] See 29 Sept. 25.
    [6] By Mrs. *Gaskell (1853).
    [7] A screw steamer built by Gibbs, Bright & co. which sank with 500 emigrants off Australia in 1859.
    [8] Justly Pearson, Liverpool attorney.
    [9] Arnold Ruge, 1802–80; German liberal; deputy to Frankfurt parliament 1848–9; fled to England 1850, naturalised 1855; propagandist for united Germany.
    [10] Published (1856), intended as the first part of a three part study.
    [11] Archer Polson, published on legal topics.
    [12] Bulkeley Owen Jones, 1824?–1909; Brasenose; warden of Ruthin, Denbighshire, from 1851.
    [13] Perhaps John C. Hudson, Manchester solicitor.

Green. Finished correcting & adding to my Q.R. MS. Saw Mr Littleboy & the pit wh at 35 feet filled with water this morning. Worked on Homer—Read Æneid—Cranford.

4. Sat.

Ch. 8½ A.M. Wrote to Duchess of Sutherland—Rev Mr Morgan[1]—S. Horswell[2]—Mr Gurney—Mr Fayerman—Saw Mr Burnett—Messrs. Robertson & Darby.[3] Sod cut at 3 P.M. for second pit. Music in evg. Worked on Homer. Read Æneid—De Tocqueville.

5. 20 S. Trin.

Hn. Ch 11 AM (H.C.) and evg. Wrote MSS. Theol. Read Birch's Tillotson—Stonehouse (finished)—Arnauld—R.C. Tract.

6. M.

Ch. 8½ A.M. Wrote to Mr S. Bannister—Earl Stanhope—Mr J. Wood (B.I.R.)—Rev H.H. Jones[4]—Mr J.H. Parker. Saw Mr Pearson (Homer).[5] Visited the pits. Worked on Homer—Walk with Mr Peel—Read Cranford—Virgil Æn XI.

7. Tu.

Ch. 8½ A.M. Wrote to Mr Fayerman—Sir S. Scott & Co—Sir T.G.—Mr J. Swift—Mr W. Deering. Worked on Homer. Read Heyne's Exc[ursus] to Il.52[6]—Cranford (finished—actionless)—Virg. Æn XI.XII. Music in evg: ended with a blue pill.

8.

In bed till noon. Wrote to Robn. G.—Willy—Rev F. Meyrick—Rev R. Greswell. Worked on Homer—Corrected Revises Q.R. Read Fraser on Perrone and on Naples[7]—Cambridge (U.S.) Speeches on the Sumner Outrage[8]—Æn. XII (finished)—De Tocqueville. Music in evg.

9. Th.

Kept the house in mg. Wrote to Rev W.M. Goalen—Mrs Bennett—Mr J. Hamilton—Sir S.H. Northcote—Scotts. Rode with Agnes in aftn. Worked

---

[1] Refusing to regard ability to speak Welsh as necessary qualification for holding a Welsh see, printed in *Liverpool Evening Mail*; see 23 Sept. 55.

[2] Unidentified.

[3] The developers of the mines.

[4] Probably Hugh Hughes Jones, d. 1887; vicar of Llanedwen, Anglesea, from 1850.

[5] George Pearson, 1791–1860; rector of Castle Camps, Cambridgeshire, from 1825. See 22 Oct. 56.

[6] C. G. Heyne, *Excursus in Homerum* (1822).

[7] *Fraser's Magazine*, liv. 398, 486 (October 1856).

[8] 'The Sumner Outrage. A full report of the speeches at the meeting of citizens in Cambridge . . . in reference to the assault on Senator Sumner' (1856).

on Homer. Read Heyne's Excursus—and Sumner's most remarkable Speech on Kansas.[1]

10. Fr.

Wrote to Duchess of Argyll—Mr A. Polson. Saw Mr G. Burnett—Mr Littleboy. Worked on Homer. Read Heyne's Excursus—Dr Ihne's Article[2] —De Tocqueville—Shakespeare's Coriolanus.

11. Sat.

Resumed Ch. 8½ AM. Wrote to J. Petheram—Rev. W. Elwin—W.B. ffolkes[3]—Mr J. Jones—Scott & Co—W. Hampton. Worked on Homer. Read Mures Greek Lit.[4]—Villoison Prolegomena[5]—De Tocqueville. Party in evg.

12. 21 S. Trin.

Hn. Ch. mg & evg. Conv. with Agnes. MSS. Theoll. Read Oxford Sermons —Birch's Tillotson—Bp of St Asaph's Charge[6]—Q.R. on Portroyal—and on Church Building.[7]

Be careful in an especial degree to cultivate the habit of inward occasional & ejaculatory prayer.

There is scarcely any place or period at which it may not be practised. To close the eyes is a help towards it, yet not essential: they may be cast downward instead. It is of course a great indeed an essential object to avoid giving outward notice of what we are about: if it is given we become pray-ers at the corners of the streets. Even so short a time is enough for this lifting up the soul to God; though it is of course desirable to have moments enough both for dwelling as it were consciously on the note, and for calling God to be present in the sanctuary of the soul & to hear, or for lifting ourselves into His presence, & the presence of the Great High Priest & of the everlasting Sacrifice.

We thus become sharers in it, in that work of Jesus the Intercessor, of which Jesus the Victim is the instrument, & which is both the foundation of all Christian prayer, & its consummation.

The material of this kind of prayer is abundant: it may be found especially in the Lord's Prayer, verses of the Psalms, as well as other parts of Scripture, & articles of the Creed, the Sanctus, the Gloria in Excelsis.

Prayer of this kind is not all petition but it is address to God and includes all thanksgiving praise contemplation of Christ and His work.

It is good to attach it as it were to recurring outward acts: as the saying of Grace, the striking of the clock: so as to build up the habit: towards which it will

---

[1] C. Sumner, 'The crime against Kansas. Speech . . . in the Senate of the United States, 19th and 20th May, 1856'; attacking Douglas as 'the squire of Slavery'. It was for this speech that he was assaulted on the Senate floor, see 4–5 July 57.

[2] Gladstone condemned W. Ihne's 'Homerus' (in *Smith's *Dictionary of classical biography and mythology* (1842)) as inaccurate and irrelevant (*Oxford Essays* 1857), 2.

[3] William B. Ffolkes of York house, Bath.   [4] See 1 Sept. 55.

[5] By J. B. C. d'Ansse de Villoison (1788).

[6] T. Short, 'A charge delivered . . . July 1856' (1856).

[7] *Quarterly Review*, xciv. 489, 371 (September 1856).

be a help, to ask ourselves at night what ejaculatory prayer we have made during the day.[1]

13. M.

Ch. 8¼ A.M. Wrote to Mr De Troy[2]—Rev. D. Williams. Worked much on my Homeric Prolegomena[3]—Read De Tocqueville—Visited all the pits & borings.

14. T.

Ch. 8½ AM. Wrote to Earl of Aberdeen (ab. Q.R.)[4]—Mr G. Arbuthnot— Bp of Brechin. Finished my Prolegomena: but I *cannot* keep my threads disentangled. Stephen's entertainment to the coal miners. We came in for the toasts, & it went all very well. Read De Tocqueville—Q.R. on Montaigne.[5] Dined at the Rectory & conv. with Miss Wynn.

15. Wed.

Ch. 8½ AM. Wrote to Ld Harris—Adam S. Gladstone—Rev Mr Hampden— J.C. Deane—Scotts. Worked on Homer: finished the Essay of Comparison.[6] Saw Mr Burnett—Ld Lyttelton—Miss Wynn(yes.)—on Homer &c. Read De Tocqueville—& Wilkin on Cambr. Bill.[7]

16. Th.

Ch. 8½ A.M. Wrote to Sir J. Graham—Canon Blomfield—J.W. Wilkins Esq—Principal St Aidans[8]—Mr F. Clifford[9]—Mrs J. Burt X—Miss Allen X.[10] Walked with Miss Wynn. Worked on Homer—ἄναξ ἀνδ. &c.[11] Read De Tocqueville. A long evening of conv. with Lady Lyttelton & Miss Wynn. Conv. with Lyttelton on Homer.

17. Fr.

Ch. 8¼ A.M. Wrote to T.C. Sandars—Rev. F. Birch[12]—Rev. C.F. Lowder —Mayor of Norwich[13]—Jas Byrn, jun.[14] Saw Mr Littleboy—& all the pits. I picked up fragments of coal yesty. at Mr Darlington's: today at Messrs. Darby's. Conv. with Miss Wynn. Worked on Homer ἀριθμὸς &c.[15] Walk with C. Read De Tocqueville.

---

[1] Dated 12 October 1856; Add MS 44746, f. 42.   [2] Unidentified.
[3] *Studies on Homer*, i. 1–89.   [4] See 19 July 56n.
[5] *Quarterly Review*, xcix. 396 (September 1856).
[6] Comparing Trojans with Greeks: *Studies on Homer*, iii. 145–247.
[7] J. W. Wilkins, 'Letter to . . . *Palmerston . . . on the Cambridge Reform Bill' (1855).
[8] J. *Baylee, see 18 Nov. 54.
[9] Frederick Clifford had written from Brixton on Naples (Hawn P).
[10] This and previous name both rescue cases.   [11] For *Studies on Homer*, i. 440.
[12] Frederick Birch, curate of Par, Cornwall; not in 1860 Crockford.
[13] Robert Chamberlin, 1804?–76; draper and mayor of Norwich 1854–7, 1871–2.
[14] Presumably James Byrne, dean of Clonfert.
[15] 'Homer's perception and use of Number', *Studies on Homer*, iii. 425.

18. Sat.

Ch. 8½ A.M. Wrote to Canon Blomfield. A telegraphic message from Hagley induced C. to go off in alarm.[1] I accompanied her to Chester. Saw Bp of Chester—Canon Blomfield—Mr Burnett—Mr Littleboy. Worked on Homer —Read De Tocqueville—Shakespeare's Tempest. Agnes was 14 today: a great epoch. We have only to wish she may grow as she has grown.

19. 22 S. Trin.

Ch. mg & evg. Conv. with A.M. & Lena. Wrote to C.G. Worked on Homeric theology. Read Birch's Tillotson—Tillotsons Sermons[2]—Astell's Xtn Religion[3]—Yorke's Letter to Chance.[4]

20. M.

Church 8½ A.M. H.S. with Mary & Lena. Rode with Agnes. Wrote to Sidney Herbert—Rev. T. Morgan[5]—Rev. Mr Chaplin[6]—Bp of Argyll—Mr E. Harford—Wm. Grogan—C.G. Worked on Homer—*Colour*.[7] Read de Tocqueville. The Powis's[8] came, the letters to stop them having miscarried: they were very kind but the evening proved *long*.

21. T.

Ch. 8½ A.M. Wrote to Lady Dunraven—Rev. Mr Sherlock[9]—Rev. Mr. Harries.[10]—C.G. Took the Powis party to the pits and borings: and then a walk in the less known part of the Park. Worked on Homer—Read de Tocqueville. Music in evening.

22. Wed.

Ch. 8½ A.M. H.S. with Agnes M. & L. Wrote to C.G.—Robn. G.—Rev. G. Pearson. Worked on Homer Theol. Saw Mr Littleboy—S.R.G. on Homer— Mr Troughton on do (colours). Much military discussion, Indian army & all the rest, in the forenoon.

[1] An illness in W. H. Lyttelton's *ménage*.
[2] *The works of* . . . *Tillotson*, ed. R. Barker, 2v. (1717).
[3] M. Astell, *The Christian religion, as profess'd by a daughter of the Church of England* (1705).
[4] G. M. Yorke, 'The school and the workshop; why should they not combine? A letter to J. T. Chance' (1856).
[5] Probably Thomas Morgan, 1827–90?; curate of Great Witley, near Hagley, 1852–7; sundry charges; vicar of Dilwyn 1873–90.
[6] William Chaplin, 1825–?1906; curate of Kendal 1850; vicar of Staveley 1858–96 (later letter in Hawn P).
[7] On Homer's perceptions and use of colour: *Studies on Homer*, iii. 457–95.
[8] 3rd earl of Powis (see 13 Apr. 43), a bachelor, his mother, the dowager, and his brother colonel (Sir) P. E. *Herbert.
[9] Edgar Sherlock, 1820?–1909; sundry curacies 1847–65; rector of Bentham 1865–84.
[10] Several; probably Gilbert Charles Frederick Harries, d. 1879; rector of Llandefar-legfach 1855–62, of Gelligaer from 1862.

23. Th.

Ch. 8¼ A.M. H.S. with A.M. & Lena. The Powis's went at 11—after another military talk with Col H[erbert]. Wrote to C.G.—Lyttelton—Mrs Wood—Mrs Haydn[1]—W.C. James—City Remembrr.—Chancr. of Exchr. —J.R. Godley. Visited pit & rode with Agnes. In evg working up letters & papers: & played chess with Stephen.

24. Fr. [Liverpool]

Wrote to C.G.—Sir T.G.—S. Herbert—Mrs J.N.G. Saw Mr Littleboy—Mr Barrow. Started for Lpool at 9¼ arr. 11½. L.N.W. & G.N. arbitration meeting 11¾–4½.[2] Read Life of Ld Herbert. Dinner party at Mr Moss's & Bank & currency conv. with him. I remained for the night.

25. Sat. [Courthey, Liverpool]

Went over the grounds with Mr M[oss] & the house with Mrs M.[3]—then to Lpool. Visited the Exhibition (1½ hour) wh pleased me much. Also shopping. Saw Mr Grant resp. T. Goalen—E. Breakenridge on Seaforth matters. Wrote to C.G.—J.G. Lacaita—J.G. Lacaita [sic]—Rev. Mr Hampden. to Courthey. Dinner party there in the evening. Saw Rob. Gladstone jun. Read Life of Ld Herbert.[4]

26. 23 S. Trin.

Walked to Seaforth Ch. mg. where Mr Ayerst[5] preached for the Jews' Society: much more fluent & clear than satisfactory but interesting & in earnest. Saw Mr Rawson—then back to aftn prayers at St Martin's: a rather sham-choral service, good catechising. I walked thro' an extraordinary district. Back by St Chrysostoms where I saw a Baptism with conduct strange enough, to C[ourt] Hey at 6. Read M'Cries Knox[6]—Coxe to Bp of Arras.[7]

27. M.

Wrote to Bp of Salisbury—Sir T. Tancred—R. Phillimore—Rev Mr Rowsell—Agnes G.—E. Breakenridge—C.G. Review of state & prospects of the Seaforth property with E. Breakenridge in aftn. Also conv. with Robn. on

---

[1] The widow of Joseph Timothy *Haydn, 1786?–1856, editor and statistical compiler; his civil list pension 1855 was transferred to her after his death.

[2] Revision of the 'six towns' arbitration made by Gladstone in 1851; see C. H. Grinling, *History of the Great Northern Railway* (1903), 149ff.

[3] See 11 Aug. 25.

[4] *Life of Edward, Lord *Herbert of Cherbury*, ed. H. *Walpole (1764).

[5] William Ayerst, 1802–83; worked with Jews in Germany; foreign sec. of Jews' Society 1841–53; vicar of Egerton from 1853.

[6] T. M'Crie, *The life of John *Knox* (1812).

[7] A. C. Coxe, 'Lettre à Mgr. Parisis, Évêque d'Arras, sur les erreurs, à l'égard de l'église anglicane' (1856).

them. Dined at Norris Green[1] where we had much conv. on Xtn & social prospects. Read Ld Herbert.

28. T. SS Simon & Jude.

Wrote to Mr Grant. Attended the Police Court mg—a sad & strange aspect of human nature & our civilisation.[2] Then to New Brighton with Arthur[3] where we saw Mr Neilson, & his Pictures. Then to the Academy 2° to meet M.E.[4] Shopping. Read Montaigne—Herbert's Life (finished). Alone with with Robn. in evg.

29. Wed.

Wrote to Agnes G.—Hon A. Gordon. Went down to Seaforth & over the ground—Also saw E. Breakenridge—Rev Mr Rawson—Mr Stanistreet—Mr Moss—Mr Geo Grant—Dr Brandreth (Homer etc.)—Shopping &c. Dinner party at Courthey. I am increasingly pleased with Mrs Heywood. Read Montaigne.

30. Th.

St Peter's Ch. 3 P.M. Wrote to Robn. G.—J. Stanistreet (2)—Mr A. Polson —E. Breakenridge—Ld De Tabley. Saw Rn. G on Seaforth matters, & on those of Miss E. R[obertson]'s Estate. Executed Memorandum to settle that affair—& prepared with some care Advt. & Particulars to be printed for Seaforth. Saw E. Breakenridge. Bid good bye to Courthey & went to W. Pattens. With him I had long conversations on political & Church matters. Read Montaigne—Marshall.[5]

31. Fr. [Hawarden]

Wrote to A.B. Hope—Mr W. Grogan. A morning conv. with Patten. Visited the Clergy Daughter's and Training Schools, & the Church. Off at 11.25. Took C. to the Lpool Exhibition to see my purchases. Then to the Town Hall to execute Jamaica conveyance. Saw Mr Stanistreet—Robn. G —& off at 2 for Hawarden: where we rejoined the dear children. Visited the D. & R. pit[6]—Read Montaigne—Emerson's Traits.[7] Worked on letters & papers.

---

[1] With John Pemberton Heywood, 1803–77; Liverpool banker, partner in A. Heywood & Sons and from 1837 in (Denison) Heywood, Kennard & Co. of Lombard Street; picture collector and friend of Robertson Gladstone; unsuccessfully ran with diarist for S. Lancs. 1865. His wife mentioned 2 Oct. 52.

[2] Robertson was a J.P.

[3] Arthur Robertson Gladstone, 1841–96, his br.'s oldest living s.; later major in the Lancashire Hussars.

[4] i.e. R. Gladstone's wife.

[5] Perhaps *Memoir of Rev. J. Marshall . . . by his son* (1856).

[6] The pit leased by Darby and Robertson.

[7] R. W. Emerson, *English Traits* (1856).

Sat. Nov. One 56. All Saints.

Hn. Church 8½ A.M. Wrote to Sir John Young—Hon Mrs Wilbraham—
Mrs Larkins—Mr J. Gibson—Mr S. Galindo[1]—Mr Williams (Manchester).[2]
Worked on Homer—Mythol. & Pol. Read Montaigne—Emerson's Traits of
England—Grote's Greece.[3]

2. 24 S. Trin.

Ch mg (with Holy Commn.) & Evg. Conv. on Gospel &c. with A. & M.
Wrote to Bp of Aberdeen: & worked on the papers. Read Birch's Tillotson
(finished)—M'Crie's Knox—Knox's Hist[4]—Tribunal Christi.[5]

3. M.

Ch. 8½ A.M. Wrote to R.G.—Sir T.G.—M. Bernard—T.C. Sandars—J.
Gaskell—Scotts—Rev. Mr Lester.[6] Worked on Hom[eric] Mythol. Read
Canti Carnascialeschi[7]—Emerson's Traits. At the pits with C. &c.

4. T.

Ch. 8½ A.M. Wrote to T.C. Sandars—Mrs Larkins—J.G. Lacaita—Lord
Canning—Rev. W. Elwin—Rev. E.C. Woollcombe—Sir W. Heathcote—
Mr Tidbury.[8] Bp of Oxford came: conv. with him (walk, & evg): on the
Scotch Clergy Bill among others.[9] Worked on Homer. Read Emerson's
Traits—and Corinne.[10]

5. Wed.

Ch. 8½ A.M. Wrote to Sir W. Heathcote—Principal of King's Coll—Mr J.M.
Knott[11]—Mr T. Hand[12]—Mr R. Phillimore. Walk & much conv. with the
Bp on Bath Judgment[13]—Gorham case—& other matters. Worked on
Homer—Pol. Visited the pit. Saw Mr [H.P.] Ffoulkes (Diocn. Assn.).

6. Th.

Ch. 8½ A.M. Wrote to Ld Lyttelton—Mr G. Patch—Bp of Aberdeen. Walk
& further conv. with Bp(O.) who saw my letter to Bp of A. Party & singing
in evg. Read Emerson's Traits—Wilsons Gateways (finished)[14]—Verka-
agen's Address[15]—Russell's Ch in Scotland[16]—Worked on Homer.

[1] Samuel Galindo, author.   [2] Not further identified.   [3] See 19 Mar. 47.
[4] J. *Knox, History of the Reformation of religioun within the realme of Scotland (1584,
Laing's ed. 1846–8).
[5] Untraced.
[6] Probably John Willian Lester, 1826–76; curate of Ashton-Hayes, Cheshire, 1853–7;
vicar of Norwood from 1858; D.D. 1860.
[7] See 4 July 55.   [8] Perhaps C. H. Tidbury, accountant in Great St. James's St.
[9] For this and next days' talks, see Wilberforce, ii. 335–6: Gladstone 'very strong
against Palmerston . . . manifestly Gladstone leans to a Conservative alliance'.
[10] By Mme. de Staël (1807).   [11] Probably sc. J. W. Knott.
[12] London solicitor.   [13] See 13 Aug. 56.
[14] G. Wilson, The five gateways of Knowledge (1856).
[15] Possibly by Pierre T. Verhaegen, Belgian politician.
[16] M. *Russell, History of the church in Scotland, 2v. (1834).

7. *Fr.*

Ch. 8½ A.M. Wrote to Mrs Hampton—Dow[age]r Lady Lyttelton—Captain Stokes.[1] Wrote & copied out draft of Scots Episc. Petition[2]—Saw Mr Littleboy—Worked on Homer (Pol &c.) Read Montaigne—Party & music in evg.

8. *Sat.*

Ch. 8½ A.M. Wrote to Joel Rowsell—Sir Jas Graham—Bp of Aberdeen. Worked on Homer Pol. Read Montaigne's Essays—Maginn's Ballads & Notes.[3]

9. *25 S. Trin.*

Hn. Ch. mg & evg. Conv. with Agnes on Gospel &c. Examined Hampden papers /36.[4] Wrote to Stephen E. G[ladstone]—Mrs T. Goalen—Bp of Hereford & draft.[5] Read Kathol. Gebetbuch[6]—M'Cries Knox—Williams's Suckling[7]—Br. Crit. on Scots Ep. Ch. &c.

10. *M.*

Ch. 8½ A.M. Wrote to Bp of St Andrews—Child & Co—Dr Acland— Macmillan & Co.[8] Worked much on Homer—Pol. Read Jay's Address on Slavery in U.S.[9]—Æneid VII.

11. *Tues.*

Ch. 8½ A.M. Wrote to Ld Aberdeen—Sir James Graham—Ld Courtenay— Bp of Glasgow. Worked much on Homer. Pol. Visited M. Williams at the Lodges:[10] & a turn with the spade. Read Dryden's Troilus & Cress.[11]

Wed. 12th.

Ch. mg.—Wrote to Rev. Mr Elwin—Robn. G—Mr Bramwell—Messrs. Davies & Co.[12] Saw Dr Moffatt[13]—Canon Blomfield. Worked much on Homer. Read Dryden Tro. & Cress.—Shakespeare do—Theocritus Idyll. Men.[14]

---

[1] Capt. L. Stokes had written from France on colonies; Hawn P.
[2] On political discrimination agst. Scottish episcopal church: Add MS 44746, f. 46.
[3] W. Maginn, *Homeric ballads; with translations and notes* (1850).
[4] This diary for 21 Mar. 36, when he was prevented from going to vote against *Hampden at Oxford; see Ward, 101.
[5] Stating that the *Maurice affair at King's, London, had made him realize the 'injustice' of his (intended) vote against *Hampden in 1836: Add MS 44386, f. 215.
[6] *Katholisches Gebetbuch* (Innsbruck, 1854).
[7] I. Suckling, *A short memoir of the Rev. R. A. Suckling* (1859).
[8] London publishers.
[9] W. Jay, 'An address delivered before the American Peace Society' (1845).
[10] Mary Williams, on the estate.   [11] Published (1679).
[12] Ashmore Davies & co., London silk merchants.
[13] Of Hawarden, see 13 Sept. 42.
[14] Probably the 1811 Leipzig ed. of Theocritus' *Idylls*.

13th Th.

Ch. mg. Wrote to A. Panizzi—E. Foster—Rev Jas Hildyard.[1] Walk to Cs ride. Worked on Homer (Trojans). Dined at the Rectory: & conv. with W. Lyttelton on the retrocession of Christianity.

14. Fr.

Ch mg. Wrote to S. Herbert—Mrs Hampton—Rev Mr Pirie[2]—James Knowles.[3] Worked on · Homer—Trojans rel. to Greeks. Dined at the Rectory—Read Hildyard.[4]

15. Sat.

Ch mg. Wrote to Mr Dorrell—M.F. Tupper—Rev. J. Marshall. Worked on with the Trojans all day. At nt corrected part of the Comparison for Q.R.[5] Read Racine's Iphigenie.

16. 26 S. Trin.

Hn. Ch. mg & evg. Conv. with daughters on Collect &c. Wrote to Rev Mr Tomline[6]—Archdeacon Jones. Read Gioberti's Post. & Massari's Preface.[7] Addl. Curates Reports & papers[8]—Hildyard (finished).

17. M.

Ch mg. Wrote to W. Grogan—J. Palmer Bookseller.[9] Corrected & sent off residue of paper on Homer Compared—Finished paper on Trojans. Saw Mr Darby—Party to dinner—singing. Read Racine's Iphigenie—Rode with my little Mary. Neuralgia at night.

18. T.

Kept my bed mg—Thought over the A[dditional] C[urates] S[ociety] subject. Off to Chester at 11. Meeting at 12. Spoke 50 m. for Addl. Curates Society[10]—To the Bps afterwards—& Luncheon. *Cathedral* 4 PM. Got a mouthful only of work on Homer—Dinner party in evg. Conv. with Dr Briscoe & Archdeacon Jones. Finished Racine's Iphigenie.

---

[1] James *Hildyard, 1809–87; fellow of Christ's, Cambridge; classicist and educationalist.
[2] William Robson *Pirie, 1804–85; professor of divinity, Aberdeen, from 1843, principal there from 1876.
[3] James Sheridan *Knowles, 1784–1862, dramatist, often on classical themes.
[4] J. *Hildyard, 'A revision of the liturgy urged, with a view chiefly to the abridgement of the morning service' (1856).
[5] Comparison between Trojans and Greeks in 'Homer and his successors [Virgil and Tasso] in epic poetry' *Quarterly Review*, ci. 80 (January 1857).
[6] Probably Alfred John Tomlin, d. 1901; curate in Liverpool 1846–72; vicar of Lower Tranmere, Cheshire, from 1883.
[7] G. Massari, preface to first v. of his ed. of *Opere inedite di V. Gioberti* (1856).
[8] See 18 Nov. 56.
[9] Joseph William Palmer, bookseller and stamp dealer in London; published verses.
[10] See *The Guardian*, 26 November 1856, 892.

19. Wed.

Ch. 8¼ A.M. Wrote to Mr Burnett—Sir Geo. Grey—Rev. E. Hawkins. Saw Archdn. Jones (Rating, Ch. Rates, &c.)—Mr Burnett. Worked on Homer (Morality). Dinner party in evg—Singing. Walk with C.G.—Recommenced Iliad.

20. Th.

Ch mg. Wrote to Chancr. of Exchequer—Mr S. Herbert—Worked on Homer (Mor.) Read Terpstra 'Antiquitas Homerica'[1]—Reimmann—Iliad II. Walk with Warburton to the pits &c. Coal is already all but proved in three places by shale at 24, 25, and 42 yards respectively. Dinner party & music in evg.

21. Fr.

Ch. mg. Wrote to J. Stuart Wortley[2]—Sir J. Graham—Bp of Oxford— M.F. Tupper—Librarian London Lib.—W. Grogan—J. MacCulloch—Rev D.C. Moore[3]—Worked on Homer (Morals) Read Il III & part IV. Dinner party & music in evg. Walk with Mr Stanley.

22. Sat.

Ch. mg. Wrote to Mons. Hippolyte Castille—J.N.G.—Mr H. Lees. Read Statius Achilleis—Racine Andromaque—Chaucer Troilus & Cress.—Max Muller Essay (part)[4] Dined at the Rectory. Walk with Stephen.

23. Last S. Trin.

Ch mg & evg. Conv. with Agnes. Visited M. Williams. Wrote on Hom Mor. & Rel. Read Suckling's Life[5]—Coxe's Letter—Manning on the Unity of the Ch.[6]—Gioberti's Riforma.[7] Mary's birthday: may she grow up dear & good as now.

24. M.

Kept at home on acct. of neuralgia. Wrote to Robn. G (with Duplicate Mema.)—T. Hughes[8]—Rev. J.O. Powell. Worked on Homer (Char.) Read Eurip. Troades &c.—Catullus—Isocrates—Dryden's Tro. & Cress.— Seneca, the Troades—Racines Andromaque (finished). A quiet evening.

---

[1] J. Terpstra (1831).

[2] Attempting to dissuade him from accepting solicitor-generalship from *Palmerston; he took it: Add MS 44386, f. 21.

[3] David Christmas Moore; licentiate priest; curate of Borley, Essex, 1853–7.

[4] F. *Max Müller, 'Comparative mythology', in *Oxford essays for 1856.*

[5] See 9 Nov. 56.   [6] See 27 Feb. 42.

[7] V. Gioberti, 'Della riforma Cattolica della Chiesa frammenti' in *Opere inedite,* i (1856).

[8] Thomas *Hughes, 1822–96; barrister; liberal M.P. Lambeth 1865, Frome 1868–74; Christian socialist and author.

25. T.

Ch. 8½ A.M. Wrote to Duchess of Sutherland—Rev B. Wilson—Rev N. Woodard—Robn. G.—Rode with Agnes. Worked on Homer—Char. and Sense of Beauty—Saw Mr Burnett—Mr Darlington—Bp of Chester. Dinner party, & singing. Read Shirley Ajax & Ul.[1]—Homer's Iliad.

26. Wed.

Ch. 8½ A.M. Wrote to Mr de Troy—Mr Burnett—Sidney Herbert—A. Panizzi—Jos. Palmer. Conv. with Sir J. Hanmer—Homer—For. & Flintsh. Politics. Took him to the pits. Worked on Homer (*Beauty*—& Plot)— Read Il. V.

27. Th. [Peckforton Castle, Cheshire]

Ch. 8½ AM. Wrote to Bp of Aberdeen (& copy)—Ed Lpool Courier—Rev N. Grieve[2]—Mr W. Grogan. Read Mr Yates on the Homeric Metre[3]—Castille's Arnaud & Canrobert[4]—Hom. Iliad. Off at 4¼ to Peckforton[5] where we found a large party a very fine house & a most kind reception. Conv. with Chancellor Thurlow.[6]

28. Fr.

Forenoon walked over the drives & to a cheese farm—Mr Armisted gave me a lecture on the process.[7] The day showed us something of the beautiful views. In aftn we rode to Cholmondeley. Read Iliad. Conv. with Mr Tolle-mache—Mr Armisted—Chancr. Thurlow.

29 Sat. [Hawarden]

Off at 10.45 to Hn. all well there D.G. Wrote to Sir J. Graham (& copy)— Mr C. Pressly—Ld A. Hervey—Mrs Hampton—J. Swift—Mr J. Masters— Mr H.W. Ellis—Mr J. Freshfield—Robn. Gladstone—Captain Crigan[8]— Jones & Yarrell—A. Panizzi. Arranging letters. Read Hom. Iliad— Arnold's Hist. of Rome.[9]

30. St Andr. & Advent S.

Ch mg & evg. Conv. with Agnes resp. her Confirmation & future life. Read Faber's Foreign Churches[10]—Manning's Unity of the Ch.—Gibbin's Carnesecchi.[11]

---

[1] J. *Shirley, *The contention of Ajax and Ulysses* (1659).
[2] Nathaniel Grieve, episcopal incumbent of Ellon, Aberdeenshire, from 1803.
[3] J. Yates, *On the irregularities in the versification of Homer* (1856).
[4] H. Castille, *Saint Arnauld et Canrobert* (1856).
[5] Seat, near Tarporley, Cheshire, of John Tollemache.
[6] Charles Augustus Thurlow, 1803–73; rector of Malpas from 1840; chancellor of Chester from 1854.
[7] i.e. John Armitstead; see 15 Apr. 52 and 5 Dec. 56.   [8] Unidentified.
[9] See 19 Feb. 45.   [10] See 11 Sept. 45.
[11] 'Report of the trial . . . of P. Carnesecchi', ed. and tr. R. Gibbings (1856).

Try not violently but steadily to keep down the number of your bodily wants—it will increase the freedom of your mind in relation to the body, and your personal freedom in relation to the opinions & practice of the world around you: it will enlarge your means of doing good: & it will open out ways of self denial, that great duty which we are so ready to find excuses for not looking in the face.

The hours of our mirth are not the hours in which we live: when we look back upon them they are as if written in water or in sand. The hours in which we live are the hours of trial sorrow care evil & struggle: those hours that leave the furrow on our faces leave their mark also on our souls: it is in them that we really labour & by labour is fruit brought forth.[1]

Mond. Decr. One 1856

Ch. 8½ AM. Wrote to Bp of Aberdeen—S. Herbert—Willy—Aunt Joh. Worked on Homer Hist.—& correcting proof-sheets. Read Iliad.

2. T.

Ch mg. Wrote to Sir Jas Graham—E. of Aberdeen (& copy)—Mr W. Elwin —(anxious letters which occupied most of my day in thought & writing)[2]— also to J.G. Davenport[3]—W.B. Donne—A. Campbell—Rev. W. James[4] —Rev. C.G. Nicolay—Rev. F.A. Marriott. Worked on Q.R. proofsheets. Read Iliad—At the [mine] borings with Lascelles.

3. Wed.

Ch mg. Wrote to J. Griffiths—R. Barker—F.R. Bonham—Mr Dorrell (P[roof] Sheets)—Messrs. Freshfield—Mrs A. Corbett.[5] Worked on Homer (Hector)—A long *sederunt* with Mr Burnett & a review of the general state of Stephen's affairs. The deadly struggle has been carried on with as much success as on the whole we could have hoped. Read Iliad—Arnold's Rome.

4. Th.

Ch mg. Wrote to Sir J. Graham—Chancr. of Exchr.—Rev O. Gordon— Station Mr. Q. Ferry. Worked on Homer (hist.) Visited Mary Williams. Saw Sherratt.[6] We burned a fire with the Hawarden coal a 2f.6. seam found at [blank] yards. Read Iliad—Armitsted on Ch. Leases.[7]

---

[1] Dated 30 November 1856; Add MS 44746, f. 50.

[2] On his 'Prospects political and financial', *Quarterly Review*, ci. 243 (January 1857); he communicated with *Aberdeen, who knew of his previous article (see 19 Sept. 56) and *Elwin, through whom *Derby was making contact; he told Elwin (1 January 1857, Elwin MSS, N.L.S.): 'Aided by . . . the lapse of time since my letter of 13th. [Dec.], I am doubtful whether Lord Derby ever had the intention of asking for a conference on the state of public affairs'. But see 4 Feb. 57.

[3] Possibly John Coltman Davenport, 1830–58; Staffordshire gentleman.

[4] William James, 1787?–1861; fellow of Oriel, Oxford, until 1837; rector of Bilton from 1853.

[5] Of Beeston, Cheshire.   [6] J. Sherratt, on the estate.

[7] J. Armitstead, 'A letter to . . . *Russell in vindication of the rights and property of the church' (1850).

5. *Fr.*

Ch mg. Wrote to Sir W. Heathcote. Worked on Homer, Hist. and Reln. Worked at the spade. Read Hom. Iliad—Armitsted on Sunday Cheese-making.[1]

6. *Sat.*

Ch. mg. Wrote to Chancr. of Exchr.—Robert Gladstone—Mrs Hampton—Mr W. Grogan—Scotts. Worked on Homer Hist. & Rel. Read Cambr. Essay on Picturesque[2]—Hom. Iliad.—Rode with A.

7. *2 S. Advent*

Hn. Ch. 11 (and H.C.) and 6½. Conv. with Agnes again resp. her confirmation. She was both earnest & tender. Worked on Hom. Theol. Read Manning's Unity—Peterhead Sermon & Appx[3]—Cambr. Ess. on French Protestm.[4]

8. *M.*

Ch mg. Wrote to Ld Aberdeen—Bp of Salisbury—Bp of Oxford—M. Van de Weyer—Rev R. Greswell—Mr G. Burnett—Mr M. Bernard—Rev J. Hamilton Gray—R. Phillimore. Worked on Homer—Religion. R. Cavendish came. Read Iliad—&c.

9. *T.*

Ch. mg. Wrote to J. Griffiths—Mr G. Applegate[5] and [blank]. Worked on Homer Rel. & Hist. Saw R. Cavendish—Mr G. Burnett. Visited the borings &c. Read Homer Iliad—Terpstra Antiq. Hom.[6]

10. *Wed.*

Ch. mg. Wrote to Bp of Aberdeen—Bp of Glasgow—Incumbent (Ep.) Peterhead[7]—Mrs Corbett (Beeston)—Mr J. Broster. Worked on Hom (Rel. & Hist). Read Hom. Iliad. The boys came home: great joy: both looking well & thoroughly good: Willy sent up: Stephy with 20 places & more.

11. *Th.*

Ch mg. Wrote to Chancr. of Exchr.—Rev Whitwell Elwin—Rev Mr Rhodes[8]—Rev Mr Greswell—Rev Mr Woollcombe—Rev Mr Rowsell.

[1] J. Armitstead, 'Sabbath Day cheese-making not a work of necessity' (1841).
[2] E. M. Cope, 'The taste for the picturesque amongst the Greeks' in *Cambridge essays, contributed by Members of the University, 1856* (1856).
[3] G. Rorison, 'The depression of the clergy the danger of the church' (1856).
[4] W. H. Waddington, 'The protestant church and religious liberty in France' in *Cambridge essays* (1856).
[5] G. Applegate of Ebbw Vale had requested a donation: Hawn P.
[6] See 20 Nov. 56.
[7] Gilbert Rorison, episcopal incumbent of Peterhead, Aberdeenshire; hymnist.
[8] Perhaps Henry Jackson Rhodes, b. 1823?; Corpus, Oxford; curate of St. Anne's, Highgate; wrote on convocation.

Corrected Revises for Q.R. Worked on Homer Rel. & Hist. Walk with Cavendish. Attended Agricultural Lecture in evg, & moved vote of thanks.[1] Read Terpstra—Cambr. Ess[ayists].

12. Fr.

Ch.. mg (with Willie) Wrote to Robn. G.—J.N.G.—Rev J. Christie[2]—J. Broster—Bp of Aberdeen. Worked on Homer (hist. & Rel.) Tasso with W. & A. Visited Mary Williams. Read Terpstra—Max Müller.

13. Sat.

Ch (with W.) mg. Wrote to Earl of Aberdeen—Dr Hook—G. Burnett— Mr Conder[3]—Rev B. Wilson—E. Allen[4]—Rev W. Elwin (for 14th). Worked on Homer & nearly finished the recast $\overset{\text{}}{\alpha}\nu\alpha\xi\ \overset{\text{}}{\alpha}\nu\delta\rho\tilde{\omega}\nu$.[5] Finished the Iliad once more. Read Max Müller—Tasso with W. & A.

14. 3 S. Adv.

Ch. mg & evg. Conv. on Ep. & Gosp. with the three eldest. Tea at the Rectory. Wrote to Ld Abn. & copy—also *sent* to Mr Elwin.[6] Read Chr. Rem. on Ch. in France[7]—Manning on the Unity of the Ch.—Woodgate's Sermons[8]—Sermons & pamphlets.

15. M.

Ch mg. Wrote to Sir J. Graham—S. Herbert. Made notes & copies from Sir J. G[raham] on my financial paper.[9] Worked on materials & set to with Article for the Q.R. Worked on 'Prolegomena' for Oxf Essays[10] & corr. proofs. Read Max Müller. Walk with C. & Stephen. Saw the two Burnetts.

16. T.

Ch mg. Wrote to Robn. G—A. Hayward—Mr Geo. Chivers[11]—Mr Dorrell. Tasso with W. & A. Worked on the projected political Article for Q.R. Walk with C.—Saw Mr Littleboy. Worked on Proof Sheets of Prolegg. Read M. Muller (finished)—O[xford] E[ssays] on Charlemagne[12]—Bopp's Grammar.[13]

[1] No account found.
[2] James Christie, episcopal incumbent of Turriff, Aberdeenshire; sending subscription to his church.
[3] G. W. Condor of the Leeds Mechanics Institute requested Gladstone to speak.
[4] Unidentified.
[5] For *Studies on Homer*, i. 440.
[6] See 2 Dec. 56.
[7] *Christian Remembrancer*, xxxii. 423 (December 1856).
[8] H. A. Woodgate, *Sermons on the Sunday historical lessons from the Old Testament* (1854).
[9] See 16 Feb. 56 for the mem. and *Graham's notes.
[10] His essay 'On the place of Homer in classical education and in historical inquiry' in *Oxford essays for 1857* (1857).
[11] Unidentified.
[12] R. J. King, 'Carolingian romance' in *Oxford essays* (1856).
[13] F. Bopp, *A comparative grammar of the Sanskrit, Zend, Greek, Latin, Lithuanian, Gothic, German and Slavonic languages*, 3v. (1845–50).

17. Wed.

Ch mg (with Stephy) Wrote to Chancr. of Exchr.—Bp of Glasgow—Mr Dowdall[1]—Mr J. Swift—Mr S. Strong.[2]—Rev Mr Greswell—Rev L. Paige —Messrs. Scott—J.N.G. Worked on Political MS. Rode with Agnes. Read Dryden's Poetry. Horace with Stephy.

18. Th.

Ch mg. Wrote to R. Barker—Scotts (2)—F. Gadaleta—J. Godley—Rev. W. Elwin—Sir W. Heathcote. Worked on Political MS. A very difficult task: not what to say, but how to say it. Visited the Borings: saw Sherratt. Children's play 6–7½: very creditably done. Read [blank]

19. Fr.

Ch. mg. I have taken to coffee to keep off morning neuralgia. Worked hard on & finished MS. for Q.R. Tasso with W. & A. Visited Mary Williams. Present at part of the 'Truant Heart['']. Read Fletchers Tamer Tamed[3]— Odyssey (began once more).

20. Sat.

Ch. mg. Wrote to Rev. Mr Elwin (2)—Scotts—Chancr. of Exr.—Robn. G. —Mr Pilgrim.[4] Tasso with W. & A. A hard day correcting MS: dispatched it all. Yesterday was the *first* day when in course of post anything cd. have come from Ld D.[5] Conv. with S. on my Prolegomena. Read Odyssey— Alexander on Opium Trade.[6]

21. 4 S. Adv. S. Thomas.

Hn Ch. mg & evg. Conv. on Ep. & Gosp. with the three eldest. Also with M. & L. on wandering eyes. Wrote to Bp of Oxford, Glasgow, Aberdeen— Mr W. Hampton. Read Manning's Unity (finished)—Suckling's Sermons[7] —Gioberti's Opere Postume[8]—Jäger's Photius.[9]

22. M.

Ch mg. with Willy. Wrote to Robert Gladstone—Mrs R. Lawley[10]— Rev. B. Wilson—Librarian of C.O.[11] Worked all the mg. on papers books &

[1] T. Dowdall of Liverpool.
[2] Solicitor in Lincoln's Inn.
[3] J. *Fletcher, *The Tamer Tamed, a comedy* (1647).
[4] William Pilgrim, London commission agent.
[5] *Elwin had tried to involve Gladstone and *Derby in political negotiations: 'The great Derby case has for the present at least ended in smoke'; Gladstone to *Aberdeen, 2 January 1857, Add MS 43071, f. 353.
[6] R. Alexander, *The rise and progress of British opium smuggling* (1856).
[7] R. A. Suckling, *Sermons, plain and practical . . . ed. by I. *Williams* (1853)
[8] In 2v., published in Italy and sent by Joseph Massari (Add MS 44385, f. 296).
[9] Abbé J. N. Jäger, *Histoire de Photius, patriarche de Constantinople* (1844).
[10] See 9 Nov. 52n.?
[11] George Mayer.

letters, towards winding up. Horace with Stephen—Tasso with W. & A. Correcting Prolegg. for Oxford Essays. Read Odyssey—Duke of Argyll's Address[1]—Carmichael's Letter to Ld P.[2]

23. T.

Ch. mg with Willy. Wrote to Earl of Aberdeen & copy part—S. Herbert—J.W. Parker—R. Daniel.[3] Finished & dispatched corr. proofs. Walk with Willy: a 3f.6. coal was reached yesterday at 70 yards by the Darlington men. Worked on Homer. Hor. with Stephy. Tasso with W. & A. Read Odyssey—Hodgson's Hunterian Oration[4]—Wilkins' State of Spain[5]—Burn's Darkening Cloud.[6]

24. Wed.

Ch mg 8½ Evg 7. Wrote to Sir W. Heathcote—C.W. Sikes—Sir A.H. Elton—Sir J. Graham (on Currency—Estimates for 1857—& the Derby Correspe.)—Rev. W. Elwin. Read Elton on the Ballot[7]—Sikes on Savings Banks[8]—Currency Self Regulating[9]—Odyssey.
Worked on the papers connected with Stephens affairs. Without the coal we can get on, & mend but only at a snail's pace. All rapid movement depends on it. Sederunt with Mr Burnett. Tasso with W. & A. Homer with S.

25. Th. Xmas day.

The children came early with carols to our doors: pure voices from pure hearts! Hn Ch. 11 AM. & H.C.—7 P.M. Read Bickersteth's Sermon[10]—Vie de Photius—Milman's hist. Xty[11]—Gilderdale's Discipl. Rediviva[12]—Ov[id] Fasti & Excursus.

26. Fr. St Stephen.

Ch. 11 A.M. Wrote to J.N.G.—Mr Petleybridge[13]—Sir T.G.—Mr Gilderdale[14]—Scotts—Mr E.S. Ffoulkes—Robn. G.—Mr Jas Burt.[15] Tasso with W. & A. Drew up Statement of Property & Income with Mem. in case of my decease.

[1] G. D. *Campbell, 'Inaugural address' (1856); as rector of Glasgow university.
[2] Perhaps an untr. letter from H. Carmichael of Liverpool.
[3] See 1 Feb. 53.
[4] J. Hodgson, 'The Hunterian Oration, delivered at the Royal College of Surgeons of England' (1855).
[5] Perhaps H. Wilkinson, *Sketches of scenery in the Basque provinces of Spain* (1838).
[6] Probably untraced work by J. Byrne; see 17 Oct. 56.
[7] Sir A. H. *Elton, 'The ballot, a conservative measure' (1856).
[8] (Sir) C. W. *Sikes, 'Good times, or the savings bank and the fireside' (1854); one of the origins of Gladstone's 1860 introduction of post-office savings banks.
[9] See 1 Aug. 56.
[10] Probably R. Bickersteth, 'Test of discipleship to Christ, a sermon' (1856).
[11] See 26 Feb. 40 and 27 Aug. 54.
[12] J. *Gilderdale, *Disciplina Rediviva: or hints and helps for youths leaving school* (1856).
[13] Unidentified.
[14] John *Gilderdale, 1802–64; principal of the Forest school, Walthamstow, 1848–63; educationalist.
[15] Probably the husband of the rescue case; see 16 Oct. 56.

Horace with Stephy. Saw Sherratt. Concocted with C. a letter for Henry to write to Lord Westminster.[1] Read Odyssey—Currency Self Regulating —Pakington's Address.[2]

The value of my Estates & goods standing at		187m[ille]+
I allow for duties to Govt. & expenses		2m.
Leaving as the disposable heritage		185m.
Of this I propose to bestow upon objects before my mind,		
& I suppose this done	=25m	
My younger sons wd have portions	=27m	
My daughters 15m. & I value their contingent		
annuities at this date 2m	=17m	
	=69m.	
And I allow for payment of £800 to my wife & small		
gifts	2m	
		71m
Leaving to pay jointure & to my heir		114m
He wd have real property Flintshire	76½m	
Lancashire	36m	
	112½m	
But the former subject to mortgages	44½m	
	68m	
Non productive personalty	6½m	
	74½m	
Productive personalty to make up the		
proper amount	39½m	
	114m.	
The income would be probably		
112½m at 3 per cent	£3400	
Less 44½m at 4%	1800	
	1600	
40m personalty at 5%	2000	
	3600	
Jointure	1600	
Available for maintenance & growth of the		
property Willy being now aged 16	2000 per ann	

These are substantial results, wh I think shd be attainable even if it please God to call me: the legal forms being accommodated to them or not as might be found desirable.[3]

[1] See 7 Apr. 57n.
[2] J. S. *Pakington, 'National Education. Address delivered . . . to the members of the Manchester Athenaeum' (1856).
[3] Headed 'Dec. 26. 1856'; Hawn P.

27. Sat.

St John Ch 11 A.M. Wrote to Author of Currency Self Regulating—G. Hogg —Rev Mr Collins[1]—Rev Mr Hewett[2]—Tasso with W. and A. Read Donaldson's Cratylus—Bopp's Grammar—Heyne's Excursus to Æn. VII —Herodotus ⎫ on the Persians.—Odyssey. Worked on Homer.
Grote ⎭

28. H. Innocents & S. aft. Xmas.

Ch. 11 AM. (& H.C.)—6½ PM. Conv. with the three eldest on the day—& MSS. Wrote on Gk religion—Read Jäger's Photius—Whiston's Josephus[3] —Lightfoot on Talmud[4]—Woodgate's O.T. Sermons.[5]

29. M.

Ch. 8½ A.M: with W., A., and S.—My birthday opened with their hymns at our door & other tokens. Verses from Willy, letters from the four next, flowers from the little ones. I replied by a note.

Wrote to Ivall—Sir S. Northcote—Horace with Stephy—Tasso with W. & A. A clergy dinner & children's dance in evg. Worked on Homer Ephyre[6] &c.

This year my blessings have abounded even more than usual: & a long unbroken country sojourn has been a great spiritual mercy. But my soul is still disturbed by the waves, & divided in the service of many masters: the anchor is not yet surely cast. Yet God still draws me to Him & I trust, nay whatever the feeling be worth I feel that He will draw me—though never did His mercy overflow on one so deeply unworthy.

30 T.

Ch. 8½ AM. Wrote to Messrs. G. & Co.—J.N.G.—my brothers jointly—Mr Emery—Scotts—Walk with Stephen. Saw Mr Burnett—Mr Barker (& went over S.s affairs)—Harry—about the County.[7] Read Dr Chapman on Homoeopathy.[8] Worked on Homer. Choir Supper at the Rectory in evg after Xmas songs. Worked on accounts.

31. Wed.

Ch. 8½ AM. with W. Wrote to Sir J. Graham—Scotts—Robn. G.—Supt. Chester Station—Lady Sarah Williams[9]—Rev Messrs. Armitstead—

---

[1] William Collins, 1817?–87; Jesus, Oxford; curate of Great Houghton, Northamptonshire, 1832–62; wrote on classics and education.

[2] John William Hewett, 1824–86; sundry curacies 1853–73; classicist and poet.

[3] *The works of Flavius Josephus translated by W.* *Whiston (1737, often reprinted).

[4] J. *Lightfoot, *Horae Hebraicae et Talmudicae* (1663).

[5] See 15 Dec. 56.

[6] Doric name for Corinth.

[7] i.e. Henry Glynne, on election preparations; see 7 Apr. 57.

[8] Perhaps E. C. Chepmell, *A domestic homoeopathy restricted to its legitimate sphere of practice* (1848).

[9] Lady Sarah Elizabeth, da. of 1st Earl Amherst, m. 1842 Sir John Hay Williams-Hay and d. 1876.

Trevitt—Lockhart—Sec. Infirmy. Saw Mr Littleboy—J. Sherratt—Worked on Homer—Arranging & packing for departure. Horace with Stephy. Tasso with W. & A. Read [blank]

And here closes a year of great blessings: would that they only had been acknowledged in corresponding fruit growing up from my heart. But while I am not conscious of any measurable progress in the warfare with particular sins I am becoming alive to a new evil and danger in this that the ties which bind me to this world are growing more numerous and stronger. It appears to me that there are few persons who are so much as I am inclosed in the invisible net of pendent steel. I have never known what tedium was, have always found time full of calls & duties, life charged with every kind of interest. But now when I look calmly around me I see that these interests are for ever growing & grown too many & powerful & that were it to please God to Call me I might answer with reluctance. For the coming of God's Kingdom, for the turning of this sad wilderness of sin & sorrow into the Garden of redeemed souls, for reunion with the beloved that have gone before, for the full accomplishment of the Conqueror's work & establishment of His supreme dominion, for all this I can pray, not indeed consistently, not with the intensity of a saintly desire, but at least with this feeling that if it lay with me to bring the consummation without doing harm to others, assuredly it would not tarry. But it is quite another question when God asks inwardly are you individually ready to come: can you willingly & freely leave the animation & action, the thoughts, desires, & designs of life, leave them as they are, see the threads of them apparently lost & broken, & yourself forbidden to gather them up even to hand them over to another—can you surrender your earthly share in the purposes of Providence & go forth elsewhere casting yourself upon Providence, without a murmur without a longing lingering look? See how I stand. Into politics I am drawn deeper every year: in the growing anxieties & struggles of the Church I have no less share than heretofore: literature has of late acquired a new & powerful hold upon me: the fortunes of my wife's family which have had with all their dry detail all the most exciting & arduous interest of romance for me now during nine years and more: seven children growing up around us and each from day [sic] the object of deeper thoughts & feelings & of higher hopes to Catherine & to me: what a network is here woven out of all that the heart & all that the mind of man can supply. How then am I to have my conversation in heaven in the sense of having my loins girt & my lamp burning & of waiting for the Lord before the morning watch? I deeply need a great access & outpouring of the Divine Grace: may He that knows my need supply it.[2]

Note of
My Godchildren[1]

+William	Selwyn
+Mary Jane	Tyler

[1] At the top of p. 135 of the MS, ruled off at the top left hand corner.
[2] Extracts in Morley, i. 557.

+Neville .. ..   Lyttelton
+   Goalen[1]
+   Farquhar
+Stafford John   .. ..   Northcote[2]
+Constance Elis[abeth]   Gladstone
+Gertrude   .. .. ..   Glynne
+George..   .. .. ..   Hampton
+Willm. Talbot Stuart..   Wortley
                              Lacaita[3]
                              Neville
+Reginald William   ..   Herbert.[4]

Rev. N. Woodward   Rev G.B. Kennaway   Rev C.T. Heartley[7]
—W.B. Heathcote   —H. Melvill
—W. Brewster   —W.E. Scudamore[6]
—J. Harris[5]   —Mr Harvey
—W. Scott [of] Hoxton   —Mr Wilbraham

[1] Robert Alexander Gladstone Goalen, s. of Rev. A. Goalen.
[2] i.e. J. S. Northcote.
[3] Charles Carmichael Lacaita, 1853–1933, oldest s. of Sir J.; liberal M.P. Dundee 1885–7.
[4] i.e. W. R. Herbert.
[5] James Harris, 1817–77; headmaster of Chester grammar school.
[6] William Edward *Scudamore, 1813–81; tractarian rector of Ditchingham from 1839.
[7] Charles Tebbott Heartley, 1824–94; headmaster in Tenbury 1856–61.

[VOLUME XX.][1]
[JANUARY 1, 1857 TO FEBRUARY 28, 1859.]

[1] Lambeth MS 1434, 161ff.

Private.

WEG

(NO 20.)[1]

Hawarden[2]

Thurs. Jan. 1. 1857. Circumcn.

No Church on acct of the accident.[3] C. & the children went. Then packing & preparing. In Chester about the Brougham. Wrote to Sec. G.P. Office[4] —T.D. Acland—Rev W. Elwin—Mr G. Burnett—Mr Petleybridge—Earl Stanhope—Mr Ffoulkes—Mr Ryman—Mr W. Hampton—Mr Laurence. Saw Mr Burnett. Visited the borings. Read Odyssey: & the Apology of Apuleius.

2. Fr. [Shrewsbury].

Wrote to C.G.—Earl of Aberdeen. Saw the Williams boy. Off at 10.15 with Willy; drove to Wrexham 12 m. then rode 28 to Shrewsbury: arriving at 6. Fox Inn: very comfortable. Read Odyssey.

3. Sat. [Hagley].

Off at 7.45. Breakfast at Bildwas:[5] the Abbey beautiful. So was the whole line of country both days. At 3.15 we reached Stewponey[6] 33 miles: the horses well & fresh. C. & Agnes met us & we found all ours well at Hagley. Read Dr Dibdin[7] in evg—a little Odyssey. Unpacked & arranged.

4. 2 S. aft Xmas.

Ch. 11 AM. and H.C.—3½ P.M. Read Church on Pascal—& on Audin.[8] Singing in evg. Conv. with the three eldest also with C. on arrangements for divers persons.

5. M.

Worked on the proof sheets of my political article. Horace with Stephen. Tasso with a class. Music in evg. Read Dr Dibdins Narrative—Pope's Dunciad—Nägelsbach Homerische Mythologie[9]—Phillimore's Preface[10] &c(proof)—

---

[1] Below this, some illegible pencil markings.
[2] Entries for 1–31 January 1857 are on four leaves of paper attached to the flyleaf (verso).
[3] Apparently minor.
[4] i.e. Rowland *Hill.
[5] Ruins of Buildwas, a Cistercian abbey by Much Wenlock.
[6] Village 4 miles NW. of Hagley.
[7] T. F. Dibdin, *Reminiscences of a literary life*, 2v. (1836).
[8] R. W. Church, 'Pascal's Ultramontanism' and 'Audin's Leo X' from *Essays and Reviews* (1854).
[9] By C. F. von Nägelsbach (1840).
[10] On current affairs, to the 3rd v. of his *International Law* (1857); see 21 Dec. 52.

6. T. Epiph.

& dearest C.s birthday. Wrote to Messrs. Hewett[1]—The Railway (G.N, LNW, & Midl.) officers were with me from 11 to 3½—on the arbitration.[2] Mr Griffiths on O.F. 4–5½. Horace with Stephy. Tasso with my class. In evg we discussed the Church here—Read Wilkins on Bolgrad[3] &c—Ferrier on Herat.[4] Worked more on my proof sheets: difficult enough: the path is herissé[5] on all sides.

7. Wed.

Wrote to Mr Elwin—J. Murray—Mr Teulon[6]—R. Phillimore. Finished my corrections & excisions & dispatched the Article to London.[7] Horace with Stephy. In the evg 6—10½ the children's play and a large party. The acting was good on the whole. Read Lauder on Milton[8]—Began to correct revise of Hom. Proleg. Herbert's 3d birthday: God bless him. He is at this moment a remarkable child whatever he may hereafter be.

8. Th.

Wrote to Scotts—Petheram—Rowsell—B. Porter[9]—& Hn. Postmaster— and Sir J.Williams. Tasso with my Class—Horace with Stephy. Read Lauder—Camelfords Pamphlets[10]—Nägelsbach—Worked on Homer— Music in evg: C. Lyttelton's admirable playing & accompaniment.

9. Fr.

Ch. 10¼ A.M. Wrote to Bonham—& draft—J. Griffiths—Scotts—Mr R. Heathfield—Rev. Mr Sweet. Tasso with my class. Walk with L[yttelto]n & Hom. conv. Horace with Stephen. Worked on Revise. Read Lauder's Essay (finish)—Montagu's Life[11]—Blakesley's Herod. Intr. & Exc.[12]

10. Sat.

Wrote to B. Porter—Rev. Mr Ffoulkes—Sir James Graham—Rev Mr Elwin—Mr J. Murray—Mr Petheram—Mr Rowsell. Rode with Ln. to

[1] W. Hewett & Co., London dealers in chinoiserie.
[2] See 22 Apr. 57.
[3] J. W. Wilkins, *The second congress and the Russian claim to the Isle of Serpents and Bolgrad* (1857).
[4] J. P. Ferrier, *Caravan journeys and wanderings in Persia, Afghanistan, Turkistan, and Beloochistan* (1856).
[5] 'rough'.
[6] Henry Teulon, Bishopsgate printer.
[7] With Gladstone's permission, *Elwin subsequently altered parts of the article, Gladstone requesting 'a print or copy of it *as it left my hands*' (to Elwin, 31 January 1857, N.L.S.).
[8] W. *Lauder, *An essay on Milton's use and imitation of the moderns in his Paradise Lost* (1750).
[9] Benjamin Porter, dealt with Gladstone's horses in London.
[10] T. Pitt, Lord Camelford, *Narrative and proof* (1785); pamphlets on a legal dispute.
[11] C. *Montagu, *The works and life of Charles, late Earl of Halifax*, 2 v. (1715).
[12] J. W. *Blakesley, *Herodotus, with a commentary* (1854).

Westwood, Sir J. Pakington's beautiful place 11¼–5.[1] Conv. with him on Foreign Policy. Horace with Stephy. Tasso with my class. Dinner party— music in evg. Saw Mr Claughton—Mr Norman[2]—Mr Boyle. Read Wharton's Life.[3]

11. 1 S. Epiph. X

Ch. 11 & 3. P.M. Conv. with the three eldest. Read Gioberti—South's Sermons[4]—Steele's Christian Hero.[5] Wrote on Gioberti.[6]

12. M. X

Saw Mr Amery—Horace with Stephy—Tasso with my class. Read & worked much on the RR. arbitration. Read Wharton's Life—Blakesley's Herodotus Intr. &c.

13. T. X

Wrote to J. Swift—Captain Huish—Mr Panizzi— Mr J. W. Wilkins. Horace with Stephy—Tasso with the Class. Again spent the morning on Railway Arbitration papers. Walk with Stephen—Finished Wharton's Life—Read Montagu's Life.

14. Wed.

Wrote to Mr Grogan—Ld Aberdeen—Tasso with my class. Worked on Homer—with Blakesley—Strabo—Selden[7]—&c. Read Montagu's Life— Saw Mr Stevens.[8]

15. Th.

Wrote to Duchess of Sutherland—Bp of Oxford—E.M. Whitty—J. Bellis[9] —Nora Glynne—Lady James—Rev E. Coleridge—Tasso with my reduced class. Worked on Homer—Read Nägelsbach—Hullah's Rudiments of Mus. Gr.[10]—Life of Montague. Saw the boys off from Stourbridge. Saw Mr Monro.[11] Attended his very eloquent Lecture & moved thanks to him.

---

[1] Westwood Park, 3 miles NW. of Droitwich.

[2] Perhaps George Norman, Birmingham brassfounder.

[3] G. W. Doane, The remains of the Rev. C. H. Wharton, with a memoir of his life, 2v. (1834).

[4] R. South, Sermons preached upon several occasions (1737–44, new ed. 1843).

[5] R. *Steele, The christian hero: an argument proving that no principles but those of religion are sufficient to make a great man (1701).

[6] Add MS 44746, f. 62.

[7] J. *Selden, Liber de nummis, in quo antiqua pecunia Romana et Graeca metitur precio ejus (1579).

[8] Probably James Stevens of Manchester, who requested employment later in the year, and corresponded on politics (Hawn P).

[9] John Bellis of Chester.

[10] J. P. *Hullah, Grammar of vocal music, for the use of public schools and adults (1843).

[11] Not further identified.

16. Fr. [London]

Ch. 10½ A.M. Wrote to J.E. Littleboy—O.W.W.Co's Secretary[1]—Lord Aberdeen—Mr Browning. Saw the Miss Rogerses,[2] & made other calls: engaged David & made household arrangements. Packed, & went off to London at 5.30. In London worked on letters & papers—went to Ld Abns.—Read N.Q. Rev. on Palmn & Derby.[3] Found Milligan gone—Also Louise ma.[R]

17. Sat. [Wilton]

An active round of visits & shopping—Wrote to S.E.G.—J. Murray— Sir W. Heathcote. Saw Ld Aberdeen—J. Murray—F.R. Bonham—Sir W. & Lady James—Scotts—Mr T. Baring. Off by 3 PM Train to Salisbury & Wilton: where we were received with the usual warmth. Conv. with Bp of Salisbury, S. Herbert. Sat up late to correct Revise.

18. 2 S.Epiph.

Ch mg & aft. Read Bp of Hereford's Charge[4]—Chr Rem. on Pitzipios.[5] Saw Bp of Salisbury—S. Herbert (on Q.R. Art. &c.).[6] Wrote to Mr J. Murray.

19. M.

Wrote to J.N.G.—& sent deed to Mr Myers. Went to Salisbury & saw the Palace & Chapterhouse: wonderful in beauty. With the Bp & S.H. on Chapters Bill.[7] Walk by the Downs & long conv. with the Bishop. Read Hardwicke's Religions of the World[8] and wrote on Mythol.[9] Read Brereton's Defence of Dundas.[10]

20. T.

Ch. 3½ P.M. Another sederunt with the Bishop & S.H. on a Chapter's Bill. Long sitting with Ld A[berdeen] & S.H. about our position: tried at a letter to Lord D.[11] Walk with C[ount] Strzelecki. Read Ed Rev on Persia[12] —Hardwicke on Religions—Reade's Never too late to mend.[13] Found Mrs

---

[1] Of the Oxford, Worcester, Wolverhampton railway.
[2] They lived in Hagley.
[3] *New Quarterly Review*, vi. 124 (January 1857).
[4] R. D. *Hampden, *Charge delivered at his third visitation of the diocese in August 1856* (1856).
[5] *Christian Remembrancer*, xxxiii. 200 (January 1857), review of *L'Eglise Orientale* by J. G. Pitzipios.
[6] See 2 December 56.
[7] Not introduced, unless as the Burial Acts Amndt. Bill: *H* cxlv. 257.
[8] C. *Hardwick, *Christ and other Masters*, 4v (1855–9); comparative studies.
[9] For *Studies on Homer*, ii, section i.
[10] W. Brereton, *The British fleet in the Black Sea, while under the command of vice-admiral J. W. D. Dundas* (1856).
[11] See 23 January 57.
[12] *Edinburgh Review*, cv. 266 (January 1857); review of J. P. Ferrier, see 6 January 57.
[13] C. *Reade, *It is never too late to mend*, 3v. (1856).

H[erbert] in conv. yest. & today only anxious that we should get out of isolation.[1] We talked over C. Wood Granville & Argyll. Saw the beautiful drawings of old masters.

21. Wed.

Ch. 10½ AM. Looking at the Pictures. Wrote to Willy—Stephy—Mr Tomlinson—Rev Mr Wilson—Mr Creed—Rev Mr Ferrar.[2] Drove to Longford[3] & saw the pictures: very fine, in bad lights. Read 'Never Too late to Mend'.

22. Th.

Wrote to S. Raleigh[4]—Rev. E. Hawkins—T. Graham—Ride with S. Herbert. Conv. on Radcliffe Trust[5]—and on politics. Read Never Too Late to Mend. Packing.

23. Fr. [Bowden Park]

Off at 10 to Bowden Park.[6] Wrote to Dowr Lady Lyttelton—Earl of Aberdeen—Earl of Derby (from draft).[7] Reached B[owden] P[ark] 12.30. Greatly pleased with the House & place. Walked with John to Spye Park.[8] His general health good: but the head is not strong. Saw his beautiful Church. Party in evg. Saw Sir J. Awdry resp. Oxford Commission.[9] Music. Read Spirit of Travel.[10]

24. Sat.

Wrote to Mr Greswell—O.W.W. Manager—Secty Inc. Tax Assocn.[11]—Secy Manchr Exhibition.[12] Settled munm. &c. with John about the L. & Y. Stock. Went to Laycock Abbey[13] mg & Bowood aftn.[14] Read Guizot's Peel[15]—Spirit of Travel.

[1] i.e. the Peelites should.
[2] Probably John Martindale Farrar, vicar of Burgh 1856, rector of Broughton Pogis 1861.
[3] Seat 3 miles SE. of Salisbury of William Pleydell-*Bouverie, 1779–1869; whig M.P. 1801–28; 3rd earl of Radnor 1828; radical, friend of *Cobbett and connoisseur. Father of E.P.*
[4] Unidentified.
[5] *Herbert was his fellow trustee.
[6] His brother John's place 3 miles S. of Chippenham.
[7] Not found in Add MS or in Derby's papers.
[8] 4 miles SW. of Calne.
[9] Awdry, a tractarian lawyer, was on the commission set up to execute the 1854 Act; see Ward, 206.
[10] C. Packe, The spirit of travel (1856).
[11] C. F. Buolt; had sent the association's pamphlet calling for a return to the 1853 tax plan (Add MS 44587, f. 56).
[12] Thomas Hamilton; see 29 June 57.
[13] Restored abbey 3 miles SW. of Chippenham, house of William Henry Fox *Talbot, 1800–77, photographer.
[14] *Lansdowne's seat, near Chippenham, with a fine picture collection.
[15] See 27 Sept. 56.

25. *3 S. Epiph. & Conv. St. Paul.*

Laycock Ch mg. Prayers aftn.
[Then, scored through:–] Wrote to Mr Jos. Howe.[1] Read Mr Howe's Letter
to W.E.G.—Manning's Sermons.[2]

25.[3] *3 S. Epiph. & Conv. St. Paul.*

Ch mg—prayers at home aft. Music in evg. Read Howe's Letter—Manning's Sermons—Gioberti's Works—Wrote to Mr Howe. Packed at night.

26. *M. [Oxford]*

Wrote to Mr C. Packe—Sec. O.W.W. Railway. Off at 8 to Chippenham.
At Oxford 10.45. Saw C. off for Hagley at 11.30 and then went to Mr
Greswell's. Saw Vice Chancr.—Master of Balliol (Homer)—Dr Acland
(Radcl[iffe] Trust)—and Mr Lake (Mil.Ed.)[4]—and made other calls. Saw
Ball. Chapel & other new buildings. Dined at Balliol with Mr Woollcombe
& a large party: we staid till 11 PM. Read William's Homerus.[5]

27. *T.*

Wrote to C.G.[6]—Rev. B. Wilson—A. Baillie Cochrane. Breakfast Trinity
(Mr Haddan). Luncheon Mr Greswell's. Dinner Mr Greswell's & evening
party. Saw Provost of Oriel (Homer)—Rev. E. Greswell(do)—Master of
Pembroke (state of Oxf—Homer.)—Vice Chancellor (New Coll.)—Mr. G.
Smith [7](New Coll.) Provost of Worcester—Mr Parker—Goalen[8]—and others.
Read Williams's Homerus—Newman on Universities.[9] Ch. Ch. service 4
P.M.

28. *Wed.*

Wrote to C.G.[10]—Special Commr. Inc. Tax—J.G. Talbot—S. Herbert &
copy. Saw Mr Meade[11]—Mr Tollemache[12]—Mr Rawlinson (Hom)—Mr
Jowett(do)—Mrs T. Goalen—Provost of Queen's—Mr Burgon (with
others) Hom. Breakf. Mr Rawlinson Ex[ete]r—Luncheon Mr Hext CCC—
Dinner Vice Chancellor. Read Williams, Homerus.

---

[1] Joseph Howe, 1804–73; Canadian politican and imperial author, including 'Letter to . . . W. E. Gladstone, M.P. . . . being a review of the debate on the Foreign Enlistment Bill and our relations with the United States' (1856).

[2] See 15 October 42.

[3] Rewritten entry for this day, following a blank page.

[4] See 29 January 57n.

[5] J. *Williams, *Homerus* (1842).

[6] Bassett, 113.

[7] Goldwin *Smith was sec. to the executive commission implementing the 1854 Oxford Act.

[8] Alexander Goalen, 1835–72; son of T. (see 19 September 27); Brasenose; lecturer in science at New Inn Hall.

[9] See 9 April 52.

[10] Bassett, 113.

[11] (Sir) Robert Henry *Meade, 1835–98; then up at Exeter; in foreign office 1859; *Granville's private secretary 1864–6; in colonial office 1868, assist. secretary 1871, permanent secretary 1892–6; G. C. B. 1897.

[12] Lionel Arthur Tollemache, 1838–1919; then at Balliol; gentleman; see his *Talks with Mr. Gladstone* (1898), 19.

29. Th.

Wrote to C.G.—Principal Alban Hall—Mrs Magarey[1]—Rev. G. Butler. Breakfast—Mr Lake. Luncheon—Mast. of Balliol. Dinner—Mr Greswell— & evening party. Read Homerus. Millingen on Vases.[2] Saw Mr Butler (Homer)—Princ. Alb. Hall.(do & printing)[3]—Princ. New Inn do (Art)— Master Univ. Univ. extension of studies—Warden All Souls—his Coll. & Law studies[4]—Mr Max Müller[5] Homer—Mr Rawlinson do—Mr Lake[,] Homer, & Army Report[6]—Mr Burgon—anc[ient] art—Bp of London &c.

30. Fr.

St Mary's 10.30 A.M. Wrote to Mr Woollcombe—Ld Abingdon—Mr Rowsell—Duke of Newcastle. Breakf. with Dr Acland to meet a party resp. Radcliffe Trust & professional Education—Dined in Ch. Ch. Hall. Busy with calls nearly all day. Saw Jacobson—Ch.Ch. scheme—Gordon with Marshall & Ley[7]—do—Mr Burgon—Mr Meyrick—Mr M. Muller (philol[ogy of] Hom)—Principal B.N.C.—Mr Murray—Master of Pembroke—& others. Finished Homerus. Much tired: as an abscess in the jaw interfered with my sleep. How much am I blessed in this fostering draft!

31. Sat. X [London]

Wrote to A. Panizzi. Ld Derby(& copy)—Rev. W. Elwin. Off at 9.30 for London. Saw Mr Lake in the train: resp. Mil. Ed. & Homer. Soon after arriving went to St Peter's Stepney meeting & spoke there.[8] Saw Mr G. Glyn—Milligan[R]. Read Q.R. on Ld Raglan.[9] Some hours work in opening letters: an accumuln. of a fortnight, over & above what follows. Found Mary pretty well. I am rather worried with my great gumboil & some neuralgia.

(4. S. Epiph.). Feb. One 1857. London.[10]

St James's & H.C. mg. Then kept at home. Mr Lavis[11] came & lanced the gum. Read Last Words of an English Catholic[12]—Newman on Universities Col. Ch. Mag. on Constantple Ch.[13]

[1] A Miss Margarey lived in Westbourne Terrace, Hyde Park.
[2] J. *Millingen, Ancient Unedited Monuments. Painted Greek Vases, 3v. (1822–6).
[3] *Cardwell had offered to have Studies on Homer and the Homeric Age printed at the University Press (Add MS 44387, f. 17).
[4] L. Sneyd, probably on next day's meeting.
[5] Friedrich Max *Müller, 1823–1900; came from Germany 1846; professor of modern European languages at Oxford 1850; wrote on philology, philosophy, mythology, etc.; see Add MS 44251.
[6] W. C. *Lake served on the commission on officers' training: PP 1857 vi. 1.
[7] i.e. O. *Gordon, G. Marshall and Jacob Lee on drafting the Christ Church Ordinance 1858; see E. G. W. Bill and J. F. A. Mason, Christ Church and Reform (1970), 66.
[8] On church extension and the spiritual condition of the London poor: The Times, 2 February 1857, 7e.
[9] Quarterly Review, ci. 168 (January 1857).
[10] First bound page of the vol. starts here.
[11] John Lavis, 1799–1867; London surgeon and medical reformer, or his son, John Samuel, 1824–88, also a surgeon.
[12] Last words of an English Catholic (1857).
[13] Colonial Church Chronicle, ix. 121 (1857).

2. M.

Wrote to J. Severn—J.G. Talbot—J. Colwell—A.B. Hope—Mrs Larkins—
Rev. E. Coleridge—Rev. Mr Burkitt—S. Wilson[1]—T. Whitehead—Govr.
Fitzgerald[2]—Ld Chancellor—Mr Turner.

Set to work on the reduction of my chaos: which is deeper & more
hopeless than usual in a new (but most promising) house.[3] Saw Lord A.
Hervey—Mr Leonard Strong[4]—Col. Tulloch—Sir W. James—Mr Lavis—
Earl of Aberdeen: with whom I discussed the topics & line of tomorrow.
Saw E. Hunt[?R].

3. T.

Saw Earl of Aberdeen—S. Herbert—Bp of Glasgow. Examining docu-
ments & papers. H of C.12–2: and $4\frac{1}{2}$–$12\frac{1}{4}$. Spoke $1\frac{1}{4}$ h. on the Address. I
think we dealt a smart blow to the boundless extravagance of govern-
ment.[5] Read Q.R. on Rats.[6]

4. W.

Wrote to J.N.G.—Ld Harrowby—Mrs James—Mr Rossetti—Mr Cowell—
Br. Museum meeting 12–2. Saw Lord Aberdeen—R. Phillimore—Ld
Stanhope—Mr Panizzi—S. Herbert—10–$11\frac{1}{2}$—Ld Derby $3\frac{1}{4}$–$6\frac{1}{2}$. Wrote
(part) Mem. Read Q.R. on Rats—&c.

This afternoon at three I called on Lord Derby and remained with him above
three hours, in prosecution of the correspondence which had passed between us.
It was understood that our conversation was to be strictly confidential: and especially I told him when he probed me as to the opinions of others than myself
that what I ventured to say of the state of their minds must not go beyond
himself.

We began by reference to the debate of last night so far as [it] touched Italian
affairs, and then went into a more general view of our subject.

I told him that I deliberately disapproved of the Government of Lord Palmerston and was prepared and desirous to aid in any proper measures which might
lead to its displacement. That so strong were my objections that I was content
to act thus without inquiring who was to follow for I was convinced that any
one who might follow would govern with less prejudice to the public interests.
That in the existing state of public affairs I did not pretend to see far but thus
far I saw clearly. I also told him that I felt the isolated position in which I
stood, and indeed in which we who are called Peelites all stand to be a great evil
as tending to prolong & aggravate that Parliamentary disorganisation which so
much clogs and weakens the working of our government: and I denounced

[1] Stephen Lea Wilson, 1818–99; curate of Prestbury, Cheshire, 1855, vicar there
1858–89.
[2] i.e. J. E. *Fitzgerald, who was superintendent of Canterbury province, N. Zealand
1853–7.
[3] 11 Carlton House Terrace.
[4] D. 1879; New College, Oxford; Scottish landowner.
[5] H cxliv. 137, notes in Add MS 44655, f. 1. He followed *Disraeli's charge, denied in
the speech following him by *Palmerston, of a British sanction to a secret French
guarantee to Austria of her Italian possessions.
[6] Quarterly Review, ci. 123 (January 1857).

myself as a public nuisance adding that it would be an advantage if my doctor sent me abroad for the Session. To this separate position I felt most anxious to put a period: but I felt that this was no matter of choice: it must depend upon the course of public affairs. The divisions which occurred long ago have cut very deep into the minds of men as well as upon the mere surface: and no union can be formed of any kind with a prospect of impressing the materials available for carrying on the Govt. unless it be founded upon a proved concurrence of senti-ment on the leading & dominant questions which for the time command the public mind. I told him that my opinions of Ld Palmerston's Govt. were I believed very much in harmony with those of Ld. Abn. Sir J. Graham & Herbert[.]

He concurred in the general sentiments which I had expressed: but said it was material for him as he had friends with & for whom to act and as I had alluded to the possibility, in the event of a change, of his being invited by the Queen to form a Govt., to consider beforehand on what strength he could rely. He said he believed his friends were stronger than any other single section (*or* something describing them as at least a numerous body) but that they were a minority in both Houses. Weak in 1852 he was weaker now: for it was natural that four years of exclusion from office should thin the ranks of a party & such had been his case.

He described the state of feeling among his friends & adverted to the offers he had made in 1851 & 1855. The fact of an overture made & not accepted had led to much bitterness or anger towards us among a portion of his adherents. He did not mean by this to imply the slightest blame but only to describe the actual state of things among a section, though they were a small minority, of those with whom he was connected. He considered that in 1855 Ld Palmerston had behaved far from well either to Herbert & me, or to him. This irritation among a portion of his party was kept up by its being observed that a small body of men, of eminence & so forth, in both houses, kept together & acted in concert apart from either great party: it was incidental to such a state of things that their support should sometimes be expected and then disappointment ensued. He said further that there was an impression among that much larger number who similarly desired the Union of the old Conservative party, that Graham, Herbert & I stood in a different position with respect to that subject: that my mind was inclined towards it but that Herbert from personal leanings to some members of the present Government, and Sir J. Graham from antecedents, leant rather in an opposite directions [*sic*].

I told him—professing to speak with entire absence of restraint under cover of his assurances—that our concert had not been the result of system & premedita-tion: that[1]

5. *Th.* X

Wrote to A. Panizzi—S. Fairbrother[2]—Mr G. Harris[3]—F. Calland[4]—E. A. Bowring—Sir C. Wood—Miss Fourdrinier.[5] H. of C.4½–7½: spoke on

[1] Holograph unfinished and undated; clearly refers to the meeting this day; Add MS 44747, f. 2, part in Morley, i. 558.
[2] Samuel Fairbrother of Hawarden.
[3] George *Harris, 1809–90; barrister on Midland circuit, and anthropologist; suggested historical MSS commission 1857; had sent a cutting (Hawn P).
[4] Frederick Calland of Park Lane, London, had written about extensions to St Stephen's, Stepney; Hawn P.
[5] Eliza Fourdrinier, *Newman's cousin; still alive 1882.

Hudsons Bay Co.[1] Saw Coalwhippers Deputn.—Sir S. Northcote (dined)—E. Cardwell (Currency)—Chancr. of Exchr.(Curr. Comm.)[2]—Mr Labouchere. Conclave at Ld Aberdeen's 12½-3½ reciting & discussing yesterday. Read Bowring on China War[3]—'Why is P. Albert unpopular?'[4] Saw Mat. and another[R].

6. Fr. X

Wrote to Mr F.W. Montague[5]—Sir C. Eastlake—Bishop of Oxford—Mr Nicolay—Dr Acland. Saw Graham. H of C. 4½-7½.[6] Dined at Lady Wenlock's. Saw Cardwell—Drew Resolutions[7]—Conclave at Ld Aberdeen's 12-3½. Saw Ld Nelson—Scotts—C.A. Wood. Read Nat Rev. on Spurgeon.[8]

7. Sat. X

Wrote to J. Macculloch—Rev Mr Lendrum—Hewett—Randolph—Mr Caldecott—Mrs Newman[9]—W. H. Lyttelton—Ld Derby(& draft). Saw Bp of Oxford—Mr J. Murray—Mr Wornum[10] & Minden Pictures.[11] Meeting at Ld Abns 1-3½. Saw one 6 P.M.[R] Breakfasted at Grillion's. Eight to dinner at home. Unpacking. This morning early Mary had her 12th child:[12] her life under God appears to have been saved by Dr Locock's skill. C. has had a time of great labour & anxiety.

8. Septa. S.

—St James's mg: St George's aft. Read Simeon's Life[13]—Last Words of an English Catholic.[14] Saw E. Hunt & another[R]. Went to Aunt J.s but she is at Lpool.

9. M. X.

Wrote to Syed Abdoollah—Robn. G.—Mr Dornbusch[15]—C. Trevor—Dr Daubeny—J. Chandler[16]—Mrs. A. Forbes.[17] Rode with Agnes. Saw Mr

[1] H cxliv. 231; he was on the consequent cttee.; see 18 Feb. 57.
[2] Setting up the select cttee. on the bank acts; see 18 Feb. 57.
[3] In the blue book on China: PP 1857 xii.
[4] F. Airplay (pseud.), 'Prince Albert; why is he unpopular?' (1856).
[5] Unidentified.
[6] Bank charter: H cxliv. 259. Gladstone had given his views on it in his speech on the address on 3 February.
[7] Against the govt.'s finance: Add MS 44747, f. 19.
[8] National Review, iv. 84 (January 1857).
[9] Maria, née Kennaway, m. 1834 Francis William *Newman, 1805-97; J. H.'s* brother, professor of Latin in London 1846; Unitarian 1876; missionary and author.
[10] Ralph Nicholson *Wornum, 1812-77; keeper of the National Gallery from 1854.
[11] Collection partly bought for the gallery when Gladstone was chancellor, see 1 Mar. 54 n. 6; the rest were sold in 1857 (Eastlake to Gladstone, 28 January 1857, Add MS 44387, f. 19).
[12] See 18 Aug. 57. Alfred *Lyttelton, d. 1913; cricketer and tory M.P. Leamington 1895-1906, St. George's, Hanover Square, from 1906; colonial secretary 1903-5.
[13] See 17 May 47.
[14] See 1 Feb. 57.
[15] G. Dornbusch of London, corresponded in 1860s on reform (Hawn P).
[16] Unidentified; but a John Chandler was a 'whip thong maker' in Clerkenwell.
[17] Not further identified; the bp. was unmarried.

Walker—Col. Tulloch—Rev Mr Lendrum—Mr Bonham—Mr Goldwin Smith—Income Tax Assn. Depn. (at H of C.)—R. Kirby[R]. Proceeded with my feeble efforts towards order. Dined with the Wortleys. H. of C. 4½–7.[1]

10. T.

Wrote to Mr J.W. Parker—J.G. Talbot—Sir E.E. Wilmot—Rev Mr Maul—Mr J. Baynes[2]—Mr Peers—Mr Boyd—Finished Revise of my Homeric Essay. Saw Mr Wetherall[3]—Sir W. Farquhar—J. Griffiths—do cum Mr Cochrane—Robn. G—do cum Lpool Deputation. Meeting at Ld Aberdeen's 12–3: and saw Ld Derby afterwards. Saw S. Herbert(evg). Read Ld. Overstone.[4]

11. Wed.

Wrote to Messrs. G. & Co—Mr Kinnear[5]—Mr Alspry[6]—Rev. H Randolph —A. Symonds. H. of C. 12¾–3.[7] Saw King of Oude's Vakeel[8]—Ld Derby on Draft Resolutions.[9] House affairs. Engaged James Kent.[10] Read Boswell's Letters[11]—Maclean's Hudson's Bay[12]—Deux Mots sur les Finances de la Gréce.[13] Dined at Mr Harcourt's: where I had much conv. with Ld Grey—Ly Grey—Ly Clarendon—C[hichester] Fortescue(resp. Oxford)— —& others.

I called on Lord Derby at two today to take a survey of the questions connected with the Budget—especially 1. the motion on Tea & Sugar Duties   2. the motion on expenditure   3. a motion to impound the outstanding ½ year of 16d Income Tax for the discharge of Exchequer Bonds or other public engagements 4. a motion—as announced in Lord D.s letter to me[14]—respecting the introduction of a descending scale into the Income Tax Act.[15]

[1] Transportation Bill: H cxliv. 352.
[2] Perhaps James Baynes of Manchester street, London; not further identified.
[3] Nathaniel Thomas Wetherell, 1800–69; antiquarian; his collection bought by the British Museum.
[4] S. J. *Loyd, Lord Overstone, 'Thoughts on the separation of the departments of the bank of England' (1844).
[5] John Boyd Kinnear, barrister.
[6] Unidentified.
[7] Misc. business: H cxliv. 496.
[8] The King's brother, wife and son came to Britain to gain support against the annexation of Oude. The King had especially requested Gladstone's intervention; he stonewalled (Add MS 44386, f. 177, 44387, f. 74).
[9] On the tea and sugar duties; correspondence on these in Derby papers, box 133.
[10] See 21 Jan. 58.
[11] Letters of James *Boswell addressed to the Rev. W.J. Temple ed. Sir P. *Francis (1856).
[12] See 14 June 50.
[13] (1856); copy in Hawn P.
[14] '...the 2d & 3rd Resolutions, and more especially the 2nd, not only point distinctly to an infraction of the implied engagement that the Income Tax should terminate in 1860, but also to an alteration of its positive enactments during the term of its continuance: and this, not to meet any sudden and unforseen emergency, but to enable the Government to reduce other Taxes, by again raising the Income Tax to its original amount: I think such a measure would be alike inconsistent with good faith and policy: and if once admitted, it would go far to make the Income Tax permanent' (Derby to Gladstone, 11 February 1857, Add MS 44140, f. 214).
[15] Holograph, undated but apparently this day: Add MS 44747, f. 16.

12. Th.

Wrote to Duke of Newcastle—Mr Tomline—Hon Mr Primrose[1]—Mrs Burnett.[2] Read Ld Overstone's Tracts—Maclean's Hudson's Bay—Saw Mr Ruttley—Mr Christie—Sir W. Heathcote—Duchess of Sutherland—Mr Labouchere—Mr Godley—Sir C. Eastlake. House & Picture business. H. of C. 4½–7.[3] Fourteen to dinner.

13. Fr.

Wrote to Scotts—Mrs Goalen. H. of C. 4¼–8. A few words on the Budget.[4] House arrangements. Dined at Stafford House: all there as kind as ever. Saw Mr Blakesley(Homer)—Ld Lyttelton—Sir W. Farquhar—Mr Grogan —Scotts—Ld Aberdeen—Duke of Argyll. Worked on the Budget at night.

14. Sat.

Wrote to J. Herbert—Mr Anderson. Saw Sir W. Heathcote—R. Phillimore —F.R. Bonham—Ld Derby—A.M. & at 5 P.M. Conclave at Argyll House 12½–4.[5] Rode with Agnes in aftn. Dined with the Herberts': & went afterwards to Lady Palmerston's. Worked on the Budget: wrote Mema: & drafted note to Lord Derby.

To maintain a steady surplus of income over expenditure—to lower indirect taxes when excessive in amount for the relief of the people and bearing in mind the reproductive power inherent in such operations—to simplify our fiscal system by concentrating its pressure on a few well chosen articles of extended consumption—and to conciliate support to the Income Tax by marking its temporary character & by associating it with beneficial changes in the laws: these aims have been for fifteen years the labour of our life. By the Budget of last night they are in principle utterly reversed[.]

I was engaged to meet Graham, Herbert & Cardwell at Ld Aberdeens and I knew from Ld Derby that he was to see his friends at noon. So I went to him on my way first to point out the *deficit* of between 5 & 6 millions for 1858–9 which is created by this Budget, with the augmentations of it in subsequent years: and secondly to say that in my opinion it was hopeless to attack the scheme in detail & that it must be resisted, on the ground of deficit, as a whole, to give a hope of success. I said that if among the Opposition there still lingered a desire to revive & extend indirect taxation, I must allow the Govt. had bid high for support for those who entertained it: that it was the worst proposition I had ever heard from a Minister of Finance, and that now the question was whether Parlt, or any portion of it would save the country from the evil.

At Ld Aberdeen's we examined the figures of the case and drafted two Resolutions which expressed our opinions. At first Graham & Cardwell inclined to narrower measures: to avoid condemnation of the plan as a whole, and to fight simply upon the Estimates[.]

[1] Bouverie Francis Primrose, 1813–98, s. of 4th earl of Rosebery; secretary to Scottish board of manufactures 1848–82.
[2] Relative of Gregory Burnett, the Hawarden agent.
[3] The alleged British sanction: *H* cxliv. 535; see 3 Feb. 57n. and *Cambridge Historical Journal*, vii (1942).
[4] *H* cxliv. 664; notes in Add MS 44655, f. 5.
[5] *Aberdeen's house.

The more serious point however was that they all wished me to insist upon taking the motion into my own hands: and announcing this to Lord J. Russell as well as to Ld Derby. As to the second I had no difficulty could I have acceded to the first. But I did not doubt that Disraeli would still keep hold of so much of his notice of Feb 3 as had not been set aside by the Budget, and I said that from motives which I could neither describe nor conquer I was quite unable to enter into any squabble or competition with him for the possession of a post of prominence.

We had much conversation on political prospects: Graham wishing to see me lead the Commons under Lord John as Prime Minister in the Lords; admitting that the same thing would do under Ld Derby but for Disraeli who could not be thrown away like a sucked orange: and I vehemently deploring our position which I said & they admitted was generally condemned by the country.

I again went to Derby as he had requested at five: and he told me that he had had with him Malmesbury—Hardwicke—Disraeli—Pakington—Walpole—Lytton: but not Henley, as I afterwards found. They had all agreed that the best motion would be a resolution (from Disraeli) on Monday, before the Speaker left the Chair corresponding with our *No 3*[1] of last Tuesday [? Wednesday]: which would virtually rest the question on deficit.

I made two verbal suggestions on the Resolution to improve its form—observed that its character would alter when detached from those which preceded & followed it—& said that it would be desirable to introduce the intermediate years (before 1860) into view by some distinct expression. I intimated doubts in short whether this Form was the best under the present circumstances: read to him as *information* our two Resolutions: and proposed to make his known at Argyll house tomorrow. I asked him whether I was to consider it as a measure decided on by him & his friends: to which he replied in the affirmative.

He said that the Resolution he proposed if it should be rejected would serve to shield from responsibility next year those who voted for it if they should then be in office. I said I took it for granted that his object in adopting it was not to provide this cover, but to act effectively against the plan that involved this deficiency: to which he replied certainly.

He also agreed that to deal rightly with the whole question there must be a further reduction of the Expenditure: while he thought the point unfavourable to take issue upon: I agreeing with him.

I[2] stated that we should be glad if the Exchequer Bond Resolution were carried before any general motion should be made on the Budget. He replied that it would perhaps be hardly fair to do this as towards the Govt.[3]

15. Sexa. S.

—St James's mg & H.C. Chapel Royal aft. Ld Aberdeen's 2–4 and consulting records in evg. Wrote to Ld Derby. Read Last Words of Engl. Catholic(finished)—Life of Simeon. MS. of 55 aloud in evg.

16. M. X.

Wrote to King of Oude(& draft)—R. Dockerill[4]—K. of Oude's Vakeel—Rev Mr Sweet—Mr Marshall—D. Bain—Rev H. Burgess—R. Lambert[5]—

---

[1] Add MS 44747, f. 19.   [2] This para. added on the opposite page.
[3] Signed and dated 14 February 1857; Add MS 44747, f. 8. See Morley, i. 560.
[4] Of Dockerill, Duchesne & Dockerill, wholesale tea dealers.
[5] Probably Richard Lambert, London commission agent.

Sir G. Sinclair—G. S. Hatton[1]—Prof Conington.[2] Read M'Lean's Hudson's Bay. Worked on papers & records in prepn. for debate: but it stood over on a point of form—not without rubbing some bloom off the Budget.[3] Saw A. Hayward—S.H. Walpole—Mr V. Corrie[4]—Saw R. Kirby[R].

17. T.

Wrote to Mr G. Hamilton—Mr Davies—Mrs Baylee[5]—Mrs Williamson[6] —T.C. Sandars. Eight to dinner. Rode with Agnes. Saw Earl of Derby— Mr H. Baillie M.P.—Sir J. Graham—S. Herbert—R. Phillimore—Mr Labouchere. Rode with Agnes. Read Ld Overstone—Col. Macdonald on do[7]—H of C. $4\frac{1}{2}$–$7\frac{1}{2}$.[8] Worked on keys & house affairs.

18. Wed.

Wrote to Mr Davidson—Ld Overstone—Mr Humphrey—Ld Derby—Jas Watson—Mrs Geare[9]—Jos Toomer[10]—Mr Weston. Saw Scotts—Sir J. Graham—Bp Edinbro—Ld Aberdeen—Mr Gibson—Bp of St Andrews— S. Herbert—Mr Laing—Mr Kingscote—Mr R. Hill—Mr Hook—Hudsons Bay Comm. 2–3.[11] Bank do 3–4.[12] H. of C. 4–6.[13] Rode with A. Dined with the Farquhars. Read Ld Overstone. Busy on House & accts.

19. Th.

Wrote to Rev Mr Troughton—Mr Ross—Rev Mr Mossman[14]—Mr Wilson —Mr Bratiano. Read Lord Overstone. Worked on the Budget. Busy on house & accts. Saw Messrs. Davison & M'Gregor—The Vicar of St Martin's —Mr Jas Wilson—Mr J. Hamilton (M.Star)[15]—Ld H. Lennox[16]—Mr R. Palmer: & various MPs. H of C. $4\frac{1}{4}$–$7\frac{1}{2}$ and 9–$10\frac{1}{4}$. Voted in 192:179 agt.

---

[1] Perhaps of Hatton, Ritchie and Cumming, Oxford street drapers.

[2] John *Conington, 1825–69; professor of Latin at Oxford 1854–69; editor and translator.

[3] H cxliv. 724; papers on the duties in Add MS 44587, f. 62.

[4] Valentine Byrom Corrie, tea broker; see Add MS 44587, f. 77.

[5] Probably the wife of Joseph *Baylee, see 18 Nov. 54.

[6] Unidentified.

[7] J. H. MacDonald, 'The errors and evils of the Bank Charter Act of 1844 as divulged by Lord *Overstone' (1855).

[8] Misc. business: H cxliv. 740.

[9] The wife of William Geare, barrister in Lincoln's Inn.

[10] Perhaps he who owned livery stables in Islington.

[11] First meeting of the select cttee. on Hudson's Bay Co., on which he sat; the cttee. supported his long-held views for removing Vancouver's Island from the Company's control: PP 1857, 2nd session, xv. 4.

[12] First meeting of the select cttee. on the bank acts, on which he sat: PP 1857, 2nd session, x part 1, 4.

[13] Education: H cxliv. 776.

[14] Thomas Wimberley *Mossman, 1826–85; ritualist vicar of Ranby 1854, of Torrington, Lincolnshire, from 1859; founded poor students' brotherhood; assumed title of bp. of Selby; joined Rome on deathbed.

[15] John Hamilton, 1821?–80, edited the Morning Star until his death.

[16] Lord Henry George Charles Gordon-Lennox, 1821–86, s. of 5th duke of Richmond; tory M.P. Chichester 1846–85; minor office 1852, 1858–9, 1866–8, 1874–6.

Mr Locke King: a bad night for Peelism.[1] C. had an evening party: the house though not quite in order showed well.

20. Fr.

Wrote to Mr Labouchere—Mr Geo. Price[2]—Mr Vernon Smith—Rev J. M. Price[3]—Mackenzie Wilson—G. Hendrie.[4] Saw Mr Cook *cum* Mr Heming[5] —Mr C. Ross of the Times[6]—The Duchess of Sutherland—Hon. A. Gordon. Hudson's Bay Commee. $12\frac{3}{4}$–2. H. of C. $4\frac{1}{2}$–7 and $7\frac{1}{2}$–$11\frac{3}{4}$. Spoke over 2 h. on the Budget.[7] Tea with C. afr. & read Ld Overstone.

21. Sat.

Wrote to D. of Newcastle—Lord Henry Lennox (and draft)—Sig. Ph. Vera[8]—Major Bird[9]—J.N.G.—C. Searle.[10] Read Six Letters[11]—R. Palmer's Lect.[12] Saw Scotts—Ld Lyndhurst—Ld Aberdeen—Sidney Herbert— R. Phillimore—J.G. Talbot. We dined at Lord Colchesters[13] where we met the Derbys & a Derby party. With him I talked over Budget motions.

22. Quinqua. S.

St Martins H.C. $8\frac{1}{2}$ AM.—St James's 11—St Andrew's $3\frac{1}{2}$ P.M. Wrote & read aloud MS for the day. Wrote to Willy—Saw S. Herbert—J.G. Talbot —on his future profession[14]—A. Hayward. Read Grinfield's Cosmos[15]— Simeon's Memoirs[16]—and Neapolitan MS.

23. M.

Wrote to Chancr. of Exchequer—H. Lees—Lord Derby (& draft)— T.C. Sandars—G. Binning House[17]—J. Kentish.[18] Saw Sir S. Northcote—

---

[1] *Graham and *Cardwell voted for *King's reform motion, Gladstone and *Herbert against: *H* cxliv. 861. Peter John Locke *King, 1811–85; liberal M.P. E. Surrey 1847–74; campaigned for church rate abolition and parliamentary reform.

[2] Perhaps George Price, 1812–90, s. of Sir R. Price, 1st bart.; worked much of his life in W. Indies.

[3] James Mansel Price; bible clerk of All Souls; vicar of Cuddington from 1855.

[4] Unidentified.   [5] See 2 Nov. 64.

[6] Charles Ross, 1800–84; chief of *The Times* parliamentary staff 1853–83; the next day's leader was on his speech against the budget.

[7] Tremendous outburst against *Lewis. 'It was thought very overstrained, and unfair in argument in the highest degree' (Argyll, ii. 73), but the brunt of the speech defended the balanced settlement of 1853; *H* cxliv. 985. Notes in Add MS 44655, f. 11.

[8] Perhaps Leon Galindo y de Vera, writer on Spanish politics.

[9] Perhaps L. J. K. Bird, private secretary in the War Office.

[10] Charles Edward Searle, 1828–1902; fellow of Pembroke, Cambridge, 1851–80; master there from 1880.

[11] Sir G. Colebrooke, *Six letters on intolerance* (1791).

[12] R. *Palmer, *The connection of poetry with history; a lecture* (1852).

[13] Charles Abbot, 1798–1867; 2nd Baron Colchester 1829; admiral and tory politician; minor office 1852, 1858–9.

[14] He became a tory M.P. eleven years later.

[15] E. W. *Grinfield, *The Christian cosmos* (1856).

[16] See 7 Feb. 57.   [17] Unidentified

[18] Joseph Kentish, cabinet maker.

Mr Travers *cum* Mr Crawfurd—Mr J. Griffiths(O.F.)—Sir W. Heathcote. Read Chinese Papers[1]—Rode with Agnes. Shopping for house & library. H of C. $4\frac{1}{4}$–7 and 9–1. Voted for D[israeli']s motion in 286:206.[2] Finished my revise of Homer Essay for *Press.*

24. T.

Wrote to S. Herbert—Mr Lathbury—Mr Kingscote—Saw Mr Lake—Sir J. Graham *cum* S. Herbert—Mr Labouchere—M. Van de Weyer. Ten to dinner: & C.s evening party afterwards—Work on house & shopping— Rode with Agnes. $5\frac{1}{4}$–$7\frac{3}{4}$: heard Lord Derby's very powerful & admirable speech.[3] Read Andrew on Euphr. Passage &c.[4]

25. Ash Wedy.

Chapel Royal mg. Sermon on the day aloud in evg. Saw Ld Derby 2–4— Bp of Oxford—Lord Alfred Hervey[5]—Sir James Graham—Lyttelton (resp. Homer & S.R.G.). Wrote to Ld Derby(& draft)—W.H.G.—Mr Don —Mr H. Lees—Mr S. Warren MP[6]—W.G. Anderson—Mr Jas Wilson MP. Read China debate. Worked $9\frac{1}{2}$–2 on bringing my papers &c. into order.

26. Th.

Wrote to Mr Scargill[7]—Mr J. Herbert—Rev E. Hawkins—Ld Derby— Wm. Gladstone—Sir S. Scott & Co—Mr V. Scully. H of C. & H of L. $4\frac{1}{2}$– $7\frac{1}{2}$ and $8\frac{1}{2}$ to 1.[8] Saw J.N.G.—The Speaker—Mr V. Scully—Mr Labouchere —Ld St Leonards[9]—Bp of Oxford. Rode with Agnes. Hudson's Bay Com. $12\frac{1}{4}$–$1\frac{3}{4}$. Attended the levee. Read China papers. do Ch. Prot Defence— & other pamphlets.

27. Fr.

Wrote to J.G. Davenport—S.R. Glynne[10]—W. Handcock—V. Corrie— Messrs. Hewett—Mr Eddy[11]—Rev Mr Barlow. H. of C. $4\frac{1}{2}$–$7\frac{1}{4}$ and $8\frac{1}{4}$–$12\frac{1}{4}$.[12] Rode with Agnes. Saw F.R. Bonham—Lord Alfred Hervey—J.N.G. (from Ld D's meeting)—Ld Henry Lennox—and various members of Parlt. abt. the China division. Worked on China papers. Read M'Lean's Hudson's Bay.[13]

---

[1] Blue Books on the bombardment of Canton and its background in *PP* 1857 xii.
[2] Apologized for excessive personal aspects of his speech of 20 February and attacked bad public reporting: *H* cxliv. 1146; the govt. majority was unexpectedly large.
[3] On *Bowring and the Canton situation: *H* cxliv. 1155.
[4] W. P. Andrew, *Memoir of the Euphrates Valley route to India* (1857).
[5] Lord Alfred Hervey, 1816–75, son of 1st marquis of Bristol; tory M.P. Brighton 1842–57, Bury St. Edmunds 1859–65; treasury lord 1852–5.
[6] Samuel *Warren, 1807–77; novelist and barrister, tory M.P. Midhurst 1856–9.
[7] E. Tudor Scargill, assistant secretary of the London Library.
[8] Canton in both houses; the govt. was defeated in the Lords: *H* cxliv. 1385.
[9] Edward Burtenshaw *Sugden, 1781–1875; tory Lord Chancellor and Baron St. Leonards 1852; legal reformer.
[10] Probably that on politics, in Bassett, 114.
[11] Perhaps Charles Wellington Eddy, chemist off Finsbury Square.
[12] *Cobden's speech on China: *H* cxliv. 1391.
[13] See 11 Feb. 57.

28. Sat. X.

Wrote to Robn. G—W.G. Anderson—Mr Deuce[1]—J. Wilson Patten—
Mr Reinagle[2]—Incumb. St Jas Cruden[3]—Sir S.H. Northcote—Mr Dun-
stan. Rode with Agnes. Saw F.R. Bonham—Rev Lord A. Hervey—Sir
Wm. Heathcote—Education Deputn.—Sir James Graham—& other MPs.
Saw Kirby[R]. Dined at the Speaker's. Read Unwin's & other pamphlets. [4]

1 S. Lent   March One 1857.

St James's mg(and H.C.) Wells St aftn. Read Life of Simeon—Life of
Romaine[5]—Church Defence Soc's papers. Read MS. of 54 in evg. Conv.
with Agnes. Saw Sir J. Maxwell—Mr J.D. Cook—Ld Lyndhurst—J. Wilson
Patten. Drafted Resolutions on Persia. [6]

2. M.

Wrote to Rev Mr Stooks—Grenside[7]—Prynne[8]—Denton—Molesworth—
Jaleesood Dowlah[9]—Mrs Salisbury.[10] Saw Bonham—Ld J. Russell—G.
Dundas MP.—W.B. Denison MP.[11]—Ld Henniker MP.—Mr Manners
Sutton M.P.—Hudson's Bay Comm. 2–3¾. H. of C. 3¾–7½ and 8½–12[12]—
Read La Bruyère.[13]

3. T.

Wrote to J. Wynne Eaton[14]—S.R.G.—Ld H. Lennox—Rode with Agnes
—Bank Commee. 12–2½. H of C. 4½–7½ and 8¼–2½. Spoke 1 h 20 m. on
Cobden's Resolution & voted in 263:247—a division doing more honour
to the H. of C. than any I ever remember.[15] Home with C. & read Ld
Ellesmere's Faust being excited wh is rare with me.[16]

4. Wed.

Wrote to Rev Mr Nugee—Rogers—Vaughan—R Harwood[17]—Mr Frere—
J. Wynne Eaton.

[1] Unidentified.
[2] Ramsay Michard *Reinagle, 1775–1862; water-colour painter and restorer of old
masters.
[3] John Burnett Pratt, episcopal incumbent at Cruden, Aberdeenshire.
[4] W. J. Unwin, *Prussian primary education, its organisation and results* (1857).
[5] Perhaps W. B. Cadogan, *The life of the rev. W. *Romaine* (1827), one of several lives.
[6] See 6 Mar. 57.
[7] Christopher Grenside, d. 1871; rector of Great Massingham.
[8] George Rundle *Prynne, 1836–1903; hymnist and vicar of St. Peter's, Plymouth,
from 1848.
[9] Untraced; probably one of the Oude emissaries.
[10] Wife of Enoch Robert Gibbon Salisbury, 1819–90, parliamentary counsel, liberal
M.P. Chester 1857–9, contested it 1859, 1868.
[11] *Sc.* E. B. Denison.   [12] China: *H* cxliv. 1589.
[13] Jean de la Bruyère, seventeenth century French moralist; perhaps *Les Caractères ou
les moeurs de ce siècle* (1688, often reprinted).
[14] John Wynne Eyton of Leeswood, Flintshire; a J.P.; supported Glynne in the
election.
[15] Denunciation of Palmerston's China policy: *H* cxliv. 1787; notes in Add MS 44655,
f. 48. Published as 'War in China'.
[16] Version in Morley, i. 564. Lord F. Leveson Gower, Earl of Ellesmere's tr. of Goethe's
Faust (1823).
[17] Richard Harwood, 1815–87; Bolton cotton spinner; mayor there 1863–4.

Rode with Agnes. Saw Ld Ward (2 h)—Sir W. Heathcote—J.N.G.—
Sir A. Elton—R. Phillimore—Ld Aberdeen—Sir J. Graham—H of C. at
3 and 5. Ten to dinner—political.

5. Th.

Wrote to Col. Wynne(2)—Sir J. Williams—Sir G. Grey—Rev Mr Haddan—
Rogers—H. Glynne.

Busy mg about Flintshire matters. H. of C. $4\frac{1}{2}$–$8\frac{1}{4}$: and in sharp debate
with Lord P.[1] Saw Ld Derby—Sir S.H. Northcote—Sir Jas Graham—
Col. Wynne—F.R. Bonham—Mr Cobden—Col. Taylor[2]—Mr Walpole.
At J. Wortley's(evg) in sad discussion whether to call in Dr Sutherland![3]

6. Fr.

Wrote to E.V. Harcourt—Sir Chas Wood—Rev. J Tweed. Read Ld
Ellesmere's Faust. Read papers on Sugar & Tea &c.[4] Rode with Agnes.
Saw Col. Rowley[5]—Mr Frere—E. Cardwell—F.R. Bonham—Sir S. North-
cote—Ld Ward—R. Phillimore—Mr Moffatt—Geo. Harcourt—Mr Ander-
son. H of C. $4\frac{1}{2}$–$11\frac{3}{4}$. Spoke on Persia & on Tea Duties, & voted in 125:187.
Times are changed, & men![6]

I saw Ld Derby yesterday, with respect primarily to a question of a County
meeting in Flintshire.[7] But two matters were touched between us that should be
noticed. He said to me that he hoped when the Dissolution came we, that is to
say Derbyites and Peelites, should not go knocking our heads against one another
at every election as we did in 1852. I replied that so far as I was concerned the
chief case for me would be that of Flintshire where upon particular grounds I
should exert myself to the uttermost against Mostyn who is a supporter of Lord
Palmerston. But that as to the question generally I gave & could give him no
answer only observing that our relative positions might be materially affected by
what was yet to happen between this time and the dissolution.

The two motions I had pending were mentioned, one as to Tea and Sugar, the
other as to Expenditure & Lord Derby said as to the latter that he would do all
he could with his friends in its favour, but he expected to have difficulty with a
portion of them who were greatly afraid of military reductions. I replied with
an apology for speaking as it were from his point of view that it seemed to me
it was high time for them to consider whether they would or would not endeavour
to attract towards themselves such a strength of public opinion as would really
put them in a condition to undertake the Government of the country: without
which they could not be a real Opposition according to the spirit of our Parliamentary system.[8]

[1] *Palmerston having announced a dissolution, Gladstone challenged him to abandon
his China policy: *H* cxliv. 1913.
[2] Thomas Edward *Taylor, 1811–83; lieut. col. in Meath militia; tory M.P. Co. Dublin
from 1841; minor office 1858–9, 1866–8, 1874–80.
[3] See 1 Dec. 41. Wortley was suffering spasms of insanity.
[4] *PP* 1857, 1st session, viii. 197 and xvi. 135.
[5] See 24 June 35n.
[6] *H* cxliv. 1974; notes in Add MS 44655, f. 62.
[7] See 7 Apr. 57n.
[8] Initialled and dated 6 March 1857: Add MS 44747, f. 14.

7. Sat.

Wrote to Rev Mr Haddan—H. Glynne—Greswell—Napier[1]—Mrs Herbert —Mr Cobden MP—J. Wilson MP—Mr Hubbard—J. Griffiths—Mr R. Hughes[2]—Ld Derby(2)—H. Raikes—Sir H. Stracey[3]—Sir T. Tancred— R. Hooper.[4] Rode with Agnes. Saw Ld A. Hervey—F.R. Bonham—Col Rowley—Sir W. Heathcote—S. Herbert—Ld Malmesbury—Ld Exmouth —Ld Lyttelton. Dined with Lyttelton. Read M'Lean's Hudson's Bay— Rode with Agnes.

8. 2 S. Lent.

St James's mg & St Paul's Kn. in aft. Read MS. Saw Lord Alfred Hervey —Sir W. James—Mrs Herbert. Wrote to Sir J. Graham—Ld Malmesbury & copy[5]—Sir Ch. Wood—& copy. Read Simeon's Memoirs—Keble on Marriage[6]—Sinclair on U.S. Education[7]—Observateur Catholique[8]— Nugee on Church Mission.[9]

9. M.

Wrote to Sir John Hanmer—Lord Ward—Mr M. Bernard—Mrs Herbert— E.V. Harcourt—V. Scully MP.—Mr A.B. Cochrane—C. Butler—Rev E. Hawkins—G. Crawshay—Rev E. Coleridge—S. Triscott [sc. Triscoll]— Rev MW Mayow—W. Stütz[10]—Ld Westminster—Jas Gladstone.[11] Arranging letters & papers. Saw Lord Malmesbury—Col. Rowley—Earl of Aberdeen—Mr J. Murray—Scotts—Major Stuart Wortley[12]—Dr Godfray[13]— Mr E.V. Harcourt—Geo. W. Hope—Sir Geo. Clerk—A. Hayward—Col. Percy Herbert and J. Griffiths(S.R.G.) Also the Speaker—a farewell.[14] Sad sad accounts of Jim Wortley. H. of C. $4\frac{1}{2}$–$8\frac{1}{4}$: spoke on Income Tax Bill.[15]

[1] Probably Henry Alfred Napier, 1797–1871; rector of Swyncombe from 1826.

[2] Hugh Robert Hughes, 1827–1911, of Kinmel Park, Denbigh; lord-lieutenant of Flintshire from 1874; contested the county as a tory 1861; see 24 May 61 ff.

[3] Sir Henry Josias Strachey, 1802–85; 5th bart. 1855; tory M.P. E. Norfolk 1855–7, Yarmouth 1859–65, Norwich, 1868–70 (unseated).

[4] Richard Hooper, 1821–94; curate in Westminster 1849–54; rector of Upton from 1862; Homeric scholar.

[5] 'I agree with Herbert in his intention to stand clear of political combination under the present circumstances' (Add MS 44387, f. 120).

[6] J. *Keble, An argument for not proceeding immediately to repeal the laws which treat the nuptial bond as indissoluble (1857).

[7] J. *Sinclair, Remarks on the Common School system of the U.S.: in a letter to Earl Granville (1857).

[8] L'Observateur catholique. Revue des sciences ecclésiastiques et des faits religieux; published in Paris, 1855–67.

[9] G. Nugee, The necessity for Christian education to elevate the native character in India (1846).

[10] Possibly Victor Stütz, German historian.

[11] James Gladstone, 1811–62, 2nd s. of Sir John's* br. James.

[12] Archibald Henry Plantagenet Stuart-Wortley-Mackenzie, 1832–90, grands. of 1st Lord Wharncliffe; tory M.P. Honiton 1857–9.

[13] Frederick Godfray, 1822?–68; domestic chaplain to earl of Limerick; D. C. L. Oxford 1855.

[14] *Shaw-Lefevre did not stand at the 1857 election; he was succeeded by J. E. *Denison.

[15] H cxliv. 2064.

10. T.

Wrote to Mr H.R. Hughes—Mrs Herbert—Mr Wynne Eyton—Rev Mr
Tweed—Sir J. Williams—S.R. Glynne—Col. Rowley—Col. Wynn—J.R.
Curtis—Ld Ward—Mr Haddan. H. of C. 4½–10½: spoke on Expenditure
for an hour: to a few corpses.[1] Saw Captain Gladstone—Mr Sandars—
Lord Alfred Hervey—Wm. Gladstone—F.R. Bonham—Lord Henry
Lennox—Geo. W. Hope(2)—Sir J. Pakington—R. Palmer M.P.—Bp of
Oxford. Nine to dinner: but I only came in at eleven o'clock. Read Sir
F. Kelly's Letter.[2]

11. Wed. X.

Wrote to Rev Mr Greswell—Wynne[3]—Dr Croly—Archdn. Sinclair[4]—Mrs
Herbert—Robn G.—Willy—S. Herbert—Mr Birkett. Rev. Osborne
Gordon—Mr. Gleig—Dr Acland. Dined with R. Cavendish. Lady Derby's
in evg. Ride with Agnes. Saw Col. Tulloch—James Gladstone—Provost
of Eton(Homer &c.)—Mr Goldwin Smith—Hon Mrs Talbot (resp. J.S.
W[ortley])—Sir Wm Heathcote—Sir A. Elton Bt.—R. Phillimore—

Ld Chelsea ⎫
G. W. Hope— ⎪
Count Freret(?) ⎬ at Ld D.s
Ld John Russell ⎭

12. Th. X.

Wrote to Mr Roundell Palmer—Rev Mr Tiddeman—Rev H Glynne—
Ed. Illustr. Times[5]—Ld Westminster—Mr D. Gladstone—Mr Treherne[6]
—Sir C. Trevelyan. Ride with Agnes—Saw Sir Wm. Heathcote—R. Philli-
more—Lord Carnarvon—Mr Jas M'Gregor MP.—Lord Elgin—Mr G.W.
Hope—Rev. Whitwell Elwin. H of C. 4½–7½.[7] Dined with Ln.: Lady
Granville's afterwards—Conv. with M. Persigny.[8] Read Facts on the
Navy[9]—M'Lean's Hudson's Bay.

Justice might for some reasons have properly been represented dumb no less
than blind: dumb, though strong. For most of her great operations are those
which She achieves in silence. She has a natural hold on man. Noisy passion

---

[1] Moving amndt., to the navy estimates: *H* cxliv. 2151. notes in Add MS 44655, f. 64.
There was no division.
[2] Sir F. *Kelly, *A Letter to Lord Lyndhurst on the late debate upon China* (1857).
[3] Perhaps Robert Wynne, 1828–81; perpetual curate of Corhampton 1856–65; vicar
of Scalford from 1865.
[4] See 3 Dec. 33.
[5] Henry Richard *Vizetelly, 1820–94; ed. *Illustrated Times* 1855–65, then worked for
Illustrated London News.
[6] Morgan Treherne, 1803–67; barrister; contested Coventry 1857 (against *Phillimore,
see 27 Mar. 57), 1859, tory M.P. there from 1863.
[7] Supply; *H* cxliv. 2215.
[8] Jean Gilbert Victor Fialin, comte de Persigny, 1808–72; Bonapartist; refugee in
Britain 1836–48, and from 1871; French ambassador here 1855–8, 1859–60; cr. duke 1863.
[9] Perhaps 'Facts and observations . . . [on] the Royal Navy' (1845).

shakes & strains but cannot destroy it. Such influences exhaust themselves: but She labours night and day in calm and as Time flows on the first mitigates & at last redresses what is wrong[.][1]

13. Fr. X.

Wrote to Col. Rowley—S.R. Glynne—Lord Ward—Mr G. Steward[2]—Rev Mr Nunn[3]—Mr T. Hamilton[4]—Geo. Wilson[5]—R. Greswell—Sir J.H. Williams—Dean of Norwich.[6] Ride with Agnes. Saw Mr Lake—Mr Bonham—Mr Hamilton Gray—Sir J. Graham—R. Phillimore—Saw Graham. Worked on books & papers. H. of C. $4\frac{1}{2}$–$6\frac{3}{4}$.[7] Read Sir R. Peel's Opinions[8]—Nat. Review on Spurgeon[9]—Dublin do on the Rambler.[10]

14. Sat.

Wrote to Rev Mr Conybeare[11]—Sir W. James—Rev G.R. Gleig—J. M'Gregor MP.—Lady Northcote—Mr Napier MP.—Mayor of Liverpool[12]—W. Lynes[13]—Hugh Hope. Saw R. Phillimore—Ld H. Lennox—F.R. Bonham—G.W. Hope—W. Hampton (House Bills &c)—Sir Geo. Clerk—Earl Jermyn—Mr Bennett MP.[14]—Mr Jas Macgregor. Worked on books & pamphlets. Read Davies on Educn.[15]—Therry's Lecture on Oratory[16]—Sketch of Livingstone's Travels[17]—Burn on Coming Danger.[18]

15. 3 S. Lent.

St James's mg & Holy Comm.—Chapel Royal aft. Read MS of 53 aloud. Saw R. Phillimore—Sir C. Trevelyan—Lady Wenlock: & Jane Wortley. Read Simeon's Life[19]—Romaine's Life[20]—Ln on Baptism[21]—E.I. Mission Conference—Report of Deputation to the East.[22]

16. M. X.

Wrote to Rev Mr Gray—Ld Stanhope—Jas Gladstone—S.R. Glynne—A.B. Cochrane—H. Glynne—S.H. Northcote—W.M. Rossetti.[23] Saw Mrs.

[1] Dated 12 March 1856; Add MS 44746, f. 5.
[2] George Steward, 1803–66; methodist minister, became congregationalist 1853, minister in Newcastle 1853–60; wrote on church and state.
[3] Probably Thomas Nunn, 1821–77; rector of Stansted 1854–73.
[4] Thomas Newte Hamilton, 1818–69; curate of All Hallows, London, 1842–58, of Thornton-le-Moor 1859–69.
[5] George Wilson; priest 1826; incumbent of Grayrigg by Kendal 1834.
[6] George *Pellew, 1793–1866; dean of Norwich from 1828; published tracts.
[7] Misc. business: H cxliv. 2304.
[8] W. T. Haly, The opinions of Sir R. *Peel expressed in parliament and in public (1843).
[9] See 6 Feb. 57.
[10] Dublin Review, xlii. 245 (March 1857); on the controversy with *Acton's Rambler.
[11] W. J. Conybeare, who d. July 1857; see 27 Sept. 42.
[12] Francis Shand.   [13] Unidentified.
[14] Philip Bennet, 1795–1866; tory M.P. W. Suffolk 1845–59.
[15] C. G. Davies, Educational difficulties; how are they to be met? (1857).
[16] R. *Therry, 'Comparison of the oratory of the House of Commons thirty years ago, and the present time. A lecture' (1856).
[17] D. *Livingstone, Missionary travels and researches in South Africa (1857).
[18] Untraced; perhaps by Richard Burn, Manchester author on cotton.
[19] See 8 Feb. 57.   [20] See 27 Feb. 57.
[21] G. W. *Lyttelton, 'Tracts. I On infant baptism. II On the Athanasian creed' (1857).
[22] Neither found.
[23] William Michael *Rossetti, 1829–1919, br. of D. G. and Christina and editor of their works; worked in Excise office 1854–94.

Herbert—G.W. Hope—Col. Rowley. Saw Lewis 34[R]. Rode with Agnes.
Worked on my books & papers. Read Ld Overstone's Tracts[1]—Life of
Sir C. Napier.[2]

17. T.

Wrote to Ld H. Lennox—Robn. G. Rode with Agnes. Worked on books
letters & pictures. Read A. Young on French Rev.[3]—Guizot's Sir R. Peel.[4]
Saw Mr G. Smith—Ld Cholmondeley—Sir Geo. Clark—Mr Hubbard.

18. Wed.

Wrote to Rev. Mr Kelly[5]—Mr Roworth[6]—Captain G—Rev. F. Burd[7]—
Rev. Mr Rogers. Rode with Agnes. Worked on books. Corrected my China
Speech.[8] Saw Sir W. Heathcote—Mr Roworth. Read Guizot's Peel. Wrote
MS on the 'situation'.[9]

19. Th.

Wrote to S.R. Glynne—Mr Darby—Tomlinson Smith[10]—Mr Brough—
Rev. Mr Witty[11]—Rev. Mr Stuart[12]—Rev. Mr MacIvor.[13] Continued my
MS. Saw F.R. Bonham—Col. Rowley—Mr Meekins.[14] Saw Clifford 42[R].
C. went to Ld Abn. about S. Herbert's letter.[15] Read Guizot's Peel.

20. Fr.

Wrote to Mr Meekins—Rev. Mr Elwin. Worked on my MS. Saw Sir Jas.
Graham—do with Ld Aberdeen—also Lord Stanhope—Read Guizot's
Peel.

[1] Collected in S. J. *Loyd, Tracts . . . on metallic and paper currency 1844–57, ed. J. R.
*M[acCulloch] (1858), especially 'Letter to the editor of The Times on the Bank Charter
Act 1855–6'.
[2] W. F. P. Napier, The life and opinions of Gen. Sir C. J. *Napier (1857).
[3] A. *Young, The example of France, a warning to Britain (1793).
[4] See 27 Sept. 56; he declined *Elwin's invitation to review it in the Quarterly: 'it
leads me over tender ground, & naturally prompts a distribution of praise and blame in
accounting for our present political evils. At the present moment looking upon dishonour
as the great characteristic of Lord Palmerston's govt. I would not willingly run the risk
of wounding Ld Derby or any friend of his' (to Elwin, 27 March 1857, N.L.S.).
[5] Perhaps John *Kelly, 1801–76; independent minister in Everton, Liverpool, 1829–
73; a director of the London missionary society.
[6] Charles Roworth, printer at Temple Bar.
[7] Frederick Burd, 1826–1915; curate of Cressage, rector there 1864–78, of Neen Savage
1878–96.
[8] See 3 Mar. 57.
[9] Not found; or perhaps see 2 Apr. 57.
[10] Unidentified.
[11] John Francis Witty; incumbent of St. Matthew's, Sheffield, 1851.
[12] Alexander Stuart, 1801–83; archdeacon of Ross from 1842.
[13] James MacIvor, d. 1886; fellow of Trinity, Dublin, from 1844; rector of Ardstraw
from 1858; wrote on Ireland, see 21 Mar. 57.
[14] T. C. Mossom Meekins, Q.C. and equity draftsman.
[15] Gladstone believed *Herbert had 'turned what is called the cold shoulder upon
Malmesbury and Co.' in the Wiltshire election campaign; Stanmore, ii. 78 ff. See 31
Mar. 57.

21. *Sat.*

Wrote to Lady Northcote—J. Griffiths—A.B. Cochrane—Mack. Wilson—
Rev. H. Roundell[1]—Dean Milman—J.N.G. Worked on books. Read
Macivor on Ir. Educn.[2]—Guizot's Peel finished. Calthorpe's Crimean
Book.[3] Saw Mrs Talbot—R. Phillimore—Col. Rowley—F.R. Bonham—
Duke of Argyll. (S[tafford] House)—Duchess of Sutherland—Lord
Wynford.[4]

22. *S.*

St Martin's 8½ a.m. H.C. St James 11 a.m. St Andrews Wells St 3½ P.M.
Wrote to S. Laing (duplicate)—S. Herbert[5]—Antonio Brady[6]—J. Hamil-
ton (M.Star.) Read aloud MS of 53 for 3 S[unday of] L[ent]. Saw Ld
Aberdeen. Read Simeons Life. Directions &c for departure.

23. *M.* [*Hawarden*].

Wrote to Robn. G (2)—P. Pickering—J. Hicklin—C.G. Up at 5. Chester
at 11¼. Canvassing there until 3. Then to Mold with Rowley & committee
work there till 6½ esp. Finance & arrangements for meetings.[7] Afterwards
home to the Rectory. Read Dryden.

24. *T.*

Ch. 8½ a.m. Wrote to C.G.—R.C. Rawlins—W. Bulkeley Hughes—F.R.
Bonham. Saw Mr Smith (canvass)[8]—Mr Littleboy and Sherratt—Mr
Burnett. Off at 2 to Rhyl: crowded meeting, canvass afterwards, & re-
turned 9 P.M. Read Disraeli's Curios. Lit.[9]

25. *W. Annunc*[*iatio*]*n.*

Ch 11 a.m. Wrote to C.G.—Mr C. Cudingley[10]—Rev. J. H. Brooks (& copy)[11]
—Rev. R. Greswell—Sir J. Hay Williams—Mackenzie Wilson. Went off
at 2 to speak at public meeting at Flint: then back & up to Buckley for a
meeting at 7.[12] Both went off decidedly well. Read Guizot on Art[13]—Disraeli's Curios Lit.

---

[1] Henry Roundell, 1825?–64; vicar of Buckingham from 1854.
[2] J. MacIvor, *A letter . . . on the present state of the education question* (1857).
[3] S. J. G. Calthorpe, *Letters from Head-Quarters*, 2v. (1856).
[4] William Samuel Best, 1798–1869; 2nd Baron Wynford 1845; active in 1857 campaign against Divorce Bill.
[5] In Stanmore, ii. 82.
[6] Not further identified.
[7] *Glynne stood as a Peelite for Flintshire against T. E. Lloyd-Mostyn, liberal; see
7 Apr. 57.
[8] H. J. Smith, *Glynne's agent in Mold.
[9] See 11 July 54.
[10] A voter?
[11] John Henry Brookes, 1823?–96; fellow of Brasenose; had written about his vote in
Flintshire (Hawn P), reply, on church rates etc. in Add MS 44387, f. 166.
[12] Resolutions agst. tea and sugar duties passed, in Add MS 44746, f. 19.
[13] F. P. G. Guizot, *Études sur les beaux arts en général* (1852, Eng. trans. by G. Grove
1853).

26. Th.

Ch 8½ a.m. Wrote to C.G.—F.R. Bonham—E. Bate[1]—Wm. Smith (Cop [Farm])—Robn. Gladstone—Robert Gladstone—Mr J. Hamilton—also draft of a second address for S.R.G.[2] Canvass morning—Attended meeting at Mold where after some rough water we got through very well; then committee Room & conv. with Mr Rawlins until 6 P.M. Read Burke's Fragm. of Speeches[3]—Sterne's Tr. Shandy, Letters &c.[4]

27. Fr.

(Ch missed) Wrote to C.G.—A. Hayward—W. Bulkeley Hughes—Rev. Whitwell Elwin. 2–7½: went to hold a meeting at Holywell & worked through it pretty well.[5] Saw Mr Littleboy.—Mr Thos Reed[6]—Mr Keats[7]—Sir W.W. Wynn. R. Phillimore came at 8 P.M. with his own news.[8] Read Burke's Speeches.

28. Sat.

Ch 8½ a.m.: & 7 P.M. Wrote to Rev. A.P. Stanley—Jones & Yarrell—C.G. —Rev. R. Greswell—Vice Chancellor of Oxford—W. Smith (Cop. Farm)— John Tollemache Esq.—Mr Meany[9]—Robn. G—Mr R. Barker—Mr W.H. Keats & Lord Ward. At Mold in afternoon to make arrangements for next week. Read Ov. Met[amorphoses] B.XIII. and Burke. Up to this time we are sanguine: but the evidences are still indefinite. Saw Mr May.[10]

29. 5 S. Lent.

Ch 11 a.m. & 6 P.M. Wrote to R. Barker—C.A. Wood—J. Davies & Son. (Holywell Observer)[11]—Read Consett's Ch of Russia[12]—Lives of Russian Saints.[13]—Sterne's Sermons.[14] A disturbed Sunday.

30. M.

Ch 8½ a.m. Wrote to W.H. Darby[15]—J. Hicklin (Chester Courant)—Provost of Oriel Coll.—Rector of Exeter Coll.—T. Edwards Moss—W.H. Keats— Captain Gladstone—G. Burnett—H. Craven.[16] Saw the Rev. Mr Lloyd (at Hope,[17] to make arrangements for meeting)—R. Phillimore (Ld Westmr.). Canvassing with Burnett. To Mold in evg. for arrangements & the Mostyn meeting but at last it was thought inexpedient. Read Ovid.—Burke's Hist.

[1] Probably of the firm involved in the Oak Farm; see 5 Feb. 50.
[2] Hawn P.   [3] See 16 Apr. 45.
[4] L. *Sterne, *Tristram Shandy* (1760–67); sundry *Letters*, some forged.
[5] See 16 Apr. 57n, for the consequences.   [6] Unidentified.
[7] W. H. Keats of Greenfield Hall, Flintshire, worked for *Glynne in the election.
[8] Last of five candidates at Coventry.
[9] Stephen J. Meaney, journalist on *Liverpool Daily Post*.
[10] Thomas Baker May, Hawarden magistrate.
[11] James Davies, published *Glynne's address.
[12] *The present state and regulations of the Church of Russia*, tr. T. Consett (1729).
[13] Not found.
[14] [L. *Sterne], *The sermons of William Yorick*, 7v. (1760–9).
[15] Of Brymbo Iron works, Wrexham, on the election (Hawn P).
[16] Of Buckley; had complained of religious discrimination in the election (Hawn P).
[17] 4 miles of SE. of Mold.

31. Tu.

Ch 8½ a.m. Wrote to Ld Aberdeen (& draft)—Archdeacon Wickham[1] (dft. for S.)—Rev. Mr Morrall (do)—C.A. Wood—J.A. Napier (Rhyl)[2]— Mr J. [P.] Roberts (Rhyl)[3]—Robert Gladstone—F.R. Bonham and [blank] Went to Chester with Henry to canvass & telegraph to C.G. Read Burke's Hist. Merry Wives of Windsor. Cic[ero] pro Leg[e] Manil[ia].

My dear Lord Aberdeen,[4]

I hope that you, who have the advantage of tranquillity, will much consider, before the new Parliament meets, what sort of figure Peelism is to cut in it. My own fear is, I confess, not only lest it should be extinguished, but lest it should have gone out, as is said, with a stench.

Its position has heretofore been so ambiguous, & there has been so little disposition in the country to make allowance for our real difficulties, that a creditable exit seems peculiarly needful: so that when we are scattered, if this we must be, we shall be scattered for a reason, & that each of us shall have a reason to give for the course he takes after the scattering.

The case is an easier, though not easy, one for Sir J. Graham & Cardwell (of whose [electoral] fate I am not yet informed) than for others; because in 1852 they went into opposition to Lord Derby. But all the rest of us, at a time when he was still a Protectionist, professed to oppose him only on Protection and its appendages.

In forming your Government, the act was done, which would probably have led to a real & final amalgamation with the Liberal party: but which had not produced any such amalgamation at the time when, the mortar being still wet, Lord John Russell's powder magazine blew the whole fabric into the air.

Since that period, the bulk of the Liberal party, in consequence of taking Lord Palmerston for its leader, has placed itself in almost continual, at least in very frequent, antagonism with us; and with its own principles also no doubt, but still with principles that are not exclusively its own, but that are recognised by all political parties.

On the one hand Lord Derby is much weaker than he was in 1852: on the other, the question, which as we declared then alone prevented our supporting him, has been finally disposed of.

How under the circumstances are men, who acted thus in 1852, to justify incorporating themselves with the Liberal party in 1857?

Foreign Policy, Expenditure, and Taxation, are now, as Protection was in 1852, the questions of the hour. Upon these questions we are sharply opposed to Lord Palmerston: &, as far as I know we are in general agreement with Lord Derby & the bulk of his party, as well as with a section of Independent Liberals, whose lights I regret to see are all put out.

What can be worse for our characters than to have it said that, having professed to quarrel with our party on a particular question in 1846, we not only continued the quarrel after that question was disposed of, but we also con-

1 Robert Wickham, 1822–80; archdeacon of St. Asaph from 1845.
2 Declining to lecture there; Hawn P.
3 On income tax; Hawn P.
4 Add MS 43071, f. 358; subsequently circulated among leading Peelites; see Stanmore, ii. 86ff., Parker, *Graham*, ii. 309. *Aberdeen replied (3 April 1857, *ibid.* f. 364) 'there is no such thing as a distinctive Peelite party . . . in this age of progress the liberal party must ultimately govern the country'.

summated the rupture just when the Conservative party had made it a main object to defend our principles & measures in finance, & the principles of Foreign policy which are peculiarly yours? Will not such conduct bear the marks both of duplicity, & of an undying hatred?

But there is an alternative: it is Lord John Russell. I cannot but regret that Sir James Graham, without at all conciliating the Liberal party at large, seems to have placed himself at Lord John's mercy, to take him or not as he pleases. For I do not believe that Sir J. Graham in his heart is persuaded that Parliamentary Reform is the present want of the country. Lord John no doubt is persuaded 1. That the country must be governed by the Liberal party, 2. That he must be at the head of it, 3. That Reform, or Education (where Graham murdered him) or some other question must be employed as an instrument for these higher purposes. But how can we become parties to such tampering with our institutions & with the public interests by this total inversion of the relative positions of means & end?

The great subjects of public policy, which may be said to lie within reach, appear to be, 1. Foreign Policy, 2. Retrenchment, 3. Taxation, 4. Reform, 5. Education, 6. Church, 7. Ecclesiastical questions in Ireland, 8. Law Reform.

In our difficult position, our whole safety, for ultimate vindication, lies in our following with perfect good faith the guidance which events afford. Upon which of these eight groups of questions shall we be naturally guided to, and justified in, party union with Liberalism at this time? Must we not, *almost* without an exception, artificially adopt certain opinions upon the questions, in order to lay the ground for the union? That is (as it will be judged against us) we have been all along covert party men, only of a new party, & likewise without the courage to say so.

What sort of light will this proceeding reflect upon the character of Sir Robert Peel, & upon his never recalled declarations that the course he took upon the Corn Law in 1846 was not a breach of his obligations rightly understood to those who had raised him to power?

Such are my dismal ruminations on the general issue, in prosecution of my late letter to Herbert.[1] As long as we held together, I had a hope, the hope of our public usefulness. If (not by my act) we are to separate, I am, for the time at least, without this last resource; & in the new H. of Commons, into which I have found my way with unusual ease, I cannot, having arrived there, find ground for the sole of my foot to rest upon. I am not, however, like 'John', or 'the young man from Northampton'. I do not look to spending in political life the last of my strength: I only await the day when the evidence of facts shall convince me that I have no reasonable expectation of doing good there, & certainly both the fact & the manner of the severance that is now hanging over us are the most significant indications that have yet been afforded me towards a proof, which I dare say the next few years will carry to demonstration.

I remain, my dear Lord Aberdeen,
always affectionately yours,
W. E. Gladstone.

Wed. Ap. One. 1857 Hawarden

Wrote to Mr Jas Beaven[2]—T. Edwards Moss—Robn. Gladstone—Roger W. Jones.[3] Off at 10 a.m. to canvass at Buckley & Bistre:[4] ended 4 P.M.

[1] See 19 Mar. 57n.
[2] James Beavan of Saltney had written about his vote in the Flintshire election.
[3] Unidentified.   [4] 3 miles E. of Mold.

& over to Hope when I spoke to a crowded meeting & home at 10 P.M. C. had arrived. Read Layard's Nineveh.[1]

2. Th.

Ch. 8½ a.m. Wrote to Rev. Mr Brown (Bodvari)[2]—Rev. Mr Hearn[3]— J.W. Parker & Son—J. Griffiths (O.F.)—E. Roberts (St Asaph)[4]—Thos Jones (Kinnerton Green)[5]—H. J. Smith (Mold).[6] Began an attempt at an Article for Q.R.[7] Saw Waters[8]—Conv. with C. on arrangements—wh hang partly on public affairs. Read Merry Wives of Windsor: and political pamphlets of Mr Pitts & the War time.

3. Fr.

Wrote to Mr Eddowes[9]—Mr Waring Perry[10]—Archdn. Wickham (dft. for Stephen). Off at 11 to Liverpool and back at 8: held a crowded meeting in a dreadful atmosphere; where a very good feeling prevailed.[11] Read St Ronan's Well.[12] Saw Robn. G.—E. Breakenridge—Mr Keats—Mr Burnett —Late dinner at Hawarden: pleased with Mr Peel's[13] manners.

4. Sat.

Ch 8.30 a.m. & 7 P.M. Wrote to Earl of Aberdeen—Messrs Williams & Co— Mr Willm. Johnson[14]—Mr Vidal[15]—Rev. E. Coleridge—Dean of Chester.[16] Off at nine to the nomination: where I nearly split my chest in speaking against some thirty roarers: but the show of hands was carried.[17] Saw Mr Smith—(Eln. Fund)—Mr Keats (resp. Lipool Commn.)—Mr E. Peel. Read St Ronan's Well—Worked on commencement of Article.

5. Palm Sunday

Ch 11 a.m. with Holy Commn.: & 6.30 P.M. Wrote (alack) drafts for Stephen to Mr Edwards (on Puseyism)—& Major Jones; and letters to

---

[1] A. H. *Layard, Nineveh and Babylon (1853).
[2] Thomas Birch Llewelyn Browne, rector of Bodvari, Denbighshire from 1850.
[3] Probably James Hearn, 1785?–1864; rector of Hatford from 1836.
[4] Edward Roberts, b. 1812; vicar of Llangwstenyn, 1846.
[5] Had written on methodism; Hawn P.
[6] Henry J. Smith, election agent in Mold; Hawn P.
[7] 'The new parliament and its work', Quarterly Review, ci. 541 (April 1857); see Add MS 44685, f. 255.
[8] A local rescue case.
[9] T. S. Eddowes of Birkenhead had written hesitating voting for *Glynne; distantly related through m. of James Gladstone.
[10] W. Warring Perry of Tranmere, writing about his vote (Hawn P).
[11] At the Clarendon Rooms, to Flintshire out-voters in Liverpool; The Guardian, 8 April 1857, 271.
[12] By *Scott (1823).
[13] Edmund Peel, who contested Flintshire in 1852 (see 21 July 52).
[14] William Johnson [*Cory], 1823–92; master at Eton 1845–72, where he tutored the Gladstone boys, taking special interest in Herbert; took name of Cory 1872.
[15] Francis Vidal, 1805–84; missionary; taught at Eton 1847–65.
[16] i.e. Frederick Anson (see above, ii. 653).
[17] Report in The Times, 6 April 1857, 7d.

Archdeacon Wickham—Sam. Holmes[1]—J. Griffiths—H. Smith (Mold)—
Mr Royle.[2] Read Consett's Russian Church—Oxf. Essay on Schemes of
Comprehension; most dangerous.[3] Chr. Remembr. on Mormonism &c.[4]
Another Sunday disturbed & such a Sunday. We all sorely lament the
thrusting of the Election into Passion Week.

6. M.

Ch 7 P.M. Wrote to Robert Gladstone—Mr T.S. Eddowes—Countess of
Dunraven—Rev. Mr. Woollcombe—W. Grogan—Sir S. Northcote—Sir
W. Heathcote—Mr J. Powell—Canvassing 10½–3. Saw Mr Littleboy—
Mr Burnett—Mr Roberts. Read St. Ronan's Well. Much uncertainty as to
the Election tomorrow with a prevailing expectn. of an extremely near
contest.

7. T.

Church at Mold 11 a.m. and at Hawarden at 7 P.M. We went off to Mold
at 8½ a.m. and soon saw the signs of a defeat which became smashing &
woeful as the day advanced.[5] Some little canvassing there—Conv. with
Mr Wynn Eyton.[6] Walked back with Phillimore & discussed Parly & Ch
prospects. Wrote to Messrs. Williams & Co—Rev. E. Coleridge. Read St
Ronan's Well.

8. Wed.

Ch 11 a.m. Wrote to Mr H. Smith—Sir W. Heathcote—Rev. Warden of
Ruthin[7]—Mr W.H. Keats—Rev. R. Greswell—G. Burnett Esq. Drove to
Northop—and saw Mr Phillips. Also to see Sherratt at the Darlington
borings. Read St Ronan's Well. Preparations for departure.

We further discussed our parting Address, wh was softened: & we
digested as well as we could the defeat of yesterday which cut us deeply
rather as a scandal & offence of the county than as a personal or family
disappointment. Wrote a little of my MS.

[1] See 20 Apr. 40.
[2] See 6 May 45?
[3] H. B. *Wilson, 'Schemes of Christian comprehension', *Oxford Essays* (1857); argued
for tolerance as basis of national church.
[4] *Christian Remembrancer*, xxxiii. 257 (June 1857).
[5] The result was: T. Lloyd Mostyn (liberal) 1171; Sir S. Glynne (Peelite) 876. Humiliation occurred thus: 'sometime before the dissolution of 1857, Lord Westminster called
on Sir S. Glynne's brother at Hawarden and of his own motion strongly urged that Sir
S. Glynne should stand for the country against Mr. Mostyn . . . When the Dissolution
came, and mainly in consequence of Lord Westminster's unsolicited offer Sir S. Glynne
offered himself, he was strongly opposed by Lord Westminster. I speak only of what
appeared; common belief said more . . . [Westminster said he] was under an erroneous
impression as to Sir S. Glynne's politics' (Gladstone to Brand, 10 May 1861, Add MS
44193, f. 36).
[6] Thomas Wynne Eyton of Leeswood; Flintshire landowner.
[7] R. Newcombe (see 1 Mar. 50) was also warden of Ruthin, Denbighshire; he d. August
1857.

9. Th. [London]

Marg. Chapel 5 P.M. Wrote to Scotts—Saw Scotts—Lord Aberdeen.
Worked on MS for Q.R. 8¼–4 Journey to London by G.W.R. Thank God
we found all the children well; & felt how much nearer they lie to the heart
than the affairs of Tuesday; though we found that bad to feed or sleep
upon. Wrote & discussed draft of a proposed farewell address for S.

10. Good Friday.

St James's & H.C. 11 a.m.—Marg. Chapel 5 P.M. Wrote to J.N.G.—
Robert Gladstone—Colonel Morgan.[1] MS on Lam. 1, aloud in evg. Revising & working on MS. Read Simeon's Memoirs. Rationale of Justifn.
for Faith.[2] After Evg. prayers worked for Q.R.

11. Easter Eve.

Marg. Chapel 8 P.M. Wrote to Mr Raikes *cum* Mr Ffoulkes.—Mr J.W.
Cowell—Mrs Elder—H. Glynne—Messrs. Carpenter & Westley.[3] Saw Mr
J. Griffiths—(S[tephen] & O[ak] F[arm])—Mr W. Grogan. Worked on MS
for Q.R. in evg. Rode with Agnes.

12. Easter Day.

St Martin's for H.C. 8½ a.m. St James 11 a.m. & Wells St 3.30. MS of 44
aloud in evg. Conv. with the elder children. Read Simeon's Memoirs—
Fleetwood on Lay Baptism[4]—Spiritual Retreat[5]—Melville on Church
Reform.[6] Saw A. Hayward—R. Cavendish.

13. M.

Marg. Chapel 5.P.M. Wrote to H. Lees—J. Murray—Sir W. Heathcote.
Worked much on MS for Q.R. Saw F.R. Bonham—Lord A. Hervey—
Mr Lacaita. Read Imaginary History &c.[7] At Benjamin's[8] & business.

14. T.

Chapel Royal at noon. Saw with pleasure the Altar ready; but I could not
remain. Wrote to Rev. W. Elwin—Mr Lancaster—Mr G.W. Gill[9]—Rev.
Mr Dowding—Sir S. Scott & Co—Rev. Mr Greswell—Mr Lataky[10]—Provost
of Oriel—Mr Phillips—Mr Marshall. Finished & dispatched my Article for

[1] Edward Morgan, 1793–1861, landowner at Golden Grove, Flintshire.
[2] *Rationale of justification by faith* (1856).
[3] Opticians in Regent Street.
[4] W. *Fleetwood, The judgement of the Church of England in the case of lay-baptism
and of dissenters' baptism* (1712).
[5] 'A spiritual retreat for one day in every month, by a priest of the Society of Jesus'
[J. Croiset] (1710).
[6] M. R. Melville, *Reform, not subversion!* (1834).
[7] *Imaginary history of the next thirty years* (1857).
[8] See 15 Apr. 56.
[9] George Wadman Gill, London chemist.
[10] Unidentified.

Q.R.: keeping apart what I have written on Eccl. Patronage.[1] Saw the Bp of Salisbury. Made inquiries but saw none[R]. Read Leake's Geography[2] and The Staff Officer.[3]

15. Wed. X.

Wrote to T.D. Acland—Dr Humphreys[4]—Mr Walter (Sec. Judic. Commn.) —Mr R. Burn. Nine to dinner. Read Ed. Rev. on China—and on the Dissolution.[5] A day on home & furnishing arrangements chiefly. Saw Kirby[R].

16. Th.

Marg. St 5 P.M. Wrote to Mr C. Butler[6] & draft.—Compton Newton & Co[7]—Sir C. Eastlake. Worked on Letters & papers. Nine to breakfast. Saw Mr J.W. Cowell—Sir Wm. Heathcote.—Rev. Mr Marshall (Ch Ch scheme).[8] Read Ed. Rev. on France & on Dilettanti Society.[9] Began reading on Tasso again with Willy and Agnes: and Virgil Æn I with Stephen: who is much come on.

17. Fr.

Wrote to T.T. Flynn—Sir J. Heron Maxwell[10]—R.W. Silk[11]—Mr H. Lees— J.N. Gladstone: & S. Herbert. Rode with Agnes. Saw Mr H. Raikes— Earl of Aberdeen—Provost of Eton—Duchess of Argyll—R. Phillimore— Read Bowring's Siam:[12] & Acct of Cheltenham Grammar School.[13] Tasso with W. & A. Virgil with S.

18. Sat.

Wrote to Col Mure—Sir C. Eastlake—H. Glynne—Rev. W. Parminter[14]— Rev. Mr Jones. Read Hansard's Deb. and Ed. Rev. on the Nature Library.[15] Tasso with W. & A.—Virgil with Stephy. Rode with Agnes. Saw Duke of Norfolk—F.R. Bonham—Mr Whitwell Elwin—Arthur Gordon—Col. Rowley. Worked at night on my proof sheets.

[1] See 2 Apr. 57.
[2] W. M. Leake, *On some disputed questions of ancient geography* (1857).
[3] Possibly *Historical record of the honourable East India Company's 1st Madras European regiment . . . by a staff officer* [J. G. Smith-Neill] (1843).
[4] E. R. Humphreys, Ll.D., educational pamphleteer; see 15 Feb. 56n.
[5] *Edinburgh Review*, cv. 517, 552 (April 1857).
[6] Charles Butler, of the City, sent extract from *The Globe*, 15 April 1857, reporting the reply to Gladstone by Sir James Hall at the Holywell meeting, 27 Mar. 57, denouncing diarist as a coward and mutineer for deserting *Palmerston. Gladstone's reply ('unequivocal slander') to Butler was printed as a broadsheet (Add MS 44387, f. 230).
[7] Unidentified.
[8] See 30 Jan. 57.
[9] *Edinburgh Review*, cv. 342, 493 (April 1857).
[10] Sir John Heron-Maxwell, 1808–85; 6th bart. 1844; contested, as Peelite, Devonport 1852, Greenwich 1859.
[11] Perhaps of Robert Silk and Sons, London coachmakers.
[12] J. *Bowring, *The kingdom and people of Siam*, 2v. (1857).
[13] Not found.
[14] William George Parminter; priest in France and Germany 1836–57; principal of Kingsbridge school, Devon, 1858.
[15] *Edinburgh Review*, cv. 360 (April 1857).

19. 1 S.E.

St Andrews & H.C. 11 a.m. St Paul's Kn[ightsbridge] 3 P.M. Stephy remained with me at St. A. *through* the service: & on the way home said 'I suppose they are not come from St James's' so little was he conscious of the length of the service. MS of [blank] in evg. Conv. with the elder children on the Ep. & Gospel. Read Simeon's Life (finished) Chalmers's do.[1] Recast the Eccl. bit of my Q.R. Art. in the proof.

20. M.

Finished working on my proofs. Rode with Stephy. Wrote to Dr. Humphrey's—Sir G. Grey—Dean Ramsay—Rev. C.H. Christie—Sig. Massari—A. Panizzi—Luke Woodward.[2] Saw Ld Abingdon[3]—Mr Grogan—Ld Aberdeen—and R. Phillimore. We had a dinner party: the ladies two to one: but it went off very well, as they were rather remarkable. It is worth recording that yesterday we saw people keeping off the sun in Piccadilly with an umbrella: at about 4 P.M. Read Remusat's Abelard[4]—Tittmann[5]—Tasso with W. & A. Virgil with S.

21. T.

Wrote to Chief Commr. Police[6]—Dr Rutherford[7]—T.T. Flynn (Coalwhippers)—Rev. Mr Bellairs and J.N.G. Saw Mr Elwin[8]—& went through the Article with him to shorten it. We cut out six pages. Saw A. Panizzi—Ld. Overstone—Sir D. Dundas—Saw Annan 27[R]. Dined for the first time at 'the Club'[9] a very good party. ½ an hour of La Figlia del Reggimento afterwards: the Piccolomini did not so very greatly strike me in what I saw.[10] Business & house arrangements. Tasso with W. & A. Virgil with Stephen.

Wednesday 22. Ap.

We went in the evening to the Princess's[11] to see Richard II; some good acting & wonderful spectacle. Worked on & settled my arbitration.[12] Busy mg. about arrangements for hanging the Murillo—lighting the Wilson & a purchase of fine china wh ought to be the last. Worked on papers. Read Ld Overstone on Decimal Coinage.[13] Wrote to Mr Willis—Rev. Mr Wood-

[1] See 18 Dec. 49.
[2] Luke Woodard, American evangelist.
[3] See 11 May 31.
[4] C. F. M. de Rémusat, *Abélard*, 2v. (1845).
[5] Probably C. C. Tittmann, *Meletemata sacra* (1816).
[6] Sir Richard *Mayne, 1796–1871; chief commissioner of police from 1850; K.C.B. 1851.
[7] George Shaw Rutherford, M.D., practiced in Devonshire Street.
[8] The *Quarterly's* editor.
[9] Dr. *Johnson's dining club, to which he had just been elected.
[10] Donizetti's opera.
[11] In Oxford Street, now demolished; managed by *Kean 1850–9; *Kean played Richard.
[12] For the G.N.R., in their demarcation dispute on routes in the Sheffield area; see C. H. Grinling, *History of the Great Northern Railway* (2nd ed. 1903), 160.
[13] S. J. *Loyd, Baron Overstone, *Decimal Association* (1857).

house[1]—Sec Royal Academy[2]—Mr J. Swift—Ld Overstone. Tasso with
W. & A. Virgil with S.

23. *Th.*

St James's 11¾–1½ for sermon & H.C. Ch Penity. Association. Wrote to
Rev. C. Onslow[3]—Speaker H. of Assembly of Newfdd.[4]—Mr J. Phillips.
Saw Mr Elwin—R. Phillimore—Mr Henry Smith. Twelve to breakfast.
Mr Elwin gave an excellent account of the new Wilson. Spent some time
in arranging 'objects' in the cases upstairs. Read Lord Overstone's Tracts
—Maclean's Hudson's Bay—Gerards Poems.[5] Saw R. Phillimore—fresh
from Court. Tasso & Virgil as usual.

24. *Fr.*

Wrote to Mr C. Buck (Hansard)[6]—Mr J. Hamilton—D. Maclean—
(stopped)—Bp of Argyll—Rev. Mr West—C. Butler. Ride with Agnes.
Saw Ld Overstone—Sir W. Farquhar. Arranging for the parties of next
week especially the arduous one of May 2 evg. when we (!) entertain the
Royal Academy. Read Q.R. on U.S. Slavery & Lord Overstone.[7] Dined
with the Goldsmith's Co. I sat by the Bp of L[ondon] whose conversation
is that of a serious minded man aiming to be comprehensive.

25. *St Mark. Sat.*

Wrote to Mr C. Kean[8]—C.C. Brooke[9]—Mr H. Smith—U.Sec. For. Off.[10]—
Mr J. W. Knott—Mrs T. Goalen—Mr J. W. Cowell. Water Colour (New)
Exhibition with Mrs Phillimore. Poor enough.[11] Tasso with W & A. Virgil
with Stephen: who spontaneously did a double lesson. Worked on papers
at home—& out shopping. Saw Hyason[12]—Lady Wenlock, also Jane
[Wortley], resp. her husband. Lady W. came to pay us a visit. C. gave a
child's Ball. Read Q.R. on Political Squibs—& on Persia.[13]

---

[1] Algernon Wodehouse, 1814–82; chaplain to duke of Northumberland; see 21 Aug. 57.
[2] John Prescott *Knight, 1803–81; secretary to Royal Academy 1848–73; see 15 Jan. 39.
[3] Charles Onslow, 1810–84; vicar of Holt from 1850.
[4] John Kent.
[5] G. Gerard, *Grace and remembrance! poems* (1856).
[6] Cornelius Buck, printer in Paternoster Row; printed *Hansard*.
[7] *Quarterly Review*, ci. 324 (April 1857).
[8] Charles John *Kean, 1811–68; at Eton with diarist; actor; see 22 Apr. 57.
[9] Charles C. Brooks of Lyall Place, London, ruined in a trust suit by the Mostyn family, requested help; Gladstone denounced that family's activities as 'highly discreditable' in Flintshire and re Brooks but could not help (Add MS 44387, f. 238).
[10] Sir Henry Thomas *Petty-Fitzmaurice, 1816–66; styled earl of Shelburne 1836; whig M.P. Calne 1847–56; foreign undersecretary 1856–8; chaired G.W. railway 1859–63; 4th marquis of Lansdowne 1863.
[11] New society of painters in watercolour, at 53 Pall Mall.
[12] Unidentified; a rescue case?
[13] *Quarterly Review*, ci. 394, 501 (April 1857), preceding his article on parliament (see 2 Apr. 57).

26. 2 S.E.

Hanover Chapel mg & Chapel Royal Evg. Sermon of the Parker series aloud in evg. Conv. with W. & S. on Br[itish] Reform[atio]n & with W. & S on Ep. & gospel. Wrote on rel. of Hom. to O.T. Scr.[1] Read Bp of Exeter's Pastoral Letter[2]—Chalmer's Life.

27. M.

Wrote to Jas. Watson—S.R. Glynne—Mr C. Kean—Rev. A.P. Stanley— Read Life of Mrs[*sic*] Bronte[3]—Neate on Capital Punishments.[4] Rode with Agnes. House arrangements and affairs. Saw B. Benjamin on extensions— Mr Walker—J. Griffiths on (O.F.)—Do *cum* Mr Cochrane—Sir John Lefevre. Tasso with W. & A. Virgil with S. Dined at Ld Overstone's— Saw Panizzi.

28. T.

Wrote to Archdeacon Grant—Rev. Mr D. Williams—Rev. Mr Gregory— Rev. Mr Barlow.[5] Tasso with W. & A. Virgil with S. Rode with Agnes. Worked on the Homeric Characters with a view to the Q.R.[6] Saw C. A. Wood—Mr Ellice—Mr G. Harcourt—Ld Stanhope—Mr Grogan—House arrangements—Read Life of Charlotte Bronte.

29. Wed.

Wrote to Jas. Watson—Dickson & Davenport[7]—Rev. Mr Elwin—Toulmin Smith—and J.W. Parker. Saw Sir F. Rogers (House)[8]—Sir J. Graham— Mr Grogan—J. Wilson Patten—Mr Walker. Finished preparations of my paper—& offered it to Q.R. Read life of Miss Bronte—C. had a large evening party—over at one. Tasso with W. & A.—Virgil with S.

30. Th. X.

Wrote to C. Butler—Mr H. Reeve—Scott & Co—Mrs Coleridge. Tasso with W. & A. Nine to breakfast. Saw Mr Kean—Mr Woodgate—Ld Aberdeen *cum* Sir J. Graham. Sir W. Heathcote—Scotts—Attended H. of C. 2–3 and again took my seat by Sir J. Graham.[9] Took Willy to see Rosa Bonheur's picture[10]—Sir W. Heathcote & S. Neville dined. Read Mure v.

---

[1] Section X of *Studies on Homer*, ii.
[2] H. *Phillpotts, *A pastoral letter to the clergy of the diocese* (1857).
[3] E. C. *Gaskell, *Life of Charlotte *Brontë*, 2v. (1857); the 1st two editions, published in spring 1857, were withdrawn on threat of legal action. She m. Rev. A. B. Nicholls a year before her death.
[4] C. *Neate, *Considerations on the punishment of death* (1857).
[5] T. W. Barlow; see 19 Feb. 53 and Hawn P.
[6] 'Homeric characters in and out of Homer', *Quarterly Review*, cii. 204 (July 1857).
[7] London auctioneers.
[8] F. *Rogers became 8th bart. in 1851 (see 26 May 27).
[9] Again sitting on the ministerial side below the gangway: 'the most nearly one of pure neutrality for ex-Ministers . . . traditionally the place of men who, having been out of office, may be either practically connected with, or wholly dissociated from the existing Government' (to Herbert, 17 April 1857, Stanmore, ii. 96).
[10] 'The horse fair' by Rosa Bonheur, 1822–99, French artist; much exhibited before being sold to U.S.A.

Grote.[1]—Neate on Capital Punishment—Humphrey's In & Out.[2]—
Burke & Laurence Corresp.[3] Saw Griffiths: a singular case[R]. The boys
returned to Eton.

Friday May One SS. Phil. & James.

Wrote to Rev. Mr Elwin—Mr W.A. Ross[4]—Mr Whitty—Mr C. Butler—
Rector of Exeter Coll. Saw Mr J. Griffiths—Mr W. Forbes—Sir C. Eastlake.
Rode with Agnes. Royal Academy private view 10½–3: & again after 4.
Read Burke & Lawr. Corresp.—Notice prefixed to S. Simon.[5] Spoke to
Agnes about a fit of remissness. She took it as I could wish.

2. Sat. X.

Wrote to Mr Madot[6]—Very Rev. Mr Torry—Rev. Mr Hinton.[7] Visited
French Exhibition[8]—when I fell in with Dss. of Sutherland an admirable
companion in such scenes. Then went with C. to the opening of the Museum
Reading Room[9]: where I had a profitable conversation with Sir H. Rawlinson.[10] Then to the Academy where I saw Sir C. Eastlake as well as Mr
Boxall[11] & others & bought Mr Madot's picture.[12] Rode—alone; by C.s
orders. Dined with Mrs Talbot's; we discussed poor Jas. Wortley's case.
Saw Bp of Oxford—Mr Hubbard—Mr Saundars. Saw Griffiths[R]: senza
gran pro[fito].[13] Read Arnold's Poems[14]—Fraser's Magazine (May).[15]

3. 3 S.E.

Chapel Royal mg; & St. A. Wells St aft. Read MS of 1840 aloud. Wrote to
Mr Stooks—Mr Joyce—Mr F.S. Williams[16]—Scott & Co. Read Chalmer's
Life—Hervey[17] and Wesley. Sims Williams's Thoughts &c. Joyce's[18] &
other Sermons—Rationale of Justifn. by Faith.[19]

---

[1] See 2 Aug. 51.
[2] Untraced pamphlet by E. R. Humphreys; see 15 Apr. 57.
[3] *The epistolary correspondence of the Rt. Hon. Edmund *Burke and Dr. French
Laurence* (1827).
[4] William Andrew Ross, colonial secretary of the Gold Coast; see Add MS 44387,
f. 258.
[5] *Historical works of St. Simon of Durham*, ed. and tr. J. Stevenson (1855).
[6] Adolphus M. Madot, d. 1861; figure painter.
[7] Zebulon Wright Hinton; Trinity, Dublin; vicar of Feckenham, 1855.
[8] Of paintings.   [9] *Panizzi's triumph.
[10] Sir Henry Creswicke *Rawlinson, 1810–95; in India; K.C.B. 1856; liberal M.P.
Reigate 1858–9, Frome 1865–8; cr. bart. 1891.
[11] (Sir) William *Boxall, 1800–79; portrait painter; directed National Gallery 1865–74;
kt. 1871.
[12] A. M. Madot, 'Slender's wooing of Anne Page', inspired by *The merry wives of
Windsor*; not noticed by *Ruskin in his 'Notes' (1857).
[13] 'without much success'.
[14] M. *Arnold, *Poems* (1856).   [15] *Fraser's Magazine*, lx (May 1857).
[16] Frederick Sims Williams, 1811?–63; barrister; wrote 'Thoughts on the doctrine of
eternal punishments' (1857); on J. F. D. *Maurice.
[17] J. *Hervey, *Eleven letters . . . to . . . John *Wesley* (1765).
[18] J. W. Joyce, 'The duty of the civil power to promote the faith of the National
Church' (1857).
[19] See 10 Apr. 57.

4. *M.*

Wrote to Rev. A. Butler[1]—D. Williams—Mr Howe—Mr Marshall—Scotts
—H. Lees—Ld Grosvenor[2]—J. Griffiths—W. Johnson. Saw Mr Read
(resp pictures)[3]—Mr G. Glyn—Messrs. Overend. Took the Oaths at H. of
C. Dined with Mrs Tyler. Read Inland Rev. Report[4]—Libretto of the
Traviata (wh leaves me with no room for doubt)[5]—Burke & Lawrence
Correspe.—and General Gardiner's Pamphlet.[6]

5. *T. X.*

Wrote to Sir D. Dundas—Sir John Young—E.R. Humphreys—Mr Bow-
man—Provost of Eton—Mr Giraud[7]—Sir H. Rawlinson—Mrs Wilkinson[8]
—J. Gilbertson[9]—Messrs. Kelly. Saw Mr G. Christie—Mr Knight R.A.—
B. Benjamin—R. Palmer (Homer)—J. R. Godley (War Dept). Tasso with
Agnes—Read Herbert's Nimrod[10]—Lady Westmeath's Statement[11]—
Burke & Laurence Corresp. (finished)—Erasmus in Biogr. Dict.[12] R.
Phillimore's party in evg. Saw Milligan: lamentable[R].

6. *Wed.*

Wrote to Mr Waring—Rev. O. Gordon—Hon. Mrs Primrose[13]—Count
Montalembert—Mr H. Wreford[14]—Sig. Terenzio Sacchi—U.Sec. For.
Affairs. Rode the young horse. Dined with Sir James Hogg. Rode the
young horse at 11: then to Christie's but could learn nothing about Read.—
thence to Lond. Libr. to study[15] 'graphic'[16]—then to Academy where I
could not find a trace of my Crome Picture.[17] Saw Mr C. Kean—Sir S.
Northcote—Sir T. Gladstone—Mr C. Pressly—Ld Grey. Read Ld Over-

---

[1] Alfred Stokes Butler; licenciate; perpetual curate of Trinity, Penn Street; low
churchman.
[2] Hugh Lupus *Grosvenor, 1825–99; liberal M.P. Chester 1847–69, Adullamite 1866;
3rd marquis of Westminster 1869, cr. duke 1874; unionist; dominant political influence
in Cheshire and Flintshire. See Add MS 44337.
[3] John Read, auctioneer in Farringdon Street; he offered 76 guineas for a Wilson, a
Rubens and two Thiers.
[4] First report of the commissioners: *PP* 1857, 1st session, iv. 65.
[5] F. M. Piave's libretto (published 1856) of Verdi's opera about a prostitute, first given
in London 1856.
[6] R. W. *Gardiner, 'Question of legislative military responsibility' (1857).
[7] Henry Arthur Giraud, 1818?–79; chaplain to King's college hospital; see 25 June 57.
[8] Unidentified.
[9] Probably J. D. Gilbertson, published his *Poems* (1856).
[10] A. *Herbert, *Nimrod; a discourse upon certain passages of history and fable* (1826).
[11] Obtained a divorce in 1827 from her husband on grounds of his adultery; see 'A
narrative of the case of the marchioness of Westmeath' (1857); a case of importance for
the 1857 Divorce Bill.
[12] Probably the entry in A. Chalmers, *General biographical dictionary* (1810).
[13] Frederica Sophia, *née* Anson, m. 1838 B. F. Primrose and d. 1867.
[14] Henry Wreford 1806–92; Neapolitan correspondent of *The Times* from 1840; had
sent documents on imprisonment of Neapolitan aristocrats; see Add MS 44387, f. 52.
[15] 'the' deleted.
[16] Perhaps a meeting of the Graphic Society; see 14 Feb. 49.
[17] Not recorded in the Academy's 1857 Catalogue.

stone—M. Arnold's Poems—Stowe Catalogue[1]—Dubl. Rev on the Union[2]
—New Quarterly on Parlt. &c.[3] Tasso with Agnes.

7. *Th. X.*

Wrote to Mr Hare—Mr Lopes[4]—J. Pearson[5]—Mrs Austin—Mrs Wilkinson
—Rev. Mr Edouart—Shannon—Berkerley. Worked on Homer as to
Numbers[6]—Fifteen to breakfast: at two tables. Saw Sir H. Rawlinson
resp. Achaeans & Pelasgians. H. of C. $4\frac{1}{2}$–$6\frac{3}{4}$. Parochial: as Sir J. Graham
observed.[7] Read Ld Overstone—Miss Bronte's Life—Various inquiries: &
saw No 65[R]. Tasso with Agnes.

I knew one who was accustomed to comfort himself with the reflection that his
heart freely desired the coming of the kingdom of the Christ and was at all times
more than willing that this visible frame should pass into the new heavens & the
new earth. He thought that this desire, felt in himself, was a ground & stay of
hope.

But is it justly so regarded? Is it much more than the saying of Balaam 'Let
me die the death of the righteous & let my last end be like his.'[8] Probably Balaam
did not mean to stipulate for an intermediate period of ungodly living: but
sought to express his desire to be in harmony with the will of God, and to pass
into a state where that harmony, which he felt did not then exist within him,
would be established, firm & fast.

It seems we are not willing to give God the thing that he desires of us but we
seek to give him some other thing instead of us.

He says to us, live here, where you are; walk onwards and upwards through
the world; ignore the foes before you, the pitfalls around you, the traitors within
you; hold fast the faith and a good conscience; my grace is sufficient for you.

We reply, this is too much, we cannot but slip this way and that, the flesh
weighs us down to one attachment & another, the world trips us up, the devil
scares us from the resolution of tone & temper which is needed in order to overcome. We therefore shuffle out of duty the one thing needful and we think to
excuse ourselves by finding that our deceitful manner professes readiness to
part in one mass with what it will not surrender in detail. It seeks to palm upon
us that which we cannot test, but the test which God applies daily and hourly it
refuses.

This is Balaam, Balaam, Balaam.[9]

8. *Fr.*

Wrote to A.B. Cochrane—Mr Read—J. Griffiths—W. Johnson—A.T.
Courroux[10]—A.A. Watts. Saw one & advised Australia[R]. Attended V.

[1] *The Stowe Catalogue; priced and annotated by H. R. Forster* (1848).
[2] *Dublin Review*, xlii 95 (March 1857); on new ultra Anglo-Catholic weekly *The Union*,
see 24 May 57.
[3] *New Quarterly Review*, vi. 260 (April 1857).
[4] Henry Charles *Lopes, 1828–99; tory M.P. Launceston 1868–74, Frome 1874–6;
judge 1876; cr. Baron Ludlow 1897.
[5] Of the family firm in Liverpool; in correspondence on church building, later on
paper duties (Hawn P).
[6] *Studies on Homer*, iii. 425.   [7] Queen's Speech: *H* cxlv. 15.
[8] Numbers xxiii. 10.   [9] Lambeth MSS; dated 7 May 1857.
[10] Of Brussels; Hawn P.

Chancellor Kindersley's Court to hear the Succession Duty agreed: but
heard only other cases.[1] Saw Mr Grogan. Dined with the Jameses: discussion on colour.[2] Read Life of Charl. Bronte. Ride with Agnes—Tasso
with Agnes—Picture-hunting (at Read's).

9. Sat.

Wrote to Jas. Watson—W. Forsyth[3]—H. Lees—W. Grogan. Revised my
paper on colour in Homer. Dined with Lady Molesworth. Rode with Agnes.
Tasso with Agnes. Saw Mr Hodgson—Mr Grogan—Mr Read. Count
Bernstorff (at dinner)—Ld Aberdeen—Mr Baillie Cochrane. Read Life of
Charlotte Bronte—Baumgarten's Letter to Lord Shaftesbury.[4]

10. 4. S.E.

St Martins H.C. 8½ a.m. Chapel Royal aft. Kept the House between. MS
of 1844 aloud in evg. Saw Bp of Oxford—Mr Oswald. Read Chalmer's Life
—Theron & Aspasio.[5]—Jerusalem Bishopric.[6]

11. M.

Wrote to Willy—Alex Goalen—Mr Cochrane (& draft)—Rev. Mr Greswell
—Brewster—R.C. Lowe[7]—E. Stuart.[8] Saw Mr J. Griffiths—S. Herbert.
Busy hanging pictures: and making arrangements for the evening. Rode
with Agnes. Tasso with her. Read Miss Bronte (finished I). Fourteen to
dinner & a party afterwards with music.

12. T.

Wrote to Mr W. Walker—Rev. Mr Mayow—Rev. Mr Owen. Went to the
Princess's Theatre when Mr Kean took me over the whole establishment
at noon. We had a long conversation on the question of Government sub-
vention to the Drama.[9] Saw Scotts. Dined with the Herberts & met
Graham only; as if Peelism were not dead. Ride with Agnes: & we finished
Canto X of the Jerusalem. Read Duncan on Currency[10]—Herbert's Nimrod
—The Staff Officer.[11] Missed seeing Griffiths (18)[R].

[1] Case of *Innes* v. *Mitchell*, testing the 1853 Succession Duty Act; judgment was
reserved, *The Times*, 9 May 1857, 10e.
[2] In Homer; see next day and *Studies on Homer*, iii. 457.
[3] Probably William *Forsyth, 1812–99; ed. *Annual Register* 1842–68; tory M.P.
Marylebone 1874–80: later a correspondent (Hawn P).
[4] M. Baumgarten, *Letter to the Earl of Shaftesbury on the oppression of the Christians
in the Duchy of Sleswick by the Danish government* (1857).
[5] *Letters on Theron and Aspasio* (1803).
[6] See 8 Apr. 45?
[7] sc. R. T. Lowe; see 6 May 52.
[8] Edward Stuart, 1821–77; founder and ritualist vicar of St. Mary Magdalen, St.
Pancras, from 1852.
[9] Nothing came of this.
[10] J. Duncan, *The principles of money demonstrated, and bullionist fallacies refuted*
(1849).
[11] See 14 Apr. 57.

13. *Wed.* X.

Wrcte to J.E. Reade[1]—Mrs Wilkinson—Dr Duke[2]—Bp of Oxford—Dr Moffatt—Rev. Mr Wayte—Mr G. Smith. Worked on accounts. Rode with Agnes. Dined with the Hubbards. Saw D. Acland—F.R. Bonham—Bp of Salisbury—Mr G. Richmond, who went over my pictures with me. Ld Lyndhurst—Mr Sandars (George St)[3]—Mr Cowell—Ld Hardwicke—D. of Newcastle. Lady Hardwicke's.[4] Music in evg. Read Inl. Rev. Report[5]— Saw one[R].

14. *Th.*

Wrote to D. of Newcastle—Mr W. Johnson—J.R.C. Thomson[6]—Robn. G —Scotts. Worked on papers relating to my property & debts. Rode with Agnes—A breakfast party. Saw Mr Goldwin Smith (resp. religious examn. at Oxford)[7]—Ld Goderich (Hudson's Bay)—Mr Lake—B. Porter (settled to sell the young horse)—Missed Kirby[R]. An early dinner & went to the Opera (Ld Ward's box) when the Lucia was beautifully sung & acted.[8] Miss Wortley[9] was of our party: with whom it is a privilege to converse. Agnes too. We came home to tea by eleven. Read Ld Overstone—The Staff Officer.

15. *Fr.* X.

Wrote to Mrs Austin—J.N.G.—Rev. R. Greswell—Sir G. Grey—Mr Cochrane—Col. Gordon—Rev. O. Gordon. Read Ld Overstone—Miss Bronte. Saw Griffiths: with better hope[R]. Saw[W.] Grogan—& agreed to let the house for 6 weeks at 100 guineas per week. Went to Christie's. Saw Scotts.
Bank Commn.—Hudson's Bay Commn. and House 2–7.[10]

16. *Sat.*

Wrote to Mr W. Lyon[11]—C.E. Walker[12]—Peter Scott[13] & Copy. Saw Ld Grey—Ld Overstone—Mr Christie—Baron Marochetti. Rode with Agnes. Music practice 11–1. In the evening behind the scenes at the Princess's (Richard II) 8–11. At Christie's Sale 2–3½. Read Ld Overstone—Miss Bronte.

[1] John Edmund *Reade, 1800–70; novelist and poet; wrote epics on Italy; requested diarist's views on his writings, see Add MS 44387, f. 278.
[2] Probably Thomas Oliver Duke, London surgeon.
[3] i.e. the dentist (see 6 Oct. 53), whose consulting room was there.
[4] Susan, da. of 1st earl of Ravensworth, m. 1833 4th earl of Hardwicke and d. 1886.
[5] See 4 May 57.
[6] Secretary of Hyde Park College in Westbourne Terrace.
[7] The row about the proposed (and rejected) division of Greats into literature and moral philosophy; see Ward, 219–20.
[8] *Lucia di Lammermoor*, at Her Majesty's.
[9] Cicely Susan, 1835–1915, da. of 2nd Baron Wharncliffe, m. 1865 Henry John Montagu-Douglas-Scott, 1832–1905, tory M.P. Selkirkshire 1861–8, S. Hampshire 1868–84, cr. Baron Montagu of Beaulieu 1885.
[10] See 18 Feb. 57.   [11] See, perhaps, 27 Feb. 43.
[12] Charles Edward Walker, unbeneficed priest; lived in London.
[13] Peter Scott wrote attacking Gladstone's pandering to his 'half Popish constituency', Add MS 44387, f. 284.

17. 5 S.E.

St James's H.C. mg—Westmr. Abbey aftn. Armstrong sermon[1] in evg. Read Alexander to Skinner[2]—Dr Steere's Account of Brotherhoods[3]— D Robertson's Sermon.[4] Wrote to Mr H.J. Newman[5]—The Primate of Ireland (& draft)[6]—J. Milligan—R. Kirby[7]—Miss Griffiths.[8] Saw S. Herbert—R. Cavendish—Aunt J.

18. M.

Wrote to W.G. Anderson—J. Griffiths—A.B. Cochrane (& copy)—Jas. Shank[9]—J. Pickering.[10] Saw Bp of Salisbury—Sir W. Heathcote—Mr Hodgson. Rode with Agnes. Read Mr Weguelin's Evidence & worked on Currency papers.[11]—Read Miss Bronte's Life. Sat to Marochetti for my Bust at C.s desire but I confess with a bad conscience:[12] I cannot desire that an image of me should remain behind me & far less that they should be multiplied.

19. T.

Read Miss Bronte. Worked on Currency Papers—At the Committee 12–3½; examining Mr Weguelin.[13] Saw Mr Wilson—Dss. of Argyll—Mr Anderson— Sir J. Graham—Bp of Oxford—Mr J. W. Patten—At Christie's I saw Redpath's 'objects': highly suggestive.[14] Music practice at 4. H. of C. 5½–7.[15] Dined with Mrs Speirs[16]—C.s music party in evg: I joined in the Choruses sustained by Sir J. Harington & Campana.[17]

20. Wed.

Wrote to Mr. G. Guthrie[18]—Rev. Mr Hewett—Rev. Mr Ansted—Provost of Oriel—Willy—Roundell Palmer—Mr Gray—Mrs Elden. Saw Sir W.

[1] J. *Armstrong, *Parochial sermons* (1854).

[2] J. Alexander, *Letter to Bp. *Skinner on . . . the Scottish Communion office* (1857).

[3] E. *Steere, *An historical sketch of the English brotherhoods which existed at the beginning of the eighteenth century* (1856).

[4] D. Robertson, 'Let all things be done decently and in order. A sermon' [on 1 Cor. xiv. 40] (1857).

[5] Henry Joseph Newman, secretary of Associate Institution for Improving & Enforcing the Laws for the Protection of Women.

[6] i.e. *Beresford.

[7] Richard Heighway Kirby, 1817–1897; vicar of Haverthwaite from 1853.

[8] Perhaps the rescue case; see 6 July 57.

[9] Provision merchant in Toxteth Park.

[10] Perhaps John Pickering, Chester auctioneer.

[11] Weguelin gave the first of five days evidence to the bank cttee. on 3 March 1857: *PP* 1857, 2nd session, x part 1, 13. See next day.

[12] Unlike many of *Marochetti's busts, not exhibited at the Academy; probably for the Mansionhouse, destroyed by German bombs 1940.

[13] Very hostile cross-examination on the bank's role: copy in Add MS 44587, f. 115; *PP* 1857, 2nd session, x part 1, 28.

[14] Sale of pictures and objects of Leopold Redpath, 1813–80?, insurance broker and bankrupt; Christie's catalogue lists nothing obviously 'suggestive'.

[15] Ireland: *H* cxlv. 540.

[16] i.e. Mrs. E. S. Speirs of Elderslie; see 17 Aug. 53.

[17] Fabio Campana, see 20 Sept. 54n.

[18] Wrote 'A safe, effective and simple reform of currency' (1857).

Heathcote—Ld Harrowby—Bps Oxford & Salisbury—Mr E. Hamilton.[1]
Visited the Govn. Offices Designs. H. of C. 3–5 conference with Univ.
Members on the Marriage Bill.[2] Sat(2d) to Marochetti—who works very
rapidly & gives me advice about art all the time. Dined with Mr Harcourt.
Read Miss Bronte—Freeport on Hudson's Bay.[3] Rode with Agnes.

21. Thurs. Ascension Day.

St James's & H.C. 11–1½. Sat to Marochetti at Brompton (3°)—an hour &
a half. Read Miss Bronte finished—Dined at Sir F. Kelly's. Saw the
Brazilian Minr.[4]—A.B. Hope—Worked on Ch. Rate Draft.[5] Wrote to Sir
Geo Grey—Mr Freshfield—Mr J.W. Cunningham.

22. Fr.

Wrote to . . . Mr Toulmin Smith—Ven. Archdn. Williams—Rev. C. Miller[6]
—Ld Ingestre[7]—Bp of St Asaph—[of] Oxford—Sir T.G.—J.J. Ffoulkes[8]—
J.N.G.—Mr Greswell—E. Hamilton—Dr Jelf. Read Mem on Financial
Controul[9]—Sat (4°) to Marochetti. Dined at Sir Geo Clerk's. Bank Com-
mittee 1–3¼. H. of C. 4½–7¼.[10]

23. Sat.

Wrote to Jas. Watson—A.B. Cochrane. Began to prepare for leaving the
house & packed books for Hawarden. Sat (5°) Marochetti: who showed us
beautiful things & who curiously combines realism with powerful imagination. Br. Museum 12½–2. Calls. Saw Ld Monteagle—Lady Lyttelton—
Dined with the Lefevres—Read.

24 S. aft. Ascension.

St James's mg. Marg. Chapel Evg. Conv. with Agnes. Read Dunlop on
Confessions[11]—Britton on Art XXIX Hist.[12] Drummond's Fate of Xtendom[13]

---

[1] i.e. E. W. T. Hamilton, the bp. of Salisbury's brother; see 2 June 34.
[2] The Divorce and Matrimonial Causes Bill, to which Gladstone was violently opposed,
was introduced on 11 May in the Lords; see above, v. xxv, xlvii, lxv.
[3] A. Freeport [pseud.] 'The case of the Hudson's Bay Company, in a letter to Lord
Palmerston' (1857).
[4] F. I. de Carvalho Moreira.
[5] See 24 May 57?
[6] See 30 Oct. 31.
[7] Charles John Chetwynd Talbot, 1830–77; styled Viscount Ingestre 1849–68; 19th
earl of Shrewsbury 1868; tory M.P. Stafford 1857–9, Staffordshire 1859–65, Stamford
1868.
[8] Of Mold, a subscriber to *Glynne's election fund.
[9] Of the banks, printed for the select cttee.: Add MS 44587, f. 129.
[10] Fraudulent Trustees Bill: H cxlv. 673.
[11] W. Dunlop, The Uses of Creeds and Confessions of Faith (1857).
[12] T. H. Britton, An examination of the principal facts and arguments advanced by Dr.
Bayford and the Rt. Hon. Dr. Lushington . . . (1857).
[13] See 16 May 55.

—The *Observateur Catholique* & the Union: both of them are remarkable as signs[1]—Mr Lake's Sermon.[2] Saw Mr Geo. Richmond—Sir W. & Lady James. Wrote Mem. on Seaforth Church.[3]

25. M. X.

Wrote to Rev Mr Kemp[4]—Mr G. Bramwell[5]—Rev. R. Wood[6]—Mr W. Grogan—Rev. Mr Ainslie—F.R. Bonham—Col. Leake[7]—Rev. O. Gordon. Rode with Agnes. Visited the Hunterian Museum[8] with Prof. Quekett & Mr Hodgson.[9] Saw Sir Thos. G.—Mr Hodgson—Rev. C. Miller—Sir B. Brodie—Rev. W. Elwin. Saw Lovell[R]. Read Nimrod. Dined at Mr Murray's: a most agreeable party. Hanging pictures, packing & making domestic arrangements.

26. T. X.

Wrote to Mr Read—H. Cole—T.G.—J.N.G.—Rode with Mazie. Saw Sir J. Lefevre—Ld Wenlock—Mr Greene—Mr Walford[10]—Mr W. Patten—Dr Waagen[11]—Lady Peel—Ld Overstone. Saw two[R]. Thirteen to breakfast. Dr W[aagen] went over the pictures &c. Dined with Wilson Patten. Read Letter to Gen. Assembly.[12] Nimrod. Attended Mr Lacaita's Lecture on Tasso.[13]

27. Wed.

Wrote to Ld Wenlock—Sir J. Lefevre—E. Lovell[R]—A. Williams—J.N.G. —Willy. Working in prepn. for departure. B. Museum Committee at 1. Then to St. Paul's School at $2\frac{1}{4}$.[14] Mercers dinner at 6—where I had to speak for H. of C.[15] Failed to see Lovell[R]. Saw Mr Walpole.

[1] The *Observateur* strongly opposed ultramontanism; for *The Union* see 6 May 57n.
[2] W. C. *Lake, 'Humility and love, the law and life of christianity: a sermon' (1856); on Rom. xii. 10.
[3] Quarrel over pew-rents: patronage had passed to the vicar (Add MS 44587, f. 135).
[4] Probably George Kemp, d.? 1880; rector of St. Alphage's, London Wall, 1856–79.
[5] George Bramwell, involved in the Radcliffe Trust; see Add MS 44532, f. 49.
[6] Richard Wood, d. 1880; fellow of St. John's, Oxford, 1828, vicar of Christ Church, Paddington, 1855–79.
[7] William Martin *Leake, 1777–1860; surveyed Levant 1800–7; collected Greek vases, coins, etc.
[8] In the royal college of surgeons in Lincoln's Fields.
[9] i.e. Joseph *Hodgson and John Thomas Quekett, 1815–61; histologist and conservator of the museum from 1856.
[10] Edward *Walford, 1823–97; priest 1846, became Roman catholic; genealogist and biographer; had requested biographical details: Add MS 44387, f. 318.
[11] Gustav Friedrich Waagen, 1794–1868; buyer abroad for the National Gallery; catalogued British art collections.
[12] 'A letter to the members of the General Assembly of the established Church of Scotland. By a heritor and vestryman of the Scottish episcopal Church' (1857).
[13] See Lacaita, 81.
[14] *The Times*, 28 May 57, 7e.
[15] No report found.

28. Th.

Wrote to Mrs Jas. Gladstone[1]—E. Lovell[R]—Rev. Mr Ainslie—F. Orsini[2]—Mr H. Raikes—J. S. Bankes[3]—Minr. of Ch.Ch.[4] Hudson's Bay Comm. 12–3½. H. of C. 4½–7.[5] Saw Ld Blandford—Ld Goderich—Sir J. Graham—S. Herbert—Sir F. Doyle—Duke of Argyll—W. Grogan. Travelling arrangements &c. Dined at Ld Aberdeen's.

29. Fr. ♄. X.

Wrote to Mr Heckley[6]—Mr Field[7]—Major Larkins[8]—Mr J. Griffiths— Dr Moffatt—Sir Geo. Grey. Continued & finished packing & went off about 11 a.m. Saw Sig. F. Orsini—Sir J. Graham—Mr Mills M.P.—Sir A. Elton— Sir G.C. Lewis—(small [bank] notes). Saw Lovell: good is there, but I was so half-hearted[R]. Dined with S. Herbert. H. of C. 4½–7½.[9] Read the Comet pamphlet.[10] Currency Commee. 12½–3.

30. Sat. [Oxford]

Wrote to Rev. Mr Stooks—Ld Goderich—Sir S. Scott & Co. Off to Oxford at 2 P.M. C. came in evg: Willy was already there. Saw Mr Hampton— Earl of Aberdeen—Duchess of Sutherland—Scotts—Mrs Wadd—Sir W. Heathcote—Mr Lygon. Dinner & evening party at Mr Greswell's. Attended Exhibn. of Women-Painters.[11] Read Book (lent by Dr Jacobson) on Homeric Medicine & Surgery.[12]

31. Whits[unday].

Ch.Ch. & H.C. mg.—Univ. sermon 10.30—Worcester Chapel 5.P.M. Went to Summertown[13] to see Mrs Goalen.[14] Dined at All Souls—Saw Sir W.H[eathcote]—Provost of Oriel. Read Melbourne Synod[15]—Letters to V.C. on Study of Theology.[16]

[1] Helen, née Monteath, wife of James Gladstone, see 9 Mar. 57.

[2] Felice Orsini, 1819–58; Italian revolutionary; with Mazzini in London 1853–4; escaped from Mantua prison 1856, again in England, where he became a popular lecturer on Italy and planned his assassination of Napoleon III with bombs made in Birmingham; its failure in January 1858 led to his execution, French anti-British outcries and *Palmerston's resignation.

[3] John Scott Bankes, 1826–94; of Soughton Hall, Flintshire; high sheriff of Flintshire 1869.

[4] Probably C. W. Page, incumbent of Christ Church, Broadway.

[5] Brazil: *H* cxlv. 932.

[6] Unidentified.

[7] G. W. Field sent suggestions on the Bank of England Charter; Hawn P.

[8] W. H. Larkins, retired as lieut. col. in Indian army; doubtless of the related family (see 22 Aug. 25).

[9] Scottish lunatics: *H* cxlv. 1020.

[10] J. Bedford, 'The great comet now rapidly approaching, will it strike the earth?' (1851).

[11] Society of female artists' exhibition at their gallery in Oxford Street.

[12] Probably C. V. Daremberg, *Collection des médicins grecs et latins*, 7v. (1851–79).

[13] Now part of north Oxford.

[14] See 26 Mar. 56.

[15] *Proceedings of the first Church of England Synod for the diocese of Melbourne*, ed. R. Perry (1857).

[16] Liberal attempts to establish a theology school at Oxford produced a spate of pamphlets; see Ward, 249.

Oxford Monday June One 57.

Wrote to Duchess of Sutherland—Bp of Salisbury—Egerton Harcourt. 11½–4½ Sir W. Heathcote & I made our usual official circuit under the guidance of the Provost of Oriel & Warden of All Souls.[1] We saw the Exeter & St John's Libraries by the way. We dined at the V. Chancellor's, & Willy was admitted in the evg. Read Keble's Praelectiones[2]—Melbourne Synod (finished). Univ. Sermon at 10.30.

2. T.

Wrote to Mr G. Sheffield[3]—Sir G. Grey—Mr G. Marshall—W. Walker[4]— Rev. G.H. Forbes—J. Griffiths. Meeting in the [Sheldonian] Theatre & prepns. 12½–5. Dinner at Exeter 5½. Spoke at both.[5] Evening party at Mr Woollcombe's. Saw Junior Proctor[6]—Master of Balliol[7]—Rev. Mr Marriott. Read Keble's Praelectiones.

3. Wed.

(N[ew] C[ollege] Chapel 4.P.M.). Wrote to D[uche]ss Sutherland—Mr Tweed—W. Hampton. At ten we went to see the [Ashmolean] Museum: the Bodleian at 11: the Radcliffe observy. at 12. At one to Luncheon in Ch.Ch. Common Room when I spoke. Willy was present & honourably mentioned. Then to the Museum there.[8] Then to see V.C. resp. Theolog. Examn.[9] New College Chapel 4.A.M.[sic]. Dined with the Prov. of Oriel. Saw Sir W. Heathcote. Rev. Mr Hobhouse. Rev. Dr Cardwell. Read S. Hawtrey on his School.[10]

4. Th. [Cliveden]

Off by early train to Eton. Breakf. with the Provost. Saw his Gallery— Saw Mr W. Johnson—Rev. S. Hawtrey—Mr Twisleton. Attended the Speeches: then with W. & S. to Cliveden.[11] We all came down in the evening to Surley Hall & the fireworks. Read [blank] v. Bryant[12]—

5. Fr. [Salisbury]

Wrote to E. Badeley—Miss Rees.[13] Read Ch. Eng. Monthly Review[14]— —Keble's Praelectiones—Tract on Confirmn.[15]—Badeley on Divorce.[16] We

[1] i.e. E. *Hawkins and L. Sneyd.
[2] J. *Keble, *De poeticae vi medica; praelectiones academicae Oxonii habitae*, 2v. (1844); quoted in *Studies on Homer*, iii. 379; the subject of his *Quarterly* article, 27 Apr. 57.
[3] George Sheffield, 1836–98; minor diplomat 1859–87.
[4] The engraver; see 30 Jan. 44.
[5] One of the speeches, to the Diocesan Spiritual Help Society, was published.
[6] W. *Ince.   [7] Robert *Scott.
[8] Dr. *Lee's Gallery; now part of the senior common room.
[9] Probably an attempt to improve the voluntary theological examination; see Ward, 249.
[10] S. T. Hawtrey, 'A letter containing an account of St. Mark's School' (1857).
[11] 3 miles NE. of Maidenhead; then owned by the duke of Sutherland, who built the present house; see 15 June 48.
[12] Untraced.
[13] Probably da. of Mrs. Edward Rees of Pembroke Square, London.
[14] *Church of England monthly review*, ii. 385 (June 1857).
[15] A. F., *Confirmation according to Scripture* (1857).
[16] [E. L. Badeley], 'Considerations on divorce a vinculo matrimonii, in connexion with holy scripture' (1857).

staid with the Duchess [of Sutherland] till the aftn: drove to Dropmore:
left Maidenhead 4.30: picked up Agnes at Reading: reached Salisbury at
8 & found the Bp. in the midst of his hallowed work & with his friends &
Chaplains round him.

6. Sat.

Conv. with Agnes in mg. Cathedral 10 a.m. The Confirmation of Agnes
then took place in the Bps Chapel: with that of two other young persons.
The Bp gave a short pointed & forcible address. We had also evg prayers
in the Chapel. Walk with the Bp & Mr [Henry] Drury. Read Fisher on
Liturgical Purity[1]—Keble's Praelectiones—Cosin's Arg. on Divorce.[2]

7. Trin. S.

At 8 C. & I went with our dear Agnes to early Communion. So this great
step onwards has been made as we trust most favorably. Morning service
& Ordination at 10½. Afternoon(for Sermon) 3¾. Evening service in the
Chapel at 8 P.M. All three sermons remarkable, two of them very parti-
cularly. Read Fisher—Pecul. of Scots Episc. Ch.[3]—Pouget Inst. Cath. on
Marriage.[4]

8. [Cuddesdon].

Chapel Prayers at 9: a conference with the Bishop, & off at 11.15 for
Oxford. There we dispatched Agnes to Hawarden; & after some business
went off to Cuddesden Palace. Here we went over the Diocesan College &
Church & found a large & congenial party. Saw R. Phillimore (resp Bills
&c)—Mr Lydden of the College[5]—Mr Butler of Wantage[6]—Mr Lloyd
(Proctor)[7]—Archdn. Bickersteth—The Bishop—Chapel prayers at nt.
Read Letter to V.C. on Theol. Study.[8] Wrote to W. Hampton—Bp of
Salisbury.

9. T.

Prayers in Chapel at 9 a.m. and in evg. Church 11-2¼: the Anniversary[9]
& a large & solemn Communion.

---

[1] J. C. Fisher 'Liturgical purity, our rightful inheritance' (1857).
[2] J. *Cosin, 'Argument proving that adultery works a dissolution of the marriage',
Works, iv. 489 (1847–55).
[3] Justitia [J. Miller], *Peculiarities of the Scottish Episcopal Church* (1847).
[4] F. A. Pouget, *Institutiones Catholicae* (1725, English tr. 1851).
[5] Henry Parry *Liddon, 1829–90; tractarian vice-principal of Cuddesdon 1854–9, of
St. Edmund Hall 1859; canon of St. Paul's 1870; biographer of *Pusey; see Add MS
44237.
[6] William John *Butler, 1818–94; Trinity, Cambridge; vicar of Wantage 1846–80;
founded St. Mary's penitentiary sisterhood at Wantage 1850, to which some of Gladstone's rescue cases were sent; dean of Lincoln from 1885.
[7] Charles Lloyd, 1809?–83; rector of Hampden 1840, of Chalfont St. Giles 1859;
proctor of Oxford diocese.
[8] See 28 May 57.
[9] Of the founding of Cuddesdon theological college in 1854.

Wrote to Rev. Dr Sewell—Captain G—Mrs Herbert—J. Collins[1]—M.F. Tupper—Ld Goderich—Ld Lyttelton—Ld Blandford. An entertainment after Ch to two or three hundred people: I had to speak & proposed the Bps health in his absence as a great Bishop. Saw Sir Wm. Heathcote—Mr Butler & others. Read Keble's Praelectiones. Certainly Cuddesden with its Bp & all that he is doing is a goodly sight.

10. Wed. [Hawarden]

Ch 8½ a.m. Saw the Bp—fresh from London—on the Divorce Bill. Also Sir W. Heathcote—Off to Oxford at 11; & by train to Chester. We reached Hawarden at 8.15 & thank God found all the children blooming. Read Friedrich's Realien[2]—Letter to C. of E. on Currency.[3] Bp of Victoria's Speeches.[4] Tyler on Opium Trade[5]—Halliday's Minute.[6]

11. Th. St Barnabas.

Ch 8½ a.m. Wrote to Lord Lyttelton—Rev. W. Elwin—W.G. Anderson— Hon. R. Lawley. Read Scotts Marmion—Keble's Praelectiones—and read up Newspaper arrears after a happy exemption. Visited the coalpits & borings & saw Sherratt. Worked on Letters & papers.

12. Fr.

Ch 8½ a.m. Wrote to Rev. J.S. Robson[7]—Sir Thos. G—Mr R.J. Congreve[8] —Captain G—Sir Jas. Graham—Mr Purdue.[9] Read Marriage Laws as to Desertion[10]—Keble's Praelectiones. Marmion. Rode with Agnes. Worked on books, letters, & papers. Saw Mr Burnett.

13. Sat.

Ch 8½ a.m. Wrote to Rev. C. Peers[11]—S. Christy M.P.—Rev. J.C. Stafford —A. Simpson[12]—Mr W. Torr[13]—C. Renton. Saw Mr Littleboy—and poor old Cree.[14] Walk to C.s ride. Read Marriage Laws. Bp Fleetwood on do[15]— Keble's Praelectiones.

[1] Probably John Coombes Collins, 1798–1867; perpetual curate of St. John's, Bridg-water, from 1846; botanist.

[2] J. B. Friedrich, *Die realien in der Iliade und Odyssee* (1851).

[3] Untraced pamphlet.

[4] George Smith, 'Our national relations with China' (1857).

[5] Capt. Tyler, R. E., 'Questions of the day: Indian revenue from Indian opium: Chinese money at the expense of Chinese life . . .' (1857).

[6] F. J. Halliday, *Minute on the state of the police, and of criminal justice in the lower provinces of Bengal* (1857).

[7] James Stuart Robson; priest 1843; naval chaplain.

[8] Probably Richard Jones Congreve, d. 1879, of Carlingwark, Kirkcudbrightshire; artist.

[9] John Purdue, inspector of taxes for the metropolitan districts.

[10] 'Observations on the marriage laws, particularly with reference to the case of desertion' (1815); see *Quarterly Review*, cii. 285.

[11] Charles Peers, 1811–58; St. Catherine's, Cambridge; perpetual curate of Walsham-le-Willows from 1852.

[12] Perhaps Adam Lind Simpson, 1817–93; presbyterian minister; wrote on non-conformity.

[13] William *Torr, 1808–74; Lincolnshire farmer, breeder and inventor of farming machinery.

[14] A tenant.

[15] W. Fleetwood, discourse xiii on husbands' duties to wives, *Works*, i (1854).

14. 1. S. Trin.

Church mg & evg. Read Dean of Wells's Sermon[1]—Milton on Divorce[2]—
Morgan on Marriage & Divorce.[3] Marriage Laws as to Desertion (finished).
Examined Seaforth Deeds.[4]

15. M.

Ch 8½ a.m. Wrote to Sir W. Heathcote—Sir W. James—Sir J. Lefevre—
C. Butler. Walk to C.s ride & with her & Wray about improvements. Read
Morgan on Divorce. Milton Tetrachordon &c.[5]—Reformatio Legum[6]—
Smith Artt. on Gr. & Rom. Marriages[7]—Lay of the Last Ministrel.[8]

16. T.

Ch 8½ a.m. Wrote to Montie. Gladstone[9]—R. Cobden & copy[10]—H. Drummond. Corrected proofs of Speech at Oxford & sent it to Mr Greswell.[11]
Rode with Mary. Read Morgan on Divorce. Bingham on do.[12] Madan's
Thelypthora[13]—Lay of the last Ministrel (finished). Searched the Gentleman's Magazine.[14]

17. Wed.

Ch 8½ a.m. Wrote to Bp of Oxford—Rev. Mr Powell—R. Cavendish—
Read Morgan on Divorce—Lawrence Empire des Nairs[15]—Symmons's
Milton[16]—Paley[17] & others. Rokeby[18]—Began, or rather re-began my
attempt at an Article for Q.R.[19] Corrected Dr Godfray's Translation[20]—
and resumed my digging.

[1] G. H. S. *Johnson, *Sermons preached in Wells Cathedral* (1857).
[2] J. *Milton, 'The doctrine and discipline of divorce' (1643), a notorious pamphlet,
supporting divorce for incompatibility of character.
[3] See 7 Feb. 50; much quoted in his *Quarterly* article.
[4] On the dispute, see 24 May 57.
[5] One of three further pamphlets on divorce by J. *Milton (1644–5); discussed in his
Quarterly article: 'The mind may well be divided between admiration of the force and
grandeur of their language, and thankfulness that England was found proof against the
seduction of the pestilent ideas they convey.'
[6] *Reformatio Legum ecclesiasticarum*, ed. E. Cardwell (1850).
[7] In *Smith's *Classical Dictionary*.
[8] By *Scott (1805).
[9] See 7 Sept. 35n.
[10] Declining, because of its counter-productivity, 'spontaneously to take up, or to
assume any leading part in, any discussion that may seem aimed against the Government'; Add MS 44135, f. 9.
[11] See 2 June 57n.
[12] W. P. S. Bingham, *A few words on the Divorce Bill* (1857).
[13] M. *Madan, *Thelypthora, or a treatise on female ruin* (1780).
[14] *Gentleman's Magazine*, xxiii. 400, on 18th. century clandestine marriages.
[15] See 17 June 52.
[16] C. *Symmons, *The prose works of J. *Milton with a life of the author* (1806).
[17] W. *Paley, *Works*, iv. 219 (1851), see *Gleanings*, vi. 96.
[18] By *Scott (1813).
[19] Add MS 44685, f. 316, 'The Bill for Divorce', *Quarterly Review* (July 1857), reprinted
in *Gleanings*, vi. 47. Bitterly hostile to the bill.
[20] Frederick Godfray, (see 9 Mar. 57) sent proofs for correction of his tr. of Gladstone's
Manual of Prayers (1845) into French; marked copy in Add MS 44388, f. 24.

18. Th.

Ch 8½ a.m. Wrote to Rev Dr Godfray—Mr A. Stafford. Worked on my Article. Read Morgan—Scott's Rokeby.

Stephen returned: & the Institution Feast was held: said to be 2000 people: a very pretty sight, & the people admirably well behaved.[1] Saw the two Mr Burnetts—and old Cree. Also Smith of the Cop[farm].

19. Fr.

Wrote to Mr H. Raikes—Goderich—S. Christy M.P.—G. Marrable and draft for Henry [Glynne] to sign to J.J. Ffoulkes about the Election expences.—after mutual consultation. Worked on my Article long. Some digging—Read Rokeby.

20. Sat.

Ch 8¼ a.m. Wrote to Sir Jas. Graham—R. Cobden—Bp of Salisbury. Finished my Article—save revision. Read Tertullian—Dr Cardwell[2]— Rokeby (finished)—and Simpson on Oregon.[3]

21. 2 S. Trin.

Ch mg & evg. Revised my Article on Marriage & Divorce—Read Chalmer's Life[4]—Reunion de l'Egl Anglicane.[5]

22. M.

Ch 8¼ a.m. Wrote to Manchr. Exec. Commee[?]—Mr Dorrell—Robn. Gladstone—Rev. W. Elwin—Duke of Newcastle—Dean Ramsay—R. Phillimore. Commenced what should be my final revision & reconstruction of my Ethnological Essay.[7]

Saw Mr Burnett—& visited the bore-holes: no news there. Read Barthe on Ceramics[8]—Scotts Lord of the Isles—Bayly on Music Poetry[9] &c. Dispatched my Article on the Divorce Bill.

23. T.

Ch 8½ a.m. Wrote to Sir Wm. Heathcote—Rev. Mr Anderson—Worked much on my Homer; C. summoned to Hagley.[10] Set out to ride with Agnes:

[1] The literary and scientific institution, founded by the Sandycroft Ironworkers, supported by *Glynne.
[2] His *Synodalia*, see *Gleanings*, vi. 94 and 6 Aug. 42.
[3] A. Simpson, *The Oregon territory* (1846).
[4] See 18 Dec. 49.
[5] Perhaps an earlier, untraced form of J. Gondon's work of this title with additional material by *Newman, *Pusey and *Manning, in 1867; or Gondon's *Du mouvement religieux* (1844), see 5 Oct. 44.
[6] See 29 June 57.   [7] *Studies on Homer*, ii, part 2.
[8] Perhaps a slip of the pen for H. G. *Bohn, *A guide to the knowledge of pottery and porcelain* (1857).
[9] A. Bayly, *The alliance of music, poetry and oratory* (1789).
[10] Mary Lyttelton's fatal illness.

who was stopped by Niger's fall. Read Empire des Nairs. Bayly on Music &c. Scott's Lord of the Isles.

24. Wed. St John Bapt.

Ch 8½ a.m. Wrote to Earl of Harrowby—Rev. Mr Stafford—C.G.—Worked on my Homer steadily. Tea at the Rectory. Read Mr Ramsay's two Lectures.[1]

25. Th.

Ch 8¼ a.m. Wrote to Sir W. Heathcote—C.G.[2]—Mr H.A. Giraud—W. Hampton—Mr Cowburn[3]—Mr Keble—Hatchards. Worked on my Homer: but the labour is considerable & progress slow: something like the boring at Mancot, now 2 inches a day. Read Bayly on Music &c—NB. Harry & Herbert have their lesson in Frere Jaques. Dined at the Rectory.

26. Fr.

Ch 8½ a.m. Wrote to Mr Gibbs (& copy)[4]—J.N.G.—Freshfields. Worked much on my Homer. Read Lord of the Isles (finished)—Freer's Marguerite of Angoulême.[5] C. returned late.

27. Sat.

Ch 8¼ a.m. Wrote to Robert Gladstone—Messrs. Hewitt—Ld Lyttelton. Went to Chester on Mr Brewster's business. Dined at the Rectory. Worked on Homer. Read Life of Marguerite; also Lewis,[6] & other Books for Homer.

28. 3. S. Trin.

Ch mg & evg. Wrote to Alex. Goalen—J.N.G.—Mr Davis. Corr. part proofs Art. on Marriage. Read Von Gurlach[sic] on Marriage[7]—Wordsworth on do.[8]—Middleton on Gk. Article.[9] Poor Helen's birthday: O that all were well with her.

29. M. [Manchester]

Wrote to Willy—Off at 8¼. Reached Manchr. at 11 and spent the day till 5 at the Exhibition:[10] a wonderful sight materially, & not less remarkable

---

[1] E. B. *Ramsay, 'Two lectures on some changes in social life and habits' (1857).

[2] Bassett, 115.

[3] George Cowburn, attorney in Lincoln's Inn.

[4] Frederick Waymouth Gibbs, 1821–98; tutor to the Prince of Wales 1852–8; to arrange the Prussian trip, see 30 June 57 and Add MS 44387, f. 326.

[5] M. W. *Freer, *The life of Marguerite d'Angoulême, Queen of Navarre*, 2v. (1854).

[6] Probably Sir G. C. *Lewis, *An enquiry into the credibility of early Roman history*, 2v. (1855).

[7] 'The law of marriage. The speech of Baron von Gerlach in the Prussian Chamber . . . with preface by H. Drummond, M.P.' (1857).

[8] Christopher *Wordsworth, *On divorce* (1857).

[9] T. F. *Middleton, *The doctrine of the Greek article* (1808); quoted in *Gleanings*, vi. 65 on difference between 'a divorced woman' and 'the divorced woman' in Matt. v. 32.

[10] Vast art exhibition housed in special buildings at Old Trafford. Gladstone lent 'Francesca da Rimini' and 'Brother and Sister', sculptures by A. *Munro.

morally, but bewildering to the mind & exhausting to the eye from vastness when viewed wholesale: it ought to be visited in compartments. We then went to Rob. Gladstone's where we were most kindly received. A dinner party there. Read Life of Marguerite.

30. T.

Wrote to Willy—on the Königswinter plan.[1] Off at 8½ for the Building.[2] The line of procession the most remarkable I ever saw for ornamentation & for feeling. At the place I saw Alderman Nield[3] & others—Ld Palmerston whom at his request I introduced to the Bp of Manchester.[4] Lady P[almerston,] the Stanhopes, Bernstorffs[5] & many more: then, during the progress Mr Gibbs with whom we settled about Willy. Besides the Spectacle & Music we got almost three hours of the pictures &c. & left at 4½. I then went to see the Harter's.[6] Another dinner party. Read Life of Marguerite.

Wed. July One 1857. X [London]

Off at 9: reached H. of C. at 4½: sent the servants to Hawarden & C. branched off at Stafford. Put up at *Usher's* [Hotel] Suffolk St[7] which seemed very nicely managed. H. of C. 4½–7.[8] Dined with the Hopes—saw Ld Goderich—R. Phillimore—Sir J. Graham—W. Hampton—Mrs Talbot —Ld Elcho. Saw Mrs Mackay—Griffiths gone; Kirby also: I hope for *good*[R]. Lady M. Hope[9] showed me her beautiful china. Wrote to V.C. Oxford—Baron Marochetti—H.G. Macleod—Rev. E.J. Smith—Rev. P. Freeman.

2. Th. X.

Wrote to J.S. Whyte—J. Griffiths—C.C. Brooke—T.D. Acland—Dr [Hugh] Jones—Dean of Ch.Ch.—J. Grant—Rev. Mr St Aubyn[10]—H.S. Dodwell[11] —A.S. Gladstone—Ld Harris—Archdn. Sinclair—Mr Raikes (2)—Mr Rowden[12]—Mr T. Young—Mr Jas. Murray—C.G.[13]—Lyttelton. Sat to Marochetti 2–4. H. of C. 5–8¾.[14] Read Marryat on Pottery.[15] Saw Lovell: & there by God's mercy there is an opening to good. Saw A. Beresford Hope —Mr Sotheron—Panizzi—S.H. Walpole.

[1] From July to October 1857 Willy and three friends accompanied the Prince of Wales, under F. W. Gibbs' supervision, to Königswinter, near Bonn, where they met Metternich, and then to Switzerland.
[2] At Old Trafford; see *The Times*, 1 July 1857, 5.
[3] William Neild, Manchester J.P., alderman and calico printer and author of articles in the *Statistical Journal*.
[4] James Prince *Lee, 1804–69; head-master, then bp. of Manchester from 1847.
[5] Anna, *née* von Könneritz, m. 1833 Albrecht von Bernstorff and d. 1893.
[6] See 12 Aug. 53.　　　[7] Used by many M.P.s.
[8] Medical Profession Bill: *H* cxlvi. 707.
[9] Lady Mildred, da. of 2nd marquis of Salisbury, m. 1842 A. J. Beresford Hope and d. 1881. They had an important collection of pictures and china at 1 Connaught Place.
[10] William John St. Aubyn, 1814–77; rector of Stoke Damerel, Devon, from 1828.
[11] Perhaps Henry John Dodwell, 1825–1900; schoolmaster; priest 1860; went mad in late 1870s.
[12] Edward Wetherell Rowden, 1814–70; Oxford university registrar from 1853.
[13] Bassett, 115.　　　[14] Supply (British Museum): *H* cxlvi. 805.
[15] J. Marryat, *A history of pottery and porcelain, mediaeval and modern* (1857).

3. Fr. X.

Wrote to Willy—Rev. Mr Heygate[1]—Mr Davies—Warden Trin. Coll[2]—G. Loveday[3]—Rev. Mr Clarke—C.G.—Rev. Mr Perry—Scotts. Sat to Marochetti 10–12. Saw J.N.G.—Sir C. Wood—Aunt J.—S. Herbert—Saw Mackay—dark[R]. Commee. on Bank $1\frac{1}{4}$–$3\frac{3}{4}$ and House 4–7.[4] Dined with Mrs Talbot. Read Report on Divorce (53)[5] Homer on Divorce[6] &c. and other works. Worked on Marryatt.

4. Sat. [Cliveden]

Wrote to Sir W. Heathcote—G.S. Harcourt[7]—Chev. Mynas[8]—Mrs Scargill[9]—Rev. Mr Webb[10]—Mr Barrow—Rev. Mr Allan[11]—Mr Walford—Mr Phelps—C.G. Saw Warden of Merton—Mrs R. Lawley[12]—Ld Aberdeen—Scotts—Bp of Oxford. Sat to Marochetti. Shopping. Off at 4 with the Sutherland party to Clifden, where were the Argylls Mr Sumner[13] Bp of Oxford the Laboucheres & Lady Blantyre with the Duchess: we had a delightful evening. Read Gondon on Naples[14]—Keble's Sequel.[15]

5. 4 S. Trin.

Taplow Ch mg & Heden aft. Bp of O[xford] preached both times. The boys came up from Eton. Wrote to Mr Woodgate—Mr Thornton—Rev. Mr Nugee. Read Woodgate on the Abnormal condition of the Church.[16] Keble's Sequel—Conv. with the Bp.

6. M. X [London]

Wrote to E.E. Wynn[17]—Rev. J. Keble—G[reat] N[orthern] Booking Clerk and Hon. Rev. S. Lawley.[18] Went with Mr Sumner to Stoke [Poges] which

[1] William Edward Heygate, 1816–1902; curate of Leigh, Essex; rector of Brightstone, Isle of Wight, from 1869; wrote devotions and novels. See above, v. lx.
[2] J. *Hannah; see 8 July 57.
[3] Probably George Beaumont Loveday, 1833–87; dramatic manager and operatic entrepreneur. His fa. Ely, 1800–92, worked with *Kean (see 25 Apr. 57).
[4] Supply: H cxlvi. 901.
[5] See 19 Mar. 53.
[6] Discussed in Studies on Homer, ii. 487.
[7] George Simon Harcourt, 1805–71; Christ Church; tory M.P. Buckinghamshire 1837–41.
[8] Minoide Mynas had written to pay respects; Hawn P.
[9] She lived in Gower Street.
[10] Benjamin *Webb, 1819–85; curate of Sheen, Staffordshire, 1851–62; vicar of St. Andrew's, Wells Street, from 1852; ed. Ecclesiologist 1842–68.
[11] Perhaps John Lloyd Allan, 1812?–66; priest 1841; headmaster in Cranbrook from 1851.
[12] See 9 Nov. 52.
[13] Charles Sumner, 1811–74; republican senator for Massachusetts from 1851; a strong advocate of slave emancipation, he was in Europe recovering from savage physical attack by representative P. S. Brooks, following an anti-slavery speech.
[14] J. Gondon, Situation et affaires du royaume de Naples (1857).
[15] J. *Keble, Sequel of the argument against immediately repealing the laws which treat the nuptial bond as indissoluble (1857).
[16] H. A. Woodgate, Anomalies in the English Church no just ground for seceding (1857).
[17] Had sent election cuttings; Hawn P.
[18] See 24 Aug. 48.

Lady Mary[1] showed us & then on with him to Slough & London. I liked him greatly. Made calls & came to H. of C. 4–7¾ and 9¼–10.[2] Saw Heathcote & Henley—W. Grogan. Saw Griffiths[R]. Worked on & I hope finished revises of Art. on Divorce Bill. C. came up.

7. Tues.

Wrote to Mr Marriott—Rev Mr Kidd—Name forgotten. Saw Bp of Oxford —Sir J. Graham—R. Phillimore—Mr Wynn M.P.—Rev. W. Scott. Sat to Marochetti. Bank Commee. 1¼–3¾, and House. Dined with Mrs Talbot and off by G.N. at 8. P.M. for the North. Read Life of Ld Arundel[3]—T. Brown's Reminiscences.[4]

8. Wed. [Glenalmond]

Wrote to C.G. Reached Edinb. 8 a.m. Perth 11. Trin Coll. at 2 walking from Methven. Chapel 5½ P.M. Much conv. with the Warden[Hannah] about the College. I was greatly pleased with him. Also a long Homeric conversation with him. Read Life of Ld Arundel. Mure Vol. V.[5]

9. Th.

Wrote to Dean Ramsay. Chapel (Choral service) 10 a.m. Examination & prizes 11–1½. Banquet at 2. I made a Speech according to order on Classical Education.[6] Left the College much pleased with all I had seen at 4¾, Perth at 6½. Read Life of Ld Arundel—Also of Lady Arundel. In the train I got from a Newcastle man a good Lecture on the Iron Trade.

10. Fr. [London]

Reached Suffolk St 10½ a.m. Wrote to Station Master G.N.R.—Rev. W. Hall[7]—Mrs Lucy Tayler[8]—Mrs Bennett—Rev. Mr Woodgate—Mr Salisbury M.P. (& copy)—Rev. Mr Woodard—Ld Powis. Bank Committee 1¾–4. House to 7½ and again after dinner.[9] Saw Sir J. Graham—Mr Gilpin[10]— Rev. Mr Elwin. Read the Molesworth Volume[11]—Life of Lady Arundel.

[1] Lady Mary Labouchere.
[2] Probates Bill: H cxlvi. 974.
[3] H. G. F. *Howard, The lives of Philip Howard, earl of Arundel, and of A. Dacres, his wife (1857).
[4] T. Brown, The reminiscences of an old traveller throughout different parts of Europe (1843).
[5] See 1 Sept. 55.
[6] Reported in The Guardian, 15 July 1857, 549.
[7] William John Hall, 1793–1861; vicar of Tottenham from 1851; ed. the Christian Remembrancer.
[8] Unidentified.
[9] Probates Bill: H cxlvi. 1288.
[10] Charles Gilpin, 1815–74; publisher; liberal M.P. Northampton from 1857; chairman of national freehold land society.
[11] Probably J. E. N. *Molesworth, The domestic chaplain or, sermons on family duties for every Sunday of the year, 2v. (1838).

11. Sat. X.

11–12½ Sat to Marochetti. 1–4¼ Br. Museum Standing Comm. Dined at Mrs Talbots—College of Physicians in evg. We returned to our house:[1] from wh & from London absence has been an advantage. Saw Smith—! [R] Rev. Mr Woodgate—Sir W. Heathcote. Read Life of Geo. Stephenson.[2] Worked on proofs of Article resp. the Homeric characters.[3]

12. 5. S. Trin.

St James's mg—Chapel Royal aft. MS of 43 aloud in evg. Read Lady Arundel's Life (finished)—Blackburn on Divorce[4]—Keble's Argument & Sequel (finished)—Dickenson on Convocation[5]—Freeman on Divine Service II.[6] Wrote to Rev. T.T. Carter—Rev Mr Cowan.

13. M.

Wrote to Inspector Parke—H. Glynne—Ld Chandos (& copy)[7]—Rev. Mr Haddan—Miss Bunbury[8]—Rev Mr Trevor—Jos. Sturge. Saw Mr Elwin— Sir Jas. Graham—Mr Grogan—Mr Leeman—Vicar of St Martin's[9]— Lyttelton. Visited Mr Munro's very beautiful collection of Pictures.[10] H. of C. 5–7½.[11] Dined with the Ralph N. Grenvilles. Read Ld Westmeath's Reply.[12] Finished proof sheets of Article on Homeric Characters.

14. T.

Wrote to Mr Labouchere—Earl of Fife[13]—Mr Goldwin Smith—Mr T. Perdue—Provost of Eton—B. Benjamin—Sir J. Lefevre—Rev. C. Lloyd— Mr C. Rogers—Saw Mr Parry[14]—Mr Roebuck—Attorney General—Coal-whipper's Agent—Sir James Graham. H. of C. & Bank Committee 12–4 and 6–9.[15] Lady Overstone's[16] Concert in evg. Began Persian papers.[17]

---

[1] 11 Carlton House Terrace.

[2] By S. *Smiles (1857).

[3] See 28 Apr. 57.

[4] P. Blackburn, *The doctrine of the New Testament law concerning divorce and separation* (1857).

[5] F. H. Dickinson, *Convocation and the laity* (1857).

[6] See 20 Jan. 56.

[7] On Gladstone's receipt of plate, 'not less than 500 guineas', for his railway arbitrations: Add MS 44388, f. 37, 61.

[8] Perhaps Emily, da. of Sir J. M. Richardson Bunbury, 2nd bart.

[9] William Gibson *Humphry, 1815–86; vicar of St. Martin-in-the-Fields from 1855; wrote extensively on liturgy.

[10] A. *Munro, the pre-raphaelite sculptor; see 18 July 51.

[11] Misc. estimates: *H* cxlvi. 1388.

[12] G. T. J. Nugent, Lord Westmeath, *A reply to the 'Narrative of the case of the Marchioness of Westmeath'* (1857).

[13] James Duff, 1814–79; liberal M.P. Banffshire 1837–57; 5th earl of Fife 1857.

[14] Probably Edward *Parry, 1830–90; bp. of London's chaplain 1857–9; rector of Acton 1859–69; archdeacon of Canterbury from 1869; suffragan bp. of Dover 1870–89.

[15] African slave trade: *H* cxlvi. 1492. At the Bank cttee. he cross-examined *Overstone: *PP* 1857, 2nd session, x part 1, 413.

[16] Harriet, *née* Wright, m. 1829 S. J. *Loyd, 1st Baron Overstone, and d. 1864.

[17] *PP* 1857, xliii. 255, on negotiations to end the British-Persian war of 1856–7; peace treaty signed in Paris, March 1857.

15. Wed. X.

Wrote to Mr Sumner—Mr G. Christie—Rev. D. Gladstone—Mr W. Baker—Sir C. Trevelyan—Read Persian papers. Dined at Lady Clinton's—Ld Lansdowne's Concert afterwards. Saw Mr S. Herbert—Ld Kinnaird. Ld Aberdeen with Sir J. Graham 1½–4. Scotts—Mr W. Walker—Rev. Mr Marriott—Mr Courtenay—Ld Lyttelton. Saw Jervis & another[R].

16. Th. X.

Wrote to Mr P. Nagle—V. Chancellor of Oxford—Spencer Lyttelton. Radcliffe Trust 12–1½. Sat to Marochetti 2¼–4½. H. of C. 6–7¾ and 10¼–12½. Spoke perforce on the Persian question & voted in 38: 352 for Parliamentary Government![1] Saw S. Herbert—Mr. Grogan. Saw two [R]. Read Stephenson's Life—Persian papers. Dined with the R. Palmer's. A party of 8 to breakfast.

17. Fr. X.

Wrote to Lady Milbank—Mr H. Lees—James (footman)—Mr H. Cole—Dr Carpenter[2]—Mr D. Lange[3]—Major Larkins. Bank Committee & House 2–4 and 6–7½ and 9¼–12½: Spoke on the new Estimates.[4] Saw Miss Eden—Mr Wilson Patten—Mr Leeman. Deputation of Proctors. Walk with C. Read Life of Stephenson.

18. Sat.

Wrote to J. G. Talbot—Mr D. Gladstone—Rev. Mr Woodgate—Robn. G.—W.P. Mann[5]—Scotts. Saw R. Phillimore—Major Larkins—Mr Franks—A. Panizzi. Sat to Marochetti. Brit. Museum 1¼–4. Dined with the Laboucheres. Read Murchison's Ld Ellesmere[6]—Lange's Letters on Suez Canal[7]—A day of anxiety about Mary Lyttelton C. settled to go tomorrow.[8]

19. 6 S. Trin. X.

St James's & H.C. mg—St Paul's Kn. Evg. Wrote to Agnes—Dr Williams.[9] C.G. went [to Hagley]. Saw S. Herbert—saw Lovell[R]. At Dr Williams's 10–11 P.M. for the chance of catching him. Read Freeman on H. Eucharist[10]—Q.R. on Ritualism.[11] Nat Rev on New Parlt. (pt.)[12] Divers Sermons on Divorce &c.

[1] Supporting *Roebuck's motion that the Persian war had been conducted unconstitutionally; H cxlvi. 1629.

[2] William Benjamin *Carpenter, 1813–85; professor of forensic medicine at Univ. college, London, 1849–59; registrar of London university 1856–79.

[3] (Sir) Daniel Adolphus Lange, 1821–94; engineer; built Suez canal 1858–76; kt. 1870.

[4] Deploring, though the vote was later agreed to, estimates for the Persian and Chinese wars: H cxlvi. 1743.

[5] Unidentified.

[6] In Sir R. I. *Murchison, 'Address to the Royal Geographical Society of London' (1857).

[7] D. A. Lange, 'Lord Palmerston and the Isthmus of Suez Canal. Two letters addressed to the Editor of The Times' (1857).

[8] Having, despite doctor's advice, had her twelfth child, she was dying.

[9] Joseph Williams, 1814–82; physician to home for gentlewomen and St. Pancras female school.

[10] See 20 Jan. 56.   [11] Quarterly review, cii. 88 (July 57).

[11] National review, v. 230 (July 57).

20. M.

Wrote to Lady M. Alford—C.G.—Hon. C. Sumner—W.H.G.—Rev. Mr Butler—W. Forbes. Sat to Marochetti 10½–12½. Hudson's Bay Comm. 1¼–3½. Drew Resolutions.[1] Saw Ld J. Russell—Robn. G.—Mr Ellice— A. Kinnaird—Aunt J. H. of C. 3¾–6½ and 9–12¼. Spoke on Shepherd's Disabilities Bill.[2] Read Wilson on Homer.[3]

21. T. X.

Wrote to Dr Dollinger—C.G.—Rev. Mr Nicolay—L. Edmunds.[4] Read Stephenson's Life. Saw Ld Kinnaird—Sir W. Heathcote—D. of Argyll— Ld J. Russell. Breakfasted with the Argyll's. Bank Committee 1–3. At Mr Barker's to see his most extraordinary collection of pictures & other objects 3¼–5½.[5] H. of Commons 7½–12¼.[6] Saw one [R].

22. Wed. X.

Wrote to Bp of Oxford—Williams & Co—Archdn. Sinclair—Scotts & Co —Provost of Oriel—G. Burnett—Freshfields—C.G.—S. Bannister—F. Curzon[7]—Dr Humphreys. Saw R. Phillimore—Mr Grogan—Rev. Dr Whiteside[8]—Sir W. Heathcote—Mr Cole.
H. of C. 12¼–6 chiefly on Burials Act Amendt. Bill—wh we fought.[9] Saw Mackay—& another [R]. Visited Kensington Museum at night.[10] Read Fortune's China[11]—Q.R. on Manchr. Exhibition.[12]

23. Th. X.

Wrote to Duke of Argyll—T.H. James[13]—Sir G. Hayter—Scotts—Rev. Mr Snape—Wing[14]—T.W. Rathbone. Read Fortune's China. Saw Sir W. Heathcote—Bp of Oxford. Sat (for the last time) to Marochetti who has made much of an intractable subject. H. of C. 12–4 and Committee of Lords on Coalwhippers, to give evidence.[15] Saw Leslie—inquired for Morgan —Clifford & Collins; & found information about the last, good [R].

[1] For the report, see 18 Feb. 57n.
[2] Bill dealing with recognition of American ordinations: *H* cxlvii. 23.
[3] J. Wilson, *Essays critical and imaginative* (1857), iv.
[4] Leonard Edmunds, 1802?–85; clerk to patents' commissioners 1852–64; played important role in the *Westbury affair (see July 1865); brought a libel action against Gladstone June 1872 when he was nonsuited; see 21–22 June 72.
[5] Thomas Jones *Barker, 1815–82; military artist and portrait painter, known as the 'English Vernet'; lived in Gloucester Road.
[6] Spoke on Oaths Bill: *H* cxlvii. 174.
[7] Frederick Emmanuel Hippolitus Curzon, 1795–1871; vicar of Mickleover, Derbyshire, from 1820.
[8] John William Whiteside, 1808?–64; D. C. L. Cambridge; friend of *Southey; vicar of Scarborough from 1848.
[9] *H* cxlvii. 225.
[10] The Victoria and Albert, called the South Kensington museum until 1899, opened though unfinished 1857.
[11] R. *Fortune, *A residence among the Chinese . . . from 1854 to 1856* (1857).
[12] *Quarterly Review*, cii. 165 (July 1857).
[13] Thomas Henry James, published on shipping.
[14] Perhaps William Wing, 1810–82; Oxfordshire antiquarian.
[15] On the introduction and working of his 1843 Act: *PP* 1857 2nd session, xii. 140.

24. Fr.

Wrote to Mr Brock—C.G.—Mr Arnold[1]—J.N.G. Hudson's Bay Committee &c. 1–4½ and House 6½–11½. Spoke for postponement of Divorce Bill.[2] Saw Phillimore—Mr Grogan—and others. Read Fortune's China—China papers.[3]

25. St James. Sat. X.

Wrote to Dr Wordsworth (& saw Mrs W.)[4] Willy—C.G.—J. Murray—T.G. —Mr Labouchere. Saw R. Phillimore—Perdue's (man)—Sir W. Heathcote —Mr Massey—Scotts—Shopping. Saw Detnore[R]. Read Wilson's Homer &c. Azeglio's G. Collegno.[5] Our Coal Fields.[6]

26. 7. S. Trin.

St Martins 8½ a.m. Chapel Royal 12. S. Mary Magd. 7 P.M. MS of 45 aloud in evg. Wrote to C.G.—Baron Marochetti. Saw J. Hope Scott. Read Chr. Rem. on Theiner—Charlotte Bronte[7]—S. Bernard Epp.[8]—Dollinger Heidenthum u. Judenthum[9] (with Iliad). Freeman on H. Eucharist.

27. M.

Wrote to Rev. C.H. Christie—Sir B. Hall—Rev. Mr Squire[10]—C.G.—D. Dickenson—Duke of Argyll. Willy came up. Worked on arranging letters &c. Read Indian papers & documents.[11] Dined with the Herberts. Read Hudson's Bay (Canada) Evidence.[12] H. of C. 4½–7¾ and 10¼–11.[13] Saw Mr Ellice—Sir W. Heathcote.

28. T. X.

Wrote to Sec. Office Woods—Messrs. Child—Rev. Mr Phillott—Union Bank—L. & Westmr. Bank—Ld Canning—A. Panizzi. Read Ellice's H.B. Evidence[14]—Our Coal Fields—Life of Stephenson. Shopping &c with

---

[1] Matthew *Arnold, 1822–88; *Lansdowne's secretary 1847–51; school inspector 1851–83; poetry professor at Oxford 1857–67; author and critic.

[2] *H* cxlvii. 383.

[3] *PP* 1857 xii; probably the correspondence with the Liverpool E.I. Association in which Robertson Gladstone was involved.

[4] Probably Susanna, *née* Frere, wife of Christopher *Wordsworth; Gladstone was not on good terms with Charles *Wordsworth.

[5] M. Tapparelli d'Azeglio, *Diario dell'assedio di Navarino. Memorie di G. Collegno* (1857).

[6] Probably [J. R. Leifchild], *Our coal and our coal-pits; the people in them and the scenes around them* (1854).

[7] *Christian Remembrancer*, xxxiv. 233, 87 (July 57).

[8] See 1 Aug. 47.

[9] J. J. I. von Döllinger, *Heidenthum und Judenthum. Vorhalle zur Geschichte Christenthums* (1857); see 6 Sept. 57n.

[10] Edward Burnard Squire; missionary in China 1836–40; vicar of Swansea 1846.

[11] News of the mutiny which began seriously in May, reached Britain in June (see, e.g., Argyll, ii. 80): *PP* 1857 xxx.

[12] See 18 Feb. 57n.

[13] Indian mutiny: *H* cxlvii. 440.

[14] Of 23 June: *PP* 1857 xv. 322.

Willy. He went off in evg.[1] Joy be with him. Saw Major Larkins—Sir W. Heathcote—Atty. General—Mr J. Wilson—Sir G. Grey—Saw Morgan's friend[R]. H. of C. 12–4 and 6–10.[2]

29. Wed.

Wrote to A. Panizzi—Major Macgregor[3]—Mr Macqueen[4]—Lyttelton— Major Larkins—Archdn. Harrison—C.G. Saw R. Phillimore—Mr Roebuck M.P.—Mr A. Finlay—Sir W. Heathcote & others—Ld Overstone—Sir C. Eastlake—Mr Dyce. Saw Leslie & another[R]. Read Villette[5]—Wilson on Homer. Attended the Royal Academy's closing Soirée.

30. Th.

Wrote to Mr W. Johnson—Mr H. Shaw[6]—Jas.[*sc.* John] Macqueen—C.G. —J. Nelson—C. Rogers—S. Williams[7]—R. Dodd[8]—Mr Madot—Provost of Oriel. Read Marriage & Divorce Debates & Evidence.[9] Ld Dufferin's Sketches.[10] H. of C. $6\frac{1}{4}$–8 and 9–$2\frac{1}{2}$ for Divorce Bill: & trying vainly to do some good in the matter of superannuations.[11] Saw Robn. G—Mr Purdue— Mr Christy.

31. Fr.

Saw Dr Wordsworth—Mr Labouchere—Sir Francis Baring. Wrote to Bp of St David's—C.G.[12]—Lambert Marshall.[13] H. of C. & H.B. Committee— 12–$2\frac{1}{2}$. Worked on Marriage question: & House 6–10 and 11–$1\frac{3}{4}$. Spoke 2 h agt. the Divorce Bill: beneath the subject ἀμήχανον ὅσον.[14] Read Wilson on Homer—Villette.

Sat. Aug. One 1857.

Wrote to A. Panizzi—Sir G. Grey—Rev. J. Baker—C.G.[15]—Rev. Mr Domvile.[16] Worked on letters—& on accounts. Read Life of Stephenson— Wilson's Homer—Ld Overstone's Introduction. Saw R. Phillimore— Geo. Hope—Scotts—Br. Museum $2\frac{1}{4}$–$3\frac{1}{2}$. Dined at S. Herberts.

[1] To the continent with the Prince of Wales.
[2] Misc. business: *H* cxlvii. 569.
[3] Major Robert MacGregor had sent a volume of *Epitaphs* (Hawn P).
[4] John Fraser *Macqueen, 1803–81; barrister; sec. of divorce commission 1851; reporter in Lords of Scottish & divorce appeals 1860; wrote on marriage law.
[5] By [Charlotte *Brontë] (1853).
[6] Probably Henry *Shaw, 1800–73; engraver and writer on Gothic architecture.
[7] Probably Stephen Frederick Williams, 1825?–97; curate of Farnham 1854–60; then schoolmaster; rector of Cold Norton from 1877.
[8] Plasterer in Toxteth Park.
[9] See 19 Mar. 53.
[10] F.T.H.T. *Blackwood, Lord Dufferin, *Letters from high latitudes* (1857).
[11] *H* cxlvii. 656, 773, discussing, without attribution, his own article on divorce in the *Quarterly*, and becoming ill-tempered with *Bethell, the attorney-general.
[12] Bassett, 116.
[13] Of Brighton; a charitable case; Hawn P.
[14] 'to a quite extraordinary degree': *H* cxlvii. 825; notes in Add MS 44655, f. 67.
[15] Bassett, 116.
[16] C. C. D. Domvile, a supporter of the Divorce Bill.

2. 8 S. Trin. X.

Chapel Royal mg. & H.C.—St Gabriel's[1] Evg. MS of 48 aloud. Wrote to
A. Kinnaird—Duke of Norfolk—Rev. Warden Trin. College—Rev. G.
Rorison—Rev. P. Freeman. Saw the Forbeses—E. Badeley—Saw Lovell:
a wavering & retrogression there by wh. I suffered[R]. Read Döllinger
Heid.u.Jnd—Rorison's Sermons.[2] Freeman on Eucharist finished[3]—
Hannah on the Fall.[4]

3. M.

Wrote to Ed. Guardian (2)[5]—C.G.—W. Grogan—T. Mahony[6]—F. Weather-
by.[7] Dined with the Herberts. Worked on accounts. Sat (stood) to Messrs.
Maull & Polyblank in a vapour bath of 92° & upwards.[8] Saw R. Phillimore
—B. Benjamin—Mr Henley—do+Walpole. H. of C. $4\frac{1}{4}$–8 and $10\frac{3}{4}$–$12\frac{1}{2}$.[9]
Read Dr Farr on Salaries.[10] Saw Lovell[R].

4. T.

Wrote to Rev. Mr Chaplin[11]—C.G.—Mackenzie Wilson—G. & Co—Mr
Wainwright. Saw Ld Overstone—A. Kinnaird—Sir W. Heathcote—
Archdn. Harrison. Read Wilson on Homer. Visited the Wellington Museum.
Designs with Ld Overstone at 11.[12] Corrected evidence before Coal-whippers
Committee.[13] H. of C. 12–3 and $6\frac{1}{4}$–$12\frac{1}{2}$: in Evg. fighting the Divorce Bill.[14]

5. Wed.

Wrote to Agnes & Stephy—C.G.—Ld Stanley—H. Rowley[15]—Mr Mar-
riott. Went at $11\frac{3}{4}$ with Ld Overstone to meet our Co-judges at St Paul's:
Then to Westmr. Hall & after this to our Committee Room. Saw R.
Phillimore—Ld Overstone—the Wortley's: poor Jim looked animally well
but not all right. Saw also the Jameses—Mr Napier M.P.+(F. Lawley).
Saw Lovell: right again[R]. Read Life of Stephenson: & 'Practical man
on new Govt. Offices.'[16]

[1] In Fenchurch Street; Henry James Newbery was the rector.
[2] G. Rorison, *The depression of the clergy the danger of the church; a sermon* (on Matt.
x. 40) (1856).
[3] See 20 Jan. 56.
[4] J. *Hannah, *Discourses on the fall and its results* (1857).
[5] Not published signed.
[6] A plumber.
[7] A linen supplier.
[8] Photographers in Piccadilly.
[9] Probate Bill: *H* cxlvii. 960.
[10] W. *Farr, 'Remarks on a proposed scheme for the conversion of the assessments
levied on public salaries . . . into a "provident fund"' (1849).
[11] George Ayscough Chaplin, rector of Raithby from 1841.
[12] He was on a cttee. to judge entries for the Wellington monument in St. Paul's.
[13] See 23 July 57.
[14] *H* cxlvii. 1062.
[15] Hercules Langford Boyle Rowley, 1828–1904, s. of 2nd Baron Langford; Irish
landlord.
[16] Not found.

6. Th.

Wrote to Freshfields—Mrs Grey—G. & Co—Oaths Committee 1–3¾.[1]
Wellington Monuments 3¾–5½. H. of C. Divorce Bill 6¼–12½.[2] Read Our
Coal Fields—Ld Dufferin. Saw Mr Slater—Mr Grogan—Scotts.

7. Fr.

Wrote to J. Gladstone—Sir H. Verney—C.G.—Oaths Comm 12¾–4.
Monuments Adjudn. 4–5. H. of C. Divorce Bill 6¼–1.[3] Saw R. Phillimore—
The Wortley's—Ld Wensleydale. Read Stephenson's Life—Br. Quart. on
Divorce.

8. Sat. X.

Wrote to Mr J. Taylor[4]—C.G.[5]—Rev. Mr Head[6]—Dean of Norwich—
Mr Greswell. Read Stephenson's Life finished—Freshfield's & Lavie's
Letters.[7] Wilson on Homer. A circle of calls on relatives. Went at 9 to
Princess's Theatre.[8] Saw the Wortley's (uncomfortable)—Robn. G.

9. 9. S. Trin.

Broad Court Ch[9] mg.—St Michael's Evg. Wrote to Mr C. Buxton[10]—Mr
W. Wainwright[11]—J.H. Parker—Rev. W. Burkitt. Saw Ld Alfred Hervey
—The Wortley's—Lady Wharncliffe—Robn. G. & M.E. Failed to get into
Exeter Hall:[12] heard a well intended sermon from a youth of twenty out-
side. Read periodicals—Pretyman's Erastianism[13]—St Bernard—Head on
Redemption.[14]

10. M.

Wrote to Rev. Mr Tweed—C.G.—Johnson L. & Co—W. Henry[15]—W.R.
Sandbach[16]—Scotts—Mr C. Kean—E. Jones—(Holywell)—Mr. Thirn-

[1] He was on the select cttee. on M.P.s' oaths: *PP* 1857 2nd session, ix. 479.
[2] *H* cxlvii. 1177.
[3] *H* cxlvii. 1258.
[4] John Taylor of the Western bank of Scotland, Glasgow.
[5] Bassett, 117.
[6] Henry Erskine Head, 1797–1860, Sir F. B.'s *brother; ecclesiastical controversialist;
rector of Feniton, Devon, from 1838; see 9 Aug. 57.
[7] Germain Lavie, 'Letter to Baron Rothschild on the proposed alteration of the law
relative to sales and pledges' (1857).
[8] 'The Tempest'.
[9] St. John's episcopal chapel in Broad Court, Long Acre.
[10] Charles *Buxton, 1822–71; brewer; liberal M.P. Newport 1857–9, Maidstone 1859–65,
E. Surrey from 1865; on the ritual commission 1867–8; pamphleteer.
[11] Of the Liverpool agency office in Westminster.
[12] Assembly rooms of evangelicals in the Strand, demolished 1907; a great series of
meetings for the working classes, controversially stopped by A. G. Edouart, incumbent
of the parish; see *The Guardian*, 11 November 1857, 854.
[13] J. R. Pretyman, *The Church of England and erastianism since the reformation* (1854).
[14] H. E. Head, *The ultimate and proximate results of redemption: chiefly deduced from
the oath sworn unto Abraham* (1854).
[15] William Henry of Dublin had written on the Divorce Bill (Hawn P).
[16] William Robertson Sandbach, d. 1891, br. of H.R.; Lancashire J.P.; trying to
arrange meeting between Gladstone and queen of the Netherlands: Add MS 44388, f. 116.

beck.[1] Oaths Comm. & House of C. 1–5¼ and 8¼–12¾. Saw Johnson L[ongden] & Co. Our old friend Hayman. Saw Wolf (Clemence)[R]—Read Ld A. Hervey's Letter[2]—Wilson on Homer—A. Clergyman on Divorce.[3] & other books.

11. T. X.

Wrote to Mr M. Bere[4]—Rev. D. Williams—Scotts—Mr Marrable—John Gibbs[5]—Sir C. Wood—Willy—Dr Briscoe—C.G.—Rev. Mr Preston.[6] Saw Mr Madot—Mr Bonham—Freshfields (Clerk)—Sir W. Heathcote—Lord Lovaine—Mr Henley—Robn. G (& M.E.)—Mr Hayter—Atty General. Saw Wolf. (Clemence) there is hope there, & others[R]. H. of C. 7½–11¾.[7] Read Wilson on Homer—Renaud &c on Divorce[8]—Villette.

12. Wed. X.

Wrote to Sir C. Wood—C.G.[9]—H. Brookes[10]—S.R. Glynne—A.B. Hope. Read Villette—also Peers & People—Campbell on Indian Mutiny[11]—Plea for Liberty of Marriage.[12] H. of C. 2½–5. Spoke on Tea & Sugar Duties Resolution.[13] Saw Mrs Talbot—Sir W. Heathcote—Mr Stanistreet (our deeds are signed at last)—Mr Henley with Sir W.H[eathcote]—Mr Malins. Saw Griffiths: inconsistent but not unhopeful[R]. In evg went off to the East & saw the Hunchback at the 'Royal Grecian'.[14]

13. Th.

Wrote to C.G.—Count A. de Meland.[15] H. of C. Working [against] Divorce Bill 12–4. and 6–12½.[16] Saw Sir W. Heathcote. Read Villette.

---

[1] Unidentified.
[2] A. C. *Hervey, 'A letter to the Rev. Christopher *Wordsworth, D. D. on the declaration of the clergy on marriage and divorce' (1857).
[3] 'Why should we petition against the new divorce bill? By a clergyman' (1857).
[4] Montagu Bere, 1824–87; recorder of Penzance 1857, of Southampton 1862, of Bristol 1870.
[5] John Gibbs, d. 1890; priest in Ireland; archdeacon of Down 1869.
[6] Probably Matthew Morris Preston, 1781?–1858; vicar of Cheshunt from 1826, wrote on morality.
[7] Troops for India: *H* cxlvii. 1392.
[8] G. Renaud, *A few words on the divorce bill, in its relation to scripture and the church services* (1857).
[9] 'This is a blacker day with us as well as you—the Cabinet is now sitting and will decide whether to make a rational concession to us or not, but all the signs at present are bad . . .' (Bassett, 117).
[10] Henry Brookes had written expressing sympathy for catholics (Hawn P).
[11] R. J. R. Campbell, 'The Indian Mutiny: its causes and its remedies' (1857).
[12] Not found.
[13] *H* cxlvii. 1494.
[14] Sheridan Knowles's 'The Hunchback' at the Grecian in the grounds of the Eagle Saloon, off the City Road.
[15] Unidentified.   [16] *H* cxlvii. 1546.

14. Fr.

Wrote to C.G.[1]—Mr Drummond. Read Villette—Documents on Moldavia.[2]
Saw Sir W. Heathcote—Pennethorne & Mr Grogan. H. of C. 12–4 and 6–
12¾: on Divorce Bill—Principalities &c.—Personal Statement.[3]

15. Sat.

Wrote to D. of Newcastle—C.G.[4]—Archdn. Williams—S. Parrell—Dr
Williamson—Mr Jebbs—Ly. M. Labouchere—H. of C. 12–2. Read Raikes
Journal[5]—Villette. Saw Baron Marochetti (on his Welln. monument)[6] and
made a round of calls among relations. Saw Mr Henley—Mr Clay[7]—&
other Members of Parliament on business. Saw Ld Wynford resp. Divorce
& Probate Bills. The account of Mary made me uneasy.

16. 10 S. Trin. [*Hagley*]

I was wakened at 8 by Hampton with a Telegraphic message & went off
at once to Hagley—arriving at 4. C. received me with the words no hope.
I saw her perfectly calm & collected, & though emaciated still not only
beautiful but young in a wonderful degree. She spoke to me a good deal &
had wished to see me, that she might give me her dying charge. She said
'I have long felt how this would end: but I wish to say one thing to you,
take care of *her*(C): for it will be a great change for her and she will feel it
more & more after a time.' She then spoke of her children: & began again
saying 'There is one thing: I cannot think *how* this is to end, for you see
the strength does not seem to give way.' The recollection & peace with
which she spoke (except an effort when she bid me take care of Catherine)
were such as would have been wonderful if in health she had been caring for
some arrangements of her day, and as it was were divine. She said she did
not desire any other end & hoped it would not be. She was already on the
wing! and to come near her or speak with her was so solemn a thing. George
was in great grief but it flowed forth like a full river in its bed, & there was
not a word of repining, only a desire for sympathy & to be allowed to talk
of his beloved & her coming departure yet with a fear lest he should wound
anyone by his own mournings; I cannot but say for it is the truth that he

[1] '. . . The Government have determined to make no concession and we have no
alternative but to tear the Bill in pieces as well as we can which is what it really deserves.'
(Bassett, 118.)
[2] 'Documents pour servir à l'histoire de l'application de l'article 24 du Traité de
Paris . . . en Moldavie' (1857).
[3] To justify a witness in a divorce case, a counsel had claimed that Newcastle had
hired Gladstone in 1849 (see 14 July 49ff.) to spy on his wife in Italy. Gladstone's claim
this day that 'As regards the statement that I either went to collect evidence, or that I
did collect evidence, it is entirely false' gives great elasticity to truth: *H* cxlvii. 1693
and *The Times*, 12 August 1857.
[4] Bassett, 118.
[5] T. *Raikes, *A portion of the journal kept by T. Raikes, Esq., from 1831 to 1847*, 4v.
(1856–7).
[6] He carved three statues of the duke.
[7] James *Clay, 1804–73; visited East with Disraeli 1830; liberal M.P. Hull 1847–53
(unseated on petition), and from 1857; played leading role in 1866–7 reform negotiations;
noted whist player.

afforded almost as edifying a spectacle as his wife. My darling C. was, as I
have seen her before, supported by the very force of the calls upon her: for
she as was natural had most to do and I well know that there is nothing for
which her heroic spirit has not force. Here were the twelve children whom
she has seen and spoken to & all there nearest to her except that Stephen
had not yet arrived; Caroline was at Ems & Willy her godson with the
Prince of Wales. Her pulse was good, & kept so through the evening: also
she slept a great deal; & a faint ray of hope gleamed on us.

Read the service as I came [from] town—Guthrie's Sermons on Cities[1]—
and Lady G. Fullerton's Conteur de Bonval.[2] Wrote to Sir J. Graham—
Mr J. W. Henley—W. Hampton.

17. M. [London]

Wrote to J.N.G.—Mr E. James. Did a Latin lesson with Stephy; and
looked with a new interest upon some of the objects in this home as if the
light in which I see them were about to be withdrawn. This morning the
little improvements continued & were visible even in the organ most
obstinately diseased. I saw her however not apparently looking better
though Dr Giles in a conversation with me seemed to think there was now
decided *hope* though many & varied dangers remained. I was permitted to
carry her from a bed to a new moveable sofa: & she took comfort in some
salts (given me in H. of C.) that I brought from town. I sent off before four,
driving C. to Stourbridge: on her return she found the evil again assuming
the mastery. For fear of causing effort or disturbance, Stephen who had
arrived was not taken to see her—until near the last. On my journey I
was hopeful enough to read some Wilson: Reached H. of C. at 10¼: we
left off at 12½ my motion for civil remarriage standing first for tomorrow.[3]
Walk & conv. with Heathcote until late. Worked on Tacitus Germania.

18. T. [Hagley]

At 7 Hampton came in with a Telegraphic message 'it is all over'. He
burst into tears. I came off at 9 reached Hagley at 3½, Agnes met me, &
then I saw C. O what a void is here! First stands George: and next I think
my Catherine: but the grievousness of the loss will long be felt by all, &
we who were of her generation cannot lose the mark of the event on this
side of the grave. C. described the deep peace of her end: & her last smile
on George. I wrote to Hampton—Mary Ellen and in evg read a little of
Marg. de Navarre[4]: but sighs & tears solitary or interchanged with prayers
were I believe the chief employment of us all. C. took me to see the very
dear remains: the deepest calm was on the face, and the refinement of her
beauty was more visible than even in life. George's grief flowed freely forth
and that gift was the best sign of its healthfulness. He fully accepts the

[1] T. *Guthrie, The City: its sins and sorrows (1857).
[2] G. C. *Fullerton, La comtesse de Bonneval, histoire du temps de Louis XIV (1857,
tr. 1858).
[3] H cxlvii. 1766.
[4] See 26 June 57.

will of God & to see his behaviour is most edifying. Meriel seems to expand under the exigencies of the time—My Catherine bears up heroically.

19. Wed.

Wrote to Willy—Sir J. Graham—Duke of Newcastle—W. Hampton— Sir W. Heathcote. George came to weep at our bedside in the morning. In the aftn. we walked in the Park. The day was gloomy, like a pall as he said. A bright one wd. have been more painful. Lesson in Virg. with Stephy. Read Marg. de Navarre. We conversed upon the future, with Geo. and with one another. We must do what we can for the Motherless. Her baby is all life & joy! Poor little thing: it consumed the last I suppose of her vital powers. Yet we do not know but that with *timely* change from the tonic treatment she might yet have been here to warm her family with her bright presence. The retrospect of her life is a blessed one. It was singularly calm & pure, and full alike of duty & of joy. For me however it has this recollection of pain, that I did not do my duty by her.

20. Th.

Wrote to Ld Canning—J.F. Macqueen—E. Badeley. Walk with C.— Virgil with Stephy. Recommenced Homer for notices bearing on religion.[1] Read Marg. de Navarre—Richard II.

21. Fr.

Ch 10½ a.m. Wrote to Aunt Johanna—Rev. A. Wodehouse—Ld Wenlock— Lady James—Rev. F.D. Legard—Hon. A. Gordon. Virgil with Stephy. Worked on my Homer—Out with C. on the hill. Read Marg. d'Angoulême[2] —Richard II—Henry IV P.1.

22. Sat.

Wrote to Scotts—Provost of Eton. Saw Sir W. Heathcote. Virgil with Stephy. Walk with Geo & the party. Worked on Homer—Mythol. Read Marg. d'Angoulême—Wilson on Homer.[3] Henry IV p. 1. but its comic force makes it unsuitable for this time.

23. 11 S. Trin.

Ch mg & aft. All the mourners were there: only going before, & leaving after, the congregation. We walked in aftn. a party of 8 or 10, wh G[eorge] likes. I shd. rather say we strolled. Wrote to Bp of Salisbury—T.D. Acland. Read Biber's Sermon[4]—Pretyman's Erastianism[5]—Hannah on the Fall[6] —Laud's Remains.[7]

[1] *Studies on Homer*, ii. 1–269.   [2] See 26 June 57.   [3] See 20 July 57.
[4] G. E. *Biber, *The Seven Voices of the Spirit* (1857).
[5] See 9 Aug. 57.   [6] See 2 Aug. 57.
[7] *The works of the most rev. father in God William *Laud, 7v. (1847–60).

24. M. St. Barthol.

We woke to the funeral bell, & gathered betimes in the Drawingroom. Ld
Wenlock came from Greenock. The funeral was at 11½. Along the short
path she had so often trodden nine of her children walked to Church in the
long train as mourners. All was calm & full of solace: especially the Communion which immediately followed & was attended by 60 or 70 including
many weeping servants. George went through it all piously and bravely.
After the Office was played the Dead March: it sounded like music from
the place of her rest greeting her arrival among the band of those who had
preceded her. When the service was over C. looked better than I have seen
her since I came.
　　Wrote to Mrs Herbert—Lady Mary Farquhar[1]—The Duchess of Argyll
—T.T. Courtenay—Dr Jephson—Read Xtn. Year[2]—Monro's Combatants[3]
—Marg. d'Angoulême—Wilson's Homer (finished)—Brougham's Speech
on Reform.[4] Walk with C. Worked (little) on Homer.

25. T.

Wrote to Rev. Mr Elliott[5]—Mr Gillies[6]—Rev. Mr Fowler—Ld Brougham—
Mr Henley—Virgil with Stephy. Worked on Homer. Today George relieved me from reading prayers: & resolutely undertook that duty himself—in a very low voice. Walk to C.s Chair drive. Read Carlyle on Germ.
Lit. & part of the two Œnones.[7] Also the Divorce Debates.

26. Wed.

Wrote to Mr Strang[8]—W. Hampton—Mr C.P. Cooper[9]—H.J.G.—H. Lees.
Worked on Homer. Read Carlyle on Germ. Lit. on Werner—Marg.
d'Angoulême (finished I). Walk with C.

27. Th.

Wrote to Bp of Salisbury—Scotts—B. Porter. Virgil with Stephy—Worked
on Homer: to end of B.XIV. Walk with G. & others. Read Carlyle on
Burns[10]—Henry IV. part I. Packed up.

----

[1] See 25 Aug. 37n.
[2] *Keble's famous series (1827).
[3] E. Monro, *The Combatants; an allegory* (1848).
[4] H. P. *Brougham, Baron Brougham and Vaux, 'Speech on Parliamentary reform,
in the House of Lords, August 3, 1857' (1857).
[5] Charles John Elliott, 1818–81, vicar of Winkfield, Windsor, had written on divorce;
Hawn P.
[6] Robert Pearse *Gillies, 1788–1858; founder and editor of *Foreign Quarterly Review*
1827; see Add MS 44388, f. 146.
[7] [T. *Carlyle], *German Romance*, 4v. (1827) and *Lyttelton's tr. of *Tennyson's
'Oenone' (1832), in the *Translations* (see 2 Sept. 57).
[8] Perhaps John *Strang, 1795–1863; Glasgow merchant and author.
[9] Charles Purton *Cooper, 1793–1873; Q.C.; contested Canterbury as a liberal 1854,
1857; wrote 52 political pamphlets 1850–57.
[10] T. *Carlyle, *Biographical Essays*, ii. (1854).

28. Fr. [Hawarden]

We parted sadly from the Hagley family soon after 11: and reached Hawarden by Stafford & Broughton at 3½. Here we found Willy & all the four children who remained here well. It was Lena's birthday: God bless her: she is a child of great promise. Read Williams's Primitive Tradition.[1] Wrote to Sir E. M'Kenzie—Mrs Hagart—Mr Saunders—Ly. Canning—Mr Healy[2]—Mr H. Brookes.

29. Sat.

Ch 8½ a.m. Wrote to Lady Lucy Grant—Messrs. G. & Co. Tasso & Italian with W. & Agnes, Virgil with Stephy. Worked on my Homer. Read Marg. d'Angouleme—Uriel & other Poems.[3]

30. 12 S. Trin.

Ch mg & evg. Conv with W. A. & S on Epistle. Wrote on Theomythology. Read Jelf Bampton Lectures[4]—Lady Verney's Isaiah[5]—Döllingers Heid.u. Jud.[6]—Horsley on the Messianic Prophecies.[7]

31. M.

Ch. 8½ a.m. (with W)—Wrote to Duchess of Sutherland—Rev. Mr Jones (mis-sent)[8]—Mr W. Grogan—Mr H. Lees. Tasso & Italian Ex. with W. & A. Virgil with Stephy. Read Marg. d' Angoulême—Ed. Rev. on Williams's Homerus[9]—Döllinger Heid.u.Jud. Worked on Homer & wrote. Saw Mr Burnett (mines & O.F.) also Mr Littleboy.

Tues. Sept. One. 1857.

Ch 8½ a.m. Wrote to Duchess of Sutherland—Robn. G—Worked on Homer. Read Döllinger H.und.J.—Twelfth Night. Walk with C. & S. The Mildmays dined. Virg. with Stephy. Tasso & Italian with W. & Agnes. Harry read well to me in French.

2. Wed.

Ch. 8½ a.m. Wrote to W. Dyce—Sec. Carlton Club[10]—Dr Goodford—Mrs Ridgway[11]—Mr J. Severn—Lyttelton—Mrs Chisholm. Tasso & It. Ex.

---

[1] J. *Williams, *Primitive tradition* (1843); reply to *Mure, see 31 Aug. 57.
[2] Probably John Healy, d. 1883?, rector of Redmile 1853–70.
[3] T. Jones, *Uriel and other poems* (1857).
[4] See 10 Nov. 44.
[5] E. Verney, *Practical thoughts on the first forty chapters of . . . Isaiah* (1858); in proof?
[6] See 26 July 57.
[7] S. Horsley, *Nine sermons on the nature of the evidence by which the fact of our Lord's resurrection is established* (1815); quoted in *Studies on Homer*, ii. 16.
[8] Jenkin Jones, perpetual curate of Gwernafield, Mold, Flintshire, 1850.
[9] [*Mure's] review of J. *Williams, *Homerus* (1842), *Edinburgh Review*, lxxvii. 44 (February 1843).
[10] W. Rainger.
[11] Sir F. Doyle's da.; see 22 Aug. 41 and next day.

with W. & A. Virgil with Stephy. Worked on my Homer (finished Mythol. Digest for Iliad & began Od.) Read Marg. d'Angoulême.

3. *Th.*

Ch 8½ a.m. Wrote to Lyttelton—Sir Jas. Graham—Sir F. Doyle. Tasso with W. & A. Virgil with Stephy. Worked on Homer. Read Marg. d'Angoulême—Döllinger's Heid.u.Jud.

4. *Fr.*

Ch 8½ a.m. Wrote to A.F.[*sc.*? T.] Courroux—J. Severn—W. Hampton—Rev. Mr Gleig—Bp of Argyll. Worked on Digest & also wrote on Homer. Tasso with W. & A. Virgil with Stephy. Read Döllinger—Marg. d'Angoulême.

5. *Sat.*

Ch 8½ a.m. Wrote to Sir W. Heathcote—Duchess of Sutherland—Rev. J. Jones (Mold)—Ld A. Hervey. Worked on Homer: Digest & Studies. Tasso with W. & A. Saw Mr Mildmay. Read Marg. d'Angoulême.

6. *13 S. Trin.*

Ch mg & (H.C. with Cath, W. & A.) and Evg. Conv. with 3 eldest on Epis. & Gosp. Wrote to Mr Leslie Foster—Archdeacon Sinclair. Thought & wrote on the Theomythology.[1] Read Outram[2]—Lyderus[3]—Johnson Serm.[4] —Sinclair's Serm.[5] Wrote draft to Sir R. Brooke.[6]

7. *M.*

Ch 8½ a.m.: a notable congregation of 26. Saw E. Griffiths (Schoolmaster). Virgil with Stephy: Tasso W. & A. also Italian exercise. Worked on Homer: Digest and my book. Read Marg. d'Angoulême. Went with C. to Buckley.

8. *T.*

Ch 8½ a.m. Wrote to J.M. Knott[7]—T.G.—Dr Pusey & Extr.—Robn. G—Scotts. Tasso with W. & A. Worked on Homer: Digest & Book. Read Marg. d'Ang.

---

[1] *Studies on Homer*, ii. 1ff. Extended exposition of the Greek 'mixture of theology and mythology' and its supposed links with the old testament, much influenced by Döllinger's *Heidenthum und Judenthum*.
[2] Sir J. *Outram, perhaps *Rough notes of the campaign in Sinde and Afghanistan 1838–39* (1840).
[3] Untraced.
[4] See 14 June 57.
[5] J. *Sinclair, 'Carthaginian and British mercenaries compared. A sermon' (1857).
[6] Sir Richard Brooke, 1785–1865, of Norton Priory, Cheshire; 6th bart. 1795.
[7] John M. Knott, of Severn Stoke, Baptist pamphleteer on church rates.

9. *Wed.*

Ch 8½ a.m. Wrote to G. Leeman—Rev. Jas. Brogden[1]—Mrs Larkins. Saw Dr. Williams[2]—Rev. Mr Mildmay[3]—Mr Jas. Darlington with Mr G. Burnett. We arranged for the immediate resuming of the borings. Made some progress in writing my Homer: but the field of work is still rather enlarging than contracting. Read Marg. d'Angoulême—Virgil with Stephy.

10. *Th.*

Ch 8½ a.m. Wrote to Ld Aberdeen—Rev. Mr Majendie.[4] Tasso with W. & A. Worked on Homer: Studies & Theomythol. Digest. Church Rate meeting 2–3. Saw Mr Burnett—Mr Brewster. Read Marg. d'Ang.

11. *Fr.*

Ch 8½ a.m. Wrote to C.J. Skeet—Tasso with W. & A. Virgil with Stephy. Worked on Homer (I am now in the stiffest part) Studies & Digest. Read Marg. d'Ang. *Heard* Bride of Lammermoor: the sublime catastrophe was resistless.[5]

12. *Sat.*

Ch 8½ a.m. Wrote to Mr Dyce—Tasso with W. & A. Virg. with S. Worked hard on Homer—Dined at the Rectory.

13. *14. S. Trin.*

Ch mg & evg. Worked on the Theology of my Homer. Read Döllinger— Jelf's Bampton Lectures. Conv. with the three eldest.

14. *M.*

Ch 8½ a.m. A threatening of neuralgia. Worked hard at Homer—Tasso with W. & A. Also It. exercise with W. Dined at the Rectory.

15. *T.*

Ch 8½ a.m. Wrote to Mr Preshaw—Dr Hook—Mr Pease M.P.[6]—Mr Wainwright—Saw Mr G. Burnett. Obliged to pull up in my work on Homer: in consequence on neuralgia at night. Read Fortunes of Nigel.[7] The boys went off at 3 to Eton. They have been *so* good: and everyone loves them.

---

[1] James Brogden, 1806?–64; Trinity, Cambridge; vicar of Deddington, Oxon., from 1848; wrote on church law.
[2] See 5 Mar. 42; a leading Homeric scholar.
[3] Charles Arundell St. John Mildmay, 1820–1904; fellow of Merton; rector of Lapworth, Birmingham, 1848–64, of Long Marston 1864–73.
[4] Probably Henry William Majendie, 1807–69; vicar of Speen, Berks., from 1819; prebendary of Salisbury from 1824.
[5] A reading of *Scott's novel.
[6] Henry *Pease, 1807–81; quaker railway and coal owner; active in Peace Society, visited Russia with it 1854; liberal M.P. S. Durham 1857–65.
[7] *Scott (1822).

16. Wed.

Ch 8½ a.m. Wrote to Mrs Larkins—J.N.G.—Rev. Mr Lowe. Again at half time on Homer, from Neuralgia. Lady Meath came. Read F. of Nigel—Dr Horner[1]—Saw Mr Burnett & visited the bore-hole. Saw Mr Keats.

17. Th.

Missed Ch. to get rid of my pain by rest. Half time, or less, on Homer. Read F. of Nigel. We had a Palmerston Conversation till ½ p. 12. Saw Sherratt with Mr B[urnett]. Wrote to Mr Darlington—Sir W. Heathcote.

18. Fr.

Ch 8½ a.m. Wrote to Mrs Surtees[2]—Ld Brougham—Mr W. Morris—Mr Jas. Stevens. Worked half time and a little more on Homer. Saw Sherratt —Read F. of Nigel.

19. Sat.

Ch 8½ a.m. Wrote to W.H. Lyttelton—R.M. Milnes—Willy—Saw Mr Burnett—Sherratt. Worked on Homer—Read Fortunes of Nigel.

20. 15 S. Trin.

Ch mg & evg. Read T.A. Kempis—Döllinger's Heid.u.Jud.[3]—Blunt's Hist Ch.[4]—Literary Churchman[5] &c.

21. St Matth. M.

Ch 8½ a.m. Dies memorabilis.[6] Wrote to Marcy & Whitcombe—Scotts— H. Lees—Tatham Upton & Co—Saw Mr Burnett—Visited the bore-hole. Worked on Homer Theomythol (finished) Digest. Read Fortunes of Nigel.

22. T.

Ch 8½ a.m. Wrote to Ld Brougham—Mr Pennethorne—Worked on Homer. Finished Fortunes of Nigel. Read Lorenzo de'Medici Poems.[7] Walk with Stephen to bore-holes &c.

23. Wed.

Ch 8½ a.m. Some bowel complaint threatened me. Worked but very little on Homer. Read Nägelsbach Hom. Theol.[8] & began Rob Roy.[9] Saw Mr Burnett on S.s. affairs.

[1] Jonah Horner, 'On health: what preserves, what destroys and what restores it' (1857).
[2] Probably Elizabeth Jane, née Fenwick, wife of Robert Smith *Surtees, 1803–64, novelist; she d. 1879.
[3] See 30 Aug. 57.
[4] J. J. *Blunt, A history of the Christian Church during the first three centuries (1856).
[5] The Literary Churchman, periodical published from 1855–92.
[6] Perhaps he meant 23 September, anniversary of his mother's death; see 23 Sept. 35.
[7] Poesie del Magnifico Lorenzo de'Medici, ed. L. Nardini and S. Buonajuti, 2v. (1801).
[8] See 6 Jan. 57.
[9] *Scott (1817).

24. Th.

Absented myself from Ch. Wrote to Marcy & Whitcombe—Mr Beavan (Buckley) and [blank]. Worked on Homer. Read Rob Roy. A political conv. in Evg. Ital. lesson to Agnes.

25. Fr.

Ch 8½ a.m. Wrote to Robn. G—C.A. Wood. Saw Mr G. Burnett—Mr Dickinson—Mr & Mrs Austin (robbed last Monday).[1] Worked on Homer— Read Nägelsbach—Rob Roy.

26. Sat.

Ch 8½ a.m. Wrote to Sir W. Heathcote—Rev. Jos. Brown[2]—W. Grogan. The Lytteltons came. Read Nägelsbach—Granville Penn on the Iliad[3]— Rob Roy. Worked on Homer. Saw R. Phillimore.

27. 16 S. Trin.

Ch mg & evg. Wrote to Robn. G. Saw R. Phillimore—Rev. E. Hawkins. Read Sewell's Sermons.[4] Blunt's Hist—Dr Döllinger.

28. M.

Ch 8½ a.m. Wrote to Ld Chandos—Messrs. Lennan & Clarke—Sir S. Scott & Co. Worked on Homer—Walked with George & S. Read G. Penn on Iliad—Rob Roy. Nägelsbach Hom. Theol.

29. T. St Michael.

Ch 8½ a.m. Wrote to Willy—Stephy. Worked on Homer. Read Ticknor's Sp.Lit.[5]—Rob Roy finished—Nägelsbach Hom.Theol.—G. Penn on Iliad.

30. Wed.

Ch 8½ a.m. Wrote to Bp of Montreal. Worked pretty well on Homer. Read Granville Penn—Ticknor's Span.Lit. Walk with C. & Phillimore.

Thurs. Octr. One. 1857.

Ch 8½ a.m. (23 pres.) Wrote to H. Lees (documents)—Robn. G.—Willy— Manager of Univ. Press Oxford.[6] A long walk with G. Read the remarkable record of Mary's illness & death.[7] It is most moving. Worked on Homer. Read Granville Penn (finished)—Music in evg. Made notes from Ticknor for Willy.[8]

[1] The priest at Broughton; see 6 Dec. 53.
[2] Joseph *Brown, 1800–1867; rector of Christ Church, Southwark 1849–67; charitable organiser (see Venn, II. ii. 407).
[3] G. *Penn, *An examination of the primary argument of the Iliad* (1821).
[4] W. *Sewell, *A year's sermons to boys preached in the Chapel of St. Peter's College, Radley* (1854).
[5] G. Ticknor, *History of Spanish literature*, 3v. (1849).
[6] James Wright, with whom Gladstone had extended correspondence over the printing and publication of *Studies on Homer*: Add MS 44388.
[7] Record of his wife's d. by George *Lyttelton, in Hawn P.
[8] Not found; see 1 Oct. 57.

2. Fr.

Ch 8½ a.m. Wrote to Rev. Mr [J.W.] Blakesley—Rev. Mr Tomlin—Rev. Mr Blakesley—Mr W. Wigan Harvey—Mr Robert (Chesterfield). Saw Rev. Canon Blomfield. Walk with George: we talked of literary employment & I recommended to him divers undertakings.[1] Music in evg. Worked on Homer: finished my ἄναξ ἀνδρῶν[2]—Read Nägelsbach—began Black Dwarf.[3]

3. Sat.

Ch 8½ a.m. Wrote to Mr Edgeley[4]—H. Lees—Canon Blomfield—Willy—Mr Jas. Wright (sent Octr. 5).[5] Worked on Homer: I am now enough advanced to begin Contents: but a good deal of licking down & filing & some rewriting remain.

4. 17. S. Trin.

Ch mg and Evg. At H.C. poor Henry could hardly get through: all the Lytteltons were before him so recalling his sister & his wife. Read Döllinger —Sewell's Sermons—Manning's Sermons[6]—Claughton's[7] & Vaughan's[8] —Tomlins's Letter.[9]

5. M.

Ch 8½ a.m. Wrote to Mr T. Chamberlayn[10]—B. Quaritch—A. Panizzi— W. Grogan—Geo. Grant. Revised the rest of the Prolegomena, & sent it off, as my first batch of 'copy', to the Clarendon Press. Worked on MS. Saw Mr Littleboy—Read Black Dwarf (finished)—Bruce on Homer[11]— Nägelsbach.

6. T.

Ch 8½ a.m. Wrote to Rev. R. Jones—Dr Pusey—G. & Co. Saw Mr Burnett —Mr Littleboy. Worked on Homer (II) for the Press. Read Nägelsbach— Heart of Midlothian—Bruce on Homer.

7. Wed. Public Fast.

Church at 11 a.m. & 6½ P.M. Read DeVere's May Carols[12]—'Lond. Quarterly' on Indian Rebellion.[13] Nägelsbach.

[1] To distract him from his grief; the start of their joint *Translations* project, published in 1861.
[2] *Studies on Homer*, i. 440–543.
[3] *Scott (1816).
[4] Possibly Edward Edgerley, chandler in Clerkenwell.
[5] Phrase added later.
[6] See 12 Mar. 43.
[7] T. L. *Claughton, 'The duty of preparing ourselves to receive the Lord's supper' (1856).
[8] C. J. *Vaughan, 'The Indian sorrow and its lessons for the young. A sermon' (1857).
[9] R. Tomlins, *A reply to a circular forwarded by the Committee of Westerton v. Liddell to . . . R. Tomlins* (1857).
[10] See 24 Nov. 31; then a Student of Christ Church.
[11] W. Bruce, *The state of society in the age of Homer* (1827).
[12] A. T. *De Vere, *May Carols* (1857).
[13] *London Quarterly Review*, ix. 208 (October 1857).

8. Th.

Ch 8¼ a.m. Wrote to Mr Jas. Wright (sent 9th)—B. Quaritch. Worked pretty fully on Homer. Dined at the Rectory: Homeric conv. with Lady L.[1] & her party there. Read Nägelsbach. Pamphlet on Bengal Army.[2]

9. Fr.

Ch 8½ a.m. Wrote to Canon Blomfield—Saw Mr Burnett—Mr Littleboy—and went with him to the outcrop of the sandstone in Broughton Brook.[3] Worked on Homer. Finished Pamphlet on Bengal Army. Read Heart of Midlothian[4]—Nägelsbach—Browne's Hist. Rom. Literature.[5]

10. Sat.

Ch 8¼ a.m. Wrote to Mr G. Burnett—Ld Granville—Post Master Chester. Went to Dee Cottage: but missed Mr B[urnett]—Visited the L. Borehole. Read H. of Midlothian—Nägelsbach—L.Q. on Univv.[6] Worked on Homer: G[eorge] & S[tephen] helped in search for Greco-Latin words. Singing in evg.

11. 18 S. Trin.

Ch mg & evg. Conv. on 2d lesson with A. Wrote to Mr Crosier[7]—Dr Godfray. Read Remusat's Abelard[8]—Lady Verney on Isaiah.[9]

12. M.

Ch 8½ a.m. Wrote to Robn. G—Worked on Homer. Saw Mr Burnett. Read some S.P.G. & E.I. papers & off at 6.15 to Chester. There was a crowded meeting: Bp of Oxford made a very powerful Speech & I a very ineffective one.[10] Home about eleven. Read Heart of Midlothian.

13. T.

Ch 8½ a.m. (28 pres.) Wrote to Mr Jas. Wright—Archdn. Denison (draft)—Worked on Homer. Saw Mr Burnett—Much conv with Bp of Oxford[11] on—

[1] i.e. Lady Sarah Lyttelton, George's mother.
[2] Probably W. Martin, 'Memorandum on the reconstruction of the Bengal army' (1857).
[3] E. of Hawarden, flowing into the Dee.
[4] *Scott (1818).
[5] R. W. Browne, *A history of Roman classical literature* (1853).
[6] *London Quarterly Review*, ix. 1 (October 1857).
[7] Robert Crozier of Manchester, who was setting up a cttee. to collect funds for W. *Bradley's (see 2 May 38) widow.
[8] See 20 Apr. 57.
[9] See 29 Aug. 57.
[10] On India; published in S.P.G. *Church missions: missionary speeches*, iii (1857) and *Chester Courant*, 14 October 1857, 5.
[11] Extracts from *Wilberforce's diary on these are in Wilberforce, ii. 349. And see above v. xxvi.

1. Bp of Brechin's Charge[1]
2. Divorce Act Movement.[2]
3. India.
Read Bp of Brechin's Charge—The Mutiny of the Bengal Army[3]—Italian
Ex. with Agnes—Singing in evg.

14. Wed.

Ch. 8½ a.m. Wrote to Miss M.N. Gladstone—Wrote off and sent letter to
Archd. D[enison]. Corrected & sent off first proof. Worked on Homer.
Conv. with Bp O[xford] on Divorce Act & his Charge. He left us. Read
Nägelsbach—Heart of Midlothian—Singing.

15. Th.

Ch 8½ a.m. Wrote to Provost of Eton. Sir W. Heathcote—Willy. Dee Trust
Meeting[4] 12¼–2¾. Saw Mr Barker—Mr Burnett. Worked on Homer. Read
Nägelsbach—Heart of Midlothian—Singing in evg.

16. Fr.

Ch 8½ a.m. Worked on Homer. Read Nägelsbach—Schönemann Hom.
Geogr.[5]—Heart of Midlothian. The Jameses came.

17. Sat.

Ch 8½ a.m. Wrote to Bp of St Davids[6]—Bp of Oxford—Ld Brougham—
Scotts. Worked on Homer. Read Nägelsbach—Döderlein[7]—Heart of Midlothian. Walk with W. James.

18. St Luke & 19. S. Trin.

Ch mg & evg. Agnes's birthday: & a day of much joy. She is full of happy
promise. Conv. with her on Ep. & Gosp. With W. James on Army Discipline.
Read Lady Verney on Isaiah—Q.R. on the Parish Priest[8]—Remusat's
Abelard.

---

[1] Distressed at the lack of ritualism amongst his Dundee parishioners, A. P. *Forbes'
Charge (1857) emphasised sacrifice and adoration in the Eucharist; his fellow Scottish
bps. and laity denounced him and he was found guilty of heresy in Edinburgh in 1860
and was censured, a result which extensive correspondence by Gladstone failed to
prevent.
[2] *Wilberforce had led opposition in the Lords to the bill, failing to amend it to
prevent inter-marriage by guilty parties.
[3] G. B. *Malleson, *The mutiny of the Bengal army. An historical narrative*, 2v. (1857–8).
[4] The Hawarden Embankment Trust, which dealt with navigation on the Dee etc.
[5] See 23 Apr. 47.
[6] Connop *Thirlwall read the proofs of *Studies on Homer*.
[7] J. C. W. von Döderlein wrote widely on the classics; probably *Homerisches Glossarium*
(1850).
[8] *Quarterly Review*, cii. 453 (Oct. 57).

19. M.

Ch. 8½ A.M. Wrote to G. Crawshay—Robn. G.—Wm. Gladstone—Mrs Webb—Capt. Norton[1]—J. Rowsell—Rev. Mr [J.S.] Howson[2]—Rev. Mr Hawkins. Italian with A. Spent the day chiefly on letters paper & accounts. Worked on Hom. proof Sheets at night. Read Q.R. on I. Mutiny[3]—and Lake Guides: meditating a little trip. Saw Mr Burnett.

20. T.

Ch. 8½ A.M. Wrote to Rev Mr Blakesley—J.N.G.—Mr Dowdall—H. Beatty[4]—Jas Wright. Worked on Homer: but I find that 'duning the hole',[5] to borrow a phrase from the borers, takes me a very long time. And all along the work has tokens of being done by an unpractised man not master of his materials. Worked also on revises. Singing in evg. Read H. of Midlothian.

21. Wed.

Ch. 8½ A.M. Wrote to V. Chancr. Oxford—J. Murray—Mayor of Oxford[6] —Ld Brougham—Rev Mr Howson—R. Andrews—Sir J. Lefevre. Corrected Speech on India for S.P.G. Worked on Homer. Walk with Lyttelton. Italian with Agnes. Read H. of Midlothian. Tidying & packing.

22. Th. [Brougham Hall]

Off at 8.25. On my journey and in Liverpool saw Mr Keats—Mr Howson— Mr G. Grant—Mr Pearson—Mr Dowdall—Robn. G—Rev Mr Carter.[7] Attended at the Lpool Collegiate Instn. Anniversary Meeting & spoke there.[8] Reached Brougham Hall[9] at 6¾. He [Lord Brougham] was full of life & good humour & knowledge & it was a very interesting evening. Read Hermann's Griechische Staats Alterthum.[10]

23. Fr.

Spent the morning chiefly with Ld Brougham—with the Bp of Oxford— & with Mr Brougham[11] & Mr Crackanthorp[12]: we discussed much Sir J. Graham's case & character. In the afternoon Ld B. the Bp & I drove to see Lowther[13] & its fine Park, & then Pooley[14] with the Patterdale Hills. We

---

[1] Edward Norton, published on Christianity and currency.

[2] Principal of Liverpool Collegiate Institution; see 8 Mar. 50 and 22 Oct. 57.

[3] *Quarterly Review*, cii. 534 (October 1857).

[4] Henry Beattie, d. 1867; priest 1848; headmaster of London orphan asylum from 1852.

[5] Not in *O.E.D.*; probably 'attacking constantly'.

[6] Isaac Grubb, Oxford baker.

[7] Thomas Carter, priest 1833; chaplain of Liverpool borough gaol.

[8] Report in *The Guardian*, 28 October 1857, 821.

[9] *Brougham's seat on the river Lowther, 2 miles SE. of Penrith.

[10] C. F. Hermann, *Lehrbuch der griechischen Staatsalterthümer* (1831).

[11] William *Brougham, 1795–1886; br. of Henry*, who greatly relied on him; barrister; 2nd Baron Brougham 1868.

[12] William Crackanthorpe, 1790–1888, of Newbiggin Hall, Westmoreland.

[13] Lowther castle, Lord Lonsdale's seat 4 miles S. of Penrith, with a splendid art collection.

[14] Pooley Bridge, at the efflux of the Eamont from Ullswater.

talked over the Eccl. Court of Appeal & were well agreed.[1] Wrote to C.G.—
Mrs T. Goalen. In evg again sat pretty late: Ld B. withdraws before 11—
Lady B.s[2] position is most singular. She seems to have everything but
recognition from him. Read πετριδης Ἱστορία.[3]—Hermann Gr. St. Alt.—
Friedrich Realien.[4]

24. Sat. [Keswick]

Wrote to C.G.[5] We had a further conversation in the forenoon about the
Court of Appeal: which went very well. Packed & bid good bye to this very
hospitable house. 12–6½ Walked by Pooley Bridge and Dockray to Keswick
(Royal Oak)[6]—the day fair tho' rather dull—the lake scenery very fine,
red fern standing for heather: distance 22 or 23 m. In evg. read Od. I–III—
the Guide Book. Corrected Lpool Speech.

25. 20 S. Trin.

Keswick Ch mg: (the one near hand—so so)—and stupidly missed New-
lands[7] in aftn. when I walked over to Buttermere 10 m. Read A Kempis
Imit. Xti a book which never loses always gains on reperusal: & Friedrich's
Realien. Hom. Theol. Buttermere is fine: the Inn rather a poor affair.
Wrote to C.G.

26. M. [Liverpool]

In mg went to see Crummock Water well: & off at 10 up the Honister pass
very savage & grand, down into Borrowdale then with a guide over into
Langdale and down to Lowwood[8] where I got at 6¼ say 24 miles: 26 for the
day, quite enough with a sore heel the sure result of inconsiderately starting
a walking tour without practice to harden the foot. On by coach & rail to
Lpool at midnight.

27. T. [Hawarden]

Wrote to T. Dowdall—G. & Co.—Bp of St David's—Scotts—Sir W.
Heathcote—J. Wright—Mr C. Sumner. Off at 7¾: home at 9¾: I found C.
not very well & the sad news of the deaths of Lady Graham & our much
esteemed Mrs Hartmann[9] who preceded her husband by a few days. She is
a great loss: but it was a signal mercy of God to keep them together.

---

[1] Discussions about a Clergy Discipline Bill; *Wilberforce, *Brougham and Gladstone
agreed to omit the abps. and the bp. of London from the final court of appeal; disagreement amongst the bps. prevented the bill being passed.
[2] *Brougham m. 1819 Mary Anne Spalding, née Eden; she d. 1865; Sidney *Smith
called her 'a showy red and white widow'.
[3] Untraced history by Plato Petrides, nineteenth century Greek author.
[4] See 10 June 57.
[5] Bassett, 119.
[6] Hotel in Keswick, on Derwentwater. He had walked over the hills from Ullswater.
[7] Perhaps a locum for J. M. Woodmason, the priest at Buttermere.
[8] i.e. he walked east from Buttermere into Borrowdale, then turned south over the
Langdale Pikes, then east to Low Wood on Lake Windermere.
[9] Miss Brown's successor as governess.

Worked on Homer Proofs and Revises. Conv. with C. on Governessing &c. Read Ed. Rev. on India[1]—Heart of Midlothian.

28. Wed. SS. Simon & Jude.

Church 8½ A.M. Wrote to Sir J. Graham—J. Murray. Worked on Homer— the Catalogue, & the 7th Section. Italian with Agnes. Read Nägelsbach— Heart of Midlothian.

29. Th.

Instead of the usual peaceful wakening for Church, we were roused about five by the announcement that the House of God was in flames. I went up immediately & was there till 11. More was saved than from a first view I hoped. There was great zeal & the measures well taken. All the different lights at dawn were struggling together: & the clock struck the chimes while the flames worked beneath & round it with a tranquillity that was really sublime. This will give us much to do & think about.[2] Wrote to C. Pressly(2)—Jas Wright—Robn. G.—T. Dowdall—Rev. Mr Maclaurin[3]—A. Lendrum—A. Gurney—Hon. A. Gordon—A.H. Monteith.[4] Worked on Homer. Read H. of Midlothian.

30. Fr.

No Church today! Wrote to J.N.G.—J. Griffiths—Rev. J.B. Sweet—Mr W. Brown M.P.[5] The Church occupies much of our thoughts & time. Saw the Bishop in the forenoon: the Detectives, & examined the gardenman in the aftn: & in evg saw the Inspector & Clerk to the Magistrates.[6] Worked on Homer, revision. Also conv. with G. [Lyttelton] on his criticisms, as he has begun to peruse the revises.[7] Read Nägelsbach—Heart of Midlothian(finished). Saw Mr Burnett on S.s affairs.

31. Sat.

Alas a blank again in that mode of opening the day. Wrote to H.S. with M. & L.—Ld Brougham—D. Meehan—Rev W.P. Pigott[8]—Glyn & Co—T. Dowdall. Worked on Homer (Cadmeans, &c.).[9] Read Engl. under Houses of York & Lancaster. Convns. about the Church & means of restoring it. Saw the Police: who have a new scent after three persons supposed local.

[1] *Edinburgh Review*, cvi. 544 (October 1857).
[2] The bulk of the church was destroyed by arson, but the registers, books, and precious objects were saved; longer description in *DLFC*, i. 58.
[3] William C. Augustine Maclaurin, dean of the diocese of Moray and Ross.
[4] Alexander H. Monteith, published on classical philology.
[5] See 18 July 45.
[6] Peter Ellis Eyton, 1827–78; solicitor and clerk to the magistrates in Mold; liberal M.P. Flint district from 1874.
[7] Of *Studies on Homer*.
[8] Wellesley Pole Pigott, 1808–90; rector of Fuggleston St. Peter, Wiltshire, from 1836.
[9] *Studies on Homer*, i. 239.

Sunday Nov One All Saints & 21 Trin.

Buckley Ch mg—Broughton aftn—together a good Sabbath day's Journey. Mr Lee[1] preached very well. Read Harvey's Prolusio—Latham on Man[2]—Taverner's Postils[3]—Letter to Ld A. Hervey.[4] Conv. with Agnes on Gospel.

2. M.

Italian with Agnes. Wrote to Bp of Oxford—Willy—Ld Wenlock—J. White. Worked on Homer (Danaans).[5] Further consultations about the Church. Saw Mr Davison. Made known to S. through C. that in my opinion he can *only* contribute 1. from his personal income 2. from *extra* wood cutting. Read Ed. Rev. on the Napiers[6]—Railways in Egypt.[7]

3. T.

Wrote to Bp of Salisbury—J. Wright—Mr W. Fraser.[8] Worked on Homer —proofs, & Achaeans. Italian with Agnes. Conv. with C. about the strange revelations as to Mrs Hartmann. She must have been mad.[9] And with Ln. on the Eccl. Court of Appeal.[10] Read Nitzsch Odysseus Erzählung[11]— Goldsmith's Poems—Watson on Chemistry of Metals.[12]

4. Wed.

Wrote to C. Sharpe—Lady M. Alford—F. Gibbs—F. Ayrton.[13] Worked on Homer—Italian Ex. with Agnes. Mr Sumner came: we walked, & had much conv. Read Ed. Rev. on Ld Campbell.[14]

5. Th.

Recommenced with the daily service, $8\frac{1}{2}$ as usual, in the poor ruined Church. Thank God. Drove with Mr Sumner[15] in the rain: he went off to Chester &

[1] Thomas Jones Lee, d. 1875; curate of Buckley, by Hawarden; vicar of Christ Church, Luton, from 1863.
[2] See 11 Mar. 52.
[3] R. Taverner, ed., *The epistles and gospels with a brief postyl from Advent till Low Sunday* (1540?).
[4] Probably W. Hanson, *Maynooth Endowments and Nunneries Bills. Letters to Lord Alfred Hervey* (1853).
[5] *Studies on Homer*, i. 355.
[6] *Edinburgh Review*, cvi. 322 (Oct. 57).
[7] *Railways in Egypt. Communication with India* (1857).
[8] Sir William *Fraser, 1816–98; Edinburgh antiquarian; deputy-keeper of sasines 1852–80, of records 1880–92; K.C.B. 1887; the Gladstone brothers had asked him to research into their genealogy, see Add MS 44388, f. 237.
[9] See 27 Oct. 57.
[10] See 23 Oct. 57n.
[11] G. W. Nitzsch, 'Des Odysseus Erzählung vor Alkinoos' from *Erklärende Anmerkungen zu Homer's Odyssee*, 3v. (1826–40).
[12] R. *Watson, *Chemical essays*, v. 1–3 (1781–7).
[13] Frederick Ayrton, 1812–73; barrister and secretary to Abbas and Ilhami Pasha; collector of Arabiana.
[14] *Edinburgh Review*, cvi. 432 (October 1857).
[15] i.e. the Senator; see 4 July 57.

Eaton, much liked by all. Worked on Homer (finished ἄναξ ἀνδρῶν for press).[1] Read Latham's Man & his Migrations. Wrote to Mr H. Lees— Mr A. Montgomery.[2] Attended prelim. meeting at Rectory, drew Resolutions & Memorandum, then Parish Meeting at 2 P.M. where we had an excellent feeling about the reparation of the Church.[3] Saw Mr Burnett.

6. Fr.

Ch. 8½ A.M. Wrote to T.G.—J.N.G.—Mr W. Fraser—Mr H. Kingscote— —Mr R.S. Holford.[4] Italian with Agnes. Saw Mr Burnett. Worked on Homer. Read Latham's Man—Q.R. on Pritchard—Malcolm's Persia.[5]

7.

Ch. 8½ A.M. Wrote to Bp of St David's—Scotts—Jas Wright. Italian with Agnes. Madlle de Romauld[6] came. Worked on Homer MS (finished preparation of 1st Vol for press) and proofs. Walk with G. & Homeric talk. Read Höck's Creta.[7] Say's picture of Mary came & quite overset C. by its beauty.[8]

8. 22 S. Trin.

Ch. 11 A.M. & H.C. 6½ P.M. Very full (in Chancel S.Aisle & Vestry). Mr Brewster preached on the fire. Read Remusat's Abélard,[9] and Sermons. Wrote on The Atonement—on Homer's Theomythol.

9. M.

Ch. 8½ A.M. Wrote to Duchess of Sutherland—Robn. G—Mr R[euben] Browning. Worked on Homer—Theomythol. and proofs. Read Grote Vol. IV (Persia &c.)[10] and Latham's Man & his Migr. Walk with G. & H. to Shotton.

10. T.

Ch. 8½ A.M. Wrote to Sir W. Heathcote—Scotts—D. Meehan. Worked on Homer as yesterday: critical conv. with G. Walk with G. H.S. with M. & L. Read N. Brit. on Alison[11]—The Crisis in India.[12] Saw Mr Burnett.

[1] *Studies on Homer*, i, section ix.
[2] Alfred Montgomery, 1814–96; commissioner of stamps 1846–82; 'the last of the dandies'; had sent some poems (Hawn P).
[3] Report in *The Guardian*, 11 November 1857, 859; MSS in Hawn P.
[4] Robert Stayner Holford, 1808–92; tory M.P. E. Gloucestershire 1854–72; built Dorchester House in Park Lane: owned splendid picture collection and library.
[5] J. Malcolm, *The history of Persia, from the most early period to the present time*, 2v. (1815).
[6] Unidentified.   [7] C. *Höck, *Kreta*, 3v. (1823–9).
[8] F. R. *Say's portrait of Mary Lyttelton, a pair with that of Catherine Gladstone, painted at the time of their marriages; both now at Hawarden.
[9] See 20 Apr. 57.
[10] See 19 Mar. 47.
[11] *North British Review*, xxvii. 277 (November 1857).
[12] Probably *The crisis of India; its causes and proposed remedies* (1857).

11. Wed.

Ch. 8½ A.M. Wrote to Sir T. Macmahon[1]—Robn. G.—Rev. R. Greswell. Saw Mr Scott[2] the Architect, come down for the poor Church. H.S. with M. & L. Worked on Homer MS. proof & revise. Read Nägelsbach.

12. Th.

Ch. 8½ AM. Wrote to Sir Jas Graham—Jas Wright—Ld Brougham—W. Grogan—Bp of St David's—J.W. Williams. H.S. with M. & L. Worked on Homer: chiefly on *dressing* for Press, which takes an hour per sheet. Read Kinglake on India—Norton on Currency[3]—Mann on Competing Examns.[4] Walk with G: whose critical assistance is of much use to me.

13. Fr.

Ch. 8½ A.M. Wrote to J.W. Macdonald[5]—Capt. Gladstone—and Sir S. Scott & Co sending our *first* fruits £298 for investment. Worked on Homer —MS. and for Press. Saw Mr Burnett resp. the Coal, & visited bore-hole. Also old G. Edwards.[6] Read Q.R. on Cornwall—Do on Euphrates Route.[7]

14. Sat.

Ch. 8½ AM. Wrote to S. Herbert. A rather stiff day on the geography of the Odyssey.[8] Also for press. Read II. 13.—Müller's Orchomenos.[9]—The Danubian Principalities.[10] We conversed on the case of T. Turner[11]: it appearing that one of the servants in the house is an unbeliever: Eli, the reading youth. C. in bed with a most severe influenza very prevalent here.

15. 23 S. Trin.

Ch. mg & aft. Conv. with Agnes on the gospel. Wrote to Sir W. Heathcote— Archdeacon Harrison—Rev. Dr Caswall—Rev. R. Campbell.[12] Read Newman's Sermons[13]—Manning,[14] aloud to C.—Heraclides Ponticus[15]—Religious Periodicals.

[1] Sir Thomas Macmahon, 1779–1860; 2nd bart. 1817; soldier; commanded at Bombay 1839–47; general 1854.
[2] i.e. (Sir) G. G. *Scott.
[3] E. Norton, 'The Bank Charter Act of 1844' (1857).
[4] H. Mann, *Civil Service competitions, considered as a means of promoting popular education* (1857).
[5] Of Penmaenmawr.
[6] A villager.
[7] *Quarterly Review*, cii. 289, 354 (October 1857).
[8] For *Studies on Homer*, iii, part 3.
[9] See 4 Aug. 56.
[10] *Westminster Review*, xi. 487 (January–April 1857).
[11] A servant.
[12] Rev. Robert Campbell of Aberdeen had asked for funds for a students' hostel: Hawn P.
[13] See 10 Oct. 43.
[14] See 12 Mar. 43.
[15] A pupil in Plato's school, wrote extensive philosophic writings almost entirely lost.

16. M.

Ch. 8½ A.M. Wrote to Bp of St David's—Mr Jas Wright—Hon. A. Gordon—Hon. S. Lyttelton—Mr Jas Greene[1]—Sir S. Scott & Co (kept back till 18th.). Worked on Homer—Crit. discussion with G. & S. H.S. with M. and Lena. Read Quest. of Principalities.

17. T.

Ch. 8½ AM. Wrote to Rev Mr Hunter[2]—Scotts—Mr Leary.[3] H.S. with M. & L. Saw Mr Burnett—Worked on Homer—Read on the Principalities. Conv. with L[yttelton] on Homer.

18. Wed.

Ch. 8½ A.M. Wrote to Sir W. James—Scotts—A. Panizzi. C. better, & walking. The Lytteltons went. H.S. with M. and L. Worked on Homer. Read Principalities(finished)—Livingstone's Travels.[4]

19. Th.

Ch 8½ AM. Wrote to Jas Wright—Bp of St David's—Worked much on Homer—the end still seems to get farther off. All will I think have been written twice & much three or four times over.
Read Cairns on Political Economy[5]—H.S. with M. & L. Attended the Vestry & Committee meetings. The rate was voted a l'unanimité.[6] I rendered an account of my intromissions for the Ch. Fund. We bought Govt. securities last week to pay 6¼ per cent.

20. Fr.

Ch. 8½ AM. Wrote to Mr Jas Wright—Sir S. Scott & Co—Mr A. Panizzi—Dow[age]r Lady Beauchamp. Worked on Homer—much. Church Fund business. H.S. with M. & L. Read Müller's Dorians.[7]

21. Sat.

Ch 8½ AM. Wrote to A.B. Cochrane—J.N.G.—Mrs Goalen—Ld Lyttelton. Worked on Homer: much. H.S. with M. & L. Read Dunlop's Rom. Lit.[8]

22. Last S. Trin.

Ch. mg & aft. Conv. with Agnes on 2d Lesson. Wrote to Mr Brewster—Jas Watson. Read Emigrants' Aid papers—Newman's Sermons. Worked a while on Homeric Theology.

[1] Smudged; perhaps James Green, chaplain in Natal; and correspondent with Gladstone 1863 on racial cooperation (Hawn P).
[2] John Hunter, priest 1816; curate of Ashton-upon-Mersey.
[3] John Frederick Leary, librarian to the House of Lords.
[4] See 14 Mar. 57.
[5] J. E. *Cairnes, *Lectures on policital economy* (1857).
[6] £1000 was voted from the rate to restore the church.
[7] See 30 Aug. 56.
[8] J. C. *Dunlop, *History of Roman literature*, 3v. (1823–8).

23. M.

Ch. 8½ AM. Mazie's birthday: may God keep her tender for ever as she is now. She is the most womanish of all the daughters: very pure & good; works well (as far as I can see) & with good powers. Worked on Homer—proofs & MS. Wrote to Lady Bath—Sir T. Gladstone—Mr T. Dowdall—Rev. G. Rorison. H.S. with M. & L. Read Dunlop's Roman Literature Vols. 2. & 3—Cic[ero] de Nat[ura] Deor[um][1]

24. T.

Ch. 8½ A.M. Wrote to Sir Jas Graham—Rev C. Badham[2]—A. Panizzi—Scotts. Church Fund business. Consultations on the Thorn & Brewster affair.[3] Worked on Homer (Outer Geogr.)[4] Read Dunlop's Rom. Lit.

25. Wed.

Ch. 8½ A.M. Wrote to Mr T. Dowdall—Mr J. Amery—Mr J. Griffiths—Mr Wm Grogan. Saw Mr R.W. Eyton. Discussed Od V.277 with S.[5] Wrote on Homer. Dined at Mr Wynn Eytons. Read Dunlop's Hist. Rom. Lit. H.S. with Agnes.

26. Th.

Ch. 8½ A.M. Wrote to Sir J. Graham—Sir S. Scott & Co—Robn. Gladstone. Worked for Church Fund. Saw Mr Brewster, and ditto with Mr Durie,[6] resp. the found Church property, wh gives a hope of discovery. Worked on Homer—still Geogr. and on proofsheets. Read Dunlop.

27. Fr.

Ch. 8½ A.M. Wrote to Sir S. Scott & Co—G. Burnett. Worked on Homer: & at length wound up, as I hope, the whole affair of the Outer Geography. Also on proofs. H.S. with Agnes. Read Dunlop. Rom. Lit.

28. Sat.

Ch. 8½ A.M. Wrote to Sir W. Heathcote—Mrs H. Gladstone[7]—Mr Jas Wright—Alex. Goalen—Sir W.C. James. Worked on Homer: Maps: Theomythol. Saw Mr Burnett. Read Dunlop Rom. Lit.

29. Adv. Sunday.

Ch. mg & evg. Conv. with Agnes: & with the little boys. Worked a little on Theomythol. & on Theol. MSS. Read Newman's Sermons—Church Periodicals—Keble on Eucharistical Adoration.[8]

[1] Cicero's philosophical dialogue on Greek philosophy, written 45 B.C.
[2] Charles *Badham, 1813–84; headmaster in Edgbaston 1854; classics professor in Sydney 1867; edited Plato and Euripides.
[3] See 26 Nov. 57.
[4] *Studies on Homer*, iii, section 3; on Homer's perception of the world beyond direct Greek experience.
[5] Discussion of the use of the Great Bear in finding Phaecia.
[6] Unidentified.
[7] See 28 May 57.
[8] J. *Keble, *On eucharistical adoration* (1857).

30. M. St Andrew.

Ch. 8½ A.M. Wrote to A. Hayward—Scotts—Jas Watson—Robn. G—Bp
of St David's—J. Amery—J. Miller—Col. Sykes.[1] Worked on Homer:
Maps: Theomythol. Read Bruce on Homer[2]—Nägelsbach Hom. Theol.—
Goldsmith's Memoirs.[3]

Tues. Dec. One 1857.

Ch. 8½ A.M. H.S. with Agnes. Wrote to Mr Primrose—Mr Chivas. Worked
on Homer: Theomythol: Proofs & revises. Read Bruce on Homer.

2. Wed. [London]

Off at 9. London at 4. Saw R. Phillimore—Bp of Oxford—S. Herbert(evg).
Dined with Farquhar: where we agreed on & framed a representn. to the
Chapters of St Paul's & the Abbey.[4] Wrote to Lyttelton. Worked on
revises and on letters & papers. Read Gleig on India.[5]

3. Th.

Saw Sir W. Heathcote—S. Herbert. Wrote to J. Griffiths—R. Phillimore.
Finished Gleig on India. Read Dossier sur les Principautés[6]—Adventures
of Mr Ledbury.[7] H. of C. 4–8.[8] Dined at Mrs Talbot's. Saw E. Lovell[R].

4. Fr.

Wrote to Sir J. Graham—Rev. E. Hawkins—R. Gregory—Bp of Brechin—
Mr A. Reeve[9]—S. Shaen[10]—G. Chivas. Saw Bp of Oxford—Sir W. Heath-
cote—Archdeacon Hale—Mr J. Hawkins[11] (intr. by Mr Kingscote)—Hon.
A. Gordon—Duchess of Sutherland—Scotts. Dined with the Herberts.
H. of C. 4¼–8 and 11–12. Spoke on Indemnity & Curr[enc]y Committee.[12]

5. Sat.

Wrote to Sir W. Farquhar—Agnes G.—J. Amery & copy—Rev Mr Anderson—J. Griffiths—J.A. Rose.[13] Read Stevenson on Caste[14]—Mommsen

[1] William Henry *Sykes, 1790–1872; chairman of E.I.C. directors 1856–7, defended
*Canning's handling of the mutiny; liberal M.P. Aberdeen from 1857; naturalist.
[2] W. Bruce, *The state of society in the age of Homer* (1827).
[3] Probably bp. T. *Percy's *Life* (1801) for which *Goldsmith supplied the materials.
[4] Presented, with signatures of other laymen, successfully requesting opening for
Sunday evg. services; see R. C. *Trench to [Gladstone], *The Guardian*, 30 December
1857, 1002.
[5] G. R. *Gleig, *The history of the British Empire in India*, 4v. (1830–35).
[6] Possibly E. Regnault, *Histoire politique et sociale des principautés Danubiennes*
(1855).
[7] A. R. Smith, *The adventures of Mr. Ledbury and his friend Jack Johnson*, 3v. (1844).
[8] Queen's Speech: *H* cxlviii. 96.
[9] Abraham Charles Reeve, 1809–89; vicar of Higham from 1835.
[10] Samuel Shaen, solicitor in Kennington Cross, Surrey.
[11] John Hawkins, 1791–1877; solicitor in Hitchin; very active in diverse charities,
hence his introduction by Kingscote (see 19 Dec. 43n).
[12] *H* cxlviii. 171.
[13] James Anderson Rose, 1819–90; London solicitor; made extensive collection of
engraved portraits.
[14] J. Stevenson, *Hindoo caste* (1858).

Röm. Geschichte.[1] Dined at Mrs Talbot's. Worked a little on Homer. Worked on Books papers letters. Saw Scotts—Lord Aberdeen.—Rev. O. Gordon (Willy[2]—& Homer)—Bp of St David's (on Homer).

6. 2 S. Adv.

St James's 11 A.M. & H.C.—Chapel Royal 5.30. Dined with the Herberts. Wrote to Rev. C.F. Lowder—Rev. Whitwell Elwin. Read Bp of Davids's Charge & Appx powerful & remarkable productions[3]—Arnold's Sermons.[4] Saw A. Gordon—Ld A. Hervey—Ld Aberdeen: who seemed to have gained since yesterday: but he has made a great stride onwards since his illness.

7. M.

Wrote to J.N.G.—J.W. Williams—The Master of Balliol. Worked in evg until late on proofs and revises. Saw Rev. Mr Gregory—Sir W. Farquhar— Lord Aberdeen—Ld Clarendon—Chancr. of Exchr.—Mr Geo. Glyn MP.— The Speaker. H. of C. $4\frac{1}{4}$–$6\frac{1}{4}$.[5] The boys came home from Eton. With C. I set about the purchase of the 500 g. plate: & we effected it to our minds with Lambert and Rawlins.[6]

8. T. X.

Wrote to Lyttelton—W.B. Clarke[7]—Capt. Cowper[8]—Rev Mr Cosens[9]— Rev. H. Howell.[10] Worked on Homer—proof Sheets. Saw Griffiths[R]— Saw Earl of Aberdeen—Sir W. Farquhar—Lady Beauchamp—Mr Grogan —Mr Bowman[11] with Stephy. He is getting on: my eyes now show the *arcus senilis.*—Mr J.A. Smith—Mr Jas Wilson. H. of C. $4\frac{1}{2}$–7.[12] Dined at Mrs Talbot's.

9. Wed.

Wrote to Mrs Herbert—A. Panizzi—Ld Stanhope—Sir W. Farquhar. Dined with Mrs Talbot. H. of C. 12–1.[13] B. Museum $1\frac{1}{2}$–$3\frac{1}{4}$. Saw A. Panizzi— Earl of Aberdeen—Scotts—Mr Bernal Osborne. Read Accession of Nicholas I[14]—Curtius's Ionier[15]—Worked on proofsheets.

[1] By T. Mommsen, 3v. (1854–5).
[2] O. *Gordon was then censor of Christ Church; Willy matriculated May 1858.
[3] C. *Thirlwall, 'Charge . . . on the Immaculate Conception' (1857).
[4] See 4 Feb. 42, 6 Apr. 49.
[5] Spoke on Bank Issues Indemnity Bill: *H* cxlviii. 274.
[6] Goldsmiths and jewellers in Coventry Street; the plate was his recompense as railway arbitrator.
[7] Perhaps William Branwhite Clarke, 1798–1878; priest in England 1833–9; vicar of Willoughby, N.S.W., from 1846–70; discovered gold in Australia 1841.
[8] Captain Thomas Alexander Cowper of the E.I.C.S.; had offered advice, from experience, on the mutiny: Add MS 44208, f. 266.
[9] Probably Edward Hyde Cosens, d. 1859; chaplain of Shepton Mallet house of correction.
[10] Probably Hugh Howell; priest 1831; rector of Llanfyrnach from 1844.
[11] The eye-surgeon.
[12] Joint Stock Banks: *H* cxlviii. 379.
[13] Spoke on lack of need for Commons' approval for pension for Havelock: *H* cxlviii. 413.
[14] By Count M. A. Korf (1857), tr. from French.
[15] E. Curtius, *Die Ionier* (1855).

10. Th.

Wrote to Mr G. Dennis[1]—Mr Rowbotham (Manchr. Ex[hibitio]n)[2]—Rev. E. Monro—Mr Jas Wright—Mrs Davenport. Dined at Mrs Talbot's. Saw Sir W. Farquhar—Capt. Cowper. Shopping & paying Bills. Saw a *wonderful* collection of Sevres China & other objects to boot at Miss Clarke's.[3] Read Crusius 'Ionier'.

11. Frid.

Wrote to J. Griffiths (& copy)—Sir Geo. Grey—Mr Pym[4]—Mr Cairnes[5]— G. Burnett. Read Höcks Creta. Dined with the Herberts. Saw Mr W. Grogan—Mr Meekin—Earl of Aberdeen—R. Phillimore. Worked on Homer— proofs. H. of C. 6–7½ and 9¾–1¼. Spoke agt. the Committee on Currency: an evasion.[6] Packing & Prepns. for departure: also shopping & paying bills.

12. Sat. [Hawarden]

Off at 8¾ to Oxford.

Saw there Dr Pusey ⎫
The Master of Balliol ⎬ resp. my Homer—also Mr Greswell.
Mr Jas Wright ⎭

Calls & shopping. Reached H[awarde]n 10 P.M. Worked on Homer.

13. 3 S. Adv.

Ch. mg & evg. Conv. with Agnes & S. on Ep. & Gosp. Read Schöttgen de Messiâ[7]—Newman's Sermons—Bp of Oxford's Charge.[8] Much conv. with Willy about his loss of ground in the race of learning.[9] He was very good.

14. M.

Ch. 8½ AM. Wrote to the Master of Balliol—Mr J. Griffiths—Mr W. Johnson. Saw Mr Burnett—Mr Littleboy. Worked on Homer—Recommenced the Poems: for Indices. Virgil with Stephy—Iliad with Willy, piecemeal. Read also the Metcalfe papers.[10]

---

[1] George Dennis, 1814–98; consul in Mediterranean and W. Africa; wrote Murray's *Handbook to Sicily* (1864); sent extracts from Sicilian journals (Hawn P).

[2] Thomas Charles Leeson *Rowbotham, 1823–75; sketcher and water-colourist.

[3] Perhaps Harriet Ludlow *Clarke, d. 1866; book illustrator and painter of stained glass.

[4] Probably Francis Pym, 1790–1860, Bedfordshire landowner.

[5] John Elliot *Cairnes, 1823–75; professor of political economy at Dublin 1856–61, at Galway 1861–70, at London 1866–72, wrote on it, and politics; see 19 Nov. 57.

[6] Outlining differences between the executive and the Bank, arguing for modification of 1844 Bank Act: *H* cxlviii. 644.

[7] C. Schöttgen, probably *Jesus, der wahre Messias aus der alten und reinen Jüdischen Theologie dargethau und erläutert* (1748).

[8] S. *Wilberforce, 'A charge delivered at his triennial visitation, Nov. 1857' (1857).

[9] Willy had done poorly in the Newcastle scholarship, and in pre-Oxford work.

[10] *Selections from the papers of Lord *Metcalfe*, ed. J. W. *Kaye (1855).

15. T.

Ch. 8¼ A.M. Wrote to Sir J. Graham—W. Grogan—Bp of St David's—
Mr J. Bellis—Robn. G.—Jas Wright. Worked on letters. On Homer: proofs,
& reperusal, with Indices. Also Olympus. Saw Mr Burnett—Ld Meath.
Worked on letters & papers. Virgil with S. Read Welsford on Engl. Lang.[1]

16. Wed.

Ch. 8½ AM. Wrote to Mr G. Burnett—Lyttelton—R. Sherlock[2]—R.
Bentley—Worked on Homer, Ind[ices] Theomythol. & Pol. Dined at the
Rectory. Read Metcalfe papers—Iliad—Virgil with Stephen.

17. Th.

Ch. 8½ A.M. Wrote to Mr W. Grogan—Rev Mr Elwin—Rev Senior Proctor.[3]
Worked on Homer: reading, proofs—Indexes. Saw Mr Griffiths sen & jun.
—Mr G. Burnett—Mr Darlington, with whom we went over the ground
to consider of further operations. Virgil with Stephy—Read Iliad—
Metcalfe papers.

18. Fr.

Ch. 8½ A.M. Willy usually accompanies me. Wrote to Robn. G.—Mr
Bickersteth—Lyttelton—R. Bentley—W.R. Farquhar—Scotts. Iliad with
W.—Virg. with S. Worked on Homer proofs revises Indexes. Read Met-
calfe papers—Iliad.

19. Sat.

Ch. 8½ A.M. Wrote to Col. Pottinger[4]—Rev. O. Gordon—Master of Balliol
—Mr W. Johnson (after conv. with W.)—Eve's[5] operations seemed today
to end in failure: no coal under the bass.[6] Virgil with S. Read Welsford—
Iliad. Worked on Homer: sheets, theomythol. & Indices.

20. 4 S. Adv.

Ch. mg & evg. Conv. on Ep. & G. with W.A. & S. Worked on Messianic
traditions.[7] Read Schöttgen's Hor. Talm.—Newman's Sermons—Law's
Letters.[8]

21. M. St Thomas.

Ch. 11 A.M. Wrote to Rev Mr Rawlinson—J.H. Parker—Ld Lyttelton—
Robn. G.—Mr Jas Darlington. Went to Chester for books &c. Worked on
Homer proofs Theomythol. & Indices. Read Iliad—letters & papers from
London.

---

[1] H. Welsford, *On the origin and ramifications of the English language* (1845).
[2] Randall Hopley Sherlock, publisher of *Liverpool Mail* and *Liverpool Daily Mail*,
had written on currency; Hawn P.
[3] E. W. Tuffnell; see 14 Jan. 60n.
[4] John Pottinger, 1815–77; lieutenant-colonel in Bombay artillery; commanded
Ahmednugger force in the mutiny.
[5] J. Eve, engineer.
[6] Black shale.
[7] *Studies on Homer*, ii. 49.
[8] W. *Law, *Three letters to the bishop of Bangor* (1717–19).

22. *T.*

Ch. 8½ A.M. Wrote to A. Panizzi—Rev. G. Rawlinson—Worked on Homer—
Conv. with & about Willy: relatively to Stephy & his claims on his care.
Virgil with Stephy. Read Iliad—Welsford.

23. *Wed.*

Ch. 8½ A.M. Wrote to Rev. Ld J. Thynne—Scotts—J.G. Talbot—J. Swift
—Lambert & Rawlins. Worked on Homer: theomythol. and Indices. Read
Iliad—Ld Metcalfe's papers. Virgil with Stephy. Hawarden Trust Meeting
12½–2½.

24. *Th.*

Ch. 8½ A.M. This is the birthday of one Saint at least with God.[1] Blessed
be her memory. Wrote to A. Panizzi—F.R. Say—Sir F.H. Doyle—Jas
Wright—Dr Pusey. Worked on Homer: *began proofs of 2d Volume.* We
have daisies and verbena in blow today. Saw Mr Burnett & visited the
Borings. Virgil with Stephy. Read Iliad—Welsford on Engl. Lang.

25. *Fr. Xmas Day.*

Ch. 11 A.M. & Holy Commn. with C. & the children: also Ch. Evg. Wrote
to Sir S. Northcote—Rev. Archer Gurney. Read Newman's Sermons.
Worked on Theomythology.

26. *Sat. St Stephen.*

Ch. 11 A.M. Wrote to Rev. Mr Marshall—J.G. Hubbard—D[uche]ss of
Sutherland. Virgil with Stephen. Visited the ground of the old coal-work-
ings: saw Mr Burnett and J. Evans.[2] Read Bunsen's Egypt.[3] Worked much
on Homer: proofs & Theomythology.

27. *Sun. & St John.*

Ch. & H.C. 11 AM. Ch. 6½ P.M. Wrote to Dss of S[utherland] in lieu of
yesterday's. Read Pratt's Life[4]—Segneri[5]—Newman—Bunsen's Egypt.
Conv. with the three eldest. Worked on Theomythology.

28. *M. H. Innocents'.*

Ch. 8½ A.M. Wrote to Vice Chancr. of Oxford—Mrs Jewson[6]—Master of
Balliol—Broadwoods[7]—J. H. Parker—Provost Fortescue.[8] Dined at the

---

[1] His sister Anne.
[2] John Evans, Chester radical; reproved diarist for half-hearted liberalism; Hawn P.
[3] C. C. J. von Bunsen, *Egypt's place in universal history*, 5v. (1848–67).
[4] J. Pratt, *Memoir of the Rev. Josiah *Pratt* (1849).
[5] P. P. Segneri, *Twelve Sermons from the Quaresimale*, 3v. (1857–60).
[6] The wife of Frederick Bowen Jewson, 1823–91, composer and professor of music
at London.
[7] John Broadwood and Sons, London piano makers.
[8] E. B. K. Fortescue had become provost of St. Ninian's, Perth, despite his earlier
resignation (see 16 Jan. 53).

Rectory. Saw Mr Burnett. Read Iliad—Grote's Hist. Vol. II. Worked on Homer. Virgil with Stephen.

29. T.

Ch. 8½ A.M. Wrote to Earl of Clarendon—Robn. G.—Mr Breakenridge—Jas Perkins[1]—Ward. of All Souls—Dr Plumptre—Lambert & Rawlins. Virgil with Stephy. Read Iliad—Ld Derby's Speech of Dec. 3.[2] Worked on Homer: Plot of Iliad, Theomythol. and Proofs. Saw Mr Burnett—Mr Littleboy.

On this day I close my 48th year. How long a time for me to cumber the ground: and still not to know *where* to work out the purpose of my life. But God I trust will clear my way: as He still contends with me & for me, my one hope amidst the depth of my sin & unworthiness, He ever saying 'Nor yet will I cast thee out: but see that thou amend thy ways.['] But so bright is the Pattern—how am I ever to come near to the slightest resemblance of that Brightness? The children were all most dear today.

30. Wed.

Ch. 8½ A.M. Wrote to Mr N.L. Torre[3]—Rev. Chas Badham—Mr Jas Darlington. Saw J. Eve—Mr Dickinson. Worked on Homer: proofs & Theomythol. Virgil with Stephy. Read Welsford.

31. Th.

Ch. 8½ A.M. Wrote to Rev. G. Nugee—J.N.G.—J. Cottingham[4]—Jas Wright—D. Williams—G. Taylor—Dean Ramsay—Lambert & Rawlins. Worked on Homer Theomythol. Virgil with Stephy.

I dismiss another year with a growing sentiment that my life must come to its crisis while I do not see in myself the inward preparation, which would be the surest sign that God was going to make His way plain before my face. I offer *that* prayer often & with warmth. But a man cannot be really sincere in a particular prayer if he blinds himself in things which that prayer touches: & it is in vain to pray with ever so great fervour for the making clear by Him of what through unfaithfulness I myself darken.

However I am quite sound in conscience as to the work on Homer which now occupies so much of my mind & time. Good night Old Year.

---

[1] Customs officer in Toxteth Park.
[2] On the Queen's speech: *H* cxlviii. 24.
[3] Nicholas Lee Torre, 1795–1867; fellow of New College 1813–18.
[4] James Cottingham, 1803–90; vicar of Shotwick, Cheshire, from 1831.

Hawarden Friday Jan One
1858. Circumcision.

Church 11 A.M. Wrote to Rev W.B. Marriott[1]—Sir W. Heathcote. Worked well on Homer MS. Read Arnold's Merope and Preface.[2] Saw Mr Burnett. Virgil with Stephen.

2. Sat.

Ch. 8½ A.M. Wrote to Dr Caswall. Worked on Homer—Proofs—Theomythol —& Woman[3]. Read Friedrich. Virgil with Stephy. Saw Mr Littleboy.

3. 2 S. aft Xm.

Ch 11 AM. & H.C.—again 6½ PM. Conv. with the three eldest. Read Covell's Gk Church[4]—Observateur Catholique[5]—Pratt's Life. Wrote to Lady Beauchamp—Sir S.H. Northcote. Worked on Lady B's Scheme.[6]

4. M.

Ch. 8½ A.M. today was almost all given to Homer—Proofs, & Section on Woman. Finished Matt. Arnold's Merope. Worked a little Homer with Willy.

5. T.

Ch. 8½ A.M. Wrote to Sir W. Farquhar—Jas Wright—A. Panizzi—Scotts —Robn. G. Attended the Rent dinner & spoke there. Worked on Homer: sent off the rest of 'Olympus'. Virgil with Stephy. Conv. with C. about Willy.

6. Wed. Epiph.

Ch. 11 A.M. Dearest C.s birthday: closing a year of tears & of somewhat broken health: may all this be blessed by God. Today she had in the evg a great Xmas tree party: very much ado. Worked on Homer—proofs, revises & Agore.[7] Wrote to Bp of Salisbury. Read Welsford[8]—Saw Mr Burnett— New Boring in Park No 4 begun. Settled to part with Jas. Kent.[9]

[1] Wharton Booth *Marriott, 1823–1871; taught at Eton 1850–60; wrote on vestments and Ovid.
[2] M. *Arnold, *Merope, a tragedy* (1858).
[3] Highly praising the Greek attitude to marriage: *Studies on Homer*, ii. 489.
[4] J. *Covel, *Some account of the present Greek Church* (1722).
[5] *L'Observateur Catholique*, v. (1858).
[6] Charitable activities.
[7] On political ideas in Homer; start of vol. iii of *Studies on Homer*.
[8] See 15 Dec. 57.
[9] A servant.

7. *Th.*

Ch. 8½ A.M. Wrote to Ld Clarendon—J.G. Talbot—Scott & Co—Robn. G. Virgil with Stephy. Worked much on Homer—Read Welsford.

8. *Fr.*

Ch. 8½ A.M. No letters: a long day on Homer, and other things as yesterday. Saw Mr Burnett: O.F. & Hn. matters.

9. *Sat.*

Ch. 8½ A.M. Again avoided letters: worked much on Homer: proofs, revises, and Agorè. All else as yesterday.

10. *1 S. Epiph.*

Ch. 11 A.M. 6½ P.M. Conv. with the 3 eldest. Read Jelf's B[ampto]n Lectures[1]—All for Jesus[2]—Keble's Euch. Adoration[3]—Pretyman's Erastianism[4]—&[blank]

11. *M.*

Ch. 8¼ A.M. Wrote to Sir J.S. Forbes—Robn. G.—Rev. E. Hawkins—Scotts—Mr W. Grogan—B. of Eng. Cashiers. Worked long on Homer. Virgil with Stephy. Saw Mr Burnett on S.s. matters: which are now rather heavy again. C had another bad night.

12. *T.*

Ch. 8¼ A.M. Wrote to Ld Stanhope—Mr Claxton[5]—Visited the Borings. Virgil with S.—finished Æn. VI. Worked much on Homer—Another bad night of C.s.

13. *Wed.*

Prevented by the broken night from attending Church. Write to Rev. E. Coleridge—Lady Beauchamp—Bp of Oxford—Mr W. Grogan—G. Burnett—Ld Lyttelton—J. Griffiths. 1–3¼ Rob[ertso]n with his three eldest kindly came over.[6] Mr Griffiths[7] came from Wrexham & thoroughly examined Catherine's case. He reports her whole system much deranged: no room thank God for anxiety but much need for care. All the arrangements were made accordingly at once. Virgil with Stephy. Worked on Homer, proofs, revises, and Thalassa—Finished Welsford.

[1] See 30 Aug. 57.
[2] By *Faber; see 12 Feb. 54.
[3] See 29 Nov. 57.
[4] See 9 Aug. 57.
[5] Perhaps Marshall *Claxton, 1813–81; historical painter.
[6] i.e. Mary Ellen Gladstone (see 1 May 40); Arthur (see 28 Oct. 56); Hugh Jones Gladstone, 1844–74; Robertson (see 13 Feb. 54).
[7] Thomas T. Griffith, physician in Wrexham.

14. Th.

Ch. 8½ A.M. Wrote to J.P. Lacaita—C.A. Wood—Miller (Books[elle]r).[1] Worked on Homer—Arranged for Stephy's allowance: & other (household) matters. A Clergy dinner. Read [blank]

15. Fr.

Ch. 8½ A.M. Wrote to Rev. F. Vidal—Bishop of Oxford. Worked on Homer. The boys went off: & leave a great blank. Read W. Hasting's Trial[2]—Half Hours[3] &c.

16. Sat.

Ch. 8½ A.M. Wrote to Scotts. Worked on Homer—finished Thalassa. Read Metcalfe's Papers[4]—Trial of Warren Hastings.

17. 2 S. Epiph.

Ch. 11 & 6½ P.M. Conv. with Agnes on Ep. & Gosp. With M. & L. on Gospel. Read Newman's Sermons—Remusat's Abelard[5]—Jelf's Bampton Lectures—and [blank] Wrote to Westell.

18. M.

Ch. 8½ A.M. Wrote to J.N.G. (on his birthday)—Robn. G.—Rev Dr Scott (Master of Balliol). Saw Mr Burnett—Do with Mr Littleboy—S.s affairs. Worked on Homer—proofs—revises—Ilium. Walk with C. Read Metcalfe's papers.

19. T.

Ch. 8½ A.M. Wrote to Rev Dr M'Pherson[6]—Robn. G.—Rev. M.T. de Burgh[7]—Mr Lacaita. Saw Mr Burnett. Worked on Homer: Map of Outer Geography[8]—Ilium: and Outer Geogr.

20. Wed.

Ch 8½ A.M. Worked much on Homer—Map of Outer Geography—Revises— Proofs—& Ilium. Read Farini's Letter to myself on the supposed Austrian Treaty.[9]

[1] See 25 Dec. 41.
[2] *The history of the trial of Warren *Hastings* (1796).
[3] *Half hours with our metropolitan ministers* (1857, 1858).
[4] See 14 Dec. 57.
[5] See 20 Apr. 57.
[6] On Homer: Alexander *M'Pherson, 1781–1861; presbyterian minister in Golspie, corresponded on Homeric links with Gaelic: Add MS 44389, ff. 14, 140.
[7] Maurice T. de Burgh, anglican priest in Limerick, had written about a Strafford memorial (Hawn P).
[8] At the end of *Studies on Homer*, iii.
[9] L. G. Farini, *La diplomazia e la quistione Italiana; lettera . . . al Signor G. Gladstone* (1856), and MS in Add MS 44389, f. 18.

21. *Th.*

Ch. 8½ A.M. Wrote to Rev. Mr Thorpe—W.H.G.—Secs. Australian Dinner[1]
—W. Hampton (2). Saw Mr Burnett—Worked on Map—Ilios. Parted with
Jas. Kent, and advised him as well as I could.

22. *Fr.*

Ch. 8½ A.M. Wrote to Vice Chancr. of Oxford—Jas Wright—Master of
Balliol—W.H.G.—Sir J. Graham—Rev Mr Woodgate. Worked much on
Homer (but not well in evg) & sent off 350 p. of 3d Volume with my map.
Read Metcalfe Papers.

23. *Sat.* [*London*]

After a doubtful morning started for London & reached George St[2] at
7.15 P.M. Worked on proofs & revises—Also on my London accumulations.
Wrote to Mr G. Burnett—Mr Crowther. Attended Mad. Bernstorffs party:
& was much pleased with the Princess of Prussia.[3] Saw Bp of Oxford—
Sir G.C. Lewis—Sir R. Murchison—Ld Stratford [de Redcliffe]—M. Tricoupi—Ld Dufferin.

24. *3 S. Epiph.* X.

Trin. Vauxhall mg and the Abbey evening. A great and unwonted scene.
The Bp of Oxford preached. We met the masses of the rejected streaming
away. Saw E. Lovell[R]: goes Tuesday D.G. Saw Aunt J—Ld Aberdeen—
with whom were Creptowitch[4] & the Speaker.—J. Talbot: resp. himself,[5] &
Willy. Read 'A Presbytn. Clergyman' &c.[6]—The Union—Sisters of Mercy[7]
—Tracts. Wrote to C.G.[8]

25. *M. Conv. St Paul.*

Wrote to Mr D. Gladstone—Mr W. Haley[9]—Rev F.W. Taylor[10]—Mr Leary
—Mr Downham[11]—Mr Burnett—Mr Aitchison—Mr Heath. Made many
calls. Saw Overends—Ld Aberdeen—Dean of Westminster—Scotts. Read
Valbezen on India[12]—Buckle's Hist. Civilisation[13]—Ld Grenville's Nugae
Metricae.[14] Concert at the Palace in evg.[15] Some very fine music: too much

---

[1] See 26 Jan. 58.
[2] Mrs Chetwynd Talbot's house in Great George Street, Westminster.
[3] [Mary Louise] Augusta Catherine of Saxe-Weimar, d. 1890; wife of Frederick, Prince
of Prussia, see 19 June 56.
[4] The Prussian ambassador.
[5] He had failed to achieve a pass degree the previous summer at Oxford.
[6] [J. Burton], 'A presbyterian clergyman looking for the church' (1855).
[7] *The sister of mercy; a tale for the times we live in* (1854).
[8] Bassett, 119.
[9] Perhaps William Haley, gold chain maker in St. James's Street.
[10] Francis William Taylor; missionary, then curate of Finningley, Lincolnshire.
[11] George Downham owned livery stables in Chester Street.
[12] E. de Valbezen, *Les anglais et l'Inde* (1857).
[13] H.T. *Buckle, *History of civilisation in England*, 2v. (1857).
[14] By W. W. Grenville, 1st Baron Grenville (1824).
[15] For the marriage this day to Victoria, the princess royal, of Frederick William of
Prussia, 1831–88, emperor as Frederick III 1888.

crash. A great deal of Homer with Sir C. Eastlake. Also Ld Stratford & Merivale. Saw Cardwell—Sir Geo. Grey—Bp of Oxford—& home at 2.45.

26. T. X

Wrote to Chancr. of Exchr.—C.G.—Master of Balliol—Willy—Overends— Rev Mr Jelf—Scotts. Saw S. Herbert (India &c.)—Lord Aberdeen (India)[1] —F.R. Bonham—Duchess of Sutherland. Dined at the Australian Anniversary & spoke—calls & shopping. Saw Lewis[R]—Read [blank]

27. Wed. [Hawarden]

Wrote to Rev Mr M'Kenzie—Mrs Lewis—Read Ruskin[2]—Voyage of Capt. Popanilla[3]—Shopping & other business—Worked on Homer revises—Saw Duchess of Sutherland & copied part of Willy's account to go to the Queen.[4] Off at 4.30: reached Hawarden 10.35. Saw Newdegate (to Rugby). Evg late with C.

28. Th.

Worked most of the day on Homer: proofs revises &c. Saw Mr Burnett— Mr Littleboy. Walk with C. who advances. Read Prichard's Eastern Origin of Celtic Nations[5]—Bp of Bangor on Divorce(!!)[6]—Scobell's Reply to Neale[7]—Dr Lee's new Crathie Gospel.[8]

29. Fr.

Ch. 8½ A.M. Wrote to Lambert & Rawlins—Robn. G.—Mr H. Merivale— Sir T.G.—Mr E. Hamilton. Read Prichard & Latham[9]—Worked on Homer.

30. Sat.

Ch. 8½ A.M. Wrote to W.H.G.—Sir Jas Graham. Worked on Homer (Comparison—& revises). Read Prichard—Renan's Etudes[10]—Pope's Odyssey.[11]

31. Septua. S.

Ch. 11 AM 6½ PM. Conv. with Agnes. Read Keble on Adoration[12]— Renan's Etudes—Christ. Remembrancer[13]—Abelard & Heloise.[14]

[1] Doubtless on E.I.C. manoeuvres to avoid losing all powers to the crown.
[2] Probably J. *Ruskin, *The political economy of art* (1857).
[3] *Disraeli's second novel (1828).
[4] Of his trip to Europe with the Prince of Wales.
[5] J. C. Prichard, *The Eastern origins of the Celtic nations proved by a comparison of their dialects with Sanscrit, Greek, Latin and Teutonic Languages* (1831).
[6] C. Bethell, 'Remarks on a petition to her majesty' (1858); attacks as 'sheer nonsense' the clergy's petition to refuse royal assent to the divorce act.
[7] J. Scobell, 'A reply to the postscript of the Rev. J. M. *Neale' (1858).
[8] R. *Lee, *Prayers for public worship* (1858).
[9] See 28 Jan. 58.
[10] E. Renan, *Études d'histoire religieuse* (1858).
[11] Tr. (1725–6).
[12] See 10 Jan. 58.
[13] *Christian Remembrancer*, xxxv (January 1858).
[14] See 20 Apr. 57.

1 Feb. Monday.

Ch. 8½ A.M. Wrote to Mr J.M. Stark[1]—Stephy—Sir W. Farquhar—Mr J. Bates—W. Hampton: & Mr Saphire.[2] Worked on my library. Worked on Homer: proofs, revises, and revising Q.R. Homer.[3] Read Renan.

2. T. Purifn. B.V.M.

Ch. 11 A.M. Wrote to Master of Balliol—Mr Howson—Mr E. Hamilton. Worked on Homer; Q.R. & Numbers. Saw Mr Burnett. Worked on Books & Letters. Read Ernest Renan—Millin Minéralogie.[4]

3. Wed.

Ch. 8½ AM. Wrote to Sir W. Heathcote—Rev Mr Jelf—B. Quaritch—J.M. Stark. C. went to Pantyochyn:[5] after two broken nights. Worked on arranging books—on Homer: numbers, & Beauty.[6] Read Millin (finished)— Prichard's Celtic Nations. H.S. with M. & Lena.

4. Th.

Ch. 8½ AM. Wrote to Sir C. Eastlake—C.G.—Mr J. Bates. H.S. with M. & Lena. Walk with Agnes. Worked on books & new bookcases. Worked on Homer: finished revises of 2d Volume. Also on Colours. Read Bechmann &c. on Metals[7]—Prantl über die Farben.[8]—Watson's Chemistry[9]—Renan's Etudes.

5. Fr.

Ch. 8½ A.M. Wrote to Ld Goderich—C.G.—S. Herbert—E. Cardwell. H.S. with M. & Lena. Walk with Agnes. Work upon books in library. Worked pretty hard on Homeric colours. Read Renan Etudes—Atkinson on Celtic.[10]

6. Sat.

Overslept H.S. with M. & L. Wrote to C.G.—Wms. & Co—Sir Jas Graham —G. Crowther—Sir T.G.—Chest. Record.[11] Worked much on Homer: proofs, revises, & 'colours'. Read Renan. H.S. with M. and L.

---

[1] Book-dealer (Hawn P).
[2] Perhaps Adolph Saphir, wrote on Jewish and biblical topics.
[3] See 15 Nov. 56 and 28 Apr. 57; sections incorporated in *Studies on Homer*, iii. 500.
[4] A. L. Millin de Grandmaison, *Minéralogie Homérique ou essai sur les minéraux dont il est fait mention dans les poëms d'Homère* (1790).
[5] Pant Iocyn, the Misses Conliffe's house near Wrexham.
[6] On the 'sense of beauty in Homer: human, animal, and inanimate': *Studies on Homer*, iii. 397.
[7] Perhaps *Des Herrn Sagens Chemische Untersuchung verschiedener mineralien . . . mit einigenanmerkungen vermehrt von J. Beckmann* (1775).
[8] C. von Prantl, *Aristoteles über die farben* (1849).
[9] See 3 Nov. 57.
[10] A. Atkinson, *Ireland exhibited to England in a political and moral survey*, 2v. (1823).
[11] Not published.

7. *Sexa. S.*

Ch. 11 AM. 6½ PM. Conv. with Agnes. C. returned: not advanced, but with good accounts from Griffith in the main. Read Newman's S.—Döllingers Judenthum[1]—Renan's Etudes—Chr. Remembrr.

8. *M.*

The daily service is stopped. H.S. with M. and L. Wrote to Mr J.W. Keats[2]—Robn. G.—Williams & Co—Jas Wright. Worked on Homer: finished 'Colour': which has been stiff. Read Renan. Walked with C: who improves.

9. *T.*

Wrote to Earl of Aberdeen—E. Hamilton—Duchess of Sutherland. H.S. with M. & L. Corrected Australian dinner Speech. Saw Mr Burnett. Worked much on Homer: proofs, revises, and Section on Beauty. Read Renan: & long debates.

10. *Wed.*

Wrote to W. Hampton—A. Banks—Rev Mr Rowsell—Rev Mr Hawkins. A deranged night threw us out of course. Griffith came: & was not discouraged. Finished this day my MS. on Homer: I wish I felt as hopeful about the execution as the design. If it were even tolerably done, it would be a good service to religion as well as to literature: and I mistrustfully offer it up to God.

Saw Mr Burnett. Read Ellis on Gr. & It. Ethnol.[3]—Renan Etudes Relig. —Cornutus[4] de Nat[ura] Deor[um]. Worked on letters & papers.

11. *Th.*

Wrote to S. Herbert—Sir W. Heathcote—D. Lange—J.M. Stark. Worked on Library—and letters and papers. Saw Mr A. Burnett[5]—Mr Troughton. Read Renan—Trench on Engl. Dictionaries[6]—N.B. Rev. on Annexn. of Oude.[7] H.S. with M. & L.

12. *Fr.*

Wrote to Mr R. Owen[8]—Sir Jas Graham—Sir Geo. Hayter. H.S. with M. and L. Saw Mr G. Burnett—Rev. Mr Lee (Buckley). Walk with C. Worked on Proofs & revises. Read Metcalfe Papers—Blackstone's Commentaries[9]— Il Pecorone.[10]

[1] See 26 July 57.
[2] *Sc.* J.A. Keats.
[3] R. Ellis, *Contributions to the ethnography of Italy and Greece* (1858).
[4] Lucius Annaeus Cornutus, a Stoic philosopher.
[5] Of Dee Bank, Queensferry; presumably a relative of G. Burnett, the Hawarden agent.
[6] R.C. *Trench, *On some deficiencies in our English dictionaries* (1857).
[7] *North British Review*, xxv. 515 (August 1856).
[8] Robert *Owen, 1771–1858, the socialist, had sent a petition on evil in society: Add MS 44389, f. 41.
[9] See 30 Apr. 50.
[10] By G. Fiorentino, based on the *Decameron*.

13. Sat.

Wrote to Sig. Farini—Rev Mr Disney[1]—Mr T.C. Sandars—Prof. Phillips[2]
—Mr T. Cannon[3]—Mr Grogan. Worked on letters & papers from London—
Read a number of pamphlets on India & other matters. In Chester 12–3
seeing Messrs Price & Son—Mr Burnett—& Mr Growcott—on O.F. affairs.
H.S. with M. & L.

14. Quinqua. S.

Ch. mg & evg. Conv. with Agnes as usual. Wrote to Sir J. Graham. Read
Renan (finished)—Newman's S. finished Vol. VI—Remusat's Abelard.

15. M.

Ch 8½ AM. H.S. with M. & L. Wrote to R. Phillimore—S.E.G.—Sir J.
Graham—Jas Wright—Bp of Salisbury—W. Hampton—Rev F. Vidal—C.
Paskin—Mr G. Burnett (2)—Mrs Talbot. Worked on Homer: Proofs Revises & rewriting note on Metals.[4] Saw Mr Littleboy. Busy on papers putting
away & preparing for departure till very late.

16. T. [London]

H.S. with M. & L.—Wrote to Mr Burnett—Saw Mr Burnett—Packed &
put away: settled accts. with C.G. & Mrs Hn. Catherine drove me into
Chester: I reached Mrs Talbot's[5] at 8 P.M. having managed to read the
debate of last night[6] (most of it) on my way. Thank God I was now able to
leave C. with some degree of comfort as to her prospects of progress. H. of C.
9–10¼.[7] Saw Sir J. Graham & S. Herbert. Inquiries for Kirby & Griffiths:
both gone[R]. Read Q.R. on Ch. Extension[8]—Disraeli's Popanilla.

17. Ash Wednesday.

Abbey 10 P.M. Wrote to Mr T. Macknight—C.G.—Mr D. Gladstone—Scotts
—Bp of Brechin—Jas Kent—Rev Mr Burgon—W. Emery. Saw Ld Abn.
with Sir J. Graham—Ld Lyndhurst with Ld Brougham: (a very remarkable
entretien)[9]—E. Cardwell—W. Grogan—Serj. Warren.[10] H. of C. 3¾–6. Voted
in 160:213 agt. Ch. Rates Abolition.[11] Worked on revises of Homer. Read
Macknight's Burke.[12]

---

[1] James William King Disney; perpetual ourate of Christ Church, Newark, from 1844;
wrote tracts.
[2] G. A. W. Phillips, professed music in Liverpool.
[3] Thomas Cannon of Covent Garden had sent clippings on his local debating society.
[4] On the low esteem for gold in Homeric times: *Studies on Homer*, iii. 84.
[5] In Great George Street.
[6] Leave to bring in an India Government Bill: *H* cxlviii. 1372.
[7] Annexation of Oude: *H* cxlviii. 1477.
[8] *Quarterly Review*, ciii. 139 (January 1858).
[9] Further described in this day's letter to his wife, in Bassett, 120.
[10] i.e. S. *Warren.
[11] *H* cxlviii. 1583.
[12] T. *MacKnight, *History of the life and times of Edmund *Burke*, 3v. (1858–60).

18. Th.

Wrote to C.G. Saw Mr Parker—Ld J. Russell—Ld Grey. Attended Levee 2. P.M. H of C. 4½–1. Voted in 173:318 agt. legislating for India *now*. Graham did not feel well: & I avoided *this* occasion wh wd. again have exhibited me as attacking Govt.[1] Read Buckle's Hist. Civilisation.[2] Worked on Homer Proofs—and on letters.

19. Fr.

Wrote to C.G. (2)—A. Banks (late)—C. Bonsall[3]—G. Burnett—Mr Macqueen—Dean Saunders—Rev[s] Mr Mayow—Stothert[4]—Woollcombe—D. M'Kenzie—W.E. Heygate. Saw Mr D. Lange—W. Hampton—Bp of St David's—Ld Jermyn. Currency Comm. & House 2 P.M. to 7¼ and 8¼–1¼. Divided in 234:215 for vote agt. Ministers. It almost revived the China night.[5] Read Macknight's Burke.

20. Sat.

Wrote to Mrs Larkins—C.G.[6]—Mr Geo. Wilson—Worked on Homer: proofs & revises. Saw Sir John Lefevre—Mr Banting—Sir Jas Graham (where I found Ld John Russell)—S. Herbert. My sister Helen (for an hour after some years: kind in her behaviour but passed prematurely into age)—J. Murray—W. Hampton. Dined at Herbert's with Graham. We sat till 12½: but did not talk quite *through* the crisis. P. has resigned. He is down: I must now cease to denounce him.

21. 1 S. Lent.

St James's mg & Holy Commn. Westmr. Abbey in evg when I sat by Sir Geo. Grey. From the sacred feast I went to Ld Aberdeen's. There Derby's letter reached me. We sent for Herbert and I wrote an answer. Graham arrived & heard it. With slight modifications it went. The case though grave was not doubtful. Made two copies: & went off before 6 with S. Herbert: we separated for the evg with the fervent wish that in public life we might never part.[7]

After evg Ch went to the Deanery: a most pleasant hour & half with the Dean & the Bp of Gloucester. Read Letters of Mere Agnès Angelique & Faugere's Preface.[8] Ah! to have like her une vertu unique—une egalitè d'âme qui ne se dementait jamais.[9]

[1] *H* cxlviii. 1717.
[2] See 25 Jan. 58.
[3] Of Tavistock Square; Gladstone had financial dealings with him (Hawn P).
[4] Samuel Kelson Stothert, b. 1826?; naval chaplain; founded St. Mary's, Constantinople, 1856–8; vicar of Ordsall 1878.
[5] Defeat of the govt. on the Conspiracy to Murder Bill; Gladstone argued in favour of friendship with France, but against Walewski's despatch: *H* cxlviii. 1806.
[6] Misdated in Bassett, 120.
[7] Version in Morley, i. 576, with copies of the letters; he declined *Derby's offer of an (unspecified) cabinet post.
[8] A. Arnauld (Mère Agnès de St. Paul), *Lettres publiées sur les textes authentiques avec une introduction par M. P. Faugère*, 2v. (1858).
[9] 'Total integrity—an inner serenity which never fails'.

22 M. X

Wrote to Mr W. Neate[1]—C.G.[2]—Rev Mr Woollcombe—W.H.G.—Rob. Phillimore. Worked on proofs of Homer. Missed Marq. Azeglio—Duchess of Sutherland. Saw Mr Hayter—A. Hayward—Earl of Aberdeen—Scotts— Ld Stratford [(]½ Homer ½ Russia & Turkey)—Sir J. Graham—Mr G. Harcourt—Ld Aberdeen (2°) cum Sir J. Gr. At London Library for Homeric searches. H. of C. 4½–6½. Palmerston died with propriety, Disraeli with bad tact anticipated his leadership.[3]

23. Tues. X

Wrote to Dean Ramsay—Sir Thos G.—Mrs Herbert—Captain G.—D.B. Chapman—Ld H. Lennox—Sir J. Maxwell—C. Bonsall—Lady F. Hotham —Rev G. Rawlinson. Saw Sir F. Thesiger (Ld Chancr)[4]—Ld Aberdeen— Do cum D. of Newcastle—Lord Lyndhurst—The Master of Trinity—Mr Slaney. Dined at the Club—Worked on Homer, proofs & revises.

24. Wed. St Matthias.

Wrote to Mrs Hampton—Robn. G—Rev Mr Mucklestone—Mr B. Shaw[5]— E L Robertson & Co—Mr Strange[6]—Rev Mr Caswall. Saw Sir W. Heath- cote—B. Benjamin—Duchess of Sutherland—Mrs Phillimore[7]—Count Vitzthum—Count Chreptowisch—& others: Poodle Byng,[8] C. Villiers (N.B.)—Lady Colchester[9]—Mr Whiteside—Mr Walpole—at Lady Col- chester's party in evg. Read Macknight's Burke. Work on Homer proof. Euston Sq. 7.30 to meet C. She arrived thank God much advanced.

25. Th.

Wrote to Helen—Mr G. Dundas—Rev W. Scott—Ld Canning—Rev J.H. Scott.[10] Calls. Saw R. Phillimore—Earl Stanhope. Attended Christie's Sale. Read Burke (Macknight's)—Welcker's Griech. Götterlehre[11]—Graham & Russell Correspondence[12]—Corrected my Homerische Erdcarte.[13]

26. Fr. X

Wrote to Sir Wm. Jolliffe[14]—Jas Watson—Mr Edw. Ellice—Rev. J. Husband[15]—Rev. H. Hayman—Rev. J.L. Ross—Lord Stanley (2)—Rev W.

---

[1] Unidentified.   [2] Bassett, 121.   [3] H cxlviii. 1855.
[4] Who became Lord Chancellor as Lord Chelmsford in *Derby's ministry.
[5] Benjamin Shaw, 1819–77; barrister; prosecuted ritualists; wrote on confession in 1858.
[6] Probably William Strange, 1801–71; London publisher.
[7] See 9 Oct. 44n.
[8] Gerald Frederick Byng, 1784–1871; s. of 5th Viscount Torrington; diplomat, and regency remnant; named Poodle by G. *Canning from his curly hair.
[9] Elizabeth Susan, da. of 1st Baron Ellenborough, m. 1836 2nd Baron Colchester, and d. 1883.
[10] John Haigh Scott, b. 1826; curate in Westmorland; vicar of Frosterley, Durham, 1866, of Whiston 1873; active in additional curates fund.
[11] F.G. Welcker, Griechische Götterlehre, 3v. (1857–63).
[12] On Indian legislation, see Parker, Graham, ii. 338.
[13] i.e. the map in Studies on Homer, iii.
[14] Sir William George Hylton *Jolliffe, 1800–76; 1st bart. 1821: tory M.P. Petersfield 1833–5, 1837–66; tory whip 1858–9; cr. Baron Hylton 1866.
[15] John Husband, d. 1869; rector of Selattyn, Shropshire, 1853–69; wrote on popery.

Field[1]—Marq. Azeglio—Mr J. Perceval.[2] Saw S. Herbert—Sir Jas Graham. Dined with the Herberts. Saw Mr Addington's Collection.[3] Saw Smith[R]. H of C. $4\frac{1}{2}$–$6\frac{1}{4}$.[4] Worked on Hom. proofsheets.

27. Sat.

Wrote to M.F. Tupper—Sir W. James—Mr A Somerville—Hon A. Gordon —Rev F.O. Morris. Saw Ld A. Hervey—J. Wilson Patten—Sir W. Heath-cote—Mr Ellice—Sir Jas Graham—E. Cardwell—Mr A. Panizzi. Worked on Homer proofs. Read Troil's Iceland.[5] Moved into No 11 C H T.

28. 2 S. Lent.

St Philips mg & H.C. St James's evg. Read Welcker's Gr. Götterlehre— Rose's Sermons[6]—Priaulx's Quaestiones[7]—Bp of Brechin's Charge.[8]

Monday March One 1858.

Wrote to Sir Jas Graham—Mr H. Lees—Sir John Forbes—Rev. E.C. Woollcombe—C.A. Wood—Master of Balliol. Read Ld Grey on Reform.[9] Saw Ld Ward—Ld Aberdeen—E. Cardwell—Sir J. Graham. Worked on (proofs & revises) Homer. H of C. & H of L. to hear Ld Derby $4\frac{1}{2}$–7.[10] Dined at Mrs Talbot's. Beginning to set in order.

2. T.

Wrote to Prov. of Oriel—Rev Whitwell Elwin—Mr Jas Wright—Mr Rowland Hill—Mr Bullock—Bp of Oxford. Continued house & room work. Saw Rev Jas Andrew[11]—Mr Ellice—Sir W. Heathcote. Read Russell & Graham Correspondence—Macknight's Burke—Sclopis on Montesquieu.[12]

3. Wed.

Wrote to Mrs Bradley[13]—Ed. Eclectic Review.[14] Worked on Homer for press. In evg at Lady Molesworth's and then Lady C. Egerton's.[15] Saw Mr Lake—

[1] Walter Field, d. 1876; curate of Romford; vicar of Godmersham from 1864.

[2] John Perceval of Canterbury had written on the Belgian press; Hawn P.

[3] Pictures and watercolours of Samuel Addington, sold in 1886; see W. Roberts, *Memorials of Christies* (1897), ii. 93.

[4] Misc. business: *H* cxlix. 4.

[5] U. von Troil, *Letters on Iceland* (1780).

[6] Probably H. J. Rose, 'The English liturgy a protest against Romish corruptions. Two sermons' (1850).

[7] O. de B. Priaulx, *Quaestiones Mosaicae* (1842).

[8] The proofs of a new ed. of *Forbes' notorious Charge, published as the heresy accusations increased; see 13 Oct. 57 and W. Perry, *A. P. *Forbes* (1939), 89.

[9] H. G. *Grey, 'Parliamentary government considered with reference to a reform of parliament. An essay' (1858).

[10] *Derby discussed his offer to Gladstone: *H* cxlix. 25.

[11] Unbeneficed anglican priest.

[12] In F. Sclopis, *La domination Française en Italie 1800–14* (n.d.).

[13] Eliza Bradley had sent thanks for help; Hawn P.

[14] Untraced: the March number had an article on 'modern deism'.

[15] Lady Charlotte Elizabeth, da. of 2nd marquess of Ely, m. 1830 William Tatton Egerton, 1806–83, Peelite M.P. N. Cheshire 1832–58, 1st Baron Egerton 1859. She d. 1878.

Mr Beaumont (pictures)—Sir E. Perry[1]—Sir T. Fremantle—and others. Read Rawlinson's Herodotus[2]—Welcker's Götterlehre.

4. Th.

Wrote to Mr J. Murray—Sir C. Eastlake[3]—Mr Jas Wright. Worked on Homer for press. Saw Ralph Neville—Mr Thackeray. Out of door business. Heathcote and Phillimore dined. Read Welcker's Götterlehre—Indian pamphlets—Iliad.

5. Fr.

Wrote to Robert Gladstone and Rev. Whitwell Elwin. Worked on Homer for press: we now advance rapidly. Walk with C. and at night. Saw Mrs Bradley. House affairs. Our China has grown almost into a collection. Read Bagehot's characters[4]—Birch on Oxygen[5]—Clanricarde's Defence (?).[6]

6. Sat.

Wrote to J.H. Parker—A. Watkin[7]—Messrs. Tatham—Baron Marochetti. Accounts; calls; & business. H.W. with M. and L[ena]. Saw Lyttelton (he looks well but older)—F.R. Bonham—The Speaker. Dined at Mr Harcourt's to meet D. & Dse d'Aumale.[8] To the latter I was not presented but I liked the Duke particularly. Read Bagehot.

7. 3 S. Lent.

St James mg: St George's aftn. Conv with Agnes. Wrote to Rev E. Hawkins —Bp of Brechin. Saw Lady Wenlock—Mr Ellison—Ld Derby (by St James's only). Read Welcker's Götterlehre[9]—Observateur Catholique—Bp of Brechin's Charge—and Tracts. Lent Sermon aloud in evg. Saw Douglas— & another[R].

8. M.

Wrote to Marq. D'Azeglio. Sat to Marochetti[10]—Saw H[elen]J.G.—Aunt J. —J.N.G.—C. Strzelecki. Dined with the Herberts—Inquiries about Lovell[11]

---

[1] Sir Edward Bindloss Perry, 1784–1859; 2nd bart. 1796.

[2] G. *Rawlinson, *The history of Herodotus* (1858).

[3] *Eastlake read the proofs of the section on 'colour': Add MS 44389, f. 87.

[4] W. Bagehot, *Estimates of some Englishmen and Scotchmen, a series of articles reprinted from the 'National Review'* (1858).

[5] S. B. Birch, *On the therapeutic action of oxygen; with cases proving its singular efficacy* (1857).

[6] U. J. de B. Clanricarde, *Inquiry into the truth of accusations against Clanricarde in Handcock v. Delacour* (1855).

[7] Perhaps Absalom Watkin, 1787–1861; Manchester cotton broker; free-trader and friend of *Bright.

[8] Henri Eugène Philippe Louis d'Orléans, s. of Louis Philippe, m. 1844 Caroline, princess of Salerno, 1822–69. They lived in England, often with Harcourt and Lady Waldegrave.

[9] See 25 Feb. 58.   [10] See 10 May 57.   [11] See 24 Jan. 58.

—Read Phillimore's Opinion[1]—Blaine's Report[2]—Pamphlets. Worked on Homer—proofs & revises. Dined with the Herberts—H.S. with M. & L[ena].

9. T.

Wrote to Rev. J. Sanders[3]—Jas Kent—Mr Geo. Harris—Lyttelton—Sir C. Trevelyan—Mr Jas Wright—Sec. of Treasury[4]—Ld Stanley—Mr J.H. Parker—Ld Nelson—Sig. Borromeo.[5] H.S. with M. Saw Ld Cremorne—Col. Rowley[6]—Mrs Malcolm. Read Jacob's Opinions[7]—Göthe Farbenlehre—Sir A. Elton on the Ministry[8]—Worked on proofs & revises.

10. Wed. X

H.S. with M. Wrote to Rev Mr Rawlinson—Worked on proofs & revises: wrote Advertisement. Sat for the last time to Marochetti. His bust of me is a product of extraordinary power: I would it were another subject. Saw R. Phillimore—Lord Stanley—E. Cardwell—Mr Ellice. Dined with the Cardwells: Lady Derby afterwards: conv. with D. of Cambridge on the Murder Bill.[9] Saw Mackay 123. Gray 20[R].

11. Th.

H.S. with my daughters. Worked on Homer: revises. Seven to dinner. Wrote to J.H. Parker. Read Bagehot's Macaulay[10]—Indian pamphlets. Visit with C. at Stafford House. Saw Sir W. Heathcote with Sir J. Awdry—Rev. Dr Godfray—Duke of Argyll—Mr Goldwin Smith—Mr J.H. Parker—Mr Pressly—Mr Hodgson.

12. Fr.

Wrote to Robn. G.—Rev M.W. Mayow. H. of C. $4\frac{1}{2}$–7 and 8–11. Witnessed sad mismanagement of the Cagliari case.[11] H.S. with my daughters. Worked on Homer proofs & revises. This day I finished them. I can expect but little fruit but I pray God it may be good. Saw S. Herbert—Sir W. Heathcote. Read Bagehot.

[1] R. J. *Phillimore, *The Cagliari. Dr. Phillimore's opinion* (1858).
[2] D. R. Blaine, *Artistic Copyright Report prepared at the request of the committee, appointed by the Society of Arts* (1858).
[3] Probably James Sanders, d. 1880; priest 1831; perpetual curate of Ripponden, Yorkshire, from 1847.
[4] Anthony Evelyn Melbourne Ashley, 1836–1907, *Shaftesbury's s.; sec. to *Palmerston as first lord 1858–65, whose life he wrote; liberal M.P. Poole 1874–80, Isle of Wight 1880–5; minor office 1880–5.
[5] C. Borromeo had written from Southwark about the Italian National League (Hawn P).
[6] See 24 June 35n.
[7] *The views and opinions of . . . J. *Jacob*, ed. L. Pelly (1858).
[8] A. H. Elton, *The case against the late ministry plainly stated* (1858).
[9] The new govt. dropped the bill.
[10] 'Mr. Macaulay' in W. *Bagehot, *Estimates of some Englishmen and Scotchmen* (1858).
[11] Supported call for papers on the *Cagliari*, captured, with released political prisoners and two Britons, by Neapolitan frigates in June 1857 and taken to Naples: *H* cxlix. 97.

13. *Sat.*

H.S. with M. & L. Wrote to J. F. Macqueen—Mr Collins[1]—Dr Dollinger—
Jas Wright—Bp of Oxford—J.H. Parker—Bp of Salisbury—B. Shaw—Bp
of Hereford—J.G. Talbot—Ld Brougham—Dr Pusey—Ld Stanhope—Mr
Hardwick[2]—Mr Pearson.[3] We learned today Ld Braybrooke's death at an
early hour this morning. It was in great resignation & peace.[4] Saw Ld
Aberdeen—A. Panizzi—Mr Greenwood—Mr [C.] Wykham Martin—Saw
Douglas & another[R]. House business. Read Debit & Credit[5]—Sharpe on
Railways[6]—Pearson on Oxford Med.—Maury Religion de la Gréce.[7]

14. *4 S.L.*

St James mg St Andr. Wells St aftn. Saw J.R. Godley—Mr Lacaita—H.J.G.
Wrote to J.H. Parker—Jas Wright—H.J.G. Read Maury Religion &c.—
Veritas on Scots Episcopacy.[8]

15. *M.*

H.S. with M. & L. Wrote to Mr Cornelius Buck—G. Burnett—E. Lovell—
Robn. G—Rev. R. Greswell—W. Heath[9]—Mr E. Sharpe. Saw Scotts—Ld
Lyndhurst—R. Phillimore—Mr Trefusis (MP). House business. Read the
Napoleon Pamphlet also the Piard.[10] H of C. $4\frac{1}{2}$–$7\frac{1}{4}$. A great day for the
Govt. Lord John was rash: Osborne might have been bribed.[11] Six to dinner.

16. *T.*

H.S. with M. & L. Wrote to Duchess of Sutherland—A. Panizzi—Mr D.
Gladstone—S. Warren—Rev. R. Hooper—W. Dyce R.A.—Mr G. Bram-
well—J.H. Parker—T. Sandars—Mr M. Arnold. Bills & house business.
Read Bagehot—Question des Principautés[12]—Q.R. on 1857 Pol.[13] Committee
$12\frac{1}{2}$–3. Dined with the Jameses. At Christie's resp. pictures. C. went to
Brighton. Saw E. Lovell—Stapylton[R].[14]

---

[1] Thomas Collins, 1825–84; Peelite/tory M.P. Knaresborough 1851–2, 1857–65, 1881–4,
for Boston 1868–74.

[2] Charles Hardwick, 1798?–1874; rector of St. Michael, Gloucester from 1839; corresponded on Homer (Hawn P).

[3] Charles Henry *Pearson, 1830–94; historian and educationalist; emigrated 1871 and
reorganized Australian education; wrote 'A letter . . . on a scheme for making Oxford
more accessible to medical students generally' (1858).

[4] See 17 May 58.

[5] G. Freytag, *Debit and credit*, tr. L.C. Cumming, 2v. (1857).

[6] E. *Sharpe, 'A letter on branch railways . . . with an appendix and map' (1857).

[7] L. F. A. Maury, *Histoire des religions de la Grèce antique depuis leur origine jusqu'à
leur complète constitution*, 3 v. (1857).

[8] Veritas [J. Carmichael], 'Romanism and Scottish episcopacy. A word with the
Scottish bishops on their recent "Declaration and Statement"' (1858).

[9] William Heath, commissioner for oaths in chancery.

[10] Perhaps 'L'Attentat du 14 Janvier 1858'; very hostile to Napoleon III; and, possibly,
P. A. J. Piard, 'Le conservateur de la santé, ou Médecine des familles' (1852).

[11] Bernal *Osborne had denounced *Russell, who replied in kind: *H* cxlix. 212.

[12] *Considérations sur la question des principautés* (1858).

[13] *Quarterly Review*, ciii. 526 (March 1858).

[14] Both prostitutes.

17.

H.S. with M. & L. Wrote to Princ. St Alban H.[1]—C.G.—Sir S. Northcote—W.H.G.—Mr Galbraith[2]—Jas Peyton[3]—Rev Mr Roberts—Mr Moffatt. Saw Mr Hawkins—Earl of Aberdeen—Mr [A.E.] Lockhart—Chas Ross—Scotts—Mr Lacaita. Saw Mackay[R]. Dined at Lady Lytteltons. Read pamphlets.

18. Th.

H.S. with M & L. Wrote to W.E. Ruskin[4]—C.G.—Robn. G.—Rev. J. Foster[5]—Geo. Grant—A Cohen[6]—Mr Bramwell—Ld C.L. Fitzroy[7]—Mr D. Lange. A busy morning on books & papers which are *coming* into order. Saw J.N.G.—J.H. Parker—C. Forster MP[8]—Col. Gilpin MP—J.G. Talbot. Christie's & business out of doors. H of C. 4½–7.[9] Read Ld Grey on Reform[10]

19. Fr.

Off at 7.20 to Audley End for Ld Braybrooke's funeral & back at 4. It seems to have been a prepared as well as peaceful end. Wrote to Earl of Derby—C.G.—Mr Stainton—M. Coronéo[11]—Prov. of Worcester—T.C. Sandars—Rev Mr Haddan. Saw Johnson Longden & Co—Sir W. Heathcote—E. Cardwell. Read Bagehot's Characters—Phillips's Curran.[12]

20. Sat.

H.S. with M. & L. Wrote to Cocks & Biddulph—C.H.—Mr Johnson—W.H.G.—Mr R. Buckley—Robn. [G.—Ld Goderich—Mr Labatz—Hansard—D. Burns.[13] Saw Sir S. Northcote—Sir W. Heathcote—Mr D.A. Lange—Ld Overstone . . . S. Herbert. Attended sale at Christie's: and shopping. Missed Mackay: saw one[R]. Dined at Lady Beauchamp's. Read Quest. des Principautés.

21. 5 S. Lent.

St James's & H.C. mg.—St Andrew's (with Harry) aft.—Pr[inted] Sermon aloud in evg. Wrote to C.G.[14] Read Agnès Arnauld's Letters[15]—Bagehot's

[1] i.e. E. *Cardwell.
[2] Possibly Joseph Allen Galbraith, 1819?–90; fellow of Trinity, Dublin, from 1844; wrote manuals; home ruler.
[3] Of the Royal Exchange Assurance Company.
[4] Unidentified; apparently not a relation of J.*
[5] Probably John Foster, 1807?–82; vicar of Oaks, Charnwood, 1856–78.
[6] Arthur *Cohen, 1829–1914; barrister 1857; junior counsel in Alabama arbitration 1872; liberal M.P. Southwark 1880–7; sat on commissions.
[7] Lord Charles Lennox Fitzroy, 1791–1865; 2nd s. of 4th duke of Grafton; soldier; whig M.P. Thetford 1818–31, Bury St. Edmunds 1832–47.
[8] (Sir) Charles Forster, 1815–91; liberal M.P. Walsall from 1852; chaired public petitions cttee. from 1865; cr. bart. 1874.
[9] Misc. business: *H* cxlix. 322.
[10] See 1 Mar. 58.
[11] P. Coroneo of Finsbury Square had sent a pamphlet in French on Greece (Hawn P).
[12] C. *Phillips, *Recollections of Curran and some of his contemporaries* (1818).
[13] Possibly Rev. Dawson Burns, nonconformist minister in Westbourne Park Road.
[14] Bassett, 121.   [15] See 21 Feb. 58.

Char[acters]—Henderson's Sermon[1]—Croesius Hist. Hebr. ab Hom.[2] Dined at Lady Lyttelton's.

22. M.

Wrote to Sir J. Lefevre—F.H. Dyke—Chief Fr[ench] Passp. Office[3]—C.G. —Ld Derby—Mr Page Legh—Johnson L. & Co. H of C. 5–7.[4] Saw Sir F. Doyle (Homer)—Baron Marochetti—Mr Butterfield—Dean of Westminster. Shopping—Missed Staplyton[R]. Read Civil Service Report[5]— Quest. des Principautés—H.S. with M. & L.

23. T.

H.S. with M. & L. Wrote to Archdn. Williams—C.G. (2)—Mr G. Richmond —Major Scott[6]—Mr H. Merritt[7]—Sir E. Cust—Rev. Mr Hinson.[8] Saw Mr Harriss (resp. China)[9]—Mr H. Cole—Mr Greswell—S. Herbert—Sir W. Heathcote. Dined at Mrs Talbot's. Saw Mackay[R]. Commee. & H of C. 12– 4, $4\frac{1}{2}$–$7\frac{1}{2}$, 8–$9\frac{1}{2}$.[10] Read Quest. des Princip.

24. Wed. X

H.S. with M. & L. Wrote to Willy . . . Rev. N. Wade—Count Hebeler. Morning chiefly spent on arranging part of our China acc. to its origin. Saw Mrs Herbert . . . Scotts—B. Quaritch (Homer &c.)—Ld Lyndhurst. Business out of doors. Dined with the Farquhars. Attempted a little Q.R.[11] Read Cagliari papers[12]—Govt. Offices papers[13]—Quest. des Principautés. At Christie's. Saw one[R].

25. Th. Annuncn.

HS. with M. & L. Wrote to Sir F. Rogers—Robn. G.—Rev. H. Roundell— C.G.—Overends. Dined at S. Herbert's. Lady Salisbury's afr. Worked on China. Saw Mr Merritt resp. pictures wh he fully examined & reported well of.—C.A. Wood—Sir S. Northcote—Rev. R. Greswell—M. Persigny—Sir W. Heathcote—Bp of Oxford (Ld Bury's bill).[14] Read Quest. des Principautés—D. of Argyll's Speech.[15] H. of C. $4\frac{1}{4}$–7 and $10\frac{1}{2}$–$11\frac{1}{2}$.[16]

[1] Perhaps E. Henderson, 'Directions to the awakened sinner' (1831); on Micah iv. 6–8.
[2] G. Croesius, *Sive historia hebraeorum ab Homero hebraicis nominibus ac sententiis conscripta in Odyssea et Iliade* (1704).
[3] In King William Street; business untraced.
[4] On an amndt. to the Oaths Bill: *H* cxlix. 483.
[5] *PP* 1857–8 xxv. 1.
[6] i.e. H. Y. D. *Scott.
[7] Henry *Merritt, 1822–77; picture cleaner and art critic.
[8] William Hinson, perpetual curate of St. Mark's, Old Street, London, from 1848 and chaplain to Lord Courtown.
[9] John Harriss, art and china dealer in Green Street, Leicester Square.
[10] Marriage Law Amndt. Bill: *H* cxlix. 603.
[11] The start of 'France and the late ministry', *Quarterly Review*, ciii. 526 (April 1858), Add MS 44689, f. 1.
[12] *PP* 1857–8 lix. 7; see 12 Mar. 58.
[13] *PP* 1857–8 xxv. 1.
[14] The Marriage Law Amnd. Bill, see 3 June, 21 July 58 etc.
[15] G. D. *Campbell, duke of Argyll, 'Speech . . . on the motion of Lord Panmure', 8 February 1858, on the mutiny.
[16] Ireland: *H* cxlix. 718.

26 Fr.

H.S. with M. & L. Wrote to C.G.[1] Saw S. Herbert. The boys returned: Willy now no longer an Etonian. Much that means. Commee. 12–2¼ and House 4½–7¼.[2] Dined at Mrs Talbot's. Lady Wensleydale's in evg. My book came from Parker's in a state fit for sale: I was weak enough to spend two hours in reading it. A little for QR. Read Q. des Princip.

27. Sat.

H.S. with M. & L. Wrote to Johnson Longden & Co—C.G.[3]—Overends— J. Murray—Rev J. Husband. Wrote for Q.R. Shopping. Saw Ld Aberdeen. Read Lyttelton on general reading[4]—Q. des Princip. Dined at Mrs Talbots. Lady Jerseys & Lady Palmerston's in evg. Br. Museum 12–1. Kensington Museum 3–5. Conv. with Willy on his measures.

28. Palm S.

St James' mg: & Marg. Chapel aftn. Printed S[ermon] aloud in evg. Conv. with S.M. & L. on Epistle. Saw Sir W. James. Wrote to Rev Mr Henderson —Col. Sykes—Rev Mr Hawkins—C.G. Scott. Read Rio's Arundel—Rio's Ansaldo Cebá[5]—Scott's Paper on Revival[6]—Rhyming Hist. of Abelard & Heloise[7]—Hawkins on Psalms.[8]

29. M.

St James's 11 AM. with Stephy and Mazie. Wrote to Lord H. Lennox— C.G.—Rev M. MacColl[9]—G. Grant—Mr Henry Lees. Saw Mr Merritt (pictures)—Bishop of Exeter—Ld De Tabley. Shopping (China). Bills & accts with Hampton. Read Gardiner on Ind. Revolt[10]—Quest. des Principautés. Worked for Q.R. Wrote to Overends—Johnson L & Co.

30. T.

H.S. with the children. Missed the Church hour in evg. Wrote to Johnson L. & Co—C.G.—Provost of Queen's—Col. Sykes—Geo. Miller—W. Brown— Rev. J. Husband—T. Barton[11]—Robn. G. Saw Earl of Aberdeen. Looking

---

[1] Bassett, 121.

[2] India Bill: *H* cxlix. 818.

[3] On India, in Bassett, 122.

[4] In MS; G.W. *Lyttelton, 'Slight hints on general reading' (?1859), published in *Ephemera* (1865).

[5] A. F. Rio, *The four martyrs* (1856), biographies of Arundel, Ansaldo, Ceba, etc.

[6] G. G. *Scott, 'The revival of gothic architecture' in 'Two lectures delivered at the meeting of the York and London architectural societies' (1857).

[7] Probably that by James Delacour (1725).

[8] E. *Hawkins, *The book of psalms* (1857).

[9] Malcolm *MacColl, 1831–1907; high churchman and ecclesiastical politician; held Scottish episcopalian incumbencies; Gladstone made him rector of St. George's, Botolph Lane, 1871 and canon of Ripon 1884; he supported most Gladstonian crusades; see Add MS 44242–5.

[10] R. W. *Gardiner, *Military analysis of the remote and proximate causes of the Indian rebellion* (1858).

[11] Perhaps Thomas Henry Barton, 1816–78; barrister in Dublin 1844; professor there 1865–8.

after pictures: busy with China & house arrangements. Worked for Q.R.: beginning anew. Read Q. des Principautés—Merritt on Picture Cleaning.[1]

31. Wed.

St Andrew's with S. 5 PM. H.S. with Stephy & Mazie. Wrote to Johnson L. & Co.—C.G.—Jas Watson—Mr Dunt.[2] Worked somewhat more effectually for the Q.R. Saw Mr Richmond: on pictures—Mr Harriss: & went over with him the China: an affair of two or three hours. Also busied in further extensions. It has become almost a 'collection'. Stafford House in evg: 10–1. Conv. with D. of Argyll—Granville—M. Persigny—& had some pleasure in the pictures.

Thurs. Ap. One. 1858.

St. And. Wells St. aftn. H.S. with S. M. and L. Wrote to C.G.—Johnson L. & Co.—Ld Braybrooke—Sir W. Heathcote. Saw Mr Harriss—Col. Sykes—Johnson Longden & Co—Overends—Went into the City. 1–3. With Mr Merritt on the pictures. Worked for Q.R. Read [blank]

2. G. Friday.

St Jamess & H.C. mg. Marg. Chapel aftn. Conv. with Harry: it being his birthday. He is good & acute & affectionate. Wrote to C.G. Read S. Bernard—Obs. Catholique[3]—Chr. Rem.[4]—Westmr. Review[5]—D'Israeli's Judaism[6]—Wiseman's Recollections.[7] Saw Jim Wortley. Schemed picture hanging. Wrote MS Theol.[8] MS. of 52 aloud in evg.

3. Easter Eve. [Brighton]

St Paul's (Brighton) 9 P.M.[9] Wrote to Jas Watson. Worked for Q.R. Arranged letters. Occupied about pictures & china with Mr Merritt & others. Read Quest. des Principautés. Off at 4 to Brighton. Found C. somewhat advanced. Dined with the De Tableys. Saw Mrs Talbot.

4. Easter Day.

St Paul's (& H.C.) 10½–1¾: and again in aft. Read Agnès Arnauld—Rio's Quatre Martyrs.[10] Walk with C. Dined with the De Tableys.

[1] H. Merritt, *Dirt and pictures separated in the works of the old masters* (1854).
[2] John E. Dunt, lamp maker, of Hancock, Rixon & Dunt (see 30 Mar. 44).
[3] See 3 Jan. 58.
[4] *Christian Remembrancer*, xxxv (April 1858).
[5] *Westminster Review*, xiii (April 1858).
[6] I. *D'Israeli, The genius of Judaism* (1833).
[7] N. P. S. *Wiseman, *Recollections of the last four Popes and of Rome in their times* (1858).
[8] Untraced.
[9] Arthur Douglas Wagner, 1825?–1902; rector of St. Paul's, Brighton from 1850; notorious ritualist.
[10] See 28 Mar. 58.

5. Easter M. [London]

St Paul's 10¼ AM. Shopping (for China). Saw Ld Ripon—Mr W. Beckett. Back to London at 3.30: C. suffering much from a *blast*. Read Quest. des Princip. Worked for Q.R. Wrote to Lady Mayoress[1]—Sec. Brighton RR. Co—Read the Cagliari Papers.

6. Easter T.

Marg. Chapel 5 PM. Wrote to Johnson L. & Co (2)—Shopping. Worked on China: busy with arrangements for pictures & other objects. Worked for Q.R. Saw Ld De Tabley—G. Christie—Mr Manson.

7. Wed.

H.S. with A.S.M. & L. Wrote to Mr T. Cannon—Lady Beauchamp—F.H. Dickinson—Johnson L. & Co.—A. Hayward—Dr Burgess—Rev Mr. Cunningham—Mr Whiteman—Dr [John] Chapman. Worked for Q.R. Saw Mr Merritt—Mr Richmond—J.N.G.

8. Th.

H.S. with A.S.M.L. Worked for Q.R. Finished in the rough, and revised part. Saw Sir W. Heathcote—Mr G. Richmond—Dr Acland—Rev. Mr Elwin—R. Phillimore—F.R. Bonham. Worked on China & pictures. Read Mazzini to Napoleon[2]—Barchester Towers.[3]

9. Fr.

H.S. as yesterday. Finished M.S. for press Q.R. It has given me a good deal of trouble. Saw Mr Whiteman—Ld Aberdeen—Mr Merritt. Working on House arrangements & China Colln. Wrote to Mr C. Edwards[4]—Queen's Proctor[5]—Sec. Brighton RR[6]—Rev Mr Rowsell—Rev Mr Mitchinson. Read Barchester Towers.

10. Sat.

H.S. with A. & S. Wrote to Ld De Tabley—Helen. Worked on proofs. Further engaged on my collection of China (for exchange &c) with Harriss. Saw Rev. Mr Elwin—Mr N. Senior. Read Mr Senior's Paris Journal[7]—Barchester Towers.

[1] Pamela Elizabeth Edith Andrews, d. 1874, m. 1827 (Sir) Robert Walter Carden, 1801–88; contested St. Albans 1850, his petition leading to its disfranchisement; lord mayor 1857–8; tory M.P. Gloucester 1857–9, Barnstaple 1880–5; cr. bart. 1887; for complex tale of earlier attempts to win patronage, see Blake, 387.
[2] G. Mazzini, *To Louis Napoleon* (1858); attack on him and his policy.
[3] A. *Trollope (1857).
[4] Charles Edwards of Dolserau, 1825–89; liberal M.P. Windsor 1866–8.
[5] F. Hart Dyke.
[6] Frederick Slight, sec. of London, Brighton & South Coast railway.
[7] Still in MS: see 30 Dec. 50 and 21 Feb. 53.

11. 1 S.E.

St James mg. Germ. Chapel[1] aft. MS. of 42 aloud in evg. Conv. with the elder children on Ep. & Gosp. Read Quatre Martyrs (finished)—Moravian Synod[2]—Gleig's Instructions.[3] At night finished proofs for Q.R. Wrote to R. Phillimore—and Johnson L[ongden] & Co.

12. M.

H.S. with A. & S. Wrote to Messrs. Overend—Mr Rice[4]—Bp of Oxford. Corrected Press and retrenched Article for Q.R. Saw Mr Dyke—Mr E.W. Pugin[5]—Rev W. Elwin—Mr S. Willson[6]—Ld Lyndhurst—Mr Ellice— Mr Geo. Glyn—Ld Aberdeen—R. Phillimore. Nine to dinner, incl. J. Wortley. I was disappointed. Wrote on Indian Govt.[7] Read Barchester Towers.

13. T.

H.S. with A. & S. Wrote to Miss Sheddon—F. Robson[8]—D.A. Lange— Robn. G.—H. Glynne—Col. Sykes. Worked on hanging pictures & arranging China. Saw Mr B. Benjamin—Ld De Tabley—Mr Jelf—Sir Thos Gladstone—Dean Milman. Went with C.G. to the Exhibition at Christie's.[9] Read Barchester Towers. Dined at the Club. Lady Granville's afr.

14. Wed. X

H.S. with A. & S. Wrote to Johnson L. & Co—Jas Watson—Scotts—H. Cole. At Christie's. Dined at Lady Wenlock's. Lady Derby's afr. Saw H.J.G on family & other affairs. Kensington Museum at 5 P.M. to receive H.M.[10] Saw Ld J. Russell—Sir C. Trevelyan—Mr Hallam. Worked on China. Read Barch. Towers.

15. Th.

H.S. with A & S. St Andrew's 5 P.M. Wrote to Robn G.—C. Butler. Dined at Mrs Stanley's. Saw Rev. Dr Vaughan[11]—Mr S. Herbert (& see inf.) Read divers pamphlets. Twelve to breakfast: incl. Bp. of Exeter & A. Kinnaird. Saw Mr Elwin—Provost of Eton: & met the Wortley party at Christie's. Inq. for Stapleton & others. Saw Winter[R].

---

[1] The German Lutheran chapel in Great Trinity Lane.
[2] *Results of the synod of the Protestant church of the United Brethren, held at Herrnhut in the year 1857* (1858).
[3] Perhaps G. *Gleig, *Directions for the study of theology* (1827).
[4] Probably Stephen Edmund Spring-Rice, 1814–65, s. of Baron Monteagle; deputy chairman of customs 1856–9.
[5] Edward Welby *Pugin, 1834–75, s. of A.W.N.*; took over his fa.'s architectural practice.
[6] Perhaps a slip of the pen for A. Willson (see 18 Dec. 31) who was tory M.P. S. Lincolnshire 1857–9.
[7] See Add MS 44747, f. 180.
[8] Francis Robson of Idle had written on finance; Hawn P.
[9] Of David Falcke's collection.
[10] To view progress on the site.
[11] Charles John *Vaughan, 1816–97; headmaster of Harrow 1844–59; vicar of Doncaster 1860–9; dean of Llandaff from 1879.

16. Fr. X

H.S. with A. & S. Wrote to Mr Stubbs[1]—B. Lancaster[2]—J. Lorimer jun.[3]—C. Fawsett[4]—Bp of Oxford—Mr Holman.[5] Worked on China & pictures. Saw Rev. Mr Hobhouse—Earl of Aberdeen—Col. Sykes & Mr Gibson—Saw Stapleton[R]. Read Q.R. on Publ. Speaking and on Lucknow.[6] Willy went off to Mr Jelf's.[7]

17. Sat.

H.S. with A & S. Wrote to J. Breakenridge—Mr Green—J. Littleboy—Sec. L[ondon] & B[righton] Co.—G. Burnett—Johnson L & Co—J.C. Pettingell.[8] Saw Sir J. Lefevre & Sir E. Ryan—Sir W. Heathcote—Mr Ellice. Dined at Mr Ellices. Read [blank] Worked on China &c.

18. 2 S. E.

Kept the house mg: service alone. Marg. Chapel aftn. Wrote MSS Theol. Read Memorial of Hedley Vicars *the 79th thousand*.[9]—Macpherson on the Romans[10]—Wilson's Bampton Lectures.[11] To bed early with influenza.

19. M.

Most of the day in bed. Wrote to Mr Burnett—Read Indophilus[12] & other Indian pamphlets. H of C. $4\frac{1}{2}$–9: spoke in aid of the Budget.[13] H. again late. Saw Mr Ellice.—Read the E. I. Bills.

20. T. X

Up at 11 AM. Wrote to Ld Braybrooke—Rev O. Gordon—Johnson L. & Co—Rev W. Elwin—Watson & Smith—F. Slight—Justice Coleridge—Rev J. James[14]—Dean [Henry] Newland—J.H. Parker—Rev. Mr D'Orsay.[15] Saw Mr Lavis—Archdeacon Hale—Sir J. Graham—Saw Stapleton[R]. Read

---

[1] William *Stubbs, 1825–1901; constitutional historian; vicar of Navestock, Essex, 1850–66; bp. of Chester 1884, of Oxford 1888; assisted in Gladstone's elections 1852–65.
[2] Of Princes Gardens, Hyde Park.
[3] James *Lorimer, 1818–90; Scottish advocate 1845; professor of law in Edinburgh from 1865; wrote on law and Scottish education.
[4] Camillus Fawsett, secretary of the United University Club.
[5] Perhaps William Henry Holman; naval chaplain 1850–70; vicar of Thanington 1870.
[6] *Quarterly Review*, ciii. 483, 505 (March 1858).
[7] W. E. Jelf tutored Willy in preparation for Oxford.
[8] Possibly John Hancock Pettingell, American religious writer.
[9] *Memorials of Captain Hedley Vicars . . . by the author of 'The Victory Won'* [C. M. Marsh] (1856); evangelical jingoism.
[10] Perhaps the untraced English tr. of A. Macpherson, 'De verklaring van Paulus aan die van Rome' (1857), on Romans i. 16.
[11] See 11 Dec. 53.
[12] Sir C.E. *Trevelyan published several pamphlets as Indophilus; this probably 'Letters . . . on the mutiny of Vellore—its parallelisms and its lessons' (?1857).
[13] Its chief proposal equalized Anglo-Irish spirit duties: *H* cxlix. 1312.
[14] Many; perhaps John James, d. 1868; vicar of St. John, Peterborough, from 1850 and canon there; author.
[15] See 11 July 47.

Athenaeum on my Homer[1]—Q.R. on Boswell[2]—Indophilus. Worked on India. Commee. & H of C. 3–7¼.[3]

21. Wed.

H.S. with A. & S. Wrote to Mrs J.E. Tyler—Ld Braybrooke (rewrote)—Ld Lyndhurst. Saw E. Cardwell—Do *cum* Sir J. Graham—Sir W. Heathcote—Lord J. Russell—Sir G.C. Lewis (Homer)—D. of Newcastle. Dined at Baron Rothschild's—Then Sir R. Murchison's—Then Lady Derby's. Saw one[R]. Read Indophilus. Visited French Exhibition[4] & met Dss of S. H of C. 1–6.[5]

22. Th. X

H.S. with A. & S. Wrote to J.H. Parker—Sir J. Graham—Hon. G.F. Boyle[6]—J.H. Turner[7]—Rev. E. Hawkins—Jas Lorimer jun. Calls & business. Nine to breakfast. Saw Ld Gifford[8]—Mr J.E. Fitzgerald—Mr E. Ellice with Sir W. Jolliffe—Mr Bright—(India & Principalities). Saw one[R] Nine to dinner; breakfast party of the same number. H of C. 4½–7½.[9] Read North Am. Rev. on Indian Revolt[10]—Letters of Indophilus.

23. Fr. X

Wrote to B. Benjamin—Ld Stanley—Mr Labouchere—T. Greene—E. of Aberdeen—J.S. Fitzgerald[11]—J.A. Franklin.[12] Read Pr. Edw. I. Papers[13]—Cagliari papers—Hayward's Essays[14]—Macknight's Burke. Framed motions on the Principalities & P.E. Island.[15] Saw Sir J. Graham—Mr Fitzgerald—Mr S. Walpole—Lord J. Russell—Saw Stapleton[R]—dined at Mrs Talbot's.

24. Sat.

Wrote to G. Burnett—G.F. Young—Rev Mr Plumptre. Dined at the Palace. Q. spoke about C.—M. Lyttelton—and Ld Abn.—Prince about the Kensington Estate. With Mr Merritt about the pictures. Meeting on

[1] *The Athenaeum*, 17 April 1858.
[2] *Quarterly Review*, ciii. 279 (March 1858).
[3] Indian railways: *H* cxlix. 1376.
[4] Private view of fifth annual French exhibition at 121 Pall Mall.
[5] Opposed Church Rates Abolition Bill amndt., arguing that 'dissenters should not be called upon to pay church rates'. *H* cxlix. 1459.
[6] George Frederick Boyle, 1825–90; tory M.P. Bute 1865; succ. his half-brother as 6th earl of Glasgow 1869.
[7] Roman catholic correspondent, who lapsed over the Vatican Council; Hawn P.
[8] Robert Francis Gifford, 1817–72; 2nd Baron Gifford 1826; a liberal-conservative.
[9] Diplomatic salaries: *H* cxlix. 1496.
[10] *North American Review*, lxxxvi. 487 (April 1858).
[11] *sc.* W. S. Fitzgerald; see 26 Apr. 58.
[12] John A. Franklin of Bow, London, corresponded on politics; Hawn P.
[13] Perhaps *Public documents on various subjects connected with the interests of Prince Edward Island* (1841).
[14] A. *Hayward, *Biographical and critical essays*, 5v. (1858).
[15] See 4 May 58 and 11 June 58n.

Col. Bprics Fund. Saw Mr Hubbard—Mr Orde[1]—Lord Aberdeen—Sir James Graham & Cardwell—Mr S. Herbert. Lady Palmerston's in Evg with Duchess of Sutherland. Some bits of Indian conversation there. Read Meade on India[2]—Hayward's Essays.

25. 3 S.E.

St James's mg St And. aft. MS. of 41 aloud in evg. Read Bp Forbes Consid[erationes][3]—Wilson B. Lectures—Letters of Mère Agnès—Alley's Vindiciae.[4] Saw J.N.G. Saw Winter[R].

26. M. X

Wrote to Watson & Smith—W.S. Fitzgerald. Dined at Mrs Talbot's. Saw Clifford—May[R]. Read Sheddon Papers.[5] Saw Hon. A. Gordon—Do *cum* Mr Waterfield[6]—Messrs. Hawkins & Baillie—Also Mr Hawkins—Ld J. Russell (Principp.)—W.S. Fitzgerald (do)—Mr Lygon (Ch. Rate).[7] Read Senior's Journal—Indian Papers &c.[8]

27. T. X

Wrote to Mr Fitzgerald—C. Pressly—Miss Sheddon—J. Petheram. Early dinner at Mr [G.G.] Harcourt's to meet D. & Dsse of d'Aumale.[9] Saw M. Bratiano—S.R. Glynne (his affairs)—Mr Bernal Osborne—Mr Seymour Fitzgerald—Sir T.G. Read Wiseman's Four Popes[10]—R. Owen's Life[11]—(Wilkins) Ed. Rev. on Thiers[12]—Bisset's Burke.[13] Saw Stapleton[R]. H of C. 10–11 and Comm. 12¾–3.[14]

28. Wed. X

Wrote to M. Bratiano—Johnson L & Co—Mr Jas Burnes[15]—Rev Mr Malet—Hon Gen Grey—Mr Nield. Saw Mr A. Gordon—Mr Fairman[16]—Scotts—Lord Aberdeen—Sir W. Heathcote—Saw May[R]. Drove with C. Dined at

[1] Leonard Shafto Orde, 1807–95; domestic chaplain to duke of Northumberland.
[2] H. Mead, *The Sepoy revolt: its causes and its consequences* (1857).
[3] See 29 Mar. 50.
[4] J. Alley, *Vindicae Christianae* (1826).
[5] Anabella Jean Shedden conducted her own legitimacy case in a lengthy trial; see *English Reports*, clxiv. 958.
[6] Thomas Nelson Waterfield, 1799–1862; sec. to Indian commissioners to 1839; assistant sec. in secret and political department 1839–58; in charge of records from 1858.
[7] See 2 Jan. 52.
[8] And spoke critically of the Government of India (No. 3) Bill: *H* cxlix. 1680.
[9] See Hewett, 128.
[10] See 2 Apr. 58.
[11] *The life of Robert Owen written by himself* (1857); only 1st v. published.
[12] *Edinburgh Review*, cvii. 358 (April 1858).
[13] R. *Bisset, *The life of Edmund Burke* (1798).
[14] *King's motion for a County Franchise Hill: H cxlix. 1816.
[15] Probably James Burnes of Montrose, 1801–62, a retired physician-general of Bombay.
[16] Perhaps F. D. Fairman, assistant clerk to the cttee. of council on education.

Mr Herrman's.[1] Lady H. Vane's[2] afterwards. Read Barch. Towers.—
Sleeman's Oude[3]—Debates on Russia &c. H of C. 3–5$\frac{1}{2}$.[4]

29. Th.

Wrote to A. Gordon—D. Meehan—Dean Newland—Scotts—Sir W.
Farquhar. Eleven to breakfast. Saw Mr Lacaita—Mrs Herbert—Mr
Bright—Sir W. Heathcote.—Robn. G. A quiet dinner at home. Euge.[5]
Read Mill & Wilson's India—Thornton's do—Richard on do[6]—and
pamphlets. H. of C. & L. 4$\frac{1}{2}$–7$\frac{1}{4}$.[7] B. Palace 3–4$\frac{1}{4}$. S.P.G. 2$\frac{1}{2}$–3.

30. Fr.

Wrote to W.S. Fitzgerald—G.F. Müller[8]—Sec. Univ. Club. Committee & H
of C. 2$\frac{1}{4}$–7$\frac{3}{4}$ and 10$\frac{1}{2}$–12.[9] Read Barchester Towers—Wilson's India. Saw
Gen Grey: then the Prince, on his plans & told him my full mind about the
H. of Commons and the method of speaking of it in our *conciliabula*.[10] Saw
Mr Arbuthnot.

Sat May One 1858. SS. Philip & James.

Wrote to Mrs Goalen—Breakfast at Grillion's—Exhibn. Commn. & Br.
Museum 11–1$\frac{3}{4}$. Royal Academy 2–5$\frac{1}{4}$: and attended the dinner. Read
Indian Hist. The Lytteltons came.

2. 4 S.E.

St James's mg & HC. Ch. Royal aft. MS of 47 aloud. Read Hampson's
Wesleys[11]—Wilson's B. Lectures—Forbes Cons. Mod.—&c. Saw W. James
—Family calls.

3. M. X

Wrote to M. Bratiano—S. Herbert—H. Ashworth[12]—F. Adams[13]—G.W.
Field—Johnson L & Co—Dr Sewell. H. of C. 4$\frac{1}{2}$–7$\frac{1}{2}$ and 9–12$\frac{1}{2}$: spoke on

[1] Hugo Hermann, of London Street; artist, never successful.
[2] Catherine Lucy Wilhelmina, *née* Stanhope, widow of Lord Dalmeny and mother of
5th earl of Rosebery, m. 1854 Lord Harry George Vane, later 4th duke of Cleveland;
beautiful, witty and malicious, she d. 1901. Vane moved a motion on India on 30 April.
[3] W. H. *Sleeman, *A Journey through the Kingdom of Oude in 1849 and 1850*, 2v.
(1858).
[4] Agricultural Statistics Bill: *H* cxlix. 1871.
[5] 'Bravo!'
[6] James *Mill, *History of British India*, 4v. (1818) ed. and continued by H. H. Wilson,
10v. (1858); E. *Thornton, *The history of the British Empire in India*, 6v. (1841–45);
H. *Richard, *The present and future of India under English rule* (1858).
[7] India in the Lords, Maynooth in the Commons: *H* cxlix. 1955, 1990.
[8] George Friedrich *Müller, 1805–98; Plymouth brother; opened many orphanages,
mostly in Bristol.
[9] Vane's motion to delay legislation on India: *H* cxlix. 2016.
[10] Presumably the meeting of the 1851 Exhibition Commissioners next day.
[11] J. *Hampson, *Memoirs of John *Wesley*, 3v. (1791).
[12] Henry *Ashworth, 1794–1880, founder of anti-corn-law-league, friend of *Cobden
and *Bright.
[13] Probably Francis Adams, 1796–1861; Aberdeenshire surgeon; translated Greek
medical works.

Finance and India.¹ Saw Ld Stanhope—Ld Stratford de Redcliffe—Sir Chas Wood—Mr [Charles] Forster M.P.—Saw one[R]. Read Ubicini²—& books on the Principalities. Barchester Towers.

4. T.

Wrote to Jas Watson—Saw Messrs Golesco³ & Bratiano—Count Montalembert. Read books & papers on the Principalities—Senior's Journal (finished). Commee. (Bank) 2–3½. H. of C. 4¾–11¾. Made my motion on the Principalities. Lost by 292:114 and with it goes another broken promise to a people.⁴

5. Wed.

Wrote to F.H. Head⁵—Johnson L. & Co.—E. Chadwick—Nathan Hayes ⁶ —Dr Jeune—Archdn. Sandford—Rev M. Osborne.⁷ Drew Resolutions on P[rince] E[dward] Island.⁸ Saw Rev. Mr Lake—Baron Brunnow—Marquis d'Azeglio—Lord Bury ⁹—Sir W. Heathcote—H of C. 1–5½.¹⁰ Ten to dinner: then evening party. Read Thornton's India.

6. Th.

Wrote to Johnson L. & Co—Rev. H. Glynne—Mr H. Bennett¹¹—Scotts. Dined at Ld Londonderry's: Lady Jersey's, also Lady Wenlock's, afterwards. Read Mill's India. Ten to breakfast. Saw Bp of Salisbury—Rev. Dr Hook—Mr A. Hayward. H of C. 4½–7.¹²

7. Fr.

Wrote to J.H. Parker—Hatchards—G. Bramwell—Read Barchester Towers—Buckle's Hist. Civilisation—Mill's India. H of C. 4½–7¼ and 9¼–11¾.¹³ Saw Mackay—Brook[R]. Saw Mr Say—Major Wortley M.P.—Sir W. Heathcote.

8. Sat. [Strawberry Hill, Twickenham].

Wrote to Mr Rawlins—Mr Giles—Rev Mr Brown—Mr Vidal—Mr Hughes— Mr Shaw—Robn G. B. Museum 12–1. Saw Mr A. Layard—Mr Stanistreet—

¹ On Exchequer bonds, and spoke and voted against the govt. on India: *H* cxlix. 2084, 2195.
² J. H. A. Ubicini, *Letters on Turkey; an account of the religious, political, social and commercial condition of the Ottoman empire*, 2v. (1856).
³ N. Golescu, co-author with Bratiano (see 30 July 56) of *The Danubian Principalities* (1858).
⁴ Resolution that Britain should keep her promise to Wallachia and Moldavia as agreed in the Paris treaty: *H* cl. 66.
⁵ Had asked for a seat in the Strangers' Gallery; Hawn P.
⁶ Had written on income tax; Hawn P.
⁷ Montagu Francis Finch Osborn, 1824–95; rector of Kibworth, Leicestershire, 1851–84.
⁸ See 11 June 58.
⁹ William Coutts *Keppel, 1832–94; styled Viscount Bury 1851–91; liberal M.P. Norwich 1857–60, Wick 1860–65, Berwick 1868–74; minor office 1878–80, 1885–6; became Roman catholic 1879; 7th earl of Albemarle 1891; wrote on Canada.
¹⁰ Marriage Law Amndt. Bill: *H* cl. 108.
¹¹ Hugh Bennett, d. 1860; vicar of Elmley Castle, Worcestershire, from 1800; Hawn P.
¹² Scottish franchise: *H* cl. 195.
¹³ Spoke on the *Cagliari*: *H* cl. 284.

Scotts—Earl of Aberdeen. At 4½ drove down to Strawberry Hill: where we found a large party.[1] The D. & Dss of Aumale dined. Read Lt Farquhar's letters [2]—Life of Sir T. Munro.[3]

9. 5 S.E.

Twickenham Ch mg & aft.[4] Read Harfords M. Angelo on Savonarola & V. Colonna[5]—Wilson's Bampton Lectures—Maitland's Eruvia.[6]

10. M.

Wrote to Mrs Hampton. Wrote resp. Ld Braybrooke.[7] Saw Orleans House[8] & drove to Bushy.[9] Conv. with Mr [J.D.] Cook, W. Harcourt, & Fleming.[10] Read Kaye's Adm. E.I. Co.[11]—Gleig's Sir T. Munro—Oldham's Sermon.[12]

11. T. [London]

Wrote to Neill Baillie[13]—Mrs Crouden—J.W. Hudson—J.A. Heraud[14]—Mrs Bennett—Dr Margoliouth.[15] Saw Sir W. Heathcote—S. Herbert—Ld Aberdeen *cum* Sir J. Graham—Mr Bright *cum* Mr Gibson—Bishop of Oxford. Came in from Strawberry Hill forenoon. Dined at Duke of Marlborough's, House of C. 4½–7¼.[16] Saw Cardwell in the Library: uttered a short but sharp warning on his motion.[17] Read Jerusalem pamphlets.

12. Wed. X

Wrote to Dr Lee—Goldwin Smith—Watson & Smith. Saw Duchess of Sutherland—Duke of Argyll—Mr G. Harcourt—Mr Reeve—Mr Bramwell—

[1] An attempt by Frances *Waldegrave, who owned H. *Walpole's Strawberry Hill, by Twickenham, to encourage Gladstone towards the liberals; see O. W. Hewett, *Strawberry Fair* (1956), 137.
[2] Untraced.
[3] By G. R. *Gleig (1830).
[4] After dinner, on being shown the full despatch on Oude, Gladstone told *Fortescue: 'There will be stormy weather about this', Hewett, (1958), 128.
[5] J. S. *Harford, *The life of Michael Angelo Buonarroti*, 2v. (1857); with memoirs of Savonarola, Colonna etc.
[6] S. R. *Maitland (1831).
[7] See 17 May 58.
[8] At Twickenham.
[9] Bushey (royal) Park, on the Thames with spendid triple avenue of trees.
[10] Henry Fleming, d. 1876; sec. to poor law board 1848–71; known as 'the Flea'; acid-tongued confidant of Lady Palmerston.
[11] J. W. *Kaye, *The administration of the East India Company, a history of Indian progress* (1853).
[12] R. S. Oldham, 'The eve of a campaign a time for self-searching' (1855).
[13] Neil Benjamin Edmonstone Baillie, d. 1883; wrote widely on Indian taxes and Mohammedan law.
[14] John Abraham *Heraud, 1799–1887; journalist and playwright; had written on Homer and demanded an acknowledgement: Add MS 44389, f. 195.
[15] Moses *Margoliouth, 1820–81; sundry curacies; vicar of Linford, Buckinghamshire from 1877; wrote on Hebraic-Christian relations and on the Jews: Add MS 44389, f. 191.
[16] Misc. business: *H* cl. 470.
[17] *Cardwell's motion condemned the tory govt.'s open attack on *Canning's proclamation on Oude. *Ellenborough, president of the board of control, had already resigned, admitting his bungling of the affair, and the ministry was seriously endangered; see 14 May 58.

Mr Brown—M. Bratiano. Saw May[R]. H. of C.[1] Oaths Comm. 4–5½. Visited Christie's. 6¼–12. To dinner at Orleans House with the D. & Dsse d'Aumale. He was agreeable & intelligent as usual: & we saw one illuminated book of astonishing beauty. Read Sullivan on India[2]—Jerusalem pamphlets: & others.

13. Ascension Day.

St James's (& H.C.) 11–1¼. H of C. 4½–7½ and 8¾–12.[3] Saw Ld Aberdeen—Sir W. Heathcote—Lord A. Hervey—Sir J. Graham—Mr Ellice—Mr Cardwell—Mr Forster M.P.—Mr Nash[4]—Mr Walpole. Read Memoirs of Mezzofanti.[5] Wrote to Archdeacon Thorp—Mr E. Sullivan[6]—Mr R. Gwynne.[7]

14. Fr.

Wrote to Vicar of St Martin's and [blank]. H of C. & H of L. 4½–7½ and 10½–12.[8] At Christie's resp. the Baillie pictures. Read Sullivan—Ritchie's Lond. Pulpit.[9] Saw Vicar of St Martins—Ld A. Hervey—Scots Univ. Deputation[10]—Ld Aberdeen—do cum Sir J. Graham—Sir W. Heathcote. Dined at the Duchess of Norfolk's.

15. Sat.

Wrote to Watson & Smith—Sir A. Elton—A. Beresford Hope—Mr Senior—Rev J. Bramston—Rev Mr Austin—Rev Mr Trevenan[11]—Lord H. Lennox. Dined with the Stanhopes. Made Mema. from Senior's Journals.[12] Breakfasted with the Bp of Oxford. Went to the Drawingroom with C. Saw Ld H. Lennox—Ld Grey—Duke of Newcastle—Bp of Oxford—Earl of Aberdeen. Attended Christie's (late). Walk with C. Read Lond Rev. on Principalities[13]—Ritchie's London Pulpit—Sullivan on India—Sleeman on Oude.[14]

16. S. aft Ascn.

St James's & H.C. mg. St Andr. aftn. Saw Ld H. Lennox—A.B. Hope—W. Harcourt—Mr Bright—Earl Nelson—Read Alley's Vind. Christ.[15]—Bp

[1] Poor Rates Bill: *H* cl. 496.
[2] E. R. Sullivan, *Letters on India . . . to J. Tremayne Esq.* (1858).
[3] Joint-stock banks: *H* cl. 534.
[4] Perhaps Charles Barnes Nash, 1815–92; prosecuted railway companies; wrote on them and on divorce law.
[5] C. W. *Russell, *The life of Cardinal Mezzofanti* (1858).
[6] (Sir) Edward Robert Sullivan, 1826–99; yachtsman and traveller; 6th bart. 1865; see previous day.
[7] Perhaps Richard Gwynne, d. 1865, Cardiganshire landowner.
[8] *Cardwell's motion on the Oude despatch (see 11 May 58): *H* cl. 686.
[9] J. E. Ritchie, *The London pulpit* (1854).
[10] On the Scottish Universities Bill.
[11] Probably Thomas John Trevenen, d. 1864; rector of St. Ewe, Cornwall, from 1836.
[12] Mema. untraced.
[13] *London Review*, x. 213 (April 1858).
[14] See 28 Apr. 58.
[15] See 25 Apr. 58.

Forbes Consid. Mod.—Chr. Rem. on Buckle[1]—Ritchie's London Pulpit. Wrote (part) MS. on Matt. XXVI. 56.[2] Finished notice of Ld Braybrooke.

17. M.

Wrote to W.H.G.—Bp of Argyll—J.H. Parker—Rev. T. Darling[3]— J. Edgar[4]—Jas Lowe[5]—C. Pressly. Dined at J.N.G.s. H of C. $4\frac{1}{2}$–$7\frac{1}{4}$ and $10\frac{1}{4}$–$12\frac{1}{2}$.[6] Read J. Symons's Sir R. Peel.[7]—Merit v. Patronage.[8] Had my notice of Lord B[raybrooke] revised by Stephen and C. and sent it to press.[9] Saw M. Tupper—S. Herbert—Earl of Aberdeen—G. Christie—Sir Jas Graham.

18. Tues. X

Wrote to S. Morley[10]—Hon R. Lawley—Jos Hyde[11]—H. of C. $4\frac{1}{2}$–$7\frac{1}{4}$.[12] Saw Shore. Missed Griffiths[R]. Saw Cardwell—Milnes Gaskell—Mr Milner Gibson. Attended Mr Lacaita's Lecture. Read Mill & Wilson's India— Symons's Peel—Sleeman's Oude.

19. Wed.

Wrote to Sir J. Graham—Mr Adams—Sec. L[ondon] & Y[ork] Comp. Dined at Ld Harry Vane's. Northumberland House afr. Shopping. Saw Mr Stansbury[13]—Mr Fitzgerald cum Ld L.[14]—Bishop of Oxford—Mr Bon- ham—Lady Dungarvan[15]—Lady Jersey—Lady M. Labouchere—Sir T. Gladstone. Much troubled in mind about this sad Indian debate. Read Kaye Adm. E.I. Co.[16]—Sleeman's Oude.

20. Th.

Wrote to Rev. O. Gordon—and [blank]. Commee. & Meeting Univ. Club $2\frac{1}{2}$–$4\frac{1}{4}$. Dined at Mrs Talbot's. H. of C. $4\frac{1}{2}$–$7\frac{1}{2}$ and $8\frac{3}{4}$–12: Graham de-

[1] *Christian Remembrancer*, xxxv. 330 (April 1858).

[2] On fulfilment of the prophets.

[3] Thomas Darling, 1816–93; St. John's, Cambridge; rector of St. Michael Royal, London, from 1848.

[4] Perhaps John Edgar, 1798–1866; American presbyterian minister and temperance advocate.

[5] Perhaps James Lowe, d. 1891; ed. *The Critic* 1843–63; translator and controversialist.

[6] *Ellenborough's despatch: *H* cl. 765.

[7] J. C. *Symons, *Sir Robert *Peel as a type of statesmanship* (1856).

[8] 'Merit v. Patronage: or the present position of the question of civil service com- petitions' (1858).

[9] For the *Gentleman's Magazine*, 2nd series, iv. 669 (June 1858), Braybrooke having d. on 13 March; this number also contained a long review of *Studies on Homer*.

[10] Samuel *Morley, 1809–86; hosier and philanthropist; liberal M.P. Nottingham 1865, Bristol 1868–85; important link between Gladstone and nonconformists.

[11] Perhaps of Hyde & Curry, Liverpool cotton brokers.

[12] Misc. business: *H* cl. 867.

[13] John Fortunatus Stansbury, 1805–94; headmaster of Oundle 1848–76.

[14] Probably *Lyttelton.

[15] Catherine, da. of 2nd earl of Howth, m. 1828 Charles, Viscount Dungarvan (d. 1834) and d. 1879.

[16] See 10 May 58.

livered a telling speech against Cardwell's motion.[1] Sixteen to Breakfast. Saw Mr G. Smith—Hon Mr Boyle—Lord Chandos—Mr Edwards—Mr Senior. Read Mill & Wilson—Ruskin's Notes.[2]

21. Fr. X

Wrote to Ld Bury—Chancr. of Exchr.[3] Saw Ld Aberdeen (mg, & night)—Mr Gerald Talbot—Robn. G. A painful morning: H of C. $4\frac{1}{2}$–$7\frac{1}{2}$ when all went off in smoke. An unexampled scene, but the operation was for good. I tried to save something out of the wreck for Canning.[4] Read Metcalfe Papers[5]—Montgomery on Land Tenures.[6] Dined at Mrs Talbot's. Saw Shore, Jewish[R].

22. Sat.

Wrote to William Gladstone—Mr V. de Montgomery[7]—B. Benjamin—Bp of Argyll—Ld Canning—Mrs Herbert—Willy—Earl of Aberdeen—Ld Derby—S.H. Walpole. Saw Mr Walpole—Sir S. Northcote—Hon A. Gordon. Wrote Memm. of conv. with W[alpole].[8] Br. Museum 12–1$\frac{1}{4}$. Mrs Marley's[9] musical party in aftn. Finished Barchester Towers.

23. Whitsunday.

Abp Tennyson's Chapel mg & H.C.—St James's Evg. MS. of 42 aloud in evg. Wrote to Bp of Oxford—Sir J. Graham (& copy).[10] Saw Ld Aberdeen on the comm[unicatio]n of yesterday. Read Holman Hunt & J. Graham on the Jerusalem controversy[11]—Maitland's Eruvia.[12] Walk with C.

Lord Aberdeen is like myself decidedly of opinion that it is impossible for me, acting alone, to join Lord Derby's administration under the present circumstances; nor does either of us forsee any circumstances in which that step would be possible or would promise public advantage. I[13] might naturally stop after having disposed of this simple question; except that the answer, turning upon sole action, might seem to blame Lord Derby for not making a more extended proposal, or to

[1] *Graham argued *Canning's proclamation was 'substantially wrong' and *Ellenborough's despatch 'substantially right'; his powerful speech made the fall of the ministry much less likely: H cl. 1001.

[2] J. *Ruskin, *Notes on some of the principal pictures exhibited in the rooms of the Royal Academy* (1858).

[3] i.e. *Disraeli.

[4] He defended *Canning's character, but supported *Cardwell's decision to withdraw his motion: H cl. 1042. It was doubtless this movement towards the govt. by *Graham and Gladstone that encouraged *Walpole to make his move next day.

[5] See 14 Dec. 57.

[6] Probably untraced pamphlet sent by Montgomery; see next day.

[7] James Hitchman, who published works, mostly religious, under pseudonym of Percy Vernon Gordon de Montgomery.

[8] *Walpole brought an offer, authorised by *Derby, of the board of control or the colonial office; Gladstone declined to act except with the Peelites; Add MS 44747, f. 170, printed in Morley i. 583–6.

[9] Catherine Louisa Augusta Tisdall m. 1828 George Marlay of Belvedere; she lived in Regent's Park.

[10] In Parker, *Graham*, ii. 344, enclosing record of his talk with *Walpole.

[11] W. H. *Hunt, 'Jerusalem. Bishop Gobat in re Hanna Hadoub', (1858).

[12] See 9 May 58.

[13] This sentence and the next inserted from opposite page.

suggest the propriety of his making one. I should not be justified in doing either the one or the other.

So far as my individual feelings are concerned they have at no time been opposed to a junction with Lord Derby as the head of an administration provided that junction could include others with whom I have been associated during my whole political life: in which case it would bear an altered aspect both with regard to probable public approval, and to the prospect of adding real strength to his ministry.

The question is not now regularly before me, whether such a junction is possible. I greatly regret that it was not understood at the critical moment in February to be Lord Derby's desire to raise it fully: for had it been then so understood the result would in all likelihood have been to give at least a decisive answer, whether affirmative or negative, to the question whether it is possible or no. But that opportunity has passed away. The difficulties in the way of such a union or reconstruction have always been great; and I apprehend that they grow with the lapse of time. At the present moment the friends of whom I speak are not I think disposed to give a fair trial and support to the Government, but I cannot say more: and though I have no authority, & no disposition, to say what Lord Derby thought of in February is *impossible*—though I am also aware that had it appeared possible Lord Aberdeen would have lent his influence to promote it—yet neither can I estimate it to be likely. My own decision as to sole action is positively taken: and I have only referred to a more extended scheme in order that it may not be supposed that I am indirectly suggesting to Lord Derby that he should make an attempt of the kind:[1] on the other point I only give an opinion which under the circumstances it appeared scarcely fair to withhold.[2]

24. *Whitm.*

St James's 11 AM. Wrote to Bp of Oxford—Mrs Goalen—Hon W.H. Merritt —Mr Purdue—G. Burnett—Mr Higgins—Sir J. Croft[3]—Jas Watson—Sig. Ricciardi—Mad. Sacrè[4]—& others. Geograph. Soc. 2—3¼. Saw Mrs H. Gladstone—Bp of Exeter—Mr A. Panizzi—Col. Sykes MP.—Saw Lovell— French & others[R]. Geograph. Socy. dinner in evg. Read Montgomery on Land Tenures.

25. *Whit T. X*

St James's 11 AM. Wrote to Chancr. of Exchr.[5]—Dean of Ch.Ch.—Willy— Rev Mr Brown—J. Durham—Mrs Keys. Saw Lord Brougham—Ld Aberdeen—Sir J. Walsh, & [blank] Dined at Lady Wenlock's—Lady Jane Walsh's[6] afr. Saw Clarke[R]. Spent the afternoon chiefly on reducing letters to order. Read Kaye's Admn. E.I. Co.

26. *Wed.*

Wrote to Lord Derby (and copy)[7]—Sir J. Graham (and copy)[8]—Warden of All Souls—Rev F.B. Zincke. Saw Ld Aberdeen: & adhered to my negative.

[1] This clause deleted with cross lines.
[2] Dated 23 May [1858]; marked 'Draft-cancelled'; Add MS 44747, f. 177.
[3] Sir John Croft, 1778–1862; diplomat; 1st bart. 1818.
[4] Madame William Sacré, who lived in Regent's Park.
[5] An arch reply, effectively declining *Disraeli's appeal to join the govt.; see Buckle, iv. 158; Add MS 44389, f. 233.
[6] Lady Jane Grey, da. of 6th earl of Stamford, m. 1825 Sir J. B. Walsh and d. 1877.
[7] Morley, i. 580: 'I have not seen, and I do not see, a prospect of public advantage or of material accession to your strength, from my entering your government single-handed'.
[8] In Parker, *Graham*, ii. 350, giving his decision not to join the govt.

Visited the National Gallery. 18 to dinner: evening party afterwards. Read Symons's Peel—&c. Missed Clarke[R]. Saw Sir F. Doyle—Sir F. Rogers.

27. Th. X

Wrote to Bp of Argyll—Mr Adams—Mr Shannon[1]—Mrs Keys (0)—Col Sykes (0). Saw Clarke[R]. Read Chandless's Mormons[2]—Kaye's Adm. E.I. Co—Macaulay's Ld Clive[3]—Symons's Peel. Willy came to us having won the Slade Exhibition.[4] I tried to press into him the *Nil actum reputans*[5] & the immense importance of *beginning* at Oxford with steady work (1) for the Schools (2) for steady independence. And he is very confiding & receptive. Visited the Scotch pictures.

28. Fr. X

Wrote to W. Gladstone—Mr Stephens (Manchr.). H of C. 4½–7½.[6] Dined at Sir J. Hogg's. Read Macaulay's Clive. Saw Ld Chandos—Mr Milligan—Mr Harriss (China Coll)—Professor Alexander (U.S.)[7]—Mr Lygon M.P. Saw Lovell[R].

29. Sat.

Wrote to H. Glynne—Dean of Ch.Ch.—Scotts—Subm. Telegr. Co.—G. Burnett—Rev Mr Chapman—S. Herbert. Princess's Theatre with a young party to see King Lear.[8] Brit. Museum 1–2¼. Worked up my Hn. Ch. accounts. Saw J.N.G.—Mr Harriss—Duke of Somerset. Read King Lear— Remarks on Ricardo's Speech[9]—Sewell's Sermon[10]—Macaulay's Warren Hastings.[11]

30. Trin. S.

St James's mg & H.C.—Marg. Chapel aft. Sermon at Westmr. Abbey evg.— MS. of 40 aloud at night. Wrote to D. of Newcastle—Rev Mr Robins. Read Forbes Cons. Mod.—Oxf. Essay on Hymnody[12]—Robins's Sermon.[13]—Amn. Ch. Rev. on El[ectio]n of Bps.[14] Saw Sir T.G.

[1] George Lidwill Shannon, incumbent of Kilkenny, a fairly regular correspondent 1847–57.

[2] W. Chandless, *Residence in the Mormon settlement at Utah* (1857).

[3] T. B. *Macaulay, *Historical Essays* (1850), iv.

[4] An in-college exhibition at Christ Church by examination with preference given to Westminster candidates.

[5] 'Nil actum reputans, dum quid superesset agendum' (Lucan); leaving no stone unturned.

[6] *Disraeli's Slough speech, taunting the liberals: *H* cl. 1069.

[7] J. B. Alexander, then in London, had sent a brochure on American banking; Hawn P.

[8] With *Kean as Lear; he went again, see 10 June 58.

[9] Not found.

[10] See 27 May 58.

[11] *Macaulay's famous denunciation of *Gleig's 'three big, bad volumes', *Edinburgh Review*, lxxiii. 160 (October 1841).

[12] C. B. *Pearson, *Hymns and hymn writers* in *Oxford Essays contributed by members of the university* (1858).

[13] S. *Robins, 'Shibboleth. A sermon' (1858); on Judges xii. 6.

[14] Probably 'St. Peter was never bishop of Rome' in [American] *Church Review*, x. 497 (January 1858).

31. *M.*

Wrote to Dean Ramsay—J. Talbot—Mrs Southey—Mrs Nimmo. Read Macaulay's W. Hastings—Ritchie's London Pulpit. H. of C. 4½–8¼.[1] Saw Sir Jas Hogg (E.I. 11–1)[2]—Duke of Newcastle—Sir Jas Graham. Parting conv. with Willy.

Tues. June One 1858.

Wrote to W.H.G.—Rev Mr McColl—Sir W. Colebrooke.[3] H of C. 4–7½ and 10½–2¼. Spoke on W. Wilks & on Suez Canal.[4] Saw Earl of Aberdeen—Mr Kingscote *cum* Mr Green—Mr S. Herbert—Mr Schneider[5]—Earl Grey—Mr Clay—Lady Sheffield[6]—Mr Gibson—Ld Clarendon. Dined at Col. Harcourt's. Read Senior's Journal—Macaulay's W. Hastings (finished).

2. *Wed.*

Wrote to Willy—V. Chancr. Oxford—and Rev Mr Martine.[7] H. of C. 4–6.[8] Saw Mr Christie—M. de Remusat[9]—Sir W. Heathcote—Mr Beresford Hope—Ld Aberdeen—D. of Newcastle. Read Senior's Journal—Westr. Rev. on Med. Reform[10]—Kaye's Adm. E.I. Co. Eighteen to dinner: & a large evening party in stewing weather. Conv. with Musurus on the Isthmus Canal.

3. *Th.* X

Wrote to Sir W. Heathcote—J. Hamilton—Rev Mr Bright[11]—Mr Macray—Rev[s] O. Gordon—W.E. Jelf—J. Jones—Mr G. Darby.[12] Univ. Club Comm. 4–5. H of C. 5–7¼.[13] Six to dinner. Saw Rob. Phillimore—Mr Schneider M.P. Made amendments in Marriage Bill for the promoters.[14] Read Dupin on Suez Canal[15]—Symons's Peel: Senior's Journal (finished). Saw May[R]. Willy's birthday: may it be ever bright.

[1] *Disraeli's Slough speech: *H* cl. 1204.
[2] *Hogg was an E.I.C. director, and was a member of council after 1858.
[3] Sir William MacBean George *Colebrooke, 1787–1870; colonial governor; colonel of R.A. from 1859.
[4] 'Let the Suez Canal stand or fall upon commercial grounds': *H* cl. 1388.
[5] Henry William Schneider, 1817–87; founded Barrow steel works; liberal M.P. Norwich 1857–60, Lancaster 1865–6.
[6] Harriet, da. of 2nd earl of Harewood, m. 1825 George Augustus Frederick Charles Holroyd, 1802–76, 2nd earl of Sheffield 1821; she d. 1889; a tory household.
[7] John Melville Martine, priest 1841, curate of Kemsing; hymnist.
[8] Property Qualification Bill: *H* cl. 1421.
[9] See 26 Mar. 52.
[10] *Westminster Review*, xiii. 478 (April 1858).
[11] William *Bright, 1824–1901; when tutor at Trinity college, Glenalmond, 1851–8, denounced with *Forbes in the 1857–8 heresy hunt and was dismissed (see Forbes to Gladstone, 22 Feb. 1858 in Perry, *Forbes*, 89); regius professor of ecclesiastical history at Oxford from 1868.
[12] Of the Brymbo iron works, Flintshire; supported *Glynne in 1857.
[13] Misc. business: *H* cl. 1447.
[14] With Lord Bury, who hoped it could thus avoid its cttee. stage; see *H* cl. 1689.
[15] F. P. C. Dupin, *Canal maritime de Suez. Institut imperial de France* (1858); sent by him: Add MS 44389, f. 247.

4. Fr.

Wrote to R. Koreah[1]—Watson & Smith—H. Glynne—A. Somerville—
Rev Mr Shaw[2]—Provost of Oriel. H. of C. 4–7¼ and 11–12½.[3] Considered &
taking counsel framed my two Resolutions resp. E.I. Government.[4] Read
Dupin (2) on Suez Canal—Kaye's Admn. E.I. Co. Dined at Sir H. Holland's.
Saw Earl of Aberdeen—Mr S. Carter[5]—Mr Collis *cum* Mr Fisher[6]—Sir W.
Heathcote—Sir J. Graham & Mr Ellice—Mr C.A. Wood—The Speaker—
Ld Macaulay.

5. Sat.

Wrote to T.S. Gladstone—Mrs Southey—Rev J.M. Neale—Mr Blackader—
Chairman E I Co—Mr Leary—Ld Lifford. Dined at Mr Hubbard's. Visited
the British Institution.[7] Read Kaye's Adm. E.I. Co. and [blank]. Saw Earl
of Aberdeen—A. Beresford Hope—Mr Atkinson. Search for Collins: saw
Colvile[R].

6. 1S. Trin.

St James's & H.C. mg. St Andrew's aft.—MS. of 47 aloud in evg. Read
Forbes Consid. Mod.[8]—Ritchie's London Pulpit[9]—Harrison's Charge[10]—
Neale's Jansenist Church[11]—MS Letters East Grinstead Sisters.[12]

7. M.

Wrote to Helen—S.R.G.—Jos Locke[13]—Mr Arbuthnot—Blackader—
Chambres. Calls with C. Dined at Mrs Talbot's. Read Kaye's E.I. Co.—Life
of Zwingli.[14] H. of C. 4¼–7 and 8¼–12. Made my motion about India and
divided in 116:265 or with 36 pairs 152:301. The Govt. acts with folly.[15]

8. T.

Wrote to V.C. Oxford[16]—Rev. W. Scott—Syed Abdoollah—Mrs Crouden.
Attended Fusco's Lecture[17]—Saw A. Gladstone—Messrs. Mathews, Collis &

---

[1] Had written about Greek philology; Hawn P.
[2] Probably Charles James Shaw, 1804–78; Trinity, Cambridge; rector of Cricket St.
Thomas from 1846.
[3] Supply: *H* cl. 1570.   [4] Moved on 7 June.
[5] Samuel Carter, 1805–78; railway solicitor; liberal M.P. Coventry 1868; doubtless
supplied 'counsel' mentioned above.
[6] W. H. Fisher, manager of the Oak Farm works from 1858, had made a report of the
works' prospects (Hawn P).
[7] For the encouragement of British artists; founded in Pall Mall in 1806.
[8] See 29 Mar. 50.   [9] See 14 May 58.
[10] B. *Harrison, *The law of church rate, and the voluntary principle* (1858).
[11] J. M. *Neale, *A history of the so-called Jansenist Church of Holland* (1858).
[12] Sent by J. M. *Neale, who founded a convent there: Add MS 44390, f. 14.
[13] Joseph *Locke, 1805–60; railway engineer; liberal M.P. Honiton from 1847.
[14] R. Christoffel, *Zwingli: or, the rise of the reformation in Switzerland* (1858).
[15] He tried to amend the bill to allow the E.I. directors to continue, under the ministers,
till the end of the next session: *H* cl. 1633.
[16] On behalf of the Radcliffe trust, offering Radcliffe library to the university; see E.
Craster, *History of the Bodleian library 1845–1945* (1952), 125.
[17] By Giuseppe Maria Fusco, Neapolitan numismatist and epigraphist.

Fisher—Prop. & Inc. Tax Deputn.[1]—Mr P. L. Foster.[2] H of C. 12–4 and 8–12. Spoke on Church Rate abolition.[3] Read Letters on Principalities—Kaye on E.I. Co.

9. Wed.

Wrote to K. M'Queen[4]—Wms Deacon & Co—Jos. Hyde[5]—Adm. Henderson—C de Morgan[6]—Bp of Brechin—Rev J. Taylor[7]—Rev. Mr Barton[8]—J.D. Carr[9]—Watson & Smith. Dined at S. Herbert's. Saw Colville[R]—Various business. Read M'Queen on E.I. and the 'Sister of Mercy'—Symons's Sir R. Peel—Idées Napoleoniennes.[10] Saw Ld Aberdeen—S. Herbert—Ld Ashburton—G. W. Hope.

10. Thursday.

Wrote to Mad. Stierling.[11] Saw Bp of Oxford—Bp of Brechin—Bp of Salisbury—Mr Geo. Coode—M. de Lesseps. H of C. $4\frac{1}{2}$–$7\frac{1}{2}$. Voted agt. L. King's Bill, for the previous question.[12] Eleven to breakfast. Mr Lacaita's Lecture 3–$4\frac{1}{4}$.[13] Princess's Theatre 8–$11\frac{1}{2}$ to see Lear for the second time. Kean's is a very considerable performance.[14] Read pamphlets.

11. Fr.

Wrote to Bp of Moray—Robn. G.—Ld Provost of Aberdeen. 9–$4\frac{1}{2}$ To Addiscombe with Col. Sykes for the Examinations there & other proceedings.[15] H of C. $4\frac{1}{2}$–$7\frac{3}{4}$ and $8\frac{1}{2}$–12.[16] Read Hayward's Essays[17]—Saw E. Cardwell—Advised Jas Wortley not to declare in his place the hostility of the French nation to England wh he was about to do.

12. Sat.

Wrote to Rev. R. Bruce[18]—Bp of Oxford—Rev M. M'Coll—Sir W. Heathcote—Mr Edmeston[19]—M. Duvergier de H.[20]—Sir T.G.—Robn. G.—J.N.G.

[1] No report found.
[2] Peter Le Neve Foster, 1809–79; fellow of Trinity, Cambridge 1830; secretary to society of arts from 1853.
[3] Opposing the bill, but arguing for a compromise settlement: *H* cl. 1727.
[4] Kenneth MacQueen of Edinburgh, probably a free-churchman, sent his 'Who is to blame for the Indian mutinies?' (1858); Hawn P.
[5] John Thomas Hyde, 1832–92; professor of fortification at Addiscombe (see 11 June 58); priest from 1869.
[6] Campbell de Morgan, London physician.
[7] Probably James Taylor, 1809–98; headmaster at Wakefield 1847–75; denounced R.I. *Wilberforce in series of pamphlets.
[8] Charles Barton, priest 1848; perpetual curate of Bromborough, Cheshire, 1850.
[9] Unidentified.
[10] Louis Napoleon Bonaparte, *Des idées napoléoniennes* (1838); promoting the legend of Bonaparte as a social reformer.
[11] Probably the wife of G. S. Stierling, a German poet.
[12] *King's County Franchise Bill eventually read 2°: *H* cl. 1857.
[13] A series at the Royal Institution on Italian literature; see Lacaita, 81–2.
[14] See 29 May 58.
[15] The East India Military College at Addiscombe, Surrey.
[16] Asked questions on Prince Edward island: *H* cl. 1948.
[17] See 23 Apr. 58.
[18] Robert B. Bruce, recently retired episcopal incumbent at Banchory.
[19] James Edmeston, London surveyor.
[20] Prosper Duvergier de Hauranne, 1798–1881; French liberal politician and historian.

—H.J.G.—Mr W. Cotton. Saw Mr Chene[1]—Mr Geo. Grant—Scotts—J.N.G.
Br. Museum 12¼–2¼. Duke of Norfolk's in evg. Read [blank]

13. 2 S. Trin.

Crown St mg: then West St[2] for a second Sermon—Chapel Royal aftn. MS
on Gospel aloud in evg. Read Forbes Cons. Mod.—Wilson's B. Lectures
(finished)[3]—Hampson's Life of Wesley.[4]

14. M.

Wrote to Mr Barber—Mr Rawson. Saw Aberdeen Univ. Depn[5]—Mr Brady
—Ld Granville—Mr Hutt—D. of Cambridge. Exhibn. Finance Comm. 11–1.
King's Coll. Hosp. meeting 3–4½. H of C. 4½–7½ and 9–11¾. Voted and
spoke agt. nominated Council.[6] Read Kaye's Adm. E.I. Co.

15. T.

Wrote to Dr Thomson—Rev Mr Kennaway—Robn. G.—Mrs Monsell—
V.C. Oxford—Mr Alexander. Saw Mr Wynne MP.—J. Stuart Wortley—M.
Duvergier de Hauranne (& fils)—do *cum* M. Odillon Barrot. H. of C.
before dinner. Ld Camden's Ball. Read Elphinstone's India[7]—Boswell's
Letters[8]—Dublin Visitation.[9] Opera 8–10¾: Lady Waldegrave's box.[10] Saw
Clarke[R].

16. Wed. X

Wrote to Mr Ryland—Mr W.H. Hillyard[11]—Sir Jas Graham—Mr Cardwell.
Dined at Col. W. Patten's. Mrs Barings & Duchess of Norfolk's after. H of
C. & Comm. at 3. Saw Mr M. Müller—Mr Hugessen[12]—Col. Wilson Patten—
Ld Wodehouse. Read Cardwell's Dft Report[13]—Reichel & Anderson on
Dublin Univ.[14]—Ryland Correspondence.[15] Thermom. 88° in shade & that
shade with draft. Saw Rigby[R].

[1] Patrick Cheyne of Aberdeen (see 23 Feb. 48) also charged with heresy; see Perry,
Forbes, 91.
[2] West Street anglican chapel; Robert William Dibdin was the incumbent.
[3] See 11 Dec. 53.
[4] See 2 May 58.
[5] The 1858 Act united the two Aberdeen universities; see W. D. Simpson, *The fusion of
1860* (1963), 10.
[6] He opposed both Crown nominated and popularly elected Council members: *H* cl.
2069.
[7] M. *Elphinstone, The history of India* (1841).
[8] See 11 Feb. 57.
[9] J. F. *Waller, 'Report of the proceedings at a visitation holden in Trinity college,
Dublin . . . 1858' (1858).
[10] Auber's 'Fra Diavolo' at the new Covent Garden.
[11] William Heard Hillyard, published *Recollections of a physician* (1861).
[12] Edward Hugessen Knatchbull-*Hugessen, 1829–93; liberal M.P. Sandwich 1857–80;
treasury lord 1859–66; under-sec. home office 1866, 1868–71, for colonies 1871–4; cr.
Baron Brabourne 1880; see Add MS 44111.
[13] Formed basis of the Hardwicke cttee.'s report on manning: *PP* 1859 session 1, vi.
[14] C. P. Reichel and W. Anderson, 'Trinity college, Dublin and university reform'
(1858).
[15] More on the Ryland case? See 22 Mar. 49.

17. Th.

Wrote to Sir T. Phillipps[1]—Scotts—Rev W. Briscoe[2]—G. & Co.—A.H. Clough.[3] H. of C. $12\frac{1}{4}$–3.[4] Sixteen to breakfast. Covent Garden Opera $8\frac{1}{2}$–$12\frac{1}{4}$ to see the Ugonotti.[5] Splendid in music acting & scenery. Saw Sir Chas Wood—E. Cardwell—Mr Philips MP.[6] Mr Lacaita's Lecture $3\frac{1}{4}$–$4\frac{1}{4}$. At Christie's to see Pictures & Drawings. Read Boswell's Lectures[7]—Cunningham's London[8] and [blank]

18. Fr.

Wrote to Overends—House of Commons $4\frac{1}{2}$–$8\frac{1}{4}$ and after dinner.[9] Queen's Concert in evg: renewed acquaintance with K of Belgians & the heir apparent.[10] Saw Aberdeen (K[ing's] C[ollege]) Deputn[11]—Rev Mr Poole[12] cum Mr Trevor—Mr Bowring (from the P. Consort)[13]—Ld Carlisle (resp. Homer) —Mr Christie—Dean of Ch.Ch. Read Idées Napoleoniennes.

19. Sat. X

Wrote to Mr Adderly. Read Senior's Journal (Greece)—Prescott on Homer[14] —Hayward's Essay on [blank]. Church Rate Bps meeting at Bounty Board 11–$1\frac{1}{4}$.[15] Saw Mr Swift. Visited Portrait Gallery with Ld Stanhope. Saw Bp of Durham. Search at Somerset House for marriage of E. C[ollins]: without success[R]. Saw Rigby Johnstone: a very singular case[R]. Lady Palmerston's in evg, then Lady Jersey's: where I vented some dissatisfaction with the Govt.

20. 3 S. Trin.

King's Coll. Chapel mg & St James's evg. MS of 46 aloud. Read Wesley's Journal[16]—Hampson's Life of Wesley—Neale's Jansenist Ch. of Holland. Wrote to J.N.G.—Rigby Johnstone.

[1] Sir Thomas *Phillipps, 1792–1872; amassed vast collection of books and MSS, including MS of the *Iliad* whose authenticity Gladstone rightly questioned; see A. N. L. Munby, *Portrait of an obsession* (1967), 213.

[2] William Kyffin Bostock Briscoe; fellow of Jesus, Oxford, 1853; curate of Mold, Flintshire; rector of Nutfield, Surrey, 1882.

[3] Arthur Hugh *Clough, 1819–61; poet; professor of English at University college, London, 1850, which this untraced letter probably discussed.

[4] India Bill cttee: *H* cl. 2221.

[5] Meyerbeer's 'Les Huguenots'.

[6] i.e. J. H. Philipps.

[7] *sc.* Letters.

[8] P. *Cunningham, *London in 1857* (1857).

[9] United States, and Irish land: *H* cli. 41, 57.

[10] Leopold I (see 6 Feb. 32) and his son, styled duc de Brabant, who succ. as Leopold II 1865 and d. 1909; annexed the Congo.

[11] Their statutes then being revised.

[12] George Ayliffe Poole, 1809–83; vicar of Welford 1843–76; rector of Winwick from 1876; strong high churchman and controversialist.

[13] i.e. E. A. Bowring; doubtless on the Bill, see 21 June 58.

[14] K. Prescot, *Letters concerning Homer the Sleeper in Horace: with additional classic amusements* (1773).

[15] Probably on capital grants; see G. F. A. Best, *Temporal Pillars* (1964), 442.

[16] *The journal of the Rev. John *Wesley,* 4v. (1827).

21. M.

Wrote to D. of Newcastle—Mr Panizzi—D. of Argyll—Mrs Walker—Mr Monsell—Mr Armitstead—Dft to Bank of E.[1] H of C. & Committees 1–7½.[2] Dined at the Ld Chancellor's. Saw Sir Jas Graham—Sir W. Williams resp. army[3]—Lady Clinton's in Evg. Prescot on Homer—Finished Senior's Journal: & made extract of Greek alphabet.

22. T. X

Wrote to Mr W.G. Clarke[4]—Willy—F.J. Morrell—P. Slater—M. Van de Weyer—Prescott & Co[5]—Rev. J. Marshall. Saw J.N.G.—Mr Thornton—Sir S. Northcote—Sir J. Graham—Scotts—Mr Niewenhuis.[6] Saw Stapleton [R]. Calls. Dined at Ld Wensleydale's. Read Tucker's Opinions E.I.[7]— Boswell's Letters—Clark's Peloponnesus—Hayward's Essays. Read & worked on E.I. Bill.

23. Wed.

Lady A. Peel's at two—Ld Ward's Concert 3½–5. Dined at the Lord Mayor's. Read Scots. Univ. Pamphlets—Clark's Peloponnesus—Prescot on Homer—Boswell's Letters. Saw Dr Bennett.[8]

Th. 24 Jun.

Wrote to Exil Polonais[9]—Mrs Walker—Mr Armitstead. Saw Mr Thornton. Read Prescott—Boswell—Scots Univ. & Suez Canal Pamphlets. B. Palace at 1 to see the King of the Belgians. 10–12 D. d'Aumale & a party to break- fast. 2–3½ Middlesex Hospital to Address the Students.[10] Then to Mr Lacaita's Lecture. Saw Mr Ellice. Dined at Mr Moffatt's.

25. Fr.

Wrote to Mr W. Brown.[11] Finished Prescott—Read Boswell. H of C. 12–3¼— 6–7¼ and 10½–12¼.[12] Dined at Ld Carysfort's. Worked on Mrs Jameson & Butler to ascertain the subject of my Murillo.[13]

[1] About a £20 note lost by Mrs. Gladstone (Bank archives).
[2] Spoke for Commissioners for Exhibition 1851 Bill: *H* cli. 93.
[3] Sir William Fenwick *Williams, 1800–83; fought in Crimea; commanded Woolwich garrison 1856–9; liberal M.P. Calne 1856–9; governed colonies 1865–76; cr. bart. 1856.
[4] William George *Clarke, 1821–78; priest 1854–70; traveller, translator, philologist; fellow of Trinity, Cambridge, from 1844; public orator from 1857; wrote *Peloponnesus* (1858) which he had sent (Hawn P).
[5] Prescott, Grote, Cave & Cave, bankers.
[6] Christian John Nieuwenhuis, 1799–1883; Belgian art dealer, in London from 1846.
[7] H. St. G. Tucker, 'A review of the financial situation of the East-India Company in 1824' (1825).
[8] Henry Bennet, society physician in Grosvenor Street.
[9] Untraced.
[10] See *The Times*, 25 June 1858, 12c.
[11] William Brown, 1819?–99: St. John's, Cambridge; rector of Little Hormead, Hert- fordshire, 1852–86; wrote on classics.
[12] Attempted to amend India Bill, but forced to report progress: *H* cli. 470.
[13] Anna Brownell *Jameson, *née* Murphy, 1794–1860; wrote widely on Italian painting. Gladstone bought Murillo's 'San Francesco di Paolo' from Louis Philippe's collection and sold it 1875.

26. Sat. X

Wrote to J.M. Knott—Shipton[1]—Mr Mitchell[2]—Adderley—Rev Mr Brown. 5½–12 to Greenwich for the Shrewsbury fête: an interesting occasion & very cordial feeling.[3] H.S. with M. & L. Saw Rigby–Johnstone—twice[R]. British Museum 12–2. Finished search for the Collins marriage: without effect. Read Boswell's Letters.

27. 4 S. Trin.

St James mg & Chapel Royal aft: Also Sermon at St Saviour's. MS of 43 aloud in evg. Wrote to Dr [J.D.] Macbride—Mr Meyrick—J.G. Talbot. Read Forbes Consid. Mod.—Hampson's Wesley (finished)—Meyrick's Sermons.[4]

28. M.

Wrote to F.J. Morrell—Overends—Gen. Jochmus[5]—Mr Geo. Nicoll—W. Dent[6]—G. Scharf[7]—Rev D Williams—Bp of Cape Town—Bp of Brechin. H of C. 1–4, 6½–11.[8] Saw Scotts—Earl of Aberdeen—Sir J. Graham—Mr Lygon MP.—Read Boswell—Kaye's Adm. E.I. Co.—Milnes on St Bartholomew.[9]

29. T. St. Peter.

Wrote to Willy—Rev Mr Chambres[10]—Bp of Moray—Rev Mr Cotham[11]—Mr Geo. Nicol. Read Boswell's Letters—Swift's Hist. Four Years.[12] Saw Bp of Brechin—Saw Rigby—gave Shakespeare for a practical purpose: & advised to think of emigration. Ten to dinner & party in evg.

30. Wed.

Wrote to Rev Mr M'Coll—Mr Bentley—Sir W. Heathcote. Saw Mr Lushington—Sir J. Graham—Mr Lygon—Ld Bury & Mr Schneider. House & Bank Comm. (on Report) 12–6¼.[13] Dined with the Wm. Gladstone's[14] at Highgate. Back late. Saw Madrid[R]. Read Boswell's Letters.

[1] George Shipton, Scottish priest 1851, permitted to hold English living by special Act 1856.

[2] Probably R. Michell, see 20 Feb. 50.   [3] Obscure.

[4] F. Meyrick, *The outcast and the poor of London . . . a course of sermons* (1858).

[5] Baron Augustus Jochmus von Cotignola; mercenary and diplomat; fought in Greece, Spain and Turkey; briefly Austrian foreign minister 1849.

[6] Wilkinson Dent, of Fitzroy Square, London.

[7] (Sir) George *Scharf, 1820–95; first secretary of National Portrait Gallery 1857, of which Gladstone was a trustee from 1860.

[8] Spoke on the funded debt: *H* cli. 539.

[9] R. Monckton *Milnes, *On the apologies for the massacre of St. Bartholomew* (1856).

[10] sc. [J.C.] Chambers.

[11] George Toulson Cotham; Trinity, Dublin; curate in Bradford, of St. John's Walworth, from 1859.

[12] J. *Swift, *The history of the four last years of the Queen* (1758).

[13] Misc. business in Commons: *H* cli. 666.

[14] He (see 31 July 32) m. 1837 Charlotte Louisa Alexandrina Kenrick, who d. 1884.

Thurs. July One 1858.

H of C. 1–4, 6–7¾ and 11–1: on Scots Univv. India Bill & other matters.[1] 4½–5¾ children's party at Dorchester House. Dined with the Sydneys.[2] Saw Mr O. Gordon—Mr Walpole—Mr Lygon—Saw Madrid[R]. Read Louis Blanc on Rev. of 48[3]—Boswell's Letters.

2. Fr.

Wrote to Dr Harvey[4]—Mr P. Buchan—Lady Heathcote—Mr G. Wilson. H of C. 1–4 and 6–7½.[5] Saw Bp of Oxford—Mr Fisher *cum* Mr Collis—Mr W. Grogan—Ld Bury—Sir J. Graham—Mr Stirling[6]—Capt? Mansfield[7]—Mr Dunlop—S.H. Northcote. Dined with the Heywoods—Lady Courtenay's[8] afterwards. Saw Lightfoot & another[R]. Read Nat. Rev. on my Homer: which ought to humble me.[9] Read Mines of Ireland.[10]

3. Sat. [Norwood]

Wrote to Mr Heraud—L. Morris—G. Curtis—Dean Ramsay—Ed. Eng Churchman—Mr Cunningham—Hannan & Co.[11] Worked on arranging letters. The children went: except Herbert. Nine to breakfast. Saw Mr Calvert— Mr Lacaita—Bp of Oxford—Mr Leeman—Ld Southesk—Captain G.—Ld Lyttelton. Went to Norwood at night.[12] Read Nat. Rev. on State of Parties —(the estimate of me there is better for me)[13]—and on Charlatan Poetry— Nat. Mag. & E. Churchman on my 'Studies' . . . &c.[14] Mr Senior's in evg to meet Mad. Ristori[15] who is very remarkable. We also heard Mad. Gold-schmidt,[16] no small matter.

---

[1] *H* cli. 730.

[2] 3rd Viscount Sydney m. 1832 Emily Caroline, 6th da. of 1st marquess of Anglesea; she d. 1893.

[3] J. J. L. Blanc, *1848. Historical revelations: inscribed to Lord *Normanby* (1858).

[4] Alexander Harvey, 1811–89, Aberdeen physician, was in correspondence on Scottish university union (Hawn P).

[5] Spoke briefly on India Bill: *H* cli. 866.

[6] (Sir) William Stirling (-*Maxwell), 1818–78; tory M.P. Perthshire 1852–68, 1874–8; on universities commission 1859; 9th bart, and took name Maxwell 1865; art connoisseur and author. See 13 Oct. 58.

[7] Unidentified.

[8] Lady Elizabeth Fortescue, da. of 1st Earl Fortescue, m. 1830 William, Lord Courtenay, 11th earl of Devon; she d. 1867.

[9] *National Review*, vii. 40 (July 1858); critical though not unsympathetic.

[10] Not traced.

[11] R. Hannan and co., Glasgow merchants.

[12] To stay with the Talbots.

[13] *National Review*, vii. 220 (July 1858); 'he has little real leadership; he convinces few, and persuades none . . . while formidable to all parties, would bring little valid strength to any.'

[14] *English Churchman* xvi. 606 (July 1 1858); favourable.

[15] (Marchesa) Adelaide Ristori, 1822–1906; Italian tragedienne; in London with her company for a season at the St. James's; see 9–10 July 58.

[16] i.e. Jenny Lind (see 28 May 47).

4. 5 S. Trin.

Ch mg & aft (Norwood). Read Neale's Ch. of Holland[1]—Nat Rev. on Mahomet—on Comte.[2] Conv. with Mr Majendie. We found E. Talbot[3] greatly better but still much shattered.

5. M. [London]

Wrote to Mr Senior. Crystal Palace 10–12. Railway Comm. 1–3½. H of C. 4½–7¾. My Clauses put into Scots Univ. Bill.[4] Dined at Lady Wenlock's. Saw J.S. Wortley—Mr Badger[5]—Sir J. Graham—Ld Advocate—Univ. Club Committee 4 P.M.

6. T. X

Wrote to Baron Dupin—Rev Dr Lee. Committee 12½–2¾ and House 6–8 and 11¼–12½. Spoke for my Clause: wh the Govt. supported handsomely.[6] Saw Mr Hodgson—Mr W. Brown—Lady Gladstone (Mulock).[7] Dined at the Duke of Newcastle's. Read Lewis's Papers in Notes & Queries.[8] Saw Lovell[R].

7. Wed.

Wrote to Sir S. Northcote—Mr J. Ramsay[9]—Dr Laycock—Mr E N Browne. Saw Mr Hodgson—Earl of Aberdeen—Count Vizthum. Busy in China exchanges and purchases. Dined at Ld Stratford's. Read Ld Ravensworth's translations: nay I actually went to work and translated the Horace and Lydia.[10]

8. Th.

Wrote to Messrs. Freshfield—Mr Burnett—Mr Morrell—W.H.G.—Rev Mr Perry—M. Guizot—Maj. Macgregor. Wrote out & considered further my translation. Saw Hon. Mr Boyle—Helen G. Worked on China &c. Dined with the Granville Vernons. Read Conington on Pope[11]—Brown's Leonardo[12]—Jeffreys on Indian Army[13]—Montoya's Chronicle.[14]

[1] See 6 June 58.
[2] National Review, vii. 137, 184 (July 1858).
[3] E. S. *Talbot had to leave Charterhouse through illness this year.
[4] Permitting unification into a national university of Scotland: H cli. 961; unpopular in Scottish universities, costing him the Edinburgh chancellorship 1868. See D. B. Horn, 'The Universities (Scotland) Act of 1858', Univ. of Edinburgh Journal, xix. 169.
[5] George Percy Badger, 1815–88, priest and Arabic scholar, wrote to request Gladstone to speak for the Indian army: Add MS 44390, f. 45.
[6] To require parliamentary consent before Indian army could be used outside India: H cli. 1007.
[7] Obscure.
[8] G. C. *Lewis, 'The amber trade of antiquity', Notes and Queries, 2nd series vi (3 July 1858).
[9] John Ramsay, 1814–92; Scottish educational reformer; liberal M.P. Stirling burghs 1868, Falkirk burghs 1874–86.
[10] For his Translations, 98.
[11] J. *Conington, 'The poetry of Pope' in Oxford essays for 1858 (1858).
[12] Reading of title uncertain; probably J. W. Brown, Leonardo da Vinci (1828).
[13] J. Jeffreys, The British army in India: its preservation by an appropriate clothing housing . . . and hopeful encouragement (1858).
[14] L. de Montoya, Coronica general de la order de los Minimos de S. Francisco de Paula su fundador (1619).

9. *Fr.* X

Wrote to J. O'Mahony[1]—Mr Morswood.[2] Saw M. Bratiano—Mr Noyes Browne[3]—Sidney Herbert—Mr Fitzgerald (resp. New Caled)[4]—Saw Rigby–Johnstone[R]. Made copies of my little Ode. H. of C. 12–2 and 6–7¼.[5] Saw Ristori's Elisabetta at the St James's Theatre: a great performance on wh much might be said.[6]

10. *Sat.*

Wrote to Mr Frith[7]—Mr Stansbury. Nine to breakfast. Saw Johnson & Co —Freshfields, with Helen—Jas Wortley—Rev Mr Elwin—Ld Powis—S. Herbert. Saw Ristori's rehearsal of Elisabetta—Attenborough's & Ramus's[8] with Helen. At the Bank to sign indemnity. Read Dubl. Rev. on Party— Do on Indemnity[9]—Netley Hospital Papers[10] and [blank]

11. *6 S. Trin.*

St James's mg Marg. Chapel aft. Saw & wrote to Rigby–Johnstone[R]. Read Close on India[11]—Forbes's Consid. Mod.—Neale's Hist. Ch. of Holland (finished). Saw Hicks[R].

12. *M.*

Wrote to Rev W. Eaton[12]—Mr Dowding—Mr Burtt[13]—J.R. Byrne—Mrs Hancock—F. Adams—G.W. Hastings[14]—Mrs Harris. Saw Mr Stansbury— Mr Grogan—Lambert & Rawlins—Mr N. Baillie—M. Musurus (Apsley House)—Ld Stanhope. Dined at Ld Bateman's.[15] Dss. of Wellington's[16] Ball afr. Saw Hicks[R]—Read [blank] H of C. & Commee. 1–3, & 6–7½.[17]

[1] *sc.* S. O. Mahony?
[2] Unidentified.
[3] E. Noyce Browne, the reporter in Naples (see 21 Dec. 50).
[4] J. E. *Fitzgerald (see 20 Sept. 48) was political agent for New Zealand in Britain 1857–60. New Caledonia was the centre of persistent British-French missionary wrangling (see W. P. Morrell, *Britain in the Pacific islands* (1960), 100ff.)
[5] Supply: *H* cli. 1172.
[6] P. Giacommetti's historic drama 'Elisabetta Regina d'Inghilterra'; first performance in London.
[7] Arthur J. Frith had sent an untraced pamphlet.
[8] Members of Ristori's 'Italian Dramatic Company'.
[9] *Dublin Review*, xliv. 336 (June 1858).
[10] Probably the catalogue of the army medical museum at the Royal Victoria Hospital at Netley, Hampshire.
[11] F. *Close, *An Indian retrospect; or what has christian England done for heathen India?* (1858).
[12] William Ray Eaton, 1828–1915; curate in Norfolk 1854–65; vicar of Longham 1869–91.
[13] Joseph Burtt, 1818–76; clerk in public record office and archaeologist.
[14] George Woodyatt Hastings, 1825–1917; liberal (–unionist) M.P. E. Worcestershire 1880–92.
[15] William Bateman-Hanbury, 1826–1901; 2nd Baron Bateman 1845; Herefordshire landowner and tory.
[16] Lady Elizabeth Hay m. 1839 Arthur Richard Wellesley, 1807–84, 2nd duke of Wellington; she d. 1904. Of great beauty, much adored by her father-in-law.
[17] Slave trade: *H* cli. 1286.

13. *T.* X

Wrote to Bp of Oxford—Dean of Peterborough—Duke of Newcastle—Rev Mr Hawkins. Saw Mr Walpole—M. Bratiano—Sir G.C. Lewis—Mrs Gibson[1]—Scotts. H of C. 4½–7.[2] Princess's to see Merchant of Venice. Saw Hicks[R]. Read Senior's Journal. Packed books for Hawarden.

14. *W.*

Wrote to Mr W. Grogan—Sir W. Heathcote—R. Heathfield—Mr T. Ponsonby[3]—Mr Gillies[4]—Mr R. Phillimore—G.P. Read[5]—Prov. of Aberdeen[6]—Dr Acland—Chairman Means Comm.—Mr C. Kean—Master Univ. Coll.—Rev. Mr Berkeley—Duc d'Aumale—M. Bratiano. Saw Mr G. Smith—Mr F. Calvert—Mr W. Hutt—M. Guizot—Ld Wodehouse. Ld Ward's Concert 3–6¼. Some preparations for departure. Read Senior's Journal. Mad Brunnow's ball in evg.

15. *Th.*

Wrote to Agnes G. Read Mr Senior's Journal. Dined with the Mildmays. H of C. 6–7¾.[7] Saw Sir E.L. Bulwer [Lytton][8]—Mr Adderley—Mr Wilson—Ld Eversley—Mr B. Benjamin. Our fright about Herbert in the morning. Worked on preparations for departure.

16. *Fr.*

Wrote to Lady Beauchamp—F. Adams—Mr Gillies—Ld Stanley—Wm. Gladstone—G. Scharf—W. Selwyn—Mr [J.C.] Robinson—Mr Jeffreys.[9] H of C. 6–9 and 12–2.[10] Dined (?) [*sic*] with the Milneses. Saw Dr Acland—Mr Grogan—Ld Stanley—Mr Hamilton—Sir E.L. Bulwer—Lord J. Manners—Ld Wharncliffe. Finished Senior's Journal. 3½–5, meeting of the Clarendon Trust.[11] Read Florine.[12]

17. *Sat.*

Wrote to W.W. Fife[13]—Sir J.B. East—G.H. Smith[14]—Mr Thos. Turner—J.

---

[1] Susanna *née* Cullum, wife of T. Milner-*Gibson; a spiritualist; her political and literary salon of great importance; became Roman catholic and d. 1885.

[2] Misc. business: *H* cli. 1371.

[3] Perhaps Thomas Henry Ponsonby, 1807–80, grand-s. of 1st Viscount Dungannon; in dragoon guards.

[4] Robert Pearse *Gillies, 1788–1858; reviewer, published reminiscences of *Scott, etc.

[5] Unidentified.

[6] John Webster of Edgehill, 1810–91, advocate, provost of Aberdeen 1856–9.

[7] Spoke on coal-whippers and New Caledonia Bill: *H* cli. 1506, 1517.

[8] Colonial secretary; but not yet about Ionia, see Morley, i. 594 and 3 Oct. 58.

[9] Probably John Gwyn *Jeffreys, 1809–85; barrister 1855–66; geologist and conchologist.

[10] Misc. business: *H* cli. 1590.

[11] He was a trustee; the trust, endowed with profits from *Clarendon's publications, was wound up 1868; see H. Carter, *A History of the O.U.P.* (1975) i. ch. 24.

[12] 'Florine; ou la belle Italienne par Mad. la comtesse de M****', in *Le cabinet des fées* (1785), i.

[13] William Wallace Fife, 1816–67; ed. *Nottingham Daily Guardian*.

[14] Possibly George Henry Smith, of Cleveland square, Hyde Park.

Slatter[1]—Rev C.H. Burton[2]—C.G. Read Quarterly Review[3] & tracts on Thames Drainage. Dined at General Peel's.[4] Saw Mr H. Merritt—Mr W.T. Young—Sir Hugh Cairns[5]—M. Guizot fils[6]—Mrs H. Gladstone. Shopping & worked on letters & papers. Saw Clarke—Rigby–Johnstone—Lovell X.

18. 7 S. Trin.

St James's & H.C. mg. St Andr. Wells St aft. Wrote to S.E.G. Saw Lord Aberdeen—Helen (& Aunt J.) to say farewell: most of the evening. Read Bp Forbes Cons. Mod.—Q.R. Wiclif & on Blunt.[7]—Moravian Life in the Black Forest.[8]

19. M.

Wrote to Lady Stratford—M. Guizot—Ld Ashburton—Lord Ward— Farquhar Matheson—H.J.G.—J.W. Gladstone[9]—Earl Nelson—C.G. (2)— Earl of Chichester. H of C. $4\frac{1}{4}$-$7\frac{1}{4}$ and 9-$2\frac{1}{2}$: spoke on Thames [drainage] & New Caledonia Bills &c.[10] Saw Mr Edwards—Mr Schneider MP.—Mr F. Matheson—Earl of Powis—Lord Wynford—Mr Akroyd MP.[11]—Earl Carnarvon. Read Pamphlets on Thames. Shopping & setting to rights.

20. T. [Hawarden]

Wrote to J.E. Fitzgerald—H.J.G.—Mrs E Southey—P. Buchan—Mr Bateman. Read Letter to Dr Lowth.[12] A good day's work in packing and putting away before my journey. Saw Ld Carnarvon—Ld Bury—Sir Jas Graham—J.W. Patten. H of C. $4\frac{1}{2}$-7: spoke on Hudson's Bay Company.[13] Off by train at 8: reached Chester at 2 AM. Hawarden 3.

21. Wed.

Found all well & a large party in the House: we spent the day in Chester on

[1] John Slatter, 1817?–99; curate at Stanford-on-Thames 1852–61, vicar of Streatley 1861–80, of Whitchurch 1880.
[2] Charles Henry Burton, 1818?–85; curate in Liverpool 1846–69; vicar of Dinton 1869–70; published on royal supremacy.
[3] Quarterly Review, civ. 1 (July 1858).
[4] The secretary for war; see 8 Jan. 35n.
[5] Sir Hugh McCalmont *Cairns, 1819–85; educated in Ireland; barrister in London; tory M.P. Belfast 1852–66; solicitor general 1858–9; attorney general 1866; appeal justice 1866–8; lord chancellor 1868, 1874–80; a strong evangelical, hostile to Irish disestablishment and land reform.
[6] Maurice Guillaume Guizot, s. of the statesman, 1833–92; brilliant promise of his youth unfulfilled as professor of language in Paris from 1866; later a diplomatist.
[7] Quarterly Review, civ. 106, 151 (July 1858).
[8] [B. B. Batty], ed. [A. Manning], An English girl's account of a Moravian settlement in the Black Forest (1858).
[9] Remnant of the Gladstone family in Biggar.
[10] H cli. 1717, 1762.
[11] Edward Akroyd, 1810–87; Halifax worsted manufacturer and volunteer colonel; liberal M.P. Huddersfield 1857–9, Halifax 1865–74; anglican benefactor of Halifax.
[12] J. Bridle, A letter to the rev. Dr. Lowth; in vindication of the conduct of the fellows of New College in Oxford in their late election of a warden of Winchester (1758).
[13] H cli. 1802.

the ploughing field, in the implement yards, & at the flower show. Began Hume's Life & Correspe.[1] Saw Bp of Oxford on the Wife's Sister Bill.[2]

22. Th.

Wrote to Rev Mr Elwin—Mr J. Murray—Rev. D. Williams—Rev W.E. Jelf. At Chester again with the stock horses & poultry. Then to the dinner at 4 P.M. when I had to propose 'the Royal Agric. Society of England' to an enthusiastic meeting.[3] Party here in evg. Bp of O. went: under remonstrance from me resp. Ld Bury's Bill.[4]

23. Fr.

Wrote to Hon. A. Gordon—Lord Bury. Church 8½ AM. Read Ewelme Hospital papers[5]—New Coll. (Golding) controversy[6]—Scott on Architecture.[7] Party continued: with some changes. Music in evg. Conv. with Dr Acland.

24. Sat.

Wrote to Agnes. Ch. 8½ AM. Read Hume's Life & Corresp. Worked on translation.[8] Music aftn. & evg. Worked on room & papers in setting to rights.

25. St James & 8 S. Trin.

Hn. Ch mg & St John's aftn. Music in evg. Read Fabiola[9]—Rorison's Speech[10]—and 'the Orthodox Confession'.[11]

26. M.

Church 8½ AM. Wrote to Sir Jas Graham—Rev Mr Rorison (& copy). Dined at Soughton[12] Mr Barker's—music in evg. He is very agreeable & pleasing. Tried my hand at translation. Read Q. Review.—Hume's Life & Correspondence & Pickering's Races of Man.[13] Saw Mr Burnett on Stephen's affairs: & visited the boring with him.

[1] J. H. *Burton, *Life and correspondence of David *Hume* (1846).
[2] The Marriage Law Amendment Bill, soon due for debate in the Lords, where *Wilberforce violently opposed it (*H* cli. 1984).
[3] At the end of the Chester show; see *Journal of the Agricultural Society* (1858), 311–420.
[4] The Marriage Bill, see previous day.
[5] Doubtless brought by H. W. *Acland; as a Radcliffe trustee Gladstone had an official interest in Ewelme whose school and almshouses are the responsibility of the regius professor of medicine.
[6] C. Golding, 'A defence of the conduct of the warden of Winchester college in accepting of that wardenship' (1759); patronage dispute, inspiring several pamphlets.
[7] G. G. *Scott, *Remarks on secular and domestic architecture, present and future* (1857).
[8] Of Homer, of which a series was published in Gladstone's and *Lyttelton's *Translations.*
[9] See 15 June 56.
[10] 'Report of the speech of G. Rorison in opening the case for the presentment of P. Cheyne before the bishop and synod of Aberdeen' (1858).
[11] P. *Lodvill, *The Orthodox Confession of the Catholic and Apostolic eastern Church* (1762).
[12] A mile N. of Mold.
[13] See 10 July 53.

27. *T.*

Ch. 8½ A.M. Wrote to Overends. Read Taylor's Germ. Poetry[1]—Horace—Greene[2]—Canti Carnascialeschi[3]—Hume's Life & Corresp. Took Dr Acland to Buckley—Conv. with Dean [Liddell] of Ch.Ch. on Hume. Music in evg: after a large party. Almost tempted to return to London for quiet. But Stephen's hospitable soul enjoys it.

28. *Wed.*

Ch. 8½ AM. Wrote to Earl of Aberdeen—L.G. Walker—Rev J.K. Walpole[4]—W. Gladstone—Rev R.W. Jelf—G. Curtis[5]—J. Hamilton. Saw Dr Acland resp. the Ewelme Mastership—Mr Acland (with Mrs) resp. the Devon seat.[6] Large party & music in evg. *Walked* Mr Peel.[7] Read Taylor's Germ. Poetry—Hume's Life & Correspe.

29. *Th.*

Church 8½ A.M. Wrote to Sir J. Graham—The Attorney General. Party: & singing in evg. Read Taylor's Germ. Poetry—Abp Herring's Letters[8]—Hume's Life & Correspe. Arranged in the shelves my year's importation of books.

30. *Fr.*

Ch. 8½ A.M. Wrote to Rev. Mr Elwin. Party & music in evg. Read Newman's Iliad—Herring's Letters—Alexander on Women.[9]

Reviewing some part of my old verses: here & there amending. On the whole I find them better than I had supposed. But that fountain is stopped. I grieve to add that they exhibit my present moral and spiritual state in a very humbling light. I fixed on a few emendations. Saw Jas. Wortley on his matters. Walk with him & others.

31. *Sat.*

Ch. 8½ AM. Resumed my operations on my MS poetry: with the same impressions. Worked on arranging letters. Wrote to Helen G.—Lord Stanley—Sir S. Scott and Co.—Mr Jas Watson. Spent the afternoon in woodcutting & the like about the old Castle: my first lesson. Read Herring's Letters & Appx—Hume's Life & Corresp.—Cicero's Epist. ad Famil[iares].[10]

[1] W. *Taylor, *Historic survey of German poetry*, 3v. (1828–30).
[2] *The dramatic works of [Robert *Greene], to which are added his poems*, ed. A. Dyce, 2v. (1831).
[3] By N. Machiavelli (1559).
[4] Joseph Kidd Walpole, d. 1869; chaplain of the *Defence*, a hulk at Woolwich, 1857–62.
[5] See 21 Aug. 58.
[6] T. D. *Acland, probably about the double-barrelled N. Devon seat, where *Northcote (as a Peelite) finished third in 1857; in 1865 Acland was elected as a liberal, joined by *Northcote (as a tory) in 1866. Acland's second wife was Mary, *née* Erskine, who d. 1892.
[7] Unidentified.
[8] T. *Herring, *Letters . . . to William *Duncombe . . . from the year 1728 to 1757* (1777).
[9] W. Alexander, *The history of women*, 2v. (1779).
[10] 'Letters to his friends'.

9 S. Trin. August One. 58.

Church Hn. 11 AM & 6½ PM. Read Taylor's Germ. Lit. (Klopstock &c.)[1]
—Remusat's Abelard[2]—Wiseman's Fabiola. Music in evg.

2. M.

Church 8½ AM. Wrote to Mrs L.A. Hamilton[3]—Robn. G.—Sir W. Heath-
cote—T.D. Acland—Rev. Jos. Hudson.[4] Read Petrarch's Sonnets—
Taylor's Germ. Lit.—Herring's Letters (finished)—Hume's Life & Correspe.
—Monti's Iliad.[5] A wood cutting afternoon about the lawn & old Castle.
Conv. with J. Wortley on politics.

3. T.

Ch. 8½ A.M. Wrote to E. Chadwick—W. Brown—E. Stanford[6]—W. Heath
—Scotts. Saw J. Davis (bis).[7] Worked on accounts & papers connected with
my affairs during the forenoon. Whist with the children. Read Chadwick on
Commns. of Inquiry[8]—Taylor's German Poetry—Hume's Life & Correspe.

4. Wed. X

Ch 8½ A.M. Wrote to Rev W.E. Jelf—Bp of Man.[9] Saw Mr Littleboy. Read
Casti Sunamitidi &c.[10]—Poètes Français du XII et XIII siecle[11]—Taylor's
Surv. Germ. Poetry—Petrarch's Sonnets & Canzoni—Hume's Life &
Correspe. The schoolfeast in aftn.

5. Th.

Ch. 8½ A.M. Convv. with Bp of Oxford. Tree-cutting while the party went to
Mold for S.P.G.[12] Read De Gassicourt's Mirabeau[13]—Rousseau Confessions[14]
—Hume's Life & Corresp.—Lessing's Nathan der Weise—Taylor's Transln.
of do.[15]

6. Fr. X

Ch. 8½ AM. Wrote to Earl Nelson—Sir G.C. Lewis—Sir Jas Graham—M. De
Tocqueville. Read Poétes Français—Rousseau's Confessions—Hume's Life

[1] On F. G. Klopstock in vol. i; see 27 July 58.
[2] See 20 Apr. 57.
[3] Unidentified.
[4] Joseph Hudson, 1793–1891; in Canada, then curate of Hexham 1845–66.
[5] V. Monti, *Iliade di Omero* (1812).
[6] Map seller at Charing Cross.
[7] Of Davies, Fenton & co., wire millers in Queen's Ferry.
[8] E. *Chadwick, Report . . . from the Poor Law Commissioners on an Inquiry into the sanitary conditions of the labouring population of Great Britain*, 2v. (1842–3).
[9] Horatio *Powys (see 3 Apr. 43).
[10] 'Le Due Sunamitidi', the 3rd of G. Casti's *Novelle*.
[11] In A. Roche, *Les Poètes français, recueil de morceaux choisis* (1844, often reprinted).
[12] *Wilberforce was on S.P.G. work in North Wales; see Wilberforce, ii. 383.
[13] C. L. Cadet de Gassicourt, *Essai sur la vie privée . . . de Mirabeau* (1820).
[14] Rousseau's autobiography published posthumously (1781–88).
[15] Tr. W. *Taylor (1791).

& Corresp.—Mirabeau's Letters to Sophie R.[1] Conv. with Bp of Oxford. Began a MS for Q.R.[2]

7. *Sat.*

Ch. 8½ A.M. Wrote to Rev W.W. Malet—W. Hampton—Dean of Raphoe[3] —J. Roberts[4]—Mrs T. Goalen. Wrote for Q.R. Read Hume's Life & Corresp.—Mirabeau's Letters—Rousseau's Confessions. Saw Mr Burnett— Mr Peel.

8. *10 S. Trin.*

Ch. mg & evg. Wrote to Willy.—Read Xavier's Life[5]—Wiseman's Fabiola— Rousseau's Emile.[6] Conv. with S. & A. on Gospel & 2d L. Evg.

9. *M.*

Worked a good deal for Q.R. Wood cutting in the afternoon. Saw Mr Burnett. Conv. with Agnes on her learning Latin. Read Mirabeau's Letters —Rousseau's Confessions—Hume's Correspondence & Life.

10. *T.*

Ch. 8½ A.M. Wrote to Mr J. Hamilton—W. Hampton—Sir J.W. Awdry— Mrs Rigby—Mr W. Grogan. Worked on MS for Q.R. Read Rousseau's Confessions—Mirabeau's Letters—Hume's Life & Corresp. Drive with C. Whist in evg with her & the children.

11. *Wed.*

Ch. 8½ AM. Wrote to Mr Ph. Rose[7]—Duchess of Sutherland. Read Rousseau's Confessions. Worked a good deal on MS. Preparations for going— visited the borehole (stopped now by sand & water)—and off by Mail at night. Dined at the Rectory.

12. *Th.* X [*London*]

Reached 11 C.H.T. at 5¾ and up at 9 A.M. Saw Mr Westell—Mr Warburton —Messrs. Ivall[8]—Scotts. Wrote to Dean Ramsay—C.G.—Jas Watson—E. Lovell—H. Merritt. Saw Stapylton Rigby +. Read Tennyson's Poems—

[1] *Choix des lettres de Mirabeau à Sophie*, 4v. (1818).
[2] Published as 'The past and present administrations', *Quarterly Review*, civ. 515 (October 1858); see Add MS 44689, f. 52.
[3] Edward Chichester, 1799–1889; dean of Raphoe 1832–73; D.D. 1852; 4th marquess of Donegal 1883.
[4] A tenant; see Hawn P.
[5] D. Bartoli and G. P. Maffei, *The life of St. Francis Xavier . . . with a preface by Dr. *Faber* (1858).
[6] Rousseau's treatise on education (1762), condemned by the parlement.
[7] Another request by Rose for employment? See 5 Oct. 53.
[8] The coachmakers; see 27 June 39.

Lendrick on Mr Senior[1]—Brimley's Essays[2]—Blackwood, North British, & Westmr. Reviews on my Book.[3] Worked little on my MS.

13. Fr. X

Wrote to Rev. J. Gillman[4]—Agnes G.—Mrs Talbot—O.B. Cole—Mrs Herbert. Saw Mr Grogan (House)—Mr Hamilton (Jobson)[5]—B. Benjamin —Saw Hicks—Lovell +. In this & another matter I ought to be most thankful. Worked on my MS. & finished the rough draft. Read Q.R. on India[6]—Q.R. Pol. of Jan & Ap. 57[7]—Mr Bright's Speech[8]—Times Reviews of my Homer: exceeding clever[9]—'Meliora' on Do.[10]

14. Sat. X

Wrote to Jas Watson—Mrs Stapleton—Rev Mr Kempe[11]—Mr W. Edwards[12]—C.G.[13]—W[estern] Br[anch] Bank Eng.[14]—Rev E. Bankes.[15] Dined at Lady Wenlocks. Correcting MS. for Q.R. Shopping and purchasing. Saw Peter MacCulloch—Mr H. Merritt. Read [blank]

15. 11 S. Trin. X [Norwood]

Ch mg: St Paul's Kn. evg. Went down to Norwood to see Mrs Talbot & Edward. Then to Ovington Square to Helen & Aunt J[ohanna].[16] Then to Stapleton[R]. Read Thérèse Lamourous[17]—Par. Lost B. III.

16. M. [Hawarden]

Wrote to Clerk Priv. Council—Mr Elwin—Mr Merritt (2)—Mr Crooke—Sir J. Young. Finished references & corrections at H. of C. Library. Shopping &

[1] Untraced pamphlet or article by W. E. Lendrick.

[2] G. *Brimley, Essays, ed. W. G. Clark, (1858).

[3] North British Review, xxix. 25 (Aug. 1858); 'he has unfolded before us the whole panorama of the age of Homer'; Blackwood's Magazine, lxxxiv. 127 (Aug. 1858), Westminster Review, xiv. 265 (July 1858), hostile.

[4] James Gillman, d. 1877; fellow of St. John's, Oxford, 1827–37; incumbent of Trinity, Lambeth, from 1847.

[5] John Hamilton (see 19 Feb. 57) recently corresponding from New York (Hawn P), about Frederick James Jobson, 1812–81, Wesleyan minister much involved in imperial and American affairs.

[6] Quarterly Review, civ. 475 (October 1858).

[7] i.e. his own articles.

[8] J. *Bright, 'Speech on legislation and policy for India, on the second reading of the India Bill, June 24 1858' (1858).

[9] 'The criticisms on style, prolixity, and want of acquaintance with much that I ought to have known, are just. The more serious arguments I think may be answered. But it is much the cleverest long review which I have seen after the National' (Bassett, 122); The Times 12 and 13 August 1858, which began with '. . . not a little amusement occasioned by the futility of his reasoning, and the insignificance of his results.'

[10] Meliora, a quarterly review of social science, ii. 136; moderately favourable, with qualifications.

[11] John Edward Kempe, 1829–1907; rector of St. James's, Piccadilly, 1853–95; published sermons etc.

[12] Perhaps William Edwards of Haverfordwest, later corresponded on Homer (Hawn P).

[13] Bassett, 122.

[14] Charles Tindal was its agent.

[15] Edward Bankes, 1795–1867; canon of Gloucester from 1821; chaplain-in-ordinary to William IV and Victoria; hugely rich on d. of his fa.-in-law, *Eldon.

[16] She then lived at 1 Ovington Square.

[17] Possibly C. Nodier, Thérèse Aubert (1819); novel of love and the Vendée risings.

business. Read Brimley's Essays.[1] Saw H.J.G.—Mr Grogan—Rigby—Mr Leitch[2]—Hicks[R]. Helen took me to the train & most kindly saw me off at 8 PM. Chester 2 A.M. & Hawarden at three—D.G.

17. T.

Up at ten. Wrote to Mr H. Merritt and Sir J. Graham. Unpacking & arranging books. Began Ariosto with W. & A. Conv. with C. & W. on the state of religious belief & about young Tollemache (Balliol) of whom it is sad to hear.[3] Read Rousseau Conf.—Mirabeau's Letters. Saw Alick Wood: resp. Ld A. Tempest especially.[4]

18. Wed.

Ch. 8½ A.M. Wrote to R.P. Gillies—Sir T.G.— Dean Ramsay—Mr M. Brown.[5] Ariosto with W. & A. Read Rousseau Conf.—Mirabeau's Letters—Who wrote the Waverley Novels[6]—Hume's Life & Corresp. Visited the boring by Manor F[arm].

19. Th.

Ch. 8½ A.M. Wrote to Ld Lyttelton—Mr Aubrey de Vere—M. Fairet (Copyright Congress). Read Rousseau—Mirabeau—Hume—Fitzpatrick on the Waverley Novels. Ariosto (Zotti)[7] with W. & A. Whist in evg.

20. Fr.

Ch. 8½ AM. 12–6. Expedition to the top of Bryn-y-auchyn,[8] a party of 16: and an open air luncheon. Ariosto with W. & A. Music in evg. Read Rousseau Conf.—finished Fitzpatrick on Waverley Novels—Read 'Our Village'[9] —'Reflections on the late Premier (Sir R. Peel)'.[10]

21. Sat.

Ch. 8½ A.M. Wrote to Ld Brougham—H.J.G.—G. Curtis[11]—O.B. Cole—

[1] See 12 Aug. 58.
[2] James Leitch.
[3] A reference to Tollemache's poor sight, which Gladstone regarded as preventing him going to the Bar, or to his agnosticism; see L. Tollemache, *Talks with Mr. Gladstone* (1898), 19.
[4] Susan, da. of 5th duke of Newcastle, loved Lord Adolphus ('Dolly') Vane-Tempest, 1825–64, tory M.P. N. Durham, wastrel, often thought insane, whom she m., despite hostility, 1860. She d. 1875.
[5] Declining Matthew Brown of Manchester's invitation to address the agricultural society there.
[6] By W. J. Fitzpatrick (1856).
[7] L. Ariosto, ed. R. Zotti, *Orlando Furioso* (1822).
[8] W. of Caerwrle, 10 miles S. of Hawarden.
[9] Possibly P. Reedpen, pseud. *Our town; or rough sketches of character, manners*, 2v. (1834).
[10] 'Reflections suggested by the career of the late premier [Sir R. *Peel]' (1847).
[11] George William Curtis, 1824–92; American traveller, poet and publicist; wrote *Prue and I* (1857), probably the work mentioned here; corresponded with diarist again 1890 (Hawn P).

Mr E. Hepple.[1] Arisoto with W. & A. Read Curtis's Poems—Rousseau Confessions—Mirabeau's Letters—Maryatt on Porcelain[2]—Hume's Life & Correspe.

22. 12 S. Trin.

Hn. Ch mg & evg. Conv. with the three eldest. Read Jerus. Commee's. Answer[3]—Report of Melanesian Mission[4]—Pritchard's Hist. Mankind[5]— Fabiola.

Study *method*, in the disposal particularly of time & money; it is the secret of independence of ease and of great results from small means.
Believe now, & hereafter you will learn that relaxation & refreshment are properly to be found in the alternation of different employments: of these some may be serious & others light but all should have an end; vacuity and dawdling have no end and should at all times & under all circumstances be avoided.[6]

23. M.

Ch. 8½ A.M. Saw Mr Burnett: & visited the boring. Read Rousseau Confessions—Duv. de Hauranne Preface[7]—Pritchard's Phys. Hist. Mankind— Mirabeau's Letters. Ariosto with W. & A.

24. T. St Barthol.

Ch 8½ AM. Wrote to Jas Leitch—C.S. Parker[8]—Jas Watson. Read Rousseau—Mirabeau—Hume's Corresp. and Jebb's MS on Homer[9]—Ariosto with W. & A. We have now also ordinarily a family song or dance after dinner. Wood cutting all the aftn.

25. Wed.

Ch. 8½ AM. Wrote to Duchess of Sutherland. Ariosto with W. & A. Dined at the Rectory. Arranging plans for Scotland; & for cases of poor persons. Read Hume—Rousseau—Mirabeau (finished Vol VI)—Jebb's Homeric MS (finished).

26. Th.

Ch. 8½ AM. Wrote to Rev J. Jebb—Ld Brougham—Rev Mr Newby[10]—

[1] Edward Hepple of Coram Street, London; not further identified.
[2] See 2 July 57.
[3] Untraced; on the Jerusalem bpric.
[4] Its annual report.
[5] J. C. *Prichard, *Researches into the physical history of mankind*, 2v. (1826).
[6] Dated 'Aug. 58'; Add MS 44747, f. 184.
[7] P. Duvergier de Hauranne, *Des principes du gouvernement représentatif et de leur application* (1838).
[8] Charles Stuart Parker, partner in the Liverpool sugar firm of Sandbach, had written about his son, Charles Stuart *Parker, 1829–1910, friend of the Gladstone boys, alpinist, biographer of *Peel and *Graham, fellow of University, Oxford 1854–64; *Cardwell's sec. 1864–6; liberal M.P. Perthshire 1868–74, Perth 1878–92; on many educational commissions.
[9] Vast MS critique of *Studies on Homer* by J. Jebb: Add MS 44390, f. 87.
[10] Perhaps George Newby, priest 1825; perpetual curate of Borrowdale, Cumberland, from 1838; Wordsworthian poet.

Rev H. Brough.[1] Woodcutting in aft. Ariosto as usual. Read Rousseau Conf. (finished II)—Ld Grey on Reform[2]—Hume's Correspondence & Life —Ariosto with W. & A. Saw Sherratt resp. the Coal.

27. Fr.

Ch. 8½ A.M. Wrote to Col. Warrington[3]—Edr. Constitutional Press.[4] Spent most of the day with Mr Darlington & Mr Burnett: and arranged for accelerating the borings, and (probably) for (myself) prosecuting with Mr D. a sinking at the point first opened. Read Rousseau Conf.—Hume's Corresp. & Life—Ld Grey on Reform—Ariosto with W. & A.

28. Sat.

Ch. 8½ A.M. Darling Lena's birthday. Horace with Stephy. Ariosto with W. & A. Saw Mr C. Butler. Finished Rousseau's Confessions & M. Musset Pathay's Preface.[5] Read Ld Grey on Reform—Law Review on Anon. Writing & Ld Brougham's Letter.[6] Finished Hume's Life & Corresp. Tree-cutting.

29. 13 S. Trin.

Ch mg & evg. Wrote to W. Hampton—Robn. G. Conv. on Ep. & Gosp. with W. A. & S. Read Abp Beaumont's Mandement[7]—Rousseau's Letter to Abp B.—Fabiola.

30. M.

Ch. 8½ AM. Wrote to J. Watson & Smith—Dr Symonds[8]—Stat. Master Warr[ingto]n—Capt. Stokes—F.B. Atkinson—Scott & Co.—Aunt J. Horace with Stephy. Saw Mr Troughton—Mr Burnett. We dined with Mr Wynn Eaton at Leeswood.[9] Finished Ld Grey on Reform (qy on *Reform*?).[10] Read Edwards's Personal Adventures.[11] Woodcutting: & worked on papers &c. in preparation for departure.

31.

Ch. 8½ AM. Wrote to Lady Canning—J.N.G.—M. Duvergier de H[auranne] —Lord Brougham. Stephen [Glynne] came: & I stated fully to him the

[1] Untraced.
[2] See 1 Mar. 58.
[3] Thornhill Warrington, colonel of 44th Foot, retired from active service 1854.
[4] *Constitutional Press*, a moderate tory journal, began April 1859.
[5] V. D. de Musset Pathay, *Oeuvres inédites de J. J. Rousseau suivies d'un supplement* (1825).
[6] H. P. *Brougham, *Letter to the Marquess of Lansdowne on the late revolution in France* (1848), or a MS.
[7] C. de Beaumont du Repaire, *Mandement* (1762); attack on Rousseau's *Emile*.
[8] Perhaps John Addington Symonds, 1807–71; physician in Bristol 1831–69; wrote on sleep and dreams; fa. of the art historian.
[9] 2 miles SE. of Mold.   [10] See 1 Mar. 58.
[11] W. Edwards, *Personal adventures during the Indian rebellion* (1858).

views & plans about the Coal: which he fully approved. Also to Henry. Read Edwards's Personal Adventures. Horace with Stephy—Ariosto with W. & A. Arrangements for departure, below & above [stairs].

Wed. Sept. One. 1858 [Brougham Hall]

Wrote to Sir Jas Graham—Bookkeeper Inverness—W.H.G. Read Edwards Personal Adv.—Ld Brougham on Rousseau—Duvergier's Parl. Gov.[1] Off at 9½ & reached Brougham Hall[2] at 4¾. The Bp of Lichfield & Hayward encountered us on our way. We found an agreeable Mrs Rose[3]: & Ld B[rougham] kind as ever.

2. Th.

Wrote to Bp of Brechin. Read Ld B.s Voltaire[4]—Mrs Crosland's Light in the Valley[5]—Mrs Behn.[6] Much interesting conversation with Ld Brougham. A visit to the Tennis Court.

3. Fr. [Netherby]

We used the fine morning in seeing, & I partly in the society of our host. In the aftn. we went 32 miles to Netherby[7] where we had a most warm reception & I had much conv. with Sir J. Graham. Read Mrs Crosland's Light in the Valley (finished)—Duvergier's Gouv. Parlem.

4. Sat.

Wrote to A. Panizzi—J. Blackwell—Dr Wolff—Cashier Lanc. & York [Railway] Co.—J. Miller. Went with Sir J. Graham to his Steamboring wh we examined: then to the old Station wh looks over Eskdale & Lidderdale. Much conv. Music in evg. Read Sir J. G[raham']s Evidence on Manning[8]—Macintyre[9]—& M. Duvergier.

5. 14 S. Trin.

Arthuret Ch[10] in mg. Aft prayers in our room. Conv. with Sir J. G[raham] on the new Kirk question.[11] Read Lessing on Ewige Strafe[12]—Williams on the Gospels[13]—Nicole La Prière.[14] The Rector dined.[15]

[1] See 23 Aug. 58.
[2] See 22 Oct. 57.
[3] Unidentified.
[4] Vol. i of H. P. *Brougham, Lives of men of letters and science, who flourished in the time of George III, 2v (1845–6).
[5] C. *Crosland, Light in the valley. My experiences of spiritualism (1857).
[6] Mrs. *A. Behn, The histories and novels of the late . . . Mrs. Behn (1696).
[7] *Graham's seat on the Esk, just in Scotland, the scene of 'Young Lochinvar'.
[8] Of ships; see 16 June 58n.
[9] Perhaps J. J. Macintyre, 'Elective franchise as it is, and as it ought to be' (1847).
[10] On the Esk, 8 miles N. of Carlisle.
[11] See 9 Sept. 58 and n. *Graham as Home Secretary was responsible for the 1844 Benefices Act.
[12] G. E. Lessing, 'Leibnitz von den ewigen Strafen' in his Works (1839) ix.
[13] I. *Williams, Thoughts on the study of the holy gospels (1842).
[14] P. Nicole, Traité de la prière (1766).
[15] William Graham, d. 1862, Sir J. G.'s br.; rector of Arthuret.

6. M. [Drumlanrig]

Wrote to Sir J. Maxwell—D. Hutcheson & Co—Sir S. Scott & Co. Went with Sir J. Graham to his Farm. More conv. on Reform: but I do not quite understand his position.[1] 2¾–5¾. 49 m. to Drumlanrig.[2] Read Buckland's Nat. Hist[3]—Duvergier Parl. Gouv.—Lettere di Jac. Ortis.[4]

7. T.

Chapel 9 A.M. Wrote to Ld Stanley. Read Wiseman's Lectures[5]—Duvergier Parl. Gouv.—Edinb. Rev. on Brougham's Sp.—on Buckle's Civilisation.[6] Went to Morton Castle: and then up the hills opposite us.

8. Wed.

Chapel 9 A.M. Wrote to Duchess of Sutherland—Jas Watson—Landlord Bannavie—Landlord Dingwall. Visited the Creil and the Farm. The Duke returned. Read Giac. Ortis—Duvergier Parl. Gouv.

9. Th. [Glasgow]

Chapel 9 A.M. Read Duvergier Parl. Gouv.—Easton & its inhabitants.[7] The Duke [of Buccleuch] showed me his maps & we discussed Cannobie[8] & Sir J. Graham's borings—Also he took us to the Gardens. 3¾–9 to Glasgow from Carron Bridge. The viaduct presents no common scene. Saw Mr Jas Watson—Do with Sir J. Campbell & others on the question of intrusion.[9]

10. Fr. [Bannavie]

Off at ¼ to 7 by Caledonian Canal to Bannavie[10] 170 miles. We enjoyed the passage notwithstanding much rain & even a little roughish water: wh affected me rather less than of yore. Read Duvergier—Giacomo Ortis. Made some steamboat acquaintances: & learned that the return of land to pasture hereabouts is diminishing the population.

11. Sat [Dunrobin Castle]

Off at 8: reached Inverness at 5. Then by Kessock Ferry to Dingwall where

[1] 'When Gladstone was here I showed him your heads of two Reform Bills. He made little comment, but thought it would be unwise prematurely to fix details. He was less hostile to Reform itself than I expected, and he expressed an opinion that no Government could now stand which blinked the question.' (Graham to Russell, 27 November 1858, in Parker, *Graham*, ii. 360).
[2] Seat of the Buccleuchs in Dumfries-shire.
[3] F. T. *Buckland, *Curiosities of natural history* (1858).
[4] U. Foscolo, *Ultime lettere di Jacopo Ortis* (1802).
[5] N. P. S. *Wiseman, *Four advent lectures on concordats* (1855).
[6] *Edinburgh Review*, cvii. 443, 465 (April 1858).
[7] E. *Eden, *Easton and its inhabitants* (1858).
[8] Cross Canonby, village on the Solway.
[9] Sale of patronage rights during vacancies; see A. L. Drummond and J. Bulloch, *The Church in Victorian Scotland* (1975), 329–30; preliminary correspondence on this in Add MS 44390 ff. 75, 80, 113. Sir James Campbell, 1790–1876; Glasgow merchant; provost 1840–3; kt. 1842.
[10] A short distance N. of the S. end of Caledonian canal.

Mrs Chisholm (at 81) came to meet us. We reached Dunrobin[1] by the
Meikle Ferry at ¼ to 3 in the morning: brought the last stage in *state* by the
Duke's carriages. Read Duvergier. We saw the noble Falls of Foyers on our
way: besides Fort Augustus of wh so much cannot be said.[2] Bed a little
before four.

12. 15 S. Trin.

The morning Prayers in our apartments. This with evg *family* prayers was
all. The Duke [of Sutherland] & the Speaker went to Golspie.[3] Walk with
the Duchess &c. Read Watson's Apology[4]—Caird's Serm.[5]—Barville's
Conversion[6]—Observateur Catholique.

13. M.

I went on the hill: missed two deer & found my shooting at a mark so bad
that I take it as a new sign of something impaired in my sight. Worked on a
Latin inscription for Mr Loch with criticisms from the Speaker and Willy.[7]
Read Duvergier Parl. Gouv. Singing in evg. Wrote to Mr J. Watson—
Scotts—Sir J. Graham.

14. T.

Wrote to Mr Hancock—Robn. G. Read Duv. de Hauranne—Sir W. Denison's Lecture.[8] The day was devoted to a trip in the yacht to Caithness: we
visited the Speaker's party at Langwell, saw the 'Man' and the grand rock
wall with one of its caverns.[9] There is in the Langwell a very curious *Via
Mala*. The sea behaved so well that we could not do otherwise. It was also
pleasant that, the Duke hearing better today, we were not so entirely cut
off from him while enjoying his hospitality.

15. Wed. X[10]

Wrote to Rev W.E. Jelf—Barnard & Dimsdale[11]—London & Co[unty]
Bank—Hon. A. Gordon. Read Lettres Persanes[12]—Poems of the Restora-

[1] Sutherland's castle; see 3 Sept. 53.
[2] Falls into Loch Ness; Fort Augustus was built to subdue the Highlands after 1715,
but decayed in the nineteenth century.
[3] Village near Dunrobin.
[4] A. *Watson, *An apology for the plain sense of the doctrine of the prayer book on holy
baptism* (1850).
[5] J. *Caird, *Sermons* (1858).
[6] J. Barville, *An account of the late conversion of Mr. John Barville alias Barton from
popery to the reformed church of England* (1710).
[7] For James *Loch's memorial; copy in Add MS 44747, f. 187.
[8] Sir W. T. *Denison, *A church a social institution. A lecture . . . to the young men's
christian association* (1858).
[9] The long sea-cliff between Helmsdale and Berriedale, 20 miles NE. of Dunrobin;
Langwell House by Berriedale was bought in 1857 by the duke of Portland, and the land
afforested.
[10] Sign used on this occasion to indicate pornography—restoration poems and the
Contes—read this day.
[11] Dimsdale, Drewett, Fowler & Barnard, London bankers.
[12] C. de S. Montesquieu, *Lettres persanes* (1761).

tion—Contes de la Reine de Navarre[1]—Froude's Reply in Fraser.[2]—We drove to Strathcarnan.[3]

16. Th.

Wrote to Bp of Oxford—Rev. Mr Claughton—Read Michelsen on Turkey[4] —Macgregor's 'genuine' Ossian.[5] Singing mg & evg. Drove to the head of Brora by S. Rifle shooting: & visited Mr Loch's[6] & the Memorial to his Father.

17. Fr.

Drove to the Batesons[7] & returned on foot. Music in evg. Read Michelsen's Turkey—Macgregor's Genuine Ossian. Visited Dr Macpherson[8]—Conversations as usual.

18. Sat.

Wrote to Watson & Smith—Music in evg. Read Michelsen. Walk with Capt. Egerton.[9] Out through the day deer-stalking on the hills over Brora.

19. 16 S. Trin.

Mg & aft prayers in our room. Wrote somewhat on Gospel. Read Lessing Ewige Strafe—Williams on the Gospels—Watson's Apology (finished)—Barville's Conversion. Walk with C. & with Duchess of S.

20. M. [Lairg]

Wrote to Mr Melly[10]—Robn. G.—Ld Lyttelton—Agnes G.—Ld Aberdeen —Mr Elwin—F. Curzon—J. Bellis (Chester)—J. Perkins (Liverpool). Read Michelsen's Turkish Empire—Wikoff's Year in Foreign Office[11]—Froude's Hist Vol III:[12] aloud, at Lairg. We set out from Dunrobin at 3 & reached Lairg at ½ past 6: visited the Mill at Pittentrail, the school house & store at Lairg.[13] Much pleased with the appearance of the country & people.

[1] See 31 May 47.
[2] J. A. *Froude in *Fraser's Magazine*, lviii. 359 (September 1858).
[3] Strathcarnach, glen SW. of Golspie.
[4] E. H. Michelsen, *The Ottoman Empire and its resources* (1853).
[5] J. Macpherson, ed. with introduction by P. MacGregor, *The genuine remains of Ossian* (1841).
[6] George, James *Loch's 1st s., 1811–77, barrister and liberal M.P. Wick burghs 1868–72.
[7] J. N. Gladstone's br.-in-law (see 30 Oct. 48), lived at Cambusmore, Golspie.
[8] See 19 Jan. 58.
[9] Arthur Frederick Egerton, 1829–66, s. of 1st earl of Ellesmere; soldier; see Add MS 44390, f. 128.
[10] George Melly, 1830–94; Liverpool merchant, contested Preston 1862, Stoke 1866; liberal M.P. Stoke 1868–74; organised Gladstone's elections in S. Lancashire.
[11] H. Wikoff, *A New Yorker in the foreign office, and his adventures in Paris* (1858).
[12] See 23 May 56.
[13] On Loch Shin, about 15 miles W. of Dunrobin.

21. *T*. [*Lochinver*]

After 20 m. yesterday we set out at 8½ A.M. for Inveran, down the Shin: then up the Oikel by Routtall (wh we stopped to see) 21 m. to Bridge of Oikel: then 18 to Inchnadampff by Altna Gallagach, & 13½ to Lochinver.[1] The falls of the Shin, the opening of the Bridge at Inveran, were beautiful: then the first sight of the Assynt Mountains, & the lower end of the Loch Assynt drive. The lights were favourable in an unusual degree. At Inchnadampff Willy & I went to see the caves & I had much conv. with my guide. The house at Lochinvar [*sic*] most appropriate & comfortable. There we made Mr Maciver's[2] acquaintance: still having the advantage of Mr Loch's presence. The Duchess's reception was most remarkable: all the people at their doors, profuse in bows & reverence: flags mounted on the eminences: one old man in a cottage opposite kept his window lighted through the evening.

After a most glorious sun, we had the Moon, the Comet,[3] the Aurora, & the Northern lights all in succession.

22. *Wed.*

Wrote to the Duchess—(resp. Albert).[4] Read Wikoff. In the forenoon we went to the bathing bays & the Duke's walks—in aft. drive to the hills northward & the hamlet of Torbrech[5]—we had a most grand view of mountains and chains from the tops.

23. *Th.* [*Scourie*]

Wrote to Mrs Chisholm. 6½–10½. To Mr Scoby's[6] to breakfast: then over the hills to the Kirkaig falls with wh I was delighted. Much pleased with Mr S. my host & guide. I managed however to sprain my ankle. Off at 11¼ to Scourie[7] 31 miles: stopping at Mr Greene's Glen Dhu[8] for luncheon. This loch & Quinag from it are very grand. Read Wikoff.

24. *Fr.* [*Dunrobin Castle*]

66 miles back to Dunrobin where we arrived at 9½ A.M. stopping at Mr Maciver's—at Arkel Lodge[9]—at Mr Reid's Lochmore lodge for luncheon[10] —we parted on reaching Loch Shin from the grand & wild scenery wh has so much delighted us. At D[unrobin] we were met by the sad news of Lady

---

[1] i.e. they crossed to Lochinver on the West coast by the spectacular road through Assynt.

[2] Probably the factor.

[3] Donati's comet, seen brilliantly in Britain in September and October 1858.

[4] Lord Albert Leveson-Gower, 1843–74, the Sutherlands' 3rd son; later captain in life guards.

[5] Just N. of Lochinver.

[6] Donald Mackay Scobie of Durness, by Lairg; or his fa.

[7] The last significant village on the West coast.

[8] Lodge at the head of the sea loch Glendhu; taken by Thomas Greene, the former M.P.?

[9] About 10 miles inland from Scourie.

[10] On the road to Loch Shin. All these lodges were owned by Sutherland.

Clanwilliam's death.[1] Finished Wikoff. Saw Dr Broomhall & had my sprain properly tended. On the way I could only douche it in a burn.

25. Sat.

Wrote to W.M. Goalen—J.N.G.—A. Gordon—Elgin Inn. Read Duv. de Hauranne—Greenwood on Papacy.[2] Singing in evg. Laid up most of the day.

26. 17 S. Trin.

Prayers in our rooms mg & aft: a Sermon of Sherlock's.[3] Wrote to Mrs Chisholm—S. Herbert—Rev Mr Grieve. Read Greenwood's Latin Patriarchate—Sherlock's Sermons—Williams on the Gospels.[4] Music in evg. We were sad at the prospect of departure. Saw Dr Broomhall: & for once determined to disobey him in going round by Dingwall to see Mrs Chisholm.

27. M. [Dingwall]

Many farewells. Saw the party off at 8.30. Followed soon after ten, by Mail, to Dingwall. I felt too much obliged to D. & Dss to say much. Saw Dr Broomhall & Dr Macpherson. Reached Dingwall 4¾. Dined & slept at Mrs Chisholms.[5] She is wonderful in strength & activity at nearly 83, & not less admirably good & kind. Met Sheriff Cameron. Read Adam Blair. Went over the scenes of 1820 in Dingwall: now entirely metamorphosed.[6]

28. T. [Haddo House]

Left Dingwall at 9 for Inverness where I went over the town, heard a cause in Court, & inquired for old China. Off by rail at 2.20, fell in with the Cranworths[7] at Keith, & reached Haddo[8] at 9¾ where I found my party & Lord Aberdeen standing in his old fashion but with a stick. My ankle weak but bears some walking. Read Adam Blair (finished) & Matthew Wald.[9] I had today some instructive or amusing fellow travellers.

29. Wed.

Wrote to Mr G. Burnett—Duke of Argyll—Sir Thos G.—Mr G. Loch—Duchess of Sutherland. Walked with Ld Aberdeen in the morning & drove with him in the afternoon. He is in good spirits & though now the old man in good health: with what degree of resisting power I know not. Finished

---

[1] Elizabeth, Sidney *Herbert's sister, m. 1830 3rd earl of Clanwilliam; she was mother of Sir R. H. *Meade.
[2] T. *Greenwood, *Cathedra Petri. A political history of the great latin patriarchate*, 4v. (1856–65).
[3] By T. *Sherlock, 1678–1761, bp. of London.
[4] See 5 Sept. 58.
[5] See 29 Aug. 53.
[6] J. G. *Lockhart, *Some passages in the life of Adam Blair* (1822).
[7] *Cranworth's wife was Laura, née Carr, who d. 1868.
[8] *Aberdeen's seat in Aberdeenshire.
[9] Also by *Lockhart (1824).

Matthew Wald: & read Sat. Rev. No 2 on Homer.[1] Singing in evg. Worked on Inscription.[2]

30. Th.
Wrote to Jas Watson—Scotts—Walk—drive—music—as yesty. Worked on my proof sheets for Q.R.[3] Read Duvergier.

Friday October One 1858.
Wrote to Mr J. Murray—Mr Elwin—Mr W. Smythe (Methven)—Finished Proofs for Q.R. Walk & drive with Ld Abn. Music practice mg: & in evg. Read Sea Margins[4]—Duvergier Parl. Gouv.

2. Sat.
Wrote to T.B. Hudson[5]—J.N.G.—F. Schnadhorst[6]—Geo. Melly—Miss Huntington—Mr J. Stirling[7]—Ld Brougham. Walk with Ld A. morning. In aftn. we drove to Tohon where both buildings and garden are curious. The *later* date is 1584–9.[8] Music at night. Read Duvergier—Accession of Nicholas.[9]

3. 18 S. Trin.
Woodhead Ch.[10] mg—& prayers in our room aftn. Walk with Ld A. Wrote to Sir E. Lytton & copy.[11] Read Edinb. Synod[12]—Bartlett's Life of Butler.[13]

4. M.
Wrote to Mr J.H. Gell[14]—Agnes G. Drive with Ld A. aftn. We talked over the Ionian I. letter.[15] Read Les Femmes Militaires[16]—Accession of Nicholas. —Hist of Dilettanti Society[17]—Music in evg. Corrected Agnes's Exercises in Italian. Went over the pictures.

[1] *Saturday Review*, ii. 307 (September 1858).
[2] The *Loch inscription; see 30 Oct. 58.
[3] See 6 Aug. 58.
[4] R. *Chambers, *Ancient sea-margins, as memorials of changes in the relative level of sea and land* (1848).
[5] Thomas B. Hudson, travel writer.
[6] Frank Schnadhorst, Birmingham, had written on Greek history (Hawn P.); the fa. of the liberal agent?
[7] Of Kippenross; see 25 Aug. 42 and 13 Oct. 58.
[8] Tolquhon Castle, 4 miles S. of Haddo.
[9] See 9 Dec. 57.
[10] 2 miles E. of Fyvie.
[11] Expressing interest in *Lytton's suggestion that he should go to Ionia: Lytton MSS D/EK 012; see Morley i. 594.
[12] The annual report, for 1858.
[13] T. *Bartlett, *Memoirs of the life, character and writings of Joseph *Butler* (1839).
[14] Of Ladywood, Birmingham; had sent a book on Homer (Hawn P)
[15] To *Lytton; see previous day.
[16] Untraced.
[17] *Historical notices of the society of Dilettanti* (1855).

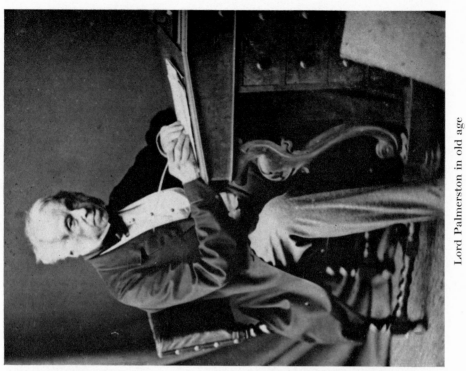

Lord Palmerston in old age

The free traders: John Bright, Richard Cobden, Michel Chevalier

Athens Dec.r 1858

In Athens. Facsimile of 18–21 December 1858, Lambeth MS 1434, f. 143

Miss Summerhayes, later Mrs. Dale, as 'Lady with the coronet of Jasmine' by *William Dyce* (see *6 Aug. 59*)

'The House of Commons debating the French Treaty of 1860'. Mezzotint by T. O. Barlow after the oil painting by J. Phillip. Gladstone is sitting third from the front on the front bench (see 4 Dec. 61)

5. *T.*

Wrote to Mr J. Calderwood[1]—Scotts—Lady Blantyre[2]—Mr Brand. Read State of England 1671[3]—Rules of Civility 1685[4]—Accession of Nicholas finished—De L'Angleterre 1811[5]—Les Femmes Militaires finished. Walk with Ld Abn. mg: we again discussed Reform. Walk with Arthur [Gordon] in aft. Music in evg.

6. *Wed. [Fasque]*

Read Wuthering Heights[6]—Cousin on Abelard—& his Ouvrages inédits.[7] Saw Ld Aberdeen: & bid him farewell with the recollection how improbable is our meeting here again.

Passed some hours in Aberdeen: saw King's Coll. Chapel with its rare carvings, the Library, the Cathedral, & St John's Chapel. Saw Mr Hutchins. Reached Laurencekirk at 6.15 and Fasque[8] soon after 7. We were most kindly received: the children are all amiable, two daughters beautiful, & the boy warm & forthcoming.[9] Music in evg.

7. *Th.*

Wrote to Earl of Aberdeen—Sir E.L. Bulwer Lytton (& copy)[10]—Mr W. Grogan. Read Hist. Earldom of Sutherland—Wuthering Heights—Ld Canning's dispatches.[11] Music in evg. Went over the house garden & part of the place & visited old friends with Louisa. Much is changed, some very well, all in the spirit of love to the place: yet I miss some marks of my Father, our foundation stone. Saw Lady H. Forbes.

8. *Fr.*

Wrote to Ld Stanley—H.J.G.—Mr Learmouth[12]—Aunt J.—Rev R. Wall[13] —Robn. G. Saw the Forbeses—Mr Ritchie[14]—Gen. Arbuthnot. Dinner party: & music. Again about the house & place. Visited the Chapel: a very sacred place to me & mine. Read Wuthering Heights.

[1] Secretary of the mechanics institute in Toxteth Park, Liverpool.

[2] Lady Evelyn Leveson-Gower, 2nd da. of 2nd duke of Sutherland, m. 1843 12th Baron Blantyre; their da. Gertrude m. 1875 Willy Gladstone.

[3] E. *Chamberlayne, *Angliae Notitia, or the Present State of England* (1669, 5th ed. with additions 1671).

[4] Probably A. de Courtin, *The rules of civility* (1671).

[5] Not found.

[6] By Emily *Brontë (1847).

[7] M. V. Cousin, *Ouvrages inédits d'Abélard* (1836).

[8] The estate in the Mearns, bought by Sir John Gladstone and inherited by the eldest son, Thomas.

[9] Sir Thomas had six daughters; Louisa and Anne were the two oldest.

[10] 'My judgment is not tied to any particular plan of proceeding. But with regard to the plan Sir J. Bowen [sic] has proposed I can *conceive* that the ultimate incorporation of the islands except Corfu, or Corfu and Paxo, with Greece might be desirable, & I can even suppose the same of an early resort to that measure'; Lytton Papers D/EK 0.12.

[11] *PP* 1857–8 xliv.

[12] Thomas Young Learmouth, lived in the Albany.

[13] Richard Wall, 1820–99; vice-principal of Chester training college 1844; taught in Birkenhead and Staffordshire; wrote on middle class religion (1858).

[14] John Ritchie of Upper Kinmouth, Fordoun.

9. Sat.

Wrote to Mr Stothert. Visited old Douglas & the Falconers: drove to Drumtouchty and Fordoun. Music in evg. Read Wuthering Heights—Earldom of Sutherland—Sinclair on Scottish Dialect[1]—Macintosh's Reply to Burke.[2] Visits to cottages: & went up the Garrol.

10. 19 S. Trin.

Chapel mg & aft. Heavy rain kept down the congregations wh were 36 mg & 52 evg. The singing was hearty & we liked the clergyman[3]—Tom collected the alms. Wrote my long letter to Willy on his going to Oxford.[4] Read Life of Rowl. Hill.[5]—Nicole on Prayer.[6]

11. M.

Wrote to Sir E. Lytton—Earl of Aberdeen—Mr J. Hamilton. We drove to the Burn & had luncheon: saw Lady H. Forbes & the Foxtons; also made Cottage visits. Music in evg. Read Wuth. Heights—Macintosh's Answer. Reviewed my letter to W. Conv. with T[om] resp. Helen & the Residuary Estate accounts.

12. T.

Wrote to W. Grogan—J. Murray. Tom & his party went off in aftn: we dined at Fettercairn House & had music. Lady H[arriet Forbes'] singing is no common object whether to ear or eye. Went on the hills: & paid visits: The blind girl at Bogindolloch went through her lessons. Read Duvergier—Macintosh on the Revolution—Wuthering Heights. Gave Willy my letter: & had a conv. with him on Oxford life.

13. Wed. [Keir]

Up at 5.30 & reached Keir[7] at one. Found a large party including Mrs Norton:[8] went over some of our host's very rich collections. Visited Dunblane Cathedral & the Kippenross trees & park. Music in evg. Read Duvergier—Agnes Grey.[9]

14. Th.

Wrote to Rn. G (missed). In aftn we saw the horse-breaking process per-

[1] J. *Sinclair, Observations on the Scottish dialect (1782).
[2] See 14 July 43.
[3] George Frederick Hardman Foxton, 1825–96; English curacies 1848–58; incumbent at Fasque 1858–71; vicar of Gedney 1871–96.
[4] Not in Lathbury.
[5] See 6 Jan. 50.
[6] See 5 Sept. 58.
[7] William *Stirling(-Maxwell's) house near Dunblane, with a fine collection of Spanish old masters.
[8] Caroline Elizabeth Sarah *Norton, née Sheridan, 1808–77; beauty, wit and novelist; separated from her husband 1836; involved in lengthy litigation (see 21 Mar. 54); m. 1877, after her husband's d., Sir W. Stirling-Maxwell, her long-standing lover.
[9] By Anne *Brontë (1847).

formed by Mr Stirling & Mr Drummond. Walks in the grounds. Willy left us for Oxford. Music in evg. Conv. with Mr Delane. Read Fabius Pictor[1]— Horne's Orion[2]—Agnes Grey—Memoirs of Mad. d'Epinay.[3]

15. Fr. X. [Liverpool]

Continued rain. Read Agnes Grey—Tom Brown's Works[4]—Morning conversations: after luncheon started for Liverpool by Stirling—met by Robn. at Broadgreen & arrived in 9 h.

16. Sat.

Wrote to Willy. Commenced Ionian I. papers.[5] St George's Hall Meeting 1–3½ and People's Concert 7–9¼. Spoke at each.[6] Visited the Exhibition of Pictures. Saw Rev Mr Tomline—Mr Macfie & others.

17. S.

Seaforth Ch mg with Robn. G. Luncheon with Mr Rawson: discussed plans for the Church. Saw Mr Stephens.[7] Visited the House. St Nicholas Lpool aftn. Music in evg. Read Williams on Gospels[8]—& at night resumed Ionian I. papers wh are pressing.

18. M.

Agnes's birthday: all blessings be upon her. Wrote to Sir E. Lytton (& copy)—Mrs Hampton—Mr F. Phillips (2)[9]—Sir J. Graham. Visited Exhibition with C. & M.E. Seaforth business with Breakenridge & Robn. G. Resid Estate do with Mr Pearson. Finished I.I. papers. Music in evg: and dancing! Finished Agnes Grey.

19. T. X. [London]

Wrote to Ld Aberdeen. S. Herbert—C.G. Off at 9¾. Reached London at 5 & went to C.O. till 7 to arrange & explain with Sir E.B. L[ytton] who is to telegraph an inquiry to Young.[10] Saw Sir R. Murchison—Rev. Mr Howson. Read Duvergier Parl. Gouv.—Carlyle's Friedrich.[11] Saw Hicks[R]. Worked on letters & papers.

[1] The oldest Roman historian, drawn upon by Livy.
[2] R. H. Horne, *Orion. An epic poem in three books* (1843).
[3] *Mémoires et correspondance de madame d'Epinay*, ed. J. P. A. Parison, 3v. (1818).
[4] *The poetical works of the late Thomas *Brown*, 4v. (1820).
[5] *PP* 1852–3 lxii. on the correspondence with banished members of the assembly, and the removal of Ionian judges; *Lytton also sent recent, unprinted papers.
[6] Addressing the National Association for the Promotion of Social Science, and the People's Saturday evening concert; *The Guardian*, 20 October 1858, 816.
[7] Thomas Stephens, Liverpool accountant.
[8] See 5 Sept. 58.
[9] Frederick Phillips, London solicitor.
[10] Sir John *Young (see 16 May 26) was lord high commissioner of Ionian islands 1855—25 January 1859. Gladstone was technically commissioner extraordinary 6 November 1858–25 January 1859.
[11] Start of T. *Carlyle, *History of Frederick II, called the Great*, 6 v. (1858–65).

20. Wed. X

Wrote to C.G.—Sir E.B. Lytton (2)—Sir J. Graham—Scotts (2)— Jas
Watson—Rev Mr Brown—F.A. Hanbury[1]—Mr Lawn—M. Bratiano &
copy—E. Lovell—Duchess of Sutherland. Saw Freshfields—Johnson
Longden & Co—Mr [Daniel] Gurney (Overends)—Ld Carnarvon[2]—Mr
Grogan 10–12—Rigby: and another[R]. Finished Duvergier Vol I.

21. Th. X

Wrote to Mr W. Moates[3]—H. Hoare—H.G. Warren[4]—A. Panizzi (2)—
Rev G. Ainslie—J. Dangerfield[5]—G.C. Brodrick[6]—Rev. E. Dodd[7]—J.E.
Kempe—C.G.—Mr D. Gurney—H.N. Sealy[8]—W. Chambres.[9] China pur-
chases. Read Q.R. on Transl. of Horace[10]—Ed. R. on WEG's Homer[11]—
Chr. Rememb. on do.[12] Potter on Reform[13]—Milne on Subscription.[14] Saw
Aunt J.—Mr H. Merritt—Scotts and E. Lovell: in whose case good was I
hope at last done[R].

22. Fr. [Hawarden]

Wrote to Mr H. Hoare—W. Fenwick—Rev Mr Kempe (2)—W. Rawson—
J.N.G.—Editor of Times—Rev G.F. Kelly[15]—Butler of ChCh[16]—Archdn.
Hale—[9th] Ld Haddington. Saw Sir E.B. Lytton—bis—Mr J. Murray.
Shop business & calls. Read Gill's Poems[17]—Off by Mail at 8 PM. &
reached Hn. at 3 A.M. of

23. Sat.

Conv. with C. on I[onian] I[slands] matters & then to bed. Pleasant greet-
ings from the children—visited the Church, & the (Rake) borehole. We
discussed further the proposal now before me—& its domestic bearings.

---

[1] Francis Alfred Hanbury, Queens', Cambridge, later a barrister, wrote about his
fa.'s death; see 15 Nov. 28.

[2] *Carnarvon played an important role in Gladstone's appointment: see Morley, i. 594.

[3] Possibly William Moates, accountant and arbitrator in Moorgate Street.

[4] Henry George Warren kept a lodging house in Gloucester Street; perhaps Rigby's
home?

[5] Perhaps John Howell Dangerfield, b. 1825?; priest without living 1853.

[6] George Charles Brodrick, 1831–1903; fellow of Merton, Oxford, 1855, warden 1881;
barrister, contested several seats as a liberal; strong liberal-unionist propagandist.

[7] Edward Dodd, d. 1868; vicar of St. Giles, Cambridge, from 1844; convocationalist.

[8] Henry Nicholas Sealy, wrote *Treatise on coins, currency and banking* (1858).

[9] Liverpool printer.

[10] *Quarterly Review*, civ. 325 (October 1858).

[11] *Edinburgh Review*, cviii. 502 (October 1858); [H. *Merivale] attacked Gladstone for
lack of critical awareness: 'we cannot regard them as anything but monuments of
ingenuity wastefully expended'.

[12] *Christian Remembrancer*, xxxvi. 331 (October 1858).

[13] E. R. Potter, 'Considerations on the questions of the adoption of a constitution and
extension of suffrage in Rhode Island' (1842).

[14] R. M. Milne, *Clerical oaths and their equivalents a hindrance to Unity* (1858).

[15] George Fitzroy Kelly, Trinity, Dublin; incumbent of Pembroke Docks chapel 1844;
published on bp. *Butler.

[16] See 19 Dec. 51.

[17] T. H. Gill, *The anniversaries: poems in commemoration of great men and great events*
(1858).

Wrote to Duke of Newcastle—W.H.G.—E. of Aberdeen—Robn. G.—
Watson & Smith—Dr Sewell—Ld Stanley—Mr Murray. Read Daru's
Venice[1] & various books on the I. Islands.

24. 21 S. Trin.

Ch. mg & evg. Read Mansell's B. Lectures[2]—Bp of Salisbury's Charge[3]—
Bp of Norwich's Charge[4]—Moore on Influences of the Soul.[5] Further
conv. with C. & S. resp. the proposal. Wrote to Messrs. Hatchard—Mr A.
Panizzi.

25. M.

Ch. 8½ A.M. Wrote to S.E.G.—Sir J.T. Coleridge. Visited the boreholes.
Read Finlay's Greece[6]—Apollodorus (Bibliotheca)[7]—Apollon[ius] Rho-
dius.[8]

26. T.

Ch. 8½ A.M. Wrote to Sir W. Farquhar—Mr Lacaita—Sir E. Lytton (part).
Spent the day principally on Bradshaw & the Handbooks. As I reflected
more, I became more disinclined to refuse. Read Lewis's Rom. Hist.[9]—
Rousseau's Letter to Dalembert[10]—Guizot's Memoires.[11]

27. Wed.

Ch 8½ A.M. Wrote to Sir E. Lytton (finished)—Mr Thos Ramsay—Sidney
Herbert—Latin with Agnes. Saw John Eve—Taylor—Mr Silline[12]—Mr H.
Hoare. Dined at the Rectory. Read Göthe's Faust—Rousseau to Dalembert
—Lewis on Rom. Hist. Busy with selecting books, & the fainter prepara-
tions. Made up my mind to go, if there be no personal obstacle *ex parte*.
Saw Mr G. Burnett—Young.

28. SS. Simon & Jude.

Church 8½ A.M. Wrote to Duke of Argyll—Sir E.B. Lytton—Jas Watson.
Attended Mr Hoare's clerical and lay meeting: I do not anticipate much

---

[1] P. A. N. B. Daru, *Histoire de la république de Venise*, 8v. (1821).
[2] H. L. *Mansel, *The limits of religious thought examined in eight lectures* (1858);
argued only supernatural revelation revealed God's nature; denounced by J. S. *Mill and
F. D. *Maurice.
[3] By W. K. *Hamilton (1858).
[4] By J. T. *Pelham (1858).
[5] G. Moore, *The power of the Soul over the body, considered in relation to health and morals*
(1845).
[6] G. *Finlay, *Greece under the Romans* (1844); see Morley, iii. 425.
[7] A compilation of myths wrongly attributed to Apollodorus of Athens.
[8] Probably his *Argonautica*, epic on Jason.
[9] See 27 June 57.
[10] *A letter from M. Rousseau . . . to M. D'Alembert concerning the effects of theatrical
entertainments on the manners of mankind* (1759).
[11] F. P. G. Guizot, *Mémoires pour servir à l'histoire de mon temps*, 8v. (1858–67).
[12] Untraced.

from his present plan.[1] Afterwards Henry [Glynne] dined near forty of us. Saw Mr Burnett—Latin with Agnes. Read Rousseau—Lewis on Rom. History.

29. Fr.

Ch. 8½ AM. Wrote to Mr W.W. Old[2]—Sir S. Scott and Co—Mr Henry Smith[3]—W. Hampton. Church Rate meeting 2–5. Saw Mr Burnett— Latin with Agnes—Read Goethe's Faust—Rousseau on the Theatre.[4]

30. Sat.

Ch. 8¼ AM. Wrote to Duchess of Sutherland (2)—Jas Watson—Sir J. Graham—Robn. G.—J.G. Lacaita—T.G.—Rev. S. Stothert—J.N.G.— Vice Chancr. Oxford—T.H. Gill[5]—Sir W. Heathcote—A. Panizzi—M. Van de Weyer—Rev. J. Stuart[6]—Sir Edw. Lytton—Rev. W. Elwin— Earl of Aberdeen—Rev. F. Meyrick—City Remembrancer. Saw Mr Burnett—Mr Littleboy. Worked on Odyssey & made the topographical extracts.[7] Finished & sent off the Loch inscription to the Duchess. Attended the Ch. Rate poll & put in my (disputed) vote. Latin with Agnes. Visited bore-holes. Busy with various arrangements for departure (wh was decided by a Telegram in aftn.) from 5 P.M. to 3 A.M. Read Goethe's Faust.

31. 22 S. Trin.

Ch. mg & evg. Wrote to Sir E. Lytton—W. Hampton—H.J.G.—J.R. Hope Scott—Mr Mansell.[8] Read Mansell's B. Lectures—Bp of Man's Letter & Charges[9]—Xt. Rem. on Scots Eccl. Affairs[10]—Liddell's Letter to Bp of London.[11] Sore throat hanging about me.

Monday Nov. One 58. [London] All Saints.

Kept my bed in mg. Wrote to Archdeacon Allen—Mrs Bennett—Lord Brougham—Willy—Sec. S.E. Co. Saw Mr Burnett. Packing & a variety of domestic arrangements. 3½–10 Hn. to C.H.T. Read Bright's speech on Foreign Policy: alike powerful & one-sided.[12] Saw A. Kinnaird—Worked on papers. Missed Stapylton[R].

[1] Henry Hoare (see 2 Mar. 52) was on tour promoting his synodal plans.
[2] William Watkins Old of Monmouth, in correspondence on Homer (Hawn P).
[3] Art dealer in New Bond Street.
[4] See 26 Oct. 58.
[5] Thomas Howard Gill, 1836–94; priest on Isle of Man 1859–63, in Lancashire 1865–81; chaplain in Paris 1883–90; wrote popular theology.
[6] Perhaps James Hilman Stuart, d. 1885; rector of Ampton, Suffolk, from 1841.
[7] Probably on Ionian Islands.
[8] Henry Longueville *Mansel, 1820–79; fellow of St. John's Oxford, 1839–55, 1864–7; Waynflete professor at Oxford 1859; dean of St. Paul's from 1868; see 24 Oct. 58.
[9] H. Powys, 'A pastoral letter to his congregation' (1848) and his 'Charge' (1857).
[10] *Christian Remembrancer*, xxxvi. 431 (October 1858).
[11] R. Liddell, 'A letter to the lord bishop of London on confession and absolution with special reference to the case of . . . A. Poole' (1858).
[12] Speech of 29 October, linking foreign policy and franchise reform; see G. M. Trevelyan, *Life of . . . Bright* (1913), 273.

2. T.

Wrote to A. Gordon—Sir J. Young—J.P. Lacaita—C.G.—D. of Newcastle
— M. Van de Weyer (kept back). Saw Ld Carnarvon—& Sir F. Rogers—
R. Phillimore—Panizzi *cum* Sig. Salvagnoli[1]—Sir E. Lytton—Ld Aberdeen
—Saw Lightfoot—Harrington[R]. Shopping &c. Dined with Panizzi &
S[alvagnoli]: most interesting & agreeable, malgré cough & headache.
Read I.I. papers.

3. Wed.

Wrote to M. Delfosse[2]—Ld Bathurst[3]—Mr Ponsonby—Mr J. Mills[4]—
M. V. de Wyer (2) (one altered)—Robn. G.—Mrs Talbot—Agnes G.—Mr
Haughton—V.C. Oxford—Ct. Bernstorff. Dined with the Wortleys. Read
Ionian Island papers. Saw R. Phillimore—Mr Grogan—J.S. Wortley—Mr
Wolf[5]—Col. Talbot[6]—Sir E. Lytton—Ld Aberdeen—Hon A. Gordon—
R. Lawley—Jane Wortley—Mr Lacaita[7]—L. Papasso.[8]

4. Th. X

Wrote to Sir E. Lytton—Johnson L. & Co—Dss of Sutherland—Ld
Carnarvon—Scotts (2)—Ld Chancellor—S.E. Gladstone—Bp of London—
Jas Watson—Mr Goldwin Smith—Rev Mr Stone[9]—Hon A. Kinnaird—
O.B. Cole.—Saw Sir H. Holland—Sir E. Lytton—Ld Carnarvon—Sir F.
Rogers—Mr Wolf—Mr Lacaita—Hon A. Gordon—Jas S. Wortley—Sir H.
Storks.[10] Dined with the Wortleys. Saw one of the most singular cases that
ever came in my way [R]. Read New Monthly on my Book.[11]

5. Fr. X

Wrote to Miss Syfret[12]—Scotts (2)—Mr Lacaita—Willy. Off early to breakfast with Sir H. Holland for conv. on I.I.[13]—then to Ld Aberdeen—A.

[1] Vincenzo Salvagnole, Piedmontese politician, propagandist and barrister, introduced
by Massari (Add MS 44390, f. 143).
[2] Maurice Delfosse, 1st secretary to Belgian embassy.
[3] Henry George Bathurst, 1790–1866; 4th Earl Bathurst 1834.
[4] Perhaps John Hillman Mills, d. 1872; St. John's, Cambridge; barrister from 1843.
[5] (Sir) Henry Drummond Charles *Wolff, 1830–1908; *Lytton's sec. 1858; as sec. to
Ionian Islands commissioner (*Storks) 1859–63 arranged islands' transfer to Greece;
tory M.P. Christchurch 1874–80, Portsmouth 1880–5; executed many diplomatic missions in Levant; member of 'fourth party' in 1880s.
[6] See 9 Dec. 52. He was then *Derby's private secretary and, as *quondam* Ionian
resident, briefed Gladstone on the islands.
[7] Persuading him to go with him to Ionia; Lacaita, 109.
[8] Unidentified; probably an Ionian.
[9] William Stone, d. 1877; rector of St. Paul's, Shoreditch, from 1858 and chaplain to a
destitute refuge at Dalston.
[10] Sir Henry Knight *Storks, 1811–74; soldier; sec. for military correspondence at war
office 1857–9; succ. Gladstone as commissioner to Ionia 1859–63; governed colonies
1864–6; under-sec. at war office 1867; helped *Cardwell's reforms; liberal M.P. Ripon
1871–4.
[11] *New Monthly Magazine*, cxiv. 300 (November 1858).
[12] The Gladstones' German governess 1857–65.
[13] *Holland often toured the Mediterranean, and published *Travels in the Ionian
Isles* (1815).

Gordon—Sir S. Scott & Co—Shopping—& by Rail to Windsor where I kissed hands & had an audience: saw Stephy—saw Lady Newry—Then to C.O. saw Mr Wolf—& examined I.I. Books at C.O. Dined with the Wortleys. Saw Hicks[R]. Worked on preparations for journey until late.

6. Sat.

Wrote to Sir S. Scott & Co—G. Moffatt MP.—C. Eborall (S.E. Co)[1]— A. Hayward—J.P. Lacaita—S. Warren MP.—Landlord H[otel] de L['Europe] (Brussels)—Ld Brougham—A. Panizzi—Watson & Smith (papers)—A.B. Cochrane—Col. Talbot (do)—Mr Westell—Rev W. Rawson —P.F. Darton[2]—Freshfield & Co—Jas Fettis—Archdn. Hale—Hon J. Fane[3]—J.R. Godley. Saw Sir C. Trevelyan—Hon. A. Gordon—Sir J. Pakington—Mr Wolf—Mr W. Grogan—Earl of Derby—R. Phillimore— Ld J. Manners. Arranged with Courier. Plans for new carpets. Much shopping, putting away & packing. Read Talbots MSS.[4] Finished a long day at 3 AM.

7. 23 S. Trin.

St James's & H.C. mg.—Wells St aft. MS on Ep. aloud in evg. Wrote to Bp of Nelson[5]—Ld Malmesbury—Dean Ramsay—Mr J. Stuart—B. Benjamin—Rev M. MacColl—E. Lovell. Saw Sir W. Farquhar—Ld Ashburton —Ld Aberdeen—The Wortleys—Mr G. Sandars—R. Phillimore. Finished packing & arrangements.

8. M. [Brussels]

Left home before 8 & reached Brussels (H. de l'Europe) at 9.20 257 m. A middling passage: Agnes & I were sick with all the servants: but by dint of immense precautions mine was slight, as nature made Agnes's. Very good hotel.

9. T.

Wrote to Consul at Trieste[6]—Sir John Young. Called at the Palace &c. Attended the opening of the Chambers. Visited the Cathedral. Also the Picture Gallery. Saw M. Niewenhuis's Pictures.[7] Went a good deal over the town. Dined with the King[8] at Laeken:[9] & had much conv. with H.M. &

[1] Manager of the S.E. Railway.
[2] Probably of the booksellers; see 30 Dec. 42.
[3] Julian Henry Charles *Fane, 1827–70, 5th s. of 11th earl of Westmoreland; attaché and embassy sec. in sundry countries, including Austria during Gladstone's visit (17 Nov. 58); friend and collaborator with *Lytton.
[4] See 9 Dec. 52; after being *Derby's secretary he was British resident in Cephalonia 1855–8.
[5] Edmund *Hobhouse; see 15 Mar. 53.
[6] H. Raven.
[7] See 22 June 58.
[8] See 6 Feb. 32. A. H. *Gordon, Gladstone's official secretary in Ionia, was badly late for the dinner, causing a lingering coolness between them; see J. B. Conacher, 'A visit to the Gladstones in 1894', Victorian Studies, ii. 155.
[9] The royal palace on the Schoonenberg, with a view of Brussels from the north.

the Duc de Brabant[1] between whom I sat. Read Perrens' Savonarola[2]—& the Seconde Incarnation.[3]

10. Wed. [*Brunswick*]

9 AM–2 A.M. 385 miles or thereabouts to Brunswick (Hotel de l'Angleterre, good). At Cöln we went to see the Cathedral wh now as ever rather disappoints me.[4] Read A. Monod's La Femme.[5]

11. Th. [*Berlin*]

We went 150 m. by Magdeburg to Berlin. In the morning we went about Brunswick[6] with much delight & saw the Martinuss Kirche, Dom, Katherine, & Andreas.[7] All have fine points, especially the outer Chapel (octagon) of the Dom. Also the fountain, the Rath Haus, the Byzantine Lion.[8] The whole character of the town too is very characteristic & archaic, the Hayhouse ([blank]) best of all. At Magdeburg A. Gordon & I spent 3 hours, saw the exterior of the various Churches, & the whole Dom:[9] the last with great delight for itself & the objects it contains.[10] The old Romaic work is most interesting & the dimensions of the centre aisle must be nearly those of Westmr. Abbey but the upper choir work is not so fine. The pulpit, font, Otho's tomb, Abps tomb 1495, & many more objects well deserve notice. We went on & rejoined the party at 10 PM. Worked on Eton Grammar, moved by its scandalous & innumerable errors.[11] Read Travelling Books.— Veneziann in Morea.[12]

12. Fr.

Wrote to Scotts. Visited the China Manufactory[13] & was desillusionné as to the various objects in the London market. We went to the Palace & left our names. Everything shut to day on account of the Elections:[14] but Berlin is chiefly seen in externals of which there are a great mass tho' not with first rate interest. In this way we profited a good deal. I went to the Schauspielhause: & thought rather poorly of the tone & the performances.[15] Read Petrizzopuli's Ital. tract—do's English[16]—also Papanicolas No. 1.[17]

[1] See 18 June 58.
[2] F. T. Perrens, *Jérôme Savonarole*, 2v. (1854).
[3] Perhaps 'The second coming of the Lord; the true hope of believers' (1834).
[4] But see 15 Aug. 38 for an earlier view of Cologne cathedral.
[5] By Adolphe Monod (1848).
[6] 35 miles E. of Hanover; then capital of its own scattered duchy.
[7] Eleventh and twelfth century churches in the city centre.
[8] Byzantine statue erected in 1166 by Henry the Lion in the square N. of the cathedral.
[9] Solid Romanesque structure begun by Henry the Lion; restored 1869.
[10] Amongst many, the coffin of Queen Caroline, which used to bear her dictated plate: 'Murdered Queen of England'.
[11] Apparently a plan for a new grammar: Add MS 44747, f. 192.
[12] Not found.
[13] The royal porcelain manufactory in the Friedrichstrasse.
[14] Consequent on resignation of Manteuffel's ministry; the liberals won.
[15] The Königliches Schauspielhaus presented alternate French and German plays.
[16] D. Petritzopoulos, 'Saggio storico sulle prime età dell'Isola di Leucadia nell'Jonio' (1814); English tract untraced.
[17] G. D. Papanikolas, *Usque adeo? or What may be said for the Ionian people* (1853); letters to British statesmen.

13. Sat. [Dresden]

To meet C.s wishes she and I staid till 7P.M. & reached Dresden at 12.45 AM. We had a most rich treat through the kindness of Dr Waagen[1] in the Picture Gallery till one o'clock. It would take long to put down all I wish to remember. I then saw the drawings & majolica: also the exceeding beautiful 'Praying Boy'.[2] We walked, and bought old China & dined at the Stadt Rom a very good Restaurant.

14. 24 S. Trin. X

Wrote to Dr Kleum—Dean Ramsay—Sir Edw. Lytton. Mr Lacaita overtook us. Prelim. conversation with him on our duties. Visited various Churches: various points observable. The Kreuz, the Frauenk[irche] & the R.C. are good in bad styles.[3] Saw one[R]. English Ch. mg (a very good congregation) & aft.[4] Read Vie de M. Arnauld[5]—Jerome Savonarola. We find the Saxe very good; but the idea of a public mission, do what we will, causes an increase of expence.

15. M.

Wrote to Captain Glasse[6]—Mr G. Burnett (Post & Telegraph)—C.A. Wood. Robertson's birthday—God bless him. Finished Usque Adeò—Read Jervis's Corfú.[7] Finished Papanicolas—Read Jervis's Hist. Corfú. 10–11 The Library:[8] 11–12 The Porcelain:[9] 12–3 The Gallery:[10] 3–4¾ The China Shops[11]—an active, most interesting, & very full day. The Porcelain Collection gave me much knowledge: but the great object, the San Sisto,[12] towers over & absorbs everything else. I might mention many pictures: the J. Van Eyck is delightful: the Rubenses very strong, especially St Jerome.[13] Mr Lacaita shows the finest intelligence. In the Porzellan there is almost nothing except Oriental & Dresden: but both there are wonderful espcy. the first wh is almost boundless. We all have colds from stove within & frost without.

[1] See 26 May 57.
[2] Giovanni Santi, Raphael's father: Madonna with saints, and a boy praying, said to represent Raphael.
[3] The Frauenkirche (Lutheran) had theatrical galleries; the Hofkirche, like the Frauenkirche, eighteenth century Italian style, was heavily decorated.
[4] Temporarily housed; rebuilt in Wiener Strasse 1869.
[5] See 21 Mar. 58.
[6] Frederick Henry Hastings Glasse, d. 1884; captain R.N. 1846; captained *Terrible* on which the Gladstones sailed to Ionia; admiral 1877.
[7] H. J. W. Jervis, *History of the island of Corfu, and of the republic of the Ionian Islands* (1852).
[8] In the eighteenth century Japanese palace.
[9] Some 90,000 pieces, chiefly Meissen, Chinese and Japanese porcelain.
[10] The picture gallery, then the finest in Germany, was housed in the rococo Zwinger.
[11] In the Augustus Strasse, often peddling forgeries, according to Murray's *Handbook for Northern Germany* (1877 ed.), 314.
[12] Raphael's 'Madonna di San Sisto': Sir D. *Wilkie thought 'the head of the Virgin is perhaps nearer the perfection of female beauty and elegance than anything in painting'.
[13] Highly finished work of Rubens' Roman period.

16. T. [Prague]

We went to the Armoury:[1] then 2° to the Gallery where we enlarged our knowledge & saw the San Sisto in new glory from a better light. Also Correggio's Ant. Then to the China & settling at the Hotel. Off at 12.45: reached Prague ½ hour late. Walk in the town: view from the Bridge by night: not clear but enough to show its peculiar character. The first half of our way from Dresden was beautiful thro' the Saxon Switz:[2] We dined well at Bodenberg.[3] Read Murray—Jervis's Hist Corfú. We were at the Goldener Engel.

17. Wed. [On train]

We went to the singularly dismal but curious Synagogue & Friedhof of the Jews[4]—to the Theinkirche & the Cathedral: debated the Inscription on the Radetzky monument with A. Gordon. Wrote to Mr Burnett. Off at 7 for Vienna travelling all night. Read Jervis Hist. Corfú—Ildegonda.[5]

18. Th. [Vienna]

We reached Erzherzog Karl[6] past eight: train late, as seems common. We went to the Grand Cathedral:[7] to the Augustinuskirche:[8] to the Picture Gallery for 2½ hours wh is very good though below what we have seen.[9] C. & I to the Theatre in evg with Ld Dunmore.[10] I sought for old Vienna China & traversed the mazy town in all possible directions. There is immense historic interest in the Glacis.[11] I dined at a Restaurant & read the papers. Read Murray's H[and] Book—Jervis Hist. Corfu—Ildegonda of Grossi. Saw Mr Dunlop—Ld Dunmore.

19. Fr.

Wrote to Duke of Newcastle—Sir Edw. Lytton—Mr G.P. James.[12] We gave up our journey in consequence of Ld A. Loftus's[13] desire to see me.

[1] Then also housed in the Zwinger.

[2] Saxon Switzerland, the mountains on the Saxon–Bohemian frontier.

[3] Bodenbach, the Austrian frontier stop.

[4] In the old town E. of the Moldau river: the chief synagogue for the large, almost completely segregated, Jewish community was twelfth century; the oldest tomb in the vast Friedhof said to be 606 A.D. George *Eliot visited them earlier in 1858, observing for *Daniel Deronda* and *The Lifted Veil*.

[5] T. Grossi, *Ildegonda* (1859 ed.).

[6] Hotel used by most wealthy English travellers in Kärnthner Strasse in the fortified inner city of Vienna.

[7] St. Stephen's gothic cathedral, by the hotel.

[8] At the S. of the fortified city.

[9] In the upper Belvedere, containing the imperial collection.

[10] Charles Adolphus Murray, 1841–1907; 7th earl of Dunmore 1845; soldier; wrote on Tibet; perhaps in Vienna with his uncle, (Sir) Charles Augustus Murray, (see 26 Aug. 42) envoy to Saxony 1859.

[11] The open, downwards sloping area encircling the city walls.

[12] G.P.R. *James, novelist; then consul in Venice.

[13] Lord Augustus William Frederick Spencer *Loftus, 1817–1904, 2nd s. of 2nd marquess of Ely; envoy extraordinary to Austria 1858–60; held many other diplomatic posts; governed New South Wales 1879–85. Loftus told him of the theft and publication in London of the despatch of 10 June 1857 of Sir J. *Young, the Ionian lord high commissioner, proposing transfer of all or most of the islands to Greece; see Morley, i. 601.

Saw Ld A. Loftus—Count Buol[1]—Prince Metternich[2]—Baron Bruck,[3] & Mr T.O.M. Bird (Times Corresp.)[4] Dined at Ld A. Loftus's. The Opera (for 20 m, quite enough) afterwards. Packing &c. Finished Jervis's Corfú. Found the Modern Vienna China & got some specimens.

20. Sat. [Trieste]

Up at 5: off at 6.10 to Trieste by what is I suppose the most beautiful & wonderful railway in the world. Its especial glories are the Semmering pass & the ascent of the Saave: then the descent upon Trieste but this arriving at 11 P.M. we saw imperfectly. We were met by the Consul[5] who had arranged all for us: & we enjoyed an admirable Austrian Band near our windows till almost 12. Wrote confidential Dispatch.[6] Read Mustoxidi[7]— Ildegonda.

21. 25 S. Trin. [On ship]

Wrote to Sir E. Lytton. We had prayers (full) in the hotel. (on other days short). Saw Captain Glasse—The British Consul. Read Savonarola. Visited the very interesting Cathedral: wh founded on a Pagan temple seems to have been enlarged into the basilican form under Byzantine influences.[8] Walk with Mr Lacaita in the town & on its eminences. We embarked on board the Terrible[9] at 8: sailed before midnight. The sea not over good: but the ship showed the utmost solidity. The Inn good but very dear.

22. M.

We came early to Pola,[10] & were greeted by the Admiral's Aid de Camp appointed our guide. We landed, visited the Admiral who said Austria had great plans at Pola: then went to the Amphitheatre—temple (so called) of Diana—the double gate (so called)—the triumphal arch—& the old Gk Ch, now a flour-store with cloister rose window & doorway.[11] A modern Gk Ch is

[1] Count Karl Ferdinand Buol-Schauenstein, 1797–1865; Austrian diplomat; foreign minister 1852–9; Gladstone told him he had no title to arrange either a 'total or partial annexation of the Islands to Greece' (to both of which Buol told him Austria was opposed) and that the theft and publication of Young's despatch was accidental (confidential despatch of next day, and cabinet paper, in Lytton Papers D/EK 011).

[2] Klement Furst von Metternich, 1773–1859; Austrian statesman, took no part in politics after 1848.

[3] Karl Ludwig von Bruck, 1798–1860; Austrian diplomat; minister of finance 1855; suicide after the 1859 Italian crisis.

[4] T. O'M. Bird, Times correspondent in Vienna from early 1850s; his liberal despatches much annoyed the Austrian government.

[5] H. Raven.

[6] See previous day.

[7] A. Mustoxidi, Notizie per servire alla Storia Corcirese dai tempi eroici fino al secolo xii (1804).

[8] On a hill near the castle; the tower reputedly stands on a temple to Jupiter; fifth century basilica, substantially added to in the fourteenth.

[9] The naval paddle-wheel steam frigate, with 21 guns, placed at the mission's disposal.

[10] On the tip of the Istrian peninsula, now in Yugoslavia, with almost land-locked harbour; developed in the 1860s as a large Austrian naval base.

[11] Pola was reputedly founded by the Greek Colchians, destroyed by Caesar and rebuilt by Augustus, destroyed again by the Venetians; the attribution of its buildings is therefore, as Gladstone suggests, probable only at best.

shut (within 20 years past) for want of congregation. The fortress is Venetian. Returned on board at one. Sailed at 3. The harbour is a noble one: & many forts are already raised. The day continued favourable. We made out to sea. Read Mustoxidi—Savonarola—Murray's (Bowen's) Handbook.[1] Bethought me of an official Address to the Senate.[2]

23. T.

More sea: I kept my room. The servants were overset. I rose & managed dinner, having escaped illness. Wrote dft of Address—Read Handbook—Mustoxidi—Savonarola. We have found the officers very agreeable: noticing especially the master, & then Lieut St John.[3] We saw Gargano[4] (of the Querceta): then struck across from the Italian side.

24. Wed. [Corfu]

The morning brought us the sight of the grand Acroceraunian range:[5] with brilliant sun & mild air. Then Corfu: which I do not think is like a ῥινὸν from the North: but Homer probably meant a *mirage* wh is common.[6] We sailed on tracking the land with glasses all the way & reached Corfú between 11 & 12. Landed with military honours and other forms at one.[7] Presented to the Senators & their Secretaries by my old friend Sir J. Young. Four hours with him on Ionian politics. We had a dinner party in the evening. Began to arrange & settle in our room:[8] & to turn my address into Italian. Wrote to Sir E. B. Lytton (disp.) Read C.O. printed papers.

25. Th.

Wrote to Sir E.B. Lytton.[9] Read C.O. papers—Ld C. Fitzroy's Letters.[10] Paid visits in uniform (after consn.) to the Pres. of the Senate[11] & the Archbishop of Corfú.[12] Saw likewise Baron Prokesch (en route)[13]—Austrian

[1] Murray's *Handbook for travellers in Greece, describing the Ionian islands* . . . (3rd ed. 1854), revised by Sir G. F. *Bowen (see 4 May 47) who as chief sec. in the Ionian islands 1854–9 recommended union of southern islands with Greece and was regarded as inspirer of *Young's despatch of 10 June 1857.

[2] See 26 Nov. 58.

[3] Charles Orlando Henry Perkins St. John, lieutenant R.N. 1846; special messenger.

[4] The mountains forming the spur of the Italian 'boot'.

[5] Mountains in Albania.

[6] *Odyssey* 5. 281: disputed passage; ῥινὸν variously given as ox-skin, hence shield, or mist, hence, in Gladstone's view, mirage.

[7] He was received with a 17 round salute, but did not know how to inspect the guard of honour; see Magnus, 136.

[8] The Gladstones stayed in the Palace for the first few days of their visit, then in lodgings.

[9] *PP* 1861 lxvii. 71.

[10] Lord C. *Fitzroy, *Letters . . . and documents . . . on past and recent events in the Ionian Islands* (1850); claims British abuses there; Gladstone's copy is marked 'worth perusing'.

[11] Sir Dionides Flamburiari, K.C.M.G. 1857; the order was created 1818 as an honour for Ionians and Britons serving there; appointments to it were suspended 1864, and it was refounded 1866; all pro-British Ionians of consequence were K.C.M.G. or G.C.M.G.

[12] Athenasius, metropolitan of Corfu, moderately hostile to the British.

[13] Baron Anton Prokesch-Osten, 1795–1876; Austrian diplomat, archaeologist, traveller and writer on the Levant.

Consul[1]—Count Bulgari[2]—Count Dusmani[3]—Dr Machariotti[4]—Count Salomons[5]—the President—Sir G. Bowen. Sir J. Young another 2 hours. He is good and judges justly but without force of character: Lady Y. not wise. Walk with Mr L. Dinner party in evg.

26. Frid.

Wrote dft dispatch to Sir E. Lytton. Wrote to Count Flamburiari—Cav. Mustoxidi.[6] Wrote out my Address to the Senate after discussing the language with Mr L[acaita] who had corrected it: & delivered it under salute in due form at a meeting at 1 P.M.[7] Walk with Sir J. Young. Saw Sir G. Bowen—Capt Glasse—Cav. Mustoxidi—Sir P. Braila[8]—Sig. Foresti[9]—The Regent (Valabili?).[10] Dinner party in evg. Found the town very curious & in creditable condition. Read Curcumelli's Reply[11]—C.O. Printed Papers: other MSS.[12]

27. Sat.

Wrote to Sir S. Scott & Co.—G. Burnett Esq—Earl of Carnarvon. We had a beautiful ride. Read Curcumelli (Ward)—Ld Lauderdale's Speech.[13] Saw Sir John Young—The Archbishop (in uniform)—The Resident of Cerigo (Col. Harvest)[14]—The Pres. of the Assembly (Count Flamburiari.)—Gen. Buller[15]—Lady Bowen[16]—Sir G. Bowen.

28. Adv. S.

Garrison Ch mg & evg. Conv. with Agnes on Gospel. Saw Rev. S. Clark[17]

[1] Not found.
[2] Spiridon Bulgari; member of the assembly; strongly pro-union with Greece. Almost everyone of consequence in Ionia called himself Count; very few had any real title to do so.
[3] Sir Antonio Lefcochilo Dusmani, d. 1889; held sundry official posts; secretary of Ionian senate 1853; K.C.M.G. 1849.
[4] Dr. Macheriotti, senator for the minor Ionian islands.
[5] D. Salomons, G.C.M.G., senator of Zante.
[6] Sir Andrea Mustoxidi, 1785–1860; sometime president of the legislative assembly; historiographer of the islands and chancellor of the university; K.C.M.G. 1857.
[7] Denying that *Young's dispatch of 10 June 1857 represented British policy: PP 1861 lxvii. 73.
[8] Sir Pietro Braila, secretary to the financial department in Ionia.
[9] Dr. Typaldo Foresti, who ed. E. Lunzi's Della condizione politica delle Isole Ionie (1858).
[10] Elias Vassilachi, regent of Corfu. Each of the seven islands had an Ionian regent and a British resident.
[11] Untraced.
[12] Queries for reform in Ionia: Add MS 44747, f. 204.
[13] J. Maitland, Lord Lauderdale, 'Substance of the Earl of Lauderdale's speech in the House of Lords . . . explanatory of Sir T. Maitland's conduct as Lord High Commissioner of the Ionian Islands' (1820).
[14] Edward Douglas Harvest of 97th foot, later in Australia; major general 1881; d. ca. 1895.
[15] Commanding forces in the islands; see 12 July 55.
[16] Diamantina, da. of Count Candiano Roma, former president of the senate, owner of most of Zante and resident of Ithaca.
[17] Gladstone's assistant in the Bedfordbury project (see 6 Apr. 49), now chaplain in Corfu.

—Mr Swinton[1]—Count Theotoky[2]—Ly. Hunter[3]—Sig Doria Prosclendi.[4] Visited the Cathedral—S. Spiridion—Chiesa τῶν στερεώτων[5]—S. Antonio. Most kindly received. The priests at the two first showed me the mortal remains of S. Theodora & S. Spiridion. Read Jerome Savonarola[6]— Encore quelque mots.[7]

29. M.

Wrote to D. of Newcastle—Sir E. Bulwer Lytton—Capt. Gladstone RN.— Maj. Gen. Portlock[8]—W.H. Gladstone. Saw Cav. Mustoxidi *cum* Papa Eustachio Valismá[9]—Sir D. Curcumelli cum Sir J.Y.—Sir J. Young— General Buller—Colonel Ormsby[10]—Mr Sargent (judge)[11]—Sig. Zambelli (judge)[12]—The President. Ball in the evg. With huge difficulty I got through a quadrille. Read I.I. papers. Held a levee at 11 A.M. attended by ab. 350 notwithstanding fearful weather.

30. T.

Wrote to Sir H. Verney—Rev. Mr Shannon—and minutes. Sir G. Bowen kindly went over the articles in Greek papers with me: an excellent lesson. Spent most of the day in long conferences with Cav. Curcumelli[13]—H.H. The President—Dr Nap. Zambelli—Saw likewise Sir J. Young—Sig. Foresti—Walk with C. Attended Ly Youngs[14] evg reception. To the Opera at 8¾: it was well got up and sung. Read Sir T. Maitland's Addresses.[15]

Corfú Wed. Dec. One, 1858.

Wrote to Cav. Mustoxidi—Sir E. Lytton. Saw Sir J. Young bis—Dr Padovan[16]—Dr Curis[17]—M. Vitali[18]—Mr Lacaita & A. G[ordon] on I.I.

[1] Unidentified.
[2] A former president of the Ionian senate, which had a right of veto on the assembly.
[3] Constance, *née* Bosanquet, m. 1852 Sir Claudius Stephen Paul Hunter, 1825–90, 2nd bart. 1852; apparently touring the islands.
[4] Stelio Doria Prossalendi, magistrate in charge of religion, public morals and political economy.
[5] 'of the wall builders'.
[6] See 28 Nov. 58.
[7] 'Deux mots sur les finances de la Grèce' (1856); copy in Hawn P.
[8] Joseph Ellison *Portlock, 1794–1864; retired as major-general in R.E., 1857; zoologist and surveyor; had sent observations on Ionia (Add MS 44390, f. 209).
[9] Not further identified.
[10] John William Ormsby, d. 1869; colonel 1858; in charge of artillery in Ionia; commandant of Woolwich academy 1867.
[11] (Sir) Charles Sargent, 1821–1900; member of Ionian council of justice 1858–60; chief justice there 1860–66; judge in Bombay 1866–95.
[12] Dr. N. Temistoc Zambelli, also on the council of justice.
[13] Sir Demetrio Curcumelli; K.C.M.G. 1857; advocate-general of the Ionian islands.
[14] Adelaide, *née* Dalton, m. 1835 Sir J. *Young, 1st Baron Lisgar.
[15] *Substance of Sir Thomas *Maitland's address to the legislative assembly of the Ionian Islands, 4th March 1822* (1822).
[16] Member of the assembly, 'one of the cleverest men in the Chamber' (*PP* 1861 lxvii. 96).
[17] Socrates Curis, president of the assembly in the extraordinary session 1859; favoured union with Greece.
[18] Unidentified.

Constn. Framing statistical queries. Walk alone through the penetralia of the town. Read Strictures on Ld Nugent[1]—Sir C. Napier on I.I.[2] Latin with Agnes. Wrote Sketch of an arrangement for the Islands.[3]

2. Th.

Wrote to Dr Hook—Mad (Marchesa) Ristori[4]—Sir E. Bulwer Lytton—Capt. Glasse C.B. Saw Count Flamburiari—Sir J. Young (on his position &c.)—Dr Lascari[5]—Sig. Polilà[6]—Sig. Giallinà.[7] Read Zambelli's Reply to Curcumelli.[8] Read Sir C. Napier. Dined at General Buller's. Further con-dered my Sketch & gave it to Mr Lacaita. Went with Sig. Doria Prosclendi to see the Platutera Church and Convent:[9] & then walked to Manduchio.[10] The senior priest of the monastic body showed it. I was much pleased with his gentle & modest yet cheerful manners. The house was very clean. 100 to 150 venerable looking books constituted the library. The monks are 20: of whom 2 are priests. They have 7 services daily including a mass: one service at midnight, which all attend. They sleep $3\frac{1}{2}$ hours in summer, 6 hours in winter. They eat no meat: but bread (which seemed very coarse & bitter) with vegetables & fruit: wine four days a week; this I believe out of Lent, or the Lents. In the cell we saw was a bed of board, on it I think a single blanket & a kind of light rug. The severity of the rule causes many to quit. Our friend was 52 but looked 70 & said he suffered from his chest. They labour with their hands. I said all this makes it easier to prepare for death. He replied that Christ gave the injunction to take up the cross & follow Him: and said whosoever loseth his life shall find it. I have not in the Latin countries seen any monastery like this.

3. Fr.

Wrote to Adm. Fanshawe[11]—Sir Thomas Wyse.[12] Walk with Mr Lacaita to Manduchio. Went to the B.V.M. τῶν στερεωτῶν at 5 P.M. to hear the vespers. Saw Count Caruso[13]—Sig Dandolo (the worst yet)[14]—Sig. Foresti—Sig.

[1] Probably 'Remarks on the office of Lord High Commissioner in the Ionian Islands [held by G. N. T. *Grenville, Baron Nugent], in reply to the statements in the "Morning Chronicle"' (1835).
[2] C. J. *Napier, *The Colonies: treating of their value generally—of the Ionian Islands in particular* (1833).
[3] The start of his Report of 28 December 1858.
[4] She toured the Levant in the early 1860s; see *Memoirs . . . of Adelaide Ristori* (1907), 66.
[5] A member of the assembly.
[6] Antonio Polita, assembly member, strongly pro-union.
[7] Untraced.
[8] Untraced.
[9] To the west of the town; with Capodistria's simple tomb.
[10] On the coast to the west of the town.
[11] (Sir) Arthur Fanshawe, 1794–1864; captain 1816; vice-admiral 1857; K.C.B. 1860.
[12] British minister in Athens; see 15 Jan. 39.
[13] Demetrio Caruso; a senator; moderately pro-union.
[14] A. Dandolo, leader of the Rizospasts (Unionists).

Valoriti.¹ We dined at the President's: where there was an evening party. Read Montalembert's Debat sur L'Inde.²

4. Sat.

Wrote to G. Burnett—Lord A. Loftus—Rev Provost of Eton. Dined at Sir G. Bowen's: music & ball afterwards, but home by 11. Saw Dr Arvinotachi³ —Dr Bisi⁴—Count Spiridion Bulgari—Sig. Teodoro Ventura⁵—Dr Putenderi⁶—Sir John Young. Read Ionian Island books & papers.

5. 2 S. Adv.

Ch (& H.C.) mg—& aft. Saw Mr Sydney Clarke—Capt Glasse. Wrote to Sir E. Lytton. Read Bp of London's Charge⁷—The Σύνοψις⁸—The Union—&c.

6. M.

On account of bad weather our departure was postponed from last night & again from tonight. Wrote to H. Glynne. Read Maitland's Dispatches— Processi verbali—Greek papers. Saw Sig. Valaoriti—The Roman Consul— Sig. Risti⁹—Sir G. Bowen. Walked with Sir G.B. to the old Byzantine Church—the Jovianus—the Teodora Convent—& the temple site.¹⁰ Dinner & evening party. At night the weather changed.

7. T. [Santa Maura]

Wrote to Cav. Dandolo—Sir J. Young. Having a tolerable day we went off to Santa Maura:¹¹ arrived at 4: saw the Resident¹²—the Regent¹³—The Archbishop—the chief Judge—& arranged for tomorrow. Then returned to the Terrible in the road. Our passage was tolerable: the coast scenery most beautiful. Read Clyde on Romaic¹⁴—and [blank]. Reflected more on Young's strange position. A giddy head reminds me that sea & work bring a double strain.

¹ (Sir) Spiridione Valaoriti, senator for Santa Maura; K.C.M.G. 1862.
² C. F. R. de Montalembert, *Un débat sur l'Inde au parlement anglais* (1858).
³ Spiridione Arvamtachi, strongly pro-union.
⁴ Alexander Calichiopulo Bisi, strongly pro-union.
⁵ Assembly member, strongly pro-union.
⁶ An assembly member.
⁷ A. C. *Tait, *Charge delivered in November 1858* (1858).
⁸ L. F. C. Tischendorf, *Synopsis Evangelica* (1851).
⁹ Both unidentified.
¹⁰ Twelfth century church on older foundations of SS. Jason and Sosipater, in the centre of the ancient city of Corcyra.
¹¹ Also known as Leukadia, an island about 60 miles S. of Corfu, part of the British group.
¹² Baron Charles Sebright D'Everton, resident of Cephalonia 1842; suppressed risings there 1843, 1848; from 1854 resident of Santa Maura; resisted brigands' invasions 1854.
¹³ Signor Condari.
¹⁴ J. Clyde, *Romaic and modern Greek compared with one another, and with ancient Greek* (1855).

8. W.

A hard day at Santa Maura: landing in form, at 9: levee, innumerable audiences, a short drive to the country, & back to a dinner party in the Fort,[1] whence to the ship before 11. I received the Legislators—the Municipality—& the district magistrates: took their addresses—the second expunged their μόνη[2]—the first, after two long conferences, in an answer to my censure, explained it & I, through Mr L. endeavoured to clinch the explanation—ending at past midnight on board. I liked much the Regent Condari: Dr Zambarlà[3] too spoke most reasonably: the post [sic] Valaoriti had more sense than most of his colleagues. In the night we sailed for Ithaca.[4]

9. Th. [Ithaca]

With rain & swell we came to Ithaca at 11. Saw the Resident (Count Roma)—The Regent[5]—The Bishop—The Members—The Municipal Councillors—and various reactionists, risospasts, & others. A correspondence with the Legislators resembling that at Santa Maura: but then avowed their personal disinclination to Union & wished me to refuse their address. In the aftn. we went to Dexia Bay[6] & staid a few minutes: then resumed business, followed by a great dinner when I was dragged out into an Italian Speech. Next came a soirée & a ball. We returned to the ship by midnight in stiff rain. I still carry a giddy head. A. Gordon remains unwell. Lacaita is invaluable. Made plans for tomorrow's journey. The salute in this beautiful harbour was one of the grandest things from its regular circles of thundering echo, that I ever heard.

10. Fr. [Cephalonia]

On acct. of the weather we were obliged to give up the journey to Opisoarto: & after seeing the Resident & Regent we sailed for Samos.[7] The floods of rain prevented seeing anything. I crossed the hill with Mr Lacaita: reached Argostoli[8] at four: received with a demonstration for Union in the streets[9]

[1] Built in the middle ages, remodelled by the Turks and the Venetians, at the end of a 4 mile long *lido*.
[2] 'delay'.
[3] Unidentified.
[4] South of Santa Maura, between Cephalonia and the Greek coast; many Homeric descriptions were then ascribed to an Ithacan setting.
[5] Constantino Inglessi.
[6] Bay to E. of the peninsula linking N. and S. parts of the island.
[7] The Homeric name for Cephalonia.
[8] On the west side of the island, capital of Cephalonia, much of it built by Sir Charles *Napier.
[9] 'I crossed the Island of Cephalonia from Samos to Argostoli. On approaching this place I was met on a long and narrow bridge leading to the town by the head of a crowd, ... the people began to raise the cry of " Ζήτω ἡ Ἕνωσις", or "Union with Greece" ... we were thus obliged to proceed to the Residency at a foot's pace ...' (to Lytton, 13 December 1858, *PP* 1861 lxvii. 74).

& at the Residency by the authorities. Saw the Resident[1]—Mr Stephens.[2] Made arrangements for tomorrow. Began a letter to Young.

11. Sat.

Went on board early to land in form. Then a solemn scene at the Abps. After this the day was occupied with 15 or 16 interviews. A short drive in aftn: & dinner at the Resident's. Walk with Mr L. Wrote to Sir Edw. Lytton. Dispatch to do.[3]

12. 3 S. Adv.

Ch on board the Terrible. Walk with C., Mr L., & others. Went round the ship before Ch. Read Synopsis—J. Savonarola. Closed letters to Young & Sir E.L. Wrote to Duke of Newcastle. We dined on board. Conversations with C. & A. Gordon about my letters—with Mr L. about a policy.

13. M.

Wrote a dispatch to Sec. of State[4]—To Sir J. Young—And Sketch of our Address to the Abp & Clergy at Zante: to anticipate theirs. Another long day of interviews: broken by a drive to Fortezza S. Giorgio,[5] which gave us a noble view down to the S. mountains of Peloponnesus: & ending with a dinner at the Regent's where the entering scene was beautiful. Levee at 12: largely attended by proprietors & independent gentlemen. At 2 C. received the ladies.

14. T.

Wrote to Sir T. Wyse. Resumed interviews of wh the general character was satisfactory. Walk to Mr Stephens's Mill with its natural wonder[6]—and to the ruins of Crani[7]—we went on board to dine & were favoured with the admirable band of the 14th.[8] Read Papa Pannà.[9]

15. Wed. [Zante]

Sailed at 5 for Zante[10] & arrived at 10. Saw the Resident[11] & others: landed at 11, and held a Levee. Recd. the Abp & Clergy—& made my Speech to

[1] Major W. C. Trevor of the 14th foot, acting resident in place of Talbot, on leave (see 24 Jan. 59).
[2] The director of police in Cephalonia and, through his friend Talbot, a chief source of *Derby's information on Ionia; see 14 Dec. 58.
[3] *PP* 1861 lxvii. 73.
[4] Describing the visit to Cephalonia: *PP* 1861 lxvii. 75.
[5] Venetian thirteenth century castle on a hill 5 m. SE. of Argostoli.
[6] Grist-mill near the harbour entrance, where the sea flows through subterranean passages.
[7] Ruined city above the harbour; it resisted attack by the Lacedaemonians at the start of the Peloponnesian war (Thucydides ii. 33).
[8] 14th (the Buckinghamshire) regiment of foot, then stationed in the islands.
[9] Untraced.
[10] Southernmost of the British islands.
[11] Berkeley Wodehouse, 1806–77, *Kimberley's uncle; colonel of E. Norfolk militia; resident of Zante since 1855.

them.[1] Then the Municipal Councillors whose Address I refused. Then the eight Members of Assembly with whom I had 3 or 4 hours: I received their Address with the change of a word. Dined at the Residency & ball in the evening: many introductions. Out after dark incog. & saw the illuminations. On board at midnight: & much rumination.

16. Th. [On ship]

A long day of incessant audiences, only interrupted by a drive to the Fort[2] (where the view was delightful) & on the plain.[3] The interviews were on the whole satisfactory. At 6.30 we went to a large dinner party at the Regent's, at 9 to the Opera. The people behaved admirably & we parted good friends. On board at midnight: & sailed at 1½.

17. Fr. [Lutraki]

Wrote to Sir J. Young—Sir E. Lytton (2). Fifteen hours sail brought us to Lutraki through the magnif. scenery of the Gulphs.[4] Here we found Prince V. Hohenlohe[5]—a most pleasing person—& Mr Locock[6] from Athens. Read Murrays Handbook—Papa Pannà &c. Worked on Report. On the way we had the harrowing incident of a boy's falling overboard: but thank God he was saved.

18. Sat. [Athens]

We landed at 7½ after having settled for our voyage to Corfu. We crossed the Isthmus,[7] I on foot, exulting in the views, & unconscious of brigands.[8] After seeing Mount Gerancian I understand why emigrants did not come this way.[9] We embarked in the Scourge[10] for Piraeus & arrived at 2½: this gulf is more diversified from its islands, but not so grand. My maimed hand,[11] being shown, persuaded a poor seaman to have a crushed finger amputated: & all went well.[12] We reached Athens at ¼ to 4 the sun showing well the beauty of the port & scenery & compensating for the cold. We

[1] Greeted with cheers of 'Long live the Phil-Hellenic Gladstone!' (Kirkwall, *Four years in the Ionian islands* (1864), i. 222); copy of speech in *PP* 1861 lxvii. 77.
[2] The town of Zante was never fortified; the Venetian fort was on a hill above the town, then occupied by British troops.
[3] The plain stretches from coast to coast, the chief British source of currants.
[4] Loutraki, a spa, is at the E. (inland) end of the gulf of Corinth.
[5] Many; perhaps Prince Louis von Hohenlohe, 1823–60.
[6] Sidney Locock, unpaid attaché in Athens 1853, from February 1858 at Constantinople.
[7] The isthmus of Corinth, about 4 miles wide at Loutraki.
[8] A real danger; in 1870 Lord Muncaster and four friends were murdered by brigands near Marathon.
[9] Mountain very dangerous to sailors, as Simonides proclaimed (Dnieper, fr. 80).
[10] A British paddle-wheel steamship. The British blockaded Piraeus 1850–7, and in 1854 a joint French-British force landed there.
[11] See 13 Sept. 42.
[12] An incident important for his views on wine, see 1860 budget speech in Bassett, *Speeches*, 290.

were received with the utmost kindness by Sir T. & Miss Wyse.[1] Saw Sir T. Wyse (on Gr. & I.I.)—Rev Mr Hill[2]—General Church.[3] Visited the Russian Church.[4] Worked on Report.

19. 4 S. Adv.

Ch mg & aft. Attended the Russian Service in the morning: it was very solemn, & the music most beautiful & devout. Saw Rev Mr Hill—M. Rangabè[5] For. Minr.—Baron Brunner & others at a party in the evg. and waited on the King & Queen[6] at the Palace. Both were affable & kind: he utters with some difficulty. Conv. with Agnes. Read Quelques Mots[7]— and Ed. Rev. on Gk Ch.[8]

20. M.

Wrote to Mr Lacaita. Saw Count H. Lunzi[9] . . . Mr Finlay (2).[10] Attended the sitting of the Senate. Saw the Univ. Library & Coins.[11] 1–5 With Sir T. Wyse to the Acropolis. The view—the ruins—& the sculptures, taken together are almost too much for one day. Among the last, a magnificent Torso and the winged Victories. Worked on report—letters—& minutes. Dined at the Palace: I sat by the Queen who conversed much. Evg party afterwards. Up late.

21. T.

Went at 9¾ to S. Irene for the Queen's birthday Te Deum. The music wholly unsatisfactory to my own ears: the demeanour generally cold. Then to the Queen's Garden[12]—Mount Lycabettus[13]—The Greek Booksellers shops—In aftn with Sir T. W[yse] The Pnyx[14]—The fountains & Ilissus[15]— Jupiter Olympius[16]—and calls. Dined at the Palace: party of 75.[17] Read

[1] Adeline, 2nd da. of Sir T. *Wyse and his wife Letitia, Napoleon's niece, m. 1861 General Estevan Türr, promoter of the Corinthian canal. Or Winifrid, *Wyse's niece (see 23 Dec. 58).
[2] Probably Pascoe Grenfell Hill, 1804–82; royal naval chaplain; ritualist rector of St. Edmund, Lombard Street from 1863; wrote on the Levant.
[3] Sir Richard *Church, 1784–1873; fought in Ionian Islands 1809–15; commander in Sicily 1820; commanded Greek army and led revolution; retired in Athens; his memorial window in the English church has an inscription by Gladstone.
[4] St. Nicodemus, restored by the Russian govt. 1852–6.
[5] The foreign minister; see 27 June 50.
[6] Otho I, Prince of Bavaria, 1815–67; elected King of Greece 1832; under a regency until 1835; m. 1836 (Maria Frederika) Amelia of Oldenburg; persistently unpopular, deposed 1862.
[7] See 29 Feb. 56.
[8] *Edinburgh Review*, cvii. 322 (April 1858).
[9] Count Ermanno Lunzi, historian of Greece and Ionia.
[10] George *Finlay, 1799–1877; friend of *Byron; fought in war of independence 1824–7; lived in Athens; wrote much on Greek history.
[11] In the university, founded 1837.
[12] In the royal palace, designed by the queen round Roman ruins.
[13] To the NE. of the city.
[14] Site of the Athenian assembly, on a hill W. of the Acropolis.
[15] The stream flowing from Mount Hymettus.
[16] Imposing ruins of the marble temple of the Olympian Zeus, built SE. of the Acropolis.
[17] Political dinner; pro-Russian Greeks not invited.

Lunzi's History.[1] Worked on Report. [Saw] Engl. Consul[2]—Mr Van Lennep[3]—Mr Ozeroff[4]—Mrs Hill: & others. Saw Sir T. Wyse (on I.I.)— General Church (on do)—Prussian Minister[5]—M. Rangabè.

22. Wed.

Saw Gen. Church—Gen. Kalergi[6]—Mr Finlay—Mr Hill—Mr Beretta (I.I.)[7] —Mr Butteni[8]—Count H. Lunzi (I.I.)—M. Ozeroff. Dinner party at the Legation. Busy in book-buying—Also ventured on the wonderful carving of the School of Mount Athos—1000 dollars. Visited Chamber of Deputies —Libr. of Adrian—Portico of Caesar—Temple of Æolus—do of Theseus, & the sculptures incl. the Assyrian.

23. Th. [On ship]

Our most kind host & his niece were up at six to see us off. Embarked in the Scourge at 7½. Reached Callamachi[9] at 12¼. Walk 11 m to Corinth: destroyed by an earthquake last winter: an appalling monument of the Divine power.[10] Then up Acrocorinth: the view upwards at the first gate is marvellous and that from the top quite satisfies.[11] This was 4 m. & then came 9 more to Lutraki[12] where we again took refuge in the Terrible. Sailed at 10 for Corfu. Read Bory St Vincent.[13]

24. Fr. [Corfu]

A delightful day past the islands & πὰρ Λευκάδα πέτρην[14] to Corfu where we arrived at 8 P.M. Then a stiff evening & night's work till 4 AM of Xmas brought me to the end of my first Report.[15] Read Greek papers: still an exercise for me. A. Gordon went ashore & reported on returning his interview with Sir J. Young.

25. Xmas Day.

Rose at 9. After breakfast landed for Ch & Holy Communion. Church again in aftn. Hearing of many deaths from England & especially of that of

[1] E. Lunzi, Della condizione politica delle Isole Ionie solto il dominio Veneto (1858).
[2] St. Vincent Lloyd.
[3] Henry J. Vanlennep, author of Brief notice of the present state of religion and education in the Levant (1852).
[4] Unidentified.
[5] Robert von der Goltz.
[6] General Dimitrios Kallergis, 1803–67; once Capodistria's private sec.; war minister.
[7] Joannes Philip Berettas, Ionian author.
[8] Unidentified.
[9] On the SE. side of the isthmus of Corinth.
[10] In February 1858; all Corinth was destroyed during the revolutionary war, and rebuilding had just begun.
[11] Mountain 1885 feet, with Roman and medieval ruins and fortifications, dominating access to the S. end of the isthmus.
[12] See 17 Dec. 58.
[13] J. B. G. M. Bory de Saint-Vincent, Histoire et description des Îles Ioniennes (1823).
[14] 'by the Leucadian rock'; Od. 24.11.
[15] See 28 Dec. 58.

Wyndham Neville,[1] now at rest in Christ, we did not dine at the Palace, but alone with Capt. Glasse. We could not however refuse to hear the songs & comic grimaces of the sailors before we landed in the evening & betook ourselves to our furnished house in Corfu. I had three hours with Sir J. Young on *the* question of his return home. Corrected my draft Report.

26. S.

Ch mg & aft. Three more hours with Sir J. Young. Wrote Confidential dispatch to Sir E. Lytton.[2] Also part of private letter. Sent Mr Lacaita to N. Zambelli. Read Question Religieuse de l'Orient et de l'Occident.[3]

27. M.

Finished private letter to Sir E. Lytton. Wrote Secret & Separate do. Wrote to Sir J. Young (2). Wrote to S.E.G. Further corrected draft Report: sat till 3 A.M. Wrote dft dispatch with Zante Speech.[4] Much consn. in regard to my course which I trust was rightly directed. Saw Sir A. Damaschino—Sir J. Young (2) for 3 hours—Mr Lacaita—Sir Geo. Bowen.

28. T.

Wrote to Sir J. Young—Read Parl. Papers on I.I.—and Gk newspapers. Today we set about arranging papers—Much conv. with Mr Lacaita on our proceedings: but this is in truth daily. Two hours with the President—Sir A. Damaschino.[5] Unpacked our China wh will do important duty here.

It is true that countries enjoying constitutional government are not wholly free from the taint of this impurity.[6] But in the Ionian Islands the checks which limit it elsewhere are generally inoperative, and as if for the purpose of raising the evil to its maximum, it is subject to incentives which elsewhere are unknown. The number of offices rendered desirable by salary, and open to direct election in proportion to the population, I suppose to be without a parallel. The smallness of the Septinsular State of itself reduces the energy of public opinion; but the existing arrangements are further calculated to keep the jobs and abuses of each Island wholly exempt from criticism by the public opinion of the others. I must add that, in part from causes creditable to the people, the Ionian press, so far as I have observed or learned, commonly shows a singular reluctance to expose in individual instances the undue predominance of personal feelings over public interests. Elsewhere the candidate for power seeks to enter into an honourable partnership, bound more or less to a political creed, subject to the action of public opinion, open in some form to impeachment, and having in view a common course of action to be pursued by the whole Executive body, with a joint responsibility. Under the Constitution of the Islands, the object presented to his desires is an office to be held in severalty, apart from all political creed and all common ties, without responsibility in any defined or intelligible sense, and likely, therefore, to have for its first, and in some cases perhaps its sole, object, the use of public patronage for private ends.

[1] See 22 Apr. 56.   [2] Sent next day.
[3] A. Popovitski, *La Question Religieuse d'Orient et d'Occident* (1853).
[4] The despatch recommended Young's transfer on the grounds that the published despatch of 10 June 1857 made his position untenable: *PP* 1861 lxvii. 75.
[5] Sir Alexander Damascino, the new president of the senate.
[6] Corruption.

By an arrangement alike strange and unfortunate the manifold temptations thus offered to the use of electioneering arts, whether vulgar or corrupt, receive a yet further enhancement. The electoral qualification is either a University degree, the exercise of a liberal profession, or the possession of a certain amount of property. It is the last-named qualification, however, on which the franchise is principally based. Thus the formation of the list or register becomes a matter of the utmost delicacy, not only involving, in any case, more or less of inquisitorial scrutiny into private affairs, which is less dreaded in the Islands than in England, but likewise affording unbounded scope for injustice . . .

The extension of the elective franchise, and the free choice of candidates, have not, under circumstances like these, produced the benefits which might otherwise have been expected from them. The electors have not had the power of choosing representatives who could determine the public expenditure, or exercise an united influence on the composition and conduct of the Executive power; they have not, therefore, been taught by experience to connect their own general as well as particular welfare with the honest and discreet exercise of the trust committed to them. This power, when thus detached from a sense of duty, is apt to become little more than an engine of corruption, and, as certainly, whenever it is thus used, to multiply electors is only to multiply the corrupt and personal claims which, in a thousand forms, are to be set up, and to prevail against the public interests. There is, indeed, a difference of opinion in the Islands upon the question whether the reforms of 1848 and 1849 ought to have been begun, but the conviction is universal that they are in hopeless contradiction with other parts, still unaltered, of the old system of 1817. Of those parts of the public law of the Islands, if the reforms were right, and if they are not to be repealed, it is impossible, in my judgment, to recommend or justify the maintenance.

. . . Notwithstanding the free press, the electoral franchise, and the secret suffrage, free institutions, properly so-called, do not, at this moment, exist in the Ionian Islands.

I proceed to consider, briefly, two objections, which may probably suggest themselves against the concession of institutions really free to the Ionian Islands, and then to explain in what form the essential conditions of those institutions might, as it would appear, with least hazard be conceded.

The objections are: first, that the Ionian people are not fit for free institutions; and secondly, that, if offered, they would not be accepted.

As respects the first, it is obvious to observe that fitness is nowhere to be found perfect, but exists only amidst various grades of imperfection; and that there are special reasons why the Ionians should not be judged in this respect by a standard to which even the most apt and experienced people can scarcely reach.

Again, that aptitude can never be found in a high degree without the aid of habit; the experience by which habit is formed can only be had by paying for it, and thus, in the Constitutional life of a people, the errors of to-day are the safeguards of to-morrow.

The Treaty of Paris declares the Seven Islands to be a free, as well as an independent State, subject only to the restraints of British Protection, which included a particular solicitude on the part of the Protecting Power for their internal affairs.

It is difficult to assign to this language any one signification so clear and indubitable as to preclude all others; but it would, perhaps, be the judgment of an impartial observer that, at any rate, among the various admissible constructions, the Constitution of 1817 adopted that which was the least favourable to liberty, and the least in harmony with the political traditions of England, or with her well-earned character for directness and fair dealing; and the reforms of 1849, if they broke up the self-consistency of the old construction, yet did not effect a transition to a new one.

While the inferences to be drawn from the Treaty of Paris are favourable, rather than otherwise, to free institutions, the changes which have taken place since its date in the views and policy of England with regard to transmarine dependencies tend powerfully in the same direction. In no one of your Majesty's Colonies did there exist, previously to the last twelve or fifteen years, any form of what is termed Responsible Government. But within that period it has been extended generally to the North American and Australian Colonies, as well as to the Cape of Good Hope, with great advantage and satisfaction on all sides, and it may now be said to form the fixed rule of the policy of the British Empire in all those of your Majesty's Possessions which are not stamped with an exceptional character, either as purely military Possessions, or as being in mere infancy, or as being too critically divided between dominant and subject races. In the absence of evidence to the contrary, presumptions of no inconsiderable weight arise out of the general tenour of British policy, in favour of the extension of similar advantages to the Ionian Islands.

Nor does any such counter-evidence exist. It cannot be said, with truth, that free institutions have failed in the Septinsular State, any more than, or indeed nearly so much as, it could have been said thirty years ago that they had failed in Canada. In neither case had they been in operation under the only conditions which, in the present age, could afford a hope of their success. But Canada at that period was much nearer to political freedom than the Ionian Islands now are; and if the concessions previously made to her were then only found available to inflame discontent and to stimulate further demands, we cannot wonder that in the Islands political arrangements, themselves rife with contradiction and disorder, should have failed to result in the establishment of harmony.

It has indeed now become a common idea in England that the race of her inhabitants has peculiar or even exclusive aptitude for popular institutions. Various nations of Europe, however, not of that race, have shown themselves to be ready and effective pupils in the school of freedom; and no one instance can probably be quoted where an European country, endowed with representative institutions, derives more evil than good from their operation. Among the countries so endowed, it is important to bear in mind that one is the Kingdom of Greece, where the principles and habits of freedom are not yet fully developed, but where its machinery is in use. The proximity of this kingdom to the Ionian Isles, with its many other points of resemblance, invests the example with considerable weight; and though, encouraged by Colonial experience, public opinion in England is now thus liberal to the British race, it must be remembered that before the change of policy was adopted, under circumstances of urgency rather than unbiassed choice, there were very many unfavourable auguries as to the result.

It is difficult, in the case of the Ionian people, to distinguish between the defects which may be due to adventitious circumstances, and those which have their roots in the groundwork of character. To be vain; to be mutable in purpose; to be liable to excitement; to want the firm tone of truthfulness and directness which only the vigour and health of freedom can confer; to substitute private for public interests as the object of pursuit—these are defects, some of which may be more prominent among the Ionian people than in the United Kingdom, and some of which, I must add, the Constitution of 1817 has contributed to extend and confirm. But I am not able to perceive that the Ionians have any such share of the infirmities of our common nature as to amount to an absolute disqualification for the discharge of the duties which political freedom must entail. On the other hand, when their character is examined from other points of view, it may, in no small degree, supply just grounds of hope. I do not rely simply or mainly on their remarkable powers of thought and expression, because I am aware that without the balance-weight of sober judgment, and the support of vigorous and resolute will, these qualities do not much avail towards the happiness of a community. But your Majesty may safely rest assured that the Ionians, if they have their defects, have also their virtues. They are a people gifted with great delicacy of feeling; eminently alive to kindly treatment; and well disposed to trust until they have been deceived. Under favourable circumstances, the influence of England, working through the medium of their free will, might be almost unbounded. Even amidst the present complications, I believe that it would be found very great, when exercised in a spirit kindly and unselfish, with the just respect to their feelings which would soothe irritation, and with a consistency which would render it intelligible: from whatever cause, this consistency, so essential to the discharge of the duties of the Protection, has not been characteristic of the British policy in the Islands, as a whole.

I do not venture to predict with confidence, especially at a time when the case has been so greatly prejudiced by antecedent events, that the working of free institutions would, in its earlier stages, be smooth and satisfactory. Rare, indeed, are the instances where this can be broadly affirmed. But I see no reason to despair, first, of a balance of advantage over evil; and, secondly, of a gradual growth and progress towards decided stability and efficiency. And it is material to observe, that if, under circumstances such as I have described, the opening prospects cannot be the brightest, on the other hand, the sphere within which incidental mischiefs could operate, is strictly circumscribed by the rights and duties of the Protecting Power, so that any risks attending the trial are limited to a more than ordinarily narrow range.

Under any construction, however favourable to popular rights, that can be given to the Treaty of Paris, England must remain responsible, in the eyes of Europe, for the order and security of the Islands. In addition, therefore, to the burden of military protection, and to the conduct of all foreign relations on behalf of the Ionian State, she can never consent to any laws which would compromise the maintenance of order, or the security of individual lives and properties; even supposing, which I see no reason to apprehend, that the representatives of the Ionian people would be likely to pass Bills of a nature to place them in jeopardy. From past experience it seems reasonable to hope that their general spirit, in matters of administrative arrangement, would, on the whole, be liberal and for-bearing. There is a further limitation, which, so long as England retains a veto upon the passing of all laws in the Ionian State, will, I take it for granted, be rigorously maintained. Your Majesty's assent will, without question, always be withheld from any measure which may impair the sanctity of contracts, or may be in any manner inconsistent with good faith. Presuming, then, that a discretion to such an extent as I have described is to remain with the Protecting Power, I submit to your Majesty that no fatal or serious danger can arise to the interests of the Ionian people from the exercise of popular rights in constitutional forms within the limits thus traced, and from the partial and casual errors by which, especially in its first stages, the exercise of such rights may possibly be marred.

The three heads under which a dangerous abuse of power might possibly be apprehended are those of democratic sentiment, of class interests, and of the spirit of Hellenic nationality.

As respects the first, I may observe that it does not appear to me that any violent democratic tendencies at present prevail in the Islands; although I do not venture to predict what form the popular dissatisfaction may take in future years, should the present system of government be continued.

As regards the second, it is probably true that the relations of proprietor and peasant, as well as those of creditor and debtor, are not in a satisfactory condition. But if it be the tendency of the present Constitution to thrust aside the more healthful class of social influences in favour of demagoguism and corruption, it is plain that any dangers arising from this source are likely to be aggravated rather than avoided by the postponement of change. But I may add generally, that I see no tendency in the mass of the people, or in their leaders, to the practical adoption of really dangerous extremes. Even were they more inclined than I suppose to push their opinions to such a point, I believe that their consciousness of weakness would still prove an amply sufficient curb.

To the third subject, that of the Hellenizing spirit, I shall presently refer . . .

The following is an outline of the constitutional changes which I recommend to be proposed by your Majesty, through the Lord High Commissioner, to the Senate and Assembly:—

1. To sever the Legislative from the Executive functions of the Senate, assigning the latter to a Ministry.

2. To provide by law for the legal or penal responsibility of the members of the Ministry, and of public functionaries.

3. Subject to a permanent provision, such as is now made for the military contribution and for the Lord High Commissioner's Civil List, to assign to the Assembly a full control over the taxation and expenditure of the country, reserving only to the other branches of the Legislative body their right of veto.

4. By means of this control over the finance, and otherwise, if possible and requisite, to provide for the due influence of the Legislative over the composition of the Executive body according to the spirit of popular institutions.

5. That any acts of government done by the Lord High Commissioner, except in matters relating to the purposes of the Protection, be countersigned by the proper Executive officer.

6. To abolish the arbitrary and extra-legal powers of the High Police.

These may be regarded as the main concessions to be made to the popular principles of government.

. . . I must not withhold from your Majesty the expression of my humble conviction that it is an error in policy to treat as if it were a crime the expression of a desire for union with Greece, whether by individuals or by bodies in authority, provided it be legal in form, respectful in terms, and in no way associated with a tendency to public disorder.

. . . It is a grave error, so far as my knowledge goes, to ascribe this desire for union with Greece either to any aversion towards your Majesty and towards England, or to foreign intrigue. In no portion of the Islands that I have visited, in no class or body whatever of their inhabitants, have I perceived any sign that would authorize me to assert the existence of the one or the other. But I have found, everywhere, signs in abundance that your Majesty is cordially venerated, and that the British nation is still viewed with admiration and regard, notwithstanding a prevailing sentiment that it has not, on the whole, been favourably represented by its protection of the Ionian Islands.

With regard to the desire in the Islands for union with Greece, it appears to be made up of the following elements. There is, first, the abstract sentiment of nationality. This is general, nay, it is universal. There is, I believe, hardly any one in the Islands—especially it would be difficult to find any one of character, education, and station—who does not say that he feels himself a Greek, and that he longs for the day when he may be united in one political society with the members of his race. But then, many, tempering their sentiment with good sense, are aware not only that this consummation is rendered impossible by the opposing authority of England, but likewise that Eastern Europe has not yet reached the state in which alone such a reunion ought to be an object of an immediate and practical desire. There are, doubtless, also persons of enthusiastic temper, who overleap these bounds of prudence, and give the reins to their sympathies without duly calling in aid their powers of observation and judgment. And lastly, there are here, as elsewhere, the traders upon popular emotion, of whom, some perhaps desire the union, and some desire it not; but all use it with the facilities afforded by the present system, as a means of advancement, through popular fame, to salary, patronage, or both. I have to add that nothing can better serve the objects of these men than the policy which has repeatedly punished the Assembly for indicating a desire to entertain the question. For by this course not only is the national grievance raised to the highest point, but the people are permitted and encouraged to believe that there would be some great efficacy for the attainment of its end in that declaration or petition of the Assembly which England shows herself so solicitous to prevent.

It would, however, be an error to suppose that the cry for union with Greece means only what it seems to mean. As the demand most in favour with the people, this cry naturally becomes the form in which all dissatisfaction with the Government finds vent. Men are apt to express their grievances, not in the form which most accurately and logically describes them, but in that form which best satisfies the feeling they have engendered; and it is not to be doubted that decided improvements in the Government would of themselves greatly diminish the available forces and enthusiasm of the unionists. But to return from this digression. Erroneous political opinions are often entitled to respect; and it does not appear to me, that the error, of which I now treat, is one which should be wholly excluded from the benefit of that indulgent view. There are five strong ties which are at once observable, as binding the Islands in feeling partly to the Kingdom of Greece, but for the most part yet more conspicuously to the Greek race at large: they are—blood, religion, language, vicinity, and predominating intercourse. Indeed, the case is even stronger than this. When it is asked, what tie binds together such Islands as Paxo and Zante, or as Cerigo and Corfu, what unites these seven small spots, severed by distances so wide in proportion to their size, into a single State, and gives them a common name and a sentiment of unity, the answer can be but one. It is this very Hellenic feeling: they are only Ionians because they are Greeks; the tie of the State subsists only in virtue of those other ties which some would so severely proscribe. Thus reasonable, under an impartial view, is the abstract sentiment which I have described, as entertained by the most moderate, judicious, and intelligent Ionians. And the exaggeration of such a sentiment, which carries it beyond the bounds of prudence, and takes no account of practicability, is not, with justice, to be treated as a guilty error, until it indicates a tendency towards illegality, but in the absence of any such tendency may be opposed by reason rather than by reproach, and by the firm maintenance of the law rather than by violence done to the freedom of opinion. I am also persuaded that a tolerant feeling towards their customs, a regard for their suscepti-bilities, and an indication of desire to touch their affections, will be found instru-ments of no mean power in the government of this people.

The case I have supposed throughout is that of a petition from the Assembly declaring, in terms of due respect, that the Ionian people desire a union with the Kingdom of Greece. Should that body attempt any resolution or vote declaratory of rights to that effect, without reference to the will of superior authority, it would, I apprehend, more or less abuse its powers, and it would be a matter for consideration, in the event of its persistence in such a course, how it should be met. Even here, however, I should hesitate to recommend the virtual suspension of free government at once, by penal prorogation, as a remedy much worse than the disease. Even were the gross error of an unseemly declaration once com-mitted, it does not follow that it would occur a second time, and the case would not of necessity be so urgent as to require the adoption of summary or predeter-mined measures; but should the Assembly proceed further still, which I do not apprehend, and attempt to bring about what is illegal, the mode of dealing with it would not be a matter of much difficulty. If, however, it confines itself to a proper petition, and should your Majesty direct that petition to be promptly answered in terms which, without rebuking the Assembly, should undeceive the country by an explicit declaration coming direct from the highest authority to the regularly elected organ of the Ionian people, I do not despair of seeing a practical stop put to the serious mischiefs of the present agitation; and the Assembly, after the delivery of its prayer, disposed to set about the business of the country, perhaps without any trace of factious or obtrusive temper or extravagant opinions. Authority would be, in the main, the basis of such a reply. But the Ionians are acute and observant, and many of them know that there are the strongest reasons against the accomplishment of their wish at the present epoch. The question of this union is, indeed, viewed with very mixed feelings, even in Greece itself, where the desire of territory and power is checquered with doubts as to the poli-tical temper of the Ionians, and as to the degree in which, with the independence of their insular position, they would prove tractable subjects to so small and poor a kingdom, destitute of an effective navy, and ill able to bear the expense of such an establishment. On the other hand, many, whose minds play with the question of union while it is remote, have, it is evident, never considered closely the changes both of general law and finance to which the measure would at once render them liable. To touch only for a moment on the latter subject: in Greece direct taxes prevail, while in the Islands they are absolutely unknown; and the attempt to equalize the two systems between the infant Kingdom and the small and disjointed Island State would require efforts to which probably neither are adequate. The experience of the United Kingdom has shown that unions of this kind between countries where differences of law and different relations of class have prevailed, are achievements which it requires the greatest effort of powerful and highly organized societies to effect. In short, it is far from improbable that if Europe and England gave permission for the union with Greece to-day, to-morrow the parties themselves would find good reasons, even in their own internal condition respectively, why it should not take effect.

But the considerations connected with that internal condition must of neces-sity be subordinate to the dictates of other and larger interests; and I am per-suaded that the Ionians of station and intelligence, though they may not be strong enough to resist the general warmth, especially when it has an ally in their own hearts, yet well know that there are many and conclusive reasons connected with the present state of Eastern Europe, which would render it an act of criminal folly on the part of England were she to give the slightest encouragement to so crude a project. What would be the position of Corfu, with its great strategical importance, in the hands of a Power so unable as Greece must be to defend it? What would be the condition of the Ottoman dominion in Albania, with Corfu an appendage to Greece? What obedience the inhabitants of Candia, Thessaly, Macedonia, the Islands, could, as Greeks, be expected to pay to Turkish sovereignty, after the Ionians of the Seven Islands had, as Greeks, been relieved of British protection? All these questions and others, when even so slightly touched, are, I believe, felt and appreciated in the Islands, and serve to show the most intelligent of their inhabitants that the union of the Seven Islands with the Kingdom of Greece is, in truth and fact, a conventional form of words, under which is hidden a far larger meaning: that this small question is the narrow corner of a very great question, one no less, in all likelihood, than the reconstruction of all political society in South-Eastern Europe. And if it be allowable to look so far into the future as to suppose possible the arrival of a day when the union of the scattered members of the Greek family may be accomplished with benefit to themselves and to Europe, it seems obvious that the best and safest means both of meeting that day when it comes, and of accelerating its tranquil arrival, will be to have trained some, at least, of the severed portions of that race in the peaceable and steady exercise of local liberty, and in the enjoyment of the happiness for which we may hope as its result. Such liberty, on a basis that would render it the ally of order, would alike prepare for the future, and turn the present to account. Even at this very late period, and when the whole case has been so seriously compromised, I believe that the force of these and other considerations would come powerfully in aid of a succinct and solemn declaration to the Assembly, proceeding directly from your Majesty, on the project of an union of the Seven Islands to Greece.

Upon these grounds I humbly and dutifully submit to your Majesty that Constitutional changes shall be proposed to the Ionian State of the nature which has been above described:

That authority be given to the Lord High Commissioner to summon the Assembly expressly, if he shall think fit, for that purpose:

That your Majesty's gracious recommendations be made known to them by Message:

That if a petition dutifully expressed respecting union be interposed, a prompt answer in the negative be dispatched:

And that opportunity be given to the Assembly to address itself thereafter, if it shall so think fit, to the consideration of the said recommendations.

But if the Assembly shall, unhappily, be seduced into a temper of political fanaticism, and shall, under the plea of desiring union with Greece, refuse to entertain propositions which aim at effecting great and necessary improvements in the condition of the Islands, it may then, I submit, be for your Majesty to consider whether the Ionian people shall have an opportunity given them, by a dissolution, of repairing the errors of its temporary Representatives. In any case, they will then better learn that England is not the friend of abuses, nor the enemy of freedom; and your Majesty's Government will cease to be responsible in the eyes of Europe for the political and administrative evils the prevalence whereof in the Seven Islands is so much to be lamented.[1]

[1] Extracted from vast dispatch to *Lytton, sent this day: printed for the cabinet, not in *PP*: Lytton MSS D/EK 011.

29. *Wed.*

Wrote to Duke of Newcastle—Sir E. Lytton (began)—Sir G. Bowen. Drove into the country with C. Saw Sir J. Young. Read Parl. papers— Finances de la Grèce[1]—Capt Glasse & Mr S. Clarke dined. My birthday brings to me no joyful sense of progress in my weakest & worst points: only the still warm ashes of hope in the mercy and boundless love of God. I am now immersed in a work of justice & mercy: Oh that my hands were cleaner that I might bear it to His altar and lay it there beside the spotless Lamb.

30. *Th.*

Wrote to Willy—Sir E. Lytton (finished & 2°). Saw Capt Glasse—Sir J. Young—The Archbishop of Corfú—Cav. Mustoxidi—Sig Curè[2] 2 hours: a material & satisfactory interview. Walk with C. Attended at 12 the interesting Girl School Meeting at the Palace—Read Parl. papers—The Leucade case.[3]

31. *Fr.*

Wrote to Sir J. Young. Wrote Queries[4]—Read Parl. Papers—Tre Costituzioni[5]—Drove with C. Saw Capt Dixon (=0)[6]—Count Salomons of Zante and Captain Stokesley[7] with the Engineers plan of the town and fortifications.

It may seem strange but so it is that my time & thoughts are as closely occupied & absorbed in the affairs of these little Islands as they have been at almost any period in Parliamentary business. Scarcely have I had a moment to collect my thoughts for any other purpose. The complexity of the case is inversely (so to speak) as the extent of the sphere.

But the stream of time flows on & we launch on a new year: it is as usual mercy & shame on looking back, hope only for the future. May the God of justice do justice here, whether through my means or through some channel less clogged with sin.

[1] See 28 Nov. 58.
[2] Unidentified.
[3] Papers on Santa Maura.
[4] On Ionian laws and police, Hawn P.
[5] *Address of Sir T. *Maitland to the Primary Council, February 3, 1817: Le tre Cotituzioni* (1849).
[6] Obscure.
[7] Probably Captain John Stokes of the royal engineers.

Corfù
Sat. Jan One 1859.
The Circumcision.

Writing to Sir E. L[ytton] for next mail: also draft of possible answer by the Queen to an address.[1] 10–1. Saw the Corfiot Members: a long debate or rather audience. Saw Cav. Mustoxidi—Sig. N. Zambelli—Sir John Young. Dined at the Palace. Walk with Mr Lacaita. Read Gk newspapers—Parliamentary Papers—V. Capodistria's Analisi del Trattato di Parigi.[2]

2. 2 S. [after] Xmas.
Church & H.C. 10½–12½: aftn. 3½. Read Encore Quelque Mots[3]—L'Orient et L'Occident[4]—Amn. Q.R. on State & Prospects of the Church.[5] Saw Capt Blomfield[6]—Mr Lacaita. Worked on Constn.

3. M.
Wrote to A. Hayward—R. Phillimore—J.S. Wortley—Ld A. Loftus—Sir Edw. Lytton (finished). Read Scarpa's Cenni[7]—Parl. Papers. Saw the L.H.C.[8]—The President of Senate—The President of Assembly[9]—Mr Sargeant—Captain Murray[10]—Sir Geo. Bowen—Mr Lacaita. Walk with C. & otherwise.

4. T. X
Wrote to L.H.C.(2) Saw Coleti[R]—Worked on plan of Constitutional changes. Saw Dr Curè—Sir P. Braila. Instr. to Mr L. for conv. with C. Caruso—Ten to dinner: and evening party. Read Parl. papers.

5. Wed.
Read Parl. Papers—West. Rev. on Myst. of Cepalonia[11]—Procès Verbal of 1821.[12] Worked on Constitn. and Queen's Message. Minutes & divers MSS. Drive with C. Mr L. reported from C. Caruso. Latin with Agnes.

[1] Start of his constitutional reforms; see 5 Feb. 59.
[2] Untraced book by the revolutionary's younger brother.
[3] See 28 Nov. 58.
[4] See 26 Dec. 58.
[5] *American Church Review*, xi. 369. (October 1858).
[6] Henry J. Blomfield, commander of the *Osprey*.
[7] G. B. Scarpa, 'Cenni sull' estratto del dispaccio indirizzato a Sua Eccellenza il Lord Alto Commissionario' (1858).
[8] The lord high commissioner; still Sir J. *Young.
[9] Flamburiari.
[10] Director of the police on Corfu.
[11] *Westminster Review*, xi. 216 (January–April 1857).
[12] 'Présentation du projet de loi sur l'organisation municipale et départementale' of Count J. J. Siméon, 22 February 1821; a moderate franchise reform; see *Archives Parlementaires de 1787 à 1860*, 2nd series, xxx. 130.

6. Th.

The Greek Christmas & my beloved Catherine's birthday. Ch at 11 AM for the Epiphany. Began a Second Report.[1] Read Parl Papers—Greek newspapers—Gk tract on Eln. of Archbishop of Cefalonìa[2]—Colquhoun's Tract on Plain of Ilium.[3] Lady Bowen's in Evg. Saw Judge Sargent. We drove to Chinopiastes[4] & saw wonderful costumes, more wonderful Greek faces: feasted the children with some sort of sweet cake to the extent of 2/6! & departed amid bows & cheers. Visited two Churches.

7. Fr. X

Again worked on Report—sitting up late. Also on Parl. papers. Saw Count Caruso—Dr Cefalà[5]—Saw Coleti[R]. Again drove to a view & village at Gasturi:[6] the former from the height is magnificent. In the latter we again saw much beauty. Mr L. & I were incensed by the Priest in the Church: the women were behind gratings at the West End. Latin for Agnes. Visited a Ch.

8. Sat. X

Wrote to C. Caruso (dft). Finished the whole mass of Parl. papers:[7] with much pain as to Cefalonia. Saw Cav. P. Braila—Cav. G. Marcoran[8]—Sig. Quartano[9]—Captain Glasse. Completed my set of Resolutions No I (vital).[10] Saw ——[R].

9. 1 S. Epiph.

Ch mg & aft.—Read Pr. of Prussia's Glaubensbekenntniss—with pain.[11]— Perrens's Savonarola.[12] Saw Sir J. Young—Mr Barr—Mr Lacaita. Wrote Resolutions II.[13]

10. M. X

Wrote to Sir Edw. Lytton. Wrote in continuance of my Report on the Constitutional Changes: & prepared the vital part for tomorrow's Mail. Dined at the Palace & saw their admirable Tableaux. Saw Sir A. Xidion[14]— Dr Colquhoun[15] (Ilium) Read [blank].

[1] See 11 Jan. 59, and notes in Add MS 44748, f. 1.
[2] Untraced.
[3] Unpublished. See 10 Jan. 59n.
[4] Kinopiastes, in the hills S. of Corfu.
[5] A. N. Cephala, of the municipal council of Cephalonia: *PP* 1861 lxvii. 81.
[6] A little further south than Kinopiastes.
[7] The background to the disturbances: *PP* 1861 lxvii. 25.
[8] (Sir) Georgio Marcoran, K.C.M.G. 1864; judge later dismissed by *Storks.
[9] Not identified.
[10] See 11 Jan. 59.
[11] Crown Prince Frederick William of Prussia, 'Glaubensbekenntniss' (1858) on confirmation.
[12] See 9 Nov. 58.
[13] See 11 Jan. 59.
[14] Sir Anastasio T. Xidian, member of the supreme court of justice, dismissed later by *Storks.
[15] (Sir) Patrick MacChombaich *Colquhoun, 1815–91, diplomat 1840–58; member of Ionian supreme court 1858; chief justice there 1861–4.

11. T. [On ship]

Wrote to Sir E. Lytton (in reply to Telegram of 8th)—Gen. Portlock—Mr
S. Herbert.[1] Sent off Corrected dft of proposed Queen's Message & covering
dispatch: with the other papers.[2] Drove with C. to Santi Deka.[3]

Saw Sig. Grollo[4]—Sig. [blank] Sir G. Bowen—Sir John Young.

Dined on board the Terrible with the Ward Room Officers: & slept:
starting at night. Read Bory de St Vincent.

12. T.[5] [Corfu]

Reached Paxo[6] at 9: left at 1½ and returned by Parga & the Albanian Coast
to Corfu at 6¼ P.M. We found Mr Lacaita suffering much pain. At Paxo I
had a Levee; then saw the Bishop—The Representatives—The Municipal
Councillors—Each of the three Judges—and various others. Then walked a
little into the country & saw two Churches. The people behaved admirably.
Read Bory de St V.—Gazette Series of Messages &c.[7] Began dispatch with
Narrative of Tour (continuance).[8]

13. Th.

Wrote to Ld Carnarvon—Mr HD Wolff—Sir E. Lytton (Telegram)—
Count Caruso (=8th). Drafts to Dusmani and N. Zambelli (in English).
Finished Narrative dispatch. Saw Abp of Corfu—Sig. Minghetti[9]—Dr N.
Zambelli—Cav. Curcumelli. Mod. Gk Grammar; MSS. and papers.

14. Fr.

Wrote to Sir T. Wyse—Admiral Fanshawe—Mad. Euphr. Samartzidou.[10]
Recast in Italian my letters to Dusmani & N. Zambelli. Began report on
the Cephalonian outbreak.[11] Saw Gen. & Lady Buller[12]—The President—
Count Caruso—Dr Cefalà. Conferences with & about A. Gordon. Drive &
walk with C.

15. Sat.

Wrote to Ld Granville—Sir J. Young. Saw Count Caruso—Dr Machariotti
—Sir J. Young (Palace arrangements). Drive with C. & discussed our plans.

[1] *Herbert was furious at Gladstone's acceptance of the lord high commissionership:
'I cannot say how much I am annoyed about Gladstone . . . What an infernal position
he has placed himself in! He really is not safe to go about out of Lord Aberdeen's room'
(Stanmore, *Herbert*, ii. 167).
[2] Giving details of proposed constitutional changes; not in *PP*, copy in Lytton Papers
D/EK 011.
[3] On the slopes of Mount Deka, S. of Corfu.
[4] Unidentified.
[5] He was this day appointed lord high commissioner by letters patent: *PP* 1861 lxvii.
99; see 25 Jan. 59.
[6] A small island in the British group, south of Corfu.
[7] Probably the *Gazette* of the Ionian senate, which was published occasionally.
[8] *PP* 1861 xlvii. 79.
[9] Unidentified.
[10] Unidentified.
[11] See next day.
[12] Henrietta, da. of Sir John *MacDonald, m. 1855 Sir George Buller.

12 to dinner and evening party till near midnight. Worked on Parl. papers and completed (with certain blanks) my report on the events of Cefalonia in 1849,[1] at 2½ A.M.

16. 2 S. Epiph.

Ch. mg. & aft. Conv. with Agnes. Walk with C. Read Nicoles Essais[2] & Vie d'Arnauld[3]—Greenwood's Latin Patriarchate[4]—S. Chrys. on reading H.S. cheap Edn. in modern Greek.

17. M. X

Heavy Mail from England and a hard day. Wrote to Sir E. Lytton (3)— Sir J. Graham—R. Phillimore—Vice Chancr. of Oxford—Provost of Oriel —Rev. Mr Greswell—Sir J. Young. Also Confidential Dispatch to Sir E. L[ytton][5]—Likewise to Sir Thos Wyse—M. Ozeroff—M. Rangabè—Lord A. Loftus—Saw Sir J. Young—& two[R]. Worked (forenoon) on MS. & Report.

18. T. X

Wrote to J.N.G.—Mr G. Burnett—Ld Carnarvon—R. Phillimore—A. Hayward[6]—Rev Mr Greswell. Saw Lt St John—just arrived from England —by Special Steamer![7]—Count Flamburiari—M. Vitalis . . . Mr Irving[8]— Sir D. Curcumelli—Cav. Valaviti.[9] Saw . . . [R]. Twelve to dinner: & party in the evening. Drove with C. to Castellanos[10] where we saw the costumes & ornaments, & the Greek dance: most curious especially for σεμνότης.[11]

19. Wed.

Wrote my letters after correction by Mr L. & discussion to Count Dusmani[12] —Sig N. Zambelli. 12–6. Expedition to Pantaleone & the Oak Tree beyond: a noble view descending towards Chorepiscopos. Saw Sir J. Young—Capt Glasse—Mr L. (resp. Senate). Wrote Mem. on the proposed Legislative Senate.[13] Read Dandolo's Tracts.[14]

[1] See 25 Jan. 59.
[2] See 27 Aug. 43.
[3] See 21 Mar. 58.
[4] See 25 Sept. 58.
[5] Sent next day, with a further Report; in Lytton Papers, D/EK 011.
[6] See A. *Hayward, Correspondence (1886), ii. 21.
[7] Gladstone was appalled at this extravagance, see Magnus, 151; the despatch brought news of the Oxford position; as L.H. Commissioner he had to resign his seat, but could not be re-elected while remaining commissioner; hence he risked losing it altogether; see 1 and 12 Feb. 59n.
[8] Mr. H. Irving; otherwise unidentified.
[9] Unidentified.
[10] Kastelani, a village high on the slopes of Mount Deka.
[11] 'dignity'.
[12] Elaborate draft in Italian in Add MS 44391, f. 62.
[13] Add MS 44748, f. 9.
[14] Probably A. Dandolo, Des Îles Ioniennes sous la protection britannique (1851).

20. Th.

Wrote to Sir Ed. Lytton—Saw Mr Barr—Col. Herbert[1]—Dr N. Zambelli
—Sir J. Young—The President—Capt. Turville.[2] 12–7. Expedition in
Osprey to Butrinto & the Mill worked by the subt[erranean] stream.
Dinner party & evg party at home. Worked on Message & Resolutions &c.
until late.

21. Fr.

Wrote Dft to Abp of Zante—Mr Lacaita (on Zambelli's paper)—Dft
Memm. on the Presidency.[3] Worked further on Resolutions. Saw Mr Barr[4]
—Capt Turville—Ct. Flamburiari cum Sir G Bowen—Mr Lacaita—Mr
Polilà—The President. Walked to Potamo.[5] Read Gk Papers. Came after
consn. to a Resolution to speak my mind to A. Gordon.[6]

22. Sat.

Wrote to Abp of Zante—Dft Dispatch to Sir E. Lytton—Part Private
Letter to do—Finished the remaining parts of my 2d Report. Saw The
President—Count Salomos—Count Roma (Sec.)—Captain Murray—Dr
Curis—A. Gordon—whom I told that he had not done his work & that his
heart was not in it. One of the most singular of men. Attended the farewell
party[7] at the Palace in evg: conv. with Lady Young. Read Zincke (in
Fraser) on my Homer.[8]

23. S. 3 Epiph.

Ch. mg & aft. Read Marcoran's Theol. Tracts.[9] Walk with C. Worked on
Speech (to accompany Resolutions). The A. Gordon affair still agitated.
Convv. with Mr Lacaita. Recd. & returned a foolish letter from C. Flam-
buriari.

24. M.

Wrote to R. Phillimore—Sir J. Graham—Sir E. Lytton (3)—Sir J. Young.
Three dispatches to C.O.—Col. Talbot—G. Burnett—Mr H. Irving—
Willy—Jas Watson. Assembly dinner of 12: and party till near midnight.
Saw Sir J. Young—Gen. Sir Geo. Buller—Mr Strachan: my new Aide de

[1] (Sir) Arthur James Herbert, 1820–97; fought in Crimea; D.Q.M.G. Corfu 1856–62;
K.C.B. 1882; general 1885.
[2] (Sir) Francis Charles Fortescue Turville, 1831–89; *Young's personal secretary in
Ionia 1854–9; governed N.S. Wales 1861–8, Canada 1868–72, K.C.M.G. 1875.
[3] Add MS 44748, f. 15.
[4] Edward Frederick Barr, assistant secretary, C.S.M.G. 1862.
[5] Along the coast to the north of the town.
[6] Gordon had been, by Gladstone's standards, slacking and there had been an argument over Strahan's appt.; see next day and *T.A.P.S.*, N.S. li, part 4, 6, 31.
[7] For the departing Youngs.
[8] *Fraser's Magazine*, lix. 50 (January 1859).
[9] G. Markoras, 'All' articolo del Drs. G. B. Scandella, su l'enciclica di Pio IX agli
Orientali' (1853) and 'Riposta all'articolo della Civiltà Cattolica' (1854).

C.[1]—A. Gordon: whose affair ends better than might have been expected—
The President—Ct. Flamburiari—Dr Dandolo—Sir Geo. Bowen (Message).

25. T.

Wrote to Sir S. Scott & Co—Rev H. Glynne. At midday I read in[2] before
the Senate & made a short address in answer to the President.[3] Assembly
met at one: & I had constant reports from it.[4] A dinner of members in the
evg: when I had conversations with Marino, Lombardo, and Linardato:[5] &
told them especially the last some sharp things: from a sense that it was
necessary. Saw Sir P. Braila . . . Mr Lacaita—Sir Geo. Bowen—C. Flamburiari. Worked on Speech for the Assembly—on Resolutions—& on
Cefalonian Report wh I corrected, to send home.[6]

26. Wed.

Wrote to Capt Glasse—Sir E. Lytton—Dispatch to ditto. Walk with Mr L.
Worked further on Speech. Saw Capt. Glasse—Sig. Polilà—Sir Geo.
Bowen—Captain Murray—The President—Mr Lacaita (whom I sent to
Foresti)—Cav. Braila—Dr Veja[7]—Conte Macrè.[8] Twelve to dinner (As-
sembly). Worked on Speech. Read Mad. de Sevigné.[9]

27. Th.

Wrote to Dr Dandolo—Sir Edw. Lytton—Earl Stanhope—Rev. Fr Vidal.
Worked on Speech—Draft Message—Saw Sir Geo. Bowen—Cav. Braila.
Drove with C. Attended the Opera in the evening.

28. Fr. X

Saw Ct. Flamburiari—Sir P. Braila (2)—The President (2)—Mr Lacaita—
Sir Geo. Bowen—Gen. Sir G. Buller. Saw [blank][R]. Finished the Speech.
Wrote & sent Message to the Assembly.[10] Minute to stop the public i.e.
Govt. illumination. Went out late to see the general one.[11] Drive with C. &
visited the Casino. Began dispatch. Read Mustoxidi's Illustrazioni.[12]

[1] (Sir) George Cumine Strahan, 1838–87; A.D.C. in Ionia 1859–64, in Malta 1864–8;
governed colonies; K.C.M.G. 1880.
[2] i.e. assumed office.
[3] Promising 'a prompt readjustment to the Ionian constitution' and summoning an
extraordinary session of the assembly: *PP* 1861 lxvii. 85. He this day, by proclamation,
assumed the duties of lord high commissioner: ibid. lxvii. 83.
[4] It passed a resolution proclaiming union with Greece the will of the Ionian people;
The Guardian, 9 February 1859, 107; Gladstone demanded a petition at most.
[5] Members of the Rizospast (unionist) group in the assembly, see ibid. lxvii. 85. Lombardo signed the pan-Hellenic declaration in *PP* 1861 lxvii. 8; MS by Lombardo,
'Considerazione sulla Questione Ionia' in Hawn P.
[6] Special Report on 1849 disturbances in Cephalonia: Lytton Papers D/EK 011.
[7] Unidentified.
[8] Demetrio Macri, legislator in Paxo.
[9] See 26 May 55.
[10] Telling it that any procedure (such as a declaration) other than a petition would be
unconstitutional: *PP* 1861 lxvii. 89, draft in Add MS 44747, f. 17.
[11] Fireworks display to support the assembly's declaration for union; only 'a very small
proportion of the inhabitants' attended: *PP* 1861 lxvii. 88.
[12] (Sir) A. Mustoxidi, *Illustrazioni Corciresi*, 2v. (1811–14).

29. Sat. X

Wrote to A.G. Dunlop[1]—Adm. Fanshawe (& copy). Saw Captain Glasse—
Papa Calagero[2]—Dr Foresti—Sir P. Braila, Sir Geo. Bowen, from time to
time. The Assembly kept me waiting all day & ended without adopting the
petition as prepared.[3] Sir G. B[owen] & I translated it. $9\frac{3}{4}$–$11\frac{1}{2}$ Attended
Ordination & Mass at St Antonio. There were noble hymns: & the whole
well deserved study. At one we went on board the Ariel[4] to see her. Saw[R].
Read Kendrick on I. Islands.[5]

30. 4 S. Epiph.

Ch mg & aftn. Read Εὐχολόγιον[6]—S. Chrys. on reading H. Scripture[7]—
Greenwood's Latin Patriarchate.[8] Walk after dusk. Corrected Speech
further. Translated in part the Rizospast (non-petitioning) petition. Waited
through aftn (except Ch) for the Assembly's Petition: we got it at six and
sent off with speed our series of Telegraphic Messages to Malta for England.[9]

31. M.

Wrote to Ld Aberdeen—Archbishop of Zante[10]—Minutes—(Dft dispatches
to) Sir E. Lytton—Sir E. Lytton (Private): & Telegram—Sir Jas Hudson[11]
—Earl Carnarvon—Duke of Newcastle. At one received the Prest. of the
Assembly with a Deputation: the petition was presented with a Greek
Speech to which I replied briefly in Italian. 2–6. To Sir P. Braila's Casino
and the Kyriake.[12] Both give most beautiful views: the former on the whole
the most lovely. C. gave a ball at the Palace at night. I used the time. Saw
Cav. Mustoxidi—Count Flamburiari—The President—Captain Murray—
Dr Curis—Dr Veja & others.

Tues. Feb. One 1859.[13] X

Saw Sir Geo. Bowen—The President—Sig. Arist. Valaoriti[14]—Cav. Curcumelli—Mr Boyd (the Treasurer)[15]—Dr Caritato.[16] 14 to dinner: a party

[1] Alexander Graham Dunlop, *Loftus' private sec. in Vienna 1858–60.
[2] Unidentified.
[3] Gladstone insisted the petition be not 'too imperious': ibid. lxvii. 88, drafts in Add
MS 44748, f. 26.
[4] A 9 gun screw steam sloop of the royal navy.
[5] T. T. C. Kendrick, The Ionian Islands (1822).
[6] The Euchologion, part of the liturgy according to the Greek Rite.
[7] One of Chrysostom's homilies, in Migne, PG, xlvii.
[8] See 25 Sept. 58.
[9] The petition declared that the 'disposition' (θέλησις—he was much concerned over
the translation) of the Ionians was for union of all the islands with Greece: PP 1861
lxvii. 89.
[10] He had refused to offer prayers for the Queen.
[11] Sir James *Hudson, 1810–85; sundry diplomatic posts; as British envoy to Turin
1851–63 played important role in Crimean and risorgimento negotiations.
[12] Kyriake, on slopes of Mount Deka, S. of the town.
[13] This day he wrote to resign as lord high commissioner, thus ensuring re-election: PP
1861 lxvii. 89. See 12 Feb. 59n.
[14] Aristos Valaorite, moderately pro-British member of the assembly.
[15] Alexander Fielding Boyd.
[16] Unidentified.

from the Assembly. Opera afr: & saw[R]. Read Kendrick—worked on Speech.

2. Wed. [Philiates, Albania]
Worked on Third Report.[1] Saw Dr Dandolo. Off at 11½ for Filates:[2] 1½ h. steam, 3 h. hard walk. We were the guests of the Validi Jaffier Pacha.[3] Visited the mosque, heard the muezzin, & went through the town. Turkish dinner, in rude abundance: after wh I smoked my first & last Chibouk.[4] Conv. by interpp. with our hostess resp. her Son whom she wants me (!) to get appointed Pacha in Albania: & with the Moodir.[5] Turkish night accommn. too. The whole impression is most saddening: it is all all indolence, decay, stagnation: the image of God seems as if it were nowhere.

But there is much of wild & picturesque.

3. Th. [Corfu]
Off at 8 instead of 7: thanks to the Turkish ideas of time. Three hours walk to the sea in pouring rain. Reached Casa Cordi[6] at 1.45: The Osprey rolled much. Saw Count Bulgari—Cavaliere Valaoriti—C. Flamburiari—The President. 14 to dinner. Worked on Resolutions & Speech. Read Kendrick's I.I.—Revue Contemp. on my Homer.[7]

4. Fr.
Wrote to Count Flamburiari—Worked upon Speech & Resolutions in finally maturing them: recd. messages in evg by Telegraph[8] & then got ready the Queen's message & all else for tomorrow. Saw Dr Foresti—Sir G. Bowen—Sir P. Braila—Mr Lacaita. Read [blank]. Up late.

5. Sat.
Going over the versions in Italian & Greek. Saw C. Flamburiari—The President—Sir P. Braila—Sir G. Bowen—Mr Lacaita. Senate met at 1½: read Message there. Then Assembly 2–4 where I read Message and Speech.[9] Party for children at the Palace in the evg. Read Kendrick on I.I. Worked on Greek Documents.

6. S 5 Epiph.
Ch & H.C. mg—Ch again aftn. Read Marcoran's Tr. of S. Chrys. Liturgy[10]

[1] See 7 Feb. 59.
[2] Philiates, an Albanian walled town on the mainland, nearly opposite Corfu. This area remained Turkish until annexed by Greece 1912–13.
[3] Civil governor of the province.
[4] The long Turkish tobacco-pipe.
[5] Governor of the village.
[6] The Gladstone's house.
[7] *Revue Contemporaine*, vi. 806 (1858); enthusiastic, with qualifications.
[8] Telegraphed 'message', read next day.
[9] Queen's message rejecting the petition for union. Gladstone proposed instead an Ionian ministerial council 'open to the influence of the chambers' with powers to the chambers to remove ministries, and other reforms, including ending elections to paid positions; all rejected, no Ionian voting for them: *PP* 1861 lxvii. 91, 99.
[10] By G. Markoras; see 8 Jan. 59.

—Greenwood's Cathedra Petri[1]—Braila's Transl.[2] Wrote (in Italian & English) a letter to Sir P. Braila.[3] Worked on proof sheets of Speech Message &c: & was disturbed with Telegrams &c. till 2½ h past midnight.

7. M.

A heavy mail—Wrote to Sir E.B. Lytton (2)—Do Telegram—Do Dispatch[4] —Do Confidential Do—Dr R. Phillimore—Sir J. Graham—Mr Wolff— Mr S. Herbert—Sir H. Storks—V. Consul Raven—Mr A. Hayward—Mr Burnett. Dined at General Buller's. Saw Col. Herbert. Saw A. Gordon— Sir Geo. Bowen—Count Dusmani—Sig. Temist. Zambelli. Walk late.

8. Tues.

Wrote to Sir H. Storks (Telegram)—Sig. Polilà—Sig. Giulio Tipaldo[5]— Williams & Norgate. Read Kendrick (finished)—Tre Costituzioni[6]— Studied Maps & Murray. Saw Count Dusmani[7]—Sir Geo. Bowen—Sig. Matteoli[8]—Mr Lacaita: whose ingatherings of rumour are all bad—General Buller—with whom I went over the Citadel—Sir P. Braila—to whom I read parts of Sir E.L.s letter.

9. Wed.

Wrote draft dispatches for tomorrow. 10–3½. Visit to Coracchiana, by invitation of the village.[9] We were met by the population, entertained; charmed with the prospects: & I had a political discussion of perhaps an hour, which ended well. Saw Sir Geo. Bowen—The Russian Consul—C. Flamburiari—Sig. Bisi—Sir P. Braila—Mr Lacaita. Read Le Tre Costituzioni. Ball at the Palace in evg. Worked on 3d Report.

10. Th. X

Wrote dispatches to Sir E.L.[10]—Telegram to do. 12–2. Visited Mr Woodhouse's[11] curious & rich collection with Cav. Mustoxidi. Saw Sir P. Braila —Mr Sergeant—Dr Veja—Sir G. Bowen. Saw [blank][R]. Fourteen to dinner. Tried Murray & Modern Greek Grammar afterwards, but at 12½ Nature beat me.

11. Fr.

Wrote to Col. Herbert. Worked long on the Cefalonian Courts Martial &

[1] See 25 Sept. 58.
[2] See 13 Feb. 59.
[3] Draft in Add MS 44391, f. 132.
[4] Sent next day: *PP* 1861 lxvii. 89.
[5] Member of the assembly.
[6] See 31 Dec. 58.
[7] Dusmani, sec. to the senate, told Gladstone the reforms would not be passed; Gladstone's influence subsequently removed him from office (Kirkwall, *Four years*, i. 236).
[8] Member of the assembly.
[9] Korakiana, about 10 miles NW. of the town.
[10] Enclosing copy of extremist Greek newspaper: *PP* 1861 lxvii. 95.
[11] See 15 Dec. 58.

made notes therefrom.[1] Drove to Garuna:[2] one of the most beautiful points among many lovely. Saw Cav. Valaoriti—Sir Geo. Bowen—The Montenegrin Bodyguard's man—Mr Wortley—Mr Lacaita. Busy packing China. Read Faust.

12. Sat.[3]

Wrote to Sir H Storks LHC.[4] Off at 10 to San Salvador:[5] we went up from Ipso[6] visiting Spartilla on the way. There we had a festive reception. Went up & along the top to the monastery where we saw the two ships of Ulysses Italy & Cephalonia: then straight to the sea & back at $7\frac{3}{4}$ by Osprey. I was on foot. Opera 9-11 (Barbiere)—Saw Sir Geo. Bowen. Worked on Third Report. Read Tennyson's Poems.[7]

13. 6 S. Epiph.

Ch mg & aft. Read Greenwood's Cath Petri[8]—Braila (Transl) μελετάι[9] —The πετρὰ σκανδάλου.[10] A quieter Sunday. Telegrams to Engl. & Malta. Draft reply to Caruso. Began with effort a letter to J. Hope Scott.[11]

14. M.

Wrote (L.H.C.) Minutes. Worked on Third Report. Wrote dispatch to C.O. Letters to Sir E.B. Lytton—Robn. G.—W. Hampton.—G. Burnett. Saw the President—Count Flamburiari—Cav. Braila. Busy packing & with plans. Ferried across the old harbour & visited the 'Ship of Ulysses' & curious old Byzantine Church on it.[12]

15. T.

Wrote to R. Phillimore—Sir James Hudson—Sir H. Storks. Finished and revised Third Report. Drive with C. & Mr L. Saw Capt. Glasse—Dr Dandolo—Dr Santorio—Conte Savini[13]—Sir D. Valsamachi—Conte Anino[14] —Dr Scalzani[15]—Conte Caruso—Dr N. Zambelli—The President—Sir Geo. Bowen—Mr Lacaita. Preparations for departure & a hard day.

[1] Not found.

[2] Apano-Garuna, on the W. shoulder of Mount Deka.

[3] He was this day returned unopposed as M.P. for Oxford university, in the by-election resulting from his appt. as lord high commissioner.

[4] *Storks was in Malta, leaving for Ionia, already appt. commissioner.

[5] On the shoulder of mount S. Salvatore, 15 miles N. of Corfu town, from which is seen the rock resembling a ship, said to be the Phaecians' galley, which, returning from taking Ulysses to Ithaca, was changed to stone by the vengeance of Neptune (*Od.* xiii. 161). See also 14 Feb. 59.

[6] Small port 9 miles N. of Corfu town.

[7] *Maud, and other poems* (1855), reviewed by Gladstone with the *Idylls* (July 1859); see 14 July 59n.

[8] See 25 Sept. 58.

[9] 'Meditations'.

[10] 'a stumbling stone'; see Romans ix. 33.

[11] *Hope-Scott's first wife and two children both died in November–December 1858.

[12] The island of Pondikonisi, linked by causeway to the peninsula south of Corfu town, is by local tradition the real Ship of Ulysses (see 12 Feb. 59).

[13] Neither identified.

[14] Unidentified.

[15] Giovanni Scalzuni, Ionian who published on Darwinism in Trieste 1879.

16. Wed.

Half invalided with a bad cold. Spent the morning in packing. Sat to Major Shakespeare[1] for Photographs: alone & in a party. Received Sir H. Storks at the door of the Palace: & made him known to the President Senators & others.[2] Dinner party of sixteen in evg, & some 30 more in evg: when I introduced him all round. Long & most satisfactory interview with him at the Palace. Saw Sir G. Bowen—Sir P. Braila—Dr N. Zambelli—Mr Sergeant. Worked on accounts.[3] Read Demiva.[4]

17. Th.

Up late. Wrote to S. Herbert—Sir E. Lytton—Dispatch to Do.[5]—R.W. Rawson—Mr T.A. Cowper—Signor Economides[6]—Count Flamburiari (& draft)—J.R. Hope-Scott (& do). Continued & nearly finished my packing. Two more interviews with Sir F. Storks [sic]: who read in today. Saw Sir P. Braila—Sir G. Bowen—Mr Lacaita—Cav. Mustoxidi. Read Demiva. Visited the University.[7]

18. Fr.

Wrote to Cav. Braila. Wrote answer to *Draft* Assembly's Reply to be left in Sir H.S.s hands.[8] Again we sat in group to Major Shakespeare. We all dined at the Presidents. Saw the L H Commr. (2)—Sir P. Braila (2)—Arthur Gordon—The President—Sir Geo. Bowen—Gen. & Ly Buller—Capt. Glasse. 4–6—Went over Vido.[9] Packing. Read Q.R. on Reform[10]—Edinb. R. on do.[11] without much light from either.

19. Sat. [*On ship*]

Saw The President—The L.H. Commissioner (3)—Dr N. Zambelli. Packing & final arrangements. Formal leave-taking of the Senate & all the authorities in the Palace at $2\frac{1}{2}$: public embarkation at 3: off a little before four with bright sun & calm: soon overcast: at 8 or 9 we were in the jaws of the *borra*.[12] Read some of Fauriel's Greek songs.[13] I bade good bye with emotion to Braila & to Strahan. The Abp came: wh I rather regretted. Visit to the very interesting Penitentiary.

[1] Major David Shakespear of the royal artillery; he and his wife were, according to Edward *Lear, the pleasantest people on Corfu (*Letters of E. Lear* (1907), 78).
[2] The assembly had spun out discussion on the Gladstone proposals, since its members stood to lose considerably by them, and later rejected them.
[3] Sent third Report, in Lytton Papers, D/EK 011.
[4] Untraced.
[5] *PP* 1861 lxvii. 97.
[6] Perhaps I. N. Oikonomides, Greek author.
[7] Founded in 1823 by Lord Guildford.
[8] Some assembly members supported a vote of thanks to Gladstone; Kirkwall, *Four years*, ii. 243 and *PP* 1861 lxvii. 99.
[9] Small island a mile N. of the town.
[10] *Quarterly Review*, cv. 255 (January 1859).
[11] *Edinburgh Review*, cix. 264 (January 1859).
[12] 'North wind'. The assembly declined to see him off, and remained in session while the departure ceremonies were gone through; Kirkwall, *Four years*, ii. 243.
[13] C. C. Fauriel, *Chants populaires de la Grèce*, 2v. (1824).

20. S & 21 M.

Sea-sickness! at the lowest depth. With the utmost effort could I get through my prayers. Monday afternoon I began slowly to mend but sore shaken. C. & Agnes suffered but less: Mr Lacaita much like me. Had some liquid.

22. T.

After 66 hours we were in Pola: & after much doubt decided on crossing to Venice even with *Borrino*[1] for daylight to try the Malamocco bar.[2] Got back to solid food: & mended well today. Read Fauriel's Gr. songs— Murray's Handbook N. Italy.

23. Wed. [*Venice*]

Reached Malamocco at 9 and the Hotel de la Ville at 12 after 2 h. rowing. A reluctant adieu to the Terrible. Found my letters & wrote Telegram to Malmesbury[3]—

Letter to S. Herbert } for Post
Sir E. Lytton

J.N.G. } for tomorrow.
H.J.G.

Saw the British Consul:[4] who dined with us. Visited St Mark's: & shops: also fed on the exterior of Venice: not what it was in 1832: but still much. Enjoyed the Austrian band: wh will I suppose play on till the Etat de Siege begins.[5]

24. Th.

A day of much interest.[6] The noble Gallery of Pictures chiefly Venetian. I must remember that miracle of power Tintoret's St Mark—The wonderful Doge's Palace—The old shops: few objects but how beautiful. The Fenice in evg: the Opera good but ballet at nauseam, chiefly mere muscle— Caffè Restaurant, sunshine, music, all the right incidents & no wrong ones: much with C. & much with Mr L. A. Gordon left us in evg. Saw the Consul & Mrs James[7]—Made all the calls of Office.

25. Fr.

Wrote to Sir J. Young—Sir E. Lytton (Telegram & Letter).[8] Breakfast at

---

[1] Probably used as a diminutive of 'borra'; see 19 Feb. 59.
[2] Part of the military cordon round the Venetian lagoon.
[3] *Malmesbury had wired that the Lord's deb. on Gladstone's resolutions had been delayed till his arrival: Add MS 44391, f. 158.
[4] G. P. R. *James, the novelist, who d. here 1860.
[5] Following the meeting of Cavour and Napoleon at Plombières in July 1858, Victor Emmanuel had made his *il grido di dolore* speech on 10 Jan. 1859; *Derby's govnt. was working to discourage a Franco-Sardinian attack on Austria; after negotiations, war began on 27 April.
[6] See 15–25 June 32 for his previous visit.
[7] An American, she d. 1891.
[8] In Lytton Papers, D/EK 012.

Florian's [café]. Much work in the China shops: settled all my purchases & the packing & junction in a vast box. Visited the Ch. of the Frari—The Santi Giovanni & Paolo—Saint Mark—Some exteriors: & the Coleone. I at last appreciated the Martyrdom of S. Pietro Inqu. as a picture. The Brostolone carvings: the Vendeamini monument: the Tintoretto of the Senators: & the interest of the Ch as a Cemetery: the Piazza too is wonderful. In the Frari the exceeding beautiful carving of the Choir: and in the opposite sense the grand Barocco monument of Vixit Devixit & Revixit (ab. 1669?).[1] Saw the English Consul. Dined at the Palace. The Archduke & Archduchess are a singularly pleasing pair.[2] She is striking too. I as the only stranger was by HRH: on the other side I had a signal Italian beauty Contessa Marcello,[3] likewise a most pleasing person. Made the acquaintance of her husband—Count Bembo[4] & others: a short but very interesting evening. Walk with C. afterwards: & up late with my packing. This visit to Venice has been in truth a surfeit.

26. Sat. [Vicenza]

Wrote to Capt Glasse. Ascended the Campanile. Saw Capt Glasse—the Consul—& his remarkable young son. ,

26 Sat. continued.[5] Off at 11. Farewell to Florians: completed the Grand Canal on the way to the Station. Reached Vicenza in evg. 5 hours at Padua: with great delight. What first what last? Take St Antonio alone. The Mantegna fresco of N.S.—The Giotto do of St A[ntonio]—The Ricci Candelabrum—The gem of San Felice—The Sister Bell towers—Not to name the bas reliefs & much beside. S. Giustina: the space & character: the Choir carvings. Eremitani: the architecture of Choir & Chapel: The horse & man of Donatello: Gatta Melata: that Giotto Chapel: The Hall: & last but not least the delightful *character* so deeply marked on this city as a whole. Dined at Stella d'Oro. Tea at Vicenza H[otel] de la V[ille]. Convn. about A. Gordon: not agreeable. Read Cusani on I. Islands.[6] He writes well. Bad signs & menacing accounts meet us of the political condition of this country.

27. Sexa[gesima] S.

Prayers morning at 10: with MS of 47 for Sexa. S. and at 8½ in evg. Went into various Churches mg: and at 5 P.M. heard a predica[7] in the Church of the Servi. It was of more sound than substance. Went up the Berici hill

---

[1] Barthel's monument to Giovanni Pesaro (1669), regarded by Murray's *Handbook for . . . Northern Italy* (1856), i. 342 as 'a curious specimen of the bad taste of the seventeenth century'.

[2] Ferdinand Maximilian Joseph, br. of Franz Joseph I; chief of the Austrian navy; m. 1857 Marie Charlotte, da. of Leopold I of Belgium. Gladstone found him 'kind, intelligent, ingenuous, & earnest' (to *Lytton, 26 Feb. 59, Lytton Papers, D/EK 012).

[3] Contessa Andriana, wife of Count Girolamo Marcello, Venetian naval officer.

[4] Salomon Pier Luigi Bembo, 1823–82, later a senator.

[5] The rest of the entries are on the back flyleaf and on a piece of paper fastened to it.

[6] F. Cusani, *La Dalmazia, le isole Ionie e la Grecia visitate nel 1840*, 2v. (1847).

[7] 'Sermon'.

with Mr Lacaita: saw the Madonna del Monte with the curious adaptation of the old Church & the new:[1] the Paolo Veronese, banquet of St Gregory, with its remarkable history:[2] & the old cloister. We went all about the town & admired the facades of the Duomo, the Corona, and San Lorenzo: the Venetian and the Palladian tribes of palaces: and the chastening effect which Palladio seems to have had on the whole architecture of Vicenza. The day was bright but the atmosphere overhung: we could however see how very grand the Berici view ought to be. A small facade on the right as we entered the city descending recalled the Wingless Victory at Athens. Read S. Chrys. on reading H.S. and Greenwood's Cathedra Petri.[3]

28. [*Milan*]

Went early to see the Palladian Theatre:[4] an effort of much interest & capable of varied development & application? 1½ hour by rail brought us to Verona at 10½. Here we were delighted, above all with the perspectives of the town and the views from the RR between the Stations, from the Anfiteatro, and from the Ponte delle Navi which must more or less compete with Prague. Then as to particular objects the Palazzo della Ragione: Ch of St Zeno; facade & general interior effect, the crypt, and the singularly beautiful & graceful 14th Century Frescoes, with some of the Greek School intermixed: here was an enthusiastic young Custode, a scraper of walls. S. Anastasia: a noble general effect: Italian Gothic Cathedral: the facade, another & simpler Titian's Assumption: old tomb of St Agata: S. Fermo Maggiore: more disclosures from the wall in progress: a second very old Crucifixion recently (1858) discovered. In San Zenone I may add we saw the palimpsest frescoes.[5] The amphitheatre: could but a cincture like that at Pola be added? After refreshment we returned to the train: again an intelligent fellow traveller gave us very sad accounts of the burdens of the country. Milan at 9.20 P.M. At Vicenza we had cavalry & artillery by the Station about to march: more cavalry on the road with a van & pickets, some with drawn swords: at Verona regiments in review: at Milan pickets in the streets; as I write I hear the tread of horse patrolling the streets. Dark omens! Read Murray on Verona—Cusani's Ionian Islands.

[The verso of p. 159 of the MS, i.e. facing the back flyleaf, contains:—]

Statesmen in the Maternal ancestry of the children.

Rt Hon Geo. Grenville......Gr Gr Grandfather to W.H. Gladstone.
Sir W. Wyndham ....Gr. Gr. Gr. Grandfather
Ld Chatham...............Gr. Gr. Grandfather in law

[1] Pilgrimage church on the monte Berico, the scene of fierce fighting 1848.
[2] Veronese's Banquet of Gregory the Great was torn to pieces in the 1848 fighting, but was restored from a copy.
[3] See 25 Sept. 58.
[4] The teatro Olimpico, the most important theatre of the Italian renaissance.
[5] Fourteenth century frescoes on the left of the choir, painted over those of the twelfth century.

Mr Pitt . . . . .1st Cousin thrice removed . .
Lord Grenville . . . . .Gr. Grand Uncle
Mr Grenville . . . . .Gr. Grand Uncle

[In the bottom left-hand corner:—]

May June 57. & after
My Print (proof before letters)
sent to
Mr Murray
Mr Elwin
Mr Greswell (framed)
Dr Jacobson
Dr Hawkins
Mr Woollcombe
Mr Haddan
Dean of Salisbury
Mr Barker Proof
Mr Burnett do
Mr Hodgson do before letters
Mr. J.W. Gladstone (Biggar)
H[elen] J.G. (Jul. 58)

[In the bottom right-hand corner:—]

Journey to Scotland: 3 maîtres
and two servants. Sep. Oct. 58.
Sep. 1 . . . . .129 m . . . .£5. 3. 7.
      3 . . . . 31 m . . . . 2. 0. 7.
      6 . . . . 49 m 1. 14. 6
      9 . . . . 79 m . . . . 2. 7. 10.
      10 and 11 ⎱ 240 m . . . .10. 5. 6.
      to Inverness ⎰
      11 . . . . 62 m . . . . 4. 8. 2.
      ————   ————

Hawarden &c.   ⎱
to Dunrobin   ⎰ 590 m. £26. 0. 2.[1]
Sutherland W.   ⎱
tour 170 m.   ⎰
Dunrobin to Haddo House . . . . ⎱
W.E.G. 178 m the rest 103 m. ∴ average ⎰ 116 m . . . .£5. 9. 10.
Dunrobin servants . . . . 2. 5. 0.
Haddo and Fasque do . . . . 1. 10. 6.
To Fasque   2. 1. 2
To Keir   98 m.   2. 4. 2.
Towards Willy's jour.   2.
Glas to Lpool   8. 12.

¹ In pencil.

[At the top of the back flyleaf:—]

Ap. 20/57. Parker J.W. for Oxf. Essay £39. 4.
                              +ten copies Vol.
    30.   Murray for Pol. Art in Q.R. £50[1]

[1] There are also traces of pencil writing on the flyleaf, mostly obscured by the attached paper and very faint but including the names 'Watson, Rigby, Lightfoot'—all rescue cases—under an address, 'Villas, Notting Hill'.

[1 MARCH 1859 TO 20 SEPTEMBER 1860]

[The inside front cover contains:—]

1859–60.

W.E.G.

Private.

(NO. 21.)

Milan March One 1859.

This town pleases more & more on each visit:² not withstanding that it is a dead flat: more completely such than any great city I know. The Cathedral, the Brera, & the great Hospital were our objects today. The interior of the first is grander to the eye & heart at each new visit. The Hospital is a most grand though half spoiled exterior, other buildings noteworthy. The Brera tho' not first is good second rate. We found the [Santa Maria] Delle grazie shut. Much engaged—once more—in the shops for China & antiquities. Read Jacini's Lombardia³—The Scala shut.

2. Wed. [Turin]

Wrote to Sir E. Lytton—Mr J.S. Wortley. To the Duomo mg: also to buy Segneri:⁴ & settling accounts. 11–6. To Turin. An intelligent engineer gave me an admirable explanation of the Alpine tunnel;⁵ and we travelled the last part with Guicialdini.⁶ The view between the Alps & the lower hills (of the Superga) was peculiar & delightful: & at Vercelli⁷ we saw admirably the beautiful facades of St Andrea—the first—& of the Cathedral (2). We met Sir Jas Hudson at the Station & were at once most agreeably impressed. I went in evg to see Ristori in Phèdre. *Great* but not *Gk*. The others I thought acted better here than in London.⁸ Europa good as ever. Read Jacini.

¹ Lambeth MS 1435, ff. 129.
² See 6 July 32, 21 Sept. 39, 30 July 49.
³ S. Jacini, *La proprietà fondiaria e le popolazioni agricole in Lombardia* (1854).
⁴ See 13 Mar. 59.
⁵ Begun 1857; see 31 Oct. 50.
⁶ Probably Enrico Guicciardi, 1812–95, commissar in Valtellina in 1859 war, later prefect and senator.
⁷ Midway between Milan and Turin.
⁸ See 9 July 58.

3. Th. X

Saw Sir J. Hudson—Count Cavour: confidential down to a certain date[1]—
Sig. Farini[2]—Sig. Massari—Gen. La Marmora[3]—Sig. Broglia.[4] Attended
the Chamber of Deputies. Visited the Collection of Sig. Della Chiesa:[5] &
shops—with the Minister. Dined with the Minister. Saw one[R]. Read
Jacini.

4. Fr. [In coach]

Wrote to Sig. Manzoni—Sir T. Fremantle—Marchesa Aranati Visconti.[6]
Saw the Mil. Inst. Quadrangle—Sig. Vela's Studio: & his Primavera.[7]—the
Archivio & Library—the Marochetti Statue. Saw Sig. Torelli[8]—Sig.
Farini—Minr. of Educn.—Conte Sclopis[9]—C. Paleocapo[10]—Gen La
Marmora—Sig. Scialoja[11]—Sir J. Hudson—C. Cavour—Sig. Massari—
Swedish Minr.[12] Visited the Picture Gallery. Attended the Senate. More
transactions in China: I have now done my work for the year in this line:
or nearly. Was much struck & pleased at the Gallery with the G. Bellini &
one of the Gaud. Ferrari's. Dined with C. Cavour $5\frac{1}{2}$–$8\frac{1}{2}$.[13] Off by train at
$9\frac{1}{2}$: from Susa at $11\frac{1}{2}$: in Diligence then traineau;[14] the latter *most* disagreeable, downhill.

5. Sat. [On train]

12 h brought us from Susa to St Jean: there we resumed the rail which gave
us fine scenery all the way to Chambery, on by the Lake of Annecy (poor
J.J!)[15] at Culoz & through the defiles of the Jura. Still on & on: Agnes as
well as C. an excellent traveller. Read Jacini. Much rumination.

[1] Gladstone spent an hour alone with Cavour; see G. Massari, *Diario 1858–60
Sull'Azione Politica di Cavour* (1931), 218ff. Massari supervised the visit, persistently
impressing Sardinian virtue upon Gladstone.
[2] Luigi Carlo Farini, 1812–66, liberal catholic whose book Gladstone translated (see
27 Nov. 50); led govt. in Modena 1859 which called for Sardinian annexation; prime
minister, though deranged, 1863.
[3] Alfonso Ferrero, marquis di Lamarmora, 1804–78; minister of war; prime minister
July 1859–60; 1864–6; chief of staff in 1866 war.
[4] Emilio Broglio; they discussed income tax, Broglio dismaying Gladstone with dirty
conversation; Massari, op. cit., 222.
[5] Perhaps Camillo della Chiesa della Torre, 1812–88; soldier, commanded a brigade
1859–60.
[6] This name added on inside of front cover.
[7] Vicenzo Vela, 1820–91; sculptor.
[8] Luigi Torelli, 1810–87; Sardinian politician; supervised troops in Florence in 1859
war.
[9] Count Federigo Sclopis, 1798–1878; Piedmontese senator; see Massari, op. cit., 223.
[10] Pietro Paleocapa, Sardinian minister of public works; see Massari, op. cit., 223.
[11] Antonio Scialoia, 1817–77; lately professor of political economy in Turin, adviser to
Cavour on fiscal policy; minister of finance 1862–6; in office again after 1870.
[12] Karl Edouard Piper.
[13] Earlier this day Nigra was told by Napoleon III that there was need for 'a moment
of truce to resettle ourselves in the saddle' and that, barring aggression by Austria, war
must be delayed till 1860; A. J. Whyte, *Political life and letters of Cavour* (1930), 280.
Account of the dinner in Massari, op. cit., 223.
[14] 'sledge'.
[15] This was where Rousseau first lived with Mme. de Warens, who sent him to a seminary in Turin.

6. Quinqua. S. [Paris]

Reached Hotel Castiglione[1] at $7\frac{1}{4}$ A.M. Two hours bed. Rue de la Madeleine Ch. & H.C. at $11\frac{1}{2}$—Ch again at $3\frac{1}{2}$. Saw Ld Chelsea[2]—Mr Wilberforce[3]— and Dr Moffatt a Scotch doctor who is in the hotel. Read S. Chrys. on reading H.S.[4]—I. Williams on Nativity.[5] Walked much.

7. M. [On train]

Saw Ld Chelsea—Ld Brougham—Sir John Young—Mr Brown (Corr. of M. Post).[6] Saw Notre Dame—the S. Chapelle—S. Germain—after much labour we got into the Louvre & much enjoyed (espy.) the room of Chef d'Œuvres. About book & China shops: but refrained from buying, as to the latter absolutely. We left by the train at 7.30 & travelled all night. A rough passage which C. A. & I withstood.

8. T. X [London]

Reached No 11 at $8\frac{3}{4}$: & had the delight of seeing the four all well. Wrote to Duchess of Sutherland—Rev. Jas Trevitt—Rev. Whitwell Elwin—Saw Sidney Herbert—Sir Jas Graham—Jas Wortley—J. Wilson Patten— E. Cardwell—Sir Edw. Lytton—Mr H.D. Wolff—Mr Lacaita. H. of C. 4–7. Took the oath. Read Bagehot on Reform.[7] Saw R. Tull—Stapylton: & made other inquiries[R].

9. Ash Wednesday

Wrote to Mr De la Pryme—Mr Jas. Watson—M.F. Tupper—G. Gowland (Coalwhippers)[8]—Rev. M. McColl. Saw Mr Lacaita—Mr Panizzi—Sir Edw. Lytton—Lord Derby cum do.—Lord Carnarvon—Ld Aberdeen—Ly. Wenlock. St James' Ch at 11. Unpacking our China: so much as has arrived. Read pamphlets: Brogniart.[9] H. of C. 4–6. Voted for 2d reading of the very feeble Ch. Rate Bill.[10]

10. Th.

Wrote to Sir E. Lytton—Saw Ld Grey—Mr Labouchere—Sir G. Lewis— Cornwall Legh—E. Cardwell—do cum Mr Langston[11]—Jas. Wilson.—B. Benjamin—Mr Lacaita—B. Quaritch—Mr Panizzi. H. of C. $4\frac{1}{2}$–8.[12] Lacaita & Panizzi dined—Saw L. Spur & R. Gray—new Chapters! the latter shd. be looked after[R]. Read Bohn on Porcelain &c[13]—Mill on Liberty.[14] Worked on papers.

---

[1] In Paris.   [2] See 16 Jan. 44.
[3] Unclear which; probably Henry, then writing for Roman catholic journals.
[4] See 30 Jan. 59.
[5] *I. Williams, Our Lord's Nativity (1851).
[6] E. N. Browne, now in Paris; see 21 Dec. 50.
[7] W. *Bagehot, Parliamentary Reform; an essay (1859).
[8] George Gowland, of Walton & Gowland, London coal shippers.
[9] A. Brongniart, Traité des arts céramiques (1854).
[10] It was defeated: H clii. 1598.
[11] James Haughton Langston, 1797–1863; tory M.P. Oxford city 1826–34, and from 1841.
[12] Spoke on exchequer bills: H clii. 1636.
[13] See 22 June 57.   [14] Just published.

11. *Fr.*

Wrote to Messrs. G. & Co—Mr Wrenfordsley—Mr Growcott—Mr Hoskins.[1] Saw Mr Wolff—Ld Elcho—Jas. Wortley—J.R. Godley—Scotts—Mr Wickens[2]—Robn. G. Sir J. Graham. Read Letters on Italy. Worked at my China. H. of C. 4–7¼.[3] Dined with the Jameses.

12. *Sat.*

Wrote to Rev. Dr Dyne[4]—Sir Edw. Lytton—H.J.G.—Jas. Watson—Sir E. Wilmot—Rev. Mr Cosens—Sir J. Young—Mr Wickens—G. Burnett—T. Hare[5]—Dr Jelf—Mr Donkin. Saw Sir Wm. Heathcote—Mr Panizzi—Lord J. Russell—Lord Stanhope—Mr Wilson. Read Ly Morgan's Diary[6]—Hare on Representation. Attended Brit. Museum. Stephy came home for his Sunday.

13. *1. S. Lent*

St Martin's H.C. 8½ a.m.—Chapel Royal at noon—Abbey 7–9. Heard Mr Butler of Wantage+MS. (finished this day) at night.[7] Saw A. Panizzi (Neap. Exiles)[8] S. Herbert—A. Hayward—G. Harcourt. Read Segneri's Quaresima[9]—S. Chrys. on reading H.S.—Greenwood's Cathedra Petri. How on this return to our home & children gratitude ought to overflow in me with shame!

14. *M.*

Wrote to Sir Jas. Hudson—Dined with the Herberts: much conv. with S.H. & Sir J. Graham on Foreign Policy & on Reform. Wrote to O. Blewitt—Robn. G.—D.A. Nagle[10]—H.J.G.—E. Lovell. Rev. E. Munro—Rev. J. Stothert. H. of C. 4½–7½.[11] Saw Mr Gregory M.P.[12]—Mr Puller—Mr Carrington[13]—and others. Sir E. Lytton.
Read D. of Buckingham's Memoirs Geo IV.[14]—Worked on papers. [In pencil:—] Imperfect.

[1] John Brownlow Hoskins, London barrister.
[2] (Sir) John *Wickens, 1815–73; equity counsel to treasury 1843–69; well known chancery lawyer, later judge; kt. 1871.
[3] Dockyards: *H* cliii. 39.
[4] John Bradley Dyne, 1809–98; fellow of Wadham, Oxford 1832–8; headmaster of Highgate school 1838–74; D.D. 1858.
[5] Thomas *Hare, 1806–91; barrister and proportional representationalist; had sent his 'Treatise on the election of representatives, parliamentary and municipal' (1859).
[6] S. *Morgan, Lady Morgan, *Diary and correspondence in France* (1859).
[7] i.e. W. J. *Butler of the Wantage rescue home (see 8 June 57).
[8] Poerio and Settembrini had been released and put on a ship for America: they escaped and landed at Queenstown, where they were assisted by a cttee. run by *Panizzi, with Gladstone, *Argyll and others; see Lacaita, 122.
[9] P. P. Segneri, *Quaresimale* (1679).
[10] David Augustine Nagle, solicitor, of Queenstown; see Add MS 44391, f. 191.
[11] Landed estates: *H* cliii. 95.
[12] (Sir) William Henry *Gregory, 1817–92; Peelite/liberal M.P. Galway 1857–72 (but voted for Derby's reform bill 1859); governed Ceylon 1872–6; involved in the Ionian question.
[13] Possibly R. Carrington, admiralty draughtsman.
[14] R. P. T. N. B. C. *Grenville, *Memoirs of the Court of George IV*, 2v. (1859).

15. T.

Wrote to Sir H. Storks (2)—H.H. Sir A. Damaschino—Sir Geo. Bowen—
Count Flamburiari—Mr Wolff—Rev. Mr Hackman. Saw Jas. Wortley—
Mr Henley M.P.—Heathcote—J. Wilson Patten M.P.—Lord Hardinge
—R. Phillimore—Mr Lacaita—D[uche]ss Sutherland—Lady Wharn-
cliffe. Neap. Exiles Committee 4–5½.[1] Saw E. Lovell—well[R]. H. of C.
One to four. Voted agt. aboln. of Church Rate.[2] Read Brodrick on Com-
petn.[3]

16. Wed.

Wrote to Rev. Mr Young—Rev. G. Rawlinson—Dr Dyne—Mr Riordon—
Mr Jus. Birch[4]—T. Rathbone—W. White—L. Heinemann.[5] Saw Duchess
of Sutherland—Mr Ellice—Baron Rothschild—C. Corti—Earl of Aberdeen
—Sir J. Graham—J. Wilson Patten—The Speaker—Mr Grenville M.P.[6]
—Mr A. Finlay M.P. H. of C. 3–5.[7] Dined at the Speaker's: Lord Stanhope's
& Cambridge House afterwards. Read Disraeli's Reform Speech.[8]

17. Th.

Wrote to Mr Woodgate—Mr Quinn—Mr Dobie[9]—Mr A. Tucker—
E.W. Keyse.[10] Saw J.N.G.—Mr Lacaita—Mr Darby—Sig. Settembrini—
E. Ellice—Hon. W. Cowper[11]—W. Patten—S.H. Northcote. Dined at
Milnes's. Read Nap. III et L'Italie.[12] Worked on accounts, & arrear of
letters.

18. Fr.

Wrote to Baron Poerio[13]—H.J.G.—Bp of Salisbury—Sir J.G.—Rev. Mr
Ridley—H. of C. 4½–8 and 11¼–1¾.[14] Read Bentley's Q.R. on my Homer.[15]
Saw Duchess of Sutherland—Mr Parker—SS. Settembrini & Spaventa[16]—

[1] He told his sister (18 March 1859, Hawn P) 'I do not think Lord Shaftesbury's
Chairmanship will give to the movement for the Neapolitan exiles any shade of the
character you anticipate . . . (on my suggestion) it was unanimously agreed that the
Sardinian Consul should not be put among those who receive subscriptions, lest it
should give offence'.
[2] The Bill was read 2°: *H* cliii. 170.
[3] G. C. Brodrick, 'Promotion by merit in relation to government and education'
(1858).
[4] Thomas Jacob Birch, 1806–68; judge on Norfolk circuit from 1847.
[5] Louis Heinemann, London agent, shipping the china.
[6] R. Neville Grenville (see 21 July 40); not yet M.P.
[7] Bankruptcy Bill: *H* cliii. 198.
[8] *Disraeli's speech of 28 February introducing his reform bill, reprinted as a pamphlet.
[9] Alexander Dobie, London solicitor.
[10] Possibly Edwin Keyse, milliner in Camden Town.
[11] William Francis *Cowper (-Temple), 1811–88; liberal M.P. Hertford 1835–63,
S. Hampshire 1868–80; cr. Baron Mount-Temple 1880; minor offices; in whig govts.;
author of eponymous clause in 1870 Education Act; (correction to 23 July 27n.).
[12] *L'Empereur Napoléon III et l'Italie* (1859).
[13] Now free, see 13 Mar. 59n.
[14] Spoke briefly on British Museum: *H* cliii. 385.
[15] *Bentley's Quarterly Review*, i. 33 (March 1859).
[16] Silvio Spaventa, Italian liberal released with Poerio, later accused of embezzling the
funds of the Neapolitan exiles cttee.; see Lacaita, 122.

J. Wilson Patten—Ld Wodehouse. Dined at Mr Ellice's. Worked on papers.

19. Sat.

Wrote to Sir E. Lytton—Rev. Mr Bramston—Vice Chancr. of Oxford—Mr Thornton—H.J.G. Saw Mr Lacaita—Mr Bonham—Christie & Manson— Sir Fred Rogers—Lord Stanhope—Mr Rainer (for H.J.G.).[1] Br. Museum Comm 12½-2. Neap. Exiles Comm 4-5. Wright's Transl. of Iliad.[2] Read Mill on Liberty—Nap. III et L'Italie—Austin's Plea for the Constitn.[3]

20. 2 S. Lent.

St James's & H.C. mg. St Andrew's aft. MS of 46 aloud at night. Lesson with each of the little pairs. Saw All Saints Church.[4] Saw Lord Aberdeen— Sir John Johnstone—Read Segneri.[5] Acct. of Penitentiaries[6]—Chr. Rememr. on Cheyne Case[7]—on Confessional & other papers. Wrote to Duchess of Sutherland.

21. M.

Wrote to Mr Sinnett[8]—Rev. Mr Harding[9]—Duke of Sutherland—Mr Loverdo.[10] Saw R. Phillimore—Sir W. Heathcote—J.W. Patten—Sir Jas. Graham. Worked on unpacking arrivals from Corfu—Willy came home: went to H.C. Dined at Mrs Talbot's. H. of C. 4-7¼ and 8½-12½: sorely puzzled.[11] Read Farini's 2d Letter.[12]

22. T.

Wrote to A. Kinnaird—Sec. of Athenaeum[13]—Vice Chancellor of Oxford— Thos. Roscoe[14]—Count B. Metaxa[15]—Rev. C. Miller.[16] Political Conv. with Willy. Saw Mr G. Harcourt—Mr J.P. Lacaita—Mr Thornton—S. Herbert. H. of C. 4¼-7¼ and 8½-12½.[17] Read Mill on Reform[18]—'The Franchise'[19]— Bagehot on Reform.[20] Dined at Mrs Talbot's.

[1] Picture dealer (see Gladstone to Helen Gladstone, 18 March 1859, Hawn P).
[2] I. C. Wright, *The Iliad . . . . translated into blank verse* (1859).
[3] J. *Austin, *A plea for the constitution* (1859).
[4] *Butterfield's masterpiece, now finished; see 4 July 45 and above, iii. 1.
[5] See 13 Mar. 59.
[6] Untraced.
[7] *Christian Remembrancer*, xxxvii. 168 (January 1859).
[8] Probably Thomas Henry Sinnott, collector and connoisseur.
[9] Probably Charles Harwick, in correspondence at this time on Homer (Hawn P); see 13 Mar. 58.
[10] S. E. Loverdo, Greek advocate; had written on Ionia in French from Moldavia (Hawn P).
[11] *Disraeli's Representation of the People Bill 2°R: *H* cliii. 389.
[12] L. C. Farini, *Il conte Buol ed il Piedmonte, lettera* (1859).
[13] James C. Webster.
[14] Thomas *Roscoe, 1791-1871; journalist, traveller, editor and critic.
[15] An Ionian.
[16] Probably Charles Miller, d. 1885; vicar of Harlow, Essex, from 1831.
[17] Reform: *H* cliii. 531.
[18] J. S. *Mill, *Thoughts on parliamentary reform* (1859).
[19] 'The Franchise. What shall we do to it?' (1858).
[20] See 8 Mar. 59.

23. Wed.

Wrote to H.J.G.—Vice Chancellor of Oxford—Mr G. Burnett (2)—Rev. R. Greswell. Saw Scotts—S.H. Walpole—Waugh & Sons (to settle carpets)[1]—Ld Harry Vane—Mr Barker—S. Herbert.—Sir J. Awdry—S.H. Northcote—A. Panizzi. At Christie's. Neap. Exiles Comm. 4. P.M. Dinner party of 17: & a small evening party. Read Farini to Ld J.R. Worked on rooms; & on China.

24. Th.

Wrote to Sir W. Heathcote—Jas. Watson & Smith—Rev. R.H. Gregory[2] —Rev. B. Price—Miss R. Gray[3]—H. of C. $4\frac{1}{2}$–$6\frac{1}{2}$ and 9–$12\frac{1}{2}$.[4] The Herbert's & Lady H. Vane dined. Attended Christie's Sale 1–$2\frac{1}{2}$. Saw Mr Grogan— Sir E. Lytton—Lord H. Vane—J. Wilson Patten—S. Herbert. Read Farini to Ld J.R.—Queens Govt. & Religions of India.[5] Meditated somewhat on the puzzled issue before us.[6]

25. Fr. Annunciation.

Wrote to A. Panizzi (with pamphlets)—Jas. Wilson. Dined at Mrs Talbot's. Saw Mr Rhodes[7]—Mr Grogan—Mr Watts.[8] H. of C. $4\frac{1}{2}$–$6\frac{3}{4}$ and 8–12[9]: then home with C. Read Bentley's Q.R. on Italy[10]—Mentor on Reform[11]— Memoirs of Pitt—Chatham—H. Pelham—Addison—and others.

26. Sat.

Wrote to C.A. Wood—Rev. Mr MacColl—Dr Angus—Syed Abdoollah— Johnson L[ongden] & Co. Rev. Mr Perry[12]—G. Burnett—Mr Pickering— Vice Chancr.—Provost of Oriel. Saw Mr Lacaita—Mr Merivale—Mr A. Montgomery—Sir Jas. Graham—Lady Heathcote—Earl of Aberdeen— Scotts—Count Vitzthum. Read Bulgari on the Ionian Treaties &c.[13] Dined at General Peel's. Speaker's Levee afterwards. Inquired for Smith. Saw Almer[R].

27. 3. S. Lent.

St Jameses mg. & Chapel Royal evg. MS. aloud in evg. Lesson with the two

---

[1] Carpet dealers in Gough Street.

[2] He has confused Rev. R. Gregory (see 25 Feb. 48) with W. H. Gregory, M.P. (see 14 Mar. 59).

[3] A rescue case; see 10 Apr. 59.

[4] Reform Bill: *H* cliii. 692.

[5] J. W. *Kaye, *Christianity in India* (1859).

[6] i.e. the Reform Bill: see 29 Mar. 59.

[7] Probably M. Rhodes of the 'engagement'; see 23 Feb. 45n.

[8] George Frederick *Watts, 1817–1904, portrait painter; his first of three portraits of Gladstone was painted later this year, see 14 June 59.

[9] Reform: cliii. 825.

[10] *Bentley's Quarterly Review*, i. 301 (March 1859).

[11] Mentor, pseud., *A treatise on political reform, or vote by lot the only way to obtain a pure election* (1837).

[12] Samuel Gideon Frederick Perry, d. 1881; priest 1843; vicar of Tottington, Lancashire from 1849.

[13] N. T. Boulgaris, *Les Sept-îles ioniennes et les traités qui les concernent* (1859).

H.s.[1] Saw Ld R. Cavendish—S. Herbert—W. Harcourt—Mr Portal. Late in evening saw Lady Heathcote: Dr Gully[2] came & reported her excellent husband's illness to be very serious though not of instant danger. Read Greenwood's Cathedra Petri—A Presbyter on the late decision of the Episcopal Synod[3]—Angus's Christ our Life[4]—& Fra Dolcino.[5]

28. M.

Wrote to J. Griffiths (Wrexham)—Sir J.E.E. Wilmot—H. of C. 4½–7½ and 8½–1.[6] Read E. Wilmot on Reform[7]—Chevalier Baisse de l'Or.[8] Saw Duke of Newcastle—J. Stuart Wortley—Sir S. Northcote—Sir John Young—Rev. Mr Lake and [blank].

29. T. X.

Wrote to E. Cardwell—Saw Sir G. Bowen—Archdeacon Hale—Duke of Newcastle—Saw Almer & another[R]. Worked on Reform—Read Chevalier —Raleigh's Tract on Trade.[9] Bentley's Q.R. on Hor. Walpole.[10] H. of C. 4–7¼; spoke 1h. 20m. agt. Ld John's Resolution.[11] H. again 10¾–11¾. Dined at Mr Harcourt's. Great anxiety about Sir W. Heathcote: mercifully relieved.

30. Wed.

Wrote to Sir S. Northcote—Mr Bentley—J.W. Parker—Sir W. James—Robn. G.—Rev. Mr Meyrick—Mr Radcliffe—Mrs Tyler—Mr Loveland[12]—Ld Chancr. of Ireland.[13] Saw Mr Lacaita—Mr Burnett 10–12½. Miss Baker[14] & Dr Saintsbury[15] at Sir W. H[eathcote']s. Duke of Cambridge—Ld Granville. Dined at Lady Molesworths. Then Sir R. Murchison's & Lady Palmerston's. Read Mill on Reform in Fraser[16]—Brodrick on Promn. by Merit.[17]

[1] i.e. Helen and Herbert Gladstone, the two youngest children.
[2] James Manby *Gully, 1808–83; society physician and playwright; discredited by the Bravo poison case 1876 involving his mistress; fa. of the Speaker.
[3] 'Synodal action in the Church of England seasonable and safe . . . by a Presbyter' (1852).
[4] J. Angus, Christ our life: in its origin, law, and end (1853).
[5] L. Mariotti [i.e. A. Gallenga] A historical memoir of Fra Dolcino and his times (1853).
[6] Reform Bill: H cliii. 915.
[7] See 21 Dec. 53.
[8] M. Chevalier, De la baisse probable de l'or, des conséquences commerciales et sociales, qu'elle peut avoir et des mesures qu'elle provoque, 2v. (1859).
[9] Sir W. *Raleigh, 'Observations touching Trade and Commerce with the Hollander and other nations' (1653, ed. J. R. *MacCulloch 1859).
[10] Bentley's Quarterly Review, i. 227 (March 1859).
[11] *Russell's resolution was designed to unite those who thought the Bill did too much, and too little; Gladstone defended 'small boroughs' as the nurseries of statesmen and supported the Bill, to end the reform controversy: H cliii. 1045.
[12] Henry Loveland, London bookseller.
[13] J. *Napier, see 8 Apr. 54n.
[14] Unidentified.
[15] Henry Sainsbury, Hampshire physician.
[16] Fraser's Magazine, lix. 489 (April 1859).
[17] See 15 Mar. 59.

31. Th.

Wrote to C.B. Cardi[1]—Syed Abdoollah—Mr Baldwin—Mr Sinnett—Sir W. Colebrooke—Mrs Southey. Saw Bp of Oxford (to breakft.)—Mr W. Forbes (Medwyn)—Sig. Porcari (*cum* Ciocci)[2]—Baron Poerio (& Mr Lacaita)—Provost of Eton—Mr Burnett—Six to dinner. H. of C. 4½–7¼ and 10¼–2. Voted in 291: 330 against Lord John's Resolution: also in 328: [98] agt. Ballot.[3] Read Newmarch.[4] Worked on China: the concluding arrival, from Venice.

Friday. Ap. One 1859.

Wrote to Lady C. Egerton—W. Bowden—R. Phillimore—Rev. Mr Stooks. Visited All Saints Church with the Jameses, Mr Butterfield & Mr Dyce.[5] Saw Mrs J.E. Tyler—Earl of Aberdeen—C.A. Wood—Ld & Lady Jersey— Lady Heathcote—Mr Dyce R.A.. Dined at Mr Wilson's: Duchess of Marlborough's afterwards. Saw A. Wright[R]. Read Chevalier, & pamphlets.

2. Sat. X.

Saw J. Wortley—Sir S.H. Northcote—Worked most of the day on examining & arranging China. Dined at the Palace. Read Burgon's Tytler[6]— Salvagnoli.[7] Visited the French Exhibition[8]—Lady Waldegrave. The Duke of Cambridge spoke with singular freedom.

3. 4. S. Lent.

St James's mg & H.C.—Ch Ch Broadway aft. Saw Lady Heathcote—Col. Wilson Patten. Read MS of 43 aloud in evg. Read Greenwood—Guillon on Salvador &c.[9] Pamphlets—Nicole.[10]

4. M.

Wrote to Stephy—on his birthday, Blessings be upon him! Saw Mr Willson:[11] & worked most of the day upon my China which is now really a collection. H. of C. 4½–7½. Universal dissatisfaction, excepting the Radicals.[12] Saw W. Patten—Newcastle—S. Herbert—Mr Newdigate—Mr Knightley[13]—Mr Trefusis—Mr C. Howard—D. of Argyll—& others: all of one mind. Kept silence in H. of C. Fifteen to dinner (for Poerio) & evening party. Read Burgon's Tytler.

[1] Unidentified; a refugee?
[2] Released Neapolitans; see *The Guardian*, 23 March 1859, 255.
[3] *Disraeli's Bill thus effectively rejected: *H* cliii. 1257.
[4] See 16 Mar. 55.
[5] See 20 Mar. 59; *Dyce painted the church's frescoes.
[6] J. W. *Burgon, *The portrait of a christian gentleman. A memoir of Patrick Fraser *Tytler* (1859).
[7] V. Salvagnoli, *Della indipendenza d'Italia: discorso* (1859).
[8] The annual exhibition of French art, in Pall Mall.
[9] M. N. S. Guillon, *Examen critique des doctrines de Gibbon, du Dr. Strauss, etc. de M. Salvador sur Jésus-Christ, son évangile et son église*, 2v. (1842).
[10] See 27 Aug. 43.
[11] Samuel Willson, art dealer off Leicester Square.
[12] *Derby announced dissolution rather than resignation: *H* cliii. 1266.
[13] (Sir) Rainald Knightley Knightley, 1819–95; tory M.P. S. Northamptonshire 1852–92; 3rd bart. 1864; rider and whist player.

5. *T.*

Wrote to Mr G. Arbuthnot—Mr G. Lock[1]—Rev. F. Scrivner—N.L. Torre—F.A. Hanbury—W.H.G.—Provost of Oriel—T. Stevens[2]—P. M'Culloch—H. of C. 4½–7.[3] Dined with the Herberts: discussed Radcliffe [trust] business. Saw Mr J. Murray—Duchess of Sutherland—Mr C.A. Wood—Sir S. Glynne—S. Herbert—Sir C. Wood—Earl of Powis. Read S.H. on Sanitary Reform in Army.[4]

6. *Wed.* X.

Wrote to Mr Hewett—Mr Donaldson[5]—Mr Allen—Watson & Smith. Read Memoir of Tytler—Mrs Elliott Journal.[6] Attended the Levee. Worked on Proofs of reprint of Neap. Letters &c—also feebly began to correct Homer. Saw Sig. Braico *cum* Duca Castromediano[7]—R. Phillimore—J. Wilson Patten—Sig. Marliano[8]—Ld Clarendon—Sir S. Northcote—C.A. Wood—Muller. Saw two Germans[R]. Mrs Jervis[R]. Dined at Lady Wenlock's—Lady Palmerston's afterwards.

7. *Th.*

Wrote to C.D. Collet[9]—M.F. Tupper—G. Lyall[10]—Rev. Mr Burgon—T.D. Acland—Rev. Mr Templer[11]—L. Heinemann—Rev. S. Perry—Rev. T.F. Stooks. Bills & business with Hampton. Saw Bishop of Oxford—Mr Lacaita—Sir S. Glynne (Flintshire)—Mr Bonham—Sir S. Northcote (2 plans)[12]—C.A. Wood—Duke of Argyll. Child's Ball at the Palace. Mazie, Lena & Harry went as Greeks. H. of C. 4½–7.[13] Finished proofs of Neap. Letters. Read Burgon's Tytler—

8. *Fr.* X.

Wrote to Mrs Canadia[14]—Dr Acland—W. Lyon—Dr Pusey—J.N.G. Radcliffe Trust Meeting at 11. H. of C. 4–8¼. A most unsatisfactory Exhibition.[15]

[1] George Lock, 1832–91, London bookseller, then in Fleet Street; partner in Ward & Lock.
[2] Thomas Stevens, 1809–88; assist. poor-law commissioner, then rector of Bradfield 1843.
[3] Misc. business: *H* cliii. 1397.
[4] *Herbert's letter to *Panmure, 22 Nov. 1856, in Stanmore, ii. 119–22.
[5] Probably John William *Donaldson, 1811–61; fellow of Trinity, Cambridge, 1835–40, 1855–61; classicist.
[6] Mrs. Elliott, *Journal of my life during the French revolution* (1859).
[7] Sigismondo Castromediano, 1811–95, duke of Morciano and Caballino, liberal imprisoned in Naples, had escaped from the ship at Queenstown.
[8] Emanuele Marliani, 1799–1873; in the constituent assembly 1859, senator 1862; historian; see Lacaita, 131.
[9] Collet Dobson Collet, 1812–98; sec. for cttee. for repeal of taxes on knowledge 1849.
[10] George Lyall, 1819–81; director of bank of England from 1857, governor 1871–3; tory M.P. Whitehaven 1857–65.
[11] William Christopher Templer, d. 1885; Trinity, Cambridge; vicar of Walditch from 1849.
[12] In the event of a contest at Oxford; Gladstone was unopposed at the general election; but see 22 June 59n.
[13] Supply: *H* cliii. 1510.
[14] Unidentified.
[15] Strongly attacked *Disraeli's handling of the Galway packet contract: *H* cliii. 1585.

Examined before Scots Central R.R. Committee.[1] Saw Earl of Carnavon—
Sir J. Graham—Mr Lock—Mr Lacaita. Saw Stapylton—Mrs Jarvis[R].
Read L[ady] of Lake aloud[2]—Tracts. Corr[ected] Homer.

9. Sat.

Wrote to C.G.[3]—Mrs Chisholm—J. Watson & Smith—E. Hayward[4]—Bp
of Brechin—R. Phillimore—Rev. Howard Rice[5]—House business. Saw Sir
J.D. Acton[6]—Mr Bohn—Sir R. Bateson—Mr D. Lange—Ld H. Lennox.
Br. Museum $12\frac{3}{4}$–$3\frac{1}{4}$: Standing Committee—there saw collection of
Majolica.[7] Attended Christies—4–5. Corrected Homer. Read Mrs Elliot—
Indian Finance—Mrs Lowe's in evg.

10. 5 S. Lent.

St M. Magd. & H.C. mg. S. Andrew Wells St with Harry aft.—MS of 41
aloud in evg. Conv. with *three* little ones[R]. Saw Lyttelton—J. Stuart
Wortley—Rev. W. Elwin—Lord Aberdeen. Wrote to Rigby—Gray—
Alma[R]. Read Guillon v. Salvador[8]—Greenwood. Also at night National
& Westm. Reviews on Italy.[9]

11. M.

Wrote to Lady Canning—Mrs Kidd[10]—Rev. Mr Greswell—C.G.—Mr
Joberns[11]—Mr Field—J.N.G. Began an Article for Q.R. on the Italian
question: to be done in haste.[12] Saw Mr Lichfield—C.A. Wood—Baron
Poerio—J. Stuart Wortley—Mr Lacaita—Rev. Whitwell Elwin—W.
Egerton—Adam S. Gladstone—D. of Argyll—Christies at 2. Attended the
luncheon at Stafford House to meet the Neapolitan Exiles. H. of C. at $5\frac{1}{2}$[13]
Geogr. Soc. 9–$10\frac{1}{2}$—Suez Canal.[14] Read Salvagnoli—Pasini—Jacini—on the
Italian question.[15]

[1] See *PP* 1859 xiii. 473.
[2] By *Scott (1810).
[3] Bassett, 123.
[4] Probably *sc.* A. Hayward.
[5] Richard John Howard Rice, vicar of Sutton Courtney from 1856.
[6] Sir John Emerich Edward Dalberg *Acton, 1834–1902; *Granville's step-son;
Roman catholic historian; 8th bart. 1837; liberal M.P. Carlow 1859–65; cr. Baron by
Gladstone 1869; see introduction above, v. lxxi and Add MS 44093–4.
[7] Italian pottery.
[8] See 3 Apr. 59.
[9] *Westminster Review*, xv. 444 (April 1859); *National Review*, viii. 488 (April 1859).
[10] Charitable worker.
[11] Charles Henry Joberns.
[12] 'Foreign affairs—War in Italy', *Quarterly Review*, cv. 527 (April 1859); see Add MS
44689, f. 72 and introduction above, v. lxxi.
[13] Misc. business: *H* cliii. 1612.
[14] Anti-de Lesseps paper by Capt. Spratt; *Journal of Royal Geographical Society*, xxix.
clxxxvi (1859).
[15] *Della Indipendenza d'Italia. Discorso di V. Salvagnoli* (1859); V. Pasini, *Sulla
Necessita di accordare al Regno Lombardo-Veneto la Perequazione della sua imposta
prediale con quella delle Provincie Tedesche del Impero* (1858); S. Jacini, *Condizioni
economiche della provincia di Sondrio* (1858); all reviewed in his *Quarterly* article.

12. T.

Wrote to A. Panizzi—Mrs Bennett—C. Addington—S. Herbert—Adjutant Gen.[1] Saw Col. Wilson Patten—Mr A. Munro—Mr Niewenhuis—W.R. Farquhar. At Christie's & Foster's. Saw Hicks[R]. Dined at Mr (Lord) Egerton's. Worked on intended Article. H. of C. $4\frac{1}{2}$–$7\frac{1}{2}$[2] & at Sir W. Heathcote's.

13. Wed.

Wrote to Robn. G.—S.E.G.—Ly Wenlock's (Dowager). Worked on intended Article. Dined with the Kerrison's. Lady Palmerston's afterwards. Attended Christie's & Foster's—Saw Duchess of Sutherland—Mr Murray— Read Mrs Elliott's Journal.

14. Th.

Wrote to Mr J. Muncas—Mr Roberts—Mr Nixon. Nine to breakfast: some examn. of China & the like. Saw Sir Jas. Hudson—Rev. Mr Greswell—Mrs Bennett. H. of C. $4\frac{1}{2}$–$7\frac{1}{2}$.[3] Worked on proposed Article. Read Ed. Rev. on Italn. Quest.[4] Toscana e Austria.[5]

15. Fr.

Wrote to Mr J. Ball—Dean of Peterborough—Master of Balliol—and Robn. G. Saw Mr Greswell—Mr Fleming—Mr Tupper—Mr S. Estcourt. Seven to dinner: Dss. of Sutherland & Sir Jas. Hudson. Worked on Article. H. of C. $4\frac{1}{2}$–7.[6] Attended Add[itiona]l Curates meeting & spoke there.

16. Sat.

Wrote to V.C. Oxford. Saw Mr Whitwell Elwin—Mr Goldwin Smith—Ld Granville—Sir R. Peel and [blank]. Dined at B. Rothschild's. Read Adam Bede[7]—Italian Tracts. Worked much on my MS & sent all to press.

17. 6. S. Lent.

St James's & H.C. mg—All Saints aft. Conv. with Stephy for his Confirmation. Read Flanagan's Hist.[8] Bp Bathurst's Life.[9] Saw Heathcote: with much joy & thankfulness: he looked better than I could have hoped.[10]

18. M.

Wrote to Mr Lacaita—Messrs. Clowes—Dr Williams—Dss. of Sutherland.

[1] Sir George Augustus *Wetherall, 1788–1868; adjutant general 1854–60; governed Sandhurst from 1866; K.C.B. 1856.
[2] Admiralty lords: *H* cliii. 1626.
[3] Indian army: *H* cliii. 1729.
[4] *Edinburgh Review*, cix. 558 (April 1859).
[5] C. Ridolfi, *Toscana e Austria* (1859).
[6] Misc. business: *H* cliii. 1808.
[7] By George *Eliot (1859).
[8] T. *Flanagan, *History of the Roman catholic church in England*, 2v. (1857).
[9] H. *Bathurst, *Memoirs of the late Dr. Henry *Bathurst* (1837).
[10] See 29 Mar. 59.

Worked on my proofsheets & sent them to the Printers. Saw Mr Niewen-
huis—Mr Elwin. Read Brooke's Liverpool.[1] H. of C. $4\frac{1}{2}$–$7\frac{1}{4}$. Spoke briefly
on the foreign complications.[2]

19. T.

All Saints Chapel 8 a.m. Wrote to The Vice Chancellor—Warden of All
Souls—Warden of New Coll—Dean of Faculty. Worked on letters. H. of C.
$1\frac{1}{2}$–$2\frac{1}{2}$: in at the death.[3] Saw Mr Elwin (Q.R., I.I., Mr Rowsell)—Mr
Lacaita—Mr Sotheron Estcourt—Col. Sykes—Sir W. Heathcote. Read
Brooke's Liverpool—Adam Bede—Final revision of my Art. in pages.

20. Wed.

All Saints (Marg.) 8 a.m. and 5 P.M. Wrote to Watson & Smith—Quaritch
—Wms. & Norgate—Robn. G—Papanicolas—G. & Co—Rev. R. Greswell
—H. Fleming—W.R. Farquhar—W.C. James—Rev. W. Beaumont.[4] Saw
Lady Heathcote—Worked on books, papers & prints &c. Lady Wenlock
dined. Arranging China. Read Q.R. on Geo. III and Fox[5]—Burgon's
Tytler.

21. Th.

St James 8 a.m. U.U.C. Committee 4–5. Wrote to Mr D. Acland—S.
Herbert—Mr Barnewall[6]—F.G. Smith—Warden All Souls—Mr Greswell—
Mast. Balliol—W. Donaldson—Gholam Mohammed[7]—Mr Rowsell—Bp of
Salisbury. Read Q.R. on Bunsen[8]—Thucyd. & construing with Willy—
Segneri on Psalm 51.[9] Maddyn, Chiefs of Parties.[10] Worked on Corr[ecting]
Hom. Studies. Saw Baron Poerio cum De'Vincenzi[11]—Mr Ellison—Sir Geo
Bowen—Muller[12]—Earl of Aberdeen—Scotts. Mazie & Lena showed me
their progress on the pianoforte. Both good: the former plays with very
great promise.

22. Good Friday.

Marg. Chapel (All Saints) with Willy 8 a.m.—St Martin's H.C. 1–2. All
Saints at 5. with W,H, & H. MS of 41 aloud in evg. Read Segneri on Ps 51.—

[1] R. Brooke, *A descriptive account of Liverpool 1775–1800*, 8v. (1854).
[2] Attacking *Disraeli on Italy: *H* cliii. 1881.
[3] Prorogation: *H* cliii. 1900.
[4] William Beresford Beaumont, d. 1901; Christ Church; then unbeneficed; rector of
Cole-Orton 1864.
[5] *Quarterly Review*, cv. 463 (April 1859).
[6] Of Robert Barnewall & sons, merchants off Throgmorton Street.
[7] Indian prince, with letter of recommendation from *Canning, and memorials on the
mutiny; Hawn P.
[8] *Quarterly Review*, cv. 463 (April 1859); review of *Bunsen on Egypt.
[9] P. P. Segneri, probably from his *Concordia tra la fatica e la quieta nell' orazione*
(1680).
[10] D. O. *Madden, *Chiefs of parties, past and present, with original anecdotes*, 2v. (1859).
[11] Guiseppi De Vincenzi, liberal friend of Panizzi and Lacaita; see Lacaita, 125.
[12] Daniel Muller, sewage rate collector; see 27 Apr. 59.

Maury, Religions de la Grece[1]—La Cretelle Hist Siècle XVIII[2]—Dubarry's Letters: what a picture![3] Picture lesson with H. & H. Conv. with Willy. Wrote to Rev. R. Greswell—S.E.G.—C.G.[4]

23. Easter Eve.

All Saints 8 a.m. and 8 P.M. Wrote to S. Herbert—C.G.—J.S. Wortley—V.C. Oxford. Saw Mr Ellison—Mr Bonham—Mr Wortley—Rev. Mr Jones. Read La Cretelle—Segneri. Worked on Corr. Homer. Read Ionian Island papers: & worked on correcting the press and text of my Report.[5]

24. Easter Day.

St Martins & H.C. 8 a.m.—St James 11 a.m.—Chapel Royal 5½ P.M. MS of 43 aloud in evg. Picture lesson with H. & H. Saw Sir Walter James—Read Horsley's Sermons[6]—Flanagan's Hist Ch.[7]—

25. Easter Monday.

St James's 8 a.m. Wrote to Ld Carnavon. Worked much on perusing & correcting my Ionian papers in type: wh I finished. Dined with C. at the Lord Mayor's & heard Lord Derby on 'the War'.[8] Saw Bp of Oxford—Gholam Mohamed—Ld & Ly Meath—Comm. Drummond[9]—and [blank]. Read La Cretelle.

26. Easter Tues. X.

All Saints at 5 P.M. Wrote to Count Flamburiari—Scotts—Sir A. Dama-schino—Sir E. Lytton—Ld High Commr.[10]—Earl of Carnavon. Saw Marq. d'Azeglio—Chev. Mass d'Azeglio—Shopping & inquiries. Saw Rigby[R]. Dined at Lady Wenlock's. Further work on I.I. papers. Corr. Homer. Read Lacretelle.

27. Wed.

Wrote to Mr Wix[11]—Mr Rees[12]—Warden Trin. Coll.—Mr May—Provost of Oriel—Mr Day[13]—Johnson L[ongden] & Co—W.H. Cooke[14]—Rev. H.

[1] See 13 Mar. 58.
[2] C. J. D. de Lacretelle, *Histoire de France pendant le XVIIIe siècle*, 4v. (1808–26).
[3] M. J. Comtesse du Barry, *Lettres originales de Madame la Comtesse du Barry* (1779).
[4] Accepting inevitability of war: Bassett, 124.
[5] For *PP*.
[6] By S. *Horsley, 2v. (1810).
[7] See 17 Apr. 59.
[8] *Derby argued the govt. had 'endeavoured studiously to maintain the strictest impartiality' between Sardinia and Austria; *The Times*, 26 April 1860, 7.
[9] (Sir) James Robert Drummond, 1812–95; sailor; commodore of Woolwich 1858–61; K.C.B. 1873.
[10] i.e. *Storks.
[11] Perhaps Horatio Nelson Wix, furniture maker.
[12] Probably (Sir) Josiah Rees, 1821–99; barrister, later on Chester circuit; chief justice, Bermuda, 1878, kt. 1891.
[13] Perhaps Philip Day, d. 1880; newspaper correspondent and author.
[14] William Henry Cooke, 1811–94; barrister; recorder of Oxford from 1866; judge 1868.

Giraud—S.R. Glynne—J.D. Glennie[1]—Scotts. Dined at Sir W. James's. Saw Mr Harcourt—Mr Grogan—Mr Isaac[2]—Mr Muller—on house business &c. Mr Lacaita. Corr. Homer—Read Lacretelle—Political Perils in 1859.[3] Worked on papers.

28. Th. [Strawberry Hill]

Wrote to Johnson L & Co—Read Thucydides with Willy—Lacretelle. Worked on letters. Seven to breakfast. We had a long Italian Convn. Saw Sir W. Heathcote. In aftn. we drove down to Strawberry Hill: found Ld Lyndhurst, Count de Paris,[4] the Bernstorffs & others. Played Whist for Ld L.—& had conv. with him. The D'Aumales dined.

29. Fr.

Visited the D'Aumale's to luncheon & saw their treasures. Then visited Mr Bohn's collection of China. Conv. with Ld Lyndhurst—Lady Waldegrave (Rel.)—Sir Hamilton Seymore[5]—Mr E.G. Vernon. Thucydides with Willy. Read Lacretelle—Toscana ed Austria—D. of Buckingham's Geo. IV.[6]

30. Sat. [London]

Returned to London after breakfast—Water colour Exhibn. 1–2—Royal Academy 2–6. The Dinner followed. My neighbours were among others Lds Granville, J. Russell, Shelburne. We talked Austria, Italy, & the Ionian Islands. Saw Sir E. Landseer—Mr Richmond, Mr Dyce—& others. Read Lacretelle & 'How shall we vote'.[7] Visited the Carlton: wh was excited & more pleased than the facts quite seem to justify.[8]

Sunday May One 1859. St Phil. & St James.

St James's (& H.C.) mg. St Andr. Wells St aft.—our whole party of nine— only darling Jessy away, at least from sight. Conv. with Stephy: & with Willy. MS for 2 S.E. of 44 aloud. Visited the Carlton. War is begun.[9] May God direct it. Read Ullathorne on Immac. Conc.[10]—Bp Bathurst's Life[11]— Segneri.

[1] John David Glennie, 1795–1874; secretary of S.P.C.K. 1842–68.
[2] William Isaac, house valuer.
[3] *Political perils in 1859* (1859).
[4] Louis Philippe Albert d'Orléans, comte de Paris, 1838–94; elder s. of Ferdinand, duc d'Orléans; heir to French throne 1842; lived in England 1849–72, 1886–94; patronized by Lady Waldegrave.
[5] See 17 Mar. 32.
[6] See 14 Mar. 59.
[7] Article in *Universal Review*, i. 432 (May 1859).
[8] 'The decisive day' of the election, according to *The Times* (2 May 1859, 9) which gave tory gains 23, liberal gains 10.
[9] i.e. between France, Piedmont and Austria.
[10] W. B. *Ullathorne, *The immaculate conception of the mother of God. An exposition* (1855).
[11] See 17 Apr. 59.

2. M. X.
Wrote to Rev. Mr Stevens—Miss Learmonth[1]—Robn. G.—Warden Trin. Coll N.B.—S.R.G.—Vice Ch. Oxford—R. Neville Gr[enville]—Sir Geo Bowen—J.N.G. Saw Sir W. Heathcote—Rev. F. Neville—Christies. Aunt J.—Sir G. Bowen. Saw Allen. Theyne: with interest[R]. Read D. Buchms. Geo. IV. Shipping Correspondence. L'Autriche dans Le Royaume L.V.[2]

3. T.
Wrote to Mr Papanicolas—Rev. Mr Littledale[3]—R. Browning—Mr H. Merritt—Univ. Club business. Read Lacretelle—T.D. Acland's Speech[4]— Busby on Federation of Colonies.[5] Seventeen to dinner & party in evening. Saw T.D. Acland—Earl of Aberdeen—Duke of Argyll—Mr Richmond who thinks well of my purchases in Italy & Greece.

4. Wed.
Wrote to Mrs T. Goalen—Edw. Ellis—Mr G. Burnett—Watson & Smith —Rev. H. Glynne—Rev. M. MacColl. Read Toscana ed Austria (finished.) —D. of Buckingham's Memoirs of Geo. IV—Thucydides with Willy. Saw A. Panizzi—B. Porter: to settle about sale of horse—Mr P. Norton (2)— Messrs. Gurney & Chapman—Messrs. Johnson Longden & Co—Mr Manson. Sir John Lawrence—two minutes are enough to know that he is a powerful man.[6] M. Ch. Remusat—Sir John D. Acton. Dined at Sir W. James's. Lady Granville's afterwards.

5. Th.
Wrote to Miss Venables[7]—Scotts. Read La Cretelle—Italian Treaties &c. Worked with Mr Merritt about the arrangements of Pictures &c. Saw Baron Poerio—Mr J.F. Stuart Wortley—Mr H. Merritt—Ld A. Paget. Nine to breakfast—incl. Sir J. Lawrence & Ld Carlisle.[8] At Christies: Tattersall's.[9] Early dinner & went to the Princess's: to see Henry V. The melodrama was admirable & Shakespeare is a mighty power.

6. Fr. [Oxford]
Wrote to G. Bramwell—Rev H. Glynne—H. Merritt—Rev. W. Elwin—

[1] Agnes, d. 1876, da. of J. Learmonth of Edinburgh (see 10 Dec. 33), m. June 1859 George Sinclair of the Bengal army, who d. 1871.
[2] L'Autriche dans le royaume Lombardo-Vénetien . . . Lettres à Lord Derby (1859).
[3] Richard Frederick *Littledale, 1833–90; curate of St. Mary, Crown Street, Soho, 1857–61; well-known confessionalist and ritualist.
[4] T. D. *Acland's nomination speech at Birmingham on 28 April 1859.
[5] J. Busby, 'The federation of colonies and the system called "representative government"' (1858); speech in Auckland.
[6] Sir John Laird Mair *Lawrence, 1811–79; in E.I.C.S.; K.C.B. 1856; relieved Delhi 1857; cr. bart. 1858; at India office in London 1858–62; viceroy 1863–9; cr. Baron 1869; chaired London school board 1870–3.
[7] Unidentified.
[8] See 13 Oct. 32.
[9] Auctioneers in Grosvenor Place.

Earl Stanhope. Saw Earl of Aberdeen—Earl of Carlisle[1]—Duchess of Sutherland—and divers of the Bishops guests. Left London at 2 for Oxford & Cuddesden with C. & with Stephy who is to be confirmed there. Corrected Homer. Read Burgon's Tytler.

7. Sat.

Wrote to Scotts. Saw Rev. Mr Burgon—The Provost of Eton—Rev. Mr King—Rev. Mr Swinney[2] and divers guests. Church 8 a.m. Conv. with Stephy: gave him the letters written for Willy.[3] Corrected Homer. Read About Question Romaine.[4]

8. 2. S. E.

H.C. 8 a.m. Morning service at 11 where our dear boy was Confirmed. The administration by the Bp [Wilberforce] was incomparably suited to take hold. Aft. service at 3. Conv. with Sir W. Farquhar resp. the Bp's position: also with Mr Lawrell.[5] Wrote Ld Carlisle and others. Read S. Bernard—Mr Drummond on the heavenly bodies.[6] Dr Forester's Letters to Dr Sewell.[7] Archd. Williams respecting Welsh Bishoprics.

9. M.

Chapel at 9 a.m. Conv. with the Bishop. Read About—Lacretelle. Went to Oxford at 12¾: & was most kindly received by the Warden of All Souls & Mrs Leighton.[8] Dinner & Evening party. We had luncheon in Willy's rooms in Peckwater. Went over the Museum with the Dean of Ch Ch & Dr Acland & made calls. Saw Mr [John] Macray.[9] conv. with Warden on the Bp's Diocesan affairs.

10. T.

All Souls Chapel 8¾ a.m. Luncheon at Balliol. Dinner & evening party at the Vice Chancellors.[10] Saw Mr Greswell—Mr Cornish—Master of Balliol— Dr Pusey—Warden of All Souls—Mast. of University—Principal of Jesus[11] and others. Read Villemain's Review in Journ. des Savants[12]—Lacretelle. Corrected Homer.

[1] For Carlisle's diary record, see Wilberforce, ii. 423.
[2] Henry Hutchinson Swinny, 1813–62; vicar and principal of Cuddesdon from May 1859.
[3] Lathbury, ii. 151.
[4] E. About, La question Romaine (1859).
[5] John Lawrell; d. 1865; barrister, then incumbent of St. Matthew's, City Road, London 1853; apparently then *Wilberforce's secretary (Wilberforce, iii. 31).
[6] H. *Drummond, On the future destinies of the celestial bodies (1855).
[7] O. W. W. Forester, 'A letter to the Rev. Dr. Sewell, in reference to a sermon preached by him in the neighbourhood of Bridgnorth' (1859).
[8] F. K. Leighton (see 11 Jan. 44) and his wife.
[9] Librarian of the Taylorian; see 30 May 45.
[10] Francis Jeune.
[11] Charles Williams, 1807–77; fellow of Jesus 1829, principal from 1857.
[12] A. F. Villemain, 'Essais sur le génie de Pindare', Journal des Savants (1859).

11. Wed. X.

All Souls Chapel mg: Ch.Ch. aft. at 4. Luncheon at Dr Aclands. Dinner in the College Hall: a most kind welcome to induct me as Hon. Fellow.[1] We then went to the Wardens. Read La Cretelle—Kempius de Osculis.[2]— P Aretino Putt. Err.[3] Saw the Vice Chancellor—Mrs Goalen[4] and made various calls.

12. Th. X.

All Souls Chapel 8¾ a.m. 10¼–4½. Made the stated round of visits: the Dean of Ch Ch was my companion, & the Warden of All Souls my host went on behalf of Sir W. H[eathcote]. I dispensed with the white neckcloth. Dinner party at All Souls: & evg. party. Conv. with the Warden (Statutes)—Vice Chancellor (Leasing)—Rev. Mr Butler & others. Read P. Aretino—Tableau de l'Amour[5]—Elegantiae[6]—all Library Books.

13. Fr. [Chevening] X.

Chapel All Souls 8¾ a.m. in surplice. Breakfast with Prof. Stanley 12–3.[7] Journey to London: 4–7. to Chevening:[8] found the Argylls & Mr Scharf. Wrote to J.S. Wortley—G. Burnett—Rev. D. Williams—Ld Chancellor— C. Fawssett. Wrote to Mr H. Lees—R. Phillimore—H. Merritt. Read Adam Bede—Lacretelle's Hist.—Elegantiae. Saw Mr Jul. Jeffreys[9]—Business in London.

14. Sat.

Read Marriage Tracts—Berni[10] &c. Friedlieb on the Sibyls[11]—Lacretelle's Hist. Political conv. with D. of A[rgyll]: who is free from all gall & guile[12]— Also with Ld Stanhope: no partisan. Rode to Knoll [sic] & saw the pictures[13] —the Amhersts dined.

15. M.

Ch mg & aft. Walk aft aftn Ch. Saw the Chancel. Wrote to Sir Jas. Lacaita

[1] Gladstone and *Heathcote were among the first honorary fellows of All Souls under the 1857 Ordinance.
[2] M. Kempius, *Opus polyhistoricum dissertationibus XXV. de osculis* (1680).
[3] The Codrington library at All Souls held (now missing) P. Aretino, *Ragionamenti* (1660) with the pseudo-Aretino *Puttana errante* bound in.
[4] The wife or mother of Alexander Goalen, a second cousin, s. of T. Goalen (see 19 Sept. 27); he was at Brasenose 1853, was lecturer in natural science at New Inn Hall 1858? and d. 1872.
[5] Probably N. Venette, *Tableau d'amour conjugal* (1751), though no record of it in the Codrington.
[6] L. Valla, *Elegantiae* (1471).
[7] i.e. A. P. *Stanley, regius professor of ecclesiastical history 1856–64.
[8] *Stanhope's seat 3½ miles NW. of Sevenoaks, Kent.
[9] Julius *Jeffreys, 1801–77; surgeon in India, returned to Britain as respiratory specialist.
[10] Probably Francesco Berni, sixteenth century Italian poet; wrote life of Aretino; see 17 Jan. 52.
[11] J. H. Friedlieb, *Oracula Sibyllina* (1852).
[12] *Argyll strongly criticised *Derby's Italian policy, see Argyll, ii. 138.
[13] Knole, Jacobean seat of the Sackvilles, 1½ miles SE. of Sevenoaks.

—Landlord Bromley.[1] Read Macbride on Mahometanism[2] & Anderdon's Life of Ken.[3]

16. M.

Wrote to R. Phillimore—W.H.G.—Rev. P. Freeman—H. Glynne—Rev. W. Richards—Scott & Co—Dean of Down[4]—E.S. Talbot—Rev. Mr Leary —H. Chester—Mrs Stapylton[R]—Rev. Mr Mayow. Read Lyell on Mt Etna[5]—Adam Bede. Drove to the Moat: much interested in it & in its inmates.[6] Mr Wimberley (& Mr Sykes) dined.[7] Herbert made me a good answer. I said 'I am afraid you have given a great deal of trouble to every-body'. He replied with truth & with acuteness for his age 'I am sure I have not given much trouble to you'.

17. T. [London]

Wrote to Mr Alex. Burnett—Mr H.D. Wolff—Rev. H. Howard—J. Hors-ley[8]—Mrs Marshall—Rev. R. Owen—P. Tomassino[9]—F.A. Neale[10]— Aristides Xenos[11]—Rev. Mr Butcher—J.S. Mastucci[12]—Revg. Edr. World[13] —Dr Macbride. Saw Stapylton[R]—Saw Mr Jas. Wortley. Dined at the Club: with M. Van de Weyer, G. Lewis, Duke of Argyll, Milman, Carlisle. Read Lacretelle—Shopping. 10½–1½ Journey to London.

18. Wed.

Wrote to S. Herbert—H. Glynne. Busy with the new arrangements in the drawingrooms. Saw Earl of Aberdeen—Duke of Argyll—R. Phillimore— Mr Wm. Lyon[14]—Mr [C.] Wykeham Martin—Mr Mavor—J.N.G.—Mr Baldock. Sir John Lawrence—at Argyll Lodge, where we dined. The Her-bert Letter caused me some reflection.[15]

19. Th. X.

Wrote to Archdn. Allen—Robn. G.—Miss Macfarlane—C. Kirk[16]—Mr

[1] Obscure.
[2] J. D. MacBride, *The Mohammedan religion explained* (1857).
[3] [J. L. Anderdon], *The life of Thomas *Ken, Bishop of Bath and Wells* (1851).
[4] Thomas Woodward, 1814–75; dean of Down from 1856; wrote widely on Irish church affairs.
[5] Sir C. *Lyell, *On lavas of Etna formed on steep slopes and on craters of elevation* (1859).
[6] Ightham Mote, 1¼ miles SW. of Swanley Junction, a fine moated manor.
[7] Charles Irvine Wimberley; Pembroke, Oxford; vicar of Hartlip, Kent, 1866–76; and Thomas Sikes, d. 1888, rector of Chevening from 1854.
[8] John Horsley, china dealer in London.
[9] Muddled with Mattiucci?
[10] Frederick Arthur Neale, published on Turkey and Islam.
[11] Greek consul in Cardiff.
[12] Possibly Leovigildo Tommasini Mattiucci, 1824–77; Italian liberal.
[13] Not published.
[14] William Lyon, 1807–92; M.P. 1831–2; contested seats as a liberal in 1837, 1859, 1862, 1865, 1874; as Middlesex magistrate consistently opposed license for Argyle Rooms (see introduction, iii. xliv–xlv).
[15] *Herbert's letter to *Russell setting out 'conditions necessary to a successful move'; *Herbert sent a copy with a covering note—'I think the future very gloomy'—to Gladstone, who replied this day: Stanmore, ii. 182–6.
[16] Perhaps Conrad A. Kirk, senior clerk in the horse guards.

Mitchinson—Dr Daubeny—Mr J. Horsley—S. Herbert—Secy. Estcourt[1]
—Rev. Mr Owen—Ld Chancellor. Covent Garden Ly Waldegrave's box in
evg. Saw Count Persigny—Baron Brunnow—At the Palace. Mr F. Peel
(Opera)—Rev. P. Freeman. Nine to breakfast. Saw Thyne. with interest[R].
Attended the Drawingroom with C. Then at Univ. Club Commee.—
Christie's & Benjamin's. Read Lacretelle.

20. Fr.

Wrote to Sig. Anartomo[2]—W. Lyon—Sec. Nat Socy.[3]—Overends. Presided & Spoke at meeting of the Deaf & Dumb Association. Saw Mr B.
Benjamin—Mr Grogan—Mr Bonham—Earl of Aberdeen—Count Persigny
—Mrs Boler—Hon. R. Lawley. Dined at J. Wortley's N. Sheen House &
saw his grounds.[4] Read Buckle, in Fraser.[5]

21. Sat.

Wrote to W.N. Goalen[6]—Rector of Exeter—N. Waterhouse[7]—Rev. N.
Woodard—Mrs Kidd—Sir H. Storks—Rev. R. Greswell—Rev. Mr Zincke
—Rev. Mr Caparn—H. Tomlinson[8]—A.F. Munro.[9] Saw Count Persigny—
Lady Jersey—Duke of Newcastle—Music in evg. Read Adam Bede.—
Lacretelle—Palmerston's Opinions.[10]

22. 4 S. E.

St James mg: Marg. St aft. MS aloud evg. Family calls—Wrote to E.
Lovell[R]—Dean Newland. Read Nicole[11]—Newland's De Dominis.[12]

23. M.

Wrote to Sir J. Lacaita—Worked on pictures, bronzes, & papers, nearly all
day. Also on accounts with Hampton. Saw Mr E. Harcourt—Mr Wade cum
Canonico del Drago[13]—Count Strzelecki—Mr Bohn. Saw E. Lovell—
J. Trelawney (44)[R]. Read Lacretelle. Attended Geogr. Soc.s dinner, the
farewell to Sir R. Murchison; thanked for Univ.[14]

24. T.

Wrote to Johnson L. & Co—Overends—Mr Lendrum—Dr Todd—V.

[1] Sotheron-*Estcourt was home secretary March–June 1859.
[2] Not found.
[3] J. G. *Lonsdale, see 6 Mar. 50.
[4] Upper Sheen House at Mortlake.
[5] *Fraser's Magazine*, lix. 509 (May 1859). H. T. Buckle on *Mill.
[6] Of London, perhaps from the related Liverpool family; assisted Gladstone in china purchasing (Hawn P).
[7] Probably Nicholas Waterhouse, archivist in Liverpool.
[8] London builder.
[9] Perhaps Alexander George Munro, perpetual curate of Woolfardisworthy, Devon, from 1854.
[10] *Opinions and policy of the Right Hon. Viscount Palmerston* (1852).
[11] See 27 Aug. 43.
[12] H. Newland, *The life . . . of Antonio de Dominis, Archbishop of Spalatro* (1859).
[13] Perhaps Raffaele Drago, Italian advocate.
[14] See *The Times*, 24 May 1859, 10.

Fergolina[1]—W.H.G.—Bp of Brechin. Read Adam Bede—Lacretelle. Saw Sir J. Lacaita—Mr Ellice—Mrs Tait (dinner)[2]—W.N. Goalen—Rev. Wm. Caparn. Drawingroom & house arrangements. Dined at Sir J. Hogg's.

25. Wed. X. ♄

Wrote to Mr Beasley[3]—Mr Taunton[4]—Mr MacColl—Ld Carlisle—Duchess of Sutherland—Lady Lyttelton dined. Saw Trelawney: ill[R]. Saw Rev. Mr Christie. Began my new picture Catalogue. Read Ad. Bede finished. Lacretelle finished Vol 5. Robinson on Ceramic Art.[5]

26. Th.

Wrote to Johnson L & Co—Mr G. Burnett—N. Waterhouse. Preparing rooms. Christies 1–2. Saw Bp of Capetown[6]—Major Ottley[7]—Sir W. Farquhar—Mr Milner Gibson—Mr Whitwell Elwin. Read Forsythes St Helena[8]—L'Affaire Mortara.[9] Sixteen to dinner to meet the Duc d'Aumale: and a large evening party till near one.

27. Fr.

Wrote to Sir J. Lacaita—Sir H. Storks—Mrs Shepheard[10]—Robn. G—J.G. Talbot—H. Kingscote—Johnson L & Co. Saw Mr C.A. Wood—Col. Wilson Patten—Rev. H. Maskew[11]—Mr W. Bagehot[12]—Ld Stanhope—Sir Chas. Wood—Ld Aberdeen. Saw Cornel[R]. Dined with the Woods.[13] Read Forsyth's St Helena—Calls.

28. Sat.

Wrote to Capt. Stokes—Sir W. Heathcote—Mr Walthew[14]—Mr Brewster. Worked on papers & letters. Still much in arrear. 12–1 Brit. Museum: 1–3 luncheon with Duke & Dss. of Galliera, the Aumales, & Granvilles. $3\frac{1}{4}$–5 with Cornel; interested were I but worthy[R]. Saw Muller—Mr Monsell—Mr Loch's Clerk—Mr Twisleton—Ld Palmerston—Dean Milman—Mr

[1] A refugee?
[2] Catherine, *née* Spooner, m. bp. A. C. *Tait and d. 1878; in 1856 five of her six daughters d. of scarlet fever. See 28 May 59.
[3] William Cole Beasley, 1816–88; treasury counsel and counsel to customs office.
[4] John Henry Taunton, civil engineer in Parliament Street.
[5] (Sir) J. C. *Robinson, 'Inventory of objects forming the collection of the museum of ornamental art' (1856).
[6] R. *Gray; St. Helena was at this time separated from Capetown as a separate bpric.
[7] F. F. Ottley, chief clerk to the receipt of exchequer.
[8] W. *Forsyth, *History of the captivity of Napoleon at St. Helena*, 3v. (1853).
[9] Pamphlet on the forcible abduction of the supposedly baptised Jewish child Edgar Mortara, on bp. of Bologna's orders, 1858.
[10] Lived in Elizabeth Terrace, Westburn Park.
[11] Henry Edward Maskew, b. 1825?; chaplain to the forces on Zante 1854–76.
[12] Walter *Bagehot, 1826–77; s. in law of J. *Wilson, Gladstone's financial sec. 1852; edited the *Economist* from 1860.
[13] He told Wood 'he would vote a condemnation of the dissolution, and is afraid of the foreign affairs at so critical a moment being left in the hands of Malmesbury' (Morley, i. 623).
[14] Richard Walthew, London solicitor.

Hayward—A. Kinnaird. Dined at Bp of London's—Lady Palmerston's afterwards. Read Mill on Liberty.

29. 5 S.E.

St Andrews & H.C. mg (this being dearest Stephen's day of first Communion at Eton). St James's evg. & MS of 1840 aloud. Saw Ld Aberdeen—Lord R. Cavendish. Wrote to S. Herbert—M. Cornelie. Read Ullathorne's Immaculate Conception.[1]

30. M. [Strawberry Hill]

Wrote to Baron Rothschild—Duchess of Sutherland—Read Lacretelle—Reeks's Catalogue[2]—Farini Hist. Italy from 1814.[3] In aftn. we went down to Strawberry Hill.[4] Saw Captain Snell—Hon. A. Kinnaird—Scotts—Lord Aberdeen—Lord Lyndhurst—Mrs Larkins—Mr Merritt—Mr G. Harcourt—Ld Clarendon: 2 hours of pretty full & very free convn. in evg.

31. Tues. [London]

Wrote to Clerk Mercers Co[5]—Rev. Mr Butcher—Mr Lambert—Mrs Williams—Rev. N. Woodard—R. Eallem—Messrs. Overend—Geo Harris —Jas. Watson—Greg. Burnett—A. Borgia[6]—C. Ekrig—Mast. Univ. Coll. Called at Orleans House. Then back to town. H. of C. 2–3. for choice of Speaker.[7] Dined at Ld Carlisle's: a formidable & highly political party. Read Leslie's Handbook[8]—Horace Walpole's Journals[9]—Lacretelle's Hist 18 Siècle—Forsythe's St Helena. Saw Gurney[R]. Saw Sir J. Graham—E. Cardwell—C.A. Wood—Mr Seward (U.S.)[10] Worked on letters.

Wed. June One. 1859. X

Wrote to Rev. Mr Meredith—Rev. R. Wood—Mr Taunton. H. of C. 2–4. Sworn in there. Queen's Concert in evg. Saw Mr Wilson—Mr Maskew—Sir Jas. Lacaita—Sir Jas. Graham—Ld Stratford de Redcliffe—Duke of Argyll—Ld Wenlock. Saw Gurney 4–6[R]. Read Lacretelle.

2. Th. Ascension Day.

All Saints 8 a.m. Holy Commn.—Breakfast party 8: and China Lectures

[1] See 1 May 59.
[2] J. and R. T. Reeks, general salesmen in London.
[3] Presumably his own tr. of Farini, see 27 Nov. 50, which starts 1815.
[4] Horace *Walpole's house at Twickenham, then owned by Lady *Waldegrave.
[5] Henry Eugene Barnes, clerk to the Mercers' company.
[6] Alessandro Borgia, an Ionian, had applied unsuccessfully in November 1855 to be Gladstone's private secretary (Hawn P).
[7] J. E. *Denison was elected: H cliv. 9.
[8] See 22 Jan. 55.
[9] H. *Walpole, *Journal of the reign of King George the III, from the year 1771 to 1783*, 2v. (1859).
[10] William Henry Seward, 1801–72; American anti-slavery statesman; in 1859 on tour in England and France; secretary of state during the civil war.

afterwards from J. Ashley[1] and others. Wrote to L. Samuel[2]—J.F. Tafe[3]—
Watson & Smith—A. Borgia—G. Burnett—C.J. Appleby[4]—H. Kingscote
—Christie & Manson. Saw Scotts—Mr Stanistreet—Ld Palmerston—D. of
Cambridge—Sir C. Wood—Ld De Tabley—A. Hayward. in evg. S. Herbert
—Sir J. Johnstone. Read Lacretelle. Dined at Gen. Malcolm's—Lady
Molesworth's afterwards.

3. Fr.

Willy's 19th birthday: God bless him. Wrote to Sir W. Heathcote—Earl
Ripon—Rev. Mr Hallward[5]—J. Busby[6]—Jane Smith[R]—Willy—Selby
Bazaar.[7] All Saints Church 5 P.M. Dined at Mr Dobree's.[8] Lady Derby's
Ball afterwards. Saw Wright & two more[R]. Humanity! Read Rich's
Pamphlet[9]—Ridolfi's Breve Nota[10]—Lacretelle Hist Siècle XVIII. Restless
half-night. A good school. How much we think of time when it is not dis-
posed of by ourselves.

4. Sat. [Cliveden]

Wrote to V.C. Oxford. Saw Scotts—Sir J. Lacaita—Mr Saunders (Dentist)
—Lord Aberdeen. Off at 1 to Cliveden.[11] We walked up from Maidenhead.
Unsuccessful drive to Eton in evg. Argyll read Tennyson aloud to us: very
high strains indeed. Read Argyll's Geolog. Lecture[12]—Lacretelle.

5. S. aft. Ascension.

Bray Ch mg & Hedsor aft. Read Haweis Reformation Sketches.[13] We
walked to Dropmore. Conv. with Argyll on public affairs & my own
position. Sang the Clock, & also Montrose: contrary to my wont, & not
without doubt but it seemed too small to fight.[14]

6. M. [London]

Wrote to Sig. Tommassini—Vic. Gen. Kildare[15]—Messrs. Overend—R.

[1] Probably A. J. Ashley (see 11 Mar. 26), known as John.
[2] Louis Samuel, 1794–1859, Liverpool business man, grand-fa. of Herbert*.
[3] See 3 May 59.
[4] Charles James Appleby, published on machinery.
[5] Probably John William Hallward, curate of St. Stephen's, Hammersmith.
[6] Marine store dealer in Chelsea.
[7] Declining to open it?
[8] Bonamy Dobree, père, 1794–1863; governor of bank of England 1859–61; china collector.
[9] Sir H. Rich, 'Yes or no? A political pamphlet' (1852).
[10] C. Ridolfi, 'Breve nota a una storia di quattro ore intorno ai fatti del 27 aprile 1859' (1859).
[11] Then owned by the Sutherlands; see 15 June 48, 4 June 57.
[12] G. D. *Campbell, Duke of Argyll, 'Geology, its past and present. A lecture' (1859).
[13] J. O. W. *Haweis, Sketches of the Reformation and Elizabethan age taken from the contemporary pulpit (1844).
[14] Untraced; probably glees. 'Montrose' may refer to *Bishop's opera from *Scott (1822).
[15] Charles Crosthwaite, 1806–92; vicar general of Kildare from 1850; controversialist.

Cheen[1]—Mr Richie—J. Parisot[2]—G.H. Wilkinson[3]—Rev. F. Vidal—Mr H. Palmer—Sir J. Lacaita. Returned from Cliveden early.[4] 11–2 Radcliffe Trust Meeting. Saw S. Herbert—Sir J. Lacaita—E. Cardwell—Col. W. Patten—Dean Ramsay—Dr Acland. Saw one[R]. C. had a downstairs dance in the evg. The Duchesse d'Aumale came with her son:[5] & was most kind, quite at her ease: I thought too Italian in feeling. Read Forsyth's Sir H. Lowe & Napoleon.[6]

7. *Tu.*

Wrote to Rev. Mr Lowder—V.C. Oxford—E. Cardwell—Mr Tatam [sc. Tatham]—Dr Acland—H. Wilberforce—G. Burnett—Robn. G. Read Univ. & other pamphlets. H. of C. 4–8 and 11–12½.[7] Saw Ld Aberdeen— S. Herbert—Milnes Gaskell.

8. *Wed.*

Wrote to Mr Dyce—Dean Ramsay—Col. Talbot—E.A. Bowring—J.F. Tafe—H.B. Ormrod[8]—Mr Rowsell—Duca di Caballino—Queens Ball in evg. Read Lacretelle. Saw Jas. Wortley—Mr Cornwall Legh—Ld Carnarvon—Duke of Argyll—Mrs Herbert: who threatened me.[9]

9. *Th.*

Party of 15 to breakfast. Dined at Ld Lyndhurst's. C.s evening party afterwards. Saw Rev. Mr Rowsell—Ld Napier—H.W. Wilberforce—Ld Harris. H. of C. 4½–7½.[10] [1851] Exhibn. Finance meeting at the Palace 11½–2¼.

10. *Fr.*

Wrote to Mrs J.E. Tyler—Rev. Mr Chaplin—Mr A[lgernon] Joy[11]—Mrs M.E. Walker[12]—Mr G.P.R. James—G. Burnett—W.H. Stone.[13] 1–4 Exhibition Finance meeting at my house. Read Lacretelle. Saw S. Herbert

[1] Probably Robert Cheere, London barrister.
[2] Unidentified.
[3] George Howard *Wilkinson, 1833–1907; M.A. Oriel, Oxford, 1859; vicar of Bishop Auckland 1863–7, incumbent of St. Peter's, Eaton Square, 1870–83, his services there often attended by the Gladstones; bp. of Truro 1883, of St. Andrews 1893; Gladstone's priestly confidant on his deathbed.
[4] But not to attend the great meeting at Willis's Rooms of anti-govt. M.P.s which decided on the amndt. which felled the govt. (see 10 June 59). *Herbert did attend.
[5] Louis Philippe Marie Léopold d'Orléans, prince de Condé, 1845–66, the Aumales' elder son; pro-English favourite of Lady *Waldegrave.
[6] See 26 May 59.
[7] Great speech moving want of confidence amndt. to Queen's speech, by Spencer Compton *Cavendish, 1833–1908; styled marquis of Hartington 1858–91; liberal M.P. N. Lancashire 1857–68, Radnor boroughs 1869–80, N.W. Lancashire 1880–5, Rossendale 1885–91; sec. for war 1866, 1882–5; P.M.G. 1868, Irish sec. 1870–4, Indian sec. 1880–2; unionist 1886; 8th duke of Devonshire 1891; lord president 1895–1903. See Add MS 44143–8. Gladstone congratulated his fa. on this speech, see Holland, i. 37.
[8] Perhaps Henry Mere Ormerod, 1816–73, of Manchester.
[9] Presumably that he must vote against the government.
[10] Queen's speech and want of confidence deb.: *H* cliv. 193.
[11] Of Bayswater, later corresponded on photographs of Italian sculpture.
[12] Unidentified.
[13] William Henry Stone, 1834–96; liberal M.P. Portsmouth 1865–74.

cum Cardwell—Ld Overstone. H. of C. $4\frac{1}{2}$–$7\frac{1}{2}$ & 10–$2\frac{1}{2}$. Voted in 310:323 agt. the Amendment.[1]

11. *St Barnabas. Sat.*

Dined with S. Herbert: learned Granville's proceedings.[2] Read Italian papers. Saw Ld Aberdeen—Duchess of Sutherland. Saw Trelawney[R]. Business.

12. *Whits.*

Chapel Royal mg. & aft. H.C. mg. MS of 47 aloud in evg. Read Haweis Sketches[3]—England Conv. & Ref. Comp.[4]—Bussy's Court. Dev. Saintes[5]— Italian papers.

13. *M.*

Wrote to Robn. G.—Rev. Mr Gregory[6]—Rev. Dr Croly—Johnson L[ongden] & Co. Read Italian papers: tracts. Saw Lovell: doing well[R]. Saw Sir J. Lacaita—Mr Algernon Joy—Mr Bonham—Sidney Herbert; bis. Went to Ld P. by his desire at night: & accepted my old office.[7]

14. *T.* X

Wrote to Rev. O. Gordon—H. Wilberforce—Willy (Student)[8]—Mrs Lane Fox. Sat to Mr Watts 5–$6\frac{3}{4}$ & found him very agreeable.[9] Meeting at Cambridge House for political arrangements $11\frac{1}{2}$–$4\frac{1}{4}$.[10] Stafford House afterwards. Saw Duke of Argyll: who was most movingly kind.[11] G.C. Lewis —Sat to Mr Watts 5–7. Read It. papers. Forsyth's St Helena. Saw [blank].

15. *Wed.*

Wrote to Watson & Smith (+Telegram)—Johnson L & Co. Saw Ld Aberdeen—S. Herbert—Adam Gladstone. Cambridge House 2–7.[12] Read Italian papers. Forsyth's St Helena. Saw Gurney[R].

---

[1] i.e. he voted with the tories against the want of confidence amndt.: *H* cliv. 417.

[2] *Granville was this day invited to form a govt., failed, and abandoned the attempt next day (*L.Q.V.* 1st Series, iii. 440). From this entry it seems clear he did not see Gladstone, though *Clarendon suggested he should, and he reported Gladstone's views to the Queen (ibid., and Fitzmaurice, i. 336).

[3] See 5 June 59.

[4] R. *Manning, *England's Conversion and Reformation compared* (1725).

[5] C. de Bussy, *Les Courtisanes devenues saintes. Étude historique* (1859).

[6] In W. H. Hutton, ed., *Robert Gregory* (1912), 79–80.

[7] As chancellor of the exchequer, which office he retained until July 1866; he told *Herbert next day 'he would not have joined the Government otherwise' (Stanmore, ii. 200).

[8] On his election as a junior student of Christ Church; Lathbury, ii. 162.

[9] *Watts painted two portraits of Gladstone from the 1859 sittings, now at Hawarden and the National Portrait Gallery.

[10] They went through the remaining cabinet offices, none to be announced immediately (Stanmore, ii. 200). Gladstone's jottings in Add MS 44748, f. 87 include 'Cobden propose B. Trade Gibson propose Poor Law'.

[11] *Argyll was lord privy seal in *Palmerston's cabinet.

[12] Jottings in Add MS 44748, f. 89 include 'B. Trade propose Cobden'.

16. Th.

Wrote to Sir W. Heathcote—Rev. Mr Cowper—Mr De Radius—Mr G. Glyn—Watson & Smith—Dr Young[1]—J. Cumberland[2]—Mr [James] Wilson. At Christies. Saw Archdn. Jones.—Mr Foster M.P.[3]—Duke of Argyll—Rev. Mr Elwin. Cambridge House 12–3.[4] Sat to Mr Watts two hours. Read Italian papers.

17. Fr.

Wrote to Mrs Coldrigh[5]—A. Tennyson—Sir T.G.—R.B. Campbell[6]— J.N.G.—Mr Rawlinson—Mr Greswell—Provost of Oriel (full) & draft[7] —Bishop of Oxford (3) & copies of 2.[8] Ld Palmerston. Saw Ld Palmerston —J. Herbert—Ld Wodehouse[9]—Count Persigny—Ld Wenlock—Count Corti: & others. Dined at Ld Braybrooke's—Lady Waldegrave's afterwards. Sat to Watts $3\frac{1}{2}$–$5\frac{1}{2}$. Then at Stafford House heard Tennyson read his Guinevere.[10] A memorable time. Up late. X.

18. Sat.

Wrote to J.N.G.—Dean of Ch.Ch.—Mr Disraeli—Mr Greswell[11]—Sir Jas. Hudson—Mr Estcourt (Radcl[iffe Trust]) & Archdn. Jones. Further consn. with colleagues of letter to Oxford: & corrections sent. Saw Northcote *cum* Phillimore—Jas. Wilson. Ld J. Russell, Granville, Herbert, D. of Argyll, Ld Palmerston, Milner Gibson, Elgin, Sir G. Lewis; on our trip to Windsor 2–$6\frac{1}{2}$. Saw J.N.G.—Rev. Mr Rawlinson—Ld Stanley, Gen. Peel in evg. Sworn in at Windsor as Chancr. of Exchequer. Lady Alice Peel's party in evg. Mr Rawlinson dined with us. Saw [blank]. Read Seniors Journal.

19. Trin. S. X.

St James's & H.C. mg. All Saints (crammed) aft. MS of 1840 aloud in evg. H.S. lesson with Mary, also with Harry & Herbert. Read Ullathorne (finished)—Soanes Hist. Mary.—Senior's Journal: secular. Saw Ld Aberdeen. Saw Stedman, Stewart: with much interest[R].

20. M. X.

Wrote to Mr Pressly—Mr Watts—Sir F. Fremantle—Ld H. Lennox—Sir

---

[1] Edward P. Young, London physician.
[2] John Cumberland, d. 1866; London publisher.
[3] William Orme Foster, 1814–99; Stourbridge ironmaster; liberal M.P. S. Staffordshire 1857–68.
[4] Minor offices—jottings in Add MS 44748, f. 90.
[5] Unidentified.
[6] Robert B. Campbell, United States consul in London.
[7] Election letter, printed in *The Guardian*, 22 June 1859, 531.
[8] 'It is quite a mistake to suppose that the formation of this Cabinet is the determining crisis of its political character. That must come in its development; & may be there six or even nine months hence'; Bodleian, MS Wilberforce d. 36, f. 177.
[9] Just appt. under-secretary for foreign affairs.
[10] In his *Idylls*; see 14 July 59.
[11] Again his chairman at Oxford.

A. Spearman—Mr Arbuthnot—Mr Blewitt—Vice Chancellor. Cabinet 3½–6½. Saw Helen—Mr Pressly—Mr Arbuthnot—Mr Anderson—C. Kielmansegge *cum* B. de Cetto.—D. of Somerset—R. Phillimore. Countess de Persigny's Ball in evg. Saw Stewart 2°[R].

I am sore about the Oxford Election; but I try to keep myself in order: it disorganises & demoralises me, while, such are the riddles of *my* 'human nature' it also quickens mere devotional sensibility.[1] O that I had wings.

21. T.

Wrote to Mr Greswell—Robn. G—F. Goulburn[2]—Rev. Dr Dyne—Mr Seward—Ld Palmerston—Dr Cureton—Bp of Oxford—Rev. J.H. Gray—R. Phillimore.[3] Dined at the Mansion Ho. & proposed the Lady Mayoress.[4] In Downing St for business. Saw Ld H. Lennox—Mr Bonham—E.G. Vernon—R. Phillimore—O. Blewitt—Sir F. Fremantle—Mr Ryan—Sir A. Spearman—Mr Pressly—Mr Wilbraham—Sir J. Coleridge[5]—Mr Stephenson. Read Senior's Journal (finished)—Lit. Fund Reports & Speeches.[6] Ld Normanby's Speech.[7]

22. Wed.

Wrote to Hon. Mr Brand[8]—S.H. Northcote (2)[9]—Mr Bignold[10]—Warden of A[ll] S[ouls]—Mr Moore—Mr V. Scully M.P.—Mr Bissett—J.H. Parker—Mr Stothert—Mr Mozley—Sir A. Gordon—Mr Greswell—Mrs Sutherland—Mr Wilkinson—Provost of Oriel. Cabinet 3½–6. Saw R. Phillimore—Mr S. Laing M.P.—Mr Hamilton—Mr Disraeli—Mr G.E. Vernon—Ld Shaftesbury (Palace)—Ld Ripon—Prince F[rederick] of Holstein.[11] 6½–11½ Presided at the Lit. Fund Dinner: in a flimsy way.[12] Palace Concert afterwards. In D. St for business.

23. Th.

Wrote to Junior Proctor[13]—Rev. Dr Dyne—H. Merivale—Rev. Mr Liddon—D. of Newcastle—Rev. Mr Gooday[14]—Sir C. Eardley—Mr Alexander—Mr Kingsmill—Mr O. Gordon—Mr Burkitt—Mr Brande. Saw Stewart 3°X.

[1] Lord *Chandos had announced his candidacy in the by-election consequent on Gladstone's acceptance of office.
[2] Frederick Goulburn, 1818–78; vice chairman of board of customs 1859, chairman 1875.
[3] Letter from *Keble to *Phillimore supporting diarist was published next day.
[4] S.P.G. dinner: *The Times*, 22 June 1859, 9.
[5] Doubtful in his support at Oxford.
[6] See next day.
[7] C. H. *Phipps, Lord Normanby, 'Speech delivered in the House of Lords . . . June 7th 1859 . . . with an appendix on Italian affairs'.
[8] H. B. W. *Brand (see 21 Nov. 53), chief liberal whip 1859–66.
[9] *Northcote declined to serve on his cttee., though he voted for him.
[10] Samuel Frederick Bignold, 1820?–73; rector of Tivetshall St. Mary from 1845.
[11] See 12 July 51.
[12] Full report in *The Times*, 23 June 1859, 10.
[13] On national defences; in *The Guardian*, 29 June 1859, 552.
[14] James Goodday, d. 1889; chaplain to Witham Union 1856–64, to Romford Union from 1864.

Saw Sir J. Coleridge *cum* J.D.C.—R. Phillimore—Mr Bonham—D. Lange—
Mr S[pring] Rice—Mr Robinson—Mr Reynolds—Provost of Eton—D. of
Argyll—Lady Campden.
In D. St for business. Sat to Mr Watts 4½–6¾. Dined at Ld Londonderry's—
Lady Johnstone's afterwards. Read Italian papers.

24. Fr. St John Baptist.

Wrote to Sir W. Heathcote—G. Hancock—Dean of Ch Ch—Mr Mozley—
Attorney General[1]—Rev. Mr Pound—Mr Greswell (2)—Dr Greenhill—
Earl of Derby—Mast. of Mint[2]—Mr Bignold—Sir F. Rogers & draft[3]—
Rect. of Exeter—Mast. of Balliol. Cabinet 4–6½. At 3½ we opened the
Treasury Commee.[4] Saw Mr Senior—Mr Scott (Hoxton)[5]—Sir S. Scott &
Co—Lord John Russell—(Suez)[6]—Mr Laing & Mr Hamilton[7]—Duchess of
Sutherland—T.D. Acland—A. Kinnaird—Lady Waldegrave's Concert in
Evg. Read Italian papers.

25. Sat.

Wrote to Rev. G.A. Jones[8]—The Speaker—Rev. T.F. Smith[9]—S. Herbert
—Rev.[J.]E.T. Rogers—Mr Cosserat—Sir H. Dymoch[10]—Rev. E. Hawkins
—D[uke of] Somerset—Jas. Wilson—Dinner party of 18 at home. Hop duty
Deputation at 2. Saw Mr Safe—Mr Stephenson—Sir J. Lacaita—Read
Italian papers. Miles on Galway Station.[11]

26. 1. S. Trin.

St Martins H.C. 8½ a.m. Whitehall 11 a.m. Chapel Royal 5½—Heard Mr
Kemp in Crown Court at 7.[12]—MS on 'Faith' in evg. Saw Earl of Aberdeen—
Sir F. Rogers. Wrote on Miracles. Wrote to Willy. Read Haweis.[13]

[1] *Bethell.
[2] Thomas *Graham, 1805–69; master of the mint from 1855, no longer a political
position; see 6 Sept. 41.
[3] Chairman of his London cttee.; on navy defences, in *The Guardian*, 29 June 1859,
552.
[4] Probably the superannuation cttee., see M. Wright, *Treasury control of the civil
service* (1969), 310.
[5] See 14 June 52.
[6] Gladstone supported building the canal, but the cab. prevented it throughout 1859;
see C. W. Halberg, *The Suez Canal* (1931), 163.
[7] S. *Laing (see 29 Oct. 41), financial sec. to the treasury, and G. A. *Hamilton (see
15 Mar. 44), assistant sec. to the treasury 1859–67. Gladstone this day appt. (Sir)
Charles Lister Ryan, 1831–1920, as private secretary, which he was until May 1865;
audit board secretary 1865, later its comptroller and auditor; K.C.B. 1887.
[8] Griffith Arthur Jones; vicar in Cardiff from 1872; voted for Gladstone 1859.
[9] Thomas Frederick Smith, 1821?–71; fellow of Magdalen 1846–56, rector of Horsing-
ton from 1856.
[10] Sir Henry Dymoke, 1801–65; King's Champion 1821; cr. bart. 1841.
[11] P. Miles, *The social, political, and commercial advantages of direct steam navigation
and rapid postal intercourse between Europe and America, via Galway, Ireland* (1858).
[12] i.e. at St. Mary's, Crown Street.
[13] See 12 June 59.

27. M.

Wrote to M.F. Tupper—Sig. Delviniotti[1]—Mr Oldfield—Mr Littleboy—
Rev. T.J. Prout[2]—Dr Goodford—Mr Lushington—Rev. Mr Wills[3]—Sir
W. Heathcote—Rev. Mr Berkeley—Mr G. Smith—Rev. Mr Greswell.
Read Italian papers. 13 to dinner: & musical party afterwards. I joined in
some choruses. Saw R. Phillimore—Mr Stephenson—Mr Laing.

28. Tu. X.

Wrote to Sir Th. Tancred—Jas Gladstone—Mr Taunton—Ed of Guardian[4]
—Sir Geo. Brown[5]—E. Cardwell and minutes. Saw Mr Laing—Sir G.
Cornewall Lewis[6]—Mr E.G. Vernon—Mr Stephenson *cum* Mr L[aing].
Dined at Mr Tollemache's: much conv. with Mr Finch[7]—Bp of London
(Gk Clergy)—Read Forsyth's St Helena.[8] Finished the Italian papers. Saw
Irish[R].

29. Wed. St Peter. X.

Wrote to Deputy Govr. of Bank—The Master of the Mint—Lord J.
Russell—Mr Jas. Wilson—Mr S. Herbert—Cabinet 4–6½. Saw Mr Stephen-
son—Mr Laing—M. Tricoupé—Sir James Graham—Ld Carlisle—Mr
Anderson—G. Berkeley. Dined at Grillion's—Queen's Ball afterwards.
Failed to see Stapleton: saw Stewart[R]. Worked on Italian papers. Read
Fraser's Mag.[9]

30. Th.[10]

Wrote to Sir F. Baring—Ld Justice Clerk[11]—O.B. Cole—Mr Woollcombe—
Rev. Dr Irons—Rev. Mr Davidson[12]—J.H. Taunton—Ld Fielding—Mr
Macfie—Mr Safe—Ld Palmerston. Nine to dinner. Saw Mr T.D. Acland—
F.R. Bonham *cum* Ld H. Lennox—Rob. Phillimore—Sir W. Farquhar—
Duke of Argyll—Mr Wilson—Mr Anderson. Read Chevalier Baisse de l'or [13]
—Bentley's Q.R. on Parties.[14] Wrote Memm. on Italian affairs.

---

[1] Achille Delvinotti Barozzi, also a correspondent with Mazzini.
[2] Thomas Jones Prout, 1824?–1909; student of Christ Church 1842; censor 1857;
proctor 1859; as leader of the movement for statute reform 1865, 'the Man who Slew the
Canons'; supported Gladstone 1859, 1865.
[3] John Wills, d. 1873; rector of South Perrott, Somerset, from 1848.
[4] Unpublished; *The Guardian* called for an explanation but supported his re-election,
22 June 1859, 527.
[5] Sir George *Brown, 1790–1865; commanded light division in Crimea; commanded
Ireland 1860–5.
[6] On his London election cttee.
[7] Perhaps George Finch, 1794–1870; tory M.P. until 1847.
[8] See 6 June 59.
[9] *Fraser's Magazine,* lix (June 1859).
[10] The Oxford poll closed this day: Gladstone 1050, Chandos 859.
[11] John *Inglis, 1810–91; lord justice clerk (known as Lord Glencorse) 1858–67; lord
justice general from 1867; encouraged Scottish university reform; defeated Gladstone
for chancellorship of Edinburgh university 1868.
[12] Jonas Pascal Fitzwilliam Davidson, curate in Dorchester; vicar of Frampton 1862.
[13] See 28 Mar. 59.
[14] *Bentley's Quarterly Review,* i (March 1859).

Lord Cowley's confidential Dispatch of the 27th [June] is so clear, able, fair, and so eminently suggestive that it might perhaps be printed at once for the use of the Cabinet?[1]

On two points I venture to dissent. With Lord Palmerston, I think he over-rates the strength of the Revolutionary party in Italy: nor can I see that *British* interests would suffer prejudice from the creation of a Kingdom of North Italy reaching from sea to sea.

There seem however to me to be two other material objections to the creation of such a Kingdom on the basis of the present Kingdom of Sardinia: first that it might be prejudicial to the internal equilibrium of Italy itself, over which the House of Savoy might seek to domineer: and secondly that it would be a bad neighbour to Austria and that the prospect of this bad neighbourship might and indeed ought to influence her adversely as to the acceptance of such terms of peace.

Though the case is far from ripe, yet with the prospect of the serious duties which may attach to England it seems to be the time for turning over alternatives and fixing the great objects which are to be had in view.

The two great objects of desire, I submit, should be

1. the cessation of the direct dominion of Austria in Italy, and
2. an essential change in the position of the Popedom with reference to its temporal prerogatives.[2]

As respects the first, the systematic domination which for near half a century Austria has carried throughout Italy in virtue of her limited Italian Sovereignty, impairs her moral if not her judicial title to that Sovereignty itself; nor can Italy ever be at peace while it continues. To take Lombardy away, and leave Venetia would leave to Austria all the dangers with half the resources: it would set free those Italians who have done little for themselves, and would leave under the yoke those who in 1848/9 did so much. There does not seem to be an argument for any scheme of this kind, except the merely material one of the fortified frontier which it would supply. No European end would be attained: the Italian question would still be an unsolved problem and a standing peril.

Lord Palmerston observes that, if Austria surrenders her Italian Provinces, she may fairly require their assumption of a portion of her debt. But though she must renounce all interference with their form of government, may she not *also* reasonably desire, and would it not be wise to assist her in obtaining, the constitution of friendly sovereignty on her borders? Is not this all the more fair, first because of the difficulty attending the constitution of a frontier, and secondly because the means of constituting such a sovereignty appear to be offered in the person of the Archduke Maximilian?

With respect to the Papal Power, it seems clear that the Emperor of the French wants his hands to be strengthened; and that he wishes to have Austria with him, as an essential condition of handling this question in a satisfactory manner. But may it not be in the power of England and other states likewise to assist him? Have we not of late professed rather too broadly the disqualification of all Powers not Roman Catholic for dealing with this subject except in a subordinate capacity? The Pope was restored in 1815 mainly by the agency of the Powers supposed to be thus disqualified. They all took part in the recommendations to Gregory XVI: and England to the last protested against the refusal of the advice

[1] PRO FO 27/1298, f. 296, advocating creation of independent Lombardo-Venetian kingdom. No printed copy found.
[2] Initialled and dated here 30 June 1859, both deleted.

then given. *At least* as far as France is willing to lead, may not we be willing to follow?

With great deference, I still venture to question Lord Palmerston's suggestion that the affairs of the Roman State may perhaps be settled between the Pope and his people: and to incline to the opinions of Lord Cowley.

If the Roman question is left to the Pope and his people, the Pope will be forthwith expelled: a republic will be almost of necessity established: the cause of temperate freedom must be discredited more or less under a government of necessity revolutionary from the incidents of its birth. The Pope will concede nothing, but will simply excommunicate his people, and will abide his time. That time will arrive in some new turn of European politics, when it may suit some powerful state to use the pleas for interference which such a condition of things cannot fail to afford, and to court some domestic interest by re-establishing the palsied Government. No pledge against foreign occupation will stand the temptation that circumstances are sure to offer.

If on the other hand *Europe* undertakes and achieves the settlement of the question, it will be settled on better terms for both Pope and people. The Pope will then have been under European guarantee [,] independence, security, dignity, and wealth: and his people will have some Government, established in order, and not in chaos. On paper, the Pope will still be bound to protest as he did in 1815: but this protest will do no more execution now than it did then, and will simply save his conscience in a harmless way.

Dissention among the Great Powers will make a settlement of this question hopeless and will leave Italy cursed with its great central volcano. But if Austria can be induced to agree, there would seem to be no insuperable difficulty in the thing proposed to be done. The internal questions between Church and State, Clergy and Laity, hopeless for any Government which the people could have strength to set up, will subside under the weight of European authority. It would have to be considered by what subventions the Pope should be supported— whether and in what degree his authority should be locally circumscribed—what should be the nature of his authority within the limits—what provision should be made for his security and independence. He need not be the subject of anybody. There is no reason to believe that the population he now rules would object to be moderately charged for his maintenance. The grand difficulty of all would perhaps be solved were his sovereignty converted into a Suzerainty, so that (within a wider or a narrower sphere) he should only have certain fixed dignities and privileges. The present hopeless problem of his army would be solved of itself, when he was guarded by European guarantee; and it would no longer be the interest, nor therefore the desire, of Italians to rise against him. In short there seem to be the elements of a solution, if there be the will to use them: but nothing will be a solution that leaves to the Pope a *constitutional* authority, which will not work, or an *absolute* authority, which will never be endured.

With respect to France I cling to the hope that Lord Cowley's expectations may be realised: but after the manner in which Austria committed herself by crossing the Ticino Sardinia will doubtless look for some extension of territory. For one I cannot wish it to be large: partly for reasons stated above; partly because after the experience of 1848/9 we cannot rely on the recent manifestation in Lombardy of a desire for annexation, while the Papers appear to show that in Tuscany *even* under present circumstances there has been much difference of opinion: partly because it seems uncertain how far Sardinia has mixed sheer ambition with those Italian aims which (I cannot but think) the absolute necessities of her position required her to adopt.

With regard to Tuscany it may deserve some inquiry whether we have in any manner committed ourselves to the Grand Duke. I infer from the Papers, that we advised the neutrality, which made the Revolution inevitable and just.[1]

Friday. July One 1859.

Wrote to J.Stuart Wortley—S. Herbert—Rev. Mr Townsend—C.A. Wood —D. of Somerset—R. Bentley—Sir G.C. Lewis—Ld Ripon[2]—Dean of Ch Ch—M. Gladstone & minutes. Saw R. Phillimore—Scotts—T.D. Acland— D. of Argyll—Ld Aberdeen—Dr Ogle[3]—Ld Overstone. Breakfast at Stafford House to meet Mr Sumner. Worked on Italian papers. Read Chevalier—Bentley No 2 on Parties. Worked on Rev. papers.

2. Sat.

Wrote to V.C. Oxford (2)—Robn. G—D. of Newcastle—Mr Burgon—Rev. A. Lendrum—J.D. Coleridge—Mr Stephenson and minutes. Saw Elgwin Bedell[4]—J.S. Wortley—Mr Laing—Mr Stephenson—Mr Gibson—Cabinet 4–6½. Dined at Ld Manners's—Lady Palmerston's afterwards. Worked on Italian papers. Read [blank.]

3. 2 S. Trin.

Chapel Royal & H.C. mg & St James's evg.—MS of 42 aloud. Read Haweis (finished)—Bentley's Q.R. on Popular Preaching.[5] Saw Ld Wenlock—Ld Carlisle. Worked at night on Italian papers.

4. M.

Wrote to Ld A. Hervey—W. Hancock—Sir E.B. Lytton—H.K. Seymer— D. of Newcastle (2)—Ld Palmerston—Mr Chapman (?)—Sidney Herbert— G. Burnett—Mr Wynne M.P.—Robn. G & minutes. Took the oaths & my seat. H. of C. 4–6¾.[6] Saw R. Phillimore—Sir F. Baring—Ld Palmerston— Sir G. Grey—Sir R. Bethell—Ld A. Hervey—H.K. Seymer—Mr Cunningham—Jas. Wilson. Deputation on Galway Harbour—Do on King of Oude. Worked on Italian Papers. Saw Stapleton—Lloyd 15.—Lovell: going back [R].

5. T.

Wrote to Rev. Mr Blackburn[7]—Sir G. Grey (2)—Atty. General—J.S. Mill— Warden of New Coll—Mr Haddan—Sir T. Fremantle—Mr Ewart—Ld

[1] Copy by Ryan, but initialled and dated 30 June 1859 by Gladstone, and docketed by him 'Copy memorandum on Italian affairs', Add MS 44748, f. 93; Gladstone's holograph in PRO 30/22/19, f. 1.

[2] *Goderich had recently succ. as 2nd. earl.

[3] John William Ogle, London physician and fellow of Merton, secretary to Gladstone's London cttee.

[4] Perhaps of H. G. Bedell & co., London printers.

[5] *Bentley's Quarterly Review*, ii. 473 (July 1859).

[6] Misc. business: *H* cliv. 591.

[7] Henry Ireland Blackburne, b. 1826; rector of Warmingham, Cheshire, from 1858.

Chancellor—Ld Granville—V. Chancellor Oxford—Mr Walpole—Mr Rawlinson—Mr G. Smith—Rev. Mr Bedford[1]—Mr Dyce & minutes. Saw Ld Palmerston—Ld John Russell—Mr Laing—D[owning] St & H.C. $2\frac{1}{4}$–$7\frac{1}{2}$.[2] Worked on Italian papers. Read Mill's Dissertations[3]—Statement resp. Unclaimed Dividends.[4]

6. Wed. X.

Wrote to J.H. Parker—Rev. J.C. Bates[5]—Mr Burnett—Rev. Mr Kempe—Mast. Balliol (& others)—Sir J. Graham. Dined at the Ld Chancellor's. Lord Lansdowne's afterwards. Read Mill's Dissertations. H. of C. $12\frac{1}{4}$–$5\frac{1}{4}$ on Endowed School's Bill. Voted in 192:210 agt Bright.[6] 10 A.M. Went to meet the Ld Chancellor & Atty. General. Saw Russell 19: almost a new phase [R]. Saw Mr M[ilner] Gibson: the chances of war gave me Mrs Gibson at dinner.

7. Th.

Wrote to Overends—Dr Wolff[7]—Mr Pressly—Dr Russell[8]—Sir T. Fremantle—Sir W. Heathcote—H. of C. $4\frac{1}{2}$–9 on business & $10\frac{3}{4}$–12.[9] Cabinet 2–4. Nine to breakfast. The Comte de Paris was the centre: a most unaffected intelligent and interesting person. Saw Mr Laing: various members of Parlt.—Mr Brand. Read Mill.

8. Fri.

Wrote to Mr G.G. Scott—Dr Wolff—Sir A. Damaschino—Mr S. Robins—Mr Cobden—Sig. Nisca.[10] Read Revision of Prayerbook[11]—Mill's Dissertations. H. of C. $4\frac{1}{4}$–7 and $9\frac{1}{2}$–$12\frac{1}{4}$.[12] Saw Mr Hamilton—Nat. Debt Commissioners—Mr Romilly (B[ank] Audit)—Mr Laing—Mr Lowe—Mr Brand—Mr W. Forbes.

9. Sat. X.

Wrote to Sir J. Lacaita—Ld J. Russell—Signor Massari—Dr Cardwell—Mr T.E. Moss—Mr Conningham M.P.[13] and minutes.[14] Cabinet $2\frac{1}{4}$–$5\frac{1}{4}$. Read Le Chevalier—Mill's Dissertations—Bentley's Q.R. on France &c.[15] Saw

[1] Probably Henry Bedford, 1824–1906; held many curacies and published sermons.
[2] Volunteers: *H* cliii. 678.
[3] J. S. *Mill, *Dissertations and Discussions*, 4v. (1859–75); i on state and church.
[4] Untraced.
[5] Joseph Chadwick Bates, b. 1826?; vicar of Castleton, Lancashire, from 1862; supported Gladstone 1859.
[6] And spoke on it: *H* cliv. 767.
[7] See 3 May 52.
[8] John Rutherford Russell of Harley Street (Hawn P).
[9] Proposed select cttee. on Galway packet contracts: *H* cliv. 800.
[10] Baron Nicola Nisco, Neapolitan nationalist.
[11] *Suggestions for a revision of the Prayer Book* (1859).
[12] Spoke on Crown securities: *H* cliv. 870.
[13] William Coningham, 1815–84; liberal M.P. Brighton 1857–64; see 9 June 49.
[14] Review of public expenditure 1854–5: Add MS 44748, f. 103.
[15] *Bentley's Quarterly Review*, ii. 508 (July 1859).

Russell: as before [R]. Close heat & bad smells. C. & her party went to Ashridge. Arranged with Mr Ryan for Willy to try his hand.[1]

10. 3. S. Trin.

Chapel Royal mg—All Saints aft. MS of 42 in evg. Saw J.N.G.—H.J.G.—Lord Aberdeen. Read Chr. Remembr.[2]—Greenwood[3]—Paradise Lost—Arnold's Sermons.[4]

11. M.

Wrote to Bp of Salisbury—Sec. of Socy. for Employing Women[5]—Bp of London—Mr Dunlop—Mr Scholefield & minutes. Cabinet $2\frac{1}{4}$–4. H. of C. $4\frac{1}{4}$–$7\frac{1}{4}$ and $10\frac{1}{2}$–$12\frac{1}{2}$.[6] Saw Bp of Brechin *cum* Mr Forbes—Rev. Mr Grieve—Duke of Argyll—Mr Laing—Mr Brand—The Speaker *cum* Mr Vardon. Sworn in before the Ld Chancellor. Read Leslie's Handbook[7]—Mill's Dissertations. C.G. went to Hn.

12. T. X.

Wrote to the Duke of Argyll—C.G. (2)—Mad. Coiffier[8]—Stephy—A. Kinnaird—Bp of Moray—Mr Mytton and minutes. H. of C. 4–$10\frac{1}{2}$ and $11\frac{1}{2}$–$1\frac{1}{2}$.[9] Working all the evening.[10] Saw Mr Taunton—Mr Gurney M.P.—Sir T. F[remantle] with Mr Pressly and Mr Anderson. Mr Laing. Saw Lovell: checquered, but yet there is good[R]. Read Narration from Perugia.[11] Westmr. Review.[12]

13. Wed.

Wrote to A.S. Gladstone—C.G.—Wm. Gladstone—Bp of Oxford—Lady Dunraven—Sir Jas. Graham—Johnson L[ongden] & Co & minutes. Ld Londonderry. Saw Sir Geo. C. Lewis—Mr Gibson—Ld Aberdeen—The Speaker—Ld Stratford—Ld Palmerston—Count Kielmansegge. Dined at Count Persignys—Ld Lansdowne's Concert afterwards. H. of C. $2\frac{1}{4}$–$5\frac{1}{2}$. Voted in 193:263 agt. abolition of Church Rate—a wretched division.[13] Read Londonderry's poems[14]—Mill's Dissertations.

14. Th.

Wrote to Mr Deedes M.P.—Rev. Mr Lowe—Ld Palmerston—H. Glynne—

[1] Helping his secretary during the holidays.
[2] *Christian Remembrancer*, xxxviii (July 1859).
[3] See 25 Sept. 58.
[4] See 4 Feb. 42.
[5] Perhaps David Conty of the S. London institution for the reformation of females.
[6] Navy estimates: *H* cliv. 989.
[7] See 22 Jan. 55.
[8] Wife of Alexandre Coiffier, optician in Hatton Garden.
[9] Spoke on Galway packet cttee. and on Roman Catholics: *H* cliv. 1080, 1116.
[10] Preparing the budget.
[11] Account of the Perugian revolution, into which there was a govt. inquiry and trial.
[12] *Westminster Review*, xvi (July 1859).
[13] Voting with the bulk of the tories: *H* cliv. 1183.
[14] *El Tih and other poems* (1859); privately printed by 4th Lord Londonderry.

O. Blewitt—C.G.—S.E.G. and minutes. Cabinet $2\frac{1}{4}$–$4\frac{1}{4}$. Saw Mr Greswell—Sir C. Wood (Indian Finance)—D. of Argyll & Elgin (Fee Jee)[1]—Seven to breakfast. H. of C. $4\frac{1}{2}$–$6\frac{1}{2}$ and 10–$2\frac{1}{2}$.[2] Read Tennyson's Idylls[3]—Discorso on Gioannetti[4]—Massingberd on Ch Law.[5]

15. Frid.

Wrote to Baron Poerio—Dean of Peterboro—Ld Torrington—R.B. Seeley[6]—Rev. R. Greswell—S. Herbert—Master of Mint—C.G. & minutes. H of C $4\frac{1}{4}$–$6\frac{1}{2}$ and $9\frac{3}{4}$–$1\frac{1}{2}$.[7] Saw R. Phillimore. Ld Kinnaird cum Packet Contract Deputation[8]—Heads of Rev. Departments. Read Q.R. on Invasion.[9]

16. Sat.

Wrote to V.C. Oxford—Sir P. Braila—Rev. N. Oxenham—G. Burnett—Mr Slaney M.P.—C.G.—Mr Brown(?) and minutes. Cabinet $2\frac{1}{4}$–$5\frac{1}{2}$: two hours took my Budget through, *pur et simple*. Saw Mr Anderson—Mr Laing—Mrs Craven.[10] Dined at Milnes Gaskell's—Lady Palmerston's aft. Saw Stewart.X. Read Q.R. on Pacific Islands.[11] MP. on Peace.[12]

17. 4. S. Trin.

Chapel Royal mg. All Saints aft. MS of 47 aloud in evg. Saw Helen—Sir Geo. Brown—Mr Wm. (Deacon) Palmer.[13] Read Guinevere—twice or thrice over & with much emotion. Also other parts of the Idylls. West. Rev. on Mr Jowett[14]—Massingberd on Ch Law.

18. M.

Wrote to Ld Torrington—C.G. (2)—Lady Lothian—Helen G.—and minutes. A day's work in preparing the figures of my Budget. Saw Mr Pressly & others. Read Questione Napolitana. Tennyson: who has grasped me with strong hand. H. of C. $4\frac{1}{4}$–9 and $10\frac{1}{2}$–$12\frac{1}{2}$. Got through my statement in 1h. 40m.[15] Met at home by the sore news of Nora's death.[16] Death, upon such a form!

[1] Probably about the increase in consuls' salaries in Fiji; see W. P. Morrell, *Britain in the Pacific islands* (1960), 132.
[2] Navy estimates: *H* cliv. 1223.
[3] Just published; reviewed by Gladstone with *In Memoriam, Maud*, and *The Princess* in the *Quarterly Review*, cvi. 454 (October 1859), reprinted in *Gleanings*, ii. 131. He asked *Elwin (16 August 1859, N.L.S.): 'Will you let me try my hand on a review of Tennyson . . . I have never been fanatical about him: but his late work has laid hold of me with a power that I have not felt, I ought to say have not suffered, for many years.'
[4] V. A. Gioanetti, *Discorso sulla fabbrica di porcellana stabilita in Vinovo* (1859).
[5] F. C. *Massingberd, *The law of the church and the law of the state* (1859).
[6] See 20 Apr. 39.
[7] Misc. business: *H* cliv. 1297.
[8] On the constitution of the cttee.
[9] *Quarterly Review*, cvi. 245; (July 1859); strongly anti-French.
[10] Preparing for meeting Helen next day; see 30 Sept. 45n.
[11] *Quarterly Review*, cvi. 174; on Fijian annexation.
[12] Untraced.
[13] i.e. William *Palmer of Magdalen: now a Roman catholic, once an anglican deacon.
[14] *Westminster Review*, xvi. 41 (July 1859).
[15] Provisional budget, meeting deficit of £5m. by raising income tax from 5d. to 9d., at the rate of 13d. on the first half of the year: *H* cliv. 1385.
[16] Henry Glynne's daughter.

19. Tues.

Wrote to Ld Stanhope 2—Dss. of Sutherland—Sir G. Lewis—W.F. Farquhar
—Rev. H. Leach[1]—Mr Pressly—C.G. & minutes. Dined with the Wenlock's.
Meditated on the future of our finance. Saw Mr Pressly & Mr Timm *bis*—
John Talbot—Mr Talmadge[2]—Ld Granville—Mr Laing. H. of C. 6–8 and
11–2$\frac{1}{4}$ a.m.[3] Read divers pamphlets. Hansard's Debates—Tennyson.

20. Wed.

Wrote to C.G. (2)—V.C. Oxford—Ld Palmerston (2)—Mrs Begbie:[4] in
answer to one received in evg. Cabinet 3–6$\frac{1}{4}$. Dined and spoke at the Kean
dinner.[5] Saw Sir J. Lacaita (Corfu Mission Accounts)—Sir C. Wood—Indian
Finance—Duke of Argyll—Duke of Somerset. Visited Mary Glynne: & saw
Miss Rose.[6] Read Westmr. Rev.

21. Th.

Wrote to C. Pressly—Sir A. Spearman—Mr Trevor—Ld Chancellor—Mr
Bignold—Profr. Robertson[7]—Mr Foxton and minutes. Saw Mrs Begbie (the
Writer)—S. Herbert—Dr Russell—Mr R. Hill[8] (*cum* Mr Baker)—Mr
Laing—Mr Pressly—Mr G. Scott—Sir G. Lewis. H. of C. 4$\frac{1}{2}$–7$\frac{1}{2}$ and like-
wise 9–1: much speaking, & slippery work.[9] Read West. Rev. on India
(finished).[10] Business in Downing St.

22. Fr.

Wrote to Mrs Malcolm—Atty. General—Mr J. Chapman—Sir A. Spearman
(2) (+over)—C.G. and minutes. Read Stapylton's Canning.[11] Worked on
Indian Finance—Cabinet 1–3$\frac{1}{2}$.[12] Saw Mr Pressly—A. Gladstone—Sir A.
Spearman—Mr Glyn. Do cum Mr Anderson—Master of the Mint—The
Lord Advocate—Mr Trevor.

23. Sat.

Wrote to Ld Carlisle—O.B. Cole—Atty General—S. Herbert—Ld Canning
—E. Cardwell and minutes. Saw Mrs Begbie; who sang—Adam Gladstone
—Mr Pressly & Mr Timm—C.G. & Willy came. Cabinet 2$\frac{1}{2}$–5. Read Photo-
grams of an Eastern Tour[13]—Kennedy on Defences.[14]

[1] Henry Leach, 1830–1921; curate of St. Thomas's, Portman Square, 1858–63; subsequently held many livings.
[2] Of J. T. Talmadge & Co., London wholesale tea dealers; the budget, despite pressure,
had not increased tea and sugar duties.
[3] Select cttee. set up on bible printing: *H* clv. 66.
[4] 'The writer' (see next day) and singer, though nothing published under her name.
[5] Dinner of Etonian contemporaries of the actor: *The Times*, 21 July 1859, 9e.
[6] H. Glynne's children's governess, probably da. of a local mine owner; see above, v. lxii.
[7] James Robertson, 1803–60; professor of church history at Edinburgh from 1843.
[8] Rowland Clegg Hill, 1833–95; tory M.P. N. Salop 1857–65; 3rd Viscount Hill 1875.
[9] Answering *Hubbard on income tax reform: *H* clv. 228.
[10] *Westminster Review*, xvi. 112 (July 1859).
[11] A. G. *Stapleton, *George *Canning and his times* (1859).
[12] Apparently on Indian finance; mem. of this day proposed 'lending funds at our
command, on the footing of other lenders' rather than a guaranteed loan: Add MS 44748,
f. 109.
[13] *Photograms of an Eastern Tour*, by Σ (1859).
[14] Sir J. S. *Kennedy, *Notes on the defences of Great Britain and Ireland* (1859).

24. 5 S. Trin.

Whitehall mg. All Saints aft.—MS for St James aloud at night. Saw Ld
Abn. (with Sir J. Graham). Read Guild of St Alban[1]—Joly to Theiner[2]—
Mrs Jameson to Ld J. Russell[3]—Tennyson's Guinevere.

25. M. St James.

Wrote to M. Rangabè—Sir S. Northcote—Mr Neate—Ld High Commissr.—
Sir T. Wyse—Ed. Sunday Times[4]—Mr Butler—Ld J. Russell—Ld Carlisle.
Wrote also to Mr Mayo[5]—Govr. Bank—Archdn. Bartholomew—Gholam
Mahomed. Saw Baron M. de Rollink—Sir A. Spearman—Mr Arbuthnot—
Mr Laing—Sir C. Wood—Mr Henley—Mr Scott—Mr Glyn. H. of C. $12\frac{1}{4}$–
$2\frac{1}{4}$, $3\frac{1}{2}$–4, 8–$12\frac{1}{2}$.[6] Read Mill's Dissertations.

26. T. X.

Wrote to O.B. Cole—R. Phillimore—Mr Baily R.A.—Sir T. Gladstone[7]—
S. Herbert—Mr Laing—and minutes. Wrote paper on Ch Rates.[8] H. of C. at
6.[9] Saw Sir J. Graham—Sir A. Spearman—D. of Sutherland & Deputation
—Mr Arbuthnot—Mr Hunt *cum* do.—Mr Brand—Saw Russell[R]. Read
Sav. Bank Report[10]—Mill's Dissertations—Russell's Mezzofanti[11]—Archd.
Hony's Charge.[12]

27. Wed.

Wrote to Ld Palmerston—W.R. Greg.—Sir F. Baring and minutes. Worked
on Italian Blue Book. Attended R. Academy in Evg. Saw Mr Bohn—Mr
Acland—Mr Grogan (At Home)—Sir A. Spearman—Sir C. Wood—Liver-
pool Deputation (P.O.)[13] Read Report on Navy & other Parl. Papers.[14]
The Italian Cause.[15] H. of C. 4–6:[16] and Cabinet 3–4. Wrote to Sir T.
Phillips—Pres. Maynooth.[17]

28. Th.

Wrote to Mr Walpole—Duke of Leinster[18]—H. Fitzroy—Sir G.F. Bowen—

[1] Untraced.
[2] Two letters from Joly to père Theiner on Clement XIV, December 1852, January
1853, reprinted in J. A. M. Crétineau-Joly, *Bonaparte, le Concordat de 1801 et le Cardinal
Consalvi* (1869).
[3] A. B. *Jameson, 'Sisters of Charity and the communion of labour. Two lectures . . .
with a prefatory letter to . . . Russell on the present condition and requirements of the
women of England' (1859).
[4] Not published.
[5] See 24 Dec. 29.
[6] Spoke on museums: *H* clv. 369, 441.
[7] Who had, as in 1852, voted against his brother at Oxford.
[8] 'Outline of a plan to alter the law of Church Rate': Add MS 44748, f. 113.
[9] Church rates: *H* clv. 464.
[10] *PP* 1859 xiv. 235.
[11] See 13 May 58.
[12] W. E. Hony, 'Church-Rates: a charge' (1859).
[13] Dispute about paying for new Liverpool Post Office; see 9 Sept. 59.
[14] Report on manning: *PP* 1859 vi. 1.
[15] 'The Italian Cause, its history and hopes' (1859).
[16] Spoke on the National Gallery: *H* clv. 505.
[17] Charles William *Russell, 1812–80; professor at Maynooth 1845, president 1857.
[18] Augustus Frederick Fitzgerald, 1791–1874; 3rd duke of Leinster 1804; Visitor of
Maynooth.

Mr Hunt & minutes. Worked Italian papers. Read 'The Italian Cause'—Mill's Dissertations. Saw Mrs Douglas—Mr Grogan—Fire Insurance Deputn.—Australian Mint Deputn.—Mr Arbuthnot—Mr Combe.[1] Drive with C. H. of C. 6–12¾. Spoke on Foreign Affairs.[2]

29. Fr.

Wrote to Duke of Newcastle—Rev. J. Mozley & minutes. H. of C. 12–3, 6–7½ and 9–12½.[3] Read Mill—Bible Bd. Reports.[4] Saw Mr Hunt—Audit Commn.—Mr Herbert—Mr Wilson—Mr Arbuthnot—Mr Laing—Mr Walpole.

30. Sat.

Wrote to Master of the Mint—Rev. Mr Robinson—Mr L. Barbar[5]—Milnes Gaskell & minutes. Ten to dinner: Lady Palmerston's afterwards. Saw Rev. Mr Liddell—Duke of Newcastle—Sir J. Lacaita—Marquis Lajatico[6] *cum do.*

> Count Fontanelli ⎫
> Cav. Malamuso ⎬ (Modena)[7]

Read Strange on Royal Academy.[8] Arranging papers. Saw Somerhayes: full in the highest degree both of interest and of beauty. (22).[9]

31. 6 S. Trin.

Chapel Royal mg & aftern. Serm. aloud in Evg. Miss Neville dined with us.[10] Saw Duchess of Sutherland—Saw H.J.G. Saw Somerhayes: briefly[R]. Wrote to G.F. Watts. Read Milton—Tennyson—Coventry Patmore[11]—Wiseman v. Turton[12]—St Bernard—Memoirs of Mrs Fry.[13]

Monday Aug. One. 1859

Wrote to Ld Clarendon—Mr. C. Kean—Ld C. Paget[14]—Mr Purdue—E. Cardwell—Sir J. Lefevre & minutes. H. of C. 12–2 and 6–12½.[15] Saw Mr M. Bernard—Mr Grogan—Mr Trevor—Mr Stephenson—Mr Bagwell.[16] Chicory

[1] Thomas *Combe, 1797–1872; printer, leading lay tractarian in Oxford and patron of pre-Raphaelites.
[2] On Prussian neutrality: *H* clv. 606.
[3] Spoke on income tax; *H* clv. 641.
[4] Board set up in 1837 to supervise bible printing in Scotland; see *H* clv. 68.
[5] Probably the consul and translator in Naples (see 18 Dec. 50).
[6] Neri Corsini, marchese Laiatico, on a mission from Tuscany to gain support against Ferdinand, in whose favour its grand duke had abdicated; see Lacaita, 127.
[7] Camillo Fontanelli, 1823–81; commanded the national guard under Farini in the Modena revolution June 1859.
[8] Sir R. *Strange, *An inquiry into the rise and establishment of the Royal Academy of Arts* (1775. ed. W. Coningham 1850).
[9] M. Summerhayes, courtesan, mentioned later as Mrs. Dale, see 6 Aug. 59, 1 Nov. 60, 17 July 61. See above, v. lx–lxi.
[10] Mirabel Jane Neville, 1821–1900, da. of 3rd Baron Braybrooke; friend of Mary Gladstone.
[11] Probably his *Angel in the house*, 2v. (1858).   [12] See 21 Mar. 47.
[13] T. Timpson, *Memoirs of Mrs. Elizabeth Fry* (1847).
[14] Lord Clarence Edward *Paget, 1811–95, 4th s. of 1st marquis of Anglesea; sailor; whig M.P. Sandwich 1847–52, 1857–66; sec. to admiralty 1859–66.
[15] East India loan: *H* clv. 769.
[16] John Bagwell, 1811–83; liberal M.P. Clonmel 1857–74; treasury commissioner 1859–62.

Deputation—Mr Pressly cum Sir T. Fremantle—Ld Palmerston (resp appts)—Mr Arbuthnot—Mr Laing—Mr Anderson—Sir C. Wood—Mr Cardwell—Sir G. Lewis—Sir J. Graham. Read Italian question.

2. T.

Wrote to V.C. Oxford—Sir G. Lewis—Ld Palmerston—H.J.G.—Mr Selwyn—Robn. G.—& minutes. H. of C. 12–1½ and 6–8½.[1] Read G. Smith on History[2]—Arnold on It. question.[3] Stapleton's Canning.[4] Saw Mr Pennethorne—Mr Scott—D. of Argyll—Mr Laing—Mr Stephenson. Saw Summerhayes: and thought as before[R]. Stafford House at night.

3. Wed.

Wrote to M. Arnold—C.G.—Mr. Locke[5]—Sir E. Lytton—Sir A. Spearman —Ld Vernon & minutes. H. of C. 12–2 and 3–6.[6] Cabinet afterwards. Dined at Grillion's—Mrs Herbert's party afr. Saw Summerhayes: briefly[R]. Saw Mr Gibson. Worked on books. Read Napoleon III in Italy[7]—La Venetie.[8]

4. Th.

Wrote to Sir G. Lewis—Rev. Mr Meredith—Mr Frewen—Rev. Mr Bloom[9] —Mr Pressly—V.C. Oxford—Mr Begbie—M. Summerhays: and minutes. Saw Ld Kinnaird—Mr Laing—Mr Trevor—Mr Herbert & a Depun. H. of C. 12–4 and 6–10½. Working Estimates.[10] Read Mill. Worked on books. Saw Summerhayes long [R].

5. Fr.

Wrote to Mr Ellice—Summerhays—G.F. Watts—Miss Heming[11]—W. Dyce[12]—Mr R. Lawley—Ld Palmerston & minutes. Saw Mr Gibson—Mr Jas. Wilson—Mr Brand—Mr Laing—Sir C. Wood—Mr Bagwell—Sir G. Lewis—Mr Leatham.[13] H. of C. with intervals from 12–12½ at night.[14] Read Tennyson—Mill's Dissertations.

[1] Misc. business: *H* clv. 871.
[2] G. *Smith, *The study of history. A lecture* (1859).
[3] M. *Arnold, *England and the Italian Question* (1859).
[4] See 22 July 59.
[5] John Locke, 1805–80; barrister; liberal M.P. Southwark 1857–80; crusader against game laws.
[6] Supply: *H* clv. 883.
[7] *Napoleon III, and Italy. What will be done? And why. By a Man in Manchester* (1859).
[8] Probably *La Vénetie devant l'Europe. Lettres de Daniel Manin* (1859).
[9] James Hague Bloom, 1805–73; Caius, Cambridge; vicar of Castle Acre, Norfolk, from 1833 and chaplain to duke of Sussex.
[10] *H* clv. 1085.
[11] Possibly a model, given juxtaposition between *Watts and *Dyce, and see 6 Aug. 59.
[12] See next day and n.
[13] Edward Aldam Leatham, 1828–1900; Yorkshire banker; liberal M.P. Huddersfield 1859–65, 1868–86.
[14] India: *H* clv. 1062.

6. Sat.

Wrote to Ld Wenlock—Sir J. Lefevre—Ld Kinnaird—Master of the Mint
& minutes. H. of C. 12–1½.[1] Then Cabinet: but the Cabinet is now some
times a λεσχή.[2] Ld P. says 'it looks well'. Princess's 7 to near 12 for The
Corsican Brothers & Midsummer Night's Dream.[3] C. knocked up & had
influenza. Saw Mr Windus[4]—Sir A. Spearman—Mr Anderson. Read Mill
on Rev. of 48[5]—Avesani on Villa Franca Peace.[6] Saw Summerhays resp.
picture &c. That is a very peculiar case: & merits what I wrote of it to
Mr Dyce.[7]

7. 7. S. Trin.

Chapel Royal & H.C. mg—All Saints aftn. MS finished today aloud in evg.
Read Nicole—Bp of Brechin[8] and divers Tracts. Also F.O. dispatches.
Visited the old man in Hart Street.

8. M.

Wrote to Master of Mint—Mr Dyce—T. W. Rathbone—Westell—Count
Flamburiari[9]—Sir E. Lytton—Christie & M[anson]—Sir A. Spearman(2)—
Ld A. Hervey and minutes. Saw Mr Pressly—Sir G. Lewis—Sir C. Wood.
Dined from House, with the Herberts. The boys went: the two elder to
Wales on an independent tour, the tinies to Hawarden. Worked much on
books, papers &c. preparing for the move. H. of C. 3¾–2 except (7½–9¼):
spoke for an *oretta*[10] on Italian affairs: my best off hand speech, or least
bad.[11] Read Grote Vol. XI:[12] & Mill's Dissertations.

9. T.

Wrote to Ld Palmerston—H.J.G.—Master of the Mint—W.C. James—Sir
· A. Spearman—Summerhays—Bp of Oxford—Warden of H. of Charity—
Count Persigny and minutes. Saw J.N.G.—Mr Anderson—Aunt J. and
Summerhayes[R]. H. of C. 12–2½.[13] Worked much on preparations to move
to D[owning] St.[14] Read Tennyson—Mill—Calls Albert Gate H. &c.[15]

[1] Spoke on the funds: *H* clv. 1090.
[2] 'just a place for conversation'.
[3] *Kean's current productions.
[4] Ansley Windus, London solicitor.
[5] His 'Vindication of the French revolution of February 1848' in *Dissertations*, i. 335.
[6] G. F. Avesani, *La Pace di Villafranca. Pensieri* (1859).
[7] Gladstone proposed she should sit to *Dyce for a commissioned portrait; Dyce painted her as *Lady with the Coronet of Jasmine*, in Aberdeen Art Gallery, reproduced in *Victorian Studies*, xix. 93 and above, v, plate 3; see Add MS 44392, f. 111 and introduction above, v. lx–lxi.
[8] A. P. *Forbes, *Mirror of young Christians* (1859).
[9] Much correspondence with him on Ionia in 1859 in Hawn P.
[10] i.e. for nearly an hour.
[11] *H* clv. 1139.
[12] Of his *History of Greece*; see 19 Mar. 47.
[13] India: *H* clv. 1260.
[14] From 11 Carlton House Terrace.
[15] The French embassy.

10. *Wed.*

Wrote to C.G. Further moving operations. H. of C.[1] & Cabinet 12½–4. Fish dinner at Greenwich: I proposed Ld Palmerston's health. Lady Palmerston's & Lady Granville's afterwards. Saw Mr Cardwell—Mr Dyce—Summerhayes—D. of Argyll—Ex. Inspector Park[2]—Mr Panizzi—D. of Newcastle—Mr Laing—Mr Hankey. Read Italian Priest (Seeleys)[3]—Tennyson.

11. *Th.*

Wrote to H.J.G.—Duchess Sutherland—C.G.[4]—Ld Lyttelton—Rev. Mr [S.W.] Wayte—Lady Beauchamp—Rev. Mr Trevor—Earl Granville—H. of C. 2–4.[5] Saw Dean of Peterborough—Sir James Lacaita—Ld Alfred Hervey—Saw Summerhayes[R]. Saw Mr Watts—Kensington Museum—at the Olympic in evg.[6] Read Tennyson—Ed. Rev. on Tennyson and on late Govt.[7]

12. *Fr.* [*Isle of Wight*]

Wrote to Mr Anderson—C.G.—& minutes. Saw Ld Palmerston—Ld Granville—Ld J. Russell. Off at 9 a.m. to Osborne for the Council. Some conv. with the Prince afterwards. Helen came to meet me & had luncheon at O[sborne]. Went over with her to the Priory & saw its beauties.[8] Much conv. in evg. She promised to write to Tom. Read [The] Princess[9]—Univ. Rev. on my wretched self[10]—Girardin's Pamphlet.[11]

13. *Sat.* [*Cliveden*]

Wrote to Atty. General—C.G.—Sir S. Scott & Co—H.J.G.—D. of Newcastle —& min.—Ld J. Russell. Left the Priory at 9¼; reached D. St (by the Direct, thro a beautiful country) at 1.35. Two hours of office work—Saw Mr Stephenson—Mr Laing—Mr Foster,[12] and off at 4 to Cliveden. The Duchess [of Sutherland] much better tho' still an invalid, met me. We drove & boated in evg with the Laboucheres. Read Tennyson, Tennyson, Tennyson.

[1] India: *H* clv. 1301.
[2] The inspector who had handled the Wilson blackmail episode; see 11 May 53.
[3] Untraced pamphlet of R. B. Seeley, who was his own publisher.
[4] Bassett, 125.
[5] Charitable trusts: *H* clv. 1353.
[6] Three plays, 'This evening', 'Payable on demand', 'Retained for the defence'.
[7] *Edinburgh Review*, cix. 247; 264 (July 1859).
[8] Priory at St. Helens, where Helen Gladstone stayed from 1858; W. G. *Ward lived nearby.
[9] By *Tennyson (1847), with added lyrics (1853); reviewed by Gladstone, see 14 July 59n.
[10] *Universal Review*, ii. 233 (August 1859); 'Mr. Gladstone', violent tory attack.
[11] E. de Girardin, *L'Empereur Napoléon III et l'Europe* (1859).
[12] Morgan Hugh Foster, 1815–91; accountant to treasury 1855–9; assistant paymaster 1859; principal clerk to treasury 1867–71; later governed Turkish banks.

14. *8 S. Trin.*

Hedsor Ch mg (a good expository sermon) & St Georges Windsor aftn.
Wrote to C.G.—G.F. Watts—Much conv. with the Duchess. Read History
of King Arthur[1]—Guinevere—Legends of Monastic Orders.[2]

15. *M.* X [*London*]

Wrote to—Duke of Argyll—C.G.—Dr Jacobson—Master of the Mint—
J. Wortley—Bp of Salisbury—Lord Thos. Clinton—Dr Jacobson—Sir D.
Brewster[3] & minutes. Saw Lord Granville *cum* Mr Lowe—Mr Arbuthnot
—Mr Stephenson—Sir A. Spearman. Sat in P.C. Commee. on Aln. case
11–3.[4] $5\frac{1}{2}$–$7\frac{1}{2}$ Sat to Watts. $7\frac{1}{2}$–9. At Kensington Museum with Mr Cole.
Then till 12 with S[ummerhayes]: no decisive issue [R]. Finished the
Princess—Read Mill on Liberty.[5]

16. *T.*

Wrote to Ld Brougham (2)—Ld J. Russell—Bp of Oxford—Mrs Peel—
Agnes—J.N.G.—Rev. W. Elwin—Sir T.G.—C.G. & minutes. Saw Mrs T.
Goalen—Signor Marliani—Duchess of Sutherland—Mrs Norton: Mr F.
Norton[6]—Mr Bratiano—Aunt J.—Mr Grogan. Summerhayes $8\frac{1}{4}$–$9\frac{1}{2}$; when
F. came[R]. Sat to Watts $5\frac{1}{2}$–$7\frac{1}{2}$. Read D. of Coburg on Russia[7]—Maud &
minor pieces—Sheridan's Gk songs[8]—Mill. Saw Pictures with Duchess of S.

17. *Wed.*

Wrote to E. Lovell—Count N. Lunzi—M. Summerhayes—Sir A. Damas-
chino—Ld Westminster[9] & minutes. Saw Committee of Cabinet 1–3.
Cabinet $3\frac{1}{2}$–$4\frac{3}{4}$. Worked on arranging papers. Saw Mr Shippard[10]—Mr Watts.
Missed Summerhayes—saw Lovell: good [R]. Preparations for departure—
C. returned. Read In Memoriam—Evidence on Printers Patent.[11]

18. *Th.* [*Hawarden*]

Wrote to Ld J. Russell—S. Herbert—Sir J. Lacaita—C. Pressly—Sir W.
Heathcote—Robn. G.—J.W. Blakesley[12]—Dss. of Sutherland—and minutes.
Read The Idylls—Comtesse d' Escarbagnas.[13] Saw Mr Neale—Sir G. Bowen

---

[1] Sir T. *Malory, The byrth, lyf and actes of King Arthur,* ed. R. *Southey, 2 v. (1817).
Gladstone's *Quarterly* article (see 14 July 59) compares Malory and Tennyson's approach.
[2] A. B. *Jameson, *Legends of the monastic orders, as represented in the fine arts: forming
the second series of sacred and legendary art* (1850).
[3] Sir David *Brewster, 1781–1868; scientist; president of peace congress 1851; principal
of Edinburgh university 1859, vice-chancellor from 1860; see 15 Apr. 60.
[4] No record in privy council archives.
[5] See 10 Mar. 59.
[6] Fletcher Cavendish Charles Conyers Norton, 1829–October 1859, s. of Caroline*;
diplomat.
[7] Ernest II, Duke of Saxe-Coburg-Gotha, 'Russia' (1859).
[8] C. B. Sheridan, *The songs of Greece, from the Romaic text* (1825).
[9] See 3 July 39n.
[10] Perhaps Captain William Henry Shippard of the 29th regiment; see Add MS 44796,
f. 160.
[11] See 19 July 59n.
[12] See 16 Dec. 31.
[13] By Molière (1671).

cum Mr R. Herbert. Saw Summerhayes to bid goodbye[R]. Saw Mr Stephenson jun.[1] to arrange for business during my absence. Off at 2.15. Reached Hawarden at 9 & found all the children well. Is there not a rod in store for me? We had some family singing.

19. *Fr.*

Wrote minutes: also to Mr Stephenson—M. Summerhayes. Visited the coal pit where they are now piercing the thick for Mr Darlington's & my account. Then the Church which is admirably rebuilt & restored: but over it & the Rectory what deep shadows hang! Began unpacking & arranging. Read Cicero pro Archiâ with the boys. Orl. Furioso I–III. Family music in evg.

20. *Sat.*

Wrote to Mr H. Lees—Sir S. Scott & Co—minutes. Read Cicero with the boys—Orl. Furioso IV–VI. Hist. of King Arthur & Introd. Most of the day at work on arranging books, letters, & papers. Visited the pit—& Mr [E.] Austin's.

21. *9 S. Trin.*

Hn. Ch mg & Broughton do aft. H.S. conv. with Stephy and Lena. Wrote Theol. MS. Read Mandeville's Fable & Essays[2]—In Memoriam.

22. *M.*

Wrote to Ld Brougham—Mr Austin—Ld J. Russell—Mr Window—Mast of the Mint—Mr Rathbone—Rev. D. Williams—Robn. G—& minutes. Read Cicero with Stephy. Read Window on El. Telegr.[3]—Orl. Fur. 7–9. Hist of King Arthur. Worked on arranging books. Saw Mr Burnett.

23. *T.*

Wrote to Lord Westminster—Mr Elwin—Mr Stephenson—A. Panizzi— S. Spring Rice and minutes. Saw Mr G. Burnett. Read Geoffrey of Monmouth[4]—Q.R. 1833 on Tennyson. Do 1842 on do.[5] Ariosto O.F. 10–12. History of King Arthur. Tennysons *first* Poems.

24. *Wed.*

St. Barthol. Ch 8½ a.m. (resumed today after interuption) Wrote to M. Summerhayes—Hon. J. Rose—Duchess of Suthd.—Rev. D. Moore & minutes. Read Feminist Love v M.[6]—Tennyson's Poems of 1830. of 1833—

---

[1] Benjamin Charles Stephenson, clerk in the treasury 1857–65; junior to W. H. Stephenson, then principal clerk.
[2] See 13 Sept. 43.
[3] *Sic*; possibly untraced pamphlet by F. B. *Winslow.
[4] *Geoffrey of Monmouth, *Historia regum Brittaniae* (1508, ed. J. A. Giles 1844), used by *Tennyson.
[5] *Quarterly Review*, cv. 385 (June 1842).
[6] Untraced.

(finished).[1] Wrote an exordium to an article on him[2]—Read also Hist King Arthur—Orl. Furioso XIII. XIV. Family music in evg.

25. Th.

Ch 8¼ a.m. Wrote to Mrs Chisholm—S. Laing—Mr Grazebrook[3]—Ld Kinnaird—A.S. Gladstone and minutes. Read Cicero with W. & S. Saw Mr Burnett with Mr Fisher[4] resp. O.F. Read Tennyson of 1842. Rowe's Jane Shore[5]—Warton's Hist Engl. Poetry.[6]—Orl. Fur. to C. XVII.—Hist King Arthur. C. on her back: with certain appearances, long disused.[7]

26. Fr.

Ch 8¼ a.m. Wrote to B.C. Stephenson—Mr Pressly—Master of mint— Johnson L & Co—G.A. Hamilton—& minutes. Saw Rogers[8] resp. his son— Mr Darlington—Mr A.S. Gladstone—Mr Griffiths resp. C. & Willy. Visited the pit. Attended the presentation to Mr Brewster.[9] Read Hist K. Arthur— Orl. Fur. XVIII. 19.

27. Sat. [London]

Ch 8½ a.m. Wrote to C.G.—Duchess of Sutherland. Off at 11 for London: arrived 8¾: by reason of summons for Cabinet. Missed Summerhayes—Saw Thynne—Rigby—Campbell[R]. Read Hist. K. Arthur—Orl. Fur.— Alfieri's Satires.[10]

28. 10. S. Trin.

Chapel R. mg. & Wells St aft. Saw Ld Palmerston—Ld Granville—Mr Edwin Palmer[11]—Marq. Azeglio. Wrote MS. Wrote to C.G.—Mrs Rigby— Lena whose happy birthday it is. Read Lee Sermons, Introd. & Dissertation[12]—Voss Idolatria Gentilium[13]—Remusat's Abelard[14]—Collection of Epitaphs. Dined at Ld Palmerston's.

29. M. X

Wrote to E. Lovell—M. Summerhayes—Hon. Mrs Gordon—Robn. G.—[W.]

[1] *Poems* (1830) and *Poems chiefly lyrical* (1833); *Tennyson's early poems were collected in 2 v. (1842); see 15 Oct. 42.
[2] See 14 July 59n.
[3] George Grazebrook, 1796–1877; Stourbridge attorney; on Oak Farm accounts.
[4] Of Fisher Brothers, brick manufacturers at Old Swinford.
[5] By N. *Rowe (1714), discussed in his *Quarterly* article (see 14 July 59), 483.
[6] By T. *Warton, 3 v. (1774–81).
[7] See 30 Aug. 59.
[8] Probably the engraver; see 15 Aug. 43.
[9] The Hawarden curate; see 22 Sept. 42.
[10] Count V. Alfieri, *Satire di Vittorio Alfieri da Asti* (1806).
[11] Edwin Palmer, 1824–95; fellow of Balliol 1845; of Corpus 1870; professor of latin literature 1870; archdeacon of Oxford 1878.
[12] S. Lee, *Six sermons on the study of the Holy Scriptures* (1830).
[13] G. J. Voss, *De theologia gentili . . . sive de origine ac progressu idolatriae*, 4 v. (1641).
[14] See 20 Apr. 57.

Fred Neville—C.G.—Duchess of Sutherland—Sir T. Fremantle—C. Pressly
—Sir John Tyrell and various minutes, Treas. & private. Saw Sir Francis
Doyle—Scotts—Mr Hamilton—Mrs Herbert—D. of Newcastle—and in evg.
E. Lovell: not laudably [R]. Shopping & various calls & inquiries. Saw Jas.
Wortley—S.P.G. Clerk—Ld Granville—Sir C. Wood. Read M. Creuzè de
Lesser.[1] Dined with S. Herberts. Cabinet 2½–5½.

30. Sat. [Hawarden]

Wrote to G.G. Scott—Duchess of Sutherland—In consequence of a note
from Agnes gave up Trentham[2] & went straight to rejoin C., sending
Hampton to Tr[entham] with a letter. 9½–6 to Hn. where I found C. going
on well: saw Griffiths & Moffatt & learned from them that this indisposition
only marks an effort of nature to regain equilibrium at a stage of transition.
Saw Mr Burnett. Read Modena Documenti[3]—Ld Campbell on Shakespeare.[4] Party at Hawarden.

31. Wed.

Church 8½ AM. Wrote to Ld John Russell—A. Turner—Dss of Sutherland
—Mrs E. Peel—Mr Arbuthnot—C. Ross—Duke of Argyll—Rev. Mr
Skinner—Rev. Mr Quekett—S. Spring Rice—Ld Westminster—Mackenzie
Wilson—Sir A. Spearman—Hon Mrs Gordon—Ld Chancellor & draft—
Johnson L[ongden] & Co.—Commr. of East Kent Militia.[5] Read A. Burnet
on Jethro Tull[6]—Hist. of King Arthur—Finished Ld Campbell on Shakes-
peare—Cicero with the boys W. & S. Saw J. Rogers—Mr. A. Burnett—Mr
G. Burnett. Dined with H. Glynne alone: always gentle he is more tender
in manner than ever.

[To 8th duke of Argyll, 31 August 1859:] . . .[7] As regards the said Cabinet I would
rather have spoken than written, but my letter will go under the double guard of
gum and sealing wax, and I trust no postmaster will presume to take liberties
with it on its way. I will try to give you a succinct account.

The Cabinet parted for the Vacation, after you had left us for Scotland, on the
17th. We had then no idea of any early proceeding of importance with respect

---

[1] A. F. Creusé de Lesser, *Les Chevaliers de la Table Ronde* (1812); see his *Quarterly*
article (14 July 59), 483.

[2] Sutherland's; see 8 Dec. 59.

[3] *Documenti risguardanti il governo degli Austro-Estensi in Modena dal 1814 al 1859*
(1859); *Elwin declined to print in the *Quarterly* extracts and notes on these documents
which Gladstone thought 'would bear immediately on the now cardinal question of the
Duchies—& which would tend on the whole I think not to irritate but to compose &
settle in the direction in which affairs are (I trust) tending' (to Elwin, 1 September 1859,
N.L.S.).

[4] J. *Campbell, *Shakespeare's legal acquirements considered* (1859), a presentation copy:
Add MS 44392, f. 157.

[5] George Brockman, 1807–64; commanded E. Kent militia 1852–60.

[6] A Burnett, *Tillage a substitute for manure, illustrated by the precepts and practice of
Jethro Tull* (1859).

[7] Letter to *Argyll, at Inverary, from copy dated 31 August 1859, not by Gladstone but
marked 'Most Private' in his hand; Add MS 44098, f. 201.

to the Italian question. But on the 21st it seems that Lord John presented to the Queen a draft dispatch with something like a new map of Italy.[1] The Queen kicked and the Minister withdrew the draft at once! no very signal proof of the deliberation with which it had been prepared. He then substituted a proposal to communicate to the French Govt. an important dispatch of July 25 written in answer to the French invitation that we received to state our views respecting a Congress or Conference. This dispatch it seems went off with a closing sentence desiring Cowley not to make it known to the French Govt. until after the proceedings at Zurich should have been completed. This prohibition Lord John had specially mentioned to the Queen as suggested by the Cabinet & approved by him. The truth, most of us thought, was this; that the Cabinet had simply thought there should be a passage inserted in the dispatch reserving our liberty to decide about a Congress after the Zurich proceedings should have come to an end. But Ld J. had understood them to desire a prohibition, & had so put it, & so stated it to the Queen. This being so, she on receiving his second proposal (at *least* the second, we could not make out quite clearly whether there was not some other or others between) not unnaturally said, this prohibition was deliberately adopted by you all & approved by me, I cannot reverse my approval unless the Cabinet is consulted and reverses too. Lord John was in a *state* upon this and imparted much of his fire to Palmerston who forthwith sent off a letter to the Queen which appeared to me one too *brusque* to address to her as a Sovereign & a woman. However it was agreed to summon a Cabinet to consider this affair. There was a general opinion when we met that the dispatch might very properly be communicated, for the prohibition was never intended to enforce secrecy but merely to reserve our freedom about a Conference entire: and besides we then thought affairs at Zurich would be over in a few days whereas they were now threatening to extend almost to months. But meantime Lord John had brought down in lieu of the proposal he had made to the Queen a new draft with a good deal of fresh matter calculated rather to raise new sores, and he proposed to administer this dose by way of sparing her scruples about the communication of a dispatch to the matter and the ultimate communication of which she had already assented. We all agreed against the new Draft and in favour of the communication. Lord John was then very desirous to know what he was to say to France after Zurich, if she proposed a Conference, as he wished to go for five weeks at least to Abergeldie distant 550 miles. Whereto we answered that in such case there should be a Cabinet.

When I look over what I have written, it does not look very kind towards the two most eminent men in the Govt. one of them particularly. But I am sorry to say first that I believe I confess the general feeling of our Colleagues: secondly that, as I learned, the Queen has undergone very great pain in this matter: thirdly that the conduct pursued has been hasty, inconsiderate, & eminently *juvenile:* fourthly, one is led to fear that it may have left behind disagreeable recollections. Sir G. Grey we trust will prove highly emollient.

I have told you a story too short to be intelligible but perhaps long enough to be wearisome so I will only subscribe myself

most sincerely yours,

W. E. Gladstone.

Thurs. Septr. One 1859.

Church 8½ A.M. Wrote to Mr B. Stephenson—Rev W. Elwin—Lord

[1] For these drafts see *L.Q.V.*, 2nd series, iii. 461 ff.

Russell—T.D. Acland—Marq Lajatico—Robn. G—Dep. Govr. Bank[1]—H. Glynne—& minutes. Cicero with the boys. Much work on Treasury papers & minutes. Read Orl. Furioso finished XX.—A. Burnett on Jethro Tull—Hist. of King Arthur. My thoughts of S[ummerhayes] require to be limited & purged.

2. Fr.

Ch. 8½ AM. Wrote to Mr Jefferies—Mr Laing—Gen. Portlock—Sig. Massari—D. of Newcastle—and minutes. Read. Orl. Fur. XXI, XXII—Hist. King Arthur—Edwards's Facts &c. on Ind. Rebell.[2] Began MS. on the duchies & Legations.[3] C. downstairs again but not strong. I had a conversation with Willy on his pursuits, with some reference to the opinion lately given by Mr Griffiths.[4]

3. Sat. [*Penmaenmawr*]

Ch. 8½ AM. Wrote to Mr Cobden—Robn. G.—Muller—Scotts and minutes. Packing & setting in order for departure. Off at 2½ for Penmaenmawr with C: where we are again in Mr Harrison's[5] house. Established myself with books & papers in a corner of the dining room. Read M. Creuzè de Lesser—Hist of King Arthur: and some Orl. Fur.

4. 11. S. Trin.

Parish Ch. mg (Welsh service, & H.C.) and aftn. Serm. of Dr Hannah's[6] aloud in evg. H.S. lesson with M[ary] & L[ena]. Read Bp Hampden B.L. & Introduction[7]—Scotch Establt. Examined 1771.[8]

5. M.

Wrote to B.C. Stephenson—S. Herbert—Hon Mrs Gordon—Sir A. Spearman—Mast. of Mint—and minutes. Saw Rev Mr Wray. Dip in the sea. Read Orl. Fur. to C.XXV incl—History of King Arthur—Nibelungenlied.[9] Wrote on Italian case.

6. T.

Wrote to B.C. Stephenson—Robn. G—Mr Ellice—Rev. Mr Tomline—Mr Maskew—D.T. Gladstone, and minutes. Cicero with W. & S. H.S. with M. & L. A second dip in the sea: & walk on the hill. Read Hist. of K. Arthur—Orl. Furioso. Wrote on Tennyson.

[1] B. *Dobree.   [2] See 30 Aug. 58.
[3] His unpublished article; see 30 Aug. 59n.
[4] The physician. This sentence added with + at foot of page.
[5] See 3 Sept. 55.   [6] See 2 Aug. 57.   [7] See 11 Feb. 49.
[8] A. Fergusson, 'The religious establishment in Scotland examined upon protestant principles' (1771).
[9] Thirteenth century German poem, the basis of Wagner's cycle; probably the 1820 ed. of F. H. von der Hagen.

7. *Wed.*

Wrote to Mr Cobden—Mr Stephenson (2) (W.H.)—Mr M.T. Gibson—Mr Muller—and minutes. Cicero with W. & S.—H.S. with M. & Lena. Wrote on Tennyson. Worked on Malta Harbour papers: a mass.[1] Read and finished Sir T. Mallory [*sic*]—on the whole a noble book. Read Tennyson.

8. *Th.*

Wrote to T.D. Acland—B.C. Stephenson—Robn. G—Duke of Somerset—Mr Anstruther[2]—and minutes. Had a third dip: I find it a very *powerful* agent. H.S. with M. and L. Wrote on Tennyson. Read Tennyson—Orl. Furioso—Saw the Dean of Westminster. H.S. with M. & L.

9. *Fr.* [*Courthey, Liverpool*]

Wrote to Lieut Strahan[3]—Mr W.H. Stephenson and minutes. Cicero with W. & S.—H.S. with M. & L. Off at $11\frac{1}{4}$ to Liverpool by Chester. There had two hours with the P.O. & Municipal authorities on the question of the new P.O.[4]—Then to Courthey for dinner & evg. Read Orl. Furioso.

10. *Sat.* [*Hawarden*]

Wrote to S. Laing MP.—C.B. Banning[5]—M.E.G.—J. Crawfurd—C.G.—G. Arbuthnot—W.H. Young[6]—Ld J. Russell—and minutes. Returned to Hawarden 11–$12\frac{1}{2}$ with the P.O. & other departmental officers. 1–3. Went down to Seaforth about site for a possible Church: & saw Mr Rawson. Read Orlando Furioso—Ramsay's Scottish Life &c.[7] Found the [Beresford-] Hopes & Dean of Westminster.[8] Visited the Bold St Picture Gallery.[9]

11. *12 S. Trin.*

Ch mg & evg. Read Dollinger Hippolytus[10]—Remusat's Abelard. Wrote to Mr. Arbuthnot—Mr Anderson—Mr G.C. Glyn (2)—C.G. A conv. with Lady M. [Beresford-Hope] on France, Peace, & War, took out of me: not the person but the subject.

12. *M.*

Ch. $8\frac{1}{2}$ A.M. Wrote to Ld Palmerston[11]—H. Glynne—Mr Horsfall MP—C.

[1] Probably those published in *PP* 1860 lx; Malta was not included in the dockyards commission's report in *PP* 1859, 2nd session, xviii.
[2] J. H. Anstruther of Manchester had urged Gladstone to challenge Shaftesbury's control of church appts; see Add MS 44392, f. 170.
[3] See 24 Jan. 59.
[4] On Victoria Street; its financing was the subject of much controversy, discussed in Gladstone's letters to his br. Robertson 1857–8 (Hawn P).
[5] Charles Barbour Banning, post-master of Liverpool.
[6] Probably the chemist's in Baker Street, London.
[7] E. B. *Ramsay, Reminiscences of Scottish life and character* (1858); typifies the episcopalian view of Scottish humour.
[8] R. Chenevix *Trench.
[9] In Liverpool.
[10] See 29 Jan. 54.
[11] On *Cobden, Guedalla, P, 111.

Pressly—Lord C. Paget—C.G.[1]—Mast. of Mint—Duke of Argyll—and minutes. Mr Cobden arrived. Several hours walk & talk with him.[2] Also with Dean of Westmr. Saw Mr Burnett. Visited the Coal Pit. Robn. arrived. Dinner Party. Conv. with Lady M. [Beresford-Hope] on farming & hop duty: with Mr C[obden] on Currency.

13. T. [Penmaenmawr]

Wrote to Rev. W. Elwin—M. Summerhayes—Mayor of Liverpool[3]— Master of Mint—Earl Granville & minutes. Church 8½ A.M. Further conv. with Mr Cobden on Tariffs & relations with France. We are closely & warmly agreed. Saw with him Mr . . . on Galway Packet Contract.[4] The party dispersed at eleven. Off at 3 for Penmaenmawr. Found C. pretty well. Read Orl. Furioso—Documenti of Modena.

14. Wed.

Wrote to C. Pressly—Rowland Hill—J.N.G.—Rev R. Greswell—and minutes. A dip in the sea: & walk on the hills. Saw Mr Hunt,[5] who came resp. the Lpool Post Office. Wrote on Tennyson. Read Orl. Furioso—Times Review of Tennyson.[6]

15. Th.

Wrote to Sir T. Fremantle—Mr Laing—Mr Arbuthnot—Sir T. Wyse— Ld Granville—M. Summerhayes—Ld Palmerston—Dr Forbes Winslow— Mr B. Stephenson—and minutes. Read The Chinese Dispatches[7]—and Orl. Furioso C[antos] 37 & 38. Another dip. Saw Rev. Mr Wray. The Vicar dined with us.—Wrote on Tennyson.

16. Fr. [London]

Wrote to Mr Merivale—S. Ogden[8]—Burnett—& minutes. Wrote on Tennyson. Bathed afternoon: & off at 2 for London. In D. St 10½. Fell in with Sheriff of Hampshire.[9] Read Tennyson's Princess 11–3½ with M S[ummerhayes]: much & variously moved[R].

17. Sat.

Wrote to Mr Brand—Johnson L[ongden] & Co—Rev A. Watson—Mr S. Spring Rice—Rev. S. Robins—Mr Sherlock (2)—Mr Herbert—Mr Bickley

[1] Bassett, 125.
[2] The talk which led to the French treaty.
[3] William Preston.
[4] On the transfer of the Galway packet contract to a Montreal company; Gladstone gave 'a virtual refusal on the part of the Treasury to entertain the question', but did not recollect the man's name when closely examined on this conversation; see 8 May 60n.
[5] Sent by Banning, see 10 Sept. 59.
[6] Moderately favourable review of the *Idylls*, *The Times*, 10 September 1859, 10.
[7] The failure of Admiral Hope to force entrance to the Peiho river (*PP* 1860 lxix); see Guedalla, *P*, 111 and Costin, *Great Britain and China*, 292–3.
[8] F. Ogden of Manchester had written in admiration; Hawn P.
[9] Thomas Smith of Droxford.

—Mr S. Laing (2)—Sir C.L. Eastlake—C. Gladstone—Duke of Buccleuch—
Ld J. Russell—Atty General & minutes. Saw Mr Stephenson—Mr Arbuthnot—Mr T.M. Gibson—Duke of Newcastle—Mr Bonham. Saw M. S[ummer-
hayes] a scene of rebuke not to be easily forgotten. 10–1¾. Read La Toscane
et les Grand Ducs.¹ Cabinet 3¼–6.²

1. *Close* concert with France, military & diplomatic. Objects to be proposed for
attainment by such concert. 2. An adequate force to be sent to China. 3. With
real equality of England & France in responsibility & as far as may be an approxi-
mation to it in force. 4. War not to be at this time declared or presumed. 5. The
determination to force a passage to Tientsin *on the 25th of June* not to be approved.
6. Object of the combined force to be, the ratification of the Treaties according
to the terms specified—(i.e. for England at Pekin &, the proper time having
passed, the earliest time to be substituted, for which the necessary *executive*
arrangements can be made): 7. And like wise disavowal & such satisfaction as
may with full knowledge be thought just and necessary by the representatives
of this country on the spot. The military measures to be taken would remain for
consn. there and on the spot. 8. With regard to the mode of access to Pekin, any
route to be accepted which shall be safe, speedy, & attended with no dishonour³.

18. 13 S. Trin.

St James's mg.—Chapel Royal aft. Wrote to Duchess of Sutherland—
Duke of Argyll⁴—Rev. T.J. Rowsell—J. Murray. Read Ecclesiastic on
Cheyne—Do on Ant. de Dominis⁵—Amr. Church Review⁶—Tennyson
Idylls, parts—China Corresp. (fresh)⁷—Trollope's Tuscany.⁸ Saw Mr
Bonham—Mr D. Tupper⁹—Rev. Mr [F.] Garden—and M. S[ummerhayes]
further. Missed Aunt J.

19. M.

Wrote to F.R. Bonham—Ld Granville—Scotts—Mr Pressly—Ld Palmerston—C.G.—Rev. W. Blackwell—S. Mason¹⁰—and minutes. Saw Mr Ham-
mond¹¹—Sir A. Spearman—D. of Somerset *cum* D. of Newcastle—Scotts—
Mrs Norton—Mr Laing—Mr Ross *cum* Mr Allen¹²—Mr. G.A. Hamilton—
Mr Hunt *cum* Mr Laing—Mr J. Stuart Wortley. Read Prince Consort's
Address. Dined at S. Herbert's. Saw M.S. 6½ and 7½ and at 11 brought
d[itt]o to D. St for 1 hour, espy. to see the pictures[R].

¹ *La Toscane et ses grand-ducs autrichiens* (1859).
² See Bassett, 126.
³ Notes, of or for the cabinet, dated 17 September 1859; Add MS 44748, f. 121.
⁴ Report of yesterday's cabinet, in Argyll, ii. 149.
⁵ *The Ecclesiastic and Theologian*, xxi. 391, 413 (1859).
⁶ *Church Review*, xii. (July 1859).
⁷ See Costin, *Great Britain and China*, 294–5.
⁸ T. A. *Trollope, *Tuscany in 1849 and in 1859* (1859).
⁹ See 26 Apr. 31.
¹⁰ Samuel Mason of Hawarden.
¹¹ *Hammond had prepared a draft of instructions to *Bruce; see Costin, *Great Britain and China*, 295.
¹² George Ross and John Allen both of the post office; on the Liverpool affair; see 10 and 14 Sept. 59?

20. T. [*Penmaenmawr*]

Wrote to Mr Arbuthnot—Gen. Grey—Max Müller—H. Lees—J.H. Whitaker—Ld Meath—Ld Carlisle—Lt Gladstone—and minutes. Wrote some verses. Read The Princess—Trollope's Tuscany—finished both. Saw Sig. Damaschino—Mr S. Laing—Mr [W.] Jackson M.P. $4\frac{1}{2}$–$12\frac{1}{4}$ Downing St to Penmaenmawr: incl. 8 miles *land*. All well.

21. Wed. St Matthew.

Day of the turn in Agnes's illness: a memorable blessing.[1] Wrote to Adam S. Gladstone—C.W. Sikes—Jas Gladstone—Rev. J.L. Ross. Wrote on Tennyson. Saw Rev. Mr Thomas—Lt Col. Macdonald. Read Lange's Pamphlet[2]—Ariosto Orl. Furioso—De Quincey on Homer[3]—Tennyson's In Memoriam.

22. Th.

Wrote to C. Pressly—Mr Hammond—J. Bullock[4]—Ld Palmerston—Rev J. Bligh[5]—Ld J. Russell: & minutes. Wrote on Tennyson. Read In Memoriam—Ariosto Orl. Furioso—The Semidetached House: *small*[6]—De Quincey's Homer. Walk to Conway to get medicines for our invalids. Saw Mr Jelf. Wrote Memm. on Ld J.R.s proposed Draft.[7]

23. Fr.

Wrote to Mr Laing—Mr Arbuthnot—W. Nield—Ld Granville—E. Cardwell —R. Wynne Williams[8]—Sir T. Fremantle—and minutes. Agnes's fever gave way. Bathe: also walk with C. Finished revision of my Tennyson MS.[9] Read De Quincey on Dr Parr[10]—Ariosto Orl. Furioso. H.S. lesson with M. & Lena.

24. Sat. [*London*]

Wrote to C.G.
Rev Mr Elwin   } from Ln.
& minutes

M. Summerhayes also. Off at $2\frac{1}{2}$ A.M. & by mail to D. St. at 11.15 AM. Cabinet 3–6 on China: anxious but went well. Saw Sir C. Wood—March[ese] Lajatico—Mr Gibson—Lord Palmerston, before the Cabinet. Out on

---

[1] Her erysipelas; see 21 Sept. 47.
[2] D. A. Lange, *The Isthmus of Suez Canal Question viewed in its political bearings* (1859).
[3] T. de *Quincey, 'Homer and the Homeridae' in *Works*, vi.
[4] Unidentified.
[5] John Bligh, d. 1876?; headmaster of Kimbolton grammar school 1827.
[6] E. *Eden, *The Semi-Detached House* (1859).
[7] Add MS 44748, f. 123 and PRO FO 17/311; strongly critical of *Bruce, partly printed in Costin, *Great Britain and China*, 295–6.
[8] Robert Wynne Williams of London; business untraced.
[9] See 14 July 59n.
[10] T. de *Quincey, 'Whiggism in its relations to literature', *Selections Grave and Gay*, 14 v. (1853–61), vi.

business. Meals at O[xford] & C[ambridge] C[lub]—8½–10¼ with M S[um-merhayes] winding up[R]. Failed to find Stewart. Read Rogers's Recollec-tions[1]—De Quincy on Parr.

25. *14 S. Trin.*

Westmr. Abbey mg.—Wells St Aftn—also a little street preaching. Saw Miss Rose & M. Glynne—Aunt J. with the Larkinses. I did not think well of her health. Dined with Lady Wenlock & heard much of Frank [Lawley]. Saw M.S. altered circc. Read Tennyson's Guin—Moore on the Body[2]—Marshall Notes on Episcopate[3]—Max Müller on the Vedas.[4]

26. *M.*

Wrote to Mr Reynolds—S. Laing—Professor Richardson[5]—H.J.G. (2)—D. of Argyll—Sir C. Wood—Lord J. Russell—S. Herbert—and minutes: incl. min. on Telegraph to Singapore. Cabinet 12¼–4½. Read F.O. St Juan Memm. Saw Aunt J. Went on to MS[ummerhayes] for an hour: all is there on the way, if there be no illusion, to order & good: the case is no common one: may God grant that all go right. To me no trivial matter, for evil or for good. Off by Mail at 9.

27. *T. [Penmaenmawr]*

Penmaenmawr 4 A.M. Wrote to Bp of Brechin—J. Binger—Ld R. Caven-dish—H. Lees—Mrs T. Goalen—Robn. G.—Sir G.C. Lewis—S. Laing and minutes. Sea bathe and hill walk. Saw Dr Edwards[6] & Mr Harrison: Agnes better, after six days in bed. Read Toscane et les Archiducs.—Ariosto Orl. Furioso.

28. *Wed.*

Wrote to R.W. Rawson—W.H. Stephenson—Mr MacColl—Attorney General—D. of Newcastle—& minutes. Read over Willy's Examn. papers and George's tr. Lotos Eaters.[7] Read La Toscane et les A.—Richardson's Roman Orthoepy[8]—Orlando Furioso—Creuzè de Lesser Pref. & C[anto] 1.[9] Went up to the quarries in the cars: a curious operation: & hill walk with C. A Sea-bathe.

29. *Th. St Michael.*

10–1. At Parish Ch & Holy Comm.—The Bp[10] preached, very good: &

[1] See 1 Mar. 56.
[2] G. *Moore, The use of the body in relation to the mind (1846).
[3] T. W. *Marshall, Notes on the episcopal polity of the holy catholic church (1844).
[4] F. M. *Müller, Rig-Veda-Sanhita, the sacred hymns of the Brahmans (1849).
[5] John F. Richardson, professor of latin at Rochester, U.S.A.; see 28 Sept. 59.
[6] James Edwards, physician in Conway.
[7] *Tennyson, into Greek; Translations, 12.
[8] J. F. Richardson, Roman Orthoëpy; a plea for the restoration of the true system of Latin pronunciation (1859).
[9] See 29 Aug. 59.
[10] James Colquhoun Campbell, 1813–95; bp. of Bangor 1859–90.

confirmed young Mr Derbyshire.[1] Wrote to Earl of Aberdeen—S. Laing—
Mr F. Goulburn—E. Cardwell—Scotts: & minutes. Saw the Bp of Bangor—
Dr Edwards. Read Orl. Furioso (finished)—Chev. de la Table Ronde[2]—
Seashore walk.

30. Fr.

Wrote to Geo. Patton—Duchess of Sutherland—J. Binger—Warden Trin.
Coll.—Mrs J. Stuart Wortley—and minutes. Seabathe in the rain. Corrected
proofsheets on Tennyson. Read Richardson's Orthoepy—Chev. de la T.
Ronde and Boaden on Portraits of Shakespeare.[3] H.S. with M. & L.

Sat. Octr. One. 1859.

In bed all the forenoon with a tight chest. Wrote to Duke of Somerset—
Scotts—G. Burnett—H. Taylor—Ld Sydney—and minutes. Read Richardson—Chev. de la Table Ronde—& Boaden on Shakespeare Portraits
(finished).

2. 15 S. Trin.

Cold on chest: but read morning prayers at 11.15. Sermon in evg & went
to Church 3 P.M. Also bathed. Read Hampden B[ampton] L[ectures][4]—
Scotch Establisht. (finished)[5]—Hannah's Sermon on the Fall.[6]

3. M. [Hawarden]

Wrote to Ld Lyttelton—E. Cardwell—Dr Molesworth—O.B. Cole—Vicar of
Conway[7]—C.G.—Ld Chancellor—Mr Arbuthnot—M. Summerhayes—and
minutes. A last sea-bathe: then off with the children at $1\frac{3}{4}$ to Hawarden.
Saw Mr Burnett—H. Glynne. Dined at the Rectory. Began Bojardo anew—
read two Cantos.

4. T.

Ch. $8\frac{1}{2}$ A.M. Wrote to Lord J. Russell—C.G.—Atty. General—Mr Ryan—
Mr Harrison—and minutes. Saw Mr Smith. Visited the coal pit. Drove
Agnes out. Read Cotton's Journey to Ireland[8]—Fauriel Hist. Poesie
Provençale[9]—Firenzuola Ragionamen.[10]—Bojardo Orl. Innam.—Cromp-
ton's Life.[11] Construed with Willy the Speech of the Corcyraeans Thuc. I.[12]

---

[1] Vernon, converted s. of Samuel Dukinfield Darbishire, 1796–1870, of Pendyffryn,
Conway, a unitarian.
[2] See 29 Aug. 59.
[3] J. *Boaden, An inquiry into the authenticity of various portraits of Shakespeare (1824).
[4] See 11 Feb. 49.   [5] See 4 Sept. 59.   [6] See 2 Aug. 57.
[7] Morgan Morgan, d. 1870; vicar of Conway from 1838.
[8] C. *Cotton, A voyage to Ireland in burlesque (1670).
[9] C. C. Fauriel, Histoire de la poésie Provençale (1846).
[10] A. Firenzuola, Ragionamenti (1552).
[11] G. J. *French, The life and times of Samuel Crompton (1859).
[12] On the dispute between Corcyra and Corinth over Epidamnus.

5. *Wed.*

Ch 8½ AM. Wrote to Mr Stephenson—C.G.—Mr Wynne Williams—Mrs Leigh—Mrs Bennett—Mr Greswell—and minutes. Saw Mr Burnett. Drive with Agnes & walk—Ariosto with W. & Agnes. Dined at the Rectory. Read Fauriel—Ticknor[1]—Taylor (Germ. Literature)[2]—Firenzuola Ragiona-menti—and Bojardo O[rlando] I[nnamorato]. Dined, with Willy, at the Rectory.

6. *Th.*

Ch. 8½ AM. Wrote to Duke of Somerset—C.G.—Mr E. Rigby[3]—Mr Laing (2)—Mr Ellice—S. Herbert—Rev Mr M'Coll—S. Ogden—Messrs. Clowes[4]—C.L. Ryan, & minutes. Ariosto with W. & A.—Speech of the Corinthians (Thuc) with W. Read Bouterwell [*sic*], Geschichte[5]—Panizzi's Essay It. Rom. Poetry[6]—Ellis's Early English Poets[7]—Raccolta di Novelle[8]—Chev. de la Table Ronde—Bojardo O.I. Visited the Coal Pit. Lena ill: stomach much deranged. Agnes nearly off the sick List.

7. *Fr.*

Ch. 8½ A.M. Wrote to Sir A. Tulloch—S. Laing—Sir G.C. Lewis—C.L. Ryan G.A. Hamilton (2)—J.N.G.—Scotts—C.G.—Sir A. Spearman—J. Murray—Duke of Argyll—and minutes. Ariosto with W. & A. Thucyd. with W. Read Chev. de la T. Ronde—Report on Indian Noneffective Charge[9]—Life of Crompton. Worked on Tennyson revises.

8. *Sat.*

Ch. 8½ A.M. Wrote to Duchess of Sutherland—Mr Pressly—Duke of Somer-set—C.G.—Earl of Elgin—H. Raikes—Messrs. Overend—Messrs. Clowes—S. Spring Rice—Drove out with Agnes. Finished Tennyson revises. Ariosto with W. & A. Dinner & Charades at the Rectory. Read Chev. de la T. Ronde (finished)—Life of Crompton.

9. *16 S. Trin.*

Ch mg & aft. Wrote to J. Murray—C.G.—Sidney Herbert. Drive with Agnes—MS. Theol. Read Crisp's Sermons[10]—Scots Episc. Synod

[1] See 29 Sept. 57.   [2] See 27 July 58.
[3] Of the Hawarden coal company.
[4] Printers of the *Quarterly*; see 8 Mar. 41.
[5] F. Bouterwek, *Geschichte der Poesie und Beredsamkeit seit dem Ende des dreizehnten Jahrhunderts*, 12 v. (1801–59).
[6] See 5 Apr. 50.
[7] G. *Ellis, *Specimens of the early English poets* (1790).
[8] Perhaps *Raccolta di Novellieri Italiani*, 2 v. (1833).
[9] Perhaps *PP* 1859 2nd session viii on Indian army reorganization.
[10] T. *Crisp, *Christ alone exalted* (1690).

Proceedings[1]—Passaglia de Immac. Concept.[2]—Bp Hampden's Charge[3]—Badger on Rel. & Ed. in India[4]—Dante's Poems. Saw Waters.[5]

Th[eology] It is perilous indeed to take the *figures* of Holy Scripture which are adaptations & reductions of the truth and using them for the whole truth to make them the foundations of dogma, & to build upon them a system, especially as that system must needs, because a system, become exclusive[,] e.g. 1. passions imputed to the Deity. 2. doctrine of substitution in the person of our Lord.

Th[eology] Command & prohibition, promise and threat give us one aspect of the various sides of the Divine method for the government of man. Of the two great forms in which it is exhibited[,] will and law[,] they belong more to the former than to the latter. For law is embedded in the providential order & works out its own results: will apparently a power standing outside it though in truth exactly parallel with it.

Th[eology]. There is many a rebel & an assassin, the guilt of whose rebellion & assassination belongs far more to him who hath provoked than to him who hath acted it: though neither side can be discharged. So in regard to heresies & perversions of the faith, pronounced and broad: the evil & mischief of these may be most of all & first done to the men who have denounced them, if they have themselves truly though less visibly violated beforehand the proposition of the faith and scheme of the Gospel by exaggeration of certain of its parts with the relative, far less if with the absolute, depression of Others.[6]

10. M.

Ch. 8½ A.M. Wrote to Rev. Sir H. Moncreiff[7]—Robn. G.—Lord John Russell—Mr Brand—A. Beresford Hope—and minutes. Drive with Agnes. Visited the Colliery. Ariosto with W. & A. Thuc. (Athenians at Sparta) with Willy. Worked on my private papers & affairs. *Sederunt* with Burnett on Estate & my own affairs. Saw Moffatt thrice resp. Lena: the bowels obstinately torpid. Arthur Gladstone came over. Read Prof. Richardson—finished—Crompton's Life & Appx. finished—Bojardo O.I.

11. T.

Ch 8½ A.M. Wrote to Ld Palmerston (2)—Mr Laing (3)—Rev. W. Elwin—Messrs Overend—Mr Murray—Dean of Ch. Ch.—Mr Ryan—D. of Somerset—C.G.—Rev Mr MacColl—Ld Brougham—Mr G. Hamilton—and minutes. Worked on papers & accts. 10–12. Miss Lyttelton came for Tennyson &c.

[1] The *Proceedings* of *Forbes's trial for heresy; Gladstone told Ewing they 'fill me with pain and even more than with pain, with shame'; see W. Perry, *A. P. *Forbes* (1939), 92.
[2] C. Passaglia, *De immaculato Deiparae semper Virginis conceptu commentarius*, 3 v. (1854–5).
[3] R. D. *Hampden's fourth and last 'Charge' (1859).
[4] G. P. Badger, *Government in its relations with education and Christianity in India* (1858).
[5] Perhaps a local rescue case.
[6] All dated 9 October 1859; Add MS 44748, ff. 128–32.
[7] Sir Henry Wellwood *Moncrieff, 1809–83; free church minister in E. Kilbride 1837–52, in Edinburgh from 1852; 10th bart. 1851; apologist for the disruption. See 9 Feb. 43.

12–2. Saw Mr Burnett. Drive with Agnes. Read Burns—Life[1]—Do Poems—The Hunchback:[2] much beautiful poetry in it & dramatic power. C. returned past midnight.

12. Wed.

No Clergyman. Wrote to M. Summerhayes—Hon C. Gore—Dean Ramsay—S. Laing—Attorney General—R. Cobden—Lord J. Russell—Robn. G.—A.S. Gladstone—Mr Ryan—Mrs Bennett—and minutes. Worked on books (i.e. manually). Visited coal pit. Read Burn's Life—do Poems and Bojardo.

13. Th.

Ch. 8½ AM. Wrote to Sir G.C. Lewis—S. Laing—Attorney General—CL Ryan—Dr Acland—Robn. G.—M. Summerhayes—G. Burnett—Rev Osborne Gordon—S.R. Glynne—Mr G.A. Hamilton—Rev M. MacColl—and minutes. Domestic & Hawarden arrangements with C. Finished working on the order of my books. Music in evg with C.L. Read Burns's Life—S. Knowles's Beggar of B. Green:[3] very inferior.

14. Fr. X [London]

Ch 8½ AM. Wrote to Duke of Somerset—HJG—Lord J. Russell—J. Baillie—J.D. Sheppard[4]—and minutes. Off with Willy at 4.25. I got to D. St. at 10¼. He went to Oxford. Read Revue Independante[5] and Tennyson's Guinevere in RR. getting by heart. Saw Mr Burnett—Mr Darlington *cum do*—Saw M. Summerhayes: for whom I wish to exert myself[R].

15. Sat. X.

Wrote to Mrs Monsell—Mr Dunlop—Sir H. Moncreiff—C.G.—Duke of Argyll—E. Cardwell—Dean of Ely[6]—E. Lovell—& minutes. Dined with the Herberts. Saw Stewart[R]. Saw J. Murray—Mr S. Laing—M. Michel Chevalier[7]—Mr C. Villiers. Cabinet 3–6. Shopping. Read National, Westminster, and Bentley's Qy Reviews on Tennyson.[8]

16. S. 17 Trin. X

Westmr. Abbey mg. Chapel Royal aftn. Wrote MS. on the Life of Christ.[9]

[1] By J. G. *Lockhart (1828).
[2] J. S. *Knowles, *The Hunchback, a play in five acts* (1832).
[3] J. S. *Knowles, *The Beggar of Bethnal Green. A comedy in three acts, in verse* (1834).
[4] Unidentified.
[5] *Revue Indépendante*, i. (1859).
[6] H. *Goodwin.
[7] Michel Chevalier, 1806–79; French economist and free trader, played a major role in the making of the 1860 treaty; see Add MS 44127.
[8] *National Review*, ix. 368 (October 1859); *Westminster Review*, xvi. 503 (October 1859); *Bentley's Quarterly Review*, ii. 159 (October 1859).
[9] Not found.

Read Chr. Remembrancer[1]—Cheyne's Reasons of Appeal &c.[2]—Franklin.[3] Saw Summerhayes—E. Lovell[R]. Saw Sir C. Wood—Dean of Westmr.

17. M. X.

Wrote to C.G.—Dean Ramsay—W.H.G.—Ld Chandos—A. Goalen—G.C. Lewis (2)—A. Latham[4]—Rev. M. MacColl—Robn. G.—Rev. G. Foxton— Rev. A.J. D'Orsay—Ld Palmerston—G.S. Hamilton—and minutes. Read Q.R. on Reform and on strikes.[5] Saw Phillips—Brook[R]. Saw Mr Laing— Scotts—Shopping. Cabinet $3\frac{1}{4}$–$6\frac{1}{4}$. Wrote minute on the question of Post Offices.[6]

18. T.

Agnes's birthday—God bless her. Wrote to Duke of Somerset—Sir T.G.— Rev. O. Gordon—Ld Taunton—Johnson L. & Co.—Ly M. Hope—Comp- troller ND Office[7]—C.G.—Sir A. Spearman—Agnes—Mrs C.W. Gladstone[8] —Mrs Nunn—R. Phillimore—Mr Laing (2)—Mr Ryan—Mrs Tull—and minutes. Cabinet $1\frac{3}{4}$–$4\frac{1}{2}$. Saw M. Summerhayes (2)[R]. Saw Mr Jas Wilson. Worked on accounts & bills. Dined with J. Herbert. Worked late on papers: to bed at 2 AM.

19. Wed. [Holyhead]

Up at 5. Left Euston $6\frac{1}{4}$. Found C. at Chester & on with her to Holyhead at $3\frac{1}{4}$: where we saw the Great Eastern[9] & then I attended the public dinner from $5\frac{1}{2}$ to midnight. Lord Chandos was marked in his attentions. C. went back to Chester: I at 2 AM started with Mr Glyn & A. Kinnaird for London to attend Cabinet. Much conv. with Lord C. Paget. Also with A.K.—Mr Glyn—Sir R. Bromley—Mr Campbell.[10] The ship of an overpower- ing vastness. At the dinner no small part of England was represented.

20. Th. [London]

Reached Downing St 11.20 A.M. Wrote to M. Summerhayes—T.D. Acland —Sir G.C. Lewis (2)—C.G.—Mr Bagwell MP—Lyttelton—Duke of Argyll— Mr Cobden—Dean Ramsay—Earl of Aberdeen—and minutes. Saw Mr Laing. Cabinet $1\frac{1}{4}$–$4\frac{3}{4}$. Saw M. Summerhayes[R]. Read Childe Harold[11]— Tennyson—Nat. Rev. on Canning[12]—Michiels on Austrian Govt.[13]

---

[1] *Christian Remembrancer*, xxxviii. (October 1859).
[2] P. Cheyne, *Reasons of appeal . . . against a judgement on the merits and sentence, pronounced by the Bishop of Aberdeen on the 26th and 27th May 1859* (1859).
[3] Perhaps J. F. Francklin, 'The indivisibility of Christ's church' (1857).
[4] See 3 Aug. 43.
[5] Articles following his review of *Tennyson, *Quarterly Review*, cvi (October 1859).
[6] Not found.
[7] Sir A. Y. Spearman.
[8] See 27 Apr. 62.
[9] *Brunel's masterpiece, 12,000 tons, launched 1857, on trials after an explosion in September.
[10] See 12 Apr. 48.   [11] See 27 Oct. 54.
[12] *National Review*, ix. 273 (October 1859).
[13] J. A. X. Michiels, *Secret history of the Austrian government and of its systematic persecutions of Protestants* (1859).

21. *Fr.*

Wrote to Subwarden Trin. Coll.[1]—Dean Ramsay—H. Fitzroy—Dean of Westmr.—C.A. Wood—Mrs T. Goalen—L. Torelli—Ld Elgin—Stephy— C.G.—Publ. Ill. News of the World—and minutes. Saw Mrs Barber— Scotts—Sir John Lawrence—Mr S. Laing—Do *cum* Mr Pennethorne—Mr T.M. Gibson. Wrote Minute on Plans for Burl[ington] House Site.[2] Read De Quincey—Tennyson—Keats. Missed M. S[ummerhayes]. Haymarket Theatre 7–11. All too long: but some very clever acting.[3] Rem[ained] in T[rafalgar] Square from 11½ to one.

22. *Sat.* [*Hawarden*]

Wrote to G. Arbuthnot—S.W. Wayte—Miss Mackenzie—C. Trevor—The Secretaries of African Mission[4]—M. Summerhayes—and minutes. Saw Aunt J—Missed M. S.[R] Went down to Council at Windsor. Saw Sir G.C. Lewis —Ld J. Russell—Ld Palmerston—Sir Geo. Grey—Duke of Newcastle— Dean of Windsor—Stephy—& fell most inopportunely in the way of *P. Alice.*[5] Went on from Windsor to Chester & reached Hn. at 1½ A.M. Read Tennyson.

23. *18 S. Trin.*

Ch mg & evg. Saw R. Phillimore—Conv with him, also with C. respecting *the Rectory.* Wrote MS on St Joh. VIII. 18. Read M'Naught on Inspiration[6] and Q.R. on B. Powell.[7]

24. *M.*

Ch. 8½ A.M. Wrote to Sir J. Maxwell—Mr Raikes—C. Lyttelton—Sir G. Lewis—Mr Ryan—and minutes. Read my own Homer! Worked on transl. of Horace—Finished yesterday's MS. Read Burns's Life—and Fraser on W. Riding.[8]

25. *T.*

Ch. 8½ A.M. Wrote to Dean of Ch.Ch.—Sir G. Lewis—Car. Lyttelton— H. Fitzroy—A.S. Gladstone—Profr. Rogers[9]—and minutes. Worked on Translations in German & English:[10] an agreeable way for a C. of E. to pass his time. Read Burns's Life—Holland's Mental Physiology.[11]

---

[1] Robert Hale Witherby, priest 1853, subwarden of Trinity college, Glenalmond.
[2] Plans for occupation of it by Messrs. Banks and Baring: Add MS 44748, f. 133.
[3] 'An unequal match', 'The rifle and how to use it' and 'Jack's return from Canton'.
[4] Arthur Tidman and Ebenezer Prout, secretaries to the London Missionary Society.
[5] Then aged 16. See 14 Nov. 59.
[6] J. MacNaught, *The doctrine of Inspiration* (1856).
[7] *Quarterly Review*, cvi. 420 (October 1859), on *Powell's *The order of nature* (1859).
[8] *Fraser's Magazine*, lx. 449 (October 1859).
[9] i.e. J. E. T. *Rogers.
[10] Work with *Lyttelton for their *Translations* (1861).
[11] H. *Holland, *Chapters on mental physiology* (1852).

26. Wed.

Ch 8½ AM. Wrote to Dean of Windsor—Mr Ryan—Ld Lyttelton—G. Burnett—J.W. Parker—and minutes. Dined at the Rectory. Walk with C. Worked on translations: a luxurious employment! Also on arranging papers. Read Mr Laing's Minute—Indian Correspondence—&c.

27. Th. [London]

Overslept Church. Wrote to Duke of Somerset—T.G.—V.C. of Cambridge —R.G.—Sir W. Dunbar—J.N.G.—Dean Ramsay—G. Burnett—Lord Hatherton[1]—E. Lovell—and minutes. House & other arrangements for departure—Worked on translations. Off at 3.20 for London arrived 10.45. Saw M. Summerhayes[R]. Read Tozer on Coinage[2]—Cunnick on Suez Canal.[3]

28. Fr. SS. Simon & Jude.

Wrote to Ld Redesdale—Rev J. Dobie[4]—Sir G. Lewis (2)—Stat Master Lichfield—Rowland Hill—J.W. Parker—S. Laing—C.G.[5]—and minutes. Cabinet 1½–4½. We now lean (as I always did) to Congress.[6] Read Life in Paris[7]—Redesdale on Prosody[8]—Livingstone (Monk's).[9] Shopping, fore-noon. Saw M. Summerhayes with much interest & satisfaction. We were on poor Mrs Pearsall's case, a most moving one[R]. Saw Mr C. Villiers—Sir Geo. C. Lewis.

29. Sat.

Wrote to Lyttelton—Mr Raikes—Miss C. Lyttelton—W. Porter—Sir T. Fremantle—C. Pressly—Sir J. Lefevre—Rev Mr Bligh—Rev W. Elwin— C.G.[10]—Master of Mint—Professor Rogers—and minutes. Cabinet 2¾–4½. Saw Mr Lowe—Mr J. Abel Smith—Sir G.C. Lewis—Mr Sumner. Dined at the Duke of Argyll's. Worked on translations. Shopping. Read various.

30. 19 S. Trin.

Westr. Abbey mg & St James's (prayers) evg. Saw Aunt J.—M. Summer-hayes[R]. Worked on translation. Read Garden on Mansell & Maurice[11]—

---

[1] See 29 Jan. 33n.
[2] Untraced.
[3] Perhaps K. Czoernig, 'Über die Durchstechung der Landenge von Suez' (1858).
[4] John Dobie, d. 1877? Chaplain of Dartmouth 1851, in Heidelberg 1865.
[5] Bassett, 126.
[6] Proposed Congress on Italy, which never met; for this cabinet, see D. Beales, *England and Italy 1859–60* (1961), 112.
[7] *Life in Paris; a drama in three acts*, in *Hodgson's Juvenile Drama*, 2 v. (1822).
[8] J. T. F. *Mitford, Lord Redesdale, *Thoughts on English prosody and translations from Horace* (1859).
[9] W. Monk, *Dr. Livingstone's Cambridge lectures . . . edited with introduction* (1858).
[10] Bassett, 127.
[11] Untraced article by F. *Garden.

Chretien on do[1]—Hymns of Adam de S. Victor[2]—Mr Monk's Vol. on Central African Mission.

31. M. [Cambridge]

Wrote to Sir J.S. Forbes—H. Fitzroy—Sir G.C. Lewis—Mr Ryan (missed) & minutes. Off to Cambridge at 4.15. found C. at the Station. Saw W. Purchase—Mr Cardwell—Sir Jas Hudson—Mr Laing—Scotts—Lord Harris. We went to Magdalen[e] lodge:[3] & met a party to dinner & in the evening. Read Sedgwick & Livingstone on the African case.[4]

Tues. Nov. One All Saints.

Magdalen[e] Chapel 8 A.M. Sermon at St Mary's 10.30. Congregation afterwards when we received our Doctor's degrees: before a crowded & very warm audience.[5] Luncheon with the Provost of Kings.[6] Then 1–5½ African Mission Meeting.[7] Spoke 30 m. The spirit of the young men was excellent especy. as indicated in whatever touched religion.

Large dinner & evening party at the Vice Chancellors.[8] Saw Mr Clark the Public Orator[9]—Professor Sedgwick—Dean of Ely, resp. Cathedrals, and others. Read Lady C. Guest's Mabinogion.[10]

2. Wed.

Magd. Chapel 8 AM.—King's Coll. Chapel 4 P.M. Wrote to Sir A. Spearman —Lyttelton—Mr Cobden MP.—C.A. Wood—Attorney General—Mr Ryan: and minutes.[11] Prof. Sedgwick's Lecture & Museum 12—2¼.[12] Saw Trin Coll. Library—Chapel—Kitchen—Various Courts. Dined at Trinity Lodge[13]— Evening party followed. Read The Master's Transln. of Plato. Saw Bp of Oxford re Bp of Brechin.[14]

[1] C. P. Chretien, A letter to F. D. *Maurice on some points suggested by his . . . criticism on *Mansel's *Bampton Lectures (1859).

[2] Twelfth century hymnist; his Elucidatorium Ecclesiasticum ed. by L. Gautier, 2 v. (1858–9).

[3] Latimer Neville, 1827–1904, 4th s. of 3rd Lord Braybrooke, (see 3 Nov. 59n.) was master from 1853.

[4] A. Sedgwick, Dr. Livingstone's Cambridge lectures, together with a prefatory letter (1858); D. *Livingstone, Cambridge lectures (1858) and see 14 Mar. 57.

[5] LL.D., which he received with S. *Wilberforce and Sir G. *Grey.

[6] Richard *Okes, see 21 Sept. 25.

[7] Gladstone, *Wilberforce and Sir G. *Grey spoke. *Sedgwick, who declined to speak, recorded 'we had a glorious meeting. It was the great event of Michaelmas term'. (J. W. Clark and T. M. Hughes, Life of Sedgwick (1890) ii. 354); report in The Times, 2 November 1859, 7.

[8] Also Latimer Neville.

[9] W. G. *Clark.

[10] Lady C. E. Guest, The Mabinogion . . . with an English translation and notes, 3v. (1838–49).

[11] Add MS 44748, f. 138, on stamps and patents.

[12] *Sedgwick's regular lecture to undergraduates in the Woodwardian Museum, now the Law Library.

[13] W. *Whewell was master, the 1st v. of his Platonic dialogues for English readers, 3 v. (1859–61) just published.

[14] See 9 Oct. 59; Gladstone was attempting to mediate between *Forbes and the synod.

3. Th. [Audley End]

Magd. Chapel 8 A.M. Wrote to Dean Ramsay—J. Aspinall Turner[1]—and minutes. Saw Jesus Chapel—Peterhouse Chapel—Univ. Library—Fitz-william Museum, & Library, with its magnificent engravings and illumi-nated Books—Pepysian Library[2]—Backs of the Colleges & divers Quad-rangles. At 4.45 started for Audley End,[3] where we were most kindly received. Found the Rosses.[4] Whist. Read Assemblea Toscana[5]—Ld J. Russell's Life of Fox.[6]

4. Fr.

Wrote to Sir J. Lefevre—C.L. Ryan—Professor Rogers—S. Herbert—Govr. of the Bank—Rev Mr Barlow—Mrs T. Goalen—Sir G.C. Lewis—Sir R. Murchison—and minutes. Add to these Messrs. Johnson Longden & Co—M. Summerhayes.[7]

A long examn. of the Audley End China which I endeavoured to bring into order. Chapel 9½ AM. Read Assemblea Toscana—Ed. Rev. on Carlyle's Frederic.[8] Whist in evg. Conv. with Ross who knows much & accurately.

5. Sat.

Chapel 9½ AM. Wrote to Sir J.S. Lefevre—S. Herbert—P[ost] Master [Saffron] Walden—J.W. Parker—Dean Ramsay—Mrs Goalen—Sir G. Lewis—and minutes. Went round this very fine & commodious house: also saw Saffron Walden Church & the Abbey Farm. Whist in evg. Read Oxoniana[9]—Ld J. Russell's Fox.

6. 20 S. Trin.

Littlebury Church and Holy C.mg.—Chapel here 5 PM. Saw Mr Wise—Wrote to Lord Palmerston—Attorney General—Mr J.S. Gregory[10]—and minutes. Read Cheyne's Answer[11]—Parker's Sermons &c[12]—Burnet's Life of Hale—do Life of Rochester.[13]

7. M. [London]

Off at 7¼: reached London before ten. Saw E. of Aberdeen—Johnson

[1] James Aspinall Turner, 1797–1867; Manchester cotton manufacturer, liberal M.P. Manchester 1857–65.
[2] In Magdalene, *Pepys's college.
[3] Braybrooke's place; see 15 Nov. 41.
[4] Unidentified.
[5] Tuscan assembly debs., which voted in September for union with Sardinia; probably supplied by Laiatico; see 30 July 59.
[6] See 19 Jan. 55.
[7] This sentence added at bottom of the page.
[8] *Edinburgh Review*, cxv. 376 (October 1859).
[9] [J. *Walker], *Oxoniana*, 4v. (1809).
[10] Unidentified.
[11] P. Cheyne, 'Answers . . . . to the appeal by the Rev. Gilbert Rorison and others against a judgement pronounced by the Bishop of Aberdeen on 15 June 1858' (1858).
[12] T. Parker, *Sermons* (1853).
[13] G. *Burnet, *Some passages in the life and death of John *Wilmot, Earl of Rochester* (1680).

Longden & Co—Sir Alex. Spearman—Mr Arbuthnot—Mr Laing *cum* Mr Stephenson—Sir Heron Maxwell—Mr Rowland Hill—M. Summerhayes [R]. Cabinet $3\frac{1}{4}$—6. Read Friends in Council[1]—Fraser's Magazine[2]—and Brown's A. Hallam.[3] Wrote to Robn. Gladstone—Rev Mr Rawlinson—W. Forbes—O.B. Cole—C. Pressly—Ld R.—and minutes.

8. *T.*

Wrote to C. Herbert[4]—J.C. Robinson—Dr Bandinel[5]—Ld Chancellor—Mr Hankey[6]—Rev Mr Mayow—Mr Corkran[7]—Bp of Brechin—E. of Meath—Ld Brougham—Robn. G—D. of Somerset—Rev S. Downe—Attorney General—& minutes. Saw Mr S. Herbert—Messrs. Johnson L. & Co—Mr T.F. Elliot—Mr Laing—Attorney General. Saw C. Herbert. Read Foresi's Tract[8]—Friends in Council—Rab & his Friends.[9] Went into the City: & hunted China in Holborn &c.

9. *Wed.* X

Wrote to Ld Elgin 2—Mr Cowper—Ld Wodehouse—Mr Lowe—A. Gibbon —and minutes. Further & I hope final minute on the Patents Stamp of £200.[10] Cabinet $1\frac{1}{4}$–$4\frac{1}{4}$. It was decided 1. to take the Budget at the opening of the Session: 2. to revise certain Civil charges: 3. (almost) to meet Jan 24. —Mema. & arrangements for meeting of committees. Saw Mr Laing—Duke of Somerset. Busy mg on porcelain. Dined at Guildhall & thanked in a roar i.e. roared my thanks for the H. of C.[11]

10. *Th.*

Wrote to D of Somerset—Mr Lane[12]—Ld Kinnaird—Ld Worsley[13]—Sec S.P. Gospel[14]—Mr T.F. Elliot—Sir T. Fremantle—and minutes. Saw Mr Cobden MP.—Sir G.C. Lewis—Mr Pressly—do *cum* Mr Timm—Sir T. Fremantle—Do *cum* Mr Pressly & Mr Dobson—Govr. & Dep. Govr. of Bank—The Master of the Mint—Aunt J.—Mrs de Pearsall. Harris & the Phillimores dined. Read Montalembert's Pamphlet[15]—Dix on the Univ of the South U.S.[16]

[1] Sir A. *Helps, Friends in Council: a series of readings and discourses thereon* (1847).
[2] *Fraser's Magazine*, lx (November 1859).
[3] J. *Brown, 'Memoir of A. H. Hallam', from *Horae Subsecivae*, i (1858).
[4] Probably a rescue case, see later this entry.
[5] Bulkeley *Bandinel, 1781–1861; Bodley's librarian 1813–60, reformed its catalogue.
[6] See 2 July 35.
[7] John Frazer Corkran, d. 1884, novelist and journalist, had sent a poem (Hawn P).
[8] A. Foresi, *Sulle porcellane medicee: lettera* (1859).
[9] J. *Brown, *Rab and his friends* (1859).
[10] Add MS 44748, f. 141.
[11] 'Incessant hubbub' made all the speeches inaudible: *The Times*, 10 November 1859, 7.
[12] Probably Richard James Lane, 1803–85; auditor of Irish friendly societies and commissioner of Irish fisheries.
[13] Charles Anderson-Pelham, 1835–75; styled Lord Worsley 1846–62; liberal M.P. Grimsby 1857–62; 3rd earl of Yarborough 1862.
[14] Ernest *Hawkins.
[15] See 3 Dec. 58.
[16] W. G. Dix, 'The university of the South. An address delivered at Beersheba Springs, Tennessee' (1859).

11. Fr.

Wrote to Mr Arbuthnot—Gen. Malcolm—Mr Pressly—Mr Cobden MP.—
R. Williams—J. Westell—Mr Greswell—Mr H. Chester, & minutes. Dined
at Duke of Argyll's. Saw Sir Charles Fox—Mr Arbuthnot—Mr Stephenson
—Lord Aberdeen—better—Mr Anderson,[1] on his sofa: how he has suf-
fered!—Mr Granville Berkeley—Duke of Argyll—Saw M. Summerhayes
[R]. Cabinet Committees 1. on Education 2. on Superannuation.[2]

12. Sat.[3] [Windsor]

Worked on Sapphics.[4] Wrote to G. Grant—Mayor of Manchr.—Master of
Mint—Duchess of Sutherland—& minutes. Court of Exchequer at 11 to
swear in. Do at 2 to make the Sheriffs Roll.[5] Then Cabinet to 5. Saw
Marquis Lajatico—Mr Cobden MP.—Provost of Eton. Tried to beg off the
Committee of Cabinet on Reform: but without success. Went to the
Deanery at Windsor in the evg: exceeding pleasant. We had music.

13. 21 S. Trin.

St George's mg & evg. Saw Stephy, C. & A. Lyttelton. Read Gerson's
Sermm[6]—Orthodoxie et Papisme[7]—Thompson's Address U.S. Conversa-
tions with the Dean,[8] & with Mr Kingsley.[9] Saw the Courtenays. Wrote to
Ryan.

14. M.

St George's Chapel mg & aft. Wrote to Attorney General—Willy—S.
Lyttelton[10]—Mr Ryan—S. Laing—Robn. G.—J.N.G.—and minutes. Read
Minghetti.[11] Walk with the Dean: also with him & Kingsley whom I much
like. We dined at the Castle: I sat by Princess Alice & was delighted with
her freshness. Also liked much Lady G. Somerset.[12] Long conv. with the
P[rince]. Queen said 'you must prepare a large Budget[']. I liked the Dean
today even better than ever.

[1] Illness of W. G. Anderson of the treasury; he lived till 1897.
[2] Apparently standing cttees. of the cabinet; possibly the first such.
[3] Gladstone was this day elected first lord rector of Edinburgh university (Gladstone
643, Lord Neaves 527); see Sir A. Grant, The story of the university of Edinburgh (1884),
ii. 106.
[4] See 21 Dec. 59.
[5] Their annual nomination, see 12 Nov. 53.
[6] J. Charlier de Gerson, Sermon inédit . . . sur le retour des Grecs à l'unité (1859);
preached 1409.
[7] Orthodoxie et papisme. Examen de l'ouvrage du père Gagarin sur la réunion des Églises
catholique greque et catholique romaine (1859).
[8] G. V. *Wellesley; see 18 Feb. 26.
[9] Charles *Kingsley, 1819–79, novelist and professor of literature and history, recently
appt. one of H.M.'s chaplains in ordinary. Gladstone made him canon of Chester August
1869.
[10] Then marshall at Windsor; see 23 Dec. 40.
[11] Probably M. Minghetti, Di alcune novità agrarie in Inghilterra (1854).
[12] Lady Geraldine Harriet Anne Somerset, da. of 7th duke of Beaufort; lady-in-
waiting to duchess of Cambridge 1856–89.

15. T. [London]

St George's 10½ AM. Wrote to Ld Brougham—S. Bright—The Speaker—
The Queen—Ld Provost of Edinb.—Sir D. Brewster—Dr L. Playfair[1]—
and minutes. Went to London at 11.30. Saw Earl of Aberdeen—S. Herbert
—Sir J. Lacaita—Duke of Argyll—S. Laing—M. de Persigny—and evg
M. Summerhayes: resp. Mrs Pearsall, & *alia*[R]. One frail hit or both.
Read (in part) Guerre a l'Anglais: a remarkable indication.[2] At Christie's—
Willson's.

16. Wed.

Wrote to S. Herbert—Ld J. Russell (2)—Mr Keats—Mr Hall & others—
Mr Pressly—Warden Tr. Coll NB—Mr S. Laing—Sir J.H. Maxwell—
Mr S. Bright—and minutes. Read Taylor's Hist. Money[3]—Luncheon at
Mr Ellison's.[4] Saw Robn. G.—His family—Mr Willson—D. of Argyll—
Mr Trevor—Sir W. Dunbar—S. Laing—Mr D. Wolff—E. Cardwell. Sat by
the Duke of Cambridge at the Guy's Hospital dinner—much pleased with
his frankness & evident *application* of mind. Saw one[R].

17. Th.

Wrote to Dss. of Sutherland—Rev Dr Lee—Marq. Lajatico—Bp Oxford—
Dean Ramsay—Sir G. Lewis—Sig. Quartano—Abp of Cefalonia (Italian)
—Sig. Scalzuni (do)—Sir Jas Graham—Earl Clarendon—Bp of Oxford—
and minutes. Saw Sir J. Lacaita—Duke of Argyll—Master of the Mint—
Mr Edwards—and two[R]. Cabinet at 1. Dined at Ld Palmerstons. She
at length seems *aging*.[5] Read Chevalier's Letters[6]—Report on Manning.[7]

18. Fr.

Wrote to Johnson L. & Co—C.A. Wood—Mr Gregson MP—Ld Ward—
C. Buxton MP—W.H.G.—T. Mainwaring MP.—C. Pressly (2)—Sir A.
Spearman—and minutes. Cabinet &c Committee on Harbours 1½–3¾.
Shopping: china &c. Saw Mr Gibson—Mr Walter Bagehot—Mr Cardwell
(widow's pensions).[8] Employed nearly all the evening on arranging papers
& the like. Read Brogniart[9]—Marryat[10]—tracts. Guided by C. Lyttelton,
corrected the German 'Lady Mary'.[11]

[1] (Sir) Lyon *Playfair, 1818–98; chemistry professor; liberal M.P. Scottish universities
1868–85, S. Leeds 1885–92; postmaster general 1873; Commons cttee.s chairman 1880–3;
K.C.B. 1883; cr. Baron 1892. See Add MS 44280.
[2] Free trade pamphlet by Louis Jourdan; strongly recommended by Gladstone to
*Russell (PRO 30/22/19, f. 39).
[3] J. *Taylor, *A view of the money system of England from the Conquest, with proposals
for establishing a secure and equitable credit currency* (1828).
[4] Probably Cuthbert Ellison, 1783–1860; Gateshead landowner and M.P. Newcastle
1812–30.
[5] Though she outlived her husband and d. 1870.
[6] M. Chevalier, *Lettres sur l'organisation du travail* (1848).
[7] Of the navy.
[8] See 21 Nov. 59.
[9] See 9 Mar. 59.
[10] J. Marryat, *Collections towards a history of pottery and porcelain, in the 15th, 16th,
17th and 18th centuries* (1850).
[11] Perhaps Schiller's 'Mary Stuart'; not included in the *Translations*.

19. Sat.

Wrote to Lyttelton—Johnson L & Co—C. Pressly—Ld Shaftesbury—
Mrs Norton—and minutes. Committee of Cabinet on Reform $2\frac{1}{2}$–$5\frac{1}{2}$. We
made progress but rating v. rent still hangs fire.[1] Saw Mr F. Boult[2]—
Mr A. Gladstone—Paper Duty Deputation[3]—Mr Milner Gibson—Duke of
Argyll—Ld Palmerston—Ld J. Russell. Cabinet dinner at Ld P.s. Walk
with C.

20. Last S. Trin.

Ch. Royal mg & aft.—Wrote a bit of Address for Edinb.[4] Read M'All on
Wife's Sister[5]—Orthodoxie et Papisme[6]—Hale's Abstract on Church
Rate[7]—Appeal of Guild of St Alban.[8] Saw Lord Aberdeen.

21. M.

Wrote to Sir R. Bromley—Sir G. Lewis—Sir J. Graham—Mr Laing—Mr
Thomas[9]—Ly Braybrooke—M. Summerhayes—and minutes. Went into
the City & saw Johnson L. & Co.—Govr. & Dep Govr. of Bank—Saw Mr
Stephenson. Eight to dinner. H. Glynne came. Read Minghetti. Wrote on
Widow's Pensions.[10]

22. T.

Wrote to Bp of Argyll—S. Herbert—Sir G. Lewis—Johnson L & Co—
R. Cobden—Ld Clarendon—Sir W. Dunbar—Dean Ramsay—Rev Dr Lee
—Mr T. Turner—Ld Granville—Mary Gladstone—Count Flamburiari.
Eight to dinner: & a small evening party. Missed M.S. &c[R]. Saw Duke
of Argyll—Mr Laing *cum* Mr Stephenson—Mr Pressly—Mr Alex. Munro—
Mr S. Herbert—A. Kinnaird. Read Brewster's Address[11]—China Quarrel.[12]

1. Clause for (voluntary) assumption of assessments & collection of taxes. 2.
Alcohol in wine. 3. Duty on British Spirits—can we venture on any increase?
4. Licences on public houses (open)[,] eating houses[,] coffee houses. 5. Paper

[1] Because rates were often compounded, rent was often thought a fairer way of
franchise extension, though never adopted for householders.
[2] Francis Boult of Liverpool, wrote *Taxation: direct and indirect* (1861).
[3] Requesting the abolition of parchment-pulp duties; Gladstone requested a detailed
statement; see C. D. *Collet, *History of the taxes on knowledge* (1933 ed.), 159.
[4] Delivered on 16 April 1860.
[5] Mr. McCaul of the marriage law defence association, pamphlet viii, 'A plea from
Leviticus XVIII for marrying a deceased wife's sister'.
[6] See 13 Nov. 59.
[7] W. H. *Hale, 'The present state of the Church Rate question exhibited in an
abstract of the evidence contained in the Report of a select committee of the House of
Lords' (1859).
[8] See 24 July 59.
[9] Perhaps Mesac Thomas, 1816–92; secretary of colonial church society 1851–63;
bp. in New South Wales from 1863.
[10] For warrant officers' widows: Add MS 44748, f. 145.
[11] Sir. D. *Brewster, 'Introductory Address . . . on the Opening of Session 1859–60
[of Edinburgh University]' (1859).
[12] *The new quarrel in China. A statement drawn from the official documents* (1859).

Duty—if abolished should the abolition be instantaneous, or should it be from a posterior date to be fixed? Should there be a drawback? Suppose the repeal *announced* on 20th February—what would be the best dates to fix? What would be the nett *loss* on the present financial year if any? What on the year 1860–1? 6. Malt Credit. If we take off another six weeks what will be the nett gain 1860–1? 7. Hop duty receivable in May 260m[ille], Novr. 260m[ille]. Offer 4% discount on 6 mo[nths] to all who pay in May? Abolish credit on all hops of the year 1860 by requiring the duty to be paid on or before Jan 1—In return for which give up the five per cent (better the foreign duty?) 8. New Stamp duties to be considered.[1]

23. Wed. [Sheen, Mortlake]

Dearest Mazie's birthday—God bless her. Wrote to S. Herbert—Ld Brougham—Robn. G.—Lyttelton—Ld Wodehouse—and minutes. Went at 6 down to the Wortleys (Sheen)[2] for dinner & night. Saw their China. Harbours Comm. 1–2¾. Ref. Bill Comm. 3–4¾. Saw Lord C. Paget—Mr Laing. Read Sup[erannuatio]n Commn. Report[3]—National Debt Tracts.

24. Th. [London]

Wrote to Ld Brougham—Dss. of Sutherland—Sir C. Wood—Sir J. Lefevre —Mr Pressly—Bp of Moray—Gen Portlock—Ld Advocate—Ld Shaftesbury—E. Cardwell—and minutes. Returned from Mortlake in the forenoon. Eccl. Comm 11–2.[4] Cabinet 2–5. Saw Bp of Oxford. Saw M. Summerhayes[R]. Read 'Out of the Depths'.[5]

25. Fr.

Wrote to Ld Brougham (2)—Sir G. Lewis—A. Kinnaird—Ld De Grey— Dean Ramsay—Mrs Summerhayes—Sir D. Brewster—Dr Brown—Clerk to Commn. Univ. Ed[6]—S. Laing Esq—J. L. Tabberner—& minutes.[7] Saw Ld Brougham—Ld Aberdeen—Mrs Westell—W. Purchas[8]—Bp of Salisbury—who dined with us—Sir G.C. Lewis. Read 'Out of the Depths'— Jones on Church Rates[9]—Tabberner on Taxation.[10]

26. Sat.

Wrote to Mrs Chisholm—Attorney General—C. Pressly—V. Chr. of Oxford—R. Cobden—Ld Palmerston[11]—Ld Brougham—Govr. of the Bank

[1] Headed 'Most Private', apparently the notes of the meeting with *Laing, the financial secretary; initialled and dated 22 November 1859: Add MS 44748, f. 180.
[2] At Mortlake, Surrey.
[3] See *PP* 1859 xix and 1860 xliii. 251.
[4] He was *ex officio* an ecclesiastical commissioner.
[5] H. G. Jebb, *Out of the depths; the story of a woman's life* (1859), the rescue of a prostitute.
[6] Eton had rejected the commission's proposals for its reform: *PP* 1860 xxvi. 697.
[7] Drew up 'experimental' plan for redistribution of seats: Add MS 44748, f. 154.
[8] A rescue case, see 29 Nov. and 8 Dec. 59.
[9] W. H. Jones, 'A letter . . . on the question of Church Rates' (1859).
[10] J. L. Tabberner, *Direct taxation and parliamentary representation . . . with remarks thereon by the Right Hon. W. Gladstone* (1860).
[11] Dated 25 in Guedalla, *P*, 113.

—Ld Clarendon—Ld Justice Clerk[1]—Mr Ellice—Sir J. Lefevre—&
minutes. British Museum 12–2¼—A divided Govt.! Harbours Commee.
3–5¼. Saw Robn. G—Ld Granville—A. Robertson—Sir G.C. Lewis—Mr
Laing. Finished 'Out of the Depths' a most remarkable book. Read
Herbert's Paper of Military proposals.[2]

27. Advent S.

St James's mg & Chapel Royal aft. MS. on St J. Baptist aloud. Saw Ld
Aberdeen: Sir J. Lacaita. Conv. with C. on State of the departed—on 'Out
of the Depths' & kindred subjects. Wrote to Ld Brougham—Bp of Oxford
—Sir W. Heathcote—S. Herbert (on Military proposals).[3] Read Rawlinson's Bampton Lectures.[4]

28. M.

Wrote (almost a Treatise) to S. Herbert on France[5]—Also to A. Robertson
—Mr Brand—and minutes. Education Vote Committee 12¼–2¼. Read Ld
Liverpool on Coins.[6] Saw Archdeacon Hale—Sir W. Snow Harris[7]—Mr
Laing. Saw M. Summerhayes. Also, two cases of interest[R].

29. T.

Wrote to Mr Arbuthnot—Sir D. Brewster (2)—Mr W. Bagehot—E. Card-
well—Ld Granville—D. of Somerset—Ld Advocate—Ld Provost Edinb.—
S. Herbert—Sir T. Fremantle—Mr Pressly—Mr Cobden MP.—Ly Blantyre
—R. Hawkins—Ld Ward—Hon. A. Kinnaird—and minutes. Saw Lord
Brougham—Lord Palmerston. Shopping & china walk. Saw Purchas: & a
case of interest.[8] Eight to dinner. Read P.O. Savings' Banks[9]—Marryat on
Porcelain.[10]

30. Wed.

Wrote to C.W. Sikes—Dr Lyon Playfair—Johnson L. & Co—Sir W. Heathcote and minutes. Dined with the Herberts. Saw Lord Ward—Sir Alex.
Spearman—Mr Byng—S. Herbert—A. Panizzi—Ld Wodehouse. Cabinet
3¼–6. I found myself very *lonely* on the question of Military Estimates.
Read Pasley on Military Policy.[11]

[1] J. Inglis.
[2] Proposal to expand the army on the assumption that the fleet could not defend the
Channel, and to reintroduce the ballot for the militia; Stanmore, ii. 211.
[3] Strongly hostile, urging colonial reductions and arguing commercial treaty would
signify France's friendship; Stanmore, 221.
[4] G. *Rawlinson, *The historical evidences of the truth of the Scripture Records stated
anew, with special reference to the doubts and discoveries of modern times* (1859).
[5] His 'second barrell', arguing sufficiency of effective Channel fleet; Stanmore, ii. 225.
[6] C. J. *Jenkinson, Lord Liverpool, *A treatise on the coins of the realm* (1805).
[7] Sir William Snow *Harris, 1791–1867; naval engineer and electrician.
[8] Apparently a male destitute; see 25 Mar. 60; or the ritualist.
[9] C. W. Sikes, 'Post Office Savings Banks. A letter to . . . Gladstone' (1859).
[10] See 18 Nov. 59.
[11] Sir C. W. *Pasley, *Essay on the military policy and institutions of the British Empire.*
pt. 1. (1810).

Thurs. Dec. One. 1859.

C.G. went to Hawarden. Wrote to E. Hamilton—Mr Pressly—Sir J.H. Maxwell—D. Maclaren—Dean Ramsay—Mr Falloon[1]—Ld Provost Edinb.[2] —and minutes. Read Pasley on Mil. Pol. 11–2. Sir T. Fremantle: and do *cum* Mr Pressly. Duke of Argyll—Mr Gibson (on Estimates &c)—R. Phillimore—Duchess of Sutherland—Mr Ellison. Dined with the Phillimores. Saw Summerhayes—Clifford[R].

Comm[itt]ee Cabt. Dec. 1. 59.[3]
For the schedule of the late Govt.: Lewis—Gladstone—Gibson.
For a Sched. A. & B.: Argyll—Villiers—Grey—Palmerston—J. Russell.

2. Fr.

Wrote to Her Majesty—Mr G. Hadfield—S. Laing (2)—Attorney Gen.— Mrs Herbert—C.G.—and minutes. Educn. Vote Committee 1–2¾. Cabinet 3¼–6¼.[4] Saw Mr Laing—S. Herbert. Dined with the Herberts. Read Fraser's Mag. on Defence & other Artt.[5] Pasley on Military Policy. Worked on Finance Bill &c.

3. Sat.

Wrote to Bp of Oxford—Mr Cobden—Bp of Brechin—Lady Heathcote— Mr Ayrton MP[6]—Subdean Chap. Royal[7]—C. Neate—Sir A. Spearman— Duchess of Sutherland—Mr Geo. Lock—C.G.—M.E.G.—& minutes.[8] Saw Mr Anderson—Earl of Aberdeen—Aunt J.—M. Summerhayes. Read Slade on States & Navies[9]—Charges agt. Duke of York[10]—Electoral abuses considered[11]—Fraser's Magazine.

4. 2 S. Adv.

Chapel Royal & H.C.mg: do aftn. Wrote to Lewis. Wrote for Edinburgh Address. Read Farrar's Sermons[12]—Maurice on Revelation[13]—Robinson on Ch. Questions[14]—Layman on Ch Extension[15]—Dr Brown on St Paul's Thorn &c.[16]—Out of the Depths.

[1] Daniel Falloon, d. 1862; anglican priest in Canada, wrote histories of anglicanism.
[2] Francis Brown Douglas; see 12 Dec. 59.
[3] Cttee. of cabinet on the Reform Bill; follows lists of county and borough seats marked 'Experimental'; Add MS 44748, f. 156.
[4] Navy estimates; figures in Add MS 44748, f. 184.
[5] *Fraser's Magazine*, lx. 643 (December 1859).
[6] Acton Smee *Ayrton, 1816–86; barrister and liberal M.P. Tower Hamlets; parliamentary sec. to treasury 1868–9; works commissioner 1869–73; judge 1873.
[7] Francis *Garden.
[8] On savings banks: Add MS 44748, f. 199.
[9] Sir A. *Slade, *Maritime states and military navies* (1859).
[10] G. L. *Wardle, *A circumstantial report of the . . . Charges preferred against . . . the Duke of York* (1809).
[11] *Electoral abuses considered, and a novel remedy suggested. By a defeated candidate* (1859).
[12] A. S. *Farrar, *Science in theology, sermons preached in St. Mary's, Oxford* (1859).
[13] J. F. D. *Maurice, *What is Revelation? A series of sermons on the Epiphany* (1859).
[14] C. Robinson, *Church questions. Practical methods for the arrangement of an abridged morning service* (1859).
[15] W. Rivington, *Church extension in the diocese of London* (1853).
[16] J. *Brown, *An exposition of the Epistle of Paul the Apostle to the Galatians* (1853).

5. M. X

Wrote to Duke of Somerset—Rev Mr Farrar[1]—Master of Mint—E. Card-well—T. Mainwaring—Bp of Moray—Lord Overstone—Scotts—R.J. Campbell—C.G.—Duchess of Suthd.—T. Turner—Hon A. Kinnaird—J. Iverach[2]—Dean Ramsay—The Queen—and minutes. Cabinet $2\frac{1}{4}$–$6\frac{1}{2}$. Stiff work: 1. on the Plenipotentiaries. 2. on the Estimates. I gained some points & lost more. We are in excess, & in fever. Saw Mr Slaney MP—Duke of Argyll—Mr T.M. Gibson—Earl of Aberdeen—Mrs Williamson: hope there[R]. Read Michiels on Austrian Government.[3] Worked on Sapphics from Heber![4]

6. T.

Wrote to Johnson Longden & Co—Mrs Stanley—J. Walpole Willis[5]—Mr Pearson—Mr Buchanan MP.[6]—J.W. Parker—Ld Palmerston—C.G.—Ld J. Russell—Dr Pusey—Duke of Somerset—T.G.—Ld Provost of Edinb.—and minutes. Saw Mr Laing—Mr Leeman—Lady Haddington[7]—Captain G.—Sir Thos Fremantle—M. Summerhayes[R]. Dined with the Fre-mantles. Worked on Wine papers &c.

7. Wed.

Wrote to Rev. E. Ffoulkes—Sir T. Fremantle—Mr Westell—M Summer-hayes—R. Cobden MP—Ld Palmerston—Count Guppi—Duchess of Sutherland—C.G.—Dean Ramsay—Sec. Statist. Soc.[8]—& minutes. Saw Mr Crafer—Mr Arbuthnot—Mr Milner Gibson—Sir W. Gibson Craig—Saw Williams 14[R]. Dined with the Rosses. Comm. of Cabinet $3\frac{1}{4}$–$6\frac{1}{2}$. Read Pasley on Mil. Policy.

8. Th. X [Trentham, Staffordshire]

Wrote to J.G. Hubbard—Rev W.M. Goalen—Mr Helmore[9]—and minutes. Cabinet 3–$4\frac{1}{2}$. Saw Mr Hamilton—Mr Stephenson—Ld Powis—Mr Laing —Sir G. Lewis. Saw Williamson: promise. Sought for Purchas & Nunn[R]. Off by Express for Trentham.[10] $9\frac{1}{2}$ & dinner & conv. till 12. Read Struthers on Scots Univv.[11]

[1] Adam Storey *Farrar, 1826–1905; fellow of Wadham 1855; divinity professor at Durham from 1864.
[2] James Iverach, published on religious topics.
[3] See 20 Oct. 59.
[4] See 28 Oct. 59.
[5] See 12 May 37.
[6] Walter Buchanan, 1797–1883; Glasgow merchant and liberal M.P. there 1857–65.
[7] Georgina, née Markham, m. 1824 10th earl of Haddington and d. 1873.
[8] William *Newmarch; see 19 Mar. 55.
[9] Thomas *Helmore, 1811–90; priest in ordinary to the Queen from 1847; precentor and hymnist.
[10] Trentham Hall, the duke of Sutherland's place in Staffordshire; the bulk of his wealth came from his estates there.
[11] J. Struthers, How to improve the teaching in the Scottish universities (1859).

9. *Fr.*

Wrote to C. Ryan (2)—Dean Ramsay—W.H.G. A morning of conversation —conv. with Count Lavradio on Congress[1]—Argyll resp. the Queen—Dss of S. resp. H.M.[2]—Dss. A. resp. Italy. Went to the gardens &c. with Mr Fleming.[3] Saw some of the books & MSS—Read Sack's Schottische Kirche.[4]

10. *Sat.* [*Edinburgh*]

Went to Minton's[5] forenoon—Out with Duc d'Aumale & the party in aftn—Saw Mr Harcourt resp. D. d'A.s son & Eton.[6] Theological conv. with Duchesses of S[utherland] & A[rgyll]. Read Sack Schott. Kirche—Mill's Political Economy[7]—Darwin's Origin of Species.[8] Off at 10 PM for Crewe 16 miles & on by Limited Mail to Edinbr.

11. *3 S. Adv.*

Arrived 7½ AM. Two hours of bed. St John's[9] mg: recalled much to me. Luncheon with Lady E. Campbell[10] then with D of Argyll to Dr Guthrie's Ch.[11] He came quite up to my expectations & his $\eta\theta os$[12] is equal to his power. Sat half an hour with him afterwards. Dinner at the Dean's. Much conv. with him & Mr A. Urquhart on the Scots Episcopal convulsions: we sat till midnight.[13] Wrote Minutes.

D 12. *M.*

Wrote to C.G.—Mr C. Cowan—Sir T.G.—Mr Westell—S. Herbert—Ld R. Cavendish—W.R. Greg—and minutes. Party to breakfast at the Dean's.[14] To dinner at the Lord Provost's.[15] Saw Mr A. Forbes Irvine[16]—Mr W. Forbes—Dr Guthrie—Professor Simpson[17]—Lord Neaves[18]—Dr J. Brown,[19]

[1] The abortive congress on Italy.
[2] She was mistress of the robes.
[3] The 'flea'; see 10 May 58.
[4] C. H. Sack, *Die Kirche von Schottland* (1844).
[5] The porcelain factory at Stoke-on-Trent.
[6] Aumale's son, never an Etonian, or, then in the fourth form: John Douglas Sutherland Campbell, 1845–1914; styled marquis of Lorne 1845; 9th duke of Argyll 1900; liberal M.P. Argyllshire 1868–78; his fa.'s private sec. 1868–71; governed Canada 1878–83; unionist M.P. S. Manchester 1895–1900. He m. 1871 Louise, Victoria's 4th da.
[7] See 7 Jan. 53.
[8] C. R. *Darwin, *On the origin of species by means of natural selection* (1859).
[9] Dean *Ramsay's church in Princes Street.
[10] Lady Emma Augusta Campbell, *Argyll's sister, m. 1870 Sir John *McNeill and d. 1893.
[11] Thomas *Guthrie, free-churchman. See 31 Dec. 49.
[12] 'charm'.
[13] The *Forbes heresy trial, which opened in Edinburgh in February 1860.
[14] i.e. Dean *Ramsay.
[15] F. B. Douglas.
[16] Alexander Forbes Irvine, 1818–92; clerk to the justiciary court; convener of Aberdeenshire 1862.
[17] See 1 Dec. 51.
[18] Charles *Neaves, 1800–76; judge of the court of Session and Lord Neaves from 1853.
[19] John *Brown, 1810–82; Edinburgh physician and essayist.

and others. Univ. Court 1–5. We started in life & chose the Curators of
Patronage:[1] W.E.G., Solr. General,[2] and Mr D. Muir.[3] Read Prof. Blackie's
pamphlets.[4]

13. T.

Wrote to Col. Biddulph[5]—Professor Balfour[6]—and Bp of Brechin at much
length[7]—and minutes. Moffat's Photogr. 11–11½. Bp of Edinb. 11½–12½
resp. the Brechin controversy. Observatory 12¾–2. Then to Holyrood—
Parl[iament] House—National Gallery (wh I enjoyed much) & Museum[8]—
Then China hunting! Saw Mr W. Forbes—Sol. Genl.—Sir D. Brewster—
Ld Provost—Sir W.G. Craig—Mr Black—Sir W. Dunbar[9]—Prof. Blackie[10]
—Sir J. M'Neill—& others. Up late with Bp of Brechin's affair.

14. Wed.

Wrote to A. Gibbon—D of Newcastle—Mr Dixon—Sir W. Heathcote—
Dr M'Donald[11]—and minutes. Saw Castle—Free Kirk Hall & College[12]—
Univ. Library Museum & apts—Bot. & Hort. Gardens[13]—Saw Dr Guthrie
—Dean Ramsay resp. Bp Forbes—W. Forbes resp. do—Dr Lee[14]—Lady
Lothian—Mrs M'Kenzie—Attended Curator's Meeting at Solr. General's.
Breakf party at the Dean's. Dined with Lady E. Campbell. China &
packing do & prep. for departure.

15. Th. [Hawarden]

After further commn. with the Dean & breakfast off at 9.30: Duke of
Argyll my travelling companion: we had much conv. We parted at N[orth-
allerton] junction & I reached Hawarden ab. 7½ & found all well but a
Telegram summoning me for tomorrow.

[1] Three of the curators, who appoint professors, were nominated by the Court, four
by the City Council. As Rector, Gladstone chaired the Court; rectors have not subsequently been curators.
[2] Edward Francis *Maitland, 1803–70; Scottish solicitor general 1855–8, 1859–62;
lord of session and Lord Barcaple 1862–70.
[3] David Mure, 1810–91; advocate; Peelite M.P. Bute 1859–65; judge 1865.
[4] J. S. *Blackie, probably University reform; eight articles reprinted from the Scotsman
newspaper (1848).
[5] Robert Myddleton-Biddulph, 1805–72; liberal M.P. Denbighshire 1830–2, 1832–4,
1852–68.
[6] John Hutton *Balfour, 1808–84; surgeon and professor of botany at Edinburgh
1845–79.
[7] Lathbury, i. 416. He was still trying to mediate.
[8] Museum of antiquities, then within the national gallery at the foot of the Mound.
[9] Sir William Dunbar, 1812–89; 7th bart. 1841; liberal M.P. Wigtown 1857–65; keeper
of Prince of Wales's seal 1859–65; auditor general 1867–88.
[10] John Stuart *Blackie, 1809–95; professor of Greek at Edinburgh 1852–82; the start
of a long friendship with Gladstone, see Add MS 44107.
[11] William MacDonald 1797–1875; physician and professor of natural history in
St. Andrews from 1850.
[12] Opposite the Church of Scotland assembly hall at the top of the High Street.
[13] At Inverleith; J. H. *Balfour their Keeper.
[14] Whose book he had reviewed, see 30 April. 49.

16. Fr. [London]

Wrote to Ld Palmerston—S. Holmes[1]—Col. Biddulph—C.G.—& minutes.
Off to London at 8. Arrived 3½. Cabinet 3½–6. Dined with S. Herbert. Saw
Ld Aberdeen—D. Newcastle—M. Summerhayes[R]. Read Parl. Hist on
Pitt's plan of 1785–6.[2] S. Herbert on Fortifications:[3] & Lord J. Russell's
drafts on S. Juan.[4] Much oppressed with cough & cold.

17. Sat. [Hawarden]

Rose late. Wrote to Lord J. Russell—Rev. Mr Neale—Rev Mr M'Coll—
W.R. Greg—Sir J. Coleridge—S. Herbert—R.C.N. Hamilton—G.C. Glyn
—Dr Pusey—Ld Palmerston—Sir G. Clerk—M. Summerhayes—Mr Cobden
—Mr Hamilton (G.A.)—and minutes. Saw Mr Galt (Canada)[5]—Mr Laing
(2): Mr. Jackson MP. Off at 4½ & reached Hawarden at 11¼ in bitter frost.
Read Debates on Fortifications in 1785–6.

18. 4 S. Adv.

Hn. Ch.mg. Read Corbet on Presb.Ch.U.S.—Inquiry resp. Septuagint[6]—
do resp. Religion & Philosophy.[7]—Milman on Love of Atonement[8]—
Mansell's Bampton Lectures.[9] Conv. with C. resp. Herbert. Considered the
case of M. Summerhayes[R].

19. M.

Church 8½ A.M. My cold better: frost intense: pr. not far from zero. Wrote
to Ld Wodehouse—S. Herbert (2)—G.A. Hamilton—C. Pressly—Rev Mr
Wayte—Mr WR Greg—Bp of Oxford—Lord J. Hay[10]—& minutes. Saw
Mr Burnett, on Stephen's matters. Visited the Coal Pit. Visitors arrived.
Read Greg on Taxation[11]—Revue Independante[12]—Ulrici on Shake-
speare.[13]

20. T.

Church 8½ AM. Wrote to M. Summerhayes—S. Laing—Sir T. Fremantle (2)
—Scotts—Rev R. Wall—Lord J. Russell—Ld Carlisle—Johnson L & Co.

[1] Samuel Holmes of Liverpool, spasmodic correspondent on politics; see Hawn P.
[2] *Pitt's bill to fortify royal dockyards was defeated by the Speaker's casting vote;
the cabinet, as in 1859–60, was openly split; see J. Ehrman, *The Younger Pitt* (1969)
i. 517–19 and *Parliamentary History*, xxv. 375, 1156.
[3] His cabinet paper, see 26 Nov. 59.
[4] Not found.
[5] (Sir) Alexander Tilloch *Galt, 1817–93; emigrated as railway contractor to Canada;
finance minister 1858–62, 1864–6, 1867–72; high commissioner in London 1880–3;
G.M.C.G. 1878.
[6] Possibly F. Field, *Vetus testamentum Graece LXX Interpretes* (1859).
[7] Untraced.
[8] See 24 Sept. 54.
[9] See 24 Oct. 58.
[10] Lord John Hay, 1827–1916, s. of 8th marquis of Tweeddale; admiral and liberal
M.P. Wick 1857–9, Ripon 1866–71; admiralty lord 1866, 1868–71.
[11] Advance copy of W. R. *Greg, 'British taxation', *Edinburgh Review*, cxi. 236
(January 1860).
[12] *Revue Indépendante*, i (1859).
[13] H. Ulrici, *Shakspeare's dramatische Kunst*, 2v. (1847).

—O.B. Cole—Govr. of the Bank—Rev Mr Rowsell—& minutes. Worked on Tariff. Visited Coal Pit. Dinner party & dance in evening. Saw Mr Burnett—Mr Thompson—Mr West—Canon Blomfield. Read Mill Pol. Economy—Ulrici on Shakespeare.

21. Wed. St Thomas.

Ch. 11 AM. Wrote to Lord J. Russell—Mr Ryan—Sir A. Spearman—S. Herbert—Provost of Eton—Mr Laing—Mr G. Harcourt—and minutes. Considered with a view to Wortley the question of my Secretariat.[1] Read Ulrici on Shakespeare. Worked upon & actually finished my translation in Sapphics from Bp Heber.[2] And so I bid to verse composition in a dead language a probably lifelong farewell. The frost broke up.

22. Th.

Ch. 8½ A.M. Wrote to Sir Geo. Lewis—Mr D. Mure—Sig. Lovardo—C. Pressly—Ld Granville—Mr Gurney—Miss M Watson[3]—Dean Ramsay—Jas Watson—and minutes. Saw Mr Darlington & had full conv. with him on the Coal Mine & Strata. Dinner party. Read La Hongrie et l'Autriche[4] —Bernard on International Law[5]: & other pamphlets.

23. Fr.

Church 8½ AM. Wrote to Dean Ramsay—Mr Ryan—Lord Palmerston[6]— Mr Pressly—Lord J. Russell—Mr Cobden—Ld Wodehouse—S. Herbert— Dr Cardwell—Sir Thos G.—J.G. Hubbard—and minutes. Worked on private accounts. Saw Wortley & settled with him. Read M'Culloch's Dictionary[7]—Mill's Pol. Economy and Ulrici on Shakespeare. Saw Mr Keats on Copper Coinage—Mr Hancock on the Mines.

24. Sat. Xmas Eve.

Church 8½ A.M. and 8 P.M. Wrote to Ld Palmerston—S. Laing—Bp of Oxford—A. Burnett—Duke of Argyll—Dr Jacobson—Dean Ramsay— Ld Hatherton—& minutes. Worked on various translations, finishing & copying out. Read Julian Fane on Hungary[8]—Ulrici on Shakespeare— Dined at the Rectory.

25. Sunday & Xmas Day.

Wrote to Mrs Walond—Mr Clifford—Mr Cobden—Lord J. Russell—Sir T.

[1] James Frederick Stuart-Wortley-Mackenzie, 1833–70, s. of 2nd Baron Wharncliffe; private secretary assisting Ryan Jan. 1860–5, though loaned to *Elgin; see 24 Mar. 60.
[2] For the *Translations*.
[3] Marion Watson of London to whom Gladstone sent donations (Hawn P).
[4] Untraced.
[5] M. *Bernard, *An introductory lecture on international law* (1859).
[6] On *Cobden, in Guedalla, *P*, 119.
[7] See 14 May 44.
[8] Unpublished; *Fane was then in Vienna.

Fremantle. Church 11 AM (& H.C.) & 6½ P.M. Read Mansell[1]—Scots Ch pamphlets—inquiry resp. Septuagint. Conv. with W. & S. on Ath[anasian] Creed.

26. M. St Stephen.
Ch 11 A.M. Wrote to Duke of Somerset—Sir G. Lewis—Bp of Oxford—Sir J. Lefevre—Bp of Brechin—Ld R. Clinton—Dean Ramsay—and minutes. Wrote on Fortifications.[2] Saw Mr Burnett—Visited the pit. We were all measured—in stockings or slippers. WEG. 5.10¾. C.G. 5.7¾. Willy 5.11⅛. Agnes 5.6⅜. Worked on Translations from Homer & writing out. Read Ulrici on Shakespeare—Page on Milford Haven.[3]

27. T. St John.
Ch 11 A.M. Wrote to Lord J. Russell—Lyttelton—Jas Pennethorne—Jas Watson—Rev R. Greswell—Sir C. Phipps—Ld Redesdale—Earl Powis—Dean Ramsay—Sir J. Graham—& minutes. Saw Mr Burnett & received from him a statement of the whole of Stephen Glynne's affairs. It is still somewhat an anxious & critical matter to consider them. Ld R. Cavendish came. Worked on translations & copying them out. Read Ulrici—Report on Public Monies.[4]

28. Wed. H.Innocents.
Church at 11 A.M. Wrote to Duke of Newcastle—Mr Ryan—Ld Brougham —Sir T.G.—& minutes. Worked on Translations & copying out. Worked on Stephen's affairs. And on arranging books. Read Ulrici—Le Pape et le Congrès.[5] Conv. with R. C[avendish] resp. A. Gordon.[6]

29. Th.
Ch. 8½ A.M. Wrote to Messrs. Overend—G. Burnett—Provost of Eton—C. Pressly—Mr Gibson—Mr Cobden—Bp of Brechin—Rev. C. Craven[7]—Rev. P. Acland[8]—& minutes. Worked on Translations: finished those from Homer. Read Ulrici—Subdivision of Exeter Diocese.[9]

Behold me then arrived at the close of half a century in this wayward world. Half a century! What do those little words enfold! Grace & glory, sin & shame, hopes, fears, joys, pains, emotions, labours, efforts; what a

[1] See 24 Oct. 58.
[2] Add MS 44748, f. 201.
[3] T. Page, *Report on the eligibility of Milford Haven for ocean steam ships and for a naval arsenal* (1859).
[4] *PP* 1860 xxxix.
[5] L.E.A. de la Gueronnière, *Le Pape et le Congrès* (1859), condemned by the Pope on 31 December.
[6] See 31 Dec. 59; his relations with *Gordon were not fully restored; see 21 Jan. 59 and *T.A.P.S.*, ns. li part 4, 32.
[7] Charles Craven, 1797–1877; vicar of Spexhall from 1847; published pamphlets.
[8] Peter Leopold Dyke Acland, 1819–99, br. of Sir T.D.*; vicar of Broadclyst, Devon, 1845.
[9] Untraced.

marvel is this life, what a miracle the construction of it for our discipline? And when will it end? When thou willest O Lord: Amen. But though I can say this, & can hope it is the truth of my heart, I have more than ever cause to hang down the head. More than ever have my besetting & peculiar dangers gathered around me during the past year. Yet as I think in a wondrous manner it has pleased the Lord whose eye slumbereth not to bring me in His own way towards a place of safety.

And what cause I have to be thankful! This morning came into my room my wife and seven children, all well, in body & in soul, all full of love. If God counts up His benefits what a reckoning it will be.

Yet there is in me a resistance to the passage of Time as if I could lay hands on it & stop it: as if youth were yet in me & life & youth were one.

But there are darker things than this: only I hope that the Image of the bound and stricken Saviour may hold me, and the desire never to bring the shadow of sin over the mind & heart of a fellow creature.

30. Fr.

Ch. 8½ A.M. Wrote to Messrs. Tatham—Scotts—Provost of Eton—Lyttelton—S. Herbert—R. Cobden—J.A. Smith—& minutes. Reviewing old papers especially poetry. Read Paper on Public Monies—Ulrici on Shakespeare.

31. Sat.

Ch. 8½ A.M. Wrote to Duke of Somerset—E. Cardwell—Treasurer L[ondon] & Y[ork] Co[1]—Mrs Goalen—Jas Watson & Smith—JG Hubbard—Rev. T. Russell[2]—Mr Ryan—Rev. G. Richards[3]—Mr Burnett, & minutes. A. Gordon came. Finished copying out my translations. Finished papers on Public Monies—&.

And so passes another year to the sum of time gone by.

[1] See 2 Jan. 60.
[2] Thomas Russell, presbyterian minister and missionary; Hawn P.
[3] George Richards, d. 1884; principal of Chester female training school 1845–51; perpetual curate of Tyldesley, Lancashire, from 1851.

Jan. One 1860.

Circumcision & S. after Xmas.
In bed most of the day with cough: no Church nor H.C. Read Tucker's Tracts[1]—Sion College Report[2]—Mansell's B. Lectures[3]—Life of Rev W. Jones[4]—Biddle on the Trinity.[5] Wrote to Ld J. Russell.

2. M. [*London*]
Up at 10.30. Wrote to Hn. Postmaster—J. Baillie[6]—Sir J. Lacaita—Mr Pressly—Bp of Brechin—Helen—Treasurer L[ondon] & Y[ork] (i.e. altered letter of Sat)—& minutes. Arranging papers—packing—& accounts. Attended rent dinner after cloth drawn & spoke. They will only just *endure* any word about ceremony. Off at 4½ for London. Reached Downing St at 11.15. Worked on papers & to bed by 2 AM. Read Suez Correspondence.[7]

I think the time is coming when great changes must be made in the Education Vote: and they will be the sharper, the longer an effective beginning is delayed, as the evil to be encountered swells with such rapidity from year to year.

On the other hand I feel the force of Ld Granville's opinion that these changes may best be made when backed by a maximum of authority, & that this we cannot have until the Report of the Commission[8]—on this account only very limited efforts can now be made & those only with great care.

Adverting to the three principal points on which we had fixed I think

1. That the adoption of a provisional resolution, for this is all we contemplate, in reduction of building grants, to operate until the Commn. shall have reported, stands wholly without objection & without any violent shock at present narrows the ground of future embarrassment.

2. That to extend the capitation grant to Scotland now, in opposition to our unanimous opinion, wd. be a great error. We may perhaps indemnify parties who prove that they have acted, for the next year, in expectation of it, if such parties should appear—but to adopt the grant in principle, while the Report of the Commission is pending, would lead to the greatest inconvenience. It seems almost absurd to start such a system in a country with the intention of probably or possibly revoking it after a year—and its existence in Scotland will seriously if not fatally prejudice any view adverse to it wh the Commission may take for England.

3. Looking always to the provisional character of our recommendations, I would rather have made some restrictive regulation with respect to the payments of pupil teachers in their first year, than have called at this time on managers for

---

[1] See 20 Feb. 47.

[2] 'Report of the committee appointed to inquire into the further union of the city benefices' (1859).

[3] See 24 Oct. 58.

[4] R. Rymer, *Memoirs of the life, ministry and character of W. Jones, late Wesleyan minister* (1842).

[5] J. Biddle, unitarian, *The apostolical and true opinion concerning the holy trinity* (1653).

[6] John Baillie, rector of Wivenhoe.

[7] See C. W. Hallberg, *The Suez Canal* (1931), 177–8.

[8] The Newcastle Commission on popular education: *PP* 1861 xxi.

voluntary contributions. For the latter though excellent is an important change in principle, & can hardly be adopted as a provisional measure—whereas the other is I think well suited to that character, for it need in no respect hamper our returning to a more costly arrangement in the improbable case of its being found needful. Nor could it operate very unfavourably in rural parishes, which are the chief object of anxiety, for in them there is nothing to compete with the pupil teachership at the age of 13. The State Endowment at such an age among the peasantry is like a pure gift & I think no great inconvenience could attend its[1] limitation or withdrawal by a regulation at once temporary and prospective. The populous places generally could bear the pressure, such as it might be.

I should very reluctantly acquiesce in the postponement of the whole matter of pupil teachers, inasmuch as the gigantic system on which we are proceeding is one that after a time unless *early* subjected to a gradual contraction, must end by exploding.[2]

3. T. [*Windsor*]

Wrote to Bp of Argyll—Duke of Newcastle—Mrs Gladstone—M. Summerhayes—Lady J. Russell—Lord J. Russell—and minutes. Saw Berkley—Mrs Pearsall: the deadly hue of consumption on her—she is much to be felt for[R]. Cabinet $1\frac{1}{2}$–$4\frac{3}{4}$.[3] Saw Mr Laing—Fremantle—J.S. Wortley who began today.[4] Off at 5.15 for Windsor. Interesting conv. with the Queen—& the P. of W. Saw C. Villiers—Sir G. Lewis—D. of Newcastle. Sat up till 2 AM with my letter to Ld J.R. about Italy & had an almost wholly sleepless night for it.[5]

4. Wed.

Castle prayers mg & St George's afternoon. Wrote to Sir A. Damaschinò—A. Gordon—J.S. Wortley—Mr Harcourt. Went over the Castle—Went to the Provost of Eton *in re* Duc d'Aumale.[6] Attended the delivery of the Victoria Cross. $2\frac{1}{2}$ hours with P. Consort a deux reprises about the Italian question, wh was largely stated on both sides. I thought he admitted so much as to leave him no standing ground.[7] Saw S. Herbert—Duke of Cambridge. Worked on Sav. B. Monies' Bill.

5. Th. X [*Pembroke Lodge*]

Castle Prayers mg. The P. Consort exulted in the Times Article on Italian

[1] 'temporary' here deleted.

[2] Signed and dated 2 January 1860, Add MS 44749, f. 1. For the annual grant system, changed to payment by results in 1861, see J. Winter, *Robert Lowe* (1976), 174.

[3] Gladstone supported *Russell's proposal to pledge help to France if Austria used force in Italy; Fitzmaurice, i. 369.

[4] As private secretary; see 21 Dec. 59.

[5] Urging swift settlement of central Italian question, which would reduce, not increase, probability of war; draft printed in D. Beales, 'Gladstone on the Italian question', *Rassegna Storica del Risorgimento*, xli (1954), 99–104; finished letter in PRO 30/22/19, f. 61, printed in K. Bourne, *The foreign policy of Victorian England* (1970), 347.

[6] A dispute between Aumale, Hawtrey and Van de Weyer: Add MS 44393, ff. 9, 120. See 10 Dec 59?

[7] See Gladstone's account to *Palmerston, in Guedalla, *P*, 120.

affairs (from S. Herbert).[1] Wrote to Dean Ramsay—Constantine S. Krokidas[2]—The Prince Consort—H.J.G.—J.N.G.—C.G.—and minutes. Back to town at 11.30. Saw Mrs Williamson: a new promise given[R]. Aunt J. (with Mr Jay). Went down to Pembroke Lodge & passed the evening with Lord John & his family. Ld J. & I had much conv. on Italy.[3] Read Booth on Taxation[4]—Suez Precis—finished.

6. Fr. Epiph. [London]

C.s birthday—God bless her. Went up from Richmond. Wrote to Ld Palmerston[5]—Mr Ayrton—Mr Cobden (2)—Mr Rigaud—Sir J. Lacaita— Mrs Walond—Dean of Windsor—C.G.—Col. Sykes—& minutes. Saw Mr Laing—Earl of Aberdeen—Scotts—Hampton resp. messengership.[6] Read The Rambler[7]—Azeglio's Droit Chrétien.[8]

7. Sat.

Wrote to Ed. Daily News[9]—Robn. G.—D. of Argyll—R. Cobden—Ld J. Russell—Dr Brown—Sir G. Lewis—Mrs De Pearsall—Bp of Oxford—M. Summerhayes—D. of Somerset—C.G.—Ld Ward—and minutes. Saw Beerseller's Deputation—M. de Persigny—Lord J. Russell—Wm. Gladstone—Mr Hammond—Mr Pressly. Saw a most interesting case.[10] Missed Hicks[R]. Read Droit Chretien (finished)—Rambler on the Pope's case— Macmillan's Mag.[11]

1. I for one agree in every particular with Lord Palmerston's paper:[12] except that I should not reckon, in the improbable event of a war, upon confining our share in it within narrow bounds.
2. It would be most illjudged of me to go over any part of his ground: but I venture to observe first that the principle which we are invited decisively to assert is a peculiarly English principle: secondly that the invitation, if it does not end so as to improve our relations with France, will probably end in serious injury to those relations.
3. I am under an impression, of which I have fully stated the grounds, to Lord John Russell,[13] that the letter which he read at the Cabinet on Tuesday last, recommending caution and procrastination, was written under an erroneous impression as to the *nature* of the proposal now apparently to be made to England.

[1] Second of a series on military organization; *The Times*, 5 January 1860, 7b.
[2] A Greek author.
[3] *Palmerston's note of his impending mem. on Italy arrived while Gladstone was with *Russell.
[4] H. *Booth, *Taxation, direct and indirect, in reply to the Report of the Financial Reform Association* (1860).
[5] On *Albert and Italy, Guedalla, *P*, 120.
[6] J. Humphreys, messenger to the chancellor since 1845, was retiring, succeeded by H. Gabbitas, probably the candidate of Hampton, the Gladstones' butler (see 22 Oct. 53).
[7] *The Rambler*, ii. 154 (January 1860).
[8] M. Tapparelli d'Azeglio, *La politique et le droit chrétien, au point de vue de la question italienne* (1860); documents.
[9] Not found published.
[10] See 14 Mar. 60.
[11] *Macmillan's Magazine*, i. 161 (January 1860).
[12] Of 5 January 1860 proposing 'common and united action' with France and Sardinia, in E. Ashley, *Palmerston* (1877) ii. 174 and Bourne, op. cit., 354.
[13] In his letter of 3 January 1860.

4. It does not appear to me that this proposal ought to involve of necessity any guarantee to secure the continuance of the state of things which may be established by the settlement of Central Italy, but that it may very well, should this be thought best[,] be limited to securing a clear stage for the settlement itself and for the free action of those who are to conduct it.

5. I cannot but think that the recent conduct and declarations of the Papal party throughout Europe, and particularly the declarations and threats in this country from the Roman Catholics generally to be governed in their conduct upon civil and domestic questions by our conduct if we presume to concur in any measure of interference with the Papal states (except of course keeping him by force upon his throne) constitutes something of a challenge to all Governments as such; and would, even if the case were doubtful which I hold it not to be, help to recommend a decisive and intelligible course.

6. I cannot avoid expressing especial concurrence with the sentiments of the Memorandum with regard to any possible danger to the Administration. The life of a Government can surely have no greater value than in the opportunities which it gives of hazarding it for the certain or probable promotion of adequate or worthy ends.

7. I have today obtained some information about Russian finance. I understand that the War cost her probably 100 millions; her debt is 400 millions; through accident or some other cause she has not got the whole of her 12 millions Loan subscribed. She has engaged herself heavily and extensively in *beginning* the construction of Railroads; and on the whole she seems bound in heavy securities to keep the peace.[1]

8. *1 S. Epiph.*

Quebec Chapel mg—Chapel Royal aft. Wrote to Ld J. Russell. Read Rawlinson's B.L.[2]—Alford Prolegomena[3]—Chr Rem. on Quakers[4]—& other Articles. Dined at the Admiralty to discuss the grave question coming on.[5] Made an unsuccessful hunt in Seymour Street.[6] Saw Williamson[R]. Saw Lord Aberdeen.

9. *M.* X

Wrote to Mr Hammond—Miss Watson—R. Cobden (2)—Robn. G.— Cesare Braico—H.J.G.—Duca di Caballino—C.G.—Sir J. Hogg—and minutes. Attended Ld Macaulay's funeral in the Abbey. It might suggest much.[7] Saw Comte de Persigny—Mr A. Munro—G. Humphries[8]—Mr Hammond—A. Kinnaird—Ld Shaftesbury—Lord J. Russell—Mr Pressly. Saw Hicks: searched Seymour St without success[R]. Attended Law

---

[1] Copy in unidentified hand, of draft by Gladstone, docketed by him 7 January 1860, Add MS 44749, f. 2.
[2] See 26 Nov. 59.
[3] See 17 Feb. 50.
[4] *Christian Remembrancer*, xxxix. 1 (January 1860).
[5] *Somerset had suggested this meeting on Italy to try to reach extra-cabinet agreement: Add MS 44304, f. 36.
[6] Off Euston Square.
[7] Described in this day's letter to his wife, Bassett, 127.
[8] Probably George Humphreys, London barrister.

Committee 2½–4. Read Indian Army Papers[1]—Chr Rememb. on Church Cause[2]—Smiles on Self Help.[3]

10. T.

Wrote to Ld Chichester—J.N.G.—Bp of Argyll—Mr Sketchley[4]—W.M. Goalen—S. Herbert—Aunt J.R.—Mr Cobden—Ld Ward—C.G.—and minutes. Began Comml Treaty Instructions.[5] Saw Mr Stephenson—Mr W.M. Goalen—Mr Laing—Sir T. Fremantle—Ld J. Russell—Ld Palmerston. Read Revue Contemporaine on French Navy.[6] Further vain search in evg[R].

11. Wed.

Wrote to Aunt J.—G. Burnett—Mr Cobden—Lord Ward—C.G.[7]—and minutes. Worked on Treaty Instructions. Saw Mr Gibson—Mr Hammond. 11–4 Conclave on the particulars of the Treaty. Read Nat. Rev. on Reform[8]—Letter to Wiseman[9]—Wine Duties Report.[10] Again searched: fruitlessly in the main[R]. Visited the Pearsalls.

Present Sir G. Lewis, Mr C. Wood, D. of Argyll, Mr Cardwell, Mr Gibson, W.E.G., Mr Laing, Sir T. Fremantle, Mr Pressly.

all wine in bottle at the 2/- rate—why not the silk trade—ascertain strictly the nature of the *ad valorem* regulations. Brandy duty. Urge 10/- as the best for British interests—If this cannot be had then 8/-—All this reduction may be immediate issue[?] in the Treaty—Reduce to 3/-—Reduction to 3/- immediately after Report of Resolution—Drawback of 2.9 to those who have complied with the Regulations.

Reductions on manufacturers to be instant—Power to make certain exceptions strictly to be such not to include brandy or silk, or wine, & not to exceed 2 years from 1st Ap. 60.[11]

12. Th.

Wrote to Mrs Davenport—Rev F. G. Lee[12]—V.C. of Oxford—[Anon.] Author of Letter to Card Wiseman—G. Harcourt—Rev F. Meyrick—Ld J. Russell—R. Cobden (2)—Johnson Longden & Co—Treasurer L.&Y.R.R.

[1] Post-mutiny reorganisation: *PP* 1859, 2nd session viii.
[2] *Christian Remembrancer*, xxxix. 80 (January 1860).
[3] S. *Smiles' classic, a best-seller from its publication (1859); see 19 Apr. 60.
[4] Alexander Sketchley, d. 1874; vicar of St. Nicholas, Deptford, from 1836.
[5] Add MS 44749, f. 5.
[6] *Revue Contemporaine*, xiii. 614 (January 1860).
[7] Morley, ii. 21.
[8] *National Review*, x. 215 (January 1860).
[9] 'The Pope, his rights and duties. A letter to . . . *Wiseman. By a Catholic layman' (1860).
[10] *PP* 1860 lxiii. 549.
[11] Notes on the 'conclave' on the French treaty; Add MS 44636, f. 19.
[12] Frederick George *Lee, 1832–1902; vicar of All Saints, Lambeth, 1867–99; advanced ritualist; involved in Order of Corporate Reunion (with Rome) in 1870s; joined Rome 1901.

Co—and minutes. Saw Mr Burn[1]—Duke of Argyll—Mr Gibson—Mr Hamilton. Reform Cabinet Comm 2½–5. Further search in vain[R]. Read Nat. Rev. on Kingsley—on Theodore Parker—on Foreign Office Architecture.[2] Saw the *Tableaux vivans:* at least one of them.[3]

£6[4]: Ld JR; WEG; Grey; Ld P agst. diversity but for uniform £8: will take £6, Wood; Granville; Gibson
£8   Boroughs: Lewis, C. Villiers.
   Only discussion: no formal vote.[5]

13. Fr.

Wrote to Baron Poerio—Ld Carlisle—C.G. and minutes. Saw Mrs Davenport—Mr Anderson—Mr Pressly—Ld Aberdeen—Aunt Johanna—Mr Gibson—Mr Laing—Mr Hammond. Cabinet 2½–5.[6] Read Western Bank[7]— Sketchley's Nk Lecture[8]—Inside Sebastopol.[9] Further search: null[R].

14. Sat. X

Wrote to Jas Watson—F. Goulburn—Mr Cobden (2)—Treasurer L.&Y.RR. —Duchess of Argyll—R. Lowe—S. Herbert—Bp of Brisbane[10]—Sir C. Wood—Rev Mr Hill—Willy—C.G.—H.J.G.—and minutes. Saw Earl Cowley—Mr Burn (F.O.)—Mr Laing. Further fruitless search: saw one, sad enough[R]. Read Inside Sebastopol—Deportment of Married Life.[11]— Rose's Diary.[12] Worked on paper resp. Fortifications.[13]

15. 2 S. Epiph. X

West. Abbey mg & Chapel Royal aft. Wrote to Mr Cobden—Mr Hammond —Mrs Williamson—Mr Stedman. Read Bp of Brechin's Answer[14]—Saint Bernard—Rawlinson's B. Lectures[15]—Robertson's Becket[16]—Deportment of Married Life. Revised Treaty Draft and Instructions. Saw one[R].

[1] Slip of the pen for John Brodribb *Bergne, 1800–73, superintendent of the foreign office treaty department (see 14 Jan. 60).
[2] *National Review*, x. 1, 144, 53 (January 1860).
[3] Probably the Chinese views at the Colosseum; Ellen *Terry read in the interval; *The Times*, 12 Jan. 1860.
[4] Notes on cabinet cttee. on reform; Add MS 44636, f, 21; £6 and £8 refer to rateable values as a criterion for franchise eligibility.
[5] Scrappy calculations on effects of this in Liverpool on f. 22.
[6] Report in Bassett, 128.
[7] Probably *How to mismanage a bank. A review of the Western Bank of Scotland* (1859).
[8] R. F. Sketchley, 'Notes on Newark. A lecture'(1860).
[9] Anon. account (1856).
[10] Edward Wyndham Tufnell, 1814–96; bp. of Brisbane 1859–75.
[11] [E. Stanhope], *The deportment of a married life* (1798).
[12] *Diaries and correspondence of George *Rose*, ed. L. V. Harcourt, 2v. (1860).
[13] See 22 Jan. 60.
[14] A. P. *Forbes, *Reply to the pleadings in the case of Henderson and others v. the bishop of Brechin* (1860); the heresy hunt.
[15] See 8 Jan. 60.
[16] J. C. *Robertson, *Becket* (1859).

16. M. X

Wrote to Robn. G.—Sir T. Fremantle—C. Pressly—Sir H. Storks—R. Cobden—Sir J. Graham[1]—Mr Kingsley—J.G. Hubbard—Earl Stanhope— & minutes. Comm. Cabinet Reform 3–5½. Saw Duke of Argyll—Mr Laing— Sir W. & Lady James—Saw Williamson[R]. C.G. came & we had a quiet evening. Read Prof. Simpson's Tracts[2]—Indian Army Papers.

Reform Comm[ittee] of Cabinet.[3] 1. arg. from tacit acquiescence in 1859. 2. If rejected then why abandon bill of 54? 3. Is the principle to be penal? Or is the transfer for enfranchisement? 4. The former will not stand—without much extension. The latter evidently points to a Schedule B. Ld J. moves that all

[schedules] A B.: Lord P., Duke of Argyll, Villiers.
[schedule] B only: Lord J.R. Granville, Gibson, Grey, Gladstone, Lewis, Wood. Lewis moves [schedule] B to take 1 from all under 7000 [population] (25 seats). Ld J. moves to strikes [sic] out County towns five. Aye: Ld J., W.E.G., Ld P. No: Argyll, Granville, Grey, Villiers, Gibson, Wood, Lewis.

Granville moved Schedule of Derby Govt. No: Ld J., Ld P., Duke of A., Villiers, Grey, Wood, Gibson, Lewis. Aye: Granville, W.E.G.

17. Tues. X

Wrote to Granville—Mr Cobden (3)—Borthwick—Sir T. Fremantle—Ld Palmerston—and minutes. Dined with the Jameses. Saw Williamson[R]. Saw Capt. Fowler[4]—Mr Bracebridge—Lord Aberdeen—Scotts—Mr H. Merritt. Read Indian Army Papers—Galt on Canada Finance.[5]

18. Wed.

Wrote to Mrs Dyke—Jas Watson—D of Newcastle—Rigby Wason[6]— S. Herbert—Mr Binger—Ld Brougham—J.N.G.—Rev W. Scott—Robn. G.—and minutes. The children came, all well D.G. Saw Sir T. Fremantle— J. Stuart Wortley—S. Herbert—do cum Col. James RE.[7]—Mr Laing— Mr H. Merritt. Attended Fine Arts Meeting: and saw afterwards Mrs Dyke & Mrs Stedman. Again I was baffled: but will not desist[R]. Read 'Select Tracts'.

[1] Arranging meeting to explain the French treaty, telling *Graham of 'the operation for which I have been living. I have seen in it not merely the increase of influence from a peaceable settlement of the Italian question, not merely the extension almost the consummation of the Tariff Reforms begun in 1842, but also the means of allaying the passions that menace danger, and of showing the fears which in my opinion have done us much discredit'; Bodley MS Film 128.
[2] Probably Sir J. Y. *Simpson, Anaesthesia (1849); essays.
[3] Add MS 44636, f. 23.
[4] (Sir) John *Fowler, 1817–98; railway engineer; cr. bart. 1890.
[5] Sir A. T. *Galt, Canada: 1849 to 1859 (1860).
[6] Peter Rigby Wason, 1789–1875; previously liberal M.P. Ipswich, prolonged legal action in 1860s on his 1842 disqualification.
[7] Sir Henry *James, 1803–77; director of topography at war office 1857; reformed ordnance survey mapping (Gladstone had reformed the dept's structure 1853–5); kt. 1860.

19. Th.

Wrote to Mr Cobden (Letter & Telegram)[1]—Sir E. Ryan—Ld Provost of Edinburgh—Mrs Williamson—Ld Chancellor of England—Rev H.P. Wright[2]—Hon. Sir C. Phipps—and minutes. Saw Williamson resp. Rose. Saw Brooks resp. China.[3] Saw Comte de Persigny—Earl of Elgin—Sir A. Spearman—Mr Arbuthnot—Duke of Newcastle—Do cum Sir C Phipps & Gen Bruce[4]—F.R. Bonham. Worked on Treaty & Revenue matters. Read Q R on gold.[5] Eight to dinner.

20. Fr. X

Wrote Mr Troughton—Sir A. Spearman—G. Burnett—Overends (2)—Mr Pressly—Sir T. Fremantle—Rev W. Scott—A. Beresford Hope—Mr Cobden—Earl Cowley, & minutes. Read Pamphlet on China. Saw Mr Hubbard—Mr Pressly cum Mr Dobson—Mr Gibson—Mr G.G. Scott— Lord Wodehouse. Saw Mrs Williamson—Turner and Watson X. Dined with the Herberts.

21. Sat.

Wrote to Ld C. Paget—Mr Cobden (Tel.)—do (Post)—Ld Granville—Mr Ayrton—Mast. of Balliol—Ld Prov. Edinb.—Incognita—& minutes. Dined at Granville's—Stafford House afterwards. Saw Ld A. Hervey—Sir G. Lewis—Ld Granville—Ld Palmerston—Mr Villiers—D. of Argyll—Mr Pressly cum Mr Laing—and Sir T. Fremantle. Cabinet $3\frac{1}{2}$–$6\frac{1}{4}$. British Museum $12\frac{1}{2}$–2. Saw Mrs Williamson[R].

Cabinet[6] Jan. 20 [sc. 21]. 60. French Treaty.
1. To grant 15° [proof] on wine if need be.
2. Not to give up the 2d on brandy
3. Not absolutely to insist upon further early instalments.

22. 3 S. Epiph.

Whitehall mg Chapel Royal aft. MS of 41 aloud at night. Wrote to Earl of Aberdeen—Earl Stanhope—Sidney Herbert—Lady Alderson[7]—Lady Bromley[8]—Earl Cowley (by Telegram). Read & wrote on the Fortifica-

[1] 'The prejudice or opinion against proceeding in the form of Treaty is strong. Two marked instances are before me today: Sir James Graham in a letter to myself and Lord Grey, whom Elgin has just seen. Do not suppose that I am therefore desponding or indifferent: although your necessary absence will be a great disadvantage, for Mr. Bright cannot supply your place, as what he says is received with an amount & kind of adverse prepossession which you would not have to encounter. But give me a Treaty carrying *bona fides* on its face (I do not have any doubt its being in the heart) and I have no fear of its fate'; Add MS 44135, f. 231.
[2] Henry Press Wright, 1814?–92; army chaplain 1846–76.
[3] Probably Brooks & Green, London auctioneers, on a china sale.
[4] Robert Bruce, 1813–62, *Elgin's br.; governor to Prince of Wales from 1858; *Phipps (see 17 Oct. 53) was treasurer to the prince, then up at Christ Church.
[5] *Quarterly Review*, cvii. 1 (January 1860).
[6] Add MS 44636, f. 24.
[7] Georgina, *née* Drewe, widow of Sir E. H. Alderson; she d. 1871.
[8] The wife of Sir R. M. *Bromley.

tions.[1] Saw Ld Aberdeen—Ld Abingdon. Read Wilson's & Rowsell's Sermons.[2]

23. M.

Wrote to Prince Consort—Overends—D. of Newcastle—H. Merritt— Resident Clerk F.O.—E. of Elgin—Sir A. Spearman—S. Herbert—Ld Palmerston—Ld Advocate—Mrs Williamson—and minutes. Saw Mrs Williamson[R]. Saw Sir C. Eastlake—Lord A. Hervey—Sir G. Lewis— Admiral Collier[3]—Ld Granville—Mr Pressly & Sir T. F[remantle] cum Mr Laing 1–4¾—Mr Laing *cum* Mr Anderson. Audit Commrs. at 2. Dined at Ld Palmerston's.[4] Went to see Granville afterwards. Read Gardner on Defences.[5]

1. Query retain the duties on all Spices, with Pepper? [The amount of duty recovered on spices is so small in each case that it is better to make them all free]. 2. List of Goods which will still be entitled to be warehoused [list sent to Mr Gladstone Jan. 26 (amended)]. 3. Query exempt corn only from the penny? [The penny duty will be made applicable to all Imports & Exports excepting Corn]. 4. Will there be any & what saving on Customs Establishments Estimates this year? [The Estimate for the year having been prepared, it is impossible to make any alterations. But if the contemplated measure be carried into effect, great reductions will be made]. 5. Plan to calculate the loss for the first financial year by reducing Tea to 1/3, also to 1/- [paper sent to Mr Gladstone 25 Jan.] 6. Likewise by reducing sugar at one step, *and* at two, to the minimum enacted in 1853 [paper sent to Mr Gladstone 25 Jan.] 7. Is the consumption of both increasing? & how much [paper sent to Mr Gladstone 26 Jan.][6]

24. T.

Wrote to Duc d'Aumale—Sir R. Gardner [*sic*]—Sir A. Spearman—Ld Carlisle—Rev E.J. Troughton[7]—Sir C. Phipps—Mr Fitzgerald—G. Burnett—& minutes. H. of C. 4¼–7½.[8] Bp of Oxford dined here to discuss Scots Ch matters.[9] Saw Mr Pressly—Sir Thos Fremantle—Mr Brand—Mr Laing—Rev Mr Simpson. Saw Mrs Murray—78 Tachbr.[10] Read Gardner on Defences—Lindsay on Shipping.[11] Worked on Treasury business.

25. Wed. Conv[ersion of] St Paul.

Wrote to Lord Cowley (2)—Mr Gibson—Ld Taunton—Mr Ayrton—and

---

[1] Report calling for further £11m. for dockyard fortifications: *PP* xxiii. 431.

[2] Probably Bp. D. Wilson, *Sermons and tracts* 2v, (1825), and T. J. Rowsell, *The English Universities and the English poor* (1859).

[3] (Sir) Edward Collier, 1783–1872; K.C.B. 1865.

[4] The Anglo-French treaty was signed in Paris at 2.00 p.m.

[5] *Political and legislative considerations on national defence: addressed to the people of England* (1860) by Sir Robert William *Gardiner, 1781–1864; soldier and courtier.

[6] Notes of talk with *Fremantle, with Fremantle's M.S. answers in [ ]; initialled and dated 23 January 1860, Add MS 44748, f. 189.

[7] i.e. J. E. Troughton.

[8] Queen's speech: *H* clvi. 80.

[9] The *Forbes heresy trial.

[10] Rescue case in Tachbrook Street, Pimlico.

[11] W. S. *Lindsay, *Our merchant shipping: its present state considered* (1860).

minutes. H of C. 12–2¼ spoke in reply to Fitzgerald on the Treaty.[1]
Revised it with Sir T. F[remantle] Mr P[ressly] & Mr Laing. Saw
Duc d'Aumale—Sir A. Spearman—Mr Bright—Sir F. Baring—Sir J.
Graham—(largely, on Loan Estimates &c.)—Duchess of Sutherland (evg).
My mind is relieved: I have now a standing ground & weapons in my hand.

26. Th.

Wrote to Sir H. Storks—S. Herbert[2]—Rev Dr Wolff—Mr J.S. Grubb[3]—
and minutes. House of Commons 4–9: and introduced my custody of S.B.
Monies Resolution.[4] Read Sir R. Gardner finished—and [blank] Saw Aunt J.
Saw Ld A. Hervey—Rev Mr Simpson—The French Ambassador[5]—Duke
of Argyll—Mr Hammond *cum* Mr Byrne[6]—Mr Milner Gibson—Mr Anderson. Saw Mrs Williamson: & others[R].

27. Fr.

Wrote to S.H. Northcote—Ld Somers—Mr Martineau[7]—Ld Warwick—
Mrs Goalen—Mr Cobden—Mr M'Coll—and minutes. Saw Sir T. Fremantle
—Mr Laing & Mr Anderson—Col. Talbot—D. of Argyll—Sir J. Graham—
S. Herbert—Sir A. Spearman. Saw Mrs Williamson[R]. Dined at Mrs
Talbot's: then to Stafford House. Finished Fortification Report[8]—Read
Parl. Deb. on Mr Pitt's plan—Also on his French Treaty.[9]

Committee of Cabinet on Indian Army[10]

1. That the native army should be officered on the irregular system. (Time for the
transition would be required.) 2. That the Indian Government in India should
be supreme over the whole force in that country: unless as to the regimental
organisation & government of the Queen's Imperial troops. 3. (W.E.G.) That if
there be a local army it should form a larger proportion of the entire force of
Europeans than was proposed by the late Administration (that was 2/5). Commee
Indian Council propose 4/5 nearly i.e. 54200 against 14600 in all = 68800. Force
before mutiny 15 m[ille]. In 1840 (ab) 9000. In the mutiny 24 m[ille]. Came home
12000. Present strength 13 m[ille]. 4. The native army to be officered by selection
out of the officers of the European force.

1. What appointments are to be retained by the Horse Guards? Favouritism
here? 2. How are officers in the extended Imperial Army to be appointed and
promoted? 3. Expense—Stanley's plan 180 m[ille] dearer than Councils plan.

[1] Delaying discussion of the treaty, not yet officially published in Britain: *H* clvi. 136;
see 10 Feb. 60n.
[2] Stanmore, ii. 281.
[3] Possibly Joseph E. Grubb, parliamentary agent, of Pritt, Sherwood etc. (see 28 Feb.
50).
[4] *H* clvi. 192.
[5] Persigny.
[6] Presumably a further rendering of *Bergne; see 12 Jan. 60.
[7] Perhaps James *Martineau, 1805–1900, unitarian minister and philosopher; but
their correspondence in 1867 does not suggest intimacy: Add MS 44412, f. 284.
[8] See 22 Jan. 60.
[9] In *Annual Register 1787*, ch. iii.
[10] Unsigned holograph, dated 27 January 1860; Add MS 44636, f. 27. See 2 May 60.

Imperial army 360 m[ille] dearer. 4. Tendency of Horse Guards to impose extra charges through the medium of the army upon Indian Revenues. 5. Is the local army to be confined to local service so exclusively that there shall be no title to claim it elsewhere in whatever circumstances of the Empire? 6. Arg. that a very large local army would be master of the Government.

28. *Sat.*

Wrote to Mr Cobden—S. Laing—Govr. of Bank—C.G.,[1] and minutes. Nine to dinner. Read Ann. Reg 1786 & 7.—Report on Col. Mil. Expenditure.[2] Saw Sir T. Fremantle—Mr Laing—Mr L. & Mr Anderson—Mr Fleming & Mr Small (Jute)—Sir J. Graham—Mr Bright—S. Herbert— Granville—Argyll—after Cabinet. Saw Mrs Williamson: & tried 29 S[eymour] Street myself in vain[R]. Cabinet $2\frac{1}{4}$–$4\frac{3}{4}$. Opened the remissions of taxes: with good effect.[3]

29. *4 S. Epiph.*

Chapel Royal mg & Marg. St aftn. Heard Dr Thompson: a striking preacher. MS of 46 aloud in evg. Conv. with C. Wrote to Sir T. Fremantle—Sir W. Heathcote—Mr Pressly—Mr Anderson—Mr Rowland Hill. Sketched slightly heads of [financial] statement.[4] Saw Lord Aberdeen: he sinks.[5] Saw Arthur Gordon. Missed Williamson[R]. Walk with C. Read Bp of Exeter's Letter[6]—Roberts on St Matthew's Gospel.[7]

30. *M.*

Wrote to Prof Walker[8]—Princ. St A. Hall—Sir J.E. Tennent: & minutes. The Herberts dined. Read Reports on Wine Countries. H. of C. $4\frac{1}{2}$–$9\frac{3}{4}$.[9] Saw Mr Laing—Sig Marliani—Gov. and Dep. Gov. Bank—Mr[S.] Morley & a Deputation[10]—Sir T. Fremantle—Mr Hammond—Lord J. Russell— J.N.G.—Mr Gibson—Ld Ward—Govr. of Bank (aft)—Granville—M. Tricoupé—Mr Brand.

1. It is requisite to devote to remissions in favour of trade & industry and consumption not less than 2100 m[ille].
2. The remissions chosen should be those which are in themselves on the whole beneficial. 3. If this is done the fund available for remission may be enlarged by the imposition of certain minor taxes.[11]

[1] Bassett, 129.
[2] *PP* 1860 xli. 573.
[3] Presentation of the budget to the cabinet.
[4] Not found.
[5] Slowly, see 21 Dec. 60.
[6] H. *Phillpotts, 'Letter on the Bill for legalising marriage with the sister of a deceased wife' (1860).
[7] A. *Roberts, *Enquiry into the original language of St. Matthew's Gospel* (1859).
[8] Robert Walker, 1801–65; professor of experimental philosophy at Oxford from 1839.
[9] Proposed select cttee. on packet and telegraphic communications: *H* clvi. 291; see 8 May 60.
[10] On silk duties, *The Times*, 31 January 1860, 9.
[11] With jottings of budget figures; holograph dated 30 January 1860: Add MS 44748, f. 194.

31. T.

Wrote to Mr Hammond (2)—Dr Guthrie—Rev Mr [J.L.] Ross—and minutes. Saw Sir T. Fremantle—Sir A. Spearman—Mr Julius Reuter[1]—Mr Gibson—Sir Jas Graham. Cabinet 1–4¼: very stiff. I carried my remissions but the Depts. carried their great Estimates. Shopping: saw Williamson & another[R]. Read Wine Duty Reports (finished) & Parl. Debates &c. on Mr Pitt's Treaty of 1786.

Wed. Feb. One. 1860.

Wrote to Anderson—Mr R. Hill—Mr Pressly—Mr G. Glyn—Jas Watson—Mr Brand—Ld J. Russell—and minutes. Saw Sir T. Fremantle—Mr Pressly—Mr Laing—Lord Brougham—Mr Glyn—Mr Arbuthnot—Sir A. Spearman—Baron de Cetto—Sir C. Wood—Count Persigny—Ld Derby (at Ld J. Russell's). Dined at Ld J. Russell's—Lady Palmerston's afterwards. Read Overstone Tracts.[2]

2. Th. Purification.

Wrote to Bp of Oxford—S. Herbert—Sir A. Spearman & minutes. H. of C. 4½–8. Eleven to dinner. Worked late & found with great vexation a new demand of 500 m[ille] upsetting all.[3] Saw Ld Palmerston 12–1½.[4] Sir T. Fremantle (2)—Mr Laing—Sir J. Lacaita—Mr Pressly—Mr Anderson. C. had news from Henry of his new attachment:[5] not quite what we could wish, & a great care to her especially because of her nieces.

3. Fr.

Wrote to Bp of Argyll—Sir J. Graham—C.S. Butler[6]—S. Herbert—Ld Kinnaird—and minutes. Unwell with cough headach sore throat & above all strife.[7] Cabinet 1¼–3½. A stiff fight: won in the main. Saw six deputations on various branches. Saw Mr Ellice—Mr Pressly—Sir T. Fremantle—Mr Laing—Mr Ryan: who has suffered very severely. Up late & early to bed: with an oppressed head & hard painful cough.

Deputations

10.15 am Feb. 3. 1860. 1. Lpool & Hull Chamber of Commerce—Sheffield, Hull, Gloucester, Leeds, Norwich—asks 750 m[ille] remission on small articles. Fruit trade: common figs. 12 to 15£ could be sold here at 3d—charge raised by duty to 5¼. Approve of French treaty.

---

[1] Baron Paul Julius de Reuter, 1816–99; moved head office of his agency to London 1851 and managed it there till 1878.
[2] S. J. *Loyd, Baron Overstone, *Tracts and other publications on metallic and paper currency* (1858).
[3] Set of new figures (marked 'Private/Night') in Add MS 44748, f. 196.
[4] On the postponement of the fortifications loan, see Guedalla, *P*, 123.
[5] Apparently an unsuccessful (or successfully foiled) attempt at marriage by H. Glynne to a Miss Lowder; see 14 Feb., 15 Mar. 60.
[6] Charles Salisbury Butler, 1812–70; liberal M.P. Tower Hamlets 1852–68.
[7] This illness delayed the budget from the 6th to the 10th.

10.45 am. Silk Coventry &c. Take off by degrees. Mr. Ellice[1]—did not believe in a Treaty—found duty was to be given up—without the *equivalent* of simultaneous admission of their goods. *Ribband* trade of Coventry the only one which will be injuriously affected by this Treaty. Requires the whole duty to compete with the finer class of goods. Difference of opinion as to immediate change—Great alarm & considerable excitement among the labouring classes of Coventry—Mr. Lynes[2] Pres. Chamber Commerce views proposed abolition with very great alarm—Mr. Browett[3] Pres. Assoc. Silk Manufacturers: The French set the fashions—we work them out 'in a manner suitable to the wants of our own people'. Some houses have competed with the French in the better class of goods—*many of these successfully*. The change will arrest progress—till we see what amount of damage we are to sustain—Raw silk very dear—even double what it has been. Have produced largely for the silk trade of the season. Parties to be relieved will not appreciate the benefit. Mayor:[4] 1000 looms out of work—meeting of operatives for Tuesday—Present range of the duty 15 to 17½ per cent—anticipates very gloomy times for Coventry for some months to come. Competition very severe—not a fortune-making trade—Swiss produce them better than we can.

Gloves 11¼. Mr Allcroft & others—Worcester, Yeovil. Effect of taking off the duty to throw all out of employment—The [blank] of gloves is extending largely— Duty about 14 per cent on the gloves that come in—Leather gloves wd. come from Naples—Belgium—Vienna. Mr Ensor—English trade at Yeovil & Worcester greatly increased within the last 20 years. Trade fell off after [18]26 when the first admission took place—gradual improvement from about [18]42—Employment now further than ever known—French have almost a monopoly in the finer kinds —our trade prospers by the lower & medium qualities which are kept out to a great extent by the duty: gloves from 6/– to 20/– a dozen—Great quantities will come in at 10/– per dozen. Duty at 36 per cent.[5] French wd have the same advantages in those.[6] French climate taste[?]—less smoke. Near Worcester wife plies the glove frame while husband bakes & washes in severe weather—sometimes. Gloves a second[?] manufacture as to the sowing. Clergy favour the manufacture. Unanimous in deprecating sudden removal. French bid up the Tuscan prices of skins against them. August or February the best time for a change.

All agreed on the general principles of Free Trade—Think their trade an exception. All admire the Treaty.[7]

4. Sat.

Sent for Dr Fergusson early who found the right lung somewhat congested: he gave me antimonial wine, James's powder in pills, more mustard plasters, and at night a hot water sponge coating round the chest wh proved very powerful. Wrote to Ld J. Russell—Mr Anderson—Saw Duke of Argyll, Mr Hammond, Mr Wortley, Mr Pressly: but this was more than was good for me.

[1] E. *Ellice, M.P. for Coventry.
[2] William Lynes, mayor of Coventry 1855.
[3] Henry Browett, ribbon manufacturer, mayor of Coventry 1856.
[4] Henry Soden, ribbon manufacturer and mayor of Coventry 1859–60.
[5] This phrase added in the margin.
[6] 'Americans buy largely at 10/– to 12/–', ibid.
[7] Add MS 44749, f. 38.

5. 5 S. Epiph.

Agnes & C. read to me. Saw Wortley and Phillimore: resp. this great mistake of Henrys. Dr F. again came twice & was satisfied. But *tomorrow* is physically impossible.

6. M.

Wrote to Overends—Johnson Longden & Co—S.R. Glynne—Ld Palmerston —Sir T. Fremantle—M. Michel Chevalier—Mr Cobden. Saw nobody but worked on letters & minutes. Read Virgil—Quintilian—and Tracts on Commerce. Saw Sir J. Graham—R. Phillimore.

7. T.

Saw R. Phillimore—Duke of Argyll—J.N.G.—Sir J. Graham. Wrote to Ld Palmerston.[1] Worked on letters & minutes—Also worked 3 or 4 hours on Budget at night. Appetite good. C. had more comfort & support respecting Henry's error.

8. Wed.

Wrote to Sir T. Fremantle—Robn. G.—Johnson L & Co—Scotts—Ld Palmerston[2]—Overends and minutes. Saw the Speaker—Duke of Argyll— Lord J. Russell—S. Herbert—Sir J. Graham—R. Phillimore—Sir T. Fremantle. Drove out with C. Dr Fergusson did not disapprove. Worked on my figures and papers. Read Mr P. Thompson's speech.[3]

9. Th.

Wrote to Ld Palmerston (2). Cabinet in my house but I did not appear. Saw D. of Newcastle, D. of Argyll, Lord John Russell, Ld Palmerston, S. Herbert, Milner Gibson—Secs. as usual—Mr Pressly to go over his part of the figures & plans. Dr F. well pleased. Did a good day's work upon the whole case.

10. Fr.

Saw Mr Anderson—Sir T. Fremantle—Secs. & Dr Fergusson as usual. Had to make changes in figures & finished all up. H of C. at 4¼. Spoke 5–9 without great exhaustion: aided by a great stock of egg & wine. Thank God. Home at 11. Saw Phillimore. This was the most arduous operation I had ever had in Parliament.[4]

11. Sat. [Stoke]

Saw Dr F. & came down at 11. Cabinet at 1½ to 3½. Off to Stoke[5] at 4:

---

[1] Guedalla, *P*, 123.
[2] *ibid.*, 125.
[3] Untraced.
[4] Budget statement, including description of the French treaty, that day laid on the Commons' table: *H* clvi. 812, Bassett, *Speeches*, 254; and Morley ii. 27 and above, v. xxxi ff.
[5] Lord Taunton's.

where we found a kind welcome & pleasant party. Saw Ld Granville—D. of Argyll—Jas S. Wortley. All my colleagues were most kind & everything looked hopeful. Arranging some papers: my affairs are in chaos after the break. Wrote to Messrs. Overend—Johnson Longden & Co—Robn. G— Duchess of Sutherland—S.R.G.—Earl Cowley—Scotts—C. Woods—Mr Hutt—Mr Brand—and minutes. Read Walsh's Essay—Bertrand sur les Dieux Prot.[1]

12. Sexa. S.

Ch mg & aft. Read Macmillan Feb.[2]—Woodward on Revision[3]—Dr Kay's Sermon[4]—Manchester Report.[5]

13. M. [London]

Wrote to Mr Horsman—Mr Christopher[6]—Sir T.G.—V.C. Oxford—H.J.G. —Ld Palmerston[7]—G. Burnett—Mr G. Wilson—& minutes. Left our kind hosts at 1¼ after conv. with Ld T[aunton] on I.I. & with Ld H Vane & Mr Merivale on Italy & Austria. Downing St in snow & great cold at 3. Saw Mr Moffatt—Mr Laing. SRG here: Phillimore dined: & we discussed the marriage. Worked on papers. Finished Sir J. Walsh. Read Robinson's Horace— T. Martin's do.[8]

14. T.

Wrote to Ld Palmerston[9]—Sir J. Walsh—D. of Newcastle—Mr Dunlop— Dean Ramsay—Robn. G.—Ld Advocate—Mr Healey[10]—Count Persigny— and minutes. Read[11] Maguire's Rome[12]—Rome et ses Provinces.[13] Saw Depns. Scots Spirits—English Spirits—English Wine Trade[14]—Mr Cook (City)[15]—Mr Wilberforce—Dr Fergusson—Earl of Aberdeen—Mrs Williamson. We conversed again on the unsatisfactory marriage: & S.s letter to Miss L. was concocted.[16]

[1] A. L. J. Bertrand, *Essai sur les dieux protecteurs des héros grecs et troyens dans l'Iliade* (1858).
[2] *Macmillan's Magazine* i. 241 (February 1860).
[3] F. B. Woodward, 'Remarks on [the] revision of the liturgy' (1860).
[4] W. *Kay, 'The influence of Christianity on the position and character of woman. A sermon' (1859).
[5] Untraced.
[6] J. S. Christopher of London had written to suggest govt. funds for telegraph research (Hawn P).
[7] Guedalla, *P*, 126.
[8] H. G. Robinson and Sir T. *Martin, both entitled *The Odes of Horace translated* (1844 and 1860).
[9] Guedalla, *P*, 127.
[10] Unidentified.
[11] Two words here smudged.
[12] J. F. *Maguire, *Rome: its ruler and its institutions* (1857).
[13] *Rome et ses provinces* (1860).
[14] Scrappy notes in Add MS 44749, f. 44.
[15] Perhaps George Cook, of Bradbury & Cook, wool brokers.
[16] See 2 Feb. 60.

15. Wed.

Wrote to S. Laing—Mr Oswald—Sir F. Baring—J.A. Wise MP[1]—Mr Farrer
—Mr Pressly—C. Wood—Mr Browne—C. Villiers—and minutes. C. went
to the marriage at Lpool.[2] Dined at Grillion's—Ld Ripon's afr. Read Maguire
on Rome. Saw Mr Farrer—Ld Elcho—Mr Brand—Mr Ridley[3]—Mr Laing—
Mr G.C. Glyn—Ld Palmerston—Bp of Oxford—Ld John Russell—Sir T.
Fremantle. Saw Lovell: & a widow[R].

16. Th. X

Wrote to Pr. Gholam Mohammed—Mr Glynn (2)—D of Newcastle—Mr
Hodgkinson—Mr Hankey[4]—and minutes on over 100 letters. C. returned
at night. Read various pamphlets. Saw Ld Granville—Mr Pressly—Mr
Horsfall—Count Persigny—Mr S. Laing—Duke of Argyll. Saw one[R].
Worked on proofs of Speech: to me the most irksome & annoying of all
occupations.

17. Frid.

Wrote to Sir S M Peto—Mr Crawfurd—Mr Gibson—Mr Th. Martin[5]—Mr
Clive[6]—Ld Palmerston—Mr H Brand—Mr Hammond & minutes. Worked
on proofs of my Speech. Saw Mr Whalley MP[7]—Mr Clay MP—Mr Laing.
The correspondence is now counted in hundreds of letters daily. Dined at
Lady Wenlock's.

18. Sat.

Wrote to Mr Baines[8]—Duc d'Aumale—Mr [blank] & minutes. Seven
deputations kept me till 2¾. Then Cabinet. Saw Mr Pressly—Sir T. Fremantle—Mr Laing—Sir J. Ogilvy.[9] and others. Fourteen to dinner—some in
the evening. Read [blank] Much exhausted: more so I think than if I had
gone to H. of C. Finished my proofs.

19. Quinqua. S.

Chapel Royal mg & St Andrew's W[ells] St aftn. No reading aloud. A day of

[1] John Ayshford Wise, 1813–70; liberal M.P. Stafford 1852–60.
[2] Next day, of Robert, s. of T. S. Gladstone, to Mary Ellen, da. of Robertson Gladstone.
[3] See 25 June 42.
[4] See 2 July 35.
[5] (Sir) Theodore *Martin, 1816–1909; parliamentary agent in London from 1846, poet
and biographer of *Albert and *Lyndhurst.
[6] George Clive, 1803–80; barrister; liberal M.P. Hereford 1857–69 (unseated), 1874–80;
under-sec. home office 1859–62.
[7] George Hammond Whalley, 1813–78; barrister and liberal M.P. Peterborough 1852–3,
1859–78; championed the Tichborne claimant.
[8] (Sir) Edward *Baines, 1800–90; economist and liberal M.P. Leeds 1859–74; owned
Leeds Mercury; abstainer and parliamentary reformer; kt. 1880; see B. ɪI. Harrison,
Drink and the Victorians (1971), 248.
[9] Sir John Ogilvy, 1803–90; 9th bart. 1823; Forfar landowner, liberal M.P. Dundee
1857–74.

peace & rest. Read Bracebridge's Vaudois[1]—Milman's fine Sermon[2]—Rowsell's Sermons &c.[3]

20. M.

Wrote to Ld Palmerston—H.J.G.—Conclave on Spirit Duties & sending off Mr Stephenson[4] $11\frac{1}{2}$–$1\frac{3}{4}$. Saw Ld Granville—The Speaker—Duke of Argyll—Mr Hodgkinson—Malt Deputation[5]—Licensed Victuallers Deputn. Then off to the House with a mezza oretta's[6] drive: and followed Disraeli.[7] Voted in 293:230 and home at one. Read Maguire.[8] The subject of debate haunted me till four.

1. To withdraw the mention of beer. 2. To withdraw the regulations for 'after midnight': (or apply them to *public houses*?). 3. To give the magistrates summary powers of withdrawal on grounds of police. 4. Strict limitation to eating houses. 5. To limit the rentals to say £25? in Parliamentary & municipal boroughs with population over 50000 £10 elsewhere. 6. All to be presented in a separate measure—Resolution to come after all the rest. 7. Eating houses to pay 10/– under £10 and 20/– over. 8. Reduce wine dealers licence from 10 g[uinea]s to 3 gs.
    W.E.G. At meeting of members of Cabinet & others.[9]

21. T.

Wrote to T. Edwards Moss[10]—Robn. G.—Mincing L[ane] Comm.—Sir R. Hill—Ld Palmerston—Mr Maguire[11]—Mr M. Chevalier—Ld Cowley—C. De Persigny—and minutes. H. of C. $4\frac{1}{2}$–$7\frac{1}{2}$ and $8\frac{1}{2}$–$12\frac{1}{2}$ following the debate.[12] Saw Dr Fergusson—Lord Palmerston—Mr Laing *cum* Sir A. Spearman—Mr Ayrton and others. Read Elden[?] on Ballot.[13]

22. Ash Wed. X

Whitehall Chapel mg. A remarkable Sermon from Mr Kingsley.[14] H of C. at 2. Palace for Council 3–$4\frac{1}{2}$. Saw Count de Persigny—Mr Pressly—R.

[1] C. H. Bracebridge, *Authentic details of the Valdenses, in Piemont and other countries* (1827).
[2] H. H. *Milman, 'Church extension in the British colonies and dependencies' (1860).
[3] See 22 Jan. 60.
[4] Sudden mission to ask France for 'a difference of 4d on behalf of the British distiller': Add MS 44749, f. 200; 44393, f. 136.
[5] The budget abridged the malt and hop credits.
[6] 'the best part of half an hour'.
[7] On *Palmerston's instructions; Guedalla, *P*, 128. *Disraeli moved the French treaty be taken before the customs acts cttee.; Gladstone's schedule excluded discussion of the treaty in principle (Guedalla, *P*, 125): *H* clvi. 1375.
[8] See 14 Feb. 60.
[9] Working out of details for the 'eating house' wine licencing scheme: see B. H. Harrison, *Drink and the Victorians* (1971), 248. Add MS 44749, f. 49.
[10] See 29 Sept. 25.
[11] John Francis *Maguire, 1815–72; liberal M.P. Dungarvan 1852–65, Cork city from 1865; wrote on catholicism and Ireland.
[12] On the French treaty: *H* clvi. 1475.
[13] Possibly Sir A. H. *Elton, *The Ballot, a conservative measure* (1856).
[14] C. *Kingsley, 'Why should we pray for fair weather?' (1860), on Matt. vii. 9.

Phillimore—Sir J. Johnstone—Mr Miller with *Cork* Manufr.[1]—Mr Crossley[2] —Duke of Newcastle—Lord J. Russell—Mr Barnes—Mr Roebuck and others. Wrote to Sir J. Shelley—Mr Ingham—Ld Brougham—Ld Ingestre —Mr Hammond—Ld J. Russell—C. de Kergoulay[3]—Mr Ridley & minutes. Saw E. Lovell: not all I cd wish[R]. Read Capps on N. Debt.[4]

23. Th.

Wrote to Bp of Oxford[5]—Messrs. Betts[6]—Ld Brougham—Sir R. Hill— & minutes. Saw Irish Newsp. Deputn.—Ld Fermoy[7]—Sir H. Cairns—M. de Persigny—Governor of the Bank—Count Lavradio—and others. Caledonian Canal Commee. at $12\frac{1}{4}$. Levee at 2. H of C. $4\frac{1}{2}$–7 and $8\frac{1}{2}$–$12\frac{1}{4}$.[8] Read Bartholony.[9]

24. Fr.

Wrote to C. Paget MP—J.W. Parker—E. Baines MP—Mr S. Bright—Mr Davy MP.[10]—G. Burnett—Mr Berkeley MP—Ld Cowley—A. Tennyson— Robn. G.—T.E. Moss & minutes. Saw Mr J.H. Parker—Mr Stephenson— Mr Mowbray Morris[11]—Mr Laing—Mr Hammond. Conclave at $2\frac{1}{2}$ to settle the Spirit duties. H of C. $4\frac{1}{2}$–$5\frac{1}{2}$ and $8\frac{3}{4}$–$2\frac{1}{2}$. Spoke $1\frac{1}{4}$ h in the debate: & greatly rejoiced in the division of 339:223.[12] Read [blank] and to bed at four.

25. Sat.

Wrote to Ld Howden[13]—Provost of Eton—J.C. Ewart—Ld Wodehouse— Mr Cogan[14]—Mr Tomlinson—and minutes. Sir T. Fremantle & Mr Laing $11\frac{1}{4}$–1. Cabinet $2\frac{3}{4}$–5. Saw Aunt J. & made various inquiries. Dined with the De Greys. Lady Waldegrave's party afterwards. Read Maguire.[15]

[1] Taverner John Miller, tory M.P. Maldon 1852–3, Colchester 1857–67; the budget reduced the cork duty from 1861, producing much complaint from Irish and British cork makers.
[2] (Sir) Francis *Crossley, 1817–72; Halifax carpet manufacturer, benefactor and liberal M.P. there 1852–59, for Yorkshire county seats from 1859; cr. bart. 1863.
[3] Louis Gabriel César, comte de Kergoulay, 1804–88; French industrialist and legitimist politician.
[4] E. Capps, *The national debt financially considered* (1859).
[5] In Wilberforce, ii. 440.
[6] Probably Thomas Betts & co., London brandy distillers; the budget hit hard at British brandy makers.
[7] Edmund Burke Roche, 1815–74; liberal M.P. Cork 1837–55, Marylebone 1859–65; cr. Baron Fermoy 1856.
[8] Answered questions: *H* clvi. 1566.
[9] F. Bartholony, *Simple exposé de quelques idées financières et industrielles* (1860).
[10] Richard Davey, 1799–1884; liberal M.P. W. Cornwall 1857–68.
[11] Mowbray Morris, 1819–74; managed *The Times* 1848–73; Gladstone was probably inquiring of the accuracy of a report of *Disraeli's speech on hops which Gladstone ridiculed this evening (*H* clvi. 1783).
[12] He announced the Cabinet decision on the spirit duties and defended his tax balance: *H* clvi. 1779.
[13] John Hobart *Caradoc, 1799–1873; 2nd Baron Howden 1839; soldier and retired ambassador.
[14] William Henry Ford Cogan, 1823–94, liberal M.P. Kildare 1852–80.
[15] See 14 Feb. 60.

26. 1 S. Lent.

Whitehall Chapel mg & aft. Saw Ld Aberdeen (with Sir J. Graham)—Sir James Lacaita. Reviewed Addl. Article.[1] Wrote to Ld Cowley—Mr Mac-Culloch. Worked on amending various Resolutions. Read Poems &c. resp. Rich. 2d & the Lollards' time.[2] Roberts on St Matthews Gospel.[3]

27. M.

Wrote to Dr Fergusson—Sir J. Ogilvy—W. Grogan—Hastings Russell—J. Murray—Sir J. Ogilvy [sic]—T.M. Gibson—Sir T. Fremantle—J.N.G.—& minutes. Saw Rectif. Distillers—Wine Trade of U.K. Saw Mr Pressly—Sir T. Fremantle—Mr Laing. H of C. 4½–12 working the Resolutions on Wine.[4] Read Pamphlets.

28. T.

Wrote to Mr Pressly—Earl Cowley—Ld Brougham—Mr Cobden—A.V. Tempest—S. Bright—Lpool W.I. Assocn.—various MPs—& minutes. Wrote Statement of the case of Wine Drawbacks.[5] Saw Mr Childers MP— Mr G. Burnett—Mr Mure—Ld Brougham—Sir J. Graham—Govr. of the Bank—Operative Cork Cutters—Baron L. Rothschild—H. of C. 4½–5: and 7–12½ on Trade Resolutions. Duncombe tonight, as Milnes last night, helped us by his mismanagement.[6] Read Army Purchase.[7]

29. Wed. X

Wrote to Rev D Morgan[8]—Duchess of Sutherland—Editor of the Guardian[9]—Ld Cowley—C. Pressly—Telegr. to do—Mr Cowell[10]—D. Taylor & Son[11]—M.J. Barry[12]—Sir G.C. Lewis—Lt Rogers[13]—Robn. G.—& minutes. Saw Mr Laing—Mr Briscoe—Ld Wodehouse—Mr James—Mr Fortescue— Mr Hadfield—Mr Dalgleish[14]—Mr Ward—Saw Turner—Lovell[R]. Dined at Count Bernstorff's. H of C. 12–1.[15] Read on Army Purchase.

[1] On foreign wine duties, introduced next day; see Add MS 44749, f. 17.
[2] *Political poems and songs relating to English history . . . from the accession of Edward III to that of Richard III*, ed. T. Wright, 2 v. (1859–61).
[3] See 29 Jan. 60.
[4] *H* clvi. 1842.
[5] Add MS 44749, f. 65.
[6] *Milnes and *Duncombe proposed amdts. to the Customs Acts Bill, the former withdrew, the latter was defeated, both outmanoeuvred by Gladstone: *H* clvi. 1874, 2002.
[7] *The Army Purchase Question, and report and minutes of evidence of the Royal Commission considered* (1858).
[8] Probably David Foscue Morgan, b. 1807?, Queens', Cambridge; vicar of St. Mary's, Leamington, 1852–6, chaplain at Mentone 1868–72.
[9] Martin Richard Sharp, 1819–89; ed. *The Guardian* 1859–83. Unpublished, unless that by 'Oxonian' supporting *Jacobson's compromise on the theological statute; *Guardian*, 7 March 1860, 216.
[10] John Wellsford Cowell had sent his book on Froissart; see Add MS 44393, f. 181.
[11] Daniel Taylor and sons, London wine merchants.
[12] Michael Joseph Barry, Irish writer, had sent a pamphlet on the papacy and Italy.
[13] Unidentified.
[14] Robert Dalgleish, 1808–80; liberal M.P. Glasgow 1857–74.
[15] Masters and Operatives Bill: *H* clvi. 2010.

Thurs. Mch One. 60.

Wrote to Sir T. Tancred—Mr Laing—V.C. of Oxford—Mr Pressly—Ld
Palmerston—Mr Byng—Mr Dalgleish—Mr Norris[1]—Mr Maguire—Letters
to MP.s—Ld Prov. Edinbro—and minutes. Saw Master Cork Cutters.[2]
Saw Sir Thos Fremantle—Mr Pressly—Mr Laing—Walk with C. H of C. 4½–
6 and 8–1½–1½ [sic] working the Customs Resolutions.[3] Read Fraser's
Magazine Mch.[4]

2. Fr.

Wrote to Ld Clancarty—Mr G. Moffatt—Sir W. Miles: letters to MP.s and
worked hard upon minutes to get down my arrears: pr[obably] 300? H of C.
4¾–12½ working Customs Resolutions.[5] Saw Paper Hangings Depn.—Paper
Makers do—Stationers' do.[6] Saw Mr Laing—M. De Persigny—Mr Grogan.
Drive with C.

3. Sat. [Brighton]

Wrote to Rev. J.L. Ross—Sir W. Heathcote—Sir G. Lewis—M. de Persigny
—Mr Burnett—Dean Ramsay—Mr Laing—Mr Cardwell—and minutes
over 100. Left Downing St 11.20 reached Brighton 1.50—we live with the
De Tableys & lodge close by.[7] Much walking & sea: also visited the China
Shops. Read Cumberworth[8]—Barry's Romagna.[9]

4. 2 S. Lent.

St George's (Mr North)[10] and H.C. mg. St Paul's aft. Walk with C. Read
Cumberworth (finished)—Cardross Case[11]—Life of Beato Angelico[12]—
Roberts on St Matthew's Gospel.[13]

5. M. [London]

Spent the forenoon in the air—saw Ld Ashburton: Also poor Granville at
his door unawares.[14] Packed up & off at 1.30 for London. Saw M. De Per-

[1] John Thomas Norris, 1808–70; Oxfordshire paper manufacturer and liberal M.P.
Abingdon 1857–65.
[2] Notes of interview in Add MS 44749, f. 54.
[3] Following introduction of English and Scottish Reform Bills: *H* clvi. 2099.
[4] *Fraser's Magazine*, lxi. 301 (March 1860); *Levi on the budget.
[5] Abolishing duties: *H* clvi. 2099.
[6] Declarations in Add MS 44749, f. 164.
[7] They owned 5 Norfolk Terrace, Brighton.
[8] F. E. Paget, *The curate of Cumberworth and the vicar of Roost. Tales* (1859).
[9] M. J. Barry, *The Pope and the Romagna* (1860).
[10] Jacob Hugo North, 1812?–84; perpetual curate of St. George's chapel, Brighton,
1851–77; rector of White Roding from 1877.
[11] R. Buchanan, *Christ and Caesar; or, the Cardross case viewed in the light of God's word*
(1860).
[12] Perhaps G. Vasari, *The life of Giovanni Angelico da Fiesole* in his *Lives* tr. G. A.
Bezzi (1850).
[13] See 29 Jan. 60.
[14] *Granville's first wife, *Acton's mother, long an invalid, d. 14 March.

signy—Mr Laing—Ld Henniker[1]—Mr Adderley, & others. H. of C. 4¾-7½ and 8-11 working Resolutions & S[avings] B[ank] Monies Bill.

6. T.

Wrote to Baron L Rothschild—Rev J.L. Ross—Mr Dodson (2)—Mr Locke —Rev Mr Trevor—Mrs Peel—Mr Holland MP[2]—Mr Whatman—Mr MacCurty[3]—Mr Clay MP. and Wads of Minutes. Cabinet 1-3. Duke of Cambridge present: he fought his battle well.[4] Saw D. of N. with C. Wood— Saw Hop Deputation—Mr Pressly—Sir T. F[remantle]—& Mr Laing. Evening's work at home.

7. Wed.

Wrote to Ld Palmerston—Sir T. Fremantle—Mr Dodson MP—Rev Mr Harvey—Mr Shaw—Mr Brand—Mr Horsfall—Mr Turner—Mr Garnett[5] and minutes. 11-4 Conclave on the new Charges in Customs & Excise.[6] Saw Duke of Argyll—Mr Hubbard—Baron L. Rothschild—R. Phillimore— Dined at D. of Argyll's. Conv. on Henry's matters.

8. Th.

Wrote to Ld Chancellor—Ld Elgin—Mr Pressly—Mr Grogan—and minutes. H. of C. 4½-7½ and 8-12¼ on [French] Treaty Debate.[7] Read Smiles on Self Help. Saw Mr Laing—Ld Elgin—Sir S. Northcote—Mr Burnett—S.R.G. & L[yttelto]n resp. H.G.—Ld Chancr. & Att. Gen with Ld Palmerston on Art. XI.[8] Museum Meeting at 1.30.

9. Fr.

Wrote to Messrs. Fearon & Co.[9]—J.C. Ewart MP—Master of Mint—E. Lovell—and many minutes. Further conclave 11¼-3¼ on the New Minor Taxes, Wine Drawbacks, and Wine Licensing. Saw R. Phillimore—Sir T. Fremantle—Mr Hadfield MP—Mr Dillwyn MP[10]—Mr Bright MP & others. C. after a consultation went to Lady and *Lord* P. about the Episcopal vacancy: *not* however to recommend.[11] H of C. 4½-8 and 8½-1½. Spoke on

[1] John Henniker–Major, 1801–70; 4th (Irish) Baron Henniker 1832; tory M.P. E. Suffolk 1832–47, 1856–66 when cr. Baron Hartismere.
[2] Edward Holland, 1806–75; liberal M.P. E. Gloucestershire 1855–68.
[3] *H* clvi. 2236.
[4] *Cambridge opposed, unsuccessfully, cabinet acceptance of *Somerset's commission's report to stop purchase at the rank of major; Royal Archives, E. 12/43.
[5] William James Garnett, 1818–73; barrister and Peelite M.P. Lancaster 1857–64.
[6] Record of it in Add MS 44749, f. 26 and see *H* clvii. 218 (9 March 1860).
[7] *H* clvi. 121.
[8] The tories denounced article xi of the French treaty, which allowed coal exports to France without the approval of a specific Resolution: *H* clvii. 175; see Guedalla, *P* 127, 130.
[9] Henry B. Fearon & son, London wine merchants.
[10] Lewis Llewelyn Dillwyn, 1814–92; Swansea pottery manufacturer and liberal M.P. there from 1855.
[11] The bpric. of Rochester, vacant by the d. of G. Murray; J.C. *Wigram (see 8 May 34) was appt. on 7 April.

various matters and in the Treaty Debate. Voted in 282:56; a most prosperous ending to a great transaction in wh I heartily thank God for having given me a share.[1] Saw M. de Persigny in leaving. Read Smiles.

10. Sat. [Cliveden]

Wrote to Ld Cowley—Mr Pressly—Ld Wodehouse—Mr L. Levi[2]—Mr Taunton—Mr O. Ricardo[3]—Rev J. Aspinall[4]—Robn. G.—Ld J. Russell—J. Locke MP.—Sir A. Spearman: & minutes. Saw R. Phillimore & had another family consultation on the H. G[lynne] matter. Saw Rev Mr Heygate—Cabinet at 3 PM. Off to Cliveden at 4.50. Read Macaulay's Biographies.[5]

11. 3 S. Lent.

Boyne Hill Ch mg. Eton afternoon. Saw Stephy: Conv. on Prayer for the Dead with the Duchess [of Sutherland]. Read Memoir of Mr Cook:[6] and Roberts on St Matthew.[7]

12. M. [London]

Worked on papers resp. Paper Duty. Returned to town by $1\frac{1}{2}$ train. H. of C. $4\frac{1}{2}$–7 and $7\frac{1}{2}$–2. Spoke in the Debate and voted in 245:192 for repeal.[8] Read Macaulay's Biographies. Wrote minutes.

13. T.

Wrote to Mr Maguire & minutes. Saw Silk Weavers Deputn.—Wine Trade Deputation—Beer Sellers Deputation—Mr Tricoupé—D. of Newcastle—Mr Horsfall—Mr Vivian[9]—Mr Bazley[10] and others. Saw H. Glynne at Lady Wenlocks: much pulled & worn. Read Maguire's Rome[11] & public papers. H. of C. $4\frac{1}{2}$–7.[12]

14. Wed.

Wrote to Ld Brougham—Sir G.C. Lewis (2)—Mr Gibson and minutes. H.

---

[1] *H* clvii. 309.

[2] Leone *Levi, 1821–88; Liverpool merchant, statistician and professor at King's, London, from 1852; sent copy of his paper, 'Revenue of the United Kingdom': Add MS 44393, f. 189; see 1 Mar. 60n.

[3] Osman Ricardo, 1795–1881, s. of D.*; liberal M.P. Worcester 1847–65.

[4] James Aspinall, 1797?–1861; rector of Althorpe, Lincolnshire, from 1839; published sermons.

[5] *Biographies of Lord *Macaulay contributed to the Encyclopaedia Britannica* (1860); with anon. memoir.

[6] W. E. Heygate, *Memoir of J. A. Cook* (1860).

[7] See 29 Jan. 60.

[8] *H* clvii. 421.

[9] (Sir) Henry Hussey *Vivian 1821–94; metal smelter and liberal M.P. Truro 1852–7, Glamorgan 1857–85, Swansea 1885–93; cr. bart. 1882, 1st Baron Swansea 1893.

[10] (Sir) Thomas *Bazley, 1797–1885; Bolton cotton merchant and free trader; liberal M.P. Manchester 1858–80; cr. bart. 1869.

[11] See 14 Feb. 60.

[12] Italian Blue Book: *H* clvii. 449.

of C. 12–1½ on Religious Worship Bill.[1] Meeting of Peers for French Treaty Debate 1½–3¼.[2] Revenue Conclave 3½–6. Saw Mr Laing—Ld Shaftesbury—Count de Persigny. Dined at Lady Molesworth's.[3] Read Macaulay's Lives. Began Dft reply to Lavradio for F.O.[4] Saw the case of Jany. 7[R].

15. Th.

Wrote to Ld J. Russell—Mr Scholefield—Ld Wodehouse—Mr Maguire—Bp of Salisbury—Sec. Carlton Club[5]—Mr Cornwall Legh—and minutes. Read Macaulay's Johnson & Bunyan. Finished draft or sketch to Count Lavradio. Consultation resp. the Lowder marriage: much offended with the L. letters.[6] H. of C. 4½–5 and 8–12: working Customs' Committee. The Opposition played foul on Hops.[7] Saw Mr Laing—Mr Barnes MP: & others.

16. Fr.

Wrote to Sir G. Lewis—Mr Woodgate—C. Villiers—Mr Anderson—Overends—D of Argyll—Mr Mitford[8]—M.P.s (signed)—Col. Talbot—and minutes. Finished Macaulay & Black's Memoir.[9] Saw Mr Anderson—Sir A. Spearman—Mrs Stewart 78. T[achbrook] St—Mrs Vincent Brewer St[R]—Mr Pressly—Mr F. Hill[10]—Mr Kingscote MP.[11]—Mr Childers MP.[12]—Mr Brand (Registration Soc) —H of C. 4½–7¾ and 10¼–1.[13]

17. Sat.

Wrote to Mr Gibson—MPs for Coventry[14]—V.C. Oxford—Rev Mr Ross—Earl of Devon—Mr Headlam[15]—Duke of Marlborough—and minutes. Cabinet 3½–6. Mr Laing on Customs New Charges. Saw Duc d'Aumale—Baron L. de Rothschild—Sir R. Peel—R. Phillimore resp. H. G[lynne]—The Earl of Aberdeen. Read Maguire's Rome. Worked on papers.

[1] In argument with Lord R. *Cecil on Jews: *H* clvii. 522.
[2] To explain details to them for next day's deb.: figures in Add MS 44749, f. 57.
[3] See Hewett, 162.
[4] Great length: Add MS 44749, f. 80.
[5] W. Rainger; reported as letter resigning from the club; *The Guardian*, 28 March 1860, 283; see 29 Mar. 60.
[6] See 2 Feb. 60.
[7] Attempting to delay business: *H* clvii. 701.
[8] William Townley Mitford, 1817–89; tory M.P. Midhurst 1859–74.
[9] See 10 Mar. 60.
[10] Perhaps Frederic Hill, 1803–96; prison inspector and 1851–75, assistant sec. to Post Office; an early suffragist.
[11] (Sir) Robert Nigel Fitzhardinge *Kingscote, 1830–1908; soldier, courtier and liberal M.P. Gloucestershire 1852–89; court office 1859–66; K.C.B. 1889.
[12] Hugh Culling Eardley *Childers, 1827–96; in Australia 1851–7; liberal M.P. Pontefract 1860–85; financial sec. to treasury 1865–6; first lord 1868–71; chancellor of duchy 1872–3; war sec. 1880–2; at exchequer 1882–5; home sec. 1886; devoted Gladstonian; see Add MS 44128–32.
[13] Supply for China: *H* clvii. 766.
[14] E. *Ellice and Sir J. *Paxton.
[15] Thomas Emerson *Headlam, 1813–75; liberal M.P. Newcastle 1847–74; judge advocate general 1859–66.

18. 4 S. Lent.

Chapel Royal mg & aft. Saw Duchess of Sutherland. Saw R. Phillimore twice & we were occupied about the delay of H.G.s marriage. Saw Sir J. Lacaita. Wrote to Rev. Dr. [J.] Robertson—Sir S. Northcote—Rev. Geo. Williams[1]—Rev. F.C. Massingberd.[2] Read Rowsell's Sermons—Curling's Do[3]—L. Davies's Do (Atonement &c).[4]

19. M. X

Wrote to Rev. Mr Gresswell—Ld E. Bruce MP.—Ld Ebury—Mr Briscoe MP.[5]—Mr Kingcote—Mrs [B.] Oliveira—Mr Liddell MP.—Ld Palmerston & minutes. Temperance Deputation at 2: debate of $1\frac{1}{2}$ hour.[6] Saw Col. Wilson Patten—Sir J. Lacaita—Mr Crawford (London) MP[7]—Mr Romilly —Mr Arbuthnot—H. of C. $4\frac{3}{4}$–$7\frac{1}{2}$ and $10\frac{1}{2}$–1.[8] Read Maguire's Rome— Dieux Protecteurs.[9]

20. T.

Wrote to Sir W. Heathcote—Mr Puseley[10]—Mr W. Rodwell[11]—L. Rose[12]— Mr T.M. Gibson (2)—Mr Pressly—Sir T. Fremantle—Robn. G—Col. Wilson Patten—Ld Henniker—Sir T. Gladstone—Mr Rawlinson & minutes. Saw Earl of Aberdeen—Sir W.R. Farquhar—Mr B. Benjamin— Mr Farrer—Mr MacCulloch—Mr Garnett[13] & Mr Sandeman—Mr Bazley MP—Sir T. Fremantle—Mr Laing—Mr Pressly—D. of Newcastle—Saw one[R]. H. of C. $5\frac{3}{4}$–8.[14] Read Ottley's [sic] Dutch Republic[15]—Maguire's Rome.

21. Wed.

Wrote to Mrs Goalen—Ld Lyttelton—Mr Greswell—Ld Brougham—Sir Jas. Hudson & minutes. H. of C. & Cabinet (on Savoy) 2–6.[16] Saw L. Rose. Mad Appony's[17] in Evg. Read Outram on Egypt.[18] Consultation on HG's

[1] See 21 Dec. 39.
[2] Frederick Charles *Massingberd, 1800–72; rector of S. Ormsby from 1825; chancellor of Lincoln from 1832; wrote on church and state.
[3] One of several by William Curling.
[4] J. L. Davies, *The work of Christ . . . Sermons . . . with a preface on the atonement controversy* (1860).
[5] John Ivatt Briscoe, 1791–1870; liberal M.P. for Surrey constituencies from 1830.
[6] The 'Alliance deputation could do little but quote formulae and testimonials: all the sophistication, subtlety, imagination and success lay with Gladstone'; Harrison, *Drink and the Victorians*, 248; brief report in *The Times*, 20 March, 1860, 9.
[7] Robert Wigram Crawford, 1813–89; E.I. merchant and banker; deputy governor Bank of England 1867–9, governor 1869–71; liberal M.P. city of London 1857–74.
[8] *Russell's Reform Bill 2°R: H clvii. 839.
[9] See 11 Feb. 60.
[10] Daniel *Puseley, 1814–82; traveller and writer on the colonies.
[11] William Rodwell, bank and stockbroker; much consulted by Gladstone in 1865.
[12] A rescue case; see 10 Apr. 60.
[13] William James Garnett, 1818–73; Christ Church; barrister and liberal M.P. Lancaster 1857–64.
[14] Voted against the ballot: H clvii. 935.
[15] J. L. *Motley, *The rise of the Dutch republic*, 3v. (1855).
[16] Clearly some disagreement, see 26 Mar. 60.
[17] Wife of Count Rudolf Apponyi, 1812–76, Austrian ambassador 1856–72.
[18] Sir James *Outram, *Memoir on Egypt* (1849).

matters & wrote draft to send for his consn. At Christie's seeing pictures. Saw Mr Laing—Mr Gibson—Duke of Marlborough.

22. Th.

Wrote to Robn. G. and minutes. More consultation on the H.G. and Lowder matters. H of C. $4\frac{1}{2}$–$7\frac{1}{2}$ and $10\frac{1}{2}$–$12\frac{1}{2}$.[1] Saw Sir W. Heathcote (2)—Sir T. Fremantle—Ld Eversley—Signor M. Marliani—Mr Cowan *cum* Yorkshire Magistrates Deputn.[2]—Mr Borthwick & Mr Rideout—Mr Glyn—Mr Horsfall—Mr Ellice—Mr Crawfurd—Mr Laing. Sir W. Heathcote came in evg & we conversed largely on the Oxford seat. Read Maguire's Rome— Crook on Income Tax.[3]

23. Fr.

Wrote to Mr Gibson—Sir T. Fremantle—Mr Cobden—Mr Pressly—Mr Oswald—& minutes. H of C. $4\frac{1}{2}$–2: got Income Tax & Stamp Resolutions.[4] Worked on papers. Saw Sir T. Fremantle—Mr Laing. A long day of $16\frac{1}{2}$ hours work.

24. Sat.

Wrote to Mr Laing—Mr Woodgate—Mr Keble—Prof. Swinton[5]—Govr. Eyre—Mrs Herbert—& minutes. Cabinet $4\frac{1}{4}$–$6\frac{1}{4}$. Drawing room at 2: when Agnes was presented, fair & simple as the snowdrops that she carried. At Christie's. Read St Stephens.[6] Saw Mr Laing—Sir A. Spearman—Lord Elgin resp. Wortley[7]—R. Phillimore resp. H.G. Saw Fairfield[R].

25. Annunc. & 5 S. Lent.

Chapel Royal mg St Margaret's evg. Made a round of duty visits: saw old Purchase lying in his rest. Occupied on H.G.'s matters. Read Pusey's letter:[8] Tracts.

26. M.

Wrote to E. Lovell—Ld Portman[9]—Mr Rodwell—Rev Mr Cooper—and minutes. Saw Sir T. Fremantle—Mr Laing—Captain G.—Count Platen[10]—

---

[1] Reform Bill: *H* clvii. 1030.
[2] Not reported.
[3] Untraced pamphlet, possibly by Charles A. Crook of Bristol.
[4] By the good majority of 55: *H* clvii. 1219.
[5] Archibald Campbell *Swinton, 1812–90; advocate; professor of civil law at Edinburgh 1842–62; a tory, but failed to win a seat.
[6] [Lord *Lytton], *St. Stephens. A poem* (1860).
[7] Loaned to Elgin for his China expedition; see 28 Mar., 14 Apr. 60.
[8] E. B. *Pusey, 'A letter . . . on some circumstances connected with the present crisis in the English church' (1842).
[9] Edward Berkeley *Portman, 1799–1888; liberal M.P. 1823–33; cr. Baron 1837, Viscount 1873; west country land owner (see 13 June 38n.).
[10] Count Baltzar Julius Ernst von Platen, 1804–75; Swedish-Norwegian minister 1857–1861.

Earl of Aberdeen—Scotts—Duke of Newcastle—Mr Pressly & conclave. H. of C. 4½–1: Income Tax. Stamps, Wine Licences. Ld J.R. used most questionable language.[1] Read St Stephen's: Ld Stanhope's Tract on Human Sacrifices in Rome.[2] Walk with C.

27. T.
Wrote to Mr Brand—Ld Belhaven[3]—Count Appony—D of Newcastle— R. Palmer—and minutes. H. of C. 4½–7½ and 8¼–1¾: on Dover Contract.[4] Finished Saint Stephen's. Saw Sir A. Spearman—Mr Arbuthnot *cum* Mr Stephenson—Mr Laing—Sir T.F., Mr P[ressly], & conclave.—Mr Crawfurd. Depn. of Tea Trade—Tobacco Trade—Manchester manufrr.[5] Saw Mr Gibson.

28. Wed. X
Wrote to Ld Portman—Col. [R.M.] Biddulph—Mrs Herbert—Rev J. Turlls[6] & others—Mr Moffatt—and minutes. Levee at 2. Saw Ld Harris— Mr Bentley—J. Wortley—on the offer—Mr Crawfurd MP.—Count Appony —M. Lavradio—and many MP.s. H of C. 12½–1¼ and 3–6.[7] Cabinet 6–7. Dined at Harcourt's. Much conv. with Ld Lyndhurst: also Duc d'Aumale & Ld Grey. Saw Mr Aniais.[8] Read Mr Wilson's Statement.[9]

29. Th.
Wrote to Mr Aniais—Sir A. Spearman—Sir T.G.—Ld Palmerston—Dean Ramsay—Col. Biddulph—Mr Mowbray Morris—Mr Hammond—Sec. Carlton Club[10]—D. of Newcastle—Professor Swinton—R. Phillimore—and minutes. Saw Mr G. Moffatt—Mr Arbuthnot (2)—Mrs Phillimore respecting H.G.—Duchess of Sutherland—Ld Aberdeen—Mr Wyn[11]—Mr Spooner[12] —Lord Clarence Paget. H of C. 4½–7¾ and 9¼–2½: Income Tax & Stamps.[13] Read Ld Overstone's Speech[14]—Union of B.N.A. Provinces.[15]

[1] *Russell's strong warning to France against annexation of Savoy and Nice: *H* clvii. 1252; see Beales, *England and Italy*, 137–8. Gladstone introduced the Refreshment Houses and Wine Licenses Bill: *H* clvii. 1302 and Harrison, *Drink and the Victorians*, 248.
[2] P. H. *Stanhope, *Were human sacrifices in use among the Romans? Correspondence between Mr. *Macaulay, Sir Robert *Peel and Lord *Mahon in Dec. 1847* (1860).
[3] See 4 Jan. 37.
[4] On telegraphic contracts: *H* clvii. 1407.
[5] For the dptns. see *Morning Chronicle*, 28 March 1860, 5c.
[6] Unidentified; nonconformist?
[7] Voted in 49:222 against Church Rates Abolition Bill: *H* clvii. 1460.
[8] Unidentified.
[9] J. *Wilson, 'Financial measures for India. Speech delivered before the legislative council of Calcutta' (1860).
[10] Allowing his membership to end by non-payment of subscription; in Sir C. Petrie, *The Carlton Club* (1955), 82.
[11] Probably H. W. W. Wynn.
[12] Richard Spooner, 1783–1864; tory M.P. Birmingham 1844–7, N. Warwickshire from 1849; leader of anti-Maynooth group in Commons (see 8 June 47n.).
[13] *H* clvii. 1528.
[14] S. J. *Loyd, Lord Overstone, 'Speech . . . on the treaty of commerce with France' (1860).
[15] J. Anderson, 'The union of the British North American Provinces' (reprinted from *Montreal Gazette*, October 1859).

30. Fr.

Wrote to Rev Mr Neale—Mr Anderson—Mr E. Baines MP—O Brien MP[1]—Crawfurd MP—F.T. Palgrave,[2] and minutes. H of C. $4\frac{1}{2}$–$7\frac{1}{2}$ and 8–$12\frac{1}{4}$. I.Tax & Stamps.[3] Read M'Laren on Scots Whisky Drinking.[4] Cabinet $12\frac{3}{4}$–2. Corn Trade Deputn. 2 hrs. Saw Mr Laing *cum* Mr Tilsley—Mr Moffatt with Mr Rush[5]—Mr Dalgleish—Mr Crawfurd.

31. Sat.

Wrote to S. Herbert—Sir J. Graham—Mr Hammond—D of Newcastle—R. Palmer—Mr Cobden—Scotts—and minutes. H of C. 12–$1\frac{1}{2}$. Passed Income Tax & Stamp Bills, the latter a little maimed.[6] Cabinet $3\frac{1}{2}$–$5\frac{1}{2}$. Saw Sir J. Graham—Mr Laing—Sir H. Holland. Presided at the Dinner of the Artists' General Benevolent Institution. $6\frac{1}{4}$–$10\frac{1}{4}$.[7] Duchess of Somerset's party afr. Read Inaugural Addresses.[8]

Palm Sunday Ap. One. 1860.

St James's & H.C. mg—Chapel Royal aft.—MS of 46 aloud in evg. Saw Sir T. Fremantle. Wrote to S. Herbert—Ld Palmerston. Read Ken's Works[9]—Therapeutes on the Healing Art & Xty[10]—Haste to the Rescue[11]—Blackburn's Tract.[12]

2. M.

Herbert came at 11 & we fought long on his proposal to augment forces.[13] Wrote minutes. Conclave on Licensing Bill & the rest at 3. H of C. $4\frac{1}{2}$–12: Customs Charges and Licensing Bill.[14]
Saw Scotts

$$\left.\begin{array}{l} \cdots\cdots\cdots \\ \cdots\cdots\cdots \\ \cdots\cdots\cdots \end{array}\right\}\ \text{forgotten[15]}$$

[1] (Sir) Patrick O'Brien, 1823–95; liberal M.P. King's Co. 1852–85; anti-Parnell; 2nd bart. 1862.
[2] Francis Turner *Palgrave, 1824–97; anthologiser, educationalist and fellow of Exeter 1847–62; first mentioned 26 June 46; see Add MS 44270.
[3] Swingeing attack on him by *Disraeli: *H* clvii. 1678.
[4] D. *McLaren, 'One year's experience of the new Public House Act in Edinburgh' (1855); Scottish Temperance League n. 56.
[5] Probably E. Rushe, clerk in assistant accountant general's branch.
[6] A procedural confusion by the treasury required withdrawal of the resolution to tax contract notes: *H* clvii. 1701.
[7] No report found.
[8] J. B. Hay, *Inaugural addresses by Lords Rectors of the University of Glasgow* (1839); preparing for 16 Apr. 60.
[9] T. *Ken, *Works*, ed. W. Hawkins, 4v. (1721).
[10] Therapeutes [pseud. of D. Brodie], *The healing art, the right hand of the Church* (1859).
[11] Mrs. J. B. Wightman, *Haste to the rescue; or work while it is day* (1859).
[12] J. Blackburn, possibly *The popular Biblical educator*, 2v. (1854–5).
[13] The start of a dispute between the treasury and the war office which lasted throughout the summer.
[14] *H* clvii. 1755.
[15] In pencil.

3. Tues. [Brighton]

Wrote to Miss C. Sinclair[1]—Dean of Windsor—Mr Hammond—Mr Horsfall MP.—Helen G.—R. Phillimore—S. Herbert & copy—Profr. Rogers[2]—Mr Torrens MP.—Mrs Bennet—Rev Mr Williams—Mr Conyngham MP.—Mr J. Gray—Rev. Dr Pusey—O.B. Cole—Ld Provost Edinb.—Robn. G—Mr Scholefield MP.—Lady Belhaven[3]—Lady Ruthven[4]—and minutes. Saw Mr Arbuthnot—Mr S. Laing—Mr Gibson. Cabinet $3\frac{3}{4}$–$6\frac{1}{2}$. I rather stiffly resisted augmentation of the Estimates (Army) & objected even to increase of force not involving charge: Ld P. at length suggested an expedient to avoid it.[5] Off to Brighton at $7\frac{1}{2}$. Tea with De Tabley's family. Read Acton's Preface, & Mamiani on Right[6]—Lord Rector's Addresses.

4. Wed.

St Paul's 10.30 A.M. We visited Lewis's: & walked. Also settled in 'Grosvenor Ho' 121.[7] Wrote to Mr Laing (2)—J.F. Stuart Wortley—Lyttelton—M. Rangabè—Scotts—W.H.G.—Rev W.B. Pusey—and minutes. We had some Brighton air: and fed on the De Tableys. Read Rev [blank] on Education—Question de l'Orient[8]—Bower's Hist Univ. Edinb.[9]

5. Th.

St George's Ch. 11 AM. Wrote to Dean of Chichester[10]—Ld Brougham—Mr Cobden—Mr Blakesley—Mr Brand—Mr Spooner—Mr Laing—Mr Ridley—Sir B. Brodie—and minutes. Walk with J. Warren[11] on the downs. Saw Mr Taylor.[12] Read Bower's Hist. Univ Ed.—Addresses of Lord Rectors.

6. Good Friday.

Parish Ch (old) 11 AM & H.C.—St Paul's aft. Read Various Tracts—Bower's Hist.—Smiles's Self Help[13]—Bp of St D[avid's] on Submerged Cities.[14] Under Mr Taylor's orders I have abstained from even the usual slight practices at this period. This change helps to show me how powerful an instrument they supply.[15]

[1] See 16 June 47.
[2] i.e. J. E. T. *Rogers, professor of statistics in London 1859–90; see 9 Feb. 48.
[3] See 4 Jan. 37.
[4] Mary Elizabeth Thornton Hore-Ruthven 1784–1864, succ. her br., 5th Baron Ruthven, 1853.
[5] A slight alteration in the Estimates.
[6] Count T. Mamiani della Rovere, *Rights of nations; or the new law of European states applied to the affairs of Italy*, tr. R. Acton (1860).
[7] Perhaps the house taken by the Grosvenors.
[8] *La question d'Orient. Un homme et une solution* (1860).
[9] A. *Bower, *The history of the university of Edinburgh*, 3v. (1817–30).
[10] W. F. *Hook.
[11] John Byrne Leicester *Warren, 1835–95; barrister, poet and liberal; 3rd Baron De Tabley 1887.
[12] The Brighton doctor; see 29 Apr. 50.
[13] See 9 Jan. 60.
[14] C. *Thirlwall, 'On some traditions relating to the submersion of ancient cities' (1860).
[15] i.e. lenten abstinences.

7. Easter Eve.

Ch (manqué) at 11 and 9 P.M. (St Paul's). Saw Sir J. Tyrell—Mr Cardwell. Wrote to Ld Grey—L. Rose—Sir J. Young—Mrs Hampton—and minutes. Worked a little on my intended Address: with sluggish & reluctant brain.[1] Read Bower's History—Ld Grey on Currency (1842)[2]—Tracts.

8. Easter Day.

St Paul's & H.C. mg. St James's aft. Wrote to Duke of Somerset—Mr Glyn MP.—Mr Cobden MP.—Sir A. Spearman—and minutes. Worked a little on Address. Read Missionary Bishops[3]—& on the Gospels.

9. M. X

St Paul's 10½ a.m. Shopping: & got much saline on the pier. Saw Mr Conyngham MP.—Mr W. Beckett—Rev Mr Wagner jun.[4] Wrote to Mr Ryan: & minutes. Worked on Address. Read Bower's Hist Edinb Univ. Saw more than one[R]. This was a fine blowing day, the very air all salt.

10. T. [London]

Busy packing & arranging for departure: goodbye to our kind friends & quasihosts the De Tableys. Off by train at 1½. Wrote to S. Herbert & copy[5] —Sir W.R. Farquhar—Mr Gibson—Robn. G.—and minutes. Examined Executor's Accounts. Nat. Debt Commn. met at 4½ in my room. Saw L. Rose—R.C. I learned. = Leary?[6] Read Addresses of Lord Rectors (finished)—Bower's History of Edinburgh University.

11. Wed.

Wrote to Sir S. Scott & Co.—Sir T. Fremantle—Mr Pressly—Mr R. Stevens[7]—Mr Laing—S. Herbert (& copy)[8]—Attorney General—and minutes. Worked on Address. Saw Ld Palmerston 1½ h.[9]—Ld Aberdeen—Mr Trevor. Saw Williamson—Inquiries resp M. S[ummerhayes][R]. Read Bower's Hist. —Bryan King's Letter.[10] C.G. returned: plenty to talk about.

12. Th.

Wrote to Dean Ramsay—L. Heyworth[11]—Rev Mr Marriott—Robn. G.—G.

[1] See 16 Apr. 60.
[2] H. G. *Grey, Speeches . . . on the second reading of the Corn Law Bill . . . and on the financial measures of the government* (1842).
[3] Probably *Missionary bishoprics* (1860).
[4] See 3 Apr. 58n.
[5] Stanmore, ii. 252.
[6] Rescue case, actually named E. Gray; see 25 Apr., 11 May 60.
[7] Probably Richard Stephens, London wine importer.
[8] Report of the *Palmerston interview; Stanmore, ii. 253.
[9] *Herbert told *Graham (12 April 1860, Bodley MS Film 128) the interview was 'not satisfactory . . . clearly he shook Palmerston as to delay'.
[10] B. King, 'Sacrilege and its encouragement, being an account of the St. George's [anti-ritualist] riots and of their successes' (1860).
[11] Lawrence Heyworth, 1786–1872; Liverpool trader and chairman of its free trade association; liberal M.P. Derby 1848–57.

Burnett—T.G. Shaw—Mr Heygate—and minutes. Worked on China. Saw Mr Lewis[1]—Mr Laing—Mr Ellison—J.F.S. Wortley—farewell: he goes on my recommendation with Ld Elgin.[2] Saw E. Lovell[R]. Worked on Address. Read Bower's Hist. Univ. Ed.

13. Fr.

Wrote to S. Herbert (2)[3]—Lord Lyttelton—Mr Laing—Ld Palmerston—Mr Morley—Mr Lendrum—and minutes. Saw Sir W. Heathcote. Worked on China, & moving. Worked on Address: finished it in rough. Worked on Paper for Cabinet.[4] Read Bower's Hist.

14. Sat.

Wrote to S. Herbert—Sir T. Fremantle—C.A. Wood—Count Platen—Ld Brougham—D. of Somerset—Ld Haddo—and minutes. Saw Mr Anderson —Mr Arbuthnot—Mr Laing—Worked on China—& on sorting clothes. Finished Bower's Hist. Univ. Edinb. Left Downing St after 8 P.M.

15. 1 S. E. [Edinburgh]

In bed at Dean Ramsay's 7.20 A.M. in Edinburgh. St John's Church mg—Dr Guthrie aftn. Sir D. Brewster[5] dined—& we discussed various matters. Saw Dr Guthrie—Mr Mackenzie. $2\frac{1}{2}$ hours revising Address. Read Foxton's Xty[6]—Binney's Ch. Life in Austra.[7] Gave Address to Dean R. for previous perusal.

16. M.

Wrote to C.G.—Mr MacColl—Dr Pusey—Mr Forsyth[8]—and minutes. Saw Mr Tait[9]—Dr Alexander[10]—Mr Clerk Maxwell[11]—Ld & Lady Meath. Met the Ld Advocate, Solr. General, & Mr Muir, on the University Act.[12] China hunting. $11\frac{1}{2}$–2 At the Music Hall:[13] for Doctor's Degree & my address, wh I

[1] Perhaps Richard Lewis, d. 1883; parliamentary reporter.
[2] See 24 Mar. 60.
[3] Stanmore, ii. 257.
[4] Finished on 20 April, draft in Add MS 44749, f. 91, printed version in Add MS 44591 f. 20. It threatened a 13 or 14d. income tax if military retrenchment, especially on expeditions, fortifications and colonial garrisons, was not achieved.
[5] The vice-chancellor; see 15 Aug. 59.
[6] F. J. Foxton, *Popular Christianity, its transition and probable development* (1844).
[7] T. *Binney, *Lights and shadows of Church Life in Australia* (1860).
[8] Perhaps William Forsyth, 1818–79, ed. the *Aberdeen Journal* from 1849.
[9] Peter Guthrie *Tait, 1860–1901; mathematician; appointed professor of natural philosophy at Edinburgh May 1860 by the curatorial board on which Gladstone sat.
[10] William Lindsay Alexander, 1808–84; minister of Augustine church, Edinburgh, and principal of Scottish congregational churches hall.
[11] James *Clerk-Maxwell, 1831–79; experimental physicist; professor in Aberdeen 1856–60, London 1860–5, Cambridge 1871.
[12] Meeting with J. *Moncrieff, lord advocate, E. F. *Maitland, solicitor general, and John *Muir, 1810–82, reformer and endower of the university, on the working of 1858 Scottish Universities Act.
[13] In George Street; scene of his first Midlothian speech 1879.

read.[1] It was a crowded & kind Assembly. The previous prayer was noteworthy. 7–11. Dinner with the Senatus Academicus, and Speeches. Read Simpson's Lecture[2]—Rectified Address for press (i.e. corrected it as actually spoken—wh is sure to vary).

17. Tu.

Wrote to S. Herbert. Attended Meeting of Curators 10–12—Of Univ. Council 12–3 when I stated as well as I could the powers & duties of the C.[3] Saw Adm. Ramsay (E P D Co)[4]—Principal Forbes[5]—Professor Christison[6] —Lady Emma Campbell. China hunting. A quiet half hour with the Dean during my dinner, after packing: then off at 6 PM.

18. Wed. [London]

In bed at 11 C.H.T. soon after five. Wrote to Robn. G.—Master of the Mint—and (many) minutes. Cabinet 3–5¼. Saw Mr Laing—Sir T. Fremantle—Mr Anderson.—Govr. & Dep. Govr. Bank[7]—Duke of Argyll— Duchess of Sutherland. Haymarket, a family party to see the Overland—7– 10¼.[8] Read Bosanquet on the Constn.[9] In much confusion on return to No 11 [Carlton House Terrace].

19. Th.

Wrote to [blank] & minutes. Six to breakfast. Mr Therry: we talked over Mr Canning's corrections.[10] Mr Smiles, a lecture on porcelain. Mrs Bennett who delighted me by telling me that Mr S[miles] wishes to write a Memoir of my father. This I now hope will be done.[11] Saw JNG & told him. Saw Mr Chapman jun—Mr Chapman sen.[12]—Governor of the Bank—Lord Clarence Paget Mr Gregson MP—Baron L. Rothschild—Lord Aberdeen—Mr Brand. Worked on paper for Cabinet resp. Expenditure. Read Stigant[13]—House 4½–7½ and 11¾–1¾.

[1] 'The work of universities', Add MS 44689, f. 115, printed in *Gleanings*, vii and in A. Stodart-Wallace, *Rectorial addresses* (1900).
[2] Sir J. Y. Simpson, probably, *Was the Roman army provided with medical officers?* (1856).
[3] The 1858 Act established a general council in each Scottish university to involve graduates; see Sir A. Grant, *The story of the university of Edinburgh* (1884) ii. 103.
[4] Sir William Ramsay, 1793–1871; rear admiral 1857; lived in Edinburgh; director of Edinburgh, Perth, Dundee railway, in which Gladstone had substantial interests.
[5] James David *Forbes (see 9 Dec. 33) was principal of St. Andrews 1859–68.
[6] (Sir) Robert *Christison, 1797–1882; professor of medical jurisprudence at Edinburgh; led opposition to Gladstone's candidacy for Chancellorship there 1868; cr. bart. 1871.
[7] Overend and Gurney's 'putsch' against the Bank; £1.5m. in £1000 notes had been withdrawn, cut in half, and later returned; see next day and Clapham, *Bank of England*, ii. 242–6.
[8] 'The overland route', 'The pilgrimage of love' and 'The boarding school'.
[9] S. R. Bosanquet, *Principia* (1843), essay ix.
[10] *Therry edited G. *Canning's *Speeches* in 6v.; see 17 July 48.
[11] Samuel *Smiles, 1812–1904; physician, journalist, railway administrator and biographer. Nothing came of this suggestion, which is not mentioned in later Smiles-Gladstone letters; they remained on good terms, Smiles often sending complimentary copies.
[12] Partners in Overend and Gurney; later in the day Gladstone made a statement but refused to make a comment: *H* clvii. 2005.
[13] William Stigand, 1825–1911, barrister and journalist, had sent his *Poems*: Add MS 44393, f. 300.

20. Fr.

Wrote to Mr Stigant—Ld Cowley—Ld Palmerston[1]—Sir F. Kelly—Robn. G.—Dr Pusey—and minutes. Saw Depn. on Customs' Bill. Finished paper for Cabinet. Saw Mr Gibson—Mr Laing & Mr Anderson—J.N.G. H of C. $4\frac{1}{2}$–$6\frac{3}{4}$ and $7\frac{1}{2}$–$1\frac{1}{2}$: working my measures. [2]

21. Sat.

Wrote to Mr Weddell[3]—C.A. Wood—Attorney General—Sir R. Mayne— Mrs Bennet—W. Brown—and minutes. Inquired in vain for M. S[ummer-hayes][R]. Saw Mr Swain[4]—Mr Laing, Mr Pressly, and Mr Anderson. Cabinet $3\frac{3}{4}$–$6\frac{1}{2}$. We are still in chaos on our return.—Read Wilson.

22. 2 S.E.

St James's mg & evg. MS of 1 S.E. aloud at night. Calls: saw Bonham. Counselled Stephy resp. H.S. Read Magee on Est. Ch.[5]—Heygate's Corresp. with Unitn.[6]—Binney's Ch. Life in Australia.[7]

23. M.

Wrote to Bp of London—Count Lavradio—Dean Ramsay—Ld Advocate— Serj. Woolrych[8]—Sir T. Fremantle—and minutes. Saw Coopers Deputa- tion. Saw Sir R. Hill—Mr Trevor—Ld Cowley—Mr Lindsay—Ld Dudley— Bp of Oxford—Mr Laing—Ald. Salomons—Mr . . . and others. Read La Coalition[9]—Hindoo Address[10]—part Q.R. on Budget.[11] H. of C. $4\frac{1}{2}$–$7\frac{1}{4}$ and $10\frac{1}{2}$–1?

24. T.

Wrote to Mackay & Chisholm—Dr Pusey—Mr Woollcombe—E. Leary— Robn. G—and minutes. H of C. at $4\frac{1}{2}$, $6\frac{3}{4}$–8 and $10\frac{1}{2}$–1.[12] Saw Mr Martin MP —Mr Kinnaird MP.—Sir T. Fremantle with Customs' party—Mr Gibson— Sir G. Lewis—Ld Palmerston—on Paper Duty! (see his note of this day)[13]— Mr E.A. Bowring—Mr Laing. Read Q.R. finished on Budget &c—National

---

[1] Guedalla, P, 132.
[2] Paper duties repeal: H clvii. 2085.
[3] William Weddell of Edinburgh had sent some biblical texts (Hawn P).
[4] Unidentified.
[5] W. C. *Magee, The voluntary system: can it supply the place of the established Church? (1860).
[6] The doctrines of original sin and the Trinity . . . correspondence between a clergyman of the Episcopal Church in England [W. E. Heygate] and a layman of Boston, U.S. (1859).
[7] See 15 Apr. 60.
[8] Humphrey William *Woolrych, 1795–1871; serjeant-at-law 1855; wrote treatises and biographies; see next day.
[9] Anon. pamphlet in French (1860).
[10] Perhaps J. Mullens, The religious aspects of Hindoo philosophy stated and discussed (1860).
[11] Quarterly Review, cvii. 514 (April 1860); [Ld. R. *Cecil].
[12] H clviii. 1.
[13] *Palmerston suggested delay of paper duties repeal till next year's budget; Guedalla, P, 133.

Review on do[1]—Paterson's Essay on Athenians[2]—Woolrych on Sir J. Barnard's Act[3]—Note sur le Budget de la G. en Angl.[4]

25. *St Mark Wed.* X

Wrote to Ld Brougham[5]—Scotts—Ld J. Russell—and minutes. Cabinet $3\frac{3}{4}$-7.[6] Worked a little on arranging my China collection: wh will be a work of *time*. Dined at Grillions. Saw Leary = Gray: in danger[R]. Wrote Mem. on Ch. Disc. Bill. Saw Mr Laing. Read Marryat.[7]

26. *Thurs.*

Wrote to Sir G.C. Lewis—Lady Beauchamp—Ld Chandos—Bp of Oxford —Mr Pressly—and minutes. H of C. $8\frac{1}{2}$-$12\frac{3}{4}$.[8] Saw Mr Hunt[9]—Mr Mure—Mr Arbuthnot—Bp of Oxford—Attorney General—Lord J. Russell (F.O.) Worked a little on China. Nipped again by the East Wind on my chest. Read Rev. F. Lee's Letter[10]—Letter to Ld Brougham[11]—The Reviews Reviewed.[12] Caledonian Canal Comme. meeting $12\frac{1}{2}$-2.[13]

27. *Fr.*

Wrote to S. Herbert—Prof. Pillans[14]—Mr Laing—Mr G. Burnett—C. Ryan—and minutes. Got up for meeting: and went to bed after disposing of my papers. Radcliffe Trust meeting 11-$12\frac{3}{4}$. Read Nichols Critical papers:[15] & various Tracts.

28. *Sat.*

Wrote to Ld Cowley—Ld Wodehouse—G. Burnett—Robn. G.—C.L. Ryan —& minutes. Spent the day in bed: improving. Saw Dss. of Sutherland & D. of Argyll. Read Scratchley on Savings Banks[16]—& divers Tracts.

29. *3 S.E.*

Got up for Chapel Royal at 12. Luncheon at Stafford House. The Duchess

[1] *National Review,* x. 313 (April 1860).

[2] J. B. *Paterson, *An essay on the national character of the Athenians* (1860).

[3] Untraced paper by H. W. *Woolrych on Sir J. *Barnard's 1734 Act on banking, repealed 1860.

[4] See perhaps 25 July 60.

[5] See Morley, ii. 181.

[6] *Herbert told *Graham (28 April 1860 Bodley MS Film 128) 'Gladstone yielded the point of an additional £130,000 for my Estimates without much resistance', Anderson having found extra Treasury funds.

[7] See 2 July 57.

[8] Reform Bill: *H* clviii. 137.

[9] Thornton Leigh *Hunt, 1810-73; a chief contributor to the *Spectator* 1840-60; acting ed. of *Daily Telegraph* 1855-72; see above, v. xlv.

[10] F. G. Lee, *The S. George's riots, a plea for justice and toleration, A letter to . . . Gladstone* (1860).

[11] Perhaps 'A letter to . . . *Brougham . . . respecting episcopacy in Scotland' (1849).

[12] One of the many pamphlets in response to *Essays and Reviews* (1860).

[13] No report found: Gladstone was a shareholder.

[14] James *Pillans, 1778-1864; professor of law at Edinburgh 1820-63; university reformer, advocated compulsory education.

[15] J. Nichol, *Fragments of criticism* (1860).

[16] A. Scratchley, 'Practical treatise on savings banks' (1860).

took us to All Saints in aftn. Drive afterwards: the wind, W[est] before, went round & caught me in the throat. Saw Ld Carlisle. Read A Word for Truth[1]—Fraser's Magazine[2]—Neale on the Psalms[3]—Thorp's Charge[4] & other Tracts. Early to bed.

30. M.
Worked in bed. Wrote to Sol. Gen. Scotland—E. Gray—Mr Scratchley[5]— Mr Ryan—Dean Ramsay—Mr Laing—& minutes. Saw J.N.G.—Mr Ryan. Worked on Reform Papers. Read MacMillan's Mag.[6]—Simpson's Lectures &c[7]—Stigant's Poems—and Tracts.

Tues. May 1. SS. Phil. & James.
Wrote to Vice Chr. Oxford—C.L. Ryan—Mr G. Burnett—Mr Brand— M. Al. Bertrand[8]—Sir J. Lacaita—and minutes. Saw Mr Gibson—Bp of Oxford—Ld Southesk.[9] Worked a little on China. Read Leslie on War[10]— La Torture en Sicile[11]—Nichol's Criticisms.[12]

Wed. May 2.
Wrote to S.E.G.—Bp of Oxford—& minutes. Saw Miss Syfret (on her affairs)—Mr Owen (reform)[13]—Mr Brand(do)—Lord Aberdeen—S. Herbert —E. Cardwell. Committee of Cabinet on Indian Army &c. $3\frac{1}{2}$–$6\frac{1}{2}$. Dined with the Cardwells: Mrs Tait's & Lady Derby's afr. Read Denison's Charge[14]—Forbes's Address[15]—& other Tracts.

Committee of Cabinet on Indian Army.[16]
1. That a maximum number being fixed for the European army in India, further charge may be incurred for a native army and a military police, but so that the total military charges shall not exceed the same charge before the mutiny. 2. That the entire native army be officered on the irregular system, by selection from the officers of the European force. 3. W.E.G.: That commissions without purchase be given only a. to meritorious soldiers advanced from the ranks b. by

[1] 'A Word for truth. By an English seaman' (1860); on Anglo-French relations.
[2] *Fraser's Magazine*, lxi. 447 (April 1860); *Peacock's *Gryll Grange* serialized.
[3] J. M. *Neale, *Commentary on the Psalms* (1860).
[4] T. Thorp, 'Church-rates and endowed schools' (1860).
[5] Arthur Scratchley, 1821–97; secretary and manager of Western life assurance co. 1846–66; had sent his pamphlet (see 28 Apr. 60).
[6] *Macmillan's Magazine*, i. 417 (April 1860).
[7] F. G. Simpson, *Lectures on the typical character of the Jewish tabernacle, priesthood and sacrifices* (1852).
[8] Alexandre Bertrand had sent his book on Homeric deities; Add MS 44530, f. 196; see 11 Feb. 60.
[9] See 13 Jan. 49.
[10] T. E. C. Leslie, *The military systems of Europe economically considered* (1856).
[11] Anon. French pamphlet (1860).
[12] See 27 Apr. 60.
[13] Probably William Owen, superintendent of Somerset House, on statistics for his speech next day.
[14] G. A. *Denison, *The Charge of the Archdeacon of Taunton, April 1860* (1860).
[15] A. P. *Forbes, 'The waning of opportunities' (1860).
[16] Dated 2 May 1860; Add MS 44636, f. 29. See 27 Jan. 60.

way of prize. 4. D. of Somerset: That a certain number of battalions (say the *nine* to begin with) shall be regulated by seniority—jointly with selection.

3. *Th.*

Wrote to Dr. Fergusson—Mr Laing—Sir W. Heathcote—Ld Palmerston—and minutes. H. of C. 4¾–7 and 8¼–12¾. Spoke at much length on Reform Bill to an adverse & difficult House.[1] Ten to breakfast: saw Mr Holman Hunt[2] for the first time: an interesting party. Saw R. Phillimore—Mr Owen (Reform Bill) (2). Read Dr Wallace on the State of Greenock.[3]

4. *Friday.*

Wrote minutes. Clergy Deputn. 3–4¼. Royal Academy 10¼–12¼, and 2¾–3. Saw Mr T.M. Gibson—Mr Laing—Mr W. Harcourt—Sir C. Eastlake—Rev Mr Lake. H of C. 4½–11¾: spoke on Fire Insurance Duties Bill.[4] Read Nichols.

5. *Sat.*

Wrote to A. Panizzi—M.F. Tupper—Sir W. Williams—and minutes. Academy Exhibition 4¼–5¾: and dinner 6 to 11. Saw Bp of Oxford—Sir R. Murchison—Mr Dyce—Mr Roberts[5]—S. Herbert (Abp York &c)[6]—Ld Overstone (Sir J. Lefevre)—Mr Richmond—and others. Cabinet 1¼–4¼. Ld P. spoke ¾ hour agt Paper Duties Bill! I had to reply. Cabinet agt. him except a few, Wood & Cardwell in particular. More wild schemes of foreign alliance are afloat! Our old men (2) are unhappily our youngest.[7] Read Pillans on Cicero.[8]

6. *4 S.E.*

Chapel Royal mg. and Holy Commn. All Saints aft.—MS of 44 aloud. Read Dante—Binney's Ch.Life in Australia[9]—Young agt Mansell[10]—Evelyns Tr. of Letter from France.[11]

7. *M.*

Wrote to Count Flamburiari—Mr Grogan—Mr Scholefield—Mr Lewis—Mr Hazlitt[12]—C.A. Wood—Mr Pressly—Mr Brand—and minutes. Worked a little on China: a little on business. Read Gairdner on Medicine[13]—Tract

---

[1] His sturdy defence of *Russell's Bill emphasized its limited intentions, but met strong tory hostility; the 2°R passed unopposed: *H* clviii. 625.

[2] He had not hitherto admired *Hunt's work, see 3 May 56.

[3] Untraced.

[4] *H* clviii. 722.

[5] David *Roberts, 1796–1864; landscape artist; see Add MS 44393, f. 302.

[6] Abp. *Musgrave died the day before; *Longley was translated on 4 June.

[7] Version in Morley, ii. 31. *Palmerston was working the Court against Gladstone, see Martin, vi. 130.

[8] *Eclogae Ciceronianae*, ed. J. *Pillans (1845).

[9] See 15 Apr. 60.

[10] J. Young, *The province of reason: a criticism of the Bampton Lecture on ' The limits of religious thought'* (1860).

[11] J. *Evelyn, *A character of England as it was lately presented in a letter to a noble man of France* (1659).

[12] William Hazlitt, 1811–93, s. of the essayist; registrar of bankruptcy in London 1845; wrote on law and classics.

[13] W. T. Gairdner, *On medicine and medical education. Three lectures* (1858).

for Gothic Architecture.[1] H. of C. 4½–7¼ and 8½–1. Replied on Wine Licenses Bill [2°R] and voted in 267:193.[2]

8. T.

Wrote to Mr Dunlop MP.—E. Gray—Mr Haddan (Rev)—and minutes. Saw Archdeacon Thorp—Mr G. Moffatt—Mr Laing—Mr G.R. Hope— Mr Henley M.P.—Mr Pressly *cum* Mr Timm. Attended Packet Contracts Committee to be examined.[3] Cabinet 2–4¼. H. of C. 4½–7¾ and 9–2. Nearly defeated on the Paper Duties Bill; 219:210. Spoke to a very adverse House.[4] Read Town & Forest.[5]

9. Wed.

Wrote to Mrs Herbert—Ld Wodehouse—and minutes. Cabinet 3½–6. Dined at Guy's & thanked for Ministers:[6] the Palace afterwards. Saw Mr Lewis—R. Phillimore—Mr Pressly—Mr Laing—Sir Rowland Hill *cum* do. —Govr. of the Bank—Sir T. Fremantle. Read [blank] on Macaulay and "a High Churchman".[7] Saw E. Gray[R].

10. Th.

Wrote to D. of Argyll—Mr Cobden—Dean of Ch.Ch.—Mr Woodgate—Ld Brougham—and minutes. Saw Mr Grogan—Mr Laing—Mr Arbuthnot— H of C. 4½–12½, working Wine Licenses Bill.[8] Seven to breakfast: incl. Mr J.R. Herbert.[9] Workmen & confusion in the House: C.s ball in evening. Read Temple's Essay[10]—The Missing Link.[11]

11. Fr.

Wrote to Rev. A. Goalen—Prof M. Müller—S.E.G.—Bp of Salisbury—Sir G. Lewis—Ld J. Russell and minutes. Saw Mr Gibson—Ld Granville. Arranged some China in Cabinet in my room. H. of C. 4¼–6¾.[12] Queen's (child) Ball 9–10. Saw E. Gray in D. St. A singular case[R]. Read divers Tracts.

[1] 'Shall Gothic architecture be denied fair play' (1860); on the new foreign office.
[2] *H* clviii. 828.
[3] On his conversation of 13 Sept. 60 (see that day): *PP* 1860 xiv. 412.
[4] On *Northcote's amndt. to the 3°R that the nation's financial state made repeal undesirable: *H* clviii. 946. The bill was then read 3°R and went to the Lords, see 21 May 60n.
[5] A. M. Powell, *Town and forest* (1860).
[6] No report found.
[7] Probably H. *Phillpotts, 'Correspondence between the bp. of Exeter and . . . *Macaulay' (1860), on *Cranmer.
[8] *H* clviii. 1015.
[9] The artist, see 17 June 53.
[10] F. *Temple, 'The education of the world' in the controversial *Essays and Reviews* (March 1860).
[11] E. *Ranyard, *The missing link; or, Bible-women in the homes of the London poor* (1859).
[12] Misc. business: *H* clviii. 1086.

12. Sat. [Cliveden]

Wrote to Mr Pressly—Sir T. Fremantle—Mr Brand—Rev Mr Cosserat—
Mr Dunlop—Rev Mr Wilson—and minutes. Cabinet $2\frac{3}{4}$–$4\frac{1}{2}$. Then off to
Cliveden. Saw Ld Brougham—Ld Lyttelton—T. Steuart Gladstone. A very
pleasant evening. The Speaker[1] is now highly approved as a member of
society. Read Ld Brougham's forthcoming Address: part of it aloud.[2]

13. 5 S.E.

Hedsor Ch m. & aft. Mr Williams[3] a pale Curate preached well & like a man
near the unseen world. We drove to Dropmore where Lady G[renville] was
well reported of by a paternal butler. Read Laurence on H.C.[4]—Madame
Swetchine.[5] Wrote to Ld Brougham—Mr Laing. A Church History conv.
I stood up for the men of 1661.[6]

14. M. [London]

Wrote minutes. Read Froude's Hist.[7] A forenoon walk. About sensitiveness
in the H of C. the Duchess [of Sutherland] gave me excellent advice in a
manner delicate beyond all conception. Back to town at $3\frac{1}{2}$. H of C. $4\frac{1}{4}$–$12\frac{1}{2}$
working the Wine Licences Bill.[8]

15. T.

Wrote to Sir W. Heathcote—Robn. G—V.C. Oxford—Ld Granville[9]—and
minutes. H of C. $4\frac{1}{4}$–7.[10] The meditated aggression of the Lords presses more
& more upon my mind.[11] Saw Sir A. Spearman *cum* Mr Anderson—Sir W.
Heathcote—Sir Jas Graham—Mr Gibson—Mr Walpole—Mr May—Dr
Ogle—The Speaker—R. Phillimore—Count Persigny—Sir T.G. Dined at
the Club: Mr Richmond one of my neighbours. C. had a ball afterwards at
which I appeared. Read [two words erased, illegibly].

16. Wed.

Wrote to Mr Laing—Ld Wodehouse—Mr Work[12]—Sir T. Fremantle—
Robn. G.—V.Chr. Oxford—Mr Gibson—Mr W. Johnson—W. Brown—
E. Gray (failed)—J.H. Parker—and minutes. Saw Sir A. Buller[13]—Lord J.

[1] J. E. *Denison.
[2] *Brougham's 'Address' on installation as Chancellor of Edinburgh university, later
published (1860).
[3] James Reynold Williams, 1828–1900; rector of Hedsor 1860–70, of Pulford from
1870.
[4] R. F. Laurence, *The Churchman's assistant at holy communion* (1860).
[5] *Madame Swetchine, sa vie et ses oeuvres, publiées par le cte. de Falloux* (1860).
[6] The Savoy conference on the prayer book when the bps. took a strong stand against
the presbyterians, effectively forcing their secession.
[7] See 23 May 56.
[8] Open disagreement on the treasury bench with *Palmerston on govt. business
programme: *H* clviii. 1210.
[9] See Fitzmaurice, i. 380.
[10] *H* clviii. 1286.
[11] On paper duties repeal, see 21 May 60n.
[12] See, perhaps, 9 Sept. 64.
[13] Sir Arthur William Buller, 1808–69; lawyer and judge in India 1840–58; liberal
M.P. Devonport 1859–65, Liskeard from 1865.

Russell—Mr Nash[1]—Mr Timm. Cabinet 3½–6¼. Worked on books about the pending *coup d'Etat*. Read Delarive on Swiss & French question.[2]

17. Th. Ascension Day.

Wrote to Sir F. Kelly—Mr Brand—and minutes. H of C. 4¼–1¼: waiting, & working W[ine] L[icences] Bill.[3] St James's 11 AM. & Holy Commn. Meeting of Peers &c. 2–3½. on the coming debate.[4] Read Forbes M'Kenzie Report.[5]

18. Fr. Queen's birthday.

Wrote to W. Johnson Esq—Brown Shipley & Co—J.H. Parker—Maj. Graham—E. Gray—and minutes. Saw Sir T. Fremantle with Mr Pressly—Duke of Argyll—Ld Granville—Mr Brand—Atty General—Mr Gibson—M. Delarive. Attended the Birthday drawingroom: in robe. Gave birthday dinner.[6] Out afterwards: saw Evelyn[R].

19. Sat.

Wrote to Mr Anderson—S. Herbert—Sir S. Northcote—Mr Laing—Watson & Smith—Mr Hankey MP.—Bp St Andrew's[7]—Lord March[8]—Ld Brougham—C. Pressly—Archdn. Thorp—Ld Granville—Mr Hodgkinson—C.A. Wood—and minutes. Saw Wm. Gladstone—Miss Syfret (her affairs)—Mr Gibson—Mr Panizzi. Cabinet 3–5. Nineteen to dinner. Lady Waldegrave told me her mind about myself.[9] Azeglio lectured a little on China when the subsequent evening party was over. The Duke of Cambridge dined: manly frank & kind as usual.

20. S. aft. Ascension.

Chapel Royal mg. All Saints aft. Dined with Ld R. Cavendish to meet the Bp of Oxford.[10] Saw Granville on Derby's Speech of yesterday.[11] Read Record[12] & weekly papers. Translated a verse still remaining of Toplady's

---

[1] E. Nash, treasury clerk 1842, senior clerk of civil list 1861.

[2] William Delarive, 1827–1900, Swiss friend of Cavour, wrote *Le droit de la Suisse* (1860) and *La question de Savoie*, 2v. (1860).

[3] *H* clviii. 1423.

[4] Whig peers preparing their tactics.

[5] Calling for full application of the 1853 Forbes Mackenzie Act, allowing police to enter Scottish public houses: *PP* 1860 xxxii.

[6] Guests in *The Times*, 21 May 1860, 8.

[7] Charles *Wordsworth.

[8] Charles Henry *Gordon-Lennox, 1818–1903; styled earl of March, succ. as 6th duke of Richmond 1860; president P.L.B. 1859, B. of T. 1867–8; tory leader in Lords 1868; lord president 1874–80; sec. for Scotland 1885–6; agriculturalist.

[9] Reflecting general whig displeasure with Gladstone at this time, see Hewett, 164.

[10] '. . . with Gladstone, he rather subdued; he said, "If the next twenty years alter as much the position of those who govern England, &c.".,' Wilberforce, ii. 449.

[11] *Derby told a dpn. that the national revenue interest required the Lords' action: *The Times*, 21 May 1860, 12.

[12] The evangelical paper.

Hymn.[1] Read Woodgate's Abnormal Condition of the Church.[2] Wrote to Ld J. Russell—& copy.[3] E. Gray[R].

21. M. X

Wrote to Rev. B. Price—Earl Granville—Mr Tite MP.[4]—A. Kinnaird— Mr Warre[5]—Mrs Marriott—Willy—Mr Dodson[6]—Dr Pusey—and minutes. Saw Ld Stratheden[7]—Mr Anderson—Mr Herries—Ld Granville[8]—Mr Pressly—Mr Timm—Mr Stephenson with Sir T. Fremantle—H of C. $4\frac{1}{4}$–$7\frac{1}{4}$: working W[ine] L[icences] Bill.[9] Saw E. Gray[R]. Read ... 1 Poems: Fortifn. Report & Papers.[10]

22. T.

Wrote to Sir T. Fremantle—Dss. of Sutherland—Mr Ryan—S. Herbert— Archdn. Thorp—and minutes. Cabinet $12\frac{3}{4}$–$4\frac{1}{4}$: rather stiff.[11] H of C. $4\frac{1}{4}$–7.[12] Evg at home. Saw Mr Gibson (2)—Rev Mr Williams. Read Sinclair Hist Rev.[13]—Capps on Nat. Debt[14]—Fortificn. Report.

23. Wed.

Wrote to Ld Palmerston—Watson & Smith—Ld J. Russell—Mr Whalley MP[15]—Dr Pusey—Rev Dr Wolff—and minutes. Eighteen to dinner: evening party afterwards. Saw Sir Jas Graham—Lord Aberdeen—failing. —Duke of Marlborough—Sir A. Spearman—Mr Hubbard—Mr Roupell[16]— Lord Clarence Paget. Worked on Memorandum resp. Fortifications.[17] Ride with Agnes.

[1] 'Rock of ages', for his *Translations* with *Lyttelton.
[2] See 5 July 57.
[3] Demanding the Commons' rights be asserted; Add MS 44291, f. 313.
[4] (Sir) William *Tite, 1798–1873; built Royal Exchange and many railway stations; vice-president administrative reform association; liberal M.P. Bath from 1855; kt. 1869.
[5] John Ashley Warre, 1787—Nov. 1860; whig M.P. sundry constituencies 1812–34, Ripon from 1857.
[6] John George *Dodson, 1825–97; Christ Church; liberal M.P. E. Sussex 1854–74, Chester 1874–80, Scarborough 1880–4; chaired cttees. and deputy speaker 1865–72; president, L.G.B. 1880, chancellor of duchy 1882–4; cr. Baron Monk Bretton 1884; unionist 1886; see Add MS 44252.
[7] See 12 Apr. 48.
[8] *Granville moved the Paper Duties Repeal Bill 2°R which the Lords then rejected in 104:183: *H* clviii. 1545.
[9] *H* clviii. 1552.
[10] See 22 Jan. 60.
[11] See *Palmerston's report in *L.Q.V.* 1 series, iii. 510. Victoria thought the Lords' rejection '*a very good thing*', ibid.
[12] Ireland: *H* clviii. 1618.
[13] See 2 Dec. 52.
[14] See 22 Feb. 60.
[15] G. H. Whalley (see 17 Feb. 60) led, with *Duncombe, Commons hostility to the Lords rejection: *H* clviii. 1614, 1724.
[16] William Roupell, 1831–*ca.* 1880; forger and defrauder; liberal M.P. Lambeth 1857–62; imprisoned 1862, released 1869.
[17] Finished next day; draft in Add MS 44749, f. 142, printed version with additions, ibid. 44591, f. 47.

24. Th.

Wrote to Mr Beckett—and minutes. Finished Memorandum on Fortifications. Eight to breakfast. Saw Mr Richards—Lord J. Russell—Mr Whalley
MP—Mr S. Herbert. Cabinet $12\frac{1}{4}$–$4\frac{1}{4}$. Read my mem. aloud.[1] H of C.
$4\frac{1}{4}$–8 and $8\frac{1}{2}$–12. W.L. Bill virtually through.[2] Read [blank space]s Poems.

25. Fr.

Wrote to S. Herbert—C.L. Ryan—M. de Hauranne—Mr W. Brown—Ld
Granville—Robn. G.—Ld J. Russell—Attorney General—and minutes.
Saw Sir A. Spearman—Duke of Marlborough—Mr Ouvry[3]—Mr T. Milner
Gibson. H of C. $4\frac{1}{4}$–7 and $8\frac{3}{4}$–$12\frac{1}{2}$. Sent up W.L. Bill.[4] Read Gairdner on
Medical Profession.[5]

26. Sat. [Cliveden]

Wrote to Mr Anderson—Watson & Smith—Mr H. Lees—D. of Argyll—
J.N.G.—S. Herbert—Bp of Oxford—Scotts—and minutes. Off at $4\frac{1}{2}$ to
Cliveden: when we were received with the usual warmth. Saw Ld Lynd-
hurst—Dr Fergusson—Scotts—Aunt J—Mr Anderson. Read Wolff's Life.[6]

Though I seldom have time to note down the hairbreadth scapes of which so
many occur in these strange times & with our strangely constructed Cabinet yet
I must put down a few words with respect to the great question now depending
between the Lords and the English Nation.

On Sunday when it was well known that the Paper Duties Bill would be
rejected I received from Lord John Russell a letter which will be found with my
reply in its due place.[7] It included one to him from Lord Palmerston with copy
of his answer. Lord Palmerston's came in sum to this that the vote of the Lords
would not be a party vote, that as to the *thing done* it was right, that we could
not help ourselves, that we should simply acquiesce, and no Minister ought to
resign.

Lord John in his reply stated that he took a much more serious view of the
question and gave reasons. Then he went on to say that though he did not agree
in the grounds stated by Lord P. he would endeavour to arrive at the same
conclusion. His letter accordingly ended with practical acquiescence. And he
stated to *me* his concurrence in Lord P.'s closing proposition.

Hereupon I wrote an immediate reply of which a copy will be found. We met
in Cabinet to consider the case. Lord P. started on the line he had marked out.
I think he proposed to use some meaningless words in the H. of C. as the value

---

[1] *Palmerston noted in his diary (Broadlands MS D 20): 'Sidney Herbert mooted
Fortification Question. Gladstone read an absurd & nonsensical Memorandum against
it . . .'

[2] *H* clviii. 1655.

[3] Frederic *Ouvry, 1814–81; antiquarian; *Newcastle's solicitor.

[4] And appt. member of select cttee. on precedents for taxation repeal: *H* clviii. 1742;
see *PP* 1860 xxii. 1.

[5] See 7 May 60.

[6] J. *Wolff, *Travels and adventures*, 2v. (1860–1).

[7] 'We have a three-fold complication—the Paper vote, the Fortifications, and the
Reform Bill: & I am afraid there will be rough weather'; to Russell, 23 May 1860, PRO
30/22/19, f. 86.

we set on our privileges & our determination to defend them if attacked by way of garniture etc. to the act of their abandonment.

Upon this I stated my opinions coming to the point that this proceeding of the H. of Lords amounted to the establishment of a reviewing power over the H. of C. in its most vital function long declared exclusively its own and of a divided responsibility in fixing the revenue and charge of the country for the year: besides aggravating circumstances on which it was needless to dwell. In this proceeding nothing would induce me to acquiesce: while I earnestly desired that the mildest means of correction should be adopted.

This was strongly backed in principle by Lord John: who thought that as public affairs would not admit of our at once confining ourselves to this subject we should take it up the first thing next Session & send up a new Bill. Practical as well as other objections were taken to this mode of proceeding and opposition was continued on the merits: Lord Palmerston keen and persevering. He was supported by the Chancellor—Wood—Granville (in substance)—Lewis & Cardwell, who thought nothing could be done, but were ready to join in resigning if thought fit.

Lord John[,] Gibson & I were for decided action. Argyll leaned the same way. Newcastle was for inquiry, to end in a declaratory Resolution. Villiers thought some step necessary.

Grey argued mildly, inclined I think to inaction. Herbert advised resignation, opposed any other course: Somerset was silent, which I conceive meant inaction.

At last Palmerston gave in & adopted with but middling grace the proposition to set out with inquiries: & with the intention to make as little of the matter as he could.

His language in giving notice on Tuesday of the General Committee went near the verge of saying we mean nothing: & an unsatisfactory impression was left on the House. Not a syllable was said in recognition of the gravity of the occasion. Lord John had unfortunately returned to F.O.—I thought I should do mischief at that stage appearing to catch at a part in the transaction.

Yesterday all was changed by the dignified declaration of Lord John. I suggested to him that he should get up: & Lord P. who had intended to keep the matter in his own hands gave way. But Lord P. was uneasy and said 'you won't pitch it into the Lords'—and other things of the same kind. On the whole I hope that in this grave matter at least we have turned the corner.[1]

27. *Whitsunday.*

Hedsor Ch & H.C. mg.—St George's Windsor aft. Saw Stephy. Received the joyful news of Meriel's coming marriage to John Talbot.[2] Read Wolff's Life. Wrote to John Talbot—Meriel Lyttelton—C.L. Ryan. Much conv.

28. *M.*

Wrote to [blank]. We drove to Bulstrode. Read Thiers' new Volume[3]— Stapylton's Canning.[4] Read Shelley &c. aloud a little.

---

[1] Initialled and dated 26 May 1860; Add MS 44778, f. 238. See Morley, ii. 32.
[2] See 19 July 60.
[3] L. A. Thiers, *History of the Consulate and the Empire of France under Napoleon,* tr. D. F. Campbell, 20 v. (1845–62), this v. just published.
[4] See 21 July 59.

29. T.

Wrote minutes. Wrote also to S.E.G.—Rev Mr Yonge.[1] Read Thiers's History. Drove to Windsor Forest & Virginia Water: 4 hours, wonderfully fine & varied woodland scenery. The bridal party came.

30. Wed.

Wrote to S. Laing—Ld R Cavendish—Prov. of Eton—Sir W. Heathcote— and minutes. The Duchess conversed & criticised on my Translations. Wrote Cabinet Mema. Read Thiers: Stapylton's Canning. We went on the water. My three fingered hand soon blisters.[2] Conv. with Dufferin.

The principal *trains* of affairs with which we have had to deal may be indicated under the following heads.
1. The Italian question, Austrian or anti-Austrian.
2. Foreign policy in general, leaning towards calm & peace, or brusqueness and war.
3. Defences & expenditure; alarm & heavy charges on the one side, modest & timid retrenchment with confidence in our position on the other.
4. Finance: as adapted to the one or the other of these groups of ideas & feelings respectively.
5. Reform: ultra Conservatism on the one side, on the other no fear of the working class & the belief that something *real* though limited should be done towards their enfranchisement.
6. Church matters may perhaps be also m ntioned though there has been no collision in regard to them whatever differences there may be: they have indeed held a very secondary place amidst the rude & constant shocks of the last twelve months.
7. Lastly the Coup d'Etat on the Paper Duties draws a new line of division.

In the many passages of argument & opinion, the only person from whom I have never to my recollection differed on a serious matter during this anxious twelvemonth is Gibson.

Let me now run through these questions noting most of those who have expressed marked opinions on them.
1. The most *Italian* members of the Cabinet have been: Lord P—Lord J R— W E G—Gibson—Argyll, and the least Italian: Lewis—Wood—Grey— Herbert—Villiers: especially.
2. In Foreign policy generally, the most combative have been: Lord Palmerston Lord John Russell—Duke of Newcastle—The Chancellor, and the *least* combative: Duke of Somerset—Duke of Argyll—Granville—Gibson—Herbert— Lewis—Grey—W.E.G.—Wood the same in feeling but not active.
3. In defence & expenditure the most alarmed, or most martial (as the case may be) have been: Lord P—Lord J R—D. of Newcastle—S. Herbert, Followed by: D. of Somerset—the Chancellor—Granville—Cardwell. Inclined the other way: Gibson—W.E.G.—Lewis—Grey—D. of Argyll—(Elgin I think).
4. In Finance some are for movement some stationary or retrograde as to be ready for immediate war. Yet here we are not divided simply as combative or anticombative. The *onward* men in finance are: Lord John Russell—D. of

[1] William Wellington Yonge, d. 1878; vicar of White Waltham, near Cliveden, from 1857.
[2] i.e. his left hand; see 13 Sept. 42.

Newcastle—Granville—Argyll—Gibson—W.E.G.—and I think the [Lord] Chancellor. The stationary men are first and foremost: Sir G. Lewis—Sir C. Wood. Next to these: Ld Palmerston—Cardwell—and I think: Villiers—Herbert.

5. On Reform I must distinguish between extension of the Franchise (a) and redistribution of seats (b). In the first the more liberal men are: Lord J Russell —D. of Somerset—D. of Newcastle—D. of Argyll—Gibson—W E G, and the fearful or opposed men are: Ld Palmerston—C. Villiers—S. Herbert. In the second, for *small* disfranchisement were I think all the first except Newcastle. For larger disfranchisement: Newcastle—Villiers and Ld Palmerston I think not greatly averse. In fact I think that larger disfranchisement of places may have been favoured by him 1. as a substitute for enlargement of the franchise which he chiefly dreads, 2. as perhaps an obstacle to the passing of any measure.

6. In Church matters Herbert Newcastle & I are the most Conservative & the most Churchlike: with a sympathy from Argyll. But as I said there is no struggle here: *patronage*, the sore subject, not being a Cabinet affair.

7. On the Paper Duties there are I think only three members of the Cabinet who have a strong feeling of the need of a remedy for the late aggression: Lord John Russell—Gibson—W E G, and Lord J. Russell leans so much upon P. in regard to foreign affairs that he is weaker on other subjects when opposed to him than might be desired.

With us in feeling are, more or less, Newcastle—Argyll—Villiers. On the other side, and pretty decidedly first and foremost, Ld Palmerston, after him: the Chancellor—Granville—Lewis—Wood—Cardwell—Herbert. It is easy to judge what an odd shifting of parts takes place in our discussions. We are not Mr Burke's famous Mosaic[1] but we are a mosaic in solution that is to say a Kaleidoscope when as the instrument turns the separate pieces readjust themselves & all come out in perfectly novel combinations.

Such a Cabinet ought not to be acephalous.[2]

31. Th.

Wrote minutes. Read Thiers. C. and I drove over to see Lady Grenville. Inspected her China. She is wonderful: to be 88 in Septr. Conv. with Sir J. Paxton—Do with Ld Dufferin.[3]

Friday June One. 1860. [London]

Wrote to Ld Granville—H.J.G.—Mr Pressly & minutes. Reached home befor_ 11. Visited Aunt J. & found her in a serious illness caused by neglect of care & nourishment. Tax Bills Comm. 3–4. Saw Mr Bright—Sir W.

---

[1] *Burke, in his 'Speech on American taxation', 19 April 1774, described *Chatham's govt. 1766–8 as a 'tessellated pavement'.

[2] Initialled and dated 30 May 1860, Add MS 44778, f. 244; parts of this mem. are in Morley, ii. 36, 635.

[3] Frederick Temple Hamilton-*Blackwood, 1826–1902, *Graham's nephew; 4th Baron Dufferin; liberally inclined; under-sec. India 1864–66; chancellor of duchy 1868; cr. earl 1871; governed Canada 1872–8, India 1884–8; ambassador at St. Petersburg 1879, Constantinople 1881, Paris 1891–6; cr. marquis 1888; see Add MS 44151. About to go on a govt. mission to Syria.

Heathcote—Missed Pearsall. Heard well in T. Square of Summerhayes. Saw Evelyn: also another[R]. H of C. 4¼–7.[1] Read M. de Kergorlay.[2]

2. Sat. [Cliveden]

Wrote to Sir J. Graham—Sir W. Dunbar—Mr Laing—Ld Palmerston— Mr Brand—Sir W. Heathcote—& minutes. Saw Ld Lyttelton—Mr Tite— Mr Pressly cum Sir T. Fremantle—Mr Laing cum Mr Anderson & Mr Arbuthnot—Mr Gibson. Cabinet 2¾–7. My resignation *all but* settled. Dined at the Palace: conv. with King of the Belgians & the P[rince] C[onsort]. Afterwards the Duchess took us back by road to Cliveden. We arrived at 2¾ AM.

3. S.

Hedsor Ch mg & aft. Mr Williams interests me much.[3] Willy's birthday: God bless him. Read Wolff's Memoirs. Wrote to Ld Palmerston[4]—S. Herbert—Ld J. Russell—Mr Pressly—Mr Arbuthnot.

4. M. [London]

Our visit ended: what courtesy, warmth, & grace. Argyll gave me to read his mediating letter to Lord P.[5] Wrote to V.C. of Oxford—H.J.G.—Sir W. Heathcote—Mr Pressly (2)—Ld J. Russell—Mr Whalley MP.—and minutes. H of C. 4¼–5¼ and 10–12¼.[6] Saw Aunt J.—better—Ld Aberdeen— J.N.G. resp. Helen. Read Duv[ergier] de Hauranne—Robinson on It. Collection[7]—Newton's Speech.[8]

5. T.

Wrote to Ld Wodehouse—Mr Pressly—Robn. G.—& minutes. H of C. 4¼–7½. Spoke on Civil Service Examnn.[9] Dined at Lady M. Alford's. Saw Ld Brougham—Mr Tite MP.—Mr Laing. Read Thiers Vol XVI.[10] Worked on Books papers & letters.

6. Wed.

Wrote to H.E. Barnes—Ld J. Russell (2)—D. of Argyll—A.B. Cochrane—

[1] Spoke on the paper duties: 'if I had any [feelings] on this particular case, I do not think the time has yet come for declaring them': *H* clviii. 1879.

[2] L. G. C. de Kergorlay, *Corps Législatif Session 1860* (1860); on tariffs.

[3] See 13 May 60.

[4] Announcing a proposal to meet the Chinese charges, and hinting at ditching the Reform Bill: Guedalla, *P*, 136.

[5] Proposing to fortify in the first instance Portsmouth only, and perhaps Plymouth, financed yearly by taxation or loan according to the state of revenue; Broadlands MSS GC/AR/22/2.

[6] Reform Bill cttee.: *H* clviii. 1951.

[7] J. C. *Robinson, *Catalogue of the various works of art forming the collection of Mathew Uzielli* (1860).

[8] Perhaps B. W. Newton, 'Regeneration in its connection with the Cross' (1860).

[9] *H* clviii. 2066.

[10] See 28 May 60.

H.J.G.—Duchess of Argyll—C. Pressly—Rev. Dr Wolff—and minutes. With Lord P. 12¼–1½: on Fortification Loan & Reform.[1] Saw Mr Gibson— Sir Jas Graham—Sir S. Northcote—Mr Tite M.P.—Mr Munro. H of C. 4–6.[2] Rode with Mary. Dined at Lady Wenlock's. Saw Chester[R]. Read Thiers.

[To 8th duke of Argyll, *Private*, 6 June 1860]

The interview with Lord Palmerston came off today. Nothing could be more kind and frank than his manner. The *matter* was first to warn me of the evils and hazards attending, for me, the operation of resigning, secondly to express his own strong sense of the obligation to persevere. Both of these I told him I could fully understand. He said he had had two great objects always before him in life: one the suppression of the Slave Trade, the other to put England in a state of defence. In short it appears that he now sees, as he considers, the opportunity of attaining a long cherished object: and it is not unnatural that he should repel any proposal which would defraud him of a glory, in & by absolving him from a duty. I understood him distinctly to adhere to 1. the whole plan, 2. the immediate commencement at all points, 3. the mode of raising the funds by one form or another of borrowing.

To every word that he said about the disadvantage of my position, I told him that I fully subscribed; but that I did not think that he was able to estimate quite adequately what it would be to me to propose or (for he said *he* would propose) to be responsible for raising money by loan to perform a service of this nature. He made no allusion to your letter.[3]

Little doubt can remain of the nature of the question which I have to decide: nor can I see such a question in any light but one.

I am now sure that Lord P. entertained this purpose when he formed the Government; but had I been in the slightest degree aware of it I should certainly but very reluctantly have abstained from joining it and helped as well as I could from another bench its Italian purposes. Still I am far indeed from regretting to have joined it, which is quite another matter.

It is the nature of one disease sometimes to drive out another: and such may be the case with our complications.

It is not yet certain whether the Fortification Loan complication, or the Reform complication or the House of Lords complication, or the China War & new Taxes complication will come uppermost. Any one of them might kill a Government: but the whole may perchance cure it.[4]

7. Th.

Wrote to Mr Pennethorne—V.C. Oxford—Mrs Wortley—Mr Cobden—

[1] *Palmerston noted in his diary, misdated 5 June (Broadlands MS D 20): 'saw Gladstone & told him nothing should turn me away from providing for Defence of Dockyards & other Points, that if he resigned nobody would believe that a man of his ability & experience & statesmanlike Position left the Govt. because he would not have the Country defended, they would say & believe however unjustly that he was afraid of the financial consequences of his Budget, & running away from them—moreover that out of office he would be thrown into Companionship with Bright which would be Ruin to him as a Public Man.'

[2] Ecclesiastical commissioners: *H* clviii. 2087.

[3] See 4 June 60.

[4] From a copy, not by Gladstone, in Add MS 44098, f. 279.

Watson & Smith—and minutes. H. of C. $4\frac{1}{4}$–8 and 10–$2\frac{1}{2}$.[1] Saw Chester[R]. Saw Aunt J—Robn. G.—Sir C. Wood (Indian I.T.).[2] Read Everett's Address[3]—Hatsell's Precedents.[4] Eleven to breakfast. Family dinner party.

8. *Fr.*

Wrote to Mr [M.J.] Barry—Mr Cobden—Mr W. Cowper—Mr Brand— Sir T. Fremantle—Saw Robn. G—S. Herbert—S. Herbert—Dss. of Sutherland—& minutes. H of C. & H. of L. $4\frac{1}{4}$–$7\frac{3}{4}$.[5] Dined with J.N.G. Saw Mr Gibson—Robn. G.—Mr Timm—Mr Dunlop. My first morning ride. Read Packet Report[6]—Thiers Hist.

9. *Sat.*

Wrote to Dr Wolff—Bp of Oxford—E. Gray—Dss. of Sutherland—J. Stenson[7]—G. Burnett. Saw Mr Barry—Mr Gibson. Failed with Gray, in Charlton St, &c[R]. Visited British Institution[8] with C. & the younger girls. Cabinet $4\frac{1}{2}$–7. Marvellous![9] Read Paper on Taxing Bills—Thiers Hist.

10. *1 S. Trin.*

Chap Royal mg & St James's (prayers) evg. MS on Gospel aloud. Wrote to D. of Argyll—Mr Westell. Missed Herbert. Saw Mr. de Beauvoir,[10] and Chester[R]. Read Thomson's Sermon[11]—Irvings Orations & argument[12]— Wolff's Memoirs.

11. *M.*

Wrote to Sir G. Sinclair—Mr Greswell—Ld Chancellor & minutes. Saw Mr Pressly—Mr W. Cowper—Ld Granville—Mr Bright—H of C.$4\frac{1}{4}$–$8\frac{1}{4}$.[13] Hatsell & worked on Taxing Bills.[14] Commee. $1\frac{1}{4}$–$3\frac{3}{4}$. Read Thiers Hist— Mitchell on Amn. Instns.[15]

[1] Govt. majority of 21 on Reform in cttee.: *H* clix. 139.
[2] *Trevelyan's refusal to collect income tax in Madras, see R. J. Moore, *Sir Charles *Wood's Indian policy* (1966), 54.
[3] E. Everett, 'Academical Education' (1857).
[4] See 24 Feb. 54.
[5] Question on French treaty: *H* clix. 178.
[6] See 8 May 60.
[7] London bookseller.
[8] For British artists, in Pall Mall.
[9] *Palmerston noted in his diary (Broadlands MS D 20): 'Gladstone urged that we ought all to resign as we had come in on Reform. This denied by John Russell . . . Gladstone's motive evidently was, to cover under a general Resignation his own failure as to Budget, & to escape from being a Party to Fortification Loan.'
[10] Possibly Ludovic de Beauvoir, travel writer.
[11] W. *Thomson, 'The power of the Atonement' (1860).
[12] E. *Irving, *For the oracles of God, four orations. For judgement to come, an argument, in nine parts* (1823).
[13] *Russell withdrew his Reform Bill: *H* clix. 226.
[14] Notes on seventeenth century Commons privileges in Add MS 44749, f. 166.
[15] S. A. Mitchell, *A general view of the United States* (1846).

12. T. X

Wrote to Mr Rowsell—Mrs L. Banks[1]—Mr Wray[2]—D of Somerset—
V.C. Oxford—and minutes. Saw Sir W. Heathcote—Mr May—The Speaker.
Tax Bills Comm. 12–4. H of C. 6–8½.[3] Visited Christie's. Read Thiers Hist—
Mitchell on Amn. Instns.—Corn Debates of 1827. Saw . . . .[R].

13. Wed.

Wrote to Robn. G.—Ld Palmerston—Mr Brand—D. of Somerset—Mr
Cobden—and minutes. P.C. Commee. on Aberdeen Ordinances 11–4¼.[4]
Read Thiers Hist.—Saw Mr Anderson—Lyttelton: about whom we had
anxiety—Mr Gibson—Lord C. Paget—Lord Aberdeen—D. of Newcastle.
Visited Phillips's. Dined at Lambeth Palace: Queen's Concert afr.

14. Th. X

Wrote to S. Herbert—Dr Bethmann[5]—S. Laing—Dss. Sutherland—Dr
Pusey—Ld Wodehouse—Sir G. Lewis—Mr Gregson—and minutes. P.C.
Committee 11 to 4½. H of C. 4½–5½ and 7–8½. Spoke on Inc. Tax.[6] Saw
Prov. of Eton—Rev Dr Russell—Mr Cardwell. Saw Williamson: singu-
lar[R]. Read Thiers Hist.—Debates on Conspir. Bill.

15. Fr.

Wrote to Col. [P.E.] Herbert—Jas Watson—Mr Gibson—and minutes.
Ten to breakfast. Tax Bills Comm. 12–4¼. H of C. 6–7½.[7] Dined at Ld
Egerton's: C.s musical party afr. Saw Mr G. Burnett (S.)—Duchess of
Sutherland—Col. Wilson Patten—Sir J. Graham—Mr. Gibson. Read Thiers
Hist.—Incidents of Ital. Priests.[8]

16. Sat.

Wrote to Mr A Court[9]—Mr E.W. Blyden[10]—Mr [A.J.H.] Banks[11]—Provost
of Oriel—Mr Hubbard—G. Harcourt—Sir J. Ogilvy—and minutes. Opera
(La Gazza Ladra)[12] & Floral Hall in evening. Saw Sir A. Spearman—Lord
Lyttelton (W.L's business)—Miss Syfret (her purchase)—Mr A'Court—

[1] Louisa Banks of Weston house, Stratford, London, wife of A. J. H., surgeon, claimed
debt of £9/11/- owed by a Miss Housley, who said diarist was her fa.; Gladstone's
denial eventually ended the affair; Hawn P.
[2] William Mark Wray, d. 1886; naval chaplain; see Add MS 44531, f. 14.
[3] European forces in India: H clix. 368.
[4] Probably on Aberdeen university reform ordinances: see PP 1861 xlviii. 735.
[5] Giving D. Bethmann permission to tr. Studies on Homer (apparently never published);
Add MS 44393, f. 363 and 44531; no application was made to the O.U.P. Studien über
Homer und das Homerische Zeitalter, frei bearbeitet von Albert Schuster in one v. was
published ?1863.
[6] H clix. 445.
[7] Annuity tax (Edinburgh) abolition: H clix. 507.
[8] L. Bianchi, priest fighting with Garibaldi, Incidents in the life of an Italian (1860).
[9] See 23 July 54?
[10] Edward Wilmot Blyden, black Liberian statesman, had written for educative books,
including Studies on Homer: Add MS 44393, f. 272; Gladstone sent many in the 1860s.
[11] The husband; see 12 June 60.
[12] Rossini, at Covent Garden.

Mr Cowper—Saw one[R]. Cabinet 3½–6. Read Thiers Hist. Rode after Cabinet.

17. 2 S. Trin.

Whitehall mg & Chapel Royal aftn. Herbert here to breakfast & we conversed a good deal on pending & Ch affairs. Read MacColls Pamphlet &c.[1] —Wolff's Memoirs—Incidents of Ital. Priest. Wrote to Willy—Rev M. MacColl—Mrs Heywood.

18. M.

Wrote to Ld Gosford[2]—E. Cardwell—and minutes. Tax Bills Comm. & H of C. 12–5¼.[3] Saw Sir W. Heathcote—Mr Pressly—Mr Deedes MP—Mr Laing—Mr Gibb[4] *cum* Mr Hadfield. Dined with the Heywoods.[5] Rode in the Park: & found a man not alarmed! (Mr Barker).[6] Read Thiers.

19. T.

Wrote to Dss. of Sutherland—Sir F. Baring—Ld Granville—Mr Cobden— Ld Stanhope—Mr Duncombe—Sir W. Heathcote—and minutes. Saw Mr Anderson—Mr Clay—The Speaker—Lord J. Russell—Mr Gibson. 11–12¾. Radcliffe Trust met at my house. Read Thiers. H of C. 6–7¾ and 8¾–12.[7] Worked a little on books.

20. Wed.

Wrote to Robn. G.—Mast. of Mint—Bp of Oxford—Watson & Smith— Mr I[saac] Butt[8]—Sir A. Spearman—Sir J. Acton—Mr G. Burnett—Mr O. Gordon—Duke of Argyll—and minutes. H of C. 5½ to forward business.[9] Saw Mr Cardwell—Mr Herbert . . . Ld Lyndhurst—Ld Lyttelton—Ld Grey —Baron Rothschild—Bp of Oxford—Rev. A. Goalen—Mr Gibson. Read Thiers Hist—The Prisoner of the Temple.[10] Attended in the evg the Apsley House Concert.

21. Th.

Wrote to Wm Gladstone—Sir A Spearman—W. Cowper—Baron Brunnow —G.G. Scott—Ld Granville—Ld Brougham—Duchess of Suthd.—and

[1] M. *MacColl, 'Mr. Cheyne and the bishop of Brechin. A letter to . . . Gladstone' (1860).
[2] Archibald Acheson, 1806–64; Christ Church; liberal M.P. Armagh 1830–47; 3rd earl of Gosford 1849.
[3] Civil service: *H* clix. 580.
[4] Possibly James Gibb of Liverpool.
[5] See 27 Oct. 56n.
[6] Obscure.
[7] Resolution in favour of harbours of refuge adopted: *H* clix. 672.
[8] Isaac *Butt sent his 2v. on Italy (see 25 June 60); Add MS 44393, f. 371.
[9] *H* clix. 728.
[10] W. A. Meves, *The 'Prisoner of the Temple'*, an introductory account of the life of *Louis Charles de Bourbon* (1860).

minutes. Ten to breakfast. Saw Rev G. Williams[1]—Sir A. Spearman. French play at $8\frac{1}{4}$. But carried off at $8\frac{3}{4}$ to H of C.[2] Staid till 11. Read Hallam's Const Hist.[3]—Thiers finished Vol. XVII. Worked on books.

22. Fr. X

Wrote to Ld Palmerston—Mr Duncombe—W. Cowper—Mr Hodgson Pratt[4]—Sir W. Heathcote—and minutes. H of C. $6\frac{3}{4}$–1: Sav. B. Monies Bill.[5] Saw Mr Anderson—Bp of Argyll—Mr Whalley MP—Mr Salt[6] & Mr Hadfield—Mr [blank]. Saw Linsell. Read Leone Levi on Taxn.[7]—Pratt on Univ. Edn. for Indians.

23. Sat. [Cliveden]

Wrote to Mr Pressly—Mr Cobden—Mr Finlay—and minutes. Wrote on the Paper Duty & Tax Bills case.[8] Attended the Volunteer Review: a very noble spectacle.[9] Off to Cliveden at 5.15. Found the Bp of Oxford & Argyll. All was kind & pleasant as usual. Read (part) Sumner's Speech.[10]

24. 3 S.Trin. St Joh. Bapt.

Taplow Ch & HC. mg. The Bp [of Oxford] preached a noble Sermon. Hedsor aft. Saw Mr Pressly. Conv. with D. of Argyll on our strange position.[11] Wrote to Sir W. Heathcote—Earl Powis. Read Vaughan's Sermons[12]—Lawrence's Assistant at H.C.[13]

25. M. [London]

Wrote to Ld Palmerston—Lady James—Mr Anderson—Sir E. Grogan—Ld Kinnaird—Mr Shand.[14] Came up by 9.55 train. Saw Ld J. Russell who showed me an ominous (but not surprising) letter from Lord P.[15] Committee 12–4. H of C. 6–$7\frac{3}{4}$.[16] Saw Ld Advocate—Ld Powis—Robn. G. Read Sumner (finished)—Butt's Hist. of Italy.[17] Saw Linsell[R].

[1] See 21 Dec. 39.
[2] To speak on the Inland Bonding Bill cttee.: H clix. 815.
[3] See 16 July 40.
[4] Had sent his 'University education for Indians in England' (1860); Hawn P.
[5] A rough ride: H clix. 894.
[6] (Sir) Titus *Salt, 1803–77; Bradford wool manufacturer and benefactor; built Saltaire; liberal M.P. Bradford 1859–61, cr. bart. 1869.
[7] L. *Levi, On taxation; how it is raised and how it is expended (1860).
[8] See 30 June 60.
[9] Review of 20,000 Volunteers in Hyde Park.
[10] 'Speech of Charles Sumner on the Bill for the admission of Kansas as a free state' (4 June 1860).
[11] See Argyll, ii. 164.
[12] C. J. *Vaughan, Five sermons on revision of the liturgy (1860).
[13] See 13 May 60.
[14] Perhaps (Sir) Charles Farquhar Shand, 1812–89, of Kincardineshire; council to treasury in Scotland 1857–60, just leaving for Mauritius as chief justice.
[15] PRO 30/22 f. 149, supporting *Walpole's rather than *Bright's report to select cttee. on Lords; see 25 May 60n.
[16] Answered questions on game licences: H clix. 953.
[17] I. *Butt, History of Italy from the abdication of Napoleon I, 2v. (1860).

26. T.

Wrote to Ld Granville (2)—Mr Laing (2)—D. of Argyll—Mr Pressly—
Sir A. Spearman—Mr Duncombe—Watson & Smith—Mr Hodgkinson MP
—and minutes. Saw Sir W. James—Bp of Oxford—R. Phillimore—Sir W.
Heathcote—Mr Ellice MP. Committee 12–4. Dined with the Duchess of
Inverness. Musical party at home afterwards. Read Canada Reformer's
Address[1]—Pitzipios on Oriental Question.[2]

27. Wed. X

Wrote to Ld Kinnaird—C. Pressly—Mr Stirling MP.—Dr Briscoe—Lady
Waldegrave—Mr Greswell—Archdn. Sinclair—and minutes. Tax Bills
Comm. 12–6 and Cabinet 6–7$\frac{1}{4}$. Saw Ld Lyttelton—Lord John Russell.
Saw Wyndham = Gray.[3] Read Cannings Speeches.[4] Dined at Mr Gibson's.

28. Th.

Wrote to Sir A. Spearman—Helen—Atty. General—S. Herbert—Vicar
St Martin's—and minutes. H of C. 4$\frac{1}{2}$–7$\frac{1}{4}$ and 10–1$\frac{3}{4}$.[5] Saw Mr Panizzi—Ld
Aberdeen ∴ Mr Hamilton[6]—The Speaker[7]—The Attorney General—Do
cum Sir G. Grey & Mr Laing—Mr Milner Gibson. Saw the Belvedere
Pictures.[8] Attended Portrait Gallery meeting.[9] Worked on Tax Bills.
Read Hazlitt's Venice.[10]

29. Fr. St Peter.

Wrote to The Speaker—Sir J. Paxton—Ld Lindsay[11]—Ld Chancellor—
Mr Everett—Dss. of Sutherland—Mr Pressly—Archd. Sandford—Dr Pusey
—Mr Potter—Scotts—Ld Glenelg[12]—Miss Chatterton[13]—and minutes. Saw
Scots Temperance Depn. Saw Mr Milner Gibson—The Speaker *cum* Mr
May. Commee. at 2.15. Dined at Mr Tomline's. Read Hazlitt's Venice—
Pamphlet on Goth. Archit. Worked on Taxing Bills.

30. Sat.

Wrote to Ld Glenelg—Heywood Kennards & Co[14]—Bp of Argyll—The

[1] Not found.
[2] Prince J. G. Pitzipios, 'The Eastern question solved, in a letter to Lord *Palmerston'
(1860).
[3] But see 25 Apr., 11 May 60.
[4] See 19 Apr. 60.
[5] Indian forces: *H* clix. 1086.
[6] Punctuation apparently thus; meaning obscure.
[7] See J. E. *Denison, *Notes from my journal* (1900), 70.
[8] Lord Eardley's pictures, from Belvedere House, sold at Christie's; see *Art Journal*
(1860), 246.
[9] As a trustee.
[10] W. C. Hazlitt, *History of the Venetian Republic*, 4 v. (1860).
[11] Sir John Trotter Bethune, 1827–94; *de jure* 10th earl of Lindsay 1851 (recognised
by Lords 1878).
[12] See 7 Sept. 30.
[13] Perhaps Elizabeth Chatterton of Toxteth Park, Liverpool.
[14] Bankers in Lombard Street; see 27 Oct. 56n.

Speaker—Ld Granville—Ld J. Russell (2)—Gladstone & Co—Prof L. Levi
—Ld Brougham—and minutes. Dined at Mr Hubbard's. Saw Mr Pressly—
Miss Chatterton—Mr T.M. Gibson. Worked on Tax Bills. Cabinet $4\frac{1}{2}$–$7\frac{1}{4}$.
Ugly![1]

Sunday Jul. 1. 1860. 4 S.Trin.

Whitehall & H.C. mg—All Saints aft. MS of 43 aloud in Evg. Saw D. of
Argyll—Dss. of Sutherland—Read Dr Vaughan's Sermons—Bp Words-
worth's Opinion[2]—Dr Wolff's Memoirs—Irving's Orations[3]—Secretan's
Life of Nelson.[4] Wrote Mem. for Box resp. Tax Bills.

1. It appears to me absolutely necessary to seek a remedy for the late act of the
Lords.
2. I see no advantage in Mr. Collier's or any other Resolution,[5] except as introductory to action: and if action can be had, a Resolution may perhaps be[6]
needless[.]
3. Lord Palmerston's objections to placing a large or considerable part of our
Taxes on the footing of annual grants appear to me conclusive.
4. I cannot agree with Sir Geo. Lewis that the Income Tax with the Tea and
Sugar Duties give us by expiring a security for next year. Those are subjects
so weighted with interests or difficulties of their own, that the odds (I think)
are greatly against its being practicable to handle them freely as tools for
operating on other questions.
5. The principle of combining in one the financial measures of the year is good:
but I fear it would often be found so inconvenient as to be unavailable.
6. Difficulty I admit surrounds us on all hands:[7] nothing can now succeed without union, effort, & determination: but even with them[8] I see no way of
ultimate hope or safety except some plan of action founded on the principle
that the Lords are not to tax the people without their consent.[9]

2. M.

Wrote to M. de la Rive[10]—V.C. Oxford—Goldwin Smith—The Queen—
Watson & Smith—Dr Adam[11]—Sir W. Heathcote—and minutes. Cabinet
$12\frac{3}{4}$–$3\frac{3}{4}$.[12] H of C. $4\frac{1}{4}$: and $10\frac{1}{4}$–1.[13] Saw Ld Granville—Mr T.M. Gibson (2)—

[1] He read the cabinet a long mem., 'Paper duty and taxing power of the two Houses.
Substance read to Cabinet Saty.', which suggested spirit duty increases to balance paper
duty repeal losses ('if there is to be any step of conciliation taken towards the Lords,
this measure would fulfil the condition in most unexceptionable form') and reminded
the cabinet that the French treaty required paper excize duty reductions: Add MS 44749,
f. 180–196.
[2] C. *Wordsworth, 'Opinion on the appeal of the Rev. P. Cheyne' (1858).
[3] See 10 June 60.
[4] C. F. Secretan, *Memoirs of . . . the pious Robert Nelson* (1860).
[5] R. P. *Collier withdrew his vague but hostile resolution: *H* clix. 1397, 5 July 60.
[6] 'seems' deleted.   [7] 'but' deleted.
[8] 'I know nothing as it seems to me will be safe or hopeful' deleted.
[9] Initialled and dated 1 July 1860; Add MS 44750, f. 1 and in Guedalla, *P*, 138.
[10] Auguste de la Rive, Swiss ambassador; about his honorary Oxford degree; Add
MS 44531, f. 24.
[11] Perhaps Andrew Mercer Adam, 1829–95; physician in Scotland and Lincolnshire;
translator and author.
[12] Only *Gibson and *Argyll voted with him on a cabinet vote on the Lords: Broadlands CAB/A/132.
[13] India; spoke briefly on supply: *H* clix. 1310.

Ld Glenelg—Ld Palmerston (afr. Cabinet)[1]—Mr Laing *cum* Mr Anderson —Mr Herbert *cum* Mr Laing. Dined at Mrs Talbots. Read Butt's Italy.

3. T.

Wrote to G.H. Christie—C. Pressly—Ld J. Russell—& draft—Ld Palmerston[2]—D. of Argyll—Mr Cobden—Dean Ramsay—and minutes. Dinner & evg party at home. Saw Rev M. MacColl—Sir A. Spearman—Mr T.M. Gibson—Ld Palmerston. H of C. 6–8.[3] Read Butt's Italy. Sat to Mr Eastham.[4]

4. Wed.

Wrote to Sir W. Heathcote—Sir T. Fremantle—The Queen[5]—Ld Palmerston (& copy)[6]—Mr Pressly—Mr Innes—Master of Mint—and minutes. Rode with Lena, W., & George. Saw Mr Bright MP—Mr Dalgleish MP— Mr Norris MP—Mr Gibson—The Master of the Mint—R. Phillimore. Dined at Ld Westminsters. Lansdowne House afr. Cabinet $4\frac{1}{2}$–7. Fortifications discussed: my knell. Further finance settled. Read Butt's History.

5. Th.

Wrote to Ld Palmerston[7]—C.L. Ryan—and minutes. Stafford House to luncheon at 2. Lady Dufferin[8] spoke to me of Agnes: & Mrs Norton of Ld Melbourne. Saw Mr Pressly [and] Sir T. Fremantle on Res[olution]s.—Sir W. Heathcote—Mr T.M. Gibson—Mr Freeland[9]—Duchess of Sutherland. H of C. $4\frac{1}{4}$–$8\frac{1}{2}$ and $9\frac{1}{2}$–$1\frac{1}{4}$. Read Senior's Journal.[10] Eleven to breakfast.

I broke the ice & spoke on the privilege question.[11]

6. Fr.

Wrote to Vicar of St Martin's—V.C. Oxford—Ld Kinnaird—E. Cardwell— B. Oliveira—J.E. Fitzgerald—D of Newcastle. Saw Sir W. Heathcote—Do *cum* Mr G. Smith—Mr S. Cave MP—Mr Eastham—Mr Milner Gibson— Dss. of Sutherland. P.C. Comm. on Cambridge Ordinance at 4 PM.[12] Ld Ward's music $4\frac{1}{2}$–6. H of C. $6\frac{1}{4}$–$8\frac{1}{4}$ and $10\frac{1}{4}$–2.[13] Read Senior's MS Journal.

[1] Threatening resignation if *Palmerston did not take some form of legislative action instead of resolution on the Lords; Palmerston delayed the resolutions to give Gladstone 'more time to think and more room to turn round in' (*L.Q.V.*, 1s., iii. 513).

[2] Guedalla, *P*, 138.

[3] Misc. business: *H* clix. 1326.

[4] Perhaps George Eastham, portrait painter or photographer in Chelsea.

[5] On *Wyon's profile for new coins: Guedalla, *Q*, i. 119.

[6] On the resolutions: Guedalla, *P*, 139.

[7] Guedalla, *P*, 140.

[8] Helen Selina, *Sheridan's da., widow of 4th Baron Dufferin; she m. 2ndly 1862 Lord Gifford, and d. 1867.

[9] Humphrey William Freeland, 1814–92; poet and liberal M.P. Chichester 1859–63.

[10] See 14 June 56.

[11] *Palmerston introduced the three govt. resolutions: Gladstone spoke later, supported the resolutions, but added: 'without in the least degree imparting blame to, or finding fault with the terms of the proposal of the Government, I reserve to myself entire freedom to adopt any words which may have the slightest hope of success for vindicating by action the rights of this House': *H* clix. 1432.

[12] Probably new statutes for professors; see *The Guardian*, 3 October 1860, 867.

[13] Resolutions on the Lords all agreed to: *H* clix. 1536.

7. Sat. X

Wrote to Sir G. Lewis—Mr Hodgkinson—C. Redding[1]—E.J. Troughton[2] —and minutes. Also[3] to Sir T. Phillipps—Dr Pusey—Dr Molesworth— Mr Brooks[4]—Mr Todd. Cabinet $3\frac{3}{4}$–$6\frac{1}{4}$. Pleased with Ld P.s words about the Census: but qy. conduct?[5] Dined with the Wortleys at Sheen. Rode with Agnes & Lena. Saw Mr Pressly—Mr T.M. Gibson. Read Senior's Journal (finished).

8. 5 S.Trin.

St James mg & All Saints' aft.—Wilson S. aloud in evg. Wrote to Dr [C.J.] Vaughan. Read Wolff (finished Vol 1)—Vaughan's 5 Sermons (finished)[6]— Arthur's Italy in Transition[7]—Roberts on St Matthew[8]—Memoirs of Italian Rebel.[9] Saw Mr Hunt's wonderful picture.[10]

9. M.

Wrote to Mr Gibson—V.C. Oxford—Mr Cardwell—Mr Pressly—Mr M'Coll —Mr Wynne—Sir C. Wood—Sir J. Lacaita—Mr Sala[11]—and minutes. N[ational] D[ebt] Commrs. met 3 P.M. H of C. $4\frac{1}{4}$–$6\frac{1}{4}$.[12] Wrote Mem. on Census & copy. Saw Mr T.M. Gibson—Mr Anderson—Sir A. Spearman— Mr Hubbard—Mr Laing—Mr A. Finlay—Mr Snelly: deranged.[13] Saw E. Lovell & found with great pleasure & thankfulness such as *I* can feel that there is to be marriage[R]. Read Roman papers[14]—Butt's Hist. Italy.

I regret that a Religious Census has been proposed on the part of the Government.[15] But I believe 1. That a religious census is not in itself mischievous. 2. That combined with a return of attendance it would be as nearly as possible fair. 3. That the opposition now offered will not materially alter the value of the return as it respects the main point, that between Church & Dissent. 4. That the Govt. may suffer from offending the Dissenters but cannot by merely conciliating

[1] Cyrus *Redding, 1785–1870; journalist and novelist, wrote influential 3v. on modern wines.

[2] i.e. Rev. J. E. Troughton.

[3] Rest of entry written at foot of next page, linked by +.

[4] H. Brooks supported his stand on the Lords: Add MS 44531, f. 26.

[5] *Palmerston's diary (Broadlands MS D 20): 'Settled arrangements of Bill for fortifications. Impossible to say whether Gladstone will go or stay. Settled to give up religious Enumeration in [1861] Census'; see 9 July 60.

[6] See 24 June 60.

[7] W. Arthur, *Italy in transition, public scenes and private opinions in the spring of 1860* (1860).

[8] See 29 Jan. 60.

[9] Count G. N. Ricciardi, *The autobiography of an Italian rebel* (1860).

[10] Holman *Hunt's 'Finding of the Saviour in the Temple', exhibited in the German Gallery, Bond St.

[11] George Augustus Henry Fairfield *Sala, 1828–95; journalist, had sent copy of his piece in the *Daily Telegraph*; then also writing weekly column in *Illustrated London News*, which observed (14 July 60) 'a rumour arose that [Palmerston] had given him [Gladstone] a letter of license to make any sort of oration which would relieve his mind and keep him *en rapport* with his free-trade admirers'.

[12] Bankruptcy Bill: *H* clix. 1618.

[13] Unidentified.

[14] Despatches on developments in papal states: *PP* 1860 lxviii. 381.

[15] This lightly deleted; a religious census was held in 1851; nonconformists prevented one in 1861, which anglicans believed would better show anglican strength.

them retain the character & strength necessary for its credit. 5. That the question whether it should have proposed the Census (and I regret it under the circs) is one thing—the question whether it can recede bodily from the proposal after the pledges which I understand to have been given, is another.[1] 6. That what is really feared is that the H. of C. would if left to itself adopt the Census, and that the Govt. is in reality required to use its influence to turn it the other way.

My constituents call for the Census as a claim of justice. I shall accept what the Cabinet may unitedly do: but my leaning for the reason I have numbered 5 is with Lord P.[2]

10. T.

Wrote to Mr Estcourt—Mr Pressly—Mr Cobden (& copy)—Mr Laing—Sir C. Wood—and minutes. H of C. 12–4 and 6–8.[3] Read Butt's Hist. Saw Mr Barry and others—V.C. Oxford—Mr Stansfield—Mr Briscoe—Mr Dunlop MP—Mr Locke King MP—Sir A. Spearman—Sir J. Graham—S. Herbert. Saw E. Porson[R]. Drive with C.

11. Wed.

A smart attack of diarrhoea came on last evening & kept me in bed all today. Saw Lavis twice. Wrote to S. Herbert, & minutes.

12. Th.

Wrote to Sir A. Spearman—D. of Argyll—Ld J. Thynne—Mr Anderson— and minutes. Rose between 3 & 4, & drove. Saw Robn. G.—Mr Lavis— S. Herbert—Duke of Argyll. H of C. 6–6½ and 9¾–12½ on China Vote &c.[4] Read Arthur on Italy—Senior's MS Journal (P.S.)

13. Frid.

Wrote to Miss Christie—Ld Brougham—Mr Laing—Sir A. Spearman— Mr W. M'Donald—and minutes. H of Commons 7½–2¼ China Vote &c.[5] Saw Mr Anderson—Duke of Argyll—Mr Gibson—Mr Lavis—Mr Anderson & Mr Pressly—Sir S. Scott & Co. Worked on finance: to be ready with my plan.[6] Read Arthur on Italy.

14. Sat.

Wrote to Rev Dr Burgess—Mr Greswell—Mr M'Coll—V.C. Oxford—Sir J. Graham—Mr Timm—Mr Laing & minutes. Radcliffe Trust 11–12¾. Cabinet 3¾–6½. Saw Duke of Argyll—Mr MacCulloch—Mr B. Quaritch & his shop. Read Chatham's Life[7]—The approved Boccaccio.[8]

[1] 'My constituents are strongly for' here deleted.
[2] Signed and dated 9 July 1860; Add MS 44636, f. 32, where Palmerston's minute (objecting to the Cabinet's decision to withdraw the religious census) is also written out.
[3] Spoke briefly on savings banks: *H* clix. 1662.
[4] Justified the small amount budgeted for: *H* clix. 1823.
[5] *H* clix. 1879.
[6] See 16 July 60.
[7] F. Thackeray, *A history of the Right Hon. William *Pitt, Earl of Chatham* (1827).
[8] Probably a bowdlerized version of Boccaccio's *Il Decamerone* (1573 ed.).

15. 6 S.Trin.

St James's mg & (prayer) evg. Wilson aloud at night. Saw Aunt J.—Made more inquiries about M. S[ummerhayes]. Looked at my MS Verses.[1] Began MS on Gospel. Read Martyn Tracts[2]—Alford's Greek Test.[3]—Babington's Pecock[4]—Vaughan's Sermons.

16. M. X

Wrote to Mr Pressly and minutes. Wrote Mem. on Fortifications for circulation: the last shot in the locker.[5] Got up the figures for this aftn. H of C. $4\frac{1}{4}$–$8\frac{1}{2}$ and $11\frac{1}{4}$–$1\frac{1}{2}$: on China: financial statement (1 hour): Wine Licences Ireland—&c.[6] Saw Sir S. Northcote—Mr Adderley—Mr Hewlett[7]—Mr Laing—Saw Wyndham[R]. Read divers.

17. T.

Wrote to Dss. of Sutherland—Baron Brunnow—Dean of Ch.Ch.—Sir J. Paxton—Dean Ramsay—Mr Barnes—Scotts.—Lady Beauchamp—Sir J. Pakington—& minutes. Dined with Ld Harris. Saw Sir T. Phillipps—Sir John Rae Reid—Col. Wilson Patten—Sir G.C. Lewis. Deputn. of 5 from Constitl. Defence Committee 4–5. H of C. $12\frac{1}{4}$–4 on Educn. &c. and 11–$2\frac{3}{4}$ on Lords' Aggression &c.[8] Rode in evg.

18. Wed.

Wrote to D. of Argyll—Sir J. Pakington—Mr Brand—Sir A. Spearman—Mr Cobden—Sir T. Fremantle—and minutes. Cabinet $2\frac{1}{4}$–$4\frac{3}{4}$. And still I am not dead. Such plans today! Ten to breakfast. Saw Sir T. Fremantle—Mr Timm—Mr Garden[9]—Mr Pressly—Mr Howes[10]—Mr Hankey—Mr Ayrton. H of C. 5–6.[11] Dined at Stafford House. Read La Politique Anglaise[12]—Q.R. on Conservative Reaction.[13]

19. Th.

Wrote to Dss. of Sutherland—Mr Pressly—Ld Palmerston (3)[14]—Mr Pease

[1] In preparation for his joint volume with *Lyttelton.
[2] H. *Martyn, *Controversial tracts on Christianity and Mohammedanism* (1824).
[3] See 17 Feb. 50.
[4] R. *Peacock, *The repressor of over much blaming of the clergy*, ed. C. Babington, 2v. (1860).
[5] Thirty eight points on the folly of the scheme, with replies by *Grey, *Wood, *Granville, *Somerset, *Herbert, *Villiers; Add MS 44749, ff. 9–31.
[6] Hansard's report clearly truncated: *H* clix. 1951; regarded by the treasury as a 'Supplementary Budget': PRO T 171/185, f. 14.
[7] Perhaps Henry Gray Hewlett, 1832–97, antiquarian and editor; later a correspondent (Hawn P).
[8] *H* clix. 2092.
[9] See 16 Dec. 31.
[10] Edward Howes, 1813–71; barrister and tory M.P. Norfolk from 1859.
[11] Misc. business: *H* clix. 2117.
[12] *La politique Anglaise* (1860).
[13] *Quarterly Review*, cviii. 265 (July 1860).
[14] Guedalla, *P*, 143, on proposed reduction of duty on imported paper.

MP—Mr Greswell—Mr Hadfield—S. Herbert—and minutes. H of C. $2\frac{1}{4}$–3 and $10\frac{1}{2}$–$2\frac{1}{4}$.[1] Attended the marriage in Westmr. Abbey. It was a beautiful sight & happily all the interior was good.[2] Read Butt's Hist. Italy. Saw Ld Granville—Mr Gibson.

20. Fr.

Wrote to C.L. Ryan—Ld Palmerston (2)—S. Herbert (& copy)—C. Townshend Wilson[3]—Dean of ChCh., & minutes. H of C. 12–4. Lost my S.B. Monies' Bill: my *first* defeat on a measure of finance in the H of C. This ought to be very good for me: & I earnestly wish to make it so.[4] H of C. again 6–8 and 11–$1\frac{1}{4}$. Saw Sir Jas Graham: who having read Herbert's letter & my reply said the latter was he thought exactly right.[5] Saw Sir C. Wood—Mr Hankey—Sir H. Willoughby—Mr Gibson. Read Nat. Rev. on myself and on H. of Lords[6]—Ionian Revenue report.[7]

21. Sat. [Cliveden]

Wrote to Ld Glenelg—D. of Argyll—and minutes. Cabinet $3\frac{1}{2}$–$5\frac{1}{4}$. I left it, that the discussion might be free & went to Stafford House & Sydenham for Sir J. Paxton's Fete.[8] There I saw, later, Argyll, & S. Herbert, who seemed to bring good news. At night we all went off to Cliveden.[9] Saw (before) Scotts—Ld Aberdeen—D. of Argyll—& did business. The little boys went off: & left us in gloomy silence.

22. 7 S. Trin.

Hedsor Ch mg. Rain aft. But we walked & went in boat afr. Wrote to Sir J. Graham[10]—Sir G. Lewis, & Copy. Saw D. of Argyll—Read Ken's Works[11]—Dean Trench's Sermons.[12]

23. M. [London]

Wrote to E. Cardwell—Sir W. Heathcote—and minutes. Read Question Irlandaise[13]—Butt's Hist. Italy. At Cliveden all day. Drive to Dropmore.

[1] Misc. business: *H* clix. 2151.
[2] Meriel Lyttelton m. John Talbot.
[3] Charles Townshend Wilson, 1823–87; captain in the guards, fought in Crimea; wrote military history.
[4] In Morley, ii. 34. Bill defeated after brief debate in 78:116; *H* clix. 2227.
[5] Long letter stating his case; Gladstone's brief reply refused support for the scheme 'as a whole' or for a recurring loan; Add MS 44211, ff. 223–9.
[6] *National Review*, xi. 219, 110 (July 1860); on budget.
[7] *PP* 1860 lxv. 477.
[8] He wrote to *Graham next day: 'I left the Cabinet yesterday purposely before the question of Fortifications was finally dealt with. I find that concessions have been made beyond my expectation, at the last moment & under great pressure.' Bodley MS Film 128. But *Palmerston's diary (Broadlands MS D 20): 'Argyll after Gladstone had gone read Letter from him agreeing to Plan about Fortifications and Loans but wishing Bill to be annual like the vote—agreed to. He evidently has throughout been playing a game of Brag & trying to bully the Cabinet & finding he has failed he has given in'.
[9] In Morley, ii. 47n.
[10] See n. 8 above.
[11] See 1 Apr. 60.
[12] R. C. *Trench, *Sermons preached in Westminster Abbey* (1860).
[13] *La question Irlandaise* (1860).

Late at night returned to London. Saw S. Herbert—T.M. Gibson—H of C. 12–1. Much dismayed at the terms of Ld P.s Resolution.[1]

24. T.

Wrote to Mrs Lyall[2]—Sir A. Spearman—M.F. Tupper—D. of Argyll— Sir G. Lewis—Ld Palmerston—Mr Cobden—Sir H. Willoughby—Sir T. Fremantle. Saw Sir J. Graham—Mr Hubbard . . . Aunt J.—Mr Evans & Mr M'Donnell[3]—Mr Sandeman & Mr [blank space]—Duke of Argyll—Ld Palmerston. Made further inquiries in T. Square[R]. Read F. Lawley's Pamphlet,[4] & Butt's History. H of C. 6–8 and $9\frac{1}{2}$–11.[5]

25. Wed. St James.

Wrote to J.G. Hubbard—S. Herbert—Mr E. Warner[6]—Mr F. Hill— Gen. Grey—& minutes. Cabinet 4.45–$7\frac{3}{4}$. We settled various things & among others the distinct basis of the Fortification Scheme. H of C. $3\frac{1}{4}$–$4\frac{3}{4}$.[7] Saw Ld Overstone—Mr Gibson—Mr Estcourt—Mr Laing—Sir H. Willoughby. —C.A. Wood. Rode. Read Butt's Hist. Italy. Dined at Ld Wensleydales. Mrs Herberts after. Visited Noble's Studio.[8]

26. Th.

Wrote to Mr Laing—Sir T. Fremantle—Scotts—Ld Wodehouse—Mr Pressly—Mr Atkinson[9]—Mr Gibson—Sig. Farini—W.A. Ross—R. Phillimore. Saw S. Herbert—Mr Puller MP.—Sir J. Graham. H. of C. 3–4. 6–8. $11\frac{1}{2}$–$1\frac{1}{2}$.[10] Saw Linsell[R]. Read Sir L. Peel[11]—P.O. Committee's Report.[12]

27. Fr.

Wrote to Mr Hubbard—Mr Laing—Mr Hamilton—Duke of Argyll—Mr Wise MP—Sir G. Lewis—Mr Brand—and minutes. Read Notes sur les Budgets[13]—Sir L. Peel on Sir R. Peel. H of C. $2\frac{1}{2}$–4. 6–9. $11\frac{1}{4}$–$12\frac{3}{4}$.[14] Saw Mr Hubbard—Mr Brand—Sir A. Spearman.

[1] His late return allowed him to miss *Palmerston's speech revealing compromise on fortifications: a £2m. loan raised by 30 year annuities; Palmerston remarked 'it would be folly to rely upon the future effects of the Commercial Treaty': *H* clx. 22.

[2] Probably Frances, *née* Cave, 2nd wife of G. Lyall, M.P. (see 7 Apr. 59).

[3] Probably (Sir) Thomas William Evans, 1821–92; Derbyshire land owner, liberal M.P. S. Derbyshire 1857–68, 1874–85; cr. bart. 1887; and E. MacDonell.

[4] Untraced.

[5] Misc. business: *H* clx. 88.

[6] Edward Warner 1818–75; barrister and liberal M.P. Norwich 1852–7, 1860–8; published on the franchise.

[7] Ecclesiastical Commission Bill: *H* clx. 152.

[8] See 20 Mar. 54.

[9] Thomas Witlam *Atkinson, 1799–1861; architect and traveller, had sent his *Travels in the regions of the upper and lower Amoor* (1860) (Hawn P).

[10] Answered *Bright's questions on spirit duties and spoke on public business: *H* clx. 210, 220.

[11] Sir L. *Peel. *A Sketch of the life and character of Sir Robert *Peel* (1860).

[12] Probably *PP* 1860 xxiii. 311.

[13] MSS sent by Chevalier: Add MS 44591, f. 61.

[14] Answered *Hubbard's criticisms of terminable annuities: *H* clx. 295.

28. Sat.

Wrote to Mr Hubbard—and minutes. Ride (cut short) with Herbert. 12–1½ Conclave on revenue matters in D.St. 1½–3. Cabinet. Saw R. Phillimore on Irish Ch Bill.[1] Read Butt's Italy Vol. II.—Sir L. Peel on Sir R.P. (finished)—Hollings on Macaulay.[2] M. de Persigny's Theatricals in evg.[3] The tone bad. Saw Mrs Barber.[4]

29. 8 S. Trin.

St James's mg—Chapel Royal aft. MS. on 'the man of God' aloud in evg. Saw Ld Derby (at Ch)—Duchess of Sutherland. Wrote to Helen. Read F. Winslow on the Brain[5]—Father Felix on Roman Ch[6]—Dr Williams's Bp of St David's.[7]

30. M.

Illness last night kept me in bed much of today. Drove with C. in aftn: & went perforce to H of C. at 9½.[8] Saw Mr J.R. Herbert—Mr Milner Gibson. Wrote to Mr Laing and Mr Cardwell: and minutes. Read Atkinson's Amoor[9]—Butt's Hist. Italy Vol II.

31. T.

Wrote to Sir W. Heathcote—Sir T. Fremantle—Lady E. Wells—W.S. Blackstone—and minutes. Saw Admiral Saurin[10]—Mr Newton.[11] H of C. 12–4: on my Bills.[12] Read Pamphlets—Butt's Hist Italy—Notes sur les Budgets. Rode: saw Mr Senior.

Wed. Aug. One. 1860.

Wrote to . . . Mast. of Mint—Mr Grub[13]—A.J.H. Banks—Dr Thorn— Scotts—W.H.G.—Sir G. Lewis (2)—Mr Cobden—Mr Herbert—and mi- nutes. Saw R. Phillimore—Ld Brougham—Mr T. Mainwaring MP.—Atty Gen. for Ireland[14]—Lord Advocate—Mr Milner Gibson—Mr Forster MP.— Mr Black MP.—Count de Persigny—Mr Hayward—Mr Chichr. Fortescue[15]—

[1] Church Temporalities (Ireland) Act Amndt. Bill, then being passed.
[2] J.F. Hollings, Lord *Macaulay. A lecture (1860).
[3] At the French embassy.
[4] See 16 Aug. 50?
[5] F. B. *Winslow, On obscure deseases of the brain and disorders of the mind (1860).
[6] M. J. J. Varnier Miritello (Father Felix), Why I left the communion of the Church of Rome (1860).
[7] R. *Williams, 'An earnestly respectful letter . . . on the difficulty of bringing theo- logical questions to an issue' (1860).
[8] The Fortifications Bill, tenth on the orders for the day, was not reached: H clx. 350.
[9] See 26 July 60n.
[10] See 1 Apr. 38; he was a commissioner of customs 1846–60.
[11] Perhaps Joseph Newton of the mint.
[12] Wine Licences (Ireland) Bill: H clx. 424.
[13] George Grub, 1819–92; church historian and professor in Aberdeen; see Add MS 44394, f. 51.
[14] Rickard *Deasy, 1812–83; liberal M.P. Cork 1855–61; attorney general, Ireland, 1860–1; exchequer baron 1861; judge from 1878.
[15] In temporary charge of colonial office while *Newcastle was in Canada.

Mr Timm. Met Audit Commrs. 3 PM. Settled C's accounts & allowance also that for Agnes. Royal Acad. $9\frac{1}{4}$–$10\frac{1}{4}$. Lady Palmerston's afr. Read Butt's Hist. Italy—Atkinson's Amoor—Rode. H of C. aftn.[1]

2. Th.

Wrote to Sir A. Spearman—& minutes. Saw Mr Milner Gibson—Sir S. Peto (Paper plot)[2]—Duke of Argyll—Bp of Oxford—Mr Brand—E. Reynolds—Lord Dalhousie—Capt J.N.G. Nine to breakfast. Went with Dss. of S[utherland] & Dss. of A[rgyll] to the Bossoli drawings[3]—& Mr Theed's Studio.[4] With C.G. to see Mr Herbert's noble cartoon.[5] Dined at Ld Crewe's. H of C. $4\frac{1}{4}$–$7\frac{1}{2}$ and $10\frac{1}{2}$–2.[6] Read Notes sur les Budgets. Missed Ld Lyndhurst.

3. Fr.

Wrote to Mr Hamilton—The Queen[7]—S. Herbert—Mr Laing—Bushell & Co[8]—Robn. G.—& minutes. Read Brialmont's D. of Wellington.[9] Saw Sir S.M. Peto—Mr Milner Gibson—Mr Pressly—Mr Hubbard—Mr Cardwell—Attorney General & conclave on Paper & Treaty 6–$7\frac{1}{2}$. H of C. $3\frac{1}{4}$–4. 6–8. $8\frac{3}{4}$–2.[10] Wrote Mem. on Lord P.s new proposal to give up the Paper Duty Resolutions.[11]

4. Sat. X

Wrote to Mr Cobden—Messrs. Rawlins—and minutes. Read Butt's Hist. Italy—Atkinson's Amoor—Thiers Consulat et l'Empire.[12] Cabinet 1–$2\frac{1}{2}$. Saw Ld Granville—Duke of Argyll—Mr Gibson—Duchess of Sutherland—Saw [blank] Rode. Evg. at home.

5. 9 S. Trin.

St James's & H.C. mg. Chapel Royal aft. The Wortleys came for 2 hours: his state is critical. Conv. with Stephy on the 'Narney'.[13] Wrote to Rev A. Goalen. Read Mant's Hist. Ireland[14]—A. Goalen's Sermons[15]—Sinclair's Charge[16]—Winslow's Obscure Diseases.[17] MS. on Gospel aloud evg.

[1] London sewage: H clx. 450.
[2] One of the leading repealers.
[3] By C. Bossoli, of the Italian war.
[4] William *Theed, 1804–91; sculptor; commissioned for statue of George IV for new Parliament buildings; see next day.
[5] J.R. *Herbert (see 17 June 53) was paid £3,500 in advance for frescoes in the peers' robing room, which he had not yet painted; see next day.
[6] Prolonged opposition by *Bright to Fortifications Bill: H clx. 485.
[7] Sending revised engravings for the coins; see Guedalla, Q. i. 119.
[8] Probably Walton and Bushell, East India merchants.
[9] A.H. Brialmont, Histoire du duc de Wellington, 3v. (1856–7).
[10] Defended proposed statues to recent monarchs, avoided commitment to a Cromwell statue, and defended J.R. *Herbert's delay: H clx. 682.
[11] Not found.
[12] See 28 May 60.   [13] Obscure.
[14] See 29 Apr. 40.
[15] A. Goalen, Four sermons on the 'Comfortable Words' in the Office for the Holy Communion (1860).
[16] J. *Sinclair, 'On school rates in England and America. A charge' (1860).
[17] See 29 July 60.

6. M.

Wrote to E. Cardwell—C. Pressly—G. Barbar[1]—Master of Mint—and minutes. Meeting of Members in Dg. Street 12–1½. Saw Mr Hayward—Ld Palmerston. Read Butt. H of C. 4¼–8 and 9½–2¼. Spoke over 1½ hour on the Paper Duty: a favourable House. Voted in 266:233. A most kind & indeed notable reception afterwards.[2]

7. T. X.

This was a day of congratulations from many kind M.P.s. Saw F.R. Bonham—Sir J. Lacaita—Duke of Argyll & Sir R. Hill—Mr Milner Gibson—Mr Gregson—Sir M. Seymour.[3] H of C. 8½–12¾.[4] With C. at Benjamins. Accounts with Hampton. Wrote minutes. Read Army Orgn. Report[5]—Brialmont's D. of Wellington—Butt's Hist. of Italy.

8. Wed.

Wrote to Bp of London[6]—D. of Argyll (2)—Bp of Oxford—Dr Wordsworth—Sir W. Heathcote—Rev Mr Mayow—Mr Puller—Mr Cobden—Author of Principles of Relig. Liberty[7]—and minutes. Read Fitzgerald's Tracts[8]—Forbes Winslow—Butt's Hist—and Thiers. Saw Mr J.E. Fitzgerald—Sir J. Lacaita—Duke of Somerset—Mr Anderson—Mr Hamilton. Saw Hunter [R]. Walk with C.

9. Th.

Wrote to D. of Somerset—E. Cardwell—and minutes. H of C. 2½–7¼ and 11–2¼.[9] Dined with the Argylls. Saw R. Phillimore—Mr Arbuthnot—Duke of Argyll—Sir James Graham—Mr Laing—Mr Bright.[10] Read Conf. Papers on Fortifns.

10. Fr.

Wrote to C. Fortescue—Ld Palmerston—Mr Pressly—and minutes. Rode. H. of Commons 12–1. 6–7¼. and 10¼–3.[11] Saw S. Herbert—Duke of Argyll—Mr Gilpin MP.—Aunt J.—& more inquiry about M. S[ummerhayes][R]. Read Brialmont—Notes sur les Budgets.

---

[1] Br. of a deceased Naples resident; subscribing to a fund; Add MS 44531 f. 47.
[2] Resolutions equalizing duties on French and Algerian paper etc. with existing British excize duties: *H* clx. 698. See introduction above, v. xxxii, xliv.
[3] Sir Michael *Seymour, 1802–87; admiral; captured Canton and forced Peiho straits 1857–8; liberal M.P. Devonport 1859–63.
[4] Indian forces: *H* clx. 847.
[5] *PP* 1860 vii. 1.
[6] *Tait, who had recently refused York.
[7] 'The ultimate principle of religious liberty' (1860); anon. pamphlet.
[8] W. *Fitzgerald, *Cautions for the times. Addressed to the parishioners of a parish in England*, No. 1–7, (1851).
[9] Fortifications Bill: *H* clx. 958.
[10] See n. next day.
[11] *Bright on Lords and paper duties: *H* clx. 1114.

11. Sat. [*The Coppice, Henley*]

Wrote to Dean of Peterboro—Sir A. Spearman—Ld Palmerston—Bp of Oxford—and minutes. Saw Duke of Argyll—Ld Granville. Cabinet 1–2½. Off at 3 to Phillimore's pleasant retreat: so adorned by the cheerful & contented spirits of the inhabitants.[1] Read Rose's Diaries &c.[2]—Thomson's Poems.[3]

12. 10 S. Trin.

Shiplake Ch & H.C.—A touching & earnest Sermon from the Vicar. Walk with R.P. Wrote to Sir A. Spearman. Read Philosophy of Evangelm[4]—Religious Liberty—Xtn. Remembr. on Sardinia and on [blank][5].

13. M. [*London*]

Wrote to Sir T. Fremantle—Robn. G (2)—J.C. Ewart—& minutes. H of C. 8½–2: on Fortification Annuities, Finance Bills, &c.[6] Off at 12 for town (C. went to Hagley after Croquet.) Read Rose's Diaries—Butt's Hist. of Italy. Saw one. X. Saw [blank].

14. T.

Wrote to Ld J. Russell—Mr Hubbard—G. Burnett—D. of Somerset (2)—C.G.—and minutes. H of C. 12–12¾, 2¾–4, 10¾–1.[7] Saw Aunt J.—Mrs Pearsall—Mr Murray (*vice*)—The Speaker—Ld Stanley—Sir Geo. Lewis—Mr Kinglake—Sir J. Graham—Mr Gibson—Duke of Argyll—Saw one[R]. Tea at Stafford House. Read Butt finished II.—Rose's Diaries.

15. Wed.

Wrote to Mr Cobden—Rev C. Miller[8]—Sir H. Storks—Sir C. Trevelyan—and minutes. Cabinet 4½–6¼: we discussed H of L. & S.B.M. Bill.[9] Saw Sir T. Fremantle—Sir A. Spearman—Duke of Argyll—Bp of Oxford—The Speaker—Sir J. Graham. Saw Godfrey, X. Dined with the Herberts. Read Rose's Diary &c. Worked on my chaos of books a little.

16. Th.

Wrote to Ld J. Russell—Scotts—G. Burnett—W. Roberts—Dean Ramsay—C.G.[10]—& minutes. H of C. 12–2¼, 6–7, & 10½–2½.[11] Read Rose's Diary.

[1] The Coppice, above Henley; *Phillimore's reaction to the visit is in Morley, ii. 35.
[2] See 14 Jan. 60.
[3] *The works of J. *Thomson*, 4v. (1757).
[4] By R. Brown, (1857).
[5] *Christian Remembrancer*, xl. 215 (July 1860).
[6] Spoke on fortifications: *H* clx. 1229.
[7] Spoke on civil service commission: ibid. 1266.
[8] See 30 Oct. 31.
[9] On the 13th the Lords had rejected *Argyll's resolution of urgency on the Savings Banks Bill; at cabinet it was decided *Palmerston should speak to *Derby; the Bill passed on 28 Aug. 60; see next day.
[10] Bassett, 130.
[11] Irish education: *H* clx. 1374.

Saw Sir C. Trevelyan—Ld Granville—The Speaker—Lord P. settled with
Ld D. Worked on books.

17. *Fr.* X.

Wrote to Mr Sanford[1]—Lord J. Russell—Mr Bright MP.—C.G.—& minutes.
H of C. 12-1¼. H of L. & H of C. 5-6¾.[2] Saw Sir J. Lacaita[3]—Dss. Sutherland—Sir Jas Graham—Mr Bazley—Ld Granville—Mr Grogan. Saw Mrs
Davis, & one—also Mrs Williamson[R]. Read Rose's Diary. Worked on
books.

18. *Sat.* X

Wrote to C.G.—S. Herbert—Bp of Oxford—C.A. Wood—Sir W. Heathcote—Dr Pusey—M. Summerhayes[R]—& minutes. Saw Ld Palmerston—
Mr Lowe (End. Sch. Salaries)[4]—Miss Dixon—Aunt J.—Mr Ryan resp.
vacation. Saw Mrs Davis, her sister, and two: in the course of inquiries[R].
H of C. 12-2¼ and 3¾-5¼.[5] Dined with the Argylls. Lady Palmerston's
afterwards.

19. *11 S. Trin.*

Chapel Royal mg St James (prayers) evg. Naaman MS aloud. Inquiries at
22 T. Square for M.S. Wrote to Mrs de Pearsall—R. Phillimore—M.
Summerhayes[R]. Saw Aunt J.—The Herberts—Mrs Wortley (sad accounts). Read Sandfords Charge[6]—Rorison's Notes[7]—F. Winslow on
Obscure Diseases[8]—Principles of Relig. Liberty.

20. *M.*

Wrote to Padre Tosti—Baron Bunsen—Lady Llanover[9]—A Roslawksy[10]—
Helen G.—F. Tatham—E. Cardwell—D. of Somerset—Ld Palmerston—
Sir R. Bromley—Mr V. Scully—Sir A. Spearman—C.G.—and minutes. H
of C. 3½-7¾ and 9¾-12¼.[11] Read Rose's Diary (finished Vol 1). Saw Ld
Granville—Attorney General *cum* Sir G. Lewis—Ld Clarence Paget—Mr
Ryan—Mr Brand resp R.P.—Ld Stanley of Alderley—Duke of Argyll.
Worked on books. Saw Jane Wortley—Scotts—Mrs J.E. Tyler.

21. *T.* X

Wrote to Editor of Times[12]—A. Lefroy MP.[13]—Sir T. Fremantle—E. Ferns[14]

[1] *Sc.* Sandford.   [2] Estimates: *H* clx. 1505.
[3] Dissuading him from becoming Neapolitan ambassador in London; Lacaita, 147.
[4] i.e. R. *Lowe, vice-president of the education board, on endowed school salaries.
[5] Spoke on historical portraits, *H* clx. 1529.
[6] J. *Sandford, 'The Church rate and the census. A charge' (1860).
[7] G. Rorison, *Notes on 'Scottish episcopacy, past and present: by Alexander Thomson'*
(1860).
[8] See 29 July 60.
[9] Augusta, wife of Sir B. *Hall, Lord Llanover: she d. 1896.
[10] A. Roslansky Petrowsky, thanking him for honorary membership of Kharhoff
university; Add MS 44531, f. 39.
[11] Misc. business: *H* clx. 1628.   [12] Not found published.
[13] Anthony Lefroy, 1800-90; tory M.P. Co. Longford 1830-2, 1833-7, 1842-7, Dublin
university 1858-70.
[14] Perhaps George Egerton Ferns, solicitor in Stockport.

—Sir W. Heathcote—D. of Argyll—V.C. of Oxford—Isaac Butt—Capt. Warburton—F.W. (£3)—E.R. Spearman[1]—Rev S. Sharpe[2]—Sir J. Lacaita—J.M. Herbert[3]—Dean Wolseley[4]—Duchess of Sutherland—Miss Godfrey—and minutes. Saw Mr Grogan—Duke of Argyll—Lord C. Paget— Miss Godfrey: singular[R]. H of C. $12\frac{1}{2}$–$2\frac{1}{4}$ and 6–$7\frac{3}{4}$.[5] Dined in B[erkeley] Square: the prospect there very dark.[6] Read Rose's memoirs. Worked on books. I have rather incautiously charged myself with my Priv. Sec's work at this *dead* time: & had 44 envelopes to open & deal with today, nearly all letters.[7]

22. Wed.

Wrote to Ed. Times—Johnson L[ongden] & Co.—Mr [P.] Ellis Eyton—Mr Berry—S.R. Glynne—Mr Mackie MP[8]—Mr Filder[9]—Mr Geo. Grant—Ld Palmerston—F.L.B.[10]—G.C. Glyn MP.—Duke of Argyll—Mr Eastham— J.G. Hubbard MP.—Mrs Bennett—Mr Pressly (2)—J. Stenson—Rev Mr Heale[11]—Mr P. Erle—Mrs Walker—Hon A. Gordon—H.J.G.—Hon W.H. Merritt—M. Tatham. Saw R. Phillimore—Sig. Manna *cum* Lacaita. H of C. 4–$5\frac{1}{2}$.[12] At No 29 in evg.[13] Also at Murray's inquiring.[14] Read L. Levi on Taxation:[15] & Rose's Diary. Worked on books—now in some order.

23. Th.

Wrote to Sir J. Lacaita—Dss. of Sutherland—Captain G.—Sig. Chiotes[16]— Mr Waldron[17]—Mrs Sullivan—Sig. Torelli—Mr Chairman[18]—and minutes. Rode: in great solitude. Eccl. Comm. 11–2. H of C. 2–$3\frac{3}{4}$.[19] Saw Mr Lefroy MP.—Ld Granville. Dined in Berkeley Square. Read Rose's Diary.

24. Frid. Saint Bartholomew.

Wrote to H. Glynne—Mr Pressly—Mr Brand—Mr Laing—Mr Hamilton—

[1] Edmund Robert Spearman, 1837–1918, 2nd s. of Sir A.Y.*; held minor diplomatic posts.
[2] Samuel Curtis Sharpe, 1814–68; anglican priest and headmaster of Pittville school, Cheltenham, 1855–60.
[3] Probably *sc.* J.R. Herbert.
[4] John Wolseley, dean of Kildare.
[5] Misc. business: *H* clx. 1688.
[6] J. Stuart-Wortley's mental breakdown; see 31 Aug. 60.
[7] Consequently there are no letter book entries until 27 August.
[8] James Mackie, 1821–67; advocate and liberal M.P. Kirkcudbrightshire from 1857.
[9] Herbert Wall Filder, London solicitor.
[10] Unidentified; probably a begging letter.
[11] Edmund Markham Heale, 1825–74; professor of classics, Sandhurst, 1851–9; rector of Yelling from 1860.
[12] Misc. business: *H* clx. 1711.
[13] Berkeley Square; the Lawleys and the Wortleys.
[14] See 24 Jan. 60.
[15] See 22 June 60.
[16] Panagiote Chiotes, Greek author; sent books, probably his περι δημοτικης ἐν Ἑλλαδι γλωσσης (1859).
[17] Laurence Waldron, 1811–75; barrister and liberal M.P. Tipperary 1857–65.
[18] Unidentified.
[19] Spoke on telegraph contracts: *H* clx. 1731.

Rev J. Conway—Mr T. Smith—Cotton & Co[1]—Sig. Rossolino[2]—Rev H. Best[3]—H.J.G.—Dr Brown—& minutes. Dined with the De Greys. H of C. 3–4¾.[4] Saw Col. Herbert—Sir A. Spearman—Messrs. Glass Elliot & Co[5]— Sir J. Lacaita *cum* Sig. Manna[6]—Mr Arbuthnot—Mr Laing MP. Worked on packing &c. Read Rose's Diary.

25. Sat.

Wrote to Ld Brougham—Messrs. Frist—W.P. Clarke[7]—J.T. Ponsonby[8]— S. Laing—C. Rossolino—& minutes. Cabinet 3–5. Haymarket 9–11½ PM to see the Critic: some well done, more overdone. Attended the Graham marriage 11.30 AM. Admiralty breakfast afr. Dined in B. Square. Read Rose's Memoirs. Making ready. St Andrew's Ch. 5 P.M.

26. 12 S. Trin.

Chapel R. mg and All Saints aft. Heard parts of 6 out of door Sermons. Wrote Latin Hymn verses. Dined at the Admiralty. Walk with C. Read A Kempis—Soames Hist.[9]—Wheatly on Am. Prayer.[10]

27. M. [Hawarden]

Wrote to Ld Brougham—Mr Spooner—Mr Potter MP[11]—Mr Fleming—and minutes. Read Everett's ans. to Ld Grey[12]—Sheridan's Critic. Saw Mr Ryder.[13] Packing: arrangements for departure: luncheon with Jane Wortley. Off at 2.45: reached Hawarden before 9. All well thank God.

28. T.

Church 8.30 A.M. Lena's birthday. She is a very dear child with much, I am sure, in the future for her. Conv. with C. on H. [Glynne']s new vagary, a sudden proposal to Miss R.[14] Had it been *later*,[15] he might have had much to say. But she is unwilling. Visited the pit & borehole: Stephens prospects there are still in the main tantalising & uncertain. Worked on letters and accounts. Archery entertainment in aftn. Read Tosti's Conc. di Costanza[16]— School for Scandal.

[1] Probably the drink shippers in Little Bush Lane.
[2] Of Zante; Hawn P.
[3] Perhaps J. H. Best, anglican missionary on Essequibo.
[4] Misc. business: *H* clx. 1783.
[5] Telegraph cable manufacturers in Greenwich (see 23 Aug. 60n.); (Sir) Richard Atwood Glass, 1820–73, was chief partner and tory M.P. Bewdley 1868–9.
[6] In London to persuade *Lacaita to be ambassador; see 17 Aug. 60n. and Lacaita, 147.
[7] See 22 June 58?
[8] Possibly James Henry Ponsonby, 1807–80; soldier.
[9] H. *Soames, *The history of the Reformation of the Church of England*, 4v. (1826–8).
[10] C. Wheatly, *The Church of England man's companion* (1710).
[11] None then of this name; perhaps E. Potter (see Mar. 65), M.P. from 1861; copy, on income tax, in Add MS 44531, f. 41.
[12] E. Everett, 'Speech . . . on American Institutions in reply to the discussion in the British House of Lords' (1860).
[13] George Lisle Ryder, treasury clerk from 1857.
[14] Miss Rose, see 29 Aug., 3, 6 Sept. 60 and introduction above, v. lxvi ff.
[15] i.e. further from his attempted second marriage earlier in the year.
[16] L. Tosti, *Storia del Concilio di Costanza*, 2v. (1853).

29. Wed.

Ch. 8½ AM. Wrote to Watson & Smith—W. Cowper MP[1]—and minutes. Read Drummonds Poems[2]—School for Scandal—The Rivals—Tosti's Conc. di Costanza. Saw Mr Burnett on the mining & other operations: & went to Plant & Rose's pits. Worked on my Will; paper of directions, & papers resp. property & Private (locked) account book.[3]

30. Th.

Ch. 8½ AM. Wrote to Mr Breakenridge—Scotts—Sig. Massari —Hampton —Ld J. Russell—Gabbitas—W. Huskisson—and minutes. Worked on papers resp. property & Seaforth Ch. Read 'the Rivals' (finished)— Hopley's Case in D. Telegraph[4]—Letter of Prince Pitzipios.[5] Mr West[6] (who dined here with Mr Austin) pleased me much.

31. Fr.

Ch 8½ A.M. Wrote to Sir W. Heathcote—G. Burnett—Gladstone & Co— Jas Watson—Count Persigny. Rode with M[eriel] & L[ena] to Soughton Archery: & saw Mr Banks's Rubens now restored.[7] Arrangements for moving. Conv. on J. Wortley's very gloomy case. What powerful warning is in it backed by the yet more awful suicide of such a man as Chancellor Martin.[8] Worked on my affairs: of which after a long desuetude I have now got some inkling. Read Count de Persigny's Speech[9]—England Policy in China[10]—Eglise Mexicaine.[11]

Sat. Sept. One 1860. [Penmaenmawr]

Ch 8½ AM. Unpacked my books from London: the stock of the season added to my library here. Wrote to Ld Palmerston—J. Harrison—Ld Brougham J. Griffiths—Mr F. Goulburn—Dr Pusey—Rev Mr Davies—Scotts—Baron Rothschild—Hon C. Gore—Dss. of Sutherland—and minutes. Off at 2.30 to Penmaenmawr:[13] reached at 5 Mr Harrisons[14] new & most excellently prepared house. Mr Thomas met us. Called on the Murray Gladstones: & arranged my table books &c. Read Mad. Sevigné Memoir & Letters[15]— Tosti's Concilio di Costanza.

[1] See 27 July 27.
[2] W. *Drummond, *Poems* (1616, often reprinted).
[3] Preserved in Hawn P.
[4] Thomas Hopley, the flagellating manslaughterer, *Daily Telegraph*, 30 August 1860.
[5] See 26 June 60.
[6] William West; Trinity, Dublin; the new curate at Hawarden.
[7] John Scott Bankes, of Soughton Hall, Northrop, Flintshire, landowner and magistrate.
[8] George Martin, 1789–1860; chancellor of Exeter diocese from 1820; cut his throat on 27 August.
[9] On Anglo–French relations; *The Guardian*, 5 September 1860, 789.
[10] Pamphlet (1860) by A. Wilson; 'I like the spirit of the book . . . above all I sympathise with his deprecations of any new assumption of territory in China' (to Elgin, 5 September 1860, Add MS 44394, f. 97).
[11] Untraced.
[12] Unidentified.
[13] On the North Wales coast, between Bangor and Conway.
[14] See 3 Sept. 59 etc.
[15] Mme de Sévigné, *Lettres . . . à Madame la Comtesse de Grignan, la fille*, 2v. (1726).

2. 13 S. Trin.

Wrote to S.R.G.—Duke of Argyll[1]—M. Summerhayes[R]. Morning service in the Hotel, Rev Mr Lease: aftn. (Welsh) at Conway, whither I walked with Willy. My ability for nine miles is the first fruit of sea-air. Conv. with M. & Lena. Read Tosti Conc. Costanza—do Storia di Abelardo[2]—Butler's Sermons.[3] One of Wilson's aloud at night.

3. M.

Wrote to Dr Tipaldo—Dss. of Sutherland—Gen. Portlock—Watson & Smith—Rev D. Morgan—J.G. Hubbard—D. of Somerset—Wynn Williams —Dean of ChCh—Warden S. Augustine's[4]—and minutes. Began the Politics of Aristotle with Willy:[5] lecturing i.e. explaining as well as I can. There came the news of Henry Glynne's engagement to Miss Rose: strictly secret, & to stand over for a year. It is startling & precipitate, & by no means what one would wish: yet it may come in lieu of worse. Read Tosti's Council of Const.—Tacitus Annales began I—Sevigne's Letters. Bathed in the sea: & visited Col. Macdonald.

4. Tues.

Wrote to Dean Ramsay—G. Burnett—Sir A. Spearman—Watson & Smith —Geo. Grant—and minutes. Bathed (2): With walk with W. on Penmaen-bach. Saw Lenton.[6] Politics of Aristotle with Willy—Tacitus Ann. I— Turkey in 1860 by R.J.C.[7]—Tosti's Council of Constance.

5. Wed.

Wrote to Earl of Elgin—Mr Laing MP—and minutes. Bathed 3°—Walk with C. & the children on the hills. Col. Macdonald dined.—A little music in evg. Politics with Willy—Congreve's Introdn. & Essays[8]—Tosti's Council of Const.—Tac. Ann. I. —Tebbs on Marriage & Divorce.[9]

6. Th.

Wrote to Watson & Smith—Mr Pressly—Duchess of Suthd.—Robn. G.— Ld Palmerston—Mr Gurney—C. J. Linton[10]—Mr Anderson—Mr F. Goulburn—Sir A. Spearman—and minutes. Bathed 4°.

Conv. on Henry's matter & on letter to Miss Rose. We now hope they are not *engaged*. Letter to Miss R framed on consultation. Hill walk with the whole party.

[1] In Morley, ii. 636, misdated?
[2] By L. Tosti (1851).
[3] J. *Butler, *Fifteen sermons preached at the Rolls Chapel* (1726).
[4] Henry Bailey, 1815–1906; warden of St. Augustine's, Canterbury, 1850–78; rector of Taring, Sussex, from 1838; wrote on anglo-catholicism.
[5] About to start his second year at Christ Church.
[6] G. Lenton; otherwise unidentified.
[7] *Turkey in 1860. By R.J.C.* (1860).
[8] R. Congreve, *The Roman Empire of the West. Four lectures* (1855).
[9] H. V Tebbs, *Essay on the 'Scripture doctrines of adultery and divorce'* (1822).
[10] Not further identified.

Read Politics with Willy—Tacitus Ann. I.—Tosti's Conc. Constance—
Mad. de Sevigné—but I begin to think this group with my business is a
little hard for pure holiday: so I may let in some lighter material.

7. *Fr.*

Wrote to Hon Rev S. Lawley—G. Burnett—Ld J. Russell—G.L. Ryder—
Mrs T. Goalen—S. Laing—& minutes. Read the Politics with Willy. Read
Tales from Blackwood[1]—Tosti's Council of Constance—Tacitus Ann. II.
Long hill walk with Willy: to Llangedynan Ch & the hill by it.[2] Bathed 5°.

8. *Sat.*

Wrote to Mr Pressly—Ld Palmerston—Mr E. Farr[3]—Mr Arbuthnot—
Robn G.—Mr C. Fortescue—Sir J. Young—Mrs MacGillivray[4]—and
minutes. Willy away. Mr Grant[5] came. Bathed 6°. Drive & walk with C. &
Mr G[rant]. Read Tacitus Ann. II—Tosti's Council of Constance—Blackwood's Tales (The Pirate of Florida). Long Railway conv. with Mr G: also on
the Lpool Churches.

9. *S. 14 Trin.*

Read mg prayers at 10—Parish Ch. 11.20 Litany & H.C. and at 3½ PM aftn.
service. Wrote to Sir J.T. Coleridge—Rev M. MacColl—and minutes. Walk
with Mr Grant. Read Irvines Memoir[6]—Mills on Future State[7]—Tebbs
on Marriage Law &c (finished).

10. *M.*

Wrote to Sir Jas Graham—H. Lees—Freshfield & Newman—Leone Levi—
Sir T. Tancred—Sir C. Wood—& minutes. Began, audacious work! a
paraphrastic translation of the Politics.[8] Read Politics with W.—Tac. Ann.
II.—Tosti's Council of Constance—Blackwood Tales. Bathed 7°. On the
top of Penmaenmawr with the party incl. Harry and Herbert.

11. *T.*

Wrote to Mr Wynn Williams—Mr Arbuthnot, & minutes. Bathed 8°.—
called on Mr Derbyshire. Aristotles Politics: read with Willy & worked on
paraphrastic Translation—Read Tosti—Tacitus (began III)—Scott's
Highland Widow: quite as fine as when I read it 30 odd years back.[9]

[1] 'The Florida Pirate', in *Tales from Blackwood* (1858ff.) x.
[2] Llangelynin, 4 miles SE. of Penmaenmawr.
[3] Had requested employment; Add MS 44531, f. 46.
[4] Unidentified.
[5] Of Gladstone & Co., Liverpool; see 5 Aug. 25.
[6] Probably J. T. Irvine, 'Historical sketches of the Church of St. Laurence in Ludlow'
(1860).
[7] W. Mills, *The belief of the Jewish people, and of the most eminent Gentile philosophers
... in a future state* (1828).
[8] Marked 'Begun Sept. 10. 60 suspended Sept. 27'. Never published; in Add MS 44750,
ff. 34–174.
[9] In *Chronicles of the Canongate* 1st. series; see 8 Dec. 27.

12. Wed.

Wrote to Mr Pressly—J.G. Hubbard—Sir Thos G.—F. Goulburn—Sir J. Graham—Watson & Smith—T.B. Horsfall—Mashfield Mason[1]—and minutes. Bathed 9°. Walk on the hill with the children. Worked on Paraphrastic Transln. of the Politics. Bible Lesson to M., L., & Gertrude Glynne. Read Tosti's Council of Const.—Tacitus Ann. III.—Scott's Aunt Margaret's Mirror.[2]

13. Th.

Wrote to Mrs Corner[3]—Mr Hamilton—Mr S. Muston[4]—Messrs. Bushell—Mr M'Coll—and minutes. 'Politics' with Willy. Worked on Transl. of do. Bathed 10°: and hill walk with Willy. 4–6¾. Read Tosti's Hist. C.C.—Scotts Two Drovers & Minor Tales.

14. Fr.

Wrote to Mr Anderson—Mr Brand—Sir A. Spearman—Duchess of Sutherland—Major Graham: & Bank of Eng(Official) & minutes. Bathed 11°. Mr Burnett here 11¼–1¾. The long struggle in Stephen's affairs is still protracted. The O[ak] F[arm] is a sad wreck. Shore walk &c. with C. Read Politics of Ar. with W. and worked on Translation. Tosti's Counc. Constance—W. Scott's Talisman.

15. Sat.

Wrote to Mr H. Lee—Sir A. Spearman—Mr M. Mason—Ld J. Russell—Mr Ryder—Rev Mr Jeffreys[5]—Mr Pressly—Mr Goulburn—Mr Laing—and minutes. Bathed 12°. Hill walk with C. & the children. The Lyttelton girls came.[6] Read Arist. Pol. (with W.): & worked on Transln.—Tosti's Counc. Constance—Tales of the Crusaders.[7]

16. 15 S. Trin.

Morning service in the Hotel. Aftn. in parish Ch. Then went to Conway. Bathed 13°. Wrote to Sir J. Coleridge—Lord J. Russell—Sir J. Lacaita:[8] —minutes. Read Thos a Kempis—Irving's Life—Tosti's Council of Constance.

17. M.

Wrote to Sir Thos G.—R. Phillimore—Robn. G.—G.A. Hamilton—and

---

[1] Of Hoddesdon, Hertfordshire; involved in Lord Lincoln's affairs; see 21 Sept. 60 and Add MS. 44394, f. 112.
[2] (1829).
[3] On the Barbar fund; Add MS 44531, f. 47, see 6 Aug. 60n.
[4] Had requested a post; ibid., f. 46.
[5] Probabl̥ Richard Jeffreys, 1808–66; rector of Cockfield, Suffolk, from 1841.
[6] Lucy, Lavinia, and Mary; Meriel, the eldest, was now married.
[7] By *Scott (1825).
[8] In Lacaita, 151.

minutes. Worked on Transln. & Notes. Read Ar. Pol. with Willy—Tosti's Counc. Constance—Talisman. Bathed 14°. Hill walk with C.

18. Tues.

Wrote to S.R. Glynne—Duke of Somerset—Rev Mr Hamilton—and minutes. Drove with W. & S. to Bangor & under the guidance of Mr Lee[1] we saw, inside & out, the wonderful Britannia Bridge. Its ugliness is much mitigated by the slant lines of the Towers. Read Ar. Pol. with Willy—Tosti Council of Constance—Talisman. Worked on Transl. Pol. Bathed 15°. Saw R. & M. Gladstone.

19. Wed.

Wrote to Ld Brougham—Watson & Smith—Mr Pressly—and minutes. W. Lyttelton here. We went up the trams. Saw Mr Templeton.[2] Bathed 16°. Worked on Transl. Politics. Read Politics with Willy—Tosti's Counc. Const.—Scott's Talisman.

20. Th.

Wrote to C. Fortescue—S. Laing—Bp of New Zealand—Bp of Argyll & Isles & minutes. Bathed 17°.—Walk with C. Saw Mr Lee. Dear Stephy left us for Eton. Worked on Transl. &c of Politics. Read Politics with Willy— The Talisman—The Headsman[3]—Tosti's Constance—Papers from London.

[The back inside cover is numbered 129 and in the top left hand corner this name is written in pencil.]

Rev Mr Tinling [4]

[1] Hedworth Lee, divisional engineer of the Chester and Holyhead railway 1847–73.
[2] William Templeton, agent for the local stone quarry.
[3] J. F. Cooper, *The Headsman; or the Abbaye des Vignerons. A tale*, 3v. (1833).
[4] Edward Douglas Tinling, 1815?–97; Christ Church; priest 1839; inspector of schools 1847–81; canon of Gloucester 1867.

[VOLUME XXII[1]]

[The inside front cover contains:—]

[In ink:—]

No. 22.
Private.
W.E.G.

21 Sept. 60 to Ap. 30., 1862.

Rich. Grenville = Lady Cobham (Temple)

E. Temple   G. Grenv.   Ly Hester = W. Pitt[2]

[In pencil]
6. Ba Feb, 3 WPL
which

           CG   JNHopken
           Anss, £39.14
      20 + 5 + 10.10 + *4.4.*
               + 10

Hazlitt

    W. Stigant Herbert Villa Howley Pl. Maida Hill
    Fitzherbert 1   Buildings C. Road. Linzell

Ballard

[Several lines erased, then:]

Herbert
Booth care of Kickburn 20 Lower Britton St
                   New Brompton
Lewis 5 James St C. Garden   Street

Brown 67

Dug M 11

[1] Lambeth MS 1436, 129ff.
[2] Glynne ancestors.

Penmaenmawr September 1860.
Frid. Sept. 21. St. Matth.

Wrote to Earl of Lincoln[1]—Mr Laing & copy—D. Graham[2]—Mr F. Goulburn—A. Simson[3]—Mr D. Gladstone—Mr Ryder and minutes. Worked on Paraphr. Transl. Bathed 18°. Read Politics with W. The Talisman (finished)—The Metempsychosis.[4]

22. Sat.

Wrote to S.W. Lawley—C. Fortescue—Rev Mr Hawkins—Sir A. Spearman—Mr A'Court—Mr Cobden—Scotts and minutes. Bathed 19°. Walk with Willy over Conway mountain which is delightful. Worked on Ar[istotle] Pol[itics]. Read Politics with Willy. Blyden on African Race[5]—Tosti's Conc[ilio] di Costanza.[6]

23. 16 S. Trin.

Reading Prayers & Sermon at home. Parish Ch. aftn. Bathed 20°. Read Tosti's Council of Constance—Remusat's St Anselm[7]—Colin Lindsay's Address[8]—Irvine's Memoir.[9]

24. M.

Wrote to G.A. Hamilton—R. Phillimore—Robn. G.—Watson & Smith—R. Cobden—Bp of Oxford—W. Grogan and minutes. Worked on Paraph. Transl. Read Politics with W. Tosti's Council of Constance—Blackwood Tales—Bathed 21°—Expedn. to Conway Hill: with the Derbyshire party. Saw Professor Newman.[10]

25. Tues.

Wrote to Mr Cobden—Lord J. Russell—Mr Pressly—Mr F. Goulburn—Rev. H. Glynne—Mrs Goalen—Ld T. Clinton and minutes. Saw Mr Burnett on Hawarden & O.F. matters: much is afloat at both. Bathed 22°. Hill with C. Read Tosti's Conc. Cost. (finished)—Arist. Pol. with W.—Horn, Finances de l'Autriche.[11]—Report of Discharged Prisoners Soc.[12] Worked on Transl. Paraph.

[1] Henry Pelham Alexander Pelham-Clinton, 1834–79; styled Earl of Lincoln; Peelite M.P. Newark 1857-9; 6th duke of Newcastle 1864; squandered remains of Newcastle fortune on horses; bankrupt 1870. In February 1861 he m., without his fa's. consent, Henrietta Adela, heiress and bastard da. of Henry Hope. As executor of the 5th duke's estate, Gladstone had many dealings with him.

[2] Perhaps a clerk in the customs office.

[3] Trying to borrow money on grounds of knowing diarist's g.-fa.; Add MS 44531, f. 49.

[4] R. Macnish, 'The Metempsychosis' in *Tales from Blackwood*, ii (1859).

[5] E.W. Blyden, 'A voice from bleeding Africa, on behalf of her exiled children' (1856).

[6] See 28 Aug. 60.

[7] By C. F. M. de Remusat (1853).

[8] C. Lindsay, 'Union and unity. An address to the members of the English Church Union and others' (1860).

[9] See 9 Sept. 60.

[10] i.e. F.W. *Newman.

[11] J. E. Horn, *Des finances de l'Autriche* (1860).

[12] Its annual report.

26. *Wed.*

Wrote to G.L. Ryder—Earl of Aberdeen—Mr Pressly—Lord Brougham—
Mr Horsfall—Mr Hamilton and minutes. Bathed 23°. Bilberry Hill with C.
& the children. PPc to the Murray Gladstones. Read the Politics with Willy
—Remusat's St Anselme—Blackwood Tales. Worked on Pol. Transl.

27. *Th.*

Wrote to Mr Anderson—Mr Pressly—Mr [G.A.] Hamilton—Mr Tomlinson
—Mr Goulburn and minutes. Worked on Paraphr. Transl. Bathed 24°.
Read Politics with Willy.—Tacitus B. III—Blackwood Tales—Sea walk
with C.

28. *Fr.* [*Llanrwst*]

Wrote to Mayor of Coventry[1]—Dr. Wolff—Mr Kingsley—Mr Pressly—Mr
Caird MP—Mr Cobden—Benj. Porter and minutes. Bathed 25° and last.
Finished Book III of the Politics of Aristotle with Willy. His intelligence is
excellent & I am struck with the easy working of his mind as well as the
justness of his ideas. He wants however solidity of scholarship.

I must not turn my back upon this place without recording my thanks
to God for the health and happiness of our large party during the month of
our stay. Read Tacitus. Gems of Engl. Poetry.[2] Off at $2\frac{1}{2}$ for Llanrwst
(Victoria [inn] excellent)

Closed Penmr. vill. . . . . . . 30 min.
Passed over ridge 65
Reached the bridge. 80
The Road 115
The 6th Milestone 121
Treffiw. 163

Thence to Ll[anrwst][3] ab 25 m. Cath. Willy & I were the party.
Saw Mr Bertie Percy.[4]

29. *Sat.* [*Hawarden*]

Saw Bp of Salisbury—9–6 Journey to Hawarden by Denbigh: went over it,
also Llansynan, during baits, & picked up what we could. Dined at the
Rectory. Saw Mr Raikes.

17. *S. Trin. Sept.* 30.60.

Parish Church mg & aft. Looked into the Quarter's Returns. Recommn. to
W. resp. his Sunday Studies, as to kind & amount. Read Tosti's Abelard[5]—
Remusat's Anselm—Anselm's Works[6]—Mills on Plato & Aristotle.[7]

[1] See 3 Feb. 60.
[2] *Gems from the poets* (1858–60).
[3] In the Conway valley, about 12 miles from the sea.
[4] Charles Greatheed Bertie Percy, 1794–1870; given precedence of duke's younger s.
1865.
[5] See 2 Sept. 60.
[6] St. *Anselm, *Opera* (1491).
[7] W. Mills, 'Lecture on the theory of moral obligation' (1830); also on *Paley and
*Butler.

M. 1.

Church 8½ a.m. Wrote to Ld Lincoln (& copy)—Mr Cobden—Sec. Lp. Fire & L[ife]—Mr Ellman[1]—Mr Hammond—Mr J. Severn—Major Trevor: and minutes. Saw Mr Burnett. Read Bp of Argyll's Charge[2]—Pol. Arist. with Willy. Peveril of the Peak.[3] Worked on papers &c (music).

2. T.

Ch 8½ a.m. Wrote to Bp of Edinburgh—Mrs Goalen—Bp of Aberdeen—Mr Gurney[4]—E. Summerhayes—Mr McColl—Watson & Smith—Mr Ryder—Warden Trin. Coll. and minutes. Ar. Pol. with Willy. Read also Tosti's Abelard—Peveril of the Peak—music. Considered the papers in the Cheyne Case.[5]

3. Wed.

Ch. 8½ a.m. Wrote to Duchess of Sutherland—Mr Ryan—Govr. of the Bank—G.A. Hamilton—Mr Arbuthnot and minutes. Mr Anderson came: much conv. with him on Bank & other matters. Dined at the Rectory. Worked on Aristotle with Willy: and read Peveril of the Peak.

4. Th.

Church 8½ a.m. Wrote to Ld Palmerston—Sir A. Spearman & Mr Anderson (Bank)—Mr G.A. Hamilton (Treas. Establishr.)—Ernest Jones[6]—Mr Paterson[7]—C.L. Ryan—Rev. Mr Newcome—Baron Rothschild—Duke of Argyll and minutes. Discussed Treasury Establt.—Irish Pay Office &c with Mr A[nderson] Arist. Politics with Willy. The *Rectory* dined here:[8] C[harles] Lyttelton gave us music. Read Peveril of the Peak. Fraser on Ld Macaulay.[9]

5. Fr.

Ch. 8½ a.m. Wrote to Mr Gibson (Telegram)—Ld J. Russell–Dr. Brown—H.E. Gurney—H.J.G.—G.A. Hamilton—Mr Cobden—E. Summerhayes—Mr Goulburn—Sir J. Lacaita—Dss. of Sutherland and minutes. Arist. Pol. with Willy. Read Peveril of the Peak—Tosti's Abelard.

6. Sat.

Ch. 8½ a.m. Wrote to Sir J. Graham—R. Barker—Govr. of the Bank—G.C.

---

[1] George Ellman of York; Hawn P.
[2] A. *Ewing, 'A charge delivered to the clergy of Argyll and the Isles' (1860).
[3] By *Scott (1823).
[4] He asked H. E. Gurney, of the bankers, about the currency (Hawn P).
[5] Case of Patrick Cheyne (see 23 Feb. 48, 12 June 58), similar to the A.P. *Forbes heresy case; in Add MS 44591, f. 193.
[6] Ernest Charles *Jones, 1819–69; barrister of Inner Temple; chartist leader till 1854; in goal 1848–50; ed. *Northern Star*; novelist and poet; Gladstone had apparently helped his family while he was on circuit in Lancashire (Hawn P).
[7] Perhaps James Paterson, 1823–94; barrister, wrote widely on licensing acts.
[8] i.e. Henry Glynne and his children.
[9] *Fraser's Magazine*, lxii. 438 (October 1860).

Glyn—Mr Hamilton. (Wrote to) Mr T.M. Gibson—Ld Chandos—Mr Goulburn and minutes. Arist. Polit. with Willy. Ride with Willy. Woodcutting. Read Peveril of the Peak—Poems of Ernest Jones[1]—Law & Liberty.

7. 18 S. Trin.
Hawarden Ch 11 a.m. (and Holy Commn.) and 6½ P.M. Wrote to Ld Palmerston[2]—Read Remusat's Anselm. Mills on Plato & Aristotle—Mgr. Parisis on Immac. Concn.[3]

8. M.
Church 8½ a.m. Wrote to Dss. of Sutherland—Mr Laing—Govr. of the Bank—Mr A'Court—J.G. Hubbard—Robn. G.—Mr J. Latimer[4]—Mr Pressly—Sir Chas. Wood—Dr. Brown—Mr. Miller[5] and minutes. Aristot. Politics with Willy—woodcutting. Saw Mr Burnett. Read Peveril of the Peak.

9. T.
Church 8½ a.m. Wrote to Ld Palmerston—Mr McColl—M. Summerhayes—Mr Brand—Jas. Darlington—W.B. Trull[6]—Sir Jas. Graham—Robn. G.—Mayor of Coventry—Mr Pressly—R. Phillimore—and minutes. Saw also Mr Burnett & Mr Moffatt: & concluded about the Mancot Pits. Music: with C. Lyttelton. Farm calls with C. Arist. Pol. with Willy. Read also E. Jones's Poems—Device for Asbury[7]—Peveril of the Peak.

10. Wed.
Ch 8½ a.m. Wrote to Ld Palmerston—Mr Brand—Duc. d'Aumale—Mr Laing—Mr Stephenson—Mr Pressly—Sidney Herbert—Mr Ryan—Col. Crombie[8]—Mr Bolton[9]—Mr E. Eyton[10] & min...es. Arist. Pol. with Willy. also conv. with him on his *avenir*.[11] Woodcutting. Worked on my tranlations. Read Tacitus—Peveril of the Peak. Dined at the Rectory. Saw Mr Darlington in evg.

11. Th.
Ch 8½ a.m. Wrote to Mr G.A. Hamilton—Mr Ryan—Watson & Smith—Mrs Waters—Dr. Holbrook[12] and minutes. Forenoon with Mr Darlington &

---

[1] E. C. *Jones, *Corayda and other poems* (1860), one on 'liberty'.
[2] On Irish volunteers' fares from Italy: Guedalla, *P*, 152.
[3] P. L. Parisis, *Démonstration de l'Immaculée Conception de la bienheureuse Vierge Marie* (1849).
[4] Perhaps the London glove seller.
[5] William Miller, first assistant cashier of the bank of England.
[6] Of Rhode Island, had requested an autograph; Hawn P.
[7] Untraced.
[8] See 1 Dec. 54.
[9] William Bolton of Birmingham; active in the savings bank movement.
[10] Had sent a broad-sheet on the injustice of the national debt; Add MS 44394, f. 140.
[11] 'future'.
[12] Dr. Erastus Holbrook of Connecticut, U.S.A. had requested an autograph; Hawn P.

Mr Burnett on the mining & boring operations. Also saw Mr D. on Savings' Banks. The Volunteers were reviewed in the afternoon: & with much company. A dinner party followed. At 10¼ P.M. I went off to London.

12. Fr. [London] X.

Arrived in C.H.T. 6¼ a.m. Wrote to Ld Shaftesbury—Robn. G.—M. Summerhayes—J.N.G.—Master of the Mint—C.G.—Mr J.C. Fisher[1]— Rev. C. Kingsley—Dr. Holbrook—Duke of Sutherland—Gray and minutes. Kings Coll. Council 2–3 P.M.—N. Debt Commn. 3–4 P.M. Saw Govr. & Dep. Govr. of the Bank—Mr Laing MP—Mr Ryan—Mr Anderson. Went to 29 B. Square in evg. Saw Clifton (2°)[R]. Read the Woman in White[2]— New Readings of Homer.[3]

13. Sat.

Wrote to Ld Palmerston—T.G. Shaw—Sidney Herbert—C.G.[4]—T.B. Horsfall—S. Lawley—Williams & Co—Author of 'New Readings of Homer' and minutes. Saw Mr Pressly—Sir Roderick Murchison—A. Panizzi (late, who detailed the King & Emperor conversations)[5]—Mr Brand —Ld Aberdeen—Hon. A. Gordon. Shopping. Dined at the Admiralty. Read Readings of Homer—arranging my tracts.

14. 19 S. Trin.

St Philips mg (late) and St George's in the East evg.: a sad spectacle, on the whole; but much the best evening yet, it was said.[6] Luncheon at 29 Berkeley Square. Saw Aunt J.—Miss Bonham.[7] Called about Mrs de Pearsall[R]. Read Fisher on Liturgy—Chr. Remembr. on Oxford. &c.[8] H. Drummond a. to Sibthorp—do Letter to Wiseman & Palmer.[9]

15. M.

Wrote to Hon. A. Gordon—C.G.—C. Hope Johnstone[10]—Mr Brand—Duc d'Aumale—Mr Pressly—Rev. Mr May[11]—Scotts—Robn. G. and minutes.

[1] Of Cockermouth, had sent his pamphlet on the liturgy.

[2] By Wilkie *Collins (1860); he found it 'far better than Adam Bede though I do not know if it rises quite as high' (Bassett, 131).

[3] Anon. (1860).

[4] Bassett, 130.

[5] After the Admiralty dinner attended by *Panizzi; *Somerset and Gladstone 'both . . . spoke [to Panizzi] against Lord John's Note [to Piedmont] which they stigmatised as "Holy Alliance Style"; Gladstone said 'certain people had reached the stage of wanting to make English policy the antechamber of Prussia's' (Beales, *England and Italy 1859–60*, 155–6).

[6] Services there had been disrupted by anti-ritualists: this night the police kept order, Gladstone sitting prominently in the church wardens' pew: *The Times*, 15 October 1860, 6.

[7] Of Albert Terrace, Knightsbridge; F. R. Bonham's sister, see 25 April. 63; Gladstone assisted her until she d. 1863.

[8] *Christian Remembrancer*, xl. 303 (October 1860).

[9] H. *Drummond, 'Remarks on the Churches of Rome and England, respectfully addressed to . . . Dr. *Wiseman and W. Palmer' (1841).

[10] Charles James Hope Johnstone, 1835–88; soldier, later major-general.

[11] Perhaps Edward Thompson May, d. 1863, curate of Princetown chapel 1858–62.

Read the Woman in White and Scarth on China.[1] Saw F.R. Bonham—Mr Arbuthnot—Mr Hamilton—Mr Hubbard—Mr C. Trevor and [blank]. Dined at 29 Berkeley Square. Shopping.

16. T.
Wrote to Mrs de Pearsall—C. Pressly (2)—A. Panizzi—Mashfield Mason— Mr Ernest Jones—Ld Palmerston[2]—Mr G. Grote—C.G.—and minutes. Dined at Mrs Stanley's. Saw R. Phillimore—Dr. Stanley—Mr Grogan resp. House.—Mr Farrar. Shopping. Read Woman in White—Scarth on China (finished)—Coleridge's Lecture.[3]

17. Wed.
Wrote to Willy—Govr. of the Bank—C.G.[4]—Chich. Fortescue—Mr Bonham —R.W. Rawson—Mr Ellacombe—Mr Arbuthnot and minutes. Saw Earl of Aberdeen—Scotts—Mrs Barber. Read Murphy's Essay[5]—Coleridge's Lecture.—The Woman in White—Mr Alexander's MS. Wrote mem. on Mr A's MS.[6]

18 TH. ST LUKE.
Agnes's 18th birthday. God bless her always & in all things). Wrote to Earl Canning—Mr Pressly—Willy—C.G.[7] & minutes. Read The Woman in White—Independence of Italy.[8] Saw Sir J. Lacaita—Mr Bagehot—Lord Kinnaird—Mr Panizzi—and Sir A. Spearman—Messrs. Overend—Gov. & Dep Gov. Bank—in the City. Visited Mrs Barber in O[ld] Jewry. Saw one[R].

19. Fr.
Wrote to Mr R. Barker—Mr Anderson—Lieut. Dunn[9]—Dss. of Sutherland —Sir Thos. G.—Wm. Gladstone—C.G.—Gray and minutes. Saw Sir E. Ryan—Mr Kinnaird—Mr Laing—A. Robertson—Read Money Pamphlets by X[10]—A.B.C.[11]—Sir J. Lubbock.[12] Saw divers[R]. Read Woman in White (finished)—Salvagnoli on Indep. Italy.[13]

20. Sat. [Hawarden]
Wrote to Mr Laing—C. Fortescue—Ld Palmerston—Bp of Oxford—Mr

[1] J. Scarth, Twelve years in China. The people, the rebels and the mandarins (1860).
[2] Guedalla, P, 153.
[3] J.T. *Coleridge, 'Public school education' (1860).
[4] Bassett, 130.
[5] J. L. Murphy, 'An essay towards a science of consciousness' (1838).
[6] On banks and discount houses, by R. D. P. Alexander of the receipt of exchequer; Add MS 44749, f. 148.
[7] Bassett, 131.
[8] V. Salvagnoli, The independence of Italy (1860).
[9] Perhaps Francis Plunkett Dunne, 1802–74; Peelite M.P. Portarlington 1847–57, Queen's co. 1859–68. a lieut.-colonel.
[10] Probably X, Monnaie et métaux précieux, de la fixité de leur valeur (1857).
[11] Untraced.
[12] J. W. *Lubbock, 'On the clearing of the London bankers' (1860).
[13] See 18 Oct. 60.

Hankey MP—Mr Herries[1]—Hon A. Kinnaird—F. Lawley—Leeman & Clark[2]—Robn. G.—Sir J. Lacaita—F. Peel—F.R. Bonham—Sir J. Young. Saw Sir A. Spearman—Duke of Argyll—Sir C. Wood—S. Herbert—Sir Geo. Lewis—Mr Ponsonby[3]—Ld J. Russell—Ld Aberdeen. Cabinet $3\frac{1}{2}$–$5\frac{1}{4}$. Off at 8: Irish Express, 4h 25 m. to Chester. Reached Hawarden at $1\frac{1}{2}$a.m.

21. 20 S. Trin.

Ch mg. & evg. Conv. with M. & L on Gospel. Read Remusat's Anselm[4]—Fisher on the Liturgy.

22. M.

Ch $8\frac{1}{2}$ a.m. Wrote to Prof. Christison—F. Peel—Rev. Mr Goodlake[5]—W.H.G.—& minutes. Worked on arranging my Library. Saw Mr Darlington with Mr Burnett at the Pit: ab. the mine & the railway. Dined at the Rectory: much conv. with [Dowager] Lady L[yttelto]n. who is excellent company. Read Condorcet Revol. Am.[6]—Peveril of the Peak.

23. Tues.

Ch $8\frac{1}{2}$ a.m. Wrote to Mr E.V. Neale[7]—Mr Horsfall MP—Mr Herries—Rev. Dr Wolff—Sir A. Spearman—Rev. Mr MacColl and minutes. Goldoni[8] lesson with Agnes, M & L. Worked on arranging books. Went over the warehouse. Saw Mr Burnett—Called at Broughton Parsonage. Read Peveril of the Peak. Company & party evg: music.

24. Wed.

Ch $8\frac{1}{2}$ a.m. Wrote to Sir Geo. Lewis—Mr Trevor—Dr Pusey—and minutes. Goldoni's Locandiera, as yesterday. Worked several hours on arranging my books. Walked to St John's [Pentrobin] with Sir G. Prevost and Mr Webb. Conv. with Lady L. resp. H. [Glynne], C., and Miss Rose. Large dinner party: & music in evg.

25. Th.

Ch. $8\frac{1}{2}$ A.M. Wrote to Sir A. Spearman—Mr Mayow—Mr Hamilton—Ld Clanricarde & minutes. Goldoni's Locandiera as yest. Rode with Agnes. Worked much on books. Family conv. with C. Party, & music in evg. Read Peveril of the Peak.

[1] (Sir) Charles John *Herries, 1815–83, s. of J.C.*; dep. chairman of I.R. board 1856, chairman 1877–81; K.C.B. 1880; involved in a row about succession duty accounts: Add MS 44394, f. 166.
[2] George Leeman, York solicitor, liberal, and mayor; dealt with the Wenlock's affairs; Hawn P. and 4 Dec. 60n.
[3] Gerald Henry Brabazon Ponsonby, 1829–1908, s. of 4th earl of Bessborough; treasury clerk from 1852.
[4] See 23 Sept. 60.
[5] Thomas William Goodlake, 1811?–75; fellow of Pembroke, Oxford, 1838–46; school inspector 1847–61; rector of Swindon from 1861.
[6] M. J. A. N. Caritat, Marquis de Condorcet, *Influence de la Révolution de l'Amerique sur l'Europe* (1788).
[7] See 21 Nov. 28.
[8] G. Goldoni, *La locandiera* (1751), Italian comedy of female coquetry.

26. Fr.

Ch. 8½ a.m. Wrote to Rev. Mr Mayow—F. Peel—S. Herbert—Mr Fowler[1] & minutes. Read Peveril of the Peak. Finished the really heavy job in the arrangement of my books. At mine & bore. Goldoni with A.M. & L. Saw Rev. Mr Wray.[2] Sir G. Prevost (Liturgy Mission).[3]

27. Sat.

Ch. 8½ a.m. Wrote to Mr Arbuthnot—M.D.[4]—Mr Caird MP—Watson & Smith—Mr G. Smith & minutes. The Company visited the 'temple of peace' in the forenoon & inspected my Library. Did some odds & ends of work upon it. Read Sull'Ipotesi del Moto della Terra.[5] Finished Peveril of the Peak. Music in evg. C.L. on H.G.

28. 21 S. Trin.

Ch mg & evg. Read Fisher on Liturgy—Remusat's Anselm—Browne on the Articles.[6] Conv. with Sir G. Prevost. Also with C. on George's possible marrying.[7] Then with C. & G. Then with C. & Lady L[yttelton]. Then with Lady L. alone.

29. M.

Wrote to Robn. G—Mr Hamilton—Mr Cobden—Lord J. Russell—Mr [J.R.] Godley[8]—Duchess of Sutherland—Sir G. Lewis & minutes. *Church 8½ a.m.* Goldoni as usual. Read Richards on Engl. Philol.[9] Tookes Letter to Dunning.[10] Dined at Mr R. Eaton's. Whist in evg at Hn. Walk with Lyttelton. Conv. with C. on his *personal* matters.[11]

30. T.

Ch 8½ a.m. Wrote to Provost of Queen's—C.A. Wood—Mr G. Hamilton— R. Bentley—Ld Chancellor—Rev C. Wray—Mr J. Harrison—S.E.G. & minutes. Read 18th Cent. Eccl. Hist. pamphlets—Ipotesi del Moto della Terra. Goldoni as usual with A.M. & L.—Whist, Music, Conv. with Sir G. Prevost—& Sir T. Wyse. Arranging letters &c.

31. Wed.

Church 8½ a.m. Wrote to Ed. Daily News[12]—Mr Laing—Mr Hamilton—

[1] William Fowler, 1829–1905; banker and author on land laws; liberal M.P. Cambridge city 1868–74, 1880–5; see Add MS 44394, f. 196.
[2] C. Wray (see 21 May 52), then in Liverpool.
[3] Probably the Anglo-Continental Society, formally constituted 1861.
[4] Anon. correspondent.
[5] Untraced.
[6] E. H. *Browne, *An exposition of the Thirty-Nine Articles* (1850).
[7] *Lyttelton remarried, but not as the Gladstones planned; see 29 July 61n.
[8] Then under-sec. to S. *Herbert.
[9] Probably T. Richards, *Antiquae linguae Brittanicae Thesaurus; being a British or Welsh–English dictionary* (1753).
[10] J. *Horne Tooke, 'A letter to J. Dunning [on the conjunction "That"]' (1778).
[11] Charles, the oldest of the Lyttelton boys, was just going up to Trinity, Cambridge, where he took a first in law 1864; or on George's remarriage.
[12] Founding with £50 a subscription fund for the bankrupt *Hullah; *Daily News*, 2 November 1860, 4d.

Willy—Sir A. Spearman—Mr Hubbard—Rev Mr Hawkins and minutes: also Freshfields. Read Goldoni as usual. Panzani's Memoirs &c:[1] Condorcet.[2] Preparations for Catalogue[3]—Party: & Music.

1. Th. All Saints.

Ch at 11 a.m. Worked on private MS.[4] Luncheon party at Rectory: & busy about H.s plan for Miss L. wh does him great credit, for the delicacy of the manner. Wrote to Sir T. Fremantle—Mr Laing—Sir A. Spearman—Mr Herries—Dss. of Sutherland—(Mrs Dale =) M. Summerhayes—Watson & Smith & minutes. Goldoni as usual. Walk with Mr T. Wyn & Mr [J.W.] Parker.[5] Read Condorcet Rev. Amer. Lyttelton's Godiva & Lotus Eaters.[6] Saw Mrs Waters. Party: whist in evg.

2. Fr.

Ch 8½ a.m. Wrote to Mr Shaw—Ld Justice Clerk—H. Glynne—Canon Stanley—Rev. C. Wray—Govr. of Bank—J.N.G.—Dep Govr. of Bank— Sir T.G. (aft)—Sir E. Lytton—Mr Ryan and minutes. Conv. with Lyttelton about *our* coming publication. Walk with him & Mr Parker. Party, whist, & music in evg. Goldoni as usual with A.M. & L. Read Panzani's Mem. H. Tooke's L to Dunning. Condorcet &c on Am. Revolution.

Be sure to think much about yourself, your motives, your acts, the consequences of your acts, and the relations between these. Be sure also to speak little of them. To do the former is absolutely of the first importance: to avoid the latter is of importance all but the first.[7]

3. Sat.

Ch 8½ a.m. Wrote to Sir W.R. Farquhar—Mr Senior—Hon. C. Lyttelton— W. Hampton—Sir G.C. Lewis—Mr Ryan and minutes. Saw H.G. on his affair resp. transmission of money. Mr Parker—resp. Copyright. Spent most of the day on the MSS of my Translations & in arranging with G. various points about publication. Read Panzani's Mem.—Senior's (1860) Journal.[8]

4. 22 S. Trin.

Ch mg (and H.C.) and evg. Wrote to Mr Hullah—Sir W.C. James. Read Nesbitt's Article[9]—Dean Elliot's Letter[10]—Bp of Argyll's Charge[11]—Mr

[1] See 15 Mar. 51.
[2] See 22 Oct. 60.
[3] i.e. the contents page of the Gladstone–Lyttelton *Translations*.
[4] Not found.
[5] The publisher.
[6] For the Gladstone–Lyttelton *Translations*.
[7] Dated 2 November 1860; Add MS 44750, f. 151.
[8] Published as N. W. Senior, *Conversations with distinguished persons during the Second Empire 1860–1863* ed. M. C. M. Simpson, 2v. 1880.
[9] Probably J. C. Nesbit, 'On agricultural chemistry' (7th ed. 1860).
[10] G. Elliot, 'Three letters to the Archbishop of Canterbury on the repeal of the Twenty-ninth Canon' (1860).
[11] See 1 Oct. 60.

Tweed's Sermon[1]—other pamphlets—& Cheyne correspondence and papers.[2]

5. M.

Ch. 8½ a.m. Wrote to Bp of Argyll—Sir W. Heathcote—Ld Palmerston and minutes.

Off at one to Chester. Luncheon at the Mayors, Then Review on the Roodee.[3] Then the Collection & crowded meeting at the Music Hall. The Bishop blew the coals. I had an uncomfortable speech to make: for I had to set up the Volunteers & yet cry down the alarms.[4] We got back before 8. Read Senior's Journal—Cavour's Speech of Oct. 11[5]—Panzani's Memoirs—

6. T.

Ch. 8½ a.m. Wrote to Lord J. Russell—Dr. Pusey—Mr Roberts (Tenant)——Mr Anderson—Leeman & Clark and minutes. Saw L[yttelton] resp. our work—H.G. resp. his remittance—Miss Syfret resp. my German version of Alfred.[6] Mr Burnett on S.s affairs &c.—Mr West. The Miss Haslems—a visit.[7] Worked on Argus.[8] Worked on Arist Pol. Read Senior's Journal—Emerton Prize Essay[9]—Stigand's Poems[10]—Goldoni as usual.

7. Wed.

Ch 8½ a.m. Wrote to Duchess of Sutherland—W.H.G.—C. Lyttelton—Sir R. Hill—Dean Ramsay—The Prince Consort[11]—Bp of Aberdeen and minutes. Worked 2 hours on arranging Stephen's China for & in the gift cabinet. Goldoni as usual. Finished Senior's Journals. Read George's (Arundines) compositions: & further prepared my own MS, & discussed matters with him. Read Stigand's Poems—Dean Goode's Letter.[12] Saw the Wests.

8. Th. [London]

Ch 8½ a.m. Wrote to Col. A. Gladstone—T.B. May—R. Phillimore—Mr Cobden—M. Summerhayes and minutes. Off at one: reached Euston 6.22. Busy mg. with arrangements for departure: & in London on letters, papers &c for 4 hours.—Also saw two [R]. Saw Cardwell—en route.

[1] H. E. Tweed, 'The apostles and the Offertory' (1860).
[2] See 2 Oct. 60.
[3] The meadow, now the race-course, below the castle.
[4] He was received 'with tremendous cheering'; he denied any 'immediate danger to the country', but praised the Volunteers' moral effect; *Chester Courant*, 7 November 1860, 5.
[5] Winding up the debate on the annexation bill.
[6] Omitted from the *Translations*.
[7] They lived in the village.
[8] 'The death of the dog Argus', for the *Translations*.
[9] J. A. Emerton, 'England and France' (1859), offering a prize for an essay on Anglo–French union.
[10] W. Stigand, *A Vision of Barbarossa, and other poems* (1859).
[11] *Albert had sent MSS on the Spanish situation; see Guedalla, Q, i. 119.
[12] See 2 May 50.

9. Fr.

Wrote to Sir W. Heathcote—W. Cowper—Mr Arbuthnot—Mrs Waters—A. Beresford Hope—Sir W. James—Mr Stephenson—C.G.—Ld Lyttelton and minutes. Saw Mr Laing—do cum Sir T. Fremantle—Sir G.C. Lewis—Mr Hamilton—Lord J. Russell—Ld Brougham—Hon. A. Gordon—Scotts—Mr Anderson—Dss. of Sutherd. Dined at the Guildhall. Conv. with my neighbour M. Chateau Renard[1]—& M. Persigny. Saw Bennet: really notable[R].

10. Sat. [Hursley]

Wrote to Mr A Court—Mr Baxter MP[2]—Mr Ellice and minutes. Went off at 3.40 to Hursely[3] and arrived for dinner. Read Hazlitt's Venice.[4] Wrote at night, tentatively, an address resigning my poor seat at Oxford![5] (Interviews or business in mg.)[6]

11. 23 S. Trin.

Read Neale's Voices[7]—Reformed Prayerbook. Hursley Ch. mg much delighted with Mr K[eble']s simple preaching, (not with the Choral Service) Ampfield aft. Saw Mr Keble. Much conv. with Sir W. H[eathcote] on the Irish Bill,[8] Oxford Seat, public affairs.

12. M. X [London]

Wrote to Mr Ellice (2)—C.G. (2)—Mr Spooner MP—Sir W. C. James—Mr Hugessen—Bp of Sodor & Man—Mr Cowell—Mr Anderson & minutes. Left Sir W.H. at 8.30 for London. Attended Court of Exchequer for [pricking the] Sheriffs List at 2 P.M. Saw the Lord Chancellor—Mr A. Panizzi—Mr Helps[9]—Governor of the Bank—Read Hazlitt's Venice. Dined with the Herberts. Saw Williamson[R].

13. T. X.

Wrote to Mr Pennethorne—Lyttelton—V.C. Oxford—Mr Hunt—Dr. Pusey—Robn. G. 2 & minutes. Cabinet $1\frac{3}{4}$–$4\frac{1}{2}$. Saw Lieut. Bonham[10]—Duke of Argyll—Mr F. Peel. Saw Vivien U.S.[R]. Dined at Stafford House: & went thence to Colleen Bawn wh is very national & also most touching.[11]

[1] Persigny's secretary; see Morning Chronicle, 10 Nov. 1860, 3.
[2] William Edward Baxter, 1825–90; Dundee merchant; liberal M.P. Montrose burghs 1855–85; minor office 1868–73.
[3] Hursley Park, *Heathcote's seat near Winchester; *Keble was the parish priest.
[4] See 28 June 60.
[5] Not sent; giving as his reason his wish not to cause another contested election: Add MS 44749, f. 166.
[6] Sentence in parenthesis added in pencil.
[7] J. M. *Neale, Voices from the East (1859).
[8] Ecclesiastical Courts (Ireland) Bill; *Heathcote was encouraging the Guardian to a moderate attitude; Add MS 44209, f. 78.
[9] (Sir) Arthur *Helps, 1813–75; clerk to the privy council from 1860; K.C.B. 1872; novelist and historian.
[10] Probably a relative of the charity case; see 14 Oct. 60.
[11] Irish drama by *Boucicault, a great success at the Adelphi; Agnes Robertson, Boucicault's wife, played Eily O'Connor, the heroine. Gladstone went thrice; see 23 Nov. 60, 17 Dec. 60.

14. Wed.

Wrote to Mr Cowper—Hon. A. Gordon—Mr Ellice—Rev. Mr Neale—Mr Cobden—Mr Arbuthnot—Mr Helps and minutes. Saw Mr Phillimore—Mr Pennethorne—Mr Cardwell

Mr Cotton & Mr Hankey⎫
Duke of Cambridge   ⎬ *at Guy's*

Lord John Russell—Saw Bennet[R]. Read Law Courts' Report.[1] Shopping. C.G. came in evg.

15. Th.

Wrote to Mr Hamilton—Sir G. Lewis—Messrs. Williams—W. Cowper—Hon. A. Gordon (& copy)—J.N.G.—Mr Ryan—Sir T.G. & minutes. Saw Mr Waters—Sir W. Farquhar—Governor of the Bank—Mr Hunt—Mr Quaritch—Mr Peel *cum* Mr Hamilton—Do *cum* Mr Stephenson. Ld. P. *cum* Chancellor & Att. General—Mr Pressly. Wrote minutes on Hop Duty.[2] Dined with Duchess of Inverness. Conv. with Corti—Lavradio—Prince of Holstein Augustenburg.[3] Read Paleario.[4]

  For Committee on Law Courts? Ld Palmerston—Chancellor—Duke of Argyll—Sir Geo. Lewis—Chancellor of Exchr.—Atty General—Mr Cowper.[5]

16. Fr.

Wrote to Ld Palmerston—W. Cowper—Goldwin Smith—S. Herbert—Mr Trevor—Mr Brand—Govr. of Bank and minutes. We dined with the Herberts. Read. Saw Duke of Argyll—Lord Aberdeen—Sir W. Farquhar—Scotts—Mr Cardwell—C. Lyttelton—Aunt J. and Bennet[R].

17. Sat. [Strawberry Hill]

Wrote to Mr Spooner—H. Glynne—Mrs Osborne[6]—Lyttelton—B. Quaritch—Mr Davison—Mr Anderson—Mr Hazlitt—Sir G. Lewis and minutes. Saw Sir A. Spearman—R. Phillimore. Cabinet 1½-4. Then off to Strawberry Hill[7] with C. Read Hazlitt.

18. 24 S. Trin.

Richm. Ch mg and Twickenham aft. Read Eucharistic Teaching[8]—Voices from the East[9]—Heartiness in Public Worship.[10] The Aumales dined. I sat by the Duchess: rather hard on her I think.

[1] On new sites for them: *PP* 1860 xxxi. 89.
[2] Not found.
[3] See 12 July 51.
[4] See 14 Sept. 56.
[5] Initialled and dated 15 November [1860]; Add MS 44750, f. 152.
[6] Mrs. C. J. Osborne of Clonmel and London, corresponded until 1865 (Hawn P).
[7] Lady *Waldegrave's; see 8 May 58.
[8] See 27 Dec. 40?
[9] See 11 Nov. 60.
[10] *Heartiness in public worship. By a London churchwarden* (1860).

19. M. [London]

Wrote to Ld Palmerston—Mr Pressly—Bp N. Zealand—Mr Woodgate—
Duke of Argyll—Sir A. Spearman—D. of Newcastle—Govr. of the Bank.—
Bp of Aberdeen and minutes. Saw C. Fortescue[1]—Duchess of Sutherland—
R. Phillimore—Sir F.H. Doyle (Homer)—Mr B. Quaritch. Saw Bickle[R].
Dined at R. Phillimore's. Read Hazlitt's Venice. Thoughts of Amn.
Independence.[2]

20.

Wrote to Mr T.S. Godfrey—Geo Grant—Duchess of Sutherland—Canon
Trevor—V. Admiral Collier[3]—Ld Wodehouse—Mr B. Quaritch (0)—Dr.
Pusey—Bennet and minutes. Saw Sir A. Spearman—Rt Hon. W. Cowper—
Rt. Hon. Sir J. Young—Mr Anderson—D. of Newcastle—Mr E.A. Bowring
—D. [of] Somerset. Saw Aunt J.—Bennet[R]. Dined with the Herberts.
Read Slack on Progress[4]—Hazlitt's Venice.

21. Wed.

Wrote to Bp of Oxford—Rev. Mr McColl—Miss Browne[5]—Rev. A. Goalen
—Mr Pressly—Sir T. Fremantle—G. Burnett—Duke of Newcastle; &
minutes. Saw R. Phillimore—Mr Anderson—Capt Gladstone—Duke of
Newcastle—Ld Stanley (Alderley)—Ld Wodehouse—Mr Booth,[6] & Mr
Bowring. Shopping. Cabinet Dinner (& Dinner Cabinet) at Ld Palmerston's.
Read account of Taxes[7]—Hazlitt's Venice. Much conv. on Henry & the
Rose affair.

1.[8] Exchequer Bills to be charged on the Consolidated Fund.
2. Bills to be *liable* to liquidation annually on demand as at present; but the
   instrument to be renewed only once in five years.
3. Interest to be paid half yearly.
4. Ten Coupons to be attached to each Bill.
x5. Four Issues of Bills in each year: about the middle of the months of March,
   June, September and December respectively.
x6. The March and June issues to be double in amount (or thereabouts) of the
   September and December issues.
7. The minimum rate of interest to be announced for each issue, as now, before
   it takes place, and before each annual period of liquidation.
x8. The minimum rate of interest may be raised for the outstanding term either
   of the half year or of the year: and either on any or all of the four sets of Bills.
9. The Bills to be receivable at par, at any period, in payment of Customs
   Duties.

[1] On the French treaty, see W. Hewett, '. . . *and Mr. Fortescue*' (1958), 174.
[2] Untraced.
[3] Henry Theodosius Browne Collier, 1791–1872; retired 1863.
[4] H. J. *Slack, *The philosophy of progress in human affairs* (1860).
[5] See 16 Aug. 47.
[6] Probably George Sclater-Booth, 1826–94; tory M.P. N. Hampshire 1857–85, Basing-
stoke 1885–7; minor office 1867–8, 1874–80; chaired cttees. 1868–74, 1880–5; cr. Baron
Basing 1887.
[7] Not found.
[8] Sketch for Exchequer Bills Bill; see 4 Mar. 61. Dated 21 Nov. 1860, Add MS 44750,
f. 154. Marked 'Private & Confidential.'

10. The Bills to be prepared and issued at the Bank.
11. The Bills to be paid at the Bank.
12. Law in other respects as now—Bill (i.e. Act) to be in force for 5 years.

22. Th.

Wrote to Mr Ellice—Mr Cobden—D. of Argyll—Scotts—Sir Geo Prevost—
Mr F. Peel—Rev. Mr Sharpe[1]—Mr Thring—Mr B.H. Cooper[2]—Miss
Browne—Mary G.—Harry N.G. and minutes. French play 8 P.M. Stifling
heat. Saw Sir J. Lacaita[3]—Mr Simner.[4] Saw Aunt J.—missed Bennet[R].
Attended Eccl. Comm. 11¼–2. Read Account of Taxes. Slack(!) on Progress.

23. Fr.

Wrote to Sir T. Fremantle—Sir G. Lewis—Hon. & Rev. F. Grey[5]—Ld
Harris—G. Burnett and minutes. Five to dinner. 12–5. To Windsor Castle,
Council. Saw Ld Palmerston—Ld Chichester—Mr Helps. Saw Williamson
[R]. At 7¼ went to Adelphi & saw the Colleen Bawn: with no diminution
of interest.[6] We were 10. Read Hazlitt's Venice—Law Courts Evidence.
My Mary's birthday: God bless her.

24. Sat. X.

Wrote to Sir J. Graham—Mr F. Peel—Duke of Argyll—Mr H. Cole—Mrs
Bickle—Mrs Dale (MS[ummerhayes])—Lord J. Russell & minutes. Saw
Sir A. Spearman: long.—Mr Godfrey (Newark Exhibition). Dined at Lady
Lyttelton's. She has much to say: but is so humble. Saw Bennett: good
hope. Also Bickle[R]. Read Hazlitt. Round of invalid & duty visits: Ly
Haddington,[7] Ld R. Clinton, Aunt J.

25. 25 S. Trin.

Ch. Royal mg & All Saints 3.30. Went to Argyll Ho. & saw A. Gordon: I
fear I shall see his father, on this side the grave, no more.[8] Saw Mr Kingsley
(who preached). Wrote to C. Lyttelton—Rev. Mr Pinder. Read Mr Pinder
on Bishops.[9] Hessey's Bampton Lectures[10]—Ch of England Review[11]—
Voices from the East (finished). Stafford Ho. 9½–11½ with the Argylls.

[1] Probably Clement Charles Sharpe, 1828?–84; perpetual curate of Ince, Cheshire,
1852–67; vicar of Bucknell, Salop, from 1867.
[2] Basil Henry Cooper, b. 1819; author and translator; had sent a copy of his pamphlet
on 'The hieroglyphical date of the exodus in the annals of Thothmes' (1860) (Hawn P).
[3] Report in Lacaita, 155–6.
[4] Possibly Abel Simnel, clerk in poor law board.
[5] See 21 Feb. 52; he was 6th s. of 2nd Earl Grey.
[6] See 13 Nov. 60.
[7] Maria, da. of 4th earl of Macclesfield, m. 1802 9th earl of Haddington and d. February
1861.
[8] See 21 Dec. 60.
[9] John Hothersall Pinder, 1811–68; principal of Wells theological college 1840–65;
wrote The candidate for the Ministry. A course of expository lectures (1837).
[10] J. A. *Hessey, Sunday, its origin, history and present obligation (1860).
[11] Church of England monthly review, ix (1860).

26. M. X.

Wrote to Master of Mint—Mr Roberts—Sir T. Fremantle—Robn. G.—Miss
Syfret—A. Panizzi—Govr. of the Bank and minutes. Cabinet $3\frac{1}{2}$–$6\frac{1}{4}$. Saw
Mr Gibson—R. Phillimore on the Rose affair, growing daily more painful:
also on Mr Cheyne. C.G. returned at 10: conv. on do. Saw Vivien[R]. Read
Public Monies Report & papers.[1] N. British R. on Macaulay & on Italy.[2]

Cabinet.[3] N. 26. 60.

1. Land Revenues Charges[4]
2. Exchequer Bills[5] removal to Bank
3. Bank remuneration.[6]
4. Chancery Monies
5. P.O. auxiliary Savings' Banks.[7]

27. T.

Wrote to Mr Espinasse[8]—Sir C. Wood—A. Panizzi—Sir C. Locock—Ld
Chancellor—Rev. Mr West—Ld Justice Clerk—Sir G. Lewis—Herbert
J.G.—Sir J. Graham & minutes. Saw Mr Anderson ($2\frac{1}{2}$ h.)—Mr Stephenson
—Mr F. Peel —Mr G. Hamilton—Mr Strutt. We dined with the Philli-
more's and discussed largely the Rose affair. I wrote a draft for C. to Miss
Rose, wh she sent: renouncing further intervention.[9] This course her posi-
tion even more than her peace requires. Cabinet $3\frac{1}{2}$–5. Wrote Mema. on
Bank & Exchequer plans.[10] Saw Godfrey[R]. Read Lunzi's Ionian I.[11]—
Watherston on the Pix.[12]

28. Wed.

Wrote to C. Trevor—Dss. of Sutherland—G. Burnett—Count Persigny—
Robn. G and minutes. Wrote Mema. on Chancery Monies—Bank.[13] Saw Mr
Anderson (2 hours on these plans)—Mr Shelley—Mr Hamilton—Sir T.
Fremantle—Do *cum* Mr Sandeman—Govr. & Dept. Govr. of the Bank—
Sir S.R.G. (come up resp. Rose)—Cabinet dinner at the Lord Chancellors.

29. Th.

Wrote to Ld Wodehouse—Ld Granville—Sir A. Spearman—Atty. General

[1] See 28 Jan. 61.
[2] *North British Review*, xxxiii. 428, 549. (November 1860).
[3] Exchequer measures for 1861; Add MS 44750, f. 155.
[4] Act for cheapening land transfers was passed 1862.
[5] See 21 Nov. 60.
[6] See next day's n.
[7] See 8 Apr. 61.
[8] Francis Espinasse, journalist, had sent proof of his article on Gladstone for *The
imperial dictionary of universal biography* (Hawn P).
[9] Not found; see 28 Aug. 60.
[10] Aiming to reduce the Bank's profits from debt management by £70,000; Add MS
44750, f. 156, 160.
[11] E. Lunzi, *Storia delle Isole Ionie sotto il reggimento dei Repubblicani Francesi* (1860).
[12] J. H. Watherston, 'The trial of the Pix' (1860).
[13] Add MS 44750, f. 164.

—Govr. Bank—Mr S. Laing and minutes. Portrait Gallery meeting at 2.15.
Saw R. Phillimore (Rose) with C. & S.—Sir W.C. James—Sir C. Eastlake—
Lord Stanhope—The Treasury Officers 4–5½—Mr Arbuthnot—Mr Stephen-
son—Hon. A. Gordon—Scotts. Read Hazlitt's Venice—Chancery Evidence
—Slack on Progress.

30. Fr. St And[rew's] X.

Wrote to Marq. Azeglio—Mr Pressly—Sir C. Locock—Master of Mint—
Lady Lyttelton and minutes. Cabinet 3¾–6¼. Much conv. & conferences on
the Rose affair. Fine Arts Deputn. at 11.30. Messrs. Johnson & Parkinson
12–2 on Chancery Funds. Saw Sir J. Lacaita. Six to dinner. Saw Vivien[R].
Read Slack on Progress.

Sat. Dec. One. 60. [Windsor]

Wrote to H.M.—Mr A. Beaumont[1]—Sir J. Lacaita & minutes. Went to
Barber Surgeons' Hall to see the great Holbein 12–1½.[2] Saw Mr Gibson—
Mr Bright—Mr Laing—Mr Stephenson—Lady Lyttelton resp. M. G[lynne].
Off at 5 to Windsor Castle: conv. with the Prince; no politics with him or
H.M. Read [blank] on events in Sicily.

2. Adv. S.

Chapel in Castle 9.30 & 12. St Georges 4½. Saw the Dean who spoke freely.
Saw Stephy. Read Jowett's Essay[3]—Watson, & Gutch's Introd.[4] Conv.
with the Prince (& co) on Sermons. Again no politics in the evg.

3. M. [London]

Wrote to Ct. Flamburiari—M. S[ummerhayes]—V.C. Oxford—Bennett—
H.J.G. and minutes. Read Pub. Monies Evidence[5]—Hazlitt's Venice. Saw
Sir J. Lacaita—Duchess of Sutherland—Dean of Windsor—Rev W. Sel-
wyn. Saw Govr. of the Bank with Messrs. Cotton & K[irkman] Hodgson
resp. the £70000; 4–5¾.[6] Dined with the Phillimores & much conv. on the
Rose affair & explosion.

4. T. X

Wrote to Rector of Exeter—R. Cobden (2)—Master of Univ.—Mrs Goalen
—Earl Granville—Mr Mitchell—Ld Chancellor—Mr Pressly—Hon A.
Gordon—Ld M[ayor] York[7]—Lord J. Russell—S. Herbert—Lady Mac-
grigor[8]—Dean of St. Paul's and minutes. Saw Capt. G.—Mr Panizzi—Sir

---

[1] Giving his opinion of the Holbein, not to be used officially; Add MS 44531, f. 85.
[2] Commemorating the uniting of the Barbers and Surgeons, 1540.
[3] B. *Jowett, 'On the interpretation of Scripture' in *Essays and Reviews* (1860).
[4] G. Watson, *Watson Redivivus. Four discourses . . . rescued from obscurity by J. M.
G[utch]* (1860).
[5] See 26 Nov. 60.
[6] Meeting between the Bank and a treasury cttee. on using exchequer bills to reduce
the debt, and reduction of Bank profits; see Clapham, *The Bank of England*, ii. 255, Add
MS 44591, f. 151, 44749, f. 172, and 21, 27 Nov. 60.
[7] George Leeman; declining to speak there; Add MS 44531, f. 88.
[8] See 28 Oct. 26.

W. Dunbar—Mr Hamilton *cum* Mr Arbuthnot. Saw Ballard[R]. Subm. Telegr. Discussion 8–9½. Read Marliani on Italy.[1]

5. Wed.

Wrote to Ld Stanhope—Ld Chancellor—Mr Robinson—Ly. Westminster[2] & minutes. Saw Sir G. Lewis—Mr Elliot (from Naples)[3]—Mr Frisark[4]— R. Phillimore—Mr Cowper—T. Goalen—The Govr. of the Bank—Mr Arbuthnot *cum* Mr Anderson.[5] Wrote Mem. on Law Courts & Suitors Fund Plan.[6] Dined at Ld Palmerston's. Called at Ld Abns. For a fortnight he has not even been out. H. Glynne came. The discussions on his affair continued. M. Glynne was brought here. Read . . .

6. Th.

Wrote to Ly Haddington—S. Herbert—Ly Lyttelton—C. Trevor—Sir C. Lewis—S.R. Glynne and minutes. Saw Bp of Sodor & Man—Mr Fowler *cum* Mr Cowper (Metrop. Railways)—Ld Granville—The Treasury Officers—Mr Peel—Mr Shelley—Mr Phillimore Q.C.—Miss Rose. Hazlitt's Venice: finished Vol. III.

7. Fr.

Wrote to Duke of Argyll—C.G.—Lady Lyttelton—W. Grogan—J. Westell and minutes. Read Lettres sur la Sicile.[7] Saw Mr Anderson (2)—Ld Chancr. *cum* Att. General—Mr F. Peel—Mr R. Phillimore. Went over the L[incoln's] Inn & M[iddle] Temple buildings with Att. General. Shopping: Woodgates[8] where are the most beautiful things. Saw Aunt J. Dined at Stafford House, and had much conversation.

8. Sat. [Hawarden]

Wrote to W. Phillimore—Bennett—Dean of St. Paul's—Ld C. Paget—Mast of Balliol—Mr Trevor—Duchess of S. (2)—M. S[ummerhayes]—Dep. Gov. Bank—H.J.G.—Mr Anderson—Mr Gilbart[9]—Mr Arbuthnot and minutes. Saw Mr Woodgate (purchases)—Sir Thomas Wyse—Sir Alex. Spearman— Hon. A. Gordon—Ld A. is dying. Off at 8 P.M. after a busy day. Detained an hour in Chester. Reached Hn. at 3 in the morning. Read Hartwig on the Sea.[10]

---

[1] E. Marliani, 'L'Unité nationale de l'Italie' (1860).
[2] Elizabeth Mary, da. of 1st duke of Sutherland, m. 2nd marquis of Westminster 1819 and d. 1891.
[3] (Sir) Henry George *Elliot, 1817–1907; s. of 2nd earl of Minto; minister in Naples (supporting unification), later Turin and Florence; ambassador to Turkey 1867, Austria 1877. He left Naples when Victor Emmanuel entered it as King on 7 November.
[4] Unidentified.
[5] Meeting of the governor of the bank on exchequer bills with a treasury cttee.: Add MS 44591, f. 151 and 44750, f. 172.
[6] See Add MS 44591, f. 180.
[7] Several; probably that by M. J. de Foresta, 2v. (1821).
[8] Probably Thomas Woodgate, curiosity dealer in High Holborn.
[9] James William *Gilbart, 1794–1863; banker and writer on banking; see next day.
[10] G. Hartwig, *The sea and its living wonders* (1860).

9. 2 S. Adv.

Hn. Ch. mg & evg. Read Scott's Univ. Sermons.[1] Aquila de Rupe! on Revision[2]—Refl. on Polygamy.[3]

10. M.

Ch. 8½ a.m. Saw Mr West on I. Tax—& on Homeric questions. Mr Burnett on O.F.—the Colliery—& my own farm. Visited the Colliery & saw Mr Dean. Conv. resp. the Rose affair—arranging books. Read Thiers Vol. XVIII[4]—Gilbart's Elements of Banking.[5]

11. T.

Ch 8½ a.m. Wrote to Ld Clanricarde—Robn. G.—Sir D. Brewster—Mr Pressly—Ld J. Russell—Mr Anderson—and minutes. Read Boswells Johnson—Gilbart's Elements of Banking—Helps on Organisation[6]—Thiers Vol XVIII. More [Miss] *Rose*. These are critical days.

12. Wed.

Ch. 8½ a.m. Wrote to Duchess of Sutherland—Mr Field—Sir T. Fremantle— Mr Burgess—Mr Arbuthnot and minutes. Read Oxford Prof. Plan.[7] Gilbart on Banking—A City for the Pope[8]—Wood on London Health[9]—London Thames Embankment.[10]

13. Th.

Ch 8½ a.m. Wrote to Ld Lyttelton—Dr Pusey—Ly Macgrigor—M.S.—Ld Palmerston—W. Cowper—V.C. Oxford—Ld C. Paget and minutes. Read Keightley's Mythology[11]—Gilbart's Elements—Thiers Vol. XVIII— Hillocks's Life.[12] Goldoni lesson with my daughters. Saw Mr Darlington on the Coal Mines. An instructing & hopeful report.

14. Fr.

Ch 8½ a.m. Wrote to Mr Stephenson—Mr Ryan—Bp of Aberdeen—Mr Acourt—Sir A. Spearman—Mr Gilbart & minutes. Went to Buckley. Goldoni with A.M. & L. Read Thiers Vol. 18—Gilbart (finished)—Hillocks's Life—finished. Went to Buckley—& walk with C.

[1] R. *Scott, Sermons preached before the University of Oxford (1860).
[2] Aquila, *Excerpta ex reliquiis versionum* (1859 ed.).
[3] [P. *Delany], *Reflections upon polygamy and the encouragement given to that practice in the Scriptures of the Old Testament* (1737).
[4] See 28 May 60.
[5] See 30 Mar. 54.
[6] Privately circulated; published as (Sir) A. *Helps, *Organization in daily life. An essay* (1862).
[7] Probably the prolonged campaign between *Max Müller and *Monier Williams for the Sanskrit chair.
[8] R. *Burgess, *A city for the Pope; or the solution of the Roman question* (1860).
[9] T. L. Wood, 'London health and London traffic' (1859); on the embankment.
[10] Report of Metropolitan board of works recommending north bank improvements.
[11] T. Keightley, *The mythology of ancient Greece and Italy* (1832).
[12] J. J. Hillocks, *Life story. A prize autobiography* (1860).

15. Sat. X. [London]

Wrote to D. of Argyll—C.G.[1]—Vice Chanc. Oxford—Bp of Argyll and minutes. Saw Duchess of Sutherland—Ld Stanley [of] A[lderley] & Ld Palmerston—E. Cardwell (*a due*[2] in the train when we had much Bank & other conv.[)]] A. Gordon—& Col. Gordon—Aunt J. Dined with C. Wood— Saw Vivien: & [blank][R]. Read Hartwig on the Sea. Began Preadamite Man.[3]

16. 3 S. Adv.

All Saints mg (with & by invitn. from Dss of S.) Chapel Royal aft. Saw Mrs Phillimore. Read Preadamite Man (through). Saw Montagu[R]. Wrote to C.E. Bennett[4]—Robn. G.

17. M.

Wrote to C.G.—Mr Godfrey—Sir W. Dunbar—Mr Anderson—Mr Arbuthnot—Mr Hamilton—Ld Palmerston—Dr J. Brown—M. S[ummerhayes]— Mr Pressly—Mr Cookson.[5]

Saunders Otley & Co[6]⎫
Professor Jowett   ⎬ and minutes
W. Cowper   ⎭

Saw Mr Grogan—Mr Field 10¾–12.—Gov. & Dep. Gov. Bank 12-2.—Mr Stephenson—Mr Scudamore.[7] Went to the Britannia Theatre to see Eily O'Connor = The Colleen Bawn: in another cast.[8] Saw Montagu[R]. Read Thiers.

18. T. X

Wrote to Mr MacColl—C.G.[9]—James Hillocks[10]—Lyttelton—Mr Arbuthnot —Govr. of Bank & minutes. Wrote Minute on Naval Force.[11] Saw R. Phillimore—Duchess of Sutherland—Hon. A. Gordon—Mr F. Peel.— Shopping. Saw Vivien[R]. Read Thiers. Dined with the Phillimores: & went to the Westmr. [school] Play: wh I saw with the greatest interest.[12]

19. Wed.

Wrote to R. Phillimore (2)—M.S.—Sir T. Fremantle—C.G.—Ld Palmerston—Agnes—Attorney General—Sir G. Lewis—and minutes. Saw Govr.

[1] Bassett, 131.
[2] 'just the two of us'.
[3] Mrs G. J. C. Duncan, *Pre-Adamite Man: or the story of our old planet* (1860).
[4] The Hawarden post-master.
[5] William Strickland Cookson, 1801–77, barrister; president of the incorporated law society 1860–1; see 19 Dec. 60.
[6] Publishers in Conduit Street.
[7] Frank Ives *Scudamore, 1823–84; in Post Office from 1841; assisted in savings bank scheme 1861; advised and negotiated for P.O. on nationalisation of telegraphs.
[8] In Hoxton; Bassett, 132.
[9] ibid.
[10] James J. Hillocks, Edinburgh missionary; correspondence in Hawn P; see 13 Dec. 60.
[11] Not found, but see 28 Dec. 60.
[12] Plautus, 'Trinummus'; *The Times*, 20 December 1860, 9.

& Dep. Govr. Bank[1]—Mr Stephenson—Professor Jowett—Mr Cookson (Law Assn.)—Mr Pressly—Do *cum* Mr Fletcher—Sir Chas Wood. Read Thiers Vol. XVIII—L'Empereur Fr. Jos. et L'Europe.[2]

20. Th.

Wrote to Ld Granville—Lyttelton—Mr Stephenson—C.G.—Govr. of Bank (2)—H. Glynne—Mr Ryan—and minutes. Wrote dft. for H.G. to Miss Rose: & revised it with R. P[hillimore]. Wrote minute on Venetia.[3] Saw Sir James Graham—Sir Geo. Lewis—Mr R. Phillimore (2)—Mr Arbuthnot—The Provost of Eton—Mr Harris[s] (porcelain). Read Thiers—Macknight's Burke Vol III.[4]

21. Fr. St Thomas [Hawarden]

Wrote to Mr Jas. Darlington—Gov. of the Bank—Mr Anderson & minutes. 9.45–4.45 *To Ld. Aberdeen's funeral: no common occasion.* Saw Sir Jas. Graham—Duke of Newcastle—Earl Clarendon (M. Bernacs)[5] Bp of Oxford (Bp)—Mr Douglas Gordon.[6] Went to D. Street for business. Saw Mr Grogan. Off at 8 for Hawarden: arr. 1¾ by Irish Mail.

22. Sat.

Wrote to C. Pressly—Dss. of Sutherland—Scotts—Sir Jas Graham. Corrected proofs Trans.[7] Visited the pit & boring. Read Bernard's Lecture[8]—Trevelyan's Statement[9]—Thiers Hist. &c.

23. 4 S. Adv.

Ch mg. & aft. Read Hook's Abps of Canterb.[10]—Hennell on Bp Butler[11]—Chr. Rem. on Oxford—on Brit Assocn.—on Mosaic & Cushite Dispens.—on Essays & Reviews.[12]

24. M.

Ch 8½ a.m.—The birthday of a Saint dear to my memory.[13] Wrote to Duke of Argyll—Corrected proofs. Read Mem. of Webster.[14]—Northward Ho.[15] Rawlinson[,] Smiths Dict. on Phoenicia. Thiers Vol. 18—Pass & Class.[16] Prof. Miller on Nephalism.[17]

[1] On discount rates; see Add MS 44394, f. 325.
[2] C. Duveyrier *L'Empereur François-Joseph I et l'Europe* (1860).
[3] Supporting *Russell's dispatch: PRO 30/22/19, f. 124.
[4] T. Macknight, *History of the life and times of Edmund *Burke*, 3v. (1858–60).
[5] Obscure.
[6] Douglas Hamilton-Gordon, 1824–1901, *Aberdeen's 3rd s., canon of Salisbury.
[7] Of his and *Lyttelton's *Translations*.
[8] M. *Bernard, 'On the principle of non-intervention. A lecture' (1860).
[9] (Sir) C. E. *Trevelyan, *Statement . . . of the circumstances connected with his recall from the Government of Madras* (1860).
[10] W. F. *Hook, *Lives of the Archbishops of Canterbury*, 12v. (1860–76).
[11] Sara S. Hennell, *Essay on the sceptical character of *Butler's 'Analogy'* (1859).
[12] *Christian Remembrancer*, xl. 303, 237, 419, 327 (October 1860).
[13] His sister Anne.
[14] Probably G. Webster, *Memoir of Dr. C. Webster* (1853).
[15] Untraced.
[16] M. Burrows, *Pass and Class. An Oxford guide-book through the courses of literae humaniores, mathematics etc.* (1860).
[17] J. Miller, *Nephalism, the true temperance of Scripture, science and experience* (1861).

25. T. Xmas Day.

Church 11 (& H.C.) and 7 P.M. Wrote on Theol. Phil. Read Watson's Sermons[1]—Miller on Nephalism (finished)—Bagot on the Atonement[2]—and [blank]. Hard frost without: all warm & happy thank God within.

26. Wed. St Stephen

Ch 11 a.m. Wrote to G.A. Hamilton—Mr Quaritch—Sir W.C. James—C.A. Wood & minutes. Corrected proof sheets. Goldoni with my daughters. Saw Mr Burnett—Bennett the Postmaster. Large dinner party. My gems examined. Read Thiers Hist.

27. Th. St John

Ch 11 a.m. Wrote to D. of Cambridge—T.G.—Ld Palmerston[3]—Mr Pressly—D. of Somerset—Mr Rorison—Gov. of Bank—Mr Ripley[4]—Dep. Gov. of Bank—Mr Briscoe—Sir G.C. Lewis—Ld Ebury—M. Gladstone—Mr Anderson and minutes. Mem. on Chancery Funds' Commn.[5] Goldoni with M & L. Saw Lord Clarence Paget—Mr G. Burnett—Col. Gladstone—Mr May—Dr. Moffatt. Read Thiers. Corr. Proofs—Large party—and Ball.

28. Fr. H. Innocents.

Ch at 11 a.m. Wrote to D. of Somerset—Mr Pressly—Sir T. Fremantle—Mr Cowper—Mr Gibson & minutes. Goldoni with my daughters. Conv. with Ld C. Paget.[6] Corr. proofs. Music in evg.—Read Falkener on Grecian Art.[7]

29. Sat.

Wrote to C. Pressly—Rev. T.W. Weare[8]—J.N.G.—Mr W. Bagehot—Robn. G—D. of Somerset—Lyttelton—Col. A. Gordon and minutes. Party reduced. Further conv. with Ld C.—on shipbuilding.

Read Falkener—Thiers: finished Vol. XVIII. and began my 52nd year. I cannot believe it. I feel within me the rebellious unspoken word, I will not be old. The horizon enlarges, the sky shifts, around me. It is an age of shocks: a discipline so strong, so manifold, so rapid & whirling, that only when it is at an end, if then, can I hope to comprehend it. But two things are ever before me, clear & unchanging: the unbounded goodness of God, and my deep deep deep unworthiness.

30. S. aft. Xmas.

Church 11 a.m. & 6½ P.M. Conv. with Ld Jermyn.[9] Read Watson Rediv.

[1] See 5 Mar. 43.
[2] D. Bagot, (1860).
[3] On *Jowett, Guedalla, *P*, 155.
[4] Probably (Sir) Henry William Ripley, 1813–82; Bradford dye merchant and liberal M.P. there 1874–80; cr. bart. 1880.
[5] Not found.
[6] On *Paget's plan to build iron-cased ships: Add MS 44591, f. 146.
[7] E. *Falkener, *Daedalus; or the causes and principles of the excellence of Greek sculpture* (1860).
[8] Thomas William Weare, d. 1871; student of Christ Church 1832–53; master at Westminster; rector of Isfield 1867.
[9] Frederick William John Hervey, 1834–1907; styled Lord Jermyn 1859–64; Peelite M.P. W. Suffolk 1859–64; 3rd marquis of Bristol 1864.

finished. Drummond on the Church.[1]—Anderson's Hist of the Birth.[2] Worked on Ugolino & thought it wd. pass muster after all.[3]

31. M.

Church 8½ a.m. Wrote to Duchess of Sutherland—R.M. Milnes—Rev. Mr Eaton—Mr Pressly—Hon. A. Gordon—Mr Brand—Ld J. Russell—and minutes. Goldoni with M. & L. Goldoni with the children. Read Pass and Class. Falkener on Greek Art. Proof Sheets of Translations. Read Young on the Province of Reason.[4]

[1] H. *Drummond, *Discourses on the true definition of the Church, One, Holy, Catholic and Apostolic, and kindred subjects* (1858).
[2] Probably W. Anderson, *Discourses* (1859).
[3] Sentence added at foot of page; for the *Translations*.
[4] See 6 May 60.

WHERE WAS HE?
1855–1860

The following list shows where the diarist was each night; he continued at each place named until he moved on to the next. Names of the owners of great houses have been given in brackets on the first mention of the house.

1	January	1855	Hawarden	14	June	Dropmore (Lady Grenville)
8	January		London	16	June	London
26	May		Hawarden	21	June	Hawarden
15	June		London	30	June	London
16	June		Oxford	13	July	Hawarden
21	June		Hawarden	22	July	London, 11 Carlton House Terrace
10	July		London			
28	July		Chevening, Kent (Stanhope)	31	July	Hawarden
31	July		London	6	September	Corwen
4	August		Hawarden	7	September	Bala
3	September		Penmaenmawr	8	September	Mallwyd
10–15	September		walking in N. Wales	9	September	Aberdovey
15	September		Penmaenmawr	10	September	Aberystwyth
27	September		Bodelwyddan	12	September	Llanidloes
29	September		Hawarden	13	September	Powis Castle (Earl of Powis)
6	October		Courthey, Liverpool (R. Gladstone)	16	September	Oteley Park (C. K. Mainwaring)
9	October		Hawarden	17	September	Bettisfield, Shropshire (Sir J. Hanmer)
23	October		Tabley (De Tabley)			
29	October		Hawarden	18	September	Hawarden
22	November		Eaton Hall (Westminster)	29	September	Courthey
				1	October	Hawarden
24	November		London	24	October	Liverpool
26	November		Hawarden	25	October	Courthey, Liverpool
3	December		Windsor			
5	December		London	31	October	Hawarden
7	December		Hawarden	27	November	Peckforton Castle, Cheshire (Tollemache)
19	January	1856	4 Carlton House Terrace, London	29	November	Hawarden
13	May		Albury (Northumberland)			
17	May		Polesden Park (Sir R. W. Farquhar)	2	January	1857 Shrewsbury
				3	January	Hagley
				16	January	London
19	May		London	17	January	Wilton (Herbert)

23	January	Bowden Park
		(J. N. Gladstone)
26	January	Oxford
31	January	London
23	March	Hawarden
9	April	London
30	May	Oxford
4	June	Cliveden
		(Sutherland)
5	June	Salisbury
8	June	Cuddesdon
10	June	Hawarden
29	June	Manchester
1	July	London
4	July	Cliveden
6	July	London
8	July	Glenalmond
10	July	London
16	August	Hagley
17	August	London
18	August	Hagley
28	August	Hawarden
22	October	Brougham Hall
		(Lord
		Brougham)
24	October	Keswick
26	October	Liverpool
27	October	Hawarden
2	November	London
12	December	Hawarden
23	January 1858	London
27	January	Hawarden
16	February	London
3	April	Brighton
5	April	London
8	May	Strawberry Hill,
		Twickenham
		(Lady
		Waldegrave)
11	May	London
3	July	Norwood (Talbot)
5	July	London
20	July	Hawarden
12	August	London
16	August	Hawarden
1	September	Brougham Hall
3	September	Netherby (Sir J.
		Graham)
6	September	Drumlanrig
		(Buccleuch)

9	September	Glasgow
11	September	Dunrobin Castle
		(Sutherland)
20	September	Lairg
21	September	Lochinver
23	September	Scourie
24	September	Dunrobin Castle
27	September	Dingwall
28	September	Haddo House
		(Aberdeen)
6	October	Fasque
13	October	Keir (Stirling-
		Maxwell)
15	October	Liverpool
19	October	London
22	October	Hawarden
1	November	London
8	November	Brussels
10	November	Brunswick
13	November	Dresden
16	November	Prague
17	November	on train
18	November	Vienna
20	November	Trieste
21	November	on ship
24	November	Corfu
9	December	Ithaca
10	December	Cephalonia
15	December	Zante
16	December	on ship
17	December	Lutraki
18	December	Athens
23	December	on ship
24	December	Corfu
11	January 1859	on ship
12	January	Corfu
1	February	Philiates, Albania
3	February	Corfu
19	February	on ship
23	February	Venice
26	February	Vicenza
28	February	Milan
2	March	Turin
4	March	in coach
5	March	on train
6	March	Paris
7	March	on train
8	March	London
28	April	Strawberry Hill
30	April	London

6	May	Oxford	3	January	Windsor
13	May	Chevening	5	January	Pembroke Lodge
17	May	London			(Russell)
30	May	Strawberry Hill	6	January	London
31	May	London	3	March	Brighton
4	June	Cliveden	5	March	London
6	June	London	10	March	Cliveden
12	August	Isle of Wight	12	March	London
13	August	Cliveden	3	April	Brighton
15	August	London	10	April	London
18	August	Hawarden	15	April	Edinburgh
27	August	London	18	April	London
30	August	Hawarden	12	May	Cliveden
3	September	Penmaenmawr	14	May	London
9	September	Courthey	26	May	Cliveden
10	September	Hawarden	1	June	London
13	September	Penmaenmawr	2	June	Cliveden
16	September	London	4	June	London
20	September	Penmaenmawr	23	June	Cliveden
24	September	London	25	June	London
27	September	Penmaenmawr	21	July	Cliveden
3	October	Hawarden	23	July	London
14	October	London	11	August	The Coppice,
19	October	Holyhead			Henley
20	October	London			(Sir R. Philli-
22	October	Hawarden			more)
27	October	London	13	August	London
31	October	Cambridge	27	August	Hawarden
3	November	Audley End	1	September	Penmaenmawr
		(Braybrooke)	28	September	Llanrwst
7	November	London	29	September	Hawarden
12	November	Windsor	12	October	London
15	November	London	20	October	Hawarden
23	November	Sheen, Mortlake	8	November	London
		(Wortley)	10	November	Hursley (Sir W.
24	November	London			Heathcote)
8	December	Trentham,	12	November	London
		Staffordshire	17	November	Strawberry Hill
		(Sutherland)	19	November	London
10	December	Edinburgh	1	December	Windsor
15	December	Hawarden	3	December	London
16	December	London	8	December	Hawarden
17	December	Hawarden	15	December	London
			21	December	Hawarden
2	January 1860	London